State
and
Metropolitan Area
Data Book
2013

State
and
Metropolitan Area
Data Book

2013

FIRST EDITION

Edited by Deirdre A. Gaquin
and Gwenavere W. Dunn

Lanham • Boulder • New York • Toronto • Plymouth, UK

Published by Bernan Press
A wholly owned subsidiary of Rowman & Littlefield
4501 Forbes Boulevard, Suite 200, Lanham, Maryland 20706
www.rowman.com
800-865-3457; info@bernan.com

10 Thornbury Road, Plymouth PL6 7PP, United Kingdom

ISBN: 978-1-59888-627-6
e-ISBN: 978-1-59888-630-6

∞™ The paper used in this publication meets the minimum requirements of American National
Standard for Information Sciences—Permanence of Paper for Printed Library Materials,
ANSI/NISO Z39.48-1992.
Manufactured in the United States of America.

CONTENTS

PREFACE

This is the first edition of the *State and Metropolitan Area Data Book* (SMADB) produced by Bernan Press. The U.S. Census Bureau terminated its Statistical Compendia program in 2011. The Statistical Compendia program included the *Statistical Abstract of the United States* and its supplemental local area products—the *State and Metropolitan Area Data Book* and the *County and City Data Book* (CCDB). The Census Bureau published seven editions of SMADB, periodically since 1979, and 14 editions of CCDB, periodically since 1944. Since 1992, Bernan Press has produced 20 editions of *County and City Extra*, a comprehensive volume that combines some of the features of both SMADB and CCDB, and five editions of *Places, Towns, and Townships,* a companion volume with details about cities and towns not included in either CCDB or *County and City Extra.* This first edition of Bernan's SMADB replaces and updates the Census Bureau's SMADB. Bernan continues to publish annual editions of *County and City Extra* that include most of the content of the former CCDB, plus many additional features. *County and City Extra* includes sections of state and metropolitan area data, but the *State and Metropolitan Area Data Book* includes a wider selection of state data, a table of data for micropolitan areas, and several tables that include the component counties of the metropolitan and micropolitan areas.

The SMADB is a convenient summary of statistics on the social and economic structure of the states, metropolitan areas, and micropolitan areas in the United States. It is designed to serve as a statistical reference and guide to other data publications and sources. The latter function is served by the source citations appearing below each table and in Appendix A, "Source Notes and Explanations." This volume includes data from a variety of statistical publications and electronic sources, including nonprofit organizations, private businesses, as well as the majority of the federal statistical agencies. Publications and Internet sites listed as sources usually contain additional detail and more comprehensive discussions of definitions and concepts than can be presented here. Data not available in printed publications issued by the contributing agency but obtained from websites are identified in the source notes. More information on the subjects covered in this publication is generally made available by its source, including additional methodological information about how the data are collected or produced.

This edition

All data have been updated to the most recent available year. All population and housing data have been updated based on the 2010 census. Detailed social and economic characteristics have been updated and expanded from the 1-year and 3-year estimates from the American Community Survey, including information on health insurance, household type, migration, and commuting. Three-year data measure the characteristics of the population for an area (or population group) over the entire data collection period (36 months for 3-year estimates).

Vital statistics on deaths have been expanded to include additional race categories and additional causes of death. Criminal justice data now include the number of prisoners removed from death row. Data on information industries have been expanded with numbers of establishments providing Internet, online publishing, and telecommunications services. The results of the 2012 elections are included, with gubernatorial and elected officials of the 113th Congress.

States. Data are presented for the United States, the 50 states, and the District of Columbia. Tables A-1 through A-84 contain 1,362 data items for these areas. The states and the District of Columbia are presented in alphabetical order under the U.S. total.

Metropolitan areas and metropolitan divisions. Data are presented for the 366 metropolitan areas and 29 metropolitan divisions defined as of December 2009. Tables B-1 through B-14 present 159 data items for these areas.

Metropolitan areas and metropolitan divisions with their component counties. Data are presented for 50 data items in Tables C-1 through C-4. The 1,100 counties and county equivalents are presented under their respective metropolitan area or metropolitan division.

Micropolitan areas with their component counties. Table D-1 includes 13 data items for 576 micropolitan areas and their 688 component counties.

Appendixes. Appendix A provides information on source notes and explanations for the data items in Parts A through D. Appendix B presents a brief introduction to central concepts of statistics and provides the methodological approach of principal sources. Appendix C presents a discussion of the geographic concepts relevant to this edition, as well as the current definitions for metropolitan areas. Appendix D offers a bibliography of the latest state specific abstracts published since 1999. For additional information on data presented, please consult the source publications available in local libraries, write to the agency indicated in the source notes, or visit the Internet site listed.

Statistics for the nation. Extensive data at the national level can be found in the *ProQuest Statistical Abstract of the United States 2013,* co-published with Bernan Press.

Statistics for counties and cities. Data for counties and cities may be found in Bernan's annual *County and City Extra* and *Places, Towns, and Townships 2012.*

GUIDE TO TABULAR PRESENTATION

Example of Table Structure:

Table A-63. Transportation and Commuting

| Geographic area | Transportation and warehousing (NAICS 48-49) | | | | | |
| | Nonfarm employment[1] (thousands) | | Earnings[2] (million dollars) | | Establishments[3] | |
	2012	2005	2012	2005	2010	2005
United States	4,414.5	4,360.9	324,865	278,340	208,474	211,150
Alabama	54.9	55.0	3,872	3,298	2,874	3,144
Alaska	19.7	19.0	1,672	1,358	1,113	1,149
Arizona	71.8	69.5	5,110	4,376	3,065	3,092
Arkansas	NA	NA	3,586	3,397	2,412	2,596
California	427.2	431.4	34,804	31,323	20,876	20,086

[1]All estimates of labor provided by the Bureau of Labor Statistics (BLS) are based on the 2007 North American Industry. Classification System (NAICS). United States totals differ from the sum of the state figures because of differing benchmarks among states and differing industrial and geographic stratification.
[2]Bureau of Economic Analysis. The estimates of earnings for 2000-2006 are based on the 2002 North American Industry Classification System (NAICS). The estimates for 2007 forward are based on the 2007 NAICS. All dollar estimates are in current dollars and not adjusted for inflation.
[3]Data for establishments in 2010 based on the 2007 North American Industry Classification System (NAICS); 2005 data are based on the 2002 NAICS.

Unit indicators show the specified quantities in which data items are presented. They are used for two primary reasons. Sometimes data are not available in absolute form. Other times, we round the numbers in order to save space to show more data, as in the case above.

If no unit indicator is shown, data presented are in absolute form (see Table B-1 for an example). When needed, unit indicators are found in the column or spanner headings for the data items as shown above.

Footnotes below the bottom rule of table pages give information relating to specific data items or figures within the table.

Further information on individual tables can be found in Appendix A, located in the back of the book.

Examples of Unit Indicator Interpretation table example:

Geographic area	Year	Item	Unit indicator	Number shown	Multiplier
United States	2012	Nonfarm employment	(thousands)	4,414.5	1,000
United States	2012	Earnings	(million dollars)	324,865	1,000,000

To determine the figure, it is necessary to multiply the number shown by the unit indicator.

Nonfarm employment, 2012 = 4,414.5 * 1,000 or 4,414,500

Earnings, 2012 = 324,865* 1,000,000 or 324,865,000,000

In many tables, details will not add to the totals shown because of rounding.

EXPLANATION OF SYMBOLS AND TERMS

The following symbols, used in the tables throughout this book, are explained in condensed form in footnotes on the tables where they appear.

0	Represents zero or rounds to zero.
D	Figure withheld to avoid disclosure pertaining to a specific individual or organization; or does not meet statistical standards for reliability of derived figure.
NA	Data not available.
X	Figure not applicable because column heading and stub line make entry impossible, or meaningless.

The following terms are also used throughout this publication:

Averages. An average is a single number or value that is often used to represent the "typical value" of a group of numbers. It is regarded as a measure of "location" or "central tendency" of a group of numbers.

The *arithmetic* mean is the type of average used most frequently. It is derived by summing the individual item values of a particular group and dividing the total by the number of items. The arithmetic mean is often referred to simply as the "mean" or "average."

The *median* of a group of numbers is the middle number or value when each item in the group is arranged according to size (lowest to highest or vice versa); it generally has the same number of items above it as well as below it. If there is an even number of items in the group, the median is taken to be the average of the two middle numbers.

Rates. A rate is a quantity or amount of an item measured in relation to a specified number of units of another item. For example, the unemployment rate is the number of unemployed people per 100 people in the civilian labor force. Examples of other rates found in this publication include birth rate, which is the number of births per 1,000 population; infant death rate, the number of infant deaths per 1,000 live births; and crime rate, which is the number of serious offenses per 100,000 population.

A *per capita* figure represents a specific type of rate computed for every person in a specified group (or population). It is derived by taking the total for a data item (such as income, taxes, or retail sales) and dividing it by the number of people in the specified population.

Ranks. Various data items in Part A, States, and Part B, Metropolitan Areas, of this publication are ranked from highest to lowest with a rank of 1 representing the highest rank. In both parts, when areas share the same rank, the next-lower rank is omitted.

In Part A, only the 50 states are ranked; the District of Columbia is not included in the state rankings. In Part B, only 366 metropolitan statistical areas (MSAs) are ranked. Not ranked are the 29 metropolitan divisions, which make up 11 metropolitan statistical areas. Areas not ranked are indicated by an "X" in the data cell.

Index numbers. An index number is a measure of difference or change, usually expressed as a percentage, relating one quantity (the variable) of a specified kind to another quantity of the same kind. Index numbers are widely used to express changes in prices over periods of time but may also be used to express differences between related subjects for a single point in time.

To compute a price index, a base year or period is selected. The base year price (of the commodity or service) is then designated as the base or reference price to which the prices for other years or periods are related. Many price indexes use the year 2000 as the base year; in tables, this is shown as "2000 = 100." A method of expressing the price relationship is: the price of a set of one or more items for a related year (e.g., 1990) divided by the price of the same set of items for the base year (e.g., 2000). The result multiplied by 100 provides the index number. When 100 is subtracted from the index number, the result equals the percentage change in price from the base year.

Current and constant dollars. Statistics in some tables are expressed in both current and constant dollars (for example, see Table A-40). Current dollar figures reflect actual prices or costs prevailing during the specified year(s). Constant dollar figures are estimates representing an effort to remove the effects of price changes from statistical series reported in dollar terms. In general, constant dollar series are derived by dividing current dollar estimates by the appropriate price index for the appropriate period (for example, the Consumer Price Index). The result is a series as it would presumably exist if prices were the same throughout, as in the base year; in other words, as if the dollar had constant purchasing power. Any changes in this constant dollar series would reflect only changes in real volume of output, income, expenditures, or other measure.

MAJOR FEDERAL DATA CONTACTS

To help *State and Metro Area Data Book* users find more data and information about statistical publications, we are including this list of contacts for federal agencies with major statistical programs. The intent is to give a single, first-contact point-of-entry for users of statistics. These agencies will provide general information on their statistical programs and publications, as well as specific information on how to order their publications. We are also including the Internet addresses for many of these agencies. These URLs were current in April 2013.

Executive Office of the President

Office of Management and Budget
Administrator
Office of Information and Regulatory Affairs
Office of Management and Budget
725 17th Street, NW
Washington, DC 20503
Information: 202-395-3080
Internet address: whitehouse.gov/omb

Department of Agriculture

Economic Research Service
U.S. Department of Agriculture
1400 Independence Avenue, SW
Washington, DC 20250
Information: 202-720-2791
Internet address: www.ers.usda.gov/

National Agriculture Statistics Service
USDA-NASS
1400 Independence Avenue, SW
Washington, DC 20250
Information: 202-720-2791 or 800-727-9540
Internet address: www.nass.usda.gov

Department of Commerce

U.S. Census Bureau
Customer Services Branch
U.S. Census Bureau
4600 Silver Hill Road
Washington, DC 20233
Information and publications: 1-800-923-8282
Internet address: www.census.gov/

Department of Commerce—Continued

Bureau of Economic Analysis
1441 L Street, NW
Washington DC 20230
Information and publications: 202-606-9900
Internet address: www.bea.gov/

International Trade Administration
1401 Constitution Avenue, NW
 Washington, DC 20230
Information: 1-800-872-8723
Internet address: http://trade.gov/

National Oceanic and Atmospheric Administration
National Oceanic and Atmospheric Administration
Central Library
U.S. Department of Commerce
1315 East-West Highway
SSMC3, 2nd Floor
Silver Spring, MD 20910
Library: 301-713-2600 x157
Internet address: www.lib.noaa.gov/

Department of Defense

Department of Defense
Office of Public Communication
1400 Defense Pentagon
Washington, DC 20301-1400
Information: 703-571-3343
Internet address: www.defenselink.mil

Department of Education

National Library of Education
U.S. Department of Education
400 Maryland Avenue, SW
Washington, DC 20202
Education information and statistics: 1-800-872-5327
Education publications: 1-877-433-7827
Internet address: www.ed.gov/

Department of Energy

Energy Information Administration
National Energy Information Center
1000 Independence Avenue, SW
Washington, DC 20585
Information and publications: 202-586-8800
Internet address: www.eia.doe.gov/

Department of Health and Human Services

Health Resources and Services Administration
HRSA Information Center
P.O. Box 2910
Merrifield, VA 22116
Information Center: 1-888-275-4772
Internet address: www.hrsa.gov/

*Substance Abuse and Mental Health Services
Administration*
1 Coke Cherry Road
Rockville, MD 20857
Information: 240-276-2130
Publications: 1-877-726-4727
Internet address: www.samhsa.gov/

Centers for Disease Control and Prevention
Public Inquiries/MASO
1600 Clifton Road
Atlanta, GA 30333
Public inquires: 1-800-232-4636
Internet address: www.cdc.gov/

Centers for Medicare and Medicaid Services (CMS)
U.S. Department of Health and Human Services
7500 Security Boulevard
Baltimore, MD 21244
Information: 1-877-267-2323
Internet address: www.cms.hhs.gov/

National Center for Health Statistics
3311 Toledo Road
Hyattsville, MD 20782
Information: 1-800-232-4636
Internet address: www.cdc.gov/nchs

Department of Homeland Security

Office of Public Affairs
245 Murray Lane, SW
Washington, DC 20528
Information and publications: 202-282-8010
Internet address: www.dhs.gov

Department of Housing and Urban Development

*Office of the Assistant Secretary for Community Planning
and Development*
451 7th Street, SW
Washington, DC 20410
Information: 202-708-0006
Publications: 1-800-767-7468
Internet address: www.hud.gov/

Department of the Interior

U.S. Geological Survey
USGS National Center
12201 Sunrise Valley Drive
Reston, VA 20192
Information and Publications: 1-888-275-8747
Internet address for minerals: http://minerals.usgs.gov/
Internet address for other materials: http://ask.usgs.gov/

Department of Justice

Bureau of Justice Statistics
Statistics Division
810 7th Street, NW
Washington, DC 20531
Information and publications: 202-307-0765
Internet address: www.ojp.usdoj.gov/bjs/

National Criminal Justice Reference Service
P.O. Box 6000
Rockville, MD 20849-6000
Publications: 1-800-851-3420
Internet address: www.ncjrs.gov/

Federal Bureau of Investigation
J. Edgar Hoover Building
935 Pennsylvania Avenue, NW
Washington, DC 20535-0001
Information: 202-324-3000
Internet address: www.fbi.gov/

Department of Labor

Bureau of Labor Statistics
Office of Publications and Special Studies Services
Bureau of Labor Statistics
Postal Square Building
2 Massachusetts Avenue, NE
Washington, DC 20212-0001
Information and publications: 202-691-5200
Internet address: www.bls.gov/

Department of Labor—Continued

Employment and Training Administration
U.S. Department of Labor
Francis Perkins Building
200 Constitution Avenue, NW
Washington, DC 20210
Information and publications: 1-877-872-5627
Internet address: www.doleta.gov/

Department of Transportation

Federal Aviation Administration
800 Independence Avenue, SW
Washington, DC 20591
Information and publications: 1-866-835-5322
Internet address: www.faa.gov/

Bureau of Transportation Statistics
1200 New Jersey Avenue, SE
Washington, DC 20590
Products and statistical information: 1-800-853-1351
Internet address: www.bts.gov/

Federal Highway Administration
Office of Public Affairs
U.S. Department of Transportation
1200 New Jersey Avenue, SE
Washington, DC 20590
Information: 202-366-0660
Internet address: www.fhwa.dot.gov/

National Highway Traffic Safety Administration
Office of Public and Consumer Affairs
1200 New Jersey Avenue, SE
West Building Washington, DC 20590
Information and publications: 1-888-327-4236
Internet address: www.nhtsa.dot.gov/

Department of the Treasury

Internal Revenue Service
Statistics of Income Division
Internal Revenue Service
P.O. Box 2608
Washington, DC 20013-2608
Information and publications: 202-874-0410
Internet address: www.irs.gov/uac/Tax-Stats-2

Department of Veterans Affairs

Department of Veterans Affairs
Office of Public Affairs
810 Vermont Avenue, NW
Washington, DC 20420
Information: 202-461-7600
Internet address: www.va.gov/

Independent Agencies

Administrative Office of the U.S. Courts
Office of Public Affairs
1 Columbus Circle, NE
Washington, DC 20544
Information: 202-502-2600
Internet address: www.uscourts.gov/

Board of Governors of the Federal Reserve System
Division of Research and Statistics
Federal Reserve System
20th & Constitution Avenue, NW
Washington, DC 20551
Information: 202-452-3000
Publications: 202-452-3245
Internet address: www.federalreserve.gov/

Environmental Protection Agency
Ariel Rios Building
1200 Pennsylvania Avenue, NW
Washington, DC 20460
Publications: 1-800-490-9198
Internet address: www.epa.gov/

National Science Foundation
Office of Legislation and Public Affairs
4201 Wilson Boulevard
Arlington, VA 22230
Information: 703-292-5111
Internet address: www.nsf.gov/

Securities and Exchange Commission
Office of Public Affairs
Securities and Exchange Commission
100 F Street, NE
Washington, DC 20549
Information: 202-551-4120
Publications: 202-551-4040
Internet address: www.sec.gov/

Social Security Administration
Office of Public Inquiries
6401 Security Boulevard
Baltimore, MD 21235
Information and Publications: 1-800-772-1213
Internet address: www.socialsecurity.gov

PART A
STATES

Note: Part A presents data for the United States, states, and the District of Columbia. Data are presented for 1,362 items, by state, listed in alphabetical order. For a more detailed listing of subjects covered in these tables, see Contents.

Table A-1.   Area and Population

Geographic area	Area, 2000 (sq. mi.) Total	Rank	2012 (thousands)	2010 (thousands)	2000[1] (thousands)	Rank 2012	Rank 2010	Rank 2000	Per sq mile 2012	Per sq mile 2010	Per sq mile 2000	Net change total[3]	Net international migration	Net domestic migration	Pct 2010–2012	Pct 2000–2010
United States..........	3,531,905	(X)	313,914	308,748	281,425	(X)	(X)	(X)	88.9	87.4	79.6	5,166.5	1,850.9	NA	1.7	9.7
Alabama..................	50,645	28	4,822	4,780	4,447	23	23	23	95.2	94.4	87.6	42.3	12.3	1.3	0.9	7.5
Alaska....................	570,641	1	731	710	627	47	47	48	1.3	1.2	1.1	21.2	4.5	-1.8	3.0	13.3
Arizona..................	113,594	6	6,553	6,392	5,131	15	16	20	57.7	56.3	45.2	161.2	24.8	48.3	2.5	24.6
Arkansas................	52,035	27	2,949	2,916	2,673	32	32	33	56.7	56.0	51.3	33.2	6.6	5.5	1.1	9.1
California...............	155,779	3	38,041	37,254	33,872	1	1	1	244.2	239.1	217.2	787.5	276.8	-104.1	2.1	10.0
Colorado................	103,642	8	5,188	5,029	4,302	22	22	24	50.1	48.5	41.5	158.4	18.3	62.3	3.1	16.9
Connecticut............	4,842	48	3,590	3,574	3,406	29	29	29	741.4	738.1	702.9	16.3	33.7	-34.5	0.5	4.9
Delaware...............	1,949	49	917	898	784	45	45	45	470.7	460.8	401.1	19.2	5.1	6.2	2.1	14.6
District of Columbia...	61	(X)	632	602	572	(X)	(X)	(X)	10,357.5	9,856.5	9,316.9	30.6	6.2	14.2	5.1	5.2
Florida..................	53,625	26	19,318	18,803	15,983	4	4	4	360.2	350.6	296.4	514.9	212.0	219.0	2.7	17.6
Georgia.................	57,513	21	9,920	9,688	8,187	8	9	10	172.5	168.4	141.4	232.3	54.7	36.1	2.4	18.3
Hawaii..................	6,423	47	1,392	1,360	1,212	40	40	42	216.8	211.8	188.6	32.0	17.4	-4.2	2.4	12.3
Idaho...................	82,643	11	1,596	1,568	1,294	39	39	39	19.3	19.0	15.6	28.1	3.9	-0.8	1.8	21.2
Illinois.................	55,519	24	12,875	12,831	12,420	5	5	5	231.9	231.1	223.4	44.6	61.1	-156.2	0.3	3.3
Indiana.................	35,826	38	6,537	6,484	6,081	16	15	14	182.5	181.0	169.5	53.5	18.8	-24.3	0.8	6.6
Iowa....................	55,857	23	3,074	3,047	2,926	30	30	30	55.0	54.5	52.4	27.3	9.3	-3.3	0.9	4.1
Kansas.................	81,759	13	2,886	2,853	2,689	33	33	32	35.3	34.9	32.9	32.8	10.7	-14.3	1.1	6.1
Kentucky...............	39,486	37	4,380	4,339	4,042	26	26	25	110.9	109.9	101.7	41.1	13.1	-1.1	0.9	7.3
Louisiana..............	43,204	33	4,602	4,533	4,469	25	25	22	106.5	104.9	102.6	68.5	13.5	6.0	1.5	1.4
Maine...................	30,843	39	1,329	1,328	1,275	41	41	40	43.1	43.1	41.3	0.8	2.3	-1.3	0.1	4.2
Maryland................	9,707	42	5,885	5,774	5,297	19	19	19	606.2	594.8	541.9	111.0	55.1	-7.5	1.9	9.0
Massachusetts..........	7,800	45	6,646	6,548	6,349	14	14	13	852.1	839.4	809.8	98.5	66.3	-9.7	1.5	3.1
Michigan...............	56,539	22	9,883	9,884	9,938	9	8	8	174.8	174.8	175.0	-0.3	37.0	-93.4	0.0	-0.6
Minnesota..............	79,627	14	5,379	5,304	4,919	21	21	21	67.6	66.6	61.8	75.2	27.2	-15.1	1.4	7.8
Mississippi............	46,923	31	2,985	2,967	2,845	31	31	31	63.6	63.2	60.6	17.6	5.8	-12.4	0.6	4.3
Missouri...............	68,742	18	6,022	5,989	5,597	18	18	17	87.6	87.1	81.2	33.1	16.3	-28.6	0.6	7.0
Montana................	145,546	4	1,005	989	902	44	44	44	6.9	6.8	6.2	15.7	1.1	7.3	1.6	9.7
Nebraska...............	76,824	15	1,856	1,826	1,711	37	38	38	24.2	23.8	22.3	29.2	6.5	-2.5	1.6	6.7
Nevada.................	109,781	7	2,759	2,701	1,998	35	35	35	25.1	24.6	18.2	58.4	18.0	2.7	2.2	35.1
New Hampshire.........	8,953	44	1,321	1,316	1,236	42	42	41	147.5	147.0	137.8	4.2	4.0	-4.3	0.3	6.5
New Jersey.............	7,354	46	8,865	8,792	8,414	11	11	9	1,205.4	1,195.5	1,134.4	72.7	101.7	-103.3	0.8	4.5
New Mexico.............	121,298	5	2,086	2,059	1,819	36	36	36	17.2	17.0	15.0	26.4	4.2	-5.3	1.3	13.2
New York...............	47,126	30	19,570	19,378	18,977	3	3	3	415.3	411.2	401.9	192.2	209.9	-224.5	1.0	2.1
North Carolina.........	48,618	29	9,752	9,535	8,046	10	10	11	200.6	196.1	165.2	216.6	50.4	72.1	2.3	18.5
North Dakota...........	69,001	17	700	673	642	48	48	47	10.1	9.7	9.3	27.0	2.1	17.4	4.0	4.7
Ohio....................	40,861	35	11,544	11,537	11,353	7	7	7	282.5	282.3	277.3	7.7	33.5	-84.5	0.1	1.6
Oklahoma	68,595	19	3,815	3,751	3,451	28	28	27	55.6	54.7	50.3	63.5	10.9	16.4	1.7	8.7
Oregon.................	95,988	10	3,899	3,831	3,421	27	27	28	40.6	39.9	35.6	68.3	14.4	24.4	1.8	12.0
Pennsylvania...........	44,743	32	12,764	12,702	12,281	6	6	6	285.3	283.9	274.0	61.2	54.5	-27.6	0.5	3.4
Rhode Island...........	1,034	50	1,050	1,053	1,048	43	43	43	1,015.9	1,018.1	1,003.2	-2.3	7.5	-13.3	-0.2	0.4
South Carolina	30,061	40	4,724	4,625	4,012	24	24	26	157.1	153.9	133.2	98.4	16.3	47.1	2.1	15.3
South Dakota	75,811	16	833	814	755	46	46	46	11.0	10.7	9.9	19.2	1.9	6.9	2.4	7.9
Tennessee..............	41,235	34	6,456	6,346	5,689	17	17	16	156.6	153.9	138.0	110.1	19.2	46.6	1.7	11.5
Texas...................	261,232	2	26,059	25,146	20,852	2	2	2	99.8	96.3	79.6	913.6	142.4	290.4	3.6	20.6
Utah....................	82,170	12	2,855	2,764	2,233	34	34	34	34.7	33.6	27.2	91.4	10.0	-0.9	3.3	23.8
Vermont................	9,217	43	626	626	609	49	49	49	67.9	67.9	65.8	0.3	1.3	-2.4	0.0	2.8
Virginia...............	39,490	36	8,186	8,001	7,079	12	12	12	207.3	202.6	178.8	184.8	66.0	22.3	2.3	13.0
Washington.............	66,456	20	6,897	6,725	5,894	13	13	15	103.8	101.2	88.6	172.5	47.0	41.1	2.6	14.1
West Virginia..........	24,038	41	1,855	1,853	1,808	38	37	37	77.2	77.1	75.1	2.4	1.9	3.7	0.1	2.5
Wisconsin..............	54,158	25	5,726	5,687	5,364	20	20	18	105.7	105.0	98.8	39.4	12.8	-21.1	0.7	6.0
Wyoming	97,093	9	576	564	494	50	50	50	5.9	5.8	5.1	12.8	0.7	5.1	2.3	14.1

[1]The April 1, 2000, Population Estimates base reflects modifications to the Census 2000 population as documented in the Count Question Resolution program and geographic program revisions.
[2]People per square mile was calculated on the basis of land area data from the 2010 census.
[3]The estimated components of population change will not sum to the numerical population change due to the process of controlling to national totals.
NA = not available
(X) = Not applicable

Table A–2. Population, by Age Group and Sex

Geographic area	Population by age, 2011[1] (thousands)										
	Total	Under 5 years	5 to 17 years	18 to 24 years	25 to 34 years	35 to 44 years	45 to 54 years	55 to 64 years	65 to 74 years	75 to 84 years	85 years and over
United States....................	311,592	20,162	53,772	31,065	41,790	40,628	44,718	38,062	22,482	13,175	5,737
Alabama.............................	4,803	304	823	485	615	608	685	610	380	215	78
Alaska................................	723	55	134	77	107	92	110	91	38	15	5
Arizona..............................	6,483	450	1,175	645	871	822	842	756	522	290	110
Arkansas............................	2,938	196	514	286	382	364	404	364	240	136	53
California............................	37,692	2,539	6,733	3,975	5,412	5,164	5,250	4,220	2,377	1,388	634
Colorado............................	5,117	342	888	501	746	701	734	629	328	174	74
Connecticut........................	3,581	197	606	331	428	469	572	462	263	165	87
Delaware............................	907	56	149	92	114	113	133	116	75	42	16
District of Columbia...........	618	36	69	84	133	82	76	67	38	21	11
Florida...............................	19,058	1,075	2,920	1,772	2,344	2,405	2,749	2,434	1,778	1,114	467
Georgia..............................	9,815	683	1,806	995	1,359	1,383	1,395	1,116	637	321	119
Hawaii................................	1,375	89	216	132	192	174	189	180	105	64	33
Idaho.................................	1,585	119	309	157	211	192	206	189	115	61	26
Illinois................................	12,869	828	2,270	1,250	1,788	1,704	1,851	1,537	873	525	243
Indiana...............................	6,517	430	1,168	658	835	830	935	803	465	274	120
Iowa..................................	3,062	199	525	311	388	360	432	389	228	153	77
Kansas...............................	2,871	204	520	293	383	343	399	346	195	126	61
Kentucky............................	4,369	281	740	419	569	570	638	560	335	186	71
Louisiana...........................	4,575	317	801	477	642	559	646	560	322	182	69
Maine.................................	1,328	68	202	116	146	166	215	200	117	70	30
Maryland............................	5,828	366	980	562	783	780	901	726	402	225	102
Massachusetts....................	6,588	366	1,039	680	868	866	1,010	838	473	298	150
Michigan............................	9,876	584	1,711	993	1,170	1,242	1,482	1,304	746	444	199
Minnesota..........................	5,345	352	925	504	730	670	800	661	367	224	111
Mississippi.........................	2,979	209	541	310	390	370	411	360	219	123	45
Missouri.............................	6,011	384	1,028	592	788	735	875	754	461	276	118
Montana.............................	998	62	161	97	125	112	145	145	84	47	21
Nebraska............................	1,843	131	329	185	249	220	254	224	126	84	41
Nevada...............................	2,723	186	477	251	389	378	375	326	207	100	33
New Hampshire...................	1,318	68	212	125	147	172	223	186	101	57	26
New Jersey	8,821	536	1,507	774	1,123	1,212	1,374	1,087	631	392	186
New Mexico	2,082	146	374	207	274	247	286	266	160	88	34
New York............................	19,465	1,164	3,122	1,986	2,714	2,561	2,865	2,389	1,397	863	405
North Carolina....................	9,656	630	1,658	954	1,263	1,316	1,370	1,187	727	398	154
North Dakota......................	684	45	106	84	94	75	95	86	48	34	17
Ohio	11,545	710	1,983	1,103	1,426	1,448	1,711	1,516	869	540	239
Oklahoma...........................	3,792	266	670	388	516	460	517	458	287	166	64
Oregon...............................	3,872	237	627	365	531	501	530	529	305	167	81
Pennsylvania......................	12,743	724	2,037	1,266	1,547	1,576	1,916	1,695	1,000	665	316
Rhode Island......................	1,051	56	163	121	129	132	160	136	76	50	28
South Carolina	4,679	303	778	481	601	593	658	607	387	198	74
South Dakota	824	60	144	83	108	93	115	103	59	40	20
Tennessee..........................	6,403	405	1,087	614	835	844	921	817	503	272	104
Texas.................................	25,675	1,960	5,001	2,630	3,695	3,492	3,456	2,735	1,539	845	323
Utah...................................	2,817	262	618	327	447	344	306	254	144	82	33
Vermont	626	31	95	66	71	76	100	94	52	29	13
Virginia..............................	8,097	510	1,343	814	1,120	1,094	1,209	995	573	310	128
Washington.........................	6,830	444	1,138	666	962	907	976	872	484	258	123
West Virginia......................	1,855	103	281	171	221	234	270	273	167	98	37
Wisconsin	5,712	355	972	555	731	709	864	733	412	259	122
Wyoming	568	40	95	57	79	67	81	77	41	22	9

[1] As of July 1 for 2011. As of April 1 for decennial census years 2010 and 2000. All years include Armed Forces stationed in area.

Table A–2. Population, by Age Group and Sex—*Continued*

Geographic area	Population under 18 years old[1] (thousands)			Population 65 years and over[1]			Percentage of population, by age[1]						Males per 100 females 2011[1]
							Under 18 years			65 years and over			
	2011	2010	2000[2]	2011	2010	2000[2]	2011	2010	2000[2]	2011	2010	2000[2]	
United States	73,934	74,181	72,294	41,394	40,268	34,992	23.7	24.0	25.7	13.3	13.0	12.4	96.8
Alabama	1,127	1,132	1,123	673	658	580	23.5	23.7	25.3	14.0	13.8	13.0	94.2
Alaska	188	187	191	58	55	36	26.1	26.4	30.4	8.1	7.7	5.7	108.0
Arizona	1,625	1,629	1,367	922	882	668	25.1	25.5	26.6	14.2	13.8	13.0	98.9
Arkansas	710	711	680	429	420	374	24.2	24.4	25.4	14.6	14.4	14.0	96.5
California	9,272	9,295	9,250	4,399	4,247	3,596	24.6	25.0	27.3	11.7	11.4	10.6	99.0
Colorado	1,230	1,226	1,101	576	550	416	24.0	24.4	25.6	11.3	10.9	9.7	100.7
Connecticut	803	817	842	515	507	470	22.4	22.9	24.7	14.4	14.2	13.8	95.0
Delaware	205	206	195	133	129	102	22.6	22.9	24.8	14.7	14.4	13.0	94.1
District of Columbia	105	101	115	70	69	70	17.0	16.8	20.1	11.4	11.4	12.2	89.7
Florida	3,994	4,002	3,646	3,360	3,260	2,808	21.0	21.3	22.8	17.6	17.3	17.6	95.7
Georgia	2,490	2,492	2,169	1,078	1,032	785	25.4	25.7	26.5	11.0	10.7	9.6	95.8
Hawaii	305	304	296	203	195	161	22.2	22.3	24.4	14.7	14.3	13.3	100.7
Idaho	428	429	369	202	195	146	27.0	27.4	28.5	12.8	12.4	11.3	100.3
Illinois	3,098	3,129	3,245	1,641	1,609	1,500	24.1	24.4	26.1	12.7	12.5	12.1	96.3
Indiana	1,598	1,608	1,574	858	841	753	24.5	24.8	25.9	13.2	13.0	12.4	96.9
Iowa	724	728	734	458	453	436	23.7	23.9	25.1	14.9	14.9	14.9	98.2
Kansas	724	727	713	383	376	356	25.2	25.5	26.5	13.3	13.2	13.3	98.6
Kentucky	1,021	1,023	995	592	578	505	23.4	23.6	24.6	13.5	13.3	12.5	96.9
Louisiana	1,118	1,118	1,220	572	558	517	24.4	24.7	27.3	12.5	12.3	11.6	95.8
Maine	269	275	301	216	211	183	20.3	20.7	23.6	16.3	15.9	14.4	95.9
Maryland	1,347	1,353	1,356	729	708	599	23.1	23.4	25.6	12.5	12.3	11.3	93.8
Massachusetts	1,405	1,419	1,500	922	903	860	21.3	21.7	23.6	14.0	13.8	13.5	93.9
Michigan	2,296	2,344	2,596	1,389	1,362	1,219	23.2	23.7	26.1	14.1	13.8	12.3	96.3
Minnesota	1,278	1,284	1,287	702	683	594	23.9	24.2	26.2	13.1	12.9	12.1	98.7
Mississippi	750	756	775	388	380	344	25.2	25.5	27.3	13.0	12.8	12.1	94.4
Missouri	1,412	1,425	1,428	855	838	755	23.5	23.8	25.5	14.2	14.0	13.5	96.0
Montana	222	224	230	151	147	121	22.3	22.6	25.5	15.2	14.8	13.4	100.9
Nebraska	460	459	450	250	247	232	25.0	25.1	26.3	13.6	13.5	13.6	98.7
Nevada	664	665	512	339	324	219	24.4	24.6	25.6	12.5	12.0	11.0	101.9
New Hampshire	280	287	310	184	178	148	21.2	21.8	25.0	14.0	13.5	12.0	97.5
New Jersey	2,043	2,065	2,088	1,208	1,186	1,113	23.2	23.5	24.8	13.7	13.5	13.2	95.1
New Mexico	519	519	509	282	272	212	24.9	25.2	28.0	13.6	13.2	11.7	97.9
New York	4,286	4,325	4,690	2,665	2,618	2,448	22.0	22.3	24.7	13.7	13.5	12.9	94.0
North Carolina	2,288	2,282	1,964	1,279	1,234	969	23.7	23.9	24.4	13.2	12.9	12.0	95.0
North Dakota	151	150	161	99	97	94	22.1	22.3	25.0	14.4	14.5	14.7	102.5
Ohio	2,693	2,731	2,888	1,648	1,622	1,508	23.3	23.7	25.4	14.3	14.1	13.3	95.5
Oklahoma	936	930	892	518	507	456	24.7	24.8	25.9	13.7	13.5	13.2	98.1
Oregon	864	866	847	553	534	438	22.3	22.6	24.7	14.3	13.9	12.8	98.0
Pennsylvania	2,761	2,792	2,922	1,982	1,959	1,919	21.7	22.0	23.8	15.6	15.4	15.6	95.2
Rhode Island	220	224	248	154	152	152	20.9	21.3	23.6	14.7	14.4	14.5	93.6
South Carolina	1,081	1,080	1,010	659	632	485	23.1	23.4	25.2	14.1	13.7	12.1	94.8
South Dakota	203	203	203	119	117	108	24.7	24.9	26.8	14.4	14.3	14.3	100.6
Tennessee	1,492	1,496	1,399	880	853	703	23.3	23.6	24.6	13.7	13.4	12.4	95.1
Texas	6,961	6,866	5,887	2,706	2,602	2,073	27.1	27.3	28.2	10.5	10.3	9.9	98.5
Utah	880	871	719	259	249	190	31.2	31.5	32.2	9.2	9.0	8.5	101.0
Vermont	126	129	148	94	91	78	20.1	20.7	24.2	15.0	14.6	12.7	97.3
Virginia	1,854	1,854	1,738	1,011	977	792	22.9	23.2	24.6	12.5	12.2	11.2	96.5
Washington	1,582	1,581	1,514	865	828	662	23.2	23.5	25.7	12.7	12.3	11.2	99.7
West Virginia	385	387	402	301	297	277	20.7	20.9	22.3	16.2	16.0	15.3	97.3
Wisconsin	1,326	1,339	1,369	793	777	703	23.2	23.6	25.5	13.9	13.7	13.1	98.6
Wyoming	135	135	129	72	70	58	23.7	24.0	26.1	12.7	12.4	11.7	104.1

[1] As of July 1 for 2011. As of April 1 for decennial census years 2010 and 2000. All years include Armed Forces stationed in area.
[2] The April 1, 2000, Population Estimates base does not reflect modifications to the Census 2000 population as documented in the Count Question Resolution program and geographic program revisions.

Table A–3.   Population, by Race and Hispanic Origin

Geographic area	All races[1]		White alone[1]		Black or African Amerian alone[1]		American Indian and Alaska Native alone[1]		Asian alone[1]		Native Hawaiian and Other Pacific Islander alone[1]	
	2011[2]	2010[3]	2011[2]	2010[3]	2011[2]	2010[3]	2011[2]	2010[3]	2011[2]	2010[3]	2011[2]	2010[3]
United States..................	311,592	308,746	243,470	223,553	40,751	38,929	3,815	2,932	15,578	14,674	692	675
Alabama..............................	4,803	4,780	3,368	3,275	1,272	1,251	33	28	57	54	5	5
Alaska.................................	723	710	490	474	26	23	107	105	40	38	8	8
Arizona...............................	6,483	6,392	5,481	4,667	290	259	340	297	195	177	17	16
Arkansas............................	2,938	2,916	2,354	2,245	458	450	28	22	40	36	7	7
California............................	37,692	37,254	27,883	21,454	2,505	2,299	637	363	5,142	4,861	185	181
Colorado	5,117	5,029	4,516	4,089	222	202	81	56	150	139	9	8
Connecticut........................	3,581	3,574	2,947	2,772	396	362	17	11	144	136	4	3
Delaware............................	907	898	651	619	199	192	6	4	30	29	1	1
District of Columbia............	618	602	262	231	313	305	3	2	23	21	1	1
Florida................................	19,058	18,801	14,959	14,109	3,142	3,000	93	71	494	455	20	19
Georgia...............................	9,815	9,688	6,198	5,787	3,045	2,950	50	32	335	314	11	10
Hawaii.................................	1,375	1,360	358	337	27	21	6	4	530	525	138	138
Idaho..................................	1,585	1,568	1,488	1,396	12	10	26	21	21	19	3	3
Illinois................................	12,869	12,831	10,042	9,178	1,906	1,866	75	44	619	587	8	7
Indiana...............................	6,517	6,484	5,656	5,468	611	591	25	18	110	102	4	4
Iowa...................................	3,062	3,046	2,848	2,782	94	89	14	11	57	53	3	2
Kansas................................	2,871	2,853	2,510	2,391	176	168	34	28	72	68	3	3
Kentucky	4,369	4,339	3,882	3,810	350	338	13	10	52	49	3	3
Louisiana	4,575	4,533	2,918	2,836	1,482	1,452	34	31	75	70	3	3
Maine..................................	1,328	1,328	1,268	1,265	17	16	9	9	14	14	(D)	(D)
Maryland.............................	5,828	5,774	3,561	3,359	1,749	1,700	31	20	338	319	6	5
Massachusetts....................	6,588	6,548	5,539	5,265	512	434	30	19	371	350	6	6
Michigan.............................	9,876	9,884	7,925	7,803	1,417	1,400	69	62	251	238	4	3
Minnesota...........................	5,345	5,304	4,646	4,524	286	274	68	61	225	214	3	3
Mississippi..........................	2,979	2,967	1,788	1,755	1,112	1,098	17	15	28	26	2	2
Missouri	6,011	5,989	5,048	4,959	704	693	31	27	103	98	7	7
Montana..............................	998	989	897	885	5	4	64	63	7	6	1	1
Nebraska............................	1,843	1,826	1,661	1,573	87	83	24	18	35	32	2	2
Nevada...............................	2,723	2,701	2,116	1,787	234	219	44	32	209	195	20	19
New Hampshire....................	1,318	1,316	1,247	1,236	17	15	4	3	30	28	1	1
New Jersey	8,821	8,792	6,540	6,029	1,289	1,205	51	29	766	726	8	8
New Mexico	2,082	2,059	1,736	1,408	52	43	210	193	32	28	3	3
New York.............................	19,465	19,378	13,910	12,741	3,401	3,074	185	107	1,518	1,420	25	24
North Carolina.....................	9,656	9,535	6,966	6,529	2,121	2,049	150	122	226	209	11	10
North Dakota.......................	684	673	618	605	9	8	38	37	7	7	(D)	(D)
Ohio....................................	11,545	11,537	9,654	9,539	1,433	1,408	30	25	202	192	6	5
Oklahoma	3,792	3,751	2,873	2,707	290	278	338	322	70	65	6	5
Oregon................................	3,872	3,831	3,429	3,205	76	69	68	53	150	141	15	15
Pennsylvania.......................	12,743	12,702	10,673	10,406	1,444	1,378	40	27	369	349	7	7
Rhode Island.......................	1,051	1,053	907	857	76	60	9	6	32	30	2	2
South Carolina	4,679	4,625	3,199	3,060	1,315	1,291	25	20	64	59	4	4
South Dakota	824	814	714	699	12	10	73	72	8	8	1	1
Tennessee	6,403	6,346	5,090	4,922	1,083	1,057	27	20	97	91	6	5
Texas..................................	25,675	25,146	20,769	17,702	3,139	2,980	263	171	1,039	965	33	31
Utah....................................	2,817	2,764	2,589	2,380	36	29	42	33	61	55	27	26
Vermont	626	626	598	596	7	6	2	2	8	8	(D)	(D)
Virginia...............................	8,097	8,001	5,773	5,487	1,600	1,551	43	29	466	440	9	8
Washington.........................	6,830	6,725	5,598	5,196	262	240	125	104	509	481	44	44
West Virginia.......................	1,855	1,853	1,745	1,740	66	63	4	4	13	12	1	0
Wisconsin	5,712	5,687	5,049	4,902	370	359	61	55	137	129	3	3
Wyoming	568	564	531	511	6	5	15	13	5	4	1	1

Note. Race numbers are in thousands, except as noted.
[1] Due to the complexities associated with the production of detailed characteristics, estimates at the state levels of geography may not necessarily sum to estimates at higher levels or geography.
[2] As of July 1 for 2011 population estimates.
[3] Population estimates for a decennial census as of April 1; and reflect changes to the Census 2010 population from the Count Question Resolution program and geographic program revisions.
(D) = Data withheld to avoid disclosure or does not meet statistical standards.

Table A–3. Population, by Race and Hispanic Origin—*Continued*

Geographic area	Two or more races[1]		Hispanic or Latino origin[1,4]		Non-Hispanic White alone[1]		Percentage of total, 2011							
	2011[2]	2010[3]	2011[2]	2010[3]	2011[2]	2010[3]	White alone	Black or African American alone	American Indian and Alaska Native alone	Asian alone	Native Hawaiian and Other Pacific Islander alone	Two or more races	Hispanic or Latino origin[4]	Non-Hispanic White alone
United States......................	7,285	6,984	52,045	50,478	197,511	197,319	78.1	13.1	1.2	5.0	0.2	2.3	16.7	63.4
Alabama...............................	67	64	194	186	3,207	3,208	70.1	26.5	0.7	1.2	0.1	1.4	4.0	66.8
Alaska.................................	51	49	42	39	461	456	67.9	3.6	14.9	5.6	1.1	7.0	5.8	63.7
Arizona................................	160	153	1,949	1,895	3,720	3,705	84.6	4.5	5.2	3.0	0.3	2.5	30.1	57.4
Arkansas.............................	52	49	195	186	2,180	2,176	80.1	15.6	0.9	1.3	0.2	1.8	6.6	74.2
California.............................	1,339	1,289	14,360	14,014	14,977	15,029	74.0	6.6	1.7	13.6	0.5	3.6	38.1	39.7
Colorado	140	132	1,071	1,039	3,568	3,529	88.3	4.3	1.6	2.9	0.2	2.7	20.9	69.7
Connecticut.........................	73	70	494	479	2,540	2,557	82.3	11.1	0.5	4.0	0.1	2.0	13.8	70.9
Delaware.............................	21	20	76	73	590	588	71.7	21.9	0.7	3.4	0.1	2.3	8.4	65.1
District of Columbia	15	14	59	55	218	210	42.4	50.7	0.6	3.7	0.1	2.5	9.5	35.3
Florida.................................	350	332	4,356	4,224	10,962	10,926	78.5	16.5	0.5	2.6	0.1	1.8	22.9	57.5
Georgia...............................	176	166	892	854	5,450	5,427	63.2	31.0	0.5	3.4	0.1	1.8	9.1	55.5
Hawaii.................................	315	314	126	121	316	311	26.0	2.0	0.4	38.5	10.1	22.9	9.2	22.9
Idaho...................................	34	32	182	176	1,325	1,318	93.9	0.8	1.7	1.3	0.2	2.1	11.5	83.6
Illinois.................................	220	211	2,080	2,028	8,147	8,182	78.0	14.8	0.6	4.8	0.1	1.7	16.2	63.3
Indiana................................	112	108	404	390	5,299	5,294	86.8	9.4	0.4	1.7	0.1	1.7	6.2	81.3
Iowa....................................	47	45	158	152	2,706	2,703	93.0	3.1	0.5	1.9	0.1	1.5	5.2	88.4
Kansas................................	76	73	310	300	2,234	2,234	87.4	6.1	1.2	2.5	0.1	2.7	10.8	77.8
Kentucky.............................	69	67	139	133	3,763	3,750	88.9	8.0	0.3	1.2	0.1	1.6	3.2	86.1
Louisiana............................	64	60	202	193	2,749	2,741	63.8	32.4	0.7	1.6	0.1	1.4	4.4	60.1
Maine..................................	20	19	18	17	1,253	1,256	95.4	1.3	0.7	1.1	(D)	1.5	1.4	94.3
Maryland..............................	143	138	491	471	3,170	3,166	61.1	30.0	0.5	5.8	0.1	2.5	8.4	54.4
Massachusetts.....................	129	123	651	628	5,033	5,037	84.1	7.8	0.5	5.6	0.1	2.0	9.9	76.4
Michigan..............................	210	203	448	436	7,546	7,580	80.2	14.3	0.7	2.5	(D)	2.1	4.5	76.4
Minnesota............................	116	111	259	250	4,425	4,411	86.9	5.4	1.3	4.2	0.1	2.2	4.9	82.8
Mississippi..........................	32	30	86	81	1,719	1,724	60.0	37.3	0.6	0.9	0.1	1.1	2.9	57.7
Missouri	117	112	221	212	4,859	4,856	84.0	11.7	0.5	1.7	0.1	1.9	3.7	80.8
Montana..............................	24	23	31	29	873	869	89.9	0.5	6.4	0.7	0.1	2.4	3.1	87.5
Nebraska.............................	34	32	175	167	1,507	1,502	90.1	4.7	1.3	1.9	0.1	1.8	9.5	81.8
Nevada................................	101	97	737	717	1,459	1,467	77.7	8.6	1.6	7.7	0.7	3.7	27.1	53.6
New Hampshire....................	20	19	39	37	1,215	1,217	94.6	1.3	0.3	2.3	(D)	1.5	2.9	92.2
New Jersey	167	160	1,601	1,555	5,194	5,238	74.1	14.6	0.6	8.7	0.1	1.9	18.1	58.9
New Mexico.........................	49	46	973	953	837	838	83.4	2.5	10.1	1.6	0.2	2.3	46.7	40.2
New York.............................	427	410	3,495	3,417	11,294	11,345	71.5	17.5	1.0	7.8	0.1	2.2	18.0	58.0
North Carolina......................	183	175	832	800	6,277	6,236	72.1	22.0	1.5	2.3	0.1	1.9	8.6	65.0
North Dakota........................	12	11	15	13	606	598	90.4	1.3	5.5	1.1	0.1	1.7	2.2	88.6
Ohio....................................	220	213	367	355	9,352	9,373	83.6	12.4	0.3	1.7	(D)	1.9	3.2	81.0
Oklahoma	215	207	348	332	2,587	2,579	75.8	7.7	8.9	1.8	0.1	5.7	9.2	68.2
Oregon................................	133	127	466	450	3,025	3,012	88.6	2.0	1.8	3.9	0.4	3.4	12.0	78.1
Pennsylvania.......................	210	202	750	720	10,092	10,109	83.8	11.3	0.3	2.9	0.1	1.6	5.9	79.2
Rhode Island.......................	25	25	135	131	804	811	86.3	7.2	0.9	3.1	0.2	2.4	12.8	76.5
South Carolina	72	68	246	236	2,994	2,968	68.4	28.1	0.5	1.4	0.1	1.5	5.3	64.0
South Dakota	17	16	24	22	695	690	86.6	1.4	8.9	1.0	0.1	2.0	2.9	84.4
Tennessee	100	96	303	290	4,830	4,807	79.5	16.9	0.4	1.5	0.1	1.6	4.7	75.4
Texas..................................	431	402	9,792	9,461	11,508	11,429	80.9	12.2	1.0	4.0	0.1	1.7	38.1	44.8
Utah....................................	62	58	373	358	2,255	2,226	91.9	1.3	1.5	2.2	1.0	2.2	13.2	80.1
Vermont	10	10	10	9	590	591	95.5	1.1	0.4	1.4	(D)	1.7	1.6	94.2
Virginia	206	197	661	632	5,222	5,199	71.3	19.8	0.5	5.8	0.1	2.5	8.2	64.5
Washington..........................	291	279	789	756	4,924	4,889	82.0	3.8	1.8	7.5	0.7	4.3	11.6	72.1
West Virginia.......................	26	25	24	22	1,725	1,728	94.1	3.5	0.2	0.7	(D)	1.4	1.3	93.0
Wisconsin............................	93	89	348	336	4,744	4,743	88.4	6.5	1.1	2.4	(D)	1.6	6.1	83.1
Wyoming	10	10	52	50	486	484	93.5	1.1	2.6	0.9	0.1	1.8	9.1	85.5

Note. Race numbers are in thousands, except as noted.
[1] Due to the complexities associated with the production of detailed characteristics, estimates at the state levels of geography may not necessarily sum to estimates at higher levels or geography.
[2] As of July 1 for 2011 population estimates.
[3] Population estimates for a decennial census as of April 1; and reflect changes to the Census 2010 population from the Count Question Resolution program and geographic program revisions.
[4] Hispanic origin is considered an ethnicity and not a race; Hispanics may be any race.
(D) = Data withheld to avoid disclosure or does not meet statistical standards.

Table A–3.   Population, by Race and Hispanic Origin—*Continued*

Geographic area	Percentage change, 2010–2011							
	White alone	Black or African American alone	American Indian and Alaska Native alone	Asian alone	Native Hawaiian and Other Pacific Islander alone	Two or more races	Hispanic or Latino origin[4]	Non-Hispanic White alone
United States.................................	8.9	4.7	30.1	6.2	2.6	4.3	3.1	0.1
Alabama..	2.8	1.6	18.0	6.6	0.4	4.6	4.5	0.0
Alaska..	3.5	11.3	2.5	5.7	2.8	3.4	7.3	0.9
Arizona...	17.4	12.0	14.5	10.3	3.0	4.8	2.9	0.4
Arkansas...	4.9	1.7	24.0	9.5	2.5	6.0	4.9	0.2
California...	30.0	8.9	75.5	5.8	2.2	3.9	2.5	-0.3
Colorado...	10.4	9.8	44.0	7.8	5.2	5.5	3.1	1.1
Connecticut.....................................	6.3	9.3	51.9	6.6	1.7	3.4	3.2	-0.7
Delaware...	5.2	3.6	45.0	6.7	3.3	3.0	4.0	0.4
District of Columbia	13.3	2.6	63.5	9.4	8.8	6.7	7.3	3.7
Florida..	6.0	4.7	30.6	8.6	5.7	5.2	3.1	0.3
Georgia...	7.1	3.2	55.9	6.5	6.8	5.9	4.5	0.4
Hawaii..	6.3	28.1	40.1	0.9	0.0	0.5	4.6	1.5
Idaho..	6.6	23.8	23.4	10.2	4.1	6.6	3.5	0.5
Illinois..	9.4	2.1	70.9	5.4	5.0	4.1	2.6	-0.4
Indiana...	3.4	3.2	35.1	7.5	3.5	3.8	3.6	0.1
Iowa...	2.4	5.5	26.7	7.1	4.4	5.2	4.3	0.1
Kansas..	5.0	5.0	20.0	6.1	0.9	4.0	3.3	0.0
Kentucky...	1.9	3.6	24.0	6.7	4.2	3.6	4.3	0.4
Louisiana..	2.9	2.0	10.0	6.5	2.7	5.9	5.0	0.3
Maine..	0.2	7.0	3.5	5.0	10.1	3.6	6.0	-0.2
Maryland...	6.0	2.9	54.0	5.9	5.0	3.9	4.3	0.1
Massachusetts................................	5.2	17.9	61.6	6.1	4.8	4.9	3.7	-0.1
Michigan...	1.6	1.2	11.1	5.4	8.0	3.5	2.6	-0.4
Minnesota.......................................	2.7	4.3	12.3	5.2	8.1	4.2	3.6	0.3
Mississippi......................................	1.9	1.2	14.7	8.3	4.8	6.9	5.1	-0.3
Missouri..	1.8	1.5	14.2	5.1	2.0	3.8	4.1	0.1
Montana..	1.4	34.1	2.4	9.9	6.3	4.7	6.8	0.4
Nebraska...	5.6	5.1	29.5	7.5	7.4	5.3	4.2	0.3
Nevada..	18.4	7.0	37.7	6.7	1.7	4.1	2.9	-0.6
New Hampshire................................	0.9	14.8	16.4	4.9	7.5	3.8	5.1	-0.2
New Jersey......................................	8.5	7.0	75.9	5.6	5.1	4.6	2.9	-0.8
New Mexico.....................................	23.3	21.8	8.9	15.0	4.6	5.8	2.1	-0.2
New York...	9.2	10.6	73.2	6.9	3.2	4.1	2.3	-0.4
North Carolina.................................	6.7	3.5	22.4	8.0	3.5	4.5	4.0	0.7
North Dakota...................................	2.1	14.3	2.6	6.6	15.9	6.5	13.7	1.2
Ohio..	1.2	1.8	19.7	5.1	3.3	3.3	3.5	-0.2
Oklahoma..	6.1	4.5	5.1	7.3	5.7	3.6	4.7	0.3
Oregon..	7.0	10.4	28.7	6.3	3.4	4.6	3.6	0.4
Pennsylvania...................................	2.6	4.8	50.6	5.6	3.2	4.0	4.3	-0.2
Rhode Island...................................	5.9	25.5	52.2	6.3	3.1	2.6	3.1	-0.8
South Carolina	4.5	1.9	27.8	8.9	1.1	5.3	4.2	0.9
South Dakota	2.0	12.9	2.0	9.3	12.6	5.4	8.6	0.8
Tennessee	3.4	2.4	34.1	6.8	4.1	4.2	4.5	0.5
Texas..	17.3	5.3	54.0	7.8	5.8	7.0	3.5	0.7
Utah..	8.8	21.8	28.0	10.7	2.8	7.3	4.1	1.3
Vermont	0.3	8.6	7.4	6.7	9.1	2.9	6.1	-0.1
Virginia...	5.2	3.1	45.7	6.0	5.5	4.6	4.6	0.5
Washington......................................	7.7	9.2	20.2	5.8	2.1	4.4	4.4	0.7
West Virginia...................................	0.3	4.3	7.9	8.5	8.5	3.1	7.3	-0.2
Wisconsin	3.0	3.1	12.1	5.7	3.2	4.5	3.6	0.0
Wyoming	4.0	26.9	10.8	12.2	5.8	6.2	3.0	0.2

Note. Race numbers are in thousands, except as noted.
[4]Hispanic origin is considered an ethnicity and not a race; Hispanics may be any race.

Table A–4. Population, by Residence

Geographic area	Inside core-based statistical area (metropolitan and micropolitan area population)[1] (thousands)						Outside core-based statistical area[1] (thousands)					Urban Population[2]			
												Number (thousands)		Percentage of total population	
	2011	2010	2000[3]	1990[4]	Percentage of total, 2010	Percentage change, 2000–2010	2011	2010	2000[3]	1990[4]	Percentage change, 2000–2010	2010	2000	2010	2000
United States............	292,139	289,261	262,299	231,020	93.7	10.3	19,453	19,484	19,125	17,779	1.9	249,253	222,361	80.7	79.0
Alabama....................	4,318	4,291	3,945	3,559	89.8	8.8	485	489	502	482	-2.6	2,822	2,466	59.0	55.4
Alaska	546	537	461	398	75.6	16.5	176	173	166	135	4.2	469	411	66.0	65.6
Arizona.....................	6,390	6,300	5,041	3,590	98.6	25.0	93	92	89	75	3.4	5,741	4,524	89.8	88.2
Arkansas	2,357	2,333	2,082	1,802	80.0	12.1	581	583	591	548	-1.4	1,638	1,404	56.2	52.5
California..................	37,435	36,995	33,629	29,594	99.3	10.0	257	258	243	218	6.2	35,374	31,990	95.0	94.4
Colorado	4,709	4,620	3,922[5]	3,013	91.9	17.8	407	409	380	306	7.6	4,333	3,633	86.2	84.4
Connecticut..............	3,581	3,574	3,406	3,287	100.0	4.9	0	0	0	0	0.0	3,145	2,988	88.0	87.7
Delaware	907	898	784	666	100.0	14.5	0	0	0	0	0.0	748	628	83.3	80.1
District of Columbia ...	618	602	572	607	100.0	5.2	0	0	0	0	0.0	602	572	100.0	100.0
Florida......................	18,637	18,380	15,620	12,645	97.8	17.7	421	421	363	293	16.0	17,140	14,270	91.2	89.3
Georgia	8,945	8,817	7,411	5,822	91.0	19.0	870	871	775	656	12.4	7,272	5,864	75.1	71.6
Hawaii	1,375	1,360	1,211	1,108	100.0	12.3	0	0	0	0	0.0	1,250	1,108	91.9	91.5
Idaho........................	1,383	1,364	1,103	846	87.0	23.7	202	203	191	161	6.3	1,106	859	70.6	66.4
Illinois	12,264	12,222	11,796	10,809	95.3	3.6	605	608	624	622	-2.6	11,354	10,910	88.5	87.8
Indiana.....................	6,149	6,116	5,715	5,198	94.3	7.0	368	368	365	346	0.8	4,697	4,304	72.4	70.8
Iowa.........................	2,258	2,240	2,090	1,939	73.5	7.2	804	807	836	838	-3.5	1,950	1,787	64.0	61.1
Kansas	2,460	2,440	2,248	2,029	85.5	8.5	411	413	440	448	-6.1	2,117	1,921	74.2	71.4
Kentucky	3,359	3,329	3,036	2,734	76.7	9.7	1,010	1,010	1,006	953	0.4	2,533	2,254	58.4	55.8
Louisiana	4,270	4,228	4,157	3,919	93.3	1.7	304	306	313	303	-2.2	3,318	3,246	73.2	72.6
Maine.......................	939	938	893	845	70.6	5.0	390	391	382	383	2.4	514	513	38.7	40.2
Maryland...................	5,745	5,690	5,218	4,708	98.6	9.0	83	83	79	73	5.1	5,034	4,559	87.2	86.1
Massachusetts..........	6,561	6,521	6,325	5,999	99.6	3.1	27	27	25	18	8.0	6,022	5,801	92.0	91.4
Michigan	9,109	9,113	9,154	8,601	92.2	-0.4	767	771	785	694	-1.8	7,370	7,419	74.6	74.6
Minnesota	4,691	4,649	4,266	3,750	87.6	9.0	654	655	653	626	0.3	3,886	3,490	73.3	70.9
Mississippi	2,346	2,331	2,196	1,969	78.6	6.1	633	636	648	606	-1.9	1,464	1,367	49.3	48.1
Missouri	5,204	5,179	4,811	4,392	86.5	7.6	807	810	786	725	3.1	4,218	3,883	70.4	69.4
Montana....................	661	654	574	495	66.1	13.9	337	335	328	304	2.1	553	488	55.9	54.1
Nebraska...................	1,493	1,476	1,339	1,198	80.8	10.2	350	351	373	381	-5.9	1,336	1,194	73.1	69.8
Nevada......................	2,673	2,651	1,950	1,157	98.1	35.9	50	50	48	44	4.2	2,544	1,829	94.2	91.5
New Hampshire.........	1,271	1,269	1,192	1,074	96.4	6.5	48	48	44	35	9.1	794	732	60.3	59.2
New Jersey	8,821	8,792	8,415	7,748	100.0	4.5	0	0	0	0	0.0	8,324	7,939	94.7	94.4
New Mexico	2,005	1,981	1,737	1,442	96.2	14.0	78	78	82	73	-4.9	1,594	1,364	77.4	75.0
New York...................	19,036	18,947	18,548	17,574	97.8	2.2	429	431	429	417	0.5	17,028	16,603	87.9	87.5
North Carolina...........	8,900	8,777	7,352	6,031	92.0	19.4	757	759	694	602	9.4	6,302	4,849	66.1	60.3
North Dakota.............	490	480	435	410	71.3	10.3	194	193	208	228	-7.2	403	359	59.9	55.9
Ohio.........................	11,032	11,023	10,849	10,377	95.5	1.6	513	514	504	470	2.0	8,990	8,782	77.9	77.4
Oklahoma	3,248	3,207	2,917	2,636	85.5	9.9	543	545	533	509	2.3	2,485	2,255	66.2	65.4
Oregon......................	3,728	3,687	3,281	2,719	96.2	12.4	144	144	140	123	2.9	3,104	2,694	81.0	78.7
Pennsylvania.............	12,355	12,314	11,898	11,518	96.9	3.5	388	388	382	365	1.6	9,991	9,464	78.7	77.1
Rhode Island.............	1,051	1,053	1,048	1,003	100.0	0.5	0	0	0	0	0.0	955	953	90.7	90.9
South Carolina	4,408	4,351	3,735	3,230	94.1	16.5	272	274	277	256	-1.1	3,068	2,427	66.3	60.5
South Dakota	604	595	527	469	73.1	12.9	220	219	228	227	-3.9	461	391	56.7	51.8
Tennessee	5,766	5,708	5,080	4,350	89.9	12.4	638	638	609	527	4.8	4,213	3,620	66.4	63.6
Texas........................	24,299	23,775	19,520	15,762	94.5	21.8	1,375	1,371	1,331	1,224	3.0	21,298	172,041	84.7	825.1
Utah.........................	2,675	2,623	2,108	1,618	94.9	24.4	142	141	126	105	11.9	2,504	1,970	90.6	88.2
Vermont	462	461	449	417	73.7	2.7	164	164	159	146	3.1	243	232	38.9	38.1
Virginia	7,263	7,166	6,269	5,434	89.6	14.3	834	835	810	755	3.1	6,037	5,170	75.5	73.0
Washington...............	6,597	6,493	5,678	4,689	96.6	14.4	233	232	216	178	7.4	5,652	4,831	84.0	82.0
West Virginia.............	1,402	1,398	1,348	1,315	75.4	3.7	453	455	460	478	-1.1	903	833	48.7	46.1
Wisconsin	4,936	4,912	4,604	4,205	86.4	6.7	776	775	759	687	2.1	3,990	3,664	70.2	68.3
Wyoming	409	405	352	320	71.9	15.1	159	159	142	133	12.0	365	321	64.8	65.0

[1]Covers metropolitan statistical areas and metropolitan divisions as defined by the Office of Management and Budget as of 2010. For information, see OMB Bulletin 10-02 at www.whitehouse.gov/sites/default/files/omb/assets/bulletins/b10-02.pdf .
[2]Resident population.
[3]The April 1, 2000, Population Estimates base reflects modifications to the Census 2000 population as documented in the Count Question Resolution program and geographic program revisions.
[4]The April 1, 1990, Census counts include corrections processed through August 1997 and results of special censuses and test censuses and do not include adjustments for census coverage errors.
[5]Colorado state total includes Broomfield city.
0 = represents zero or rounds to 0.

Table A–5.   Households

Geographic area	Total households (thousands)		Family households Total¹		Husband-wife families		Female householder, no husband present		Nonfamily households Total	Householder living alone		Households with one or more people—		People per household	
	2010	2000	Family households, total	With own children under 18 years	Total	With own children under 18 years	Total	With own children under 18 years		Total	65 years and over	under 18 years	65 years and over	2010	2000
United States	116,716	105,480	66.4	29.8	48.4	20.2	13.1	7.2	33.6	26.7	9.4	33.4	24.9	2.58	2.59
Alabama	1,884	1,737	67.8	28.6	47.9	18.5	15.3	8.1	32.2	27.4	9.9	33.1	25.5	2.48	2.49
Alaska	258	222	66.2	33.0	49.4	22.7	10.7	6.8	33.8	25.6	5.4	36.4	16.0	2.65	2.74
Arizona	2,381	1,901	66.2	29.7	48.1	19.5	12.4	7.1	33.8	26.1	9.1	33.6	26.4	2.63	2.64
Arkansas	1,147	1,043	67.6	29.0	49.5	18.9	13.4	7.7	32.4	27.1	10.1	33.0	26.2	2.47	2.49
California	12,577	11,503	68.7	33.0	49.4	23.4	13.3	6.8	31.3	23.3	8.1	37.5	24.7	2.90	2.87
Colorado	1,973	1,658	63.9	29.9	49.2	21.4	10.1	6.0	36.1	27.9	7.8	32.7	20.2	2.49	2.53
Connecticut	1,371	1,302	66.3	30.0	49.0	20.9	12.9	7.1	33.7	27.3	10.5	32.7	26.5	2.52	2.53
Delaware	342	299	67.4	28.3	48.3	18.3	14.2	7.6	32.6	25.6	9.6	32.5	27.0	2.55	2.54
District of Columbia	267	248	42.3	17.2	22.0	7.9	16.4	7.9	57.7	44.0	9.7	20.7	20.4	2.11	2.16
Florida	7,421	6,338	65.2	26.0	46.6	16.6	13.5	7.1	34.8	27.2	11.1	29.8	31.4	2.48	2.46
Georgia	3,586	3,006	68.5	32.3	47.8	21.1	15.8	8.9	31.5	25.4	7.5	36.8	21.2	2.63	2.65
Hawaii	455	403	68.9	27.7	50.5	20.1	12.6	5.2	31.1	23.3	8.1	34.3	30.3	2.89	2.92
Idaho	579	470	69.6	32.7	55.3	24.0	9.6	5.9	30.4	23.8	8.8	35.7	23.9	2.66	2.69
Illinois	4,837	4,592	65.8	30.1	48.2	21.0	12.9	6.9	34.2	27.8	9.7	33.5	24.2	2.59	2.63
Indiana	2,502	2,336	66.9	29.8	49.6	19.9	12.4	7.3	33.1	26.9	9.5	33.3	23.9	2.52	2.53
Iowa	1,222	1,149	64.7	28.4	51.2	20.0	9.3	5.9	35.3	28.4	11.0	30.6	25.5	2.41	2.46
Kansas	1,112	1,038	66.0	30.4	51.1	21.3	10.4	6.5	34.0	27.8	10.0	33.2	23.7	2.49	2.51
Kentucky	1,720	1,591	66.9	28.7	49.3	19.1	12.7	7.1	33.1	27.5	9.8	32.6	24.4	2.45	2.47
Louisiana	1,728	1,656	67.1	29.5	44.4	17.6	17.2	9.3	32.9	26.9	9.0	34.7	23.7	2.55	2.62
Maine	557	518	62.9	25.4	48.5	16.7	10.0	6.0	37.1	28.6	11.3	27.8	27.1	2.32	2.39
Maryland	2,156	1,981	67.1	30.2	47.6	20.4	14.6	7.6	32.9	26.1	8.8	34.3	23.9	2.61	2.61
Massachusetts	2,547	2,444	63.0	28.3	46.3	19.7	12.5	6.8	37.0	28.7	10.7	30.8	25.6	2.48	2.51
Michigan	3,873	3,786	66.0	28.6	48.0	18.9	13.2	7.3	34.0	27.9	10.2	31.6	25.4	2.49	2.56
Minnesota	2,087	1,895	64.6	29.5	50.8	21.2	9.5	5.9	35.4	28.0	9.7	31.6	22.8	2.48	2.52
Mississippi	1,116	1,046	69.0	30.1	45.4	17.8	18.5	10.0	31.0	26.3	9.5	35.8	25.1	2.58	2.63
Missouri	2,376	2,195	65.3	28.5	48.4	18.9	12.3	7.1	34.7	28.3	10.1	31.8	25.0	2.45	2.48
Montana	410	359	62.8	25.9	49.2	17.8	9.0	5.4	37.2	29.7	10.7	28.4	25.6	2.35	2.45
Nebraska	721	666	64.8	29.7	50.8	21.2	9.8	6.2	35.2	28.7	10.5	32.0	23.9	2.46	2.49
Nevada	1,006	751	65.3	30.0	46.0	19.6	12.7	7.0	34.7	25.7	8.0	33.9	24.0	2.65	2.62
New Hampshire	519	475	66.3	28.6	52.1	20.4	9.7	5.7	33.7	25.6	9.2	31.0	24.4	2.46	2.53
New Jersey	3,214	3,065	69.3	31.9	51.1	23.3	13.3	6.6	30.7	25.2	10.1	35.0	26.9	2.68	2.68
New Mexico	791	678	65.5	29.1	45.3	17.9	14.0	7.8	34.5	28.0	9.3	33.7	25.3	2.55	2.63
New York	7,318	7,057	63.5	28.3	43.6	18.7	14.9	7.5	36.5	29.1	10.5	31.7	26.3	2.57	2.61
North Carolina	3,745	3,132	66.7	29.6	48.4	19.6	13.7	7.8	33.3	27.0	9.1	33.3	23.9	2.48	2.49
North Dakota	281	257	60.8	26.1	48.6	18.6	8.2	5.2	39.2	31.5	11.0	27.9	23.9	2.30	2.41
Ohio	4,603	4,446	65.0	28.1	47.2	18.2	13.1	7.5	35.0	28.9	10.4	31.3	25.3	2.44	2.49
Oklahoma	1,460	1,342	66.8	29.4	49.5	19.7	12.3	7.0	33.2	27.5	9.9	33.3	25.0	2.49	2.49
Oregon	1,519	1,334	63.4	27.3	48.3	18.7	10.5	6.1	36.6	27.4	9.8	30.1	25.3	2.47	2.51
Pennsylvania	5,019	4,777	65.0	26.9	48.2	18.3	12.2	6.5	35.0	28.6	11.4	29.9	27.9	2.45	2.48
Rhode Island	414	408	62.8	27.4	44.5	17.6	13.5	7.7	37.2	29.6	11.3	30.1	26.6	2.44	2.47
South Carolina	1,801	1,534	67.5	28.3	47.2	17.7	15.6	8.4	32.5	26.5	9.3	32.8	25.5	2.49	2.53
South Dakota	322	290	64.2	28.5	50.1	19.7	9.7	6.2	35.8	29.4	10.9	31.1	24.9	2.42	2.50
Tennessee	2,494	2,233	67.3	28.4	48.7	18.7	13.9	7.5	32.7	26.9	9.3	32.6	24.9	2.48	2.48
Texas	8,923	7,393	69.9	34.2	50.6	23.7	14.1	8.0	30.1	24.2	7.1	38.9	21.2	2.75	2.74
Utah	878	701	75.2	39.5	61.0	31.7	9.7	5.5	24.8	18.7	6.4	43.3	20.0	3.10	3.13
Vermont	256	241	62.5	26.2	48.5	17.6	9.6	6.0	37.5	28.2	10.3	28.3	25.4	2.34	2.44
Virginia	3,056	2,699	67.0	29.9	50.2	21.1	12.4	6.7	33.0	26.0	8.5	33.4	23.3	2.54	2.54
Washington	2,620	2,271	64.4	29.1	49.2	20.4	10.5	6.2	35.6	27.2	8.7	31.9	22.8	2.51	2.53
West Virginia	764	736	65.8	25.0	49.8	17.0	11.2	5.7	34.2	28.4	11.6	28.6	28.5	2.36	2.40
Wisconsin	2,280	2,085	64.4	28.4	49.6	19.4	10.3	6.4	35.6	28.2	10.2	30.6	24.0	2.43	2.50
Wyoming	227	194	64.6	28.1	50.9	19.6	8.9	5.6	35.4	28.0	8.8	30.9	22.0	2.42	2.48

¹ Total includes male householder with no wife present (not shown separately).

Table A–6.   Marital Status, 2010

Geographic area	Males 15 years and over						Females 15 years and over					
	Total (thousands)	Percentage					Total (thousands)	Percentage				
		Never married	Now married, except separated[1]	Separated[2]	Widowed	Divorced		Never married	Now married, except separated[1]	Separated[2]	Widowed	Divorced
United States..................	120,743	35.4	50.5	1.9	2.5	9.6	127,313	29.0	47.1	2.5	9.3	12.1
Alabama............................	1,845	32.5	50.6	2.5	3.0	11.4	2,004	26.1	45.9	3.1	11.2	13.6
Alaska	291	35.5	49.7	1.7	1.8	11.4	268	27.3	50.2	2.6	6.1	13.7
Arizona............................	2,493	35.3	50.1	1.4	2.5	10.7	2,559	28.0	48.0	2.2	8.3	13.5
Arkansas..........................	1,129	29.5	53.3	2.2	3.1	12.0	1,201	23.5	48.8	2.9	11.2	13.6
California..........................	14,662	39.8	48.2	1.9	2.1	8.0	15,043	32.3	45.7	2.7	8.1	11.2
Colorado	2,004	34.4	51.7	1.6	2.0	10.3	2,017	26.9	50.8	2.0	7.0	13.3
Connecticut......................	1,399	36.3	50.6	1.1	2.7	9.3	1,512	29.9	46.5	1.8	9.3	12.5
Delaware	350	35.3	50.4	1.9	2.9	9.4	381	30.8	45.3	2.0	9.8	12.1
District of Columbia	243	58.9	28.2	2.4	2.1	8.4	277	55.8	22.8	3.1	7.5	10.8
Florida..............................	7,535	33.9	49.3	2.2	3.2	11.5	8,021	26.6	45.1	3.0	10.8	14.5
Georgia	3,683	35.4	50.5	2.1	2.2	9.9	3,955	29.7	46.1	2.9	8.6	12.7
Hawaii	554	37.8	49.1	1.2	2.7	9.2	557	28.7	48.5	1.8	10.1	11.0
Idaho................................	602	28.3	57.0	1.4	2.4	10.9	609	22.4	55.3	1.6	7.6	13.1
Illinois..............................	4,978	37.2	50.0	1.4	2.6	8.8	5,290	31.1	46.3	2.1	9.5	11.0
Indiana.............................	2,514	32.6	52.3	1.1	2.5	11.4	2,644	26.7	49.1	1.8	9.2	13.2
Iowa.................................	1,200	31.3	55.2	1.1	2.6	9.7	1,251	24.7	52.4	1.5	10.2	11.2
Kansas.............................	1,106	31.6	53.9	1.4	2.6	10.5	1,145	25.1	51.4	1.7	9.2	12.6
Kentucky..........................	1,702	30.8	52.0	2.1	2.8	12.3	1,794	24.2	48.9	2.6	10.6	13.7
Louisiana	1,752	37.0	47.2	2.2	2.8	10.8	1,861	30.8	42.6	3.2	10.1	13.3
Maine...............................	534	31.0	52.5	1.2	2.9	12.5	570	24.2	49.3	1.6	9.9	15.0
Maryland...........................	2,232	36.8	50.2	2.3	2.7	8.0	2,442	32.2	45.3	2.9	9.0	10.7
Massachusetts..................	2,579	38.7	49.1	1.6	2.7	8.0	2,820	33.2	44.1	2.4	9.1	11.1
Michigan	3,875	34.9	50.5	1.3	2.7	10.6	4,099	29.0	47.2	1.6	9.7	12.5
Minnesota.........................	2,091	34.6	53.5	0.9	2.2	8.7	2,155	28.2	51.5	1.2	8.4	10.7
Mississippi........................	1,121	34.9	48.3	2.5	2.7	11.7	1,224	29.8	43.8	3.4	10.8	12.3
Missouri...........................	2,333	32.1	52.5	1.7	2.6	11.0	2,492	26.8	48.2	2.2	10.0	12.8
Montana...........................	404	30.5	53.4	1.5	2.3	12.4	404	23.5	52.9	1.6	9.7	12.3
Nebraska..........................	709	32.4	54.0	1.4	2.3	9.9	736	25.3	52.7	1.5	9.5	10.9
Nevada.............................	1,082	35.0	47.6	2.0	2.9	12.5	1,069	27.2	47.2	2.8	8.0	14.8
New Hampshire.................	529	30.5	54.7	1.3	2.6	10.9	556	25.4	51.4	1.3	8.6	13.4
New Jersey	3,419	36.4	52.1	1.8	2.6	7.1	3,691	30.2	47.6	2.2	10.2	9.8
New Mexico	802	35.4	48.4	1.6	2.6	11.9	833	29.9	45.0	2.6	8.5	14.1
New York..........................	7,587	40.5	47.6	2.2	2.6	7.2	8,284	34.8	42.8	3.1	9.6	9.7
North Carolina...................	3,679	33.3	51.8	2.9	2.5	9.6	3,976	27.3	47.3	3.5	9.8	12.1
North Dakota.....................	278	35.8	53.1	0.6	2.1	8.4	271	26.6	52.5	0.7	10.1	10.2
Ohio.................................	4,488	33.5	51.2	1.7	2.9	10.8	4,810	27.9	46.9	2.1	10.1	12.9
Oklahoma.........................	1,458	30.7	52.2	1.8	3.0	12.3	1,522	23.8	49.7	2.7	10.1	13.7
Oregon.............................	1,533	32.6	51.4	1.6	2.7	11.8	1,588	25.8	48.9	1.9	8.5	14.9
Pennsylvania.....................	5,032	35.9	50.6	2.0	3.1	8.5	5,406	29.8	46.2	2.7	11.2	10.2
Rhode Island.....................	415	39.8	45.2	1.6	3.1	10.3	456	32.4	41.8	2.4	10.4	13.0
South Carolina	1,797	35.2	49.4	3.0	2.8	9.5	1,939	29.1	45.2	3.9	10.6	11.2
South Dakota	323	33.5	52.5	0.9	2.8	10.3	326	26.0	52.1	1.0	9.5	11.4
Tennessee........................	2,462	31.4	52.2	2.1	2.7	11.7	2,653	25.3	47.9	2.7	10.3	13.7
Texas...............................	9,587	34.6	51.6	2.3	2.2	9.4	9,903	27.6	48.5	3.3	8.1	12.5
Utah.................................	1,015	31.3	58.0	1.3	1.8	7.6	1,019	25.8	56.6	1.6	5.8	10.1
Vermont	254	34.2	51.3	1.3	2.5	10.7	267	27.7	49.7	1.4	8.2	13.0
Virginia	3,156	34.2	52.6	2.3	2.3	8.5	3,331	28.0	49.0	2.9	8.7	11.4
Washington.......................	2,687	33.8	52.0	1.6	2.1	10.5	2,746	26.4	50.6	2.1	7.8	13.2
West Virginia.....................	751	30.3	52.1	1.6	3.4	12.6	785	22.6	49.7	1.7	12.8	13.2
Wisconsin.........................	2,261	34.1	52.1	1.0	2.6	10.2	2,329	28.1	50.1	1.2	9.2	11.4
Wyoming	229	29.0	56.2	1.3	2.4	11.2	220	20.7	55.1	2.0	8.6	13.6

[1] Includes people whose current marriage has not ended through widowhood, divorce, or separation (regardless of previous marital history). The category may also include couples who live together or people in common-law marriages, if they consider this category the most appropriate. In certain tabulations currently married people are further classified as "spouse present" or "spouse absent." For federal definitions, "now married" does not include same-sex married people even when the marriage was performed in a state issuing marriage certificates for same-sex couples.
[2] Includes people legally separated or otherwise absent from their spouse because of marital discord. Those without a final divorce decree are classified as "separated." This category also includes people who have been deserted or who have parted because they no longer want to live together but who have not obtained a divorce.

Table A–7.   Residence One Year Ago, People Obtaining Legal Permanent Resident Status, and Language Spoken at Home

Geographic area	Residence 1 year ago, 2011		People obtaining legal permanent resident status											Language spoken at home, population 5 years old and over in the United States, 2011		
	Population 1 year old and over (thousands)	Percentage of population who lived in same house 1 year ago	Total			Leading countries of birth, 2011								All languages other than English		Spanish (thousands)
			2011	2010	2000	Mexico	China	India	Phillippines	Dominican Republic	Cuba	Vietnam	Total (thousands)	Percentage of population	
United States................	307,900	84.8	1,062,040	1,042,625	841,002	143,446	87,016	69,013	57,011	46,109	36,452	34,157	60,577	20.8	37,580
Alabama.........................	4,745	84.8	4,063	3,740	1,894	375	317	317	242	18	39	178	236	5.2	154
Alaska..........................	712	80.3	1,799	1,703	1,364	70	47	21	690	98	5	25	111	16.6	25
Arizona.........................	6,402	79.8	20,333	18,243	11,935	8,347	687	988	842	61	267	602	1,630	27.0	1,243
Arkansas.......................	2,907	83.3	2,874	2,684	1,594	946	171	278	151	7	8	125	205	7.5	149
California.......................	37,223	83.9	210,591	208,446	216,447	49,774	23,117	15,061	22,797	146	354	12,213	15,390	43.8	10,125
Colorado.......................	5,048	80.2	13,547	12,489	8,167	3,372	734	481	337	25	71	503	799	16.7	559
Connecticut...................	3,549	88.5	12,577	12,222	11,263	263	734	1,108	300	779	53	140	724	21.4	368
Delaware	897	86.4	2,355	2,198	1,563	158	222	362	126	58	14	26	116	13.6	61
District of Columbia.......	612	80.1	2,724	2,897	2,528	53	122	48	59	87	9	25	88	15.0	42
Florida..........................	18,864	83.5	109,229	107,276	94,474	3,434	1,910	1,855	2,274	3,248	29,700	1,384	4,959	27.6	3,647
Georgia	9,700	83.5	27,015	24,833	14,707	2,763	1,260	2,311	423	236	254	1,113	1,215	13.3	715
Hawaii..........................	1,358	85.5	7,296	7,037	6,047	53	864	19	4,399	3	0	158	324	25.2	27
Idaho............................	1,560	82.4	2,602	2,556	1,914	715	134	89	114	(D)	(D)	33	153	10.4	115
Illinois..........................	12,718	87.1	38,325	37,909	36,052	7,334	2,816	4,532	2,260	146	120	574	2,730	22.7	1,614
Indiana.........................	6,437	85.1	8,262	8,539	4,105	1,198	561	643	350	96	22	146	502	8.2	283
Iowa.............................	3,028	85.0	4,624	4,245	3,035	780	245	242	127	15	14	277	208	7.3	114
Kansas.........................	2,834	83.7	5,086	5,501	4,554	1,348	273	308	166	26	59	318	304	11.4	198
Kentucky.......................	4,316	85.4	5,403	4,930	2,902	382	302	269	148	18	561	115	197	4.8	98
Louisiana	4,519	85.5	4,226	4,397	2,981	337	337	221	232	121	115	401	372	8.7	157
Maine...........................	1,316	85.1	1,467	1,349	1,123	10	124	54	72	10	4	32	84	6.6	13
Maryland.......................	5,759	87.0	25,778	26,450	17,565	450	1,494	1,744	1,372	436	37	485	914	16.7	379
Massachusetts..............	6,515	86.9	32,236	31,069	23,302	202	2,959	2,139	335	3,889	48	1,033	1,370	22.0	498
Michigan.......................	9,767	85.4	18,347	18,579	16,655	1,113	1,010	1,602	524	95	99	387	847	9.1	265
Minnesota.....................	5,277	85.4	12,389	12,408	8,554	779	578	767	284	27	24	593	541	10.8	196
Mississippi....................	2,943	86.1	1,666	1,709	1,074	265	128	154	119	23	11	144	105	3.8	62
Missouri........................	5,938	83.6	7,048	7,151	5,988	617	516	525	341	34	180	303	362	6.4	152
Montana........................	987	83.9	511	457	488	27	49	18	60	0	0	18	44	4.7	15
Nebraska.......................	1,817	82.8	4,535	4,400	2,201	911	162	139	91	18	186	280	176	10.3	116
Nevada.........................	2,688	77.5	10,449	10,803	7,757	2,444	689	221	1,950	57	690	157	755	29.7	529
New Hampshire..............	1,306	87.4	2,478	2,556	1,992	42	126	231	74	122	8	87	97	7.8	27
New Jersey	8,720	89.7	55,547	56,920	39,778	861	2,503	8,341	2,352	7,229	798	466	2,521	30.4	1,288
New Mexico	2,055	85.3	3,767	3,528	3,951	1,981	137	96	204	6	104	147	708	36.5	561
New York.......................	19,249	88.6	148,426	147,999	105,521	1,784	27,358	4,805	2,527	22,154	442	547	5,507	30.1	2,699
North Carolina...............	9,539	84.6	17,571	16,112	9,193	1,996	1,119	1,325	587	292	167	952	966	10.7	655
North Dakota.................	675	82.9	948	1,058	414	19	34	37	42	7	0	20	32	5.1	9
Ohio.............................	11,419	85.5	13,857	13,585	9,201	558	1,065	1,557	525	156	43	235	722	6.7	240
Oklahoma	3,743	82.5	4,503	4,627	4,550	1,251	276	281	196	24	27	311	329	9.3	223
Oregon.........................	3,829	81.7	7,694	7,997	8,479	1,462	722	487	363	18	81	643	540	14.9	324
Pennsylvania.................	12,610	88.0	25,397	24,130	17,970	838	2,227	2,396	584	2,024	170	940	1,238	10.3	518
Rhode Island.................	1,040	86.9	3,681	4,027	2,513	51	134	78	61	1,028	0	15	211	21.2	107
South Carolina	4,624	84.3	4,216	4,401	2,253	467	294	301	236	57	30	150	289	6.6	187
South Dakota................	814	84.6	1,337	987	445	42	51	37	56	3	6	22	50	6.6	18
Tennessee.....................	6,333	84.4	8,279	8,156	4,837	887	510	613	257	43	108	228	415	6.9	246
Texas............................	25,327	82.9	94,481	87,750	63,391	36,648	3,365	5,907	2,475	285	1,137	4,546	8,221	34.7	6,989
Utah.............................	2,770	82.9	6,426	6,085	3,667	1,422	298	141	164	28	13	176	380	14.9	258
Vermont	621	86.5	943	867	802	3	51	51	26	6	0	16	29	4.9	6
Virginia.........................	7,997	84.9	27,767	28,607	19,985	802	1,405	2,909	1,385	180	127	902	1,132	14.9	511
Washington...................	6,748	82.5	23,789	22,283	18,245	2,446	1,962	2,168	2,025	24	61	1,838	1,187	18.6	518
West Virginia.................	1,837	87.6	830	729	569	28	74	54	65	15	0	20	40	2.3	16
Wisconsin.....................	5,647	85.8	6,245	6,189	5,034	1,146	431	647	226	59	21	91	468	8.7	236
Wyoming	561	82.4	420	452	247	107	27	19	21	0	(D)	7	34	6.4	26

0 = zero.
(D) = Figure withheld to avoid disclosure pertaining to a specific organization or individual.

Table A–8. Place of Birth, 2011

Geographic area	Total population (thousands)	Percentage			Foreign born											
		Born in state of residence	Born in different state	Foreign born	Total (thousands)	Not a citizen	Entered the U.S. in 2000 or later	Europe	Asia					Latin America		
									Total	China	India	Philippines	Vietnam	Total	Mexico	El Salvador
United States.............	311,592	58.9	26.8	13.0	40,378	55.1	25.7	12.1	28.6	5.5	4.6	4.5	3.1	52.6	28.9	3.1
Alabama......................	4,803	70.2	25.6	3.4	163	64.6	17.9	11.8	26.7	3.9	4.5	3.3	3.6	54.9	39.0	2.7
Alaska	723	39.8	50.9	7.1	52	48.4	27.2	21.1	52.0	3.7	1.3	26.1	1.4	16.1	6.9	1.2
Arizona......................	6,483	38.4	47.0	13.4	872	62.4	22.5	10.1	17.8	2.8	2.7	2.8	2.2	65.3	58.7	0.9
Arkansas	2,938	61.2	33.8	4.4	129	71.8	18.7	7.3	21.2	3.9	2.8	2.9	2.9	64.4	47.9	8.9
California...................	37,692	54.3	17.5	27.0	10,195	53.2	24.7	6.5	36.6	7.5	3.7	8.0	4.8	53.4	41.8	4.2
Colorado	5,117	42.4	46.6	9.7	495	64.1	21.6	13.7	21.6	3.2	2.8	2.1	3.3	55.9	48.0	1.5
Connecticut................	3,581	55.5	27.5	13.4	478	50.6	25.5	27.6	23.3	4.4	6.6	2.2	1.3	41.0	5.2	1.6
Delaware	907	45.4	44.4	8.4	76	57.4	33.1	15.2	30.0	6.4	11.6	2.6	0.9	41.1	19.6	0.2
District of Columbia	618	38.2	46.6	13.5	84	62.2	19.8	20.3	18.8	3.7	1.9	1.8	1.3	44.9	3.3	16.3
Florida......................	19,058	35.5	41.8	19.4	3,703	50.3	31.3	10.4	10.0	1.3	1.8	1.8	1.4	75.0	7.8	1.2
Georgia	9,815	55.8	33.2	9.6	943	60.4	26.2	8.9	26.8	4.2	5.6	1.7	3.9	54.0	28.9	2.8
Hawaii.......................	1,375	54.6	24.7	17.9	246	44.1	29.1	5.0	78.6	10.2	0.2	45.6	3.0	4.4	1.9	0.2
Idaho........................	1,585	46.5	46.4	6.0	95	67.5	19.9	13.9	19.5	4.3	2.7	0.8	0.3	58.6	54.6	0.7
Illinois......................	12,869	67.0	18.1	14.0	1,799	53.5	21.7	20.8	27.4	4.1	7.1	4.7	1.2	47.6	39.5	0.5
Indiana......................	6,517	68.9	25.7	4.7	307	64.9	23.5	14.4	29.4	6.6	7.1	2.3	1.4	48.1	37.2	1.9
Iowa.........................	3,062	72.5	22.7	4.4	134	62.4	33.5	15.7	33.6	5.2	7.3	2.0	3.9	39.9	28.8	3.1
Kansas	2,871	59.0	33.2	6.9	199	66.1	30.8	7.5	30.0	4.6	5.0	2.6	6.2	54.9	43.4	2.4
Kentucky	4,369	70.1	25.9	3.2	140	64.4	25.7	15.4	32.9	4.9	6.7	1.8	3.0	38.4	21.0	1.8
Louisiana	4,575	78.0	17.7	3.8	174	59.9	20.8	10.1	32.1	4.7	3.6	3.3	11.5	52.5	18.0	2.4
Maine.......................	1,328	64.3	31.4	3.2	43	44.3	22.2	24.0	26.1	4.4	2.6	5.0	2.6	9.3	1.5	0.2
Maryland...................	5,828	48.0	36.8	13.9	812	54.1	28.4	10.4	32.4	6.1	6.0	4.9	2.2	40.2	4.0	11.5
Massachusetts...........	6,588	62.9	19.6	14.9	983	49.0	32.4	23.3	29.3	8.3	4.8	1.1	3.9	35.7	1.2	3.1
Michigan	9,876	76.6	16.5	6.1	604	49.1	26.7	24.1	46.1	5.4	8.0	3.5	2.4	18.5	11.4	0.6
Minnesota..................	5,345	68.6	23.6	7.3	389	54.1	20.4	11.8	35.8	4.8	5.3	1.9	4.3	28.1	16.7	1.2
Mississippi................	2,979	71.5	25.9	2.2	65	67.9	22.6	9.6	31.0	5.5	5.5	4.4	9.2	53.3	35.7	1.1
Missouri....................	6,011	66.2	29.1	4.0	243	58.4	21.9	22.1	36.0	7.2	6.2	3.6	3.8	30.8	19.4	1.5
Montana....................	998	55.5	41.8	2.0	20	51.8	13.5	31.5	24.3	3.9	1.5	7.4	0.8	10.5	6.3	0.0
Nebraska...................	1,843	65.8	27.3	6.3	116	64.5	15.7	7.6	27.0	3.6	2.6	1.3	6.6	57.0	41.1	3.7
Nevada.....................	2,723	25.3	53.9	19.2	522	59.1	22.8	8.3	28.1	3.8	1.3	12.3	2.2	58.9	45.8	4.1
New Hampshire..........	1,318	42.5	50.6	5.6	74	48.2	23.7	25.8	34.8	5.3	9.0	2.1	2.3	20.3	4.3	0.8
New Jersey	8,821	52.1	23.9	21.5	1,893	49.3	22.7	17.1	31.3	4.9	11.1	4.6	1.1	46.1	6.7	2.3
New Mexico	2,082	52.2	36.6	10.1	211	67.6	20.8	7.7	10.1	2.0	2.2	1.7	0.7	79.5	71.4	0.9
New York...................	19,465	63.6	11.7	22.2	4,318	48.2	21.0	18.0	27.2	9.5	3.4	2.0	0.6	49.2	5.8	2.4
North Carolina............	9,656	58.0	33.6	7.3	708	66.9	25.5	11.1	22.6	3.6	6.1	1.3	2.8	58.1	34.7	4.9
North Dakota..............	684	67.7	29.3	2.4	17	64.9	15.7	16.0	43.7	7.5	5.9	5.5	6.5	8.3	4.3	0.0
Ohio.........................	11,545	75.1	20.2	4.0	456	50.5	25.2	25.2	38.3	7.6	10.1	3.0	2.4	20.6	11.0	1.1
Oklahoma	3,792	61.1	32.5	5.5	209	66.3	23.4	8.3	25.4	3.0	3.5	2.2	6.6	59.3	50.2	0.9
Oregon	3,872	46.2	43.0	9.8	378	62.0	18.7	15.0	29.4	6.3	3.3	2.8	4.9	46.8	40.3	0.9
Pennsylvania..............	12,743	74.0	18.6	5.9	756	47.7	28.4	24.1	37.5	7.6	9.0	2.6	5.1	29.5	7.1	0.8
Rhode Island..............	1,051	58.5	25.8	13.5	142	49.9	27.4	23.2	17.4	3.8	3.5	1.9	0.4	46.0	2.7	1.4
South Carolina	4,679	59.4	34.9	4.7	222	66.3	26.0	18.3	22.2	3.5	4.3	4.0	2.2	53.7	33.0	1.3
South Dakota	824	64.7	32.1	2.7	22	69.6	24.6	15.0	29.1	5.6	4.3	3.3	0.8	33.8	20.2	1.1
Tennessee	6,403	61.4	33.0	4.8	307	65.4	22.5	12.7	27.0	3.3	6.3	2.3	2.7	47.6	31.7	3.4
Texas.......................	25,675	60.6	21.8	16.4	4,202	66.8	28.6	4.5	18.5	2.6	3.9	2.1	3.6	72.2	59.6	4.3
Utah.........................	2,817	61.7	28.9	8.4	238	63.8	27.9	11.5	16.7	2.7	1.7	1.7	3.1	61.5	44.2	3.3
Vermont	626	50.7	44.5	3.9	24	38.8	11.1	30.3	25.6	5.7	1.0	1.4	4.8	12.3	2.7	0.0
Virginia	8,097	50.3	37.0	11.1	900	53.0	24.9	11.4	40.7	3.8	8.0	5.7	4.8	36.4	6.2	10.8
Washington................	6,830	47.3	37.7	13.3	909	54.1	23.9	17.2	39.8	7.0	4.9	7.0	6.4	30.7	25.8	1.1
West Virginia..............	1,855	71.0	27.3	1.3	24	55.5	12.1	24.4	41.7	7.1	9.3	3.7	3.3	22.6	10.6	0.6
Wisconsin..................	5,712	71.8	22.7	4.7	270	55.7	28.7	19.9	32.4	5.3	6.1	2.4	1.0	39.4	33.3	0.5
Wyoming	568	40.7	55.3	3.2	18	67.5	25.8	11.9	17.1	5.0	4.0	2.9	0.4	62.1	52.8	0.1

Table A–9.   Live Births and Birth Rates

Geographic area	Total			Rate[2]			Percentage with low birth weight[3]			Percentage to teenage mothers[4]			Percentage to unmarried women		
	2011, preliminary[1]	2010	2000	2011	2010	2000	2011	2010	2000	2011	2010	2000	2011	2010	2000
United States..............	3,953,593	3,999,386	4,058,814	12.7	13.0	14.4	8.1	8.1	7.6	8.3	9.3	11.8	40.7	40.8	33.2
Alabama......................	59,347	60,050	63,299	12.4	12.6	14.2	9.9	10.3	9.7	11.1	10.5	15.7	42.1	41.9	34.3
Alaska	11,455	11,471	9,974	15.8	16.2	15.9	6.0	5.7	5.6	7.7	8.0	11.8	36.8	37.6	33.0
Arizona.......................	85,543	87,477	85,273	13.2	13.7	16.6	7.0	7.1	7.0	9.8	7.9	14.3	44.7	44.9	39.3
Arkansas....................	38,713	38,540	37,783	13.2	13.2	14.1	9.1	8.8	8.6	12.5	10.9	17.3	44.9	45.3	35.7
California....................	502,118	510,198	531,959	13.3	13.7	15.7	6.8	6.8	6.2	7.6	8.6	10.6	40.4	40.5	32.7
Colorado	65,055	66,355	65,438	12.7	13.2	15.2	8.7	8.8	8.4	7.3	6.1	11.7	23.7	23.9	25.0
Connecticut.................	37,280	37,708	43,026	10.4	10.6	12.6	7.7	8.0	7.4	5.4	5.2	7.8	38.0	37.4	29.3
Delaware	11,257	11,364	11,051	12.4	12.7	14.1	8.4	8.9	8.6	8.0	6.9	12.3	48.7	47.4	37.9
District of Columbia	9,314	9,165	7,666	15.1	15.2	13.4	10.5	10.2	11.9	9.4	14.7	14.2	53.5	54.8	60.3
Florida.......................	213,344	214,590	204,125	11.2	11.4	12.8	8.7	8.7	8.0	8.0	7.4	12.6	47.6	47.5	38.2
Georgia......................	132,488	133,947	132,644	13.5	13.8	16.2	9.4	9.7	8.6	9.8	8.6	13.9	45.4	45.8	37.0
Hawaii........................	18,957	18,988	17,551	13.8	14.0	14.5	8.2	8.3	7.5	6.3	7.0	10.3	37.5	37.8	32.2
Idaho.........................	22,305	23,198	20,366	14.1	14.8	15.7	6.1	6.8	6.7	7.1	5.8	11.6	26.8	26.5	21.6
Illinois.......................	161,312	165,200	185,036	12.5	12.9	14.9	8.2	8.3	7.9	8.1	9.0	11.4	40.0	40.5	34.5
Indiana......................	83,702	83,940	87,699	12.8	12.9	14.4	8.1	8.0	7.4	9.5	8.9	12.5	42.8	43.0	34.7
Iowa..........................	38,213	38,719	38,266	12.5	12.7	13.1	6.5	7.0	6.1	7.0	6.7	10.0	33.8	34.2	28.0
Kansas	39,642	40,649	39,666	13.8	14.2	14.8	7.2	7.1	6.9	8.8	8.0	12.0	37.3	37.8	29.0
Kentucky	55,377	55,784	56,029	12.7	12.9	13.9	9.1	9.0	8.2	11.0	10.4	14.1	41.5	41.2	31.0
Louisiana	61,889	62,379	67,898	13.5	13.8	15.2	10.9	10.7	10.3	11.3	12.7	17.0	52.9	53.3	45.6
Maine.........................	12,704	12,970	13,603	9.6	9.8	10.7	6.7	6.3	6.0	6.8	6.8	9.4	41.8	41.2	31.0
Maryland....................	73,086	73,801	74,316	12.5	12.8	14.0	8.9	8.8	8.6	6.6	6.5	9.9	41.2	41.9	34.6
Massachusetts.............	73,225	72,865	81,614	11.1	11.1	12.9	7.6	7.7	7.1	4.8	4.9	6.6	34.6	34.7	26.5
Michigan.....................	114,004	114,531	136,171	11.5	11.6	13.7	8.3	8.4	7.9	8.5	9.8	10.5	42.3	41.8	33.3
Minnesota...................	68,411	68,610	67,604	12.8	12.9	13.7	6.4	6.4	6.1	5.1	4.7	8.3	32.7	33.2	25.8
Mississippi..................	39,856	40,036	44,075	13.4	13.5	15.5	11.8	12.1	10.7	13.4	14.4	18.8	54.4	54.8	46.0
Missouri.....................	76,117	76,759	76,463	12.7	12.8	13.7	7.9	8.2	7.8	9.1	8.7	13.1	40.1	40.2	34.6
Montana.....................	12,069	12,060	10,957	12.1	12.2	12.1	7.2	7.5	6.2	7.7	7.9	11.6	36.5	36.4	30.8
Nebraska....................	25,720	25,918	24,646	14.0	14.2	14.4	6.6	7.1	6.8	6.7	5.7	10.2	33.2	33.6	27.2
Nevada......................	35,295	35,934	30,829	13.0	13.3	15.4	8.2	8.3	7.2	8.7	5.2	12.7	44.2	44.3	36.4
New Hampshire............	12,852	12,874	14,609	9.7	9.8	11.8	7.1	6.9	6.3	4.9	5.1	6.8	34.5	33.2	24.7
New Jersey	105,886	106,922	115,632	12.0	12.2	13.7	8.5	8.2	7.7	5.1	5.0	7.1	35.9	35.4	28.9
New Mexico.................	27,289	27,850	27,223	13.1	13.5	15.0	8.8	8.7	8.0	12.6	11.5	17.4	51.3	52.3	45.6
New York....................	241,290	244,375	258,737	12.4	12.6	13.6	8.1	8.2	7.7	5.7	6.1	8.2	41.2	41.7	36.6
North Carolina..............	120,385	122,350	120,311	12.5	12.8	14.9	9.0	9.1	8.8	9.2	7.7	13.0	40.9	42.0	33.3
North Dakota................	9,527	9,104	7,676	13.9	13.5	12.0	6.7	6.7	6.4	6.8	6.9	9.2	33.4	32.7	28.3
Ohio..........................	137,916	139,128	155,472	11.9	12.1	13.7	8.6	8.6	7.9	8.9	9.6	12.1	43.4	43.8	34.6
Oklahoma	52,274	53,238	49,782	13.8	14.2	14.4	8.5	8.4	7.5	11.5	9.8	15.9	41.8	41.8	34.3
Oregon.......................	45,157	45,540	45,804	11.7	11.9	13.4	6.1	6.3	5.6	6.9	6.3	11.3	35.7	35.7	30.1
Pennsylvania...............	143,148	143,321	146,281	11.2	11.3	11.9	8.2	8.3	7.7	7.6	7.0	9.9	41.8	41.5	32.7
Rhode Island...............	10,960	11,177	12,505	10.4	10.6	11.9	7.4	7.7	7.2	7.6	7.1	10.2	44.5	45.0	35.5
South Carolina	57,368	58,342	56,114	12.3	12.6	14.0	9.9	9.9	9.7	10.5	9.9	15.3	47.2	47.6	39.8
South Dakota	11,849	11,811	10,345	14.4	14.5	13.7	6.3	6.8	6.2	8.1	7.4	11.6	38.9	37.6	33.5
Tennessee..................	79,588	79,495	79,611	12.4	12.5	14.0	9.0	9.0	9.2	10.7	10.0	14.7	44.1	44.1	34.5
Texas.........................	377,449	386,118	363,414	14.7	15.4	17.4	8.5	8.4	7.4	11.3	9.9	15.3	42.0	42.4	30.5
Utah..........................	51,223	52,258	47,353	18.2	18.9	21.2	6.9	7.0	6.6	5.0	4.2	8.9	18.7	19.2	17.3
Vermont	6,078	6,223	6,500	9.7	9.9	10.7	6.7	6.1	6.1	6.3	5.8	8.0	39.5	39.2	28.1
Virginia......................	102,648	103,002	98,938	12.7	12.9	14.0	8.0	8.2	7.9	6.4	6.3	9.9	35.5	35.5	29.9
Washington.................	86,976	86,539	81,036	12.7	12.9	13.7	6.1	6.3	5.6	6.4	5.5	10.2	32.8	33.0	28.2
West Virginia...............	20,720	20,470	20,865	11.2	11.0	11.5	9.6	9.2	8.3	11.9	12.2	15.9	43.9	43.9	31.7
Wisconsin...................	67,811	68,487	69,326	11.9	12.0	12.9	7.2	7.0	6.5	6.6	6.4	10.2	36.9	36.7	29.3
Wyoming	7,398	7,556	6,253	13.0	13.4	12.7	8.1	9.0	8.3	8.5	7.7	13.5	34.5	34.0	28.8

[1]Total births are per 1,000 total population, estimated as of July 1.
[2]Per 1,000 estimated population.
[3]Less than 2,500 grams (5 pounds, 8 ounces).
[4]Defined as mothers who are 15 to 19 years of age.

Table A–10. Births and Birth Rates, by Race and Hispanic Origin and Fertility Rate, 2010

Geographic area	Births								Birth rates[3]						
	All Races[1]	White		Black		American Indian	Asian or Pacific Islander	Hispanic[2]	All races	White non-Hispanic	Black non-Hispanic	American Indian	Asian or Pacific Islander	Hispanic[2]	Fertility rate[4]
		Total	Non-Hispanic	Total	Non-Hispanic										
United States............	3,999,386	3,069,315	2,162,406	636,425	589,808	46,760	246,886	945,180	13.0	10.8	15.0	11.0	14.5	18.7	64.1
Alabama......................	60,050	40,571	35,819	18,297	18,203	205	977	4,840	12.6	11.0	14.4	5.7	15.1	26.1	62.5
Alaska	11,471	7,051	6,264	467	409	2,899	1,054	661	16.2	13.1	14.4	24.1	20.7	16.8	80.1
Arizona.......................	87,477	73,690	39,211	4,447	4,058	5,999	3,341	35,092	13.7	10.4	15.1	16.7	14.9	18.5	69.3
Arkansas	38,540	30,172	26,113	7,447	7,354	285	636	4,047	13.2	11.8	16.0	9.8	13.6	21.8	67.7
California....................	510,198	404,691	145,931	32,930	30,336	3,652	68,925	257,588	13.7	9.4	12.8	4.9	12.5	18.4	64.8
Colorado	66,355	59,487	40,164	3,579	3,201	714	2,575	19,458	13.2	11.2	14.9	7.7	15.1	18.7	64.7
Connecticut.................	37,708	29,789	22,021	5,262	4,742	281	2,376	8,235	10.6	8.5	13.2	14.0	15.8	17.2	54.5
Delaware	11,364	7,709	6,338	3,117	3,054	15	523	1,427	12.7	10.6	15.7	2.3	16.5	19.5	63.4
District of Columbia	9,165	3,288	2,492	5,346	4,870	18	513	1,359	15.2	11.7	15.8	4.5	20.9	24.8	56.5
Florida........................	214,590	153,289	97,984	53,859	49,489	379	7,063	59,605	11.4	8.9	16.8	3.8	13.1	14.1	60.3
Georgia	133,947	78,629	59,700	49,201	44,824	335	5,782	21,217	13.8	10.9	15.1	6.2	16.4	24.9	64.6
Hawaii........................	18,988	5,868	4,758	610	508	71	12,439	2,968	14.0	13.2	17.5	12.2	13.7	24.6	72.4
Idaho.........................	23,198	22,097	18,616	191	158	466	444	3,639	14.8	13.9	12.7	15.6	17.1	20.7	75.7
Illinois.......................	165,200	126,270	89,165	29,019	28,267	258	9,653	37,356	12.9	10.8	14.9	3.0	15.0	18.4	62.8
Indiana	83,940	71,629	64,304	10,224	9,952	127	1,960	7,569	12.9	12.0	16.0	4.4	16.7	19.4	65.2
Iowa..........................	38,719	35,360	32,511	1,967	1,841	274	1,118	3,092	12.7	11.9	18.0	17.8	18.7	20.4	67.1
Kansas	40,649	35,722	29,551	3,238	3,045	359	1,330	6,429	14.2	13.0	16.6	8.8	17.0	21.4	73.3
Kentucky	55,784	49,157	46,607	5,484	5,233	102	1,041	2,858	12.9	12.3	14.7	7.9	18.1	21.5	65.3
Louisiana	62,379	36,178	32,894	24,424	24,167	490	1,287	3,586	13.8	11.9	16.5	13.6	16.2	18.6	67.2
Maine	12,970	12,236	12,026	396	378	112	226	210	9.8	9.5	20.3	10.7	14.9	12.4	53.6
Maryland.....................	73,801	42,307	33,568	25,706	24,432	200	5,588	10,263	12.8	10.4	14.2	5.5	15.8	21.8	61.8
Massachusetts	72,865	57,343	48,934	9,423	7,059	143	5,956	10,618	11.1	9.6	15.9	4.1	15.6	16.9	54.0
Michigan	114,531	87,230	79,979	22,592	22,133	845	3,864	7,808	11.6	10.4	15.3	9.9	14.5	17.9	59.7
Minnesota	68,610	54,961	50,093	6,934	6,523	1,583	5,132	5,139	12.9	11.2	21.8	20.3	22.1	20.5	65.6
Mississippi	40,036	21,780	20,345	17,535	17,509	269	452	1,426	13.5	11.7	15.8	15.2	15.0	17.5	66.3
Missouri	76,759	62,642	58,471	11,741	11,381	407	1,969	4,334	12.8	11.9	15.8	10.4	16.9	20.4	65.2
Montana......................	12,060	10,416	9,952	75	64	1,430	139	433	12.2	11.3	10.3	20.6	17.3	15.2	67.1
Nebraska	25,918	22,672	19,205	1,940	1,723	553	753	3,943	14.2	12.7	18.9	21.4	19.8	23.6	73.0
Nevada	35,934	28,782	15,750	3,760	3,541	438	2,954	13,398	13.3	10.5	15.4	8.8	12.2	18.7	65.3
New Hampshire.............	12,874	12,055	11,511	264	224	23	532	529	9.8	9.4	13.2	5.1	17.0	14.4	51.5
New Jersey	106,922	75,529	50,455	19,443	16,332	236	11,714	28,003	12.2	9.5	13.9	4.0	15.1	18.0	61.5
New Mexico	27,850	23,006	7,859	623	486	3,679	542	15,478	13.5	9.2	11.6	16.7	14.2	16.2	69.9
New York.....................	244,375	172,593	118,223	47,678	39,266	796	23,308	58,583	12.6	10.3	13.5	3.7	14.9	17.1	60.4
North Carolina..............	122,350	86,234	68,699	29,883	29,007	1,821	4,412	18,731	12.8	10.9	13.9	11.6	18.3	23.4	62.8
North Dakota................	9,104	7,738	7,440	224	193	967	175	305	13.5	12.3	20.1	24.7	21.9	22.6	70.5
Ohio..........................	139,128	110,895	105,356	24,355	22,957	285	3,593	6,323	12.1	11.1	15.6	7.3	16.4	17.8	62.2
Oklahoma	53,238	40,578	34,096	5,008	4,802	6,341	1,311	6,931	14.2	12.7	15.7	16.4	16.6	20.9	72.3
Oregon.......................	45,540	40,644	31,680	1,257	1,141	895	2,744	9,257	11.9	10.3	13.8	10.9	15.4	20.6	60.4
Pennsylvania................	143,321	110,878	101,136	25,752	21,025	415	6,276	13,736	11.3	9.9	15.1	8.8	16.4	19.1	58.7
Rhode Island...............	11,177	8,998	7,003	1,459	955	164	556	2,435	10.6	8.5	14.9	15.6	15.8	18.6	52.1
South Carolina	58,342	37,412	33,190	19,523	18,677	208	1,199	4,947	12.6	11.1	14.3	7.8	17.0	21.0	62.8
South Dakota	11,811	9,460	9,003	262	259	1,937	152	509	14.5	12.9	20.4	25.1	17.1	23.0	77.5
Tennessee	79,495	59,964	53,921	17,468	16,629	218	1,845	7,139	12.5	11.1	15.4	7.7	17.3	24.6	62.4
Texas.........................	386,118	320,637	134,920	47,482	44,560	1,181	16,818	189,126	15.4	11.6	15.0	4.3	15.4	20.0	72.5
Utah..........................	52,258	49,181	41,473	720	584	723	1,634	8,054	18.9	18.4	17.6	15.7	17.4	22.5	86.8
Vermont	6,223	5,973	5,896	122	112	18	110	77	9.9	9.9	14.5	5.9	12.6	8.4	52.6
Virginia......................	103,002	72,203	60,375	22,983	22,366	172	7,644	12,506	12.9	11.4	14.1	3.7	15.5	19.8	62.3
Washington..................	86,539	70,375	55,083	4,865	4,087	2,217	9,082	16,219	12.9	11.0	14.4	15.0	15.5	21.5	63.8
West Virginia................	20,470	19,505	19,236	755	745	21	189	210	11.0	11.0	10.7	5.0	13.2	9.4	59.9
Wisconsin	68,487	57,374	51,038	6,983	6,861	1,238	2,892	6,545	12.0	10.7	18.2	18.3	20.4	19.5	62.4
Wyoming	7,556	7,067	6,047	105	86	296	88	939	13.4	12.4	14.7	18.7	15.4	18.7	70.9

[1]Includes other races not shown separately.
[2]People of Hispanic origin may be of any race. Births by Hispanic origin of mother.
[3]Per 1,000 estimated population, using the bridged-race April 1, 2010, census counts.
[4]Number of births per 1,000 women age 15–44 years estimated.

Table A–11. Deaths and Death Rates, by Race and Hispanic Origin

Geographic area	All races				Infant deaths, 2010[3]					
	Number (thousands)		Crude rate per 1,000 population[2]		Number			Mortality rate[2,4]		
	2011[1]	2010	2011[1]	2010	All races	White	Black	All races	White	Black
United States......................	2,513	2,468	8.1	8.0	24,586	15,954	7,401	6.2	5.2	11.6
Alabama...............................	49	48	10.1	10.1	523	269	250	8.7	6.6	13.7
Alaska.................................	4	4	5.3	5.2	43	23	5	3.8	3.3	(D)
Arizona...............................	48	47	7.5	7.3	522	403	54	6.0	5.5	12.1
Arkansas.............................	30	29	10.1	9.9	282	201	77	7.3	6.7	10.3
California............................	239	234	6.3	6.3	2,420	1,853	324	4.7	4.6	9.8
Colorado.............................	33	31	6.4	6.3	392	330	47	5.9	5.6	13.1
Connecticut.........................	30	29	8.3	8.0	199	134	61	5.3	4.5	11.6
Delaware.............................	8	8	8.6	8.6	87	49	37	7.7	6.4	11.9
District of Columbia	5	5	7.4	7.8	72	16	56	7.9	(D)	10.5
Florida................................	174	174	9.1	9.2	1,403	773	610	6.5	5.0	11.3
Georgia...............................	70	71	7.2	7.4	860	397	448	6.4	5.1	9.1
Hawaii................................	10	10	7.2	7.1	117	23	11	6.2	3.9	(D)
Idaho..................................	12	11	7.6	7.3	112	105	1	4.8	4.8	(D)
Illinois................................	102	100	7.9	7.8	1,118	680	394	6.8	5.4	13.6
Indiana...............................	58	57	8.9	8.8	640	476	153	7.6	6.7	15.0
Iowa...................................	28	28	9.2	9.1	189	163	22	4.9	4.6	11.2
Kansas................................	25	25	8.7	8.6	253	204	40	6.2	5.7	12.4
Kentucky.............................	43	42	9.8	9.7	379	316	61	6.8	6.4	11.1
Louisiana	41	41	8.9	9.0	474	176	287	7.6	4.9	11.8
Maine..................................	13	13	9.8	9.6	70	66	3	5.4	5.4	(D)
Maryland.............................	44	43	7.5	7.5	498	184	297	6.8	4.4	11.6
Massachusetts.....................	54	53	8.2	8.0	323	231	68	4.4	4.0	7.2
Michigan.............................	89	88	9.1	8.9	817	481	318	7.1	5.5	14.1
Minnesota...........................	40	39	7.5	7.3	308	231	44	4.5	4.2	6.4
Mississippi..........................	29	29	9.8	9.8	387	144	242	9.7	6.6	13.8
Missouri	56	55	9.3	9.2	507	362	139	6.6	5.8	11.8
Montana..............................	9	9	9.1	8.9	71	61	0	5.9	5.9	(X)
Nebraska.............................	15	15	8.4	8.3	136	107	26	5.3	4.7	13.4
Nevada................................	20	20	7.5	7.3	201	137	52	5.6	4.8	13.8
New Hampshire....................	11	10	8.2	7.7	51	47	3	4.0	3.9	(D)
New Jersey	71	69	8.0	7.9	514	275	202	4.8	3.6	10.4
New Mexico	16	16	7.9	7.7	157	126	5	5.6	5.5	(D)
New York.............................	149	146	7.7	7.6	1,243	731	439	5.1	4.2	9.2
North Carolina.....................	80	79	8.3	8.3	858	461	367	7.0	5.4	12.3
North Dakota.......................	6	6	8.7	8.8	62	42	3	6.8	5.4	(D)
Ohio...................................	111	109	9.7	9.4	1,072	695	360	7.7	6.3	14.8
Oklahoma	37	37	9.8	9.7	404	255	62	7.6	6.3	12.4
Oregon................................	33	32	8.5	8.3	225	192	14	4.9	4.7	(D)
Pennsylvania.......................	128	125	10.1	9.8	1,039	696	325	7.3	6.3	12.6
Rhode Island........................	10	10	9.1	9.1	79	60	17	7.1	6.7	(D)
South Carolina	42	42	9.0	9.0	430	199	221	7.4	5.3	11.3
South Dakota	7	7	8.9	8.7	82	57	1	6.9	6.0	(D)
Tennessee...........................	61	60	9.5	9.4	630	393	232	7.9	6.6	13.3
Texas..................................	169	167	6.6	6.6	2,368	1,788	533	6.1	5.6	11.2
Utah...................................	15	15	5.4	5.3	254	223	8	4.9	4.5	(D)
Vermont	5	5	8.7	8.6	26	26	0	4.2	4.4	(X)
Virginia...............................	61	59	7.5	7.4	700	347	328	6.8	4.8	14.3
Washington..........................	50	48	7.3	7.2	389	283	40	4.5	4.0	8.2
West Virginia.......................	22	21	11.8	11.5	149	138	11	7.3	7.1	(D)
Wisconsin	48	47	8.5	8.3	400	280	102	5.8	4.9	14.6
Wyoming.............................	4	4	7.7	7.9	51	45	1	6.8	6.4	(D)

[1]Preliminary.
[2]Estimated resident population as of July 1.
[3]Infants are considered under 1 year of age.
[4]Per 1,000 live births. Infant deaths are based on decedent. Live births are based on races of mother.
0 = zero or rounds to zero
(D) = Data withheld to avoid disclosure or does not meet statistical standards for reliability
(X) = Not applicable

Table A–11. Deaths and Death Rates, by Race and Hispanic Origin—*Continued*

Geographic area	Deaths by race, 2010									
	Number					Crude rate per 1,000 population				
	White	Black	American Indian	Asian or Pacific Islander	Hispanic	White	Black	American Indian	Asian or Pacific Islander	Hispanic
United States......................	2,114,749	286,959	15,550	51,162	144,490	8.6	6.8	3.7	3.0	2.9
Alabama............................	36,852	10,981	77	128	254	10.8	8.6	2.1	2.0	1.4
Alaska...............................	2,630	100	865	133	63	5.2	3.2	7.2	2.6	1.6
Arizona..............................	42,819	1,398	2,012	533	5,595	7.8	4.4	5.6	2.4	3.0
Arkansas............................	25,008	3,748	51	109	236	10.5	8.0	1.7	2.3	1.3
California............................	194,086	17,800	1,472	20,654	38,444	6.9	6.5	2.0	3.7	2.7
Colorado............................	29,703	1,188	197	377	3,377	6.6	4.8	2.1	2.2	3.3
Connecticut........................	26,346	2,073	23	250	1,244	8.8	5.0	1.1	1.7	2.6
Delaware............................	6,363	1,281	12	50	103	9.7	6.3	(D)	1.6	1.4
District of Columbia..............	1,042	3,590	(D)	39	106	4.1	11.3	(D)	1.6	1.9
Florida...............................	153,505	18,729	238	1,319	19,288	10.2	5.9	2.4	2.4	4.6
Georgia..............................	51,547	18,929	44	743	935	8.3	6.2	0.8	2.1	1.1
Hawaii................................	2,747	87	32	6,751	447	6.7	2.6	5.5	7.4	3.7
Idaho.................................	11,177	34	131	87	312	7.5	2.3	4.4	3.4	1.8
Illinois...............................	83,184	15,118	61	1,568	3,926	8.2	7.7	0.7	2.4	1.9
Indiana..............................	52,170	4,363	31	179	695	9.2	6.8	1.1	1.5	1.8
Iowa..................................	27,127	489	41	88	202	9.5	4.6	2.7	1.5	1.3
Kansas...............................	22,846	1,222	279	155	652	9.0	6.3	6.9	2.0	2.2
Kentucky............................	39,239	2,636	26	82	192	10.0	7.2	2.0	1.4	1.4
Louisiana...........................	28,411	11,950	94	212	428	9.7	8.0	2.6	2.7	2.2
Maine................................	12,633	42	58	17	44	9.8	2.1	5.5	(D)	2.6
Maryland............................	30,636	11,802	26	861	684	8.5	6.6	0.7	2.4	1.5
Massachusetts.....................	49,467	2,318	47	751	1,300	8.8	4.3	1.3	2.0	2.1
Michigan............................	75,080	12,067	423	451	1,320	9.3	8.1	4.9	1.7	3.0
Minnesota...........................	37,076	926	434	536	314	7.9	3.0	5.6	2.3	1.3
Mississippi.........................	19,745	9,078	76	66	108	10.9	8.1	4.3	2.2	1.3
Missouri.............................	49,455	5,465	118	243	312	9.7	7.4	3.0	2.1	1.5
Montana.............................	8,308	24	480	15	73	9.2	3.5	6.9	(D)	2.6
Nebraska............................	14,476	534	93	68	262	8.7	5.6	3.6	1.8	1.6
Nevada..............................	17,270	1,413	151	789	1,410	8.0	5.5	3.0	3.3	2.0
New Hampshire....................	10,101	63	(D)	31	44	8.0	3.2	(D)	1.0	1.2
New Jersey	58,943	8,957	47	1,548	4,074	8.9	6.7	0.8	2.0	2.6
New Mexico	14,349	302	1,172	108	5,046	8.2	5.2	5.3	2.8	5.3
New York............................	121,568	20,668	264	3,932	11,769	8.6	5.9	1.2	2.5	3.4
North Carolina.....................	61,805	15,862	737	369	827	8.8	7.4	4.7	1.5	1.0
North Dakota.......................	5,604	17	311	12	28	9.1	(D)	7.9	(D)	2.1
Ohio..................................	96,372	11,791	71	477	791	9.9	7.8	1.8	2.2	2.2
Oklahoma...........................	31,455	2,366	2,481	227	549	10.6	7.4	6.4	2.9	1.7
Oregon..............................	30,660	411	312	507	702	8.8	4.4	3.8	2.8	1.6
Pennsylvania.......................	112,051	11,707	61	777	1,705	10.4	7.8	1.3	2.0	2.4
Rhode Island.......................	9,174	306	26	73	251	9.9	3.6	2.5	2.1	1.9
South Carolina	30,558	10,827	61	168	323	9.6	8.1	2.3	2.4	1.4
South Dakota.......................	6,499	19	565	17	33	9.1	(D)	7.3	(D)	1.5
Tennessee..........................	51,073	8,232	42	231	346	10.0	7.5	1.5	2.2	1.2
Texas................................	144,289	19,959	243	2,036	32,147	7.0	6.3	0.9	1.9	3.4
Utah..................................	14,237	114	163	262	682	5.5	2.7	3.5	2.8	1.9
Vermont	5,340	17	(D)	15	26	8.8	(D)	(D)	(D)	2.8
Virginia..............................	46,131	11,786	81	1,034	941	7.9	7.2	1.7	2.1	1.5
Washington.........................	44,233	1,313	819	1,781	1,196	7.8	4.2	5.5	3.0	1.6
West Virginia.......................	20,644	589	15	27	38	11.7	8.3	(D)	1.9	1.7
Wisconsin	44,422	2,241	383	262	486	8.7	5.7	5.7	1.9	1.4
Wyoming	4,293	27	104	14	160	8.0	3.9	6.6	(D)	3.2

[1]Preliminary.
[2]Estimated resident population as of July 1.
[3]Infants are considered under 1 year of age.
[4]Per 1,000 live births. Infant deaths are based on decedent. Live births are based on races of mother.
0 = zero or rounds to zero
(D) = Data withheld to avoid disclosure or does not meet statistical standards for reliability
(X) = Not applicable

Table A–12. Age-Adjusted Death Rates, by Cause, 2010

Geographic area	Age-adjusted rates, 2010[1]									
	All causes	Diseases of the heart	Malignant neoplasms	Chronic lower respiratory diseases	Cerebro-vascular diseases	Accidents and adverse effects		Alzheimer's disease	Diabetes mellitus	Nephritis, nephrotic syndrome, and nephrosis
						Total	Motor vehicle			
United States..............................	747.0	179.1	172.8	42.2	39.1	38.0	11.3	25.1	20.8	15.3
Alabama..	939.7	236.0	191.7	55.4	51.6	49.6	19.4	31.2	25.0	23.1
Alaska...	771.5	151.5	176.9	41.5	40.9	58.7	10.4	25.9	19.6	13.5
Arizona...	693.1	146.7	154.2	43.1	31.9	46.7	12.3	35.3	20.3	7.9
Arkansas.......................................	892.7	222.5	194.7	53.5	53.8	49.4	20.7	29.6	25.8	22.8
California......................................	646.7	161.9	156.9	37.0	38.1	27.8	7.7	30.1	19.7	8.7
Colorado.......................................	682.7	132.8	149.5	49.7	36.1	43.5	9.5	31.1	15.2	9.6
Connecticut..................................	652.9	155.7	163.4	29.4	29.4	33.6	9.1	17.1	15.4	13.4
Delaware.......................................	769.9	175.7	185.7	44.0	40.7	39.2	12.5	21.9	19.2	15.4
District of Columbia.....................	792.4	222.4	178.3	25.7	32.7	35.1	6.0	18.7	24.9	14.4
Florida..	701.1	162.3	165.6	40.1	32.8	43.1	13.0	18.1	20.1	12.9
Georgia...	845.4	192.6	174.8	46.7	46.3	40.7	13.9	28.3	23.1	21.3
Hawaii	589.6	134.7	140.9	18.0	35.8	29.6	9.1	10.5	16.6	12.8
Idaho..	731.6	159.3	159.9	47.0	42.0	42.1	13.8	26.8	22.5	12.1
Illinois..	736.9	181.7	178.6	39.3	39.2	30.4	7.9	20.9	18.5	19.3
Indiana...	820.6	191.8	188.6	55.3	44.5	38.5	11.8	27.8	22.7	22.0
Iowa...	721.7	173.3	171.9	44.7	38.0	37.2	12.7	32.9	19.3	8.1
Kansas..	762.2	164.9	171.3	50.0	41.2	44.0	16.6	24.2	20.5	17.7
Kentucky.......................................	915.0	210.1	208.3	60.0	44.1	60.5	18.8	33.5	26.0	23.8
Louisiana	903.8	229.4	197.6	43.6	44.9	44.4	15.8	30.7	26.4	27.3
Maine...	749.6	151.1	187.9	47.4	34.5	36.5	12.2	28.5	21.8	15.8
Maryland......................................	728.6	182.2	171.2	35.0	38.8	24.7	8.8	16.8	19.9	13.6
Massachusetts..............................	675.0	150.0	171.3	31.0	31.3	28.5	5.5	21.2	13.3	17.5
Michigan.......................................	786.2	204.2	182.9	45.6	39.5	36.2	10.3	24.0	24.0	15.3
Minnesota.....................................	661.5	119.4	167.2	35.1	36.1	36.7	9.5	23.4	17.7	15.0
Mississippi....................................	962.0	251.1	201.4	55.2	51.2	56.8	22.9	32.6	30.3	24.7
Missouri..	819.5	201.8	185.6	52.6	44.0	47.9	14.4	28.8	21.2	19.2
Montana..	754.7	154.2	161.0	51.3	41.8	53.2	19.6	25.2	19.1	11.3
Nebraska.......................................	717.8	154.2	167.4	48.8	40.5	35.8	11.3	24.9	21.7	13.4
Nevada..	795.4	197.3	174.2	49.5	33.3	41.3	10.7	14.2	13.8	19.5
New Hampshire.............................	690.4	152.7	167.9	41.7	33.5	37.2	10.1	26.9	16.1	14.2
New Jersey	691.1	182.0	169.5	31.4	33.3	26.7	6.5	17.7	21.0	15.6
New Mexico	749.0	151.2	152.4	47.7	38.4	60.7	16.4	16.8	29.8	13.1
New York.......................................	665.5	199.9	163.1	31.4	27.9	24.2	6.6	11.3	16.7	11.0
North Carolina..............................	804.9	174.9	179.0	46.1	44.7	43.2	14.5	30.3	20.5	19.5
North Dakota.................................	704.3	158.0	157.1	43.1	42.9	38.8	14.5	37.2	22.2	11.5
Ohio...	815.7	192.4	187.7	50.5	42.6	42.4	10.6	29.7	25.8	15.4
Oklahoma	915.5	235.2	191.3	67.4	50.0	60.3	19.0	26.1	26.9	15.0
Oregon...	723.1	137.9	173.9	45.3	40.1	37.8	8.1	28.5	23.7	8.9
Pennsylvania.................................	765.9	187.0	181.6	37.9	39.3	41.1	11.0	20.0	20.0	17.8
Rhode Island.................................	721.7	167.1	178.3	38.5	31.4	40.0	8.2	22.6	16.0	14.5
South Carolina..............................	854.8	189.9	183.6	46.3	47.9	48.9	17.5	34.7	22.6	19.9
South Dakota................................	715.1	155.2	171.0	46.0	39.9	44.5	17.3	35.9	24.5	7.3
Tennessee.....................................	890.8	217.4	195.7	52.7	48.7	54.9	17.1	38.5	24.7	14.8
Texas..	772.3	181.1	165.9	43.0	44.4	39.0	13.4	26.8	21.6	18.4
Utah..	703.2	143.2	133.7	33.1	37.1	40.6	10.6	19.3	22.7	13.1
Vermont	718.7	153.6	183.2	45.3	35.3	42.7	11.8	30.8	20.7	6.7
Virginia...	741.6	168.5	172.4	38.1	42.1	31.6	9.0	24.4	18.8	20.2
Washington...................................	692.3	151.5	170.5	40.4	37.0	37.6	7.9	43.6	21.6	8.0
West Virginia.................................	933.6	211.2	198.0	62.7	47.8	63.7	16.2	26.0	32.9	20.3
Wisconsin.....................................	719.0	165.1	174.5	38.0	38.7	40.8	10.6	25.3	17.7	17.5
Wyoming	778.8	169.8	172.6	59.5	37.2	59.8	23.1	27.2	18.5	12.5

[1]Causes of death classified according to tenth revision of International Classification of Diseases. Rates per 100,000 population; age-adjusted rates per 100,000 U.S. standard population. Rates for the United States and each state are based on populations enumerated in the 2010 census as of April 1.
(D) = Data withheld to avoid disclosure or does meet statistical standards.

Table A–12. Age-Adjusted Death Rates, by Cause, 2010—*Continued*

Geographic area	Influenza and pneumonia	Drug-induced causes	Intentional self-harm (suicide)	Injury by firearms	Chronic liver diseases and cirrhosis	Essential hypertension and hypertensive renal disease	Alcohol-induced causes	Parkinson's disease	Assault (homicide)	HIV[2]
United States......................	15.1	12.9	12.1	10.1	9.4	8.0	7.6	6.8	5.3	2.6
Alabama............................	18.7	12.6	14.0	16.2	9.4	10.6	5.0	6.9	8.3	3.2
Alaska..............................	15.8	11.9	22.8	20.4	9.8	6.4	16.3	9.2	6.1	(D)
Arizona.............................	11.4	18.2	17.0	14.6	12.7	7.6	14.7	7.4	6.7	1.6
Arkansas...........................	19.9	13.3	15.5	14.4	9.9	6.8	5.7	6.4	6.6	2.2
California...........................	16.4	11.1	10.3	7.7	11.3	10.4	11.2	6.5	5.1	1.9
Colorado	12.3	13.1	16.8	10.8	11.2	5.9	13.5	7.2	3.4	1.2
Connecticut.......................	12.1	10.3	9.4	5.9	7.3	7.0	4.8	5.3	4.2	2.0
Delaware...........................	13.8	16.8	11.3	9.9	8.8	6.2	7.3	5.8	7.0	4.9
District of Columbia	13.5	15.0	6.9	14.2	8.9	9.6	14.1	4.6	17.2	20.4
Florida..............................	8.9	17.0	13.7	11.5	10.6	7.1	7.8	6.7	6.2	5.4
Georgia.............................	18.3	11.4	11.7	12.6	7.5	12.9	6.2	6.3	6.6	5.0
Hawaii...............................	17.0	11.1	15.0	3.2	6.5	5.9	5.5	5.0	1.7	(D)
Idaho................................	13.5	12.2	18.8	12.8	9.3	7.6	9.9	8.3	1.5	(D)
Illinois..............................	16.1	10.4	9.0	8.2	8.2	6.3	5.0	6.9	6.1	2.3
Indiana..............................	16.8	14.9	13.1	10.8	9.0	6.5	6.3	7.2	4.9	1.5
Iowa.................................	13.7	8.8	12.1	6.8	7.9	7.8	6.7	8.1	1.9	(D)
Kansas	16.4	10.2	13.9	10.5	7.8	4.6	6.5	7.9	3.8	0.9
Kentucky	21.0	24.2	14.2	12.4	9.4	6.5	6.2	6.8	4.7	1.2
Louisiana	20.2	13.7	12.3	19.2	7.9	8.9	4.8	6.2	12.0	5.0
Maine...............................	13.4	10.7	13.2	7.9	8.8	5.0	7.6	8.2	2.0	(D)
Maryland...........................	15.7	11.4	8.3	9.3	7.0	7.3	4.5	6.9	7.7	5.0
Massachusetts....................	16.0	12.5	8.8	4.1	7.7	5.3	6.5	5.9	3.2	1.6
Michigan...........................	13.6	17.3	12.5	11.0	10.0	7.1	8.3	7.4	6.4	1.5
Minnesota.........................	9.7	7.9	11.2	6.8	7.0	7.3	7.3	8.9	2.1	0.9
Mississippi........................	19.2	12.0	13.0	16.1	9.0	17.6	5.3	6.1	9.8	4.2
Missouri	17.4	17.4	14.0	14.0	7.8	6.3	6.0	7.2	7.5	1.8
Montana............................	13.6	13.3	21.8	15.4	10.7	6.3	13.0	8.1	3.0	(D)
Nebraska...........................	11.9	7.3	10.4	8.2	8.1	8.0	7.4	8.7	3.4	(D)
Nevada.............................	19.8	20.8	19.8	14.5	11.1	5.7	11.4	6.6	6.1	2.2
New Hampshire....................	12.6	12.1	14.1	8.2	6.4	5.4	7.9	8.0	(D)	(D)
New Jersey	11.0	10.1	7.7	5.2	7.3	7.2	5.6	6.5	4.6	3.9
New Mexico	14.2	24.3	20.1	14.9	17.0	5.7	19.7	8.3	7.6	1.6
New York...........................	20.6	8.8	7.7	5.1	6.6	9.1	5.7	4.5	4.6	4.7
North Carolina.....................	17.7	11.7	12.0	11.6	8.9	8.7	6.3	6.8	5.7	3.3
North Dakota.......................	13.9	3.9	15.6	9.5	10.1	7.0	11.4	7.0	(D)	(D)
Ohio.................................	14.6	16.7	12.2	9.9	9.4	8.9	6.5	6.9	5.1	1.1
Oklahoma	19.7	19.7	16.5	14.4	12.5	8.6	11.1	6.4	5.7	1.4
Oregon..............................	9.2	14.6	17.1	11.4	11.3	9.8	12.9	8.3	2.9	1.2
Pennsylvania......................	13.6	15.8	11.9	10.1	7.8	5.7	5.0	7.1	5.6	1.9
Rhode Island......................	13.8	16.3	12.3	4.6	9.7	4.9	8.2	7.1	2.6	1.8
South Carolina	15.9	15.0	13.5	14.0	10.8	8.5	7.5	8.3	7.1	3.9
South Dakota......................	15.8	6.6	17.5	9.2	10.1	9.1	10.7	8.3	(D)	(D)
Tennessee	20.5	17.7	14.6	14.4	10.2	9.0	7.5	6.9	6.5	3.2
Texas...............................	14.6	10.0	11.7	11.0	11.7	8.3	6.3	7.6	5.4	3.2
Utah.................................	17.1	17.9	18.3	12.2	7.3	6.1	7.7	8.9	1.9	(D)
Vermont	7.9	10.3	15.7	10.3	7.2	6.5	7.9	9.6	(D)	(D)
Virginia.............................	15.5	7.0	11.7	10.8	7.9	7.5	4.7	7.0	4.7	1.7
Washington........................	8.3	13.8	13.9	8.9	10.5	7.1	11.4	7.9	2.7	1.0
West Virginia.......................	19.0	29.3	14.1	14.1	10.7	11.3	6.3	6.2	5.0	(D)
Wisconsin..........................	13.3	11.0	13.4	8.6	8.2	5.9	7.8	7.4	2.8	0.8
Wyoming	19.5	15.5	22.4	15.6	12.5	(D)	(D)	6.8	(D)	(D)

[1]Causes of death classified according to tenth revision of International Classification of Diseases. Rates per 100,000 population; age-adjusted rates per 100,000 U.S. standard population. Rates for the United States and each state are based on populations enumerated in the 2010 census as of April 1.
[2]Human immunodeficiency virus.
(D) = Data withheld to avoid disclosure or does meet statistical standards.

Table A–13.　Marriages and Divorces—Number and Rate

Geographic area	Marriages[1]						Divorces[2]					
	Number (thousands)			Rates per 1,000 population[3]			Number (thousands)			Rates per 1,000 population[3]		
	2009	2005	2000	2009	2005	2000	2009	2005	2000	2009	2005	2000
United States[4]	2,080.0	2,249.0	2,315.0	6.8	7.6	8.2	840.0	847.0	944.0	3.5	3.6	4.0
Alabama	37.3	43.3	45.0	8.3	9.2	10.1	20.2	22.1	23.5	4.4	4.9	5.5
Alaska	5.5	5.5	5.6	7.8	8.2	8.9	3.3	3.9	2.7	4.4	4.3	3.9
Arizona	35.3	37.5	38.7	5.6	6.6	7.5	23.1	24.5	21.6	3.6	4.2	4.6
Arkansas	31.6	35.1	41.1	10.7	12.9	15.4	16.3	16.6	17.9	5.7	6.0	6.4
California[5]	213.9	227.9	196.9	5.8	6.4	5.8	NA	NA	NA	NA	NA	NA
Colorado	37.4	29.7	35.6	6.9	7.6	8.3	21.2	20.5	NA	4.3	4.4	4.7
Connecticut	19.8	19.2	19.4	5.9	5.8	5.7	10.8	9.4	6.5	3.0	3.0	3.3
Delaware	5.1	4.7	5.1	5.4	5.9	6.5	3.4	3.3	3.2	3.6	3.8	3.9
District of Columbia	1.9	2.4	2.8	4.7	4.1	4.9	1.3	1.1	1.5	2.7	2.0	3.2
Florida	141.2	158.8	141.9	7.5	8.9	8.9	79.9	81.3	81.9	4.2	4.6	5.1
Georgia	63.6	62.9	56.0	6.6	7.0	6.8	NA	NA	30.7	NA	NA	3.3
Hawaii	22.2	28.6	25.0	17.2	22.6	20.6	NA	NA	4.6	NA	NA	3.9
Idaho	13.9	15.1	14.0	8.9	10.5	10.8	7.7	7.0	6.9	5.0	5.0	5.5
Illinois	72.7	74.1	85.5	5.7	5.9	6.9	32.7	32.4	39.1	2.5	2.6	3.2
Indiana	52.9	48.5	34.5	7.9	6.9	7.9	NA	NA	NA	NA	NA	NA
Iowa	21.2	20.4	20.3	7.0	6.9	6.9	7.3	8.1	9.4	2.4	2.7	3.3
Kansas	18.5	19.1	22.2	6.4	6.8	8.3	10.3	8.6	10.6	3.6	3.1	3.6
Kentucky	33.4	36.8	39.7	7.6	8.7	9.8	19.9	18.9	21.6	4.6	4.6	5.1
Louisiana	28.7	36.6	40.5	7.1	8.0	9.1	NA	NA	NA	NA	NA	NA
Maine	9.4	10.5	10.5	7.1	8.2	8.8	5.3	4.7	5.8	4.1	4.1	5.0
Maryland	32.4	37.6	40.0	5.8	6.9	7.5	15.2	17.1	17.0	2.8	3.1	3.3
Massachusetts	36.7	39.1	37.0	5.6	6.2	5.8	12.7	14.3	18.6	2.2	2.2	2.5
Michigan	53.1	61.5	66.4	5.4	6.1	6.7	32.5	34.7	39.4	3.3	3.4	3.9
Minnesota	28.4	30.3	33.4	5.3	6.0	6.8	NA	NA	14.8	NA	NA	3.2
Mississippi	14.5	17.2	19.7	4.8	5.8	6.9	12.2	13.0	14.4	4.1	4.4	5.0
Missouri	39.8	47.0	43.7	6.5	7.0	7.8	23.3	21.0	26.5	3.8	3.6	4.5
Montana	7.1	6.8	6.6	7.3	7.4	7.3	3.9	3.5	2.1	4.0	4.5	4.2
Nebraska	12.5	12.3	13.0	6.6	7.0	7.6	5.4	6.0	6.4	3.4	3.3	3.7
Nevada	108.2	147.3	144.3	40.3	57.4	72.2	17.7	18.6	18.1	6.6	7.4	9.9
New Hampshire	8.5	9.5	11.6	6.5	7.3	9.4	4.9	4.4	7.1	3.7	3.9	4.8
New Jersey	46.3	43.9	50.4	5.0	5.7	6.0	24.0	25.3	25.6	2.7	2.9	3.0
New Mexico	10.2	12.8	14.5	5.0	6.6	8.0	8.0	8.8	9.2	3.9	4.6	5.1
New York	120.1	135.6	162.0	6.5	6.8	7.1	46.1	53.5	62.8	2.6	2.9	3.0
North Carolina	65.8	58.6	65.6	6.6	7.3	8.2	36.7	32.7	36.9	3.8	4.1	4.5
North Dakota	4.3	4.1	4.6	6.4	6.8	7.2	1.6	1.5	2.0	2.8	2.9	3.4
Ohio	64.8	76.3	88.5	5.8	6.5	7.8	36.9	41.7	49.3	3.3	3.5	4.2
Oklahoma	23.5	25.8	15.6	6.9	7.3	NA	16.9	20.0	12.4	4.8	5.6	...
Oregon	23.5	26.8	26.0	6.6	7.3	7.6	13.3	15.5	16.7	3.9	4.2	4.8
Pennsylvania	64.2	58.4	73.2	5.3	5.8	6.0	28.8	29.1	37.9	2.7	2.3	3.1
Rhode Island	6.5	7.5	8.0	5.9	7.0	7.6	3.3	3.1	3.1	3.0	3.0	2.9
South Carolina	29.2	35.4	42.7	7.3	8.3	10.6	12.2	12.4	14.4	3.0	2.9	3.8
South Dakota	5.9	6.5	7.1	7.3	8.4	9.4	2.6	2.4	2.7	3.3	2.8	3.5
Tennessee	55.2	61.3	88.2	8.4	10.9	15.5	25.8	27.6	33.8	3.9	4.6	5.9
Texas	179.8	169.3	196.4	7.1	7.8	9.4	76.9	74.0	85.2	3.3	3.3	4.0
Utah	23.9	21.4	24.1	8.4	9.8	10.8	10.7	10.0	9.7	3.7	4.1	4.3
Vermont	4.7	5.5	6.1	8.7	8.9	10.0	2.1	2.1	5.1	3.5	3.6	4.1
Virginia	54.1	62.1	62.4	6.9	8.2	8.8	28.5	29.1	30.2	3.7	4.0	4.3
Washington	40.4	41.5	40.9	6.0	6.5	6.9	26.3	25.3	27.2	3.9	4.3	4.6
West Virginia	12.4	13.5	15.7	6.7	7.4	8.7	9.2	9.2	9.3	5.1	5.1	5.1
Wisconsin	30.3	33.9	36.1	5.3	6.1	6.7	17.3	16.5	17.6	2.9	2.9	3.2
Wyoming	4.7	4.8	4.9	8.0	9.3	10.0	2.8	2.7	2.8	5.1	5.2	5.8

[1]Data are accounts of marriages performed, except as noted.
[2]Includes annulments.
[3]Based on provisional counts of marriages by state occurrence; total population residing in area; population enumerated as of April 1 for 2000 and estimated as of July 1 for all other years.
[4]U.S. total for the number of divorces is an estimate that includes states not reporting. Beginning in 2000, divorce rates are based solely on the combined counts and populations for reporting states and the District of Columbia. Divorce data for the year 2000 excludes data for California, Indiana, and Oklahoma; and for years 2005 and 2009 exclude data for California, Georgia, Hawaii, Indiana, Louisiana, and Minnesota.
[5]Marriage data include nonlicensed marriages registered.
NA = Not available

Table A–14. Health Care Services, Physicians, and Nurses

Geographic area	Health care services and social assistance, 2010[1] (NAICS 62)									Physicians[2]		Nurses[3]	
	Establishments				Employees				Annual payroll (NAICS 62) (millions of dollars)	Number	Rate per 100,000 population[4]	Number	Rate per 100,000 population[4]
	Total (NAICS 62)	Ambulatory Health Care services (NAICS 621)	Hospitals (NAICS 622)	Nursing and residential care facilities (NAICS 623)	Total (NAICS 62)	Ambulatory Health Care services (NAICS 621)	Hospitals (NAICS 622)	Nursing and residential care facilities (NAICS 623)		2012	2012	2012	2012
United States[5]...............	812,860	568,257	6,792	79,047	17,787,859	6,184,324	5,650,848	3,234,545	752,852	834,769	266	2,633,950	839
Alabama.........................	10,238	7,210	133	876	236,266	81,826	86,763	43,018	9,541	10,446	217	43,760	908
Alaska	2,222	1,425	28	285	43,303	15,554	15,077	3,374	2,095	1,652	226	5,350	731
Arizona.........................	16,400	12,431	119	1,570	308,087	112,937	101,078	46,917	14,017	15,269	233	45,600	696
Arkansas.......................	7,439	5,033	106	564	170,323	49,571	60,333	31,133	6,214	5,747	195	23,480	796
California......................	101,157	75,046	481	8,569	1,685,434	654,617	514,186	256,194	83,637	95,041	250	249,980	657
Colorado.......................	14,542	10,875	113	874	250,442	98,912	74,269	40,968	10,967	12,838	247	41,380	798
Connecticut...................	10,257	6,910	47	1,152	262,337	84,861	69,521	63,569	11,796	12,268	342	34,820	970
Delaware	2,485	1,642	16	222	58,369	19,546	18,657	11,247	2,687	2,657	290	9,660	1,053
District of Columbia	2,142	1,234	18	140	65,170	13,128	30,087	7,547	3,375	6,238	987	11,310	1,789
Florida..........................	54,241	42,922	315	3,328	950,331	369,502	296,934	176,746	41,505	46,830	242	163,720	848
Georgia	22,038	15,986	196	1,461	437,942	158,602	152,450	62,158	18,389	21,558	217	64,180	647
Hawaii..........................	3,508	2,686	28	137	65,125	25,106	20,841	7,149	3,005	3,464	249	10,060	723
Idaho...........................	4,741	3,253	62	399	79,920	27,574	24,858	14,491	2,833	2,738	172	11,420	716
Illinois.........................	32,304	23,682	230	2,669	741,655	244,202	244,514	137,566	31,676	35,643	277	114,730	891
Indiana.........................	15,073	9,866	162	1,825	384,458	124,102	127,498	81,066	14,918	14,654	224	58,430	894
Iowa............................	8,011	4,730	134	1,217	207,653	49,756	68,700	55,288	7,240	7,133	232	32,170	1,046
Kansas.........................	7,751	4,767	152	988	186,820	57,648	58,541	40,841	6,872	6,439	223	26,380	914
Kentucky	10,960	7,460	133	1,016	241,385	76,778	85,351	46,489	9,386	10,192	233	42,920	980
Louisiana......................	11,902	8,141	234	925	279,436	86,242	102,069	43,668	10,100	11,169	243⸰	40,180	873
Maine...........................	4,786	2,429	49	973	106,197	30,298	33,797	24,465	4,093	4,109	309	14,260	1,073
Maryland.......................	15,551	11,036	79	1,660	332,605	106,895	103,032	71,162	14,670	20,060	341	45,630	775
Massachusetts...............	18,102	11,116	136	2,636	564,011	164,032	186,244	108,764	26,344	30,091	453	79,570	1,197
Michigan.......................	26,197	18,295	189	3,283	562,949	194,170	202,291	100,095	23,858	31,172	315	90,540	916
Minnesota	14,682	7,710	145	3,108	431,296	134,346	116,381	101,372	16,583	15,412	287	54,940	1,021
Mississippi....................	6,092	4,117	111	406	155,636	43,293	67,232	23,897	6,121	5,681	190	28,200	945
Missouri........................	16,133	10,255	164	1,697	380,717	109,720	136,172	72,781	14,545	16,824	279	65,260	1,084
Montana........................	3,381	1,999	65	361	64,545	17,997	22,931	11,717	2,316	2,072	206	8,400	836
Nebraska.......................	5,189	3,280	103	483	120,265	32,868	41,879	28,448	4,610	4,495	242	18,590	1,002
Nevada.........................	6,234	5,032	59	329	98,544	42,585	30,098	11,153	4,590	5,221	189	16,790	609
New Hampshire...............	3,562	2,277	32	300	86,333	29,147	28,643	14,679	3,893	3,683	279	12,530	949
New Jersey	26,267	19,983	123	1,864	524,392	203,375	152,444	90,789	23,552	25,117	283	74,700	843
New Mexico	4,853	3,293	59	350	109,432	39,550	31,039	13,526	4,319	4,841	232	14,780	709
New York.......................	56,042	39,375	274	5,378	1,388,458	478,507	421,403	242,894	61,707	68,898	352	166,950	853
North Carolina...............	22,888	14,730	153	2,734	541,331	184,796	174,108	102,942	21,137	23,253	238	86,240	884
North Dakota..................	1,835	1,024	50	254	54,873	11,907	19,206	15,232	2,055	1,649	236	7,580	1,083
Ohio.............................	28,094	19,220	232	3,132	789,118	252,409	264,613	165,776	30,930	34,656	300	120,460	1,043
Oklahoma	10,587	7,088	157	1,154	209,144	68,914	68,043	39,669	7,797	8,064	211	26,850	704
Oregon.........................	12,200	7,544	62	2,107	207,944	75,689	56,981	44,088	9,201	10,380	266	28,840	740
Pennsylvania..................	35,980	23,791	285	4,214	929,267	303,850	267,273	201,522	37,519	41,437	325	125,220	981
Rhode Island.................	3,268	2,151	16	491	83,998	26,655	24,760	19,368	3,446	4,055	386	11,840	1,127
South Carolina	9,724	6,777	87	943	215,865	73,647	73,656	41,322	8,784	10,424	221	41,870	886
South Dakota	2,310	1,300	65	309	61,993	15,194	25,869	13,978	2,443	1,874	225	11,030	1,324
Tennessee	14,869	10,608	173	1,182	367,826	128,296	132,063	64,279	15,663	16,526	256	55,580	861
Texas...........................	59,193	44,559	640	3,995	1,280,332	555,626	367,671	176,491	51,168	54,508	209	187,290	719
Utah.............................	6,812	5,306	55	463	118,505	48,037	38,015	20,960	4,530	5,741	201	17,920	628
Vermont	2,138	1,261	17	208	50,747	16,421	19,172	7,614	1,756	2,022	323	6,310	1,008
Virginia.........................	18,101	12,728	131	1,442	387,252	141,602	114,332	67,297	16,847	20,688	253	58,650	716
Washington....................	19,178	12,385	113	2,172	370,406	136,385	106,972	63,374	16,750	18,773	272	51,060	740
West Virginia..................	4,905	3,038	75	654	124,688	35,334	47,774	19,808	4,552	4,750	256	17,440	940
Wisconsin	14,486	8,096	155	2,428	382,914	123,332	113,651	79,893	15,519	15,256	266	54,640	954
Wyoming	1,810	1,155	31	120	31,820	8,983	11,376	5,761	1,302	1,061	184	4,460	774

[1]Data for 2010 is based on the 2007 North American Industry Classification System (NAICS).
[2]As of November. Data includes currently active allopathic physicians (MDs) and osteopathic physicians (DOs).
[3]As of May. Estimates for detailed occupations do not sum to the totals because the totals include occupations not shown separately. Estimates do not include self-employed workers.
[4]Based on U.S. Census Bureau estimates as of July 1 for 2012. As of April 1 for 2000.
[5]National total includes state employment figures that are not offered discretely at the state level. The national total will therefore differ from the sum of the state total.

Table A-15. Health Care, Employment, and Type of Health Insurance

Geographic area	Employment in health care occupations, 2006–2010[1]								
	Physicians and surgeons		Physician assistants	Registered nurses, nurse practitioners, midwives, and anesthetists	Other health diagnosing and treating practitioners	Dentists	Pharmacists	Physical, speech, respiratory, and other therapists	Health technologists and technicians
	Number	Rate per 1,000 residents							
United States................................	812,560	2.67	99,105	2,624,550	314,460	161,305	244,525	611,320	2,378,655
Alabama...	9,325	1.98	1,130	42,010	4,205	1,940	4,300	7,080	41,590
Alaska	1,785	2.58	155	5,230	625	705	440	1,040	5,010
Arizona..	14,585	2.33	2,530	48,175	6,175	2,875	4,675	11,640	42,615
Arkansas.......................................	5,585	1.94	410	24,200	2,005	1,090	2,460	6,375	25,210
California.......................................	91,690	2.50	9,230	249,435	37,930	24,050	23,285	61,090	215,625
Colorado..	13,055	2.67	1,770	39,320	6,695	3,115	4,250	11,140	31,305
Connecticut....................................	12,585	3.55	1,575	34,780	4,335	2,410	2,770	8,930	28,195
Delaware	2,785	3.16	375	9,715	975	385	615	1,810	7,370
District of Columbia	6,825	11.68	430	10,155	1,165	660	465	1,950	7,265
Florida...	44,775	2.42	6,720	154,765	18,085	8,800	14,540	32,585	150,745
Georgia..	19,500	2.06	3,205	68,955	9,990	3,525	7,345	15,990	70,055
Hawaii...	3,660	2.74	275	9,695	1,240	1,170	995	2,575	8,415
Idaho...	2,905	1.90	485	10,590	1,575	810	1,250	3,575	10,270
Illinois...	35,335	2.77	3,135	111,715	12,175	7,955	9,600	26,935	91,615
Indiana..	13,555	2.11	1,335	60,400	5,485	2,745	5,440	13,355	55,130
Iowa..	6,630	2.20	955	32,260	3,545	1,480	2,895	5,495	24,145
Kansas..	5,935	2.11	1,060	27,270	3,065	1,360	2,535	6,575	24,390
Kentucky..	9,960	2.32	1,340	41,175	3,765	1,720	4,335	9,345	39,045
Louisiana.......................................	11,080	2.50	1,045	39,090	3,180	2,035	3,905	8,685	41,470
Maine..	4,200	3.16	515	14,195	1,490	575	780	3,770	10,920
Maryland..	19,335	3.39	2,625	51,875	6,340	3,195	4,800	12,195	45,975
Massachusetts...............................	27,460	4.24	2,295	74,135	7,430	4,610	5,985	18,415	59,485
Michigan..	27,075	2.72	3,780	83,785	10,625	5,230	8,160	20,575	76,695
Minnesota......................................	14,940	2.85	1,850	57,800	6,635	2,955	4,895	11,255	49,155
Mississippi.....................................	5,455	1.85	615	26,715	1,790	1,400	2,500	5,200	26,855
Missouri...	16,935	2.86	1,280	60,230	5,495	2,520	5,090	13,165	56,445
Montana...	2,130	2.19	440	9,065	1,015	525	765	2,429	7,400
Nebraska..	4,055	2.25	805	19,850	2,410	775	2,465	4,880	16,595
Nevada..	4,800	1.82	465	17,300	2,030	1,255	2,170	3,555	15,935
New Hampshire...............................	3,745	2.85	575	13,720	1,725	695	1,000	3,670	12,310
New Jersey	25,460	2.92	2,260	71,805	8,080	5,950	7,475	17,950	61,295
New Mexico....................................	4,430	2.20	405	14,235	2,330	700	1,245	4,270	14,270
New York..	77,365	4.02	9,530	179,785	25,755	14,195	16,670	49,415	139,605
North Carolina................................	23,370	2.52	4,205	84,205	10,725	3,545	7,630	17,260	80,640
North Dakota..................................	1,410	2.14	235	7,830	1,060	200	705	1,695	6,830
Ohio..	31,460	2.73	3,480	121,410	11,535	5,360	10,330	25,235	106,615
Oklahoma	7,530	2.05	1,185	27,440	3,640	1,360	2,715	6,315	32,690
Oregon	10,390	2.76	1,020	30,400	4,365	2,650	2,555	7,825	24,485
Pennsylvania..................................	40,375	3.20	4,775	131,585	14,945	6,855	12,890	34,215	116,760
Rhode Island..................................	4,235	4.01	355	11,585	1,165	385	780	2,555	8,075
South Carolina	9,625	2.13	795	37,735	3,285	1,805	3,970	8,845	37,840
South Dakota	1,750	2.19	320	9,990	1,180	365	840	1,870	7,280
Tennessee......................................	16,300	2.61	1,925	61,180	5,960	2,400	5,980	12,045	65,625
Texas..	53,260	2.19	7,255	170,380	20,230	9,670	15,725	37,375	180,155
Utah..	5,770	2.17	930	17,370	2,915	1,590	1,610	5,150	17,325
Vermont	1,885	3.02	335	6,354	890	425	320	1,535	5,360
Virginia..	19,820	2.53	2,340	61,145	6,465	4,205	6,330	13,315	61,340
Washington.....................................	16,855	2.57	2,315	53,655	8,105	3,610	5,605	11,860	44,545
West Virginia..................................	4,420	2.40	650	18,185	1,760	490	1,605	3,385	18,850
Wisconsin	14,210	2.52	2,200	56,710	6,275	2,735	4,335	12,715	48,160
Wyoming..	945	1.73	170	3,960	555	245	485	1,240	3,700

[1]Employment data represent the workplace state.

Table A-15.   Health Care, Employment, and Type of Health Insurance—*Continued*

Geographic area	Type of health insurance coverage for all persons, 2009–2011 (thousands)						
	Employer-based	Direct Purchase	Medicare	Medicaid	TRICARE	VA	No health insurance
United States...................................	168,706	38,655	44,897	51,335	7,913	6,346	46,282
Alabama..............................	2,540	618	804	845	205	123	668
Alaska.................................	373	47	62	106	64	20	137
Arizona...............................	3,111	792	974	1,264	199	165	1,059
Arkansas.............................	1,355	383	513	593	92	98	492
California.............................	18,615	4,483	4,618	6,947	652	518	6,695
Colorado..............................	2,779	716	605	630	195	97	770
Connecticut..........................	2,282	457	533	525	42	60	313
Delaware.............................	554	100	146	163	30	16	87
District of Columbia	363	102	72	151	9	9	42
Florida................................	8,603	2,574	3,537	2,864	647	543	3,901
Georgia...............................	5,007	1,059	1,213	1,511	369	189	1,846
Hawaii................................	839	207	204	207	105	25	96
Idaho..................................	810	260	222	217	52	42	265
Illinois................................	7,398	1,525	1,729	2,184	136	207	1,686
Indiana................................	3,777	792	940	950	93	139	924
Iowa...................................	1,854	542	484	456	48	80	268
Kansas................................	1,651	429	411	344	103	68	369
Kentucky.............................	2,317	524	714	780	114	115	625
Louisiana	2,172	540	662	934	111	98	779
Maine.................................	728	170	243	293	42	44	135
Maryland..............................	3,690	697	756	778	201	97	623
Massachusetts......................	4,305	882	967	1,300	72	98	275
Michigan..............................	5,873	1,225	1,578	1,872	107	171	1,172
Minnesota............................	3,327	846	739	743	66	119	472
Mississippi...........................	1,324	350	478	668	106	76	521
Missouri..............................	3,377	812	960	867	148	151	779
Montana..............................	498	177	163	122	35	37	172
Nebraska.............................	1,056	314	262	230	56	52	208
Nevada................................	1,469	304	357	287	94	73	590
New Hampshire......................	874	154	198	141	29	31	136
New Jersey	5,569	1,009	1,260	1,132	79	96	1,123
New Mexico	913	216	312	464	83	58	399
New York..............................	11,101	2,277	2,836	4,040	162	276	2,214
North Carolina.......................	4,822	1,286	1,445	1,565	411	225	1,540
North Dakota.........................	406	134	102	64	26	20	64
Ohio...................................	6,960	1,307	1,794	1,845	170	240	1,365
Oklahoma.............................	1,849	463	584	614	145	114	690
Oregon................................	2,050	585	596	560	73	106	632
Pennsylvania.........................	7,678	1,865	2,133	2,046	169	254	1,246
Rhode Island.........................	621	139	168	171	24	21	119
South Carolina	2,344	564	757	780	217	126	775
South Dakota	437	158	125	111	30	32	96
Tennessee............................	3,315	808	1,028	1,176	210	148	897
Texas..................................	12,214	2,417	2,913	4,089	757	493	5,796
Utah...................................	1,737	341	275	303	66	39	410
Vermont	356	79	105	146	14	15	48
Virginia...............................	4,775	1,028	1,105	819	636	170	975
Washington...........................	3,778	890	923	1,053	288	144	923
West Virginia.........................	1,028	199	368	344	38	64	264
Wisconsin	3,510	731	846	969	73	128	518
Wyoming	322	78	76	68	22	20	84

[1]Employment data represent the workplace state.

Table A–16. Health Risks, Chronic Conditions, and Cardiovascular Disease

Geographic area	Health risk (percent)									
	No exercise in the past month[1]		Cigarette smoking[2]		Binge drinking[3]		Overweight[4]		Obesity[4]	
	2011	2000	2011	2000	2011	2001	2011	2000	2011	2000
United States[7]	26.2	26.7	21.2	23.2	18.3	14.8	35.7	36.7	27.8	20.0
Alabama	32.6	31.6	24.3	25.2	13.7	11.6	34.7	36.8	32.0	23.9
Alaska	22.0	20.0	22.9	25.0	20.8	18.2	38.9	38.2	27.4	21.0
Arizona	24.1	34.2	19.3	18.6	17.6	16.8	37.2	36.8	25.1	19.2
Arkansas	30.9	28.1	27.0	25.1	14.1	11.3	34.0	36.6	30.9	23.3
California	19.1	26.5	13.7	17.2	18.6	15.5	36.4	37.4	23.8	19.9
Colorado	16.5	19.8	18.3	20.0	20.1	16.7	35.4	33.8	20.7	14.2
Connecticut	25.5	25.2	17.1	19.9	17.9	13.8	35.2	36.3	24.5	17.4
Delaware	27.0	28.0	21.8	22.9	20.3	15.7	35.0	39.2	28.8	16.6
District of Columbia	19.8	20.8	20.8	20.9	25.0	14.8	29.1	31.7	23.8	21.5
Florida	26.9	28.8	19.3	23.2	17.1	12.0	36.7	35.2	26.6	18.7
Georgia	26.7	29.0	21.2	23.5	16.6	11.9	34.7	37.9	28.0	21.5
Hawaii	21.3	23.2	16.8	19.7	21.5	10.4	33.8	34.5	21.9	15.7
Idaho	21.4	19.8	17.2	22.3	16.6	12.8	35.2	36.8	27.1	18.9
Illinois	25.1	30.9	20.9	22.3	23.0	17.3	36.9	37.2	27.1	21.7
Indiana	29.2	25.4	25.6	26.9	17.8	13.8	34.8	36.5	30.8	21.8
Iowa	25.9	27.3	20.4	23.2	23.1	16.2	35.8	38.5	29.0	21.5
Kansas	26.8	30.4	22.0	21.0	17.0	14.7	34.8	37.9	29.6	20.8
Kentucky	29.3	41.1	29.0	30.5	16.1	8.7	36.1	38.0	30.4	23.0
Louisiana	33.8	36.2	25.7	24.1	16.1	13.8	34.1	36.5	33.4	23.6
Maine	23.0	27.2	22.8	23.8	17.3	15.4	37.2	36.3	27.8	20.0
Maryland	26.2	24.2	19.1	20.5	18.0	11.9	36.1	36.5	28.3	20.2
Massachusetts	23.5	24.6	18.2	19.9	20.6	18.1	36.6	36.1	22.7	16.8
Michigan	23.6	22.9	23.3	24.1	19.7	18.0	34.2	38.7	31.3	22.4
Minnesota	21.9	24.8	19.1	19.8	22.1	19.6	36.8	37.6	25.7	17.4
Mississippi	36.0	33.3	26.0	23.5	14.2	11.8	34.0	36.7	34.9	25.0
Missouri	28.4	28.8	25.0	27.2	19.2	14.1	34.6	34.4	30.3	22.1
Montana	24.4	23.3	22.1	18.8	20.8	16.7	35.6	37.2	24.6	15.9
Nebraska	26.3	29.6	20.0	21.2	22.7	14.6	36.5	37.4	28.4	21.1
Nevada	24.3	24.9	22.9	29.0	18.6	16.7	35.7	35.3	24.5	17.9
New Hampshire	22.5	26.7	19.4	25.3	18.7	15.8	35.4	36.5	26.2	18.1
New Jersey	26.4	28.6	16.8	21.0	18.2	13.5	37.8	38.3	23.7	18.5
New Mexico	25.3	24.4	21.5	23.6	16.4	15.8	35.9	36.2	26.3	19.3
New York	26.3	29.4	18.1	21.6	19.6	14.4	35.8	39.2	24.5	17.7
North Carolina	26.7	30.4	21.8	26.1	15.2	9.8	36.0	37.4	29.1	21.8
North Dakota	27.1	24.3	21.9	23.2	23.8	22.3	36.0	40.0	27.8	20.4
Ohio	27.0	31.3	25.1	26.2	20.1	16.2	36.2	35.7	29.7	21.5
Oklahoma	31.2	34.4	26.1	23.3	16.5	11.0	34.4	36.6	31.1	19.7
Oregon	19.8	20.1	19.7	20.7	16.5	14.7	34.8	36.1	26.7	21.5
Pennsylvania	26.2	23.0	22.4	24.3	18.3	15.6	36.0	36.4	28.6	21.2
Rhode Island	26.2	27.5	20.0	23.4	19.7	15.1	37.1	36.6	25.4	17.1
South Carolina	27.2	28.1	23.1	24.9	15.4	12.3	35.0	36.9	30.8	22.0
South Dakota	27.0	26.7	23.0	21.9	22.1	18.5	36.3	38.9	28.1	19.8
Tennessee	35.1	32.7	23.0	25.7	10.0	6.8	37.3	36.5	29.2	22.9
Texas	27.2	28.5	19.2	21.9	18.9	15.1	35.4	36.7	30.4	23.1
Utah	18.9	15.5	11.8	12.9	12.0	9.7	34.5	35.0	24.4	19.1
Vermont	21.0	23.2	19.1	21.5	18.5	15.7	34.3	34.6	25.4	18.2
Virginia	25.1	25.0	20.9	21.4	17.9	14.3	34.2	38.0	29.2	18.2
Washington	22.0	16.9	17.5	20.7	17.8	14.9	34.5	36.3	26.5	18.8
West Virginia	35.1	33.6	28.6	26.1	10.1	9.4	36.5	36.5	32.4	23.2
Wisconsin	22.7	22.1	20.9	24.1	24.3	25.7	36.3	37.8	27.7	20.0
Wyoming	25.5	22.6	23.0	23.8	18.9	16.0	36.3	37.2	25.0	18.0

[1]For those of the age 18 and over.
[2]Current cigarette smoking is defined as persons 18 years and older who reported having smoked 100 or more cigarettes during their lifetime and who currently smoke every day or some days.
[3]For 2011, binge drinking is considered for males having five or more drinks on one occasion, females having four or more drinks on one occasion. For 2001, binge drinking is considered for adults (both male and female ages 18 and over) having five or more drinks on one occasion.
[4]Weight classification by Body Mass Index (BMI). Overweight is considered BMI between 25.0 and 29.9; obese between 30.0 and 99.8.
[7]Represents median value of states and the District of Columbia.

Table A–16. Health Risks, Chronic Conditions, and Cardiovascular Disease—*Continued*

Geographic area	Chronic condition (percent)								Cardiovascular disease (percent)			
	Hypertension		Diabetes		Asthma[5]		Skin Cancer[6]	Other Cancers[6]	Angina or coronary heart disease		Stroke	
	2011	2001	2011	2000	2011	2000	2011	2011	2011	2005	2011	2005
United States[7]	30.8	25.6	9.5	6.1	9.1	7.3	5.8	6.6	4.1	4.4	2.9	2.6
Alabama	40.1	31.6	11.8	7.4	8.0	6.1	8.3	7.1	5.6	4.8	4.6	3.4
Alaska	29.4	21.8	7.9	3.8	8.2	6.9	3.0	6.4	2.6	3.2	2.4	1.7
Arizona	27.5	23.6	9.5	5.9	9.7	8.6	6.9	6.3	3.8	5.0	3.0	2.1
Arkansas	35.8	29.7	11.2	6.2	9.5	6.6	6.0	6.3	5.7	5.1	4.1	3.1
California	27.8	23.3	8.9	6.8	8.4	7.3	5.8	5.8	3.6	4.1	2.2	2.4
Colorado	25.0	21.6	6.7	5.1	8.3	6.6	6.1	6.1	2.5	2.6	2.0	1.4
Connecticut	29.8	24.0	9.3	5.5	9.9	7.8	5.7	6.0	3.4	4.3	2.3	1.7
Delaware	34.8	27.2	9.7	6.4	9.8	7.1	6.5	7.6	3.9	5.0	3.2	2.7
District of Columbia	30.0	29.0	9.1	7.2	10.1	7.9	2.8	4.7	3.0	3.0	3.7	3.1
Florida	34.2	26.9	10.4	6.9	7.6	5.7	9.0	7.4	5.3	6.0	3.8	3.2
Georgia	32.4	26.9	10.2	6.8	9.6	6.2	5.6	6.2	4.4	3.7	3.4	2.5
Hawaii	28.7	24.1	8.4	5.2	9.6	7.3	3.8	5.4	3.0	3.4	2.5	2.9
Idaho	29.4	24.6	9.4	4.9	9.3	7.7	6.1	6.5	4.1	5.0	2.4	2.4
Illinois	31.0	24.8	9.7	6.2	8.1	7.9	4.2	6.5	3.4	3.6	3.1	2.9
Indiana	32.8	25.8	10.2	6.0	9.6	8.1	5.4	6.3	4.8	4.8	3.4	2.6
Iowa	29.9	25.5	8.2	6.1	8.3	6.3	5.8	6.2	3.8	4.6	2.4	2.9
Kansas	30.8	23.9	9.5	5.9	8.8	7.8	6.2	6.9	4.5	4.6	2.7	2.4
Kentucky	38.0	30.1	10.8	6.5	10.5	7.8	6.6	7.1	5.9	5.6	3.9	3.2
Louisiana	38.4	27.6	11.8	6.6	6.4	5.0	4.7	6.8	4.9	5.3	3.8	3.2
Maine	32.2	25.2	9.6	6.0	12.1	8.9	5.9	7.4	5.2	4.6	2.8	2.6
Maryland	31.3	26.3	9.5	6.4	8.5	7.3	4.5	6.3	4.0	3.7	2.6	2.1
Massachusetts	29.2	23.6	8.0	5.8	10.7	8.5	5.3	6.7	3.8	4.0	2.2	2.2
Michigan	34.2	27.3	10.0	7.0	9.9	7.3	5.6	7.3	5.0	4.6	3.3	3.0
Minnesota	26.3	22.3	7.3	4.9	7.0	7.2	4.5	6.5	3.2	3.3	2.1	1.7
Mississippi	39.3	31.3	12.4	7.6	7.7	6.8	5.7	6.2	4.6	5.2	4.0	4.2
Missouri	34.3	26.5	10.2	6.7	9.2	7.2	6.6	7.3	4.7	4.8	3.6	3.4
Montana	30.2	26.8	8.0	4.9	9.1	8.3	7.1	8.0	4.0	3.6	3.2	2.2
Nebraska	28.6	22.6	8.4	4.9	7.3	6.6	5.6	6.6	3.9	3.6	2.6	2.4
Nevada	30.8	25.6	10.3	6.8	8.1	8.3	5.4	6.9	4.1	4.1	3.2	2.9
New Hampshire	30.7	22.8	8.7	4.4	11.0	8.3	5.9	7.6	3.9	4.5	2.6	2.6
New Jersey	30.6	26.1	8.8	5.8	9.0	6.2	4.8	5.5	4.1	4.6	2.3	2.2
New Mexico	28.4	20.0	10.0	6.5	10.0	6.9	5.7	6.0	3.7	3.4	2.6	2.3
New York	30.7	26.0	10.5	6.3	9.7	7.7	4.4	6.9	4.1	4.4	2.1	2.5
North Carolina	32.4	27.2	10.9	6.4	8.8	7.1	6.6	6.5	4.5	4.3	3.1	2.8
North Dakota	29.1	24.1	8.2	5.2	8.1	7.4	4.0	5.7	4.1	4.3	2.2	2.0
Ohio	32.7	26.6	10.0	6.4	9.8	8.6	5.1	6.6	5.0	4.5	3.1	2.4
Oklahoma	35.5	28.5	11.1	5.5	9.6	6.3	5.9	6.7	4.9	5.0	3.4	3.6
Oregon	29.9	24.9	9.3	6.0	10.5	8.5	6.8	7.1	3.6	3.8	2.9	2.6
Pennsylvania	31.4	28.1	9.5	7.1	9.0	6.5	5.7	6.8	5.3	5.1	3.1	2.5
Rhode Island	32.9	25.4	8.4	6.0	11.9	8.5	6.1	7.4	4.2	4.3	2.4	2.2
South Carolina	36.4	28.8	12.1	7.1	8.2	6.8	6.6	6.7	4.3	4.2	3.7	3.0
South Dakota	31.0	24.1	9.5	5.7	6.9	5.6	5.9	7.1	4.3	4.4	2.6	2.8
Tennessee	38.7	29.3	11.2	7.2	7.2	7.3	6.7	5.9	5.0	4.7	3.8	3.2
Texas	31.3	25.6	10.2	6.2	7.4	6.5	5.5	6.0	4.1	4.5	2.7	2.8
Utah	22.9	22.3	6.7	5.4	8.8	7.6	6.4	5.1	3.0	2.7	2.3	2.1
Vermont	29.3	21.4	7.7	4.4	11.1	7.2	5.8	6.7	4.0	4.4	2.6	2.2
Virginia	31.2	25.8	10.4	6.2	8.8	7.1	5.7	6.4	3.8	4.7	3.2	2.6
Washington	30.0	24.4	8.9	5.5	9.7	8.2	5.7	6.8	3.8	3.6	2.4	2.3
West Virginia	37.0	32.5	12.0	7.6	9.2	8.5	6.3	7.8	6.7	8.2	3.9	3.4
Wisconsin	28.9	24.1	8.4	6.1	9.2	7.7	5.1	6.8	4.0	4.0	2.5	1.9
Wyoming	28.6	22.4	8.2	5.0	9.1	8.6	6.0	6.4	3.6	3.8	2.9	1.9

[5]Adults (aged 18 and over) who have been told they currently have asthma.
[6]Data for earlier years not available.
[7]Represents median value of states and the District of Columbia.

Table A–17. People With and Without Health Insurance Coverage

Geographic area	Total people covered (thousands)			Number not covered (thousands)			Percentage of people not covered			Number not covered (thousands)			Percentage of children not covered		
	2011	2010	2000	2011	2010	2000¹	2011	2010	2000	2011	2010	2000	2011	2010	2000
United States...............	260,214	256,603	242,932	48,613	49,951	36,586	15.7	16.3	13.1	6,964	7,270	7,756	9.4	9.8	10.7
Alabama.........................	4,143	3,985	3,833	622	732	547	13.0	15.5	12.5	86	103	95	7.3	9.0	8.4
Alaska...........................	584	570	516	130	126	108	18.2	18.1	17.4	20	27	27	10.7	14.0	14.2
Arizona..........................	5,424	5,207	4,346	1,137	1,232	853	17.3	19.1	16.4	219	253	199	13.5	15.3	13.9
Arkansas.......................	2,401	2,348	2,278	508	533	373	17.5	18.5	14.1	56	51	80	8.1	7.3	11.5
California.......................	30,209	30,064	28,048	7,425	7,228	5,956	19.7	19.4	17.5	1,008	1,003	1,332	10.8	10.7	14.0
Colorado........................	4,239	4,356	3,782	788	644	559	15.7	12.9	12.9	131	96	133	10.4	7.8	11.8
Connecticut....................	3,215	3,149	3,071	303	397	300	8.6	11.2	8.9	43	51	49	5.3	6.2	5.9
Delaware........................	812	790	712	90	101	66	10.0	11.3	8.5	13	12	12	6.4	5.8	6.1
District of Columbia	567	527	483	52	78	71	8.4	12.8	12.8	5	5	10	4.3	5.3	8.8
Florida...........................	15,247	14,890	13,426	3,765	3,885	2,591	19.8	20.7	16.2	516	566	594	13.0	14.3	15.8
Georgia	7,821	7,779	6,998	1,862	1,879	1,126	19.2	19.5	13.9	278	249	229	10.9	10.0	10.3
Hawaii...........................	1,235	1,213	1,108	105	102	95	7.8	7.7	7.9	13	7	19	4.1	2.2	6.2
Idaho.............................	1,308	1,250	1,092	266	295	198	16.9	19.1	15.4	48	40	55	11.3	9.3	14.5
Illinois...........................	10,837	10,894	10,827	1,873	1,898	1,474	14.7	14.8	12.0	191	236	274	6.2	7.7	8.7
Indiana..........................	5,589	5,553	5,407	764	856	608	12.0	13.4	10.1	88	98	149	5.6	6.0	9.9
Iowa..............................	2,730	2,620	2,628	303	365	233	10.0	12.2	8.1	36	54	50	4.9	7.4	6.9
Kansas..........................	2,434	2,420	2,397	380	350	256	13.5	12.6	9.6	68	54	62	9.4	7.5	9.2
Kentucky........................	3,689	3,653	3,494	621	634	509	14.4	14.8	12.7	47	69	81	4.6	6.8	8.0
Louisiana.......................	3,568	3,542	3,631	938	875	736	20.8	19.8	16.8	131	103	188	11.6	9.0	15.2
Maine............................	1,196	1,179	1,138	133	121	131	10.0	9.3	10.4	17	12	25	6.3	4.3	8.6
Maryland........................	5,009	5,048	4,788	802	741	473	13.8	12.8	9.0	136	124	103	10.0	9.2	7.4
Massachusetts...............	6,304	6,180	5,843	219	362	450	3.4	5.5	7.1	35	54	66	2.5	3.8	4.6
Michigan........................	8,493	8,498	9,069	1,209	1,266	767	12.5	13.0	7.8	123	122	107	5.4	5.2	4.3
Minnesota......................	4,798	4,713	4,502	487	508	393	9.2	9.7	8.0	82	77	75	6.4	5.9	6.1
Mississippi.....................	2,458	2,315	2,431	476	614	368	16.2	21.0	13.2	69	101	67	9.0	13.4	8.6
Missouri	5,020	5,115	5,049	877	828	474	14.9	13.9	8.6	162	123	84	11.5	8.9	5.9
Montana.........................	806	803	748	180	178	144	18.3	18.2	16.1	27	20	34	12.3	9.2	15.2
Nebraska........................	1,600	1,567	1,553	225	239	134	12.3	13.2	7.9	38	49	24	8.2	10.5	5.6
Nevada..........................	2,077	2,120	1,727	607	578	321	22.6	21.4	15.7	139	115	84	21.0	17.5	15.2
New Hampshire..............	1,138	1,166	1,135	163	131	97	12.5	10.1	7.9	21	15	16	7.4	5.4	5.5
New Jersey	7,316	7,378	7,536	1,336	1,364	857	15.4	15.6	10.2	190	191	144	9.4	9.3	7.2
New Mexico....................	1,640	1,599	1,385	399	435	415	19.6	21.4	23.0	51	72	91	9.9	14.0	18.0
New York........................	16,986	16,249	16,057	2,355	2,886	2,730	12.2	15.1	14.5	284	352	402	6.6	8.1	8.7
North Carolina...............	7,955	7,776	7,032	1,550	1,606	964	16.3	17.1	12.1	215	213	180	9.3	9.1	8.9
North Dakota..................	614	566	562	61	88	61	9.1	13.4	9.8	7	18	13	4.7	11.3	9.2
Ohio..............................	9,771	9,810	10,077	1,549	1,547	1,101	13.7	13.6	9.8	230	223	245	8.7	8.2	8.8
Oklahoma.......................	3,131	3,062	2,797	636	641	587	16.9	17.3	17.4	60	119	130	6.4	12.5	14.9
Oregon...........................	3,324	3,166	3,022	532	604	398	13.8	16.0	11.6	64	87	78	7.4	10.2	9.0
Pennsylvania..................	11,341	11,173	11,148	1,375	1,372	915	10.8	10.9	7.6	206	230	158	7.6	8.3	5.6
Rhode Island..................	913	923	965	125	120	71	12.0	11.5	6.9	13	12	8	5.8	5.4	3.2
South Carolina	3,736	3,633	3,547	877	936	426	19.0	20.5	10.7	142	155	74	13.3	14.5	7.3
South Dakota	706	696	658	105	105	80	13.0	13.1	10.8	15	13	18	7.5	6.7	9.7
Tennessee	5,495	5,403	5,042	841	921	603	13.3	14.6	10.7	88	118	93	5.9	8.0	6.6
Texas............................	19,513	19,018	16,166	6,080	6,208	4,555	23.8	24.6	22.0	1,073	1,131	1,353	15.4	16.3	22.3
Utah..............................	2,402	2,389	1,999	412	381	243	14.6	13.8	10.8	95	99	62	10.7	11.4	8.5
Vermont	563	567	557	53	58	44	8.6	9.3	7.4	5	5	5	4.0	4.2	3.6
Virginia	6,910	6,743	6,322	1,066	1,102	670	13.4	14.0	9.6	111	157	139	5.9	8.4	7.8
Washington....................	5,831	5,793	5,105	986	935	767	14.5	13.9	13.1	143	97	133	8.8	6.0	8.7
West Virginia..................	1,553	1,579	1,536	273	243	239	14.9	13.4	13.4	37	11	39	9.7	2.7	9.8
Wisconsin......................	5,097	5,110	4,942	589	528	378	10.4	9.4	7.1	77	61	54	5.8	4.7	4.0
Wyoming	463	457	415	100	95	71	17.8	17.2	14.7	14	14	16	10.0	10.4	12.4

¹Children are considered anyone under the age of 18.

Table A–18. Immunizations, HIV, AIDS, STDs, and Lyme Disease

Geographic area	Percentage of children aged 19 to 35 months who are immunized[1]		Percentage of adults aged 65 years and over who received influenza vaccine[2]		Diagnosed with HIV infection (not AIDS) 2011[3]		Stage 3 (AIDS), 2011[3]			Sexually transmitted disease cases, 2011			Lyme disease cases, 2011
	2011	2010	2011	2010	Total	Adults or adolescents	Total	Adults or adolescents	Cumulative total[4]	Total[5]	Chlamydia	Gonorrhea	
United States...............	77.0	76.3	59.4	69.6	49,273	49,081	32,052	32,037	1,155,792	1,748,618	1,412,791	321,849	24,364
Alabama......................	79.2	78.2	60.2	65.3	843	837	391	391	10,596	38,986	29,626	9,132	9
Alaska	73.2	71.4	45.7	60.7	27	27	29	29	793	6,728	5,739	984	9
Arizona......................	68.1	76.9	53.9	69.4	709	708	430	430	13,073	34,090	29,251	4,564	8
Arkansas....................	79.1	79.7	55.9	74.2	244	243	138	138	4,727	20,921	16,052	4,687	0
California....................	80.4	72.3	55.9	67.5	5,973	5,965	3,623	3,622	168,692	196,733	166,773	27,516	79
Colorado	75.8	72.8	63.9	74.1	411	404	257	256	10,381	24,307	21,811	2,363	0
Connecticut.................	81.2	82.2	62.1	72.6	430	430	327	327	16,709	16,163	13,649	2,449	2,004
Delaware	72.1	75.7	65.0	68.5	127	127	105	105	4,337	5,362	4,508	827	767
District of Columbia	81.4	81.2	54.1	61.1	962	959	510	508	21,431	9,319	6,585	2,569	NA
Florida.......................	77.8	85.8	54.8	65.9	5,408	5,394	3,440	3,440	126,839	96,979	76,033	19,689	78
Georgia	83.9	76.4	57.6	66.0	2,522	2,520	2,234	2,234	42,068	71,509	54,403	16,428	32
Hawaii	80.7	77.2	58.9	74.1	78	78	44	44	3,408	6,700	6,001	685	0
Idaho.........................	68.8	65.1	55.7	60.8	38	38	23	23	776	4,874	4,699	162	3
Illinois.......................	77.3	77.4	53.3	67.2	2,142	2,137	1,304	1,304	40,818	82,857	64,939	17,037	194
Indiana.......................	73.4	74.8	59.2	67.6	513	512	353	353	10,137	34,543	27,801	6,569	81
Iowa..........................	78.9	82.1	72.2	73.5	131	128	93	93	2,177	12,645	10,705	1,920	72
Kansas	81.1	80.8	67.0	70.0	151	146	105	105	3,440	12,831	10,598	2,209	11
Kentucky	82.4	75.2	61.6	71.5	344	342	173	173	5,867	21,279	16,629	4,521	3
Louisiana	79.5	75.7	64.4	70.0	1,381	1,376	842	842	22,242	41,230	31,614	9,169	1
Maine........................	79.1	75.4	63.5	74.9	59	59	22	22	1,318	3,378	3,094	272	801
Maryland.....................	81.1	73.3	64.6	70.1	1,783	1,771	1,170	1,169	38,418	34,122	27,212	6,458	938
Massachusetts...............	80.3	80.4	63.3	75.0	1,267	1,262	668	666	23,627	25,385	22,764	2,353	1,801
Michigan.....................	76.4	85.5	56.2	68.6	802	793	508	506	18,058	62,756	49,568	12,901	89
Minnesota	79.0	77.9	65.7	75.9	322	318	215	215	6,069	19,325	16,902	2,284	1,185
Mississippi..................	73.8	80.6	61.8	70.6	617	617	399	399	8,538	27,221	21,216	5,814	3
Missouri	72.7	71.7	66.5	68.8	563	562	361	361	13,339	35,825	27,887	7,802	5
Montana......................	71.0	66.0	55.6	69.2	22	22	12	12	510	3,498	3,406	85	9
Nebraska.....................	82.9	81.6	63.6	74.9	78	77	47	47	1,870	8,142	6,780	1,352	7
Nevada	66.7	68.7	48.3	62.3	398	398	244	244	7,199	12,643	10,507	2,000	3
New Hampshire...............	75.4	84.1	58.2	74.3	55	51	31	31	1,288	3,158	3,010	130	887
New Jersey	79.1	67.0	58.5	65.2	1,567	1,557	959	956	56,970	33,789	26,209	7,348	3,398
New Mexico	80.0	72.4	56.9	72.6	147	146	181	181	3,268	13,284	11,374	1,839	2
New York......................	70.3	70.2	59.1	71.9	4,960	4,944	3,574	3,574	205,198	124,552	102,763	20,706	3,118
North Carolina...............	75.3	81.6	66.9	72.7	1,672	1,664	941	941	21,421	72,704	54,819	17,454	18
North Dakota.................	84.1	78.4	61.6	66.7	15	15	4	4	186	2,697	2,445	251	22
Ohio..........................	80.6	77.8	63.2	67.8	1,222	1,218	661	660	18,829	69,819	52,653	16,726	36
Oklahoma	77.3	70.8	64.7	69.9	335	332	175	175	5,837	18,895	14,596	4,215	2
Oregon	67.0	74.0	54.3	68.3	259	259	186	186	7,141	15,229	13,643	1,489	9
Pennsylvania.................	75.4	80.4	63.6	70.0	1,545	1,539	1,198	1,198	40,554	67,027	52,884	13,770	4,739
Rhode Island.................	79.5	76.7	57.2	70.0	127	126	67	67	3,055	4,552	4,146	360	111
South Carolina	74.1	78.8	61.1	71.2	862	858	641	641	17,022	37,505	28,932	8,350	24
South Dakota	71.0	73.5	69.7	74.6	26	26	22	22	352	4,011	3,409	602	2
Tennessee	73.9	83.4	70.1	70.7	926	921	577	576	15,668	39,050	31,105	7,667	5
Texas.........................	76.3	74.9	59.2	70.9	5,065	5,044	3,393	3,393	86,106	156,982	124,882	30,930	28
Utah..........................	71.1	73.0	59.5	70.0	92	92	72	72	2,690	7,377	7,086	277	6
Vermont	76.7	71.0	65.8	73.2	12	12	3	3	530	1,540	1,483	48	476
Virginia	77.0	75.4	58.9	73.2	1,100	1,096	637	637	20,710	43,045	36,314	6,518	756
Washington...................	76.0	73.7	58.6	71.5	546	539	348	348	13,796	26,345	23,280	2,737	17
West Virginia.................	69.3	73.4	70.3	67.7	105	104	90	90	1,909	5,095	4,295	796	107
Wisconsin	81.5	83.3	51.7	69.7	273	272	203	202	5,498	29,473	24,619	4,789	2,408
Wyoming	70.3	69.8	54.0	70.6	16	16	22	22.0	307.0	2,138	2,092	46	1

[1]Immunized children are those who received 4:3:1:3:3:1, which is four or more doses of diphtheria, tetanus, and pertussis, three or more doses of poliovirus vaccine, one or more doses of any measles, mumps, and rubella containing vaccine (MMR), three or more doses of Haemophilius Influenza of any type (Hib), three or more doses of hepatitis B vaccine (HepB), and one or more doses of varicella vaccine.
[2]Refers to the number of persons aged 65 years and over who reported receiving influenza vaccine during the preceding year.
[3]These numbers do not represent reported case counts but are point estimates, which result from adjustments of reported case counts. The reported case counts have been adjusted for reporting delays, but not for incomplete reporting. Adults and adolescents refers to people aged 18 years and older. Total includes children or people less than 13 years of age.
[4]From the beginning of the epidemic through 2011.
[5]Total includes cases of syphilis and chancroid not shown separately.
NA = Not available

Table A–19. Public and Private School Fall Enrollment

| Geographic area | Total enrollment (public and private) 2009–2011 | | | | | | | Public school enrollment | | | | | | | | |
| | 3 to 4 years of age | | | 5 to 17 years of age | | | | Total (thousands) | | | Pre-kindergarten through grade 8 (thousands) | | | Grades 9 through 12 (thousands) | | |
	Total enrollment (thousands)	Percent enrolled[1]	Percent enrolled in public school[2]	Total enrollment (thousands)	Public (thousands)	Private (thousands)	Percent enrolled in public school[2]	2011	2008	2000	2011	2008	2000	2011	2008	2000
United States..............	3,964	47.8	55.8	52,203	46,563	5,641	89.2	49,484	49,291	46,857	34,548	34,065	33,071	14,818	14,995	13,166
Alabama.....................	55	43.4	49.5	799	706	94	88.3	756	743	741	534	526	539	222	217	202
Alaska........................	7	35.0	67.0	128	117	11	91.5	132	131	134	92	89	96	40	42	39
Arizona......................	64	33.9	61.6	1,124	1,048	76	93.2	1,072	1,087	853	752	771	620	320	316	229
Arkansas....................	40	48.5	69.1	492	456	36	92.7	482	479	451	345	340	317	136	139	133
California...................	518	49.3	58.6	6,583	5,992	591	91.0	6,290	6,343	6,039	4,290	4,324	4,281	1,994	2,012	1,676
Colorado	70	49.5	54.7	850	777	73	91.4	843	802	708	601	566	506	242	236	201
Connecticut................	53	61.7	51.3	600	534	66	89.0	561	571	554	387	394	404	173	177	150
Delaware....................	12	50.1	52.5	144	117	27	81.4	129	123	113	90	85	80	39	38	33
District of Columbia	9	69.1	72.5	67	55	12	82.4	71	78	77	53	53	57	18	20	16
Florida.......................	222	50.1	51.0	2,827	2,490	337	88.1	2,643	2,667	2,381	1,858	1,856	1,725	785	811	656
Georgia......................	138	49.9	57.4	1,753	1,580	172	90.2	1,677	1,650	1,423	1,202	1,179	1,044	475	471	379
Hawaii.......................	20	55.1	41.4	208	168	40	80.7	180	180	186	127	125	133	52	54	53
Idaho.........................	17	35.2	47.8	295	271	24	91.7	276	272	245	194	191	169	82	81	76
Illinois.......................	187	54.6	59.5	2,222	1,966	256	88.5	2,092	2,113	2,028	1,455	1,473	1,460	637	640	564
Indiana......................	72	40.1	51.0	1,125	990	135	88.0	1,047	1,047	989	729	730	697	318	317	287
Iowa..........................	39	47.4	64.5	511	457	54	89.5	496	485	497	348	330	330	148	156	156
Kansas......................	38	46.3	63.7	504	448	56	88.9	484	468	472	340	325	318	140	141	143
Kentucky....................	50	42.9	63.7	720	638	82	88.6	673	666	648	480	469	453	193	197	187
Louisiana...................	69	53.4	63.1	779	638	141	82.0	697	681	757	512	500	540	184	181	205
Maine........................	12	43.1	48.1	199	179	21	89.6	189	196	209	129	131	147	60	66	60
Maryland....................	78	52.0	46.4	957	814	143	85.1	852	846	847	588	576	604	264	269	236
Massachusetts............	89	59.7	45.8	1,022	896	126	87.7	956	963	971	666	666	702	289	296	265
Michigan....................	116	47.6	65.9	1,687	1,517	170	89.9	1,587	1,693	1,726	1,070	1,124	1,177	509	549	454
Minnesota..................	67	46.3	58.3	897	795	102	88.6	838	838	854	570	558	580	268	279	274
Mississippi.................	45	52.6	71.0	523	468	55	89.4	491	494	501	346	348	356	136	137	129
Missouri.....................	73	45.1	58.9	993	854	139	86.0	919	917	914	643	632	642	276	285	263
Montana.....................	11	43.6	52.6	155	139	16	89.7	142	143	158	98	96	107	43	46	50
Nebraska....................	25	47.9	56.3	319	276	43	86.5	299	291	288	210	200	197	88	91	91
Nevada......................	25	31.9	57.7	456	428	28	93.8	437	429	326	307	306	239	130	122	86
New Hampshire............	16	53.0	36.7	211	187	24	88.6	195	201	207	132	134	146	63	66	60
New Jersey	143	63.4	51.1	1,476	1,294	181	87.7	1,403	1,382	1,289	941	914	883	405	411	313
New Mexico................	23	39.7	70.6	359	330	29	91.9	338	329	324	239	230	229	99	99	96
New York....................	269	57.7	52.5	3,068	2,636	432	85.9	2,735	2,765	2,888	1,856	1,804	1,954	852	852	781
North Carolina.............	112	43.7	50.1	1,593	1,440	153	90.4	1,491	1,489	1,276	1,058	1,072	935	432	417	341
North Dakota..............	6	35.0	64.3	99	90	9	91.1	96	95	113	66	63	75	30	32	38
Ohio..........................	136	45.7	56.5	1,934	1,665	270	86.1	1,754	1,827	1,837	1,223	1,241	1,287	531	586	540
Oklahoma..................	45	42.3	76.2	647	597	50	92.2	660	642	627	482	460	445	176	178	179
Oregon......................	40	40.9	43.9	604	544	61	90.0	571	566	545	393	383	376	178	182	166
Pennsylvania..............	149	49.7	45.7	1,985	1,688	297	85.0	1,793	1,802	1,817	1,209	1,204	1,247	582	596	541
Rhode Island..............	12	48.1	46.0	160	140	20	87.2	144	148	156	98	99	110	46	48	43
South Carolina	62	49.5	56.3	755	685	70	90.7	726	712	667	516	505	484	210	208	183
South Dakota	10	40.6	63.1	139	126	12	91.1	126	122	131	88	83	89	38	38	41
Tennessee.................	68	40.8	58.1	1,051	925	126	88.0	987	964	916	702	669	650	286	283	252
Texas........................	342	42.7	60.6	4,787	4,462	325	93.2	4,936	4,675	3,992	3,587	3,375	2,896	1,349	1,300	1,096
Utah..........................	43	40.7	48.2	587	549	38	93.6	586	576	480	425	410	323	161	166	146
Vermont	6	48.1	56.1	94	85	9	90.7	97	94	105	68	63	72	29	31	32
Virginia	101	49.0	42.2	1,301	1,161	140	89.2	1,251	1,231	1,134	871	850	795	380	380	317
Washington................	74	41.8	45.2	1,097	983	114	89.6	1,044	1,030	1,004	714	697	695	330	333	309
West Virginia..............	16	37.2	70.5	272	253	19	93.1	283	283	292	201	199	203	81	84	88
Wisconsin..................	65	44.4	64.3	952	824	128	86.6	872	875	878	598	585	596	274	289	281
Wyoming	7	40.9	54.5	92	87	6	93.6	89	86	92	63	59	62	26	27	30

[1]As a percentage of all 3 and 4 year olds, including those not enrolled.
[2]As a percentage of those enrolled.

Table A–20. Public Elementary and Secondary Schools—Finances and Teachers, 2011–2012

Geographic area	Total enrollment (thousands)[1]	Receipts (millions of dollars)				Expenditures						Teachers[4]				Pupil–teacher ratio[5]
		Revenue receipts				Total (millions of dollars)[2]	Per capita (dollars)[3]	Current expenditures				Number (thousands)		Average salary (thousands of dollars)		
		Total	Source					Elementary and secondary day schools (millions of dollars)	Average per pupil in average daily attendance		Capital outlay (millions of dollars)	Elementary	Secondary	Elementary	Secondary	
			Federal	State	Local				Amount (dollars)	Rank						
United States	47,388	587,991	61,597	269,520	256,873	609,977	1,943.1	533,285	11,254	(X)	46,469	1,791.1	1,317.5	54.7	56.2	15.4
Alabama	705	7,037	822	3,929	2,286	7,114	1,475.4	6,330	8,983	46	527	24.9	21.5	47.5	48.6	15.5
Alaska	118	2,326	342	1,436	548	2,515	3,438.1	2,175	18,433	3	297	4.0	5.6	61.1	63.8	14.4
Arizona	1,048	10,765	842	5,717	4,205	8,623	1,315.8	7,170	6,844	51	808	43.1	17.9	48.7	48.7	17.5
Arkansas	465	5,093	686	2,544	1,863	5,199	1,762.7	4,420	9,511	39	618	14.0	17.2	45.0	47.4	15.0
California	6,131	65,364	9,215	36,557	19,592	67,883	1,784.4	56,164	9,160	42	6,916	131.7	117.0	68.3	68.6	25.3
Colorado	792	8,728	758	3,625	4,344	9,902	1,908.7	8,543	10,783	27	851	25.7	23.5	48.6	49.5	16.5
Connecticut	578	9,868	717	3,645	5,506	9,853	2,744.4	8,754	15,137	11	835	28.6	13.1	68.4	69.8	13.9
Delaware	114	2,164	159	1,346	659	2,374	2,588.1	1,870	16,399	6	316	4.6	4.6	58.8	58.8	12.8
District of Columbia	77	952	107	0	845	1,393	2,203.2	1,075	13,952	13	315	4.0	2.1	68.7	68.7	12.7
Florida	2,576	24,099	3,122	8,702	12,274	25,770	1,334.0	22,456	8,718	49	1,837	89.0	80.2	46.5	46.5	15.3
Georgia	1,617	18,104	1,826	7,651	8,627	16,579	1,671.2	16,148	9,986	35	138	66.2	42.5	52.6	53.5	14.6
Hawaii	163	2,676	303	2,330	42	2,588	1,858.7	2,116	13,013	15	189	5.9	5.3	54.1	54.1	14.4
Idaho	271	2,621	246	1,874	501	3,046	1,909.0	2,409	8,888	47	549	8.5	7.7	48.6	48.6	17.1
Illinois	2,001	26,328	3,418	5,629	17,281	29,284	2,274.4	26,001	12,991	17	1,933	96.9	33.8	57.6	57.6	15.6
Indiana	1,000	11,746	1,046	6,534	4,166	13,382	2,047.0	11,256	11,255	22	818	34.6	29.0	49.8	50.0	16.0
Iowa	451	5,696	464	2,628	2,604	5,747	1,869.3	4,680	10,376	33	922	23.1	11.4	50.5	49.8	13.2
Kansas	422	5,672	444	3,157	2,071	5,672	1,965.4	4,595	10,901	26	874	17.5	17.6	46.7	46.7	12.4
Kentucky	628	5,999	958	2,812	2,228	7,273	1,660.3	6,490	10,340	34	541	29.9	12.1	49.6	50.1	15.2
Louisiana	659	7,856	1,212	3,532	3,112	8,208	1,783.5	7,033	10,672	29	1,025	35.5	15.7	50.2	50.2	13.3
Maine	172	2,980	345	1,092	1,543	2,070	1,557.0	1,924	11,182	24	0	10.3	5.0	48.0	46.5	11.1
Maryland	804	13,631	923	5,960	6,747	13,876	2,358.1	12,483	15,528	9	936	35.1	24.1	63.3	62.2	13.8
Massachusetts	898	16,282	928	6,867	8,487	15,072	2,267.8	14,226	15,838	7	526	45.2	23.2	71.7	71.7	13.0
Michigan	1,524	15,024	1,949	10,263	2,812	20,906	2,115.3	20,550	13,487	14	0	46.6	37.5	61.6	61.6	18.1
Minnesota	764	10,779	661	8,690	1,428	12,284	2,283.7	9,571	12,525	19	1,751	26.9	26.0	55.0	55.0	14.4
Mississippi	450	4,319	682	2,211	1,426	4,540	1,521.1	4,440	9,859	36	15	19.8	13.9	41.6	41.6	13.5
Missouri	840	11,314	1,196	3,416	6,702	10,114	1,679.4	8,840	10,529	31	754	35.1	33.6	46.4	46.4	12.2
Montana	111	1,574	203	756	615	1,480	1,472.8	1,440	12,992	16	28	7.2	3.5	48.5	48.5	10.4
Nebraska	271	3,075	236	1,114	1,725	3,083	1,661.7	2,830	10,461	32	168	21.6	9.3	48.2	48.2	9.6
Nevada	473	3,513	286	1,229	1,999	5,071	1,838.1	3,876	8,195	50	865	15.3	11.1	54.6	54.6	18.4
New Hampshire	182	3,022	166	1,012	1,844	2,893	2,190.7	2,785	15,335	10	53	10.6	5.0	54.2	54.2	11.6
New Jersey	1,445	25,642	798	8,589	16,255	25,924	2,924.5	25,173	17,416	5	97	44.0	69.4	67.1	67.1	12.8
New Mexico	321	3,714	634	2,450	631	4,127	1,978.9	3,404	10,608	30	651	14.6	6.7	45.4	46.3	15.0
New York	3,125	51,078	4,570	22,917	23,591	54,429	2,781.2	48,729	15,592	8	2,923	95.8	119.9	73.4	73.4	15.2
North Carolina	1,347	13,089	1,781	7,575	3,734	12,760	1,308.4	12,144	9,015	45	616	66.3	26.7	45.9	46.0	14.3
North Dakota	86	1,195	121	481	593	1,025	1,464.9	839	9,743	38	88	5.7	2.4	46.1	46.1	11.0
Ohio	1,642	19,182	1,778	8,806	8,598	18,458	1,598.9	18,458	11,239	23	0	68.6	37.9	56.7	56.7	15.2
Oklahoma	624	6,164	1,127	2,813	2,224	6,180	1,620.0	5,517	8,835	48	577	29.5	12.2	44.0	45.2	15.1
Oregon	500	6,523	840	3,002	2,681	6,800	1,743.8	6,113	12,232	20	375	18.0	9.8	57.0	58.0	18.0
Pennsylvania	1,680	30,492	1,849	11,939	16,704	29,169	2,285.4	24,333	14,487	12	2,714	62.2	62.2	61.9	61.9	13.9
Rhode Island	115	2,287	172	700	1,416	2,391	2,276.7	2,288	19,940	2	28	6.2	3.8	62.2	62.2	10.4
South Carolina	669	7,896	993	3,460	3,443	7,837	1,659.1	6,331	9,467	40	995	33.3	14.4	45.7	45.9	14.1
South Dakota	118	1,292	210	395	687	1,357	1,627.9	1,150	9,753	37	175	6.5	2.7	38.8	38.7	13.0
Tennessee	902	8,790	1,260	4,090	3,440	8,745	1,354.6	8,228	9,122	44	92	46.2	19.9	47.1	47.1	13.9
Texas	4,634	50,054	5,725	20,661	23,668	52,521	2,015.4	42,303	9,128	43	6,557	161.8	152.0	47.9	48.8	14.3
Utah	443	4,926	551	2,523	1,853	5,104	1,787.4	4,091	9,234	41	760	15.6	12.2	48.2	48.2	16.3
Vermont	65	1,842	143	1,617	82	1,711	2,732.9	1,560	24,056	1	62	4.7	4.3	51.3	51.3	7.2
Virginia	1,163	15,614	999	6,006	8,609	16,669	2,036.3	14,105	12,125	21	987	62.1	41.7	48.7	48.7	11.2
Washington	979	12,132	1,488	6,991	3,653	13,320	1,931.3	10,460	10,682	28	2,334	30.1	23.4	52.1	52.4	18.5
West Virginia	305	3,585	492	2,128	965	4,043	2,178.8	3,322	10,907	25	186	14.4	5.5	45.3	45.3	15.3
Wisconsin	838	12,272	1,659	5,270	5,344	11,873	2,073.3	10,603	12,653	18	603	40.1	16.7	53.6	54.4	14.9
Wyoming	83	1,614	147	848	619	1,742	3,021.6	1,483	17,958	4	247	4.0	3.4	56.9	57.5	11.4

Note. Figures may not sum to totals because of rounding.

[1] Enrollment represents average daily attendance (ADA) in school year 2011–2012. The ADA for the school year is the total number of students that actually were present in school divided by the number of days school was in session.

[2] Includes interest on school debt and other current expenditures not shown separately.

[3] Based on U.S. Census Bureau estimated resident population as of July 1, 2012.

[4] Full-time equivalent. Schools classified by type of organization rather than by grade-group; elementary includes kindergarten.

[5] Students in average daily attendance in K-12 schools.

(0) = zero or rounds to zero

(X) = No applicable

Table A–21. Public High School Graduates and Educational Attainment

Geographic area	Public high school graduates (thousands)[1]			18- to 24-year-olds who completed high school, 2009–2011 (percent)	Population 25 years and over (thousands)	Educational attainment, 2009–2011					
						Percentage of people 25 years and over, by highest level completed					
	2010 projected	2005	2000			Not a high school graduate	High school graduate	Some college, but no degree	Associate's degree	Bachelor's degree	Advanced degree[2]
United States....................	3,013.4	2,799.3	2,553.8	83.6	204,348	14.4	28.4	21.3	7.6	17.7	10.5
Alabama...........................	40.6	37.5	37.8	80.9	3,169	17.7	31.0	21.9	7.2	14.1	8.0
Alaska..............................	8.4	6.9	6.6	81.5	449	8.5	26.7	29.7	7.8	17.9	9.4
Arizona.............................	60.6	59.5	38.3	80.4	4,149	14.6	24.6	26.4	8.1	16.8	9.5
Arkansas..........................	28.5	26.6	27.3	82.8	1,923	16.9	35.1	22.3	6.1	13.0	6.5
California..........................	383.7	355.2	309.9	83.2	24,114	19.2	20.9	22.2	7.6	19.2	10.9
Colorado...........................	47.7	44.5	38.9	84.0	3,329	10.2	22.6	22.8	8.0	23.3	13.1
Connecticut.......................	37.8	35.5	31.6	86.4	2,431	11.3	28.0	17.7	7.3	20.2	15.6
Delaware...........................	8.1	6.9	6.1	82.9	603	12.8	31.7	19.9	7.2	16.9	11.5
District of Columbia..........	3.0	2.8	2.7	88.0	417	12.6	19.2	14.6	2.8	22.5	28.2
Florida..............................	144.3	133.3	106.7	81.7	13,100	14.4	30.2	21.1	8.6	16.5	9.2
Georgia............................	85.4	70.8	62.6	79.7	6,243	15.7	29.2	21.0	6.7	17.6	9.8
Hawaii..............................	10.7	10.8	10.4	90.9	928	9.8	28.7	22.5	9.7	19.5	9.9
Idaho...............................	17.2	15.8	16.2	84.6	986	11.5	28.4	27.1	8.5	16.9	7.7
Illinois..............................	133.7	123.6	111.8	84.7	8,466	13.1	27.4	21.3	7.3	19.2	11.7
Indiana.............................	62.4	55.4	57.0	80.9	4,229	13.0	35.6	21.0	7.6	14.6	8.2
Iowa.................................	33.5	33.5	33.9	88.0	2,014	9.4	33.3	21.7	10.3	17.5	7.8
Kansas.............................	30.1	30.4	29.1	85.7	1,842	10.4	27.9	24.5	7.3	19.5	10.3
Kentucky...........................	41.0	38.4	36.8	83.5	2,903	17.8	34.1	20.4	6.8	12.4	8.5
Louisiana..........................	34.6	36.0	38.4	79.0	2,944	17.9	34.3	21.4	5.0	14.3	7.1
Maine...............................	14.0	13.1	12.2	87.5	938	9.4	33.9	20.1	8.9	17.7	10.0
Maryland...........................	58.2	54.2	47.8	86.1	3,872	11.7	26.1	19.7	6.3	19.9	16.3
Massachusetts...................	63.7	59.7	53.0	88.3	4,461	10.9	26.1	16.5	7.7	22.1	16.7
Michigan...........................	112.7	101.6	97.7	85.0	6,571	11.4	30.9	24.1	8.4	15.6	9.7
Minnesota.........................	59.7	58.4	57.4	86.9	3,528	8.3	27.3	22.5	10.0	21.5	10.4
Mississippi........................	26.0	23.5	24.2	80.7	1,905	19.1	30.5	22.7	8.0	12.5	7.1
Missouri...........................	63.7	57.8	52.8	84.0	3,981	12.9	31.8	22.9	6.9	16.1	9.6
Montana...........................	9.9	10.3	10.9	84.8	672	8.3	30.6	24.8	8.1	19.6	8.7
Nebraska..........................	20.1	19.9	20.1	86.8	1,187	9.6	28.5	24.4	9.3	19.2	9.0
Nevada.............................	18.5	15.7	14.6	77.7	1,791	15.7	29.2	25.7	7.3	14.6	7.5
New Hampshire..................	14.5	13.8	11.8	87.1	908	8.5	29.6	19.3	9.8	20.8	12.1
New Jersey........................	94.7	86.5	74.4	86.4	5,968	12.1	29.4	17.2	6.2	22.0	13.2
New Mexico.......................	18.1	17.4	18.0	78.3	1,337	16.8	26.6	24.0	7.3	14.6	10.8
New York...........................	177.3	153.2	141.7	84.9	13,096	15.2	27.6	16.4	8.3	18.6	14.0
North Carolina...................	85.5	75.0	62.1	82.4	6,329	15.5	27.4	21.9	8.6	17.7	8.9
North Dakota......................	6.8	7.6	8.6	91.3	443	9.6	27.0	24.2	12.5	19.4	7.2
Ohio.................................	120.2	116.7	111.7	83.9	7,718	11.9	35.0	20.8	7.6	15.5	9.1
Oklahoma.........................	38.1	36.2	37.6	81.9	2,442	13.9	31.8	24.4	6.8	15.5	7.6
Oregon.............................	34.9	32.6	30.2	83.6	2,614	11.0	24.7	27.2	8.1	18.5	10.6
Pennsylvania.....................	121.9	124.8	114.0	86.7	8,662	11.7	37.5	16.6	7.4	16.5	10.4
Rhode Island.....................	9.5	9.9	8.5	88.1	709	15.5	27.2	18.5	8.1	18.6	12.2
South Carolina...................	38.6	33.4	31.6	81.5	3,077	16.1	30.5	20.7	8.5	15.7	8.6
South Dakota.....................	8.6	8.6	9.3	82.9	532	10.0	31.8	22.4	9.8	18.2	7.8
Tennessee.........................	58.2	48.0	41.6	84.3	4,253	16.3	33.3	21.0	6.1	15.0	8.2
Texas...............................	265.7	239.7	212.9	80.3	15,773	19.4	25.5	22.8	6.4	17.4	8.6
Utah.................................	26.4	30.3	32.5	86.7	1,579	9.5	24.1	27.8	9.1	19.9	9.5
Vermont...........................	7.1	7.2	6.7	90.4	432	8.7	31.2	17.8	8.4	20.4	13.6
Virginia.............................	78.4	73.7	65.6	87.2	5,354	13.0	25.5	20.3	6.8	20.2	14.3
Washington........................	64.5	61.1	57.6	82.9	4,512	10.2	23.8	25.2	9.5	20.0	11.3
West Virginia......................	17.5	17.1	19.4	83.8	1,295	16.6	41.2	18.2	6.1	11.1	6.8
Wisconsin.........................	64.0	63.2	58.5	87.0	3,803	9.9	33.4	21.2	9.3	17.4	8.8
Wyoming...........................	5.4	5.6	6.5	86.3	371	7.8	30.2	27.7	10.0	16.1	8.2

[1] For school year ending in year shown.
[2] Graduate or professional degree.

Table A–22. Institutions of Higher Education

Geographic area	Fall enrollment (thousands)[1]									State appropriations for higher education, FY 2012			Degrees conferred from degree-granting institutions, 2010–2011[4]	
	Total			Public			Private			Full-time equivalent enrollment (thousands)[2]	Educational appropriations (millions of dollars)[3]	Educational appropriations per full-time equivalent enrollment (dollars)[3]	Total	Bachelor's
	2011	2006	2000	2011	2006	2000	2011	2006	2000					
United States............	20,994	17,759	15,312	15,110	13,180	11,753	5,884	4,579	3,560	11,549	68,204	5,906	3,552,640	1,715,913
Alabama....................	319	258	234	261	231	207	58	28	27	205	1,202	5,855	53,075	27,248
Alaska	35	30	28	32	29	27	3	1	1	22	260	11,909	4,032	1,770
Arizona.....................	797	567	342	366	331	285	431	236	58	275	1,257	4,567	149,087	50,928
Arkansas...................	179	147	115	159	131	102	21	16	13	126	866	6,873	29,046	13,259
California...................	2,686	2,435	2,257	2,179	2,048	1,928	507	387	329	1,496	9,839	6,577	361,877	169,623
Colorado...................	366	308	264	269	232	218	97	76	46	193	491	2,551	62,101	29,540
Connecticut...............	202	177	161	126	112	101	75	64	60	86	630	7,354	36,753	19,735
Delaware	57	51	44	41	38	34	16	13	10	35	162	4,663	10,948	5,877
District of Columbia	90	110	73	5	6	5	85	104	67	n.a.	n.a.	n.a.	22,493	8,402
Florida......................	1,144	886	708	803	652	557	340	234	151	638	3,273	5,130	213,598	86,281
Georgia	565	435	346	429	346	272	137	89	74	379	2,518	6,644	84,562	45,075
Hawaii......................	79	67	60	60	50	45	19	17	16	41	280	6,898	12,108	5,751
Idaho.......................	90	78	66	66	59	54	24	19	12	59	334	5,661	15,201	9,171
Illinois......................	893	831	744	577	553	534	316	278	210	422	3,612	8,554	162,446	71,580
Indiana.....................	458	368	314	340	272	240	118	96	74	262	1,114	4,258	79,845	43,519
Iowa	372	239	189	178	151	135	194	88	54	132	581	4,390	68,650	36,266
Kansas.....................	217	193	180	186	171	160	30	23	20	143	664	4,647	36,395	18,191
Kentucky...................	294	249	188	233	204	152	60	45	36	159	1,109	6,959	44,269	21,078
Louisiana	266	224	224	225	193	189	41	32	35	182	1,008	5,551	37,998	21,509
Maine	72	66	58	50	48	41	22	18	18	38	230	6,071	12,789	7,347
Maryland...................	380	319	274	314	261	224	66	59	50	243	1,620	6,668	62,795	29,247
Massachusetts	509	452	421	227	192	183	282	259	238	170	802	4,712	108,191	53,749
Michigan...................	686	634	568	555	512	468	131	123	100	423	1,771	4,185	114,135	56,217
Minnesota	458	376	293	274	244	219	184	132	75	214	986	4,607	80,041	33,386
Mississippi................	179	151	137	161	137	125	18	15	12	142	857	6,033	30,516	13,230
Missouri	457	377	321	261	218	202	196	159	120	196	979	4,984	85,535	41,648
Montana....................	54	48	42	49	43	37	5	5	5	41	164	4,007	9,128	5,512
Nebraska...................	143	125	112	107	94	89	36	30	24	84	581	6,933	24,916	13,510
Nevada.....................	121	112	88	105	102	83	16	10	5	65	432	6,676	16,112	7,556
New Hampshire..........	77	71	62	43	42	36	34	29	26	39	62	1,583	16,655	9,479
New Jersey	444	386	336	359	308	267	84	77	69	279	1,687	6,051	75,739	37,087
New Mexico	158	132	111	147	122	101	11	10	9	98	726	7,430	18,580	8,179
New York...................	1,318	1,160	1,043	732	636	583	586	525	460	586	4,421	7,542	278,304	127,205
North Carolina...........	585	496	405	471	406	329	114	90	75	412	3,602	8,735	94,166	48,670
North Dakota.............	56	50	40	49	43	36	7	7	4	38	260	6,938	10,254	5,674
Ohio	735	620	550	543	453	411	192	167	138	456	1,669	3,663	126,030	63,882
Oklahoma	230	206	178	197	178	154	33	28	24	147	1,027	7,008	38,188	19,511
Oregon.....................	259	198	183	215	160	155	44	38	28	170	656	3,851	39,662	19,542
Pennsylvania.............	788	707	610	428	388	339	360	319	270	369	1,430	3,875	162,778	88,205
Rhode Island.............	85	82	75	43	40	38	41	41	37	32	166	5,226	17,578	10,863
South Carolina	260	212	186	208	176	156	52	36	30	176	796	4,515	40,260	23,034
South Dakota	56	49	43	44	38	35	12	11	8	34	141	4,195	9,539	5,211
Tennessee	350	291	264	242	205	203	108	85	61	204	1,136	5,582	57,592	31,026
Texas.......................	1,564	1,253	1,034	1,367	1,094	897	197	159	137	973	7,723	7,938	217,791	107,438
Utah	264	202	164	179	148	123	85	54	41	127	611	4,830	44,941	24,461
Vermont	45	41	35	27	24	20	18	17	15	22	55	2,512	10,088	6,100
Virginia	588	456	382	414	358	314	175	98	68	326	1,391	4,272	98,890	49,077
Washington...............	373	348	321	317	297	274	56	51	47	254	1,216	4,788	70,705	31,398
West Virginia.............	162	101	88	96	87	76	67	14	12	80	447	5,575	24,557	12,978
Wisconsin	377	340	307	297	272	250	80	68	57	233	1,315	5,639	62,404	35,279
Wyoming	38	35	30	36	33	29	2	2	1	26	369	14,105	5,746	1,860

[1]Data for 2000–2012 are for 4-year and 2-year degree-granting institutions that participated in Title IV federal financial aid programs. Represents opening fall enrollment of resident and extension students attending full-time or part-time. Excludes students taking courses for credit by mail, radio, or TV, and students in branches of U.S. institutions operated in foreign countries.
[2]Full-time equivalent enrollment equates student credit hours to full-time, academic year students, but excludes medical students.
[3]Educational appropriations measure state and local support available for public higher education operating expenses, including ARRA funds and excludes appropriations for independent institutions, financial aid for students attending independent institutions, research, hospitals, and medical education.
[4]Totals include Associate's, Bachelor's, Master's, Ph.D., Ed.D., and comparable degrees at the doctoral level. Also includes most degrees formerly classified as first-professional, such as M.D., D.D.S., and law degrees conferred.

Table A–23   Violent Crimes and Crime Rates

Geographic area	Number[1]				Rates (per 100,000)[2]							
					2011					Total		
	2011	2010	2005	2000	Total	Murder[3]	Rape	Robbery	Assualt	2010	2005	2000
United States...............	1,203,564	1,251,248	1,390,745	1,425,486	386.3	4.7	26.8	113.7	241.1	404.5	469.0	506.5
Alabama[4]........................	20,174	18,056	19,678	21,620	420.1	6.3	28.5	102.2	283.0	377.8	431.7	486.2
Alaska	4,383	4,537	4,194	3,554	606.5	4.0	58.1	79.7	464.6	638.8	631.9	566.9
Arizona...........................	26,311	26,085	30,478	27,281	405.9	6.2	34.9	109.9	254.8	408.1	513.2	531.7
Arkansas	14,129	14,735	14,659	11,904	480.9	5.5	41.3	82.6	351.5	505.3	527.5	445.3
California........................	154,944	164,133	190,178	210,531	411.1	4.8	20.3	144.0	242.0	440.6	526.3	621.6
Colorado	16,383	16,133	18,498	14,367	320.2	2.9	44.5	64.6	208.1	320.8	396.5	334.0
Connecticut....................	9,767	10,057	9,635	11,058	272.8	3.6	19.2	102.7	147.3	281.4	274.5	324.7
Delaware[5]......................	5,075	5,575	5,332	5,363	559.5	4.5	31.9	169.5	353.5	620.9	632.1	684.4
District of Columbia[6].......	7,429	8,004	8,032	8,626	1,202.1	17.5	28.0	662.3	494.3	1,330.2	1,459.0	1,507.9
Florida............................	98,199	101,969	125,957	129,777	515.3	5.2	27.7	134.4	348.0	542.4	708.0	812.0
Georgia	36,634	39,072	40,725	41,319	373.2	5.6	20.9	123.8	222.9	403.3	448.9	504.7
Hawaii	3,949	3,574	3,253	2,954	287.2	1.2	31.6	75.8	178.6	262.7	255.1	243.8
Idaho..............................	3,184	3,465	3,670	3,267	200.9	2.3	27.4	11.6	159.6	221.0	256.8	252.5
Illinois[4,7]........................	55,247	55,835	70,392	81,567	429.3	5.6	28.8	157.4	237.5	435.2	551.5	656.8
Indiana...........................	21,626	20,389	20,302	21,230	331.8	4.8	27.0	107.1	193.0	314.5	323.7	349.1
Iowa...............................	7,826	8,333	8,642	7,796	255.6	1.5	27.2	26.9	199.9	273.5	291.3	266.4
Kansas[7].........................	10,162	10,531	10,634	10,470	353.9	3.8	37.8	50.8	261.5	369.1	387.4	389.4
Kentucky[7]......................	10,406	10,528	11,134	11,903	238.2	3.5	33.5	84.5	116.7	242.6	266.8	294.5
Louisiana	25,406	24,886	26,889	30,440	555.3	11.2	27.7	114.5	401.9	549.0	594.4	681.1
Maine.............................	1,636	1,621	1,483	1,397	123.2	2.0	29.6	27.8	63.8	122.0	112.2	109.6
Maryland.........................	28,797	31,620	39,369	41,663	494.1	6.8	20.5	177.5	289.3	547.7	703.0	786.6
Massachusetts	28,219	30,553	29,237	30,230	428.4	2.8	24.7	102.7	298.1	466.6	456.9	476.1
Michigan.........................	43,983	48,460	55,877	55,159	445.3	6.2	44.0	105.2	289.9	490.3	552.1	555.0
Minnesota.......................	11,825	12,515	15,243	13,813	221.2	1.4	31.1	63.4	125.4	236.0	297.0	280.8
Mississippi.....................	8,036	8,003	8,131	10,267	269.8	8.0	29.0	83.7	149.1	269.7	278.4	360.9
Missouri	26,889	27,252	30,477	27,419	447.4	6.1	24.3	104.3	312.7	455.0	525.4	490.0
Montana[4,7].....................	2,670	2,693	2,634	2,171	267.5	2.8	35.8	16.9	212.0	272.2	281.5	240.6
Nebraska........................	4,665	5,104	5,048	5,606	253.2	3.6	37.7	54.1	157.7	279.5	287.0	327.6
Nevada...........................	15,309	17,841	14,654	10,474	562.1	5.2	33.5	157.9	365.6	660.6	606.8	524.2
New Hampshire...............	2,478	2,198	1,729	2,167	188.0	1.3	32.5	36.0	118.2	167.0	132.0	175.4
New Jersey	27,203	27,055	30,919	32,298	308.4	4.3	11.4	138.4	154.3	307.7	354.7	383.8
New Mexico	11,817	12,126	13,541	13,786	567.5	7.5	41.2	82.7	436.2	588.9	702.2	757.9
New York.........................	77,490	75,977	85,839	105,111	398.1	4.0	14.1	145.9	234.1	392.1	445.8	553.9
North Carolina................	33,774	34,653	40,650	40,051	349.8	5.3	20.7	98.9	224.9	363.4	468.1	497.6
North Dakota...................	1,689	1,513	625	523	247.0	3.5	37.9	13.3	192.3	225.0	98.2	81.4
Ohio...............................	35,484	36,366	40,273	37,935	307.4	4.4	31.5	139.1	132.4	315.2	351.3	334.1
Oklahoma	17,243	17,987	18,044	17,177	454.8	5.5	37.0	86.6	325.7	479.5	508.6	497.8
Oregon[4].........................	9,586	9,655	10,444	12,000	247.6	2.1	31.4	57.4	156.6	252.0	286.8	350.7
Pennsylvania...................	45,240	46,514	52,761	51,584	355.0	5.0	26.1	126.6	197.3	366.2	424.5	420.0
Rhode Island..................	2,602	2,701	2,703	3,121	247.5	1.3	28.9	71.0	146.3	256.6	251.2	297.7
South Carolina	26,760	27,648	32,384	32,293	571.9	6.8	34.5	92.2	438.4	597.7	761.1	804.9
South Dakota	2,094	2,186	1,363	1,259	254.1	2.5	60.2	20.3	171.1	268.5	175.7	166.8
Tennessee	38,944	38,921	44,891	40,233	608.2	5.8	31.6	126.2	444.5	613.3	752.8	707.2
Texas.............................	104,873	113,231	121,091	113,653	408.5	4.4	29.0	110.6	264.5	450.3	529.7	545.1
Utah...............................	5,494	5,879	5,612	5,711	195.0	1.9	30.3	38.4	124.4	212.7	227.2	255.7
Vermont	847	815	746	691	135.2	1.3	19.0	13.6	101.4	130.2	119.7	113.5
Virginia	15,923	17,087	21,400	19,943	196.7	3.7	19.0	67.1	106.9	213.6	282.8	281.7
Washington.....................	20,121	21,101	21,745	21,788	294.6	2.4	33.5	82.5	176.1	313.8	345.8	369.7
West Virginia...................	5,861	5,830	4,957	5,723	315.9	4.3	20.9	49.0	241.6	314.6	272.8	316.5
Wisconsin.......................	13,532	14,142	13,371	12,700	236.9	2.4	20.4	78.2	135.9	248.7	241.5	236.8
Wyoming	1,246	1,104	1,172	1,316	219.3	3.2	25.7	12.5	177.9	195.9	230.1	266.5

[1]Includes murder and nonnegligent manslaughter, forcible rape, robbery, and aggravated assault.
[2]Populations are U.S. Census Bureau estimates as of July 1 for each year except 2000 and 2010, which are decennial census counts.
[3]Includes nonnegligent manslaughter.
[4]Because of changes in the state's reporting practices, figures are not comparable to previous years' data for Minnesota (2011), and Illinois and Oregon (2010).
[5]The data collection methodology for the offense of forcible rape does not comply with the national Uniform Crime Reporting (UCR) Program guidelines; therefore, it was necessary that the forcible rape count be estimated for Delaware for 2000, and for Ilinois and Minnesota for 2005 and 2010.
[6]Includes offenses reported by the police at the National Zoo and by Metro Transit Police.
[7]Limited data for 2005 were available for Illinois; limited data for 2000 were available for Illinois, Kansas, Kentucky, and Montana; therefore, it was necessary that their crime counts be estimated.

Table A–24. Property Crimes and Crime Rates

Geographic area	Number[1]				Rate (per 100,000)[2]						
					2011				Total		
	2011	2010	2005	2000	Total	Burglary	Larceny	Motor vehicle theft	2010	2005	2000
United States[3,4,5]	9,063,173	9,112,625	10,166,159	10,181,462	2,908.7	702.2	1,976.9	229.6	2,945.9	3,429.8	3,618.3
Alabama[5]	173,190	168,828	177,393	180,539	3,606.1	1,064.3	2,319.7	222.0	3,528.0	3,892.1	4,059.7
Alaska	19,028	20,259	23,975	23,087	2,632.8	391.0	2,056.0	185.8	2,836.8	3,612.5	3,682.5
Arizona	230,422	226,802	287,345	271,811	3,554.5	847.3	2,401.3	305.9	3,536.5	4,838.0	5,297.8
Arkansas	110,295	103,820	112,775	98,115	3,754.1	1,173.3	2,383.0	197.8	3,553.5	4,057.9	3,670.0
California	973,901	981,939	1,200,531	1,056,183	2,583.8	610.4	1,583.8	389.6	2,629.9	3,322.6	3,118.2
Colorado	133,361	135,001	188,449	156,937	2,606.3	503.6	1,886.8	215.9	2,674.5	4,039.5	3,648.6
Connecticut	77,609	78,259	89,794	99,033	2,167.4	437.9	1,542.1	187.4	2,188.8	2,558.0	2,908.0
Delaware	30,939	31,078	26,245	29,727	3,410.6	830.2	2,411.8	168.7	3,453.9	3,111.4	3,793.6
District of Columbia[4]	29,636	28,802	26,133	33,000	4,795.5	623.0	3,451.5	721.0	4,761.4	4,747.0	5,768.6
Florida	671,200	669,035	712,998	780,377	3,522.0	892.9	2,421.1	207.9	3,551.4	4,007.9	4,882.7
Georgia	355,952	353,449	378,534	347,630	3,626.5	974.6	2,351.7	300.3	3,639.2	4,172.3	4,246.4
Hawaii	45,889	45,667	61,115	60,033	3,337.8	728.0	2,305.6	304.3	3,349.6	4,792.6	4,955.1
Idaho	32,787	31,436	38,556	37,961	2,068.6	436.6	1,547.9	84.1	2,000.9	2,697.9	2,933.7
Illinois	346,025	349,064	393,148	450,748	2,688.8	604.1	1,861.1	223.5	2,718.1	3,080.3	3,629.4
Indiana	206,055	199,274	216,778	206,905	3,161.8	775.7	2,158.8	227.3	3,070.2	3,456.3	3,402.8
Iowa	71,361	68,740	84,056	86,834	2,330.3	568.2	1,633.6	128.5	2,253.6	2,833.7	2,967.3
Kansas	88,438	89,109	103,941	108,057	3,080.1	654.4	2,193.2	232.5	3,116.6	3,787.0	4,019.4
Kentucky	118,358	111,170	105,608	107,723	2,708.8	745.0	1,811.1	152.7	2,557.3	2,530.5	2,665.2
Louisiana	168,744	165,667	166,611	211,904	3,688.5	1,012.5	2,476.6	199.4	3,644.8	3,683.1	4,741.7
Maine	33,809	32,900	31,889	32,003	2,545.5	591.3	1,873.0	81.2	2,478.6	2,413.1	2,510.2
Maryland	166,699	173,309	198,483	213,422	2,860.2	614.0	1,970.5	275.7	2,995.5	3,544.1	4,029.5
Massachusetts	148,790	154,496	151,241	161,901	2,258.7	554.6	1,540.3	163.7	2,356.8	2,363.6	2,550.0
Michigan	257,979	271,501	312,843	353,297	2,612.1	724.9	1,629.0	258.2	2,748.8	3,091.1	3,554.9
Minnesota	136,264	136,431	158,301	157,798	2,549.4	481.3	1,915.1	153.1	2,569.0	3,084.1	3,207.6
Mississippi	90,115	88,596	95,231	103,644	3,025.5	1,037.7	1,822.5	165.4	2,983.0	3,260.1	3,643.5
Missouri	198,882	200,858	227,809	225,919	3,308.8	745.7	2,308.3	254.8	3,350.0	3,927.5	4,037.7
Montana	NA	NA	29,407	29,707	NA	NA	NA	NA	NA	3,142.9	3,292.7
Nebraska	50,726	48,827	60,207	64,479	2,752.9	472.9	2,057.3	222.7	2,667.9	3,423.2	3,767.9
Nevada	69,731	75,004	102,424	74,823	2,560.5	742.3	1,470.0	348.3	2,773.5	4,241.5	3,744.4
New Hampshire	30,106	29,230	23,532	27,901	2,283.9	436.1	1,773.9	73.9	2,219.8	1,796.4	2,257.8
New Jersey	189,719	183,042	203,391	233,637	2,150.7	490.2	1,463.1	197.4	2,080.1	2,333.0	2,776.6
New Mexico	73,534	70,776	79,995	86,605	3,531.5	1,028.9	2,242.9	259.7	3,425.9	4,148.3	4,761.0
New York	372,255	379,710	405,990	483,078	1,912.4	336.0	1,477.2	99.2	1,957.8	2,108.5	2,545.7
North Carolina	340,562	329,202	353,855	355,921	3,526.8	1,099.2	2,251.2	176.4	3,443.5	4,075.1	4,421.8
North Dakota	13,246	12,010	12,595	14,171	1,936.7	355.7	1,437.7	143.3	1,780.2	1,978.2	2,206.6
Ohio	387,297	376,836	419,899	420,939	3,354.7	976.3	2,195.9	182.5	3,266.1	3,662.7	3,707.7
Oklahoma	127,252	129,464	143,406	140,125	3,356.2	958.5	2,106.8	290.9	3,443.0	4,042.0	4,060.8
Oregon	120,594	116,657	160,199	153,780	3,114.6	528.1	2,352.8	233.7	3,039.3	4,399.8	4,494.7
Pennsylvania	283,179	276,366	300,444	316,274	2,222.3	454.0	1,636.1	132.2	2,173.1	2,417.2	2,575.3
Rhode Island	28,141	26,959	29,260	33,323	2,676.8	662.4	1,796.8	217.5	2,561.4	2,718.9	3,178.7
South Carolina	182,685	181,098	184,646	177,189	3,904.2	1,002.8	2,609.4	292.0	3,905.4	4,339.4	4,416.5
South Dakota	14,979	15,188	13,784	16,252	1,817.7	351.8	1,351.1	114.8	1,859.9	1,776.4	2,153.0
Tennessee	230,261	232,855	254,948	237,985	3,595.9	979.9	2,396.8	219.2	3,662.7	4,275.5	4,183.0
Texas	891,499	951,246	990,293	919,658	3,472.3	838.3	2,387.3	246.7	3,766.8	4,332.0	4,410.4
Utah	83,758	88,316	95,546	94,247	2,973.1	465.8	2,287.8	219.5	3,182.0	3,868.9	4,220.3
Vermont	14,464	14,160	14,210	17,494	2,309.0	581.5	1,647.7	79.7	2,262.3	2,280.7	2,873.4
Virginia	182,141	187,403	199,644	194,405	2,249.6	377.9	1,751.6	120.1	2,335.5	2,638.2	2,746.4
Washington	244,146	249,426	307,661	279,144	3,574.6	827.7	2,383.3	363.6	3,699.1	4,893.0	4,736.0
West Virginia	42,189	41,301	47,696	41,344	2,273.9	603.2	1,549.2	121.5	2,227.2	2,625.2	2,286.3
Wisconsin	138,949	142,781	147,275	159,424	2,432.7	466.7	1,821.9	144.1	2,508.6	2,660.2	2,972.3
Wyoming	12,877	13,869	16,070	14,969	2,266.4	327.9	1,846.8	91.7	2,456.6	3,155.3	3,031.5

[1]Property crimes include burglary, larceny-theft, and motor vehicle theft.
[2]Populations are U.S. Census Bureau estimates as of July 1 for each year except 2000 and 2010, which are decennial census counts.
[3]The crime figures have been adjusted
[4]Includes offenses reported by the police at the National Zoo and by Metro Transit Police.
[5]Because of changes in the state's reporting practices, figures are not comparable to previous years' data.
NA = Not available

Table A–25. Juvenile Arrests, Child Abuse Cases, and Prisoners

Geographic area	Juvenile arrest rate, 2010 (except as noted)[1]				Child abuse and neglect cases reported and investigated, 2011			Prisoners under jurisdiction of federal or state authorities (Dec. 31)			Prisoners executed		Prisoners under death sentence (Dec. 31)		
	Violent crime index[2]	Property crime index[3]	Drug abuse	Weapons	Number of reports[4]	Number of children subjects of investigation[5]	Number of victims[6]	2011 Number	2011 Rate[7]	2000	2011	1977 to 2011	2010	2005	2000
United States............	226	1,091	508	93	1,647,214	3,049,679	676,569	[8] 1,598,780	518	1,391,261	43	1,277	[9] 3,158	3,245	3,557
Alabama....................	158	951	NA	103	18,700	26,221	8,601	32,270	675	26,332	6	55	201	189	191
Alaska	239	1,332	393	35	5,669	7,989	2,898	5,412	[ ] 762	4,173	([10])	([10])	([10])	([10])	([10])
Arizona....................	178	1,402	780	47	31,364	59,923	8,708	[11] 40,020	626	26,510	4	28	133	109	120
Arkansas	120	898	314	42	33,670	59,713	11,105	16,108	552	11,915	0	27	42	38	40
California..................	307	923	548	159	238,139	381,196	80,100	149,569	401	163,001	0	13	699	646	614
Colorado	164	1,373	668	87	31,603	42,099	10,604	21,978	437	16,833	0	1	3	2	5
Connecticut..............	205	852	408	67	29,780	37,073	10,012	[12] 18,324	513	18,355	([10])	1	10	7	7
Delaware	374	1,461	640	128	7,347	14,382	2,466	[12] 6,739	751	6,921	1	15	17	16	14
District of Columbia ...	NA	NA	NA	NA	6,190	13,187	2,377	([13])	NA	7,456	([10])	([10])	([10])	([10])	([10])
Florida......................	407	1,851	NA	82	167,212	291,929	51,920	103,055	548	71,319	2	71	392	372	366
Georgia	286	1,441	NA	140	22,194	51,060	18,541	55,944	577	44,232	4	52	100	107	112
Hawaii......................	203	1,262	430	22	NA	3,329	1,346	[12] 6,037	444	5,053	([10])	([10])	([10])	([10])	([10])
Idaho.......................	92	1,447	495	75	6,545	9,018	1,470	7,739	494	5,535	1	2	16	18	20
Illinois.....................	924	1,732	NA	291	NA	114,849	25,832	48,427	377	45,281	([10])	12	15	7	159
Indiana.....................	231	1,574	NA	58	61,473	79,963	17,930	28,906	446	20,125	0	20	13	20	36
Iowa........................	193	1,500	399	39	28,810	31,143	11,028	9,116	299	7,955	([10])	([10])	([10])	([10])	([10])
Kansas	145	1,198	NA	51	20,566	25,436	1,729	9,327	327	8,344	0	0	8	0	5
Kentucky	86	542	169	24	49,459	61,912	16,994	21,545	497	14,919	0	3	34	36	36
Louisiana	627	1,749	NA	95	26,255	37,994	9,545	39,710	876	35,207	0	28	84	83	86
Maine	55	1,345	440	44	6,513	9,518	3,118	2,145	161	1,679	([10])	([10])	([10])	([10])	([10])
Maryland...................	481	1,566	971	175	27,315	32,950	13,740	22,558	391	23,538	([10])	5	5	7	15
Massachusetts.........	246	439	103	33	37,799	62,443	20,262	11,623	178	10,722	([10])	([10])	([10])	([10])	([10])
Michigan..................	176	888	308	59	83,320	156,168	33,366	42,940	434	47,718	([10])	([10])	([10])	([10])	([10])
Minnesota	180	1,507	498	92	18,186	23,016	4,342	9,800	185	6,238	([10])	([10])	([10])	([10])	([10])
Mississippi..............	136	1,582	NA	130	19,774	27,138	6,712	21,386	721	20,241	2	15	60	68	66
Missouri	228	1,506	511	74	58,782	69,037	5,826	[11] 30,833	515	27,543	1	68	49	46	66
Montana...................	111	1,612	385	21	7,536	10,413	1,066	3,678	372	3,105	0	3	2	4	6
Nebraska..................	99	1,734	696	77	13,489	24,856	4,307	4,616	253	3,895	0	3	12	10	7
Nevada	334	1,467	752	104	13,667	23,323	5,355	12,778	473	10,063	0	12	81	82	83
New Hampshire.........	85	826	625	14	8,671	11,022	876	2,614	199	2,257	0	0	1	0	0
New Jersey	243	733	519	118	NA	71,517	8,238	23,834	271	29,784	([10])	([10])	([10])	10	14
New Mexico	237	1,359	766	113	16,992	22,752	5,601	6,998	340	5,342	([10])	1	2	2	2
New York..................	428	1,205	627	112	NA	222,195	72,625	55,436	286	70,199	([10])	([10])	([10])	1	5
North Carolina...........	203	1,137	333	164	NA	123,198	22,940	39,440	414	31,266	0	43	158	174	206
North Dakota.............	95	1,601	554	20	3,798	6,146	1,295	1,423	212	1,076	([10])	([10])	([10])	([10])	([10])
Ohio........................	145	1,001	NA	62	80,875	103,554	30,601	50,964	442	45,833	5	46	157	199	205
Oklahoma	148	1,160	432	69	29,736	44,188	7,836	25,977	692	23,181	2	96	71	86	112
Oregon.....................	152	1,637	735	56	32,169	NA	NA	14,510	379	10,580	0	2	34	31	26
Pennsylvania............	352	865	410	97	NA	21,570	3,287	51,578	406	36,847	0	3	215	218	241
Rhode Island............	196	895	458	145	6,477	8,263	3,131	[12] 3,337	317	3,286	([10])	([10])	([10])	([10])	([10])
South Carolina	194	1,090	572	110	17,444	36,011	11,324	22,914	495	21,778	1	43	56	68	72
South Dakota	95	1,497	686	81	3,907	6,334	1,353	3,535	434	2,616	0	1	2	4	5
Tennessee	312	1,094	494	96	59,288	80,005	9,243	28,479	449	22,166	0	6	86	103	95
Texas......................	145	1,040	533	40	178,605	272,553	63,474	172,224	685	166,719	13	477	315	411	450
Utah........................	90	1,735	550	98	18,821	25,571	10,586	6,879	249	5,637	0	7	9	9	11
Vermont	67	484	213	14	3,385	3,716	630	[12] 2,053	328	1,697	([10])	([10])	([10])	([10])	([10])
Virginia....................	113	766	314	53	32,566	61,602	5,964	38,130	477	30,168	1	109	9	22	23
Washington...............	240	1,517	NA	100	35,798	42,554	6,541	17,847	265	14,915	0	5	8	10	10
West Virginia.............	55	335	153	7	17,225	33,816	4,000	6,826	368	3,856	([10])	([10])	([10])	([10])	([10])
Wisconsin.................	233	1,907	677	150	27,060	33,333	4,750	22,654	398	20,754	([10])	([10])	([10])	([10])	([10])
Wyoming	95	1,640	1,062	81	3,040	5,393	703	2,183	387	1,680	0	1	1	2	2

[1]Arrest rate is defined as the number of arrests of persons under age 18 for every 100,000 persons ages 10–17. Arrest rate data for 2010 for the following states were unavailable at the time of publication. The data shown for these states are from 2009: Alabama, Florida, Georgia, Illinois, Indiana, Kansas, Louisiana, Mississippi, Ohio, and Washington.
[2]Violent crime includes murder or nonnegligent manslaughter, forcible rape, robbery, and aggravated assault.
[3]Property crime includes burglary, larceny-theft, motor vehicle theft, and arson.
[4]The number of investigations includes assessments; and is based on the total number of investigations that received a disposition in 2011.
[5]The number of "Children subjects of investigation" is based on the "Unique count," counting a child once, regardless of the number of reports concerning that child, that received a CPS response in the year shown.
[6]Victims are defined as children for whom the state determined at least one maltreatment was substantiated or indicated; and a disposition of "substantiated," "indicated," or "alternative response victim" was assigned for a child in a specific report.
[7]Per 100,000 resident population counted in the census as of April 1, 2010.
[8]U.S. total includes federal prisoners not distributed by state. This total includes inmates held in nonsecure privately operated community corrections centers and juveniles held in contract facilities.
[9]Includes federal cases not distributed by state. Excludes persons held under Armed Forces jurisdiction with a military death sentence for murder.
[10]State did not have death penalty as of December 31 of year shown. The following states abolished the death penalty in recent years: Connecticut (2012), Illinois (2011), Maryland (2013), and New Mexioco (2009).
[11]Prison population based on custody counts.
[12]Prisons and jails form one integrated system. Data include total jail and prison populations.
[13]The District of Columbia transferred responsibility for sentenced felons to the Federal Systems. The District of Columbia inmates sentenced to more than 1 year are now under the responsibility of the Bureau of Prisons.
NA = Not available

Table A–26. State and Local Justice Employment and Expenditures

Geographic area	Full-time equivalent employment (March)							Expenditures						
	2009 preliminary		2000	Per 10,000 population, 2009 preliminary[1]				2009 preliminary		2000 (million dollars)	Per capita, 2009 preliminary[1] (dollars)			
	Number	Percentage of total state and local		Total justice system	Police protection	Judicial and legal	Corrections	Total (million dollars)	Percentage of total state and local[2]		Total justice system	Police protection	Judicial and legal	Corrections
United States............	2,153,228	12.8	1,940,571	70	32	14	25	211,244	7.1	132,636	688	303	140	245
Alabama......................	27,668	9.5	25,298	59	30	10	19	2,211	5.6	1,322	470	227	90	152
Alaska	5,346	9.9	4,693	77	25	24	28	772	5.4	482	1,105	397	327	380
Arizona.......................	48,724	15.7	39,345	74	32	16	25	5,029	9.4	2,662	762	327	150	285
Arkansas	19,293	11.4	15,172	67	29	11	26	1,146	5.6	836	397	179	68	149
California....................	256,981	13.9	226,448	70	29	14	27	40,103	9.4	22,129	1,085	439	258	388
Colorado	33,660	12.2	26,869	67	31	14	22	3,263	7.3	1,979	649	289	120	241
Connecticut................	24,469	12.5	23,986	70	32	15	23	2,391	6.4	1,666	680	281	193	206
Delaware	7,353	14.8	6,353	83	29	20	33	715	7.6	485	807	328	171	308
District of Columbia	8,225	18.1	7,235	137	78	35	24	950	7.6	680	1,585	955	193	437
Florida........................	148,844	16.7	127,600	80	36	18	26	13,946	8.7	8,407	752	381	123	248
Georgia	70,060	13.1	60,195	71	28	14	30	5,584	7.3	3,180	568	236	102	230
Hawaii	9,500	12.6	8,701	73	30	24	19	932	6.5	556	720	286	256	178
Idaho..........................	10,434	13.2	7,365	68	30	14	23	891	7.7	500	576	232	117	228
Illinois........................	86,498	13.1	86,731	67	37	12	17	7,746	6.3	5,777	600	333	108	158
Indiana.......................	38,727	11.1	33,189	60	28	12	20	2,742	5.3	1,895	427	186	77	164
Iowa...........................	15,681	8.6	14,919	52	25	11	17	1,394	5.0	977	463	207	111	145
Kansas	19,790	9.7	18,906	70	32	14	24	1,464	5.8	985	519	247	103	170
Kentucky	24,671	10.1	22,371	57	24	15	19	1,818	5.0	1,389	422	150	107	165
Louisiana	37,916	13.7	36,601	84	39	15	30	3,265	7.0	1,968	727	301	149	277
Maine.........................	6,119	8.3	5,724	46	22	8	17	603	5.1	356	457	184	79	194
Maryland.....................	43,974	14.5	37,870	77	33	15	29	4,628	8.6	2,714	812	347	141	324
Massachusetts............	45,471	13.2	44,731	69	40	16	14	4,251	6.0	2,901	645	292	149	204
Michigan....................	56,586	11.7	61,472	57	23	12	22	5,968	6.9	4,551	599	248	105	246
Minnesota	28,555	10.0	24,272	54	24	12	19	3,263	6.0	1,907	620	313	129	178
Mississippi.................	18,398	9.4	17,786	62	33	10	20	1,347	5.2	850	456	207	75	175
Missouri.....................	43,084	13.1	38,350	72	33	12	27	2,915	6.1	1,917	487	248	88	150
Montana......................	6,243	11.0	4,841	64	27	16	20	601	7.1	326	617	238	141	237
Nebraska....................	11,631	9.8	9,309	65	29	11	25	909	4.9	563	506	205	98	204
Nevada.......................	19,199	16.5	14,702	73	33	14	25	2,422	10.8	1,259	917	436	175	305
New Hampshire...........	7,521	10.2	7,146	57	31	10	16	656	6.2	395	496	230	104	161
New Jersey	74,823	14.6	69,960	86	42	24	19	7,024	7.3	4,660	807	360	172	274
New Mexico	16,241	12.4	14,096	81	31	19	31	1,528	7.4	865	761	305	170	285
New York....................	182,574	14.6	177,474	93	46	18	30	18,337	6.7	12,372	938	433	207	299
North Carolina.............	63,694	11.3	52,656	68	30	9	30	4,879	6.4	3,010	520	233	80	208
North Dakota...............	3,419	8.1	3,019	53	23	13	17	291	4.9	164	450	203	103	144
Ohio...........................	80,070	12.9	80,094	69	28	19	22	7,049	6.6	5,220	611	284	151	176
Oklahoma	23,543	10.6	22,213	64	31	12	21	1,824	6.2	1,223	495	212	88	194
Oregon.......................	23,927	12.0	21,554	63	25	13	25	2,603	6.9	1,799	680	273	110	297
Pennsylvania...............	84,245	13.9	74,925	67	27	15	25	7,553	6.5	5,510	599	231	126	242
Rhode Island...............	7,479	14.1	6,426	71	38	12	21	648	6.1	456	616	314	115	187
South Carolina	30,136	11.7	28,447	66	32	10	24	2,130	5.1	1,391	467	216	78	174
South Dakota	4,518	9.6	3,813	56	25	11	19	389	6.0	209	479	189	88	201
Tennessee	41,682	12.6	34,375	66	32	12	23	3,139	6.1	1,943	499	239	100	159
Texas.........................	172,156	12.0	150,718	69	29	11	29	14,102	7.0	8,314	569	246	95	229
Utah...........................	15,242	10.8	12,318	55	23	12	20	1,534	6.4	935	551	227	120	203
Vermont	3,252	8.2	2,934	52	23	11	18	329	5.2	184	529	227	110	192
Virginia......................	54,687	12.2	48,070	69	29	12	29	4,787	7.4	2,935	607	261	104	243
Washington.................	39,489	11.0	34,250	59	24	12	23	4,025	5.6	2,530	604	221	126	258
West Virginia..............	9,854	9.6	7,519	54	21	14	19	841	5.8	463	462	192	108	162
Wisconsin	36,654	12.9	34,031	65	28	10	26	3,745	7.1	2,594	662	288	105	269
Wyoming	4,922	9.5	3,499	90	38	19	33	563	6.8	247	1,034	429	193	412

[1]Based on Census Bureau estimated population on July 1, 2009.
[2]Justice system expenditure of independent school districts (primarily for special police forces) are not available.

Table A-27. Civilian Labor Force and Employment

Geographic area	Civilian noninstitutionalized population 16 years and over[1] (thousands)						Civilian labor force[1,2] (thousands)											
	2012[3]			2010	2005	2000	2012[3]			Total			Employed					
	Total	Male	Female				Total	Male	Female	2010	2005	2000	2012[3]			2010	2005	2000
													Total	Male	Female			
United States............	243,284	117,343	125,941	237,532	226,082	209,699	154,975	82,327	72,648	153,700	149,320	140,863	142,469	75,555	66,914	138,894	141,730	135,208
Alabama..................	3,752	1,776	1,977	3,646	3,521	3,401	2,178	1,151	1,028	2,180	2,179	2,154	2,003	1,056	947	1,952	2,086	2,055
Alaska....................	536	272	264	518	473	438	365	197	168	360	341	322	338	180	158	331	318	301
Arizona...................	4,987	2,428	2,558	5,027	4,433	3,626	3,011	1,629	1,382	3,180	2,832	2,347	2,764	1,495	1,268	2,850	2,697	2,256
Arkansas................	2,271	1,095	1,176	2,221	2,132	1,977	1,354	718	636	1,343	1,371	1,238	1,252	663	588	1,228	1,301	1,183
California................	29,297	14,316	14,980	28,293	26,935	25,489	18,454	10,110	8,344	18,195	17,666	17,091	16,529	9,056	7,473	15,976	16,724	16,246
Colorado	3,975	1,959	2,017	3,899	3,526	3,141	2,725	1,474	1,251	2,720	2,530	2,276	2,505	1,353	1,152	2,482	2,406	2,213
Connecticut.............	2,841	1,363	1,478	2,765	2,714	2,537	1,881	983	898	1,892	1,815	1,746	1,722	893	828	1,719	1,724	1,707
Delaware................	718	340	378	693	655	588	446	226	220	428	440	409	414	208	206	392	421	393
District of Columbia	523	242	281	496	437	413	363	179	183	341	296	279	330	164	166	310	277	263
Florida....................	15,431	7,391	8,040	14,736	13,868	11,960	9,358	4,898	4,460	9,089	8,704	7,490	8,572	4,460	4,111	8,083	8,390	7,221
Georgia	7,456	3,537	3,919	7,396	6,769	5,967	4,803	2,520	2,283	4,744	4,583	4,173	4,365	2,307	2,057	4,238	4,334	4,019
Hawaii....................	1,060	515	545	989	958	889	642	340	301	623	635	595	603	319	284	579	616	570
Idaho.....................	1,194	588	606	1,163	1,073	951	772	430	342	759	751	658	717	402	316	691	721	626
Illinois...................	10,007	4,828	5,179	9,936	9,700	9,199	6,616	3,492	3,124	6,645	6,460	6,419	6,039	3,177	2,862	5,970	6,097	6,140
Indiana...................	5,043	2,443	2,600	4,939	4,760	4,529	3,159	1,677	1,481	3,153	3,214	3,084	2,898	1,542	1,356	2,818	3,032	2,984
Iowa......................	2,397	1,177	1,221	2,348	2,329	2,193	1,650	863	787	1,673	1,667	1,563	1,565	815	750	1,571	1,592	1,522
Kansas...................	2,182	1,062	1,120	2,146	2,089	2,001	1,482	781	701	1,497	1,481	1,411	1,400	736	663	1,385	1,406	1,359
Kentucky.................	3,394	1,633	1,761	3,354	3,222	3,082	2,074	1,090	984	2,056	2,008	1,982	1,908	995	913	1,844	1,885	1,900
Louisiana	3,500	1,661	1,839	3,420	3,344	3,289	2,078	1,106	972	2,092	2,098	2,030	1,932	1,027	904	1,928	1,973	1,917
Maine.....................	1,084	525	559	1,066	1,063	998	704	366	338	690	712	689	650	336	314	633	677	665
Maryland.................	4,585	2,168	2,417	4,443	4,261	4,015	3,110	1,569	1,541	3,055	2,922	2,805	2,893	1,455	1,438	2,819	2,800	2,697
Massachusetts..........	5,320	2,540	2,780	5,282	5,027	4,804	3,476	1,762	1,715	3,493	3,357	3,237	3,245	1,629	1,616	3,194	3,193	3,151
Michigan	7,787	3,752	4,035	7,780	7,771	7,548	4,673	2,474	2,200	4,821	5,112	5,201	4,247	2,239	2,008	4,232	4,773	5,016
Minnesota...............	4,188	2,061	2,128	4,112	3,985	3,648	2,946	1,562	1,383	2,935	2,929	2,739	2,776	1,466	1,311	2,721	2,815	2,649
Mississippi..............	2,256	1,061	1,195	2,211	2,185	2,086	1,329	691	637	1,296	1,333	1,326	1,211	632	578	1,155	1,241	1,251
Missouri..................	4,679	2,249	2,430	4,642	4,479	4,166	3,018	1,578	1,441	3,032	3,020	2,930	2,810	1,466	1,344	2,745	2,855	2,828
Montana..................	793	394	399	773	741	691	506	265	241	490	499	479	476	246	229	452	476	456
Nebraska.................	1,417	695	722	1,375	1,344	1,254	1,027	538	489	976	987	924	986	517	468	929	948	897
Nevada...................	2,108	1,047	1,061	2,015	1,826	1,408	1,363	744	619	1,322	1,220	986	1,214	654	559	1,131	1,167	946
New Hampshire..........	1,065	521	544	1,063	1,030	939	739	387	352	747	736	686	697	363	335	702	708	666
New Jersey	6,958	3,338	3,620	6,812	6,687	6,292	4,584	2,425	2,160	4,520	4,440	4,188	4,150	2,194	1,956	4,100	4,244	4,030
New Mexico	1,594	773	822	1,535	1,463	1,318	952	500	452	921	947	833	884	462	422	843	897	792
New York.................	15,554	7,408	8,146	15,431	14,971	14,163	9,556	5,019	4,536	9,654	9,414	8,941	8,726	4,545	4,181	8,832	8,943	8,533
North Carolina...........	7,485	3,530	3,955	7,200	6,567	5,809	4,693	2,475	2,218	4,573	4,318	3,958	4,262	2,257	2,005	4,094	4,092	3,814
North Dakota.............	542	272	270	510	501	477	394	211	183	372	361	339	381	203	178	358	349	329
Ohio......................	9,042	4,342	4,700	8,976	8,859	8,624	5,729	3,013	2,716	5,853	5,910	5,783	5,317	2,792	2,525	5,263	5,558	5,546
Oklahoma	2,897	1,400	1,497	2,802	2,704	2,558	1,818	994	825	1,745	1,745	1,648	1,726	945	781	1,621	1,665	1,598
Oregon...................	3,097	1,513	1,584	3,039	2,848	2,608	1,958	1,032	926	2,000	1,857	1,803	1,785	936	849	1,780	1,745	1,715
Pennsylvania............	10,193	4,886	5,307	9,987	9,747	9,290	6,521	3,451	3,070	6,317	6,282	5,972	6,012	3,177	2,835	5,774	5,972	5,722
Rhode Island.............	846	402	443	845	843	753	558	285	273	572	570	505	499	253	246	508	541	484
South Carolina	3,646	1,720	1,926	3,530	3,251	3,032	2,161	1,104	1,057	2,134	2,079	1,985	1,958	1,007	951	1,899	1,939	1,909
South Dakota	633	313	320	625	593	552	440	235	206	443	433	401	420	223	197	420	414	392
Tennessee	5,021	2,395	2,626	4,913	4,631	4,284	3,094	1,658	1,437	3,077	2,878	2,798	2,853	1,523	1,330	2,788	2,717	2,688
Texas.....................	19,287	9,360	9,927	18,419	16,736	15,132	12,640	6,915	5,725	12,122	11,237	10,325	11,797	6,475	5,323	11,149	10,629	9,987
Utah......................	2,028	1,005	1,023	2,007	1,774	1,527	1,365	768	597	1,385	1,268	1,104	1,285	721	564	1,271	1,216	1,068
Vermont	513	250	262	510	503	471	356	183	173	361	355	332	338	173	165	339	342	322
Virginia	6,298	3,008	3,290	6,077	5,704	5,299	4,184	2,202	1,982	4,108	3,918	3,610	3,934	2,078	1,856	3,800	3,781	3,530
Washington..............	5,377	2,639	2,739	5,247	4,862	4,434	3,469	1,851	1,618	3,541	3,298	3,045	3,181	1,696	1,485	3,180	3,114	2,888
West Virginia............	1,492	725	767	1,458	1,456	1,445	811	436	375	795	801	825	751	398	353	724	759	779
Wisconsin................	4,495	2,206	2,289	4,440	4,317	4,031	3,084	1,602	1,482	3,082	3,022	2,935	2,866	1,482	1,384	2,813	2,881	2,831
Wyoming	441	222	219	422	400	371	305	169	136	298	283	267	288	160	128	278	273	257

[1]Annual averages of monthly figures.
[2]Civilian labor force includes all persons in the civilian noninstitutional population classified as either employed or unemployed.
[3]Preliminary

Table A-28. Civilian Labor Force and Unemployment

Geographic area	Civilian labor force participation, 2012[1,2,3]		Employment/ population ratio, 2012[3,4]		Unemployment[1]											
					Total (thousands)						Rate[5]					
					2012[3]			2010	2005	2000	2012[3]			2010	2005	2000
	Male	Female	Male	Female	Total	Male	Female				Total	Male	Female			
United States[6]	70.2	57.7	64.4	53.1	12,506	6,771	5,734	14,808	7,591	5,692	8.1	8.2	7.9	9.6	5.1	4.0
Alabama	64.8	52.0	59.5	47.9	175	95	81	228	92	99	8.0	8.2	7.9	10.5	4.2	4.6
Alaska	72.6	63.6	66.3	59.8	27	17	10	29	23	21	7.4	8.6	6.1	8.0	6.7	6.6
Arizona	67.1	54.0	61.6	49.6	248	134	114	331	133	91	8.2	8.2	8.2	10.4	4.8	3.9
Arkansas	65.6	54.1	60.6	50.0	102	54	48	116	70	55	7.6	7.6	7.6	8.6	5.1	4.4
California	70.6	55.7	63.3	49.9	1,925	1054	871	2,219	951	845	10.4	10.4	10.4	12.2	5.3	4.9
Colorado	75.2	62.0	69.1	57.1	220	121	99	238	124	63	8.1	8.2	7.9	8.7	4.9	2.7
Connecticut	72.1	60.7	65.6	56.0	159	89	69	173	91	39	8.4	9.1	7.7	9.2	5.0	2.3
Delaware	66.5	58.3	61.3	54.5	32	18	15	37	19	16	7.2	7.8	6.6	8.5	4.3	4.0
District of Columbia	74.0	65.3	67.6	59.2	33	15	17	31	18	16	9.0	8.6	9.3	9.2	6.2	5.8
Florida	66.3	55.5	60.3	51.1	786	438	348	1,006	314	269	8.4	8.9	7.8	11.1	3.6	3.6
Georgia	71.2	58.3	65.2	52.5	438	212	226	506	245	154	9.1	8.4	9.9	10.7	5.4	3.7
Hawaii	66.2	55.2	62.0	52.1	39	21	17	43	19	26	6.0	6.3	5.7	7.0	2.9	4.3
Idaho	73.0	56.5	68.2	52.1	55	28	27	68	30	32	7.1	6.5	7.8	9.0	4.0	4.9
Illinois	72.3	60.3	65.8	55.3	577	315	262	675	363	279	8.7	9	8.4	10.2	5.6	4.4
Indiana	68.7	57.0	63.1	52.2	261	136	125	334	182	100	8.3	8.1	8.5	10.6	5.7	3.2
Iowa	73.3	64.5	69.3	61.4	85	48	37	102	74	41	5.1	5.5	4.7	6.1	4.5	2.6
Kansas	73.6	62.5	69.3	59.2	82	45	37	111	75	52	5.6	5.8	5.3	7.4	5.1	3.7
Kentucky	66.8	55.8	61.0	51.8	166	95	71	212	123	82	8.0	8.7	7.2	10.3	6.1	4.1
Louisiana	66.6	52.9	61.3	49.2	147	79	68	164	125	112	7.1	7.1	7.0	7.8	6.0	5.5
Maine	69.7	60.5	64.0	56.1	54	30	24	57	35	24	7.7	8.2	7.1	8.2	5.0	3.5
Maryland	72.4	63.7	67.1	59.5	217	114	103	236	123	108	7.0	7.3	6.7	7.7	4.2	3.9
Massachusetts	69.3	61.7	64.1	58.1	231	133	99	298	165	86	6.7	7.5	5.8	8.5	4.9	2.6
Michigan	65.9	54.5	59.7	49.8	426	235	192	589	340	185	9.1	9.5	8.7	12.2	6.6	3.6
Minnesota	75.8	65.0	71.1	61.6	169	97	73	214	114	90	5.8	6.2	5.3	7.3	3.9	3.3
Mississippi	65.2	53.3	59.6	48.4	118	59	59	141	92	75	8.9	8.5	9.2	10.9	6.9	5.7
Missouri	70.2	59.3	65.2	55.3	208	112	96	287	164	101	6.9	7.1	6.7	9.5	5.5	3.5
Montana	67.4	60.3	62.5	57.4	31	19	12	38	22	24	6.1	7.2	4.8	7.7	4.4	4.9
Nebraska	77.4	67.7	74.5	64.9	41	20	21	47	39	28	4.0	3.8	4.2	4.8	4.0	3.0
Nevada	71.0	58.4	62.5	52.7	150	90	60	191	53	40	11.0	12	9.7	14.4	4.3	4.1
New Hampshire	74.2	64.7	69.6	61.5	42	24	17	44	27	19	5.6	6.2	4.9	5.9	3.7	2.8
New Jersey	72.6	59.7	65.7	54.0	434	231	204	420	197	157	9.5	9.5	9.4	9.3	4.4	3.8
New Mexico	64.8	55.0	59.7	51.4	68	39	29	79	50	40	7.1	7.7	6.5	8.5	5.3	4.9
New York	67.8	55.7	61.4	51.3	830	474	356	822	470	408	8.7	9.4	7.8	8.5	5.0	4.6
North Carolina	70.1	56.1	63.9	50.7	431	218	213	479	225	144	9.2	8.8	9.6	10.5	5.2	3.6
North Dakota	77.6	67.6	74.8	65.7	13	8	5	14	12	10	3.2	3.6	2.8	3.8	3.4	3.0
Ohio	69.4	57.8	64.3	53.7	412	221	191	590	352	237	7.2	7.3	7.0	10.1	6.0	4.1
Oklahoma	71.0	55.1	67.5	52.1	93	48	44	125	80	50	5.1	4.9	5.4	7.2	4.6	3.0
Oregon	68.2	58.5	61.9	53.6	173	96	77	221	111	87	8.9	9.3	8.4	11.0	6.0	4.9
Pennsylvania	70.6	57.9	65.0	53.4	509	273	236	543	310	250	7.8	7.9	7.7	8.6	4.9	4.2
Rhode Island	70.8	61.6	62.9	55.5	59	32	27	65	30	21	10.5	11.1	9.9	11.3	5.2	4.1
South Carolina	64.2	54.9	58.6	49.4	203	97	106	235	140	77	9.4	8.8	10.0	11.0	6.7	3.9
South Dakota	75.1	64.2	71.5	61.4	20	11	9	23	19	9	4.6	4.8	4.4	5.1	4.3	2.3
Tennessee	69.2	54.7	63.6	50.6	242	135	107	289	161	110	7.8	8.1	7.5	9.4	5.6	3.9
Texas	73.9	57.7	69.2	53.6	843	440	402	974	608	437	6.7	6.4	7.0	8.0	5.4	4.2
Utah	76.5	58.3	71.8	55.1	80	47	33	114	51	36	5.8	6.1	5.5	8.2	4.1	3.2
Vermont	73.0	66.1	69.1	62.9	18	10	8	22	13	10	5.1	5.4	4.9	6.2	3.5	2.9
Virginia	73.2	60.2	69.1	56.4	251	124	126	308	138	80	6.0	5.6	6.4	7.5	3.5	2.2
Washington	70.2	59.1	64.3	54.2	288	155	133	361	184	158	8.3	8.4	8.2	10.2	5.6	5.2
West Virginia	60.1	48.9	54.9	46.0	60	38	22	71	42	46	7.4	8.7	5.9	9.0	5.3	5.5
Wisconsin	72.6	64.7	67.2	60.5	219	120	98	268	142	104	7.1	7.5	6.6	8.7	4.7	3.5
Wyoming	75.9	62.3	71.8	58.8	17	9	8	20	10	10	5.5	5.4	5.6	6.6	3.6	3.9

[1] Annual averages of monthly figures.
[2] Percent of each specified group which is classified as either employed or unemployed.
[3] Preliminary data.
[4] Percent of civilian noninstitutionalized population classified as employed.
[5] Percent unemployed of the civilian labor force.

Table A-29. Employed Civilians, by Occupation, 2011

Geographic area	Total[1] (thousands)	Management, professional, and related occupations (thousands)		Service occupations (thousands)	Sales and office occupations (thousands)		Natural resources, construction, and maintenance occupations (thousands)			Production, transportation, and material moving occupations (thousands)	
		Management, business, and financial operations occupations	Professional and related occupations		Sales and related occupations	Office and administrative support occupations	Farming, fishing, and forestry occupations	Construction and extraction occupations	Installation, maintenance, and repair occupations	Production occupations	Transportation and material moving occupations
United States............	139,869	21,589	30,957	24,787	15,330	17,736	1,001	7,125	4,883	8,142	8,318
Alabama.....................	2,006	236	437	303	221	263	(D)	108	92	197	137
Alaska	342	49	70	62	30	49	(D)	24	18	(D)	25
Arizona......................	2,732	432	620	495	345	358	(D)	146	86	105	131
Arkansas....................	1,247	157	241	223	131	174	(D)	73	50	98	82
California...................	16,239	2,557	3,618	2,866	1,816	2,064	243	784	501	869	922
Colorado	2,507	465	607	419	274	294	(D)	139	75	98	123
Connecticut...............	1,745	299	456	291	186	213	(D)	78	60	90	68
Delaware	412	65	88	77	43	55	4	22	13	19	26
District of Columbia ...	312	78	114	52	17	30	(D)	6	3	3	9
Florida.......................	8,366	1,336	1,802	1,636	1,096	1,111	36	369	316	250	415
Georgia	4,263	694	862	702	527	536	(D)	228	175	209	308
Hawaii	619	88	115	132	73	95	(D)	37	19	19	36
Idaho.........................	702	98	137	120	79	97	23	39	24	41	44
Illinois.......................	5,925	924	1,257	1,044	670	758	(D)	225	198	397	437
Indiana......................	2,913	414	536	515	299	347	26	140	143	296	198
Iowa..........................	1,570	244	307	250	164	204	(D)	80	64	131	110
Kansas	1,399	225	334	234	127	173	(D)	75	47	92	83
Kentucky	1,859	250	393	308	192	234	20	102	55	159	146
Louisiana	1,893	236	399	341	191	263	(D)	128	70	125	131
Maine........................	643	96	143	118	68	82	9	34	22	38	34
Maryland....................	2,873	532	804	492	271	342	(D)	143	80	69	128
Massachusetts..........	3,207	566	914	546	327	358	(D)	159	71	140	123
Michigan....................	4,181	598	935	763	444	521	35	155	134	351	245
Minnesota.................	2,764	464	632	460	305	335	32	117	88	181	149
Mississippi................	1,206	134	243	211	130	161	(D)	73	56	106	86
Missouri	2,812	454	580	453	315	366	(D)	154	111	193	170
Montana....................	466	75	92	94	51	59	8	26	16	18	27
Nebraska...................	963	165	198	154	99	124	(D)	52	28	77	51
Nevada......................	1,197	164	183	324	155	153	(D)	54	37	46	78
New Hampshire..........	697	117	179	107	76	86	(D)	31	26	40	31
New Jersey	4,159	729	922	712	454	569	(D)	192	134	167	271
New Mexico	858	141	212	159	80	104	(D)	61	31	30	33
New York....................	8,707	1,313	2,178	1,721	939	1,086	(D)	409	231	339	483
North Carolina...........	4,145	623	934	708	439	462	(D)	247	180	286	244
North Dakota..............	377	66	75	69	37	50	(D)	24	15	16	20
Ohio..........................	5,265	699	1,093	958	550	675	27	262	184	470	347
Oklahoma	1,657	244	345	272	162	223	(D)	116	92	94	98
Oregon......................	1,818	310	418	316	201	227	33	73	52	93	95
Pennsylvania.............	5,895	905	1,253	1,011	632	769	43	300	198	377	407
Rhode Island.............	497	75	127	95	49	61	(D)	20	15	28	25
South Carolina	1,941	269	408	349	226	222	16	80	81	169	120
South Dakota	421	73	81	68	40	58	9	23	15	29	27
Tennessee	2,854	393	580	473	334	406	(D)	147	111	208	194
Texas........................	11,476	1,635	2,343	2,066	1,272	1,466	68	793	456	661	716
Utah..........................	1,244	189	256	176	149	183	(D)	84	47	86	71
Vermont	340	52	83	61	31	41	4	20	12	20	17
Virginia	3,954	715	941	684	409	459	(D)	195	137	184	206
Washington...............	3,127	512	762	559	300	374	42	125	114	160	178
West Virginia.............	742	84	159	143	74	102	(D)	60	30	36	52
Wisconsin	2,848	431	607	497	296	360	28	104	84	253	188
Wyoming	290	40	53	51	23	36	(D)	32	15	14	22

[1]Due to separate processing and weighting procedures, totals for the United States differ from the results obtained by aggregating the totals for the States.
(D) = Data withheld to avoid disclosure or does not meet statistical standards.

Table A-30. Private Industry Employment and Wages

Geographic Area	Employment							Average annual wages per employee								
	Total (thousands)					Percent change		Total (dollars)					Rank			Percent change	
	2011	2010	2009	2005	2000	2000–2009	2009–2011	2011	2010	2009	2005	2000	2011	2005	2000	2000–2009	2009–2011
United States............	108,185	106,201	106,947	110,611	110,015	-2.8	1.2	47,815	46,455	45,155	40,505	35,337	(X)	(X)	(X)	27.8	5.9
Alabama...................	1,449	1,444	1,463	1,548	1,542	-5.1	-1.0	40,103	39,270	38,332	34,009	28,491	35	32	35	34.5	4.6
Alaska	243	237	235	226	207	13.6	3.5	48,199	47,150	46,304	38,817	33,500	13	18	18	38.2	4.1
Arizona....................	1,993	1,958	1,994	2,108	1,904	4.7	-0.1	44,091	42,860	42,149	37,706	32,432	19	20	20	30.0	4.6
Arkansas	937	929	931	957	952	-2.2	0.6	36,801	35,814	35,131	30,778	26,032	46	44	46	35.0	4.8
California.................	12,265	12,045	12,206	12,878	12,632	-3.4	0.5	54,345	52,553	50,680	45,684	41,175	5	5	5	23.1	7.2
Colorado	1,840	1,802	1,829	1,844	1,868	-2.1	0.6	49,245	47,916	46,820	41,593	37,553	12	10	7	24.7	5.2
Connecticut..............	1,375	1,354	1,369	1,409	1,461	-6.3	0.4	62,031	60,396	58,377	53,678	46,068	2	1	2	26.7	6.3
Delaware	343	339	342	361	353	-3.1	0.1	50,535	48,592	47,365	44,592	36,607	8	6	10	29.4	6.7
District of Columbia ...	461	448	446	436	419	6.6	3.3	74,710	73,072	70,984	61,598	49,828	(X)	(X)	(X)	42.5	5.2
Florida......................	6,151	6,045	6,117	6,695	6,084	0.5	0.5	41,377	40,562	39,856	36,096	30,031	30	25	29	32.7	3.8
Georgia	3,136	3,085	3,119	3,289	3,292	-5.2	0.5	45,580	44,311	43,177	39,514	34,686	17	16	16	24.5	5.6
Hawaii......................	472	465	470	487	443	5.9	0.6	39,838	39,294	38,836	34,564	29,179	37	30	31	33.1	2.6
Idaho.......................	497	493	500	505	463	8.1	-0.7	35,406	34,611	33,688	30,440	27,623	47	46	38	22.0	5.1
Illinois	4,765	4,686	4,730	4,943	5,139	-8.0	0.7	50,921	49,523	48,360	43,852	38,246	6	7	6	26.4	5.3
Indiana	2,359	2,305	2,296	2,476	2,553	-10.0	2.7	40,272	39,226	38,138	35,463	31,022	33	28	25	22.9	5.6
Iowa........................	1,218	1,201	1,208	1,218	1,219	-0.9	0.8	38,554	37,429	36,309	32,651	27,501	42	37	39	32.0	6.2
Kansas	1,058	1,047	1,067	1,067	1,083	-1.5	-0.8	40,507	39,431	38,519	34,265	29,646	32	31	30	29.9	5.2
Kentucky	1,427	1,404	1,409	1,464	1,479	-4.7	1.3	39,323	38,373	37,599	33,736	28,773	39	33	33	30.7	4.6
Louisiana	1,509	1,481	1,497	1,483	1,515	-1.2	0.8	42,458	41,470	40,491	33,517	28,013	23	35	36	44.5	4.9
Maine	482	479	483	496	496	-2.7	0.0	37,389	36,582	35,753	32,104	27,280	45	40	41	31.1	4.6
Maryland..................	1,991	1,969	1,984	2,049	1,972	0.6	0.4	50,620	49,496	48,315	42,779	35,407	7	8	13	36.5	4.8
Massachusetts..........	2,778	2,733	2,721	2,758	2,866	-5.1	2.1	60,196	58,359	56,659	50,425	45,049	3	3	3	25.8	6.2
Michigan..................	3,284	3,180	3,175	3,664	3,959	-19.8	3.4	45,285	43,631	42,835	41,125	37,227	18	11	9	15.1	5.7
Minnesota................	2,236	2,184	2,196	2,266	2,260	-2.8	1.8	48,091	46,984	45,253	40,965	35,513	14	13	12	27.4	6.3
Mississippi...............	838	833	838	878	916	-8.5	-0.1	34,217	33,537	33,047	29,201	24,833	50	48	47	33.1	3.5
Missouri...................	2,162	2,143	2,173	2,247	2,270	-4.3	-0.5	41,723	40,852	40,182	36,205	31,598	28	24	22	27.2	3.8
Montana...................	340	335	339	334	306	10.6	0.2	34,518	33,244	32,247	27,936	23,184	49	50	50	39.1	7.0
Nebraska..................	743	737	743	740	737	0.8	0.1	37,567	36,686	36,069	32,005	27,471	44	41	40	31.3	4.2
Nevada....................	970	958	986	1,075	902	9.3	-1.6	41,657	40,899	41,124	37,881	31,387	29	19	23	31.0	1.3
New Hampshire.........	520	514	518	536	530	-2.3	0.5	47,642	46,287	45,112	41,023	35,250	15	12	14	28.0	5.6
New Jersey	3,157	3,135	3,158	3,309	3,320	-4.9	-0.1	56,885	55,736	54,543	49,119	43,646	4	4	4	25.0	4.3
New Mexico	597	593	602	597	564	6.7	-0.9	38,674	37,927	37,021	31,343	26,518	40	43	43	39.6	4.5
New York..................	7,051	6,906	6,901	6,929	7,073	-2.4	2.2	63,081	61,548	58,821	52,979	46,224	1	2	1	27.3	7.2
North Carolina...........	3,158	3,102	3,137	3,209	3,260	-3.8	0.7	41,933	40,874	39,365	35,764	30,998	27	27	26	27.0	6.5
North Dakota.............	313	291	284	265	254	11.7	10.2	42,098	38,028	35,666	29,577	24,319	26	47	48	46.7	18.0
Ohio	4,248	4,170	4,199	4,555	4,775	-12.1	1.2	42,244	41,040	40,128	36,830	32,191	25	22	21	24.7	5.3
Oklahoma	1,190	1,161	1,173	1,159	1,173	0.0	1.4	40,157	39,011	38,936	31,558	26,617	34	42	42	38.8	8.7
Oregon	1,342	1,318	1,329	1,387	1,363	-2.5	1.0	42,421	40,984	40,002	36,230	32,488	24	23	19	23.1	6.0
Pennsylvania.............	4,825	4,742	4,741	4,837	4,860	-2.5	1.8	46,662	45,325	44,395	39,264	33,629	16	17	17	32.0	5.1
Rhode Island.............	389	387	388	415	405	-4.1	0.3	43,532	42,525	41,315	37,067	31,206	20	21	24	32.4	5.4
South Carolina	1,451	1,424	1,429	1,501	1,507	-5.2	1.5	37,734	36,785	35,779	32,420	27,776	43	39	37	28.8	5.5
South Dakota	322	317	318	307	305	4.1	1.3	35,086	33,887	32,847	28,655	24,291	48	49	49	35.2	6.8
Tennessee................	2,186	2,138	2,149	2,287	2,288	-6.1	1.7	42,622	41,760	40,282	35,859	30,527	22	26	27	32.0	5.8
Texas.......................	8,634	8,363	8,366	7,927	7,748	8.0	3.2	49,534	47,610	46,207	40,880	35,681	11	14	11	29.5	7.2
Utah	969	946	955	925	870	9.8	1.4	39,937	38,936	37,975	32,828	28,925	36	36	32	31.3	5.2
Vermont	243	240	240	250	249	-3.7	1.4	39,502	38,636	37,963	33,648	28,691	38	34	34	32.3	4.1
Virginia	2,889	2,850	2,863	2,931	2,823	1.4	0.9	50,261	49,138	47,662	41,938	34,967	9	9	15	36.3	5.5
Washington...............	2,325	2,283	2,311	2,265	2,248	2.8	0.6	49,827	47,861	46,794	40,225	37,249	10	15	8	25.6	6.5
West Virginia.............	560	550	552	559	551	0.2	1.3	38,565	36,991	36,033	30,545	26,292	41	45	45	37.0	7.0
Wisconsin	2,284	2,247	2,258	2,365	2,379	-5.1	1.1	40,627	39,556	38,626	35,115	30,304	31	29	28	27.5	5.2
Wyoming	209	205	210	195	176	19.2	-0.4	42,911	41,258	39,786	32,620	26,502	21	38	44	50.1	7.9

(X) = Not applicable

Table A-31.   Industry Employment and Wages

| Geography area | Private industry employment, 2011[1] (thousands) | | | | | | | | |
	Total[2]	Construction (NAICS 23)	Manufacturing (NAICS 31-33)	Wholesale trade (NAICS 42)	Retail trade (NAICS 44-45)	Transportation and warehousing (NAICS 48-49)	Information (NAICS 51)	Finance and insurance (NAICS 52)	Real estate and rental and leasing (NAICS 53)
United States...............	108,185	5,473	11,701	5,546	14,667	4,056	2,675	5,507	1,910
Alabama.......................	1,449	81	237	72	225	50	23	69	21
Alaska..........................	243	16	14	6	36	19	6	9	5
Arizona........................	1,993	111	150	96	295	67	37	121	45
Arkansas.....................	937	47	159	47	131	50	15	35	13
California.....................	12,265	558	1,238	656	1,528	399	425	512	246
Colorado	1,840	112	129	92	240	58	72	98	41
Connecticut..................	1,375	52	166	63	180	40	31	115	19
Delaware	343	19	26	12	51	9	6	37	5
District of Columbia	461	12	1	5	18	2	18	15	10
Florida.........................	6,151	334	311	308	956	205	134	323	151
Georgia	3,136	145	349	197	440	156	98	150	56
Hawaii.........................	472	28	13	17	67	24	8	15	11
Idaho...........................	497	30	55	26	75	17	9	20	7
Illinois.........................	4,765	196	573	290	596	220	100	278	71
Indiana........................	2,359	120	464	115	308	107	34	92	32
Iowa............................	1,218	62	206	67	174	52	28	88	13
Kansas	1,058	53	161	59	142	40	28	56	15
Kentucky	1,427	68	212	72	201	81	27	67	18
Louisiana	1,509	122	140	72	221	68	24	58	31
Maine..........................	482	25	51	19	81	15	8	24	6
Maryland......................	1,991	143	113	86	281	63	42	95	42
Massachusetts..............	2,778	111	254	123	343	70	84	167	40
Michigan	3,284	124	510	154	446	95	53	131	49
Minnesota....................	2,236	92	301	126	280	74	54	136	36
Mississippi...................	838	49	135	34	133	38	12	32	11
Missouri	2,162	103	246	116	302	79	56	119	35
Montana.......................	340	23	17	16	55	11	7	15	5
Nebraska......................	743	40	94	41	105	38	17	53	9
Nevada.........................	970	52	38	33	129	46	13	30	22
New Hampshire.............	520	22	67	26	93	12	11	27	7
New Jersey	3,157	129	252	209	439	147	75	184	53
New Mexico	597	42	30	21	90	16	13	21	10
New York......................	7,051	307	457	330	890	219	255	497	177
North Carolina...............	3,158	174	435	168	441	104	69	148	47
North Dakota.................	313	24	24	23	45	14	7	17	4
Ohio............................	4,248	176	638	218	555	158	76	207	58
Oklahoma	1,190	68	130	58	171	41	24	55	22
Oregon	1,342	67	168	74	184	46	32	55	23
Pennsylvania.................	4,825	223	565	228	629	205	91	251	58
Rhode Island.................	389	16	40	16	47	9	10	23	6
South Carolina	1,451	77	215	65	226	47	26	65	26
South Dakota	322	20	39	19	50	9	6	24	3
Tennessee	2,186	105	304	118	310	128	43	101	31
Texas...........................	8,634	564	836	516	1,161	369	195	453	174
Utah............................	969	65	113	46	139	43	28	52	17
Vermont	243	14	31	10	38	7	5	9	3
Virginia	2,889	178	230	112	402	97	74	123	51
Washington...................	2,325	127	266	120	308	81	104	87	43
West Virginia................	560	33	49	23	87	17	10	19	7
Wisconsin	2,284	93	443	114	294	86	47	125	24
Wyoming	209	21	9	9	29	9	4	7	4

[1]All estimates of labor and earnings provided by the Bureau of Labor Statistics (BLS) are based on the 2007 North American Industry Classification System (NAICS). National total may differ from sum of state total due to rounding. Annual employment data are the average employment by industry for the calendar year.
[2]Includes data for industries and unclassified establishments not shown separately.

Table A-31.   Industry Employment and Wages—*Continued*

Geography area	Private industry employment, 2011[1] (thousands)						Government employment, 2008[3] (thousands) (NAICS 92)
	Professional and technical services (NAICS 54)	Management of companies and enterprises (NAICS 55)	Educational services (NAICS 61)	Health care and social assistance (NAICS 62)	Arts, entertainment, and recreation (NAICS 71)	Accommodation and food services (NAICS 72)	
United States....................	7,673	1,915	2,546	16,489	1,923	11,372	21,226
Alabama............................	94	16	18	192	16	153	364
Alaska	14	1	2	41	5	28	79
Arizona..............................	123	25	52	300	33	226	386
Arkansas............................	39	26	12	154	10	91	203
California............................	1,053	198	294	1,495	246	1,279	2,302
Colorado............................	172	30	30	240	46	226	373
Connecticut.......................	88	29	55	251	24	113	238
Delaware............................	26	8	4	58	9	34	60
District of Columbia	102	2	39	61	7	55	246
Florida...............................	444	81	130	944	189	765	1,045
Georgia	223	54	64	404	40	340	656
Hawaii	24	7	14	61	11	93	121
Idaho.................................	32	6	6	76	8	51	111
Illinois...............................	354	98	138	699	76	445	801
Indiana..............................	98	28	48	355	41	237	397
Iowa..................................	43	15	25	177	20	111	234
Kansas	60	14	13	165	14	101	246
Kentucky	69	20	17	223	18	151	307
Louisiana	81	24	25	236	28	173	340
Maine	23	7	12	99	8	52	97
Maryland............................	229	22	61	330	36	197	487
Massachusetts	257	59	128	511	49	266	411
Michigan............................	234	53	63	538	47	330	571
Minnesota..........................	128	73	47	400	38	202	367
Mississippi.........................	32	10	10	120	11	108	239
Missouri	124	61	41	349	41	229	423
Montana............................	19	2	4	59	11	46	83
Nebraska	43	17	10	112	12	70	158
Nevada	47	18	9	94	27	289	145
New Hampshire..................	30	8	17	84	11	52	86
New Jersey	276	77	72	499	53	281	578
New Mexico	54	5	8	104	8	76	184
New York...........................	572	133	303	1,301	141	623	1,393
North Carolina....................	188	77	64	458	56	343	680
North Dakota......................	13	4	2	52	4	32	67
Ohio	245	113	95	736	63	420	721
Oklahoma	65	15	15	182	15	129	318
Oregon	73	30	27	200	22	143	274
Pennsylvania......................	308	123	183	904	92	418	710
Rhode Island......................	21	10	19	78	8	43	59
South Carolina	79	15	21	173	26	184	330
South Dakota	11	4	3	57	6	37	72
Tennessee	109	30	41	331	30	237	417
Texas.................................	588	83	128	1,212	110	931	1,788
Utah..................................	68	17	24	120	18	96	208
Vermont	14	1	9	47	4	29	52
Virginia..............................	391	73	62	383	47	301	689
Washington........................	163	33	35	327	45	222	519
West Virginia......................	25	6	6	112	7	66	142
Wisconsin	96	51	34	357	35	217	381
Wyoming	9	1	2	24	3	30	66

[1]All estimates of labor and earnings provided by the Bureau of Labor Statistics (BLS) are based on the 2007 North American Industry Classification System (NAICS). National total may differ from sum of state total due to rounding. Annual employment data are the average employment by industry for the calendar year.
[3]Includes local, state, and federal.

Table A-31. Industry Employment and Wages—*Continued*

Geography area	Private industry average annual pay, 2011[1] (dollars)								
	Total[2]	Construction (NAICS 23)	Manufacturing (NAICS 31-33)	Wholesale trade (NAICS 42)	Retail trade (NAICS 44-45)	Transportation and warehousing (NAICS 48-49)	Information (NAICS 51)	Finance and insurance (NAICS 52)	Real estate and rental and leasing (NAICS 53)
United States..................	47,815	50,693	59,210	66,142	27,118	45,336	78,331	88,292	45,861
Alabama............................	40,103	43,518	49,139	56,153	24,706	40,694	50,956	61,808	36,618
Alaska..............................	48,199	70,151	38,512	52,189	28,663	58,926	58,491	59,526	37,803
Arizona............................	44,091	45,076	68,488	65,649	29,981	46,543	58,431	61,410	43,493
Arkansas..........................	36,801	39,893	40,512	56,604	23,394	40,835	50,477	53,034	31,716
California..........................	54,345	56,206	74,882	66,794	31,552	47,426	106,238	95,702	51,329
Colorado	49,245	48,864	61,668	71,428	27,113	43,761	84,138	74,312	43,918
Connecticut......................	62,031	58,311	77,228	83,435	31,121	46,074	78,965	154,171	58,224
Delaware..........................	50,535	52,472	56,202	82,543	25,962	40,214	57,402	84,398	41,530
District of Columbia	74,710	63,460	104,661	107,660	31,629	53,783	106,836	136,656	74,712
Florida..............................	41,377	40,875	52,372	63,101	27,079	44,663	64,536	68,450	40,332
Georgia	45,580	46,116	51,970	68,190	26,306	49,803	78,148	74,060	47,242
Hawaii..............................	39,838	63,597	40,444	49,748	28,158	42,653	57,758	60,131	42,403
Idaho................................	35,406	38,482	50,227	47,382	25,268	34,676	42,881	47,243	27,554
Illinois..............................	50,921	59,702	61,119	71,447	26,685	46,594	71,042	95,354	52,108
Indiana.............................	40,272	51,475	55,398	55,410	23,826	39,465	50,613	56,974	35,472
Iowa.................................	38,554	45,120	51,131	53,967	23,191	38,406	46,781	61,364	39,324
Kansas.............................	40,507	45,111	52,010	58,574	23,903	40,036	63,206	58,782	34,215
Kentucky	39,323	44,006	51,329	53,679	24,085	46,101	44,555	58,890	35,370
Louisiana	42,458	50,963	62,438	55,684	24,885	55,309	49,710	55,934	47,110
Maine................................	37,389	41,473	50,253	53,025	24,202	35,905	43,793	59,224	34,177
Maryland...........................	50,620	54,849	67,194	71,067	27,835	46,546	75,328	82,889	55,021
Massachusetts	60,196	63,230	77,572	82,215	27,877	42,720	95,930	120,502	63,050
Michigan...........................	45,285	52,004	62,305	67,050	26,009	47,673	60,398	64,051	36,256
Minnesota.........................	48,091	53,455	57,549	71,781	24,845	43,715	66,179	82,337	46,875
Mississippi.......................	34,217	41,424	41,815	48,617	22,908	38,484	42,237	47,168	30,500
Missouri	41,723	48,685	50,457	58,829	24,647	40,011	68,419	62,650	35,367
Montana............................	34,518	42,757	42,773	47,887	24,663	38,762	41,965	50,633	28,439
Nebraska..........................	37,567	41,083	42,962	51,215	22,995	37,242	52,352	54,951	32,866
Nevada.............................	41,657	53,087	51,704	62,944	28,161	41,306	56,947	59,400	40,172
New Hampshire.................	47,642	50,118	63,208	77,868	27,353	37,660	74,526	81,587	47,030
New Jersey	56,885	61,722	75,068	79,534	30,367	48,638	89,799	107,138	54,216
New Mexico	38,674	41,036	53,848	48,930	25,547	42,207	44,259	53,032	35,075
New York..........................	63,081	61,511	60,066	73,836	30,272	44,467	95,966	201,446	56,628
North Carolina..................	41,933	41,311	52,585	61,217	24,649	41,341	64,354	75,194	38,483
North Dakota.....................	42,098	51,202	44,778	57,560	25,653	51,688	50,933	49,664	44,504
Ohio.................................	42,244	48,671	55,317	60,854	24,714	43,253	58,613	62,773	37,778
Oklahoma	40,157	41,518	48,162	50,992	25,020	50,458	50,306	50,075	38,302
Oregon.............................	42,421	49,110	60,223	67,982	26,298	40,958	66,049	61,872	33,016
Pennsylvania....................	46,662	54,652	55,239	68,717	25,287	39,788	65,805	75,016	48,648
Rhode Island.....................	43,532	52,767	50,822	63,775	26,672	37,184	64,106	78,240	38,696
South Carolina	37,734	41,959	51,153	56,596	24,506	38,436	50,549	54,808	34,997
South Dakota	35,086	38,999	41,474	48,936	23,713	37,636	41,939	47,947	28,123
Tennessee	42,622	45,583	52,895	59,682	27,690	48,470	57,070	68,149	39,868
Texas...............................	49,534	50,947	66,032	71,447	27,868	53,474	70,784	71,740	49,150
Utah.................................	39,937	42,932	50,134	57,294	26,379	41,624	56,584	56,532	37,691
Vermont	39,502	43,298	53,818	54,660	26,714	36,448	49,349	64,057	34,459
Virginia	50,261	47,542	52,645	70,558	25,722	44,031	80,196	76,209	45,312
Washington......................	49,827	52,303	68,062	65,832	30,917	49,628	119,966	73,147	39,817
West Virginia....................	38,565	47,014	51,733	51,233	23,700	44,725	48,595	46,850	35,049
Wisconsin	40,627	50,197	51,435	55,813	23,202	37,561	54,551	60,113	32,924
Wyoming	42,911	47,613	54,913	56,171	25,887	46,730	40,476	49,078	42,214

[1]All estimates of labor and earnings provided by the Bureau of Labor Statistics (BLS) are based on the 2007 North American Industry Classification System (NAICS). National total may differ from sum of state total due to rounding. Annual employment data are the average employment by industry for the calendar year.
[2]Includes data for industries and unclassfied establishments not shown separately.

Table A-31. Industry Employment and Wages—*Continued*

Geography area	Private industry average annual pay, 2011[1] (dollars)						Government employment, 2008[3] (thousands) (NAICS 92)
	Professional and technical services (NAICS 54)	Management of companies and enterprises (NAICS 55)	Educational services (NAICS 61)	Health care and social assistance (NAICS 62)	Arts, entertainment, and recreation (NAICS 71)	Accommodation and food services (NAICS 72)	
United States.....................	79,807	103,075	43,663	44,494	32,943	17,545	49,205
Alabama..............................	68,269	78,601	31,433	42,327	16,876	14,091	45,490
Alaska	67,672	77,107	30,362	44,361	18,698	20,595	53,028
Arizona...............................	68,582	74,522	39,610	47,509	33,929	17,961	47,115
Arkansas............................	55,047	88,418	30,014	36,287	17,852	13,260	39,489
California............................	93,421	100,545	45,413	53,506	51,591	19,422	58,575
Colorado.............................	81,381	130,514	37,978	44,852	30,733	18,042	48,281
Connecticut........................	89,807	139,193	54,053	47,736	26,211	18,641	56,020
Delaware	89,587	127,273	40,696	48,901	28,071	16,716	50,293
District of Columbia	120,124	201,791	53,936	57,588	64,185	28,904	94,297
Florida................................	65,198	91,942	38,702	45,245	32,964	19,078	47,827
Georgia	72,853	90,947	46,042	44,339	32,550	16,669	42,748
Hawaii	63,632	79,822	37,012	46,880	24,567	27,030	52,719
Idaho..................................	56,255	83,954	35,418	36,235	16,165	13,466	36,615
Illinois................................	84,600	114,051	45,596	43,870	32,309	17,701	50,356
Indiana...............................	57,182	81,539	34,670	40,742	29,167	13,611	40,104
Iowa...................................	54,014	71,651	32,672	37,539	18,195	12,906	42,587
Kansas...............................	58,532	84,958	32,345	38,236	15,779	13,319	37,757
Kentucky	52,912	92,006	32,540	42,125	20,234	14,024	41,151
Louisiana	61,394	67,869	40,758	37,561	31,513	16,735	42,009
Maine.................................	56,401	68,313	38,522	40,554	21,656	16,120	41,147
Maryland.............................	86,836	101,183	49,085	47,356	28,269	18,069	62,761
Massachusetts....................	104,065	123,026	59,420	52,290	35,302	19,669	56,123
Michigan.............................	73,315	112,442	32,735	44,531	28,100	14,817	48,947
Minnesota	76,286	109,617	36,984	43,816	29,656	14,942	46,436
Mississippi..........................	51,404	74,560	31,615	38,228	20,556	16,054	37,636
Missouri..............................	67,399	87,142	40,878	41,359	34,651	14,909	40,120
Montana..............................	51,834	59,497	25,739	39,288	17,767	14,392	40,990
Nebraska............................	58,252	77,616	40,822	39,808	15,836	12,726	41,569
Nevada...............................	68,430	110,933	37,796	49,622	31,342	30,429	52,766
New Hampshire...................	77,067	88,538	47,760	48,032	19,121	17,299	45,085
New Jersey	91,186	137,037	45,155	47,652	32,758	20,356	61,157
New Mexico	70,041	60,668	33,327	38,052	19,020	15,380	44,429
New York............................	94,074	145,872	48,799	45,381	45,792	22,812	55,267
North Carolina.....................	66,951	88,777	43,575	40,562	28,502	14,871	42,994
North Dakota.......................	55,999	65,950	29,123	41,423	14,460	13,791	40,282
Ohio...................................	64,486	93,048	33,549	40,294	27,945	13,849	47,261
Oklahoma	54,415	93,321	34,468	38,839	25,631	14,137	39,923
Oregon...............................	62,125	78,085	31,855	44,874	22,696	16,400	46,368
Pennsylvania.......................	79,112	106,940	49,667	43,369	29,452	15,485	49,569
Rhode Island.......................	64,889	103,190	46,172	41,865	24,447	16,592	59,965
South Carolina	59,825	66,659	33,134	40,964	18,012	15,308	41,477
South Dakota	49,216	88,051	29,655	41,750	15,965	12,945	36,880
Tennessee	66,118	82,232	40,589	45,685	39,732	16,273	41,571
Texas.................................	79,622	106,879	41,321	41,799	30,086	17,013	44,876
Utah...................................	61,595	76,082	37,787	38,070	22,457	14,939	41,870
Vermont	64,756	78,315	39,901	39,477	21,362	18,388	43,969
Virginia...............................	94,547	104,202	40,737	44,383	23,639	16,647	52,317
Washington.........................	77,178	102,014	35,567	45,853	25,015	18,062	52,174
West Virginia.......................	50,720	81,769	32,958	37,644	17,073	15,422	41,165
Wisconsin	60,244	84,333	43,912	42,556	26,545	12,566	43,258
Wyoming	54,718	102,665	29,137	39,480	18,953	16,625	44,927

[1]All estimates of labor and earnings provided by the Bureau of Labor Statistics (BLS) are based on the 2007 North American Industry Classification System (NAICS). National total may differ from sum of state total due to rounding. Annual employment data are the average employment by industry for the calendar year.
[3]Includes local, state, and federal.

Table A–32. Union Membership

Geographic area	Union members[1] (thousands)			Workers covered by union[2] (thousands)			Percentage of workers								
							Union members			Covered by union			Percentage of private sector union members		
	2012	2010	2000	2012	2010	2000	2012	2010	2000	2012	2010	2000	2012	2010	2000
United States............	14,349.4	14,715.1	16,258.2	15,905.9	16,289.5	17,944.1	11.2	11.9	13.5	12.5	13.1	14.9	6.6	6.9	9.0
Alabama[3].................	166.7	183.3	180.8	190.4	202.8	197.6	9.2	10.1	9.6	10.5	11.2	10.5	5.7	5.7	5.8
Alaska	66.8	67.6	56.8	71.4	73.0	64.3	22.4	22.9	21.9	23.9	24.8	24.8	10.3	11.2	12.8
Arizona[3]....................	125.6	161.0	129.7	159.2	203.0	147.8	5.2	6.4	6.4	6.5	8.1	7.3	3.2	3.6	4.2
Arkansas[3]	36.7	43.6	61.5	42.6	58.6	70.9	3.2	4.0	5.8	3.7	5.4	6.7	1.4	2.7	4.0
California..................	2,485.0	2,431.3	2,295.1	2,662.1	2,577.8	2,546.0	17.2	17.5	16.0	18.4	18.6	17.7	8.9	9.3	9.7
Colorado	169.3	140.4	173.2	190.2	170.9	193.0	7.8	6.6	9.0	8.8	8.0	10.0	4.9	3.8	6.0
Connecticut..............	216.1	258.3	245.8	232.1	269.7	262.5	14.0	16.7	16.3	15.1	17.4	17.4	6.6	8.3	9.4
Delaware	39.4	40.2	46.9	44.5	43.9	51.7	10.4	11.4	13.3	11.8	12.5	14.6	5.6	5.8	8.9
District of Columbia ...	26.6	25.9	35.9	31.7	30.0	40.2	8.6	9.0	14.7	10.3	10.5	16.5	5.6	5.9	9.5
Florida[3].....................	438.8	391.8	433.6	553.5	488.0	553.6	5.8	5.6	6.8	7.3	6.9	8.7	2.4	2.3	3.3
Georgia[3]...................	170.7	153.3	228.1	210.0	191.3	267.0	4.4	4.0	6.3	5.4	5.0	7.4	3.1	2.5	4.6
Hawaii	116.6	111.3	123.5	124.8	120.3	129.1	21.7	21.8	24.8	23.2	23.5	26.0	14.6	14.6	14.4
Idaho[3]......................	29.2	41.5	40.7	35.7	50.1	48.0	4.8	7.1	7.6	5.8	8.6	9.0	3.2	3.6	5.5
Illinois	800.4	843.8	1,046.3	851.1	891.2	1,100.6	14.6	15.5	18.6	15.5	16.4	19.5	9.3	9.5	14.1
Indiana[4]....................	245.4	278.6	418.4	268.3	312.8	460.6	9.1	10.9	15.6	9.9	12.2	17.1	7.2	8.2	13.1
Iowa[3].......................	144.4	158.2	181.8	171.4	191.8	215.1	10.4	11.4	13.6	12.3	13.8	16.1	5.5	7.1	10.5
Kansas[3]....................	85.4	83.7	108.5	104.6	111.0	134.5	6.9	6.8	9.0	8.4	9.1	11.2	4.0	4.5	8.0
Kentucky...................	173.7	146.5	208.0	198.1	166.1	234.6	10.0	8.9	12.0	11.3	10.1	13.6	7.1	7.2	10.1
Louisiana[3]	107.7	75.6	121.9	130.0	96.0	154.8	6.2	4.3	7.1	7.5	5.5	9.0	3.7	3.2	5.5
Maine.......................	64.2	62.9	78.1	77.6	70.7	92.2	11.5	11.6	14.0	13.9	13.0	16.6	5.4	5.1	8.0
Maryland...................	278.8	296.1	353.3	324.5	328.8	405.5	10.6	11.6	14.6	12.3	12.9	16.7	5.5	6.1	7.8
Massachusetts...........	416.3	414.8	406.3	470.2	446.4	444.9	14.3	14.5	14.3	16.2	15.6	15.7	7.4	7.0	7.9
Michigan[4].................	628.8	627.3	938.3	647.9	658.7	985.3	16.6	16.5	20.8	17.1	17.3	21.8	11.3	11.1	15.7
Minnesota	350.5	384.6	419.0	367.5	397.3	434.3	14.2	15.6	18.2	14.9	16.1	18.8	7.7	8.4	12.3
Mississippi[3]..............	47.9	46.3	67.7	63.8	58.3	104.3	4.3	4.5	6.0	5.7	5.6	9.3	3.0	3.7	5.4
Missouri	224.1	244.3	337.9	253.1	274.4	365.3	8.9	9.9	13.2	10.1	11.1	14.2	7.2	8.5	12.1
Montana...................	54.5	46.1	51.2	64.7	52.2	57.8	13.9	12.7	13.9	16.5	14.4	15.7	5.8	5.6	8.2
Nebraska[3].................	51.4	75.3	64.9	70.0	95.6	89.4	6.0	9.3	8.4	8.1	11.8	11.5	3.4	4.8	4.6
Nevada[3]....................	162.3	151.3	150.9	181.0	169.9	165.3	14.8	15.0	17.1	16.5	16.8	18.8	11.1	10.8	13.8
New Hampshire..........	65.3	63.2	59.8	74.4	72.6	66.7	10.5	10.2	10.4	12.0	11.7	11.6	4.2	4.4	6.3
New Jersey	611.2	636.9	762.0	636.4	660.0	800.7	16.1	17.1	20.8	16.8	17.7	21.8	8.5	9.0	13.1
New Mexico	50.3	54.8	56.2	68.1	72.4	69.7	6.5	7.3	8.1	8.7	9.7	10.1	2.8	2.6	5.5
New York	1,836.4	1,958.7	1,958.0	1,970.0	2,098.6	2,036.4	23.2	24.2	25.5	24.8	26.0	26.5	13.3	13.7	15.3
North Carolina[3]..........	111.5	116.7	124.1	161.4	179.6	148.4	2.9	3.2	3.6	4.2	4.9	4.4	1.8	1.8	2.4
North Dakota[3]............	20.0	23.0	17.6	26.9	28.4	21.1	6.1	7.4	6.5	8.2	9.1	7.8	3.4	4.6	3.7
Ohio	604.3	654.9	879.0	664.7	701.9	955.1	12.6	13.7	17.3	13.9	14.7	18.8	8.4	8.4	12.3
Oklahoma[3]................	114.5	77.4	93.8	139.3	98.5	108.0	7.5	5.5	6.8	9.1	6.9	7.8	4.3	3.5	4.4
Oregon	240.7	245.1	234.4	250.5	267.9	251.0	15.8	16.2	16.1	16.4	17.7	17.2	8.6	9.1	9.8
Pennsylvania............	732.2	770.2	869.6	785.3	831.4	925.7	13.4	14.7	16.9	14.4	15.9	18.0	7.8	9.3	11.2
Rhode Island.............	81.1	74.9	79.6	83.9	79.4	82.5	17.8	16.4	18.2	18.4	17.4	18.8	10.1	8.4	9.9
South Carolina[3]	58.4	79.6	70.3	81.7	106.8	88.8	3.3	4.6	4.0	4.6	6.2	5.1	1.3	2.7	2.5
South Dakota[3]	19.5	20.0	18.2	23.6	23.5	22.2	5.6	5.6	5.5	6.7	6.6	6.7	3.1	3.0	2.5
Tennessee[3]...............	124.3	115.5	211.5	151.7	142.5	238.8	4.8	4.7	8.9	5.9	5.8	10.0	2.9	2.2	6.7
Texas[3].....................	598.1	545.4	505.4	719.3	676.7	645.1	5.7	5.4	5.8	6.8	6.7	7.4	3.4	3.2	3.8
Utah[3]	60.8	74.6	69.3	77.7	95.6	84.9	5.2	6.5	7.3	6.6	8.4	9.0	2.9	3.9	4.5
Vermont	31.0	34.2	28.2	37.6	39.5	33.9	10.7	11.8	10.3	13.1	13.6	12.4	4.1	5.3	5.1
Virginia[3]	159.5	160.6	179.1	197.2	196.4	227.0	4.4	4.6	5.6	5.5	5.7	7.1	3.0	2.9	3.9
Washington...............	512.9	551.8	470.8	540.9	605.2	516.1	18.5	19.4	18.2	19.5	21.3	19.9	11.1	10.7	11.8
West Virginia.............	83.9	99.9	102.9	91.2	111.4	111.4	12.0	14.8	14.3	13.1	16.5	15.5	8.4	11.2	12.4
Wisconsin	292.8	354.9	446.0	311.8	379.8	473.1	11.2	14.2	17.6	12.0	15.1	18.7	6.9	8.4	11.7
Wyoming[3]	17.0	18.1	17.9	20.5	20.7	21.6	6.7	7.4	8.3	8.1	8.4	10.0	4.7	4.9	5.5

[1]Members are employed workers who are union members.
[2]Covered members are workers covered by a collective bargaining agreement.
[3]Right-to-work state.
[4]Indiana and Michigan passed the right-to-work law in 2012.

Table A-33. Median Income of Households in Constant (2011) Dollars and Distribution by Income Level, 2009–2011

Geographic area	Median household income (in 2011 constant dollars)	Total number of households (thousands)	Percentage of households by income level (in 2011 constant dollars)									
			Under $10,000	$10,000–$14,999	$15,000–$24,999	$25,000–$34,999	$35,000–$49,999	$50,000–$74,999	$75,000–$99,999	$100,000–$149,999	$150,000–$199,999	$200,000 and over
United States..................	51,484	114,932	7.4	5.6	11.0	10.6	13.9	18.3	12.0	12.3	4.5	4.3
Alabama............................	41,973	1,837	10.2	7.2	13.5	11.6	14.7	17.3	10.5	9.6	3.0	2.4
Alaska	68,211	255	4.0	3.7	7.4	8.3	12.1	19.3	15.2	18.1	7.0	4.9
Arizona..............................	48,518	2,343	7.8	5.5	11.4	11.4	15.2	18.8	11.7	11.4	3.6	3.2
Arkansas	39,588	1,126	9.7	8.1	14.2	12.9	15.4	17.6	9.7	8.2	2.4	1.9
California............................	59,641	12,433	5.7	5.3	9.8	9.3	12.6	17.4	12.3	14.7	6.4	6.5
Colorado	56,345	1,959	6.5	4.7	9.6	9.8	13.7	18.8	12.8	14.0	5.4	4.7
Connecticut.......................	67,427	1,359	5.7	4.2	8.4	8.0	11.5	16.8	13.3	16.4	7.4	8.3
Delaware	58,580	332	5.6	4.3	9.5	9.6	13.3	19.4	13.7	15.0	5.3	4.3
District of Columbia	62,214	260	10.9	4.9	7.5	7.3	11.0	15.2	11.2	13.8	7.2	10.9
Florida...............................	45,736	7,082	7.9	6.0	12.3	12.1	15.5	18.4	10.9	10.0	3.4	3.4
Georgia	47,690	3,494	8.9	6.0	11.6	11.1	14.1	18.3	11.3	11.1	3.9	3.5
Hawaii...............................	64,909	447	5.9	3.9	7.5	8.4	12.5	18.4	14.6	17.2	6.4	5.2
Idaho.................................	45,254	577	7.1	6.0	12.4	13.0	16.0	20.3	11.5	9.3	2.4	1.9
Illinois...............................	55,044	4,758	7.1	4.8	10.5	9.9	13.3	18.5	12.8	13.4	5.0	4.8
Indiana..............................	46,815	2,469	7.4	5.8	12.0	12.0	15.5	19.7	12.0	10.4	2.8	2.3
Iowa..................................	50,028	1,222	6.3	5.7	11.3	11.2	15.4	20.4	13.1	11.1	3.1	2.4
Kansas	49,929	1,105	6.6	5.4	11.5	11.3	15.3	19.6	12.4	11.4	3.5	3.0
Kentucky	41,479	1,683	10.3	7.5	13.3	12.0	14.9	17.7	10.6	9.2	2.5	2.2
Louisiana	43,484	1,694	10.0	7.2	12.9	11.3	14.0	16.8	11.1	10.6	3.3	2.8
Maine................................	47,206	554	6.9	6.7	12.5	11.4	14.8	19.7	12.4	10.3	3.0	2.3
Maryland............................	71,294	2,131	5.3	3.5	7.1	7.6	11.1	17.8	13.5	17.8	8.3	8.0
Massachusetts..................	64,504	2,528	6.7	5.3	8.7	8.0	11.2	16.5	12.9	16.4	7.2	7.1
Michigan	46,847	3,804	8.3	6.0	12.2	11.3	14.9	18.7	11.7	10.8	3.4	2.7
Minnesota.........................	57,439	2,098	5.9	4.8	9.6	9.6	13.6	19.8	14.0	14.0	4.7	4.0
Mississippi........................	37,813	1,085	11.5	8.4	14.6	12.1	14.6	16.8	10.0	7.9	2.2	1.8
Missouri	46,123	2,355	8.1	6.2	12.2	11.7	15.3	18.9	11.6	10.4	3.1	2.7
Montana............................	44,392	405	7.1	6.6	13.4	12.3	16.0	19.1	11.8	9.3	2.4	2.0
Nebraska...........................	50,365	721	6.3	5.7	11.2	11.5	14.8	20.1	13.1	11.2	3.2	2.8
Nevada..............................	52,276	989	6.5	4.6	10.5	11.2	14.8	19.8	12.8	12.6	4.0	3.2
New Hampshire.................	63,168	517	4.7	4.2	8.5	9.1	13.4	18.5	14.4	16.3	6.0	4.8
New Jersey	69,911	3,177	5.3	4.0	8.2	8.1	10.9	16.5	13.1	17.1	8.1	8.7
New Mexico	43,715	764	9.6	6.4	13.2	11.6	14.8	17.5	10.9	10.1	3.3	2.6
New York...........................	55,972	7,219	8.1	5.3	10.2	9.4	12.2	17.0	11.9	13.7	5.8	6.4
North Carolina...................	44,942	3,686	8.6	6.6	12.3	12.1	15.0	18.3	11.0	10.0	3.2	2.9
North Dakota.....................	50,671	281	7.4	5.6	10.8	11.4	14.1	19.7	13.6	11.6	2.9	2.9
Ohio..................................	46,595	4,546	8.5	6.0	12.1	11.5	14.9	18.9	11.7	10.6	3.3	2.6
Oklahoma	43,530	1,440	8.4	6.8	12.8	12.5	15.3	18.7	11.0	9.4	2.6	2.4
Oregon..............................	48,377	1,514	7.5	5.7	11.7	11.5	15.0	19.2	12.1	11.0	3.5	2.9
Pennsylvania.....................	51,016	4,955	7.2	5.8	11.3	10.7	14.0	18.8	12.3	11.9	4.1	3.8
Rhode Island.....................	54,525	410	7.8	6.0	10.2	9.2	12.6	18.0	12.9	14.0	5.1	4.2
South Carolina	43,304	1,767	9.4	6.9	13.1	11.8	14.9	18.2	10.8	9.8	2.8	2.3
South Dakota	48,208	319	7.3	6.1	11.5	11.8	14.8	20.8	12.9	10.1	2.4	2.4
Tennessee	42,661	2,461	9.2	6.9	13.1	12.2	15.2	18.1	10.9	8.9	2.8	2.7
Texas................................	50,266	8,768	7.7	5.7	11.3	11.0	14.1	18.1	11.6	12.0	4.4	4.2
Utah..................................	56,610	881	5.3	4.3	9.1	10.0	14.8	22.1	14.0	13.3	3.9	3.2
Vermont	52,941	258	6.1	5.7	10.8	10.1	14.6	20.3	13.6	11.8	4.0	3.0
Virginia	62,391	2,996	5.8	4.3	8.6	8.9	12.7	18.0	13.0	15.1	6.7	6.9
Washington.......................	57,742	2,617	6.2	4.4	9.4	9.6	13.7	19.3	13.4	14.4	5.2	4.3
West Virginia.....................	39,453	740	10.3	7.9	14.9	12.3	15.0	17.5	10.2	8.1	2.1	1.8
Wisconsin	51,009	2,285	6.2	5.5	11.3	11.0	15.0	20.1	13.3	11.7	3.3	2.6
Wyoming	56,290	223	5.1	4.7	9.8	10.4	14.4	20.5	14.4	14.4	3.7	2.7

Table A-34. Family Income and Families and Individuals below Poverty, 2009–2011

Geographic area	Median family income (in 2011 inflation-adjusted dollars)	Total number of families (thousands)	Percentage of families, by income level						Families below poverty		Individuals below poverty		Children below poverty	
			Under $25,000	$25,000–$49,999	$50,000–$74,999	$75,000–$99,999	$100,000–$199,999	$200,000 and over	Number	Percent	Number	Percent	Number	Percent
United States	62,735	76,428	16.6	22.7	19.5	14.2	21.3	5.6	8,515,185	11.1	45,768,084	15.2	15,569,283	21.4
Alabama	52,664	1,248	21.7	25.6	19.7	13.2	16.7	3.2	177,510	14.2	859,893	18.4	297,458	26.6
Alaska	79,617	172	10.0	17.7	18.8	17.0	30.1	6.2	11,452	6.7	68,189	9.8	24,366	13.2
Arizona	57,477	1,547	18.1	24.8	20.4	13.7	18.8	4.2	197,549	12.8	1,104,797	17.6	398,665	24.9
Arkansas	49,212	768	22.6	28.1	20.5	12.3	14.0	2.5	111,070	14.5	538,029	19.0	193,281	27.7
California	67,745	8,519	16.2	20.9	17.5	13.2	24.3	7.9	988,708	11.6	5,676,189	15.5	1,971,754	21.6
Colorado	70,461	1,256	13.6	20.3	19.4	15.0	25.2	6.5	115,171	9.2	651,642	13.2	211,156	17.5
Connecticut	84,558	904	10.9	16.6	16.4	14.9	30.0	11.2	65,513	7.2	350,440	10.1	107,411	13.3
Delaware	70,218	225	12.3	21.3	19.6	16.2	24.9	5.6	17,751	7.9	102,356	11.7	36,051	17.9
District of Columbia	75,807	108	19.8	16.9	13.0	9.5	23.6	17.3	15,982	14.8	108,037	18.9	31,329	30.7
Florida	55,043	4,587	18.5	26.4	20.2	13.2	17.2	4.4	536,282	11.7	2,969,987	16.1	912,158	23.2
Georgia	57,018	2,396	19.7	24.2	19.5	13.2	18.9	4.6	327,262	13.7	1,686,034	17.8	603,820	24.6
Hawaii	77,385	310	11.3	18.6	18.3	16.8	28.8	6.2	24,371	7.9	147,400	11.1	45,310	15.2
Idaho	53,805	403	17.0	28.7	22.8	14.4	14.7	2.4	44,324	11.0	235,881	15.3	79,573	18.9
Illinois	67,892	3,135	14.9	21.0	19.2	15.0	23.6	6.3	320,533	10.2	1,749,315	14.0	611,177	19.9
Indiana	57,996	1,654	16.6	25.6	22.1	15.0	17.6	3.1	182,007	11.0	955,418	15.2	339,432	21.6
Iowa	63,433	795	13.1	23.9	23.4	16.9	19.4	3.3	63,029	7.9	364,270	12.4	118,448	16.6
Kansas	63,317	727	14.2	23.9	21.7	15.8	20.2	4.2	66,898	9.2	375,695	13.6	130,590	18.4
Kentucky	52,123	1,132	21.7	26.2	20.3	13.4	15.6	2.9	162,424	14.3	790,525	18.8	264,693	26.4
Louisiana	54,730	1,129	21.6	24.3	18.4	13.8	18.2	3.7	163,007	14.4	824,906	18.7	293,711	26.7
Maine	59,547	353	16.0	25.3	22.1	15.7	17.7	3.2	30,982	8.8	168,372	13.0	47,561	17.8
Maryland	86,056	1,425	10.1	16.2	16.8	14.7	31.6	10.6	94,367	6.6	546,487	9.7	167,939	12.6
Massachusetts	82,009	1,597	12.3	16.9	16.5	14.5	30.0	9.8	125,699	7.9	709,307	11.2	201,281	14.4
Michigan	58,632	2,511	17.6	24.3	20.8	14.5	19.1	3.7	299,669	11.9	1,613,406	16.7	538,355	23.5
Minnesota	71,826	1,364	11.9	19.9	20.8	17.1	24.8	5.5	102,022	7.5	601,199	11.6	189,404	15.0
Mississippi	47,003	750	25.8	26.8	19.4	12.5	13.1	2.4	131,243	17.5	638,370	22.2	236,185	31.8
Missouri	57,917	1,545	17.3	25.1	21.4	14.6	18.1	3.6	168,351	10.9	881,478	15.2	295,957	21.3
Montana	56,895	257	17.3	26.1	22.3	15.8	16.0	2.7	25,326	9.9	144,321	14.9	44,289	20.3
Nebraska	63,618	469	13.7	23.0	22.9	16.6	19.9	3.8	39,798	8.5	224,416	12.7	77,253	17.3
Nevada	60,964	643	15.5	24.8	20.9	14.8	20.2	3.9	68,717	10.7	385,122	14.5	135,552	20.7
New Hampshire	77,178	347	9.6	19.3	19.5	17.1	28.4	6.2	18,964	5.5	107,800	8.4	30,420	10.8
New Jersey	85,005	2,197	11.2	16.4	16.1	14.3	30.7	11.2	164,331	7.5	858,982	10.0	288,304	14.2
New Mexico	53,054	501	22.4	25.0	19.0	13.0	17.3	3.4	76,785	15.3	407,406	20.2	147,228	28.8
New York	68,161	4,644	16.6	20.1	17.6	13.5	24.0	8.1	536,145	11.5	2,845,024	15.1	902,006	21.2
North Carolina	55,338	2,459	19.4	25.7	20.2	13.5	17.3	3.9	312,058	12.7	1,596,887	17.2	547,235	24.3
North Dakota	67,126	173	12.5	21.5	22.9	18.3	20.8	4.0	12,622	7.3	80,691	12.4	21,901	14.9
Ohio	59,193	2,958	17.3	24.3	21.2	14.8	18.8	3.6	341,521	11.5	1,777,415	15.8	619,154	23.1
Oklahoma	54,263	960	19.1	26.5	21.4	13.9	15.9	3.1	119,763	12.5	612,305	16.8	216,354	23.7
Oregon	59,494	966	17.0	24.5	21.2	14.8	18.6	3.9	105,482	10.9	594,816	15.8	180,643	21.3
Pennsylvania	64,331	3,225	14.4	22.9	20.9	15.1	21.4	5.2	295,170	9.2	1,621,222	13.2	509,461	18.6
Rhode Island	70,360	255	14.6	20.3	18.4	15.5	25.3	5.9	24,337	9.5	136,371	13.5	42,550	19.4
South Carolina	53,345	1,191	21.0	25.6	20.2	13.5	16.7	3.1	163,696	13.7	816,485	18.2	281,259	26.5
South Dakota	61,794	208	14.7	23.2	24.7	17.0	17.2	3.2	18,742	9.0	110,442	14.0	35,749	18.1
Tennessee	52,889	1,649	20.7	26.1	20.7	13.4	15.4	3.6	220,034	13.3	1,097,580	17.7	373,424	25.4
Texas	58,929	6,131	19.0	23.7	18.7	13.3	20.1	5.3	843,338	13.8	4,379,172	17.8	1,732,276	25.5
Utah	64,095	663	13.0	23.1	23.5	16.1	20.4	3.9	61,981	9.4	345,730	12.7	125,019	14.6
Vermont	65,959	163	13.2	22.4	22.0	16.9	21.4	4.1	12,366	7.6	70,871	11.8	18,484	14.7
Virginia	74,766	2,018	12.3	19.4	18.3	14.6	26.2	9.0	156,845	7.8	861,951	11.1	268,246	14.7
Washington	69,979	1,688	13.3	20.4	20.1	15.6	24.9	5.7	150,307	8.9	876,844	13.3	274,559	17.7
West Virginia	50,295	485	21.6	28.2	20.9	13.2	13.8	2.4	64,191	13.2	322,674	17.9	93,030	24.7
Wisconsin	64,492	1,473	14.0	22.8	22.2	16.9	20.4	3.7	129,161	8.8	716,249	12.9	237,861	18.2
Wyoming	68,694	147	11.6	21.1	22.7	17.6	23.4	3.6	10,329	7.0	59,686	10.8	19,961	14.9

Table A-35. Housing—Units and Characteristics, 2009–2011

Geographic area	Total housing units (thousands)	Characteristics												
		Total units						Occupied units						
		Units in structure (percent)			Year built (percent)			Total units (thousands)	Vehicles available (percent)				House heating fuel (percent)	
		1-unit detached	1-unit attached	Mobile home	2005 or later	1990 to 2004	Before 1950		None	1	2	3 or more	Utility gas	Electricity
United States	131,827	61.5	5.8	6.5	6.0	22.6	19.3	114,932	9.1	33.8	37.6	19.6	49.4	35.5
Alabama	2,174	68.3	1.7	14.0	7.3	27.7	10.9	1,837	6.4	32.6	37.5	23.5	30.6	59.6
Alaska	308	62.8	7.9	5.4	6.2	22.5	3.5	255	9.8	31.4	38.1	20.7	48.5	10.6
Arizona	2,849	62.8	5.2	10.7	9.8	36.1	3.5	2,343	6.9	38.1	38.2	16.8	35.2	58.3
Arkansas	1,318	69.5	1.7	13.1	7.4	27.4	10.0	1,126	6.4	33.9	39.3	20.4	41.3	45.4
California	13,688	57.9	7.1	3.8	4.8	17.5	16.0	12,433	7.8	32.3	37.3	22.6	66.6	24.9
Colorado	2,215	62.7	7.0	4.3	6.6	29.2	11.5	1,959	5.8	31.9	39.8	22.5	73.8	17.9
Connecticut	1,489	59.2	5.2	0.9	2.9	11.4	30.0	1,359	8.9	32.9	38.1	20.2	31.8	15.1
Delaware	407	58.5	14.7	9.2	8.0	27.8	14.5	332	6.8	33.3	40.3	19.6	40.1	30.2
District of Columbia	297	12.0	25.6	0.1	4.4	6.7	50.8	260	36.5	44.5	15.3	3.6	62.2	32.6
Florida	8,997	54.0	6.3	9.3	7.1	30.8	4.6	7,082	6.9	41.4	38.0	13.7	4.5	92.3
Georgia	4,092	66.4	3.7	9.4	9.2	34.4	7.7	3,494	6.7	33.8	39.0	20.5	41.7	50.9
Hawaii	520	54.1	7.2	0.1	5.9	21.4	7.6	447	9.0	34.0	36.3	20.7	2.0	31.5
Idaho	669	72.1	3.0	9.3	9.7	31.5	13.7	577	4.3	27.5	39.6	28.5	51.2	32.4
Illinois	5,296	58.3	5.9	2.7	4.7	17.4	29.9	4,758	10.7	34.9	37.2	17.2	80.2	14.1
Indiana	2,797	72.8	3.4	5.1	4.9	22.7	25.0	2,469	6.6	32.9	39.3	21.2	62.1	26.4
Iowa	1,337	73.9	3.6	4.1	5.2	17.4	33.7	1,222	5.9	30.0	39.5	24.6	64.8	17.8
Kansas	1,234	72.5	4.6	5.0	4.9	19.5	24.3	1,105	5.2	30.6	39.3	24.9	68.8	20.7
Kentucky	1,928	67.0	2.3	12.4	5.8	26.3	16.2	1,683	7.8	33.2	38.3	20.8	39.4	49.0
Louisiana	1,968	65.2	3.1	13.3	7.8	21.1	12.8	1,694	8.6	36.7	38.2	16.5	36.9	59.3
Maine	723	69.6	2.3	8.9	4.1	19.3	31.9	554	7.2	33.6	40.5	18.7	4.6	4.8
Maryland	2,381	51.4	21.1	1.8	4.8	21.5	18.4	2,131	9.6	32.7	36.7	21.0	44.5	39.2
Massachusetts	2,811	52.0	5.1	0.8	3.1	11.3	41.3	2,528	12.6	36.1	36.8	14.5	48.7	13.6
Michigan	4,531	71.8	4.5	5.5	3.1	19.7	23.9	3,804	7.7	35.1	38.8	18.4	77.6	7.5
Minnesota	2,348	67.3	7.4	3.7	5.2	22.8	22.8	2,098	7.1	30.3	40.9	21.7	67.4	15.0
Mississippi	1,276	69.6	1.3	15.3	8.1	27.7	8.9	1,085	7.0	34.0	37.1	21.9	31.6	52.8
Missouri	2,715	70.1	3.5	6.7	5.9	22.6	20.4	2,355	7.3	33.4	38.7	20.7	52.8	32.3
Montana	484	69.3	3.0	11.1	6.4	22.8	21.6	405	4.9	28.2	37.7	29.2	56.0	20.0
Nebraska	798	72.7	3.9	3.7	5.2	18.4	28.2	721	5.7	30.0	39.7	24.6	64.0	25.0
Nevada	1,176	58.9	4.8	6.2	11.7	46.1	2.5	989	7.6	36.5	38.1	17.8	63.3	30.5
New Hampshire	615	63.4	5.1	5.9	4.1	18.1	25.8	517	5.0	30.8	42.1	22.1	19.6	7.8
New Jersey	3,556	53.6	9.3	1.0	3.7	14.8	27.2	3,177	11.8	35.0	36.3	17.0	73.8	10.9
New Mexico	903	64.3	3.7	16.7	6.5	27.2	10.1	764	5.6	33.6	37.9	22.8	67.5	14.9
New York	8,111	41.9	4.8	2.4	2.8	9.8	42.2	7,219	29.0	32.6	26.8	11.6	55.1	9.3
North Carolina	4,335	65.2	3.7	13.9	8.7	32.6	9.9	3,686	6.6	32.6	38.7	22.1	25.0	58.1
North Dakota	318	61.3	5.5	7.8	6.3	17.1	22.0	281	5.4	29.4	37.6	27.6	41.3	37.2
Ohio	5,129	68.3	4.7	3.9	3.5	18.1	28.1	4,546	8.3	33.8	38.1	19.7	67.8	20.9
Oklahoma	1,666	73.2	2.1	9.5	6.5	18.9	14.8	1,440	5.6	33.3	39.2	21.9	55.6	33.4
Oregon	1,677	63.7	4.3	8.3	6.4	26.4	17.9	1,514	7.8	32.6	38.3	21.3	38.2	48.8
Pennsylvania	5,570	57.0	18.2	4.2	3.3	14.1	36.1	4,955	11.7	34.0	36.6	17.7	51.2	20.1
Rhode Island	464	54.8	3.4	1.0	2.4	10.5	41.4	410	9.5	36.8	36.7	17.0	50.2	8.4
South Carolina	2,142	62.0	2.6	17.4	9.0	32.4	8.5	1,767	7.1	33.7	38.4	20.8	23.9	67.9
South Dakota	364	68.7	3.7	8.7	6.8	22.2	25.4	319	5.7	27.9	37.2	29.2	49.3	26.4
Tennessee	2,816	68.4	3.2	10.1	7.3	28.5	11.6	2,461	6.3	33.0	38.4	22.3	33.9	58.4
Texas	10,002	65.3	2.6	7.6	10.0	27.3	8.3	8,768	6.0	34.6	40.5	18.9	37.9	57.2
Utah	982	68.4	6.0	3.8	10.0	31.0	12.1	881	4.5	26.1	41.9	27.5	85.7	9.9
Vermont	323	66.1	3.4	7.1	3.4	17.6	31.6	258	6.6	32.9	40.5	20.0	15.4	4.5
Virginia	3,369	62.4	10.4	5.6	6.5	25.1	13.2	2,996	6.2	30.5	38.5	24.8	34.1	51.0
Washington	2,890	63.4	3.6	7.0	7.4	26.6	16.4	2,617	6.7	31.0	38.0	24.3	35.5	53.0
West Virginia	882	71.0	1.9	15.1	4.3	19.1	25.2	740	8.6	35.4	37.4	18.6	42.5	41.2
Wisconsin	2,625	66.3	4.3	3.8	4.6	22.1	27.5	2,285	7.0	32.2	40.4	20.4	65.5	14.0
Wyoming	263	66.6	3.8	13.7	7.4	19.2	17.1	223	3.6	25.4	38.3	32.7	60.6	20.8

Table A-36.   Owner- and Renter-Occupied Units—Value and Gross Rent, 2009–2011

Geographic Area	Owner-occupied units									Renter-occupied units					
	Total units (thousands)	Median value	Value—percent distribution				Housing units with a mortgage			Total units (thousands)	Median gross rent (dollars)	Gross rent—percent distribution			Gross rent 30 percent or more of household income (percent of rental units paying rent)
			Less than $100,000	$100,000–$199,999	$200,000–$299,999	$300,000 and over	Total (thousands)	Median selected monthly owner costs (dollars)	Monthly owner costs 30 percent or more of household income			Less than $500	$500–$999	$1,000 or more	
United States............	75,124	179,500	23.9	31.2	18.5	26.4	50,469	1,539	37.5	37,622	878	13.7	47.5	38.8	52.7
Alabama......................	1,288	122,200	40.8	34.4	13.9	10.9	778	1,157	31.1	487	687	23.8	59.0	17.2	53.2
Alaska........................	163	237,300	12.2	24.3	33.0	30.4	110	1,827	32.2	82	1,041	8.2	38.6	53.2	44.2
Arizona......................	1,528	169,500	23.2	36.2	19.7	20.8	1,065	1,469	40.5	773	870	9.9	53.1	37.0	52.4
Arkansas....................	755	105,800	47.4	34.2	10.9	7.3	441	1,004	27.4	332	644	25.7	62.8	11.5	49.8
California...................	6,929	370,400	8.0	14.1	16.6	61.3	5,204	2,305	50.9	5,327	1,191	6.5	28.8	64.8	56.8
Colorado....................	1,288	235,800	10.2	28.1	28.2	33.5	971	1,629	36.1	646	893	9.8	50.9	39.4	52.0
Connecticut................	928	285,800	4.1	20.3	29.6	46.0	663	2,122	40.8	414	1,029	11.9	35.5	52.6	54.0
Delaware...................	242	243,100	9.9	24.9	32.3	32.9	170	1,613	36.2	87	978	10.0	42.6	47.3	54.0
District of Columbia......	110	431,300	2.7	6.2	17.0	74.1	85	2,303	36.9	146	1,191	12.1	26.8	61.0	50.0
Florida.......................	4,813	165,600	25.8	35.0	19.3	19.8	3,073	1,556	48.3	2,150	972	7.5	45.7	46.8	60.5
Georgia......................	2,309	155,800	26.7	39.1	17.4	16.8	1,632	1,419	37.1	1,109	838	13.4	55.2	31.4	54.0
Hawaii.......................	258	510,600	2.9	5.5	11.4	80.1	177	2,306	49.4	176	1,316	7.4	22.7	70.0	56.8
Idaho.........................	403	165,600	19.7	44.0	20.7	15.7	277	1,236	36.8	160	707	19.4	61.3	19.4	50.2
Illinois......................	3,232	191,100	21.1	31.4	22.3	25.2	2,227	1,705	39.0	1,460	866	13.4	51.6	35.0	52.3
Indiana......................	1,738	123,200	37.0	42.2	12.6	8.1	1,212	1,132	27.1	687	709	18.4	65.7	16.1	50.9
Iowa..........................	886	123,000	37.7	40.5	14.0	7.8	555	1,168	23.8	312	645	26.3	61.2	12.6	45.9
Kansas......................	752	127,500	38.6	37.2	14.7	9.4	482	1,266	26.2	329	708	21.2	59.1	19.7	45.7
Kentucky...................	1,158	120,000	40.4	37.8	13.1	8.8	715	1,108	28.8	472	633	28.1	59.4	12.5	49.2
Louisiana	1,141	137,900	36.0	36.8	16.2	11.1	637	1,192	29.7	494	754	19.0	57.5	23.4	53.4
Maine........................	400	175,600	21.6	36.8	23.3	18.4	262	1,329	35.0	142	745	21.5	56.0	22.5	51.9
Maryland....................	1,444	301,400	6.5	16.6	26.7	50.3	1,105	2,062	38.0	661	1,159	8.8	27.5	63.8	52.6
Massachusetts............	1,585	332,800	3.4	12.9	25.6	58.0	1,144	2,110	39.4	910	1,036	16.4	31.1	52.5	50.7
Michigan....................	2,763	124,600	37.8	38.7	14.1	9.4	1,824	1,334	35.6	984	746	16.9	60.3	22.8	55.7
Minnesota..................	1,532	193,000	15.7	37.0	26.2	21.1	1,081	1,543	33.1	538	790	18.4	53.1	28.6	50.2
Mississippi.................	760	99,700	50.2	31.7	11.3	6.9	419	1,068	34.1	280	689	25.0	59.3	15.7	54.9
Missouri....................	1,621	138,300	32.7	40.1	16.0	11.3	1,070	1,216	29.4	684	704	21.0	60.9	17.9	49.1
Montana.....................	279	181,500	23.5	32.5	23.1	20.9	163	1,262	35.8	113	657	26.1	58.1	15.8	45.6
Nebraska...................	487	126,600	35.0	43.7	13.7	7.5	312	1,265	25.1	219	680	22.9	61.3	15.7	43.4
Nevada......................	570	178,200	19.6	36.7	22.8	20.9	430	1,681	45.2	405	981	5.5	46.6	47.9	52.6
New Hampshire............	373	243,000	9.3	24.3	35.6	30.9	261	1,924	40.2	138	958	11.9	43.5	44.6	50.1
New Jersey	2,096	337,800	4.6	13.2	23.3	58.8	1,484	2,451	46.9	1,045	1,145	8.7	27.4	63.9	53.8
New Mexico	526	160,800	28.7	34.2	19.6	17.4	316	1,230	35.1	218	722	20.6	57.2	22.2	49.6
New York....................	3,917	294,400	17.4	20.2	13.0	49.3	2,539	2,009	41.2	3,189	1,047	13.0	33.7	53.3	53.3
North Carolina.............	2,474	154,300	27.8	38.1	17.4	16.7	1,667	1,278	33.7	1,118	751	16.2	61.6	22.1	52.1
North Dakota...............	187	122,800	39.8	39.7	14.0	6.6	103	1,168	20.5	86	605	32.0	57.4	10.6	40.9
Ohio..........................	3,086	133,200	32.7	43.4	14.9	9.1	2,094	1,284	31.3	1,380	699	20.5	62.6	17.0	51.2
Oklahoma...................	972	110,600	44.8	36.9	11.2	7.1	579	1,112	27.6	424	673	22.3	62.4	15.3	47.6
Oregon.......................	941	244,600	11.0	24.5	29.7	34.8	653	1,613	42.0	548	843	10.3	58.0	31.7	53.8
Pennsylvania..............	3,475	165,200	27.1	33.8	20.2	19.0	2,189	1,430	32.9	1,388	783	18.0	54.3	27.6	50.3
Rhode Island...............	251	256,200	4.3	23.2	36.8	35.9	181	1,899	42.6	153	902	17.5	43.8	38.7	51.1
South Carolina	1,226	137,200	34.9	35.3	15.0	14.9	771	1,196	33.7	485	743	17.2	61.2	21.5	53.1
South Dakota..............	219	130,000	36.2	40.0	13.9	9.9	130	1,193	25.4	91	602	35.2	52.8	12.0	40.8
Tennessee	1,680	138,600	32.5	39.2	15.3	12.9	1,058	1,193	33.1	713	717	19.7	61.6	18.7	52.2
Texas........................	5,579	127,500	36.8	38.0	13.6	11.7	3,486	1,432	31.8	3,003	823	11.5	57.9	30.6	49.9
Utah..........................	617	216,600	7.9	36.0	30.9	25.3	456	1,466	35.0	251	823	12.0	56.7	31.3	49.5
Vermont	183	215,700	11.9	32.8	29.7	25.6	123	1,519	37.9	70	847	15.1	52.0	32.9	52.5
Virginia.....................	2,032	247,900	12.9	24.8	23.4	38.9	1,467	1,769	34.9	909	1,055	10.4	35.8	53.9	50.0
Washington.................	1,658	272,000	8.5	21.5	27.2	42.7	1,197	1,795	40.5	921	938	10.0	46.2	43.8	50.6
West Virginia..............	546	96,700	51.7	31.1	11.0	6.2	271	949	25.4	163	591	33.9	56.7	9.4	48.8
Wisconsin	1,565	169,000	18.5	43.5	23.0	14.8	1,061	1,443	34.1	689	738	16.4	64.4	19.4	49.0
Wyoming	158	182,300	19.9	37.1	24.7	18.2	96	1,322	27.3	58	740	19.8	56.6	23.6	38.3

Table A-37. Home Ownership and Vacancy Rates

Geographic area	Homeownership rate[1]					Homeowner vacancy rates[2]					Rental vacancy rates[2]				
	2012	2011	2010	2005	2000	2012	2011	2010	2005	2000	2012	2011	2010	2005	2000
United States...............	65.4	66.1	66.9	68.9	67.4	2.0	2.5	2.6	1.9	1.6	8.7	9.5	10.2	9.8	8.0
Alabama........................	71.9	72.9	73.2	76.6	73.2	2.1	2.8	2.9	2.0	2.3	11.1	14.2	12.1	13.2	14.4
Alaska	63.7	64.4	65.7	66.0	66.4	1.4	1.3	1.9	1.5	1.5	4.7	5.8	5.6	7.9	6.9
Arizona........................	65.3	66.0	66.6	71.1	68.0	2.4	3.2	3.2	1.2	1.6	11.4	12.4	14.9	11.6	10.7
Arkansas......................	66.0	67.6	67.9	69.2	68.9	3.3	3.0	3.1	2.3	2.4	10.6	12.6	11.4	13.7	11.4
California.....................	54.5	55.3	56.1	59.7	57.1	1.6	2.1	2.5	1.2	1.2	5.2	6.1	7.5	6.0	4.5
Colorado	65.3	65.9	68.5	71.0	68.3	1.7	2.4	2.7	2.7	1.6	5.8	7.4	7.9	13.5	5.4
Connecticut..................	68.8	70.6	70.8	70.5	70.0	1.7	2.2	1.7	1.3	0.7	7.4	9.5	10.7	8.3	8.6
Delaware	73.4	74.2	74.7	75.8	72.0	2.1	2.7	2.4	1.7	1.6	9.3	11.2	9.9	11.3	10.6
District of Columbia	45.0	44.8	45.6	45.8	41.9	1.9	1.4	2.3	2.0	1.9	7.8	8.4	9.0	7.7	11.7
Florida........................	67.0	69.0	69.3	72.4	68.4	2.2	3.3	4.5	2.0	2.6	13.1	14.9	15.1	10.1	10.8
Georgia	64.3	66.2	67.1	67.9	69.8	2.7	3.6	2.9	2.7	1.9	9.9	10.0	12.3	14.6	9.7
Hawaii	57.2	55.4	56.1	59.8	55.2	2.3	2.2	1.9	0.6	0.9	10.2	9.4	8.1	5.1	5.3
Idaho..........................	73.0	72.4	72.4	74.2	70.5	2.2	3.8	3.3	1.4	1.8	7.1	8.9	8.8	7.0	6.7
Illinois	66.8	68.4	68.8	70.9	67.9	2.8	3.4	2.9	1.9	1.1	9.5	10.2	11.0	13.4	7.8
Indiana........................	72.1	72.1	71.2	75.0	74.9	2.1	2.6	3.0	2.4	1.1	12.5	13.0	11.8	14.2	10.6
Iowa...........................	70.2	71.2	71.1	73.9	75.2	2.3	2.4	2.0	2.4	1.6	6.3	7.2	8.1	13.1	6.9
Kansas	63.2	65.4	67.4	69.5	69.3	2.0	2.1	2.4	2.7	1.7	8.0	8.7	11.3	12.8	9.2
Kentucky	68.7	69.1	70.3	71.6	73.4	2.0	2.2	2.2	2.2	1.5	7.2	10.5	10.4	11.2	9.5
Louisiana	68.7	70.1	70.4	72.5	68.1	1.9	1.7	1.5	1.3	1.7	12.6	11.7	12.5	8.8	11.2
Maine	74.1	73.9	73.8	73.9	76.5	1.9	2.2	2.2	1.4	1.3	5.3	6.1	6.2	6.8	6.0
Maryland.....................	68.5	69.7	68.9	71.2	69.9	1.9	2.7	2.8	1.3	1.5	9.3	10.1	10.5	8.8	4.6
Massachusetts.............	65.8	65.3	65.3	63.4	59.9	1.6	1.6	1.2	1.1	0.6	6.5	5.8	6.6	5.7	3.5
Michigan	74.8	74.1	74.5	76.4	77.2	1.6	2.4	2.7	2.7	1.3	11.9	13.2	13.1	13.1	9.6
Minnesota	72.0	71.3	72.6	76.5	76.1	1.7	2.0	2.0	1.5	0.9	5.9	7.3	8.3	10.5	5.2
Mississippi..................	74.2	74.8	74.8	78.8	75.2	1.7	1.7	2.3	1.8	2.0	11.0	14.5	15.6	13.2	11.6
Missouri	70.8	71.1	71.2	72.3	74.2	2.4	2.2	2.5	2.6	1.8	10.4	10.8	11.6	13.8	15.0
Montana......................	67.8	68.4	68.1	70.4	70.2	1.6	1.6	1.6	1.2	1.9	5.9	4.9	5.7	10.3	7.5
Nebraska.....................	69.3	68.9	70.4	70.2	70.2	1.3	2.1	2.5	1.8	2.0	7.5	8.1	7.2	10.3	7.4
Nevada	55.7	56.2	59.7	63.4	64.0	3.4	3.6	4.5	3.0	2.3	11.9	11.0	13.4	8.4	11.6
New Hampshire.............	74.8	74.1	74.9	74.0	69.2	2.0	1.9	1.7	1.0	0.7	7.2	7.5	7.2	5.1	3.2
New Jersey	66.6	66.4	66.5	70.1	66.2	2.1	2.1	1.6	1.2	1.0	11.2	8.8	9.1	6.2	4.3
New Mexico	66.8	69.1	68.6	71.4	73.7	2.1	1.4	1.8	1.5	2.4	7.0	7.4	6.3	7.7	13.2
New York.....................	53.6	53.6	54.5	55.9	53.4	2.0	2.7	2.1	2.0	1.5	5.5	6.5	6.8	5.1	5.5
North Carolina..............	67.2	68.3	69.5	70.9	71.1	2.4	2.5	3.4	2.4	1.9	11.2	11.3	12.0	13.8	11.2
North Dakota................	66.2	68.3	67.1	68.5	70.7	1.4	1.5	1.5	1.3	1.8	6.9	9.8	7.4	8.5	11.7
Ohio	67.9	68.9	69.7	73.3	71.3	1.7	2.8	3.3	2.6	1.3	9.3	10.5	11.5	13.4	9.0
Oklahoma	68.8	69.4	69.2	72.9	72.7	2.3	2.6	2.0	2.5	2.2	9.5	10.1	10.9	12.6	15.2
Oregon........................	66.1	66.4	66.3	68.2	65.3	2.2	2.1	3.3	1.6	2.4	4.9	4.0	5.5	8.3	6.8
Pennsylvania................	71.0	71.1	72.2	73.3	74.7	1.7	2.0	1.6	1.6	1.4	9.1	8.6	8.8	10.0	8.3
Rhode Island................	62.1	63.4	62.8	63.1	61.5	1.8	2.3	1.8	1.6	1.1	6.8	7.9	7.1	7.7	5.3
South Carolina	71.5	74.2	74.8	73.9	76.5	2.1	3.3	3.2	2.1	1.4	9.7	11.6	13.9	10.0	15.5
South Dakota	69.2	69.3	70.6	68.4	71.2	1.0	1.8	1.5	1.9	1.6	8.9	9.2	9.5	8.8	7.7
Tennessee	67.9	69.3	71.0	72.4	70.9	2.6	2.8	2.6	1.7	1.9	11.6	12.0	12.5	10.3	7.1
Texas..........................	64.3	64.3	65.3	65.9	63.8	2.0	1.8	2.0	2.6	1.6	10.4	12.3	13.3	13.6	10.8
Utah...........................	71.1	71.4	72.5	73.9	72.7	1.5	1.9	2.0	1.6	1.8	7.7	6.4	7.2	7.0	7.6
Vermont	73.4	74.6	73.6	74.2	68.7	1.6	1.7	1.9	0.5	0.9	4.2	4.2	6.1	4.4	3.8
Virginia.......................	67.8	67.9	68.7	71.2	73.9	1.9	2.2	2.3	1.3	2.2	9.5	9.9	10.5	7.8	7.7
Washington..................	63.5	64.2	64.4	67.6	63.6	2.0	2.3	2.7	1.0	1.9	5.9	6.0	7.0	6.8	4.9
West Virginia................	75.8	78.7	79.0	81.3	75.9	2.0	2.4	2.1	1.7	2.4	8.1	7.9	8.2	11.9	10.0
Wisconsin	67.5	68.5	71.0	71.1	71.8	1.5	2.1	1.6	1.6	1.2	6.3	6.6	8.6	9.0	4.7
Wyoming	70.3	71.1	73.4	72.8	71.0	1.4	1.3	2.0	1.1	2.3	5.4	6.5	8.3	6.0	8.1

[1]Proportion of owner households to occupied households.
[2]Proportion of the homeowner inventory that is vacant for sale.
[3]Proportion of the rental inventory that is vacant for rent.

Table A-38. Cost of Living Indicators—Housing, Public University, Energy Expenditures, and Sales Taxes

Geographic area	Housing price indexes for single-family homes[1]				Average costs per full-time-equivalent student in public colleges and universities (dollars)					
					Public 4-year institutions[2]			Public 2-year institutions[3]		
	2012	2010	2005	2000	2010–2011	2005–2006	2000–2001	2010–2011	2005–2006	2000–2001
United States............................	190.3	184.9	217.0	144.1	15,918	12,108	8,655	2,439	1,935	1,359
Alabama................................	181.7	176.5	182.7	142.6	14,416	9,625	7,338	3,422	2,764	1,671
Alaska..................................	227.4	219.8	207.5	136.6	14,053	10,620	8,386	3,894	2,353	2,088
Arizona.................................	202.5	171.1	303.5	155.7	17,083	11,480	7,872	1,671	1,344	924
Arkansas...............................	184.0	175.0	185.8	141.5	12,580	9,192	6,789	2,311	1,780	1,159
California..............................	170.5	159.0	283.0	123.6	18,933	13,685	9,592	723	718	316
Colorado...............................	286.7	266.3	271.7	217.3	16,208	11,569	8,360	2,727	1,991	1,655
Connecticut............................	165.4	170.0	195.6	118.1	19,400	14,658	10,512	3,401	2,536	1,867
Delaware...............................	178.2	188.3	208.8	121.5	19,541	14,326	10,290	2,942	2,240	1,680
District of Columbia	386.6	328.0	327.1	136.0	(X)	(X)	(X)	(X)	(X)	(X)
Florida.................................	187.1	175.5	298.7	139.7	12,774	10,141	7,944	2,497	1,844	1,438
Georgia................................	160.1	152.9	191.2	151.5	14,019	10,062	7,455	2,480	1,645	1,374
Hawaii..................................	194.8	178.2	204.7	92.8	15,133	9,042	8,286	2,172	1,226	1,067
Idaho...................................	208.4	189.3	229.7	154.7	11,773	8,982	6,763	2,557	1,891	1,316
Illinois................................	169.1	178.2	204.1	145.8	20,054	13,976	9,533	2,947	2,104	1,534
Indiana................................	161.1	157.7	165.6	142.4	16,912	12,388	9,232	3,256	2,589	2,125
Iowa....................................	200.7	196.1	191.5	157.8	14,855	12,329	7,589	3,769	3,032	2,149
Kansas.................................	193.3	189.7	187.9	154.0	13,229	9,980	6,650	2,463	1,938	1,379
Kentucky...............................	189.3	189.4	184.4	150.6	15,002	10,663	6,921	3,148	2,404	1,376
Louisiana	234.3	226.7	212.8	156.9	11,856	8,506	6,304	2,132	1,469	929
Maine	202.8	204.6	221.2	133.5	17,767	12,568	9,361	3,334	3,039	2,599
Maryland...............................	211.8	209.8	254.9	122.3	16,963	14,793	10,846	3,237	2,833	2,271
Massachusetts.........................	217.7	218.3	254.5	157.6	19,164	14,651	9,206	3,759	2,925	1,891
Michigan...............................	153.5	144.5	202.1	174.0	18,333	13,693	9,841	2,486	2,076	1,739
Minnesota..............................	210.5	208.4	254.2	172.8	16,385	12,777	8,146	4,965	4,085	2,512
Mississippi............................	176.1	172.0	177.6	142.4	12,051	9,461	7,181	2,141	1,660	1,134
Missouri...............................	186.3	180.8	197.9	150.4	15,110	11,861	8,201	2,440	2,247	1,482
Montana................................	309.5	284.1	277.4	179.9	12,891	10,613	7,607	3,173	2,721	2,007
Nebraska...............................	202.4	188.3	195.0	162.7	14,081	11,286	7,335	2,391	1,899	1,425
Nevada.................................	131.1	125.9	270.9	128.5	14,172	10,865	8,252	2,243	1,635	1,371
New Hampshire..........................	190.2	195.8	238.6	146.9	21,481	15,479	11,717	6,687	5,720	3,935
New Jersey.............................	207.8	221.9	254.5	133.7	22,592	17,708	11,998	3,553	2,712	2,295
New Mexico	203.6	211.8	215.4	145.7	12,520	9,579	7,085	1,462	1,179	866
New York...............................	204.3	208.9	214.7	128.9	16,606	13,275	10,254	3,848	3,181	2,557
North Carolina.........................	178.4	185.1	183.0	146.5	12,874	9,675	7,080	1,832	1,295	891
North Dakota...........................	260.9	224.2	190.8	138.0	12,503	9,829	6,405	3,929	3,084	1,903
Ohio....................................	154.8	153.6	175.3	148.5	17,964	16,032	10,449	3,227	3,127	2,294
Oklahoma...............................	198.7	192.3	177.8	144.1	11,938	9,404	6,000	2,578	2,111	1,250
Oregon.................................	264.7	255.6	298.1	184.4	16,402	12,720	9,397	3,314	2,635	1,637
Pennsylvania...........................	188.0	189.4	190.2	121.4	19,916	15,464	11,087	3,577	2,976	2,285
Rhode Island...........................	179.7	187.9	237.6	120.5	19,815	14,315	11,104	3,652	2,470	1,806
South Carolina	175.4	181.3	185.4	144.9	17,641	13,145	9,065	3,643	2,932	1,466
South Dakota...........................	232.5	219.3	210.3	160.9	12,603	9,493	6,979	4,700	3,154	2,861
Tennessee..............................	187.8	181.7	186.0	147.4	13,759	9,956	7,661	3,128	2,395	1,441
Texas...................................	202.6	187.4	172.5	143.2	14,585	10,973	7,634	1,585	1,273	931
Utah....................................	265.7	249.7	256.8	194.4	10,768	8,745	6,623	2,860	2,224	1,563
Vermont	208.7	205.3	208.3	127.1	21,530	16,571	12,836	5,020	4,012	3,004
Virginia...............................	216.3	209.3	234.6	131.3	18,110	12,279	8,744	3,384	2,049	1,132
Washington.............................	225.0	223.7	243.5	154.9	16,253	12,384	8,917	3,266	2,554	1,745
West Virginia..........................	198.2	188.1	180.4	138.0	12,799	9,992	7,287	2,871	2,509	1,667
Wisconsin	199.9	208.3	223.8	166.9	13,819	10,560	7,385	3,695	2,965	2,262
Wyoming................................	302.3	282.1	258.7	169.3	11,467	8,946	7,017	2,164	1,772	1,442

[1]The housing price indexes reflect fluctuation from a base of 100. 100 represents the average price of a sample of local single-family homes in 1991. The indexes represent the change in value as of the end of the year shown.
[2]Costs include in-state tuition, required fees, and room and board.
[3]Costs include in-state tuition and required fees only and do not include room or board.
(X) = Not applicable

Table A-38. Cost of Living Indicators—Housing, Public University, Energy Expenditures, and Sales Taxes—*Continued*

Geographic area	Energy expenditures, per capita[4] (dollars)				State tax rates							
					General sales tax[5] (cents per dollar)				Gasoline (cents per gallon)			
	2010	2007	2005	2000	2013	2008	2005	2000	2013	2008	2005	2000
United States	3,895	4,093	3,537	2,443	(X)	(X)	(X)	(X)	(X)	(X)	(X)	(X)
Alabama	4,494	4,670	4,025	2,718	4.00	4.00	4.00	4.00	18.0	18.0	18.0	18.0
Alaska	8,807	9,191	7,806	4,520	(X)	(X)	(X)	(X)	8.0	8.0	8.0	8.0
Arizona	3,021	3,179	2,789	2,065	6.60	5.60	5.60	5.00	19.0	18.0	18.0	18.0
Arkansas	4,128	4,428	3,874	2,729	6.00	6.00	6.00	4.63	21.8	21.5	21.7	19.5
California	3,134	3,349	2,886	2,019	7.50	7.25	7.25	6.00	43.0	18.0	18.0	18.0
Colorado	3,319	3,517	3,152	2,006	2.90	2.90	2.90	3.00	22.0	22.0	22.0	22.0
Connecticut	3,977	4,340	3,577	2,394	6.35	6.00	6.00	6.00	25.0	25.0	25.0	32.0
Delaware	4,019	4,465	3,673	2,543	(X)	(X)	(X)	(X)	23.0	23.0	23.0	23.0
District of Columbia	4,033	4,069	3,496	2,684	6.00	5.75	5.75	5.75	23.5	20.0	20.0	20.0
Florida	3,194	3,338	2,832	1,918	6.00	6.00	6.00	6.00	16.9	15.6	14.5	13.3
Georgia	3,844	3,746	3,591	2,413	4.00	4.00	4.00	4.00	19.5	7.5	8.0	7.5
Hawaii	4,191	4,833	3,951	2,255	4.00	4.00	4.00	4.00	17.0	17.0	16.0	16.0
Idaho	3,622	3,621	3,167	2,399	6.00	6.00	6.00	5.00	26.0	25.0	25.0	25.0
Illinois	3,503	3,766	3,317	2,345	6.25	6.25	6.25	6.25	20.1	19.0	19.0	19.0
Indiana	4,217	4,518	4,052	2,773	7.00	6.00	6.00	5.00	18.0	18.0	18.0	15.0
Iowa	4,841	4,805	4,224	2,803	6.00	5.00	5.00	5.00	22.0	21.0	20.7	20.0
Kansas	4,357	4,610	3,481	2,714	6.30	5.30	5.30	4.90	25.0	24.0	24.0	20.0
Kentucky	4,526	4,796	4,114	2,716	6.00	6.00	6.00	6.00	29.9	22.5	18.5	16.4
Louisiana	8,661	7,688	6,673	4,440	4.00	4.00	4.00	4.00	20.1	20.0	20.0	20.0
Maine	4,746	5,090	4,238	2,979	5.00	5.00	5.00	5.50	30.0	28.4	25.9	19.0
Maryland	3,719	3,825	3,158	2,185	6.00	6.00	5.00	5.00	23.5	23.5	24.0	23.5
Massachusetts	3,739	3,998	3,371	2,305	6.25	5.00	5.00	5.00	21.0	21.0	21.0	21.0
Michigan	3,497	3,670	3,217	2,260	6.00	6.00	6.00	6.00	19.0	19.0	19.0	19.0
Minnesota	3,930	4,189	3,587	2,482	6.88	6.50	6.50	6.50	28.6	22.5	20.0	20.0
Mississippi	4,446	4,585	3,929	2,622	7.00	7.00	7.00	7.00	18.4	18.4	18.0	18.4
Missouri	3,817	3,971	3,433	2,359	4.23	4.23	4.225	4.225	17.3	17.0	17.0	17.0
Montana	4,610	5,504	4,318	2,819	(X)	(X)	(X)	(X)	27.0	27.8	27.8	27.0
Nebraska	4,421	4,451	3,667	2,512	5.50	5.50	5.50	5.00	25.5	26.0	25.3	23.9
Nevada	3,437	4,138	3,534	2,355	6.85	6.50	6.50	6.50	23.8	24.0	24.0	24.0
New Hampshire	3,971	4,065	3,530	2,624	(X)	(X)	(X)	(X)	19.6	19.6	20.0	19.5
New Jersey	4,246	4,577	3,730	2,467	7.00	7.00	6.00	6.00	14.5	10.5	11.0	10.5
New Mexico	3,599	4,010	3,383	2,241	5.13	5.00	5.00	5.00	18.9	18.9	18.9	18.5
New York	3,177	3,276	2,929	2,120	4.00	4.00	4.25	4.00	26.6	24.5	23.3	21.5
North Carolina	3,451	3,603	3,270	2,386	4.75	4.50	4.50	4.00	37.8	30.2	26.6	22.0
North Dakota	6,740	6,442	5,192	3,222	5.00	5.00	5.00	5.00	23.0	23.0	23.0	21.0
Ohio	3,907	4,199	3,656	2,600	5.50	5.50	6.00	5.00	28.0	28.0	28.0	22.0
Oklahoma	4,268	4,719	4,036	2,683	4.50	4.50	4.50	4.50	17.0	17.0	17.0	17.0
Oregon	3,281	3,527	2,957	2,221	(X)	(X)	(X)	(X)	30.0	24.0	24.0	24.0
Pennsylvania	3,829	3,969	3,465	2,367	6.00	6.00	6.00	6.00	31.2	30.0	30.0	25.9
Rhode Island	3,506	3,387	2,919	2,076	7.00	7.00	7.00	7.00	33.0	30.0	30.0	29.0
South Carolina	4,034	4,116	3,751	2,527	6.00	6.00	5.00	5.00	16.8	16.0	16.0	16.0
South Dakota	4,651	4,506	3,717	2,558	4.00	4.00	4.00	4.00	24.0	22.0	22.0	22.0
Tennessee	3,956	4,141	3,667	2,417	7.00	7.00	7.00	6.00	21.4	20.0	20.0	20.0
Texas	5,446	5,899	5,019	3,471	6.25	6.25	6.25	6.25	20.0	20.0	20.0	20.0
Utah	3,002	3,274	2,794	2,013	5.95	4.65	4.75	4.75	24.5	24.5	25.0	24.5
Vermont	4,344	4,329	3,656	2,684	6.00	6.00	6.00	5.00	26.7	21.0	19.0	19.0
Virginia	3,717	3,963	3,488	2,330	5.00	5.00	5.00	3.50	17.5	17.5	18.0	17.5
Washington	3,395	3,601	2,945	2,196	6.50	6.50	6.50	6.50	37.5	37.5	31.0	23.0
West Virginia	4,251	4,624	3,873	2,428	6.00	6.00	6.00	6.00	34.7	32.2	27.0	25.4
Wisconsin	3,774	4,011	3,478	2,419	5.00	5.00	5.00	5.00	32.9	30.9	29.1	25.8
Wyoming	7,904	8,687	7,244	4,381	4.00	4.00	4.00	4.00	14.0	14.0	14.0	14.0

[4]Expenditures are in nominal dollars and include taxes where data are available. Population enumerated as of April 1 for 2000; estimated as of July 1 for all other years.
[5]As of January 1 of the year shown. States vary in taxation of food and in local/state taxation practices. See the source for details.
(X) = Not applicable

Table A-39.   Personal Income

Geographic area	Personal income													
	Current dollars (billion dollars)					Constant (2005) dollars[1]								
						Amount (billion dollars)					Percent change		Percent distribution	
	2012	2011	2010	2009	2005	2012	2011	2010	2009	2005	2005–2009	2009–2012	2012	2005
United States..............	13,401.9	12,949.9	12,308.5	11,852.7	10,476.7	11,574.4	11,380.5	11,080.1	10,873.7	10,476.7	3.8	6.4	100.0	100.0
Alabama.......................	171.8	167.5	161.3	154.2	135.6	148.4	147.2	145.2	141.5	135.6	4.3	4.9	1.3	1.3
Alaska.........................	34.2	33.0	31.2	29.9	24.6	29.5	29.0	28.1	27.4	24.6	11.2	7.9	0.3	0.2
Arizona........................	235.8	227.3	216.6	212.9	188.2	203.6	199.7	195.0	195.3	188.2	3.8	4.3	1.8	1.8
Arkansas.....................	102.4	99.1	94.6	91.8	77.5	88.4	87.1	85.1	84.2	77.5	8.7	5.0	0.8	0.7
California.....................	1,711.1	1,645.1	1,564.2	1,516.7	1,387.7	1,477.8	1,445.8	1,408.1	1,391.4	1,387.7	0.3	6.2	12.8	13.2
Colorado......................	234.1	225.4	212.5	204.6	179.7	202.2	198.1	191.3	187.7	179.7	4.5	7.7	1.7	1.7
Connecticut..................	211.5	207.3	198.2	188.4	168.8	182.7	182.2	178.4	172.9	168.8	2.4	5.7	1.6	1.6
Delaware......................	38.5	37.6	35.5	34.5	31.1	33.2	33.0	31.9	31.7	31.1	1.9	4.9	0.3	0.3
District of Columbia.......	47.2	45.6	43.1	40.3	32.0	40.8	40.1	38.8	37.0	32.0	15.7	10.3	0.4	0.3
Florida.........................	779.3	755.4	722.4	687.3	633.2	673.1	663.8	650.3	630.6	633.2	-0.4	6.7	5.8	6.0
Georgia........................	365.7	353.1	335.4	326.0	292.5	315.9	310.3	301.9	299.1	292.5	2.2	5.6	2.7	2.8
Hawaii.........................	61.3	59.0	55.8	54.2	45.3	52.9	51.9	50.3	49.7	45.3	9.7	6.5	0.5	0.4
Idaho...........................	53.9	52.1	49.6	47.9	42.2	46.5	45.8	44.6	43.9	42.2	4.1	5.9	0.4	0.4
Illinois.........................	577.0	562.7	539.7	522.9	472.1	498.3	494.5	485.8	479.7	472.1	1.6	3.9	4.3	4.5
Indiana........................	241.2	232.6	220.9	214.2	195.5	208.3	204.4	198.8	196.5	195.5	0.5	6.0	1.8	1.9
Iowa............................	129.5	126.0	115.5	112.1	95.5	111.8	110.8	104.0	102.9	95.5	7.8	8.7	1.0	0.9
Kansas........................	120.7	117.4	110.2	107.6	90.9	104.3	103.2	99.2	98.7	90.9	8.6	5.6	0.9	0.9
Kentucky......................	153.5	148.5	141.3	137.1	119.2	132.6	130.5	127.2	125.8	119.2	5.5	5.4	1.1	1.1
Louisiana.....................	181.4	176.4	168.7	162.0	135.3	156.6	155.0	151.9	148.6	135.3	9.8	5.4	1.4	1.3
Maine..........................	52.5	50.9	48.6	47.8	42.0	45.3	44.7	43.8	43.9	42.0	4.5	3.3	0.4	0.4
Maryland......................	305.8	295.2	281.3	271.7	237.1	264.1	259.5	253.2	249.3	237.1	5.1	6.0	2.3	2.3
Massachusetts..............	363.5	352.2	335.3	323.1	282.4	313.9	309.6	301.8	296.4	282.4	5.0	5.9	2.7	2.7
Michigan......................	370.6	358.2	339.0	328.9	325.7	320.1	314.7	305.2	301.8	325.7	-7.4	6.1	2.8	3.1
Minnesota....................	248.7	238.2	225.9	216.3	194.0	214.8	209.3	203.3	198.4	194.0	2.3	8.2	1.9	1.9
Mississippi...................	98.7	95.3	91.6	88.8	77.7	85.3	83.8	82.5	81.5	77.7	4.8	4.7	0.7	0.7
Missouri......................	235.2	228.2	218.3	213.6	186.8	203.1	200.6	196.5	196.0	186.8	4.9	3.6	1.8	1.8
Montana.......................	37.6	36.0	34.1	32.8	28.2	32.4	31.6	30.7	30.1	28.2	6.9	7.7	0.3	0.3
Nebraska......................	80.1	78.2	72.2	69.7	60.1	69.1	68.7	65.0	63.9	60.1	6.4	8.2	0.6	0.6
Nevada........................	103.1	100.7	96.8	96.4	91.8	89.0	88.5	87.1	88.5	91.8	-3.7	0.6	0.8	0.9
New Hampshire.............	62.2	60.5	57.9	55.8	50.0	53.7	53.2	52.1	51.2	50.0	2.4	4.8	0.5	0.5
New Jersey	475.4	462.5	443.7	431.0	379.7	410.6	406.4	399.5	395.4	379.7	4.1	3.8	3.5	3.6
New Mexico..................	73.2	71.1	68.1	65.6	55.3	63.2	62.5	61.3	60.2	55.3	8.7	5.0	0.5	0.5
New York......................	1,019.5	995.2	952.7	902.4	786.5	880.5	874.6	857.6	827.8	786.5	5.3	6.4	7.6	7.5
North Carolina..............	361.3	347.9	330.8	321.3	277.7	312.0	305.7	297.8	294.8	277.7	6.1	5.9	2.7	2.7
North Dakota................	36.3	32.3	28.6	26.2	20.5	31.4	28.4	25.8	24.0	20.5	16.9	30.5	0.3	0.2
Ohio............................	453.6	436.8	414.6	403.5	371.9	391.7	383.9	373.2	370.2	371.9	-0.5	5.8	3.4	3.6
Oklahoma	148.8	142.9	133.6	126.7	107.6	128.5	125.5	120.3	116.2	107.6	8.0	10.6	1.1	1.0
Oregon........................	151.2	145.3	137.8	133.9	117.6	130.6	127.7	124.1	122.8	117.6	4.4	6.3	1.1	1.1
Pennsylvania................	556.7	538.9	514.4	496.7	432.2	480.8	473.6	463.0	455.6	432.2	5.4	5.5	4.2	4.1
Rhode Island................	47.3	46.1	44.2	42.6	38.6	40.8	40.5	39.8	39.1	38.6	1.4	4.3	0.4	0.4
South Carolina	161.9	156.2	149.3	144.3	124.4	139.8	137.3	134.4	132.4	124.4	6.5	5.6	1.2	1.2
South Dakota	36.4	36.4	32.3	30.8	25.8	31.4	32.0	29.1	28.2	25.8	9.4	11.3	0.3	0.2
Tennessee....................	243.3	234.2	223.2	212.6	187.7	210.1	205.8	200.9	195.0	187.7	3.9	7.7	1.8	1.8
Texas..........................	1,080.7	1,030.7	965.2	907.6	756.7	933.3	905.8	868.9	832.7	756.7	10.0	12.1	8.1	7.2
Utah............................	98.8	94.4	89.2	86.5	71.5	85.3	83.0	80.3	79.4	71.5	11.0	7.5	0.7	0.7
Vermont	26.9	26.0	24.9	24.1	20.7	23.2	22.9	22.4	22.1	20.7	6.7	5.2	0.2	0.2
Virginia	385.4	373.3	354.1	340.3	294.7	332.9	328.1	318.8	312.1	294.7	5.9	6.6	2.9	2.8
Washington..................	313.2	299.7	283.4	276.7	230.1	270.5	263.4	255.1	253.9	230.1	10.4	6.6	2.3	2.2
West Virginia................	64.0	62.0	59.0	57.2	48.1	55.2	54.5	53.1	52.5	48.1	9.1	5.2	0.5	0.5
Wisconsin	232.1	226.0	216.3	209.0	186.5	200.5	198.6	194.7	191.7	186.5	2.8	4.6	1.7	1.8
Wyoming	28.1	27.2	25.6	24.0	20.0	24.2	23.9	23.0	22.0	20.0	10.2	10.1	0.2	0.2

[1]Constant dollar estimates are computed using the national implicit price deflator for personal consumption expenditures from the Bureau of Economic Analysis. Any regional differences in the rate of inflation are not reflected in these constant dollar estimates.

Table A-39. Personal Income—*Continued*

Geographic area	Current dollars (billion dollars)					Constant (2005) dollars[1]						
						Amount (billion dollars)					Percent change	
	2012	2011	2010	2009	2005	2012	2011	2010	2009	2005	2005–2009	2009–2012
United States.................	11,928.7	11,553.4	11,114.9	10,709.3	9,269.4	10,302.1	10,153.2	10,005.6	9,824.7	9,269.4	6.0	4.9
Alabama..........................	156.6	153.0	148.8	142.0	122.9	135.2	134.4	133.9	130.3	122.9	6.0	3.8
Alaska	30.9	29.9	28.7	27.4	22.5	26.7	26.3	25.8	25.1	22.5	11.8	6.3
Arizona............................	214.9	207.5	200.0	196.8	168.2	185.6	182.4	180.0	180.5	168.2	7.3	2.8
Arkansas..........................	93.4	90.5	87.2	84.4	70.4	80.7	79.6	78.5	77.4	70.4	10.0	4.2
California..........................	1,499.4	1,443.9	1,389.7	1,355.3	1,210.2	1,295.0	1,268.9	1,251.0	1,243.4	1,210.2	2.7	4.1
Colorado..........................	207.9	200.7	191.6	184.7	159.2	179.5	176.4	172.5	169.4	159.2	6.4	5.9
Connecticut.....................	177.9	175.0	170.7	162.2	141.5	153.7	153.8	153.7	148.8	141.5	5.2	3.3
Delaware..........................	33.9	33.3	31.8	31.0	27.1	29.3	29.3	28.7	28.4	27.1	4.9	3.1
District of Columbia	41.5	40.3	38.4	35.8	27.6	35.9	35.4	34.6	32.9	27.6	18.9	9.2
Florida.............................	710.1	689.4	666.7	633.8	564.2	613.3	605.8	600.2	581.4	564.2	3.1	5.5
Georgia............................	329.0	318.3	305.6	297.1	260.7	284.2	279.7	275.1	272.5	260.7	4.6	4.3
Hawaii..............................	55.6	53.7	51.2	49.5	40.2	48.0	47.2	46.1	45.4	40.2	12.8	5.9
Idaho...............................	49.3	47.7	45.8	44.1	37.9	42.6	41.9	41.2	40.5	37.9	6.8	5.3
Illinois.............................	505.2	499.3	486.3	471.5	417.9	436.4	438.8	437.8	432.6	417.9	3.5	0.9
Indiana............................	217.1	209.8	201.2	195.6	175.2	187.5	184.4	181.1	179.4	175.2	2.4	4.5
Iowa................................	117.6	114.5	105.7	102.6	86.4	101.6	100.7	95.1	94.1	86.4	8.9	8.0
Kansas	108.3	105.7	100.0	97.8	81.5	93.6	92.9	90.0	89.7	81.5	10.1	4.3
Kentucky..........................	138.8	134.4	128.9	125.2	106.7	119.8	118.1	116.1	114.8	106.7	7.6	4.4
Louisiana.........................	165.9	161.5	156.1	149.0	123.9	143.2	142.0	140.5	136.7	123.9	10.3	4.8
Maine...............................	47.6	46.1	44.5	43.7	37.6	41.1	40.5	40.0	40.1	37.6	6.5	2.7
Maryland..........................	266.7	258.8	249.3	240.2	205.4	230.3	227.4	224.5	220.4	205.4	7.3	4.5
Massachusetts	312.0	302.8	293.4	283.9	242.3	269.5	266.1	264.1	260.4	242.3	7.5	3.5
Michigan..........................	332.8	322.5	309.5	301.0	291.9	287.4	283.4	278.6	276.1	291.9	-5.4	4.1
Minnesota........................	218.8	209.8	202.1	193.5	170.1	188.9	184.4	181.9	177.5	170.1	4.4	6.4
Mississippi.......................	90.9	87.9	85.1	82.9	71.9	78.5	77.3	76.6	76.0	71.9	5.7	3.2
Missouri	212.1	206.7	199.5	194.9	167.7	183.2	181.6	179.6	178.8	167.7	6.6	2.4
Montana..........................	33.9	32.6	31.2	29.9	25.4	29.3	28.6	28.1	27.5	25.4	8.0	6.7
Nebraska..........................	72.1	70.9	66.0	63.7	54.2	62.3	62.3	59.4	58.5	54.2	7.8	6.5
Nevada............................	93.4	91.3	88.8	88.4	81.3	80.7	80.3	79.9	81.1	81.3	-0.3	-0.4
New Hampshire...............	56.1	54.7	53.0	51.2	45.0	48.5	48.0	47.7	47.0	45.0	4.4	3.2
New Jersey	415.4	404.4	393.4	381.3	328.7	358.7	355.4	354.1	349.8	328.7	6.4	2.5
New Mexico	67.4	65.4	63.1	60.4	50.3	58.2	57.4	56.8	55.4	50.3	10.1	5.1
New York..........................	868.0	847.2	825.0	781.1	668.8	749.7	744.5	742.7	716.6	668.8	7.1	4.6
North Carolina.................	325.1	313.9	301.2	292.1	247.5	280.7	275.8	271.2	267.9	247.5	8.3	4.8
North Dakota...................	32.5	29.1	26.2	24.0	18.8	28.1	25.5	23.6	22.0	18.8	16.9	27.4
Ohio................................	405.8	391.9	375.8	366.3	329.6	350.5	344.4	338.3	336.0	329.6	2.0	4.3
Oklahoma	135.3	130.2	123.0	116.3	96.9	116.8	114.4	110.8	106.7	96.9	10.0	9.5
Oregon............................	134.4	129.2	124.0	120.7	103.1	116.1	113.5	111.6	110.7	103.1	7.4	4.8
Pennsylvania....................	494.4	479.7	462.7	447.5	382.6	427.0	421.6	416.6	410.5	382.6	7.3	4.0
Rhode Island...................	42.4	41.4	40.2	38.7	34.2	36.6	36.4	36.1	35.5	34.2	3.8	3.1
South Carolina	148.1	142.8	137.8	133.1	112.2	127.9	125.5	124.0	122.1	112.2	8.8	4.8
South Dakota	33.7	33.9	30.2	28.8	23.9	29.1	29.8	27.2	26.4	23.9	10.5	10.3
Tennessee	225.3	217.4	209.2	199.1	172.7	194.6	191.1	188.3	182.7	172.7	5.8	6.5
Texas..............................	983.0	940.5	891.5	838.5	688.1	849.0	826.5	802.5	769.3	688.1	11.8	10.4
Utah	89.5	85.7	81.7	79.0	63.9	77.3	75.3	73.5	72.4	63.9	13.4	6.7
Vermont	24.4	23.6	22.8	22.0	18.5	21.1	20.8	20.5	20.2	18.5	9.2	4.3
Virginia............................	338.6	328.8	316.0	303.5	257.5	292.5	288.9	284.5	278.4	257.5	8.1	5.1
Washington......................	284.6	272.9	261.2	255.3	208.0	245.8	239.9	235.1	234.2	208.0	12.6	4.9
West Virginia....................	58.0	56.3	54.2	52.4	43.7	50.1	49.5	48.8	48.1	43.7	9.9	4.2
Wisconsin.........................	207.5	202.0	195.6	188.4	165.5	179.2	177.5	176.1	172.9	165.5	4.5	3.6
Wyoming	25.2	24.5	23.4	22.0	17.9	21.8	21.6	21.0	20.2	17.9	12.6	8.1

[1]Constant dollar estimates are computed using the national implicit price deflator for personal consumption expenditures from the Bureau of Economic Analysis. Any regional differences in the rate of inflation are not reflected in these constant dollar estimates.

Table A-40. Personal Income Per Capita

Geographic area	Personal income per capita[1]											
	Current dollars					Constant (2005) dollars[2]					Income rank	
	2012	2011	2010	2009	2005	2012	2011	2010	2009	2005	2012	2005
United States....................	42,693	41,560	39,791	38,637	35,452	36,871	36,523	35,820	35,445	35,452	(X)	(X)
Alabama............................	35,625	34,880	33,710	32,406	29,681	30,767	30,653	30,346	29,729	29,681	43	42
Alaska...............................	46,778	45,665	43,749	42,713	36,911	40,399	40,131	39,383	39,185	36,911	11	15
Arizona.............................	35,979	35,062	33,773	33,560	32,223	31,073	30,813	30,402	30,788	32,223	42	33
Arkansas..........................	34,723	33,740	32,373	31,688	27,858	29,988	29,651	29,142	29,070	27,858	46	49
California..........................	44,980	43,647	41,893	41,034	38,731	38,847	38,358	37,712	37,644	38,731	16	10
Colorado...........................	45,135	44,053	42,107	41,154	38,795	38,980	38,714	37,905	37,755	38,795	14	9
Connecticut......................	58,908	57,902	55,427	52,900	48,134	50,875	50,885	49,895	48,530	48,134	2	2
Delaware..........................	41,940	41,449	39,425	38,695	36,771	36,221	36,426	35,490	35,499	36,771	24	16
District of Columbia..........	74,710	73,783	71,220	68,093	56,362	64,523	64,841	64,112	62,468	56,362	1	1
Florida..............................	40,344	39,636	38,345	36,849	35,489	34,843	34,833	34,518	33,805	35,489	28	19
Georgia............................	36,869	35,979	34,531	33,887	32,775	31,842	31,619	31,085	31,088	32,775	41	28
Hawaii..............................	44,024	42,925	40,952	40,242	35,067	38,021	37,723	36,865	36,918	35,067	18	20
Idaho................................	33,749	32,881	31,556	30,809	29,544	29,147	28,896	28,407	28,264	29,544	50	44
Illinois..............................	44,815	43,721	42,025	40,865	37,437	38,704	38,423	37,831	37,489	37,437	17	14
Indiana.............................	36,902	35,689	34,028	33,163	31,141	31,870	31,364	30,632	30,424	31,141	40	39
Iowa.................................	42,126	41,156	37,882	36,977	32,204	36,382	36,168	34,101	33,923	32,204	23	34
Kansas.............................	41,835	40,883	38,545	37,988	33,102	36,130	35,928	34,698	34,850	33,102	25	27
Kentucky..........................	35,041	33,989	32,504	31,754	28,486	30,263	29,870	29,260	29,131	28,486	45	48
Louisiana.........................	39,413	38,549	37,116	36,062	29,567	34,039	33,877	33,412	33,083	29,567	30	43
Maine...............................	39,481	38,299	36,629	35,981	31,834	34,097	33,658	32,973	33,009	31,834	29	36
Maryland..........................	51,971	50,656	48,621	47,419	42,405	44,884	44,517	43,768	43,502	42,405	6	5
Massachusetts..................	54,687	53,471	51,143	49,578	44,097	47,230	46,991	46,039	45,483	44,097	3	3
Michigan...........................	37,497	36,264	34,326	33,221	32,409	32,384	31,869	30,900	30,477	32,409	36	31
Minnesota.........................	46,227	44,560	42,528	40,950	37,892	39,923	39,160	38,284	37,567	37,892	12	12
Mississippi.......................	33,073	32,000	30,841	30,013	26,755	28,563	28,122	27,763	27,534	26,755	51	50
Missouri...........................	39,049	37,969	36,406	35,837	32,253	33,724	33,368	32,773	32,877	32,253	32	32
Montana...........................	37,370	36,016	34,405	33,364	29,975	32,274	31,651	30,971	30,608	29,975	37	41
Nebraska..........................	43,143	42,450	39,445	38,438	34,098	37,260	37,306	35,508	35,263	34,098	21	22
Nevada.............................	37,361	36,964	35,777	35,919	37,760	32,266	32,484	32,206	32,952	37,760	38	13
New Hampshire.................	47,058	45,881	43,968	42,418	38,528	40,641	40,321	39,580	38,914	38,528	10	11
New Jersey	53,628	52,430	50,428	49,221	43,880	46,315	46,076	45,395	45,155	43,880	4	4
New Mexico.......................	35,079	34,133	32,940	32,200	28,641	30,296	29,996	29,652	29,540	28,641	44	47
New York...........................	52,095	51,126	49,119	46,739	41,108	44,991	44,930	44,217	42,878	41,108	5	6
North Carolina...................	37,049	36,028	34,604	34,001	31,905	31,997	31,662	31,150	31,192	31,905	39	35
North Dakota.....................	51,893	47,236	42,462	39,372	31,795	44,817	41,512	38,224	36,120	31,795	7	37
Ohio.................................	39,289	37,836	35,931	35,001	32,445	33,932	33,251	32,345	32,110	32,445	31	30
Oklahoma	39,006	37,679	35,535	34,082	30,333	33,687	33,113	31,988	31,267	30,333	33	40
Oregon.............................	38,786	37,527	35,906	35,159	32,557	33,497	32,979	32,322	32,255	32,557	34	29
Pennsylvania.....................	43,616	42,291	40,444	39,210	34,719	37,669	37,166	36,408	35,971	34,719	20	21
Rhode Island.....................	44,990	43,875	42,001	40,460	36,117	38,855	38,558	37,809	37,118	36,117	15	18
South Carolina	34,266	33,388	32,193	31,448	29,131	29,593	29,342	28,980	28,850	29,131	49	45
South Dakota	43,659	44,217	39,558	38,147	33,306	37,706	38,858	35,610	34,996	33,306	19	25
Tennessee........................	37,678	36,567	35,103	33,711	31,327	32,540	32,136	31,600	30,926	31,327	35	38
Texas...............................	41,471	40,147	38,222	36,595	33,220	35,816	35,282	34,407	33,572	33,220	26	26
Utah.................................	34,601	33,509	32,121	31,778	29,104	29,883	29,448	28,915	29,153	29,104	47	46
Vermont	42,994	41,572	39,736	38,530	33,317	37,131	36,534	35,770	35,347	33,317	22	24
Virginia............................	47,082	46,107	44,134	42,929	38,898	40,662	40,519	39,729	39,383	38,898	9	7
Washington.......................	45,413	43,878	42,024	41,504	36,766	39,220	38,561	37,830	38,076	36,766	13	17
West Virginia.....................	34,477	33,403	31,806	30,968	26,443	29,776	29,355	28,632	28,410	26,443	48	51
Wisconsin.........................	40,537	39,575	38,010	36,859	33,635	35,009	34,779	34,216	33,814	33,635	27	23
Wyoming	48,670	47,898	45,353	42,828	38,839	42,033	42,093	40,827	39,290	38,839	8	8

[1]Per capita personal income (or disposable personal income) is total (disposable) personal income divided by total midyear population.
[2]Constant dollar estimates are computed using the national implicit price deflator for personal consumption expenditures from the Bureau of Economic Analysis. Any regional differences in the rate of inflation are not reflected in these constant dollar estimates.
(X) = Not applicable

Table A-40. Personal Income Per Capita—*Continued*

Geographic area	Disposable personal income per capita[1]											
	Current dollars					Constant (2005) dollars[2]					Disposable income index (U.S. = 100)	
	2012	2011	2010	2009	2005	2012	2011	2010	2009	2005	2012	2005
United States..................	38,000	37,078	35,932	34,910	31,367	32,818	32,585	32,346	32,026	31,367	100.0	100.0
Alabama............................	32,467	31,854	31,087	29,848	26,885	28,040	27,994	27,984	27,382	26,885	85.4	85.7
Alaska	42,306	41,420	40,167	39,196	33,701	36,537	36,400	36,158	35,958	33,701	111.3	107.4
Arizona..............................	32,797	32,015	31,187	31,019	28,814	28,325	28,135	28,074	28,457	28,814	86.3	91.9
Arkansas	31,675	30,819	29,843	29,128	25,299	27,356	27,084	26,865	26,722	25,299	83.4	80.7
California..........................	39,416	38,308	37,218	36,669	33,779	34,041	33,666	33,503	33,640	33,779	103.7	107.7
Colorado...........................	40,069	39,221	37,957	37,145	34,373	34,605	34,468	34,169	34,077	34,373	105.4	109.6
Connecticut......................	49,562	48,873	47,753	45,535	40,346	42,804	42,950	42,987	41,774	40,346	130.4	128.6
Delaware	36,983	36,721	35,378	34,746	32,052	31,940	32,271	31,847	31,876	32,052	97.3	102.2
District of Columbia	65,677	65,233	63,532	60,477	48,727	56,721	57,328	57,191	55,481	48,727	172.8	155.3
Florida..............................	36,760	36,173	35,392	33,978	31,622	31,747	31,789	31,860	31,171	31,622	96.7	100.8
Georgia	33,168	32,430	31,462	30,880	29,203	28,645	28,500	28,322	28,329	29,203	87.3	93.1
Hawaii...............................	39,956	39,073	37,586	36,719	31,110	34,508	34,338	33,835	33,686	31,110	105.1	99.2
Idaho.................................	30,913	30,111	29,148	28,383	26,528	26,698	26,462	26,239	26,038	26,528	81.4	84.6
Illinois..............................	39,242	38,797	37,872	36,848	33,141	33,891	34,095	34,092	33,804	33,141	103.3	105.7
Indiana..............................	33,217	32,199	30,994	30,275	27,902	28,688	28,297	27,901	27,774	27,902	87.4	89.0
Iowa..................................	38,257	37,406	34,640	33,816	29,150	33,040	32,873	31,183	31,023	29,150	100.7	92.9
Kansas	37,539	36,807	34,964	34,511	29,676	32,420	32,346	31,474	31,660	29,676	98.8	94.6
Kentucky	31,676	30,758	29,659	28,994	25,509	27,357	27,030	26,699	26,599	25,509	83.4	81.3
Louisiana	36,042	35,308	34,341	33,172	27,082	31,127	31,029	30,914	30,432	27,082	94.8	86.3
Maine................................	35,834	34,713	33,492	32,842	28,520	30,948	30,506	30,149	30,129	28,520	94.3	90.9
Maryland...........................	45,324	44,404	43,097	41,923	36,722	39,144	39,023	38,796	38,460	36,722	119.3	117.1
Massachusetts.................	46,947	45,960	44,751	43,558	37,838	40,545	40,390	40,285	39,960	37,838	123.5	120.6
Michigan...........................	33,672	32,651	31,333	30,398	29,038	29,080	28,694	28,206	27,887	29,038	88.6	92.6
Minnesota.........................	40,670	39,257	38,051	36,642	33,217	35,124	34,500	34,253	33,615	33,217	107.0	105.9
Mississippi.......................	30,449	29,514	28,669	28,013	24,746	26,297	25,937	25,808	25,699	24,746	80.1	78.9
Missouri	35,229	34,383	33,268	32,703	28,965	30,425	30,216	29,948	30,002	28,965	92.7	92.3
Montana............................	33,734	32,618	31,488	30,410	27,039	29,134	28,665	28,345	27,898	27,039	88.8	86.2
Nebraska..........................	38,883	38,457	36,042	35,167	30,795	33,581	33,796	32,445	32,262	30,795	102.3	98.2
Nevada..............................	33,866	33,536	32,842	32,910	33,419	29,248	29,472	29,564	30,192	33,419	89.1	106.5
New Hampshire................	42,502	41,472	40,244	38,915	34,669	36,706	36,446	36,227	35,701	34,669	111.8	110.5
New Jersey	46,856	45,850	44,705	43,552	37,994	40,467	40,294	40,243	39,954	37,994	123.3	121.1
New Mexico	32,314	31,392	30,551	29,634	26,028	27,908	27,588	27,502	27,186	26,028	85.0	83.0
New York...........................	44,355	43,524	42,539	40,458	34,957	38,307	38,249	38,293	37,116	34,957	116.7	111.4
North Carolina..................	33,333	32,505	31,509	30,907	28,428	28,788	28,566	28,364	28,354	28,428	87.7	90.6
North Dakota.....................	46,460	42,492	38,873	36,106	29,174	40,125	37,342	34,993	33,124	29,174	122.3	93.0
Ohio..................................	35,153	33,943	32,572	31,769	28,751	30,360	29,830	29,321	29,145	28,751	92.5	91.7
Oklahoma	35,461	34,327	32,720	31,274	27,312	30,626	30,167	29,454	28,691	27,312	93.3	87.1
Oregon..............................	34,466	33,361	32,300	31,688	28,530	29,766	29,318	29,076	29,070	28,530	90.7	91.0
Pennsylvania.....................	38,739	37,647	36,386	35,325	30,730	33,457	33,085	32,755	32,407	30,730	101.9	98.0
Rhode Island.....................	40,361	39,383	38,152	36,747	32,052	34,857	34,610	34,344	33,712	32,052	106.2	102.2
South Carolina	31,346	30,528	29,717	28,991	26,282	27,072	26,828	26,751	26,596	26,282	82.5	83.8
South Dakota	40,427	41,133	36,958	35,634	30,793	34,914	36,148	33,269	32,691	30,793	106.4	98.2
Tennessee	34,898	33,954	32,899	31,580	28,832	30,139	29,839	29,616	28,971	28,832	91.8	91.9
Texas................................	37,723	36,631	35,301	33,809	30,207	32,579	32,192	31,778	31,016	30,207	99.3	96.3
Utah..................................	31,329	30,405	29,436	28,993	25,990	27,057	26,720	26,498	26,598	25,990	82.4	82.9
Vermont	38,981	37,714	36,454	35,255	29,798	33,666	33,144	32,816	32,343	29,798	102.6	95.0
Virginia.............................	41,369	40,608	39,382	38,288	33,980	35,728	35,687	35,451	35,125	33,980	108.9	108.3
Washington.......................	41,259	39,960	38,731	38,295	33,237	35,633	35,117	34,865	35,132	33,237	108.6	106.0
West Virginia....................	31,270	30,369	29,223	28,360	24,028	27,006	26,689	26,306	26,017	24,028	82.3	76.6
Wisconsin	36,230	35,359	34,364	33,239	29,839	31,290	31,074	30,934	30,493	29,839	95.3	95.1
Wyoming	43,788	43,194	41,408	39,256	34,826	37,817	37,959	37,275	36,013	34,826	115.2	111.0

[1]Per capita personal income (or disposable personal income) is total (disposable) personal income divided by total midyear population.
[2]Constant dollar estimates are computed using the national implicit price deflator for personal consumption expenditures from the Bureau of Economic Analysis. Any regional differences in the rate of inflation are not reflected in these constant dollar estimates.

Table A-41. Earnings by Industry, 2012

Geographic area	Private earnings[1] (millions dollars)								
	Mining (NAICS 21)	Utilities (2007, NAICS 22)	Construction (2007, NAICS 23)	Manufacturing (2007, NAICS 31-33)	Wholesale trade (2007, NAICS 42)	Retail trade (2007, NAICS 44-45)	Transportation and warehousing (2007, NAICS 48-49)	Information (2007, NAICS 51)	Finance and insurance (2007, NAICS 52)
United States.................	119,203	85,813	525,353	987,242	504,818	601,407	324,865	322,511	700,584
Alabama...........................	847	1,870	7,132	15,942	5,404	8,078	3,872	1,558	5,537
Alaska.............................	2,340	289	2,184	776	464	1,560	1,672	493	864
Arizona............................	1,260	1,722	9,508	14,182	8,644	12,921	5,110	3,133	11,061
Arkansas.........................	856	904	3,762	8,751	3,598	4,907	3,586	1,061	2,516
California.........................	5,447	10,743	60,842	131,959	60,913	77,145	34,804	69,802	75,488
Colorado..........................	5,345	1,358	10,545	11,240	9,177	10,218	4,884	10,663	11,995
Connecticut.....................	127	1,139	7,049	17,551	7,047	8,265	2,832	4,367	22,900
Delaware..........................	(D)	292	1,505	1,995	1,264	1,795	704	563	3,977
District of Columbia	4	253	1,184	137	684	799	417	2,414	2,597
Florida.............................	463	3,121	22,992	23,726	27,339	38,198	15,310	12,920	33,365
Georgia............................	406	2,534	12,658	25,621	18,245	17,052	12,475	12,460	16,706
Hawaii.............................	34	482	3,112	778	1,154	2,701	1,485	677	1,346
Idaho...............................	247	351	2,351	3,830	1,813	2,939	1,173	589	1,699
Illinois.............................	1,064	3,884	19,096	51,372	28,490	23,179	17,924	10,275	37,111
Indiana............................	727	1,841	11,210	38,007	8,590	10,741	7,275	2,531	7,351
Iowa................................	137	833	5,819	14,863	5,098	6,017	3,592	1,814	8,034
Kansas............................	1,336	1,007	4,705	12,440	4,757	5,308	3,204	2,433	4,952
Kentucky.........................	1,917	739	5,573	15,666	5,330	7,206	5,768	1,703	5,357
Louisiana.........................	6,154	1,155	10,550	13,166	5,736	8,489	6,868	1,715	4,715
Maine..............................	15	218	2,266	3,569	1,418	2,930	893	500	1,970
Maryland..........................	181	2,023	14,216	10,137	7,965	11,580	4,659	5,674	11,445
Massachusetts.................	112	1,795	13,488	26,264	12,995	13,325	4,855	10,567	28,480
Michigan..........................	828	3,151	11,423	44,335	13,845	16,211	7,672	4,472	12,890
Minnesota........................	720	1,781	9,034	24,442	12,380	10,022	5,595	4,756	15,620
Mississippi.......................	913	840	4,254	8,267	2,283	4,866	2,522	764	2,353
Missouri..........................	410	1,552	9,710	18,501	9,408	11,343	6,135	6,588	10,753
Montana..........................	953	405	1,895	1,094	1,092	2,097	1,062	394	1,121
Nebraska.........................	119	633	3,783	5,702	2,933	3,639	4,260	1,314	4,241
Nevada............................	1,656	594	4,493	2,882	2,717	5,460	3,259	1,012	3,648
New Hampshire.................	41	414	2,699	5,459	2,639	3,959	713	1,275	2,939
New Jersey	222	2,669	15,495	26,401	22,919	20,831	11,180	11,066	27,271
New Mexico......................	2,348	498	2,914	2,300	1,430	3,461	1,388	843	1,540
New York..........................	784	6,294	32,251	37,794	33,586	39,977	15,514	43,118	135,500
North Carolina.................	198	1,743	13,808	32,215	13,627	16,898	6,847	6,397	16,973
North Dakota....................	2,669	450	2,613	1,551	2,033	1,761	1,789	518	1,099
Ohio................................	1,688	2,721	16,367	50,672	18,258	20,664	11,526	5,926	18,026
Oklahoma	9,608	1,683	5,708	10,279	4,346	7,192	5,245	1,830	4,349
Oregon............................	139	723	6,215	14,436	7,106	7,293	3,310	2,927	4,940
Pennsylvania....................	3,863	3,496	22,593	43,261	20,573	23,297	13,814	11,714	25,569
Rhode Island....................	(D)	162	1,653	2,826	1,476	1,841	569	1,070	2,673
South Carolina	87	1,525	6,090	15,639	4,926	8,157	2,935	1,919	5,714
South Dakota	67	214	1,478	2,354	1,350	1,790	727	379	1,573
Tennessee.......................	316	370	10,505	22,832	9,471	12,970	9,746	3,283	9,959
Texas..............................	53,138	9,543	61,133	81,657	53,472	50,154	40,172	19,689	50,243
Utah................................	1,234	551	5,486	8,256	3,702	5,950	3,070	2,302	4,738
Vermont	43	295	1,287	2,251	687	1,457	391	304	756
Virginia............................	1,169	1,717	14,135	16,958	9,942	14,715	7,105	8,162	14,087
Washington......................	193	647	12,966	25,456	11,140	15,576	6,803	18,094	9,849
West Virginia....................	3,363	624	2,993	3,618	1,521	2,979	1,437	696	1,142
Wisconsin........................	233	1,644	8,739	33,064	9,135	10,295	5,655	3,565	10,961
Wyoming	3,149	322	1,885	770	695	1,197	1,061	222	588

[1] All data estimates are in current dollars (not adjusted for inflation).
(D) = Data withheld to avoid disclosure or does not meet statistical standards, but the estimates for this item are included in the total.

Table A-41. Earnings by Industry, 2012—*Continued*

Geographic area	Private earnings[1] (million dollars)									Government and government enterprises		
	Real estate and rental and leasing (2007, NAICS 53)	Professional, scientific, and technical services (2007, NAICS 54)	Management of companies and enterprises (2007, NAICS 55)	Administrative and waste services (2007, NAICS 56)	Educational services (2007, NAICS 61)	Health care and social assistance (2007, NAICS 62)	Arts, entertainment, and recreation (2007, NAICS 71)	Accommodation and food services (2007, NAICS 72)	Other services (except public administration) (2007, NAICS 81)	Federal, civilian	Military	State and local
United States.............	163,876	980,724	253,378	388,154	162,363	1,071,467	108,849	301,274	355,615	328,158	182,256	1,164,165
Alabama.....................	1,447	9,580	1,548	3,875	950	12,264	458	3,239	5,247	6,633	2,468	16,893
Alaska	406	1,815	160	780	129	2,952	225	917	833	1,834	2,886	4,340
Arizona	4,094	13,328	2,435	9,328	2,882	20,292	1,952	6,192	5,795	6,088	2,778	20,126
Arkansas	1,114	3,268	3,411	1,998	521	7,931	291	1,813	2,522	2,036	1,124	9,922
California...................	22,187	157,092	25,513	52,236	19,874	119,586	21,101	38,942	46,035	28,421	19,785	158,046
Colorado	4,609	21,874	4,983	7,422	2,038	15,683	2,314	6,166	6,539	6,088	5,346	19,643
Connecticut................	2,628	13,518	5,559	5,202	4,181	17,178	1,063	3,336	4,833	1,928	1,097	16,207
Delaware	525	3,672	1,103	994	354	3,811	341	807	967	554	579	3,567
District of Columbia	1,269	20,219	497	2,549	2,850	4,527	534	2,212	6,881	30,836	1,962	3,246
Florida......................	11,806	44,148	10,184	25,139	6,996	61,451	10,489	21,825	19,964	14,273	9,012	56,002
Georgia	4,909	26,331	6,656	12,810	4,267	26,084	2,211	8,447	9,423	11,144	9,636	29,577
Hawaii	956	2,608	702	1,856	714	4,081	476	3,661	1,687	3,797	6,449	5,505
Idaho	424	3,096	640	1,380	377	4,236	308	1,048	1,339	1,187	617	4,977
Illinois	7,575	50,216	14,267	18,876	8,796	43,987	4,046	11,863	16,668	9,180	3,255	50,981
Indiana	2,062	9,807	2,945	6,573	2,602	21,764	1,812	4,725	6,660	3,880	1,074	20,133
Iowa	872	4,090	1,432	2,526	1,206	9,427	603	2,152	3,209	1,675	559	12,581
Kansas	891	5,779	1,365	3,745	757	9,586	427	2,281	3,176	2,583	3,894	11,194
Kentucky	1,144	5,881	2,107	3,753	1,023	13,298	639	3,304	3,806	3,828	6,004	14,512
Louisiana	2,366	9,289	2,059	4,449	1,740	14,029	1,345	4,412	5,178	3,202	3,125	17,140
Maine	466	2,312	661	1,232	661	5,654	360	1,287	1,218	1,569	523	4,393
Maryland...................	3,658	29,262	2,995	8,132	4,339	22,994	1,965	5,561	7,807	25,231	5,144	23,719
Massachusetts............	4,050	41,600	8,227	9,323	10,790	37,150	3,115	7,602	8,376	5,472	1,223	26,697
Michigan	2,807	26,011	7,009	12,205	3,028	33,116	2,039	7,104	9,573	5,737	994	33,441
Minnesota	3,105	15,205	9,858	5,675	2,686	23,072	2,044	4,367	6,150	3,309	1,042	20,814
Mississippi................	664	2,864	967	1,996	717	7,033	323	2,548	2,504	2,573	2,056	11,086
Missouri	2,136	13,952	6,814	6,846	2,803	21,078	2,311	5,046	6,549	5,783	2,734	19,691
Montana	318	1,722	169	773	162	3,399	295	1,026	1,066	1,304	543	3,722
Nebraska...................	543	3,962	1,746	1,813	716	6,576	313	1,347	2,195	1,641	1,046	7,703
Nevada	1,351	5,378	2,452	3,082	462	6,616	1,316	11,997	2,480	1,836	1,532	8,847
New Hampshire..........	610	3,695	814	1,772	1,210	5,523	375	1,352	1,685	827	224	4,555
New Jersey	4,829	38,842	13,555	13,710	4,726	35,895	2,835	8,504	9,824	6,028	1,585	42,040
New Mexico	642	5,104	412	1,872	485	5,622	312	1,831	1,820	3,386	1,628	8,692
New York...................	16,823	91,492	22,311	25,451	20,197	84,460	13,166	21,381	24,057	13,066	4,629	98,148
North Carolina............	3,344	19,829	8,967	11,280	4,096	26,455	2,568	7,618	9,249	6,973	14,519	34,423
North Dakota..............	482	1,263	395	552	116	3,053	89	710	821	883	884	3,050
Ohio.........................	5,249	25,048	16,301	13,420	4,506	43,041	2,869	9,067	11,201	8,603	2,238	39,290
Oklahoma	1,573	5,781	1,479	4,126	825	10,675	661	2,997	3,696	4,975	3,172	14,567
Oregon	1,665	8,181	3,110	3,811	1,438	13,607	915	3,639	4,076	2,914	625	14,710
Pennsylvania..............	5,383	38,997	17,086	12,672	12,435	56,507	4,461	9,776	14,293	10,822	1,952	38,347
Rhode Island..............	383	2,418	1,345	1,090	1,232	4,605	304	1,038	1,078	1,203	645	3,957
South Carolina	1,596	7,665	1,454	6,100	1,120	10,386	790	4,252	4,422	3,271	4,658	17,080
South Dakota	240	936	426	492	262	3,476	221	701	866	1,075	559	2,859
Tennessee	2,657	12,662	3,653	9,843	2,444	26,265	2,203	5,886	7,550	5,461	1,111	19,310
Texas........................	16,366	77,510	10,984	36,230	7,858	77,584	5,984	24,018	30,883	21,886	17,778	85,797
Utah.........................	1,362	6,625	1,677	3,004	1,515	6,542	649	2,194	3,704	3,410	1,004	9,760
Vermont	241	1,439	174	471	551	2,600	155	766	675	679	195	2,513
Virginia	4,317	51,471	10,033	10,728	3,827	24,605	1,876	7,367	11,312	25,323	16,468	30,878
Washington................	3,333	20,887	4,646	8,219	2,053	23,034	1,890	6,388	7,555	7,846	8,208	29,261
West Virginia..............	517	2,332	529	1,246	289	5,958	247	1,463	1,505	2,505	433	6,547
Wisconsin	1,505	9,800	5,452	5,152	2,474	21,299	1,402	4,327	6,000	2,704	800	20,182
Wyoming	379	871	113	346	82	1,417	164	769	664	697	453	3,494

[1]All data estimates are in current dollars (not adjusted for inflation).
(D) = Data withheld to avoid disclosure or does not meet statistical standards, but the estimates for this item are included in the total.

Table A-42. Gross Domestic Product, by State

Geographic area	Current dollars (million dollars)						Chained (2005) dollars[1] (million dollars)					
	2012	2011	2010	2009	2005	2000	2012	2011	2010	2005	2000	1990
United States.............	15,566,077	14,959,778	14,388,813	13,869,678	12,539,116	9,884,171	13,430,576	13,108,318	12,897,088	12,592,668	12,539,116	11,225,406
Alabama.....................	183,547	178,533	172,842	166,315	150,968	116,009	157,272	155,390	153,839	149,843	150,968	132,699
Alaska.......................	51,859	51,237	47,910	45,149	37,774	25,911	44,732	44,232	43,472	44,215	37,774	34,192
Arizona......................	266,891	255,989	247,329	245,216	222,569	161,792	230,641	224,787	221,016	221,405	222,569	178,845
Arkansas...................	109,557	106,557	103,170	99,530	88,501	68,335	93,892	92,684	92,075	89,776	88,501	77,539
California....................	2,003,479	1,908,985	1,845,249	1,818,627	1,688,949	1,319,472	1,751,002	1,692,301	1,672,473	1,667,152	1,688,949	1,472,323
Colorado....................	274,048	264,733	254,551	245,362	217,329	172,037	239,884	234,929	230,976	225,984	217,329	195,300
Connecticut...............	229,317	225,409	221,767	217,103	196,307	163,455	197,202	197,452	197,613	195,237	196,307	184,776
Delaware	65,984	64,377	62,832	60,201	54,422	40,614	56,110	56,004	55,496	55,352	54,422	46,453
District of Columbia	109,793	107,201	103,745	98,355	82,488	58,267	92,106	91,442	89,968	87,172	82,488	69,866
Florida.......................	777,164	746,439	727,972	721,175	681,225	481,239	672,287	656,346	650,291	648,642	681,225	549,269
Georgia	433,569	417,438	402,006	393,964	363,177	293,966	374,000	366,342	358,843	353,817	363,177	329,292
Hawaii	72,424	70,006	67,274	64,787	56,901	41,450	61,877	60,899	59,673	57,902	56,901	48,819
Idaho.........................	58,243	57,096	55,639	54,285	48,683	36,147	50,976	50,759	50,734	49,949	48,683	39,402
Illinois	695,238	670,247	642,769	625,423	568,114	474,520	594,201	583,055	571,228	561,154	568,114	537,369
Indiana......................	298,625	284,344	270,739	252,488	239,321	198,238	255,380	247,222	241,927	227,383	239,321	222,254
Iowa..........................	152,436	146,057	138,378	134,659	119,998	93,312	129,799	126,792	124,011	121,742	119,998	105,338
Kansas......................	138,953	134,767	126,640	121,967	104,869	85,722	118,523	116,907	113,324	110,420	104,869	97,940
Kentucky	173,466	168,019	161,064	152,040	138,772	113,233	146,829	144,779	141,977	135,180	138,772	128,522
Louisiana...................	243,264	237,389	227,373	204,370	196,917	131,289	198,548	195,640	200,944	189,853	196,917	168,033
Maine........................	53,656	52,489	51,343	50,048	45,520	36,438	45,986	45,763	45,564	44,770	45,520	41,715
Maryland....................	317,678	305,175	295,981	284,724	247,241	182,923	274,930	268,418	264,321	255,757	247,241	209,712
Massachusetts...........	403,823	388,575	376,908	360,675	323,314	273,006	353,717	345,961	340,159	327,739	323,314	301,565
Michigan....................	400,504	385,123	367,107	349,195	375,753	337,459	348,867	341,194	329,812	314,260	375,753	372,148
Minnesota..................	294,729	279,987	268,578	257,596	237,813	188,818	252,971	244,305	240,418	233,758	237,813	211,529
Mississippi.................	101,490	97,533	95,763	92,614	81,360	65,625	86,396	84,402	85,363	83,702	81,360	76,050
Missouri	258,832	249,546	243,876	237,774	216,336	180,967	221,702	217,401	216,681	212,591	216,336	204,918
Montana.....................	40,422	38,933	36,521	35,027	30,054	21,633	33,374	32,683	31,918	31,271	30,054	25,816
Nebraska...................	99,557	96,230	90,910	86,323	72,505	57,333	83,393	82,172	80,638	77,625	72,505	65,318
Nevada......................	133,584	129,421	124,838	123,115	114,478	75,895	113,197	111,574	109,610	110,001	114,478	88,043
New Hampshire..........	64,697	63,333	61,147	58,951	53,693	44,161	56,735	56,443	55,242	53,475	53,693	48,814
New Jersey	508,003	493,175	483,007	471,957	430,246	350,110	438,173	432,415	431,409	424,871	430,246	394,422
New Mexico	80,600	79,555	77,686	75,308	67,763	50,294	70,699	70,529	70,785	70,239	67,763	58,461
New York....................	1,205,930	1,169,436	1,136,417	1,080,441	959,867	769,291	1,038,541	1,024,985	1,013,251	974,078	959,867	862,501
North Carolina............	455,973	436,144	426,875	412,912	354,664	281,542	392,905	382,655	380,693	372,219	354,664	316,598
North Dakota..............	46,016	39,992	35,357	32,204	24,670	18,266	38,654	34,092	31,618	29,497	24,670	21,276
Ohio...........................	509,393	490,265	465,679	451,574	444,083	380,895	435,104	425,913	413,991	405,483	444,083	429,017
Oklahoma	160,953	156,058	147,649	142,078	120,529	91,273	138,296	135,454	132,917	132,059	120,529	110,354
Oregon.......................	198,702	188,981	181,523	171,535	143,429	113,180	187,440	180,326	174,165	164,711	143,429	121,134
Pennsylvania..............	600,897	581,256	558,818	540,231	482,200	395,602	511,345	502,769	493,530	482,665	482,200	452,415
Rhode Island..............	50,956	49,423	48,572	47,443	44,189	33,584	43,774	43,168	43,153	42,741	44,189	38,457
South Carolina	176,217	168,716	162,292	157,825	141,877	115,443	150,596	146,669	143,407	139,913	141,877	130,940
South Dakota	42,464	41,667	38,297	37,040	31,549	24,038	35,985	35,898	34,371	34,354	31,549	26,878
Tennessee.................	277,036	263,626	253,602	246,617	224,288	177,540	240,523	232,891	227,360	221,902	224,288	198,052
Texas........................	1,397,369	1,321,005	1,226,714	1,140,218	968,553	731,064	1,211,692	1,156,013	1,116,268	1,071,959	968,553	870,111
Utah..........................	130,486	124,454	118,225	112,995	90,616	69,489	111,808	108,106	105,199	102,863	90,616	79,679
Vermont	27,296	26,545	25,809	24,394	22,743	18,039	23,912	23,639	23,341	22,108	22,743	19,952
Virginia......................	445,876	433,611	422,763	404,005	356,370	261,759	385,772	381,493	377,466	363,730	356,370	298,266
Washington................	375,730	357,056	342,702	332,600	279,333	227,704	325,165	313,783	307,685	300,785	279,333	259,155
West Virginia..............	69,380	66,109	62,732	59,575	51,857	41,386	56,384	54,597	53,575	51,881	51,857	49,564
Wisconsin	261,548	253,349	245,415	237,237	218,689	177,355	225,094	221,874	219,080	212,592	218,689	198,885
Wyoming	38,422	38,190	36,459	34,432	26,250	17,050	31,302	31,231	32,004	32,439	26,250	23,172

[1]For chained (2005) dollar estimates, states will not add to U.S. total.

Table A-43. Science and Engineering Indicators

Geographic area	Employment 2006–2010[1]			Science & Engineering doctorates awarded 2010[2]	Federal R&D obligations[3] (million dollars)		Total R&D expenditures[3] (million dollars)		Industry R&D expenditures[3,4] (million dollars)	
	Engineers	Life and physical scientists	Computer specialists		2009	2007	2008	2007	2009	2007
United States......................	2,269,000	776,935	3,569,860	32,741	138,769	124,768	372,661	359,737	266,884	265,919
Alabama...........................	36,580	7,490	37,370	382	3,023	2,248	4,870	3,289	1,562	1,771
Alaska	6,500	3,900	5,059	42	247	264	269	311	71	58
Arizona............................	51,905	9,315	69,980	572	3,142	2,422	7,010	5,006	4,682	3,846
Arkansas	11,360	4,365	18,285	128	171	178	747	632	709	339
California..........................	324,605	108,730	480,745	4,352	26,989	26,987	81,323	77,608	64,939	64,187
Colorado	53,190	16,285	91,255	548	3,862	2,798	5,810	6,828	3,960	5,223
Connecticut.......................	32,445	11,805	51,620	468	2,365	2,117	11,322	10,228	10,638	9,444
Delaware	5,735	4,720	10,220	158	225	131	1,594	1,607	2,046	1,472
District of Columbia	2,575	3,145	13,400	307	4,268	4,278	5,946	3,862	672	379
Florida.............................	99,690	24,340	162,295	1,410	3,734	4,078	6,515	7,158	4,329	4,569
Georgia	55,840	18,800	111,930	882	1,958	1,686	5,232	4,425	3,905	2,788
Hawaii	7,345	3,100	10,575	124	387	379	663	592	240	218
Idaho..............................	12,150	5,620	13,725	63	388	287	1,375	1,115	1,015	726
Illinois.............................	86,855	28,240	162,780	1,540	2,746	2,145	11,961	14,287	9,188	11,362
Indiana............................	48,825	15,430	50,635	852	1,109	597	6,111	5,980	5,220	4,939
Iowa...............................	20,155	7,730	30,304	456	683	662	2,136	1,882	1,943	1,202
Kansas	22,175	6,325	29,385	261	464	318	2,029	1,697	1,616	1,304
Kentucky	21,885	6,035	28,420	259	319	222	1,463	1,406	986	890
Louisiana	27,695	9,825	19,970	393	406	419	1,193	1,073	416	373
Maine..............................	8,304	3,500	10,785	40	194	379	516	485	530	265
Maryland...........................	54,915	32,455	138,360	874	15,971	11,906	16,605	14,130	4,492	3,665
Massachusetts	65,295	38,400	119,985	1,787	9,047	7,529	20,090	24,557	14,422	19,488
Michigan...........................	110,605	19,635	90,940	1,150	2,427	1,726	15,507	17,402	11,999	15,736
Minnesota	46,035	15,795	83,320	585	1,551	1,387	6,697	7,533	6,880	6,636
Mississippi.........................	13,340	4,670	12,500	212	385	434	808	838	260	279
Missouri	31,645	14,220	62,485	514	1,285	1,221	3,884	3,754	3,136	2,736
Montana	4,863	4,085	6,510	75	171	654	401	859	144	134
Nebraska	8,985	4,565	21,370	194	220	230	988	900	602	489
Nevada	14,235	4,275	17,185	130	558	321	913	794	619	567
New Hampshire....................	16,845	3,530	23,480	131	458	340	2,496	2,146	772	1,814
New Jersey	61,275	31,785	154,755	685	2,492	2,192	20,713	19,552	18,404	17,892
New Mexico	18,340	7,875	17,620	199	3,696	3,478	5,906	5,663	623	568
New York...........................	99,870	38,540	203,455	2,603	6,242	5,368	16,486	15,939	10,919	10,916
North Carolina.....................	55,380	24,890	96,870	1,076	2,022	1,828	8,612	9,204	5,531	6,829
North Dakota......................	3,870	2,490	5,795	77	101	116	511	327	231	126
Ohio...............................	86,670	24,445	117,575	1,269	4,460	3,661	10,164	10,041	6,811	7,265
Oklahoma	21,670	7,210	28,860	294	370	253	1,030	921	509	527
Oregon	30,745	11,150	44,480	308	635	506	4,802	4,333	4,080	3,629
Pennsylvania......................	87,450	38,900	137,595	1,581	4,298	3,360	13,068	13,510	9,989	10,387
Rhode Island......................	8,090	2,850	12,080	211	679	628	1,233	1,081	460	411
South Carolina	33,410	7,560	31,720	274	662	422	2,086	2,291	1,254	1,426
South Dakota	4,064	2,065	6,530	49	79	62	254	240	143	132
Tennessee	37,105	11,230	46,810	468	2,081	1,908	3,871	3,659	1,487	1,638
Texas..............................	190,865	54,080	269,395	2,194	6,031	6,693	20,316	17,853	15,307	13,889
Utah...............................	20,634	6,550	36,105	316	1,169	991	2,522	2,337	2,083	1,764
Vermont	5,534	1,428	7,420	57	151	108	546	534	418	413
Virginia	72,870	19,795	178,450	809	9,381	9,088	11,472	9,473	6,159	4,840
Washington........................	71,475	22,295	115,340	576	4,157	4,751	16,696	15,061	16,471	12,687
West Virginia......................	7,790	3,785	9,635	123	263	219	778	650	349	233
Wisconsin	45,250	15,160	61,595	639	886	671	4,967	4,555	3,616	3,411
Wyoming	4,085	2,545	2,960	44	65	37	154	129	47	37

[1]The employment data represent the state of residence; technicians are included.
[2]Does not include health fields. Data are classified by the state where the doctorate holder resides.
[3]Research and Development. National totals may include data for outlying areas, offices abroad, and/or undistributed funds and may differ from the sum of state totals.
[4]Industrial R&D statistics represent the expenditures in R&D performed by both private and public companies. The reliability varies by state because the sample allocation was not based on geography and several values were modeled or imputed.
NA = Not available

Table A-44.   Employer Establishment Births and Deaths, and Business Bankruptcies

Geographic area	Births of Establishments[1]					Deaths of Establishments					Business bankruptcies[2]				
	2010	2009	2008	2007	2006	2010	2009	2008	2007	2006	2012	2011	2010	2005	2000
United States[3]	646,740	641,759	728,180	905,761	824,921	719,225	813,353	765,160	753,330	702,201	40,075	47,806	56,282	39,201	35,472
Alabama	7,580	7,862	9,219	12,380	10,454	9,472	10,607	9,908	9,483	9,128	549	641	751	331	445
Alaska	1,770	1,809	1,852	2,343	2,116	1,640	1,941	1,998	1,941	1,789	51	58	76	83	118
Arizona	13,286	13,197	15,991	20,336	18,821	16,157	18,919	16,505	14,670	12,408	1,134	1,351	1,636	525	765
Arkansas	5,328	5,467	5,916	7,635	7,024	5,665	6,593	6,349	6,276	6,169	363	424	537	426	261
California	79,161	80,625	90,546	112,236	104,649	91,682	101,698	95,395	93,065	83,407	6,127	7,558	8,814	4,236	4,595
Colorado	15,148	14,894	17,334	20,888	19,025	17,164	18,757	16,994	16,552	15,477	906	1,162	1,361	1,120	373
Connecticut	6,751	6,550	7,908	9,263	8,630	8,020	8,960	8,235	8,513	8,116	372	388	459	156	139
Delaware	2,062	2,073	2,395	2,979	2,632	2,383	2,635	2,572	2,644	2,603	834	645	973	218	2,320
District of Columbia	2,038	2,028	1,973	2,399	2,126	1,808	1,985	1,911	1,978	1,730	55	68	115	46	58
Florida	55,315	52,989	58,121	73,549	69,335	58,701	70,621	68,583	61,984	53,992	3,285	4,016	4,880	1,622	1,447
Georgia	20,286	20,818	24,568	30,703	26,918	24,049	28,565	25,800	23,127	21,393	1,899	2,242	2,650	2,232	1,012
Hawaii	2,403	2,608	2,731	3,559	3,347	2,930	3,079	2,983	3,065	2,434	79	165	156	81	63
Idaho	4,033	3,791	4,862	6,589	6,209	4,818	5,879	5,307	4,430	4,001	230	305	351	141	269
Illinois	25,712	25,150	28,979	35,031	31,508	28,943	32,412	30,087	29,738	28,087	1,905	2,135	2,197	1,042	1,270
Indiana	10,370	10,630	12,444	16,242	14,605	12,260	14,417	13,981	13,884	12,961	689	729	918	758	398
Iowa	5,453	5,420	6,234	7,777	7,597	5,825	6,530	6,792	6,834	6,903	255	356	381	455	214
Kansas	5,458	5,512	6,260	8,168	7,260	6,164	6,735	6,792	6,955	6,998	249	298	329	410	169
Kentucky	6,977	6,969	7,789	9,977	8,829	7,687	8,656	8,410	8,613	7,996	403	480	530	409	355
Louisiana	8,410	8,654	9,612	13,476	10,120	8,556	9,258	9,143	8,856	13,053	486	622	760	718	619
Maine	3,200	2,896	3,528	4,475	4,180	3,411	4,184	4,029	3,807	3,669	178	220	232	144	162
Maryland	11,519	11,367	12,581	15,776	14,927	12,982	14,692	13,973	13,754	12,270	614	658	832	760	677
Massachusetts	13,345	12,365	14,121	17,609	16,463	14,634	16,329	15,446	15,934	14,549	460	529	577	406	393
Michigan	16,369	16,477	19,161	23,893	21,899	20,523	24,138	22,940	23,346	21,398	1,290	1,599	1,876	1,071	577
Minnesota	11,143	11,240	12,639	15,924	15,101	12,394	14,285	14,223	14,484	12,984	596	691	788	1,721	1,492
Mississippi	4,651	4,825	5,514	7,426	6,154	5,218	5,961	5,729	5,603	6,458	323	406	465	200	203
Missouri	13,552	12,729	13,795	17,508	16,127	14,699	15,654	14,922	15,650	16,140	717	639	772	438	369
Montana	2,993	2,916	3,530	4,528	4,262	3,354	4,104	3,614	3,259	3,146	103	115	162	129	141
Nebraska	3,829	3,757	4,229	5,172	4,796	3,772	4,185	4,327	4,420	4,356	166	225	315	296	115
Nevada	6,707	6,757	7,824	9,715	9,097	7,593	8,548	7,725	7,171	6,203	624	989	982	333	332
New Hampshire	2,966	2,863	3,346	4,093	3,890	3,344	3,954	3,703	3,750	3,566	349	479	632	586	302
New Jersey	20,089	19,704	22,661	27,396	26,254	24,024	27,191	25,164	25,421	23,420	1,043	1,215	1,422	765	660
New Mexico	3,586	3,756	4,450	5,592	5,068	4,475	4,776	4,621	4,313	4,199	182	203	279	828	513
New York	49,665	47,381	51,213	56,997	53,634	48,472	52,603	48,980	50,776	48,758	2,192	2,116	2,711	2,112	1,960
North Carolina	19,581	18,184	21,811	28,039	24,570	21,828	25,165	21,876	21,404	19,523	967	1,147	1,409	612	445
North Dakota	1,630	1,517	1,665	2,127	1,908	1,415	1,625	1,600	1,712	1,736	33	47	70	95	92
Ohio	17,535	17,790	20,264	27,186	23,800	21,775	24,872	24,699	25,361	23,471	1,069	1,372	1,779	2,099	1,471
Oklahoma	7,159	7,639	8,773	10,483	9,100	7,877	8,315	8,101	8,332	8,115	311	406	541	944	876
Oregon	9,704	8,960	10,849	13,756	12,477	10,740	12,802	11,159	10,473	9,694	424	549	575	1,160	1,453
Pennsylvania	21,448	21,909	24,703	29,735	27,391	24,314	26,172	25,300	27,402	25,312	1,058	1,208	1,401	1,356	1,455
Rhode Island	2,343	2,050	2,512	3,071	3,012	2,650	3,258	2,973	2,916	2,614	173	144	169	136	74
South Carolina	8,689	8,741	9,959	13,056	11,243	10,222	12,063	10,373	10,024	9,277	309	388	389	176	138
South Dakota	1,990	1,961	2,189	2,758	2,467	1,900	2,156	2,177	2,165	2,251	55	99	100	196	133
Tennessee	10,503	10,835	13,054	16,176	14,200	12,490	14,257	12,813	12,907	12,371	756	961	1,101	574	641
Texas	49,590	50,177	54,842	66,939	57,950	48,786	52,374	50,612	51,816	48,358	2,813	3,513	4,109	3,590	2,592
Utah	7,367	7,070	8,502	10,603	9,507	8,092	9,387	8,007	6,863	6,372	378	597	670	449	451
Vermont	1,534	1,553	1,752	2,227	1,979	1,687	2,100	1,991	2,002	1,849	54	46	69	78	71
Virginia	16,538	17,088	18,651	23,561	22,001	18,384	20,434	19,942	19,074	17,033	736	892	1,104	476	815
Washington	16,286	15,712	19,178	23,484	21,182	18,020	21,303	18,524	18,095	16,685	884	1,124	1,188	786	717
West Virginia	2,506	2,784	3,059	4,106	3,683	3,103	3,394	3,548	3,727	3,742	143	193	235	282	277
Wisconsin	9,626	9,913	11,033	14,288	13,116	11,174	12,840	12,385	12,930	12,193	693	796	930	820	685
Wyoming	1,556	1,797	2,058	2,532	2,278	1,949	1,985	1,939	1,831	1,844	83	83	73	84	47

[1]Births represent an employing unit, which is determined, for the first time, as meeting the definition of "employer" in the state unemployment compensation law or a previously terminated employing unit, which again is determined as meeting the definition of employer.
[2]For the calendar year (12-month period ending December). A business bankruptcy is the legal recognition that a company is insolvent (that is, not able to satisfy creditors or discharge liabilities) and must restructure or completely liquidate under Chapter 7, 9, 11, 12, 13, or 15 of the federal bankruptcy laws.
[3]National total includes data for outlying territories and will differ from sum of state totals.

Table A-45. Employer Firms and Nonemployer Establishments

Geographic area	Firms (thousands)				Employment, 2010 (thousands)			Annual payroll, 2010 (million dollars)			Nonemployer establishments[1]			
			By employment-size of enterprise, 2007		Total	By employment-size of enterprise		Total	By employment-size of enterprise		Number (thousands)		Receipts (million dollars)	
	2010	2000	Fewer than 20 employees	Fewer than 500 employees		Fewer than 20 employees	Fewer than 500 employees		Fewer than 20 employees	Fewer than 500 employees	2010	2005	2010	2005
United States......................	5,734.5	5,652.5	5,160.4	5,717.3	111,970.1	20,573.8	54,996.7	4,940,983	721,827	2,106,533	22,110.6	20,392.1	950,814	951,206
Alabama	75.5	79.9	64.2	73.2	1,568.1	284.4	768.3	57,448	8,578	25,631	320.6	282.6	12,111	12,405
Alaska	16.5	15.9	14.4	15.9	254.7	56.7	135.4	12,821	2,497	5,940	53.3	50.9	2,412	2,125
Arizona	102.2	93.0	88.2	99.2	2,065.2	338.1	926.0	84,030	11,339	32,552	396.0	358.1	16,864	17,982
Arkansas	51.1	52.4	43.8	49.4	965.5	183.7	482.6	33,735	5,161	14,336	192.0	186.8	7,499	7,767
California	690.5	664.6	615.8	685.0	12,536.4	2,396.1	6,323.5	635,620	97,386	273,208	2,814.4	2,609.3	138,315	142,439
Colorado	125.8	116.2	111.5	122.8	1,955.3	395.2	961.4	89,245	14,135	37,676	426.4	401.1	18,688	18,551
Connecticut...........................	72.7	78.5	62.2	70.6	1,437.0	261.8	713.6	79,919	11,179	33,942	255.8	252.0	14,243	15,074
Delaware	19.7	20.2	15.9	18.3	359.0	63.5	168.9	17,167	2,438	6,834	53.9	52.3	2,792	2,772
District of Columbia	16.9	16.3	12.5	15.6	463.1	55.5	217.1	30,987	3,621	13,238	46.0	39.5	2,230	1,898
Florida...................................	400.8	354.0	366.8	396.5	6,626.6	1,225.8	2,840.1	252,973	41,504	101,247	1,686.1	1,473.4	68,162	72,084
Georgia	170.2	160.4	148.5	166.4	3,315.3	568.4	1,483.9	137,539	18,888	53,141	771.2	657.3	28,043	29,640
Hawaii	25.4	24.3	21.5	24.5	478.8	92.8	258.9	17,542	3,050	8,802	92.1	87.7	4,066	4,026
Idaho	36.7	32.2	32.1	35.5	487.9	123.6	281.5	16,236	3,345	8,121	112.3	106.3	4,269	4,527
Illinois	253.6	254.1	221.2	249.2	4,980.0	849.4	2,388.7	235,718	32,406	99,709	903.0	835.2	35,305	35,032
Indiana	111.0	116.3	94.6	108.1	2,400.4	409.9	1,156.6	90,399	12,182	38,419	380.1	363.9	13,839	14,091
Iowa	63.4	65.6	54.4	61.6	1,253.1	228.7	643.5	44,905	6,461	20,573	201.4	192.9	7,607	7,055
Kansas	59.2	61.6	50.0	57.2	1,127.2	208.7	594.6	42,686	6,232	19,692	183.6	179.0	7,326	7,243
Kentucky	69.6	72.3	58.9	67.2	1,456.8	258.3	696.7	52,247	7,331	21,939	272.5	263.7	10,454	10,714
Louisiana	81.3	81.7	68.9	79.2	1,599.6	306.9	871.4	62,266	9,903	30,569	340.6	269.8	14,084	10,868
Maine.....................................	33.8	34.1	29.7	32.8	480.9	111.9	282.5	17,279	3,426	9,177	110.4	114.0	4,477	4,750
Maryland................................	108.2	106.0	92.7	105.6	2,075.5	381.0	1,071.7	97,807	14,845	46,131	424.2	400.0	17,833	17,572
Massachusetts......................	137.4	148.2	118.9	134.4	2,928.5	486.3	1,357.4	158,404	20,856	64,794	472.5	471.3	23,388	24,234
Michigan	174.3	193.9	152.5	171.4	3,288.5	626.5	1,699.8	138,810	21,295	62,850	679.8	638.5	25,659	26,708
Minnesota	117.7	116.2	101.6	115.2	2,358.0	400.5	1,180.7	105,548	13,271	42,693	381.8	373.4	15,550	15,532
Mississippi............................	45.8	48.3	39.1	44.2	882.2	170.4	437.0	28,607	4,633	12,934	196.2	163.8	7,299	6,911
Missouri	117.8	118.1	101.9	115.0	2,292.6	405.1	1,110.3	88,577	12,149	36,950	390.2	375.4	15,298	15,466
Montana	31.4	28.0	28.0	30.6	338.4	105.5	231.6	10,716	2,831	6,649	83.7	80.9	3,324	3,215
Nebraska...............................	42.0	41.4	35.9	40.6	769.4	146.7	391.4	28,033	4,150	12,479	123.9	116.2	4,653	4,215
Nevada..................................	47.4	40.3	39.7	45.3	1,003.0	152.7	418.4	37,910	5,663	15,177	177.2	163.5	8,796	9,779
New Hampshire......................	31.0	32.1	26.3	29.8	562.5	110.8	284.9	24,224	4,135	11,208	102.8	106.6	5,164	5,662
New Jersey	193.7	202.2	171.2	190.5	3,367.2	654.6	1,689.3	178,657	26,629	75,106	604.7	573.1	32,500	32,092
New Mexico	35.7	35.5	30.1	34.1	600.2	127.1	330.7	21,319	3,805	10,602	120.5	116.6	4,434	4,473
New York...............................	444.9	424.8	401.1	440.7	7,266.2	1,443.7	3,737.7	418,438	59,562	177,641	1,575.8	1,443.5	71,776	67,082
North Carolina......................	168.9	163.6	147.4	165.5	3,234.6	594.2	1,545.4	125,174	18,183	50,801	640.7	583.5	24,682	25,128
North Dakota.........................	18.2	17.2	15.2	17.4	294.9	64.8	182.5	10,543	1,938	5,758	47.8	44.1	2,021	1,689
Ohio.......................................	190.2	212.5	162.5	186.5	4,352.5	719.6	2,074.8	174,516	22,875	72,004	730.4	693.7	28,739	28,560
Oklahoma	72.0	70.2	62.2	70.0	1,241.2	256.1	673.4	46,094	7,810	22,140	263.0	256.4	11,313	11,307
Oregon	88.0	85.1	77.4	85.9	1,351.2	309.8	750.3	54,368	9,231	25,422	258.8	246.1	11,019	11,274
Pennsylvania.........................	231.2	237.5	199.8	227.3	4,976.2	861.7	2,419.0	211,638	28,663	89,171	762.4	731.0	34,263	33,547
Rhode Island	24.6	25.2	20.9	23.5	399.0	82.7	221.0	16,832	2,945	8,298	71.9	69.3	3,113	3,153
South Carolina	78.9	78.4	67.8	76.5	1,502.9	283.7	727.8	52,548	8,139	22,323	295.6	259.6	11,400	11,782
South Dakota	21.6	20.6	18.5	20.9	329.2	78.7	203.9	10,843	2,115	5,971	60.2	55.5	2,376	2,063
Tennessee............................	98.0	102.4	82.9	95.0	2,264.0	366.8	1,017.6	87,536	11,533	35,941	465.5	422.8	19,008	19,916
Texas.....................................	394.4	369.0	343.0	389.1	8,785.2	1,456.0	4,076.2	386,654	52,503	155,421	1,934.5	1,686.3	85,935	81,313
Utah	57.7	46.2	49.9	55.8	1,021.1	183.4	491.9	38,022	5,642	16,498	192.0	175.1	8,005	8,008
Vermont	18.6	19.1	16.1	17.9	264.1	64.2	157.7	9,308	2,024	5,401	59.9	59.6	2,304	2,378
Virginia	149.3	139.7	129.3	146.0	2,998.3	530.3	1,437.5	139,059	18,895	58,841	510.3	469.9	21,157	20,705
Washington............................	144.4	138.2	127.6	141.6	2,326.7	506.3	1,249.6	111,399	16,995	48,430	405.3	386.9	18,134	17,598
West Virginia	29.6	33.5	25.0	28.4	560.5	113.6	297.7	19,324	2,966	8,845	90.1	89.9	3,153	3,153
Wisconsin	110.4	115.6	94.0	108.0	2,320.7	410.0	1,201.8	90,916	12,496	40,591	331.7	322.0	13,829	13,919
Wyoming	17.6	15.9	15.3	16.9	205.0	61.3	132.9	8,398	1,986	4,720	45.6	41.9	1,901	1,729

[1]Nonemployer business defined as a firm with no payroll or paid employees.

Table A-46. Private Nonfarm Establishments, Employment, and Payroll

Geographic area	Establishments[1]							Employment[1,2] (thousands)						Annual payroll[1] (billion dollars)	
	2010	2005	Net change, 2005–2010	By employment-size class of establishment, 2010				2010	2005	By employment-size class of establishment, 2010				2010	2005
				Under 20	20 to 99	100 to 499	500 or more			Under 20	20 to 99	100 to 499	500 or more		
United States	7,396,628	7,499,702	-103,074	6,407,787	823,778	147,750	17,313	111,970	116,317	28,958	32,730	27,718	22,564	4,941	4,483
Alabama	99,251	101,976	-2,725	85,071	11,845	2,078	257	1,568	1,668	423	465	401	279	57	53
Alaska	19,985	19,808	177	17,744	1,876	318	47	255	231	77	73	62	44	13	10
Arizona	131,849	131,651	198	113,649	15,106	2,751	343	2,065	2,160	512	596	525	433	84	76
Arkansas	65,158	66,039	-881	56,394	7,381	1,233	150	965	1,017	268	287	239	171	34	30
California	849,875	860,866	-10,991	737,169	95,031	15,819	1,856	12,536	13,382	3,238	3,768	2,915	2,616	636	588
Colorado	151,973	151,070	903	134,726	14,495	2,474	278	1,955	1,936	548	571	461	375	89	76
Connecticut	89,234	93,561	-4,327	76,642	10,426	1,970	196	1,437	1,530	360	413	363	301	80	76
Delaware	24,290	25,319	-1,029	21,133	2,629	464	64	359	393	93	104	88	74	17	17
District of Columbia	21,502	20,481	1,021	17,683	3,038	699	82	463	440	86	124	135	118	31	25
Florida	491,150	504,662	-13,512	438,508	43,493	8,208	941	6,627	7,107	1,714	1,740	1,511	1,661	253	239
Georgia	217,099	220,528	-3,429	187,814	24,300	4,463	522	3,315	3,489	835	970	838	673	138	129
Hawaii	31,939	32,244	-305	27,511	3,741	615	72	479	491	132	151	117	78	18	16
Idaho	43,450	43,346	104	38,994	3,852	540	64	488	519	169	146	99	74	16	15
Illinois	314,171	318,927	-4,756	271,464	35,018	6,843	846	4,980	5,236	1,193	1,410	1,274	1,103	236	217
Indiana	145,019	149,871	-4,852	123,586	17,697	3,348	388	2,400	2,611	605	710	628	458	90	88
Iowa	80,801	82,087	-1,286	69,894	9,125	1,586	196	1,253	1,261	335	366	311	242	45	39
Kansas	74,301	76,173	-1,872	64,015	8,612	1,513	161	1,127	1,116	301	342	289	195	43	37
Kentucky	90,771	92,176	-1,405	77,573	10,895	2,084	219	1,457	1,514	383	427	396	250	52	48
Louisiana	103,365	102,790	575	88,081	12,980	2,069	235	1,600	1,618	438	517	377	268	62	51
Maine	40,571	41,933	-1,362	36,111	3,783	614	63	481	497	155	146	112	67	17	16
Maryland	134,579	138,481	-3,902	115,075	16,274	2,931	299	2,076	2,168	528	651	532	363	98	89
Massachusetts	169,790	175,291	-5,501	145,673	19,562	4,090	465	2,929	2,996	672	781	765	711	158	141
Michigan	219,119	237,523	-18,404	189,935	24,244	4,466	474	3,288	3,797	883	962	831	612	139	148
Minnesota	145,464	150,231	-4,767	125,042	16,736	3,290	396	2,358	2,431	566	672	621	499	106	97
Mississippi	59,300	60,542	-1,242	51,435	6,673	1,060	132	882	927	251	261	205	165	29	26
Missouri	149,903	154,306	-4,403	129,580	16,969	2,992	362	2,293	2,425	592	676	567	457	89	82
Montana	36,011	35,736	275	32,679	2,968	337	27	338	327	136	114	59	29	11	9
Nebraska	51,886	51,440	446	45,087	5,719	961	119	769	773	207	225	188	150	28	24
Nevada	59,207	58,561	646	51,155	6,667	1,181	204	1,003	1,089	232	266	223	282	38	39
New Hampshire	37,452	39,224	-1,772	32,485	4,139	751	77	563	562	152	162	135	114	24	21
New Jersey	228,937	242,128	-13,191	200,035	23,731	4,646	525	3,367	3,595	851	949	865	702	179	166
New Mexico	44,221	45,006	-785	38,417	4,951	788	65	600	595	185	192	145	78	21	18
New York	519,504	514,265	5,239	459,997	49,247	8,933	1,327	7,266	7,417	1,859	1,945	1,724	1,739	418	371
North Carolina	218,104	216,994	1,110	187,798	25,689	4,152	465	3,235	3,410	867	1,017	777	573	125	116
North Dakota	21,832	21,061	771	18,883	2,519	404	26	295	270	89	100	78	28	11	8
Ohio	253,491	270,968	-17,477	214,062	32,526	6,210	693	4,352	4,763	1,061	1,310	1,139	842	175	168
Oklahoma	90,050	88,548	1,502	78,044	10,266	1,575	165	1,241	1,220	361	403	302	175	46	38
Oregon	107,397	108,571	-1,174	94,727	10,895	1,602	173	1,351	1,410	429	420	295	207	54	50
Pennsylvania	297,023	303,333	-6,310	253,251	36,167	6,790	815	4,976	5,083	1,221	1,450	1,286	1,019	212	190
Rhode Island	28,521	30,331	-1,810	24,891	3,024	551	55	399	442	110	119	98	72	17	16
South Carolina	102,045	103,416	-1,371	88,352	11,543	1,933	217	1,503	1,585	419	457	367	260	53	49
South Dakota	25,622	25,205	417	22,572	2,603	408	39	329	311	105	101	77	46	11	9
Tennessee	131,582	133,098	-1,516	111,202	16,761	3,272	347	2,264	2,379	558	666	621	419	88	81
Texas	522,146	497,758	24,388	443,599	65,240	11,879	1,428	8,785	8,305	2,133	2,604	2,270	1,779	387	316
Utah	68,820	65,549	3,271	60,074	7,301	1,281	164	1,021	975	254	289	245	234	38	31
Vermont	21,451	22,273	-822	19,205	1,919	293	34	264	262	84	73	52	55	9	8
Virginia	193,042	193,067	-25	165,473	23,078	4,011	480	2,998	3,060	772	920	758	548	139	122
Washington	175,914	175,658	256	155,187	17,441	3,016	270	2,327	2,316	689	683	548	407	111	95
West Virginia	38,676	40,735	-2,059	33,463	4,410	731	72	560	565	173	173	139	75	19	16
Wisconsin	139,554	145,159	-5,605	118,377	17,475	3,302	400	2,321	2,449	573	698	616	433	91	86
Wyoming	20,231	19,736	495	18,270	1,718	225	18	205	192	80	64	44	17	8	6

[1]Data provided by County Business Patterns is based on the North American Industry Classification System (NAICS). Data for 2005 is based on NAICS 2002. Data for 2010 is based on NAICS 2007.
[2]Employment is measured in March.

Table A-47. Foreign Direct Investment in the United States and U.S. Exports

| Geographic area | U.S. Foreign Majority-owned Affliates[1] | | | | | | U.S. exports[2] (million dollars) | | | | | U.S. agriculture exports[3] (million dollars) | | |
| | Number of affiliates with assets, sales, or net income greater than $15 million[4] | | | Employment of affiliates[5] (thousands) | | | 2012 | | | 2010 | 2005 | 2011 | 2010 | 2005 |
	2010	2009	2008	2010	2009	2008	Total exports	Rank	Percent change 2005–2012					
United States	4,596	4,594	4,330	5,270.4	5,290.3	5,636.2	1,547,138	(X)	117.5	1,278,115	711,401	136,374	115,820	63,182
Alabama	538	538	542	81.2	77.7	80.5	19,526	21	107.5	15,505	9,408	1,349	1,047	734
Alaska	139	136	132	13.6	13.0	14.2	4,596	40	518.4	4,152	743	12	12	9
Arizona	725	705	709	73.1	74.3	76.3	18,357	23	70.1	15,652	10,795	1,692	1,277	898
Arkansas	410	413	406	34.8	32.8	35.5	7,621	35	114.0	5,156	3,562	3,481	3,088	1,893
California	1,941	1,936	1,910	567.0	562.7	600.5	161,700	2	90.0	143,269	85,108	17,844	15,021	9,467
Colorado	737	732	732	77.3	81.6	85.1	8,164	34	62.1	6,670	5,037	2,198	1,660	952
Connecticut	691	684	674	101.2	101.5	106.6	15,866	26	85.9	16,033	8,536	258	206	182
Delaware	316	317	322	25.2	29.1	31.6	5,157	39	134.8	4,965	2,196	265	215	136
District of Columbia	293	301	289	19.6	19.6	15.6	2,015	47	197.7	1,501	677	(X)	(X)	(X)
Florida	1,148	1,143	1,146	223.6	235.2	255.6	66,398	6	147.7	55,227	26,806	3,085	2,727	1,885
Georgia	1,091	1,078	1,075	183.4	170.1	179.6	35,892	12	100.4	28,704	17,909	3,195	2,455	1,456
Hawaii	268	266	264	26.2	26.7	27.6	726	51	-17.2	685	877	499	434	222
Idaho	284	291	298	13.7	13.9	18.0	6,113	38	126.1	5,150	2,703	2,170	1,563	918
Illinois	1,259	1,271	1,253	245.9	251.8	273.1	68,026	5	119.2	49,767	31,041	8,238	7,206	3,428
Indiana	725	719	751	133.6	132.1	140.4	34,385	13	75.4	28,670	19,602	4,655	4,133	1,823
Iowa	403	407	398	43.9	45.4	48.8	14,604	27	119.4	10,895	6,655	10,577	9,124	4,178
Kansas	495	494	506	54.8	55.5	55.6	11,660	31	100.4	9,927	5,819	5,265	4,924	2,375
Kentucky	572	586	612	89.5	86.0	94.9	22,092	19	74.4	19,320	12,671	2,434	2,144	1,466
Louisiana	487	491	495	51.7	49.1	50.6	63,156	7	453.1	41,348	11,419	1,574	1,361	767
Maine	303	294	296	30.4	29.9	30.3	3,058	44	72.4	3,148	1,774	215	181	128
Maryland	688	686	682	99.2	103.5	108.6	11,781	29	97.7	10,168	5,958	654	531	290
Massachusetts	872	875	876	177.5	182.9	184.8	25,549	16	31.5	26,256	19,435	226	188	118
Michigan	926	929	938	141.7	138.9	150.2	56,902	8	76.1	44,504	32,316	2,777	2,294	1,067
Minnesota	680	676	694	89.3	92.8	97.0	20,565	20	58.1	18,929	13,004	6,738	5,995	2,604
Mississippi	362	368	382	25.9	26.9	28.1	11,779	30	246.6	8,267	3,399	2,017	1,625	1,001
Missouri	635	621	630	79.9	84.0	92.7	13,910	28	49.4	12,920	9,308	3,879	3,510	1,683
Montana	212	203	197	(D)	6.8	8.0	1,573	48	224.4	1,422	485	1,632	1,162	685
Nebraska	305	315	317	24.2	24.8	26.4	7,449	36	204.3	5,804	2,448	6,930	5,520	2,595
Nevada	456	444	460	37.9	34.1	38.0	10,190	33	225.2	5,911	3,134	158	126	84
New Hampshire	413	418	419	39.7	39.3	40.4	3,485	43	65.6	4,368	2,105	64	56	34
New Jersey	1,036	1,036	1,024	223.4	227.2	239.0	37,035	11	130.7	32,156	16,054	468	422	259
New Mexico	291	291	292	14.9	15.8	17.6	2,980	45	28.5	1,562	2,319	1,028	825	462
New York	1,562	1,563	1,505	388.5	390.4	410.6	79,189	3	135.4	67,686	33,646	1,312	1,103	566
North Carolina	886	877	876	188.2	185.6	202.4	28,747	15	70.0	24,817	16,908	3,735	3,233	1,976
North Dakota	177	182	171	11.6	11.1	12.0	4,288	42	343.4	2,522	967	3,948	3,616	1,641
Ohio	1,016	1,014	1,013	206.5	212.5	229.4	48,535	9	55.9	41,437	31,136	3,734	3,275	1,550
Oklahoma	438	442	441	36.0	34.9	37.9	6,576	37	94.1	5,360	3,389	1,987	1,721	1,109
Oregon	578	583	588	41.8	42.9	47.6	18,300	24	93.0	17,683	9,481	1,976	1,460	1,172
Pennsylvania	965	970	953	251.0	253.6	272.8	38,869	10	100.7	34,826	19,368	1,645	1,403	812
Rhode Island	297	299	289	26.0	24.2	22.0	2,376	46	158.1	1,946	921	24	21	15
South Carolina	603	599	616	104.3	101.5	112.3	25,247	17	155.1	20,316	9,897	959	775	445
South Dakota	177	175	171	7.2	7.3	8.0	1,550	49	80.3	1,263	860	3,644	2,923	1,418
Tennessee	699	698	713	112.5	119.8	129.7	31,126	14	111.6	25,924	14,710	1,627	1,350	819
Texas	1,457	1,476	1,449	428.1	413.3	444.8	265,352	1	154.7	206,643	104,175	7,553	6,986	3,980
Utah	438	437	441	29.0	28.9	33.4	18,939	22	269.7	13,572	5,123	462	359	241
Vermont	195	187	190	11.0	10.7	10.6	4,306	41	50.2	4,376	2,866	150	121	64
Virginia	750	756	763	140.8	151.3	163.4	18,239	25	90.0	17,090	9,598	1,033	836	548
Washington	800	803	804	92.3	93.5	93.9	75,525	4	146.4	53,244	30,652	3,307	2,651	1,618
West Virginia	283	288	284	24.8	22.4	22.2	11,362	32	341.0	6,427	2,576	121	102	63
Wisconsin	626	623	622	76.0	72.7	82.0	23,097	18	73.7	19,783	13,298	3,176	2,579	1,207
Wyoming	148	156	150	7.2	8.8	10.8	1,421	50	142.2	983	587	404	276	142

[1]For calendar year. U.S. business enterprises that are more than 50 percent owned by foreign direct investors.
[2]For calendar year. National total includes Puerto Rico and US Virgin Islands. Foreign Trade Zone shipments are included in the U.S. total and distributed among individual states and territories. Unreported and estimated shipments are included in national totals.
[3]For calendar year. The U.S. totals include unallocated exports not included in states.
[4]National total includes data for territories as well as unspecified data (aircraft, railroad rolling stock, satellites, undersea cable, and trucks engaged in interstate transportation) and will differ from sum of state totals.
[5]National total includes data for territories and will differ from sum of state totals.
(X) = Not applicable

Table A-48. Farms and Farm Earnings

Geographic Area	Farms (USDA)[1] (as of June 1)												Farm earnings (BEA)[2] (million dollars)			
	Number (thousands)				Land in farms (million acres)				Average acreage per farm							
	2012	2010	2005	2000	2012	2010	2005	2000	2012	2010	2005	2000	2012	2010	2005	2000
United States	2,170.0	2,200.9	2,101.0	2,172.1	914.0	920.0	933.4	943.0	421	418	444	434	99,737	75,843	71,394	52,468
Alabama	46.5	48.5	43.5	47.0	8.9	9.0	8.6	9.0	190	186	198	191	505	819	1,775	957
Alaska	0.7	0.7	0.6	0.6	0.9	0.9	0.9	0.9	1,294	1,294	1,406	1,586	10	9	14	21
Arizona	15.5	15.5	10.1	7.5	26.1	26.1	26.2	26.7	1,684	1,684	2,594	3,560	877	702	967	807
Arkansas	47.8	49.3	47.0	48.0	13.5	13.7	14.4	14.6	282	278	306	304	1,765	1,306	1,883	1,699
California	80.5	81.7	76.5	87.5	25.4	25.4	26.4	27.8	316	311	345	318	15,618	13,089	10,768	8,872
Colorado	36.3	36.1	30.5	29.0	31.3	31.2	30.7	31.6	862	864	1,007	1,090	1,027	973	1,140	775
Connecticut	4.9	4.9	4.2	3.9	0.4	0.4	0.4	0.4	82	82	86	92	188	170	200	226
Delaware	2.5	2.5	2.3	2.6	0.5	0.5	0.5	0.6	196	198	226	223	126	151	292	148
District of Columbia	(X)	(X)	(X)	(X)	(X)	(X)	(X)	(X)	(X)	(X)	(X)	(X)	(X)	(X)	(X)	(X)
Florida	47.5	47.5	42.5	44.0	9.3	9.3	10.0	10.3	195	195	235	234	2,404	2,250	2,701	2,589
Georgia	47.0	47.4	49.0	50.0	10.4	10.3	10.5	11.1	221	217	214	222	2,536	1,847	2,478	1,842
Hawaii	7.5	7.5	5.5	5.7	1.1	1.1	1.3	1.4	148	148	236	253	264	265	259	241
Idaho	24.5	25.7	25.0	24.5	11.4	11.4	11.8	11.9	465	444	472	486	2,310	1,594	1,209	1,012
Illinois	74.3	76.0	72.5	78.0	26.6	26.7	27.3	27.7	358	351	377	355	3,981	3,697	1,830	1,794
Indiana	60.0	62.0	59.0	64.0	14.7	14.8	15.0	15.5	245	239	254	242	2,311	2,010	1,386	864
Iowa	92.2	92.4	89.0	95.0	30.7	30.8	31.6	32.8	333	333	355	345	7,936	4,746	3,982	2,443
Kansas	65.5	65.5	64.5	64.0	46.0	46.2	47.2	47.5	702	705	732	742	2,648	2,165	1,943	1,007
Kentucky	85.5	85.7	84.0	90.0	14.0	14.0	13.8	13.6	164	163	164	151	976	676	1,580	1,485
Louisiana	29.0	30.0	26.8	29.5	8.0	8.1	7.8	8.1	274	268	291	275	1,425	863	714	619
Maine	8.1	8.1	7.1	6.8	1.4	1.4	1.4	1.3	167	167	193	187	209	199	187	207
Maryland	12.8	12.8	12.1	12.4	2.1	2.1	2.0	2.1	160	160	169	169	496	331	408	415
Massachusetts	7.7	7.7	6.1	6.1	0.5	0.5	0.5	0.6	68	68	85	93	150	134	126	131
Michigan	54.7	54.9	53.0	52.0	9.9	10.0	10.1	10.4	181	182	191	200	2,702	1,780	1,060	602
Minnesota	79.4	81.0	79.6	79.0	26.8	26.9	27.5	28.6	338	332	345	362	6,152	4,239	3,089	1,437
Mississippi	42.3	42.4	42.2	43.0	11.2	11.2	11.1	11.1	264	263	262	258	1,794	1,250	1,250	788
Missouri	106.0	108.0	105.0	109.0	29.0	29.1	30.1	30.0	274	269	287	275	1,608	1,675	1,419	778
Montana	28.6	29.4	28.0	27.6	58.8	60.8	60.1	56.7	2,056	2,068	2,146	2,054	746	444	599	256
Nebraska	46.7	47.2	48.0	54.0	45.5	45.6	45.7	46.4	974	966	952	859	4,869	3,472	2,926	1,441
Nevada	3.0	3.1	3.0	3.0	5.8	5.9	6.3	6.8	1,980	1,903	2,100	2,267	178	140	135	104
New Hampshire	4.2	4.2	3.4	3.1	0.5	0.5	0.5	0.4	113	113	132	135	30	32	51	44
New Jersey	10.2	10.3	9.8	9.6	0.7	0.7	0.8	0.8	72	71	81	86	396	353	346	338
New Mexico	23.8	21.0	17.5	15.2	43.9	43.2	44.5	44.0	1,845	2,057	2,543	2,895	1,367	991	834	541
New York	36.0	36.3	35.6	38.0	7.0	7.0	7.6	7.7	194	193	212	203	1,605	1,259	1,066	774
North Carolina	50.0	52.4	50.0	57.0	8.5	8.6	8.9	9.2	170	164	178	161	2,541	2,549	3,148	2,965
North Dakota	31.6	31.9	30.3	30.3	39.6	39.6	39.4	39.4	1,253	1,241	1,300	1,300	3,644	2,662	1,208	1,090
Ohio	73.4	74.7	76.5	80.0	13.6	13.7	14.3	14.9	185	183	187	186	2,885	1,976	1,145	1,199
Oklahoma	85.5	86.5	83.0	85.0	34.8	35.2	33.7	34.0	407	407	406	400	1,442	720	1,322	827
Oregon	38.1	38.8	40.0	40.0	16.5	16.4	17.1	17.2	433	423	428	430	1,407	1,115	1,251	822
Pennsylvania	62.1	63.2	58.2	59.0	7.7	7.8	7.7	7.7	124	123	132	131	1,773	1,191	1,342	1,097
Rhode Island	1.2	1.2	0.9	0.7	0.1	0.1	0.1	0.1	57	57	71	86	18	18	23	17
South Carolina	26.7	27.0	24.3	24.0	4.8	4.9	4.8	4.7	180	181	199	196	349	434	649	525
South Dakota	31.0	31.8	31.4	32.5	43.7	43.7	43.7	44.0	1,408	1,374	1,392	1,354	3,521	2,387	1,731	1,336
Tennessee	76.0	78.3	84.0	90.0	10.8	10.9	11.6	11.7	142	139	138	130	527	164	546	321
Texas	244.7	247.5	230.0	226.0	128.0	130.4	129.8	130.0	523	527	564	575	5,266	3,785	5,005	3,335
Utah	16.4	16.6	15.2	15.5	11.1	11.1	11.6	11.6	677	669	763	748	230	205	287	205
Vermont	7.0	7.0	6.3	6.8	1.2	1.2	1.3	1.3	174	174	198	197	206	165	200	150
Virginia	46.2	47.3	47.0	49.0	8.1	8.1	8.5	8.7	174	170	181	178	598	277	594	564
Washington	39.3	39.5	34.5	40.0	14.8	14.8	15.1	15.7	377	375	438	393	3,172	2,557	1,875	1,736
West Virginia	22.1	23.0	20.8	20.5	3.6	3.7	3.6	3.6	164	159	173	176	-71	-67	13	18
Wisconsin	76.8	78.0	76.5	77.0	15.0	15.2	15.4	16.2	195	195	201	210	2,805	1,944	1,671	880
Wyoming	10.8	11.0	9.2	9.2	30.2	30.2	34.4	34.6	2,796	2,745	3,739	3,761	216	126	232	123

[1] U.S. Department of Agriculture.
[2] Bureau of Economic Analysis. The estimates of earnings for 2000–2006 are based on the 2002 North American Industry Classification System (NAICS). The estimates for 2007 forward are based on the 2007 NAICS. All numbers provided are in current dollars (not adjusted for inflation).
(X) = Not applicable

Table A-49. Farm Finances and Income

Geographic Area	Value of agricultural sector productions[1] (million dollars)				Farm marketings[2] (million dollars)				Net farm income[3] (million dollars)			
	2011	2010	2005	2000	2011	2010	2005	2000	2011	2010	2005	2000
United States	418,051	353,250	274,109	218,446	374,252	321,149	240,898	192,098	117,908	80,404	78,763	50,685
Alabama	5,675	5,259	4,877	3,720	4,850	4,623	4,189	3,184	547	841	2,073	1,128
Alaska	40	39	46	60	32	32	36	53	9	10	18	23
Arizona	5,080	3,938	3,731	2,746	4,314	3,440	3,174	2,350	1,581	804	1,190	767
Arkansas	9,165	8,462	6,838	5,290	8,416	7,848	6,470	4,547	1,423	1,281	2,074	1,722
California	47,423	41,123	34,562	27,185	43,544	38,003	32,298	25,185	16,305	10,950	9,853	5,567
Colorado	8,176	6,907	6,374	5,150	7,076	6,079	5,474	4,673	1,670	1,170	1,376	816
Connecticut	665	623	603	597	560	515	507	505	144	114	183	194
Delaware	1,232	1,186	1,073	834	1,081	1,058	938	732	197	189	390	160
District of Columbia	(X)	(X)	(X)	(X)	(X)	(X)	(X)	(X)	(X)	(X)	(X)	(X)
Florida	8,949	8,335	8,053	7,101	8,262	7,842	7,449	6,780	2,261	2,056	3,117	2,719
Georgia	9,824	8,663	7,280	5,806	8,354	7,564	6,194	5,032	2,463	2,191	2,900	2,074
Hawaii	819	770	655	567	720	690	584	524	231	239	175	117
Idaho	8,020	6,347	4,994	3,854	7,328	5,890	4,517	3,395	2,441	1,587	1,180	956
Illinois	21,156	16,285	9,207	7,960	19,820	15,981	8,980	7,026	6,100	3,387	1,602	1,691
Indiana	12,892	10,437	6,370	5,304	11,836	9,736	5,358	4,529	3,804	2,364	1,534	952
Iowa	32,657	24,563	16,066	11,733	29,892	24,031	14,487	10,778	10,813	4,983	4,043	2,434
Kansas	17,312	15,024	11,213	8,741	15,859	14,726	10,150	8,040	5,191	2,844	2,492	1,136
Kentucky	6,127	5,210	4,892	4,542	4,918	4,453	3,987	3,642	1,509	913	2,027	1,751
Louisiana	3,801	3,359	2,401	1,984	3,461	3,082	2,175	1,655	1,192	908	742	557
Maine	801	751	616	635	718	627	543	573	236	232	184	189
Maryland	2,499	2,192	1,890	1,741	2,091	1,835	1,520	1,443	551	369	560	434
Massachusetts	660	626	538	500	516	473	408	395	129	106	120	96
Michigan	9,030	7,365	5,107	3,939	8,046	6,632	4,231	3,354	3,348	2,033	1,243	428
Minnesota	19,777	17,031	11,256	8,413	18,536	15,822	9,444	7,368	5,785	4,639	3,381	1,407
Mississippi	6,288	5,730	4,718	3,331	5,358	4,961	4,171	2,715	1,255	1,303	1,963	811
Missouri	11,064	9,274	6,764	5,511	9,710	8,491	5,951	4,561	3,333	2,207	1,973	1,056
Montana	4,156	3,678	3,000	1,993	3,542	3,043	2,290	1,838	847	749	836	290
Nebraska	23,767	18,126	12,903	9,530	21,815	17,116	11,593	8,956	7,457	3,993	2,972	1,453
Nevada	809	676	578	461	680	559	475	387	224	150	149	103
New Hampshire	245	225	212	182	189	175	170	153	29	24	52	30
New Jersey	1,311	1,218	1,059	960	1,121	1,044	909	814	387	316	332	262
New Mexico	4,236	3,493	2,901	2,214	4,106	3,270	2,608	2,108	1,347	1,026	876	494
New York	5,717	4,985	3,898	3,401	5,261	4,416	3,562	3,129	1,776	1,187	1,042	560
North Carolina	11,941	10,614	9,107	8,428	10,543	9,730	8,147	7,309	3,007	3,326	3,743	3,347
North Dakota	8,238	7,661	4,482	3,403	7,337	6,919	3,883	2,771	2,171	2,618	1,194	1,043
Ohio	10,949	8,823	6,168	5,409	9,648	7,987	5,157	4,404	3,886	2,247	1,483	1,449
Oklahoma	7,462	6,779	6,230	4,688	7,056	6,156	5,428	4,251	1,510	1,216	1,735	1,057
Oregon	5,572	4,591	4,592	3,504	4,624	3,739	3,670	3,036	1,029	520	1,179	407
Pennsylvania	7,619	6,674	5,578	4,904	6,690	5,833	4,818	4,131	2,042	1,397	1,706	1,120
Rhode Island	81	79	78	59	63	59	63	46	11	14	27	10
South Carolina	3,049	2,803	2,127	1,797	2,595	2,416	1,827	1,502	446	515	787	593
South Dakota	10,835	8,129	5,443	4,368	9,410	7,475	4,833	3,731	4,620	2,536	1,813	1,420
Tennessee	4,467	3,904	3,336	2,714	3,501	3,137	2,594	1,927	799	448	942	591
Texas	26,126	24,272	19,831	15,140	22,681	20,370	16,619	12,969	5,344	5,518	6,557	4,102
Utah	1,995	1,649	1,658	1,211	1,607	1,349	1,355	1,020	294	180	397	244
Vermont	826	702	635	575	757	612	572	503	261	163	211	135
Virginia	4,240	3,689	3,399	2,925	3,304	2,898	2,638	2,300	753	397	953	740
Washington	9,670	8,363	6,449	5,746	8,666	7,508	5,943	5,064	2,985	1,903	1,037	1,021
West Virginia	804	706	642	519	564	521	464	397	32	-12	91	60
Wisconsin	12,991	10,508	8,397	6,007	11,741	9,224	7,071	5,357	3,803	2,100	1,961	822
Wyoming	1,810	1,406	1,280	1,063	1,450	1,159	971	959	330	151	297	145

[1]The sum of the value of crop production, the value of livestock production, and revenues from services and forestry.
[2]Represents gross receipts from commercial market sales as well as net Commodity Credit Corporation loans. Excludes value of home consumption and value of inventory adjustment.
[3]Represents the value of agricultural sector production plus net government transactions (such as direct government payments) minus capital consumption, employee compensation, net rent received by nonoperator landlords, and interest payments.
(X) = Not applicable

Table A-50. Farm Marketings and Government Payments

Geographic area	Government payments (million dollars)			Farm marketings										
				Crops (million dollars)				Livestock and livestock products (million dollars)				Principal commodities, 2011[1]		
	2011	2010	2009	2011	2010	2009	2008	2011	2010	2009	2008	Top	2nd	3rd
United States...............	10,421	12,392	12,178	208,254	179,595	168,858	175,027	165,998	141,554	120,260	141,638	Corn	Cattle	Dairy products
Alabama........................	116	135	169	1,168	927	840	908	3,683	3,697	3,316	3,560	Broilers	Cattle	Chicken eggs
Alaska	11	10	6	25	24	25	25	7	7	6	6	Greenhouse	Hay	Potatoes
Arizona.........................	58	70	112	2,494	2,019	1,792	1,950	1,819	1,421	1,184	1,505	Dairy products	Lettuce	Cattle
Arkansas.......................	365	389	482	4,002	3,420	3,314	3,905	4,414	4,428	3,964	4,479	Broilers	Soybeans	Rice
California......................	259	364	568	31,186	28,184	26,725	26,431	12,358	9,820	7,863	10,623	Dairy products	Almonds	Grapes
Colorado	235	272	192	2,922	2,318	2,230	2,270	4,154	3,761	3,338	4,040	Cattle	Corn	Dairy products
Connecticut..................	11	15	13	363	342	363	387	197	173	152	188	Greenhouse	Dairy products	Aquaculture
Delaware	21	24	16	320	230	243	262	761	828	772	781	Broilers	Corn	Soybeans
District of Columbia	(X)	(X)	(X)	(X)	(X)	(X)	(X)	(X)	(X)	(X)	(X)	(X)	(X)	(X)
Florida..........................	175	93	77	6,764	6,497	6,035	6,417	1,498	1,345	1,105	1,388	Greenhouse	Oranges	Tomatoes
Georgia	222	262	383	3,528	3,049	2,510	2,779	4,826	4,515	4,294	4,758	Broilers	Cotton	Chicken eggs
Hawaii	17	16	13	630	616	560	541	90	74	71	68	Cane for sugar	Greenhouse	Cattle
Idaho............................	113	164	140	3,347	2,673	2,645	2,807	3,981	3,217	2,499	3,410	Dairy products	Cattle	Potatoes
Illinois..........................	627	698	567	17,220	13,713	13,098	13,077	2,600	2,268	1,851	2,121	Corn	Soybeans	Hogs
Indiana.........................	300	372	304	8,545	6,868	6,564	6,607	3,292	2,868	2,377	2,852	Corn	Soybeans	Hogs
Iowa.............................	812	1,025	767	17,542	13,839	13,374	13,498	12,350	10,192	8,522	9,869	Corn	Hogs	Soybeans
Kansas	543	632	475	6,945	7,181	6,249	5,637	8,914	7,545	6,343	7,192	Corn	Wheat	Soybeans
Kentucky......................	274	320	337	2,170	1,857	1,920	1,793	2,748	2,596	2,430	2,924	Horses	Broilers	Corn
Louisiana	210	210	247	2,402	2,103	1,838	1,985	1,058	979	870	1,019	Cane for sugar	Corn	Soybeans
Maine...........................	17	49	20	373	325	304	333	345	303	252	344	Potatoes	Dairy products	Aquaculture
Maryland.......................	41	54	53	980	806	849	769	1,111	1,030	911	1,109	Broilers	Greenhouse	Corn
Massachusetts..............	21	20	16	398	362	366	442	118	111	96	116	Greenhouse	Cranberries	Dairy products
Michigan.......................	157	185	180	5,027	4,163	3,729	4,023	3,019	2,469	1,905	2,529	Dairy products	Corn	Soybeans
Minnesota.....................	488	566	528	11,535	9,654	8,606	9,560	7,001	6,168	5,182	6,102	Corn	Soybeans	Hogs
Mississippi....................	246	251	481	2,448	1,934	1,766	1,978	2,910	3,027	2,732	2,941	Broilers	Soybeans	Corn
Missouri........................	367	436	479	5,510	4,803	4,342	4,633	4,199	3,688	3,294	3,675	Soybeans	Corn	Cattle
Montana........................	299	327	256	2,122	1,779	1,662	1,641	1,420	1,264	1,069	1,181	Wheat	Cattle	Hay
Nebraska.......................	470	509	419	11,754	8,656	8,807	8,201	10,061	8,460	7,271	8,321	Cattle	Corn	Soybeans
Nevada..........................	10	10	11	281	215	252	273	399	344	273	296	Cattle	Hay	Dairy products
New Hampshire..............	13	20	9	93	90	94	109	96	85	75	94	Dairy products	Greenhouse	Apples
New Jersey	17	22	17	995	917	876	926	127	127	134	171	Greenhouse	Blueberries	Horses/mules
New Mexico	88	91	82	808	781	645	653	3,298	2,490	1,991	2,408	Cattle	Dairy products	Pecans
New York.......................	57	66	149	2,053	1,838	1,760	2,006	3,208	2,578	2,010	2,759	Dairy products	Corn	Greenhouse
North Carolina..............	401	438	456	3,612	3,383	3,409	3,349	6,932	6,347	5,695	6,296	Broilers	Hogs	Turkeys
North Dakota.................	461	845	442	6,209	5,964	5,858	5,951	1,128	955	785	905	Wheat	Soybeans	Corn
Ohio	257	373	288	6,528	5,245	4,893	4,897	3,120	2,742	2,238	2,748	Corn	Soybeans	Dairy products
Oklahoma	342	319	229	1,301	1,423	1,242	1,774	5,755	4,732	3,640	3,892	Cattle	Hogs	Broilers
Oregon	111	150	102	3,273	2,685	2,912	3,201	1,351	1,054	907	1,142	Greenhouse	Cattle	Dairy products
Pennsylvania.................	74	81	161	2,312	2,128	1,927	2,159	4,377	3,705	3,061	3,927	Dairy products	Corn	Cattle
Rhode Island.................	4	6	6	51	49	49	54	11	10	9	10	Greenhouse	Dairy products	Aquaculture
South Carolina	114	125	151	1,177	1,046	939	996	1,418	1,370	1,250	1,369	Broilers	Turkeys	Greenhouse
South Dakota	303	401	256	5,958	4,452	5,042	4,973	3,453	3,023	2,338	2,698	Corn	Cattle	Soybeans
Tennessee	140	153	262	2,096	1,806	1,847	1,621	1,405	1,332	1,148	1,346	Cattle	Soybeans	Broilers
Texas............................	917	1,018	1,407	6,864	8,612	6,471	8,048	15,818	11,758	10,640	11,403	Cattle	Cotton	Dairy products
Utah	35	39	44	510	361	323	469	1,097	988	758	1,004	Dairy products	Cattle	Hay
Vermont	18	21	45	120	107	111	110	637	505	399	568	Dairy products	Cattle	Maple products
Virginia	100	111	115	1,182	942	1,045	1,097	2,122	1,956	1,637	1,964	Broilers	Cattle	Dairy products
Washington...................	231	314	189	6,311	5,516	5,255	5,950	2,355	1,992	1,646	2,022	Apples	Dairy products	Wheat
West Virginia.................	14	17	18	104	92	94	90	460	429	410	425	Broilers	Cattle	Turkeys
Wisconsin.....................	196	259	406	4,330	3,330	2,771	3,177	7,410	5,894	4,800	6,340	Dairy products	Corn	Cattle
Wyoming	41	43	34	362	269	286	288	1,087	890	751	748	Cattle	Hay	Hogs

[1]As determined by cash receipts; "Cattle" includes calves; "Greenhouse" includes nursery.
(X) = Not applicable

Table A-51.   Natural Resource Industries and Minerals

Geographic Area	Natural resource industries[1] Establishments 2010	Establishments 2005	Number of employees[2] 2010	2005	Annual payroll (million dollars) 2010	2005	Value of nonfuel mineral production[3] (million dollars) 2011	2010	2005	Crude oil production[4] 2012 Quantity (million barrels)	Value (million dollars)	Natural gas production[5] 2010 Quantity (billion cubic feet)	Value (million dollars)	Coal production[6] 2011 Quantity (thousand short tons)	Value[7] (million dollars)
United States..........................	71,506	71,673	1,453,024	1,675,924	83,032	75,712	74,000	64,000	55,400	2,381	225,059	21,316	95,493	1,095,628	44,932
Alabama.................................	1,715	1,751	38,685	48,998	1,887	2,007	964	1,010	1,130	10	1,003	204	909	19,071	1,958
Alaska	493	483	11,984	6,780	1,260	621	3,790	3,240	1,500	192	18,987	353	1,120	2,149	(D)
Arizona...................................	714	728	18,412	24,222	955	932	8,250	6,700	4,350	0	NA	0	1	8,111	(D)
Arkansas................................	1,521	1,556	32,328	35,371	1,555	1,382	771	630	597	7	584	926	3,557	133	(D)
California................................	4,576	4,606	87,734	107,221	4,613	4,589	2,870	2,710	4,290	196	20,370	274	1,332	(X)	(X)
Colorado.................................	1,763	1,686	29,228	24,036	2,394	1,501	1,940	1,930	1,750	49	4,204	1,496	5,923	26,890	1,072
Connecticut............................	359	356	5,363	6,354	331	300	125	141	161	(X)	(X)	(X)	(X)	(X)	(X)
Delaware	98	97	1,328	703	62	19	7	13	20	(X)	(X)	(X)	(X)	(X)	(X)
District of Columbia	10	10	0	0	0	0	(X)	(X)	(X)	(X)	(X)	(X)	(X)	(X)	(X)
Florida....................................	2,019	1,999	33,886	52,050	1,348	1,795	3,270	2,080	2,910	2	NA	12	NA	(X)	(X)
Georgia...................................	1,960	2,028	42,363	59,112	1,984	2,410	1,440	1,500	1,770	(X)	(X)	(X)	(X)	(X)	(X)
Hawaii....................................	93	93	759	693	23	18	95	112	125	(X)	(X)	(X)	(X)	(X)	(X)
Idaho......................................	902	887	10,518	13,232	438	466	1,290	1,200	896	(X)	(X)	(X)	(X)	(X)	(X)
Illinois....................................	1,645	1,688	34,457	43,338	1,724	1,889	894	910	1,210	10	869	1	NA	37,770	1,919
Indiana...................................	1,305	1,321	30,029	38,500	1,325	1,476	772	837	894	2	209	7	28	37,426	1,795
Iowa.......................................	680	684	16,035	19,799	742	781	565	542	659	(X)	(X)	(X)	(X)	(X)	(X)
Kansas....................................	1,358	1,329	13,850	13,843	656	573	1,180	1,040	873	44	3,827	298	1,263	37	(D)
Kentucky.................................	1,451	1,491	42,272	44,895	2,169	1,898	836	742	782	3	278	131	584	108,766	6,921
Louisiana................................	2,448	2,449	66,134	67,493	4,377	3,762	498	492	397	71	7,499	2,108	8,915	3,865	(D)
Maine......................................	1,033	1,040	14,371	14,774	709	707	94	114	141	(X)	(X)	(X)	(X)	(X)	(X)
Maryland.................................	485	496	4,445	11,789	349	462	276	438	580	(X)	(X)	0	NA	2,937	145
Massachusetts........................	880	920	13,751	18,916	701	842	196	194	250	(X)	(X)	(X)	(X)	(X)	(X)
Michigan.................................	1,729	1,726	28,145	34,506	1,339	1,468	2,470	1,960	1,740	7	659	128	486	(X)	(X)
Minnesota...............................	1,073	1,085	29,438	36,263	1,569	1,756	5,120	3,860	2,190	(X)	(X)	(X)	(X)	(X)	(X)
Mississippi..............................	1,456	1,480	22,083	28,393	984	1,086	195	183	221	24	2,435	55	231	2,747	(D)
Missouri..................................	1,163	1,179	19,593	24,817	789	871	2,220	2,140	1,860	0	11	0	0	465	(D)
Montana..................................	894	865	9,634	11,634	576	544	1,360	1,120	847	26	2,193	86	314	42,008	673
Nebraska................................	393	393	4,970	4,600	206	151	259	181	115	3	NA	2	9	(X)	(X)
Nevada...................................	357	341	12,862	12,027	1,100	661	10,400	7,550	3,890	0	0	0	NA	(X)	(X)
New Hampshire.......................	355	371	3,701	5,636	158	213	79	100	88	(X)	(X)	(X)	(X)	(X)	(X)
New Jersey	728	737	14,327	20,549	675	919	221	232	356	(X)	(X)	(X)	(X)	(X)	(X)
New Mexico............................	874	874	15,900	18,258	1,110	917	1,290	1,010	1,150	84	7,409	1,200	6,385	21,922	750
New York................................	1,865	1,877	29,796	37,337	1,384	1,494	1,140	1,290	1,290	0	NA	36	167	(X)	(X)
North Carolina........................	2,015	2,033	40,667	51,459	1,674	1,960	883	908	862	(X)	(X)	(X)	(X)	(X)	(X)
North Dakota..........................	386	365	10,404	6,326	802	335	98	88	35	242	20,381	70	276	28,231	444
Ohio.......................................	2,046	2,072	40,338	54,138	1,837	2,149	1,160	1,080	1,210	5	452	78	362	28,166	1,307
Oklahoma	2,954	2,906	47,128	38,820	3,588	2,205	749	646	616	90	8,064	1,707	8,039	1,145	81
Oregon	2,147	2,197	37,798	52,966	1,523	2,076	297	292	439	(X)	(X)	1	7	(X)	(X)
Pennsylvania..........................	2,789	2,802	68,240	75,094	3,591	3,117	1,590	1,530	1,560	4	376	568	NA	59,182	4,703
Rhode Island..........................	143	143	1,581	2,069	71	75	28	34	35	(X)	(X)	(X)	(X)	(X)	(X)
South Carolina	1,052	1,053	24,049	29,461	1,172	1,229	502	440	659	(X)	(X)	(X)	(X)	(X)	(X)
South Dakota	264	268	3,407	2,517	145	87	320	298	217	2	145	2	NA	(X)	(X)
Tennessee...............................	1,238	1,237	27,517	36,204	1,114	1,327	848	814	771	0	NA	5	20	1,547	115
Texas......................................	9,221	9,125	204,728	180,281	16,743	10,905	2,810	2,560	2,710	735	67,966	6,282	29,524	45,904	887
Utah.......................................	714	685	13,868	13,514	831	670	4,570	4,420	2,800	30	2,503	422	1,785	19,648	664
Vermont	318	302	2,690	3,664	108	126	123	119	98	(X)	(X)	(X)	(X)	(X)	(X)
Virginia...................................	1,635	1,690	34,096	44,334	1,646	1,866	1,030	952	1,150	0	NA	147	NA	22,523	3,044
Washington.............................	2,370	2,333	36,168	47,150	1,805	2,088	727	665	638	(X)	(X)	(X)	(X)	(X)	(X)
West Virginia...........................	1,237	1,258	36,905	34,866	2,314	1,644	350	230	209	2	191	257	0	134,662	11,421
Wisconsin...............................	1,595	1,603	52,280	70,669	2,446	3,062	599	651	570	(X)	(X)	(X)	(X)	(X)	(X)
Wyoming	987	975	23,790	20,143	1,848	1,204	1,950	1,860	1,300	58	4,696	2,213	9,515	438,673	5,948

[1]Includes Agriculture, forestry, fishing, and hunting (NAICS 11), Mining, quarrying, and oil and gas extraction (NAICS 21), Wood product manufacturing (NAICS 321), and Paper manufacturing (NAICS 322). Data provided by County Business Patterns is based on the North American Industry Classification System (NAICS). Data for 2010 is based on NAICS 2007. Data for 2005 is based on NAICS 2002, adjusted to match 2007.
[2]Covers full- and part-time employees who are on the payroll in the pay period including March 12.
[3]Data for 2010 and 2011 are preliminary. Partial data only for Connecticut, Delaware, Massachusetts, Maine, North Dakota, Rhode Island, Vermont in all years; for New Jersey in 2010 and 2011; for Maine and Mississippi in 2011; for Maryland, New Hampshire, and Wisconsin in 2005 and 2011; for Nebraska and Pennsylvania in 2005 and 2010; for North Carolina in 2005; excludes values withheld to avoid disclosing individual company data. Concealed data included in U.S. total.
[4]U.S. totals include offshore production.
[5]Excludes nonhydrocarbon gases. U.S. total includes natural gas extracted from the Gulf of Mexico that is not distributed to states. The national total will therefore differ from the sum of state totals.
[6]Includes both surface and underground mines. U.S. total includes refuse recovery not distributed by state.
[7]The United States average sales price includes both open and captive market sales. Captive coal is coal produced and consumed by the mine operator, a subsidiary, or parent company.
(D) = Data withheld to avoid disclosure
NA = Not available
(X) = Not applicable

Table A-52. Agricultural Census

Geographic area	Number of farms (thousands\)		Land in farm (millions of acres)		Average size of farm (acres)		Value of land and buildings[1] (million dollars)		Market value of agricultural products sold and government payment 2007 (million dollars)	
	2007	2002	2007	2002	2007	2002	2007	2002	Total	Products sold
United States	2,204.8	2,129.0	922.1	938.3	418	441	1,744,295	1,144,906	305,204	297,220
Alabama	48.8	45.0	9.0	8.9	185	197	20,704	15,126	4,540	4,416
Alaska	0.7	1.0	0.9	0.9	1,285	1,479	345	331	59	57
Arizona	15.6	7.0	26.1	26.6	1,670	3,645	19,545	10,626	3,290	3,235
Arkansas	49.3	47.0	13.9	14.5	281	305	32,506	21,226	7,778	7,509
California	81.0	80.0	25.4	27.6	313	346	162,533	96,129	34,125	33,885
Colorado	37.1	31.0	31.6	31.1	853	991	33,058	23,757	6,217	6,061
Connecticut	4.9	4.0	0.4	0.4	83	85	5,138	3,533	556	552
Delaware	2.5	2.0	0.5	0.5	200	226	5,279	2,344	1,092	1,083
District of Columbia	(X)	(X)	(X)	(X)	(X)	(X)	(X)	(X)	(X)	(X)
Florida	47.5	44.0	9.2	10.4	195	236	52,054	29,330	7,831	7,785
Georgia	47.8	49.0	10.2	10.7	212	218	31,636	22,553	7,337	7,113
Hawaii	7.5	5.0	1.1	1.3	149	241	8,621	4,584	516	514
Idaho	25.3	25.0	11.5	11.8	454	470	22,675	15,342	5,788	5,689
Illinois	76.9	73.0	26.8	27.3	348	374	101,538	66,667	13,816	13,329
Indiana	60.9	60.0	14.8	15.1	242	250	52,937	38,441	8,532	8,271
Iowa	92.9	91.0	30.7	31.7	331	350	104,187	64,154	21,124	20,418
Kansas	65.5	64.0	46.3	47.2	707	733	42,205	32,581	14,840	14,413
Kentucky	85.3	87.0	14.0	13.8	164	160	37,533	25,463	4,928	4,825
Louisiana	30.1	27.0	8.1	7.8	269	286	16,687	12,163	2,787	2,618
Maine	8.1	7.0	1.3	1.4	166	190	2,968	2,298	626	617
Maryland	12.8	12.0	2.1	2.1	160	170	14,432	8,453	1,868	1,835
Massachusetts	7.7	6.0	0.5	0.5	67	85	6,377	4,590	494	490
Michigan	56.0	53.0	10.0	10.1	179	190	34,200	27,144	5,872	5,753
Minnesota	81.0	81.0	26.9	27.5	332	340	69,165	41,777	13,626	13,180
Mississippi	42.0	42.0	11.5	11.1	273	263	21,418	15,634	5,108	4,877
Missouri	107.8	107.0	29.0	29.9	269	280	63,237	45,299	7,832	7,513
Montana	29.5	28.0	61.4	59.6	2,079	2,139	47,568	23,281	3,025	2,803
Nebraska	47.7	49.0	45.5	45.9	953	930	52,693	35,727	15,893	15,506
Nevada	3.1	3.0	5.9	6.3	1,873	2,118	3,597	2,849	517	513
New Hampshire	4.2	3.0	0.5	0.4	113	132	2,326	1,354	202	199
New Jersey	10.3	10.0	0.7	0.8	71	81	11,255	7,359	994	987
New Mexico	20.9	15.0	43.2	44.8	2,066	2,954	14,569	10,631	2,218	2,175
New York	36.4	37.0	7.2	7.7	197	206	16,322	12,871	4,481	4,419
North Carolina	52.9	54.0	8.5	9.1	160	168	34,715	27,977	10,461	10,314
North Dakota	32.0	31.0	39.7	39.3	1,241	1,283	30,597	15,824	6,444	6,084
Ohio	75.9	78.0	14.0	14.6	184	187	49,244	39,618	7,302	7,070
Oklahoma	86.6	83.0	35.1	33.7	405	404	40,582	23,796	6,016	5,806
Oregon	38.6	40.0	16.4	17.1	425	427	31,002	20,383	4,463	4,386
Pennsylvania	63.2	58.0	7.8	7.7	124	133	37,290	26,332	5,885	5,809
Rhode Island	1.2	1.0	0.1	0.1	56	71	1,141	565	67	66
South Carolina	25.9	25.0	4.9	4.8	189	197	13,973	10,081	2,420	2,353
South Dakota	31.2	32.0	43.7	43.8	1,401	1,380	39,127	19,617	6,841	6,570
Tennessee	79.3	88.0	11.0	11.7	138	133	37,057	28,534	2,713	2,617
Texas	247.4	229.0	130.4	129.9	527	567	165,573	100,496	21,722	21,001
Utah	16.7	15.0	11.1	11.7	664	768	13,858	8,966	1,438	1,416
Vermont	7.0	7.0	1.2	1.2	177	189	3,581	2,543	680	674
Virginia	47.4	48.0	8.1	8.6	171	181	34,141	23,329	2,961	2,906
Washington	39.3	36.0	15.0	15.3	381	426	29,822	22,414	6,931	6,793
West Virginia	23.6	21.0	3.7	3.6	157	172	8,820	4,817	595	592
Wisconsin	78.5	77.0	15.2	15.7	194	204	48,994	35,799	9,163	8,967
Wyoming	11.1	9.0	30.2	34.4	2,726	3,651	15,471	10,195	1,186	1,158

(X) = Not applicable

Table A-52. Agricultural Census—*Continued*

Geographic area	Total number of farm operators	Farms by value of sales						Cropland (thousand acres)
		Less than $2,500	2,500–9,999	$10,000–$24,999	$25,000–$49,999	$50,000–$99,999	$100,000 or more	
United States...................................	3,337,450	900,327	418,833	248,285	154,732	125,456	357,159	406,425
Alabama..	70,959	22,582	11,160	6,457	2,538	1,287	4,729	3,143
Alaska	1,146	231	172	91	68	47	77	86
Arizona...	26,183	9,632	3,098	1,063	433	358	1,053	1,205
Arkansas.......................................	75,308	17,810	11,616	7,147	3,018	1,685	8,070	8,432
California.......................................	130,756	23,965	13,756	10,481	7,578	6,212	19,041	9,465
Colorado.......................................	60,684	17,566	6,124	3,600	2,383	2,283	5,098	11,484
Connecticut....................................	7,913	1,933	1,280	652	329	231	491	164
Delaware.......................................	3,928	683	360	272	127	115	989	433
District of Columbia	(X)	(X)	(X)	(X)	(X)	(X)	(X)	(X)
Florida..	73,146	21,529	9,507	5,404	3,355	2,435	5,233	2,953
Georgia...	69,060	23,391	8,977	4,906	2,308	1,491	6,773	4,478
Hawaii..	11,412	2,932	2,008	1,143	557	353	528	178
Idaho...	40,427	10,772	4,473	2,617	1,666	1,505	4,316	5,919
Illinois..	111,089	26,879	9,155	5,910	5,381	6,245	23,290	23,708
Indiana...	91,590	22,470	10,657	6,325	4,531	4,273	12,682	12,716
Iowa..	136,068	26,730	9,086	6,663	7,514	9,805	33,058	26,316
Kansas...	97,150	22,731	9,061	7,844	6,097	5,609	14,189	28,216
Kentucky.......................................	123,971	35,800	20,937	12,642	6,296	3,663	5,922	7,278
Louisiana......................................	43,774	14,626	6,229	3,167	1,771	1,091	3,222	4,691
Maine...	13,063	3,924	1,684	949	479	328	772	529
Maryland.......................................	20,241	4,985	2,520	1,469	910	691	2,259	1,405
Massachusetts................................	12,265	3,329	1,608	1,035	518	398	803	187
Michigan.......................................	85,339	24,150	10,521	6,094	3,941	3,342	7,966	7,804
Minnesota.....................................	119,650	30,678	9,246	6,677	5,737	6,490	22,164	21,949
Mississippi....................................	60,669	22,205	7,688	4,520	1,930	1,070	4,546	5,531
Missouri.......................................	163,553	39,479	23,044	16,261	10,563	6,634	11,844	16,406
Montana.......................................	46,903	11,977	3,718	2,770	2,215	2,464	6,380	18,242
Nebraska......................................	71,924	11,042	3,978	3,878	3,977	5,261	19,576	21,486
Nevada...	5,117	1,184	602	334	217	179	615	754
New Hampshire...............................	7,022	2,068	935	466	263	148	286	129
New Jersey	16,182	4,948	2,006	1,108	656	462	1,147	489
New Mexico....................................	32,109	10,496	4,772	2,064	1,065	844	1,689	2,334
New York.......................................	57,984	13,004	6,845	4,706	2,694	2,253	6,850	4,315
North Carolina................................	76,832	22,608	11,668	5,828	2,765	1,718	8,326	4,895
North Dakota..................................	45,114	11,386	2,083	1,967	2,163	2,891	11,480	27,527
Ohio..	114,172	27,556	15,150	9,045	6,501	5,565	12,044	10,833
Oklahoma.....................................	131,232	34,669	19,790	13,494	6,886	4,563	7,163	13,008
Oregon...	64,503	17,450	8,585	3,730	2,272	1,838	4,678	5,010
Pennsylvania..................................	94,500	27,495	11,355	6,488	4,103	3,067	10,655	4,870
Rhode Island..................................	1,912	487	287	179	93	56	117	24
South Carolina	37,082	14,336	5,484	2,289	1,289	664	1,805	2,151
South Dakota.................................	46,710	8,277	2,510	2,515	2,515	3,409	11,943	19,094
Tennessee.....................................	117,044	38,522	20,756	9,488	4,712	2,001	3,801	6,047
Texas...	372,563	116,887	58,886	30,100	15,210	8,774	17,580	33,667
Utah..	26,424	7,059	3,808	1,994	1,363	860	1,616	1,838
Vermont	11,392	2,581	1,536	902	497	390	1,078	517
Virginia..	71,281	20,191	11,582	6,597	3,399	1,886	3,728	3,274
Washington....................................	63,645	18,443	7,534	3,423	2,190	1,729	5,965	7,609
West Virginia..................................	34,720	12,433	6,444	2,538	1,033	421	749	942
Wisconsin	123,217	30,296	12,687	7,732	5,704	5,397	16,647	10,116
Wyoming	18,522	3,920	1,865	1,261	922	975	2,126	2,576

(X) = Not applicable

Table A-53.   Utilities

Geographic area	Utilities[1] (NAICS 22)						Public water systems, 2012[3]							
	Establishments		Number of employees		Annual payroll[2] (million dollars)		Number of systems				Population served (thousands)			
	2010	2005	2010	2005	2010	2005	Total	Community[4]	Non-transient, non-community[5]	Transient, non-community[6]	Total	Community[4]	Non-transient, non-community[5]	Transient, non-community[6]
United States.............	17,600	17,326	638,058	633,106	55,396	46,293	150,669	50,803	17,922	81,944	319,186	300,203	6,235	12,748
Alabama......................	417	413	16,546	20,254	1,241	1,330	606	528	22	56	5,556	5,537	13	6
Alaska	91	85	1,988	1,721	155	120	1,515	426	268	821	772	607	63	101
Arizona.......................	265	244	(D)	10,415	(D)	752	1,547	763	209	575	6,491	6,246	127	118
Arkansas....................	344	370	7,362	7,059	518	421	1,092	706	34	352	2,752	2,722	9	21
California....................	1,117	1,140	(D)	59,422	(D)	5,026	7,538	2,955	1,484	3,099	42,553	41,341	363	849
Colorado	385	370	8,837	8,013	713	548	2,030	872	172	986	5,772	5,457	80	235
Connecticut.................	169	140	(D)	9,947	1,163	1,000	2,558	542	572	1,444	2,835	2,663	113	59
Delaware	46	47	2,632	2,593	250	206	492	216	83	193	975	900	22	53
District of Columbia	45	33	(D)	1,164	(D)	98	6	5	1		646	646	0	0
Florida........................	585	645	26,859	32,240	2,113	2,100	5,458	1,703	847	2,908	19,713	19,226	238	248
Georgia	598	572	25,127	27,291	1,879	1,693	2,419	1,778	187	454	8,580	8,436	64	80
Hawaii	53	46	3,163	2,730	253	188	116	97	17	2	1,438	1,427	11	0
Idaho..........................	192	184	2,887	3,451	206	200	1,945	741	228	976	1,349	1,198	52	99
Illinois........................	483	481	28,851	27,688	2,722	2,437	5,583	1,745	421	3,417	12,625	12,139	143	343
Indiana.......................	626	529	16,176	14,401	1,234	919	4,149	803	564	2,782	5,455	4,880	196	379
Iowa...........................	271	255	(D)	7,963	(D)	501	1,885	1,116	132	637	2,879	2,754	50	75
Kansas	197	254	6,502	6,545	513	430	1,018	886	45	87	2,715	2,689	22	4
Kentucky	341	330	8,310	8,179	663	530	460	400	20	40	4,553	4,537	11	5
Louisiana	537	567	(D)	11,382	(D)	738	1,388	1,040	139	209	5,035	4,931	57	47
Maine.........................	96	109	2,311	2,345	153	130	1,868	376	354	1,138	937	691	65	181
Maryland.....................	139	108	10,494	10,181	1,123	888	3,427	473	550	2,404	5,642	5,200	160	282
Massachusetts.............	281	251	12,861	11,601	1,319	949	1,750	528	272	950	9,431	9,209	76	147
Michigan.....................	396	401	(D)	23,935	1,942	1,609	11,145	1,383	1,348	8,414	8,943	7,624	308	1,012
Minnesota...................	295	276	(D)	11,988	(D)	866	7,036	961	491	5,584	4,881	4,275	73	534
Mississippi..................	596	576	9,338	8,693	639	496	1,245	1,089	81	75	3,193	3,114	66	12
Missouri	357	384	16,665	15,112	1,355	1,066	2,740	1,455	219	1,066	5,526	5,345	72	109
Montana......................	200	217	2,972	2,645	231	171	2,136	700	278	1,158	1,030	709	139	183
Nebraska....................	105	128	(D)	1,172	(D)	93	1,311	589	150	572	1,915	1,579	49	287
Nevada.......................	120	103	(D)	5,324	(D)	448	564	211	121	232	2,697	2,594	80	22
New Hampshire.............	113	103	3,492	3,434	298	234	2,431	695	441	1,295	1,172	858	93	221
New Jersey	375	340	18,018	18,164	1,823	1,546	3,810	603	747	2,460	9,787	9,014	350	424
New Mexico..................	231	225	5,017	4,134	379	255	1,154	597	148	409	1,959	1,836	51	72
New York.....................	613	584	42,155	40,341	3,811	3,296	8,856	2,434	742	5,680	21,007	17,882	303	2,822
North Carolina..............	472	368	19,636	19,722	1,726	1,384	6,019	2,067	396	3,556	8,113	7,688	114	311
North Dakota................	113	115	(D)	3,250	(D)	230	591	339	39	213	661	627	10	25
Ohio...........................	696	593	(D)	27,291	(D)	2,040	4,822	1,236	712	2,874	10,812	10,206	218	387
Oklahoma	353	390	7,850	8,833	583	514	1,667	1,093	101	473	3,630	3,570	25	36
Oregon.......................	291	263	7,395	8,051	614	560	2,570	876	323	1,371	3,715	3,448	69	197
Pennsylvania...............	783	709	31,133	33,510	2,956	2,725	9,052	2,034	1,193	5,825	12,015	10,793	482	740
Rhode Island...............	31	34	1,136	1,444	99	110	484	86	77	321	1,093	1,009	29	56
South Carolina	329	302	11,831	11,279	892	664	1,426	597	120	709	3,842	3,757	43	41
South Dakota	154	155	2,198	2,018	138	109	650	457	25	168	772	739	9	24
Tennessee..................	150	163	3,536	3,183	218	157	838	475	40	323	6,522	6,445	25	53
Texas.........................	1,911	2,207	47,548	41,610	3,995	2,889	6,958	4,691	901	1,366	26,150	25,361	515	274
Utah...........................	218	208	4,633	4,725	380	315	1,006	468	67	471	2,868	2,763	27	79
Vermont	59	54	2,067	1,885	182	131	1,347	429	247	671	582	441	45	96
Virginia	360	309	15,050	15,625	1,430	1,212	2,751	1,161	532	1,058	7,090	6,614	312	164
Washington..................	302	305	8,291	5,637	686	375	4,092	2,230	322	1,540	7,041	6,517	147	378
West Virginia................	254	238	6,444	6,251	467	401	1,023	484	114	425	1,573	1,507	35	31
Wisconsin	317	286	13,484	14,874	1,168	1,043	11,432	1,055	864	9,513	4,957	4,034	206	717
Wyoming	128	117	2,492	2,391	196	151	799	315	92	392	549	451	23	75

[1]Data provided by County Business Patterns is based on the North American Industry Classification System (NAICS). Data for 2005 is based on NAICS 2002. Data for 2010 is based on NAICS 2007. Utilities data is for private use and excludes government employees, railroad employees, self-employed persons, and so on.
[2]National payroll figures include undisclosed data found at the State level and will therefore differ from the sum of the state totals.
[3]As of October. Covers public drinking water systems that provide water for human consumption through pipes and other constructed conveyances to at least 15 service connections or serve an average of at least 25 persons for at least 60 days a year. National totals differ from the sum of the state figures because national totals include water systems for Tribes and Territories.
[4]Includes any public water system that supplies water to the same population year-round.
[5]Includes any public water system that regularly supplies water to at least 25 of the same people at least six months per year but not year-round.
[6]Includes any public water system that provides water in a place, such as a gas station or a campground, where people do not remain for long periods of time and is open at least 60 days per year.
0 = Represents or rounds to zero
(D) = Data withheld to avoid disclosure or does not meet statistical standards.

Table A-54. Energy Consumption

Geographic area	Total Primary Energy Consumption[1]					End-use sector, 2010[3] (trillion Btu)				Selected source, 2010 (trillion Btu)				
	2010[1] (trillion Btu)	Per capita[2] (million Btu)	Percent change, 2000–2010	2005[1] (trillion Btu)	2000[1] (trillion Btu)	Residential	Commercial	Industrial[1]	Transportation	Petroleum[4]	Natural gas (dry)[5]	Coal	Hydro-electric power[6]	Nuclear electric power
United States............	97,711	316	-1.2	100,465	98,866	21,836	18,040	30,391	27,444	36,021	24,249	20,869	2,539	8,434
Alabama..................	1,960	410	-8.5	2,126	2,142	418	271	786	486	554	547	719	85	397
Alaska.....................	642	899	0.6	798	638	52	66	313	211	274	335	15	14	0
Arizona...................	1,400	218	4.7	1,486	1,336	381	332	209	478	508	337	458	65	326
Arkansas................	1,126	385	-3.4	1,135	1,166	254	177	400	294	341	275	294	36	157
California................	7,826	210	-2.2	8,332	7,998	1,463	1,501	1,765	3,097	3,463	2,326	55	326	337
Colorado................	1,517	301	21.6	1,428	1,248	351	288	448	430	485	506	383	15	0
Connecticut.............	754	211	-12.0	897	857	247	187	76	245	329	204	29	4	175
Delaware.................	256	285	-16.5	313	307	73	64	53	67	91	56	30	0	0
District of Columbia ...	186	307	-0.7	190	187	39	124	3	20	21	34	0	0	0
Florida....................	4,382	233	5.8	4,553	4,142	1,299	1,002	523	1,559	1,737	1,181	637	2	250
Georgia	3,156	325	5.5	3,172	2,990	821	587	763	984	1,052	541	768	32	350
Hawaii	272	200	-1.5	329	276	34	40	64	134	234	0	17	1	0
Idaho......................	534	340	-0.6	505	537	126	85	186	137	165	85	9	89	0
Illinois....................	3,937	307	-1.6	4,116	4,000	982	775	1,188	992	1,230	935	1,069	1	1,005
Indiana...................	2,871	442	-1.2	2,913	2,906	581	382	1,292	617	763	565	1,450	4	0
Iowa.......................	1,492	489	30.0	1,200	1,148	244	203	733	312	421	279	494	9	47
Kansas...................	1,165	408	6.5	1,029	1,094	258	222	417	268	383	288	360	0	100
Kentucky	1,977	455	5.0	1,999	1,883	408	264	831	474	627	239	1,010	25	0
Louisiana	4,065	894	2.4	3,610	3,971	385	282	2,704	694	1,929	1,468	260	11	195
Maine.....................	407	307	-21.5	481	519	79	62	140	126	195	81	2	37	0
Maryland.................	1,481	256	2.5	1,565	1,445	447	438	153	443	505	214	266	16	146
Massachusetts...........	1,397	213	-9.8	1,556	1,548	427	284	228	459	584	445	84	10	62
Michigan.................	2,798	283	-13.8	3,170	3,245	762	600	694	741	813	759	749	12	310
Minnesota................	1,867	352	4.6	1,854	1,785	396	340	649	483	612	427	315	8	141
Mississippi..............	1,189	400	-3.1	1,183	1,227	242	167	412	368	422	438	149	0	101
Missouri..................	1,928	322	7.8	1,930	1,788	557	421	378	572	658	282	802	15	94
Montana..................	401	405	-1.6	412	408	88	77	126	112	168	73	203	92	0
Nebraska.................	844	461	33.6	655	632	165	144	352	182	217	170	255	13	116
Nevada....................	646	239	3.0	730	627	152	115	168	211	236	268	80	21	0
New Hampshire.........	296	224	-9.7	334	327	83	66	40	107	153	63	34	14	114
New Jersey	2,448	278	-2.8	2,724	2,519	596	639	259	953	1,077	670	72	0	343
New Mexico	680	329	0.5	677	677	123	126	232	199	249	246	268	2	0
New York.................	3,728	192	-12.2	4,163	4,248	1,118	1,222	346	1,042	1,324	1,224	167	249	438
North Carolina...........	2,705	283	1.0	2,724	2,679	809	614	561	722	825	309	749	46	426
North Dakota.............	481	713	27.1	407	378	67	67	244	103	150	64	410	20	0
Ohio.......................	3,834	332	-10.1	4,059	4,262	945	701	1,230	959	1,169	809	1,355	4	165
Oklahoma	1,552	413	5.1	1,549	1,476	329	251	551	420	491	697	346	27	0
Oregon...................	977	255	-14.6	1,075	1,144	240	184	234	320	343	243	43	298	0
Pennsylvania............	3,759	296	-4.7	4,044	3,946	944	687	1,135	993	1,271	889	1,311	23	814
Rhode Island............	197	187	-11.8	227	224	61	45	26	64	92	96	0	(Z)	0
South Carolina	1,662	358	2.9	1,709	1,614	403	275	523	461	508	226	405	23	543
South Dakota	380	465	46.7	274	259	71	63	150	95	115	72	39	51	0
Tennessee	2,251	354	2.4	2,352	2,197	607	400	634	610	681	260	516	79	290
Texas......................	11,770	466	-2.5	11,559	12,068	1,689	1,479	5,787	2,816	5,752	3,459	1,609	12	432
Utah.......................	764	275	1.8	759	750	166	154	209	234	266	229	356	7	0
Vermont	148	236	-10.3	167	165	43	29	23	52	79	9	0	13	50
Virginia...................	2,502	312	4.9	2,605	2,385	683	633	439	747	818	386	346	15	278
Washington..............	2,037	302	-8.4	1,969	2,223	479	380	565	613	739	295	95	666	97
West Virginia............	739	398	-4.7	806	775	173	113	278	175	201	122	848	13	0
Wisconsin................	1,800	316	-5.3	1,870	1,901	428	352	577	443	537	377	458	21	139
Wyoming	535	948	24.0	462	432	48	64	300	123	166	149	484	10	0

[1]U.S. total energy and U.S. industrial sector include 60.8 trillion Btu of net imports of coal coke that is not allocated to the states. U.S. total includes energy losses and co-products from the production of fuel ethanol, which is not allocated to State figures.
[2]Based on estimated resident population as of July 1.
[3]End-use sector data include electricity sales and associated electrical system energy losses.
[4]Includes fuel ethanol blended into motor gasoline.
[5]Includes supplemental gaseous fuels.
[6]Conventional hydroelectric power. Does not include pumped-storage hydroelectricity.
0 = Represents zero or rounds to zero

Table A-55. Energy Expenditures

Geographic area	Total[1,2,3]				Per capita[4] (dollars)			End-use sector, 2010[3] (million dollars)				Selected source, 2010 (million dollars)				
	2010		2005 (million dollars)	2000 (million dollars)	2010	2005	2000	Residential	Commercial	Industrial[2]	Transportation	Petroleum products		Natural gas[6]	Coal	Retail electricity
	Amount (million dollars)	Percentage change, 2000–2010										Total	Motor gasoline[5]			
United States............	1,204,827	75.2	1,045,465	687,587	3,895	3,535	2,449	249,739	178,128	216,172	560,787	709,471	376,512	159,821	50,407	365,900
Alabama..................	21,507	77.9	18,264	12,089	4,494	4,024	2,720	4,707	2,873	4,243	9,683	11,224	6,990	3,181	2,136	7,833
Alaska	6,289	121.9	5,219	2,834	8,807	7,817	4,520	729	825	509	4,227	5,119	979	479	43	912
Arizona...................	19,374	82.9	16,628	10,594	3,021	2,785	2,065	4,346	3,267	1,872	9,889	11,130	7,227	2,203	829	7,059
Arkansas.................	12,061	65.3	10,726	7,295	4,128	3,875	2,732	2,292	1,364	2,323	6,083	7,177	3,864	1,785	490	3,393
California.................	117,003	71.1	103,558	68,399	3,134	2,888	2,019	18,930	18,653	12,598	66,822	72,077	44,744	14,919	161	33,382
Colorado	16,751	94.1	14,695	8,632	3,319	3,139	2,012	3,383	2,393	2,408	8,567	9,805	5,656	2,573	607	4,786
Connecticut.............	14,221	74.4	12,443	8,153	3,977	3,579	2,394	4,839	2,914	1,059	5,409	7,724	4,303	1,744	99	5,284
Delaware	3,616	81.4	3,080	1,993	4,019	3,673	2,545	1,002	702	476	1,437	1,838	1,221	524	101	1,390
District of Columbia ...	2,439	58.9	2,035	1,535	4,033	3,496	2,684	510	1,512	32	387	478	330	416	0	1,586
Florida.....................	60,172	96.3	50,128	30,648	3,194	2,832	1,918	14,662	10,214	4,673	30,623	34,694	21,780	7,969	2,219	24,460
Georgia	37,338	89.0	32,655	19,754	3,844	3,590	2,413	8,661	5,215	4,593	18,868	20,793	12,456	4,544	2,994	12,410
Hawaii.....................	5,714	109.2	4,996	2,732	4,191	3,900	2,138	916	1,012	866	2,920	4,238	1,408	95	40	2,473
Idaho......................	5,691	83.3	4,510	3,105	3,622	3,162	2,401	1,024	589	1,144	2,934	3,584	1,968	572	20	1,492
Illinois	44,989	54.5	42,133	29,122	3,503	3,306	2,350	10,078	6,528	7,835	20,548	24,163	13,404	7,594	1,978	13,115
Indiana....................	27,374	62.3	25,321	16,861	4,217	4,043	2,772	5,021	2,836	6,863	12,653	14,801	8,195	3,512	3,791	8,036
Iowa.......................	14,766	80.0	12,467	8,204	4,841	4,117	2,830	2,532	1,737	3,975	6,523	9,016	4,605	2,151	744	3,480
Kansas	12,457	70.7	9,546	7,298	4,357	3,481	2,742	2,402	1,665	3,206	5,185	7,459	3,234	1,777	547	3,352
Kentucky.................	19,675	79.2	17,139	10,977	4,526	4,108	2,720	3,357	1,922	4,655	9,742	11,817	6,081	1,497	2,383	6,224
Louisiana	39,369	98.4	29,998	19,840	8,661	6,673	4,514	3,557	2,443	21,431	11,938	28,680	6,035	5,446	621	6,436
Maine......................	6,300	65.9	5,556	3,798	4,746	4,242	2,979	1,550	976	1,032	2,743	4,256	1,932	624	9	1,481
Maryland..................	21,517	86.0	17,606	11,571	3,719	3,157	2,185	5,936	4,629	1,482	9,470	11,261	7,385	2,097	894	8,300
Massachusetts..........	24,512	67.5	21,689	14,635	3,739	3,374	2,305	7,114	4,284	3,276	9,838	13,176	7,735	4,211	269	8,146
Michigan	34,540	53.8	32,472	22,461	3,497	3,216	2,262	8,740	5,335	5,163	15,302	17,833	12,158	6,594	1,788	10,172
Minnesota	20,869	70.9	18,313	12,208	3,930	3,586	2,484	4,027	2,813	3,864	10,166	12,473	7,129	2,796	572	5,653
Mississippi...............	13,206	77.0	11,387	7,459	4,446	3,928	2,624	2,500	1,587	2,151	6,968	7,872	4,324	2,179	477	4,147
Missouri	22,885	73.3	19,862	13,204	3,817	3,432	2,362	5,086	3,138	2,832	11,829	13,633	8,321	2,664	1,287	6,699
Montana	4,568	79.6	4,037	2,544	4,610	4,313	2,819	816	625	754	2,374	2,979	1,429	496	289	1,046
Nebraska..................	8,091	88.2	6,422	4,299	4,421	3,667	2,519	1,428	1,006	1,796	3,862	4,734	2,366	1,112	366	2,244
Nevada....................	9,294	97.5	8,488	4,706	3,437	3,534	2,357	2,020	1,225	1,562	4,487	5,164	3,109	1,886	196	3,235
New Hampshire.........	5,229	61.3	4,591	3,242	3,971	3,532	2,628	1,452	956	484	2,338	3,330	1,990	504	129	1,616
New Jersey	37,362	80.0	32,206	20,755	4,246	3,731	2,466	8,792	7,690	2,545	18,335	20,697	11,134	6,214	299	11,590
New Mexico	7,435	82.4	6,471	4,076	3,599	3,378	2,241	1,258	1,027	978	4,172	5,008	2,506	898	550	1,834
New York..................	61,619	53.2	56,645	40,232	3,177	2,933	2,121	18,634	17,838	3,276	21,871	28,401	16,144	11,722	541	23,736
North Carolina...........	32,989	71.8	28,321	19,202	3,451	3,268	2,393	8,240	5,027	4,105	15,618	18,588	12,234	2,743	2,650	11,823
North Dakota............	4,547	119.8	3,298	2,069	6,740	5,110	3,234	582	485	1,490	1,990	3,038	1,105	269	722	913
Ohio	45,081	52.7	41,866	29,519	3,907	4,952	2,602	10,118	6,374	8,178	20,411	23,981	13,807	6,731	3,389	13,980
Oklahoma	16,049	73.4	14,246	9,258	4,268	4,035	2,687	3,083	1,947	3,004	8,015	9,065	5,024	3,941	598	4,363
Oregon....................	12,592	65.7	10,710	7,599	3,281	2,968	2,224	2,355	1,569	1,621	7,047	7,819	4,465	1,677	73	3,479
Pennsylvania.............	48,701	67.5	42,803	29,072	3,829	3,467	2,368	12,589	6,942	8,395	20,776	26,775	14,410	7,054	3,604	15,222
Rhode Island.............	3,690	69.6	3,107	2,176	3,506	2,922	2,077	1,204	732	353	1,400	2,062	1,120	840	0	1,098
South Carolina	18,705	84.5	15,938	10,139	4,034	3,750	2,529	4,108	2,371	2,966	9,261	10,344	6,836	1,543	1,500	7,004
South Dakota	3,798	96.7	2,896	1,931	4,651	3,716	2,563	640	458	729	1,971	2,474	1,206	435	78	888
Tennessee	25,153	82.9	21,943	13,751	3,956	3,666	2,418	5,324	3,549	3,872	12,409	14,071	8,441	1,976	1,418	8,851
Texas......................	137,532	90.0	114,495	72,369	5,446	5,019	3,513	18,992	13,171	51,756	53,613	96,090	32,378	14,759	2,949	32,698
Utah........................	8,332	85.3	6,989	4,496	3,002	2,791	2,017	1,365	1,085	944	4,938	5,401	2,940	1,184	608	1,925
Vermont	2,719	66.4	2,264	1,634	4,344	3,660	2,683	812	451	259	1,198	1,861	946	97	0	741
Virginia	29,826	80.8	26,326	16,496	3,717	3,488	2,331	7,071	4,666	2,868	15,222	17,397	10,786	2,996	1,220	9,894
Washington..............	22,893	76.8	18,422	12,946	3,395	2,956	2,195	4,161	2,940	2,596	13,196	14,643	8,041	2,486	220	5,959
West Virginia............	7,882	79.5	6,987	4,391	4,251	3,873	2,430	1,573	919	1,922	3,468	4,510	2,471	700	2,253	2,360
Wisconsin	21,483	65.6	19,264	12,975	3,774	3,476	2,424	4,784	3,165	3,677	9,858	11,695	7,233	3,061	1,023	6,669
Wyoming	4,462	106.3	3,665	2,163	7,904	7,239	4,379	439	489	1,328	2,206	3,026	928	351	636	1,035

[1]Total expenditures are the sum of purchases for each source (including retail electricity sales) less electric power sector purchases of fuel.
[2]Includes sources not shown separately, such as electricity imports and exports and coal coke net imports ($347 million in 2007), which are not included in the States.
[3]Excludes expenditures on energy sources such as hydroelectric, geothermal, wind, photovoltaic, or solar thermal. Also excluded are expenditures for reported amounts of energy consumed by the energy industry for production, transportation, and processing operations.
[4]Based on estimated resident population as of July 1.
[5]Includes fuel ethanol blended into motor gasoline.
[6]Includes supplemental gaseous fuels.
0 = Represents zero or amounts to zero

Table A-56. Construction

Geographic area	Construction (NAICS 23) Nonfarm employment (BLS)[1]			Earnings (BEA)[2] (million dollars)			Establishments		New private housing units authorized by building permits[3] Units (thousands)		Value (million dollars)	
	2012	2010	2005	2012	2010	2005	2010	Net change, 2005–2010	2012	2005	2012	2005
United States..................	5,599	5,520	7,353	525,353	489,548	562,591	682,684	-104,988	572.2	2,155.3	905.4	2,070.1
Alabama............................	79.1	87.2	105.5	7,132	7,157	6,856	8,235	-1,717	12.2	30.6	17.5	27.4
Alaska	16.6	16.1	18.6	2,184	2,012	1,945	2,461	-312	0.9	2.9	0.9	3.1
Arizona............................	115.7	111.5	219.4	9,508	8,623	13,453	12,091	-2,991	14.1	90.9	26.1	90.6
Arkansas..........................	47.4	48.7	54.7	3,762	3,636	3,518	5,539	-809	6.6	17.9	8.8	15.9
California.........................	587.5	559.8	905.3	60,842	55,141	81,130	66,999	-8,152	33.8	205.0	62.7	207.4
Colorado	115.1	115.1	160.0	10,545	9,807	12,989	16,747	-2,406	9.4	45.9	19.0	46.5
Connecticut......................	51.1	50.0	65.9	7,049	6,795	8,276	8,187	-1,624	3.3	11.9	5.2	11.8
Delaware	18.4	19.3	28.0	1,505	1,551	(D)	2,375	-334	3.1	8.2	3.3	7.9
District of Columbia	13.5	10.6	12.6	1,184	916	(D)	421	45	1.1	2.9	0.5	1.9
Florida.............................	341.5	350.8	633.2	22,992	23,139	37,097	45,041	-12,305	35.9	287.3	61.0	255.9
Georgia............................	141.0	149.7	208.8	12,658	12,593	15,419	17,482	-4,984	17.2	109.3	35.4	108.4
Hawaii.............................	29.5	28.9	33.4	3,112	2,950	2,878	2,738	-15	2.6	9.8	4.1	9.0
Idaho...............................	31.3	31.3	45.0	2,351	2,314	2,808	6,358	-1,339	5.3	21.6	6.5	18.1
Illinois.............................	187.9	198.3	268.5	19,096	19,548	24,033	29,175	-3,376	10.9	66.9	22.5	59.8
Indiana............................	124.4	115.7	148.2	11,210	9,530	10,607	13,756	-2,686	12.4	38.5	16.6	39.2
Iowa................................	64.4	61.6	71.4	5,819	5,143	5,036	8,609	-446	7.1	16.8	8.4	16.3
Kansas............................	55.1	54.1	62.4	4,705	4,347	4,223	7,064	-968	6.8	14.0	8.2	13.3
Kentucky..........................	67.3	67.9	84.2	5,573	5,277	5,636	7,770	-1,548	6.9	21.2	10.5	22.6
Louisiana.........................	126.5	121.5	118.8	10,550	10,006	7,286	8,441	-174	12.6	22.8	16.3	23.0
Maine...............................	25.6	24.4	30.7	2,266	2,080	2,394	5,023	-513	2.8	9.0	3.6	8.8
Maryland..........................	145.2	144.8	185.3	14,216	13,657	13,998	14,516	-2,372	11.1	30.2	13.0	27.4
Massachusetts..................	114.6	107.1	139.5	13,488	12,070	14,459	16,844	-2,482	7.1	24.5	9.9	22.5
Michigan..........................	127.3	121.6	189.1	11,423	10,386	15,597	18,895	-7,273	7.0	45.3	10.9	54.7
Minnesota........................	94.8	87.6	129.4	9,034	7,909	10,575	16,368	-1,916	9.3	36.5	11.6	41.8
Mississippi.......................	48.3	49.5	52.2	4,254	4,006	3,390	4,389	-587	6.7	13.4	11.4	14.5
Missouri	104.0	106.2	143.1	9,710	9,394	10,766	13,846	-3,204	8.3	33.1	13.3	32.8
Montana	22.9	22.6	27.6	1,895	1,733	1,851	5,111	-256	1.7	4.8	2.4	5.0
Nebraska..........................	42.9	42.6	47.8	3,783	3,594	3,036	5,810	-268	5.2	9.9	6.3	10.9
Nevada............................	51.8	59.3	134.7	4,493	5,312	8,712	5,003	-710	6.8	47.7	14.9	44.6
New Hampshire.................	22.2	21.4	29.4	2,699	2,551	3,268	4,059	-854	2.2	7.6	3.2	8.7
New Jersey	130.4	129.5	169.1	15,495	14,923	16,815	20,865	-4,590	12.2	38.6	18.4	35.9
New Mexico	40.7	43.6	54.4	2,914	2,948	3,015	4,738	-718	4.6	14.2	6.1	12.6
New York..........................	311.9	306.6	325.3	32,251	30,832	27,291	45,293	-1,155	17.4	61.9	51.6	53.5
North Carolina..................	171.9	176.5	231.1	13,808	12,908	14,996	23,107	-4,095	33.8	97.9	54.7	93.1
North Dakota....................	29.6	21.6	17.5	2,613	1,645	1,122	2,570	271	3.1	4.0	2.8	4.0
Ohio................................	179.8	168.8	232.9	16,367	14,586	17,414	20,620	-5,702	13.1	47.7	17.7	51.7
Oklahoma	69.1	67.0	66.1	5,708	5,234	4,298	8,086	-169	8.8	18.4	10.5	17.1
Oregon............................	69.5	67.6	90.9	6,215	5,527	6,301	11,797	-2,021	7.7	31.0	11.7	27.3
Pennsylvania....................	225.8	215.9	255.7	22,593	20,838	22,044	26,835	-2,993	18.7	44.5	24.6	49.7
Rhode Island....................	15.8	15.9	21.8	1,653	1,568	1,787	3,091	-606	1.0	2.8	1.1	2.5
South Carolina	77.8	79.4	116.9	6,090	5,742	6,980	9,688	-2,597	15.8	54.2	25.9	43.2
South Dakota	21.0	21.0	21.9	1,478	1,411	1,278	3,158	-93	3.5	5.7	3.9	5.8
Tennessee	109.2	105.1	125.2	10,505	9,633	9,835	10,025	-1,393	14.6	46.6	22.4	44.8
Texas..............................	585.2	564.4	567.1	61,133	53,313	45,467	39,321	-311	82.9	210.6	129.5	188.8
Utah................................	69.0	65.0	81.5	5,486	4,908	4,898	8,822	-1,184	10.6	27.8	10.9	24.3
Vermont	14.2	13.5	16.9	1,287	1,199	1,286	2,784	-283	1.2	2.9	1.4	3.6
Virginia	175.9	183.1	243.6	14,135	14,031	17,026	20,779	-3,748	21.1	61.5	27.6	63.2
Washington......................	138.5	140.7	177.4	12,966	12,395	13,269	21,027	-2,971	16.8	53.0	28.9	50.1
West Virginia....................	35.6	32.8	36.8	2,993	2,496	2,234	3,659	-966	2.0	6.1	3.5	5.7
Wisconsin........................	93.0	94.6	127.5	8,739	8,421	9,942	14,325	-3,039	10.8	35.3	15.5	40.0
Wyoming	21.7	22.3	20.7	1,885	1,815	1,263	2,741	-49	2.0	4.0	2.7	3.3

[1]All estimates of labor and earnings provided by BLS are based on the 2007 North American Industry Classification System (NAICS). Figure includes logging and mining with construction for Delaware, the District of Columbia, Hawaii, Maryland, Nebraska, South Dakota, and Tennessee.
[2]Bureau of Economic Analysis. The estimates of earnings for 2000–2006 are based on the 2002 North American Industry Classification System (NAICS). The estimates for 2007 forward are based on the 2007 NAICS. All dollars estimates are in current dollars and not adjusted for inflation.
[3]Data based on 20,000 places in the United States having building permits systems; see Source in Appendix A for details.
(D) = Data withheld to avoid disclosure or does not meet statistical standards.

Table A-57. Manufactures (2007, NAICS 31-33)

Geographic area	Nonfarm employment in manufacturing (BLS)[1] (thousands)			Earnings (BEA)[2] (million dollars)			Establishments[3] 2010		Average hourly earnings of production workers[1,4] (dollars)		Value of shipments[5] (million dollars)		
	2012	2010	2005	2012	2010	2005	Total	Net change 2005–2010	2012	2010	2011	2010	2005
United States..................	11,926	11,509	14,212	987,242	895,864	942,254	299,982	-33,478	19.08	18.61	5,498,599	4,905,446	4,735,384
Alabama............................	243	236	299	15,942	14,843	15,769	4,402	-551	18.31	15.71	113,195	104,370	87,841
Alaska...............................	14	13	13	776	690	661	525	11	17.89	20.44	8,323	7,260	6,571
Arizona.............................	155	149	182	14,182	12,550	12,737	4,356	-502	18.17	17.00	50,048	47,925	43,234
Arkansas..........................	156	160	202	8,751	8,401	9,149	2,774	-331	15.20	13.87	59,897	54,953	58,188
California..........................	1,253	1,242	1,505	131,959	119,621	120,967	38,937	-5,888	20.20	18.95	497,755	447,921	434,238
Colorado...........................	132	126	150	11,240	10,158	10,827	4,809	-380	25.13	22.07	49,230	44,774	37,420
Connecticut......................	165	166	195	17,551	16,322	16,600	4,473	-564	23.94	23.68	51,946	51,393	46,549
Delaware..........................	26	26	33	1,995	2,021	2,406	601	-51	15.74	16.53	20,626	21,006	23,362
District of Columbia	1	1	2	137	142	207	89	-53	NA	NA	182	216	261
Florida..............................	317	309	416	23,726	21,970	23,989	12,616	-1,670	19.64	19.42	92,182	87,431	91,573
Georgia............................	355	345	450	25,621	23,461	25,513	7,683	-940	17.89	16.63	144,395	129,684	143,960
Hawaii..............................	13	13	15	778	735	767	844	-102	19.15	18.58	7,695	6,399	6,407
Idaho...............................	57	53	64	3,830	3,525	3,668	1,757	-92	20.92	20.70	22,895	21,775	18,232
Illinois..............................	583	561	688	51,372	46,199	47,039	14,210	-1,863	19.17	16.92	275,279	242,760	231,332
Indiana.............................	482	447	571	38,007	33,715	36,544	8,222	-748	18.50	18.52	232,142	209,047	199,872
Iowa.................................	211	201	229	14,863	13,431	12,809	3,596	-204	17.41	16.73	102,091	88,995	86,427
Kansas.............................	163	160	180	12,440	11,769	11,122	2,955	-173	18.46	18.87	84,277	77,713	62,064
Kentucky..........................	223	209	262	15,666	13,729	14,961	3,778	-374	18.43	18.94	118,970	106,193	106,365
Louisiana	142	138	152	13,166	11,944	10,293	3,257	-120	20.43	21.31	270,123	202,423	163,163
Maine...............................	51	51	61	3,569	3,475	3,443	1,630	-220	20.50	20.18	15,853	15,090	14,918
Maryland...........................	109	114	139	10,137	10,111	10,084	3,191	-551	16.64	20.06	41,836	39,256	39,774
Massachusetts..................	252	253	305	26,264	24,595	24,485	6,907	-1,008	20.90	20.50	80,477	78,100	80,702
Michigan...........................	537	474	678	44,335	37,274	50,066	12,378	-1,655	20.71	21.79	221,204	195,137	222,075
Minnesota.........................	305	293	347	24,442	22,127	22,164	7,377	-580	19.19	18.87	121,021	107,312	97,999
Mississippi.......................	137	136	178	8,267	7,583	8,206	2,356	-273	15.90	14.83	60,471	55,908	49,661
Missouri	248	243	309	18,501	16,921	18,616	6,222	-713	18.05	18.45	107,703	101,201	107,661
Montana...........................	18	17	20	1,094	1,003	1,021	1,210	-73	17.88	17.10	11,706	9,526	7,949
Nebraska..........................	95	92	101	5,702	5,315	5,082	1,845	-140	16.64	16.13	52,946	45,039	38,258
Nevada.............................	39	38	48	2,882	2,582	2,818	1,704	-159	16.00	15.51	14,923	13,845	12,281
New Hampshire.................	66	66	80	5,459	5,205	5,394	1,894	-261	18.13	17.81	19,653	18,454	16,872
New Jersey	246	257	330	26,401	26,530	27,505	8,088	-1,487	19.33	18.80	107,436	98,724	103,236
New Mexico	30	29	36	2,300	2,086	2,103	1,400	-131	15.70	15.76	28,594	21,127	26,748
New York..........................	458	457	579	37,794	36,559	40,766	16,933	-2,416	18.54	18.39	151,374	147,368	154,682
North Carolina..................	440	432	565	32,215	29,904	32,569	8,963	-1,175	16.55	15.85	200,420	178,838	186,665
North Dakota....................	25	23	26	1,551	1,294	1,269	738	-10	18.06	15.93	13,403	10,281	8,978
Ohio.................................	656	621	812	50,672	45,471	51,951	14,729	-1,888	19.35	18.66	292,737	259,529	278,577
Oklahoma	135	123	145	10,279	8,705	10,067	3,625	-240	16.89	14.33	69,833	58,783	55,096
Oregon.............................	172	164	204	14,436	12,457	12,995	5,281	-278	18.67	17.60	59,665	55,609	61,770
Pennsylvania....................	567	560	679	43,261	40,150	42,627	14,167	-1,457	18.26	16.88	237,600	220,008	214,876
Rhode Island....................	40	40	55	2,826	2,706	3,167	1,554	-402	18.26	14.71	11,175	11,047	11,548
South Carolina	220	207	260	15,639	13,753	14,650	3,966	-323	17.01	16.52	90,737	82,596	87,499
South Dakota	41	37	40	2,354	2,010	1,818	1,007	43	16.95	15.28	16,152	13,581	10,361
Tennessee	314	299	409	22,832	20,519	23,191	5,961	-710	16.64	15.33	132,135	119,024	137,388
Texas...............................	863	812	897	81,657	70,993	69,909	19,593	-959	18.55	14.50	671,372	567,060	463,953
Utah.................................	117	111	118	8,256	7,436	6,515	3,150	-15	17.99	18.46	50,788	45,406	33,572
Vermont	32	31	37	2,301	2,090	2,208	986	-140	18.22	16.63	10,550	9,960	10,686
Virginia	232	231	296	16,958	15,941	17,046	5,313	-485	18.54	19.11	94,688	92,758	88,966
Washington.......................	280	258	273	25,456	21,955	20,222	7,050	-354	24.14	23.48	115,059	103,720	93,099
West Virginia....................	49	49	62	3,618	3,398	3,612	1,299	-107	18.61	18.11	23,977	21,862	21,573
Wisconsin	455	431	505	33,064	29,824	30,100	9,033	-721	18.05	18.10	163,107	149,261	144,244
Wyoming	9	9	10	770	668	558	548	5	22.69	20.49	8,757	7,800	6,660

[1] All estimates of labor and earnings provided by the Bureau of Labor Statistics (BLS) are based on the 2007 North American Industry Classification System (NAICS). Earning estimates are in current dollars and not adjusted for inflation.
[2] Bureau of Economic Analysis. The estimates of earnings for 2000–2006 are based on the 2002 North American Industry Classificataion System. The estimates for 2007 forward are based on the 2007 NAICS. All dollars estimates are in current dollars and not adjusted for inflation.
[3] 2010 data for establishments are based on the 2007 North American Industry Classification System (NAICS); 2005 data are based on the 2002 NAICS.
[4] Data for average hourly earnings of production workers are provided in current dollars and not adjusted for inflation. United States totals differ from the sum of the state figures because of differing benchmarks among states and differing industrial and geographic stratification.
[5] Includes extensive and unmeasurable duplication from shipments between establishments in the same industry classification.
NA = Not available

Table A-58. Manufactures Summary and Export-Related Shipments and Employment

Geographic area	Manufactures summary, 2011 (2007, NAICS 31-33)										Export-related, 2009[4,5]			
	All employees[1]				Production workers[1]			Value added by manufactures[2]		Value of shipments[3] (million dollars)	Export related shipments (million dollars)	Export related manufacturing employment (thousands)	Export related as a percentage of all manufacturers	
	Number	Percent change, 2010–2011	Payroll		Total	Hours (million)	Wages (million dollars)	Total (million dollars)	Per production worker (dollar)				Shipments	Employment
			Total (million dollars)	Per employee (dollar)										
United States................	10,649,378	1.4	559,518	52,540	7,440,140	14,867	313,710	2,295,220	308,491	5,498,599	983,813	2,419.1	22.2	21.9
Alabama........................	213,473	-0.4	10,001	46,850	161,347	327	6,469	43,374	268,826	113,195	24,372	51.8	26.9	23.1
Alaska	11,140	4.2	469	42,066	8,999	19	329	1,740	193,334	8,323	474	0.8	7.6	7.3
Arizona.........................	126,847	-1.4	7,829	61,720	71,540	145	3,185	27,192	380,100	50,048	12,315	34.4	26.0	25.6
Arkansas......................	145,777	0.0	5,977	41,004	116,553	231	4,224	23,737	203,654	59,897	7,949	21.6	16.1	14.2
California......................	1,114,193	0.1	66,869	60,015	693,571	1,374	29,834	231,029	333,100	497,755	89,477	268.2	20.2	22.4
Colorado	110,187	2.3	6,068	55,068	73,770	149	3,191	23,270	315,441	49,230	8,215	26.3	20.0	22.9
Connecticut...................	154,580	-0.4	9,488	61,381	94,715	185	4,510	29,885	315,524	51,946	10,893	36.7	22.5	22.2
Delaware......................	27,248	-4.9	1,452	53,295	18,714	38	776	7,421	396,547	20,626	2,287	5.5	11.5	18.8
District of Columbia	977	-27.5	41	41,648	660	1	22	104	157,435	182	4	NA	1.6	NA
Florida..........................	254,670	-0.7	12,893	50,628	169,661	333	6,489	46,016	271,226	92,182	12,980	38.2	15.2	14.2
Georgia	313,230	1.1	14,318	45,712	240,374	487	9,075	65,055	270,641	144,395	23,783	61.4	19.7	18.8
Hawaii	10,676	-0.5	431	40,367	6,691	13	232	1,457	217,692	7,695	595	0.7	10.0	6.0
Idaho............................	48,378	-4.0	2,375	49,098	36,377	72	1,475	11,428	314,153	22,895	2,946	8.4	18.0	16.1
Illinois..........................	535,485	0.5	29,008	54,171	366,486	744	15,654	115,314	314,648	275,279	51,233	131.0	23.7	23.8
Indiana.........................	428,843	3.5	21,509	50,156	321,256	645	14,017	100,287	312,170	232,142	38,584	95.4	21.7	22.7
Iowa.............................	192,249	4.8	9,502	49,427	140,042	283	5,701	39,521	282,211	102,091	16,210	40.6	19.6	21.2
Kansas.........................	150,994	1.4	7,645	50,631	107,759	216	4,628	31,534	292,630	84,277	15,792	41.0	22.9	26.3
Kentucky.......................	201,792	2.5	9,293	46,054	155,931	309	6,354	38,181	244,861	118,970	19,321	44.4	21.6	22.1
Louisiana......................	124,910	2.1	7,594	60,793	90,507	186	4,765	61,561	680,175	270,123	33,061	25.7	21.0	19.9
Maine...........................	47,949	0.4	2,325	48,486	33,665	66	1,452	7,866	233,641	15,853	2,313	8.8	15.1	17.1
Maryland.......................	104,199	0.0	5,998	57,564	65,683	128	2,774	23,203	353,257	41,836	3,838	11.3	10.2	10.3
Massachusetts	223,998	-0.6	13,638	60,885	138,618	278	6,270	45,417	327,643	80,477	20,923	70.8	28.3	27.6
Michigan	461,459	6.2	25,129	54,457	336,239	680	15,665	84,244	250,548	221,204	41,537	117.9	26.0	26.9
Minnesota	290,103	1.2	15,214	52,444	191,634	381	7,811	53,376	278,531	121,021	16,744	57.1	16.8	19.2
Mississippi...................	127,596	-0.5	5,461	42,800	99,587	194	3,593	20,323	204,070	60,471	9,271	16.7	17.7	11.9
Missouri	230,627	1.8	11,388	49,381	170,348	331	7,192	45,121	264,874	107,703	19,447	44.5	20.1	18.8
Montana	13,244	3.0	638	48,196	9,596	19	403	3,354	349,474	11,706	1,326	2.2	16.0	15.6
Nebraska......................	90,223	2.0	3,817	42,301	69,138	143	2,630	19,174	277,322	52,946	5,471	13.1	12.9	14.5
Nevada.........................	38,525	-1.7	2,080	53,978	25,801	52	1,062	8,172	316,727	14,923	1,953	6.2	13.9	14.7
New Hampshire..............	70,323	1.4	3,947	56,132	43,258	86	1,781	10,637	245,891	19,653	4,055	17.3	23.8	24.5
New Jersey	234,549	-2.2	14,357	61,210	150,390	302	6,552	47,285	314,414	107,436	18,115	44.1	18.7	17.3
New Mexico	25,471	0.7	1,294	50,820	17,105	34	731	18,400	1,075,704	28,594	2,411	3.5	16.4	13.7
New York.......................	418,843	0.4	22,260	53,147	277,512	543	11,376	77,618	279,691	151,374	32,563	95.6	22.3	21.4
North Carolina...............	388,032	0.7	17,342	44,692	292,549	581	10,832	102,559	350,571	200,420	27,751	72.5	16.7	17.7
North Dakota.................	21,621	6.4	968	44,761	16,264	32	629	4,238	260,557	13,403	1,616	3.2	16.6	14.5
Ohio.............................	598,564	2.7	30,907	51,635	432,629	871	18,968	118,817	274,638	292,737	60,127	162.2	26.4	26.9
Oklahoma	125,433	6.7	5,951	47,444	93,665	192	3,807	23,715	253,185	69,833	9,898	28.7	17.5	22.5
Oregon	129,355	3.3	6,543	50,578	91,633	181	3,692	37,150	405,420	59,665	12,779	31.7	25.4	23.3
Pennsylvania.................	530,464	0.8	27,231	51,335	371,848	738	15,800	100,737	270,908	237,600	34,463	94.1	17.0	17.4
Rhode Island.................	36,202	-2.2	1,997	55,166	23,655	48	1,000	5,652	238,929	11,175	1,776	5.9	18.5	15.1
South Carolina	194,423	2.3	9,408	48,388	146,600	293	6,069	37,582	256,358	90,737	23,267	55.8	31.6	28.5
South Dakota	38,676	3.8	1,633	42,226	28,825	58	1,023	6,164	213,853	16,152	1,594	5.5	13.0	14.5
Tennessee	276,641	0.3	13,121	47,431	203,177	408	8,039	54,420	267,843	132,135	22,741	57.5	20.1	19.6
Texas...........................	700,761	1.8	38,534	54,988	488,835	994	21,946	216,794	443,491	671,372	137,668	208	28.6	27.6
Utah.............................	100,373	1.7	5,290	52,699	65,450	130	2,732	26,720	408,245	50,788	7,575	18.5	20.0	17.9
Vermont	28,030	0.7	1,537	54,817	18,096	37	748	5,017	277,224	10,550	2,121	6.8	23.9	23.2
Virginia	222,000	-0.8	11,189	50,400	157,615	312	6,476	54,557	346,143	94,688	16,123	41	18.9	17.4
Washington...................	230,154	3.3	13,306	57,813	152,903	303	7,370	52,683	344,552	115,059	44,128	94.7	45.0	40.2
West Virginia.................	49,600	1.0	2,527	50,946	37,570	74	1,678	10,140	269,902	23,977	4,872	9.2	22.3	18.1
Wisconsin	427,906	3.6	21,168	49,470	309,396	611	12,331	72,804	235,311	163,107	24,123	81.7	18.4	19.4
Wyoming	8,386	10.1	557	66,372	5,903	11	349	3,180	538,737	8,757	737	0.9	9.0	10.3

[1]Includes employment and payroll at administrative offices and auxiliary units. All employees represents the average of production workers plus all other employees for the payroll period ended nearest the 12th of March. Production workers represents the average of the employment for the payroll periods ended nearest the 12th of March, May, August, and November.
[2]Adjusted value added; takes into account (a) value added by merchandising operations (that is, difference between the sales value and cost of merchandise sold without further manufacture, processing, or assembly), plus (b) net change in finished goods and work-in-process inventories between beginning and end of year.
[3]Includes extensive and unmeasurable duplication from shipments between establishments in the same industry classification.
[4]Exports includes both "direct" exports (exports manufactured in the United States and consumed in foreign markets) and "indirect" exports (intermediate goods and services required to manufacture export goods).
[5]Preliminary data.
NA = Not available

Table A-59.   Major Manufacturing Sectors, 2011

| Geographic area | Food manufacturing[1] (2007 NAICS 311) | | | | Fabricated metal products[1] (2007 NAICS 332) | | | |
| | Employment | | | Value of shipments (million dollars) | Employment | | | Value of shipments (million dollars) |
	Total	Percent of total manufacturing	Percent change, 2010–2011		Total	Percent of total manufacturing	Percent change, 2010–2011	
United States......................	1,358,996	12.8	-0.4	710,366	1,285,707	12.1	4.0	326,797
Alabama.............................	28,377	13.3	-4.7	10,519	21,327	10.0	2.1	5,249
Alaska................................	7,905	71.0	7.6	2,487	NA	NA	NA	NA
Arizona..............................	8,994	7.1	0.9	5,927	17,592	13.9	3.0	4,299
Arkansas............................	39,851	27.3	-3.1	15,460	13,290	9.1	6.1	4,827
California...........................	149,019	13.4	0.8	71,271	125,189	11.2	2.4	27,139
Colorado...........................	16,491	15.0	2.1	8,825	13,390	12.2	10.9	3,721
Connecticut.......................	5,995	3.9	0.9	2,556	30,454	19.7	1.9	7,125
Delaware...........................	8,084	29.7	-2.8	2,960	2,214	8.1	-1.0	437
District of Columbia.............	NA	NA	NA	NA	NA	NA	NA	NA
Florida...............................	24,184	9.5	-4.7	12,620	24,531	9.6	-6.0	5,430
Georgia.............................	57,721	18.4	-0.6	28,739	20,899	6.7	-5.0	5,862
Hawaii...............................	4,515	42.3	-0.5	1,035	NA	NA	NA	NA
Idaho.................................	14,575	30.1	-2.1	7,751	4,618	9.5	-2.7	976
Illinois...............................	70,461	13.2	-1.8	42,315	84,750	15.8	5.6	22,293
Indiana..............................	33,163	7.7	-0.4	20,403	49,666	11.6	7.6	14,083
Iowa..................................	47,685	24.8	0.5	37,526	17,787	9.3	7.7	4,126
Kansas..............................	27,689	18.3	0.5	21,611	14,247	9.4	3.9	3,288
Kentucky............................	25,561	12.7	5.5	11,806	20,129	10.0	3.8	5,152
Louisiana...........................	15,085	12.1	3.5	9,186	18,761	15.0	-0.6	4,480
Maine................................	5,864	12.2	-4.3	1,758	4,936	10.3	2.7	1,224
Maryland............................	14,628	14.0	3.0	7,633	8,221	7.9	-1.5	1,984
Massachusetts....................	19,437	8.7	0.8	7,125	29,494	13.2	1.7	8,339
Michigan............................	24,635	5.3	1.6	15,224	64,316	13.9	9.2	15,392
Minnesota..........................	46,378	16.0	1.9	26,827	38,179	13.2	5.7	10,269
Mississippi.........................	20,776	16.3	-1.3	5,566	9,342	7.3	0.8	2,594
Missouri............................	36,142	15.7	-4.9	21,334	28,036	12.2	3.8	6,588
Montana............................	2,094	15.8	-6.4	873	1,393	10.5	6.8	317
Nebraska...........................	34,193	37.9	2.1	26,678	7,629	8.5	5.2	2,120
Nevada..............................	3,764	9.8	-4.4	1,638	4,778	12.4	-4.2	1,057
New Hampshire...................	2,647	3.8	-4.4	1,303	11,283	16.0	0.2	2,620
New Jersey.........................	26,164	11.2	-4.8	11,926	20,995	9.0	-0.8	4,664
New Mexico........................	4,828	19.0	-1.8	3,170	2,335	9.2	-0.1	472
New York............................	42,143	10.1	-0.6	18,497	49,869	11.9	3.7	10,808
North Carolina....................	48,871	12.6	-2.4	21,138	32,563	8.4	1.1	8,870
North Dakota......................	4,751	22.0	-2.4	4,215	2,163	10.0	13.8	511
Ohio..................................	48,622	8.1	2.5	28,127	97,406	16.3	6.0	28,705
Oklahoma..........................	16,003	12.8	3.6	7,330	21,409	17.1	9.6	6,838
Oregon..............................	19,816	15.3	2.2	7,390	14,484	11.2	4.1	2,726
Pennsylvania......................	65,370	12.3	0.4	32,036	72,589	13.7	2.5	18,846
Rhode Island......................	2,152	5.9	6.8	459	7,207	19.9	5.7	1,935
South Carolina....................	17,015	8.8	0.3	6,365	20,582	10.6	1.0	5,904
South Dakota......................	7,837	20.3	1.1	4,475	3,734	9.7	5.6	785
Tennessee.........................	33,906	12.3	0.6	17,852	26,955	9.7	-1.8	7,544
Texas................................	83,615	11.9	-3.4	43,304	107,657	15.4	8.4	28,529
Utah..................................	14,142	14.1	0.2	7,564	10,241	10.2	6.3	2,394
Vermont	4,017	14.3	-3.1	2,434	1,448	5.2	-23.9	286
Virginia..............................	25,045	11.3	-2.1	12,385	18,318	8.3	2.5	4,708
Washington........................	31,372	13.6	2.3	12,358	18,158	7.9	1.1	4,240
West Virginia......................	3,669	7.4	1.9	902	6,369	12.8	0.1	2,224
Wisconsin..........................	63,000	14.7	0.3	39,324	63,015	14.7	8.0	14,333
Wyoming	NA	NA	NA	NA	NA	NA	NA	NA

[1]Data may not be available for all NAICS industries or geographies.
NA = Not available

Table A-59. Major Manufacturing Sectors, 2011—*Continued*

Geographic area	Computer and electronic products[1] (2007 NAICS 334)				Transportation equipment[1] (2007 NAICS 336)			
	Employment			Value of shipments (million dollars)	Employment			Value of shipments (million dollars)
	Total	Percent of total manufacturing	Percent change, 2010–2011		Total	Percent of total manufacturing	Percent change, 2010–2011	
United States...............	816,676	7.7	0.0	337,861	1,235,431	11.6	3.9	690,437
Alabama.......................	9,827	4.6	-12.2	3,421	37,851	17.7	1.4	31,478
Alaska.........................	NA	NA	NA	NA	NA	NA	NA	NA
Arizona.......................	21,197	16.7	-3.3	7,315	28,435	22.4	-6.8	12,282
Arkansas.....................	2,619	1.8	-3.1	650	11,088	7.6	4.4	4,860
California....................	177,413	15.9	3.9	67,614	111,979	10.1	-4.2	43,477
Colorado.....................	16,144	14.7	1.5	5,638	6,403	5.8	-2.4	2,235
Connecticut..................	15,687	10.1	2.6	5,006	38,853	25.1	-2.2	17,131
Delaware.....................	2,212	8.1	(D)	844	NA	NA	NA	NA
District of Columbia........	NA	NA	NA	NA	NA	NA	NA	NA
Florida........................	33,776	13.3	-3.9	12,897	21,253	8.3	-0.4	6,781
Georgia.......................	5,917	1.9	0.8	2,107	37,266	11.9	16.7	22,082
Hawaii.........................	NA	NA	NA	NA	NA	NA	NA	NA
Idaho..........................	7,607	15.7	-17.4	(D)	(D)	(D)	(D)	505
Illinois........................	26,659	5.0	-2.4	9,819	35,288	6.6	7.2	21,307
Indiana........................	14,010	3.3	-0.1	5,481	94,550	22.0	6.3	54,952
Iowa...........................	12,493	6.5	5.8	3,041	10,000	5.2	8.3	3,129
Kansas........................	6,722	4.5	8.5	3,494	36,112	23.9	-0.6	20,528
Kentucky......................	2,626	1.3	-8.3	741	39,383	19.5	2.2	34,677
Louisiana.....................	986	0.8	2.9	(D)	18,851	15.1	4.2	5,315
Maine..........................	3,610	7.5	2.1	1,117	8,057	16.8	-1.1	2,418
Maryland......................	18,351	17.6	-5.0	7,485	5,233	5.0	7.1	1,702
Massachusetts...............	46,857	20.9	3.3	21,188	5,609	2.5	-6.2	2,052
Michigan......................	15,245	3.3	-3.6	4,323	121,057	26.2	9.4	94,980
Minnesota....................	38,450	13.3	-1.4	11,531	10,866	3.7	12.4	6,784
Mississippi...................	1,774	1.4	-12.7	662	22,684	17.8	-0.1	7,143
Missouri......................	6,299	2.7	-1.8	2,601	28,424	12.3	6.5	24,369
Montana.......................	NA	NA	NA	NA	NA	NA	NA	NA
Nebraska.....................	4,441	4.9	13.8	806	6,857	7.6	2.7	2,252
Nevada........................	3,438	8.9	6.2	1,764	1,013	2.6	-6.5	355
New Hampshire..............	14,513	20.6	-2.1	4,259	1,979	2.8	0.5	434
New Jersey..................	23,266	9.9	4.0	8,142	3,010	1.3	-0.9	796
New Mexico..................	5,401	21.2	9.8	(D)	NA	NA	NA	NA
New York.....................	49,269	11.8	0.0	15,694	21,689	5.2	-3.2	8,817
North Carolina...............	14,119	3.6	-5.2	5,776	25,633	6.6	10.2	16,738
North Dakota.................	1,530	7.1	4.2	(D)	1,626	7.5	25.8	404
Ohio...........................	20,569	3.4	2.9	5,619	94,866	15.8	3.1	61,063
Oklahoma.....................	3,083	2.5	-0.4	1,340	11,505	9.2	13.1	4,625
Oregon........................	12,521	9.7	3.5	22,459	8,563	6.6	3.1	2,624
Pennsylvania.................	28,346	5.3	0.7	9,946	34,891	6.6	-2.2	17,152
Rhode Island.................	3,153	8.7	-3.7	715	NA	NA	NA	NA
South Carolina..............	5,239	2.7	1.9	1,915	29,277	15.1	15.0	15,253
South Dakota................	2,330	6.0	3.4	458	3,410	8.8	10.6	938
Tennessee...................	5,789	2.1	6.8	3,109	36,141	13.1	4.2	25,316
Texas..........................	58,349	8.3	-8.2	29,427	73,944	10.6	4.4	44,186
Utah...........................	15,620	15.6	1.5	5,033	9,165	9.1	2.4	3,611
Vermont......................	7,504	26.8	4.9	(D)	1,679	6.0	-9.6	502
Virginia.......................	11,739	5.3	0.6	3,739	37,019	16.7	6.3	10,397
Washington..................	17,182	7.5	-0.4	5,207	69,247	30.1	9.6	38,765
West Virginia.................	NA	NA	NA	NA	4,424	8.9	4.8	2,899
Wisconsin....................	21,529	5.0	0.9	8,780	25,374	5.9	8.6	12,280
Wyoming.....................	NA	NA	NA	NA	NA	NA	NA	NA

[1]Data may not be available for all NAICS industries or geographies.
0 = Zero or rounds to zero.
NA = Not available
(D) = Data withheld to avoid disclosure or does not meet statistical standards.

Table A-60.   Information Industries

Geographic area	Information industries (2007, NAICS 51)														
	Nonfarm Employment (BLS)[1] (thousands)			Earnings (BEA)[2] (million dollars)			Establishments[3]								
	2012	2010	2005	2012	2010	2005	Total, 2010	Publishing, 2010	Motion Picture/ Sound Recording, 2010	Broadcasting, 2010	Tele-communications, 2010	Data Processing, hosting and related, 2010	Other Informa-tion services, 2010	Total, 2005	Net change, 2005–2010
United States............	2,691.2	2,717.1	3,042.5	322,511	294,804	277,711	135,431	28,109	24,039	9,940	51,996	12,377	8,970	141,290	-5,859
Alabama....................	22.5	24.0	29.2	1,558	1,526	1,796	1,587	308	140	213	780	101	45	1,702	-115
Alaska......................	6.2	6.5	7.0	493	470	458	385	56	39	62	186	25	17	380	5
Arizona.....................	38.2	36.4	45.3	3,133	2,856	2,978	2,060	505	268	159	745	257	126	2,224	-164
Arkansas..................	14.5	15.3	19.3	1,061	1,062	1,414	1,052	202	105	134	490	81	40	1,034	18
California..................	430.4	427.8	473.6	69,802	61,112	53,571	20,287	3,480	7,463	1,029	5,129	1,706	1,480	20,837	-550
Colorado...................	69.7	72.0	76.9	10,663	10,013	10,204	2,940	761	414	220	993	353	199	3,222	-282
Connecticut..............	31.1	31.7	38.1	4,367	4,066	3,579	1,649	429	224	89	587	162	158	1,778	-129
Delaware...................	5.5	6.0	6.7	563	569	488	402	74	46	26	169	47	40	407	-5
District of Columbia ...	17.3	18.7	22.6	2,414	2,359	2,604	726	172	123	76	197	57	101	723	3
Florida......................	133.4	137.1	163.2	12,920	12,167	13,116	7,806	1,578	1,343	599	3,025	736	525	8,693	-887
Georgia	100.5	99.8	112.2	12,460	10,970	11,476	4,064	789	612	350	1,684	425	204	4,198	-134
Hawaii......................	8.3	9.8	10.8	677	722	678	543	94	108	55	212	55	19	631	-88
Idaho........................	9.3	9.6	10.3	589	543	508	702	159	75	62	296	62	48	698	4
Illinois......................	100.1	101.8	118.2	10,275	9,486	10,167	5,535	1,164	826	344	2,362	530	309	5,697	-162
Indiana.....................	35.5	35.6	40.3	2,531	2,305	2,362	2,297	411	291	196	1,095	238	66	2,334	-37
Iowa.........................	27.1	28.7	33.0	1,814	1,766	1,686	1,585	423	172	151	702	99	38	1,582	3
Kansas.....................	28.3	30.6	39.6	2,433	2,362	3,138	1,437	313	121	138	694	102	69	1,519	-82
Kentucky	26.3	26.4	29.3	1,703	1,585	1,443	1,487	304	160	205	628	142	48	1,688	-201
Louisiana	24.9	24.7	29.1	1,715	1,597	1,802	1,393	223	151	142	729	108	40	1,498	-105
Maine.......................	7.9	8.7	11.2	500	567	625	719	169	93	59	224	52	122	770	-51
Maryland...................	39.9	44.0	50.5	5,674	5,595	4,663	2,417	505	332	149	1,018	291	122	2,631	-214
Massachusetts..........	86.8	85.0	86.9	10,567	9,753	8,430	3,492	946	417	206	1,276	370	277	3,720	-228
Michigan	53.1	54.8	64.9	4,472	4,242	4,621	3,451	667	450	253	1,627	321	133	3,895	-444
Minnesota.................	53.7	54.1	59.1	4,756	4,444	4,142	2,568	721	398	192	836	275	146	2,725	-157
Mississippi...............	12.5	12.3	14.3	764	691	807	918	162	49	121	509	49	28	1,106	-188
Missouri	58.2	60.1	63.8	6,588	6,636	4,727	2,537	562	286	197	1,171	224	97	2,570	-33
Montana....................	6.9	7.3	7.8	394	396	373	575	149	83	76	205	41	21	613	-38
Nebraska..................	17.2	17.0	20.2	1,314	1,184	1,226	934	250	103	99	346	92	44	899	35
Nevada.....................	12.5	12.5	14.7	1,012	964	1,159	1,119	219	173	79	387	136	125	1,155	-36
New Hampshire.........	12.0	11.4	12.7	1,275	1,169	1,007	723	226	65	46	259	70	57	777	-54
New Jersey	77.7	79.2	97.1	11,066	10,501	10,549	3,841	847	511	101	1,707	451	224	4,059	-218
New Mexico..............	13.6	14.4	14.7	843	783	755	791	168	110	102	314	56	41	793	-2
New York..................	260.6	253.2	269.3	43,118	39,055	35,219	11,014	2,016	3,148	646	3,156	699	1,349	11,199	-185
North Carolina...........	69.3	68.3	71.4	6,397	5,656	5,418	3,576	751	433	297	1,611	314	170	3,356	220
North Dakota.............	6.9	7.3	7.6	518	475	391	352	106	40	82	91	20	13	374	-22
Ohio.........................	74.4	77.6	89.9	5,926	5,697	5,895	4,055	834	443	377	1,896	362	143	4,216	-161
Oklahoma	22.5	24.3	30.2	1,830	1,768	1,903	1,543	326	177	125	747	111	57	1,540	3
Oregon.....................	32.5	32.1	33.6	2,927	2,784	2,362	1,977	550	283	134	684	199	127	1,953	24
Pennsylvania............	90.2	93.3	109.5	11,714	11,297	8,942	5,010	927	522	310	2,168	442	641	5,315	-305
Rhode Island............	9.6	10.0	10.8	1,070	1,024	930	415	85	46	35	151	46	52	403	12
South Carolina	25.7	25.9	27.0	1,919	1,854	1,661	1,393	287	135	138	690	80	63	1,354	39
South Dakota	6.2	6.5	6.8	379	365	347	419	136	50	59	135	22	17	422	-3
Tennessee	43.0	45.0	49.4	3,283	3,075	2,992	2,421	437	519	276	916	190	83	2,574	-153
Texas.......................	197.0	195.7	223.1	19,689	17,926	18,558	8,911	1,780	989	685	4,042	940	475	9,486	-575
Utah.........................	31.4	29.3	32.0	2,302	1,989	1,877	1,375	325	258	68	406	193	125	1,349	26
Vermont	4.7	5.4	6.2	304	318	325	484	124	63	56	144	25	72	527	-43
Virginia	71.8	76.0	92.7	8,162	8,116	9,416	3,819	844	376	242	1,660	454	243	4,099	-280
Washington...............	104.7	103.0	94.7	18,094	14,742	11,097	3,199	833	455	170	1,148	345	248	3,226	-27
West Virginia............	9.5	10.3	11.7	696	700	585	747	104	44	80	466	34	19	718	29
Wisconsin	46.2	46.7	49.7	3,565	3,295	3,057	2,399	547	270	193	1,166	170	53	2,284	115
Wyoming	3.9	3.9	4.3	222	206	180	300	61	37	37	137	17	11	337	-37

[1]All employment estimates provided by the Bureau of Labor Statistics are based on the 2007 North American Industry Classification System (NAICS).
[2]The estimates of earnings provided by the Bureau of Economic Analysis for 2000–2006 are based on the 2002 North American Industry Classification System (NAICS). The estimates for 2007 forward are based on the 2007 NAICS. All dollar estimates are in current dollars (not adjusted for inflation).
[3]Data provided by County Business Patterns is based on the North American Industry Classification System (NAICS). Data for 2010 is based on NAICS 2007. Data for 2005 is based on NAICS 2002.

Table A-61. Wholesale and Retail Trade

Geographic area	Wholesale and retail nonfarm employment[1] (thousands)			Wholesale trade					Retail trade				
				Earnings (BEA)[2] (million dollars)			Establishments (NAICS 42)		Earnings (BEA)[2] (million dollars)			Establishments (NAICS 44 and 45)	
	2012	2010	2005	2012	2010	2005	2010	Net change, 2005–2010	2012	2010	2005	2010	Net change, 2005-2010
United States........................	20,536	19,970	21,043	504,818	454,320	418,386	414,608	-15,215	601,407	549,657	544,190	1,067,984	-55,223
Alabama................................	296	295	315	5,404	5,089	4,920	5,335	-198	8,078	7,601	7,444	18,484	-967
Alaska...................................	42	42	42	464	447	410	743	7	1,560	1,440	1,413	2,515	-160
Arizona..................................	394	387	407	8,644	7,993	7,210	6,504	-142	12,921	11,822	11,910	17,993	-235
Arkansas...............................	181	176	179	3,598	3,310	2,780	3,386	-87	4,907	4,476	3,955	11,006	-874
California...............................	2,239	2,157	2,333	60,913	54,538	52,747	58,023	-1,229	77,145	68,698	75,246	106,265	-6,117
Colorado...............................	338	328	339	9,177	8,144	7,031	7,140	-129	10,218	9,241	8,948	18,521	-687
Connecticut...........................	245	241	259	7,047	6,626	6,136	4,418	-253	8,265	7,763	8,167	12,940	-988
Delaware...............................	63	62	68	1,264	1,206	1,197	1,023	24	1,795	1,708	1,741	3,654	-188
District of Columbia	24	23	22	684	576	458	413	-35	799	731	651	1,762	-151
Florida...................................	1,297	1,249	1,350	27,339	24,563	23,487	30,212	-1,497	38,198	34,685	34,853	70,627	-1,842
Georgia.................................	646	630	671	18,245	16,813	15,974	13,125	-848	17,052	15,657	15,677	33,720	-1,303
Hawaii...................................	86	84	87	1,154	1,072	1,029	1,749	-112	2,701	2,494	2,433	4,694	-230
Idaho....................................	105	101	103	1,813	1,647	1,425	2,019	36	2,939	2,713	2,757	5,910	-154
Illinois..................................	891	874	929	28,490	25,231	23,160	19,194	-807	23,179	21,188	21,516	40,670	-2,499
Indiana.................................	429	418	453	8,590	7,854	7,560	7,771	-382	10,741	9,920	10,202	22,076	-1,418
Iowa.....................................	244	239	247	5,098	4,515	3,912	4,801	-14	6,017	5,515	5,154	12,343	-1,300
Kansas..................................	201	199	208	4,757	4,548	3,846	4,432	-109	5,308	4,843	4,641	10,727	-835
Kentucky...............................	276	272	287	5,330	4,881	4,665	4,284	-276	7,206	6,695	6,409	15,579	-987
Louisiana..............................	295	288	293	5,736	5,171	4,439	5,536	-68	8,489	7,752	6,953	16,687	-739
Maine....................................	101	100	107	1,418	1,311	1,267	1,591	-78	2,930	2,783	2,795	6,513	-467
Maryland...............................	371	362	392	7,965	7,433	7,329	5,761	-282	11,580	10,834	10,874	18,356	-1,205
Massachusetts.......................	466	461	488	12,995	12,503	11,478	8,161	-657	13,325	12,567	13,188	24,412	-1,427
Michigan...............................	607	597	677	13,845	12,438	12,416	11,511	-470	16,211	15,250	16,179	35,017	-3,658
Minnesota.............................	412	400	432	12,380	11,024	10,026	8,249	-494	10,022	9,213	9,571	19,547	-1,403
Mississippi............................	168	167	174	2,283	2,159	2,093	2,829	-24	4,866	4,476	4,222	11,744	-685
Missouri................................	420	415	438	9,408	8,747	8,073	7,940	-336	11,343	10,550	10,325	21,799	-1,708
Montana................................	72	70	72	1,092	958	819	1,455	-36	2,097	1,932	1,746	4,939	-253
Nebraska...............................	147	145	148	2,933	2,664	2,464	3,024	119	3,639	3,370	3,128	7,417	-663
Nevada.................................	165	160	168	2,717	2,508	2,581	2,858	46	5,460	4,929	5,059	8,084	78
New Hampshire......................	121	118	125	2,639	2,374	2,268	1,865	-153	3,959	3,610	3,693	6,166	-521
New Jersey	657	645	703	22,919	21,117	19,867	14,871	-1,476	20,831	19,552	19,201	32,408	-2,855
New Mexico	112	111	116	1,430	1,394	1,280	1,957	-3	3,461	3,198	3,146	6,813	-419
New York...............................	1,247	1,201	1,232	33,586	30,345	28,727	32,975	-2,462	39,977	36,506	32,727	76,763	-1,371
North Carolina.......................	623	599	612	13,627	12,348	11,243	11,651	-215	16,898	15,513	15,248	34,339	-1,536
North Dakota.........................	72	65	61	2,033	1,417	1,018	1,500	48	1,761	1,421	1,205	3,199	-236
Ohio.....................................	783	767	847	18,258	16,539	15,708	14,310	-1,235	20,664	18,981	19,416	37,035	-3,914
Oklahoma	233	224	226	4,346	3,676	3,291	4,594	-22	7,192	6,391	5,727	12,964	-763
Oregon..................................	262	257	271	7,106	6,292	5,728	5,505	-132	7,293	6,751	6,720	13,835	-653
Pennsylvania.........................	861	849	895	20,573	18,615	16,645	15,077	-813	23,297	21,813	21,624	44,430	-2,793
Rhode Island.........................	64	62	69	1,476	1,343	1,268	1,409	-10	1,841	1,782	1,843	3,886	-315
South Carolina	292	287	299	4,926	4,458	4,164	4,899	104	8,157	7,715	7,479	17,708	-882
South Dakota	71	68	67	1,350	1,185	984	1,406	128	1,790	1,617	1,457	3,973	-309
Tennessee	434	424	455	9,471	8,605	8,375	6,939	-397	12,970	11,982	11,675	22,813	-985
Texas....................................	1,725	1,633	1,587	53,472	45,300	36,937	31,526	393	50,154	44,545	40,480	76,787	452
Utah......................................	192	182	179	3,702	3,151	2,644	3,522	88	5,950	5,309	4,547	8,816	362
Vermont	47	47	51	687	638	608	865	-10	1,457	1,374	1,360	3,657	-248
Virginia.................................	516	508	536	9,942	9,293	8,530	7,415	-375	14,715	13,714	13,747	27,747	-1,588
Washington............................	443	428	438	11,140	10,035	8,701	9,382	-112	15,576	13,440	12,520	21,770	-1,021
West Virginia.........................	111	110	114	1,521	1,413	1,273	1,552	-89	2,979	2,764	2,603	6,557	-686
Wisconsin	411	406	435	9,135	8,211	7,721	7,074	-198	10,295	9,724	9,680	19,591	-1,628
Wyoming	39	38	38	695	599	475	827	57	1,197	1,115	936	2,726	-249

[1]All estimates of labor provided by the Bureau of Labor Statistics (BLS) are based on the 2007 North American Industry Classification System (NAICS). Includes Wholesale trade (NAICS 42) and Retail trade (NAICS 44).
[2]Bureau of Economic Analysis. The estimates of earnings for 2000–2006 are based on the 2002 North American Industry Classification System (NAICS). The estimates for 2007 forward are based on the 2007 NAICS. All dollars estimates are in current dollars and not adjusted for inflation.

Table A-62. Retail Trade Earnings, 2011

Geographic area	Total retail sales plus food services and drinking places (2007, NAICS 44-45, 722) (million dollars)	Food services and drinking places (2007, NAICS 722) (million dollars)	All retail stores (2007, NAICS 44, 45) (million dollars)	Motor vehicle and parts dealers (2007, NAICS 441) Earnings (million dollars)	Percentage of all retail	Furniture and Home furnishings (2007, NAICS 442) Earnings (million dollars)	Percentage of all retail	Electronics and appliances (2007, NAICS 443) (million dollars) Earnings (million dollars)	Percentage of all retail	Building material and garden equipment and supplies dealers (2007, NAICS 444) (million dollars) Earnings (million dollars)	Percentage of all retail	Food and beverage stores (2007, NAICS 445) (million dollars) Earnings (million dollars)	Percentage of all retail
United States	793,746	221,632	572,114	102,311	17.9	19,022	3.3	27,647	4.8	46,025	8.0	91,352	16.0
Alabama	10,519	2,721	7,798	1,514	19.4	220	2.8	295	3.8	732	9.4	877	11.2
Alaska	2,098	601	1,496	230	15.4	37	2.5	35	2.3	165	11.0	229	15.3
Arizona	17,007	4,449	12,558	2,213	17.6	415	3.3	1,094	8.7	822	6.5	1,942	15.5
Arkansas	6,152	1,491	4,661	981	21.1	129	2.8	172	3.7	365	7.8	634	13.6
California	100,861	28,712	72,149	10,649	14.8	2,463	3.4	5,151	7.1	4,849	6.7	13,600	18.8
Colorado	14,072	4,455	9,617	1,836	19.1	386	4.0	393	4.1	790	8.2	1,637	17.0
Connecticut	10,753	2,740	8,012	1,340	16.7	338	4.2	386	4.8	676	8.4	1,301	16.2
Delaware	2,451	692	1,758	368	20.9	78	4.4	80	4.5	169	9.6	266	15.1
District of Columbia	2,054	1,292	762	10	1.4	36	4.8	25	3.3	35	4.6	212	27.8
Florida	51,184	14,833	36,351	6,889	19.0	1,317	3.6	1,848	5.1	2,595	7.1	5,828	16.0
Georgia	23,049	6,853	16,196	3,103	19.2	523	3.2	604	3.7	1,520	9.4	2,360	14.6
Hawaii	4,081	1,501	2,580	356	13.8	63	2.4	63	2.4	181	7.0	469	18.2
Idaho	3,593	810	2,783	536	19.3	93	3.3	124	4.5	274	9.9	326	11.7
Illinois	31,598	9,499	22,100	3,726	16.9	814	3.7	1,563	7.1	1,558	7.1	3,374	15.3
Indiana	14,216	3,961	10,256	1,909	18.6	312	3.0	399	3.9	1,078	10.5	1,357	13.2
Iowa	7,347	1,597	5,750	1,095	19.0	160	2.8	254	4.4	548	9.5	933	16.2
Kansas	6,995	1,924	5,070	958	18.9	202	4.0	220	4.3	439	8.7	774	15.3
Kentucky	9,680	2,796	6,884	1,222	17.8	174	2.5	204	3.0	647	9.4	998	14.5
Louisiana	11,362	3,275	8,087	1,484	18.3	259	3.2	245	3.0	798	9.9	1,021	12.6
Maine	3,774	930	2,844	497	17.5	60	2.1	101	3.6	286	10.0	497	17.5
Maryland	15,479	4,361	11,118	2,051	18.4	418	3.8	494	4.4	994	8.9	2,449	22.0
Massachusetts	18,763	5,872	12,891	2,129	16.5	420	3.3	472	3.7	1,116	8.7	2,586	20.1
Michigan	21,253	5,603	15,650	3,131	20.0	471	3.0	665	4.3	1,527	9.8	2,116	13.5
Minnesota	13,062	3,494	9,568	1,713	17.9	346	3.6	383	4.0	890	9.3	1,319	13.8
Mississippi	6,134	1,497	4,637	808	17.4	125	2.7	131	2.8	448	9.7	570	12.3
Missouri	14,978	4,112	10,866	2,063	19.0	321	3.0	348	3.2	999	9.2	1,395	12.8
Montana	2,673	674	2,000	364	18.2	66	3.3	57	2.8	214	10.7	300	15.0
Nebraska	4,558	1,112	3,447	662	19.2	131	3.8	123	3.6	336	9.7	492	14.3
Nevada	7,903	2,759	5,144	841	16.3	143	2.8	187	3.6	279	5.4	817	15.9
New Hampshire	4,816	1,047	3,769	715	19.0	94	2.5	269	7.1	382	10.1	535	14.2
New Jersey	25,981	5,782	20,199	3,166	15.7	671	3.3	1,151	5.7	1,423	7.0	4,205	20.8
New Mexico	4,711	1,402	3,308	653	19.7	83	2.5	102	3.1	293	8.8	447	13.5
New York	53,619	15,387	38,232	4,902	12.8	1,378	3.6	2,029	5.3	2,528	6.6	7,223	18.9
North Carolina	22,165	6,222	15,943	3,332	20.9	540	3.4	623	3.9	1,421	8.9	1,890	11.9
North Dakota	2,030	477	1,552	337	21.7	61	3.9	79	5.1	160	10.3	151	9.7
Ohio	27,445	7,727	19,718	3,714	18.8	552	2.8	769	3.9	1,740	8.8	2,974	15.1
Oklahoma	9,282	2,532	6,749	1,423	21.1	204	3.0	221	3.3	607	9.0	749	11.1
Oregon	9,818	2,837	6,982	1,310	18.8	220	3.1	334	4.8	541	7.8	1,153	16.5
Pennsylvania	30,223	7,738	22,484	4,037	18.0	678	3.0	796	3.5	1,894	8.4	3,923	17.4
Rhode Island	2,636	849	1,786	294	16.5	46	2.6	59	3.3	153	8.6	339	19.0
South Carolina	11,147	3,250	7,897	1,497	19.0	224	2.8	288	3.6	682	8.6	1,340	17.0
South Dakota	2,188	493	1,695	354	20.9	49	2.9	70	4.1	181	10.7	186	11.0
Tennessee	17,032	4,541	12,491	2,580	20.7	333	2.7	659	5.3	1,015	8.1	1,613	12.9
Texas	66,243	19,208	47,035	10,537	22.4	1,753	3.7	2,139	4.5	3,645	7.7	6,593	14.0
Utah	7,028	1,549	5,479	1,011	18.4	187	3.4	281	5.1	418	7.6	714	13.0
Vermont	1,841	411	1,430	255	17.8	38	2.7	38	2.6	141	9.9	269	18.8
Virginia	19,862	5,725	14,138	2,816	19.9	582	4.1	658	4.7	1,166	8.2	2,012	14.2
Washington	19,200	5,045	14,155	2,167	15.3	434	3.1	453	3.2	1,051	7.4	2,417	17.1
West Virginia	3,826	958	2,867	538	18.8	72	2.5	95	3.3	277	9.7	364	12.7
Wisconsin	13,461	3,438	10,023	1,748	17.4	281	2.8	375	3.7	863	8.6	1,424	14.2
Wyoming	1,546	397	1,149	247	21.5	28	2.4	42	3.6	111	9.6	153	13.3

Table A-62. Retail Trade Earnings, 2011—*Continued*

Geographic area	Gasoline stations (2007, NAICS 447) (million dollars)		Clothing and clothing accessories (2007, NAICS 448) (million dollars)		Sporting goods, hobby, book, music stores (2007, NAICS 451)		General merchandise stores (2007, NAICS 452) (million dollars)		Miscellaneous stores (2007, NAICS 453)		Non-store retailers (2007, NAICS 454)	
	Earnings (million dollars)	Percentage of all retail	Earnings (million dollars)	Percentage of all retail	Earnings (million dollars)	Percentage of all retail	Earnings (million dollars)	Percentage of all retail	Earnings (million dollars)	Percentage of all retail	Earnings (million dollars)	Percentage of all retail
United States.............	30,650	5.4	37,488	6.6	16,905	3.0	85,492	14.9	33,967	5.9	35,405	6.2
Alabama............................	552	7.1	421	5.4	236	3.0	1,569	20.1	412	5.3	214	2.7
Alaska..............................	65	4.3	67	4.5	74	4.9	343	22.9	119	8.0	80	5.4
Arizona............................	748	6.0	518	4.1	304	2.4	1,781	14.2	902	7.2	955	7.6
Arkansas..........................	349	7.5	181	3.9	103	2.2	986	21.1	249	5.3	143	3.1
California..........................	3,910	5.4	5,439	7.5	2,297	3.2	9,295	12.9	4,471	6.2	4,468	6.2
Colorado	511	5.3	500	5.2	482	5.0	1,443	15.0	686	7.1	459	4.8
Connecticut......................	401	5.0	557	7.0	231	2.9	770	9.6	419	5.2	981	12.2
Delaware	62	3.5	121	6.9	48	2.7	245	13.9	103	5.9	79	4.5
District of Columbia	17	2.3	106	13.9	32	4.2	42	5.5	55	7.2	86	11.3
Florida..............................	1,571	4.3	2,726	7.5	941	2.6	5,431	14.9	1,995	5.5	1,876	5.2
Georgia............................	896	5.5	934	5.8	457	2.8	2,834	17.5	867	5.4	826	5.1
Hawaii..............................	91	3.5	342	13.3	96	3.7	444	17.2	233	9.0	38	1.5
Idaho................................	167	6.0	90	3.2	113	4.1	467	16.8	187	6.7	263	9.4
Illinois..............................	884	4.0	1,400	6.3	628	2.8	3,535	16.0	1,264	5.7	1,219	5.5
Indiana.............................	557	5.4	513	5.0	307	3.0	1,803	17.6	615	6.0	537	5.2
Iowa.................................	439	7.6	208	3.6	168	2.9	907	15.8	331	5.7	340	5.9
Kansas.............................	354	7.0	234	4.6	164	3.2	848	16.7	301	5.9	207	4.1
Kentucky	468	6.8	270	3.9	187	2.7	1,328	19.3	440	6.4	211	3.1
Louisiana	766	9.5	428	5.3	214	2.6	1,419	17.5	511	6.3	176	2.2
Maine...............................	214	7.5	121	4.2	78	2.8	352	12.4	161	5.6	295	10.4
Maryland..........................	396	3.6	657	5.9	319	2.9	1,441	13.0	692	6.2	416	3.7
Massachusetts..................	518	4.0	1,010	7.8	434	3.4	1,362	10.6	696	5.4	1,006	7.8
Michigan	642	4.1	773	4.9	525	3.4	2,851	18.2	955	6.1	589	3.8
Minnesota........................	588	6.1	484	5.1	306	3.2	1,588	16.6	557	5.8	706	7.4
Mississippi.......................	467	10.1	214	4.6	109	2.4	953	20.6	270	5.8	123	2.7
Missouri...........................	815	7.5	531	4.9	302	2.8	1,924	17.7	619	5.7	685	6.3
Montana...........................	176	8.8	61	3.1	94	4.7	330	16.5	176	8.8	71	3.5
Nebraska..........................	233	6.8	133	3.9	112	3.3	531	15.4	204	5.9	214	6.2
Nevada.............................	275	5.4	564	11.0	130	2.5	795	15.5	351	6.8	445	8.7
New Hampshire.................	184	4.9	166	4.4	142	3.8	417	11.1	240	6.4	453	12.0
New Jersey	725	3.6	1,838	9.1	638	3.2	2,050	10.2	951	4.7	1,712	8.5
New Mexico	235	7.1	162	4.9	88	2.7	613	18.5	277	8.4	150	4.5
New York..........................	908	2.4	4,813	12.6	1,045	2.7	4,120	10.8	2,648	6.9	2,764	7.2
North Carolina..................	1,221	7.7	825	5.2	416	2.6	2,727	17.1	923	5.8	626	3.9
North Dakota....................	154	9.9	59	3.8	55	3.5	205	13.2	92	6.0	92	5.9
Ohio.................................	1,091	5.5	1,144	5.8	546	2.8	3,026	15.3	1,164	5.9	1,440	7.3
Oklahoma	575	8.5	262	3.9	159	2.4	1,233	18.3	480	7.1	312	4.6
Oregon.............................	341	4.9	427	6.1	294	4.2	1,222	17.5	381	5.5	396	5.7
Pennsylvania.....................	1,155	5.1	1,429	6.4	656	2.9	2,807	12.5	1,198	5.3	1,981	8.8
Rhode Island.....................	92	5.1	111	6.2	42	2.4	223	12.5	103	5.8	107	6.0
South Carolina	516	6.5	441	5.6	189	2.4	1,399	17.7	408	5.2	229	2.9
South Dakota	167	9.9	55	3.3	59	3.5	249	14.7	126	7.4	104	6.1
Tennessee........................	713	5.7	681	5.5	310	2.5	2,122	17.0	721	5.8	545	4.4
Texas...............................	2,468	5.2	3,163	6.7	1,226	2.6	7,440	15.8	2,713	5.8	1,944	4.1
Utah	303	5.5	253	4.6	206	3.8	834	15.2	277	5.1	747	13.6
Vermont............................	122	8.6	71	5.0	60	4.2	82	5.7	89	6.2	175	12.2
Virginia	862	6.1	768	5.4	396	2.8	2,431	17.2	772	5.5	679	4.8
Washington.......................	555	3.9	649	4.6	456	3.2	2,383	16.8	836	5.9	1,990	14.1
West Virginia.....................	260	9.1	95	3.3	75	2.6	544	19.0	152	5.3	98	3.4
Wisconsin.........................	739	7.4	430	4.3	320	3.2	1,564	15.6	495	4.9	1,093	10.9
Wyoming	131	11.4	43	3.7	34	3.0	184	16.0	76	6.6	59	5.1

Table A-63. Transportation and Commuting

Geographic area	Transportation and warehousing (NAICS 48-49)							Workers 16 years and over, 2009–2011			
	Nonfarm employment (BLS)[1] (thousands)		Earnings (BEA)[2] (million dollars)		Establishments[3]			Total workers (thousands)	Percentage of workers who		Mean travel time to work (minutes)
	2012	2005	2012	2005	2010	2005	Net change 2005–2010		Drove alone to work	Used public transportation[4]	
United States..............................	4,414.5	4,360.9	324,865	278,340	208,474	211,150	-2,676	138,077	76.4	5.0	25.3
Alabama.....................................	54.9	55.0	3,872	3,298	2,874	3,144	-270	1,965	84.5	0.4	23.9
Alaska..	19.7	19.0	1,672	1,358	1,113	1,149	-36	343	67.8	1.5	18.3
Arizona......................................	71.8	69.5	5,110	4,376	3,065	3,092	-27	2,645	76.1	1.9	24.5
Arkansas....................................	NA	NA	3,586	3,397	2,412	2,596	-184	1,223	82.0	0.5	21.2
California...................................	427.2	431.4	34,804	31,323	20,876	20,086	790	16,063	73.1	5.2	26.9
Colorado....................................	63.4	65.7	4,884	4,209	3,340	3,285	55	2,450	75.0	3.1	24.3
Connecticut................................	42.7	43.6	2,832	2,580	1,641	1,694	-53	1,717	78.8	4.6	24.7
Delaware....................................	NA	NA	704	612	652	740	-88	413	80.4	3.4	24.4
District of Columbia	NA	NA	417	366	182	188	-6	300	34.6	38.2	29.5
Florida.......................................	217.8	225.5	15,310	13,357	12,538	12,668	-130	7,956	79.6	2.0	25.6
Georgia.....................................	167.4	161.9	12,475	10,335	5,831	5,986	-155	4,166	79.1	2.2	27.0
Hawaii.......................................	24.8	28.0	1,485	1,448	856	850	6	658	66.8	6.3	25.7
Idaho...	18.7	17.4	1,173	1,021	1,602	1,645	-43	675	77.5	0.9	20.0
Illinois.......................................	240.6	234.2	17,924	15,542	12,151	10,924	1,227	5,841	73.6	8.7	28.0
Indiana......................................	118.0	115.3	7,275	6,430	5,016	5,090	-74	2,873	83.5	1.0	23.2
Iowa..	56.0	52.0	3,592	3,088	3,620	3,702	-82	1,517	79.7	1.1	18.8
Kansas.......................................	47.8	45.7	3,204	2,728	2,615	2,632	-17	1,370	81.6	0.4	18.8
Kentucky....................................	88.4	84.6	5,768	5,267	2,951	3,167	-216	1,812	82.3	1.2	22.7
Louisiana...................................	73.9	70.4	6,868	4,636	3,819	3,652	167	1,946	81.8	1.3	24.7
Maine..	15.2	16.7	893	824	1,217	1,274	-57	634	79.2	0.6	23.1
Maryland....................................	69.2	69.1	4,659	3,991	3,307	3,712	-405	2,857	73.1	8.9	31.8
Massachusetts............................	74.5	72.3	4,855	4,252	3,565	3,675	-110	3,190	72.3	9.1	27.7
Michigan....................................	102.0	107.6	7,672	7,347	5,482	5,557	-75	4,085	82.9	1.3	23.9
Minnesota..................................	79.0	83.2	5,595	5,584	4,549	4,666	-117	2,662	77.9	3.5	22.8
Mississippi.................................	40.2	39.2	2,522	2,206	2,077	2,342	-265	1,172	83.6	0.5	23.7
Missouri.....................................	81.6	90.6	6,135	5,880	4,704	5,114	-410	2,721	81.4	1.5	23.1
Montana.....................................	13.6	12.4	1,062	855	1,309	1,237	72	466	75.6	0.9	17.9
Nebraska....................................	51.1	50.6	4,260	3,454	2,302	2,330	-28	928	80.9	0.7	18.1
Nevada......................................	49.0	41.5	3,259	2,279	1,392	1,447	-55	1,202	78.6	3.3	23.5
New Hampshire............................	12.3	12.8	713	728	811	839	-28	672	81.5	0.7	26.1
New Jersey	151.0	160.1	11,180	10,364	6,697	7,228	-531	4,078	71.8	10.9	30.2
New Mexico	NA	NA	1,388	1,179	1,283	1,281	2	866	78.9	1.1	21.7
New York	226.2	228.5	15,514	13,559	11,985	12,004	-19	8,777	54.1	26.7	31.4
North Carolina............................	108.6	115.2	6,847	6,660	5,342	5,819	-477	4,167	81.3	1.1	23.4
North Dakota..............................	21.0	10.1	1,789	691	1,175	1,040	135	361	79.1	0.5	16.5
Ohio..	169.5	175.4	11,526	10,870	7,029	7,583	-554	5,115	83.3	1.7	22.9
Oklahoma	44.5	43.5	5,245	3,121	2,596	2,591	5	1,661	81.7	0.5	20.8
Oregon	49.5	52.4	3,310	3,238	2,936	3,106	-170	1,682	71.8	4.2	22.3
Pennsylvania..............................	219.1	204.2	13,814	12,408	7,907	7,779	128	5,752	76.8	5.3	25.7
Rhode Island..............................	9.7	9.7	569	491	640	703	-63	496	80.0	3.0	23.2
South Carolina	50.1	51.9	2,935	2,775	2,474	2,688	-214	1,964	82.4	0.6	23.4
South Dakota	NA	NA	727	648	1,134	1,055	79	409	77.8	0.6	16.9
Tennessee..................................	137.8	139.9	9,746	8,980	4,161	4,259	-98	2,715	83.6	0.8	24.1
Texas...	401.0	361.3	40,172	27,662	15,745	15,245	500	11,216	79.8	1.5	24.7
Utah..	46.4	43.4	3,070	2,624	2,051	1,851	200	1,230	76.6	2.3	21.3
Vermont	6.8	7.2	391	392	496	536	-40	316	74.5	1.2	21.8
Virginia......................................	104.9	110.5	7,105	6,397	4,779	5,348	-569	3,869	77.5	4.4	27.5
Washington................................	88.0	87.7	6,803	5,917	4,847	4,767	80	3,081	72.8	5.7	25.4
West Virginia..............................	NA	NA	1,437	1,278	1,249	1,433	-184	738	82.4	0.8	25.4
Wisconsin	89.0	97.0	5,655	5,583	5,189	5,493	-304	2,779	80.1	1.8	21.6
Wyoming	12.3	10.4	1,061	732	890	858	32	284	76.9	1.7	18.3

[1]All estimates of labor provided by the Bureau of Labor Statistics (BLS) are based on the 2007 North American Industry. Classification System (NAICS). United States totals differ from the sum of the state figures because of differing benchmarks among states and differing industrial and geographic stratification.

[2]Bureau of Economic Analysis. The estimates of earnings for 2005 are based on the 2002 North American Industry Classification System (NAICS). The estimates for 2012 are based on the 2007 NAICS. All dollars estimates are in current dollars and not adjusted for inflation.

NA Not available

Table A-63. Transportation and Commuting—*Continued*

Geographic area	Vehicle miles of travel (billions)		Railroad shipments[5] (thousand tons)		Waterborne shipments[6]	
	2011	2005	2010	2005	2010	2006
United States..........................	2,946	2,990	1,802,184	2,005,739	2,334,399	2,588,440
Alabama..................................	65	60	32,783	44,871	72,696	80,646
Alaska....................................	5	5	6,194	8,157	45,032	50,974
Arizona...................................	60	60	2,546	5,498	NA	NA
Arkansas................................	33	32	18,214	24,094	14,334	14,785
California................................	321	329	56,270	67,773	212,285	237,954
Colorado................................	47	48	24,807	41,238	NA	NA
Connecticut............................	31	32	1,639	2,022	16,229	19,340
Delaware................................	9	10	421	1,287	8,510	35,182
District of Columbia	4	4	22	197	108	651
Florida...................................	192	202	40,079	68,573	101,455	128,737
Georgia..................................	108	114	28,294	38,878	37,120	36,472
Hawaii....................................	10	10	0	0	18,386	27,770
Idaho.....................................	16	15	7,460	11,465	654	975
Illinois....................................	103	108	109,467	109,119	108,083	120,350
Indiana...................................	76	72	52,576	54,830	60,805	73,520
Iowa.......................................	31	31	47,004	43,464	10,470	13,847
Kansas...................................	30	30	22,398	24,078	239	2,002
Kentucky................................	48	47	74,416	92,682	91,357	108,661
Louisiana...............................	47	45	27,221	38,341	483,050	489,935
Maine.....................................	14	15	2,329	3,947	20,907	28,103
Maryland................................	56	56	6,167	8,195	45,277	54,407
Massachusetts........................	55	55	1,759	2,632	22,661	27,411
Michigan................................	95	104	22,030	36,128	59,067	71,251
Minnesota..............................	57	57	89,568	77,407	40,408	43,008
Mississippi.............................	39	42	7,759	12,076	54,210	50,677
Missouri.................................	69	69	14,521	19,185	32,953	30,738
Montana.................................	12	11	47,925	44,035	NA	NA
Nebraska................................	19	19	32,830	25,856	46	22
Nevada...................................	24	21	2,009	2,516	NA	NA
New Hampshire.......................	13	13	50	647	2,964	4,823
New Jersey	73	74	10,637	13,258	155,130	134,666
New Mexico	26	24	11,357	14,647	NA	NA
New York................................	128	138	7,323	10,479	50,492	102,185
North Carolina........................	104	101	10,093	15,670	12,011	13,369
North Dakota..........................	9	8	35,585	26,031	NA	NA
Ohio.......................................	112	110	63,031	68,936	98,986	117,000
Oklahoma...............................	47	47	17,727	26,323	5,020	4,480
Oregon...................................	33	35	8,374	18,270	30,198	34,898
Pennsylvania..........................	99	108	54,535	66,979	90,373	105,011
Rhode Island..........................	8	8	148	464	8,315	11,016
South Carolina........................	49	49	10,810	17,573	18,110	27,546
South Dakota..........................	9	8	19,053	15,326	NA	NA
Tennessee..............................	71	71	17,337	18,719	34,314	51,106
Texas.....................................	237	235	88,871	122,901	486,658	488,357
Utah.......................................	26	25	17,960	23,064	NA	NA
Vermont	7	8	615	830	0	0
Virginia..................................	81	80	37,009	49,705	69,095	55,437
Washington............................	57	55	20,817	27,870	112,314	121,233
West Virginia..........................	19	21	100,262	119,318	69,704	71,379
Wisconsin...............................	54	60	15,044	16,115	34,494	46,649
Wyoming	9	9	476,841	424,070	NA	NA

[5]Rail shipments of all commodities originating in state.
[6]Includes domestic and foreign shipments terminating and originating in state and intrastate shipments. National and state totals exclude duplication. National total includes Guam, the Virgin Islands, the Pacific Islands, Puerto Rico, other territories, and trans-shipments.
NA Not available
0 = Represents zero or rounds to zero

Table A-64.   Motor Vehicle and Motorcycle Registrations, Highway Mileage, Bridges, and Drivers Licenses

Geographic area	Motor vehicle registrations								Motorcycle registrations[5] (thousands)	
	Total[1]				Automobile[3] (thousands)		Trucks[4] (thousands)			
	Number (thousands)		Rate per 1,000 persons[2]							
	2011	2005	2011	2005	2011	2005	2011	2005	2011	2005
United States	244,778	241,194	786	814	125,657	135,192	118,456	103,819	8,410	6,184
Alabama	4,685	4,545	975	997	2,308	1,745	2,365	2,774	127	93
Alaska	727	673	1006	1,014	216	248	509	421	31	22
Arizona	4,930	3,972	761	669	2,363	2,103	2,556	1,846	179	98
Arkansas	2,372	1,940	807	698	1,022	942	1,347	980	76	50
California	28,358	32,487	752	899	14,550	19,438	13,771	12,793	802	659
Colorado	4,159	1,808	813	388	1,799	849	2,350	943	173	117
Connecticut	2,731	3,059	763	871	1,720	2,016	1,004	1,020	98	65
Delaware	899	737	991	873	491	419	405	307	30	19
District of Columbia	313	237	506	431	239	181	71	49	4	1
Florida	14,895	15,691	782	882	7,982	8,201	6,878	7,332	574	510
Georgia	7,334	8,063	747	889	3,430	4,180	3,877	3,834	200	141
Hawaii	1,118	948	813	743	535	510	580	424	30	24
Idaho	1,563	1,374	986	961	611	577	947	787	63	56
Illinois	10,095	9,458	784	741	5,564	5,633	4,498	3,736	350	291
Indiana	5,928	4,955	910	790	2,882	2,670	3,025	2,229	204	147
Iowa	3,322	3,398	1085	1,145	1,646	1,831	1,667	1,548	174	146
Kansas	2,365	2,368	824	863	1,142	857	1,218	1,499	81	66
Kentucky	3,665	3,428	839	821	1,883	1,888	1,771	1,499	98	56
Louisiana	3,984	3,819	871	844	1,801	1,910	2,169	1,838	67	55
Maine	1,121	1,075	844	813	530	583	586	483	50	40
Maryland	3,786	4,322	650	772	2,088	2,583	1,683	1,713	120	76
Massachusetts	5,536	5,420	840	847	3,180	3,348	2,345	2,041	159	140
Michigan	8,874	8,247	899	815	4,743	4,704	4,111	3,468	308	263
Minnesota	4,669	4,647	874	905	2,249	2,493	2,403	2,124	240	201
Mississippi	2,008	1,978	674	677	1,051	1,109	948	850	28	27
Missouri	5,029	4,589	837	791	2,441	2,532	2,572	2,039	141	81
Montana	1,172	1,009	1174	1,078	436	427	732	573	47	48
Nebraska	1,836	1,703	996	968	766	823	1,065	860	51	31
Nevada	2,083	1,349	765	559	1,079	663	1,001	674	69	50
New Hampshire	1,199	1,174	910	897	595	648	601	520	79	69
New Jersey	7,609	6,262	863	718	4,417	3,914	3,172	2,281	330	158
New Mexico	1,707	1,548	820	803	718	671	984	859	65	37
New York	10,085	11,863	518	616	5,867	8,891	4,170	2,822	346	190
North Carolina	6,026	6,148	624	708	3,264	3,552	2,743	2,531	223	105
North Dakota	753	695	1101	1,092	329	337	422	351	33	23
Ohio	9,827	10,634	851	928	5,412	6,303	4,386	4,229	390	308
Oklahoma	3,302	3,725	871	1,050	1,523	1,920	1,771	1,774	127	82
Oregon	3,020	2,897	780	796	1,472	1,364	1,543	1,489	108	72
Pennsylvania	9,898	9,864	777	794	5,485	5,840	4,388	3,938	404	305
Rhode Island	886	812	843	754	528	512	356	293	33	29
South Carolina	3,719	3,339	795	785	1,984	1,922	1,726	1,389	108	63
South Dakota	926	854	1123	1,100	385	380	539	466	69	46
Tennessee	5,134	4,980	802	835	2,637	2,809	2,484	2,128	168	122
Texas	19,175	17,470	747	764	8,965	8,793	10,156	8,468	439	328
Utah	1,824	2,210	647	895	858	1,079	961	1,118	59	48
Vermont	575	508	918	815	286	267	287	237	30	22
Virginia	6,803	6,591	840	871	3,827	4,031	2,954	2,506	196	77
Washington	5,660	5,598	829	890	3,037	3,040	2,611	2,527	221	171
West Virginia	1,401	1,352	755	744	663	686	732	649	56	17
Wisconsin	4,927	4,725	863	854	2,419	2,546	2,493	2,149	317	303
Wyoming	768	646	1352	1,269	242	226	522	411	30	33

[1]Automobiles, trucks, and buses (excludes motorcycles). Excludes vehicles owned by military services.
[2]Based on population as enumerated July 1.
[3]Includes private and commercially owned (including taxis). Excludes publicly owned.
[4]Includes private, commercial, and publicly owned trucks.
[5]Includes private and commercially owned. Excludes publicly owned.

Table A-64. Motor Vehicle and Motorcycle Registrations, Highway Mileage, Bridges, and Drivers Licenses—*Continued*

Geographic area	Highway mileage, 2011					Bridges (as of December)		Drivers licenses[8] (thousands)	
	Total	Interstate	Arterial[6]	Collector	Local	Number	Number deficient and obsolete[7]	2011	2005
						2012	2012		
United States.........................	4,077,756	46,960	414,922	800,948	2,814,925	605,132	150,283	211,875	200,549
Alabama.........................	101,668	906	9,426	22,171	69,164	16,070	3,653	3,799	3,637
Alaska.........................	16,675	1,084	1,575	3,282	10,733	1,173	275	521	487
Arizona.........................	65,092	1,168	6,022	8,097	49,804	7,835	968	4,592	3,943
Arkansas.........................	100,082	656	7,296	20,963	71,168	12,696	2,929	1,956	2,024
California.........................	172,202	2,453	29,048	32,299	108,402	24,812	7,156	23,857	22,896
Colorado.........................	88,415	953	9,233	16,259	61,971	8,591	1,473	3,670	3,341
Connecticut.........................	21,445	346	3,004	3,207	14,888	4,208	1,476	2,986	2,740
Delaware.........................	6,358	41	675	1,044	4,598	862	175	716	610
District of Columbia......................	1,501	13	285	156	1,046	239	185	395	330
Florida.........................	121,759	1,495	13,556	14,523	92,185	11,982	2,026	13,882	13,374
Georgia.........................	123,546	1,248	14,283	23,072	84,943	14,739	2,749	6,506	5,940
Hawaii.........................	4,405	55	789	828	2,733	1,131	505	912	856
Idaho.........................	48,553	612	4,242	10,505	33,194	4,214	837	1,084	978
Illinois.........................	139,498	2,182	14,776	21,927	100,614	26,514	4,287	8,374	7,871
Indiana.........................	97,066	1,172	8,693	22,447	64,754	18,789	4,224	6,570	4,246
Iowa.........................	114,387	782	9,745	31,619	72,241	24,496	6,475	2,192	2,033
Kansas.........................	140,513	874	9,707	33,591	96,341	25,176	4,617	2,026	1,974
Kentucky.........................	79,220	801	6,148	16,551	55,720	14,031	4,463	2,960	2,861
Louisiana.........................	61,635	898	5,658	9,983	45,096	13,175	3,815	3,186	3,084
Maine.........................	22,874	369	2,199	5,930	14,377	2,408	792	1,015	1,004
Maryland.........................	32,321	481	4,112	5,078	22,650	5,294	1,467	3,857	3,710
Massachusetts.........................	36,303	574	6,475	4,837	24,417	5,120	2,707	4,683	4,613
Michigan.........................	122,086	1,244	15,007	24,483	81,351	11,000	3,026	7,060	7,105
Minnesota.........................	138,702	914	13,600	30,453	93,735	13,121	1,613	3,306	3,084
Mississippi.........................	75,119	702	7,617	15,559	51,240	17,061	3,774	1,927	1,965
Missouri.........................	131,667	1,206	10,658	25,308	94,495	24,334	6,893	4,277	4,135
Montana.........................	74,880	1,192	6,038	16,193	51,457	5,120	908	752	716
Nebraska.........................	93,600	482	8,139	20,780	64,199	15,393	3,837	1,356	1,321
Nevada.........................	36,839	571	3,518	5,569	27,182	1,798	256	1,701	1,596
New Hampshire.........................	16,076	225	1,589	2,742	11,520	2,429	807	1,057	998
New Jersey.........................	39,213	431	6,158	4,143	28,480	6,554	2,368	5,977	5,871
New Mexico.........................	68,384	1,000	5,142	8,556	53,686	3,924	657	1,419	1,305
New York.........................	114,592	1,704	14,597	20,765	77,526	17,420	6,887	11,211	11,072
North Carolina.........................	105,869	1,174	10,071	17,343	77,282	18,165	5,488	6,569	6,228
North Dakota.........................	86,851	571	5,937	11,901	68,442	4,453	993	490	467
Ohio.........................	123,247	1,574	11,452	22,652	87,569	27,045	6,773	7,982	7,708
Oklahoma.........................	112,808	933	8,420	25,309	78,146	23,781	6,986	2,371	2,234
Oregon.........................	59,148	730	7,110	17,699	33,610	7,633	1,774	2,774	2,693
Pennsylvania.........................	119,771	1,855	13,766	19,845	84,305	22,669	9,910	8,797	8,461
Rhode Island.........................	6,485	71	918	887	4,609	757	411	750	746
South Carolina.........................	65,997	851	7,232	15,086	42,829	9,271	1,981	3,408	2,988
South Dakota.........................	82,459	679	6,412	19,010	56,359	5,870	1,445	603	566
Tennessee.........................	95,492	1,104	9,272	17,982	67,134	19,985	3,864	4,544	4,352
Texas.........................	312,911	3,237	33,270	65,137	211,266	52,260	10,052	15,123	14,659
Utah.........................	45,635	937	3,754	8,190	32,754	2,947	469	1,747	1,600
Vermont.........................	14,290	320	1,321	3,110	9,539	2,727	931	522	563
Virginia.........................	74,461	1,119	8,752	14,399	50,190	13,769	3,671	5,467	5,178
Washington.........................	83,743	764	8,306	17,315	57,357	7,840	2,059	5,179	4,682
West Virginia.........................	38,646	555	3,512	8,602	25,977	7,093	2,547	1,199	1,328
Wisconsin.........................	115,018	742	12,743	23,405	78,127	14,057	1,936	4,147	3,993
Wyoming.........................	28,253	914	3,663	10,156	13,520	3,101	713	422	383

[6]Includes other freeways and expressways.
[7]Bridges are structurally deficient if they have been restricted to light vehicles, require immediate rehabilitation to remain open, or are closed. Bridges are functionally obsolete if they have deck geometry, load carrying capacity, clearance or approach roadway alignment that no longer meet the criteria for the system of which the bridge is carrying a part.
[8]Include restricted drivers and graduated driver licenses.

Table A-65. Traffic Fatalities and Seat Belt Use

Geographic area	Traffic fatalities[1] Number 2010	2005	2000	Fatality rate[2] 2010	2005	2000	Traffic fatalities in alcohol involved crashes 2010[3]	2005[3]	Percent of all persons killed in crashes 2010	2005	By highest driver BAC in crash[4] Low alcohol: BAC 0.01 to 0.07 2010	2005	Alcohol impaired driving fatalities: BAC 0.08 or more 2010	2005	Rate of seat belt use[5] 2011	2010	2005
United States	32,885	43,510	41,945	1.11	1.46	1.53	11,948	16,885	36.3	38.9	1,720	2,346	10,228	14,539	84.0	85.0	82.0
Alabama	862	1,148	996	1.34	1.92	1.76	314	423	36.4	37.4	35	42	279	382	88.0	91.4	81.8
Alaska	56	73	106	1.17	1.45	2.30	17	35	30.4	48.6	1	4	16	31	89.3	86.8	78.4
Arizona	762	1,179	1,036	1.27	1.97	2.11	231	492	30.3	41.8	38	58	194	434	82.9	81.8	94.2
Arkansas	563	654	652	1.68	2.05	2.24	196	233	34.8	36.0	23	25	173	208	78.4	78.3	68.3
California	2,715	4,333	3,753	0.84	1.32	1.22	924	1,719	34.0	39.7	133	254	791	1,466	96.6	96.2	92.5
Colorado	448	606	681	0.95	1.26	1.63	142	244	31.7	40.3	15	31	127	213	82.1	82.9	79.2
Connecticut	319	278	341	1.02	0.88	1.11	138	120	43.3	43.8	16	19	121	101	88.4	88.2	81.6
Delaware	101	133	123	1.13	1.40	1.49	43	66	42.6	49.3	7	6	36	59	90.3	90.7	83.8
District of Columbia	24	48	48	0.67	1.29	1.37	9	26	37.5	54.2	4	5	5	21	95.2	92.3	88.8
Florida	2,445	3,518	2,999	1.25	1.75	1.99	751	1,471	30.7	41.5	91	201	660	1,271	88.1	87.4	73.9
Georgia	1,244	1,729	1,541	1.11	1.52	1.47	346	545	27.8	31.5	48	82	298	463	93.0	89.6	89.9
Hawaii	113	140	132	1.13	1.39	1.55	48	71	42.5	50.7	6	13	42	58	96.0	97.6	95.3
Idaho	209	275	276	1.32	1.85	2.04	82	89	39.2	32.4	11	5	71	85	79.1	77.9	76.0
Illinois	927	1,363	1,418	0.88	1.27	1.38	366	580	39.5	42.6	69	103	298	477	92.9	92.6	86.0
Indiana	754	938	886	1.00	1.31	1.25	220	320	29.2	34.1	25	47	195	273	93.2	92.4	81.2
Iowa	390	450	445	1.24	1.45	1.51	103	118	26.4	26.2	13	16	90	102	93.5	93.1	87.1
Kansas	431	428	461	1.44	1.44	1.64	192	151	44.5	35.3	25	30	168	122	82.9	81.8	69.0
Kentucky	760	985	820	1.58	2.08	1.75	210	313	27.6	31.8	39	47	171	267	82.2	80.3	66.7
Louisiana	710	963	938	1.56	2.14	2.30	280	394	39.4	41.3	55	47	225	347	77.7	75.9	77.7
Maine	161	169	169	1.11	1.13	1.19	48	59	29.8	34.9	10	8	38	50	81.6	82.0	75.8
Maryland	493	614	588	0.88	1.09	1.17	188	235	38.1	38.3	34	44	154	191	94.2	94.7	91.1
Massachusetts	314	441	433	0.58	0.80	0.82	141	171	44.9	38.7	26	21	115	150	73.2	73.7	64.8
Michigan	942	1,129	1,382	0.97	1.09	1.41	285	421	30.3	37.3	55	58	230	363	94.5	95.2	92.9
Minnesota	411	559	625	0.73	0.98	1.19	135	201	32.8	36.0	8	26	127	176	92.7	92.3	83.9
Mississippi	641	931	949	1.61	2.32	2.67	259	371	40.4	39.8	23	40	236	331	81.9	81.0	60.8
Missouri	819	1,257	1,157	1.16	1.83	1.72	313	515	38.2	41.0	55	81	258	434	79.0	76.0	77.4
Montana	189	251	237	1.69	2.26	2.40	84	124	44.4	49.4	11	12	73	112	76.9	78.9	80.0
Nebraska	190	276	276	0.98	1.43	1.53	59	91	31.1	33.0	7	13	51	78	84.2	84.1	79.2
Nevada	257	427	323	1.22	2.06	1.83	85	159	33.1	37.2	17	16	69	143	94.1	93.2	94.8
New Hampshire	128	166	126	0.98	1.24	1.05	53	60	41.4	36.1	9	5	44	55	75.0	72.2	NA
New Jersey	556	747	731	0.76	1.01	1.08	187	263	33.6	35.2	35	46	153	217	94.5	93.7	86.0
New Mexico	346	488	432	1.37	2.04	1.90	121	189	35.0	38.7	10	17	111	172	90.5	89.8	89.5
New York	1,200	1,434	1,460	0.91	1.03	1.13	428	524	35.7	36.7	64	91	364	434	90.5	89.8	85.0
North Carolina	1,319	1,547	1,557	1.29	1.53	1.74	453	549	34.3	35.8	65	65	388	484	89.5	89.7	86.7
North Dakota	105	123	86	1.27	1.62	1.19	51	58	48.6	47.2	4	13	47	46	76.7	74.8	76.3
Ohio	1,080	1,321	1,366	0.97	1.20	1.29	413	505	38.2	38.2	71	96	341	409	84.1	83.8	78.7
Oklahoma	668	803	650	1.40	1.71	1.50	248	283	37.1	35.3	29	34	220	249	85.9	85.9	83.1
Oregon	317	487	451	0.94	1.38	1.33	91	177	28.7	36.3	20	38	71	139	96.6	97.0	93.3
Pennsylvania	1,324	1,616	1,520	1.32	1.50	1.49	502	636	37.9	39.4	69	77	433	559	83.8	86.0	83.3
Rhode Island	66	87	80	0.80	1.05	0.96	30	43	45.5	49.4	4	10	25	34	80.4	78.0	74.7
South Carolina	810	1,094	1,065	1.65	2.21	2.34	410	464	50.6	42.5	53	68	357	396	86.0	85.4	69.7
South Dakota	140	186	173	1.58	2.22	2.05	46	80	32.9	43.0	9	4	37	76	73.4	74.5	68.8
Tennessee	1,031	1,270	1,307	1.46	1.79	1.99	340	464	33.0	36.5	57	67	283	397	87.4	87.1	74.4
Texas	2,998	3,536	3,779	1.28	1.50	1.72	1,450	1,569	48.4	44.8	190	198	1,259	1,371	93.7	93.8	89.9
Utah	236	282	373	0.89	1.12	1.65	49	37	20.8	13.1	5	2	44	35	89.2	89.0	86.9
Vermont	71	73	76	0.98	0.95	1.12	25	29	35.2	39.7	7	1	18	28	84.7	85.2	84.7
Virginia	740	947	929	0.90	1.18	1.24	253	347	34.2	36.6	41	63	211	284	81.8	80.5	80.4
Washington	458	649	631	0.80	1.17	1.18	194	294	42.4	45.4	25	41	170	253	97.5	97.6	95.2
West Virginia	315	374	411	1.64	1.82	2.14	101	126	32.1	33.7	13	11	88	116	84.9	82.1	84.9
Wisconsin	572	815	799	0.96	1.36	1.40	240	369	42.0	45.3	34	41	205	328	79.0	79.2	73.3
Wyoming	155	170	152	1.62	1.88	1.88	59	65	38.1	38.2	5	9	54	56	82.6	78.9	NA

[1]Traffic fatalities pertain to a police-reported crash involving a motor vehicle in transport on a trafficway in which at least one person dies within 30 days of the crash. Data include fatalities in crashes in which there was no driver or motorcycle rider present at the scene.
[2]Deaths per 100 million vehicle miles traveled.
[3]Data represents all fatalities (both operators and passengers) in which the operator of the crash had a BAC of .01 or above.
[4]BAC stands for blood alcohol concentration and is measured in grams per deciliter (g/dl).
[5]Seat belt use pertains to both drivers and passengers in front seat.
NA = Not available

Table A-66. Communications

Geographic area	Mobile wireless telephone subscribers[1] (thousands)			Percent of households[2]								Telecommunications revenue (million dollars)	
				Using Internet anywhere		Using Internet in the home				No Internet use			
						Total		Broadband	Dial-up				
	2011	2010	2005	2010	2007	2010	2007	2010	2010	2010	2007	2007	2005
United States	294,990	281,848	201,373	80.2	71.0	71.1	61.7	68.2	2.8	19.8	29.0	296,467	294,966
Alabama	4,491	4,328	3,071	74.2	60.6	60.0	49.8	55.5	4.5	25.8	39.4	4,619	4,587
Alaska	634	608	377	88.6	84.3	78.7	73.4	73.4	5.3	11.4	15.8	835	831
Arizona	5,532	5,285	3,849	83.5	71.7	75.4	62.5	74.1	1.3	16.5	28.3	5,685	5,127
Arkansas	3,340	2,673	1,781	70.9	62.0	58.8	51.2	52.4	6.4	29.1	38.0	2,771	2,709
California	34,892	33,839	25,564	84.2	73.6	75.8	66.1	73.1	2.7	15.8	26.4	35,322	35,042
Colorado	4,767	4,687	3,260	82.7	78.9	74.7	69.1	71.6	3.1	17.3	21.1	5,067	5,013
Connecticut	3,360	3,230	2,466	81.9	73.4	76.5	66.3	74.8	1.7	18.1	26.6	3,745	3,929
Delaware	893	851	751	79.1	72.8	71.8	65.7	68.4	3.4	20.9	27.3	971	1,014
District of Columbia	1,347	1,249	819	81.0	74.7	73.4	58.9	71.7	1.7	19.0	25.3	1,380	1,397
Florida	17,923	17,251	12,522	79.9	69.7	72.0	64.8	70.2	1.8	20.1	30.3	18,969	19,918
Georgia	9,655	9,063	6,103	79.9	72.0	70.4	61.7	68.6	1.8	20.1	28.1	9,487	9,657
Hawaii	1,296	1,252	984	78.6	72.5	71.1	64.1	69.2	1.9	21.4	27.5	1,261	1,229
Idaho	1,323	1,277	838	84.1	69.9	75.6	57.9	72	3.6	15.9	30.1	1,390	1,300
Illinois	12,705	12,057	9,027	79.9	73.4	70.7	63.0	68.7	2.0	20.1	26.6	11,794	12,113
Indiana	5,580	5,410	3,540	74.7	68.0	61.3	58.1	58.9	2.4	25.3	32.0	5,524	5,389
Iowa	2,658	2,535	1,768	79.4	73.6	70.6	62.4	67.4	3.2	20.6	26.4	2,872	2,630
Kansas	2,653	2,560	1,666	84.8	76.7	76.3	62.8	74.6	1.7	15.2	23.3	2,631	2,488
Kentucky	3,813	3,726	2,658	72.0	66.7	61.3	54.9	57.8	3.5	28.0	33.3	3,894	3,856
Louisiana	5,676	4,340	3,258	74.9	63.2	62.8	53.9	60.5	2.3	25.1	36.9	4,369	4,430
Maine	1,179	1,124	823	81.7	74.5	73.4	65.1	67.4	6.0	18.3	25.5	1,411	1,425
Maryland	6,153	5,560	4,471	83.3	76.8	76.3	66.4	74.1	2.2	16.7	23.2	6,266	6,441
Massachusetts	6,534	6,316	4,545	83.8	72.9	77.6	66.4	76	1.6	16.2	27.1	6,963	6,962
Michigan	9,253	8,861	6,613	80.8	70.7	69.7	58.5	66.3	3.4	19.2	29.3	8,745	9,089
Minnesota	4,943	4,704	3,370	83.4	78.6	73.7	66.6	70.6	3.1	16.6	21.4	4,722	4,629
Mississippi	2,658	2,440	1,817	71.4	59.7	57.7	46.0	51.7	6.0	28.6	40.3	2,695	2,834
Missouri	5,650	5,309	3,733	78.2	67.3	67.9	56.1	64.4	3.5	21.8	32.7	5,925	5,750
Montana	864	846	527	75.7	68.6	65.4	56.9	61.4	4.0	24.3	31.4	957	912
Nebraska	1,648	1,523	1,169	82.5	73.9	71.2	63.8	68.9	2.3	17.5	26.2	1,745	1,749
Nevada	2,571	2,453	1,778	84.3	73.4	76.6	65.4	74.2	2.4	15.7	26.6	2,591	2,407
New Hampshire	1,207	1,170	989	86.4	80.6	81.0	74.9	77.8	3.2	13.6	19.4	1,412	1,474
New Jersey	8,926	8,601	7,724	82.9	74.1	74.7	68.4	73.2	1.5	17.1	25.9	9,535	10,493
New Mexico	1,691	1,689	1,170	76.8	67.4	62.6	54.8	57.7	4.9	23.2	32.6	1,891	1,775
New York	20,221	19,504	12,634	79.3	68.0	71.0	61.5	69	2.0	20.7	32.0	20,465	19,724
North Carolina	9,114	8,526	5,784	76.5	67.8	69.3	56.8	65.1	4.2	23.5	32.2	8,757	8,558
North Dakota	641	623	454	79.9	72.6	73.1	59.3	70.9	2.2	20.1	27.4	642	645
Ohio	11,134	10,511	7,560	78.4	69.1	67.5	58.6	63.9	3.6	21.6	30.9	10,789	10,736
Oklahoma	3,433	3,188	2,187	77.3	63.7	66.2	53.1	62.5	3.7	22.7	36.3	3,297	3,185
Oregon	3,427	3,340	2,418	86.2	75.3	78.3	68.2	74.7	3.6	13.8	24.7	3,456	3,292
Pennsylvania	11,595	11,424	7,882	78.1	69.3	70.3	60.1	67.4	2.9	21.9	30.7	12,260	12,166
Rhode Island	959	920	710	79.8	72.5	72.1	66.1	70.8	1.3	20.2	27.5	1,047	963
South Carolina	3,787	3,935	2,768	74.4	66.8	63.8	54.7	59.5	4.3	25.6	33.3	4,314	4,306
South Dakota	725	728	483	81.0	73.6	69.0	60.8	65.5	3.5	19.0	26.4	757	712
Tennessee	6,373	6,193	4,114	72.2	65.9	63.3	53.5	59.5	3.8	27.8	34.2	5,902	5,738
Texas	23,752	23,030	15,620	80.2	68.1	69.6	57.3	66.9	2.7	19.8	31.9	22,941	22,162
Utah	2,328	2,251	1,532	90.1	82.0	82.3	69.5	79.7	2.6	9.9	18.0	2,217	2,062
Vermont	509	485	315	83.5	79.4	74.7	70.2	69.2	5.5	16.5	20.6	691	663
Virginia	7,785	7,595	5,127	79.8	75.0	73.0	68.0	69.5	3.5	20.2	25.0	8,324	8,134
Washington	6,259	6,022	4,177	88.4	81.7	79.7	71.6	76.7	3.0	11.6	18.3	5,827	6,005
West Virginia	1,662	1,500	859	72.9	58.2	65.1	49.1	59.1	6.0	27.1	41.8	1,794	1,732
Wisconsin	4,939	4,730	3,356	83.2	76.6	73.7	65.0	70.5	3.2	16.8	23.4	4,949	5,000
Wyoming	533	526	359	84.3	76.4	74.4	61.4	72.9	1.5	15.7	23.6	594	584

[1]As of December. All facilities-based wireless carriers are required to report, and to use the area codes of telephone numbers provided to subscribers to determine subscriber counts by state.
[2]As of October.

Table A-67. Financial Activities

Geographic area	Financial activities[1]								FDIC-insured financial institutions[2]						Assets, 2012[6] (billion dollars)			
	Nonfarm employment (BLS)[3] (thousands)			Earnings (BEA) (million dollars)			Establishments[4]		Number of institutions[5]		Number of offices		Deposits (billion dollars)				By asset-size of bank,	
	2012	2010	2005	2012[3]	2010[3]	2005[7]	2010	Net change 2005–2010	2012	2010	2012	2010	2012	2010	Total[8]	Less than $1 billion	$1 billion to $10 billion	Greater than $10 billion
United States	7,753.0	7,610.8	8,192.2	864,459	842,581	787,272	820,821	-26,636	8,659	9,107	96,823	97,955	8,888.8	7,621.9	14,438.8	1,404.3	1,449.8	11,584.7
Alabama	92.5	92.0	98.3	6,984	6,760	6,457	11,175	377	172	173	1,573	1,578	84.8	82.1	229.4	25.9	14.0	189.5
Alaska	13.3	13.6	13.6	1,270	1,344	1,047	1,606	-14	8	8	132	133	10.1	8.9	5.4	1.2	4.2	0.0
Arizona	176.5	167.6	176.4	15,155	14,229	15,001	17,405	-648	74	81	1,360	1,381	86.8	86.1	12.4	5.3	7.1	0.0
Arkansas	49.1	48.8	51.4	3,630	3,645	3,031	7,270	-17	144	146	1,447	1,483	53.4	50.9	61.3	25.4	22.7	13.2
California	774.6	760.2	920.3	97,675	93,715	109,336	95,762	-6,064	295	324	7,295	7,176	953.5	845.7	509.1	55.7	110.2	343.2
Colorado	146.1	144.3	158.5	16,604	16,373	14,827	19,126	-1,061	156	190	1,623	1,662	99.6	91.2	45.7	18.6	14.2	12.8
Connecticut	132.3	134.2	141.0	25,528	26,299	22,936	9,571	-118	71	68	1,293	1,296	102.7	95.8	81.5	15.9	15.5	50.2
Delaware	42.3	42.7	45.2	4,502	4,425	4,599	3,102	-195	41	39	293	274	363.7	290.3	981.6	3.8	16.8	961.0
District of Columbia	28.1	26.9	30.2	3,866	3,734	3,335	2,153	214	35	33	244	244	33.1	27.4	1.9	1.9	0.0	0.0
Florida	497.5	478.0	539.8	45,171	42,989	42,111	59,517	-7,403	292	339	5,602	5,666	423.9	409.9	142.5	49.5	53.0	40.0
Georgia	227.2	218.3	237.2	21,615	20,866	20,109	25,292	-1,027	278	321	2,651	2,758	186.2	180.9	267.0	38.2	33.3	195.5
Hawaii	27.0	26.9	29.3	2,302	2,293	2,273	3,382	-329	13	12	280	284	33.2	28.3	42.7	1.3	11.0	30.4
Idaho	30.3	29.2	29.7	2,123	2,084	1,818	4,955	152	35	35	536	541	19.5	18.7	6.7	5.6	1.0	0.0
Illinois	366.1	363.7	401.9	44,687	44,102	41,569	34,830	-1,951	624	665	4,887	4,942	393.0	361.8	400.8	99.7	80.5	220.7
Indiana	130.3	130.9	138.8	9,412	9,156	9,267	15,527	-671	180	186	2,352	2,400	102.2	98.4	68.5	28.6	39.9	0.0
Iowa	101.6	101.3	98.3	8,906	8,477	6,808	8,809	16	362	381	1,598	1,621	72.8	66.5	72.6	51.9	20.7	0.0
Kansas	74.6	72.0	70.5	5,843	5,451	4,833	8,922	11	348	367	1,533	1,561	62.9	60.0	63.6	41.2	22.3	0.0
Kentucky	86.7	85.7	85.7	6,501	6,263	5,550	9,997	74	221	227	1,781	1,827	70.9	68.9	55.4	36.7	18.8	0.0
Louisiana	94.0	93.0	98.4	7,081	6,927	6,265	11,974	-135	158	164	1,631	1,650	88.8	82.8	70.3	33.9	10.1	26.3
Maine	31.4	31.7	34.2	2,436	2,403	2,224	3,530	-135	33	33	517	511	33.6	27.6	34.5	11.4	8.1	15.0
Maryland	143.0	143.8	158.8	15,104	14,447	14,680	13,714	-965	123	134	1,752	1,804	120.8	112.8	33.7	21.7	12.0	0.0
Massachusetts	206.2	207.8	221.4	32,531	32,963	29,150	15,803	-890	185	191	2,210	2,217	271.5	205.2	331.1	42.6	69.9	218.7
Michigan	196.2	188.1	216.1	15,697	14,949	18,679	21,222	-1,893	160	165	2,949	3,008	166.6	155.7	67.2	27.9	25.2	14.1
Minnesota	177.1	172.6	179.6	18,726	17,161	15,618	15,574	-1,410	428	444	1,801	1,842	201.0	129.7	63.1	50.3	12.8	0.0
Mississippi	44.2	44.5	45.8	3,017	2,966	2,647	7,142	88	104	105	1,202	1,209	46.2	45.1	60.1	21.3	25.4	13.4
Missouri	164.1	162.2	163.4	12,889	12,266	10,866	16,989	-626	377	386	2,423	2,436	141.8	129.0	151.8	54.4	43.9	53.5
Montana	21.4	21.2	21.4	1,439	1,446	1,519	3,725	61	72	78	394	392	18.9	17.5	26.7	8.9	17.8	0.0
Nebraska	70.9	68.9	64.5	4,783	4,677	3,970	6,177	213	229	242	1,082	1,092	51.7	43.0	62.5	28.6	19.4	14.5
Nevada	54.2	52.9	64.3	4,999	4,860	5,744	7,853	-1,017	48	50	544	550	113.0	183.5	125.2	3.4	19.9	101.8
New Hampshire	34.9	35.2	39.4	3,548	3,536	3,240	3,247	-287	41	40	429	433	27.9	26.4	10.3	6.9	3.5	0.0
New Jersey	249.0	251.6	279.7	32,100	32,752	30,804	21,071	-1,056	161	170	3,276	3,338	268.4	246.5	155.1	30.4	55.4	69.3
New Mexico	33.0	33.0	34.9	2,182	2,200	2,177	5,042	-136	64	65	512	514	26.2	25.8	15.3	10.2	5.1	0.0
New York	682.7	669.5	713.3	152,323	150,262	117,832	59,732	-97	236	242	5,441	5,479	1,065.7	854.8	896.9	44.0	152.6	700.3
North Carolina	203.1	199.9	198.4	20,316	19,495	16,423	23,366	377	119	129	2,720	2,779	341.8	207.4	1,717.4	21.7	22.7	1,673.0
North Dakota	21.9	20.6	18.8	1,582	1,416	1,005	2,513	180	98	100	439	444	21.3	17.6	29.9	15.3	14.7	0.0
Ohio	279.3	276.7	308.5	23,274	23,455	21,957	27,375	-1,609	264	268	4,026	4,015	244.0	226.4	2,609.4	43.5	35.4	2,530.5
Oklahoma	79.9	79.9	83.1	5,923	5,698	4,595	10,535	431	255	264	1,397	1,411	74.4	69.0	94.3	37.7	28.7	27.9
Oregon	90.2	93.2	102.1	6,605	6,537	6,465	11,582	-855	61	59	1,125	1,124	66.2	53.7	34.6	5.0	6.3	23.3
Pennsylvania	310.2	311.0	335.7	30,952	30,497	29,012	27,109	-1,283	242	258	4,648	4,720	312.6	285.8	216.6	59.2	76.7	80.8
Rhode Island	31.5	30.7	34.3	3,056	2,959	2,579	2,472	-306	26	25	259	259	44.9	39.8	134.1	2.9	5.9	125.2
South Carolina	98.8	97.3	97.9	7,310	7,074	6,235	12,055	310	94	107	1,401	1,458	67.4	70.3	37.7	18.2	19.5	0.0
South Dakota	28.7	28.9	28.5	1,813	1,801	1,605	2,827	92	92	93	475	487	315.0	107.4	2,625.2	12.7	14.6	2,597.8
Tennessee	137.6	137.1	143.3	12,616	12,535	11,966	15,445	117	227	229	2,275	2,298	118.4	114.7	86.7	44.3	17.1	25.3
Texas	659.5	625.4	609.5	66,609	62,928	53,959	63,969	3,824	648	679	6,854	6,965	599.0	499.2	436.6	107.7	99.7	229.2
Utah	69.4	68.0	67.5	6,100	5,872	4,646	9,163	239	66	74	598	602	339.6	271.9	426.1	11.8	26.5	387.8
Vermont	12.0	12.2	13.2	997	1,021	929	1,687	-103	24	23	257	266	11.7	10.6	6.3	4.6	1.7	0.0
Virginia	188.2	179.1	192.5	18,404	17,486	18,707	20,201	-236	149	153	2,644	2,684	248.8	214.3	634.5	27.5	43.0	564.1
Washington	142.9	140.5	157.3	13,182	12,920	13,696	19,730	-723	103	111	1,876	1,891	113.3	109.2	63.9	15.6	35.2	13.1
West Virginia	28.0	28.4	29.7	1,659	1,706	1,428	3,583	-65	82	85	671	664	30.3	28.8	27.5	12.3	15.3	0.0
Wisconsin	162.6	158.8	159.8	12,466	12,207	10,935	13,921	-281	295	299	2,287	2,351	132.8	126.7	98.6	54.7	20.6	23.3
Wyoming	10.8	10.8	10.8	967	955	812	2,092	194	46	47	228	235	13.0	12.0	7.3	7.3	0.0	0.0

[1]Includes Finance and Insurance (NAICS 52) and Real Estate and Rental and Leasing (NAICS 53).
[2]Includes insured U.S. branches of foreign banks. As of June 30.
[3]Based on the 2007 North American Industry Classification System (NAICS).
[4]2010 data for establishments are based on the 2007 North American Industry Classification System (NAICS); 2005 data are based on the 2002 NAICS.
[5]Includes commercial banks, savings institutions, and insured U.S. branches of foreign banks. As of June 30.
[6]Data are based on the location or each reporting institution's main office and reported data may include assets located outside of the reporting institution's home state.
[7]Based on the 2002 North American Industry Classification System (NAICS).
[8]As of December 31.

Table A-67. Financial Activities—*Continued*

Geographic area	Credit unions				Life insurance and annuity benefit payments, 2011 (million dollars)					
	Number		Assets (million dollars)		Total payments	Policy and contract dividends	Death payments	Annuity payments[9]	Surrender values	Other payments[10]
	2010	2000	2010	2000						
United States.................	7,320	10,291	913,509	437,649	436,254	19,189	79,704	79,754	255,647	1,960
Alabama..........................	125	186	15,177	6,990	5,165	204	1,354	732	2,853	22
Alaska............................	12	13	6,275	2,594	806	24	216	111	453	2
Arizona..........................	52	68	11,954	6,608	7,990	267	1,573	1,678	4,447	26
Arkansas........................	62	82	2,307	1,188	2,772	115	753	475	1,419	10
California.......................	426	632	121,241	64,356	43,055	1,512	7,352	8,444	25,617	129
Colorado........................	102	175	14,994	8,393	6,888	285	1,152	1,212	4,210	29
Connecticut....................	134	195	8,586	4,817	14,868	398	1,305	2,357	10,786	22
Delaware........................	26	41	1,766	985	4,406	63	793	1,430	2,113	6
District of Columbia........	50	75	6,303	3,341	1,490	54	182	203	899	152
Florida...........................	176	250	42,015	22,032	29,399	1,017	5,066	5,421	17,795	101
Georgia..........................	153	224	16,636	8,822	10,106	477	2,555	1,396	5,634	42
Hawaii............................	85	102	9,070	4,104	2,372	88	343	399	1,533	8
Idaho.............................	40	50	4,121	1,540	1,611	77	361	329	839	5
Illinois...........................	363	548	31,422	14,237	18,063	1,064	3,340	3,598	9,978	82
Indiana..........................	172	236	17,072	9,659	8,391	426	1,531	1,442	4,955	37
Iowa..............................	134	193	8,913	3,731	5,483	347	1,094	937	3,078	27
Kansas...........................	102	134	4,457	2,245	4,524	202	796	653	2,855	19
Kentucky........................	86	128	6,031	3,176	4,381	202	1,071	819	2,240	49
Louisiana.......................	222	284	8,444	4,290	5,160	212	1,154	829	2,940	25
Maine............................	64	82	5,396	2,756	1,763	92	342	340	977	11
Maryland........................	108	128	18,023	8,608	8,327	399	1,712	1,602	4,584	30
Massachusetts...............	217	285	28,442	14,643	12,953	677	1,698	2,429	8,111	38
Michigan........................	324	465	39,987	22,317	14,648	626	2,363	2,767	8,847	45
Minnesota......................	152	189	15,636	8,599	9,509	446	2,104	1,467	5,456	35
Mississippi.....................	92	131	4,026	1,770	2,412	93	664	322	1,319	13
Missouri.........................	139	188	10,608	6,045	9,033	358	1,645	1,422	5,558	50
Montana.........................	57	76	3,896	1,614	976	61	209	222	479	5
Nebraska........................	72	86	3,180	1,855	3,150	164	732	746	1,494	13
Nevada...........................	16	23	1,837	1,897	2,808	90	629	510	1,570	9
New Hampshire...............	23	32	5,025	2,275	2,308	117	318	439	1,424	10
New Jersey	207	284	11,800	6,384	19,738	825	3,087	2,977	12,739	111
New Mexico	51	56	6,895	2,947	2,371	86	466	720	1,009	91
New York........................	441	643	53,675	22,780	32,476	2,045	4,912	6,172	19,202	145
North Carolina................	99	171	32,466	12,774	13,475	609	2,645	1,786	8,389	47
North Dakota..................	47	65	2,342	1,053	938	57	186	157	534	4
Ohio..............................	324	509	19,130	10,865	16,530	699	3,080	3,511	9,164	76
Oklahoma	74	94	9,905	4,604	3,801	160	889	723	2,015	14
Oregon	81	114	16,175	7,246	4,840	178	876	1,145	2,622	19
Pennsylvania..................	541	776	33,761	15,876	21,727	1,069	3,960	4,386	12,204	107
Rhode Island..................	24	39	4,345	2,274	1,872	85	459	398	921	9
South Carolina	77	99	9,595	4,482	5,329	218	1,282	790	3,016	23
South Dakota	50	61	2,274	1,008	1,135	68	269	202	592	4
Tennessee	181	249	15,672	7,791	7,945	292	1,581	1,246	4,800	27
Texas.............................	549	714	67,634	32,585	24,930	894	5,286	4,420	14,252	79
Utah..............................	94	137	14,333	5,940	3,192	119	752	536	1,777	8
Vermont	27	44	2,683	1,016	1,056	68	203	206	573	6
Virginia..........................	193	256	81,676	25,668	10,475	511	2,167	1,630	6,129	39
Washington....................	112	167	30,145	14,639	7,791	333	1,249	1,934	4,238	36
West Virginia..................	106	132	2,771	1,665	1,959	111	391	402	1,041	13
Wisconsin.......................	225	343	21,469	9,796	9,271	571	1,435	1,577	5,642	46
Wyoming	31	37	1,921	769	588	32	122	104	326	4

[9]Excludes payments from deposit-type contracts.
[10]Includes matured endowments, disability payments, and payments on guaranteed interest contracts (GICs).

Table A-68. Professional and Business Services and Education and Health Services

Geographic area	Professional and business services[1]								
	Nonfarm employment (BLS)[3] (thousands)			Earnings (BEA)[4] (million dollars)			Establishments		
	2012	2010	2005	2012	2010	2005	2010	2005	Net change, 2005–2010
United States...................	17,888	16,721	16,954	1,622,256	1,444,093	1,213,332	1,284,153	1,243,201	40,952
Alabama............................	218	209	209	15,002	14,002	11,246	14,067	13,770	297
Alaska...............................	29	27	24	2,755	2,429	1,791	3,175	2,956	219
Arizona..............................	354	340	366	25,091	22,997	20,317	25,374	23,937	1,437
Arkansas............................	123	119	111	8,678	7,723	6,041	9,423	8,790	633
California............................	2,235	2,074	2,160	234,840	205,902	177,462	159,144	154,323	4,821
Colorado............................	355	329	317	34,279	30,241	24,672	32,874	30,297	2,577
Connecticut........................	203	191	200	24,279	21,525	19,638	15,435	16,240	-805
Delaware............................	56	55	63	5,768	5,146	4,516	5,126	5,665	-539
District of Columbia...........	153	148	148	23,265	21,220	16,470	6,292	5,783	509
Florida...............................	1,068	1,006	1,156	79,471	72,384	68,992	103,692	99,433	4,259
Georgia..............................	562	526	536	45,797	40,780	36,170	41,307	39,144	2,163
Hawaii...............................	76	72	74	5,166	4,714	4,125	5,429	5,207	222
Idaho.................................	76	74	78	5,116	4,948	4,264	6,614	5,977	637
Illinois...............................	862	802	827	83,360	74,221	66,103	57,382	56,250	1,132
Indiana...............................	298	275	274	19,324	17,051	14,679	20,926	20,586	340
Iowa..................................	130	122	113	8,048	7,051	5,598	10,297	9,935	362
Kansas...............................	153	144	133	10,890	9,741	7,593	11,233	10,972	261
Kentucky............................	191	180	174	11,741	10,620	8,716	12,782	12,305	477
Louisiana	203	194	188	15,797	14,478	10,904	16,704	15,980	724
Maine................................	58	56	50	4,205	3,829	3,048	5,676	5,648	28
Maryland............................	410	388	389	40,389	36,308	29,247	28,700	27,816	884
Massachusetts....................	491	464	461	59,150	52,466	43,486	32,205	32,191	14
Michigan............................	577	516	589	45,224	39,249	42,404	34,708	36,285	-1,577
Minnesota..........................	336	314	308	30,738	27,851	22,771	24,553	24,737	-184
Mississippi.........................	97	92	88	5,827	5,347	4,322	7,320	7,090	230
Missouri.............................	338	322	320	27,612	25,184	22,143	21,844	21,879	-35
Montana.............................	41	39	35	2,664	2,239	1,728	5,347	4,903	444
Nebraska............................	106	101	98	7,521	6,769	5,391	7,384	6,878	506
Nevada...............................	144	136	146	10,912	9,990	9,376	12,775	12,033	742
New Hampshire...................	68	64	59	6,281	5,691	4,922	6,320	6,249	71
New Jersey.........................	617	586	593	66,107	58,985	50,165	44,536	46,403	-1,867
New Mexico........................	97	100	93	7,387	7,220	5,516	6,860	6,770	90
New York............................	1,168	1,098	1,083	139,253	127,284	104,287	86,697	84,273	2,424
North Carolina....................	533	485	449	40,076	34,487	27,651	35,726	33,313	2,413
North Dakota......................	33	28	27	2,210	1,678	1,245	2,579	2,349	230
Ohio..................................	671	626	644	54,769	46,890	41,210	39,917	41,218	-1,301
Oklahoma	177	171	170	11,385	10,203	8,266	14,275	13,457	818
Oregon...............................	195	182	186	15,102	13,220	11,505	17,523	16,660	863
Pennsylvania.......................	730	690	661	68,756	60,658	49,191	46,684	45,955	729
Rhode Island......................	56	53	55	4,853	4,415	3,839	4,885	4,920	-35
South Carolina	234	216	205	15,218	13,471	10,727	15,732	14,999	733
South Dakota	29	28	25	1,854	1,663	1,242	3,031	2,779	252
Tennessee	337	304	313	26,157	22,399	18,766	18,858	18,317	541
Texas.................................	1,406	1,275	1,162	124,724	108,100	80,810	89,234	83,056	6,178
Utah..................................	167	152	146	11,305	9,888	7,875	13,082	11,374	1,708
Vermont	26	23	22	2,084	1,805	1,457	3,338	3,164	174
Virginia..............................	678	650	606	72,232	66,363	48,808	40,413	36,856	3,557
Washington.........................	349	326	316	33,752	30,187	23,426	29,891	27,680	2,211
West Virginia......................	65	61	59	4,107	3,644	2,854	4,671	4,678	-7
Wisconsin	290	272	263	20,404	18,246	15,423	19,045	19,068	-23
Wyoming	18	17	16	1,331	1,190	930	3,068	2,653	415

[1]Professional, scientific and technical services; management of companies and enterprises; administrative and support and waste management and remediation services.
[3]Bureau of Labor Statistics.
[4]Bureau of Economic Analysis.

Table A-68. Professional and Business Services and Education and Health Services—*Continued*

Geographic area	Education and health services[2]								
	Nonfarm employment (BLS)[3] (thousands)			Earnings (BEA)[4] (thousand dollars)			Establishments		
	2012	2010	2005	2012	2010	2005	2010	2005	Net change, 2005–2010
United States......................	20,298	19,566	17,372	1,233,829	1,161,549	886,472	902,972	827,086	75,886
Alabama..............................	219	214	200	13,214	12,620	10,070	11,073	10,605	468
Alaska.................................	46	42	36	3,081	2,741	2,048	2,478	2,183	295
Arizona...............................	366	345	276	23,175	21,791	14,916	18,307	15,468	2,839
Arkansas.............................	172	166	146	8,452	8,081	6,313	8,006	7,335	671
California............................	1,879	1,788	1,587	139,460	130,195	100,114	112,953	104,038	8,915
Colorado.............................	282	265	225	17,722	16,568	12,417	16,700	14,603	2,097
Connecticut.........................	318	307	273	21,359	20,280	15,699	11,553	10,833	720
Delaware.............................	68	65	54	4,166	3,870	2,930	2,760	2,505	255
District of Columbia.............	115	108	92	7,377	6,991	5,384	2,671	2,584	87
Florida................................	1,110	1,071	968	68,447	64,370	48,603	60,038	53,173	6,865
Georgia...............................	496	476	424	30,351	28,451	21,828	24,746	21,643	3,103
Hawaii.................................	77	75	70	4,796	4,599	3,627	4,030	3,905	125
Idaho..................................	89	84	68	4,613	4,391	3,070	5,143	4,514	629
Illinois................................	864	833	745	52,783	50,318	38,978	36,141	32,769	3,372
Indiana...............................	438	424	378	24,366	22,598	17,592	16,671	15,652	1,019
Iowa...................................	221	214	195	10,633	10,021	7,999	8,758	8,213	545
Kansas...............................	186	180	164	10,342	9,651	7,438	8,451	8,111	340
Kentucky.............................	257	251	235	14,321	13,441	10,565	11,834	10,948	886
Louisiana............................	282	271	246	15,768	14,825	11,039	12,975	12,313	662
Maine.................................	121	119	112	6,315	6,044	4,907	5,261	5,086	175
Maryland.............................	415	398	354	27,333	25,439	19,487	17,535	16,427	1,108
Massachusetts.....................	688	664	590	47,940	45,280	33,613	20,771	19,780	991
Michigan.............................	632	612	576	36,144	34,148	28,071	28,400	27,429	971
Minnesota...........................	478	458	391	25,757	24,545	18,457	16,519	15,084	1,435
Mississippi..........................	133	131	122	7,750	7,327	5,526	6,674	6,169	505
Missouri..............................	413	408	369	23,881	21,911	17,290	17,642	16,689	953
Montana..............................	68	64	56	3,561	3,331	2,491	3,723	3,494	229
Nebraska.............................	140	136	124	7,292	6,778	5,333	5,713	5,117	596
Nevada................................	107	101	84	7,078	6,694	5,014	6,852	5,808	1,044
New Hampshire....................	115	112	98	6,732	6,489	4,950	4,167	3,922	245
New Jersey	621	601	558	40,621	38,862	30,611	29,598	27,793	1,805
New Mexico	122	120	105	6,107	5,780	4,349	5,447	4,982	465
New York.............................	1,763	1,703	1,544	104,657	100,251	78,849	63,220	58,460	4,760
North Carolina.....................	549	537	472	30,551	29,246	22,011	25,309	21,900	3,409
North Dakota.......................	58	55	49	3,169	2,769	2,070	1,980	1,838	142
Ohio....................................	866	841	762	47,547	44,882	35,718	31,030	29,786	1,244
Oklahoma	224	222	184	11,500	10,791	8,011	11,285	10,433	852
Oregon................................	238	229	199	15,045	14,052	10,634	13,591	11,811	1,780
Pennsylvania.......................	1,169	1,135	1,030	68,941	64,806	49,648	39,477	37,464	2,013
Rhode Island.......................	104	103	95	5,838	5,735	4,643	3,671	3,493	178
South Carolina	210	214	187	11,505	10,839	8,106	10,781	9,825	956
South Dakota.......................	67	65	57	3,738	3,450	2,602	2,529	2,373	156
Tennessee...........................	394	374	330	28,710	26,611	19,258	16,059	14,782	1,277
Texas..................................	1,462	1,385	1,184	85,443	78,860	56,114	64,826	56,338	8,488
Utah....................................	155	129	8,057	7,633	5,464	7,065	7,718	6,657	1,061
Vermont	59	54	3,151	3,023	2,395	2,538	2,495	2,417	78
Virginia...............................	460	394	28,432	26,548	19,340	19,966	20,663	18,566	2,097
Washington..........................	375	329	25,087	23,636	17,226	20,752	21,596	19,590	2,006
West Virginia.......................	121	113	6,247	5,906	4,662	5,124	5,187	5,003	184
Wisconsin	408	373	23,773	22,630	17,954	15,863	15,995	15,411	584
Wyoming	26	22	1,499	1,452	1,035	1,870	1,970	1,764	206

[2]Education services; health care and social assistance.
[3]Bureau of Labor Statistics.
[4]Bureau of Economic Analysis.

Table A-69. Leisure and Hospitality Services

Geographic area	Leisure and hospitality employees (BLS)[1] (includes Arts, Entertainment, and Recreation and Accommodations and Food Services) (thousands)			Arts, entertainment, and recreation services						Accommodations and food services					
				Earnings (BEA)[2] (million dollars)			Establishments			Earnings (BEA)[2] (million dollars)			Establishments[3]		
	2012	2010	2005	2012	2010	2005	2010	2005	Net change, 2005–2010	2012	2010	2005	2010	2005	Net change, 2005–2010
United States................	13,762	13,050	12,817	108,849	100,520	89,303	123,151	121,777	1,374	301,274	271,451	243,256	643,960	603,435	40,525
Alabama.........................	174	168	165	458	442	426	1,105	1,130	-25	3,239	2,979	2,489	8,123	7,529	594
Alaska...........................	33	32	31	225	191	215	548	522	26	917	826	763	1,993	1,966	27
Arizona..........................	267	254	254	1,952	1,756	1,488	1,695	1,782	-87	6,192	5,667	5,163	11,438	10,688	750
Arkansas........................	103	99	94	291	268	252	809	856	-47	1,813	1,656	1,381	5,290	4,878	412
California........................	1,599	1,502	1,475	21,101	19,574	17,863	20,205	18,817	1,388	38,942	34,629	32,397	75,463	71,625	3,838
Colorado........................	280	263	258	2,314	2,116	2,030	2,417	2,349	68	6,166	5,459	4,757	12,207	11,697	510
Connecticut....................	143	134	129	1,063	994	1,028	1,607	1,678	-71	3,336	3,011	2,671	8,004	7,579	425
Delaware........................	43	42	41	341	321	271	410	376	34	807	775	687	1,910	1,722	188
District of Columbia........	65	60	54	534	590	434	309	285	24	2,212	2,029	1,715	2,264	1,956	308
Florida...........................	998	932	934	10,489	9,474	8,105	7,462	7,515	-53	21,825	19,199	17,983	35,543	33,049	2,494
Georgia..........................	395	374	372	2,211	2,106	1,843	2,696	2,693	3	8,447	7,763	7,038	18,567	17,218	1,349
Hawaii............................	107	100	106	476	436	480	494	490	4	3,661	3,188	3,176	3,483	3,393	90
Idaho..............................	61	58	57	308	293	290	737	670	67	1,048	959	844	3,512	3,256	256
Illinois............................	535	515	512	4,046	3,697	3,443	4,450	4,537	-87	11,863	10,725	9,592	26,879	25,595	1,284
Indiana...........................	286	273	278	1,812	1,789	1,696	2,140	2,103	37	4,725	4,280	3,964	12,718	12,316	402
Iowa...............................	134	130	131	603	542	553	1,457	1,441	16	2,152	1,925	1,731	6,918	6,771	147
Kansas...........................	120	113	112	427	330	302	1,018	1,109	-91	2,281	2,072	1,957	5,898	5,776	122
Kentucky........................	175	167	165	639	591	574	1,274	1,301	-27	3,304	3,030	2,719	7,517	6,965	552
Louisiana.......................	208	194	198	1,345	1,241	1,396	1,390	1,329	61	4,412	4,033	3,231	8,657	7,886	771
Maine.............................	62	60	59	360	331	336	876	899	-23	1,287	1,190	1,066	3,960	3,909	51
Maryland........................	245	230	226	1,965	1,779	1,606	2,037	2,172	-135	5,561	5,057	4,484	10,986	10,230	756
Massachusetts...............	324	307	293	3,115	2,897	2,393	3,050	3,058	-8	7,602	6,904	6,125	16,437	15,562	875
Michigan........................	387	378	405	2,039	2,068	2,278	3,520	3,647	-127	7,104	6,395	6,005	19,449	19,297	152
Minnesota......................	244	235	242	2,044	1,913	1,524	2,679	2,668	11	4,367	3,966	3,677	11,165	10,812	353
Mississippi.....................	122	118	123	323	346	384	668	660	8	2,548	2,379	2,339	4,956	4,649	307
Missouri.........................	275	272	273	2,311	2,151	2,014	2,111	2,134	-23	5,046	4,813	4,318	12,313	11,811	502
Montana.........................	58	56	55	295	281	233	1,150	1,034	116	1,026	902	770	3,391	3,375	16
Nebraska........................	84	81	79	313	292	251	855	839	16	1,347	1,223	1,098	4,243	4,108	135
Nevada...........................	318	309	327	1,316	1,152	1,265	1,224	1,286	-62	11,997	11,233	11,337	5,733	4,915	818
New Hampshire...............	65	62	63	375	353	386	721	747	-26	1,352	1,255	1,186	3,538	3,369	169
New Jersey	346	334	333	2,835	2,736	2,246	3,418	3,601	-183	8,504	8,099	7,669	19,543	18,872	671
New Mexico	86	84	84	312	284	291	654	666	-12	1,831	1,702	1,483	4,089	3,944	145
New York........................	801	736	671	13,166	12,003	10,052	11,378	10,837	541	21,381	18,502	14,977	47,433	42,300	5,133
North Carolina................	416	392	362	2,568	2,326	1,791	3,391	3,232	159	7,618	6,965	5,882	19,120	16,903	2,217
North Dakota..................	38	34	31	89	79	65	421	395	26	710	537	422	1,833	1,795	38
Ohio...............................	499	475	500	2,869	2,563	2,343	3,860	4,080	-220	9,067	8,204	7,519	23,143	23,337	-194
Oklahoma.......................	148	139	132	661	552	391	1,074	1,057	17	2,997	2,658	2,110	7,131	6,676	455
Oregon...........................	170	162	159	915	826	705	1,639	1,564	75	3,639	3,262	2,923	10,319	9,433	886
Pennsylvania..................	521	501	485	4,461	3,977	3,071	4,508	4,749	-241	9,776	8,864	7,883	27,683	26,115	1,568
Rhode Island..................	51	50	50	304	286	269	543	536	7	1,038	951	906	2,945	2,901	44
South Carolina	218	208	203	790	720	750	1,546	1,512	34	4,252	3,881	3,443	9,532	8,913	619
South Dakota..................	44	43	42	221	215	239	666	643	23	701	644	557	2,359	2,285	74
Tennessee......................	277	262	262	2,203	1,943	1,733	2,282	2,257	25	5,886	5,381	4,950	11,689	10,892	797
Texas.............................	1,087	1,008	907	5,984	5,504	4,440	6,101	6,117	-16	24,018	21,203	17,364	46,045	39,989	6,056
Utah...............................	119	111	104	649	584	482	863	802	61	2,194	1,956	1,652	4,851	4,360	491
Vermont	33	32	33	155	141	130	436	497	-61	766	702	668	1,896	1,963	-67
Virginia..........................	358	341	329	1,876	1,746	1,421	2,739	2,650	89	7,367	6,773	5,933	16,219	14,670	1,549
Washington.....................	277	267	264	1,890	1,906	1,920	2,696	2,706	-10	6,388	5,691	4,924	16,039	14,963	1,076
West Virginia..................	75	72	69	247	315	293	689	688	1	1,463	1,269	1,049	3,682	3,501	181
Wisconsin	257	251	255	1,402	1,346	1,137	2,716	2,620	96	4,327	3,987	3,698	14,130	13,972	158
Wyoming	34	33	32	164	156	180	417	441	-24	769	698	580	1,724	1,749	-25

[1]All estimates of labor and earnings provided by Bureau of Labor Statistics (BLS) are based on the 2007 North American Industry Classific System.
[2]Bureau of Economic Analysis. The estimates of earnings for 2005 are based on the 2002 North American Industry Classification System (NAICS). The estimates for 2010 forward are based on the 2007 NAICS. All dollars estimates are in current dollars and not adjusted for inflation.
[3]Data provided by County Business Patterns is based on the North American Industry Classification System (NAICS). Data for 2005 is based on NAICS 2002. Data for 2010 is based on NAICS 2007.

Table A–70. Travel and Tourism Indicators

Geographic area	International visitors for pleasure by primary state of destination[1]			National parks[2]				State parks[3]			
				Visits			Acreage	Visits			Acreage
	2011	2010	2009	2012	2011	2010	2012	2012	2011	2009	2012
United States............	23,806,138	19,144,042	12,680,504	280,573,548	276,626,130	276,626,130	84,422,725	741,280,263	720,603,895	727,069,354	14,960,010
Alabama......................	17,385	15,649	13,715	717,724	755,264	781,550	17,786	4,006,561	4,410,121	5,461,542	48,154
Alaska........................	19,476	18,917	20,082	2,412,524	2,333,919	2,274,843	54,654,073	5,593,600	5,405,238	5,224,650	3,386,702
Arizona......................	1,400,783	1,169,975	625,398	9,979,972	10,134,892	10,546,150	2,010,257	2,156,475	2,051,265	2,072,574	64,088
Arkansas...................	16,934	14,649	10,849	2,727,454	2,879,494	3,125,664	105,004	8,681,384	8,241,768	8,192,134	54,370
California...................	6,000,010	4,479,084	2,768,686	35,991,200	35,448,424	34,915,676	8,250,874	67,987,208	63,964,034	72,748,218	1,596,267
Colorado	247,044	236,579	158,125	5,811,546	5,819,069	5,635,307	729,042	12,235,771	12,338,520	11,955,691	1,045,523
Connecticut...............	60,678	59,202	54,826	21,465	22,415	19,313	74	7,481,711	7,757,499	7,261,173	206,633
Delaware	8,119	8,072	7,345	(X)	(X)	(X)	(X)	4,758,602	4,652,806	4,649,252	25,866
District of Columbia	73,295	62,059	53,264	34,286,073	30,579,692	33,140,005	9,098	(X)	(X)	(X)	(X)
Florida.......................	3,252,468	2,815,714	2,430,265	10,366,613	10,580,858	9,222,981	2,709,652	24,983,179	20,442,212	21,458,588	785,395
Georgia	137,362	129,723	114,347	7,350,309	7,167,680	6,776,556	65,263	8,928,321	8,858,751	10,270,601	92,880
Hawaii........................	115,592	98,836	79,772	5,119,035	4,784,285	4,493,123	369,203	11,087,175	10,278,329	10,207,904	39,824
Idaho.........................	8,262	6,703	6,015	553,554	601,668	530,977	483,280	5,007,714	4,381,523	4,031,348	58,922
Illinois.......................	282,252	245,889	226,579	295,464	296,214	354,125	13	41,345,970	42,001,147	41,873,139	480,353
Indiana......................	38,573	33,542	27,950	2,148,903	2,094,529	2,395,485	15,540	16,828,007	15,833,775	16,146,266	171,441
Iowa..........................	13,976	12,553	10,219	207,352	216,830	222,295	2,713	14,933,483	13,908,470	13,971,344	71,081
Kansas	46,504	42,143	29,892	101,752	90,383	100,361	11,636	6,403,567	6,208,064	7,019,423	32,900
Kentucky	15,445	14,768	10,992	1,717,853	1,666,505	1,797,894	203,032	6,976,640	6,922,313	7,123,887	45,180
Louisiana	49,461	43,237	28,900	625,913	577,755	496,329	24,785	2,150,652	2,241,983	2,078,920	43,919
Maine.........................	21,134	15,399	6,731	2,431,052	2,374,645	2,504,208	283,798	2,992,843	2,554,057	2,238,813	98,065
Maryland....................	106,121	100,351	95,229	6,658,643	6,064,410	3,541,570	88,979	11,082,366	10,776,396	10,728,037	134,539
Massachusetts...........	186,613	168,505	150,207	10,487,447	10,231,394	9,913,501	46,442	30,361,566	30,180,480	31,209,357	353,889
Michigan	122,022	97,506	70,690	2,192,477	1,961,506	1,796,006	718,148	25,083,369	19,582,601	21,076,506	292,721
Minnesota	49,769	43,095	35,704	601,274	572,795	540,195	365,716	8,195,518	8,867,858	5,598,985	284,131
Mississippi.................	7,836	6,807	5,455	6,449,713	6,990,401	6,588,026	1,912	1,125,008	1,256,873	1,268,165	24,591
Missouri	35,085	30,783	25,016	4,171,826	3,913,220	4,140,544	83,577	19,328,653	16,706,158	15,054,451	204,331
Montana	8,983	8,056	5,909	4,451,755	4,061,967	4,584,011	1,141,577	1,965,323	1,798,267	5,523,273	46,035
Nebraska...................	11,777	10,729	8,341	304,046	276,058	290,323	35,375	10,883,859	12,193,783	9,873,401	135,484
Nevada......................	899,385	696,943	412,558	4,808,929	4,888,963	5,399,439	77,180	3,093,056	2,931,594	3,110,856	144,683
New Hampshire..........	10,220	9,556	8,698	33,663	32,695	30,941	191	1,082,880	957,547	1,669,228	233,071
New Jersey	327,809	312,188	275,632	4,885,202	5,357,781	5,858,443	140,401	17,296,524	17,169,906	18,357,358	441,110
New Mexico	566,221	486,392	204,183	1,502,808	1,491,144	1,657,550	391,077	4,218,251	4,572,200	4,519,423	196,677
New York....................	1,504,524	1,372,232	1,128,708	12,633,278	16,206,130	17,506,355	99,688	58,249,970	56,277,311	55,588,000	1,351,569
North Carolina............	66,782	61,121	55,607	17,706,032	17,191,874	17,093,464	156,085	14,668,084	14,574,394	13,346,341	215,404
North Dakota..............	7,435	5,746	3,389	669,242	591,668	659,927	72,636	1,079,109	1,052,589	891,107	19,842
Ohio	58,702	53,226	47,448	2,611,158	2,417,080	2,738,275	34,744	51,073,033	51,814,701	47,871,225	174,342
Oklahoma	53,529	47,322	30,423	1,497,654	1,223,134	1,266,189	10,214	8,794,915	9,907,267	12,244,696	70,031
Oregon	39,887	34,242	27,721	875,271	839,614	888,358	201,184	42,905,777	42,303,613	42,516,571	108,613
Pennsylvania..............	106,828	97,513	87,380	8,768,869	8,526,173	8,970,475	16,464	38,531,951	37,629,620	36,592,426	297,055
Rhode Island..............	12,853	12,113	10,561	51,944	50,909	51,559	5	5,288,257	6,078,584	5,134,909	9,475
South Carolina	20,621	18,251	16,990	1,566,756	1,589,650	1,529,172	32,618	7,193,773	7,291,493	7,418,433	90,167
South Dakota	2,352	1,762	1,524	3,950,666	3,807,375	4,199,267	313,269	7,682,641	7,469,361	8,083,947	101,943
Tennessee	36,209	31,329	25,692	8,414,094	7,767,864	7,898,557	598,524	32,372,652	31,719,369	29,960,369	190,144
Texas.........................	4,863,837	3,363,979	1,692,449	3,939,160	4,211,655	5,495,156	1,245,833	8,028,429	7,699,177	7,450,532	638,391
Utah..........................	46,823	42,735	31,928	9,503,304	9,281,567	8,975,525	855,550	5,050,684	4,820,957	4,655,467	150,758
Vermont	10,895	8,757	6,993	32,403	29,049	31,209	643	894,682	814,677	678,201	69,349
Virginia	127,233	119,689	108,635	23,398,517	23,459,706	22,708,338	253,883	8,280,911	8,062,354	7,264,392	71,637
Washington................	438,881	288,960	177,034	7,529,549	7,419,258	7,281,785	1,965,551	35,338,161	38,895,704	41,535,327	119,548
West Virginia..............	3,302	2,870	2,737	1,543,425	1,477,886	1,811,722	15,869	8,546,655	7,507,885	7,400,392	177,133
Wisconsin..................	33,203	29,126	25,346	273,933	312,905	251,145	69,372	15,886,544	14,260,697	13,863,077	146,183
Wyoming	4,308	3,968	3,102	6,194,752	5,955,778	6,307,997	416,385	3,158,799	2,978,604	2,599,445	119,480

[1]Admissions represent counts of events (for example, arrivals) not unique individuals. Admission totals exceed the number of nonimmigrants admitted. Also, the majority of short-term admissions from Canada and Mexico are excluded.
[2]Visits represent the entry of a person onto lands or waters administered by the National Park Service for recreational purposes, excluding government personnel, through traffic (commuters), trades-persons residing within park boundaries.
[3]For year ending June 30. Data are shown as reported by state park directors. In some states, park agency has under its control forests, fish and wildlife areas, and/or other areas. In other states agency is responsible for state parks only. Includes overnight visitors.
(X) = Not applicable

Table A-71. Government

Geographic area	Government employees (BLS)[1] (thousands)			Government earnings (BEA)[2] (million dollars)			Federal tax collections[3] (million dollars)			State tax collections (million dollars)		
	2012	2010	2005	2012	2010	2005	2012	2010	2005	2012	2010	2005
United States......................	22,172	22,658	21,865	1,674,579	1,645,002	1,332,972	[4] 2,524,320	[4] 2,345,055	[4] 2,268,895	794,570	703,444	650,629
Alabama................................	377	387	363	25,994	25,529	20,012	20,883	19,895	20,399	9,053	8,397	7,774
Alaska..................................	84	85	81	9,060	8,412	6,567	4,899	4,685	3,520	7,049	4,523	1,858
Arizona................................	411	416	403	28,992	28,391	23,099	34,850	31,678	29,177	12,973	10,720	11,008
Arkansas..............................	216	218	204	13,082	12,871	10,433	25,300	28,250	24,012	8,288	7,560	6,539
California.............................	2,375	2,448	2,420	206,252	204,908	171,747	292,564	273,353	265,784	112,372	104,841	98,435
Colorado..............................	395	394	363	31,078	29,781	22,895	41,253	39,288	37,769	10,251	8,575	7,648
Connecticut..........................	239	244	244	19,233	19,158	16,021	47,263	43,998	46,131	15,420	12,304	11,585
Delaware.............................	64	64	59	4,699	4,628	3,818	21,835	15,328	13,227	3,360	2,763	2,590
District of Columbia.............	243	247	234	36,043	35,560	27,273	20,748	18,400	18,189	(X)	(X)	(X)
Florida.................................	1,079	1,112	1,081	79,287	80,012	66,926	122,250	111,365	115,562	32,997	31,487	33,895
Georgia................................	682	699	647	50,357	49,809	39,909	65,498	60,506	66,064	16,577	14,783	15,666
Hawaii.................................	126	125	120	15,751	14,651	11,167	6,512	6,281	6,680	5,516	4,838	4,434
Idaho..................................	117	119	115	6,781	6,670	5,634	7,622	6,217	7,809	3,374	2,952	2,934
Illinois.................................	832	854	846	63,417	62,420	50,378	124,431	111,039	119,182	36,438	26,551	26,412
Indiana................................	429	437	426	25,087	24,794	20,761	51,239	43,320	37,752	15,705	13,796	12,854
Iowa...................................	254	253	245	14,815	14,340	11,648	18,754	17,576	17,168	7,832	6,809	5,778
Kansas................................	259	262	251	17,672	16,898	12,714	21,905	18,821	18,798	7,418	6,493	5,638
Kentucky..............................	337	331	314	24,344	23,226	17,631	25,086	23,383	19,036	10,473	9,531	9,091
Louisiana.............................	350	366	374	23,467	24,072	19,690	34,811	34,563	25,647	8,994	8,759	8,639
Maine..................................	101	104	105	6,485	6,523	5,639	6,229	5,896	5,717	3,777	3,490	3,216
Maryland..............................	505	502	466	54,094	50,325	38,905	48,107	47,672	46,825	17,064	15,247	13,367
Massachusetts.....................	437	439	425	33,392	31,335	26,391	79,827	71,418	64,373	22,806	20,091	18,035
Michigan..............................	610	636	674	40,172	40,876	37,029	59,210	53,797	68,500	23,969	22,626	23,525
Minnesota............................	412	417	415	25,165	24,859	20,937	78,685	68,010	67,149	20,561	17,209	15,881
Mississippi...........................	246	249	241	15,715	15,441	12,591	10,459	9,093	8,860	6,953	6,269	5,432
Missouri...............................	437	448	429	28,209	28,191	22,727	48,413	46,100	39,555	10,801	9,703	9,544
Montana...............................	90	92	86	5,568	5,436	4,356	4,384	4,000	3,596	2,459	2,143	1,876
Nebraska.............................	168	170	161	10,389	10,058	8,177	19,795	17,642	16,122	4,358	3,809	3,797
Nevada................................	149	154	144	12,215	12,379	9,542	13,727	12,881	16,711	6,775	5,836	5,670
New Hampshire....................	91	96	91	5,606	5,575	4,412	8,808	8,377	8,205	2,206	2,272	2,011
New Jersey	620	640	642	49,654	48,926	40,791	111,377	118,943	101,997	27,456	25,928	24,248
New Mexico..........................	194	200	201	13,707	13,507	11,662	7,866	7,613	6,642	5,088	4,295	4,478
New York..............................	1,460	1,511	1,489	115,844	115,228	95,175	201,168	200,210	198,562	71,546	63,808	51,326
North Carolina......................	714	721	656	55,914	53,972	40,512	61,600	57,549	60,526	22,713	21,515	18,640
North Dakota........................	80	80	75	4,817	4,544	3,572	5,665	4,283	2,929	5,620	2,646	1,403
Ohio....................................	757	780	800	50,131	49,692	43,625	111,094	106,483	96,837	25,924	23,584	24,011
Oklahoma	347	349	312	22,714	22,154	16,946	27,087	23,398	28,510	8,826	7,082	6,859
Oregon................................	292	300	285	18,248	17,887	14,846	22,717	21,139	19,714	8,700	7,475	6,523
Pennsylvania.......................	722	761	745	51,122	50,891	43,099	108,962	101,859	95,088	32,950	30,169	27,263
Rhode Island........................	60	62	65	5,805	5,682	4,876	10,992	10,510	9,713	2,805	2,569	2,629
South Carolina	347	347	328	25,009	23,999	18,987	18,557	17,361	16,972	8,036	7,313	7,318
South Dakota	78	79	75	4,492	4,353	3,492	5,136	4,305	3,844	1,521	1,321	1,110
Tennessee	424	433	413	25,881	25,154	20,784	47,010	44,557	42,061	11,982	10,514	10,007
Texas..................................	1,795	1,857	1,684	125,461	122,787	91,546	219,460	189,142	169,393	48,597	39,399	32,785
Utah....................................	224	218	202	14,174	13,595	10,796	15,642	13,528	11,648	5,810	5,092	4,703
Vermont	54	55	53	3,387	3,305	2,739	3,525	3,209	3,311	2,757	2,511	2,243
Virginia................................	712	705	662	72,669	70,314	55,445	64,297	57,955	54,430	18,138	16,411	15,919
Washington..........................	541	550	527	45,315	44,246	33,705	52,444	48,437	45,997	17,625	16,106	14,840
West Virginia........................	154	153	144	9,485	9,163	7,690	6,499	6,001	5,470	5,356	4,804	4,301
Wisconsin............................	411	420	415	23,686	24,002	20,422	41,498	38,213	37,973	14,748	14,369	13,152
Wyoming	74	73	65	4,644	4,470	3,234	3,828	3,830	3,086	2,551	2,158	1,740

[1]All estimates of labor and earnings provided by BLS are based on the 2007 North American Industry Classification System (NAICS). Government employment covers only civilian employees; military personnel are excluded. Employees of the Central Intelligence Agency, the National Security Agency, the National Imagery and Mapping Agency, and the Defense Intelligence Agency also are excluded.
[2]The estimates of earnings provided by the Bureau of Economic Analysis (BEA) for 2005 are based on the 2002 North American Industry Classification System (NAICS). The estimates for 2010 and 2012 are based on the 2007 NAICS. All dollar estimates are in current dollars (not adjusted for inflation). Includes Government enterprises.
[3]Excludes excise taxes collected by the Customs Service and the Alcohol and Tobacco Tax and Trade Bureau.
[4]Sum of State totals will differ from national total as the totals for the United States include revenue received from U.S. Armed Services overseas, Puerto Rico, and tax and excess withholding payments not classified by state, which contribute to the total amount of internal revenue collected by the federal government.

Table A-72. State Government Employment and Finances

Geographic area	Employment (full-time equivalent) Number (thousands)		Finances											
			Revenue (million dollars)					Expenditures (million dollars)						
			Total		General, 2011			Total		General, 2011				
												Direct		
	2011	2005	2011	2005	Total¹	Intergovernmental from federal government	Taxes	2011	2005	Total¹	Intergovernmental	Education	Public welfare	Highway
United States	4,359	4,209	2,265,533	1,642,468	1,652,590	593,679	757,869	2,002,719	1,472,542	1,652,902	497,512	592,335	496,762	109,330
Alabama	90	85	26,305	22,297	23,277	8,882	8,636	28,061	20,346	24,290	6,801	10,938	5,962	1,616
Alaska	27	25	14,921	9,185	12,666	3,041	5,538	11,320	8,056	9,956	1,723	2,475	1,918	1,412
Arizona	69	69	36,611	25,453	27,049	12,360	10,848	32,875	24,114	28,123	8,668	9,122	9,511	2,038
Arkansas	63	54	22,808	14,918	17,454	6,313	7,976	18,862	13,077	16,860	5,152	7,508	4,494	1,081
California	407	387	334,233	250,278	211,358	68,431	116,695	280,213	210,407	224,992	91,502	74,993	77,465	10,624
Colorado	72	66	30,248	22,453	21,864	7,008	9,468	29,169	18,734	23,030	7,091	9,250	5,663	1,436
Connecticut	62	60	28,928	20,457	23,508	6,561	13,432	28,094	19,926	22,249	4,486	6,748	6,362	1,013
Delaware	26	25	9,106	6,166	7,310	1,891	3,018	7,936	5,964	7,058	1,293	2,544	1,762	461
District of Columbia	(X)	(X)	(X)	(X)	(X)	(X)	(X)	(X)	(X)	(X)	(X)	(X)	(X)	(X)
Florida	184	186	106,166	77,356	75,290	27,804	32,558	84,633	71,155	71,985	19,725	24,883	22,303	5,449
Georgia	124	121	52,295	36,112	37,168	15,266	16,003	44,750	35,659	37,410	10,600	17,429	10,367	1,641
Hawaii	58	54	12,932	9,092	10,204	2,918	4,858	11,476	8,405	9,963	208	3,345	2,087	357
Idaho	22	23	10,776	7,204	7,344	2,805	3,262	8,733	6,144	7,405	2,036	2,701	2,175	836
Illinois	131	133	79,512	58,791	58,202	19,587	29,433	74,655	55,373	59,505	15,711	17,131	19,508	5,110
Indiana	90	93	38,895	27,122	31,450	10,858	14,909	35,262	26,363	30,902	9,265	14,055	8,397	2,680
Iowa	50	53	24,089	15,631	18,097	7,044	7,236	19,937	13,898	17,219	5,152	6,270	4,901	1,591
Kansas	44	44	18,613	12,522	15,019	4,941	6,828	16,687	11,765	14,527	4,209	5,966	3,531	1,239
Kentucky	81	79	31,056	21,273	23,573	9,025	10,203	29,370	20,435	24,676	5,069	9,415	7,334	1,936
Louisiana	84	91	33,975	24,852	26,939	12,533	8,865	33,396	21,411	29,135	6,580	8,904	6,426	2,185
Maine	21	21	10,611	8,456	8,249	3,241	3,676	9,099	7,470	8,005	1,302	2,121	2,905	647
Maryland	87	91	41,717	28,648	32,999	11,336	16,003	37,673	26,763	32,306	8,124	11,213	9,274	2,196
Massachusetts	92	89	56,637	42,054	44,898	14,137	22,090	52,551	37,625	43,181	8,826	12,334	14,716	1,908
Michigan	145	131	64,440	55,482	54,727	19,914	23,540	63,109	51,563	52,202	19,878	23,146	14,927	2,464
Minnesota	80	74	45,684	31,724	33,452	9,819	18,953	38,488	29,560	32,671	11,102	12,406	10,872	2,565
Mississippi	58	57	23,606	15,518	17,807	8,727	6,714	20,157	14,705	17,546	5,253	5,519	5,437	1,378
Missouri	87	92	38,607	26,821	27,083	12,015	10,110	30,647	23,151	25,773	5,948	8,855	7,587	2,033
Montana	21	20	7,951	5,692	5,769	2,415	2,304	7,105	4,809	6,082	1,353	1,841	1,390	709
Nebraska	32	32	11,523	8,740	9,389	3,402	4,153	9,356	7,240	8,617	2,307	3,330	2,091	602
Nevada	28	26	17,597	11,535	10,444	2,827	6,332	13,203	9,158	9,991	3,905	4,148	2,128	773
New Hampshire	19	19	8,521	6,137	6,252	2,159	2,320	7,638	5,781	6,376	1,191	2,016	1,945	553
New Jersey	147	154	70,798	52,662	51,676	14,793	27,183	67,114	50,964	48,733	11,167	15,710	14,214	3,179
New Mexico	47	50	19,867	13,344	14,949	6,364	4,980	17,865	12,463	15,594	4,326	5,392	4,329	806
New York	244	245	205,546	144,260	148,841	60,200	67,945	184,009	135,811	146,078	59,698	45,219	51,132	4,880
North Carolina	154	135	63,199	44,892	45,858	16,049	22,406	53,089	39,778	44,335	13,633	19,311	11,619	3,433
North Dakota	19	18	7,806	3,877	6,683	1,737	3,822	5,516	3,491	5,032	1,301	1,781	913	717
Ohio	139	136	98,560	72,208	61,984	24,133	25,177	79,153	60,491	60,491	18,412	22,408	18,412	3,494
Oklahoma	68	65	26,225	17,874	20,190	7,874	7,766	22,378	15,712	19,012	4,478	7,491	5,457	2,049
Oregon	66	58	34,991	22,603	20,817	7,609	8,112	27,335	19,217	21,110	5,775	7,102	6,027	1,672
Pennsylvania	169	160	91,705	69,760	69,499	23,843	32,352	90,792	63,881	73,458	19,945	22,849	23,707	7,790
Rhode Island	19	20	9,372	7,252	7,141	2,732	2,738	8,271	6,408	6,408	1,074	1,815	2,403	255
South Carolina	77	76	31,733	22,991	22,792	8,690	7,687	29,352	22,710	23,659	5,586	8,081	6,831	1,171
South Dakota	14	13	6,017	4,059	4,124	1,879	1,380	4,498	3,266	4,062	775	1,300	966	607
Tennessee	86	83	34,681	25,847	27,520	12,117	11,235	30,841	23,954	27,566	7,105	9,177	10,747	1,705
Texas	318	274	134,345	95,821	107,190	42,859	43,188	125,940	81,277	108,599	29,666	48,809	31,269	6,558
Utah	54	49	16,985	13,053	13,835	4,365	5,476	16,683	11,126	14,708	3,106	6,516	2,812	1,514
Vermont	14	14	6,506	4,599	5,628	2,035	2,688	5,854	4,429	5,391	1,553	2,323	1,463	419
Virginia	125	120	50,782	37,037	39,194	10,513	17,409	45,549	32,709	40,350	11,489	14,372	9,348	3,328
Washington	121	117	50,420	36,802	34,993	10,944	17,411	46,000	33,048	36,889	9,347	14,886	8,669	3,030
West Virginia	40	38	15,329	12,019	12,646	4,749	5,143	13,000	9,668	11,446	2,534	4,162	3,288	1,224
Wisconsin	71	70	44,807	34,243	32,133	10,536	15,347	39,350	28,828	33,041	10,429	11,345	8,969	2,432
Wyoming	13	12	7,494	5,297	6,056	2,401	2,462	5,674	4,000	4,905	1,653	1,679	740	537

¹Includes categories not shown separately.
(X) = Not applicable

Table A-73.   State Government Tax Collections: 2012 and Federal Aid to State and Local Governments

Geographic area	State government tax collections, 2012[1]												
	Total[3] (million dollars)	Percent change, 2011–2012	Property taxes (million dollars)	Sales and gross receipts (million dollars)									
				Total	General sales and gross receipts	Selective sales taxes							
						Total	Alcoholic beverages	Amusements	Insurance premiums	Motor fuels	Public utilities	Tobacco products	Other selective sales
United States..............	794,570	4.5	12,994	374,763	242,697	132,066	6,019	6,755	16,660	39,915	14,478	17,086	31,154
Alabama......................	9,053	4.8	325	4,626	2,275	2,352	173	(D)	278	541	737	126	496
Alaska	7,049	27.3	215	248	(X)	248	40	8	62	41	4	67	26
Arizona.......................	12,973	5.8	754	8,066	6,211	1,855	68	1	426	897	21	319	122
Arkansas.....................	8,288	4.2	1,009	3,983	2,809	1,173	49	28	157	467	(X)	247	226
California....................	112,372	-3.7	2,080	38,624	28,536	10,088	346	(X)	2,416	5,545	766	896	119
Colorado	10,251	8.3	(X)	4,091	2,302	1,788	39	93	198	631	12	203	612
Connecticut.................	15,420	15.0	(X)	6,677	3,759	2,918	61	379	206	487	251	418	1,116
Delaware	3,360	3.0	(X)	491	(X)	491	18	(X)	92	113	60	121	88
District of Columbia	(X)	(X)	(X)	(X)	(X)	(X)	(X)	(X)	(X)	(X)	(X)	(X)	(X)
Florida........................	32,997	1.3	(D)	27,267	19,404	7,863	527	157	705	2,274	3,163	381	657
Georgia	16,577	3.6	69	7,254	5,304	1,950	175	(X)	309	881	(X)	227	358
Hawaii........................	5,516	13.6	(X)	3,582	2,698	884	49	(X)	122	93	151	122	347
Idaho..........................	3,374	3.5	(X)	1,665	1,225	440	8	(X)	70	237	3	48	74
Illinois	36,438	19.1	65	14,296	8,034	6,261	279	547	369	1,290	1,750	606	1,419
Indiana.......................	15,705	5.3	(D)	9,173	6,622	2,551	44	823	203	784	216	465	15
Iowa...........................	7,832	8.2	(X)	3,533	2,423	1,110	15	295	101	440	(X)	225	33
Kansas	7,418	9.1	74	3,686	2,826	860	118	(D)	166	435	(X)	104	36
Kentucky	10,473	2.7	530	5,035	3,052	1,982	118	(D)	133	790	65	277	599
Louisiana	8,994	1.5	51	4,889	2,816	2,073	57	671	357	575	13	133	267
Maine.........................	3,777	2.8	38	1,749	1,064	684	17	29	109	242	29	140	119
Maryland.....................	17,064	6.5	756	7,174	4,077	3,097	31	28	428	733	127	411	1,338
Massachusetts.............	22,806	3.3	4	7,319	5,079	2,240	78	3	342	668	24	574	551
Michigan.....................	23,969	1.9	1,798	13,119	9,566	3,553	149	118	298	974	26	951	1,037
Minnesota	20,561	8.5	808	9,139	4,942	4,197	79	42	361	849	(D)	422	2,444
Mississippi..................	6,953	6.2	24	4,397	3,072	1,324	42	152	189	417	2	157	364
Missouri	10,801	6.8	29	4,764	3,103	1,661	34	391	270	708	(X)	105	152
Montana......................	2,459	6.8	257	545	(X)	545	34	54	71	212	50	87	37
Nebraska.....................	4,358	4.9	(D)	2,085	1,457	629	28	3	46	300	56	34	162
Nevada	6,775	7.0	235	5,232	3,434	1,798	42	911	238	291	23	103	191
New Hampshire............	2,206	-5.8	381	875	(X)	875	10	(D)	74	144	84	215	348
New Jersey	27,456	1.0	6	12,010	8,100	3,910	135	239	532	540	958	792	713
New Mexico	5,088	4.2	60	2,651	1,991	661	41	59	118	235	27	75	106
New York.....................	71,546	5.3	(X)	22,869	11,904	10,965	239	1	1,339	1,605	943	1,632	5,207
North Carolina.............	22,713	1.4	(X)	9,539	5,574	3,966	323	14	480	1,862	382	295	611
North Dakota...............	5,620	47.0	2	1,595	1,123	472	8	6	43	205	40	28	141
Ohio...........................	25,924	3.6	(X)	13,120	8,273	4,847	98	20	478	1,684	1,052	843	672
Oklahoma	8,826	13.5	(X)	3,724	2,416	1,308	104	19	229	445	39	293	180
Oregon........................	8,700	7.2	16	1,399	(X)	1,399	17	(D)	101	533	94	256	398
Pennsylvania...............	32,950	1.8	38	17,152	9,167	7,985	324	1,500	791	2,074	1,337	1,119	841
Rhode Island...............	2,805	1.8	2	1,475	839	635	13	(X)	86	118	102	131	186
South Carolina	8,036	4.5	9	4,198	2,926	1,272	154	39	144	532	46	26	332
South Dakota	1,521	10.3	(X)	1,197	838	359	15	9	67	136	4	60	67
Tennessee	11,982	6.9	(X)	8,962	6,512	2,450	133	(X)	639	838	9	279	551
Texas.........................	48,597	12.6	(X)	37,432	24,501	12,931	938	39	1,508	3,178	620	1,470	5,178
Utah...........................	5,810	6.1	(X)	2,722	1,857	865	46	(X)	104	372	26	124	193
Vermont	2,757	2.6	949	968	342	626	22	(X)	59	108	13	80	343
Virginia......................	18,138	4.2	34	5,853	3,487	2,366	191	(D)	391	866	151	192	575
Washington.................	17,625	1.2	1,897	14,171	10,614	3,557	349	(X)	430	1,178	460	471	669
West Virginia...............	5,356	2.8	6	2,630	1,277	1,352	87	78	145	387	156	110	390
Wisconsin	14,748	-3.9	156	6,395	3,872	2,523	50	(D)	152	894	385	598	445
Wyoming	2,551	3.6	317	1,120	994	126	2	(X)	26	66	4	26	1

[1]The tax revenue data pertain to state fiscal years that end on June 30 in all but four states (NY, TX, AL, MI). Amounts shown for these four states reflect the different timing of their respective fiscal years, which were the 12-month periods ending on March 31 for New York, August 31 for Texas, and September 30 for Alabama and Michigan.
[3]Includes items not shown separately.
(D) = Data withheld to avoid disclosure or does not meet statistical standards.
(X) = Not applicable

Table A-73. State Government Tax Collections: 2012 and Federal Aid to State and Local Governments—*Continued*

Geographic area	State government tax collections, 2012[1]						Federal aid to state and local governments[2] (million dollars)								
	Licenses (million dollars)			Other taxes (thousand dollars)			Total[2]			2010					
	Corporation	Motor vehicle	Occupation and business, NEC[4]	Individual income	Corporate net income tax	Severance	2010	2008	2005	Centers for Medicare and Medicaid Services[5]	Highway trust fund[6]	Community development block grant[7]	Title 1 programs[8]	Office of Special Education programs	Childrens nutrition program[9]
United States............	10,944	22,596	13,304	280,360	41,741	18,753	630,170	469,773	403,660	278,041	30,273	7,361	18,110	16,695	16,281
Alabama....................	131	202	124	3,017	413	116	8,609	6,994	6,306	3,980	675	99	343	274	290
Alaska......................	(X)	58	39	(X)	663	5,787	3,326	2,604	2,671	911	352	15	50	57	46
Arizona.....................	11	146	129	3,094	648	41	13,370	9,940	7,965	7,403	512	74	374	261	359
Arkansas..................	25	154	125	2,402	404	83	6,418	4,733	4,179	3,338	341	39	186	176	211
California..................	53	3,529	4,293	55,024	7,949	37	66,565	53,818	46,029	29,247	1,881	1,268	2,236	1,792	1,990
Colorado...................	16	456	39	4,876	492	175	7,651	5,321	4,538	2,723	416	52	195	217	172
Connecticut...............	28	209	144	7,371	625	(D)	7,673	5,279	4,539	3,464	584	55	165	229	119
Delaware...................	625	50	375	1,312	262	(X)	3,325	1,363	1,142	834	1,547	13	48	44	48
District of Columbia ...	(X)	(X)	(X)	(X)	(X)	(X)	9,942	11,946	3,450	1,493	154	202	40	19	38
Florida......................	276	1,305	204	(X)	2,003	50	27,731	20,659	19,046	12,297	1,269	212	905	953	947
Georgia	44	308	74	8,142	591	(X)	15,879	10,675	8,914	6,075	1,135	128	602	480	686
Hawaii	2	206	31	1,541	80	(X)	2,520	2,120	1,731	933	138	22	53	50	51
Idaho........................	2	128	70	1,213	189	8	3,057	2,688	1,814	1,179	286	19	65	86	77
Illinois......................	321	1,621	391	15,692	3,495	(X)	23,194	16,267	14,616	9,835	859	202	830	769	620
Indiana.....................	12	320	32	4,766	959	2	10,400	8,272	6,483	4,570	722	120	311	374	335
Iowa.........................	35	521	112	3,030	426	(X)	5,871	4,014	3,594	2,469	349	107	121	217	143
Kansas	21	185	52	2,892	318	133	4,980	3,514	2,872	1,823	398	35	129	182	156
Kentucky	100	189	88	3,512	575	346	9,756	6,867	5,779	4,666	497	46	303	261	260
Louisiana	105	132	110	2,475	290	886	13,437	12,457	7,148	5,538	604	644	392	293	346
Maine.......................	9	99	105	1,442	232	(X)	3,581	2,695	2,623	1,840	151	29	76	87	55
Maryland...................	96	444	145	7,117	880	(X)	10,832	7,473	6,800	4,574	418	80	264	300	211
Massachusetts..........	26	377	259	11,933	2,002	(X)	15,121	11,402	9,989	7,860	623	144	3	14	247
Michigan	22	916	150	6,828	609	64	19,646	13,587	12,113	8,701	809	150	705	603	436
Minnesota.................	7	631	374	7,988	1,066	46	10,872	7,533	5,878	4,842	511	67	196	315	235
Mississippi...............	146	134	92	1,501	396	116	8,611	7,484	5,168	3,715	377	699	244	171	261
Missouri	63	268	134	5,132	302	(D)	12,717	8,273	7,407	6,152	939	105	294	364	301
Montana....................	3	143	100	900	132	306	2,810	2,109	2,021	807	342	19	61	59	47
Nebraska..................	26	123	12	1,838	234	5	3,122	2,439	2,256	1,232	131	25	76	108	102
Nevada.....................	67	161	225	(X)	(X)	303	3,610	2,450	2,213	1,020	290	31	113	104	91
New Hampshire.........	47	94	88	82	521	(X)	2,355	1,692	1,483	835	161	23	46	69	34
New Jersey	214	606	472	11,128	1,929	(X)	16,309	11,580	10,479	6,840	622	125	354	537	327
New Mexico	22	93	26	1,150	281	768	6,811	5,381	4,097	3,187	305	32	169	141	162
New York...................	52	1,419	186	38,772	4,568	(X)	61,341	44,454	43,438	32,737	1,632	691	1,518	1,019	1,000
North Carolina...........	523	569	219	10,384	1,220	2	15,522	12,906	11,568	8,369	376	82	489	486	520
North Dakota.............	(X)	105	63	433	216	3,187	2,169	1,467	1,363	523	192	9	48	44	36
Ohio.........................	1,682	715	861	9,030	117	10	23,072	15,230	13,726	11,299	968	187	725	710	513
Oklahoma	51	665	96	2,774	446	849	8,022	5,922	4,935	3,218	653	45	174	205	262
Oregon......................	19	477	302	5,826	433	14	7,849	5,498	4,808	3,193	513	41	194	218	172
Pennsylvania.............	656	838	890	10,102	1,837	(X)	26,291	18,832	18,103	12,688	1,235	251	732	659	483
Rhode Island.............	5	56	40	1,064	122	(X)	2,944	2,037	1,937	1,280	175	24	71	67	44
South Carolina	101	135	129	3,097	253	(X)	8,296	6,035	5,326	4,119	456	54	249	256	276
South Dakota	4	65	125	(X)	60	14	2,145	1,473	1,336	626	214	18	NA	1	47
Tennessee	626	262	297	182	1,226	2	12,514	9,201	9,083	6,346	660	57	353	353	343
Texas.......................	4,544	1,833	620	(X)	(X)	3,656	43,732	30,580	25,622	20,095	1,611	515	1,810	1,503	1,907
Utah.........................	1	158	48	2,466	259	107	4,212	3,160	2,633	1,490	248	29	81	149	129
Vermont	2	64	18	598	97	(X)	2,044	1,441	1,213	890	163	11	48	43	25
Virginia	57	432	184	10,216	839	2	10,647	7,724	6,330	4,221	854	71	279	386	239
Washington...............	30	471	253	(X)	(X)	36	11,945	8,668	7,681	4,474	479	85	250	356	265
West Virginia.............	4	3	13	1,756	192	626	4,830	3,557	3,482	2,224	396	47	130	124	99
Wisconsin	19	455	323	6,261	890	5	10,710	7,000	6,563	4,942	660	119	270	323	232
Wyoming	13	66	24	(X)	(X)	969	2,356	2,334	2,243	365	239	6	39	36	25

[1]The tax revenue data pertain to state fiscal years that end on June 30 in all but four states (NY, TX, AL, MI). Amounts shown for these four states reflect the different timing of their respective fiscal years, which were the 12-month periods ending on March 31 for New York, August 31 for Texas, and September 30 for Alabama and Michigan.
[2]National totals include federal government grants and payments to outlying areas as well as undistributed aid and will differ from the sum of state total.
[3]Includes items not shown separately.
[4]NEC means not elsewhere classified.
[5]Program of the Department of Health and Human Services.
[6]Program of the Department of Transportation.
[7]Program of the Department of Housing and Urban Development.
[8]Program of the Department of Education.
[9]Program of the Department of Agriculture.
(D) = Data withheld to avoid disclosure or does not meet statistical standards.
(X) = Not applicable

Table A–74   State Resources, Expenditures, and Balances

Geographic area	Expenditures by fund source (millions of dollars)					State general fund (millions of dollars)								
	2012 estimate[1]			2010 total	2000 total	Resources[2,3]			Expenditures[3]			Balances[4]		
	Total[5]	General fund	Federal fund			2012	2010	2,000	2012	2010	2000	2012	2010	2000
United States............	1,664,751	662,780	519,437	1,617,118	945,271	695,675	638,354	504,076	666,856	623,394	468,216	28,819	14,960	35,860
Alabama....................	20,849	7,076	8,307	20,604	14,730	7,445	6,751	5,317	7,598	7,457	5,215	-153	-706	102
Alaska......................	11,884	7,394	3,135	9,761	5,245	9,917	5,635	2,262	7,013	6,603	2,262	2,904	-968	0
Arizona....................	27,595	8,421	11,287	27,946	14,924	8,817	7,846	6,216	8,421	7,852	6,012	396	-6	204
Arkansas..................	20,686	4,578	6,296	19,922	10,093	4,606	4,323	3,177	4,606	4,323	3,177	0	0	0
California..................	213,344	87,027	78,235	206,089	122,167	83,944	81,894	75,861	87,027	87,237	66,494	-3,083	-5,343	9,367
Colorado...................	28,079	7,240	7,621	31,064	12,267	8,032	6,853	6,791	7,168	6,716	5,992	864	137	799
Connecticut...............	26,875	18,781	2,562	24,359	18,096	18,562	17,689	11,214	18,705	17,208	10,913	-143	481	301
Delaware.................	8,942	3,592	1,777	8,720	5,015	4,157	3,614	2,584	3,592	3,077	2,246	565	537	338
District of Columbia ...	NA	NA	NA	NA	NA	NA	NA	NA	NA	NA	NA	NA	NA	NA
Florida....................	69,368	23,170	25,111	62,050	48,808	24,749	22,796	19,044	23,749	21,223	18,554	1,000	1,573	490
Georgia....................	39,433	16,511	11,099	40,748	25,865	18,559	17,110	15,581	17,428	15,971	13,782	1,131	1,139	1,799
Hawaii......................	11,513	5,509	1,953	10,948	6,784	5,787	4,816	3,473	5,511	4,838	3,201	276	-22	272
Idaho........................	6,944	2,548	2,708	6,393	3,636	2,644	2,336	1,863	2,545	2,507	1,681	99	-171	182
Illinois......................	51,352	29,163	9,937	49,315	35,084	34,092	32,609	24,600	29,272	25,165	23,084	4,820	7,444	1,516
Indiana.....................	26,304	13,579	9,272	26,656	16,881	15,382	13,656	10,426	13,590	12,877	8,967	1,792	779	1,459
Iowa.........................	19,123	6,010	6,514	17,637	11,652	6,693	5,634	4,939	6,004	5,298	4,763	689	336	178
Kansas.....................	14,734	6,129	3,891	14,044	8,416	6,593	5,241	4,746	6,126	5,268	4,368	467	-27	378
Kentucky...................	25,649	9,334	8,687	25,941	12,653	9,683	8,604	7,141	9,435	8,452	6,549	248	152	592
Louisiana..................	32,755	8,374	11,871	31,684	15,636	8,401	8,575	5,868	8,249	8,683	5,811	152	-108	57
Maine.......................	8,106	3,087	2,649	8,351	4,846	3,191	2,921	2,610	3,130	2,849	2,317	61	72	293
Maryland...................	35,800	15,041	9,438	33,159	18,316	15,487	13,773	9,958	14,935	13,429	9,022	552	344	936
Massachusetts...........	52,187	24,486	11,238	51,278	26,532	34,447	31,327	21,326	32,458	30,424	20,838	1,989	903	488
Michigan...................	48,628	8,855	19,550	47,759	34,947	9,111	7,892	9,788	8,383	7,705	9,576	728	187	212
Minnesota.................	32,680	18,073	9,009	29,950	18,447	17,900	15,067	13,602	16,802	14,627	11,476	1,098	440	2,126
Mississippi...............	23,965	4,309	12,813	22,758	9,655	4,812	4,499	3,557	4,803	4,320	3,515	9	179	42
Missouri...................	23,364	7,938	7,539	23,390	16,015	8,143	7,755	7,520	7,938	7,570	7,350	205	185	170
Montana....................	5,919	1,764	2,131	6,049	2,783	2,222	2,026	1,281	1,775	1,716	1,105	447	310	176
Nebraska...................	9,877	3,446	2,988	9,606	5,801	3,944	3,610	2,660	3,446	3,313	2,344	498	297	316
Nevada.....................	7,949	3,105	2,351	8,284	4,594	3,357	3,362	1,744	3,114	3,212	1,608	243	150	136
New Hampshire..........	5,108	1,280	1,648	5,468	3,395	1,404	1,436	1,032	1,241	1,405	1,028	163	31	4
New Jersey	49,681	29,929	12,344	48,520	29,672	30,560	29,284	21,147	29,991	28,480	19,459	569	804	1,688
New Mexico	15,198	5,432	5,660	15,373	8,269	6,392	5,930	3,614	5,687	5,358	3,390	705	572	224
New York...................	133,504	56,489	40,311	128,937	73,573	58,276	54,504	38,337	56,489	52,202	37,170	1,787	2,302	1,167
North Carolina...........	52,987	18,893	17,781	48,747	25,837	20,116	18,750	14,100	19,576	18,513	13,854	540	237	246
North Dakota.............	6,191	2,223	1,980	4,866	2,256	3,517	1,898	833	2,223	1,585	773	1,294	313	60
Ohio..........................	57,905	31,011	13,144	57,630	38,816	28,030	25,685	20,272	26,395	25,175	19,244	1,635	510	1,028
Oklahoma	21,102	5,018	8,326	20,874	10,595	6,232	5,163	4,825	5,797	5,119	4,545	435	44	280
Oregon.....................	30,082	6,897	7,448	32,547	10,655	6,899	5,982	5,222	6,897	6,371	4,849	2	-389	373
Pennsylvania.............	68,227	27,161	25,382	68,091	38,465	27,690	27,346	20,014	27,186	27,641	19,295	504	-295	719
Rhode Island.............	8,228	3,139	2,838	7,813	4,271	3,246	2,881	2,344	3,117	2,864	2,231	129	17	113
South Carolina	21,904	5,456	9,324	19,702	16,892	6,581	5,363	5,730	5,517	5,117	5,156	1,064	246	574
South Dakota	3,698	1,215	1,488	3,834	2,109	1,282	1,132	800	1,207	1,132	771	75	0	29
Tennessee	31,077	12,067	13,125	28,449	15,809	11,969	10,004	6,682	11,458	9,451	6,593	511	553	89
Texas........................	92,300	44,164	30,847	92,056	49,465	44,486	40,916	31,259	43,911	39,465	27,493	575	1,451	3,766
Utah.........................	13,227	4,743	3,638	12,598	6,561	4,859	4,435	3,477	4,830	4,441	3,364	29	-6	113
Vermont	4,849	756	1,741	4,667	2,231	1,250	1,090	905	1,250	1,088	855	0	2	50
Virginia.....................	43,372	16,986	9,212	40,774	22,364	17,027	14,919	11,935	16,351	14,787	11,282	676	132	653
Washington...............	43,238	15,114	6,710	33,587	21,481	14,910	14,475	10,705	15,325	15,036	10,220	-415	-561	485
West Virginia.............	22,517	4,053	4,402	20,378	6,482	4,902	4,240	2,802	4,140	3,677	2,639	762	563	163
Wisconsin	41,324	13,381	10,572	40,085	26,185	13,795	12,963	12,166	13,868	12,824	11,271	-73	139	895
Wyoming	6,128	2,833	1,547	7,657	1,594	1,580	1,750	733	1,580	1,750	518	0	0	215

[1]Capital inclusive.
[2]Includes funds budgeted, adjustments, and balances from previous year.
[3]May or may not include budget stabilization fund transfers, depending on state accounting practices.
[4]Resources less expenditures.
[5]Includes bonds and other state funds not shown separately.
0 = zero or rounds to zero.
NA = Not applicable

Table A-75. Federal Government

Geographic area	Nonfarm employees in the federal government (BLS)[1] (thousands)			Federal earnings (BEA)[2] (million dollars)						Federal funds and grants[3]						
				Civilian			Military			Total (million dollars)		Defense, 2010		Selected object categories, 2010[4] (million dollars)		
	2012	2010	2005	2012	2010	2005	2012	2010	2005	2010	2008	Percent	Per capita[5] (dollars)	Direct payments for individuals	Grants to state and local government	Salaries and wages
United States.............	2,815.2	2,980.9	2,735.9	328,158	320,431	253,023	182,256	178,261	131,338	3,251,309	2,771,784	17.0	1,773	1,719,574	675,281	341,628
Alabama	56.0	58.5	51.4	6,633	6,252	4,691	2,468	2,525	2,162	56,496	47,966	23.1	2,726	31,128	9,273	5,613
Alaska	16.3	17.5	17.0	1,834	1,831	1,529	2,886	2,548	1,749	12,615	9,423	41.3	7,338	2,631	3,465	4,055
Arizona......................	56.3	60.0	51.8	6,088	5,792	4,444	2,778	2,825	2,184	64,427	54,314	22.1	2,231	32,273	14,361	4,980
Arkansas	20.6	22.9	20.9	2,036	2,067	1,727	1,124	1,143	1,038	28,904	23,857	10.3	1,018	17,893	6,843	2,418
California...................	249.8	268.4	250.4	28,421	28,272	22,657	19,785	20,090	14,528	333,809	299,923	16.7	1,496	172,819	78,869	24,585
Colorado	54.5	56.2	52.7	6,088	5,909	4,837	5,346	4,908	3,140	49,687	38,015	24.6	2,428	22,008	8,793	8,519
Connecticut................	17.6	19.7	19.9	1,928	1,969	1,673	1,097	1,117	884	55,978	38,879	21.4	3,352	33,820	8,299	1,903
Delaware	5.6	6.1	5.4	554	568	417	579	578	465	8,076	6,623	10.1	910	4,951	2,055	708
District of Columbia	208.0	210.6	193.8	30,836	29,836	22,544	1,962	2,356	2,002	61,920	47,203	14.0	14,457	6,769	10,872	23,030
Florida.......................	132.7	142.3	128.7	14,273	14,047	11,229	9,012	8,895	7,188	186,704	149,872	12.1	1,205	127,692	28,066	12,964
Georgia......................	102.4	107.6	93.9	11,144	10,965	8,382	9,636	9,303	6,590	92,387	74,165	24.7	2,353	45,804	16,751	17,372
Hawaii	34.0	34.8	31.3	3,797	3,543	2,683	6,449	5,818	4,040	20,855	15,009	48.0	7,354	7,187	3,026	7,898
Idaho.........................	12.5	13.7	13.1	1,187	1,234	1,044	617	657	534	14,252	11,227	7.6	688	7,393	2,980	1,245
Illinois.......................	83.0	91.7	89.0	9,180	9,475	7,975	3,255	3,623	2,835	109,967	100,672	9.5	814	66,357	24,060	7,949
Indiana......................	37.5	42.2	36.3	3,880	3,909	3,055	1,074	1,117	869	58,603	52,813	12.2	1,102	36,780	11,965	4,360
Iowa..........................	17.7	19.1	18.1	1,675	1,683	1,373	559	633	563	28,379	23,927	9.1	847	17,710	6,394	1,902
Kansas	26.4	28.2	25.8	2,583	2,562	2,066	3,894	3,487	1,869	29,046	25,129	23.8	2,426	15,431	4,736	5,818
Kentucky	39.7	42.5	37.3	3,828	3,703	2,889	6,004	5,482	3,475	57,271	52,264	23.1	3,054	31,077	9,502	9,205
Louisiana	30.4	33.6	34.0	3,202	3,210	2,872	3,125	3,085	2,355	53,214	44,496	17.5	2,051	26,134	15,088	4,703
Maine........................	14.5	15.6	14.1	1,569	1,489	1,220	523	595	575	14,644	11,974	14.7	1,620	7,987	3,787	1,134
Maryland....................	146.2	139.9	125.8	25,231	22,687	17,302	5,144	4,428	3,414	96,261	77,905	19.4	3,235	40,256	14,441	15,041
Massachusetts...........	46.7	50.5	49.9	5,472	5,433	4,699	1,223	1,251	1,009	82,454	72,115	17.7	2,224	39,608	22,352	4,506
Michigan....................	52.7	57.3	54.7	5,737	5,647	4,598	994	1,131	921	90,921	82,933	6.7	613	59,079	20,577	4,798
Minnesota	31.5	34.8	33.2	3,309	3,290	2,832	1,042	1,044	966	44,376	38,246	7.0	587	27,529	10,528	3,368
Mississippi................	25.7	27.3	25.6	2,573	2,515	2,111	2,056	2,178	1,834	31,419	30,098	13.0	1,372	17,865	7,871	3,017
Missouri	54.9	59.5	54.3	5,783	5,983	4,689	2,734	2,699	1,973	70,348	60,829	21.5	2,527	36,022	14,003	7,321
Montana.....................	13.4	14.8	13.5	1,304	1,315	1,086	543	528	452	10,758	8,843	8.8	956	5,805	2,939	1,195
Nebraska....................	16.7	17.3	16.3	1,641	1,569	1,278	1,046	1,046	931	16,532	15,739	12.8	1,156	9,935	3,507	1,783
Nevada......................	18.0	18.5	16.8	1,836	1,757	1,446	1,532	1,409	928	19,771	17,260	14.6	1,072	11,720	3,702	1,942
New Hampshire..........	7.4	8.0	7.9	827	820	718	224	237	165	11,335	10,311	14.1	1,218	6,709	2,311	880
New Jersey	50.7	60.5	61.6	6,028	6,467	5,711	1,585	1,614	1,313	80,990	72,085	12.8	1,177	49,719	15,457	5,578
New Mexico	31.5	33.7	30.0	3,386	3,342	2,576	1,628	1,475	1,120	27,959	23,846	11.6	1,572	10,972	6,720	2,768
New York....................	118.1	132.5	128.6	13,066	13,351	11,048	4,629	4,429	4,429	202,266	174,071	7.5	787	111,343	63,104	13,936
North Carolina............	69.6	72.0	61.1	6,973	6,570	4,956	14,519	13,951	8,650	90,737	70,203	19.4	1,846	49,198	20,099	15,349
North Dakota..............	9.4	10.2	10.0	883	870	704	884	859	726	8,696	7,323	11.9	1,545	4,690	2,237	1,083
Ohio..........................	78.2	84.6	77.3	8,603	8,576	6,979	2,238	2,295	1,957	106,449	90,592	9.4	863	66,245	24,399	6,975
Oklahoma	48.4	50.4	45.9	4,975	4,802	3,832	3,172	3,259	2,380	38,475	31,758	18.2	1,868	21,669	7,855	5,575
Oregon.......................	28.1	30.5	29.7	2,914	3,004	2,556	625	666	562	33,974	27,530	6.4	564	20,664	8,694	2,569
Pennsylvania..............	100.3	109.6	106.7	10,822	10,856	9,164	1,952	2,069	1,855	145,934	121,551	11.1	1,280	88,367	29,411	8,803
Rhode Island..............	10.3	10.6	9.9	1,203	1,193	959	645	633	505	11,759	9,841	12.7	1,414	6,609	3,152	997
South Carolina	32.9	34.4	28.6	3,271	3,094	2,327	4,658	4,433	3,282	46,578	38,832	19.0	1,914	25,579	8,210	4,618
South Dakota	11.4	11.9	11.2	1,075	1,034	837	559	576	441	9,507	8,552	12.4	1,449	5,313	2,250	1,031
Tennessee	49.9	52.4	49.2	5,461	5,322	4,298	1,111	1,320	1,032	68,866	58,672	8.2	890	40,793	14,094	3,837
Texas.........................	199.2	209.7	181.9	21,886	21,146	15,761	17,778	16,278	11,230	225,725	210,005	24.0	2,157	110,580	44,624	29,926
Utah..........................	35.2	38.0	35.3	3,410	3,428	2,828	1,004	1,063	917	23,545	17,117	20.3	1,730	11,606	4,987	3,195
Vermont	6.4	6.8	6.1	679	639	504	195	212	164	7,405	6,080	14.9	1,760	3,369	2,380	724
Virginia......................	174.1	174.5	151.8	25,323	23,734	17,138	16,468	16,894	13,485	136,083	118,527	42.7	7,263	44,405	12,228	21,112
Washington................	73.0	75.6	69.5	7,846	7,801	6,017	8,208	7,681	5,427	70,437	56,436	21.2	2,225	34,133	14,725	11,539
West Virginia..............	23.3	24.4	21.9	2,505	2,430	1,897	433	517	422	21,511	18,002	5.2	609	12,822	4,970	1,936
Wisconsin	29.0	31.4	29.2	2,704	2,742	2,288	800	848	742	54,866	40,137	18.2	1,755	30,143	11,992	2,926
Wyoming	7.5	8.1	7.5	697	697	574	453	451	362	6,211	5,969	10.0	1,102	2,678	2,254	709

[1]All employment estimates provided by the Bureau of Labor Statistics are based on the 2007 North American Industry Classification System (NAICS).
[2]The estimates of earnings for 2005 are based on the 2002 North American Industry Classification System (NAICS). The estimates for 2010 forward are based on the 2007 NAICS. All dollar estimates are in current dollars (not adjusted for inflation).
[3]Data pertains to year ending September 30.
[4]Data for grants, salaries and wages, and direct payments to individuals are on an expenditures basis.
[5]Based on U.S. Census Bureau estimated resident population as of July 1.

Table A-76. Federal Individual Income Tax Returns

Geographic area	Federal individual income tax returns								Deductions, 2010 (million dollars)		Federal buildings, 2010 (million square feet)		Federal lands, 2010[4]
	Number of returns[1] (thousands)		Adjusted gross income[2] (million dollars)		Adjusted gross income per return (dollars)		Income tax[3] (million dollars)		Total itemized deductions	Mortgage interest paid	Owned	Leased	Total, owned or leased (acres)
	2010	2000	2010	2000	2010	2000	2010	2000					
United States[5]	144,002	130,122	8,090,663	6,307,009	56,184	48,470	1,002,111	980,064	1,232,542	390,779	2,487.5	308.4	39,974,200
Alabama	2,102	1,904	98,932	72,591	47,060	38,125	10,778	9,476	12,591	4,052	48.1	4.5	201,400
Alaska	374	329	21,508	13,964	57,544	42,444	2,754	2,064	1,951	903	44.3	3.3	2,151,200
Arizona	2,719	2,153	135,801	98,821	49,952	45,899	15,144	14,165	21,794	8,602	50.5	3.9	4,063,100
Arkansas	1,224	1,118	55,981	39,706	45,723	35,515	5,720	5,087	6,761	1,783	19.3	1.6	658,100
California	16,684	14,867	1,026,911	864,645	61,551	58,159	133,458	146,454	204,887	71,921	269.4	21.2	2,886,200
Colorado	2,370	2,096	142,647	112,909	60,190	53,869	17,803	18,243	22,446	9,124	50.3	7.3	855,100
Connecticut	1,728	1,672	145,642	117,734	84,305	70,415	22,652	22,682	24,243	6,498	11.4	1.0	12,400
Delaware	428	378	23,888	18,647	55,844	49,331	2,699	2,794	3,568	1,417	5.1	0.4	12,000
District of Columbia	323	279	23,964	16,271	74,223	58,318	3,703	2,839	4,121	1,223	65.7	24.9	4,800
Florida	9,631	7,499	467,521	348,609	48,542	46,487	59,914	56,618	60,525	20,903	95.5	11.8	905,500
Georgia	4,590	3,637	216,008	168,486	47,065	46,326	24,703	24,693	36,793	11,982	104.0	10.8	983,700
Hawaii	653	572	33,362	23,929	51,062	41,834	3,502	3,124	5,239	2,281	49.0	0.8	235,300
Idaho	663	559	29,569	22,572	44,580	40,379	2,937	2,922	4,836	1,719	18.8	2.8	1,264,100
Illinois	6,044	5,787	362,262	302,994	59,939	52,358	46,803	49,472	51,347	16,575	62.0	6.0	222,900
Indiana	2,982	2,837	143,180	119,554	48,022	42,141	15,191	16,416	16,470	5,270	31.5	3.2	315,900
Iowa	1,400	1,351	72,095	54,016	51,499	39,982	7,572	6,896	9,270	2,453	12.1	1.9	228,500
Kansas	1,307	1,223	70,710	53,410	54,096	43,671	8,025	7,491	9,914	2,470	32.7	2.8	597,500
Kentucky	1,856	1,747	86,693	66,933	46,698	38,313	8,893	8,617	11,351	3,353	44.7	5.6	552,300
Louisiana	1,991	1,874	98,239	69,184	49,344	36,918	11,668	9,261	10,639	3,186	32.9	6.0	289,300
Maine	625	606	29,966	24,374	47,941	40,220	3,047	3,151	4,299	1,331	11.6	0.9	389,400
Maryland	2,787	2,563	189,301	139,963	67,914	54,609	23,632	20,950	38,349	12,766	101.6	22.2	61,500
Massachusetts	3,203	3,110	233,487	202,426	72,893	65,089	33,218	36,438	36,185	11,438	30.4	3.1	55,100
Michigan	4,607	4,620	227,557	217,648	49,396	47,110	25,396	31,781	30,767	9,978	22.5	4.6	172,700
Minnesota	2,561	2,386	152,396	120,028	59,505	50,305	18,219	17,687	24,651	8,184	14.7	2.0	99,300
Mississippi	1,283	1,173	53,325	39,170	41,547	33,393	5,592	4,666	6,411	1,686	33.5	2.6	784,900
Missouri	2,689	2,565	135,415	108,519	50,361	42,307	15,114	15,270	18,318	5,577	42.4	8.5	631,400
Montana	475	424	21,570	14,523	45,425	34,253	2,258	1,766	3,179	1,000	15.5	2.2	474,800
Nebraska	854	809	45,209	33,605	52,934	41,539	4,952	4,561	5,971	1,520	12.3	1.6	179,800
Nevada	1,264	954	66,772	48,858	52,829	51,214	8,423	7,845	10,062	3,792	29.7	2.1	4,898,100
New Hampshire	664	629	41,350	34,469	62,281	54,800	5,047	5,673	6,376	2,055	2.6	0.6	22,800
New Jersey	4,286	4,067	308,540	253,294	71,995	62,280	43,545	44,470	57,100	15,717	39.1	5.1	88,800
New Mexico	913	728	41,429	23,655	45,377	32,493	4,388	2,721	5,089	1,887	55.4	4.8	3,964,700
New York	9,272	8,577	628,370	474,337	67,770	55,303	91,175	80,907	111,991	22,735	81.0	9.7	169,800
North Carolina	4,203	3,636	207,775	156,022	49,438	42,910	22,165	21,231	33,352	10,714	77.5	5.3	494,400
North Dakota	330	303	18,586	10,735	56,241	35,428	2,266	1,333	1,462	394	20.5	1.0	629,800
Ohio	5,437	5,575	267,042	231,057	49,112	41,445	29,269	31,612	35,068	10,512	60.7	5.0	146,800
Oklahoma	1,590	1,465	79,531	54,835	50,007	37,430	8,856	7,150	9,870	2,448	51.5	11.5	1,086,200
Oregon	1,743	1,562	88,462	70,282	50,744	44,995	9,325	9,723	16,776	5,774	19.9	2.6	303,400
Pennsylvania	6,130	5,806	339,678	262,961	55,413	45,291	41,103	39,214	44,122	13,418	68.6	9.8	193,600
Rhode Island	509	494	28,279	23,015	55,548	46,589	3,344	3,316	4,476	1,457	13.0	0.5	4,700
South Carolina	2,052	1,802	94,103	69,543	45,863	38,592	9,463	8,804	14,013	4,587	48.9	2.3	460,700
South Dakota	394	355	19,818	13,233	50,327	37,275	2,278	1,824	1,741	525	14.8	2.0	550,000
Tennessee	2,847	2,567	136,096	103,066	47,810	40,150	15,292	14,590	15,031	5,228	58.2	5.0	375,100
Texas	10,996	9,052	620,581	417,263	56,439	46,096	80,302	67,590	67,161	19,892	175.9	22.3	1,674,600
Utah	1,135	942	58,858	40,270	51,875	42,750	5,769	4,964	10,934	3,771	32.1	3.3	2,459,000
Vermont	318	299	15,678	12,632	49,315	42,247	1,677	1,705	2,127	660	2.6	1.2	18,700
Virginia	3,729	3,338	245,073	171,060	65,713	51,246	31,185	26,051	41,417	15,585	142.3	30.5	467,000
Washington	3,169	2,773	190,783	149,598	60,201	53,948	23,868	25,254	27,076	12,078	77.8	7.1	1,364,200
West Virginia	783	750	35,604	25,645	45,457	34,193	3,639	3,102	3,132	956	16.0	2.9	156,200
Wisconsin	2,742	2,597	143,792	116,346	52,447	44,800	15,934	18,900	21,952	6,260	18.9	2.6	104,200
Wyoming	276	235	17,685	11,020	63,975	46,894	2,284	1,820	1,893	581	13.4	0.8	1,053,200

[1]Includes returns constructed by Internal Revenue Service for certain self-employment tax returns.

[2]Less deficit.

[3]Includes additional tax for tax preferences, self-employment tax, tax from investment credit recapture, and other income-related taxes. Total is before earned income credit.

[4]Federal real property is defined as any real property owned, leased, or otherwise managed by the federal government, within the United States, and improvements of federal lands. Federal real property shall exclude: interest in real property assets that have been disposed of for public benefit purposes pursuant to section 484 of title 40, United States Code, and are now held in private ownership; land easements or rights-of-way held by the federal government; public domain land (including lands withdrawn for military purposes) or land reserved or dedicated for national forest, national park, or national wildlife refuge purposes except for improvements on those lands; land held in trust or restricted fee status for individual Indians or Indian tribes; and land and interests in land that are withheld from the scope of this order by agency heads for reasons of national security, foreign policy, or public safety.

[5]For federal individual income tax returns, the states will not sum to U.S. totals. Totals include returns filed from Army Post Office and Fleet Post Office addresses by members of the armed forces stationed overseas; returns by other U.S. citizens abroad; and returns filed by residents of Puerto Rico with income from sources outside of Puerto Rico or with income earned as U.S. government employees.

Table A-77. Social Security, Supplemental Nutrition Assistance (Food Stamps), and School Lunch Programs

Geographic area	Social security benefits								Supplemental Nutrition Assistance Program						National school lunch program			
	Recipients Dec 31[1] (thousands)				Payments, month of December[2] (million dollars)				Participants (annual average, year ending Sept 30) (thousands)			Annual benefits[3] (million dollars)			Participants (thousands)		Federal cost[4] (million dollars)	
	Total		Retired workers and dependents[1]		Total		Retired workers and dependents[1]											
	2011	2005	2011	2005	2011	2005	2011	2005	2012	2010	2008	2012	2010	2008	2012	2008	2012	2008
United States.............	53,972	47,237	37,536	32,709	61,210	43,658	44,848	31,590	46,541	40,245	28,181	74,453	64,562	34,525	30,658	30,000	11,412	9,161
Alabama....................	1,037	904	623	516	1,112	6,942	720	499	910	805	572	1,390	1,226	664	563	587	204	180
Alaska	82	65	56	35	87	465	63	39	91	76	57	186	159	94	54	52	32	26
Arizona.....................	1,105	923	808	575	1,283	7,163	980	644	1,124	1,018	628	1,707	1,588	772	662	648	266	210
Arkansas...................	647	566	397	332	673	4,250	445	315	502	467	378	733	686	432	349	349	129	113
California..................	5,130	4,464	3,745	3,046	5,761	38,138	4,346	3,043	3,964	3,239	2,220	7,090	5,692	2,995	3,333	3,119	1,495	1,225
Colorado...................	721	585	525	376	816	4,698	616	393	492	405	253	809	688	325	390	377	130	102
Connecticut...............	630	585	471	436	788	5,711	617	462	403	336	225	697	570	285	297	317	92	77
Delaware	177	150	127	96	215	1,268	162	108	148	113	74	227	171	86	96	88	32	23
District of Columbia	76	71	52	52	78	579	56	41	141	118	89	233	196	112	48	43	21	16
Florida......................	3,894	3,430	2,884	2,381	4,429	28,700	3,407	2,426	3,353	2,603	1,455	5,592	4,417	1,779	1,654	1,558	688	505
Georgia	1,524	1,233	1,016	712	1,685	9,503	1,192	749	1,913	1,591	1,021	3,119	2,565	1,277	1,287	1,284	479	397
Hawaii......................	234	201	184	143	268	1,628	217	148	177	138	97	453	358	185	115	101	44	32
Idaho........................	279	226	199	140	307	1,697	230	150	233	194	100	361	300	117	170	168	55	42
Illinois......................	2,065	1,893	1,470	1,320	2,407	17,530	1,793	1,337	1,870	1,646	1,299	3,129	2,784	1,718	1,142	1,138	437	354
Indiana.....................	1,220	1,064	830	695	1,429	9,380	1,036	741	909	813	623	1,444	1,291	773	801	763	262	197
Iowa.........................	592	552	434	396	672	4,891	514	384	408	340	258	593	526	306	396	392	103	85
Kansas.....................	499	452	352	317	575	4,057	430	318	305	270	188	457	403	211	362	351	108	83
Kentucky...................	914	798	534	438	954	6,203	599	418	849	778	633	1,299	1,186	742	550	549	189	155
Louisiana	809	715	482	429	827	5,906	522	374	949	826	791	1,550	1,286	1,025	588	586	214	179
Maine.......................	307	271	204	170	320	2,075	225	159	253	230	173	377	356	196	107	109	36	29
Maryland...................	873	771	628	519	1,027	6,622	774	538	716	561	360	1,104	878	432	434	441	156	114
Massachusetts...........	1,161	1,067	803	759	1,325	9,696	970	727	862	749	506	1,370	1,166	587	534	558	170	136
Michigan...................	2,017	1,749	1,366	1,138	2,419	15,892	1,742	1,231	1,828	1,776	1,256	2,980	2,809	1,506	908	901	314	235
Minnesota.................	905	787	665	545	1,051	6,633	809	554	539	430	294	750	625	330	627	612	159	129
Mississippi................	610	549	363	303	625	4,101	404	283	660	576	447	980	847	497	399	405	164	145
Missouri....................	1,188	1,063	792	687	1,314	8,881	931	674	948	901	701	1,462	1,361	810	639	639	212	174
Montana....................	198	169	143	111	214	1,376	161	110	126	114	80	193	177	94	87	86	27	22
Nebraska...................	313	292	227	209	351	2,533	266	199	176	163	121	259	238	141	251	240	69	54
Nevada.....................	425	346	314	212	489	2,609	373	246	355	278	144	525	415	170	219	196	90	66
New Hampshire..........	263	221	182	145	308	1,849	227	155	117	104	64	166	152	71	105	113	26	21
New Jersey	1,500	1,376	1,105	1,000	1,889	13,521	1,456	1,079	826	622	438	1,321	1,030	533	729	670	248	185
New Mexico	371	311	253	191	388	2,303	279	185	438	357	240	674	542	269	227	217	93	78
New York..................	3,337	3,062	2,362	2,147	3,935	28,691	2,933	2,196	3,077	2,758	1,953	5,444	4,985	2,573	1,796	1,818	665	571
North Carolina...........	1,808	1,510	1,230	906	2,028	11,651	1,466	959	1,669	1,346	947	2,430	2,072	1,104	943	966	369	300
North Dakota.............	121	115	88	81	129	972	96	72	59	60	48	91	95	59	85	80	20	16
Ohio.........................	2,166	1,961	1,474	1,334	2,425	17,724	1,739	1,300	1,808	1,607	1,151	3,007	2,734	1,495	1,114	1,105	369	281
Oklahoma..................	717	636	474	408	775	5,141	543	392	615	582	419	947	900	491	446	424	162	133
Oregon......................	735	619	540	420	845	5,200	645	439	815	705	469	1,254	1,067	542	307	308	111	89
Pennsylvania.............	2,618	2,419	1,829	1,708	3,044	22,121	2,243	1,687	1,799	1,575	1,188	2,773	2,333	1,387	1,127	1,148	346	290
Rhode Island.............	207	193	144	139	236	1,739	174	133	173	139	85	289	238	108	80	84	30	25
South Carolina	956	778	640	448	1,074	5,908	764	482	870	797	590	1,371	1,256	707	493	499	194	163
South Dakota	156	141	115	97	166	1,124	128	90	104	95	63	165	153	78	107	106	29	25
Tennessee	1,288	1,090	837	642	1,411	8,537	983	657	1,317	1,224	911	2,089	1,966	1,115	687	695	248	205
Texas........................	3,552	2,952	2,385	1,811	3,839	22,883	2,721	1,821	4,038	3,552	2,532	6,007	5,447	3,068	3,374	3,173	1,333	1,046
Utah.........................	335	273	241	178	380	2,152	287	190	277	247	134	405	367	151	349	328	100	73
Vermont	132	112	93	73	148	918	110	75	97	86	56	141	124	62	54	55	16	12
Virginia.....................	1,319	1,140	917	704	1,499	9,060	1,100	734	914	786	545	1,404	1,213	610	749	752	227	183
Washington................	1,127	938	814	618	1,330	7,898	1,005	671	1,108	956	581	1,685	1,387	681	540	529	195	150
West Virginia.............	451	414	266	233	488	3,488	304	224	347	341	277	500	487	304	199	211	66	58
Wisconsin	1,086	954	784	665	1,265	8,347	961	686	835	715	423	1,168	1,000	430	590	597	169	136
Wyoming	94	81	68	56	107	690	82	56	34	35	23	52	52	26	57	55	15	12

[1]Includes special benefits for persons age 72 and over not insured under regular or transitional provisions of Social Security Act.
[2]Unnegotiated checks not deducted.
[3]Includes benefits only and excludes administrative expenditures.
[4]Includes cash payments and commodity costs.

Table A-78. Social Insurance Programs and Workers' Compensation

| Geographic area | Supplemental Security Income (SSI)[1] | | | | Temporary Assistance for Needy Families (TANF) | | | | State unemployment insurance[6] | | | | | | | | Workers' compensation payments[8] (million dollars) | |
| | Recipients[2] (thousands) | | Annual payments[3] (million dollars) | | Recipients[4] (thousands) | | Annual payments[5] (million dollars) | | Beneficiaries, first payments (thousands) | | Benefits paid (million dollars) | | Extended benefits, first payments (thousands) | | Extended benefits paid[7] (million dollars) | | | |
	2011	2010	2011	2010	2011	2010	2011	2010	2011	2010	2011	2010	2011	2010	2011	2010	2010	2009
United States............	8,112	7,911	49,514	48,189	4,316	4,361	35,307	33,255	9,475	10,727	46,648	57,890	1,917	2,293	10,672	9,015	57,542	57,946
Alabama....................	175	172	1,009	996	56	53	190	191	126	140	373	466	22	21	88	63	629	626
Alaska......................	13	12	73	70	10	9	101	62	37	35	168	182	1	13	17	38	221	221
Arizona....................	113	110	670	644	40	60	359	350	155	179	580	750	22	38	79	125	698	658
Arkansas..................	110	107	623	603	18	19	187	233	93	103	364	431	0	0	0	0	204	215
California.................	1,286	1,269	8,951	8,870	1,463	1,437	8,761	7,239	1,344	1,524	7,196	8,968	280	307	1,950	1,576	9,396	9,393
Colorado..................	69	66	402	377	32	29	322	323	129	153	673	918	26	33	159	169	810	836
Connecticut..............	60	58	356	340	32	34	576	500	162	174	867	1,022	30	78	199	227	789	843
Delaware..................	16	16	94	91	15	15	97	75	26	27	129	157	4	5	24	18	212	206
District of Columbia	26	24	169	153	23	19	303	251	28	28	165	187	8	6	49	29	106	105
Florida......................	506	484	2,911	2,760	94	105	976	901	376	522	1,630	2,248	141	129	497	451	2,527	2,821
Georgia....................	239	228	1,384	1,317	37	38	586	563	269	300	926	1,152	71	70	282	237	1,411	1,527
Hawaii......................	25	25	160	157	27	26	357	378	36	41	262	325	0	0	0	0	242	244
Idaho.......................	28	27	160	155	3	3	31	35	64	75	216	280	6	8	22	21	246	258
Illinois.....................	276	273	1,676	1,662	88	66	1,349	1,255	418	476	2,422	3,176	91	86	541	417	2,916	3,025
Indiana....................	122	118	746	716	58	86	292	344	197	222	817	1,040	41	44	172	196	603	598
Iowa........................	49	48	273	266	44	46	243	194	108	126	471	593	0	0	1	0	555	549
Kansas....................	47	46	279	269	37	38	259	207	85	91	403	518	9	14	33	80	408	416
Kentucky..................	193	192	1,119	1,116	63	62	304	281	122	135	544	678	24	18	147	96	651	686
Louisiana	179	175	1,022	989	24	24	277	264	102	107	385	351	0	0	1	153	840	832
Maine.......................	36	35	203	196	26	26	171	141	44	48	191	214	6	6	17	22	254	261
Maryland...................	111	107	689	658	61	60	462	564	139	155	814	919	30	0	80	2	954	896
Massachusetts...........	198	193	1,246	1,211	99	97	1,350	1,022	255	270	1,717	1,957	54	45	381	316	1,013	952
Michigan..................	265	254	1,657	1,581	158	179	1,469	1,703	361	387	1,591	2,120	79	134	404	402	1,272	1,510
Minnesota................	89	86	535	516	49	50	487	475	172	185	891	1,218	31	69	115	132	1,038	1,072
Mississippi...............	126	126	710	699	25	25	118	106	71	80	219	279	0	0	0	0	338	322
Missouri	137	134	800	785	86	86	380	405	168	189	671	853	29	25	115	85	811	850
Montana...................	18	18	102	98	9	9	46	47	31	34	138	173	0	2	0	2	267	246
Nebraska..................	27	26	150	144	15	18	121	98	46	54	173	202	0	0	0	0	313	299
Nevada.....................	44	41	259	241	28	27	140	108	107	128	567	785	44	36	157	107	430	431
New Hampshire..........	19	18	110	103	10	11	97	86	33	42	138	186	0	8	0	0	237	239
New Jersey	173	169	1,024	1,001	84	81	1,324	1,446	360	385	2,591	2,967	98	97	692	607	2,000	1,987
New Mexico	62	60	346	340	51	54	192	237	50	54	278	349	5	17	43	101	277	246
New York...................	690	681	4,497	4,445	279	272	5,448	5,347	628	666	3,505	3,947	163	174	904	797	4,606	4,137
North Carolina...........	225	219	1,270	1,243	44	46	629	563	309	379	1,241	1,666	109	143	908	8	1,316	1,399
North Dakota.............	8	8	44	43	4	5	43	37	16	18	69	81	0	0	0	0	115	111
Ohio........................	295	286	1,855	1,784	215	238	1,326	1,331	270	308	1,387	1,773	73	77	362	321	2,269	2,353
Oklahoma	96	94	554	541	20	21	207	179	65	76	290	417	0	0	0	0	846	785
Oregon.....................	78	75	459	439	79	72	439	392	174	200	845	1,042	20	62	163	294	633	617
Pennsylvania.............	367	358	2,287	2,229	163	130	974	964	530	587	3,033	3,589	102	93	537	416	2,909	2,901
Rhode Island.............	32	33	192	201	16	17	141	149	45	49	286	313	5	15	38	76	160	161
South Carolina	115	112	654	635	40	44	239	180	128	149	450	581	25	25	103	96	891	892
South Dakota	14	14	77	75	7	7	37	31	11	13	41	52	0	0	0	0	100	94
Tennessee	179	175	1,054	1,023	153	157	383	338	176	194	611	725	41	58	135	141	782	781
Texas.......................	640	617	3,486	3,316	111	117	873	908	494	545	2,392	2,902	120	139	617	568	1,484	1,606
Utah........................	29	28	170	160	14	18	121	132	63	75	270	370	0	0	0	0	258	290
Vermont	16	15	90	87	6	6	93	78	25	29	116	146	0	2	0	4	138	145
Virginia....................	151	148	857	832	73	79	337	299	136	178	629	753	12	27	34	69	790	859
Washington...............	143	137	905	881	139	162	1,161	1,494	236	264	1,296	1,820	38	50	435	314	2,309	2,312
West Virginia.............	81	80	477	472	23	23	201	199	49	58	199	246	7	5	31	21	362	342
Wisconsin	111	107	642	625	63	53	683	524	284	325	1,085	1,367	49	47	111	143	1,071	1,114
Wyoming	7	6	36	35	1	1	45	29	18	22	92	126	0	0	1	0	163	135

[1]Data cover federal SSI payments and/or federally administered state supplementation. National figures include data not distributed by state.
[2]As of December.
[3]Total payments for calendar year.
[4]Represents the average number of recipients for the calendar year.
[5]National figure includes expenditure for assistance and non-assistance. Data pertains to year ending September 30.
[6]Includes unemployment compensation for state and local government employees where covered by state law. National totals include data for territories.
[7]Extended benefits are paid during an extended benefit period to claimants following exhaustion of their rights to regular benefits.
[8]Calendar-year data. Payments represent compensation and medical benefits and include insurance losses paid by private insurance carriers (compiled from state workers' compensation agencies and A.M. Best Co.); disbursements of state funds (compiled from the A.M. Best Co. and state workers' compensation agencies); and self-insurance payments (compiled from state workers' compensation agencies and authors' estimates). National total includes federal benefits not distributed by state. Federal benefits include: those paid under the Federal Employees Compensation Act for civilian employees; the portion of the Black Lung benefit program that is financed by employers; and a portion of benefits under the Longshore and Harbor Workers Compensation Act (LHWCA) that are not reflected in state data, namely, benefits paid by self-insured employers and by special funds under the LHWCA.

Table A-79. Government Transfer Payments to Individuals

Geographic area	Total government transfer payments (million dollars) 2011					Program area 2011 (million dollars)						
	Total	Percent change, 2005–2011	Per capita[1] (dollars)	2005	2000	Retirement and disability insurance benefits	Medical payments	Income maintenance benefits	Unemployment insurance benefits	Veterans benefits	Federal education and training assistance payments[2]	Other[3]
United States.................	2,319,212	53.7	7,443	1,508,471	1,082,982	749,880	974,728	278,037	108,555	63,263	71,291	4,206
Alabama.........................	38,248	53.8	7,964	24,875	17,674	13,496	14,534	5,376	935	1,452	1,269	41
Alaska	5,166	53.1	7,148	3,375	3,069	1,035	2,041	613	268	244	78	731
Arizona..........................	47,519	67.6	7,330	28,350	16,958	15,373	19,578	5,095	1,335	1,505	2,972	230
Arkansas........................	23,871	55.5	8,125	15,347	10,693	8,238	9,794	2,785	709	903	765	28
California........................	261,743	55.9	6,944	167,921	121,521	74,826	112,081	34,586	17,694	5,588	8,290	372
Colorado	29,542	70.5	5,773	17,326	11,988	10,044	11,236	2,878	1,831	1,341	1,039	50
Connecticut....................	28,961	52.6	8,088	18,981	14,890	9,262	13,280	2,540	1,966	422	662	37
Delaware	7,370	62.7	8,125	4,529	3,061	2,549	3,294	665	264	178	211	9
District of Columbia	5,744	59.7	9,294	3,597	2,807	943	3,168	902	304	91	193	8
Florida...........................	153,284	56.3	8,043	98,055	67,717	52,278	64,484	17,695	4,467	4,830	4,904	169
Georgia	62,981	64.2	6,417	38,351	25,792	20,175	23,157	9,871	2,557	2,412	2,567	83
Hawaii	9,417	65.3	6,850	5,698	4,116	3,108	3,643	1,304	489	408	161	12
Idaho.............................	10,093	65.1	6,368	6,115	4,122	3,813	3,625	1,157	443	356	330	20
Illinois...........................	87,461	42.1	6,796	61,528	44,726	29,168	34,361	11,030	5,490	1,497	2,946	125
Indiana..........................	46,177	51.4	7,086	30,495	21,668	17,240	17,705	4,889	2,030	997	1,813	61
Iowa..............................	22,176	57.1	7,242	14,119	10,816	8,051	8,710	2,082	852	491	1,285	27
Kansas	19,310	52.8	6,725	12,636	9,617	7,032	7,663	2,105	839	528	483	30
Kentucky........................	35,720	54.9	8,175	23,059	16,849	11,983	14,335	4,488	1,377	1,109	1,429	39
Louisiana	34,843	27.0	7,616	27,439	17,617	10,181	15,681	5,145	658	954	1,040	38
Maine............................	11,701	44.4	8,810	8,104	5,601	3,827	5,262	1,224	363	486	231	15
Maryland........................	39,464	53.1	6,771	25,773	18,175	12,469	17,572	4,253	1,702	1,124	1,016	47
Massachusetts................	55,951	43.7	8,493	38,931	27,823	15,685	26,592	6,425	3,733	987	1,008	64
Michigan	81,711	56.5	8,274	52,206	38,941	28,834	32,247	10,459	3,875	1,484	2,508	119
Minnesota......................	38,651	61.6	7,231	23,915	17,075	12,553	16,755	3,768	1,846	1,104	1,384	59
Mississippi.....................	24,768	42.1	8,316	17,426	11,472	7,601	10,886	3,673	508	622	720	37
Missouri.........................	46,044	48.5	7,660	30,999	22,219	15,921	19,929	4,719	1,500	1,279	1,316	53
Montana.........................	6,917	53.5	6,930	4,506	3,374	2,764	2,492	651	248	323	196	24
Nebraska........................	11,897	44.9	6,456	8,210	6,088	4,385	4,760	1,152	307	532	340	15
Nevada..........................	16,552	74.0	6,078	9,515	5,974	5,734	5,815	1,885	1,475	608	398	38
New Hampshire...............	8,934	51.9	6,777	5,882	4,246	3,606	3,450	861	223	284	207	12
New Jersey	69,895	52.2	7,924	45,910	35,165	23,104	29,244	6,476	6,316	999	1,715	92
New Mexico	15,990	66.1	7,679	9,624	6,390	4,677	6,671	2,224	640	698	480	141
New York........................	182,843	41.1	9,393	129,589	100,304	48,653	93,403	22,178	7,544	2,208	4,366	189
North Carolina.................	71,211	61.7	7,374	44,049	29,902	23,909	27,985	8,636	4,113	2,592	1,760	107
North Dakota...................	4,510	44.2	6,594	3,127	2,464	1,702	1,827	414	95	161	123	38
Ohio..............................	93,528	50.3	8,101	62,236	46,135	32,311	38,965	11,120	3,350	1,841	3,274	113
Oklahoma	27,882	53.1	7,354	18,217	12,737	9,590	11,225	3,274	619	1,480	817	44
Oregon	29,487	65.8	7,616	17,782	13,003	10,551	10,782	3,324	2,011	1,090	811	61
Pennsylvania...................	110,439	45.3	8,667	76,000	57,781	37,144	48,884	10,190	6,567	1,970	2,712	153
Rhode Island...................	9,515	45.6	9,051	6,536	4,908	2,950	4,205	1,065	609	190	251	11
South Carolina	36,270	59.6	7,751	22,729	15,383	12,860	13,592	4,572	1,232	1,426	1,513	46
South Dakota	5,369	51.3	6,515	3,548	2,646	1,977	2,129	563	61	226	155	75
Tennessee	50,835	56.1	7,939	32,575	23,093	16,925	21,027	6,805	1,633	1,532	1,445	55
Texas.............................	160,440	66.5	6,249	96,378	64,333	46,450	69,084	22,904	5,671	5,962	4,494	189
Utah	13,437	69.3	4,770	7,937	5,465	4,704	4,711	1,762	522	380	699	36
Vermont	5,371	58.1	8,574	3,396	2,427	1,737	2,412	602	165	135	176	7
Virginia	50,329	61.0	6,216	31,266	21,604	17,979	19,272	5,601	1,259	2,614	1,782	59
Washington.....................	49,152	64.9	7,196	29,803	22,341	17,718	17,420	5,853	3,225	1,822	1,524	94
West Virginia...................	17,034	42.9	9,181	11,924	9,263	6,352	6,918	1,850	411	625	452	16
Wisconsin.......................	39,852	52.1	6,977	26,204	19,240	14,938	15,507	4,079	2,079	1,040	866	79
Wyoming	3,606	51.8	6,346	2,376	1,709	1,475	1,335	270	144	131	118	9

[1]Based on estimated resident population as of July 1.
[2]Consists largely of federal fellowship payments (National Science Foundation fellowships and traineeships, subsistence payments to state maritime academy cadets, and other federal fellowships), interest subsidy on higher education loans, Pell grants, Job Corps payments, education exchange payments, and state education assistance.
[3]Consists largely of Bureau of Indian Affairs payments, Alaska Permanent Fund dividend payments, compensation of survivors of public safety officers, compensation of victims of crime, disaster relief payments, compensation for Japanese internment, the American Recovery and Reinvestment Act of 2009, funded Federal Additional Compensation for unemployment, COBRA premium reduction, and the Economic Recovery lump sum payment; and other special payments to individuals.

Table A-80. Medicare, Medicaid, and Children's Health Insurance Program

| Geographic area | Medicare enrollment (thousands) | | | Medicaid | | | | | | Children's Health Insurance Program (CHIP) | | | | | |
| | | | | Beneficiaries[1] (thousands) | | | Payments[2] (million dollars) | | | Enrollment[3] (thousands) | | | Expenditures[4] (million dollars) | | |
	2010	2005	2000	2009	2005	2000	2009	2005	2000	2010	2005	2000	2010	2005	2000
United States	46,585	41,003	38,762	60,119	57,643	42,887	308,238	275,569	168,443	7,706	6,151	3,357	7,913	6,359	1,929
Alabama	845	740	685	877	839	619	3,626	4,154	2,393	138	82	38	128	101	32
Alaska	66	51	42	119	125	96	1,067	1,004	473	13	22	13	19	35	18
Arizona	930	777	675	1,588	1,203	681	8,617	4,449	2,112	40	88	60	58	80	29
Arkansas	531	464	439	825	977	489	3,579	2,662	1,543	101	1	2	86	77	2
California	4,757	4,158	3,901	11,519	10,509	7,918	35,224	28,638	17,105	1,732	1,223	484	1,187	1,202	187
Colorado	625	513	467	678	593	381	3,288	2,595	1,809	107	60	35	116	53	14
Connecticut	568	520	515	558	521	420	5,289	3,787	2,839	21	22	20	30	32	13
Delaware	149	125	112	209	165	115	1,264	885	529	13	10	4	13	10	2
District of Columbia	78	72	75	175	158	139	1,940	1,316	793	8	7	2	11	9	6
Florida	3,375	3,008	2,804	3,261	3,166	2,373	14,054	13,154	7,433	403	385	227	309	343	126
Georgia	1,236	1,016	916	1,805	2,038	1,369	7,376	6,821	3,624	248	307	121	225	279	49
Hawaii	206	180	165	261	224	194	1,201	931	600	27	21	(D)	31	18	0
Idaho	230	188	165	253	201	131	1,351	1,072	594	42	22	12	34	21	7
Illinois	1,839	1,674	1,635	2,626	2,239	1,519	11,774	10,788	7,807	329	281	63	259	318	33
Indiana	1,006	893	852	1,109	984	706	5,390	4,780	2,977	141	130	44	90	103	54
Iowa	517	484	477	482	400	314	2,877	2,350	1,477	64	47	20	72	55	15
Kansas	433	397	390	355	385	263	2,316	2,080	1,227	56	47	26	53	59	13
Kentucky	760	668	623	942	857	764	5,017	4,044	2,921	79	64	56	123	90	60
Louisiana	687	630	602	1,184	1,146	761	5,430	4,420	2,632	157	146	50	176	138	25
Maine	265	233	216	315	294	194	1,481	2,366	1,310	33	31	23	34	27	11
Maryland	785	687	645	846	750	626	6,325	4,949	3,003	119	120	93	160	188	92
Massachusetts	1,061	961	961	NA	1,110	1,060	NA	8,308	5,413	142	163	113	301	188	44
Michigan	1,651	1,468	1,403	1,890	1,856	1,352	10,171	7,654	4,881	70	89	55	115	90	36
Minnesota	786	691	654	802	708	558	7,029	5,234	3,280	5	5	(D)	19	58	(D)
Mississippi	497	449	419	932	716	605	3,198	3,470	1,808	96	79	12	152	134	21
Missouri	1,004	901	861	1,101	1,156	890	5,771	5,263	3,274	86	115	73	107	122	41
Montana	170	146	137	113	116	104	714	621	422	25	16	8	37	16	4
Nebraska	279	259	254	256	248	229	1,590	1,450	960	48	45	11	37	47	6
Nevada	357	294	240	281	257	138	1,196	1,090	516	32	39	16	23	38	9
New Hampshire	223	185	170	141	121	97	995	818	651	11	12	4	12	10	2
New Jersey	1,327	1,215	1,203	1,151	966	822	8,293	7,010	4,714	187	130	89	562	160	47
New Mexico	313	261	234	562	491	376	2,913	2,415	1,249	10	24	8	231	25	3
New York	2,988	2,758	2,715	4,985	4,938	3,420	44,883	39,348	26,148	540	619	769	499	558	401
North Carolina	1,490	1,255	1,133	1,782	1,549	1,214	9,665	8,415	4,834	254	196	104	359	283	65
North Dakota	109	103	103	77	74	63	588	557	358	7	6	3	14	11	2
Ohio	1,901	1,731	1,701	2,238	1,955	1,305	13,972	12,114	7,115	254	216	118	264	240	53
Oklahoma	603	531	508	809	686	507	3,574	2,561	1,604	123	108	58	113	80	51
Oregon	621	532	489	564	547	558	2,797	2,444	1,714	65	53	37	86	41	13
Pennsylvania	2,283	2,108	2,095	2,716	1,990	1,492	14,207	11,902	6,366	273	180	120	306	208	71
Rhode Island	183	171	172	203	209	179	1,556	1,638	1,070	23	27	12	29	35	10
South Carolina	774	637	568	906	870	689	4,712	4,248	2,765	73	81	60	93	73	47
South Dakota	137	123	119	141	131	102	732	627	402	16	14	6	19	16	3
Tennessee	1,058	903	829	1,479	1,610	1,568	7,262	7,698	3,491	81	NA	15	127	NA	42
Texas	3,001	2,491	2,265	4,283	3,753	2,633	18,543	14,365	9,277	928	526	131	776	396	41
Utah	283	231	206	NA	314	225	NA	1,501	960	62	44	25	60	36	13
Vermont	112	95	89	171	151	139	970	859	480	7	7	4	6	5	1
Virginia	1,141	981	893	917	778	627	5,548	4,061	2,479	174	124	38	165	123	19
Washington	972	807	736	1,177	1,178	896	5,734	5,335	2,435	36	16	3	43	51	1
West Virginia	382	351	338	386	374	342	2,589	2,339	1,394	38	39	22	39	40	10
Wisconsin	911	818	783	NA	949	577	NA	4,580	2,968	161	57	47	98	33	21
Wyoming	80	70	65	72	69	46	552	398	215	8	6	3	9	8	1

[1]Persons who had payments made on their behalf at any time during the fiscal year.
[2]Payments are for fiscal year and reflect federal and state contribution payments. Data exclude disproportionate hospital share payments. Disproportionate share hospitals receive higher Medicaid reimbursement than other hospitals because they treat a disproportionate share of Medicaid patients.
[3]Number of children ever enrolled in CHIP.
[4]Expenditures for which states are entitled to federal reimbursement under Title XXI.
0 = Zero or rounds to zero.
(D) = Data withheld to avoid disclosure or does not meet statistical standards.
NA = Not available

Table A-81. Department of Defense and Veterans

Geographic area	Department of Defense												Number of veterans[8] (thousands)	
	Personnel[1]						Expenditures[4] (million dollars)							
	Total			2009			Total			2009			2010	2000
	2009	2005	2000	Active duty military[2]	Civilian[3]	Reserve and National Guard	2009	2005	2000	Payroll[5]	Contracts[6]	Grants[7]		
United States..................	2,617,048	2,847,783	2,791,331	1,088,465	709,265	819,318	527,824	381,290	229,072	195,170	327,462	5,192	23,032	26,745
Alabama...........................	58,789	61,943	63,333	11,896	24,794	22,099	14,292	10,571	5,704	4,724	9,502	66	424	447
Alaska.............................	33,281	28,733	25,986	23,178	5,356	4,747	4,888	3,370	1,750	2,660	2,180	49	74	72
Arizona............................	44,662	50,624	48,126	21,343	9,591	13,728	15,308	12,075	6,598	3,138	12,065	106	541	563
Arkansas.........................	23,936	26,960	25,015	6,717	4,168	13,051	2,674	1,964	1,146	1,622	986	66	257	282
California.........................	236,963	295,517	263,173	117,806	61,365	57,792	56,743	46,381	29,821	14,568	41,698	477	1,943	2,570
Colorado	59,480	60,211	61,230	35,404	11,585	12,491	10,726	6,881	4,638	5,125	5,544	56	405	446
Connecticut.....................	10,908	17,617	17,712	1,914	2,625	6,369	12,638	9,574	2,745	720	11,818	100	231	310
Delaware.........................	10,373	10,595	10,941	3,870	1,622	4,881	876	605	436	537	315	24	33	84
District of Columbia........	35,890	37,335	35,171	13,424	16,088	6,378	8,406	5,483	3,176	3,599	4,741	66	80	44
Florida.............................	105,724	134,621	127,677	42,642	28,429	34,653	22,802	19,234	13,454	9,418	13,189	195	1,588	1,876
Georgia	140,358	138,753	133,663	73,988	37,012	29,358	18,608	12,600	8,642	11,495	7,039	74	778	769
Hawaii.............................	68,550	70,208	62,111	40,874	18,400	9,276	8,801	5,583	3,731	6,344	2,377	79	117	121
Idaho..............................	12,575	12,630	12,489	4,967	1,716	5,892	935	699	632	709	166	59	139	137
Illinois............................	50,965	73,180	84,045	10,111	15,770	25,084	9,237	6,809	4,018	3,129	5,937	172	804	1,004
Indiana............................	35,113	32,896	36,929	3,108	10,932	21,073	9,188	5,823	2,591	2,338	6,795	55	517	591
Iowa................................	15,419	16,837	18,556	1,296	1,733	12,390	2,089	1,386	905	747	1,285	57	248	292
Kansas............................	44,761	36,523	37,255	25,482	7,800	11,479	6,868	3,414	2,044	3,668	3,158	42	233	267
Kentucky	65,226	63,579	60,709	43,138	8,962	13,126	12,285	6,921	2,779	5,681	6,534	70	348	381
Louisiana	42,056	47,209	50,968	17,398	6,647	18,011	9,150	4,877	3,386	2,688	6,408	54	326	393
Maine..............................	11,829	14,270	14,918	730	6,946	4,153	2,382	2,569	1,366	847	1,407	128	135	155
Maryland.........................	80,126	84,264	87,002	29,160	34,966	16,000	19,926	16,284	8,786	6,538	12,912	477	464	524
Massachusetts...............	25,458	27,878	33,039	3,205	6,918	15,335	15,082	9,573	5,713	1,491	13,347	244	416	559
Michigan..........................	29,448	32,824	36,976	2,858	8,972	17,618	7,289	5,339	2,418	1,827	5,332	130	719	914
Minnesota	23,905	28,686	25,948	1,897	2,752	19,256	2,807	2,465	1,943	1,208	1,530	69	387	465
Mississippi......................	36,351	39,252	42,834	9,895	9,124	17,332	5,690	5,072	2,993	2,224	3,447	18	231	249
Missouri	51,676	51,245	53,743	17,925	9,982	23,769	14,281	9,213	6,123	3,787	10,454	40	522	592
Montana	9,967	10,854	10,654	3,623	1,596	4,748	854	682	392	541	289	24	104	108
Nebraska.........................	18,128	19,515	20,120	6,845	3,785	7,498	2,142	1,431	907	1,152	931	59	145	173
Nevada............................	18,440	18,221	16,118	10,034	2,319	6,087	3,268	1,658	1,106	1,415	1,819	35	233	238
New Hampshire...............	5,973	6,521	6,809	675	1,047	4,251	2,014	1,421	693	411	1,568	36	118	139
New Jersey	39,202	41,135	44,016	6,673	15,217	17,312	11,020	8,160	4,514	2,671	8,227	122	476	672
New Mexico	23,266	24,516	26,303	11,038	7,029	5,199	3,271	2,625	1,777	1,626	1,604	40	174	191
New York..........................	72,233	77,295	79,443	29,553	12,318	30,362	13,562	8,666	5,721	4,819	8,545	199	984	1,361
North Carolina.................	159,041	148,014	137,176	116,073	20,426	22,542	14,678	9,883	5,901	10,558	3,995	125	777	793
North Dakota....................	13,788	14,516	14,474	7,209	1,910	4,669	1,100	805	549	631	437	32	57	61
Ohio................................	61,785	64,979	71,679	8,261	25,001	28,523	10,256	8,598	5,300	3,834	6,249	172	943	1,144
Oklahoma	59,428	62,850	66,529	21,673	22,115	15,640	7,104	5,099	3,810	4,100	2,880	124	347	376
Oregon	15,646	17,605	18,447	1,615	3,561	10,470	2,696	1,415	857	1,051	1,546	99	340	389
Pennsylvania...................	64,619	72,405	78,642	5,215	27,107	32,297	16,789	10,707	6,311	4,210	12,363	216	1,036	1,281
Rhode Island	10,300	12,282	13,683	1,490	4,372	4,438	1,431	1,044	939	743	662	26	76	103
South Carolina	62,026	68,752	73,865	32,518	10,406	19,102	9,021	5,351	3,538	3,683	5,299	39	422	421
South Dakota...................	10,280	10,083	10,451	3,910	1,388	4,982	1,026	798	360	514	445	68	76	79
Tennessee	32,084	31,751	37,243	3,511	7,967	20,606	5,362	4,354	2,273	2,235	3,083	44	534	560
Texas..............................	235,972	225,990	228,792	131,548	48,057	56,367	42,083	31,754	20,901	19,299	22,484	300	1,690	1,755
Utah................................	33,054	34,554	31,556	6,237	14,818	11,999	4,361	3,890	2,023	2,116	2,206	39	154	161
Vermont	5,246	4,919	5,509	565	729	3,952	828	551	348	262	550	17	52	63
Virginia............................	177,982	243,871	198,005	63,160	89,713	25,109	56,934	43,272	25,106	18,071	38,732	131	828	786
Washington......................	93,611	98,534	84,071	46,161	27,980	19,470	13,524	9,795	6,271	8,224	5,174	127	617	671
West Virginia....................	12,648	12,756	13,937	1,199	2,146	9,303	1,063	826	361	617	396	50	180	202
Wisconsin........................	20,689	23,571	26,331	2,046	2,810	15,833	8,898	3,240	1,253	1,152	7,674	72	437	514
Wyoming	7,818	7,904	7,841	3,407	1,193	3,218	567	500	326	405	140	21	56	58

[1]As of September 30.

[2]Military personnel include active duty personnel based ashore or afloat. Excluded are personnel temporarily shore-based in a transient status. Before 2005, active duty military strength data for U.S. Navy and Marine Corps service members were only enumerated for those who were shore-based; members who were not shore-based (afloat) did have their payroll included in the payroll outlay figures for their home port. Beginning with 2005 Service members in afloat status are included in the strength counts of their homeport locations. Reserve and National Guard personnel called to active duty under Title 10, United States Code 12304, are not included in the active duty military personnel counts.

[3]Civilian personnel includes United States citizens and foreign national direct hire civilians subject to Office of Management and Budget (OMB) ceiling controls and civilian personnel involved in civil functions in the United States. Excludes indirect-hire civilians and those direct-hire civilians not subject to OMB ceiling controls.

[4]For year ending September 30.

[5]Includes the gross earnings of civilian, active duty military personnel, reserve and national guard, and retired military for services rendered to the government and for cash allowances for benefits. Excludes employer's share of employee benefits, accrued military retirement benefits and most permanent change of stations costs.

[6]Refer to awards made in year 2009; expenditures relating to awards may extend over several years. Military awards are for supplies, services, and construction. For years before 2005, procurement data were only reported for contract awards with obligations exceeding $25,000. As of 2005, all contract dollars are accounted for. Figures reflect impact of prime contracting on state distribution of defense work. Often the state in which a prime contractor is located in is not the state where the subcontracted work is done. Undistributed civilians and military personnel, their payrolls, and prime contract awards for performance in classified locations are excluded.

[7]Includes all financial data related to obligations of funds by grants, cooperative agreements, or other nonprocurement instruments. Obligations of any dollar value are listed at the location reported as the place of performance.

[8]Includes only those veterans living as of September of the stated year. Veterans serving in more than one period of service are counted only once in the total. Veterans are considered any civilian honorably discharged from active duty, other than for training only without service-connected disability.

Table A-82. Elections

Geographic area	Voting-age population[1] (thousands)		Percent of voting-age population casting votes for president		Electoral votes cast for president[2]		Popular vote for president					
							2012			2008		
							Total[3] (thousands)	Percent of total		Total[3] (thousands)	Percent of total	
	2012	2008	2012	2008	2012	2008		Democratic	Republican		Democratic	Republican
United States...............	240,186	230,118	53.8	57.1	D-332	D-365	129,140	50.9	47.0	131,407	52.9	45.6
Alabama..........................	3,698	3,540	56.1	59.3	R-9	R-9	2,074	38.4	60.5	2,100	38.7	60.3
Alaska...........................	544	506	55.2	64.4	R-3	R-3	300	40.8	54.8	326	37.9	59.4
Arizona..........................	4,932	4,793	46.6	47.9	R-11	R-10	2,299	44.6	53.7	2,293	45.1	53.6
Arkansas........................	2,238	2,153	47.8	50.5	R-6	R-6	1,069	36.9	60.6	1,087	38.9	58.7
California........................	28,801	27,392	45.3	49.5	D-55	D-55	13,039	60.2	37.1	13,562	61.0	37.0
Colorado........................	3,956	3,732	64.9	64.3	D-9	D-9	2,570	51.5	46.1	2,401	53.7	44.7
Connecticut....................	2,797	2,689	55.7	61.2	D-7	D-7	1,558	58.1	40.7	1,647	60.6	38.2
Delaware........................	712	667	58.1	61.8	D-3	D-3	414	58.6	40.0	412	61.9	36.9
District of Columbia..........	523	480	56.2	55.4	D-3	D-3	294	90.9	7.3	266	92.5	6.5
Florida...........................	15,315	14,324	55.3	58.6	D-29	D-27	8,474	50.0	49.1	8,391	51.0	48.2
Georgia...........................	7,430	7,137	52.5	55.0	R-16	R-15	3,898	45.5	53.3	3,924	47.0	52.2
Hawaii...........................	1,089	1,003	40.1	45.5	D-4	D-4	437	70.1	27.7	456	71.5	26.4
Idaho............................	1,169	1,111	55.8	59.0	R-4	R-4	652	32.6	64.5	655	36.1	61.5
Illinois...........................	9,811	9,722	53.4	56.8	D-20	D-21	5,242	57.6	40.7	5,522	61.9	36.8
Indiana..........................	4,946	4,792	53.1	57.4	R-11	D-11	2,625	43.9	54.1	2,751	49.9	48.9
Iowa.............................	2,351	2,290	67.3	67.1	D-6	D-7	1,582	52.0	46.2	1,537	53.9	44.4
Kansas..........................	2,162	2,102	53.7	58.8	R-6	R-6	1,160	38.0	59.7	1,236	41.7	56.6
Kentucky........................	3,362	3,261	53.5	56.0	R-8	R-8	1,797	37.8	60.5	1,827	41.2	57.4
Louisiana........................	3,484	3,303	57.2	59.4	R-8	R-9	1,994	40.6	57.8	1,961	39.9	58.6
Maine............................	1,063	1,042	68.2	70.2	D-4	D-4	725	55.4	40.3	731	57.7	40.4
Maryland........................	4,541	4,293	59.6	61.3	D-10	D-10	2,707	62.0	35.9	2,632	61.9	36.5
Massachusetts.................	5,245	5,071	60.7	61.2	D-11	D-12	3,184	60.3	37.3	3,103	61.4	35.7
Michigan........................	7,616	7,613	62.1	65.7	D-16	D-17	4,731	54.2	44.7	5,002	57.4	41.0
Minnesota......................	4,103	3,966	71.6	73.4	D-10	D-10	2,937	52.7	45.0	2,910	54.1	43.8
Mississippi.....................	2,240	2,172	57.4	59.4	R-6	R-6	1,286	43.8	55.3	1,290	43.0	56.2
Missouri.........................	4,619	4,490	59.7	65.1	R-10	R-11	2,757	44.4	53.8	2,925	49.3	49.4
Montana.........................	783	747	61.8	65.6	R-3	R-3	484	41.7	55.4	490	47.3	49.5
Nebraska........................	1,392	1,336	57.1	60.0	R-5	R-4/D-1	794	38.0	59.8	801	41.6	56.5
Nevada..........................	2,095	1,932	48.4	50.1	D-6	D-5	1,015	52.4	45.7	968	55.1	42.7
New Hampshire................	1,046	1,022	68.0	69.5	D-4	D-4	711	52.0	46.4	711	54.1	44.5
New Jersey	6,838	6,635	53.2	58.3	D-14	D-15	3,638	58.3	40.6	3,868	57.3	41.7
New Mexico	1,571	1,482	49.9	56.0	D-5	D-5	784	53.0	42.8	830	56.9	41.8
New York........................	15,307	15,082	46.5	51.2	D-29	D-31	7,117	60.8	31.2	7,722	62.2	35.6
North Carolina.................	7,466	6,979	60.3	61.6	R-15	D-15	4,505	48.4	50.4	4,298	49.8	49.5
North Dakota...................	545	498	59.3	63.5	R-3	R-3	323	38.7	58.3	317	44.6	53.3
Ohio.............................	8,881	8,756	62.8	65.2	D-18	D-20	5,581	50.7	47.7	5,708	51.5	46.9
Oklahoma	2,877	2,736	46.4	53.5	R-7	R-7	1,335	33.2	66.8	1,463	34.4	65.6
Oregon..........................	3,039	2,922	58.9	62.5	D-7	D-7	1,789	54.2	42.1	1,828	56.7	40.4
Pennsylvania...................	10,024	9,686	57.3	62.1	D-20	D-21	5,742	52.1	46.7	6,013	54.5	44.2
Rhode Island...................	834	822	53.5	57.4	D-4	D-4	446	62.7	35.2	472	62.9	35.1
South Carolina	3,644	3,414	53.9	56.3	R-9	R-8	1,964	44.1	54.6	1,921	44.9	53.9
South Dakota	629	606	57.8	63.0	R-3	R-3	364	39.9	57.9	382	44.7	53.2
Tennessee	4,962	4,736	49.5	54.9	R-11	R-11	2,459	39.1	59.5	2,600	41.8	56.9
Texas............................	19,074	17,601	41.9	45.9	R-38	R-34	7,994	41.4	57.2	8,078	43.7	55.5
Utah.............................	1,967	1,887	51.7	50.5	R-6	R-5	1,017	24.7	72.8	952	34.4	62.6
Vermont	502	492	59.6	66.0	D-3	D-3	299	66.6	31.0	325	67.5	30.4
Virginia..........................	6,329	5,946	60.9	62.6	D-13	D-13	3,854	51.2	47.3	3,723	52.6	46.3
Washington.....................	5,312	5,008	58.8	60.6	D-12	D-11	3,126	56.2	41.3	3,037	57.7	40.5
West Virginia...................	1,471	1,428	45.6	50.0	R-5	R-5	670	35.5	62.3	713	42.6	55.7
Wisconsin.......................	4,409	4,314	69.7	69.2	D-10	D-10	3,071	52.8	45.9	2,983	56.2	42.3
Wyoming	441	404	56.9	63.1	R-3	R-3	251	27.6	68.2	255	32.5	64.7

[1]Estimated population for those 18 years and over as of July 1 for the listed year. Includes armed forces stationed in each state, aliens, and institutionalized population.
[2]By major political party. D=Democratic, R=Republican.
[3]Includes other parties not shown separately.
(X) = Not applicable

Table A-82. Elections—*Continued*

Geographic area	Votes cast for U.S. senators					
	2012			2010		
	Total (thousands)	Percent of total		Total[1] (thousands)	Percent of total	
		Democratic	Republican		Democratic	Republican
United States	93,561	53.4	41.8	66,191	44.0	49.4
Alabama	(X)	(X)	(X)	1,485	34.7	65.2
Alaska	(X)	(X)	(X)	256	23.5	35.6
Arizona	2,243	46.2	49.2	1,708	34.7	58.9
Arkansas	(X)	(X)	(X)	780	36.9	57.9
California	12,579	62.5	37.5	10,000	52.2	42.2
Colorado	(X)	(X)	(X)	1,772	48.1	46.4
Connecticut	1,512	52.5	40.0	1,153	52.5	43.2
Delaware	400	66.4	29.0	307	56.6	40.0
District of Columbia	(X)	(X)	(X)	(X)	(X)	(X)
Florida	8,190	55.2	42.2	5,411	20.2	48.9
Georgia	(X)	(X)	(X)	2,555	39.0	58.3
Hawaii	437	61.6	36.8	371	74.8	21.6
Idaho	(X)	(X)	(X)	450	24.9	71.2
Illinois	(X)	(X)	(X)	3,704	46.4	48.0
Indiana	2,560	50.0	44.3	1,744	40.0	54.6
Iowa	(X)	(X)	(X)	1,116	33.3	64.4
Kansas	(X)	(X)	(X)	838	26.4	70.1
Kentucky	(X)	(X)	(X)	1,356	44.2	55.7
Louisiana	(X)	(X)	(X)	1,265	37.7	56.6
Maine	725	12.8	29.7	(X)	(X)	(X)
Maryland	2,633	56.0	26.3	1,834	62.2	35.8
Massachusetts	3,184	53.3	45.8	(X)	(X)	(X)
Michigan	4,653	58.8	38.0	(X)	(X)	(X)
Minnesota	2,843	65.2	30.5	(X)	(X)	(X)
Mississippi	1,242	40.6	57.2	(X)	(X)	(X)
Missouri	2,726	54.8	39.1	1,944	40.6	54.2
Montana	486	48.6	44.9	(X)	(X)	(X)
Nebraska	789	42.2	57.8	(X)	(X)	(X)
Nevada	998	44.7	45.9	721	50.3	44.5
New Hampshire	(X)	(X)	(X)	455	36.8	60.1
New Jersey	3,377	58.9	39.4	(X)	(X)	(X)
New Mexico	776	51.0	45.3	(X)	(X)	(X)
New York	7,117	62.1	21.3	4,764	64.0	26.0
North Carolina	(X)	(X)	(X)	2,660	43.0	54.8
North Dakota	321	50.2	49.3	239	0.0	76.2
Ohio	5,449	50.7	44.7	3,815	39.4	56.8
Oklahoma	(X)	(X)	(X)	1,017	26.1	70.6
Oregon	(X)	(X)	(X)	1,443	57.2	39.2
Pennsylvania	5,627	53.7	44.6	3,978	49.0	51.0
Rhode Island	418	64.8	35.0	(X)	(X)	(X)
South Carolina	(X)	(X)	(X)	1,319	27.6	61.5
South Dakota	(X)	(X)	(X)	228	0.0	100.0
Tennessee	2,321	30.4	64.9	(X)	(X)	(X)
Texas	7,865	40.6	56.5	(X)	(X)	(X)
Utah	1,007	30.0	65.3	585	32.8	61.6
Vermont	293	0.0	24.9	235	64.3	30.9
Virginia	3,802	52.9	47.0	(X)	(X)	(X)
Washington	3,069	60.5	39.5	2,511	52.4	47.6
West Virginia	660	60.6	36.5	(X)	(X)	(X)
Wisconsin	3,009	51.4	45.9	2,171	47.0	51.9
Wyoming	251	21.1	73.9	(X)	(X)	(X)

[1]Includes other parties not shown separately.
(X) = Not applicable

Table A–83 Composition of the Congress and Public Officials

Geographic area	Votes cast for U.S. representatives[1] 2012 — Total[4]	Votes cast for U.S. representatives[1] 2012 — Percentage of total Democratic	Votes cast for U.S. representatives[1] 2012 — Percentage of total Republican	Composition of the 113th Congress, 2013[2] Senate[3] Democratic	Composition of the 113th Congress, 2013[2] Senate[3] Republican	Composition of the 113th Congress, 2013[2] House of Representatives Democratic	Composition of the 113th Congress, 2013[2] House of Representatives Republican	Composition of the 112th Congress, 2012 Senate[3] Democratic	Composition of the 112th Congress, 2012 Senate[3] Republican	Composition of the 112th Congress, 2012 House of Representatives Democratic	Composition of the 112th Congress, 2012 House of Representatives Republican
United States	122,346	48.4	47.1	55	45	196	235	51	47	193	242
Alabama	1,934	35.9	63.8	0	2	1	6	0	2	1	6
Alaska	290	28.6	63.9	1	1	0	1	1	1	0	1
Arizona	2,173	43.6	52.1	0	2	5	4	0	2	3	5
Arkansas	1,038	29.4	61.4	1	1	0	4	1	1	1	3
California	12,204	60.6	37.1	2	0	37	15	2	0	34	19
Colorado	2,450	44.1	46.7	2	0	2	4	2	0	3	4
Connecticut	1,467	60.3	33.5	2	0	5	0	1	0	5	0
Delaware	388	64.4	33.4	2	0	1	0	2	0	1	0
District of Columbia	(X)	(X)	(X)	(X)	(X)	(X)	(X)	(X)	(X)	(X)	(X)
Florida	7,514	45.2	50.9	1	1	10	17	1	1	6	19
Georgia	3,553	40.8	59.2	0	2	5	9	0	2	5	8
Hawaii	437	65.2	31.5	2	0	2	0	2	0	2	0
Idaho	635	32.8	64.0	0	2	0	2	0	2	0	2
Illinois	5,058	54.2	43.6	1	1	11	6	1	1	7	11
Indiana	2,554	44.7	52.9	1	1	2	7	0	2	3	6
Iowa	1,537	50.3	47.3	1	1	2	2	1	1	3	2
Kansas	1,058	18.5	70.1	0	2	0	4	0	2	0	4
Kentucky	1,745	39.2	58.9	0	2	1	5	0	2	2	5
Louisiana	1,706	21.1	67.0	1	1	1	5	1	1	1	6
Maine	725	59.0	36.7	1	1	2	0	0	1	2	0
Maryland	2,586	62.9	33.2	2	0	7	1	2	0	6	2
Massachusetts	3,184	65.3	21.9	3	0	9	0	1	1	10	0
Michigan	4,575	50.9	45.6	2	0	4	9	2	0	7	8
Minnesota	2,813	55.5	43.0	2	0	5	3	2	0	4	4
Mississippi	1,208	34.1	58.2	0	2	1	3	0	2	1	3
Missouri	2,676	41.8	54.7	1	1	2	5	1	1	3	6
Montana	480	42.7	53.3	2	0	0	1	2	0	0	1
Nebraska	773	35.8	64.2	0	2	0	3	1	1	0	3
Nevada	974	46.6	47.0	1	1	2	2	1	2	1	2
New Hampshire	682	50.0	45.7	1	1	2	0	1	1	0	2
New Jersey	3,282	54.7	43.6	2	0	6	6	2	0	7	6
New Mexico	766	55.1	44.8	2	0	2	1	2	0	2	1
New York	7,116	54.8	24.4	2	0	21	6	2	0	21	8
North Carolina	4,384	50.6	48.7	1	1	4	9	1	1	7	6
North Dakota	316	41.7	54.9	1	1	0	1	1	1	0	1
Ohio	5,142	46.9	51.0	1	1	4	12	1	1	5	13
Oklahoma	1,326	30.9	64.6	0	2	0	5	0	2	1	4
Oregon	1,708	49.9	32.0	2	0	4	1	2	0	4	1
Pennsylvania	5,556	50.3	48.8	1	1	5	11	1	1	7	12
Rhode Island	428	54.4	37.9	2	0	2	0	2	0	2	0
South Carolina	1,803	39.6	56.9	0	2	1	6	0	2	1	5
South Dakota	361	42.6	57.4	0	1	0	1	1	1	0	1
Tennessee	2,284	34.9	60.0	0	2	2	11	0	2	2	7
Texas	7,664	38.5	57.8	0	2	11	24	0	2	9	23
Utah	999	32.5	64.9	0	2	1	3	0	2	1	2
Vermont	290	71.9	23.3	1	0	1	0	1	0	1	0
Virginia	3,740	48.3	50.2	2	0	3	8	2	0	3	8
Washington	3,006	54.4	45.6	2	0	6	4	2	0	5	4
West Virginia	641	40.1	59.9	2	0	1	2	2	0	1	2
Wisconsin	2,866	50.4	48.9	1	1	3	5	1	1	3	5
Wyoming	251	23.0	66.4	0	2	0	1	0	2	0	1

[1]In each state, totals represent the sum of votes cast in each Congressional District or votes cast for Representative at Large in states where only one member is elected. In all years there are numerous districts within the state where either the Republican or Democratic party had no candidate. In some states the Republican and Democratic vote includes votes cast for the party candidate by endorsing parties.
[2]As of May 6, 2013.
[5]Vermont had one independent.
[4]Includes votes cast for minor parties not shown separately.
X = not applicable

Table A–83   Composition of the Congress and Public Officials—*Continued*

Geographic area	Black elected officials[5]		Hispanic public officials, 2012[6]		Women holding state public offices, 2010		
	Total, 2002	U.S. and state legislatures, 2012[5]	Total	State executives and legislatures	Total	Statewide elective executives offices[7]	State legislatures
United States	9,430	630	5,928	292	1,880	71	1,809
Alabama	757	33	0	0	24	6	18
Alaska	2	1	2	0	13	0	13
Arizona	13	1	345	15	32	3	29
Arkansas	535	13	1	0	32	1	31
California	234	9	1,353	29	33	1	32
Colorado	17	2	165	9	40	2	38
Connecticut	69	13	40	9	64	4	60
Delaware	29	6	3	1	18	2	16
District of Columbia	[8] 174	25	(X)	(X)	(X)	(X)	(X)
Florida	275	56	164	20	39	1	38
Georgia	640	0	7	2	46	0	46
Hawaii	1	1	2	2	26	1	25
Idaho	1	30	3	2	28	1	27
Illinois	619	12	109	12	51	1	50
Indiana	94	5	17	2	33	1	32
Iowa	12	7	2	0	36	1	35
Kansas	16	8	12	5	51	1	50
Kentucky	62	27	0	0	23	1	22
Louisiana	739	0	7	1	23	0	23
Maine	2	44	0	0	54	0	54
Maryland	1,912	7	8	3	59	0	59
Massachusetts	79	21	32	5	52	1	51
Michigan	353	2	15	2	39	2	37
Minnesota	20	49	6	2	73	3	70
Mississippi	950	18	0	0	25	0	25
Missouri	206	0	3	2	46	2	44
Montana	0	2	4	0	43	4	39
Nebraska	9	7	1	0	11	1	10
Nevada	13	2	20	11	23	3	20
New Hampshire	5	17	4	4	156	0	156
New Jersey	269	3	119	9	35	1	34
New Mexico	4	30	701	51	37	3	34
New York	328	25	143	24	51	0	51
North Carolina	523	0	2	2	50	6	44
North Dakota	1	17	0	0	24	1	23
Ohio	305	6	12	1	31	2	29
Oklahoma	115	2	1	1	21	4	17
Oregon	5	20	13	1	28	2	26
Pennsylvania	215	3	10	1	39	0	39
Rhode Island	8	37	12	5	26	1	25
South Carolina	547	0	0	0	17	0	17
South Dakota	0	18	0	0	21	0	21
Tennessee	195	19	4	1	25	0	25
Texas	466	0	2,518	44	45	2	43
Utah	5	1	9	5	23	0	23
Vermont	1	18	1	1	68	1	67
Virginia	248	1	5	1	27	0	27
Washington	24	3	41	4	49	1	48
West Virginia	19	8	0	0	23	1	22
Wisconsin	33	1	8	1	31	2	29
Wyoming	1	0	4	2	16	1	15

[5]U.S. and state legislatures includes elected state administrators.
[6]State executives and legislators includes U.S. senators and representatives not shown separately.
[7]Excludes women elected to the judiciary, women appointed to state cabinet-level positions, women elected to executive posts by the legislature, and elected members of university Board of Trustees or Board of Education.
[8]Includes one shadow senator (an elected official who lobbied Congress on DC issues, but was not sworn in at the federal level and had no voting privileges).
X = not applicable

Table A–84   Composition of Governors and State Legislatures

Geographic area	Current governor[1]	Year of election	Votes cast for governor				Composition of state legislatures, 2012			
			Total (thousands)[2]	Republican (thousands)	Democrat (thousands)	Percent for leading party	Lower House[3]		Upper House[4]	
							Democratic	Republican	Democratic	Republican
United States...............		(X)	(X)	(X)	(X)	(X)	(X)	(X)	(X)	(X)	(X)
Alabama..........................	Robert Bentley	2011	1,485	860	625	R-57.9	40	65	12	22
Alaska............................	Sean Parnell[5]	2009	256	151	97	R-59.1	16	24	10	10
Arizona..........................	Jan Brewer[6]	2009	1,728	939	734	R-54.3	20	40	9	21
Arkansas........................	Mike Beebe	2007	781	263	503	D-33.6	54	46	20	15
California........................	Edmund Gerald "Jerry" Brown[7]	1975	10,095	4,127	5,428	D-40.9	52	28	25	15
Colorado........................	John Hickenlooper	2011	1,788	199	912	D-11.1	32	33	20	15
Connecticut....................	Dan Malloy	2011	1,146	561	567	D-49.0	99	52	22	14
Delaware........................	Jack Markell	2009	395	127	267	D-32.0	26	15	14	7
District of Columbia[8]......		(X)	(X)	(X)	(X)	(X)	(X)	(X)	11	0
Florida............................	Rick Scott	2011	5,360	2,619	2,558	R-48.9	39	81	12	28
Georgia..........................	Nathan Deal	2011	2,576	1,366	1,107	R-53.0	63	115	20	36
Hawaii............................	Neil Abercrombie	2010	383	157	223	D-58.2	42	8	24	1
Idaho..............................	C.L. "Butch" Otter	2007	453	267	149	R-59.1	13	57	7	28
Illinois............................	Patrick Quinn[9]	2009	3,730	1,713	1,745	D-46.8	64	54	35	24
Indiana..........................	Mitch Daniels	2005	2,704	1,564	1,082	R-57.8	40	60	13	37
Iowa..............................	Terry Branstad[10]	1983	1,122	592	485	R-52.8	40	60	26	24
Kansas	Sam Brownback	2011	839	531	270	R-63.3	33	92	8	32
Kentucky	Steven L. Beshear	2007	833	294	464	D-55.7	59	40	15	22
Louisiana	Bobby Jindal	2008	1,023	673	288	R-65.8	45	58	15	24
Maine............................	Paul LePage	2011	573	218	109	R-38.1	72	77	14	20
Maryland........................	Martin O'Malley	2007	1,858	776	1,045	D-56.2	98	43	35	12
Massachusetts...............	Deval L. Patrick	2007	2,297	965	1,112	D-48.4	125	33	36	4
Michigan	Rick Snyder	2011	3,226	1,875	1,287	R-58.1	46	62	12	26
Minnesota	Mark Dayton	2011	2,107	910	919	D-43.6	[11] 62	72	[11] 30	37
Mississippi......................	Phil Bryant	2012	893	545	349	R-61.0	58	64	21	31
Missouri	Jay Nixon	2009	2,878	1,136	1,681	D-58.4	56	106	8	26
Montana	Brian Schweitzer	2005	487	158	319	D-65.5	32	68	22	28
Nebraska........................	Dave Heineman[12]	2005	488	361	127	R-73.9	[13]	[13]	[13]	[13]
Nevada..........................	Brian Sandoval	2011	717	382	298	R-53.4	26	16	11	10
New Hampshire..............	John Lynch	2005	457	206	240	D-52.6	104	292	5	19
New Jersey	Christopher J. Christie	2010	2,424	1,174	1,088	R-48.5	47	32	24	16
New Mexico	Susana Martinez	2011	603	321	281	R-53.2	36	33	28	14
New York........................	Andrew Cuomo	2011	4,654	1,548	2,912	D-62.6	96	49	29	32
North Carolina................	Beverly Perdue	2009	4,269	2,001	2,146	D-50.3	52	68	19	31
North Dakota..................	Jack Dalrymple[14]	2010	316	235	74	R-74.4	25	69	12	35
Ohio..............................	John Kasich	2011	3,852	1,889	1,812	R-49.0	40	59	10	23
Oklahoma	Mary Fallin	2011	1,035	626	409	R-60.4	33	68	15	31
Oregon	John Kitzhaber[15]	1995	1,454	694	717	D-49.3	30	30	16	14
Pennsylvania..................	Tom Corbett	2011	3,988	2,173	1,815	R-54.5	87	110	20	30
Rhode Island..................	Lincoln Chafee	2011	342	115	79	R-33.6	65	10	29	8
South Carolina	Nikki Haley	2011	1,344	691	631	R-51.4	48	76	19	27
South Dakota	Dennis Daugaard	2011	317	195	122	R-61.5	19	50	5	30
Tennessee	Bill Haslam	2011	1,602	1,042	530	R-65.0	34	64	13	20
Texas..............................	Rick Perry[16]	2000	4,980	2,737	2,106	R-55.0	49	101	12	19
Utah..............................	Gary Herbert[17]	2009	643	412	205	R-64.1	17	58	7	22
Vermont	Peter Shumlin	2011	242	115	120	D-49.5	94	48	21	8
Virginia	Robert McDonnell	2010	1,982	1,164	819	R-58.7	32	67	20	20
Washington....................	Christine Gregoire	2005	3,003	1,404	1,599	D-53.2	56	42	27	22
West Virginia..................	Earl Ray Tomblin[18]	2010	301	142	149	D-49.6	65	35	28	6
Wisconsin	Scott Walker	2011	2,133	1,129	1,004	R-52.3	39	59	16	17
Wyoming	Matt Mead	2011	188	124	43	R-65.7	10	50	4	26

[1]As of January 2012.
[2]Includes minor party and scattered votes.
[3]In general, Lower House refers to the body consisting of State Representatives.
[4]In general, Upper House refers to the body consisting of State Senators.
[5]Lieutenant Governor Sean Parnell was sworn in as Governor on July 26, 2009, after Governor Palin resigned. He was elected to a full term in the November 2010 general election.
[6]Secretary of State Jan Brewer succeeded to the office of governor on January 21, 2009, upon Governor Napolitano's appointment as U.S. Secretary of Homeland Security. Her partial term will serve as the first of two terms allowed by Arizona law.
[7]Governor Brown previously served two terms as governor of California from 1975–1983. He was elected again in November 2010 and was inaugurated on January 3, 2011, to begin serving his third term.
[8]Council of the District of Columbia. The District functions as a unicameral legislature, having no representation in the Lower House.
[9]Lieutenant Governor Patrick Quinn became governor on January 29, 2009, after Governor Blagojevich was removed from office. He was elected to a full term in November 2010.
[10]Governor Branstad was first elected in 1983 and served for four terms until 1999. He was elected to a 5th term in November of 2010.
[11]The Minnesota arm of the national Democratic Party is the Democratic-Farmer-Labor Party.
[12]Governor Heineman, as lieutenant governor, was sworn in as Nebraska's governor on Friday, January 21, 2005, after Governor Johanns resigned on January 20, 2005, upon being confirmed as the United States Secretary of Agriculture. He was then elected to full terms in the 2006 and 2010 general elections.
[13]Members serve 4-year terms; Nebraska is the only state to have a nonpartisan legislature.
[14]Lt. Gov. Dalrymple was sworn in on December 21, 2010, to complete Governor Hoeven's term as governor of North Dakota after Hoeven was elected to the Senate.
[15]John Kitzhaber previously served two terms as governor of Oregon from 1995–2003 and was elected again in November 2010 and was inaugurated on January 10, 2011, to begin serving his third term.
[16]Lieutenant Governor Perry was sworn in on December 21, 2000, to complete President George W. Bush's term as governor of Texas. He was elected to serve four-year terms in 2002, 2006, and 2010.
[17]Lieutenant Governor Gary Herbert was sworn in as Governor on August 10, 2009, after Governor Huntsman resigned to accept President Obama's appointment as ambassador to China. Utah law states that a replacement governor elevated in a term's first year will face a special election at the next regularly scheduled general election, November 2010, instead of serving the remainder of the term. Utah's next regular scheduled gubernatorial election was held in November 2012.
[18]Senate President Earl Ray Tomblin was sworn in as Governor on November 15, 2010, after Governor Manchin was elected in the November election to fill Senator Robert Byrd's seat.
D=Democrat
R=Republican
(X) = Not applicable

PART B

METROPOLITAN AREAS

Note: Part B covers 366 metropolitan statistical areas including 11 metropolitan statistical areas with 29 metropolitan divisions defined by the Office of Management and Budget as of December 2009. For more information, see OMB Bulletin 10-02 at http://www.whitehouse.gov/sites/default/files/omb/assets/bulletins/b10-02.pdf .

For additional information, see Appendix C, Geographic Concepts.

Table B-1.   Area and Population

Metropolitan statistical area and division	Area, 2010 (square miles) Total	Area, 2010 (square miles) Land	2011 Estimate (July 1)	2010 Census (April 1)	2000[1] (estimates base)	1990[2] (April 1)	Rank 2010	Rank 2000	Rank 1990	Persons per square mile of land area[3] 2010	Persons per square mile of land area[3] 2000	Persons per square mile of land area[3] 1990
Abilene, TX	2,757.7	2,743.5	166,416	165,252	160,245	148,004	240	230	222	60.2	58.4	53.9
Akron, OH	924.1	900.1	701,456	703,200	694,960	657,575	72	67	65	781.2	772.1	730.6
Albany, GA	1,958.0	1,932.5	157,688	157,308	157,833	146,583	252	233	226	81.4	81.7	75.9
Albany–Schenectady–Troy, NY	2,878.2	2,811.5	871,478	870,716	825,875	809,642	58	56	52	309.7	293.7	288.0
Albuquerque, NM	9,297.1	9,282.4	898,642	887,077	729,649	599,416	57	65	70	95.6	78.6	64.6
Alexandria, LA	2,026.3	1,961.0	154,505	153,922	145,035	149,082	257	252	221	78.5	74.0	76.0
Allentown–Bethlehem–Easton, PA–NJ	1,475.9	1,453.2	824,916	821,173	740,395	686,718	64	64	58	565.1	509.5	472.6
Altoona, PA	527.1	525.8	127,099	127,089	129,144	130,542	301	276	254	241.7	245.6	248.3
Amarillo, TX	3,682.3	3,649.2	253,823	249,881	226,522	196,111	185	179	176	68.5	62.1	53.7
Ames, IA	573.6	572.8	89,663	89,542	79,981	74,252	356	358	354	156.3	139.6	129.6
Anchorage, AK	27,218.5	26,312.4	387,516	380,821	319,605	266,021	133	143	149	14.5	12.1	10.1
Anderson, IN	452.9	451.9	131,235	131,636	133,358	130,669	293	268	253	291.3	295.1	289.2
Anderson, SC	757.4	715.4	188,488	187,126	165,740	145,177	222	224	228	261.6	231.7	202.9
Ann Arbor, MI	722.4	706.0	347,962	344,791	322,895	282,937	146	140	139	488.4	457.4	400.8
Anniston–Oxford, AL	612.3	605.9	117,797	118,572	112,249	116,032	315	305	274	195.7	185.3	191.5
Appleton, WI	1,041.7	955.8	227,403	225,666	201,602	174,801	194	191	197	236.1	210.9	182.9
Asheville, NC	2,041.4	2,033.0	429,017	424,858	369,171	308,005	117	124	128	209.0	181.6	151.5
Athens–Clarke County, GA	1,035.0	1,024.8	193,317	192,541	166,079	136,025	219	223	241	187.9	162.1	132.7
Atlanta–Sandy Springs–Marietta, GA	8,481.0	8,338.5	5,359,205	5,268,860	4,247,981	3,068,975	9	11	12	631.9	509.4	368.0
Atlantic City–Hammonton, NJ	671.8	555.7	274,338	274,549	252,552	224,327	166	165	165	494.1	454.5	403.7
Auburn–Opelika, AL	615.8	607.5	143,468	140,247	115,092	87,146	276	297	336	230.9	189.5	143.5
Augusta–Richmond County, GA–SC	3,324.8	3,270.3	561,858	556,877	499,684	435,799	92	89	88	170.3	152.8	133.3
Austin–Round Rock–San Marcos, TX	4,280.1	4,219.9	1,783,519	1,716,289	1,249,763	846,227	35	40	48	406.7	296.2	200.5
Bakersfield–Delano, CA	8,162.6	8,131.9	851,710	839,631	661,645	544,981	62	70	75	103.3	81.4	67.0
Baltimore–Towson, MD	3,105.0	2,601.5	2,729,110	2,710,489	2,552,994	2,382,172	20	19	19	1,041.9	981.4	915.7
Bangor, ME	3,557.1	3,397.3	153,786	153,923	144,919	146,601	256	253	225	45.3	42.7	43.2
Barnstable Town, MA	1,305.5	393.7	215,769	215,888	222,230	186,605	197	184	186	548.4	564.5	474.0
Baton Rouge, LA	4,214.5	4,026.9	808,242	802,484	705,973	623,850	65	66	68	199.3	175.3	154.9
Battle Creek, MI	718.3	706.2	135,490	136,146	137,985	135,982	287	265	242	192.8	195.4	192.6
Bay City, MI	630.7	442.3	107,110	107,771	110,157	111,723	333	310	280	243.7	249.1	252.6
Beaumont–Port Arthur, TX	2,389.7	2,100.5	390,535	388,745	385,090	361,218	132	117	109	185.1	183.3	172.0
Bellingham, WA	2,503.5	2,106.8	203,663	201,140	166,814	127,780	210	222	256	95.5	79.2	60.7
Bend, OR	3,054.8	3,018.2	160,338	157,733	115,367	74,976	251	296	353	52.3	38.2	24.8
Billings, MT	4,711.2	4,682.1	160,097	158,050	138,904	121,499	250	264	264	33.8	29.7	25.9
Binghamton, NY	1,238.4	1,224.4	250,074	251,725	252,320	264,497	182	166	150	205.6	206.1	216.0
Birmingham–Hoover, AL	5,369.7	5,279.5	1,132,264	1,128,047	1,052,238	956,668	49	48	45	213.7	199.3	181.2
Bismarck, ND	3,613.7	3,558.9	110,879	108,779	94,719	83,831	332	343	339	30.6	26.6	23.6
Blacksburg–Christiansburg–Radford, VA	1,089.5	1,072.5	162,487	162,958	151,272	140,715	241	242	234	151.9	141.0	131.2
Bloomington, IN	1,345.1	1,322.3	194,193	192,714	175,506	156,669	218	211	210	145.7	132.7	118.5
Bloomington–Normal, IL	1,186.3	1,183.4	170,556	169,572	150,433	129,180	235	244	255	143.3	127.1	109.2
Boise City–Nampa, ID	11,833.3	11,765.5	627,664	616,561	464,840	319,596	86	97	125	52.4	39.5	27.2
Boston–Cambridge–Quincy, MA–NH	4,512.4	3,487.4	4,591,112	4,552,402	4,391,344	4,133,895	10	10	6	1,305.4	1,259.2	1,185.4
Boston–Quincy, MA	1,657.8	1,113.3	1,903,947	1,887,792	1,812,937	1,715,269	(X)	(X)	(X)	1,695.7	1,628.4	1,540.7
Cambridge–Newton–Framingham, MA	847.1	817.8	1,518,171	1,503,085	1,465,396	1,398,468	(X)	(X)	(X)	1,838.0	1,791.9	1,710.0
Peabody, MA	828.5	492.6	748,930	743,159	723,419	670,080	(X)	(X)	(X)	1,508.6	1,468.6	1,360.3
Rockingham County–Strafford County, NH	1,179.1	1,063.7	420,064	418,366	389,592	350,078	(X)	(X)	(X)	393.3	366.3	329.1
Boulder, CO	740.4	726.3	299,378	294,567	269,814	225,339	160	159	164	405.6	371.5	310.3
Bowling Green, KY	855.6	844.5	127,607	125,953	104,166	88,077	304	325	334	149.1	123.3	104.3
Bremerton–Silverdale, WA	565.9	394.9	254,633	251,133	231,969	189,731	183	177	180	635.9	587.4	480.5
Bridgeport–Stamford–Norwalk, CT	836.9	624.9	925,899	916,829	882,567	827,645	56	51	51	1,467.2	1,412.3	1,324.4
Brownsville–Harlingen, TX	1,276.5	890.9	414,123	406,220	335,227	260,120	126	137	151	456.0	376.3	292.0
Brunswick, GA	1,606.3	1,286.4	112,923	112,370	93,044	82,207	325	344	341	87.4	72.3	63.9
Buffalo–Niagara Falls, NY	2,366.5	1,565.0	1,134,039	1,135,509	1,170,111	1,189,340	47	42	37	725.6	747.7	760.0
Burlington, NC	434.7	423.9	153,291	151,131	130,800	108,213	264	272	289	356.5	308.6	255.3
Burlington–South Burlington, VT	1,505.9	1,252.1	212,535	211,261	198,889	177,059	199	193	193	168.7	158.8	141.4
Canton–Massillon, OH	979.5	969.9	403,869	404,422	406,934	394,106	128	110	98	416.4	419.6	406.3
Cape Coral–Fort Myers, FL	1,212.5	784.5	631,330	618,754	440,888	335,113	85	103	122	788.7	562.0	427.2
Cape Girardeau–Jackson, MO–IL	1,460.1	1,431.9	97,024	96,275	90,312	82,878	350	349	340	67.2	63.1	57.9
Carson City, NV	157.2	144.7	55,439	55,274	52,457	40,443	366	365	365	382.0	362.5	279.5
Casper, WY	5,375.6	5,340.3	76,366	75,450	66,533	61,226	364	363	361	14.1	12.5	11.5
Cedar Rapids, IA	2,020.0	2,008.8	260,575	257,940	237,230	210,640	176	174	168	128.4	118.1	104.9
Champaign–Urbana, IL	1,924.1	1,921.1	232,336	231,891	210,275	202,848	191	187	174	120.7	109.5	105.6
Charleston, WV	2,546.9	2,527.7	303,674	304,284	309,635	307,689	154	147	129	120.4	122.5	121.7
Charleston–North Charleston–Summerville, SC	3,163.0	2,588.2	682,121	664,607	549,033	506,877	79	85	81	256.8	212.1	195.8
Charlotte–Gastonia–Rock Hill, NC–SC	3,146.9	3,085.2	1,795,472	1,758,038	1,330,448	1,024,096	33	37	42	569.8	431.2	331.9
Charlottesville, VA	1,657.7	1,644.0	203,882	201,559	174,021	144,151	209	215	229	122.6	105.9	87.7
Chattanooga, TN–GA	2,137.8	2,089.0	533,372	528,143	476,531	433,039	97	94	89	252.8	228.1	207.3
Cheyenne, WY	2,687.5	2,685.9	92,680	91,738	81,607	73,142	354	356	356	34.2	30.4	27.2
Chicago–Joliet–Naperville, IL–IN–WI	9,578.5	7,196.8	9,504,753	9,461,105	9,098,316	8,181,939	3	3	3	1,314.6	1,264.2	1,136.9
Chicago–Joliet–Naperville, IL	5,342.9	4,602.6	7,922,566	7,883,147	7,628,412	6,894,440	(X)	(X)	(X)	1,712.8	1,657.4	1,497.9
Gary, IN	2,113.2	1,878.5	708,672	708,070	675,971	642,900	(X)	(X)	(X)	376.9	359.8	342.2
Lake County–Kenosha County, IL–WI	2,122.5	715.7	873,515	869,888	793,933	644,599	(X)	(X)	(X)	1,215.4	1,109.3	900.7

[1]The April 1, 2000, population estimates base reflects modifications to the Census 2000 population as documented in the Count Question Resolution program and geographic program revisions.
[2]The April 1, 1990, census counts include corrections processed through August 1997, results of special censuses and test censuses, and do not include adjustments for census coverage errors.
[3]Persons per square mile were calculated on the basis of land area data from the 2010 census.
(X) = Not applicable

Table B-1.   Area and Population—*Continued*

Metropolitan statistical area and division	Area, 2010 (square miles)		Population				Rank			Persons per square mile of land area[3]		
	Total	Land	2011 Estimate (July 1)	2010 Census (April 1)	2000[1] (estimates base)	1990[2] (April 1)	2010	2000	1990	2010	2000	1990
Chico, CA	1,677.1	1,636.5	220,266	220,000	203,171	182,120	195	190	189	134.4	124.1	111.3
Cincinnati–Middletown, OH–KY–IN	4,465.7	4,391.9	2,138,038	2,130,151	2,009,632	1,844,888	27	24	23	485.0	457.6	420.1
Clarksville, TN–KY	2,242.2	2,157.4	277,701	273,949	232,000	189,279	168	176	182	127.0	107.5	87.7
Cleveland, TN	773.8	763.4	116,834	115,788	104,015	87,355	319	326	335	151.7	136.3	114.4
Cleveland–Elyria–Mentor, OH	3,979.4	1,997.3	2,068,283	2,077,240	2,148,143	2,102,207	28	23	21	1,040.0	1,075.5	1,052.5
Coeur d'Alene, ID	1,315.6	1,244.1	141,132	138,494	108,685	69,795	279	316	359	111.3	87.4	56.1
College Station–Bryan, TX	2,133.4	2,100.1	231,623	228,660	184,885	150,998	192	204	216	108.9	88.0	71.9
Colorado Springs, CO	2,688.5	2,683.8	660,319	645,613	537,484	409,482	82	86	95	240.6	200.3	152.6
Columbia, MO	1,162.5	1,149.3	175,831	172,786	145,666	122,010	232	251	263	150.3	126.7	106.2
Columbia, SC	3,834.0	3,702.7	777,116	767,598	647,158	548,935	70	73	74	207.3	174.8	148.3
Columbus, GA–AL	1,959.8	1,936.1	301,439	294,865	281,768	266,452	159	154	148	152.3	145.5	137.6
Columbus, IN	409.5	406.9	77,870	76,794	71,435	63,657	363	362	360	188.7	175.6	156.4
Columbus, OH	4,014.1	3,967.2	1,858,464	1,836,536	1,612,690	1,405,178	32	31	33	462.9	406.5	354.2
Corpus Christi, TX	2,401.5	1,784.0	431,381	428,185	403,280	367,786	114	111	106	240.0	226.1	206.2
Corvallis, OR	678.6	675.9	85,928	85,579	78,153	70,811	358	360	358	126.6	115.6	104.8
Crestview–Fort Walton Beach–Destin, FL	1,082.1	930.2	183,482	180,822	170,498	143,777	225	217	231	194.4	183.3	154.6
Cumberland, MD–WV	759.1	752.0	102,884	103,299	102,008	101,643	339	334	302	137.4	135.6	135.2
Dallas–Fort Worth–Arlington, TX	9,285.2	8,927.5	6,526,548	6,371,773	5,161,544	3,989,294	4	5	9	713.7	578.2	446.9
Dallas–Plano–Irving, TX	5,815.7	5,531.3	4,345,590	4,235,751	3,451,226	2,622,562	(X)	(X)	(X)	765.8	623.9	474.1
Fort Worth–Arlington, TX	3,469.4	3,396.2	2,180,758	2,136,022	1,710,318	1,366,732	(X)	(X)	(X)	628.9	503.6	402.4
Dalton, GA	637.7	634.9	142,741	142,227	120,031	98,609	275	290	312	224.0	189.1	155.3
Danville, IL	901.3	898.4	81,509	81,625	83,919	88,257	359	353	331	90.9	93.4	98.2
Danville, VA	1,022.1	1,011.9	105,696	106,561	110,156	108,728	336	311	288	105.3	108.9	107.4
Davenport–Moline–Rock Island, IA–IL	2,313.8	2,269.9	381,342	379,690	376,019	368,145	134	121	105	167.3	165.7	162.2
Dayton, OH	1,716.7	1,706.0	845,388	841,502	848,153	843,837	61	54	49	493.3	497.2	494.6
Decatur, AL	1,316.2	1,270.0	154,070	153,829	145,867	131,556	258	250	250	121.1	114.9	103.6
Decatur, IL	585.9	580.7	110,730	110,768	114,706	117,206	330	299	272	190.7	197.5	201.8
Deltona–Daytona Beach–Ormond Beach, FL	1,432.4	1,101.0	494,804	494,593	443,343	370,737	103	101	102	449.2	402.7	336.7
Denver–Aurora–Broomfield, CO[4]	8,402.8	8,346.0	2,599,504	2,543,482	2,179,240	1,650,489	21	22	24	304.8	261.1	197.5
Des Moines–West Des Moines, IA	2,911.8	2,883.7	580,255	569,633	481,394	416,346	88	93	94	197.5	166.9	144.4
Detroit–Warren–Livonia, MI	4,235.6	3,888.4	4,285,832	4,296,250	4,452,557	4,248,699	12	9	5	1,104.9	1,145.1	1,092.7
Detroit–Livonia–Dearborn, MI	672.7	611.2	1,802,096	1,820,584	2,061,162	2,111,687	(X)	(X)	(X)	2,974.3	3,367.4	3,449.9
Warren–Troy–Farmington Hills, MI	3,562.9	3,276.3	2,483,736	2,475,666	2,391,395	2,137,012	(X)	(X)	(X)	755.6	729.9	652.3
Dothan, AL	1,728.9	1,716.0	146,562	145,639	130,861	120,352	270	271	266	84.9	76.3	70.1
Dover, DE	798.3	586.2	164,834	162,310	126,697	110,993	242	279	282	276.9	216.1	189.3
Dubuque, IA	616.6	608.3	94,648	93,653	89,143	86,403	353	350	337	154.0	146.5	142.0
Duluth, MN–WI	9,214.4	8,412.9	279,815	279,771	275,486	269,249	165	156	145	33.3	32.7	32.0
Durham–Chapel Hill, NC	1,813.2	1,758.4	512,979	504,357	426,493	344,665	102	105	116	286.8	242.5	196.0
Eau Claire, WI	1,686.5	1,646.3	162,657	161,151	148,337	137,543	245	246	240	97.9	90.1	83.5
El Centro, CA	4,481.7	4,176.6	177,057	174,528	142,361	109,303	231	258	287	41.8	34.1	26.2
Elizabethtown, KY	893.8	884.8	121,771	119,736	107,547	100,919	314	320	305	135.3	121.5	114.1
Elkhart–Goshen, IN	468.0	463.2	198,941	197,559	182,791	156,198	215	205	211	426.5	394.6	337.2
Elmira, NY	410.8	407.3	88,840	88,830	91,070	95,195	357	346	318	218.1	223.6	233.7
El Paso, TX	1,015.0	1,012.7	820,790	800,647	679,622	591,610	66	69	71	790.6	671.1	584.2
Erie, PA	1,558.2	799.1	280,985	280,566	280,843	275,575	164	155	143	351.1	351.4	344.9
Eugene–Springfield, OR	4,721.8	4,553.1	353,416	351,715	322,959	282,912	143	139	140	77.2	70.9	62.1
Evansville, IN–KY	2,347.8	2,283.9	359,879	358,676	342,815	324,858	142	133	124	157.0	150.1	142.2
Fairbanks, AK	7,443.6	7,338.2	99,192	97,581	82,840	77,720	346	355	350	13.3	11.3	10.6
Fargo, ND–MN	2,820.5	2,810.3	212,171	208,777	174,367	153,296	204	214	213	74.3	62.0	54.5
Farmington, NM	5,538.4	5,513.0	128,200	130,044	113,801	91,605	296	300	325	23.6	20.6	16.6
Fayetteville, NC	1,050.7	1,043.1	374,157	366,383	336,609	297,569	139	136	132	351.2	322.7	285.3
Fayetteville–Springdale–Rogers, AR–MO	3,213.1	3,163.0	473,830	463,204	347,045	239,495	109	130	158	146.4	109.7	75.7
Flagstaff, AZ	18,661.2	18,618.8	134,511	134,421	116,320	96,591	289	293	315	7.2	6.2	5.2
Flint, MI	649.6	637.0	422,080	425,790	436,141	430,459	115	104	92	668.4	684.7	675.8
Florence, SC	1,370.5	1,361.1	206,161	205,566	193,155	176,195	206	198	194	151.0	141.9	129.5
Florence–Muscle Shoals, AL	1,343.1	1,260.3	147,293	147,137	142,950	131,327	268	257	252	116.7	113.4	104.2
Fond du Lac, WI	765.8	719.5	102,079	101,633	97,296	90,083	341	340	328	141.3	135.2	125.2
Fort Collins–Loveland, CO	2,633.9	2,596.0	305,525	299,630	251,494	186,136	156	167	187	115.4	96.9	71.7
Fort Smith, AR–OK	4,092.7	3,996.3	300,087	298,592	273,170	234,078	158	158	159	74.7	68.4	58.6
Fort Wayne, IN	1,368.2	1,361.0	419,453	416,257	390,156	354,435	121	116	113	305.8	286.7	260.4
Fresno, CA	6,011.2	5,958.0	942,904	930,450	799,407	667,479	55	58	62	156.2	134.2	112.0
Gadsden, AL	548.6	535.0	104,303	104,430	103,459	99,840	338	329	308	195.2	193.4	186.6
Gainesville, FL	1,324.0	1,224.7	266,369	264,275	232,392	191,263	173	175	179	215.8	189.8	156.2
Gainesville, GA	429.3	392.8	183,052	179,684	139,277	95,434	226	262	317	457.4	354.6	243.0
Glens Falls, NY	1,777.5	1,698.1	128,996	128,923	124,345	118,539	298	281	271	75.9	73.2	69.8
Goldsboro, NC	556.8	553.1	123,697	122,623	113,329	104,666	311	301	297	221.7	204.9	189.2
Grand Forks, ND–MN	3,437.3	3,407.5	98,054	98,461	97,478	103,272	345	339	300	28.9	28.6	30.3
Grand Junction, CO	3,341.1	3,329.0	147,083	146,723	116,255	93,145	269	294	324	44.1	34.9	28.0
Grand Rapids–Wyoming, MI	2,890.7	2,784.5	779,604	774,160	740,482	645,918	69	63	67	278.0	265.9	232.0
Great Falls, MT	2,711.5	2,698.1	81,837	81,327	80,357	77,691	360	357	351	30.1	29.8	28.8

[1]The April 1, 2000, population estimates base reflects modifications to the Census 2000 population as documented in the Count Question Resolution program and geographic program revisions.
[2]The April 1, 1990, census counts include corrections processed through August 1997, results of special censuses and test censuses, and do not include adjustments for census coverage errors.
[3]Persons per square mile were calculated on the basis of land area data from the 2010 census.
[4]The Denver–Aurora metropolitan statistical area includes Broomfield County. Broomfield County, CO, was formed from parts of Adams, Boulder, Jefferson, and Weld counties on November 15, 2001, and is coextensive with Broomfield city. For the purposes of defining and presenting data for the Denver–Aurora metropolitan statistical area, Broomfield city is treated as if it were a county when data are available to do so. In many cases, the data will not be available.
(X) = Not applicable

Table B-1. Area and Population—*Continued*

Metropolitan statistical area and division	Area, 2010 (square miles)		Population				Rank			Persons per square mile of land area[3]		
	Total	Land	2011 Estimate (July 1)	2010 Census (April 1)	2000[1] (estimates base)	1990[2] (April 1)	2010	2000	1990	2010	2000	1990
Greeley, CO	4,016.8	3,987.2	258,638	252,825	180,926	131,821	179	208	249	63.4	45.4	33.1
Green Bay, WI	2,848.8	1,870.2	309,469	306,241	282,599	243,698	153	153	157	163.7	151.1	130.3
Greensboro–High Point, NC	2,019.7	1,993.8	730,966	723,801	643,430	540,041	71	74	77	363.0	322.7	270.9
Greenville, NC	921.2	917.9	192,690	189,510	152,772	123,864	220	238	260	206.5	166.4	134.9
Greenville–Mauldin–Easley, SC	2,030.7	1,995.3	647,401	636,986	559,940	472,155	83	84	85	319.2	280.6	236.6
Gulfport–Biloxi, MS	1,976.7	1,493.2	253,511	248,820	246,190	207,875	186	171	171	166.6	164.9	139.2
Hagerstown–Martinsburg, MD–WV	1,018.5	1,008.0	271,488	269,140	222,771	192,774	172	181	178	267.0	221.0	191.2
Hanford–Corcoran, CA	1,391.5	1,389.4	153,765	152,982	129,461	101,469	259	274	303	110.1	93.2	73.0
Harrisburg–Carlisle, PA	1,664.0	1,621.9	552,911	549,475	509,074	474,242	93	87	84	338.8	313.9	292.4
Harrisonburg, VA	870.8	866.5	126,562	125,228	108,193	88,189	306	318	332	144.5	124.9	101.8
Hartford–West Hartford–East Hartford, CT	1,606.7	1,514.6	1,213,255	1,212,381	1,148,618	1,123,678	45	44	38	800.5	758.4	741.9
Hattiesburg, MS	1,620.9	1,610.6	145,428	142,842	123,812	109,603	274	283	286	88.7	76.9	68.1
Hickory–Lenoir–Morganton, NC	1,666.4	1,637.4	364,567	365,497	341,851	292,405	140	135	136	223.2	208.8	178.6
Hinesville–Fort Stewart, GA	1,006.3	890.1	80,587	77,917	71,914	58,947	361	361	362	87.5	80.8	66.2
Holland–Grand Haven, MI	1,631.4	563.5	266,300	263,801	238,314	187,768	174	173	185	468.1	422.9	333.2
Honolulu, HI	2,128.1	600.7	963,607	953,207	876,156	836,231	53	52	50	1,586.8	1,458.6	1,392.1
Hot Springs, AR	734.6	677.8	97,124	96,024	88,068	73,397	351	351	355	141.7	129.9	108.3
Houma–Bayou Cane–Thibodaux, LA	3,556.4	2,300.0	208,583	208,178	194,477	182,842	205	195	188	90.5	84.6	79.5
Houston–Sugar Land–Baytown, TX	10,071.7	8,827.4	6,086,538	5,946,800	4,715,407	3,767,218	6	8	10	673.7	534.2	426.8
Huntington–Ashland, WV–KY–OH	1,773.9	1,744.6	287,599	287,702	288,649	288,189	161	151	137	164.9	165.5	165.2
Huntsville, AL	1,419.9	1,361.5	425,480	417,593	342,376	293,047	120	134	135	306.7	251.5	215.2
Idaho Falls, ID	3,006.2	2,959.6	132,073	130,374	101,677	88,750	295	335	330	44.1	34.4	30.0
Indianapolis–Carmel, IN	3,887.8	3,854.4	1,778,568	1,756,241	1,525,104	1,294,217	34	34	34	455.6	395.7	335.8
Iowa City, IA	1,194.1	1,182.9	154,893	152,586	131,676	115,731	260	270	276	129.0	111.3	97.8
Ithaca, NY	491.6	474.6	101,723	101,564	96,501	94,097	342	341	321	214.0	203.3	198.3
Jackson, MI	723.5	701.7	159,748	160,248	158,422	149,756	247	232	219	228.4	225.8	213.4
Jackson, MS	3,795.1	3,726.1	545,394	539,057	497,197	446,941	96	90	86	144.7	133.4	119.9
Jackson, TN	844.6	842.8	115,396	115,425	107,377	90,801	321	321	326	137.0	127.4	107.7
Jacksonville, FL	3,698.4	3,201.1	1,360,251	1,345,596	1,122,750	925,213	40	45	47	420.4	350.7	289.0
Jacksonville, NC	905.9	762.7	179,719	177,772	150,355	149,838	227	245	218	233.1	197.1	196.5
Janesville, WI	726.1	718.1	160,092	160,331	152,307	139,510	246	240	237	223.3	212.1	194.3
Jefferson City, MO	2,278.6	2,247.7	150,480	149,807	140,052	120,704	266	261	265	66.6	62.3	53.7
Johnson City, TN	863.9	853.8	199,818	198,716	181,607	160,390	214	206	205	232.7	212.7	187.9
Johnstown, PA	693.6	688.3	143,728	143,679	152,598	163,062	272	239	200	208.7	221.7	236.9
Jonesboro, AR	1,476.3	1,465.6	122,829	121,026	107,762	93,620	312	319	322	82.6	73.5	63.9
Joplin, MO	1,267.9	1,263.2	176,849	175,518	157,322	134,910	230	234	244	138.9	124.5	106.8
Kalamazoo–Portage, MI	1,670.2	1,169.1	328,205	326,589	314,866	293,471	148	146	134	279.4	269.3	251.0
Kankakee–Bradley, IL	681.4	676.6	113,698	113,449	103,833	96,255	324	327	316	167.7	153.5	142.3
Kansas City, MO–KS	7,950.4	7,827.3	2,052,676	2,035,334	1,836,038	1,636,527	29	26	25	260.0	234.6	209.1
Kennewick–Pasco–Richland, WA	3,025.4	2,942.5	264,133	253,340	191,822	150,033	178	201	217	86.1	65.2	51.0
Killeen–Temple–Fort Hood, TX	2,858.5	2,815.9	411,595	405,300	330,714	268,820	127	138	146	143.9	117.4	95.5
Kingsport–Bristol–Bristol, TN–VA	2,047.1	2,009.8	309,793	309,544	298,484	275,678	151	149	142	154.0	148.5	137.2
Kingston, NY	1,160.8	1,124.2	182,448	182,493	177,749	165,380	224	210	199	162.3	158.1	147.1
Knoxville, TN	1,931.7	1,856.8	704,500	698,030	616,079	534,910	75	76	79	375.9	331.8	288.1
Kokomo, IN	554.5	553.6	98,588	98,688	101,541	96,946	344	336	314	178.3	183.4	175.1
La Crosse, WI–MN	1,048.8	1,003.7	134,488	133,665	126,838	116,401	291	278	273	133.2	126.4	116.0
Lafayette, IN	1,284.8	1,278.4	203,608	201,789	178,541	158,848	208	209	208	157.8	139.7	124.3
Lafayette, LA	1,085.7	1,006.4	277,307	273,738	239,086	208,859	169	172	170	272.0	237.6	207.5
Lake Charles, LA	3,030.9	2,348.5	200,822	199,607	193,568	177,394	213	197	192	85.0	82.4	75.5
Lake Havasu City–Kingman, AZ	13,460.6	13,311.0	202,351	200,186	155,032	93,497	211	236	323	15.0	11.6	7.0
Lakeland–Winter Haven, FL	2,010.5	1,797.8	609,492	602,095	483,924	405,382	87	92	96	334.9	269.2	225.5
Lancaster, PA	983.8	943.8	523,594	519,445	470,658	422,822	99	96	93	550.4	498.7	448.0
Lansing–East Lansing, MI	1,714.7	1,697.7	465,138	464,036	447,728	432,684	108	99	90	273.3	263.7	254.9
Laredo, TX	3,375.6	3,361.5	256,496	250,304	193,117	133,239	184	199	247	74.5	57.4	39.6
Las Cruces, NM	3,814.4	3,807.5	213,598	209,233	174,682	135,510	203	213	243	55.0	45.9	35.6
Las Vegas–Paradise, NV	8,060.8	7,891.4	1,969,975	1,951,269	1,375,765	741,368	30	36	56	247.3	174.3	93.9
Lawrence, KS	474.6	455.9	112,211	110,826	99,962	81,798	329	337	344	243.1	219.3	179.4
Lawton, OK	1,083.7	1,069.3	125,815	124,098	114,996	111,486	310	298	281	116.1	107.5	104.3
Lebanon, PA	362.5	361.8	134,311	133,568	120,327	113,744	292	288	278	369.2	332.6	314.4
Lewiston, ID–WA	1,496.9	1,484.3	61,476	60,888	57,961	51,359	365	364	363	41.0	39.0	34.6
Lewiston–Auburn, ME	497.1	467.9	107,398	107,702	103,793	105,259	334	328	295	230.2	221.8	225.0
Lexington–Fayette, KY	1,484.3	1,468.5	479,244	472,099	408,326	348,428	106	109	115	321.5	278.1	237.3
Lima, OH	406.8	402.5	106,094	106,331	108,473	109,755	337	317	285	264.2	269.5	272.7
Lincoln, NE	1,422.3	1,409.0	306,503	302,157	266,787	229,091	155	160	162	214.4	189.3	162.6
Little Rock–North Little Rock–Conway, AR	4,198.5	4,085.2	709,901	699,757	610,518	534,943	74	77	78	171.3	149.4	130.9
Logan, UT–ID	1,841.4	1,828.4	127,549	125,442	102,720	79,415	305	332	347	68.6	56.2	43.4
Longview, TX	1,806.8	1,780.3	216,666	214,369	194,042	180,053	198	196	190	120.4	109.0	101.1
Longview, WA	1,166.2	1,140.1	102,478	102,410	92,948	82,119	340	345	343	89.8	81.5	72.0
Los Angeles–Long Beach–Santa Ana, CA	5,699.0	4,848.4	12,944,801	12,828,837	12,365,627	11,273,720	2	2	2	2,646.0	2,550.5	2,325.2
Los Angeles–Long Beach–Glendale, CA	4,750.9	4,057.9	9,889,056	9,818,605	9,519,338	8,863,052	(X)	(X)	(X)	2,419.6	2,345.9	2,184.1
Santa Ana–Anaheim–Irvine, CA	948.1	790.6	3,055,745	3,010,232	2,846,289	2,410,668	(X)	(X)	(X)	3,807.5	3,600.2	3,049.2
Louisville/Jefferson County, KY–IN	4,196.1	4,110.8	1,294,849	1,283,566	1,161,975	1,056,156	42	43	40	312.2	282.7	256.9

[1]The April 1, 2000, population estimates base reflects modifications to the Census 2000 population as documented in the Count Question Resolution program and geographic program revisions.
[2]The April 1, 1990, census counts include corrections processed through August 1997, results of special censuses and test censuses, and do not include adjustments for census coverage errors.
[3]Persons per square mile were calculated on the basis of land area data from the 2010 census.
(X) = Not applicable

Table B-1. Area and Population—*Continued*

Metropolitan statistical area and division	Area, 2010 (square miles)		Population				Rank			Persons per square mile of land area[3]		
	Total	Land	2011 Estimate (July 1)	2010 Census (April 1)	2000[1] (estimates base)	1990[2] (April 1)	2010	2000	1990	2010	2000	1990
Lubbock, TX	1,802.4	1,795.8	290,002	284,890	249,700	229,940	162	169	160	158.6	139.0	128.0
Lynchburg, VA	2,146.7	2,120.3	254,171	252,634	228,616	206,226	180	178	173	119.2	107.8	97.3
Macon, GA	1,737.7	1,722.6	232,920	232,293	222,368	206,786	190	183	172	134.9	129.1	120.0
Madera–Chowchilla, CA	2,153.3	2,137.1	152,925	150,865	123,109	88,090	265	284	333	70.6	57.6	41.2
Madison, WI	2,802.1	2,725.3	576,467	568,593	501,774	432,323	89	88	91	208.6	184.1	158.6
Manchester–Nashua, NH	892.2	876.1	401,696	400,721	380,841	335,838	129	119	121	457.4	434.7	383.3
Manhattan, KS	1,888.3	1,835.4	130,240	127,081	108,999	113,720	302	315	279	69.2	59.4	62.0
Mankato–North Mankato, MN	1,232.3	1,196.3	97,204	96,740	85,712	82,120	348	352	342	80.9	71.6	68.6
Mansfield, OH	500.1	495.3	123,510	124,475	128,852	126,137	308	277	258	251.3	260.1	254.7
McAllen–Edinburg–Mission, TX	1,582.9	1,570.9	797,810	774,769	569,463	383,545	68	81	100	493.2	362.5	244.2
Medford, OR	2,801.6	2,783.5	204,822	203,206	181,269	146,387	207	207	227	73.0	65.1	52.6
Memphis, TN–MS–AR	4,699.4	4,577.8	1,325,605	1,316,100	1,205,204	1,067,263	41	41	39	287.5	263.3	233.1
Merced, CA	1,978.5	1,935.0	259,898	255,793	210,554	178,403	177	186	191	132.2	108.8	92.2
Miami–Fort Lauderdale–Pompano Beach, FL	6,137.0	5,077.2	5,670,125	5,564,635	5,007,564	4,056,228	8	6	8	1,096.0	986.3	798.9
Fort Lauderdale–Pompano Beach–Deerfield Beach, FL	1,322.9	1,209.8	1,780,172	1,748,066	1,623,018	1,255,531	(X)	(X)	(X)	1,444.9	1,341.6	1,037.8
Miami–Miami Beach–Kendall, FL	2,431.2	1,897.7	2,554,766	2,496,435	2,253,362	1,937,194	(X)	(X)	(X)	1,315.5	1,187.4	1,020.8
West Palm Beach–Boca Raton–Boynton Beach, FL	2,383.0	1,969.8	1,335,187	1,320,134	1,131,184	863,503	(X)	(X)	(X)	670.2	574.3	438.4
Michigan City–La Porte, IN	613.3	598.3	111,374	111,467	110,106	107,066	327	312	291	186.3	184.0	179.0
Midland, TX	902.0	900.3	140,308	136,872	116,009	106,611	284	295	294	152.0	128.9	118.4
Milwaukee–Waukesha–West Allis, WI	3,322.0	1,454.7	1,562,216	1,555,908	1,500,741	1,432,149	39	35	31	1,069.6	1,031.6	984.5
Minneapolis–St. Paul–Bloomington, MN–WI	6,363.7	6,027.1	3,318,486	3,279,833	2,968,806	2,538,776	16	16	16	544.2	492.6	421.2
Missoula, MT	2,618.3	2,593.4	110,138	109,299	95,802	78,687	331	342	348	42.1	36.9	30.3
Mobile, AL	1,644.0	1,229.4	412,577	412,992	399,843	378,643	124	113	101	335.9	325.2	308.0
Modesto, CA	1,514.7	1,494.8	518,522	514,453	446,997	370,522	100	100	103	344.2	299.0	247.9
Monroe, LA	1,537.1	1,487.4	177,651	176,441	170,053	162,987	229	219	201	118.6	114.3	109.6
Monroe, MI	680.0	549.4	151,560	152,021	145,945	133,600	262	249	245	276.7	265.6	243.2
Montgomery, AL	2,786.4	2,713.1	378,608	374,536	346,528	305,175	136	131	130	138.0	127.7	112.5
Morgantown, WV	1,017.3	1,008.9	132,251	129,709	111,200	104,546	297	307	298	128.6	110.2	103.6
Morristown, TN	792.6	715.9	137,494	136,608	123,081	100,591	285	285	306	190.8	171.9	140.5
Mount Vernon–Anacortes, WA	1,920.1	1,731.2	118,109	116,901	102,979	79,545	317	331	346	67.5	59.5	45.9
Muncie, IN	395.9	392.1	117,660	117,671	118,769	119,659	316	292	268	300.1	302.9	305.2
Muskegon–Norton Shores, MI	1,460.0	499.2	171,302	172,188	170,200	158,983	234	218	207	344.9	340.9	318.5
Myrtle Beach–North Myrtle Beach–Conway, SC	1,255.0	1,133.9	276,340	269,291	196,629	144,053	171	194	230	237.5	173.4	127.0
Napa, CA	788.6	748.4	138,088	136,484	124,279	110,765	286	282	284	182.4	166.1	148.0
Naples–Marco Island, FL	2,305.0	1,998.3	328,134	321,520	251,377	152,099	149	168	214	160.9	125.8	76.1
Nashville–Davidson—Murfreesboro—Franklin, TN	5,762.6	5,688.6	1,617,142	1,589,934	1,311,789	1,048,216	38	39	41	279.5	230.6	184.3
New Haven–Milford, CT	862.1	604.5	861,113	862,477	824,008	804,219	60	57	53	1,426.8	1,363.1	1,330.4
New Orleans–Metairie–Kenner, LA	7,623.3	2,960.2	1,191,089	1,167,764	1,316,510	1,264,383	46	38	35	394.5	444.7	427.1
New York–Northern New Jersey–Long Island, NY–NJ–PA	9,211.6	6,686.9	19,015,900	18,897,109	18,323,002	16,863,671	1	1	1	2,826.0	2,740.1	2,521.9
Edison–New Brunswick, NJ	2,208.4	1,708.3	2,349,499	2,340,249	2,173,869	1,898,329	(X)	(X)	(X)	1,369.9	1,272.5	1,111.2
Nassau–Suffolk, NY	2,826.4	1,196.8	2,843,252	2,832,882	2,753,913	2,609,212	(X)	(X)	(X)	2,367.0	2,301.1	2,180.2
Newark–Union, NJ–PA	2,256.7	2,181.0	2,153,014	2,147,727	2,098,843	1,959,933	(X)	(X)	(X)	984.7	962.3	898.6
New York–White Plains–Wayne, NY–NJ	1,920.2	1,600.8	11,670,135	11,576,571	11,296,377	10,396,197	(X)	(X)	(X)	7,231.5	7,056.7	6,494.4
Niles–Benton Harbor, MI	1,581.5	567.7	156,941	156,813	162,453	161,378	254	229	203	276.2	286.2	284.3
North Port–Bradenton–Sarasota, FL	1,618.0	1,298.8	709,355	702,281	589,959	489,483	73	79	82	540.7	454.2	376.9
Norwich–New London, CT	771.7	664.9	273,502	274,055	259,088	254,957	167	161	155	412.2	389.7	383.5
Ocala, FL	1,662.6	1,584.5	332,529	331,298	258,916	194,835	147	162	177	209.1	163.4	123.0
Ocean City, NJ	620.4	251.4	96,601	97,265	102,326	95,089	347	333	319	386.9	407.0	378.2
Odessa, TX	901.8	897.7	140,111	137,130	121,123	118,934	283	287	269	152.8	134.9	132.5
Ogden–Clearfield, UT	1,904.2	1,484.1	555,916	547,184	442,656	351,799	94	102	114	368.7	298.3	237.0
Oklahoma City, OK	5,581.7	5,511.5	1,278,053	1,252,987	1,095,421	971,042	44	47	44	227.3	198.8	176.2
Olympia, WA	773.5	722.0	256,591	252,264	207,355	161,238	181	189	204	349.4	287.2	223.3
Omaha–Council Bluffs, NE–IA	4,407.2	4,349.6	877,110	865,350	767,041	685,797	59	60	59	198.9	176.3	157.7
Orlando–Kissimmee–Sanford, FL	4,011.4	3,478.5	2,171,360	2,134,411	1,644,561	1,224,844	26	30	36	613.6	472.8	352.1
Oshkosh–Neenah, WI	578.6	434.5	167,699	166,994	156,763	140,320	238	235	236	384.3	360.8	322.9
Owensboro, KY	931.7	898.5	115,333	114,752	109,875	104,681	323	313	296	127.7	122.3	116.5
Oxnard–Thousand Oaks–Ventura, CA	2,208.4	1,843.1	831,771	823,318	753,197	669,016	63	61	61	446.7	408.7	363.0
Palm Bay–Melbourne–Titusville, FL	1,557.0	1,015.7	543,566	543,376	476,230	398,978	95	95	97	535.0	468.9	392.8
Palm Coast, FL	570.8	485.5	97,376	95,696	49,832	28,701	352	366	366	197.1	102.6	59.1
Panama City–Lynn Haven–Panama City Beach, FL	1,033.1	758.5	169,856	168,852	148,217	126,994	236	247	257	222.6	195.4	167.4
Parkersburg–Marietta–Vienna, WV–OH	1,386.1	1,360.8	162,248	162,056	164,624	161,907	244	225	202	119.1	121.0	119.0
Pascagoula, MS	1,527.0	1,201.5	162,790	162,246	150,564	131,916	243	243	248	135.0	125.3	109.8
Pensacola–Ferry Pass–Brent, FL	2,048.5	1,668.1	453,218	448,991	412,153	344,406	110	108	117	269.2	247.1	206.5
Peoria, IL	2,518.0	2,470.8	379,556	379,186	366,899	358,552	135	127	111	153.5	148.5	145.1
Philadelphia–Camden–Wilmington, PA–NJ–DE–MD	4,870.1	4,602.1	5,992,414	5,965,343	5,687,147	5,435,550	5	4	4	1,296.2	1,235.8	1,181.1
Camden, NJ	1,384.3	1,341.8	1,251,921	1,250,679	1,186,999	1,127,972	(X)	(X)	(X)	932.1	884.6	840.6
Philadelphia, PA	2,201.6	2,155.8	4,030,926	4,008,994	3,849,647	3,728,991	(X)	(X)	(X)	1,859.6	1,785.7	1,729.7
Wilmington, DE–MD–NJ	1,284.2	1,104.5	709,567	705,670	650,501	578,587	(X)	(X)	(X)	638.9	589.0	523.8

[1]The April 1, 2000, population estimates base reflects modifications to the Census 2000 population as documented in the Count Question Resolution program and geographic program revisions.
[2]The April 1, 1990, census counts include corrections processed through August 1997, results of special censuses and test censuses, and do not include adjustments for census coverage errors.
[3]Persons per square mile were calculated on the basis of land area data from the 2010 census.
(X) = Not applicable

Table B-1. Area and Population—*Continued*

Metropolitan statistical area and division	Area, 2010 (square miles) Total	Land	Population 2011 Estimate (July 1)	2010 Census (April 1)	2000[1] (estimates base)	1990[2] (April 1)	Rank 2010	2000	1990	Persons per square mile of land area[3] 2010	2000	1990
Phoenix–Mesa–Glendale, AZ	14,598.5	14,565.7	4,263,236	4,192,887	3,251,876	2,238,498	14	14	20	287.9	223.3	153.7
Pine Bluff, AR	2,084.7	2,030.0	98,924	100,258	107,341	106,958	343	322	292	49.4	52.9	52.7
Pittsburgh, PA	5,342.4	5,281.4	2,359,746	2,356,285	2,431,087	2,468,289	22	20	18	446.1	460.3	467.4
Pittsfield, MA	946.4	926.8	130,458	131,219	134,953	139,352	294	267	238	141.6	145.6	150.4
Pocatello, ID	2,590.1	2,516.2	91,457	90,656	83,103	73,112	355	354	357	36.0	33.0	29.1
Portland–South Portland–Biddeford, ME	2,857.2	2,079.6	515,807	514,098	487,568	441,257	101	91	87	247.2	234.5	212.2
Portland–Vancouver–Hillsboro, OR–WA	6,821.3	6,683.7	2,262,605	2,226,009	1,927,881	1,523,741	23	25	27	333.1	288.4	228.0
Port St. Lucie, FL	1,440.9	1,115.4	427,824	424,107	319,426	251,071	118	144	156	380.2	286.4	225.1
Poughkeepsie–Newburgh–Middletown, NY	1,664.0	1,607.3	672,871	670,301	621,517	567,033	78	75	73	417.0	386.7	352.8
Prescott, AZ	8,127.9	8,123.5	211,888	211,033	167,517	107,714	200	220	290	26.0	20.6	13.3
Providence–New Bedford–Fall River, RI–MA	2,236.1	1,586.9	1,600,224	1,600,852	1,582,997	1,509,789	37	32	28	1,008.8	997.5	951.4
Provo–Orem, UT	5,550.5	5,395.7	540,834	526,810	376,774	269,407	98	120	144	97.6	69.8	49.9
Pueblo, CO	2,397.8	2,386.1	160,545	159,063	141,472	123,051	249	260	261	66.7	59.3	51.6
Punta Gorda, FL	858.3	680.3	160,511	159,978	141,627	110,975	248	259	283	235.2	208.2	163.1
Racine, WI	792.1	332.5	195,388	195,408	188,831	175,034	217	202	196	587.7	567.9	526.4
Raleigh–Cary, NC	2,147.3	2,118.2	1,163,515	1,130,490	797,071	544,031	48	59	76	533.7	376.3	256.8
Rapid City, SD	6,267.1	6,247.5	128,361	126,382	112,818	103,221	303	303	301	20.2	18.1	16.5
Reading, PA	865.8	856.5	412,778	411,442	373,638	336,523	125	123	120	480.4	436.2	392.9
Redding, CA	3,847.4	3,775.4	177,774	177,223	163,256	147,036	228	228	224	46.9	43.2	38.9
Reno–Sparks, NV	6,805.8	6,565.2	429,606	425,417	342,885	257,193	116	132	154	64.8	52.2	39.2
Richmond, VA	5,839.6	5,684.9	1,269,380	1,258,251	1,096,957	949,244	43	46	46	221.3	193.0	167.0
Riverside–San Bernardino–Ontario, CA	27,408.1	27,263.3	4,304,997	4,224,851	3,254,821	2,588,793	13	13	13	155.0	119.4	95.0
Roanoke, VA	1,896.8	1,868.7	308,861	308,707	288,309	268,513	152	152	147	165.2	154.3	143.7
Rochester, MN	1,644.0	1,615.6	187,612	186,011	163,618	141,945	223	227	233	115.1	101.3	87.9
Rochester, NY	4,870.0	2,928.1	1,055,278	1,054,323	1,037,831	1,002,410	51	49	43	360.1	354.4	342.3
Rockford, IL	801.3	794.1	348,360	349,431	320,204	283,719	144	142	138	440.0	403.2	357.3
Rocky Mount, NC	1,049.4	1,045.7	152,157	152,392	143,026	133,369	261	256	246	145.7	136.8	127.5
Rome, GA	518.5	509.9	95,989	96,317	90,565	81,251	349	347	345	188.9	177.6	159.3
Sacramento—Arden-Arcade—Roseville, CA	5,306.4	5,094.2	2,176,235	2,149,127	1,796,857	1,506,792	24	27	29	421.9	352.7	295.8
Saginaw–Saginaw Township North, MI	816.0	800.1	199,088	200,169	210,039	211,946	212	188	167	250.2	262.5	264.9
St. Cloud, MN	1,803.0	1,751.4	190,014	189,093	167,392	149,509	221	221	220	108.0	95.6	85.4
St. George, UT	2,429.9	2,426.3	141,666	138,115	90,354	48,560	281	348	364	56.9	37.2	20.0
St. Joseph, MO–KS	1,675.2	1,655.5	127,574	127,329	122,336	115,816	300	286	275	76.9	73.9	70.0
St. Louis, MO–IL[5]	8,844.3	8,623.2	2,817,355	2,812,896	2,698,687	2,580,720	18	18	14	326.2	313.0	299.3
Salem, OR	1,936.4	1,923.1	394,865	390,738	347,214	278,024	131	129	141	203.2	180.5	144.6
Salinas, CA	3,771.2	3,280.6	421,898	415,057	401,762	355,660	122	112	112	126.5	122.5	108.4
Salisbury, MD	1,010.6	694.2	125,529	125,203	109,391	97,779	307	314	313	180.4	157.6	140.9
Salt Lake City, UT	9,975.4	9,555.3	1,145,905	1,124,197	968,858	768,075	50	50	54	117.7	101.4	80.4
San Angelo, TX	2,592.2	2,573.5	113,443	111,823	105,781	100,087	326	323	307	43.5	41.1	38.9
San Antonio–New Braunfels, TX	7,370.8	7,312.6	2,194,927	2,142,508	1,711,703	1,407,745	25	29	32	293.0	234.1	192.5
San Diego–Carlsbad–San Marcos, CA	4,525.7	4,206.6	3,140,069	3,095,313	2,813,833	2,498,016	17	17	17	735.8	668.9	593.8
Sandusky, OH	626.0	251.6	76,751	77,079	79,551	76,781	362	359	352	306.4	316.2	305.2
San Francisco–Oakland–Fremont, CA	3,426.1	2,470.5	4,391,037	4,335,391	4,123,740	3,711,756	11	12	11	1,754.9	1,669.2	1,502.4
Oakland–Fremont–Hayward, CA	1,625.1	1,454.9	2,595,971	2,559,296	2,392,557	2,108,078	(X)	(X)	(X)	1,759.1	1,644.5	1,449.0
San Francisco–San Mateo–Redwood City, CA	1,801.0	1,015.6	1,795,066	1,776,095	1,731,183	1,603,678	(X)	(X)	(X)	1,748.8	1,704.6	1,579.0
San Jose–Sunnyvale–Santa Clara, CA	2,694.5	2,678.8	1,865,450	1,836,911	1,735,819	1,534,274	31	28	26	685.7	648.0	572.7
San Luis Obispo–Paso Robles, CA	3,615.5	3,298.5	271,969	269,637	246,681	217,162	170	170	166	81.7	74.8	65.8
Santa Barbara–Santa Maria–Goleta, CA	3,789.1	2,735.1	426,878	423,895	399,347	369,608	119	114	104	155.0	146.0	135.1
Santa Cruz–Watsonville, CA	607.2	445.2	264,298	262,382	255,602	229,734	175	163	161	589.4	574.1	516.0
Santa Fe, NM	1,910.9	1,909.4	145,648	144,170	129,292	98,928	271	275	311	75.5	67.7	51.8
Santa Rosa–Petaluma, CA	1,767.9	1,575.8	488,116	483,878	458,614	388,222	104	98	99	307.1	291.0	246.4
Savannah, GA	1,569.6	1,340.1	355,576	347,611	293,000	257,899	145	150	153	259.4	218.6	192.4
Scranton—Wilkes-Barre, PA	1,776.2	1,746.7	563,223	563,631	560,625	575,322	91	83	72	322.7	321.0	329.4
Seattle–Tacoma–Bellevue, WA	6,309.6	5,872.3	3,500,026	3,439,809	3,043,878	2,559,136	15	15	15	585.8	518.3	435.8
Seattle–Bellevue–Everett, WA	4,503.1	4,202.8	2,692,122	2,644,584	2,343,058	1,972,933	(X)	(X)	(X)	629.2	557.5	469.4
Tacoma, WA	1,806.4	1,669.5	807,904	795,225	700,820	586,203	(X)	(X)	(X)	476.3	419.8	351.1
Sebastian–Vero Beach, FL	617.0	502.9	138,894	138,028	112,947	90,208	282	302	327	274.5	224.6	179.4
Sheboygan, WI	1,271.2	511.3	115,149	115,507	112,646	103,877	320	304	299	225.9	220.3	203.2
Sherman–Denison, TX	979.2	932.8	121,419	120,877	110,595	95,019	313	309	320	129.6	118.6	101.9
Shreveport–Bossier City, LA	2,698.6	2,594.2	403,595	398,604	375,965	360,009	130	122	110	153.7	144.9	138.8
Sioux City, IA–NE–SD	2,095.2	2,073.9	144,062	143,577	143,053	131,350	273	255	251	69.2	69.0	63.3
Sioux Falls, SD	2,586.2	2,575.7	232,433	228,261	187,093	153,500	193	203	212	88.6	72.6	59.6
South Bend–Mishawaka, IN–MI	969.7	947.9	318,688	319,224	316,663	296,529	150	145	133	336.8	334.1	312.8
Spartanburg, SC	819.2	807.9	286,868	284,307	253,791	226,793	163	164	163	351.9	314.1	280.7
Spokane, WA	1,780.7	1,763.8	473,761	471,221	417,939	361,333	107	107	108	267.2	237.0	204.9
Springfield, IL	1,192.5	1,182.7	211,547	210,170	201,437	189,550	201	192	181	177.7	170.3	160.3
Springfield, MA	1,904.0	1,843.7	693,204	692,942	680,014	672,964	76	68	60	375.8	368.8	365.0
Springfield, MO	3,020.7	3,006.8	440,142	436,712	368,374	298,818	112	125	131	145.2	122.5	99.4
Springfield, OH	402.5	397.5	137,691	138,333	144,742	147,538	280	254	223	348.0	364.1	371.2
State College, PA	1,113.0	1,109.9	154,722	153,990	135,758	124,812	255	266	259	138.7	122.3	112.5
Steubenville–Weirton, OH–WV	591.5	580.1	123,243	124,454	132,008	142,523	309	269	232	214.5	227.6	245.7

[1]The April 1, 2000, population estimates base reflects modifications to the Census 2000 population as documented in the Count Question Resolution program and geographic program revisions.

[2]The April 1, 1990, census counts include corrections processed through August 1997, results of special censuses and test censuses, and do not include adjustments for census coverage errors.

[3]Persons per square mile were calculated on the basis of land area data from the 2010 census.

[4]The Denver–Aurora metropolitan statistical area includes Broomfield County. Broomfield County, CO, was formed from parts of Adams, Boulder, Jefferson, and Weld counties on November 15, 2001, and is coextensive with Broomfield city. For the purposes of defining and presenting data for the Denver–Aurora metropolitan statistical area, Broomfield city is treated as if it were a county when data are available to do so. In many cases, the data will not be available.

[5]The portion of Sullivan city in Crawford County, MO, is legally part of the St. Louis, MO–IL MSA. That portion is not included in these figures for the St. Louis MSA.

(X) = Not applicable

Table B-1.   Area and Population—*Continued*

Metropolitan statistical area and division	Area, 2010 (square miles)		Population				Rank			Persons per square mile of land area[3]		
	Total	Land	2011 Estimate (July 1)	2010 Census (April 1)	2000[1] (estimates base)	1990[2] (April 1)	2010	2000	1990	2010	2000	1990
Stockton, CA	1,426.5	1,391.3	696,214	685,306	563,598	480,628	77	82	83	492.6	405.1	345.5
Sumter, SC	682.1	665.1	107,460	107,456	104,646	101,276	335	324	304	161.6	157.3	152.3
Syracuse, NY	2,779.0	2,384.9	662,553	662,577	650,154	659,924	80	72	64	277.8	272.6	276.7
Tallahassee, FL	2,602.6	2,387.7	369,758	367,413	320,304	259,107	137	141	152	153.9	134.1	108.5
Tampa–St. Petersburg–Clearwater, FL	3,331.3	2,513.4	2,824,724	2,783,243	2,395,997	2,067,959	19	21	22	1,107.4	953.3	822.8
Terre Haute, IN	1,484.8	1,464.9	172,663	172,425	170,943	166,578	233	216	198	117.7	116.7	113.7
Texarkana, TX–Texarkana, AR	1,560.6	1,510.6	136,552	136,027	129,749	120,132	288	273	267	90.0	85.9	79.5
Toledo, OH	2,208.6	1,618.4	650,266	651,429	659,188	654,157	81	71	66	402.5	407.3	404.2
Topeka, KS	3,289.9	3,232.6	234,647	233,870	224,551	210,257	189	180	169	72.3	69.5	65.0
Trenton–Ewing, NJ	228.9	224.6	367,063	366,513	350,761	325,759	138	128	123	1,631.8	1,561.7	1,450.4
Tucson, AZ	9,189.0	9,187.0	989,569	980,263	843,746	666,957	52	55	63	106.7	91.8	72.6
Tulsa, OK	6,460.1	6,269.2	946,962	937,478	859,532	761,019	54	53	55	149.5	137.1	121.4
Tuscaloosa, AL	2,667.7	2,612.8	221,553	219,461	192,034	176,151	196	200	195	84.0	73.5	67.4
Tyler, TX	949.7	921.4	213,381	209,714	174,706	151,309	202	212	215	227.6	189.6	164.2
Utica–Rome, NY	2,715.6	2,623.9	298,447	299,397	299,896	316,645	157	148	126	114.1	114.3	120.7
Valdosta, GA	1,628.9	1,589.3	142,307	139,588	119,560	99,244	278	291	310	87.8	75.2	62.4
Vallejo–Fairfield, CA	906.2	821.8	416,471	413,344	394,542	339,469	123	115	119	503.0	480.1	413.1
Victoria, TX	2,780.9	2,241.0	116,230	115,384	111,663	99,394	322	306	309	51.5	49.8	44.4
Vineland–Millville–Bridgeton, NJ	677.6	483.7	157,095	156,898	146,438	138,053	253	248	239	324.4	302.7	285.4
Virginia Beach–Norfolk–Newport News, VA–NC	3,897.6	2,629.6	1,679,894	1,671,683	1,576,370	1,450,855	36	33	30	635.7	599.5	551.7
Visalia–Porterville, CA	4,838.6	4,824.2	449,253	442,179	368,021	311,932	111	126	127	91.7	76.3	64.7
Waco, TX	1,060.2	1,037.1	238,564	234,906	213,517	189,123	188	185	183	226.5	205.9	182.4
Warner Robins, GA	379.9	375.5	143,925	139,900	110,765	89,208	277	308	329	372.6	295.0	237.6
Washington–Arlington–Alexandria, DC–VA–MD–WV	6,030.3	5,598.3	5,703,948	5,582,170	4,796,183	4,122,259	7	7	7	997.1	856.7	736.3
Bethesda–Rockville–Frederick, MD	1,174.3	1,151.5	1,226,539	1,205,162	1,068,618	913,083	(X)	(X)	(X)	1,046.6	928.0	793.0
Washington–Arlington–Alexandria, DC–VA–MD–WV	4,856.0	4,446.8	4,477,409	4,377,008	3,727,565	3,209,176	(X)	(X)	(X)	984.3	838.3	721.7
Waterloo–Cedar Falls, IA	1,514.0	1,503.1	168,289	167,819	163,706	158,640	237	226	209	111.6	108.9	105.5
Wausau, WI	1,576.3	1,545.0	134,400	134,063	125,834	115,400	290	280	277	86.8	81.4	74.7
Wenatchee–East Wenatchee, WA	4,842.5	4,739.8	112,448	110,884	99,219	78,455	328	338	349	23.4	20.9	16.6
Wheeling, WV–OH	962.4	943.4	147,197	147,950	153,172	159,301	267	237	206	156.8	162.4	168.9
Wichita, KS	4,181.3	4,149.0	625,526	623,061	571,166	511,111	84	80	80	150.2	137.7	123.2
Wichita Falls, TX	2,675.3	2,619.6	150,261	151,306	151,524	140,375	263	241	235	57.8	57.8	53.6
Williamsport, PA	1,243.8	1,228.6	116,747	116,111	120,044	118,710	318	289	270	94.5	97.7	96.6
Wilmington, NC	2,310.8	1,908.3	369,685	362,315	274,532	200,124	141	157	175	189.9	143.9	104.9
Winchester, VA–WV	1,069.4	1,063.0	130,065	128,472	102,997	84,168	299	330	338	120.9	96.9	79.2
Winston–Salem, NC	1,472.9	1,455.9	482,025	477,717	421,961	361,426	105	106	107	328.1	289.8	248.2
Worcester, MA	1,579.2	1,510.8	801,227	798,552	750,963	709,711	67	62	57	528.6	497.1	469.8
Yakima, WA	4,311.3	4,295.4	247,141	243,231	222,581	188,823	187	182	184	56.6	51.8	44.0
York–Hanover, PA	910.7	904.2	436,770	434,972	381,751	339,574	113	118	118	481.1	422.2	375.6
Youngstown–Warren–Boardman, OH–PA	1,744.4	1,702.5	562,739	565,773	602,964	613,604	90	78	69	332.3	354.2	360.4
Yuba City, CA	1,252.3	1,234.2	167,497	166,892	139,149	122,643	239	263	262	135.2	112.7	99.4
Yuma, AZ	5,519.1	5,514.0	200,870	195,751	160,026	106,895	216	231	293	35.5	29.0	19.4

[1]The April 1, 2000, population estimates base reflects modifications to the Census 2000 population as documented in the Count Question Resolution program and geographic program revisions.
[2]The April 1, 1990, census counts include corrections processed through August 1997, results of special censuses and test censuses, and do not include adjustments for census coverage errors.
[3]Persons per square mile were calculated on the basis of land area data from the 2010 census.
(X) = Not applicable

Table B-2. Components of Population Change

Metropolitan statistical area and division	Components of population change, April 1, 2010 (estimates base) to July 1, 2011								Population change, April 1, 2000 to April 1, 2010	
	Number							Percent change	Number	Percent change
	Total population change[1]	Natural increase			Total migration	Net international migration	Net domestic migration			
		Total	Births	Deaths						
Abilene, TX	1,164	994	3,033	2,039	179	176	3	0.7	5,007	3.1
Akron, OH	-1,744	1,338	9,631	8,293	-3,064	541	-3,605	-0.2	8,240	1.2
Albany, GA	380	1,141	2,852	1,711	-764	123	-887	0.2	-525	-0.3
Albany–Schenectady–Troy, NY	760	1,984	11,337	9,353	-1,186	1,654	-2,840	0.1	44,841	5.4
Albuquerque, NM	11,563	6,490	14,631	8,141	5,084	1,903	3,181	1.3	157,428	21.6
Alexandria, LA	583	813	2,718	1,905	-220	175	-395	0.4	8,887	6.1
Allentown–Bethlehem–Easton, PA–NJ	3,743	1,740	10,994	9,254	2,047	1,595	452	0.5	80,778	10.9
Altoona, PA	23	-254	1,763	2,017	294	17	277	0.0	-2,055	-1.6
Amarillo, TX	3,942	2,265	4,856	2,591	1,650	546	1,104	1.6	23,359	10.3
Ames, IA	121	597	1,184	587	-489	461	-950	0.1	9,561	12.0
Anchorage, AK	6,695	5,201	7,336	2,135	1,453	983	470	1.8	61,216	19.2
Anderson, IN	-401	277	1,991	1,714	-677	32	-709	-0.3	-1,722	-1.3
Anderson, SC	1,366	433	2,807	2,374	941	182	759	0.7	21,386	12.9
Ann Arbor, MI	3,171	2,203	4,649	2,446	975	1,566	-591	0.9	21,896	6.8
Anniston–Oxford, AL	-775	24	1,709	1,685	-797	72	-869	-0.7	6,323	5.6
Appleton, WI	1,737	1,622	3,454	1,832	124	165	-41	0.8	24,064	11.9
Asheville, NC	4,158	-129	5,447	5,576	4,293	739	3,554	1.0	55,687	15.1
Athens–Clarke County, GA	776	1,378	2,901	1,523	-619	668	-1,287	0.4	26,462	15.9
Atlanta–Sandy Springs–Marietta, GA	90,345	53,218	92,228	39,010	36,686	21,826	14,860	1.7	1,020,879	24.0
Atlantic City–Hammonton, NJ	-211	1,049	4,221	3,172	-1,270	1,074	-2,344	-0.1	21,997	8.7
Auburn–Opelika, AL	3,221	901	1,954	1,053	2,291	342	1,949	2.3	25,155	21.9
Augusta–Richmond County, GA–SC	4,981	2,067	8,013	5,946	2,865	737	2,128	0.9	57,193	11.4
Austin–Round Rock–San Marcos, TX	67,230	22,576	32,447	9,871	44,117	7,668	36,449	3.9	466,526	37.3
Bakersfield–Delano, CA	12,079	11,189	17,828	6,639	897	2,531	-1,634	1.4	177,986	26.9
Baltimore–Towson, MD	18,621	13,795	42,120	28,325	4,888	6,647	-1,759	0.7	157,495	6.2
Bangor, ME	-135	105	1,882	1,777	-232	126	-358	-0.1	9,004	6.2
Barnstable Town, MA	-119	-1,234	2,188	3,422	1,140	394	746	-0.1	-6,342	-2.9
Baton Rouge, LA	5,758	6,450	14,114	7,664	-730	1,044	-1,774	0.7	96,511	13.7
Battle Creek, MI	-656	421	2,065	1,644	-1,083	200	-1,283	-0.5	-1,839	-1.3
Bay City, MI	-661	32	1,434	1,402	-690	44	-734	-0.6	-2,386	-2.2
Beaumont–Port Arthur, TX	1,790	1,894	6,637	4,743	-90	661	-751	0.5	3,655	0.9
Bellingham, WA	2,523	1,154	2,855	1,701	1,385	499	886	1.3	34,326	20.6
Bend, OR	2,605	782	2,219	1,437	1,831	190	1,641	1.7	42,366	36.7
Billings, MT	2,047	830	2,511	1,681	1,224	75	1,149	1.3	19,146	13.8
Binghamton, NY	-1,651	60	3,180	3,120	-1,720	322	-2,042	-0.7	-595	-0.2
Birmingham–Hoover, AL	4,214	5,362	18,893	13,531	-1,133	1,656	-2,789	0.4	75,809	7.2
Bismarck, ND	2,100	782	1,833	1,051	1,311	51	1,260	1.9	14,060	14.8
Blacksburg–Christiansburg–Radford, VA	-471	269	1,809	1,540	-741	335	-1,076	-0.3	11,686	7.7
Bloomington, IN	1,479	578	2,359	1,781	899	625	274	0.8	17,208	9.8
Bloomington–Normal, IL	984	1,298	2,638	1,340	-314	403	-717	0.6	19,139	12.7
Boise City–Nampa, ID	11,103	5,853	10,628	4,775	5,255	1,346	3,909	1.8	151,721	32.6
Boston–Cambridge–Quincy, MA–NH	38,710	22,896	64,756	41,860	16,137	19,290	-3,153	0.9	161,058	3.7
Boston–Quincy, MA	16,155	9,521	27,044	17,523	6,725	9,161	-2,436	0.9	74,855	4.1
Cambridge–Newton–Framingham, MA	15,086	8,735	22,051	13,316	6,488	7,441	-953	1.0	37,689	2.6
Peabody, MA	5,771	3,246	10,846	7,600	2,591	2,444	147	0.8	19,740	2.7
Rockingham County–Strafford County, NH	1,698	1,394	4,815	3,421	333	244	89	0.4	28,774	7.4
Boulder, CO	4,811	1,947	3,828	1,881	2,863	905	1,958	1.6	24,753	9.2
Bowling Green, KY	1,654	784	1,976	1,192	873	415	458	1.3	21,787	20.9
Bremerton–Silverdale, WA	3,500	1,199	3,615	2,416	2,294	220	2,074	1.4	19,164	8.3
Bridgeport–Stamford–Norwalk, CT	9,070	5,230	12,923	7,693	3,947	4,754	-807	1.0	34,262	3.9
Brownsville–Harlingen, TX	7,903	6,928	9,821	2,893	990	1,452	-462	1.9	70,993	21.2
Brunswick, GA	555	474	1,739	1,265	94	221	-127	0.5	19,326	20.8
Buffalo–Niagara Falls, NY	-1,470	348	14,876	14,528	-1,714	1,451	-3,165	-0.1	-34,602	-3.0
Burlington, NC	2,160	497	2,285	1,788	1,666	474	1,192	1.4	20,331	15.5
Burlington–South Burlington, VT	1,273	931	2,584	1,653	359	278	81	0.6	12,372	6.2
Canton–Massillon, OH	-553	472	5,603	5,131	-998	78	-1,076	-0.1	-2,512	-0.6
Cape Coral–Fort Myers, FL	12,576	511	7,817	7,306	12,119	2,560	9,559	2.0	177,866	40.3
Cape Girardeau–Jackson, MO–IL	749	329	1,443	1,114	416	51	365	0.8	5,963	6.6
Carson City, NV	165	65	827	762	106	140	-34	0.3	2,817	5.4
Casper, WY	916	452	1,286	834	461	27	434	1.2	8,917	13.4
Cedar Rapids, IA	2,635	1,534	4,067	2,533	1,110	211	899	1.0	20,710	8.7
Champaign–Urbana, IL	445	1,471	3,375	1,904	-1,036	983	-2,019	0.2	21,616	10.3
Charleston, WV	-608	-112	4,428	4,540	-467	106	-573	-0.2	-5,351	-1.7
Charleston–North Charleston–Summerville, SC	17,514	5,610	11,641	6,031	11,778	1,277	10,501	2.6	115,574	21.1
Charlotte–Gastonia–Rock Hill, NC–SC	37,434	16,246	30,650	14,404	21,068	5,785	15,283	2.1	427,590	32.1
Charlottesville, VA	2,323	1,113	2,847	1,734	1,205	703	502	1.2	27,538	15.8
Chattanooga, TN–GA	5,229	1,473	7,820	6,347	3,750	408	3,342	1.0	51,612	10.8
Cheyenne, WY	942	702	1,582	880	242	88	154	1.0	10,131	12.4
Chicago–Joliet–Naperville, IL–IN–WI	43,648	77,631	160,436	82,805	-34,206	30,468	-64,674	0.5	362,789	4.0
Chicago–Joliet–Naperville, IL	39,419	67,410	135,691	68,281	-28,169	27,652	-55,821	0.5	254,735	3.3
Gary, IN	602	3,006	11,080	8,074	-2,398	468	-2,866	0.1	32,099	4.7
Lake County–Kenosha County, IL–WI	3,627	7,215	13,665	6,450	-3,639	2,348	-5,987	0.4	75,955	9.6

[1]Includes residual not shown separately.

Table B-2. Components of Population Change—*Continued*

Metropolitan statistical area and division	Components of population change, April 1, 2010 (estimates base) to July 1, 2011								Population change, April 1, 2000 to April 1, 2010	
	Number							Percent change	Number	Percent change
	Total population change[1]	Natural increase			Total migration	Net international migration	Net domestic migration			
		Total	Births	Deaths						
Chico, CA	266	290	3,009	2,719	-3	309	-312	0.1	16,829	8.3
Cincinnati–Middletown, OH–KY–IN	7,887	13,408	35,743	22,335	-5,512	2,771	-8,283	0.4	120,519	6.0
Clarksville, TN–KY	3,752	3,534	6,027	2,493	168	705	-537	1.4	41,949	18.1
Cleveland, TN	1,046	283	1,656	1,373	767	143	624	0.9	11,773	11.3
Cleveland–Elyria–Mentor, OH	-8,957	4,336	29,308	24,972	-13,301	2,373	-15,674	-0.4	-70,903	-3.3
Coeur d'Alene, ID	2,638	704	2,150	1,446	1,920	57	1,863	1.9	29,809	27.4
College Station–Bryan, TX	2,963	2,351	3,845	1,494	611	1,144	-533	1.3	43,775	23.7
Colorado Springs, CO	14,706	6,714	11,383	4,669	7,871	1,223	6,648	2.3	108,129	20.1
Columbia, MO	3,045	1,421	2,675	1,254	1,611	475	1,136	1.8	27,120	18.6
Columbia, SC	9,512	4,794	12,222	7,428	4,702	1,550	3,152	1.2	120,440	18.6
Columbus, GA–AL	6,574	2,036	5,384	3,348	4,472	452	4,020	2.2	13,097	4.6
Columbus, IN	1,076	453	1,262	809	624	366	258	1.4	5,359	7.5
Columbus, OH	21,928	15,555	32,300	16,745	6,408	4,134	2,274	1.2	223,842	13.9
Corpus Christi, TX	3,196	3,187	7,501	4,314	9	559	-550	0.7	24,905	6.2
Corvallis, OR	347	266	944	678	81	327	-246	0.4	7,426	9.5
Crestview–Fort Walton Beach–Destin, FL	2,660	1,238	3,138	1,900	1,407	542	865	1.5	10,324	6.1
Cumberland, MD–WV	-415	-239	1,296	1,535	-167	39	-206	-0.4	1,291	1.3
Dallas–Fort Worth–Arlington, TX	154,774	79,464	124,562	45,098	74,789	28,732	46,057	2.4	1,210,229	23.4
Dallas–Plano–Irving, TX	110,038	54,874	83,523	28,649	54,718	21,571	33,147	2.6	784,525	22.7
Fort Worth–Arlington, TX	44,736	24,590	41,039	16,449	20,071	7,161	12,910	2.1	425,704	24.9
Dalton, GA	514	1,190	2,538	1,348	-682	321	-1,003	0.4	22,196	18.5
Danville, IL	-116	200	1,340	1,140	-310	59	-369	-0.1	-2,294	-2.7
Danville, VA	-865	-317	1,357	1,674	-544	50	-594	-0.8	-3,595	-3.3
Davenport–Moline–Rock Island, IA–IL	1,652	1,701	5,971	4,270	-44	492	-536	0.4	3,671	1.0
Dayton, OH	3,886	2,835	12,833	9,998	1,149	694	455	0.5	-6,651	-0.8
Decatur, AL	241	415	2,274	1,859	-160	220	-380	0.2	7,962	5.5
Decatur, IL	-38	380	1,781	1,401	-413	70	-483	0.0	-3,938	-3.4
Deltona–Daytona Beach–Ormond Beach, FL	207	-1,430	5,912	7,342	1,723	712	1,011	0.0	51,250	11.6
Denver–Aurora–Broomfield, CO[2]	56,022	24,998	43,696	18,698	30,765	6,742	24,023	2.2	364,242	16.7
Des Moines–West Des Moines, IA	10,622	5,399	10,363	4,964	5,190	1,131	4,059	1.9	88,239	18.3
Detroit–Warren–Livonia, MI	-10,415	15,050	62,764	47,714	-25,680	8,906	-34,586	-0.2	-156,307	-3.5
Detroit–Livonia–Dearborn, MI	-18,488	7,925	29,904	21,979	-26,718	3,610	-30,328	-1.0	-240,578	-11.7
Warren–Troy–Farmington Hills, MI	8,073	7,125	32,860	25,735	1,038	5,296	-4,258	0.3	84,271	3.5
Dothan, AL	923	337	2,256	1,919	595	103	492	0.6	14,778	11.3
Dover, DE	2,524	982	2,752	1,770	1,544	305	1,239	1.6	35,613	28.1
Dubuque, IA	995	434	1,485	1,051	565	51	514	1.1	4,510	5.1
Duluth, MN–WI	44	132	3,647	3,515	-62	107	-169	0.0	4,285	1.6
Durham–Chapel Hill, NC	8,622	4,015	8,199	4,184	4,608	2,850	1,758	1.7	77,864	18.3
Eau Claire, WI	1,506	826	2,366	1,540	686	109	577	0.9	12,814	8.6
El Centro, CA	2,529	2,703	3,771	1,068	-171	757	-928	1.4	32,167	22.6
Elizabethtown, KY	2,029	1,037	2,250	1,213	958	191	767	1.7	12,189	11.3
Elkhart–Goshen, IN	1,380	2,008	3,831	1,823	-638	458	-1,096	0.7	14,768	8.1
Elmira, NY	10	47	1,222	1,175	-26	25	-51	0.0	-2,240	-2.5
El Paso, TX	20,143	11,552	17,270	5,718	8,533	2,707	5,826	2.5	121,025	17.8
Erie, PA	419	645	3,989	3,344	-217	183	-400	0.1	-277	-0.1
Eugene–Springfield, OR	1,701	563	4,375	3,812	1,163	562	601	0.5	28,756	8.9
Evansville, IN–KY	1,203	1,025	5,516	4,491	211	258	-47	0.3	15,861	4.6
Fairbanks, AK	1,611	1,604	2,082	478	3	317	-314	1.7	14,741	17.8
Fargo, ND–MN	3,394	2,070	3,695	1,625	1,327	392	935	1.6	34,410	19.7
Farmington, NM	-1,844	1,488	2,611	1,123	-3,377	46	-3,423	-1.4	16,243	14.3
Fayetteville, NC	7,774	5,492	8,455	2,963	2,246	1,045	1,201	2.1	29,774	8.8
Fayetteville–Springdale–Rogers, AR–MO	10,623	4,732	8,549	3,817	5,831	1,318	4,513	2.3	116,159	33.5
Flagstaff, AZ	93	1,365	2,238	873	-1,286	193	-1,479	0.1	18,101	15.6
Flint, MI	-3,710	1,449	6,543	5,094	-5,223	89	-5,312	-0.9	-10,351	-2.4
Florence, SC	595	619	3,292	2,673	-11	179	-190	0.3	12,411	6.4
Florence–Muscle Shoals, AL	156	-176	1,930	2,106	352	85	267	0.1	4,187	2.9
Fond du Lac, WI	446	367	1,446	1,079	89	146	-57	0.4	4,337	4.5
Fort Collins–Loveland, CO	5,895	2,053	4,227	2,174	3,826	343	3,483	2.0	48,136	19.1
Fort Smith, AR–OK	1,495	1,265	4,878	3,613	241	314	-73	0.5	25,422	9.3
Fort Wayne, IN	3,196	3,484	7,614	4,130	-265	436	-701	0.8	26,101	6.7
Fresno, CA	12,454	12,196	19,885	7,689	266	3,234	-2,968	1.3	131,043	16.4
Gadsden, AL	-127	-280	1,530	1,810	163	96	67	-0.1	971	0.9
Gainesville, FL	2,094	1,408	3,751	2,343	695	1,076	-381	0.8	31,883	13.7
Gainesville, GA	3,368	1,793	3,314	1,521	1,578	1,074	504	1.9	40,407	29.0
Glens Falls, NY	75	26	1,566	1,540	56	53	3	0.1	4,578	3.7
Goldsboro, NC	1,074	505	2,005	1,500	578	220	358	0.9	9,294	8.2
Grand Forks, ND–MN	-407	582	1,591	1,009	-1,001	151	-1,152	-0.4	983	1.0
Grand Junction, CO	360	815	2,413	1,598	-459	187	-646	0.2	30,468	26.2
Grand Rapids–Wyoming, MI	5,444	6,274	13,254	6,980	-818	1,126	-1,944	0.7	33,678	4.5
Great Falls, MT	510	547	1,444	897	-28	60	-88	0.6	970	1.2

[1]Includes residual not shown separately.
[2]The Denver–Aurora metropolitan statistical area includes Broomfield County. Broomfield County, CO, was formed from parts of Adams, Boulder, Jefferson, and Weld counties on November 15, 2001, and is coextensive with Broomfield city. For the purposes of defining and presenting data for the Denver–Aurora metropolitan statistical area, Broomfield city is treated as if it were a county when data are available to do so. In many cases, the data will not be available.

Table B-2.   Components of Population Change—*Continued*

Metropolitan statistical area and division	Components of population change, April 1, 2010 (estimates base) to July 1, 2011								Population change, April 1, 2000 to April 1, 2010	
	Number							Percent change	Number	Percent change
	Total population change[1]	Natural increase			Total migration	Net international migration	Net domestic migration			
		Total	Births	Deaths						
Greeley, CO	5,813	3,069	4,735	1,666	2,716	412	2,304	2.3	71,899	39.7
Green Bay, WI	3,228	2,391	5,014	2,623	850	468	382	1.1	23,642	8.4
Greensboro–High Point, NC	7,168	2,870	10,701	7,831	4,308	2,032	2,276	1.0	80,371	12.5
Greenville, NC	3,180	1,328	3,024	1,696	1,839	237	1,602	1.7	36,738	24.0
Greenville–Mauldin–Easley, SC	10,413	5,311	12,031	6,720	5,097	1,710	3,387	1.6	77,046	13.8
Gulfport–Biloxi, MS	4,691	1,628	4,231	2,603	3,037	605	2,432	1.9	2,630	1.1
Hagerstown–Martinsburg, MD–WV	2,348	993	3,965	2,972	1,362	257	1,105	0.9	46,369	20.8
Hanford–Corcoran, CA	783	2,171	3,128	957	-1,416	670	-2,086	0.5	23,521	18.2
Harrisburg–Carlisle, PA	3,436	1,923	7,873	5,950	1,522	844	678	0.6	40,401	7.9
Harrisonburg, VA	1,334	623	1,728	1,105	722	320	402	1.1	17,035	15.7
Hartford–West Hartford–East Hartford, CT	874	3,154	15,407	12,253	-2,198	3,850	-6,048	0.1	63,763	5.6
Hattiesburg, MS	2,586	1,142	2,546	1,404	1,430	227	1,203	1.8	19,030	15.4
Hickory–Lenoir–Morganton, NC	-930	420	4,857	4,437	-1,345	608	-1,953	-0.3	23,646	6.9
Hinesville–Fort Stewart, GA	2,670	1,539	1,978	439	1,063	348	715	3.4	6,003	8.3
Holland–Grand Haven, MI	2,499	1,979	3,965	1,986	535	184	351	0.9	25,487	10.7
Honolulu, HI	10,400	8,080	16,566	8,486	2,409	4,279	-1,870	1.1	77,051	8.8
Hot Springs, AR	1,102	-151	1,380	1,531	1,246	146	1,100	1.1	7,956	9.0
Houma–Bayou Cane–Thibodaux, LA	405	1,572	3,724	2,152	-1,168	168	-1,336	0.2	13,701	7.0
Houston–Sugar Land–Baytown, TX	139,699	80,133	121,794	41,661	59,340	30,016	29,324	2.3	1,231,393	26.1
Huntington–Ashland, WV–KY–OH	-101	1	4,097	4,096	-78	121	-199	0.0	-947	-0.3
Huntsville, AL	7,887	2,435	6,414	3,979	5,395	482	4,913	1.9	75,217	22.0
Idaho Falls, ID	1,699	2,011	3,058	1,047	-309	143	-452	1.3	28,697	28.2
Indianapolis–Carmel, IN	22,327	16,106	32,209	16,103	6,155	3,724	2,431	1.3	231,137	15.2
Iowa City, IA	2,307	1,440	2,488	1,048	866	472	394	1.5	20,910	15.9
Ithaca, NY	159	410	1,139	729	-260	693	-953	0.2	5,063	5.2
Jackson, MI	-500	414	2,268	1,854	-916	92	-1,008	-0.3	1,826	1.2
Jackson, MS	6,337	3,631	9,327	5,696	2,709	490	2,219	1.2	41,860	8.4
Jackson, TN	-29	616	1,897	1,281	-648	110	-758	0.0	8,048	7.5
Jacksonville, FL	14,655	8,282	21,871	13,589	6,334	2,710	3,624	1.1	222,846	19.8
Jacksonville, NC	1,947	4,192	5,239	1,047	-2,304	686	-2,990	1.1	27,417	18.2
Janesville, WI	-239	802	2,428	1,626	-1,045	212	-1,257	-0.1	8,024	5.3
Jefferson City, MO	673	642	2,186	1,544	40	118	-78	0.4	9,755	7.0
Johnson City, TN	1,102	-74	2,577	2,651	1,187	185	1,002	0.6	17,109	9.4
Johnstown, PA	49	-589	1,662	2,251	625	50	575	0.0	-8,919	-5.8
Jonesboro, AR	1,803	639	2,084	1,445	1,156	102	1,054	1.5	13,264	12.3
Joplin, MO	1,331	1,049	3,103	2,054	295	128	167	0.8	18,196	11.6
Kalamazoo–Portage, MI	1,616	1,670	5,030	3,360	-39	508	-547	0.5	11,723	3.7
Kankakee–Bradley, IL	249	519	1,867	1,348	-266	111	-377	0.2	9,616	9.3
Kansas City, MO–KS	17,342	15,885	35,289	19,404	1,456	3,858	-2,402	0.9	199,296	10.9
Kennewick–Pasco–Richland, WA	10,793	3,286	5,242	1,956	7,403	601	6,802	4.3	61,518	32.1
Killeen–Temple–Fort Hood, TX	6,295	6,090	9,048	2,958	142	1,441	-1,299	1.6	74,586	22.6
Kingsport–Bristol–Bristol, TN–VA	249	-606	3,801	4,407	886	132	754	0.1	11,060	3.7
Kingston, NY	-48	154	2,035	1,881	-193	323	-516	0.0	4,744	2.7
Knoxville, TN	6,470	1,862	10,020	8,158	4,624	780	3,844	0.9	81,951	13.3
Kokomo, IN	-100	73	1,353	1,280	-165	67	-232	-0.1	-2,853	-2.8
La Crosse, WI–MN	823	519	1,903	1,384	315	122	193	0.6	6,827	5.4
Lafayette, IN	1,819	1,527	3,144	1,617	292	755	-463	0.9	23,248	13.0
Lafayette, LA	3,569	2,503	5,068	2,565	1,078	317	761	1.3	34,652	14.5
Lake Charles, LA	1,215	1,227	3,567	2,340	-3	115	-118	0.6	6,039	3.1
Lake Havasu City–Kingman, AZ	2,165	-506	2,588	3,094	2,673	283	2,390	1.1	45,154	29.1
Lakeland–Winter Haven, FL	7,397	2,120	9,196	7,076	5,304	2,229	3,075	1.2	118,171	24.4
Lancaster, PA	4,146	3,311	8,918	5,607	898	765	133	0.8	48,787	10.4
Lansing–East Lansing, MI	1,102	2,261	6,399	4,138	-1,166	1,074	-2,240	0.2	16,308	3.6
Laredo, TX	6,192	5,640	7,041	1,401	551	1,218	-667	2.5	57,187	29.6
Las Cruces, NM	4,364	2,340	4,079	1,739	2,011	559	1,452	2.1	34,551	19.8
Las Vegas–Paradise, NV	18,706	17,954	34,395	16,441	699	9,894	-9,195	1.0	575,504	41.8
Lawrence, KS	1,385	834	1,539	705	553	427	126	1.2	10,864	10.9
Lawton, OK	1,717	1,451	2,580	1,129	233	351	-118	1.4	9,102	7.9
Lebanon, PA	738	297	2,021	1,724	459	193	266	0.6	13,241	11.0
Lewiston, ID–WA	588	-4	855	859	594	43	551	1.0	2,927	5.0
Lewiston–Auburn, ME	-306	431	1,659	1,228	-741	151	-892	-0.3	3,909	3.8
Lexington–Fayette, KY	7,145	3,569	7,869	4,300	3,560	1,720	1,840	1.5	63,773	15.6
Lima, OH	-237	362	1,669	1,307	-602	61	-663	-0.2	-2,142	-2.0
Lincoln, NE	4,346	2,932	5,361	2,429	1,426	595	831	1.4	35,370	13.3
Little Rock–North Little Rock–Conway, AR	10,142	4,883	12,019	7,136	5,240	1,308	3,932	1.4	89,239	14.6
Logan, UT–ID	2,107	2,643	3,321	678	-544	225	-769	1.7	22,722	22.1
Longview, TX	2,288	1,239	3,904	2,665	1,060	387	673	1.1	20,327	10.5
Longview, WA	68	326	1,533	1,207	-253	108	-361	0.1	9,462	10.2
Los Angeles–Long Beach–Santa Ana, CA	115,964	118,726	212,915	94,189	-3,197	68,197	-71,394	0.9	463,210	3.7
Los Angeles–Long Beach–Glendale, CA	70,451	92,391	165,146	72,755	-22,519	52,981	-75,500	0.7	299,267	3.1
Santa Ana–Anaheim–Irvine, CA	45,513	26,335	47,769	21,434	19,322	15,216	4,106	1.5	163,943	5.8
Louisville/Jefferson County, KY–IN	11,284	6,761	20,673	13,912	4,572	2,143	2,429	0.9	121,591	10.5

[1]Includes residual not shown separately.

Table B-2. Components of Population Change—*Continued*

Metropolitan statistical area and division	Components of population change, April 1, 2010 (estimates base) to July 1, 2011								Population change, April 1, 2000 to April 1, 2010	
	Number							Percent change	Number	Percent change
	Total population change[1]	Natural increase			Total migration	Net international migration	Net domestic migration			
		Total	Births	Deaths						
Lubbock, TX	5,112	2,525	5,437	2,912	2,570	387	2,183	1.8	35,190	14.1
Lynchburg, VA	1,533	487	3,361	2,874	1,060	289	771	0.6	24,018	10.5
Macon, GA	627	1,059	3,980	2,921	-427	214	-641	0.3	9,925	4.5
Madera–Chowchilla, CA	2,060	1,857	2,961	1,104	212	636	-424	1.4	27,756	22.5
Madison, WI	7,874	4,505	8,755	4,250	3,359	1,301	2,058	1.4	66,819	13.3
Manchester–Nashua, NH	975	2,174	5,555	3,381	-1,204	896	-2,100	0.2	19,880	5.2
Manhattan, KS	3,159	2,212	3,068	856	909	576	333	2.5	18,082	16.6
Mankato–North Mankato, MN	464	550	1,400	850	-82	196	-278	0.5	11,028	12.9
Mansfield, OH	-965	289	1,858	1,569	-1,263	13	-1,276	-0.8	-4,377	-3.4
McAllen–Edinburg–Mission, TX	23,041	16,347	20,909	4,562	6,694	4,270	2,424	3.0	205,306	36.1
Medford, OR	1,616	360	2,865	2,505	1,272	227	1,045	0.8	21,937	12.1
Memphis, TN–MS–AR	9,505	10,791	24,186	13,395	-1,288	2,341	-3,629	0.7	110,896	9.2
Merced, CA	4,105	3,412	5,283	1,871	698	1,134	-436	1.6	45,239	21.5
Miami–Fort Lauderdale–Pompano Beach, FL	105,490	25,220	81,921	56,701	80,259	43,538	36,721	1.9	557,071	11.1
Fort Lauderdale–Pompano Beach–Deerfield Beach, FL	32,106	8,175	26,039	17,864	23,899	11,988	11,911	1.8	125,048	7.7
Miami–Miami Beach–Kendall, FL	58,331	16,255	38,820	22,565	41,972	24,919	17,053	2.3	243,073	10.8
West Palm Beach–Boca Raton–Boynton Beach, FL	15,053	790	17,062	16,272	14,388	6,631	7,757	1.1	188,950	16.7
Michigan City–La Porte, IN	-93	256	1,669	1,413	-347	72	-419	-0.1	1,361	1.2
Midland, TX	3,436	1,557	2,774	1,217	1,849	108	1,741	2.5	20,863	18.0
Milwaukee–Waukesha–West Allis, WI	6,308	10,579	26,115	15,536	-4,194	2,316	-6,510	0.4	55,167	3.7
Minneapolis–St. Paul–Bloomington, MN–WI	38,653	30,470	54,901	24,431	8,224	9,892	-1,668	1.2	311,027	10.5
Missoula, MT	839	539	1,475	936	303	79	224	0.8	13,497	14.1
Mobile, AL	-413	2,023	7,099	5,076	-2,445	383	-2,828	-0.1	13,149	3.3
Modesto, CA	4,069	5,269	9,588	4,319	-1,216	1,743	-2,959	0.8	67,456	15.1
Monroe, LA	1,210	1,105	3,262	2,157	123	98	25	0.7	6,388	3.8
Monroe, MI	-461	520	2,079	1,559	-986	65	-1,051	-0.3	6,076	4.2
Montgomery, AL	4,072	2,097	6,156	4,059	1,970	530	1,440	1.1	28,008	8.1
Morgantown, WV	2,542	406	1,579	1,173	2,112	295	1,817	2.0	18,509	16.6
Morristown, TN	884	104	1,963	1,859	788	289	499	0.6	13,527	11.0
Mount Vernon–Anacortes, WA	1,208	493	1,848	1,355	729	475	254	1.0	13,922	13.5
Muncie, IN	-11	199	1,597	1,398	-203	125	-328	0.0	-1,098	-0.9
Muskegon–Norton Shores, MI	-886	751	2,774	2,023	-1,654	47	-1,701	-0.5	1,988	1.2
Myrtle Beach–North Myrtle Beach–Conway, SC	7,049	708	3,870	3,162	6,312	794	5,518	2.6	72,662	37.0
Napa, CA	1,604	449	1,941	1,492	1,161	727	434	1.2	12,205	9.8
Naples–Marco Island, FL	6,614	755	4,174	3,419	5,941	2,503	3,438	2.1	70,143	27.9
Nashville–Davidson—Murfreesboro—Franklin, TN	27,208	12,427	26,966	14,539	14,699	3,886	10,813	1.7	278,145	21.2
New Haven–Milford, CT	-1,364	2,389	11,460	9,071	-3,728	2,361	-6,089	-0.2	38,469	4.7
New Orleans–Metairie–Kenner, LA	23,325	7,033	19,364	12,331	16,006	2,138	13,868	2.0	-148,746	-11.3
New York–Northern New Jersey–Long Island, NY–NJ–PA	118,791	140,465	306,195	165,730	-21,038	103,521	-124,559	0.6	574,107	3.1
Edison–New Brunswick, NJ	9,248	9,489	34,134	24,645	-173	9,651	-9,824	0.4	166,380	7.7
Nassau–Suffolk, NY	10,370	12,104	39,231	27,127	-1,495	4,782	-6,277	0.4	78,969	2.9
Newark–Union, NJ–PA	5,289	11,963	31,100	19,137	-6,651	9,692	-16,343	0.2	48,884	2.3
New York–White Plains–Wayne, NY–NJ	93,884	106,909	201,730	94,821	-12,719	79,396	-92,115	0.8	279,874	2.5
Niles–Benton Harbor, MI	128	399	2,377	1,978	-260	128	-388	0.1	-5,640	-3.5
North Port–Bradenton–Sarasota, FL	7,074	-2,484	7,717	10,201	9,619	2,134	7,485	1.0	112,322	19.0
Norwich–New London, CT	-553	585	3,414	2,829	-1,148	754	-1,902	-0.2	14,967	5.8
Ocala, FL	1,231	-962	4,210	5,172	2,244	368	1,876	0.4	72,382	28.0
Ocean City, NJ	-664	-401	1,171	1,572	-255	104	-359	-0.7	-5,061	-4.9
Odessa, TX	2,981	1,900	3,340	1,440	1,056	107	949	2.2	16,007	13.2
Ogden–Clearfield, UT	8,732	8,988	12,580	3,592	-256	728	-984	1.6	104,528	23.6
Oklahoma City, OK	25,066	11,240	23,482	12,242	13,730	2,922	10,808	2.0	157,566	14.4
Olympia, WA	4,327	1,504	3,763	2,259	2,811	321	2,490	1.7	44,909	21.7
Omaha–Council Bluffs, NE–IA	11,760	8,901	16,449	7,548	2,887	1,810	1,077	1.4	98,309	12.8
Orlando–Kissimmee–Sanford, FL	36,949	14,308	32,418	18,110	22,629	12,360	10,269	1.7	489,850	29.8
Oshkosh–Neenah, WI	705	707	2,403	1,696	14	117	-103	0.4	10,231	6.5
Owensboro, KY	578	537	1,942	1,405	52	63	-11	0.5	4,877	4.4
Oxnard–Thousand Oaks–Ventura, CA	8,453	7,394	13,769	6,375	1,089	2,528	-1,439	1.0	70,121	9.3
Palm Bay–Melbourne–Titusville, FL	194	-1,151	6,140	7,291	1,415	751	664	0.0	67,146	14.1
Palm Coast, FL	1,680	-129	1,057	1,186	1,807	153	1,654	1.8	45,864	92.0
Panama City–Lynn Haven–Panama City Beach, FL	1,004	743	2,745	2,002	267	396	-129	0.6	20,635	13.9
Parkersburg–Marietta–Vienna, WV–OH	192	-127	2,139	2,266	339	41	298	0.1	-2,568	-1.6
Pascagoula, MS	544	748	2,576	1,828	-191	352	-543	0.3	11,682	7.8
Pensacola–Ferry Pass–Brent, FL	4,227	1,848	7,065	5,217	2,391	714	1,677	0.9	36,838	8.9
Peoria, IL	370	1,617	6,175	4,558	-1,225	383	-1,608	0.1	12,287	3.3
Philadelphia–Camden–Wilmington, PA–NJ–DE–MD	27,071	28,694	93,001	64,307	-1,284	14,618	-15,902	0.5	278,196	4.9
Camden, NJ	1,242	5,158	17,997	12,839	-3,886	2,357	-6,243	0.1	63,680	5.4
Philadelphia, PA	21,932	19,791	64,204	44,413	2,413	10,385	-7,972	0.5	159,347	4.1
Wilmington, DE–MD–NJ	3,897	3,745	10,800	7,055	189	1,876	-1,687	0.6	55,169	8.5

[1]Includes residual not shown separately.

Table B-2. Components of Population Change—*Continued*

Metropolitan statistical area and division	Components of population change, April 1, 2010 (estimates base) to July 1, 2011								Population change, April 1, 2000 to April 1, 2010	
	Number							Percent change	Number	Percent change
	Total population change[1]	Natural increase			Total migration	Net international migration	Net domestic migration			
		Total	Births	Deaths						
Phoenix–Mesa–Glendale, AZ	70,349	40,513	73,940	33,427	29,778	19,701	10,077	1.7	941,011	28.9
Pine Bluff, AR	-1,334	176	1,503	1,327	-1,523	44	-1,567	-1.3	-7,083	-6.6
Pittsburgh, PA	3,461	-3,864	29,699	33,563	7,513	1,805	5,708	0.1	-74,802	-3.1
Pittsfield, MA	-761	-319	1,387	1,706	-432	155	-587	-0.6	-3,734	-2.8
Pocatello, ID	801	1,110	1,955	845	-312	132	-444	0.9	7,553	9.1
Portland–South Portland–Biddeford, ME	1,707	612	6,198	5,586	1,116	319	797	0.3	26,530	5.4
Portland–Vancouver–Hillsboro, OR–WA	36,596	17,135	35,976	18,841	19,477	6,213	13,264	1.6	298,128	15.5
Port St. Lucie, FL	3,767	-290	5,245	5,535	4,107	1,169	2,938	0.9	104,681	32.8
Poughkeepsie–Newburgh–Middletown, NY	2,570	4,038	9,970	5,932	-1,460	1,340	-2,800	0.4	48,784	7.8
Prescott, AZ	855	-545	2,322	2,867	1,460	427	1,033	0.4	43,516	26.0
Providence–New Bedford–Fall River, RI–MA	-628	3,783	21,302	17,519	-4,369	3,266	-7,635	0.0	17,855	1.1
Provo–Orem, UT	14,024	12,761	15,202	2,441	1,266	1,284	-18	2.7	150,036	39.8
Pueblo, CO	1,482	506	2,447	1,941	978	161	817	0.9	17,591	12.4
Punta Gorda, FL	533	-1,527	1,217	2,744	2,093	179	1,914	0.3	18,351	13.0
Racine, WI	-20	1,276	3,180	1,904	-1,301	185	-1,486	0.0	6,577	3.5
Raleigh–Cary, NC	33,025	11,956	19,396	7,440	20,866	4,012	16,854	2.9	333,419	41.8
Rapid City, SD	1,979	1,232	2,319	1,087	753	135	618	1.6	13,564	12.0
Reading, PA	1,339	1,840	6,241	4,401	-501	757	-1,258	0.3	37,804	10.1
Redding, CA	551	234	2,577	2,343	342	140	202	0.3	13,967	8.6
Reno–Sparks, NV	4,189	2,986	6,860	3,874	1,237	1,420	-183	1.0	82,532	24.1
Richmond, VA	11,129	6,992	19,090	12,098	4,188	2,615	1,573	0.9	161,294	14.7
Riverside–San Bernardino–Ontario, CA	80,146	44,249	76,738	32,489	35,708	11,161	24,547	1.9	970,030	29.8
Roanoke, VA	154	168	4,172	4,004	-4	311	-315	0.0	20,398	7.1
Rochester, MN	1,601	1,821	3,286	1,465	-215	473	-688	0.9	22,393	13.7
Rochester, NY	955	3,408	14,424	11,016	-2,425	1,543	-3,968	0.1	16,492	1.6
Rockford, IL	-1,071	1,953	5,556	3,603	-3,061	506	-3,567	-0.3	29,227	9.1
Rocky Mount, NC	-235	433	2,361	1,928	-668	187	-855	-0.2	9,366	6.5
Rome, GA	-328	352	1,604	1,252	-687	237	-924	-0.3	5,752	6.4
Sacramento—Arden-Arcade—Roseville, CA	27,108	15,818	34,428	18,610	11,339	7,732	3,607	1.3	352,270	19.6
Saginaw–Saginaw Township North, MI	-1,081	505	2,967	2,462	-1,598	119	-1,717	-0.5	-9,870	-4.7
St. Cloud, MN	921	1,690	3,124	1,434	-773	130	-903	0.5	21,701	13.0
St. George, UT	3,551	1,807	3,029	1,222	1,750	246	1,504	2.6	47,761	52.9
St. Joseph, MO–KS	245	566	2,052	1,486	-320	84	-404	0.2	4,993	4.1
St. Louis, MO–IL[5]	4,464	12,842	43,490	30,648	-8,311	3,513	-11,824	0.2	114,209	4.2
Salem, OR	4,127	2,918	6,856	3,938	1,243	1,229	14	1.1	43,524	12.5
Salinas, CA	6,841	5,640	8,471	2,831	1,237	2,292	-1,055	1.6	13,295	3.3
Salisbury, MD	326	406	1,876	1,470	-75	303	-378	0.3	15,812	14.5
Salt Lake City, UT	21,708	17,150	24,576	7,426	4,587	3,820	767	1.9	155,339	16.0
San Angelo, TX	1,620	785	1,969	1,184	831	150	681	1.4	6,042	5.7
San Antonio–New Braunfels, TX	52,419	21,841	39,699	17,858	30,253	5,050	25,203	2.4	430,805	25.2
San Diego–Carlsbad–San Marcos, CA	44,756	30,790	54,908	24,118	14,154	12,757	1,397	1.4	281,480	10.0
Sandusky, OH	-328	-105	967	1,072	-217	12	-229	-0.4	-2,472	-3.1
San Francisco–Oakland–Fremont, CA	55,646	29,674	64,440	34,766	26,124	22,305	3,819	1.3	211,651	5.1
Oakland–Fremont–Hayward, CA	36,675	19,388	39,392	20,004	17,317	12,777	4,540	1.4	166,739	7.0
San Francisco–San Mateo–Redwood City, CA	18,971	10,286	25,048	14,762	8,807	9,528	-721	1.1	44,912	2.6
San Jose–Sunnyvale–Santa Clara, CA	28,539	19,085	30,763	11,678	9,525	13,711	-4,186	1.6	101,092	5.8
San Luis Obispo–Paso Robles, CA	2,332	717	3,301	2,584	1,629	380	1,249	0.9	22,956	9.3
Santa Barbara–Santa Maria–Goleta, CA	2,983	3,718	7,269	3,551	-736	1,903	-2,639	0.7	24,548	6.1
Santa Cruz–Watsonville, CA	1,916	1,850	3,984	2,134	73	856	-783	0.7	6,780	2.7
Santa Fe, NM	1,480	598	1,766	1,168	893	715	178	1.0	14,878	11.5
Santa Rosa–Petaluma, CA	4,238	2,095	6,777	4,682	2,188	1,266	922	0.9	25,264	5.5
Savannah, GA	7,960	2,774	6,202	3,428	5,134	606	4,528	2.3	54,611	18.6
Scranton–Wilkes-Barre, PA	-407	-1,518	7,051	8,569	1,178	602	576	-0.1	3,006	0.5
Seattle–Tacoma–Bellevue, WA	60,217	28,062	55,592	27,530	32,130	15,251	16,879	1.8	395,931	13.0
Seattle–Bellevue–Everett, WA	47,538	21,662	41,930	20,268	25,933	13,692	12,241	1.8	301,526	12.9
Tacoma, WA	12,679	6,400	13,662	7,262	6,197	1,559	4,638	1.6	94,405	13.5
Sebastian–Vero Beach, FL	866	-564	1,578	2,142	1,453	350	1,103	0.6	25,081	22.2
Sheboygan, WI	-358	386	1,652	1,266	-747	127	-874	-0.3	2,861	2.5
Sherman–Denison, TX	542	400	1,923	1,523	151	199	-48	0.4	10,282	9.3
Shreveport–Bossier City, LA	4,991	2,522	7,265	4,743	2,460	418	2,042	1.3	22,639	6.0
Sioux City, IA–NE–SD	485	1,249	2,722	1,473	-769	188	-957	0.3	524	0.4
Sioux Falls, SD	4,172	2,692	4,631	1,939	1,482	296	1,186	1.8	41,168	22.0
South Bend–Mishawaka, IN–MI	-534	1,504	5,057	3,553	-2,033	472	-2,505	-0.2	2,561	0.8
Spartanburg, SC	2,561	1,477	4,800	3,323	1,107	419	688	0.9	30,516	12.0
Spokane, WA	2,540	2,409	7,336	4,927	166	587	-421	0.5	53,282	12.7
Springfield, IL	1,377	600	3,158	2,558	787	106	681	0.7	8,733	4.3
Springfield, MA	262	1,726	9,125	7,399	-1,433	2,088	-3,521	0.0	12,928	1.9
Springfield, MO	3,430	2,179	7,000	4,821	1,272	229	1,043	0.8	68,338	18.6
Springfield, OH	-642	95	2,089	1,994	-732	64	-796	-0.5	-6,409	-4.4
State College, PA	737	444	1,580	1,136	285	513	-228	0.5	18,232	13.4
Steubenville–Weirton, OH–WV	-1,211	-716	1,441	2,157	-473	21	-494	-1.0	-7,554	-5.7

[1]Includes residual not shown separately.
[3]The portion of Sullivan city in Crawford County, MO, is legally part of the St. Louis, MO–IL MSA. That portion is not included in these figures for the St. Louis MSA.

Table B-2. Components of Population Change—*Continued*

Metropolitan statistical area and division	Components of population change, April 1, 2010 (estimates base) to July 1, 2011								Population change, April 1, 2000 to April 1, 2010	
	Number							Percent change	Number	Percent change
	Total population change[1]	Natural increase			Total migration	Net international migration	Net domestic migration			
		Total	Births	Deaths						
Stockton, CA	10,908	7,441	13,131	5,690	3,504	2,409	1,095	1.6	121,708	21.6
Sumter, SC	4	741	1,952	1,211	-745	158	-903	0.0	2,810	2.7
Syracuse, NY	-26	2,512	9,325	6,813	-2,518	911	-3,429	0.0	12,423	1.9
Tallahassee, FL	2,345	2,169	5,167	2,998	187	762	-575	0.6	47,109	14.7
Tampa–St. Petersburg–Clearwater, FL	41,481	2,761	38,448	35,687	38,564	8,642	29,922	1.5	387,246	16.2
Terre Haute, IN	240	165	2,389	2,224	92	135	-43	0.1	1,482	0.9
Texarkana, TX–Texarkana, AR	525	531	2,229	1,698	3	137	-134	0.4	6,278	4.8
Toledo, OH	-1,163	2,647	10,167	7,520	-3,848	553	-4,401	-0.2	-7,759	-1.2
Topeka, KS	777	1,102	3,806	2,704	-310	214	-524	0.3	9,319	4.2
Trenton–Ewing, NJ	552	2,050	5,462	3,412	-1,526	1,981	-3,507	0.2	15,752	4.5
Tucson, AZ	9,306	4,944	15,169	10,225	4,496	3,444	1,052	0.9	136,517	16.2
Tulsa, OK	9,484	6,824	16,952	10,128	2,698	1,715	983	1.0	77,946	9.1
Tuscaloosa, AL	2,095	1,085	3,425	2,340	1,005	427	578	1.0	27,427	14.3
Tyler, TX	3,667	1,532	3,845	2,313	2,136	325	1,811	1.7	35,008	20.0
Utica–Rome, NY	-950	195	4,030	3,835	-1,124	317	-1,441	-0.3	-499	-0.2
Valdosta, GA	2,723	1,288	2,674	1,386	1,410	205	1,205	1.9	20,028	16.8
Vallejo–Fairfield, CA	3,127	2,767	6,343	3,576	380	1,545	-1,165	0.8	18,802	4.8
Victoria, TX	846	880	2,121	1,241	-25	243	-268	0.7	3,721	3.3
Vineland–Millville–Bridgeton, NJ	197	1,177	2,867	1,690	-992	587	-1,579	0.1	10,460	7.1
Virginia Beach–Norfolk–Newport News, VA–NC	8,204	12,495	28,276	15,781	-4,380	4,024	-8,404	0.5	95,313	6.0
Visalia–Porterville, CA	7,074	6,752	10,053	3,301	337	1,674	-1,337	1.6	74,158	20.2
Waco, TX	3,658	1,792	4,197	2,405	1,855	477	1,378	1.6	21,389	10.0
Warner Robins, GA	4,014	1,234	2,493	1,259	2,743	256	2,487	2.9	29,135	26.3
Washington–Arlington–Alexandria, DC–VA–MD–WV	121,911	60,573	98,139	37,566	60,963	31,536	29,427	2.2	785,987	16.4
Bethesda–Rockville–Frederick, MD	21,377	11,672	19,959	8,287	9,771	8,119	1,652	1.8	136,544	12.8
Washington–Arlington–Alexandria, DC–VA–MD–WV	100,534	48,901	78,180	29,279	51,192	23,417	27,775	2.3	649,443	17.4
Waterloo–Cedar Falls, IA	470	681	2,559	1,878	-192	183	-375	0.3	4,113	2.5
Wausau, WI	337	734	2,031	1,297	-395	166	-561	0.3	8,229	6.5
Wenatchee–East Wenatchee, WA	1,564	794	1,935	1,141	779	293	486	1.4	11,665	11.8
Wheeling, WV–OH	-753	-428	1,899	2,327	-305	40	-345	-0.5	-5,222	-3.4
Wichita, KS	2,465	5,530	11,892	6,362	-3,080	776	-3,856	0.4	51,895	9.1
Wichita Falls, TX	-1,045	752	2,512	1,760	-1,821	386	-2,207	-0.7	-218	-0.1
Williamsport, PA	639	-78	1,517	1,595	723	33	690	0.5	-3,933	-3.3
Wilmington, NC	7,370	889	4,832	3,943	6,429	647	5,782	2.0	87,783	32.0
Winchester, VA–WV	1,593	648	1,927	1,279	939	191	748	1.2	25,475	24.7
Winston–Salem, NC	4,308	2,327	7,357	5,030	2,015	1,242	773	0.9	55,756	13.2
Worcester, MA	2,675	3,301	11,362	8,061	-591	2,183	-2,774	0.3	47,589	6.3
Yakima, WA	3,910	3,255	5,536	2,281	653	771	-118	1.6	20,650	9.3
York–Hanover, PA	1,798	1,887	6,309	4,422	-66	381	-447	0.4	53,221	13.9
Youngstown–Warren–Boardman, OH–PA	-3,034	-1,226	7,191	8,417	-1,764	37	-1,801	-0.5	-37,191	-6.2
Yuba City, CA	605	1,777	3,181	1,404	-1,191	807	-1,998	0.4	27,743	19.9
Yuma, AZ	5,120	2,266	3,930	1,664	2,844	840	2,004	2.6	35,725	22.3

[1]Includes residual not shown separately.

Table B-3. Population by Age, Race, and Sex

Metropolitan statistical area and division	Population characteristics, 2011																
	Age (percent)										One race (percent)					Hispanic or Latino origin[1] (percent)	Males per 100 females
	Under 5 years	5 to 14 years	15 to 24 years	25 to 34 years	35 to 44 years	45 to 54 years	55 to 64 years	65 to 74 years	75 to 84 years	85 years and over	White alone	Black or African American alone	Asian alone	American Indian, Alaska Native alone	Native Hawaiian and Other Pacific Islander alone		
Abilene, TX	7.0	12.8	16.6	14.1	11.4	13.3	11.2	7.1	4.7	1.8	87.3	7.9	1.5	1.0	0.1	21.8	100.8
Akron, OH	5.6	12.3	14.8	11.9	12.3	15.2	13.6	7.4	4.8	2.2	83.5	12.2	2.1	0.2	0.0	1.6	94.1
Albany, GA	7.2	14.2	15.7	12.8	12.2	13.5	12.3	6.9	3.8	1.5	44.9	52.5	1.1	0.3	0.2	2.4	91.4
Albany–Schenectady–Troy, NY	5.3	11.7	15.0	12.3	12.6	15.4	13.5	7.4	4.6	2.3	85.6	8.3	3.4	0.3	0.1	4.4	95.4
Albuquerque, NM	6.7	13.6	13.8	13.9	12.6	14.1	12.6	7.1	3.9	1.6	85.1	3.1	2.2	6.7	0.2	47.1	96.8
Alexandria, LA	7.0	14.0	13.2	13.6	12.3	14.2	12.2	7.7	4.4	1.6	66.6	29.8	1.1	0.9	0.0	2.9	97.4
Allentown–Bethlehem–Easton, PA–NJ	5.6	12.6	13.2	11.4	13.0	15.7	13.2	7.7	5.2	2.6	88.8	6.1	2.7	0.5	0.1	13.5	95.2
Altoona, PA	5.7	11.6	13.0	11.2	12.0	14.5	14.3	8.8	6.1	2.9	96.2	1.8	0.6	0.1	0.0	1.0	94.5
Amarillo, TX	7.6	14.5	14.9	14.2	12.3	13.3	11.4	6.4	4.0	1.5	87.7	6.7	2.8	1.1	0.1	26.2	99.7
Ames, IA	5.2	9.5	33.0	13.6	9.1	10.0	9.5	5.1	3.3	1.7	89.2	2.8	6.2	0.2	0.0	3.1	107.5
Anchorage, AK	7.5	14.4	15.1	15.2	13.1	15.0	12.0	5.0	2.1	0.7	71.8	4.8	6.8	7.6	1.7	6.9	103.6
Anderson, IN	6.1	12.7	13.0	12.5	12.9	14.2	13.0	8.4	5.1	2.2	89.1	8.4	0.4	0.4	0.0	3.4	99.9
Anderson, SC	6.3	13.3	12.5	11.6	13.1	14.6	13.2	8.8	4.8	1.8	80.9	16.6	0.8	0.3	0.0	3.1	93.3
Ann Arbor, MI	5.3	11.3	22.0	13.8	12.3	13.2	11.6	5.9	3.1	1.4	75.2	12.9	8.3	0.4	0.1	4.2	97.3
Anniston–Oxford, AL	6.1	12.9	14.5	12.5	12.2	14.1	13.3	8.2	4.8	1.6	76.2	20.9	0.8	0.5	0.1	3.4	92.8
Appleton, WI	6.5	14.2	12.6	13.3	13.6	16.0	11.9	6.3	3.9	1.8	93.3	1.0	2.9	1.5	0.0	3.7	99.8
Asheville, NC	5.4	11.3	11.3	12.1	12.7	14.1	14.5	10.1	6.0	2.6	91.9	4.8	1.0	0.6	0.1	6.6	93.2
Athens–Clarke County, GA	5.9	11.3	25.6	13.9	11.4	11.5	10.0	6.1	3.1	1.3	74.8	19.8	3.4	0.3	0.1	8.1	94.0
Atlanta–Sandy Springs–Marietta, GA	7.1	14.7	13.6	14.4	15.4	14.6	10.9	5.6	2.7	1.0	59.4	33.0	5.0	0.5	0.1	10.6	95.1
Atlantic City–Hammonton, NJ	6.0	12.7	13.6	11.5	12.7	16.0	13.0	7.9	4.6	2.0	71.8	17.3	7.9	0.7	0.1	17.3	94.5
Auburn–Opelika, AL	5.9	12.1	25.6	13.6	11.9	11.9	9.8	5.5	2.8	0.9	72.3	23.0	2.7	0.4	0.1	3.4	97.6
Augusta–Richmond County, GA–SC	6.6	13.6	14.2	13.4	12.3	14.4	12.7	7.4	4.0	1.4	59.9	35.6	1.9	0.4	0.1	4.7	94.8
Austin–Round Rock–San Marcos, TX	7.3	14.1	15.1	17.0	15.1	13.1	10.0	4.9	2.4	1.0	83.5	7.9	5.0	1.3	0.1	31.8	100.4
Bakersfield–Delano, CA	8.6	16.3	16.3	14.7	12.8	12.7	9.5	5.3	2.8	1.1	80.0	6.3	4.7	2.7	0.3	50.0	106.7
Baltimore–Towson, MD	6.2	12.6	13.8	13.7	13.0	15.4	12.6	6.9	4.0	1.9	63.4	29.1	4.8	0.4	0.1	4.8	93.0
Bangor, ME	5.1	10.9	16.5	11.6	11.9	15.5	13.9	7.8	5.0	2.0	95.5	0.8	1.0	1.2	0.0	1.1	97.3
Barnstable Town, MA	4.1	9.4	10.1	8.5	10.0	15.5	17.0	12.8	8.7	3.9	94.2	2.3	1.2	0.7	0.1	2.3	90.9
Baton Rouge, LA	6.8	13.4	16.2	14.6	12.5	13.7	11.7	6.4	3.3	1.3	60.8	35.8	1.9	0.3	0.0	3.6	96.5
Battle Creek, MI	6.3	13.3	13.6	11.6	12.1	14.6	13.5	7.7	5.0	2.2	83.6	11.1	1.6	0.7	0.1	4.6	95.6
Bay City, MI	5.6	12.3	12.3	11.6	11.8	15.3	14.5	8.7	5.2	2.6	95.2	1.7	0.6	0.6	0.0	4.7	96.2
Beaumont–Port Arthur, TX	6.8	13.3	14.1	13.6	12.4	14.6	12.1	6.9	4.5	1.7	70.3	24.8	2.6	0.8	0.1	13.5	102.3
Bellingham, WA	5.5	11.4	18.7	12.8	11.6	13.1	13.2	7.7	4.1	2.0	88.0	1.2	3.9	3.1	0.3	8.2	98.2
Bend, OR	5.9	12.8	11.1	12.5	13.2	14.1	14.7	9.2	4.4	2.0	94.8	0.4	1.0	1.1	0.2	7.7	97.5
Billings, MT	6.5	12.8	12.5	13.4	11.8	14.7	13.5	7.7	4.7	2.2	92.0	0.7	0.7	4.1	0.1	4.6	96.2
Binghamton, NY	5.2	11.5	15.5	11.5	11.0	15.5	13.4	8.1	5.7	2.7	90.3	4.3	3.0	0.2	0.1	3.1	96.5
Birmingham–Hoover, AL	6.6	13.2	12.9	13.8	13.2	14.5	12.8	7.3	4.3	1.7	68.5	28.6	1.3	0.4	0.1	4.4	93.0
Bismarck, ND	6.6	12.3	13.3	14.4	12.0	14.5	13.0	7.0	4.8	2.2	93.4	0.7	0.5	4.0	0.1	1.4	97.6
Blacksburg–Christiansburg–Radford, VA	4.5	9.1	29.1	11.5	10.9	11.2	11.0	7.1	3.9	1.6	89.6	4.6	3.7	0.3	0.0	2.3	102.1
Bloomington, IN	4.9	10.0	26.5	13.1	10.6	11.9	11.0	6.5	3.8	1.6	91.1	2.6	4.1	0.3	0.0	2.5	99.6
Bloomington–Normal, IL	6.2	12.4	21.8	13.4	12.1	13.1	10.7	5.4	3.3	1.6	85.5	7.6	4.5	0.3	0.0	4.6	94.5
Boise City–Nampa, ID	7.4	15.7	13.4	14.1	13.5	13.3	11.3	6.4	3.3	1.5	93.2	1.0	1.9	1.2	0.2	12.8	99.7
Boston–Cambridge–Quincy, MA–NH	5.6	11.9	14.1	13.9	13.4	15.4	12.4	6.9	4.3	2.1	82.3	8.5	6.8	0.4	0.1	9.3	94.0
Boston–Quincy, MA	5.6	11.6	15.2	14.9	13.2	14.5	11.9	6.8	4.2	2.0	76.7	13.9	6.8	0.4	0.1	9.9	93.1
Cambridge–Newton–Framingham, MA	5.7	11.7	13.1	14.8	13.8	15.4	12.3	6.8	4.4	2.1	82.8	5.2	9.8	0.3	0.1	6.8	94.9
Peabody, MA	5.8	12.8	13.0	11.5	13.1	16.1	13.3	7.3	4.6	2.4	88.1	5.6	3.4	0.8	0.1	16.9	92.6
Rockingham County–Strafford County, NH	5.0	12.3	14.1	10.7	13.5	17.7	13.8	7.3	4.0	1.7	95.4	0.9	2.1	0.2	0.0	2.1	97.0
Boulder, CO	5.4	11.9	18.6	13.0	13.5	14.5	12.5	6.0	3.0	1.4	91.2	1.1	4.3	0.9	0.1	13.7	100.9
Bowling Green, KY	6.2	12.5	19.6	13.5	12.2	13.1	11.2	6.7	3.6	1.5	86.7	8.5	2.6	0.3	0.1	4.3	96.1
Bremerton–Silverdale, WA	5.8	12.1	14.6	13.0	11.7	14.8	14.3	8.0	3.9	1.8	83.8	3.0	5.1	1.7	1.0	6.6	103.5
Bridgeport–Stamford–Norwalk, CT	6.0	14.0	12.4	11.7	13.9	16.2	12.1	7.0	4.4	2.3	80.9	11.8	4.9	0.5	0.1	17.4	95.0
Brownsville–Harlingen, TX	8.8	18.5	15.5	12.6	12.8	11.2	9.4	6.2	3.8	1.3	97.4	0.8	0.8	0.6	0.1	88.1	92.9
Brunswick, GA	6.5	13.2	12.6	11.7	12.3	14.6	13.9	9.1	4.6	1.6	72.8	24.0	1.0	0.5	0.2	5.2	92.4
Buffalo–Niagara Falls, NY	5.3	11.9	14.3	12.0	11.9	15.4	13.4	7.8	5.4	2.6	82.5	12.6	2.4	0.8	0.0	4.3	93.5
Burlington, NC	6.2	13.2	14.4	11.3	13.4	14.4	12.2	7.8	4.9	2.2	76.2	19.2	1.3	1.4	0.1	11.4	90.9
Burlington–South Burlington, VT	5.1	11.5	17.6	12.8	12.7	15.6	12.8	6.6	3.7	1.7	93.4	1.8	2.4	0.5	0.0	1.7	96.2
Canton–Massillon, OH	5.7	12.7	12.8	11.1	12.0	15.1	14.5	8.5	5.4	2.6	89.7	7.2	0.7	0.3	0.0	1.6	94.3
Cape Coral–Fort Myers, FL	5.2	10.8	10.9	10.5	11.1	13.0	14.3	13.4	7.8	2.9	87.6	8.8	1.5	0.5	0.1	18.6	96.4
Cape Girardeau–Jackson, MO–IL	6.1	12.1	16.8	12.3	11.4	13.7	12.7	7.8	4.9	2.2	88.1	8.8	1.1	0.4	0.0	1.9	95.1
Carson City, NV	5.8	11.7	12.2	12.0	12.2	15.1	14.0	9.1	5.5	2.5	90.1	2.2	2.3	2.6	0.3	22.0	107.3
Casper, WY	7.0	12.9	13.3	14.7	12.0	14.3	13.3	6.5	4.2	1.7	94.9	1.1	0.7	1.3	0.1	7.1	101.6
Cedar Rapids, IA	6.5	13.7	13.2	13.4	12.7	14.6	12.2	7.1	4.5	2.1	92.4	3.6	1.7	0.3	0.1	2.5	98.3
Champaign–Urbana, IL	5.6	10.7	25.9	14.0	10.6	11.7	10.4	5.7	3.7	1.7	77.9	11.1	8.2	0.4	0.1	5.0	99.3
Charleston, WV	5.8	12.0	11.1	12.1	12.8	15.0	15.1	8.8	5.3	2.0	92.4	5.0	0.9	0.2	0.0	0.9	94.5
Charleston–North Charleston–Summerville, SC	6.9	12.6	14.4	15.4	12.9	14.0	12.1	7.1	3.4	1.3	67.8	27.8	1.7	0.6	0.1	5.4	95.8
Charlotte–Gastonia–Rock Hill, NC–SC	7.1	14.5	13.0	14.4	15.4	14.3	10.9	6.0	3.1	1.3	69.4	24.6	3.3	0.7	0.1	10.1	94.3
Charlottesville, VA	5.7	11.2	17.6	13.6	11.8	13.7	12.6	7.6	4.4	1.9	80.5	12.7	4.0	0.4	0.1	4.9	91.9
Chattanooga, TN–GA	6.0	12.3	13.3	12.6	13.0	14.4	13.6	8.3	4.8	1.9	82.4	14.1	1.5	0.5	0.1	3.7	93.9
Cheyenne, WY	7.1	13.1	13.3	13.7	12.2	14.4	13.2	7.2	4.1	1.7	92.3	2.7	1.2	1.2	0.2	13.3	100.6
Chicago–Joliet–Naperville, IL–IN–WI	6.6	13.8	13.7	14.5	13.7	14.4	11.6	6.3	3.7	1.7	74.0	17.6	5.9	0.7	0.1	21.1	95.7
Chicago–Joliet–Naperville, IL	6.6	13.6	13.7	15.0	13.9	14.2	11.4	6.2	3.6	1.7	72.5	18.7	6.3	0.7	0.1	22.0	95.4
Gary, IN	6.4	14.1	13.3	12.5	12.7	14.7	13.0	7.2	4.3	1.8	77.7	19.0	1.3	0.4	0.0	14.3	94.5
Lake County–Kenosha County, IL–WI	6.5	15.2	14.2	11.7	13.7	16.0	11.8	6.0	3.4	1.6	84.2	7.3	5.6	0.8	0.1	18.7	99.5

[1] Persons of Hispanic origin may be any race.

Table B-3.   Population by Age, Race, and Sex—*Continued*

Metropolitan statistical area and division	Population characteristics, 2011																
	Age (percent)										One race (percent)					Hispanic or Latino origin[1] (percent)	Males per 100 females
	Under 5 years	5 to 14 years	15 to 24 years	25 to 34 years	35 to 44 years	45 to 54 years	55 to 64 years	65 to 74 years	75 to 84 years	85 years and over	White alone	Black or African American alone	Asian alone	American Indian, Alaska Native alone	Native Hawaiian and Other Pacific Islander alone		
Chico, CA	5.5	11.2	19.5	11.9	10.3	12.5	13.4	8.1	4.9	2.6	87.0	1.8	4.4	2.3	0.3	14.7	98.0
Cincinnati–Middletown, OH–KY–IN	6.7	13.8	13.6	13.0	13.0	15.0	12.4	6.7	4.0	1.7	83.8	12.2	2.0	0.2	0.1	2.7	95.8
Clarksville, TN–KY	8.6	14.8	15.9	16.7	12.7	12.1	9.5	5.6	3.0	1.0	75.2	18.6	1.8	0.7	0.4	7.0	98.5
Cleveland, TN	5.8	13.0	13.9	12.1	13.3	14.4	12.7	8.8	4.6	1.5	92.9	4.1	0.9	0.5	0.1	4.4	95.3
Cleveland–Elyria–Mentor, OH	5.7	12.8	12.7	11.8	12.5	15.5	13.7	7.8	5.1	2.5	75.6	20.3	2.0	0.2	0.0	4.8	92.7
Coeur d'Alene, ID	6.4	13.7	12.9	12.3	12.2	14.1	13.6	8.6	4.5	1.8	95.2	0.4	0.8	1.4	0.1	4.0	97.5
College Station–Bryan, TX	6.4	11.2	31.6	14.0	9.9	9.9	8.2	4.9	2.8	1.2	80.9	12.0	4.6	0.7	0.1	23.2	102.0
Colorado Springs, CO	7.0	14.2	15.2	14.3	12.8	14.6	11.6	6.0	3.2	1.2	84.6	6.5	2.8	1.3	0.4	15.0	100.1
Columbia, MO	6.1	11.4	24.3	14.8	11.2	12.1	10.4	5.2	3.0	1.5	84.0	9.2	3.7	0.5	0.1	3.1	94.2
Columbia, SC	6.4	13.0	15.7	13.9	12.9	14.1	12.2	6.8	3.5	1.4	62.3	33.6	1.8	0.5	0.1	5.2	95.0
Columbus, GA–AL	7.3	13.6	15.4	14.7	12.3	13.5	11.4	6.5	3.8	1.4	54.2	40.9	1.8	0.5	0.2	6.1	96.2
Columbus, IN	6.6	13.9	12.3	13.1	13.4	14.1	12.4	8.0	4.4	1.8	92.0	2.2	3.7	0.5	0.1	6.3	97.9
Columbus, OH	6.9	13.6	14.2	14.8	13.9	14.3	11.4	6.0	3.4	1.4	78.8	15.2	3.3	0.3	0.1	3.7	96.5
Corpus Christi, TX	6.9	14.4	14.3	13.3	12.0	13.8	12.3	7.2	4.3	1.6	92.1	3.9	1.7	0.9	0.1	58.2	96.8
Corvallis, OR	4.3	9.6	27.8	11.7	9.7	11.7	12.8	6.6	3.8	1.9	88.7	1.1	5.5	0.9	0.3	6.7	100.7
Crestview–Fort Walton Beach–Destin, FL	6.5	11.8	14.1	14.3	11.6	15.4	12.2	7.9	4.8	1.5	82.7	9.8	3.1	0.7	0.2	7.2	101.0
Cumberland, MD–WV	4.8	10.3	15.6	11.6	12.1	14.1	13.5	9.6	5.8	2.5	90.7	6.9	0.7	0.2	0.0	1.3	105.1
Dallas–Fort Worth–Arlington, TX	7.7	15.5	13.8	14.9	14.8	14.1	10.2	5.3	2.7	1.1	75.9	15.5	5.6	1.0	0.1	28.1	97.4
Dallas–Plano–Irving, TX	7.7	15.5	13.7	15.1	15.1	14.0	10.0	5.2	2.6	1.0	74.2	16.5	6.3	1.0	0.1	29.3	97.6
Fort Worth–Arlington, TX	7.6	15.5	13.8	14.3	14.2	14.3	10.6	5.6	2.9	1.1	79.3	13.3	4.2	0.9	0.2	25.6	97.0
Dalton, GA	7.6	15.7	14.0	13.0	14.0	13.6	10.7	6.9	3.5	1.1	92.5	3.5	1.2	1.2	0.2	27.1	99.5
Danville, IL	6.7	13.4	12.4	11.9	11.6	14.2	13.4	8.6	5.5	2.3	83.6	13.3	0.8	0.3	0.0	4.4	98.2
Danville, VA	5.6	11.9	11.9	10.4	11.6	15.4	15.0	9.9	5.9	2.5	65.1	32.8	0.6	0.3	0.0	2.6	91.2
Davenport–Moline–Rock Island, IA–IL	6.4	13.0	12.6	12.7	12.1	14.5	13.5	8.0	4.9	2.4	88.6	7.0	1.7	0.4	0.1	7.8	96.6
Dayton, OH	6.0	12.6	14.2	12.3	11.8	14.4	13.2	8.1	5.1	2.2	80.5	15.1	1.9	0.3	0.1	2.2	93.9
Decatur, AL	6.2	13.2	12.5	12.3	13.1	15.2	12.9	8.5	4.6	1.5	82.7	12.3	0.5	2.1	0.1	6.5	96.7
Decatur, IL	6.3	12.5	13.2	11.7	11.4	14.2	14.1	8.3	5.6	2.6	79.8	16.4	1.1	0.3	0.0	2.0	91.8
Deltona–Daytona Beach–Ormond Beach, FL	4.9	10.3	12.4	10.4	11.1	14.7	14.7	11.1	7.2	3.2	85.2	10.9	1.6	0.4	0.1	11.5	95.4
Denver–Aurora–Broomfield, CO[2]	7.0	13.8	12.4	15.5	14.7	14.4	11.8	5.9	3.1	1.3	85.8	5.9	3.9	1.5	0.2	22.7	99.1
Des Moines–West Des Moines, IA	7.5	14.4	12.5	15.2	13.8	13.9	11.4	6.1	3.6	1.7	89.6	4.9	3.2	0.4	0.1	6.8	96.4
Detroit–Warren–Livonia, MI	5.9	13.4	13.2	11.9	13.4	15.5	13.1	7.1	4.3	2.0	71.2	22.9	3.5	0.4	0.0	4.0	94.1
Detroit–Livonia–Dearborn, MI	6.5	13.8	14.5	12.1	13.1	14.6	12.6	6.6	4.2	2.0	54.3	40.3	2.7	0.4	0.0	5.4	92.6
Warren–Troy–Farmington Hills, MI	5.6	13.1	12.3	11.7	13.6	16.2	13.5	7.5	4.4	2.1	83.4	10.3	4.0	0.4	0.0	3.0	95.2
Dothan, AL	6.3	13.4	12.1	12.2	12.7	14.3	13.3	8.9	5.1	1.8	73.7	23.5	0.7	0.6	0.1	3.1	92.4
Dover, DE	6.7	13.7	15.0	12.5	12.3	14.2	11.7	8.1	4.3	1.5	69.2	24.6	2.2	0.7	0.1	6.0	93.0
Dubuque, IA	6.3	13.1	14.4	12.2	11.3	14.4	12.9	7.6	5.2	2.5	94.5	2.7	1.1	0.2	0.3	2.0	97.5
Duluth, MN–WI	5.5	11.1	15.4	11.9	11.0	14.8	14.6	8.0	5.2	2.5	92.7	1.4	0.9	2.7	0.0	1.3	101.4
Durham–Chapel Hill, NC	6.5	12.0	15.9	15.1	13.5	13.4	12.0	6.5	3.5	1.6	64.7	27.6	4.5	0.9	0.1	11.3	91.6
Eau Claire, WI	6.0	11.9	17.5	13.2	11.5	13.9	12.5	7.0	4.4	2.1	94.2	1.2	2.6	0.6	0.0	1.7	100.5
El Centro, CA	7.9	15.9	16.2	14.0	12.9	12.6	9.9	5.6	3.7	1.3	89.3	3.8	2.4	2.6	0.2	80.6	106.0
Elizabethtown, KY	7.0	14.0	13.9	13.6	13.2	15.1	11.6	6.5	3.8	1.4	83.1	11.3	1.9	0.5	0.3	4.9	99.1
Elkhart–Goshen, IN	8.0	15.8	13.4	12.8	12.9	13.3	11.4	6.6	4.0	1.8	90.1	6.0	1.1	0.6	0.1	14.5	97.4
Elmira, NY	5.9	12.3	13.1	12.0	12.1	15.4	13.6	7.9	5.3	2.5	88.9	6.9	1.3	0.3	0.0	2.7	99.1
El Paso, TX	8.1	16.5	16.6	13.7	12.9	12.4	9.5	5.5	3.5	1.2	92.8	3.6	1.2	1.0	0.2	81.4	94.7
Erie, PA	5.9	12.4	15.8	11.9	11.7	14.4	13.2	7.4	4.8	2.5	89.2	7.4	1.2	0.2	0.0	3.5	96.7
Eugene–Springfield, OR	5.1	10.8	16.9	12.8	11.4	13.1	14.5	8.4	4.7	2.3	90.6	1.1	2.7	1.3	0.3	7.6	96.5
Evansville, IN–KY	6.4	12.8	13.5	12.5	12.1	14.9	13.3	7.6	4.7	2.1	90.6	6.3	1.0	0.3	0.1	2.1	95.1
Fairbanks, AK	8.0	13.4	17.3	17.1	12.4	13.4	11.5	4.5	1.7	0.6	78.2	5.0	2.8	7.2	0.4	6.3	111.4
Fargo, ND–MN	6.8	11.7	20.2	16.1	11.8	12.3	10.6	5.1	3.5	1.8	92.5	2.2	2.1	1.4	0.1	2.6	100.6
Farmington, NM	8.2	15.9	14.3	13.9	11.4	13.5	11.4	6.3	3.6	1.4	58.6	0.9	0.5	37.2	0.1	19.6	98.7
Fayetteville, NC	8.6	14.4	16.4	16.6	12.4	12.6	9.8	5.4	3.0	0.9	54.1	36.5	2.3	2.8	0.4	10.2	94.6
Fayetteville–Springdale–Rogers, AR–MO	7.5	14.9	14.9	15.1	13.3	12.7	10.2	6.4	3.6	1.4	89.9	2.4	2.6	1.7	1.1	15.2	98.9
Flagstaff, AZ	6.6	12.6	22.7	13.2	11.1	12.7	11.6	5.9	2.6	0.9	66.6	1.6	1.6	27.4	0.2	13.9	97.8
Flint, MI	6.3	13.8	13.5	11.7	12.7	15.0	13.0	7.5	4.8	1.8	75.2	20.9	0.9	0.6	0.0	3.1	93.0
Florence, SC	6.6	13.6	13.6	11.9	12.7	14.1	13.5	8.3	4.2	1.6	55.9	41.7	1.0	0.4	0.0	2.2	88.9
Florence–Muscle Shoals, AL	5.6	12.0	13.7	11.3	12.1	14.3	13.7	9.4	5.7	2.1	84.9	12.5	0.7	0.5	0.0	2.3	92.0
Fond du Lac, WI	5.9	12.6	12.9	12.3	12.3	15.5	13.3	7.7	5.1	2.6	95.7	1.4	1.2	0.5	0.0	4.5	96.8
Fort Collins–Loveland, CO	5.6	11.7	18.3	13.9	12.0	13.5	12.8	6.9	3.7	1.7	93.5	1.0	2.1	1.0	0.1	10.8	98.4
Fort Smith, AR–OK	6.8	14.2	13.2	12.3	12.5	14.2	12.5	8.2	4.4	1.7	82.9	3.9	2.3	6.5	0.1	8.5	97.6
Fort Wayne, IN	7.2	14.7	13.6	13.0	12.7	14.1	12.2	6.6	4.0	1.9	84.3	10.4	2.5	0.4	0.1	6.0	95.7
Fresno, CA	8.5	16.1	16.6	14.4	12.2	12.2	9.8	5.5	3.3	1.5	77.7	5.9	10.3	3.0	0.3	50.9	100.0
Gadsden, AL	6.0	12.8	12.7	11.6	13.1	14.1	14.0	8.8	5.2	1.9	81.5	15.5	0.7	0.6	0.3	3.5	93.8
Gainesville, FL	5.3	9.4	27.2	13.9	10.1	11.5	11.1	6.4	3.5	1.6	72.6	19.3	5.2	0.4	0.1	8.6	94.7
Gainesville, GA	7.7	15.6	13.8	13.4	14.0	13.3	10.7	6.7	3.5	1.3	87.4	8.1	2.0	1.0	0.2	26.8	100.4
Glens Falls, NY	5.0	11.4	12.2	11.2	12.7	16.2	14.7	9.0	5.3	2.3	95.7	2.2	0.6	0.2	0.1	2.2	101.1
Goldsboro, NC	6.9	13.7	14.0	13.4	12.3	14.1	12.2	7.6	4.3	1.4	63.9	32.0	1.3	0.7	0.1	10.1	95.9
Grand Forks, ND–MN	6.3	10.9	21.9	13.6	10.2	12.9	11.6	6.2	4.1	2.1	92.2	1.7	1.6	2.4	0.0	3.9	103.9
Grand Junction, CO	6.8	12.7	13.7	13.3	11.2	13.7	13.4	8.1	4.9	2.2	94.5	0.9	0.9	1.5	0.1	13.6	98.9
Grand Rapids–Wyoming, MI	7.0	14.2	14.3	13.7	12.6	14.5	11.8	6.3	3.8	1.8	86.3	8.5	2.0	0.7	0.1	8.6	98.2
Great Falls, MT	6.8	12.1	14.1	13.1	10.9	14.3	13.0	8.3	5.2	2.2	89.9	1.4	0.8	4.5	0.1	3.6	99.7

[1]Persons of Hispanic origin may be any race.
[2]The Denver–Aurora metropolitan statistical area includes Broomfield County. Broomfield County, CO, was formed from parts of Adams, Boulder, Jefferson, and Weld counties on November 15, 2001, and is coextensive with Broomfield city. For the purposes of defining and presenting data for the Denver–Aurora metropolitan statistical area, Broomfield city is treated as if it were a county when data are available to do so. In many cases, the data will not be available.

Table B-3.   Population by Age, Race, and Sex—*Continued*

Metropolitan statistical area and division	Population characteristics, 2011																
	Age (percent)										One race (percent)					Hispanic or Latino origin[1] (percent)	Males per 100 females
	Under 5 years	5 to 14 years	15 to 24 years	25 to 34 years	35 to 44 years	45 to 54 years	55 to 64 years	65 to 74 years	75 to 84 years	85 years and over	White alone	Black or African American alone	Asian alone	American Indian, Alaska Native alone	Native Hawaiian and Other Pacific Islander alone		
Greeley, CO	7.7	15.6	15.1	13.8	13.7	13.3	11.0	5.8	2.9	1.2	93.5	1.3	1.3	1.7	0.1	28.5	100.6
Green Bay, WI	6.6	13.5	13.4	13.2	12.8	15.4	12.4	6.8	4.1	1.8	91.2	2.0	2.4	2.6	0.1	6.4	99.1
Greensboro–High Point, NC	6.1	13.1	14.4	12.5	13.6	14.5	12.4	7.4	4.3	1.7	68.2	26.1	3.1	0.8	0.1	7.8	92.3
Greenville, NC	6.6	12.2	21.2	14.1	12.2	12.4	10.8	5.8	3.3	1.3	61.1	34.7	1.6	0.7	0.2	6.6	92.0
Greenville–Mauldin–Easley, SC	6.7	12.8	15.1	12.7	13.1	14.1	12.2	7.7	4.1	1.7	79.0	17.1	1.8	0.5	0.1	7.0	95.4
Gulfport–Biloxi, MS	7.1	13.1	14.3	13.7	12.4	12.3	7.3	4.0	1.3		74.5	20.2	2.4	0.6	0.1	4.8	99.1
Hagerstown–Martinsburg, MD–WV	6.2	13.1	12.1	12.8	13.9	15.4	12.9	7.6	4.3	1.7	87.6	8.5	1.2	0.3	0.1	3.5	101.0
Hanford–Corcoran, CA	8.4	14.9	15.9	16.8	14.2	13.2	8.7	4.6	2.5	0.9	81.2	7.9	4.2	2.9	0.3	51.4	129.6
Harrisburg–Carlisle, PA	5.8	12.0	13.4	12.6	12.6	15.1	13.7	7.7	4.9	2.2	83.9	10.6	3.0	0.3	0.1	4.9	95.5
Harrisonburg, VA	5.5	11.2	25.1	11.6	10.8	12.2	10.6	6.6	4.3	2.0	91.4	4.1	2.0	0.6	0.1	9.7	93.2
Hartford–West Hartford–East Hartford, CT	5.3	12.5	13.8	12.0	12.8	15.9	13.1	7.4	4.7	2.5	81.4	11.9	4.1	0.4	0.1	12.9	95.0
Hattiesburg, MS	7.3	13.3	18.2	14.5	12.1	12.5	10.4	6.6	3.7	1.3	68.7	28.7	1.0	0.3	0.1	2.9	92.4
Hickory–Lenoir–Morganton, NC	5.7	12.8	12.4	11.1	13.8	15.2	13.6	8.9	4.8	1.7	87.8	7.2	2.7	0.6	0.2	6.5	97.9
Hinesville–Fort Stewart, GA	10.4	15.6	17.9	17.3	12.0	11.8	8.5	4.2	1.7	0.5	54.2	38.6	2.0	0.7	0.6	10.7	98.2
Holland–Grand Haven, MI	6.6	14.6	17.1	11.9	12.3	14.0	11.4	6.5	3.8	1.8	93.3	1.8	2.7	0.6	0.0	8.8	96.1
Honolulu, HI	6.5	11.9	13.9	14.6	12.8	13.4	12.1	7.4	4.9	2.5	22.2	2.5	43.6	0.4	9.6	8.5	100.7
Hot Springs, AR	5.6	11.5	11.5	10.9	11.2	13.7	14.6	11.4	7.0	2.7	88.1	8.3	0.8	0.7	0.1	5.0	94.0
Houma–Bayou Cane–Thibodaux, LA	7.2	13.8	14.2	13.9	12.4	14.9	11.5	6.9	3.8	1.4	76.3	16.6	1.0	4.3	0.1	4.1	97.3
Houston–Sugar Land–Baytown, TX	7.9	15.3	14.0	15.1	14.3	13.8	10.7	5.3	2.6	1.0	72.8	17.6	6.8	1.0	0.1	35.9	99.0
Huntington–Ashland, WV–KY–OH	5.8	11.9	13.2	12.2	12.7	14.1	13.7	9.0	5.4	2.0	94.8	2.9	0.6	0.2	0.0	1.0	95.6
Huntsville, AL	6.2	13.1	13.9	13.4	13.1	16.0	11.9	7.1	4.0	1.4	72.4	22.2	2.2	0.8	0.1	4.9	97.3
Idaho Falls, ID	9.6	17.8	12.9	14.5	11.5	12.3	10.6	6.1	3.4	1.4	95.5	0.6	0.8	1.1	0.1	11.5	99.8
Indianapolis–Carmel, IN	7.2	14.5	13.0	14.3	13.8	14.6	11.4	6.1	3.4	1.5	79.9	15.3	2.4	0.4	0.1	6.4	95.3
Iowa City, IA	6.1	11.0	23.4	15.9	11.3	11.7	10.7	5.3	3.1	1.6	88.6	4.4	4.7	0.3	0.1	4.9	99.4
Ithaca, NY	4.1	8.3	31.9	12.8	9.6	11.2	11.1	5.9	3.4	1.8	82.4	4.3	9.7	0.5	0.1	4.6	97.4
Jackson, MI	5.7	12.9	13.5	11.7	12.9	15.4	13.4	7.6	4.7	2.1	88.3	8.2	0.7	0.4	0.0	3.1	104.3
Jackson, MS	7.1	14.3	14.5	14.2	12.8	13.9	11.8	6.4	3.6	1.4	49.7	48.0	1.1	0.3	0.1	2.2	91.2
Jackson, TN	6.6	12.9	15.9	12.3	12.0	14.0	12.5	7.5	4.3	1.8	65.0	32.4	0.9	0.3	0.0	3.3	90.8
Jacksonville, FL	6.4	13.1	13.6	13.6	13.3	15.0	12.6	7.1	3.8	1.6	71.5	22.1	3.6	0.4	0.1	7.2	94.9
Jacksonville, NC	9.7	12.3	25.7	17.1	10.1	9.8	7.6	4.5	2.4	0.7	76.8	16.2	2.1	0.8	0.3	10.5	116.3
Janesville, WI	6.4	13.9	12.9	12.7	13.0	14.9	12.5	7.3	4.6	2.0	91.2	5.1	1.1	0.5	0.1	7.8	96.5
Jefferson City, MO	6.3	13.0	13.6	13.3	13.0	15.0	12.8	7.0	4.1	1.8	89.4	7.7	0.9	0.4	0.1	2.3	104.5
Johnson City, TN	5.3	11.2	13.7	12.1	12.9	14.4	13.7	9.4	5.1	2.0	94.3	3.1	0.9	0.3	0.0	2.7	95.7
Johnstown, PA	4.9	10.8	13.4	10.6	11.8	14.8	14.9	8.9	6.6	3.3	94.1	4.0	0.6	0.1	0.0	1.5	98.6
Jonesboro, AR	7.1	13.7	15.8	14.0	12.4	12.8	11.2	7.3	4.1	1.6	84.7	12.3	1.0	0.5	0.0	4.2	95.3
Joplin, MO	7.2	14.1	13.9	13.0	12.2	13.6	11.9	7.7	4.6	1.8	91.6	1.9	1.2	1.8	0.6	6.2	96.3
Kalamazoo–Portage, MI	6.1	12.8	18.2	12.5	11.7	13.5	12.3	6.8	4.1	1.9	84.9	9.6	2.0	0.7	0.0	5.6	96.5
Kankakee–Bradley, IL	6.6	14.1	14.5	12.5	12.4	14.0	12.2	7.2	4.5	2.0	81.3	15.5	1.0	0.4	0.0	9.2	96.6
Kansas City, MO–KS	7.0	14.2	12.3	14.2	13.3	14.7	12.1	6.6	3.9	1.8	81.6	12.7	2.4	0.6	0.2	8.3	96.0
Kennewick–Pasco–Richland, WA	8.4	16.0	14.0	14.4	12.5	12.9	11.3	6.0	3.1	1.3	91.4	1.9	2.6	1.2	0.2	28.8	103.1
Killeen–Temple–Fort Hood, TX	8.7	15.1	16.0	17.2	12.8	12.1	9.0	5.1	2.8	1.1	71.1	20.2	2.8	1.1	0.8	21.0	97.5
Kingsport–Bristol-Bristol, TN–VA	5.1	11.5	11.4	10.6	13.1	15.0	14.6	10.5	5.9	2.2	95.9	2.2	0.5	0.3	0.0	1.4	94.8
Kingston, NY	4.8	11.0	14.0	11.1	12.8	16.6	14.5	8.3	4.8	2.2	88.8	6.6	1.8	0.4	0.0	9.0	99.0
Knoxville, TN	5.7	12.1	14.2	12.5	12.9	14.4	13.2	8.4	4.7	2.0	89.6	6.7	1.5	0.4	0.1	3.5	94.6
Kokomo, IN	5.9	13.0	12.1	11.3	12.2	14.9	13.8	9.3	5.3	2.3	90.7	6.0	0.9	0.3	0.0	2.6	93.7
La Crosse, WI–MN	5.8	11.6	18.4	12.5	11.1	13.8	12.5	7.0	4.7	2.4	93.0	1.4	3.7	0.4	0.0	1.5	96.1
Lafayette, IN	6.3	11.3	26.3	13.5	10.8	11.3	10.0	5.6	3.3	1.6	88.4	3.9	5.6	0.3	0.1	7.2	103.7
Lafayette, LA	7.1	13.5	15.5	15.1	12.5	14.1	11.4	6.0	3.5	1.2	69.8	27.0	1.4	0.4	0.0	3.7	95.4
Lake Charles, LA	7.1	13.8	14.2	13.6	11.9	14.3	12.3	7.2	4.2	1.4	72.3	24.5	1.1	0.5	0.1	2.7	95.1
Lake Havasu City–Kingman, AZ	5.3	11.3	10.4	9.3	9.7	13.8	16.1	14.4	7.5	2.1	92.5	1.2	1.2	2.7	0.2	15.2	100.3
Lakeland–Winter Haven, FL	6.3	13.0	12.8	11.9	12.0	13.1	12.5	10.2	6.0	2.2	80.4	15.3	1.8	0.6	0.1	18.1	96.1
Lancaster, PA	6.8	13.6	13.9	11.9	11.9	14.3	12.4	7.6	5.1	2.6	91.5	4.4	2.0	0.4	0.1	8.9	95.5
Lansing–East Lansing, MI	5.6	12.0	20.2	12.7	11.4	13.6	12.4	6.6	3.7	1.7	83.2	9.3	3.9	0.6	0.1	6.2	94.9
Laredo, TX	9.8	19.3	16.7	13.8	13.7	10.9	7.7	4.5	2.5	1.0	97.8	0.6	0.7	0.6	0.0	95.4	94.7
Las Cruces, NM	7.5	14.5	17.4	13.5	11.1	12.4	11.0	7.1	4.2	1.4	92.5	2.1	1.3	2.2	0.1	65.9	96.5
Las Vegas–Paradise, NV	7.0	13.7	14.0	15.0	14.5	13.5	11.3	7.2	3.5	1.1	73.8	11.0	9.1	1.2	0.8	29.7	103.1
Lawrence, KS	5.4	10.1	28.9	15.4	10.7	10.7	9.8	4.8	2.8	1.5	85.3	4.2	4.1	2.8	0.1	5.5	100.7
Lawton, OK	7.7	13.5	17.4	16.7	12.0	12.7	9.7	5.7	3.4	1.1	67.2	17.7	2.4	6.2	0.6	11.5	106.5
Lebanon, PA	6.2	12.6	12.3	11.3	12.3	14.6	13.5	8.6	5.7	2.8	94.3	2.8	1.3	0.3	0.0	9.7	95.4
Lewiston, ID–WA	5.7	12.2	12.8	11.9	11.0	14.0	13.8	9.6	6.0	2.9	92.2	0.5	0.8	4.1	0.1	3.1	96.0
Lewiston–Auburn, ME	6.3	12.2	13.0	12.2	12.9	15.7	13.3	7.5	4.8	2.0	93.1	3.8	0.8	0.4	0.0	1.6	96.2
Lexington–Fayette, KY	6.5	12.4	15.9	14.9	13.5	13.8	11.7	6.3	3.5	1.5	84.1	11.0	2.4	0.3	0.1	5.9	96.3
Lima, OH	6.3	13.3	14.8	11.7	11.5	14.2	13.2	7.6	4.9	2.4	84.4	12.1	0.7	0.2	0.1	2.5	101.5
Lincoln, NE	6.9	12.5	18.6	14.8	11.9	12.6	11.4	5.9	3.7	1.8	89.7	3.5	3.5	0.9	0.1	5.8	100.5
Little Rock–North Little Rock–Conway, AR	6.8	13.6	13.7	14.6	13.1	13.8	12.1	7.0	3.8	1.5	73.6	22.4	1.6	0.6	0.1	5.0	94.5
Logan, UT–ID	9.7	17.1	22.4	14.0	10.3	9.2	7.6	4.5	2.7	1.2	94.1	0.8	2.0	0.9	0.5	9.7	98.9
Longview, TX	7.1	13.7	13.6	13.2	12.1	13.9	12.2	7.6	4.7	1.9	78.7	17.6	0.9	0.9	0.1	14.9	99.8
Longview, WA	6.2	13.4	12.4	11.3	12.0	14.4	14.2	9.0	4.8	2.2	92.2	0.8	1.6	1.8	0.3	8.1	98.1
Los Angeles–Long Beach–Santa Ana, CA	6.5	13.2	15.0	14.8	14.4	14.1	10.8	6.1	3.6	1.6	72.5	7.6	15.2	1.4	0.4	44.8	97.5
Los Angeles–Long Beach–Glendale, CA	6.6	13.1	15.2	15.1	14.4	13.9	10.7	6.0	3.5	1.6	71.8	9.3	14.2	1.5	0.4	48.1	97.4
Santa Ana–Anaheim–Irvine, CA	6.3	13.4	14.5	13.8	14.3	14.7	11.1	6.4	3.8	1.7	74.9	2.1	18.4	1.1	0.4	34.1	98.0
Louisville/Jefferson County, KY–IN	6.4	13.3	12.6	13.5	13.2	15.1	12.9	7.1	4.2	1.7	82.2	13.9	1.6	0.3	0.1	4.1	95.4

[1] Persons of Hispanic origin may be any race.

Table B-3.   Population by Age, Race, and Sex—*Continued*

Metropolitan statistical area and division	Population characteristics, 2011																
	Age (percent)										One race (percent)					Hispanic or Latino origin[1] (percent)	Males per 100 females
	Under 5 years	5 to 14 years	15 to 24 years	25 to 34 years	35 to 44 years	45 to 54 years	55 to 64 years	65 to 74 years	75 to 84 years	85 years and over	White alone	Black or African American alone	Asian alone	American Indian, Alaska Native alone	Native Hawaiian and Other Pacific Islander alone		
Lubbock, TX	7.3	13.3	21.1	14.3	10.8	12.0	10.1	6.0	3.7	1.5	87.3	7.8	2.2	1.1	0.1	33.0	97.6
Lynchburg, VA	5.4	11.6	16.4	11.0	11.7	14.5	13.4	8.8	5.1	2.1	78.9	17.7	1.4	0.4	0.0	2.2	93.1
Macon, GA	6.8	13.7	14.2	12.5	12.2	14.4	12.8	7.4	4.2	1.6	53.1	43.8	1.4	0.3	0.1	2.7	92.3
Madera–Chowchilla, CA	7.8	15.6	15.3	13.8	12.5	12.6	10.8	6.7	3.6	1.3	86.3	4.4	2.2	4.5	0.2	54.5	93.1
Madison, WI	6.0	12.1	16.2	15.4	13.0	14.1	12.1	6.0	3.5	1.7	88.2	4.7	4.4	0.5	0.0	5.6	98.6
Manchester–Nashua, NH	5.8	12.9	12.9	12.4	13.9	17.0	12.9	6.7	3.8	1.8	92.2	2.4	3.4	0.3	0.1	5.5	98.0
Manhattan, KS	8.2	12.1	27.4	17.4	9.6	9.2	7.9	4.2	2.7	1.3	82.6	8.9	3.4	0.9	0.3	8.3	105.2
Mankato–North Mankato, MN	6.0	10.9	23.8	13.7	10.3	12.0	11.1	6.0	3.9	2.1	93.5	2.6	2.0	0.4	0.0	3.0	100.5
Mansfield, OH	5.9	12.3	12.4	11.9	12.3	14.7	13.8	8.7	5.6	2.4	87.9	9.4	0.7	0.2	0.0	1.5	102.7
McAllen–Edinburg–Mission, TX	9.7	19.3	16.3	13.8	13.2	10.4	7.9	5.2	3.2	1.1	97.2	0.8	1.0	0.5	0.0	90.7	95.2
Medford, OR	5.8	11.9	12.4	11.6	11.2	13.7	15.2	9.7	5.7	2.8	93.0	0.8	1.3	1.5	0.3	11.2	95.1
Memphis, TN–MS–AR	7.1	14.5	14.4	13.7	13.3	14.2	11.9	6.1	3.3	1.3	50.4	45.9	1.9	0.4	0.1	5.2	92.2
Merced, CA	8.5	17.2	17.4	13.8	12.3	12.1	9.1	5.3	3.1	1.2	82.1	4.3	7.9	2.4	0.4	55.7	101.6
Miami–Fort Lauderdale–Pompano Beach, FL	5.8	11.7	12.9	12.9	13.9	15.0	11.8	8.0	5.4	2.6	74.1	21.5	2.4	0.4	0.1	41.8	94.3
Fort Lauderdale–Pompano Beach–Deerfield Beach, FL	5.9	12.2	12.5	13.1	14.0	15.8	12.2	7.3	4.6	2.5	66.7	27.4	3.5	0.4	0.1	25.8	94.3
Miami–Miami Beach–Kendall, FL	5.9	11.6	13.8	13.7	14.7	14.9	11.2	7.5	4.8	2.0	77.5	19.3	1.7	0.3	0.1	64.5	94.6
West Palm Beach–Boca Raton–Boynton Beach, FL	5.3	11.2	11.7	11.2	12.2	14.1	12.4	10.0	7.8	4.0	77.4	17.8	2.5	0.6	0.1	19.6	93.9
Michigan City–La Porte, IN	6.0	12.5	12.5	13.0	12.8	15.0	13.8	8.0	4.5	2.0	86.2	10.9	0.6	0.4	0.0	5.6	106.9
Midland, TX	8.2	14.8	14.3	15.0	11.7	13.8	11.3	5.5	3.9	1.5	89.1	7.0	1.4	1.1	0.1	38.8	97.1
Milwaukee–Waukesha–West Allis, WI	6.6	13.5	13.7	13.7	12.6	14.8	12.3	6.4	4.3	2.1	77.2	17.0	3.1	0.7	0.1	9.7	94.9
Minneapolis–St. Paul–Bloomington, MN–WI	6.8	13.7	13.1	14.8	13.6	15.3	11.8	5.9	3.4	1.6	83.0	7.6	5.9	0.9	0.1	5.5	97.7
Missoula, MT	5.6	10.6	18.9	15.8	11.5	12.9	13.0	6.7	3.5	1.6	92.8	0.5	1.3	2.7	0.1	2.8	101.6
Mobile, AL	6.8	13.7	14.3	13.0	12.2	14.2	12.5	7.5	4.1	1.6	60.8	34.9	1.9	0.9	0.1	2.5	92.2
Modesto, CA	7.7	15.6	15.5	13.7	12.8	13.3	10.5	5.9	3.5	1.5	84.5	3.3	5.7	1.9	0.8	42.6	98.0
Monroe, LA	7.2	14.2	15.1	13.4	12.0	13.2	11.8	7.1	4.4	1.6	62.1	35.6	0.9	0.3	0.0	2.2	92.4
Monroe, MI	5.7	13.5	12.9	10.9	12.8	16.3	14.1	7.6	4.4	1.8	95.1	2.3	0.6	0.4	0.1	3.1	97.4
Montgomery, AL	6.6	13.5	15.4	13.6	13.1	13.9	11.7	6.9	3.9	1.4	53.6	43.0	1.6	0.4	0.1	3.2	92.2
Morgantown, WV	4.8	9.1	24.6	14.9	11.3	12.1	11.6	6.5	3.7	1.5	92.8	3.1	2.3	0.2	0.1	1.7	106.2
Morristown, TN	6.0	12.7	12.6	11.2	13.2	14.5	13.4	9.9	5.0	1.5	94.2	3.2	0.6	0.6	0.1	6.7	96.5
Mount Vernon–Anacortes, WA	6.4	12.8	12.5	12.1	11.7	13.6	14.2	9.2	5.0	2.4	91.4	0.9	2.0	2.6	0.3	17.3	98.5
Muncie, IN	5.4	10.8	23.6	10.7	10.6	12.4	11.5	8.0	4.8	2.2	89.4	7.1	1.1	0.3	0.1	1.9	92.4
Muskegon–Norton Shores, MI	6.5	13.6	13.4	12.4	12.2	14.9	13.2	7.4	4.5	2.0	81.3	14.6	0.6	0.9	0.1	4.9	98.6
Myrtle Beach–North Myrtle Beach–Conway, SC	5.6	11.1	12.7	12.4	12.1	13.5	14.7	11.0	5.2	1.6	82.5	13.9	1.1	0.6	0.1	6.3	95.5
Napa, CA	5.9	12.9	13.0	12.4	12.8	14.4	13.3	8.0	4.7	2.6	85.8	2.3	7.2	1.3	0.4	32.9	99.7
Naples–Marco Island, FL	5.2	10.7	10.3	10.1	10.7	12.5	13.3	14.6	9.3	3.3	90.2	6.9	1.2	0.5	0.1	26.3	97.5
Nashville–Davidson—Murfreesboro—Franklin, TN	6.8	13.5	13.6	14.9	14.1	14.6	11.7	6.3	3.3	1.3	79.8	15.5	2.4	0.4	0.1	6.8	95.6
New Haven–Milford, CT	5.5	12.4	14.0	12.7	12.8	15.3	12.7	7.3	4.7	2.6	79.9	13.7	3.7	0.4	0.1	15.4	93.0
New Orleans–Metairie–Kenner, LA	6.6	12.7	13.4	14.6	12.5	14.7	12.9	6.9	3.9	1.6	60.4	34.7	2.8	0.5	0.1	8.0	94.7
New York–Northern New Jersey–Long Island, NY–NJ–PA	6.2	12.4	13.3	14.4	13.8	14.7	11.9	7.0	4.3	2.0	66.7	19.6	10.5	1.0	0.1	23.3	93.2
Edison–New Brunswick, NJ	6.0	13.1	12.6	11.8	13.3	15.7	12.5	7.7	5.0	2.4	78.3	8.0	11.6	0.4	0.1	13.2	94.9
Nassau–Suffolk, NY	5.6	13.2	13.2	11.0	13.3	16.3	12.8	7.5	4.8	2.3	82.0	10.0	5.8	0.5	0.1	16.1	95.4
Newark–Union, NJ–PA	6.1	13.5	12.7	12.1	14.2	16.1	12.3	6.8	4.0	1.9	69.6	22.4	5.6	0.5	0.1	18.4	94.9
New York–White Plains–Wayne, NY–NJ	6.4	11.8	13.6	16.2	13.9	13.9	11.4	6.7	4.1	1.9	60.0	23.7	12.4	1.3	0.2	28.0	92.0
Niles–Benton Harbor, MI	6.1	12.9	12.6	11.1	11.9	14.9	13.9	8.8	5.4	2.5	79.9	15.6	1.7	0.6	0.1	4.7	95.0
North Port–Bradenton–Sarasota, FL	4.6	9.9	9.6	9.1	10.3	13.4	15.0	14.1	9.7	4.2	89.6	7.0	1.6	0.4	0.1	11.4	92.4
Norwich–New London, CT	5.3	11.9	14.0	12.1	12.6	16.2	13.3	7.7	4.6	2.2	84.8	6.5	4.3	1.0	0.1	8.8	99.7
Ocala, FL	5.1	10.6	10.6	9.8	10.5	13.1	14.1	14.4	8.8	3.0	83.6	12.8	1.4	0.5	0.1	11.2	92.0
Ocean City, NJ	4.8	10.0	11.7	9.7	10.1	15.3	16.3	11.7	7.3	3.0	92.0	5.1	1.0	0.3	0.1	6.4	94.7
Odessa, TX	9.0	15.8	15.4	14.8	11.9	12.8	10.2	5.5	3.4	1.1	91.5	4.8	0.9	1.4	0.2	53.9	98.4
Ogden–Clearfield, UT	9.4	18.1	14.5	15.5	12.4	11.6	9.3	5.0	3.0	1.2	93.2	1.4	1.7	0.9	0.5	12.1	100.8
Oklahoma City, OK	7.3	13.7	14.6	14.9	12.5	13.5	11.6	6.6	3.8	1.5	76.8	10.6	2.9	4.6	0.1	11.7	97.4
Olympia, WA	6.1	12.5	13.3	13.8	12.8	14.2	13.9	7.6	4.0	1.8	84.3	3.0	5.4	1.6	0.8	7.4	95.5
Omaha–Council Bluffs, NE–IA	7.5	14.4	13.4	14.9	12.9	14.0	11.6	6.0	3.6	1.6	86.6	8.0	2.2	0.9	0.1	9.2	97.5
Orlando–Kissimmee–Sanford, FL	6.1	12.9	15.0	14.1	13.7	14.3	11.3	7.0	4.0	1.6	75.8	17.0	4.2	0.6	0.2	25.9	96.0
Oshkosh–Neenah, WI	5.9	11.8	15.2	13.5	12.5	15.2	12.4	6.8	4.6	2.2	93.7	1.9	2.4	0.7	0.0	3.6	101.1
Owensboro, KY	6.7	13.5	12.5	12.2	12.4	14.7	13.0	8.0	4.8	2.0	93.2	4.4	0.6	0.2	0.1	2.4	95.0
Oxnard–Thousand Oaks–Ventura, CA	6.6	14.1	14.6	12.9	13.2	14.8	11.8	6.5	3.8	1.8	85.3	2.2	7.2	1.8	0.3	40.9	98.8
Palm Bay–Melbourne–Titusville, FL	4.8	10.8	11.7	10.2	10.9	16.4	14.4	10.8	7.2	2.8	84.4	10.5	2.2	0.4	0.1	8.4	95.8
Palm Coast, FL	4.8	11.0	9.9	9.2	11.0	13.1	15.7	14.6	7.9	2.8	83.8	11.7	2.3	0.3	0.1	9.0	92.5
Panama City–Lynn Haven–Panama City Beach, FL	6.2	11.8	13.1	13.3	12.4	15.4	12.9	8.2	4.8	1.8	83.1	11.2	2.1	0.7	0.1	5.1	97.9
Parkersburg–Marietta–Vienna, WV–OH	5.4	11.9	12.0	11.1	12.4	15.3	14.6	9.7	5.5	2.1	96.7	1.2	0.5	0.2	0.0	0.8	95.2
Pascagoula, MS	6.8	14.2	13.2	12.9	13.2	14.8	12.2	7.7	3.9	1.1	75.9	20.2	1.9	0.4	0.1	4.5	97.9
Pensacola–Ferry Pass–Brent, FL	6.2	12.1	15.2	12.9	11.9	14.9	12.8	8.0	4.5	1.6	76.2	17.3	2.6	0.9	0.2	4.8	99.0
Peoria, IL	6.5	13.2	12.9	12.9	12.4	14.0	13.2	7.7	4.9	2.3	86.4	9.4	2.0	0.3	0.1	3.0	95.6
Philadelphia–Camden–Wilmington, PA–NJ–DE–MD	6.1	12.7	14.1	13.2	12.9	15.1	12.4	6.9	4.4	2.1	70.9	21.4	5.2	0.4	0.1	8.1	93.3
Camden, NJ	6.0	13.3	13.2	12.3	13.4	15.9	12.6	7.0	4.3	2.0	75.7	17.2	4.5	0.4	0.1	9.6	94.7
Philadelphia, PA	6.2	12.6	14.3	13.5	12.6	14.8	12.3	6.9	4.5	2.2	69.1	22.9	5.6	0.4	0.1	7.6	92.6
Wilmington, DE–MD–NJ	6.1	12.9	14.5	12.9	13.2	15.3	12.4	6.9	4.0	1.8	72.8	20.9	3.7	0.4	0.1	8.0	94.8

[1]Persons of Hispanic origin may be any race.

Table B-3. Population by Age, Race, and Sex—*Continued*

Metropolitan statistical area and division	Under 5 years	5 to 14 years	15 to 24 years	25 to 34 years	35 to 44 years	45 to 54 years	55 to 64 years	65 to 74 years	75 to 84 years	85 years and over	White alone	Black or African American alone	Asian alone	American Indian, Alaska Native alone	Native Hawaiian and Other Pacific Islander alone	Hispanic or Latino origin[1] (percent)	Males per 100 females
Phoenix–Mesa–Glendale, AZ	7.2	14.5	13.9	14.2	13.5	13.0	10.9	7.1	4.0	1.6	85.2	5.4	3.6	3.0	0.3	29.9	99.0
Pine Bluff, AR	6.1	13.0	14.6	12.9	12.2	14.5	13.0	7.6	4.3	1.8	50.1	47.6	0.7	0.4	0.0	2.0	103.2
Pittsburgh, PA	5.1	11.0	12.8	12.0	12.0	15.4	14.4	8.4	6.0	2.9	88.0	8.5	1.8	0.1	0.0	1.4	93.7
Pittsfield, MA	4.5	10.6	13.5	10.0	11.2	15.8	15.4	9.4	6.3	3.3	93.4	3.0	1.3	0.3	0.0	3.5	93.1
Pocatello, ID	8.1	15.1	16.7	14.6	11.0	11.6	11.4	6.3	3.6	1.5	92.1	0.8	1.3	3.3	0.3	9.0	99.5
Portland–South Portland–Biddeford, ME	5.1	11.7	12.2	11.6	13.1	16.5	14.6	8.1	4.9	2.2	94.7	1.7	1.6	0.4	0.0	1.6	94.6
Portland–Vancouver–Hillsboro, OR–WA	6.4	13.0	12.5	15.1	14.5	14.1	12.7	6.5	3.4	1.8	85.6	3.0	5.9	1.3	0.5	11.1	97.7
Port St. Lucie, FL	5.2	11.6	10.9	10.1	11.4	14.3	13.6	11.7	8.0	3.2	81.2	14.7	1.6	0.7	0.1	15.3	96.2
Poughkeepsie–Newburgh–Middletown, NY	6.1	13.8	15.1	11.0	13.2	16.1	12.3	6.8	3.9	1.7	82.8	11.0	3.1	0.6	0.1	15.1	99.7
Prescott, AZ	4.7	10.4	10.4	8.8	9.4	13.6	17.6	14.4	7.9	2.9	94.1	0.8	0.9	2.0	0.1	13.9	96.2
Providence–New Bedford–Fall River, RI–MA	5.4	11.9	14.8	12.1	12.9	15.4	12.8	7.3	4.7	2.6	88.0	6.2	2.7	0.8	0.1	10.6	93.7
Provo–Orem, UT	10.9	19.1	21.4	16.1	11.1	8.3	6.4	3.7	2.1	0.8	93.8	0.7	1.5	0.8	0.8	10.9	100.7
Pueblo, CO	6.5	13.5	13.6	12.1	11.7	13.6	13.3	8.1	5.2	2.2	91.1	2.4	1.0	2.9	0.1	41.6	96.8
Punta Gorda, FL	3.3	7.7	8.2	7.0	8.4	12.9	17.3	18.5	12.0	4.6	91.0	6.0	1.3	0.3	0.1	5.9	94.5
Racine, WI	6.5	13.8	12.4	12.2	12.8	16.0	12.9	7.1	4.3	2.1	84.7	11.5	1.2	0.6	0.1	11.7	98.2
Raleigh–Cary, NC	7.1	14.8	13.2	14.5	15.9	14.6	10.6	5.5	2.7	1.1	71.6	20.8	4.6	0.9	0.1	10.3	95.4
Rapid City, SD	7.3	13.3	13.4	13.9	11.4	14.1	13.0	7.2	4.5	1.9	85.9	1.4	1.0	8.3	0.1	3.9	101.2
Reading, PA	6.0	13.2	14.4	11.3	12.7	15.1	12.6	7.4	5.0	2.3	89.5	6.3	1.5	0.7	0.1	16.8	96.4
Redding, CA	5.7	12.2	13.1	11.5	10.8	14.5	14.9	9.7	5.3	2.3	89.1	1.0	2.7	3.0	0.2	8.8	96.5
Reno–Sparks, NV	6.5	12.8	14.3	13.5	12.8	14.3	13.1	7.6	3.6	1.4	86.2	2.5	5.4	2.1	0.7	22.6	101.8
Richmond, VA	6.1	12.9	13.7	13.4	13.4	15.2	12.9	7.0	3.8	1.7	63.9	30.1	3.3	0.6	0.1	5.2	93.7
Riverside–San Bernardino–Ontario, CA	7.5	15.6	16.1	13.5	13.2	13.4	10.1	5.9	3.4	1.3	79.4	8.2	6.7	1.9	0.4	47.9	99.1
Roanoke, VA	5.7	11.8	12.2	11.3	12.6	15.2	14.6	8.9	5.4	2.3	83.0	13.2	1.7	0.3	0.1	3.3	93.3
Rochester, MN	7.1	14.0	11.6	14.4	12.4	15.2	11.8	7.1	4.3	2.1	89.4	4.0	4.5	0.3	0.1	4.2	96.6
Rochester, NY	5.6	12.3	15.1	12.0	12.1	15.3	13.2	7.5	4.6	2.3	82.6	12.3	2.6	0.4	0.1	6.4	94.6
Rockford, IL	6.6	14.2	12.9	12.2	13.1	14.7	12.5	7.5	4.4	2.0	83.9	10.9	2.3	0.5	0.1	12.7	96.1
Rocky Mount, NC	6.2	13.2	13.1	11.4	12.4	15.0	14.1	8.3	4.6	1.7	52.0	45.1	0.7	0.8	0.0	5.5	90.9
Rome, GA	6.6	13.3	14.4	12.2	12.8	13.9	12.3	7.8	4.8	1.8	81.2	14.8	1.4	0.8	0.3	9.7	94.3
Sacramento—Arden-Arcade—Roseville, CA	6.5	13.6	14.8	13.6	12.9	14.2	11.9	6.7	3.9	1.8	72.2	7.8	12.6	1.5	0.9	20.5	96.2
Saginaw–Saginaw Township North, MI	5.9	12.9	14.9	11.1	11.7	14.4	13.6	8.2	5.1	2.3	76.9	19.4	1.1	0.5	0.1	7.8	93.7
St. Cloud, MN	6.5	12.8	18.8	13.6	11.4	13.7	10.9	6.2	4.2	1.9	93.1	3.0	1.9	0.4	0.1	2.7	101.6
St. George, UT	8.7	16.8	13.8	13.1	10.1	9.5	9.4	6.0	2.1	—	93.9	0.8	0.8	1.7	0.8	10.0	97.8
St. Joseph, MO–KS	6.4	12.5	14.1	13.3	12.3	14.7	12.3	7.4	4.7	2.2	91.2	5.4	0.8	0.6	0.2	4.4	105.1
St. Louis, MO–IL[3]	6.2	13.1	13.3	13.4	12.5	15.3	12.7	7.1	4.5	1.9	77.4	18.3	2.2	0.3	0.0	2.7	94.0
Salem, OR	7.2	14.3	14.6	13.2	12.2	12.7	12.2	7.2	4.2	2.0	90.3	1.2	2.1	2.5	0.7	22.4	98.7
Salinas, CA	8.0	14.4	15.5	15.1	13.0	12.6	10.6	5.7	3.5	1.7	82.5	3.7	6.9	2.7	0.6	56.1	105.9
Salisbury, MD	6.0	11.6	18.7	12.4	11.4	14.0	12.3	7.4	4.3	1.8	66.6	28.6	2.3	0.3	0.1	4.4	96.1
Salt Lake City, UT	8.6	16.2	16.9	16.9	13.4	11.9	9.7	5.0	2.7	1.1	89.9	1.8	3.3	1.3	1.5	17.0	101.4
San Angelo, TX	7.0	12.8	17.1	13.9	10.8	12.8	11.7	7.2	4.8	1.9	91.1	4.6	1.1	1.1	0.1	36.1	96.4
San Antonio–New Braunfels, TX	7.3	14.9	14.8	14.1	13.2	13.5	11.0	6.2	3.5	1.4	87.3	7.1	2.3	1.2	0.2	54.2	96.7
San Diego–Carlsbad–San Marcos, CA	6.6	12.5	15.8	15.4	13.4	13.7	11.0	6.0	3.7	1.8	77.0	5.6	11.4	1.4	0.6	32.5	100.9
Sandusky, OH	5.3	12.3	11.8	10.6	11.7	15.5	15.2	9.4	5.7	2.6	87.8	8.7	0.6	0.3	0.0	3.5	95.5
San Francisco–Oakland–Fremont, CA	5.9	11.6	12.2	15.1	14.9	14.8	12.5	6.9	4.0	2.0	60.9	8.8	24.0	1.0	0.8	22.0	97.5
Oakland–Fremont–Hayward, CA	6.3	12.9	13.2	14.0	14.5	14.9	12.2	6.6	3.6	1.8	59.4	11.6	22.1	1.1	0.8	23.6	95.9
San Francisco–San Mateo–Redwood City, CA	5.4	9.7	10.8	16.7	15.4	14.7	13.0	7.4	4.5	2.3	63.0	4.6	26.6	0.9	0.9	19.6	99.7
San Jose–Sunnyvale–Santa Clara, CA	6.9	13.3	12.6	15.0	15.4	14.7	10.8	6.1	3.5	1.6	59.3	2.9	32.0	1.5	0.5	28.0	100.8
San Luis Obispo–Paso Robles, CA	4.9	10.1	19.3	11.5	10.7	13.7	14.1	8.2	5.0	2.5	89.1	2.4	3.7	1.4	0.2	21.3	104.9
Santa Barbara–Santa Maria–Goleta, CA	6.4	12.2	20.2	13.2	11.6	12.6	10.8	6.5	4.3	2.2	86.1	2.4	5.5	2.2	0.3	43.4	100.7
Santa Cruz–Watsonville, CA	5.7	11.4	18.4	12.4	12.3	14.2	14.0	6.4	3.3	1.9	88.0	1.4	4.8	1.7	0.2	32.7	99.2
Santa Fe, NM	5.5	11.6	11.0	11.5	12.3	15.0	17.0	9.9	4.5	1.6	91.5	1.1	1.3	4.0	0.2	50.9	95.3
Santa Rosa–Petaluma, CA	5.8	12.1	13.2	12.8	12.3	14.8	14.6	7.8	4.2	2.4	87.9	1.9	4.1	2.2	0.4	25.4	96.7
Savannah, GA	7.0	13.1	15.6	15.4	12.5	13.3	11.4	6.7	3.6	1.5	61.2	34.1	2.2	0.4	0.1	5.3	94.9
Scranton—Wilkes-Barre, PA	5.2	11.2	13.4	11.3	12.3	14.9	13.9	8.7	6.1	3.0	93.5	3.5	1.3	0.3	0.0	6.2	95.0
Seattle–Tacoma–Bellevue, WA	6.5	12.3	13.0	15.5	14.6	14.9	12.1	6.2	3.3	1.7	75.2	5.9	11.8	1.3	0.9	9.2	99.6
Seattle–Bellevue–Everett, WA	6.3	12.0	12.6	15.8	15.0	15.0	12.2	6.1	3.3	1.7	74.6	5.5	13.5	1.2	0.7	9.2	99.8
Tacoma, WA	6.9	13.3	14.5	14.5	13.2	14.4	11.9	6.3	3.5	1.5	77.3	7.1	6.2	1.6	1.4	9.4	98.8
Sebastian–Vero Beach, FL	4.6	10.4	10.2	9.0	9.9	13.4	14.7	13.4	9.9	4.3	87.6	9.3	1.3	0.4	0.1	11.6	93.3
Sheboygan, WI	6.1	13.3	11.9	12.0	12.6	16.0	13.4	7.4	4.9	2.4	92.0	1.6	4.7	0.4	0.0	5.6	101.0
Sherman–Denison, TX	6.4	13.5	13.3	11.4	11.8	14.7	13.2	8.8	5.1	2.0	88.9	6.1	1.0	1.7	0.1	11.8	94.8
Shreveport–Bossier City, LA	7.2	13.7	13.7	14.3	12.0	13.6	12.3	7.2	4.4	1.7	57.5	39.1	1.3	0.6	0.1	3.6	92.5
Sioux City, IA–NE–SD	7.7	14.8	14.0	12.7	12.0	13.5	12.2	6.8	4.3	2.0	90.6	2.4	2.3	2.3	0.2	15.9	98.5
Sioux Falls, SD	7.9	13.9	12.9	15.8	12.9	14.0	11.3	5.8	3.7	1.9	91.4	3.0	1.4	2.2	0.1	3.6	99.5
South Bend–Mishawaka, IN–MI	6.4	13.5	14.9	12.3	12.1	13.9	13.0	7.0	4.6	2.2	83.2	11.8	1.8	0.6	0.1	6.8	95.2
Spartanburg, SC	6.7	13.4	14.1	11.9	13.2	14.2	12.7	8.0	4.2	1.6	75.1	20.9	2.1	0.4	0.0	6.1	94.1
Spokane, WA	6.3	12.6	15.1	13.5	12.0	14.1	13.0	7.1	4.1	2.0	90.3	1.8	2.2	1.7	0.4	4.7	97.9
Springfield, IL	6.2	13.2	12.3	12.9	12.4	15.1	13.8	7.5	4.5	2.1	84.7	11.3	1.6	0.2	0.0	1.9	92.3
Springfield, MA	5.3	11.9	17.2	11.4	11.8	14.8	13.4	7.2	4.5	2.5	86.5	7.9	2.7	0.6	0.1	15.8	91.9
Springfield, MO	6.4	12.7	15.8	13.4	12.1	13.5	11.9	7.6	4.6	2.0	93.5	2.3	1.2	0.7	0.1	2.8	95.8
Springfield, OH	6.2	13.0	13.2	11.1	11.8	14.3	14.0	8.8	5.2	2.4	87.6	8.9	0.7	0.3	0.1	2.8	94.0
State College, PA	4.2	8.5	33.2	11.6	10.0	11.2	9.9	6.0	3.8	1.6	89.5	3.3	5.4	0.1	0.1	2.7	107.9
Steubenville–Weirton, OH–WV	4.8	11.1	12.5	10.0	11.8	15.2	15.9	9.5	6.5	2.6	94.0	4.0	0.4	0.1	0.0	1.1	93.2

[1]Persons of Hispanic origin may be any race.
[3]The portion of Sullivan city in Crawford County, MO, is legally part of the St. Louis, MO–IL MSA. That portion is not included in these figures for the St. Louis MSA.

Table B-3. Population by Age, Race, and Sex—*Continued*

Metropolitan statistical area and division	Under 5 years	5 to 14 years	15 to 24 years	25 to 34 years	35 to 44 years	45 to 54 years	55 to 64 years	65 to 74 years	75 to 84 years	85 years and over	White alone	Black or African American alone	Asian alone	American Indian, Alaska Native alone	Native Hawaiian and Other Pacific Islander alone	Hispanic or Latino origin[1] (percent)	Males per 100 females
Stockton, CA	7.8	16.1	15.5	13.3	13.1	13.3	10.4	5.8	3.3	1.5	68.7	8.2	15.5	2.0	0.7	39.4	99.5
Sumter, SC	7.3	13.8	15.1	13.2	11.7	13.8	11.8	7.5	4.2	1.6	49.5	46.9	1.2	0.5	0.1	3.5	93.1
Syracuse, NY	5.7	12.5	15.8	11.8	11.9	15.4	12.9	7.1	4.6	2.2	86.0	8.5	2.5	0.8	0.0	3.6	94.7
Tallahassee, FL	5.5	10.9	23.6	13.6	11.3	12.6	11.7	6.2	3.2	1.4	62.5	32.8	2.4	0.4	0.1	6.2	94.3
Tampa–St. Petersburg–Clearwater, FL	5.6	11.6	12.3	12.3	12.8	14.9	13.2	9.0	5.9	2.5	81.8	12.5	3.1	0.5	0.1	16.6	94.1
Terre Haute, IN	5.6	12.2	16.2	12.6	12.4	13.9	12.7	7.6	4.6	2.1	91.6	5.2	1.2	0.3	0.0	2.0	103.1
Texarkana, TX–Texarkana, AR	6.6	13.4	13.0	13.5	12.8	14.0	12.4	7.9	4.4	1.9	72.0	24.4	0.8	0.9	0.1	5.8	100.4
Toledo, OH	6.3	12.7	15.7	12.2	12.0	14.4	13.1	7.1	4.5	2.0	82.2	13.7	1.4	0.4	0.0	5.9	94.7
Topeka, KS	6.7	13.9	12.3	12.5	11.5	14.6	13.6	7.9	4.9	2.2	87.0	6.9	1.0	1.7	0.1	9.0	95.7
Trenton–Ewing, NJ	5.9	12.5	14.9	12.7	13.8	15.1	12.1	6.7	4.2	2.1	66.9	21.0	9.3	0.6	0.2	15.5	95.7
Tucson, AZ	6.3	12.5	14.8	13.0	11.6	13.1	12.8	8.6	5.1	2.1	86.2	4.0	2.8	4.2	0.2	35.1	96.9
Tulsa, OK	7.0	14.1	13.3	13.5	12.7	14.0	12.2	7.3	4.1	1.7	74.8	8.6	1.8	8.5	0.1	8.7	96.5
Tuscaloosa, AL	6.0	11.9	22.6	13.0	11.3	12.2	11.5	6.2	3.8	1.4	63.5	34.0	1.2	0.3	0.1	2.9	93.5
Tyler, TX	7.1	14.2	14.8	13.0	12.0	12.8	11.6	7.7	4.8	1.9	78.2	18.1	1.4	0.8	0.1	17.9	93.7
Utica–Rome, NY	5.6	12.0	13.9	11.4	11.9	15.2	13.5	8.2	5.4	3.0	90.0	5.5	2.4	0.3	0.0	4.1	98.6
Valdosta, GA	7.6	13.0	20.3	14.3	11.7	12.3	10.2	6.1	3.3	1.1	61.4	34.6	1.4	0.6	0.1	5.9	96.6
Vallejo–Fairfield, CA	6.4	13.3	14.2	13.5	12.8	15.1	12.9	6.6	3.6	1.5	60.8	15.2	15.2	1.2	1.0	24.6	99.8
Victoria, TX	7.2	14.6	13.2	12.6	11.5	14.0	12.6	7.8	4.7	1.8	90.1	6.0	1.7	0.8	0.1	44.4	97.1
Vineland–Millville–Bridgeton, NJ	6.9	13.1	13.4	14.4	13.8	14.1	11.4	6.9	4.0	1.9	72.9	21.5	1.4	1.5	0.1	27.6	105.6
Virginia Beach–Norfolk–Newport News, VA–NC	6.5	12.7	15.9	14.5	12.4	14.7	11.5	6.6	3.7	1.5	61.2	31.4	3.6	0.5	0.1	5.6	96.2
Visalia–Porterville, CA	9.2	17.8	16.1	14.0	12.3	11.7	9.3	5.3	3.0	1.2	88.5	2.2	3.9	2.8	0.2	61.3	100.7
Waco, TX	7.0	13.8	19.3	12.8	11.2	12.5	10.9	6.5	4.2	1.8	80.3	15.1	1.6	1.1	0.1	24.2	94.8
Warner Robins, GA	7.1	14.6	14.3	14.6	13.2	15.0	10.8	6.0	3.4	1.0	65.1	29.2	2.6	0.4	0.2	6.2	95.0
Washington–Arlington–Alexandria, DC–VA–MD–WV	6.7	13.0	13.1	15.6	14.8	15.1	11.5	5.9	3.0	1.3	60.1	26.4	9.6	0.7	0.1	14.1	95.1
Bethesda–Rockville–Frederick, MD	6.5	13.3	11.9	13.4	14.3	15.7	12.5	6.6	3.8	2.0	67.5	16.5	12.4	0.7	0.1	15.6	93.5
Washington–Arlington–Alexandria, DC–VA–MD–WV	6.8	12.9	13.4	16.1	14.9	14.9	11.3	5.7	2.8	1.2	58.1	29.1	8.8	0.7	0.1	13.7	95.5
Waterloo–Cedar Falls, IA	6.2	11.8	18.8	12.6	10.7	12.6	12.6	7.4	4.9	2.4	89.4	7.0	1.3	0.3	0.2	3.3	95.2
Wausau, WI	6.4	13.4	12.1	12.4	12.7	15.5	13.1	7.4	4.7	2.3	92.0	0.7	5.5	0.5	0.0	2.3	100.7
Wenatchee–East Wenatchee, WA	7.1	14.1	13.0	12.0	11.5	13.8	13.3	8.2	4.8	2.3	94.4	0.6	1.0	1.7	0.2	27.4	100.0
Wheeling, WV–OH	5.1	10.9	12.6	11.2	11.8	15.0	15.7	8.9	6.1	2.9	94.7	3.2	0.5	0.1	0.0	0.8	97.1
Wichita, KS	7.6	14.8	13.7	13.7	12.1	14.0	11.9	6.3	4.1	1.9	84.0	7.9	3.5	1.3	0.1	11.8	98.0
Wichita Falls, TX	6.6	12.7	16.6	13.6	11.3	13.8	11.6	7.2	4.8	1.8	85.0	9.6	1.9	1.3	0.1	15.8	104.5
Williamsport, PA	5.5	11.5	14.5	11.5	11.7	15.0	13.8	8.2	5.7	2.6	92.9	4.7	0.6	0.2	0.0	1.5	96.2
Wilmington, NC	5.5	11.0	13.4	12.7	12.5	13.4	14.6	10.3	4.9	1.8	82.1	14.4	1.0	0.7	0.1	5.5	95.0
Winchester, VA–WV	6.2	13.4	12.9	12.3	13.2	15.4	12.7	8.0	4.3	1.6	90.9	5.4	1.4	0.5	0.1	7.6	99.4
Winston–Salem, NC	6.4	13.3	13.3	12.1	13.3	14.7	12.8	7.7	4.6	1.8	74.7	21.2	1.6	0.7	0.1	10.6	91.7
Worcester, MA	5.8	13.0	14.0	11.8	13.7	16.3	12.6	6.6	4.1	2.2	88.8	4.8	4.2	0.3	0.1	9.6	97.3
Yakima, WA	8.9	16.7	14.9	13.2	11.9	12.1	10.6	6.4	3.6	1.7	88.6	1.4	1.4	5.6	0.2	45.8	100.5
York–Hanover, PA	6.0	13.0	12.5	11.7	13.5	15.7	13.3	7.7	4.6	2.0	90.4	6.2	1.3	0.3	0.1	5.8	97.5
Youngstown–Warren–Boardman, OH–PA	5.3	12.1	12.7	10.6	11.8	15.0	14.7	8.8	6.1	3.0	86.3	11.1	0.6	0.2	0.0	2.8	94.7
Yuba City, CA	7.8	15.4	14.6	14.0	12.2	13.2	11.0	6.5	3.8	1.4	77.1	3.1	11.9	2.6	0.4	27.9	99.9
Yuma, AZ	7.6	15.2	16.2	12.7	11.4	11.4	9.6	8.8	5.5	1.5	91.6	2.6	1.5	2.2	0.2	60.1	102.6

[1]Persons of Hispanic origin may be any race.

Table B-4.   Migration and Commuting, 2009–2011

Metropolitan statistical area and division	Migration, 2009–2011			Commuting, 2009–2011				
	Total population age 1 year and older	Number who lived in the same house in prior year	Number who lived outside this metro area in prior year	Resident population age 16 and older	Lived and worked in this metro area	Total who worked in this metro area	Number who drove alone to work	Mean travel time to work
Abilene, TX.............................	163,096	129,569	19,557	72,189	69,280	73,552	57,746	16.6
Akron, OH..............................	695,280	607,947	58,955	324,436	246,958	320,336	281,508	23.0
Albany, GA............................	154,834	129,200	17,597	59,063	52,532	59,983	46,217	20.1
Albany–Schenectady–Troy, NY..........	861,792	752,765	72,149	427,485	400,342	438,487	343,297	22.2
Albuquerque, NM......................	876,528	745,251	89,915	395,797	381,147	390,191	315,654	23.5
Alexandria, LA........................	152,188	131,735	13,502	59,541	53,757	61,667	50,501	22.9
Allentown–Bethlehem–Easton, PA–NJ....	812,649	707,734	71,485	374,265	290,083	334,652	306,338	27.0
Altoona, PA...........................	126,039	111,335	9,955	56,396	49,478	62,435	46,883	19.1
Amarillo, TX..........................	247,334	200,155	32,763	118,479	112,093	116,529	94,516	18.7
Ames, IA.............................	88,593	61,649	13,578	47,211	37,697	48,454	34,100	18.4
Anchorage, AK........................	375,433	300,172	47,679	187,618	181,790	185,962	141,114	21.3
Anderson, IN..........................	130,535	110,944	13,034	53,199	33,181	43,272	44,733	25.3
Anderson, SC.........................	185,498	159,451	17,325	76,646	51,655	65,280	65,916	23.7
Ann Arbor, MI........................	341,747	261,683	43,097	164,154	127,322	198,746	120,483	23.1
Anniston–Oxford, AL..................	117,079	97,898	12,230	45,753	37,586	49,697	39,594	21.7
Appleton, WI.........................	223,324	201,018	13,936	116,860	78,755	111,039	98,167	19.6
Asheville, NC.........................	420,693	360,621	37,600	186,413	177,109	190,295	149,080	21.3
Athens–Clarke County, GA.............	190,878	159,947	17,190	81,152	70,411	88,208	62,375	20.3
Atlanta–Sandy Springs–Marietta, GA....	5,219,598	4,321,655	687,895	2,396,364	2,303,433	2,409,028	1,862,460	30.3
Atlantic City–Hammonton, NJ..........	271,575	241,865	18,486	123,995	103,145	130,600	93,769	23.9
Auburn–Opelika, AL...................	139,274	106,382	15,863	61,609	41,171	52,083	50,505	20.4
Augusta–Richmond County, GA–SC.......	549,334	465,028	52,978	232,069	218,738	235,428	194,363	23.4
Austin–Round Rock–San Marcos, TX....	1,706,559	1,332,361	252,891	856,549	822,999	861,374	646,348	25.3
Bakersfield–Delano, CA...............	829,161	659,920	124,150	304,238	283,962	307,225	229,457	23.6
Baltimore–Towson, MD................	2,679,883	2,332,546	246,080	1,318,062	1,140,978	1,283,672	1,007,758	30.1
Bangor, ME..........................	152,340	127,772	13,914	71,677	64,574	74,460	58,113	21.9
Barnstable Town, MA.................	214,637	195,705	10,205	98,448	84,117	93,421	81,669	24.8
Baton Rouge, LA.....................	792,361	675,708	84,627	367,419	342,527	369,283	303,072	25.9
Battle Creek, MI.....................	134,238	114,668	13,310	54,369	44,624	61,302	44,002	19.5
Bay City, MI.........................	106,324	91,822	9,414	45,896	27,443	36,637	39,622	20.4
Beaumont–Port Arthur, TX............	384,622	324,039	41,258	157,398	148,921	167,502	130,970	20.9
Bellingham, WA......................	199,543	165,442	22,276	94,429	85,008	89,635	69,938	21.0
Bend, OR............................	156,865	130,678	15,861	67,035	63,237	67,877	52,549	18.5
Billings, MT..........................	156,174	131,310	15,497	80,826	77,973	81,866	64,697	18.8
Binghamton, NY......................	248,764	219,131	18,953	111,627	99,445	112,555	88,721	19.4
Birmingham–Hoover, AL...............	1,116,186	943,889	132,984	486,545	457,134	490,423	409,139	26.2
Bismarck, ND........................	107,514	90,682	10,706	60,184	55,918	58,103	48,408	18.9
Blacksburg–Christiansburg–Radford, VA..	161,324	122,227	19,885	72,835	64,391	75,975	56,982	20.0
Bloomington, IN......................	190,872	140,726	26,175	86,127	73,203	86,086	64,039	21.7
Bloomington–Normal, IL...............	167,498	134,316	19,620	85,833	77,194	91,297	68,144	17.8
Boise City–Nampa, ID.................	609,569	501,228	76,354	269,532	260,545	266,817	212,586	21.1
Boston–Cambridge–Quincy, MA–NH......	4,510,012	3,874,996	456,163	2,284,979	2,145,895	2,440,017	1,573,258	28.8
Boston–Quincy, MA..................	1,869,751	1,590,598	198,850	930,385	874,677	1,087,957	575,406	30.4
Cambridge–Newton–Framingham, MA....	1,488,977	1,277,172	144,500	778,054	737,469	850,456	544,093	27.9
Peabody, MA.......................	736,255	644,953	75,192	356,028	347,200	305,405	273,272	27.6
Rockingham County–Strafford County, NH..	415,029	362,273	37,621	220,512	186,549	196,199	180,487	27.8
Boulder, CO.........................	292,752	225,771	37,082	152,818	120,669	181,023	99,234	22.3
Bowling Green, KY...................	124,610	96,897	16,054	57,025	49,777	61,949	47,589	19.8
Bremerton–Silverdale, WA............	248,845	207,305	22,833	114,585	93,836	105,681	77,983	29.6
Bridgeport–Stamford–Norwalk, CT......	908,614	816,284	57,490	431,076	336,881	455,133	319,124	27.7
Brownsville–Harlingen, TX............	400,416	354,492	33,847	137,413	125,914	135,038	108,699	19.9
Brunswick, GA.......................	110,617	92,630	11,755	46,160	41,934	47,920	37,436	21.4
Buffalo–Niagara Falls, NY.............	1,123,661	988,411	101,962	516,703	501,197	522,593	422,290	21.0
Burlington, NC.......................	149,734	126,531	13,692	67,811	45,983	59,908	55,086	23.2
Burlington–South Burlington, VT........	209,165	174,687	22,977	112,376	106,163	118,578	82,411	21.7
Canton–Massillon, OH................	399,773	348,528	37,412	176,994	137,392	166,824	150,091	21.7
Cape Coral–Fort Myers, FL............	614,725	492,772	79,875	234,406	206,634	224,791	176,220	26.5
Cape Girardeau–Jackson, MO–IL........	95,562	78,243	10,685	43,584	38,109	47,063	35,788	20.3
Carson City, NV.....................	54,852	44,599	5,117	22,405	16,610	29,223	18,730	16.6
Casper, WY.........................	75,072	60,069	9,984	38,556	36,118	38,632	31,289	18.4
Cedar Rapids, IA.....................	255,322	215,674	27,025	133,260	119,589	137,448	109,740	19.4
Champaign–Urbana, IL................	229,341	171,955	35,884	110,638	102,736	115,578	77,213	18.0
Charleston, WV......................	300,731	270,088	21,478	127,376	116,960	139,169	106,060	23.4
Charleston–North Charleston–Summerville, SC...	660,355	539,132	76,304	308,392	299,095	312,528	248,758	24.7
Charlotte–Gastonia–Rock Hill, NC–SC....	1,743,623	1,452,672	202,063	812,811	761,811	861,332	650,538	25.2
Charlottesville, VA....................	200,222	164,431	18,091	92,160	83,948	103,173	68,831	23.6
Chattanooga, TN–GA..................	522,540	442,969	57,550	232,259	212,805	240,013	195,578	22.6
Cheyenne, WY.......................	90,502	73,115	10,632	46,753	45,040	49,012	39,430	15.2
Chicago–Joliet–Naperville, IL–IN–WI.....	9,348,734	8,181,288	941,818	4,330,406	4,251,334	4,371,951	3,074,676	30.8
Chicago–Joliet–Naperville, IL..........	7,789,758	6,810,184	798,799	3,615,596	3,566,836	3,701,388	2,496,238	31.3
Gary, IN...........................	699,426	617,387	66,995	301,448	290,826	263,555	257,911	27.3
Lake County–Kenosha County, IL–WI....	859,550	753,717	76,024	413,362	393,672	407,008	320,527	29.1

Table B-4.   Migration and Commuting, 2009–2011—*Continued*

Metropolitan statistical area and division	Migration, 2009–2011			Commuting, 2009–2011				
	Total population age 1 year and older	Number who lived in the same house in prior year	Number who lived outside this metro area in prior year	Resident population age 16 and older	Lived and worked in this metro area	Total who worked in this metro area	Number who drove alone to work	Mean travel time to work
Chico, CA	217,600	170,749	34,574	83,281	75,369	81,968	61,331	21.0
Cincinnati–Middletown, OH–KY–IN	2,103,322	1,798,696	242,293	985,151	937,155	988,657	812,986	24.1
Clarksville, TN–KY	269,740	209,723	28,721	114,565	101,831	113,955	95,066	23.1
Cleveland, TN	114,677	96,604	12,551	47,651	35,718	43,310	40,218	22.2
Cleveland–Elyria–Mentor, OH	2,053,899	1,776,038	223,466	932,678	877,284	981,612	766,805	24.4
Coeur d'Alene, ID	136,954	113,498	15,424	60,395	48,375	55,057	47,015	20.9
College Station–Bryan, TX	225,579	157,684	36,649	101,890	93,326	102,072	78,903	19.4
Colorado Springs, CO	638,709	501,782	75,469	307,630	291,396	304,370	237,445	22.0
Columbia, MO	170,825	125,892	27,099	88,834	78,309	90,783	69,275	19.1
Columbia, SC	759,721	621,567	88,122	353,690	330,353	362,938	287,335	23.5
Columbus, GA–AL	293,343	224,657	37,580	127,076	117,333	140,299	99,581	20.9
Columbus, IN	76,343	63,355	8,025	36,333	30,546	44,042	30,653	19.3
Columbus, OH	1,816,863	1,495,947	242,337	875,570	845,147	917,614	725,185	22.8
Corpus Christi, TX	423,001	341,124	55,126	183,565	173,982	186,580	143,718	19.6
Corvallis, OR	84,951	66,889	7,777	39,043	30,047	39,790	24,322	18.4
Crestview–Fort Walton Beach–Destin, FL	179,386	143,376	20,119	86,614	77,234	93,855	70,861	22.9
Cumberland, MD–WV	102,150	88,904	7,929	40,348	35,786	41,569	31,926	22.3
Dallas–Fort Worth–Arlington, TX	6,315,249	5,228,199	850,078	3,013,987	2,950,509	3,045,816	2,451,761	26.4
Dallas–Plano–Irving, TX	4,199,168	3,472,603	567,253	2,018,595	1,977,241	2,117,915	1,628,346	26.5
Fort Worth–Arlington, TX	2,116,081	1,755,596	282,825	995,392	973,268	927,901	823,415	26.3
Dalton, GA	140,538	118,496	17,132	57,397	50,427	65,274	48,058	20.9
Danville, IL	80,627	70,747	6,784	32,524	27,522	31,763	26,606	20.5
Danville, VA	105,284	91,745	9,530	42,817	34,589	40,894	35,332	23.5
Davenport–Moline–Rock Island, IA–IL	374,674	324,886	35,260	178,198	168,232	182,862	150,244	19.3
Dayton, OH	833,205	698,419	94,361	370,364	327,807	382,755	308,989	21.0
Decatur, AL	151,499	133,300	12,998	64,129	44,059	56,043	55,850	24.1
Decatur, IL	109,258	93,926	10,372	46,622	42,148	52,715	40,268	17.7
Deltona–Daytona Beach–Ormond Beach, FL	490,307	422,355	35,993	194,082	152,198	172,021	161,141	25.7
Denver–Aurora–Broomfield, CO[1]	2,518,539	2,049,774	340,095	1,271,588	1,195,774	1,261,974	968,746	26.6
Des Moines–West Des Moines, IA	563,772	472,071	65,481	296,177	283,547	311,556	241,931	19.9
Detroit–Warren–Livonia, MI	4,246,833	3,664,805	483,126	1,751,931	1,655,239	1,764,703	1,478,626	26.2
Detroit–Livonia–Dearborn, MI	1,796,080	1,532,222	226,727	651,999	613,081	706,641	531,766	25.0
Warren–Troy–Farmington Hills, MI	2,450,753	2,132,583	256,399	1,099,932	1,042,158	1,058,062	946,860	26.9
Dothan, AL	143,751	123,566	12,565	60,418	50,830	61,032	52,420	21.4
Dover, DE	160,700	138,407	12,349	71,976	52,329	64,200	58,677	25.5
Dubuque, IA	92,437	80,119	7,445	48,382	44,535	55,589	40,113	17.1
Duluth, MN–WI	276,887	233,667	28,999	129,047	123,599	130,818	101,948	19.8
Durham–Chapel Hill, NC	499,795	392,236	62,203	238,307	193,700	282,027	176,315	22.5
Eau Claire, WI	159,664	133,445	16,554	81,432	74,217	85,429	66,087	18.2
El Centro, CA	172,429	144,870	19,718	57,099	52,715	56,392	45,036	21.1
Elizabethtown, KY	117,742	94,634	9,228	52,297	44,285	57,626	43,239	22.2
Elkhart–Goshen, IN	195,178	164,717	20,769	85,338	72,250	102,841	69,723	19.6
Elmira, NY	88,095	74,558	8,507	38,244	29,821	39,077	32,266	19.3
El Paso, TX	793,066	661,284	85,139	320,948	304,044	320,322	253,823	23.0
Erie, PA	277,124	237,681	27,354	124,974	119,878	130,136	101,303	18.7
Eugene–Springfield, OR	348,852	271,215	53,749	148,344	141,523	149,215	106,246	19.9
Evansville, IN–KY	354,306	306,557	34,665	168,187	159,962	177,625	143,236	20.6
Fairbanks, AK	96,096	71,730	13,438	49,646	48,088	48,862	36,731	18.5
Fargo, ND–MN	206,562	162,488	26,424	119,018	112,938	121,273	97,041	17.1
Farmington, NM	127,169	111,125	11,056	51,338	47,936	50,766	43,044	26.0
Fayetteville, NC	362,097	278,338	43,050	161,223	145,363	177,472	132,468	22.2
Fayetteville–Springdale–Rogers, AR–MO	459,415	360,315	69,136	211,754	202,392	214,782	165,839	20.9
Flagstaff, AZ	132,576	106,165	14,136	63,215	58,291	63,330	41,884	18.7
Flint, MI	419,719	356,634	48,735	153,857	114,753	140,873	131,263	25.7
Florence, SC	202,788	174,509	19,950	82,913	74,064	87,091	69,522	21.9
Florence–Muscle Shoals, AL	145,688	126,258	12,956	59,764	50,440	56,240	52,455	23.4
Fond du Lac, WI	100,700	88,486	8,013	51,873	36,419	47,043	42,626	19.7
Fort Collins–Loveland, CO	297,627	234,671	34,682	151,814	124,813	142,559	116,110	22.6
Fort Smith, AR–OK	294,925	251,974	31,374	121,092	114,491	122,015	100,865	19.9
Fort Wayne, IN	411,388	358,705	38,841	186,109	168,095	194,950	160,826	20.7
Fresno, CA	918,858	768,280	119,797	341,798	314,825	346,313	266,107	21.8
Gadsden, AL	102,708	87,796	9,886	38,175	27,820	33,730	0	23.7
Gainesville, FL	261,730	192,095	39,657	117,427	109,770	130,368	85,446	20.7
Gainesville, GA	177,706	153,731	14,516	77,379	53,195	77,273	61,006	25.0
Glens Falls, NY	127,798	111,043	9,669	58,429	43,351	54,918	47,506	24.0
Goldsboro, NC	121,068	99,109	12,610	53,535	41,948	49,502	44,888	21.7
Grand Forks, ND–MN	97,089	76,619	11,248	52,297	49,392	54,199	42,272	14.6
Grand Junction, CO	145,104	117,974	17,653	66,459	61,626	64,061	52,486	21.2
Grand Rapids–Wyoming, MI	765,225	653,808	78,792	345,799	302,439	372,287	286,071	22.0
Great Falls, MT	80,235	66,069	8,143	39,001	37,569	39,366	30,917	16.0

[1]The Denver–Aurora metropolitan statistical area includes Broomfield County. Broomfield County, CO, was formed from parts of Adams, Boulder, Jefferson, and Weld counties on November 15, 2001, and is coextensive with Broomfield city. For the purposes of defining and presenting data for the Denver–Aurora metropolitan statistical area, Broomfield city is treated as if it were a county when data are available to do so. In many cases, the data will not be available.

Table B-4. Migration and Commuting, 2009–2011—*Continued*

Metropolitan statistical area and division	Migration, 2009–2011			Commuting, 2009–2011				
	Total population age 1 year and older	Number who lived in the same house in prior year	Number who lived outside this metro area in prior year	Resident population age 16 and older	Lived and worked in this metro area	Total who worked in this metro area	Number who drove alone to work	Mean travel time to work
Greeley, CO	249,825	202,594	27,489	116,152	71,343	94,777	92,265	26.0
Green Bay, WI	303,462	263,800	28,073	152,514	137,543	160,235	125,765	19.6
Greensboro–High Point, NC	715,659	612,249	69,193	321,850	284,740	353,185	267,034	22.2
Greenville, NC	187,646	148,212	22,547	84,762	69,560	81,871	71,076	20.3
Greenville–Mauldin–Easley, SC	631,579	526,352	63,159	276,885	237,895	289,100	233,268	22.0
Gulfport–Biloxi, MS	246,687	200,699	25,567	109,779	96,663	123,908	88,707	23.5
Hagerstown–Martinsburg, MD–WV	266,493	227,898	25,007	120,677	79,329	99,795	98,571	29.3
Hanford–Corcoran, CA	151,040	123,698	15,302	55,240	44,246	54,833	43,258	21.2
Harrisburg–Carlisle, PA	544,425	460,163	53,972	267,150	238,516	316,085	218,131	21.9
Harrisonburg, VA	123,605	98,698	13,538	57,468	51,412	62,763	45,491	20.2
Hartford–West Hartford–East Hartford, CT	1,199,971	1,049,194	100,822	586,724	512,893	619,057	474,068	22.8
Hattiesburg, MS	141,288	113,860	16,674	61,783	53,201	64,498	51,166	22.9
Hickory–Lenoir–Morganton, NC	361,167	320,328	28,760	151,800	134,529	149,366	130,189	22.0
Hinesville–Fort Stewart, GA	77,950	57,861	6,007	34,325	26,711	34,776	27,865	21.0
Holland–Grand Haven, MI	261,177	224,876	18,915	121,637	73,416	107,009	101,995	20.0
Honolulu, HI	942,055	798,326	82,660	472,037	467,953	472,514	307,887	26.9
Hot Springs, AR	95,790	79,748	10,457	38,167	32,458	37,301	30,909	21.8
Houma–Bayou Cane–Thibodaux, LA	205,475	178,624	20,830	89,793	79,763	92,485	71,933	24.7
Houston–Sugar Land–Baytown, TX	5,883,067	4,893,211	765,553	2,737,238	2,678,327	2,745,875	2,177,497	27.7
Huntington–Ashland, WV–KY–OH	285,077	245,795	28,115	109,507	96,636	111,258	93,975	22.0
Huntsville, AL	414,019	352,290	41,006	192,318	181,019	217,277	166,274	21.7
Idaho Falls, ID	128,255	108,526	11,663	56,530	50,061	58,040	43,655	20.1
Indianapolis–Carmel, IN	1,736,507	1,456,637	215,553	816,747	778,501	842,276	689,022	24.5
Iowa City, IA	151,214	112,072	20,987	83,419	72,615	90,995	57,286	18.2
Ithaca, NY	100,908	72,249	12,827	47,978	43,411	58,021	27,611	19.1
Jackson, MI	158,025	130,526	18,276	63,499	46,855	58,532	53,302	23.6
Jackson, MS	533,235	457,434	56,400	233,205	221,270	242,681	199,217	23.1
Jackson, TN	113,945	98,340	8,916	46,842	41,581	58,597	39,042	20.4
Jacksonville, FL	1,332,247	1,099,368	167,230	610,309	588,715	616,388	495,041	25.1
Jacksonville, NC	172,892	127,078	17,230	87,587	80,524	90,263	63,035	23.4
Janesville, WI	158,368	136,461	15,461	73,519	51,078	60,917	59,362	22.7
Jefferson City, MO	148,213	125,536	12,405	71,488	63,047	75,640	57,398	19.4
Johnson City, TN	196,695	167,516	20,000	83,418	66,852	80,285	72,006	21.2
Johnstown, PA	143,165	127,400	8,795	59,782	45,836	57,161	49,329	22.5
Jonesboro, AR	119,551	92,254	18,566	50,123	44,746	52,460	42,374	17.9
Joplin, MO	173,833	144,371	21,733	77,279	69,866	81,843	63,691	18.9
Kalamazoo–Portage, MI	323,351	261,928	40,349	144,657	121,832	144,049	120,582	21.1
Kankakee–Bradley, IL	111,759	96,138	10,401	47,800	36,512	44,330	38,804	23.0
Kansas City, MO–KS	2,010,093	1,675,012	253,670	979,839	950,234	995,825	813,427	22.7
Kennewick–Pasco–Richland, WA	251,399	209,388	25,086	110,224	100,318	109,215	84,217	22.1
Killeen–Temple–Fort Hood, TX	398,185	301,520	45,977	179,001	165,238	178,239	145,346	19.3
Kingsport–Bristol–Bristol, TN–VA	306,379	265,536	27,977	124,946	104,650	125,906	108,889	22.8
Kingston, NY	180,661	158,306	12,689	84,170	56,494	68,087	64,988	26.9
Knoxville, TN	693,154	599,125	66,013	316,886	298,448	345,625	272,008	22.3
Kokomo, IN	97,474	81,146	11,565	40,100	31,694	41,083	34,487	21.7
La Crosse, WI–MN	132,225	109,605	14,392	70,272	62,723	74,034	56,233	19.1
Lafayette, IN	199,277	146,891	31,763	93,409	83,800	99,288	71,215	18.3
Lafayette, LA	270,352	233,297	23,636	129,514	111,166	145,000	109,687	23.2
Lake Charles, LA	196,937	163,941	24,508	85,322	80,334	92,212	71,745	20.7
Lake Havasu City–Kingman, AZ	199,202	159,370	23,023	69,365	55,412	58,065	52,777	19.2
Lakeland–Winter Haven, FL	595,418	493,676	64,685	231,456	181,039	204,200	186,919	25.8
Lancaster, PA	513,153	453,606	39,293	245,497	205,025	231,697	194,017	22.4
Lansing–East Lansing, MI	458,951	367,427	58,190	210,277	188,718	221,223	166,246	21.1
Laredo, TX	246,795	200,938	37,092	94,685	92,102	95,608	73,787	21.6
Las Cruces, NM	206,766	167,626	24,409	84,522	70,294	80,312	68,871	19.8
Las Vegas–Paradise, NV	1,927,641	1,469,877	361,341	873,743	859,248	882,784	690,543	23.9
Lawrence, KS	109,844	77,402	19,090	58,626	44,090	53,693	44,025	19.5
Lawton, OK	122,113	87,800	15,627	57,773	55,219	62,619	42,246	16.6
Lebanon, PA	131,693	116,918	9,105	62,829	38,628	52,987	51,967	22.5
Lewiston, ID–WA	60,253	51,149	6,014	26,928	25,050	27,046	22,265	15.9
Lewiston–Auburn, ME	106,228	90,072	10,569	49,833	36,468	48,067	39,833	23.1
Lexington–Fayette, KY	467,954	359,873	73,528	228,594	212,492	252,853	184,709	20.8
Lima, OH	105,107	88,188	12,221	44,004	35,889	51,080	38,328	19.3
Lincoln, NE	298,109	232,949	42,490	158,385	147,994	163,253	128,859	18.5
Little Rock–North Little Rock–Conway, AR	693,006	574,430	83,655	325,679	309,589	338,983	273,484	22.3
Logan, UT–ID	123,508	98,095	14,640	57,244	52,509	54,787	42,744	17.2
Longview, TX	211,945	174,906	21,002	91,798	77,759	97,620	76,131	22.6
Longview, WA	100,780	82,657	13,020	38,226	29,140	35,927	30,477	25.1
Los Angeles–Long Beach–Santa Ana, CA	12,701,843	10,880,085	1,482,058	5,728,515	5,532,791	5,958,622	4,218,661	28.2
Los Angeles–Long Beach–Glendale, CA	9,716,300	8,365,157	1,103,544	4,327,711	4,180,417	4,486,378	3,123,948	28.9
Santa Ana–Anaheim–Irvine, CA	2,985,543	2,514,928	378,514	1,400,804	1,352,374	1,472,244	1,094,713	26.0
Louisville/Jefferson County, KY–IN	1,270,173	1,101,480	126,945	581,365	554,263	581,615	483,687	23.7

Table B-4. Migration and Commuting, 2009–2011—*Continued*

Metropolitan statistical area and division	Migration, 2009–2011			Commuting, 2009–2011				
	Total population age 1 year and older	Number who lived in the same house in prior year	Number who lived outside this metro area in prior year	Resident population age 16 and older	Lived and worked in this metro area	Total who worked in this metro area	Number who drove alone to work	Mean travel time to work
Lubbock, TX	281,931	209,422	44,565	134,635	128,212	136,948	109,336	15.8
Lynchburg, VA	250,097	214,610	21,758	112,392	96,724	106,071	91,458	22.3
Macon, GA	229,956	194,731	24,257	90,902	76,894	98,153	77,633	23.2
Madera–Chowchilla, CA	148,972	128,283	10,692	42,029	27,901	40,357	31,626	26.0
Madison, WI	564,175	459,224	69,346	311,601	292,433	338,833	229,858	21.4
Manchester–Nashua, NH	397,080	342,621	34,809	206,705	138,872	189,266	171,728	26.7
Manhattan, KS	125,004	96,977	11,858	64,905	61,870	69,560	48,112	17.1
Mankato–North Mankato, MN	95,432	77,898	9,478	53,672	46,674	55,320	42,392	17.0
Mansfield, OH	123,175	105,117	11,799	51,874	41,447	51,966	45,435	21.4
McAllen–Edinburg–Mission, TX	763,215	661,450	75,972	276,502	255,580	265,062	215,141	21.5
Medford, OR	201,631	159,970	28,667	82,326	78,689	82,277	63,926	19.3
Memphis, TN–MS–AR	1,299,744	1,084,416	172,000	568,767	557,114	586,339	472,734	23.7
Merced, CA	252,730	205,287	35,185	90,382	67,540	79,215	71,282	25.7
Miami–Fort Lauderdale–Pompano Beach, FL	5,523,233	4,697,296	620,707	2,471,541	2,432,251	2,487,355	1,936,319	27.1
Fort Lauderdale–Pompano Beach– Deerfield Beach, FL	1,736,435	1,444,862	225,062	816,269	805,178	749,095	651,283	26.8
Miami–Miami Beach–Kendall, FL	2,478,692	2,143,576	253,167	1,095,107	1,082,372	1,161,086	842,743	28.8
West Palm Beach–Boca Raton– Boynton Beach, FL	1,308,106	1,108,858	142,478	560,165	544,701	577,174	442,293	24.0
Michigan City–La Porte, IN	110,349	94,191	9,360	45,890	32,794	41,573	39,578	22.2
Midland, TX	135,851	111,404	15,140	66,714	57,884	71,594	56,391	18.1
Milwaukee–Waukesha–West Allis, WI	1,536,366	1,292,089	196,735	737,573	708,605	781,321	588,078	22.4
Minneapolis–St. Paul–Bloomington, MN–WI	3,246,474	2,757,654	383,007	1,678,765	1,630,885	1,706,027	1,312,506	24.7
Missoula, MT	108,637	84,327	13,953	55,010	52,950	59,210	40,646	16.8
Mobile, AL	407,439	350,552	43,728	168,696	152,845	178,436	141,873	23.6
Modesto, CA	507,184	405,156	77,864	194,087	151,023	179,410	154,935	26.3
Monroe, LA	174,187	150,382	16,400	74,370	66,350	77,248	64,459	21.1
Monroe, MI	149,577	131,866	11,866	65,057	32,245	44,306	56,777	24.7
Montgomery, AL	370,692	298,408	48,362	159,178	150,920	167,842	136,487	22.3
Morgantown, WV	128,679	105,482	11,950	58,589	49,985	65,327	46,670	23.0
Morristown, TN	135,432	116,375	12,390	53,908	38,679	47,575	45,561	24.4
Mount Vernon–Anacortes, WA	115,655	97,007	12,594	49,938	39,292	50,895	40,046	25.2
Muncie, IN	116,481	84,352	19,735	47,279	38,134	48,659	37,845	19.8
Muskegon–Norton Shores, MI	169,800	142,929	18,513	64,857	48,502	59,687	53,840	20.7
Myrtle Beach–North Myrtle Beach–Conway, SC	268,652	225,450	25,310	118,493	109,233	121,011	97,905	21.0
Napa, CA	135,085	115,015	12,490	62,963	47,943	67,147	47,834	23.9
Naples–Marco Island, FL	320,200	274,443	27,224	125,583	111,655	131,507	95,366	23.2
Nashville–Davidson—Murfreesboro— Franklin, TN	1,574,665	1,297,477	205,576	743,748	713,361	766,269	607,419	26.0
New Haven–Milford, CT	852,595	748,600	69,673	410,426	301,528	383,172	325,973	24.0
New Orleans–Metairie–Kenner, LA	1,156,388	981,735	122,320	527,151	504,085	560,508	414,653	25.2
New York–Northern New Jersey–Long Island, NY–NJ–PA	18,688,192	16,819,333	1,471,801	8,637,945	8,441,029	8,824,025	4,345,711	34.7
Edison–New Brunswick, NJ	2,314,742	2,087,980	182,532	1,074,645	1,007,158	964,353	819,680	32.2
Nassau–Suffolk, NY	2,803,763	2,609,595	160,319	1,340,256	1,331,536	1,177,517	1,008,770	31.8
Newark–Union, NJ–PA	2,122,324	1,918,639	163,231	992,052	959,079	987,933	702,152	31.3
New York–White Plains–Wayne, NY–NJ	11,447,363	10,203,119	965,719	5,230,992	5,143,256	5,694,222	1,815,109	36.5
Niles–Benton Harbor, MI	155,336	136,798	13,556	65,814	52,896	65,446	54,195	19.8
North Port–Bradenton–Sarasota, FL	697,300	581,631	70,550	271,364	246,609	265,754	219,357	22.5
Norwich–New London, CT	271,434	230,688	21,842	135,801	109,866	139,147	106,832	22.8
Ocala, FL	328,567	279,165	29,504	114,309	94,358	105,995	91,620	25.1
Ocean City, NJ	96,232	85,895	5,177	42,701	31,953	41,093	32,454	21.9
Odessa, TX	135,887	111,014	15,973	62,468	50,331	60,790	49,214	19.5
Ogden–Clearfield, UT	537,828	459,651	53,083	244,939	185,841	206,912	195,111	21.9
Oklahoma City, OK	1,240,176	1,000,470	175,344	587,703	565,495	593,713	486,299	21.5
Olympia, WA	250,167	203,877	24,766	115,847	82,000	100,966	90,670	25.1
Omaha–Council Bluffs, NE–IA	853,629	708,665	108,973	442,074	423,515	446,188	366,268	20.0
Orlando–Kissimmee–Sanford, FL	2,115,674	1,735,136	264,475	974,729	933,144	1,033,297	791,504	26.7
Oshkosh–Neenah, WI	164,850	140,165	13,255	81,298	58,540	91,755	68,050	18.3
Owensboro, KY	113,356	98,645	10,360	48,704	42,568	48,654	41,415	19.0
Oxnard–Thousand Oaks–Ventura, CA	814,164	697,406	76,667	378,846	293,306	334,429	287,664	24.3
Palm Bay–Melbourne–Titusville, FL	538,470	455,614	53,891	223,676	206,667	216,605	186,120	23.9
Palm Coast, FL	94,742	83,681	5,000	33,621	19,110	23,039	0	26.3
Panama City–Lynn Haven–Panama City Beach, FL	166,250	132,857	20,977	76,653	73,013	78,698	64,313	20.8
Parkersburg–Marietta–Vienna, WV–OH	161,391	142,679	13,063	66,087	60,821	67,721	55,479	20.8
Pascagoula, MS	159,564	136,166	14,117	66,929	45,433	59,349	54,905	24.8
Pensacola–Ferry Pass–Brent, FL	444,845	358,828	47,536	193,166	172,603	179,939	149,205	23.3
Peoria, IL	374,626	323,931	36,883	171,499	160,252	177,027	144,761	20.4
Philadelphia–Camden–Wilmington, PA–NJ– DE–MD	5,901,178	5,232,395	505,257	2,733,769	2,544,829	2,706,901	2,017,067	28.4
Camden, NJ	1,237,223	1,111,870	95,097	587,500	516,668	499,343	474,930	28.1
Philadelphia, PA	3,966,278	3,521,961	336,465	1,815,724	1,725,673	1,882,623	1,275,888	29.0
Wilmington, DE–MD–NJ	697,677	598,564	73,695	330,545	302,488	324,935	266,249	25.4

Table B-4. Migration and Commuting, 2009–2011—*Continued*

Metropolitan statistical area and division	Migration, 2009–2011			Commuting, 2009–2011				
	Total population age 1 year and older	Number who lived in the same house in prior year	Number who lived outside this metro area in prior year	Resident population age 16 and older	Lived and worked in this metro area	Total who worked in this metro area	Number who drove alone to work	Mean travel time to work
Phoenix–Mesa–Glendale, AZ	4,151,285	3,272,801	675,254	1,799,764	1,764,771	1,788,393	1,372,708	25.7
Pine Bluff, AR	98,621	82,040	9,371	37,083	30,543	36,748	31,044	22.4
Pittsburgh, PA	2,335,627	2,065,190	204,934	1,088,444	1,047,639	1,104,920	836,557	25.8
Pittsfield, MA	129,771	114,453	11,223	60,093	55,985	63,049	48,321	20.2
Pocatello, ID	89,568	73,380	9,041	39,883	35,688	38,394	31,707	19.2
Portland–South Portland–Biddeford, ME	509,022	436,015	48,922	263,688	233,930	264,188	210,118	23.9
Portland–Vancouver–Hillsboro, OR–WA	2,206,852	1,816,741	279,971	1,034,023	998,598	1,036,646	738,442	24.9
Port St. Lucie, FL	420,723	351,137	42,531	160,734	125,846	137,729	129,946	26.2
Poughkeepsie–Newburgh–Middletown, NY	663,719	588,560	45,896	306,220	211,714	259,363	225,506	32.3
Prescott, AZ	208,849	167,802	23,420	79,121	72,716	76,102	58,878	22.2
Providence–New Bedford–Fall River, RI–MA	1,584,345	1,379,899	149,540	752,336	632,304	687,914	607,280	24.3
Provo–Orem, UT	517,450	403,799	68,885	219,180	182,295	198,704	160,925	21.0
Pueblo, CO	157,638	129,995	19,487	63,553	57,233	63,049	50,963	20.2
Punta Gorda, FL	159,126	132,529	13,290	52,613	37,825	48,918	41,794	23.5
Racine, WI	193,091	171,680	13,053	89,050	57,075	75,195	75,340	23.0
Raleigh–Cary, NC	1,122,578	948,259	107,523	547,445	456,726	529,290	443,651	24.4
Rapid City, SD	125,074	101,265	14,876	62,820	59,425	62,950	51,565	18.0
Reading, PA	407,017	347,431	41,341	189,491	140,254	167,747	152,845	24.2
Redding, CA	175,790	144,548	21,143	64,818	60,553	66,201	51,830	20.1
Reno–Sparks, NV	421,246	325,419	70,947	198,207	184,989	198,059	155,329	21.0
Richmond, VA	1,246,261	1,067,336	124,359	591,234	553,238	586,428	481,876	24.7
Riverside–San Bernardino–Ontario, CA	4,179,555	3,413,131	552,301	1,621,411	1,270,379	1,387,415	1,228,264	30.6
Roanoke, VA	304,952	261,465	29,619	142,524	133,342	154,871	118,607	21.8
Rochester, MN	183,925	161,362	14,325	98,091	90,105	104,888	75,617	18.5
Rochester, NY	1,043,223	891,632	111,859	485,645	467,084	497,500	398,402	20.6
Rockford, IL	345,499	303,790	30,096	150,570	127,104	147,588	126,610	23.6
Rocky Mount, NC	150,159	130,808	12,110	60,591	46,970	59,056	50,585	21.2
Rome, GA	95,197	81,027	9,101	38,064	31,642	41,925	30,231	22.2
Sacramento—Arden-Arcade—Roseville, CA	2,129,363	1,706,236	324,035	906,056	842,624	902,830	684,261	25.8
Saginaw–Saginaw Township North, MI	197,812	169,878	18,920	77,323	61,801	88,838	66,583	21.5
St. Cloud, MN	186,542	151,554	20,382	97,106	83,103	101,203	77,571	20.9
St. George, UT	136,848	113,538	14,611	51,214	48,399	51,672	41,496	17.5
St. Joseph, MO–KS	125,762	100,890	15,498	57,964	50,474	58,464	47,280	19.2
St. Louis, MO–IL[1]	2,776,986	2,401,178	294,641	1,311,131	1,276,553	1,317,411	1,086,914	24.8
Salem, OR	386,729	318,222	48,705	160,301	135,212	157,782	118,065	22.1
Salinas, CA	410,240	338,156	46,744	174,314	156,640	173,378	123,508	22.2
Salisbury, MD	123,864	100,335	13,901	54,349	43,088	52,855	44,365	22.2
Salt Lake City, UT	1,110,103	921,248	129,916	535,391	502,627	599,215	409,442	22.4
San Angelo, TX	110,641	83,173	13,473	53,075	50,801	53,594	41,199	16.5
San Antonio–New Braunfels, TX	2,121,937	1,730,851	281,318	960,466	924,153	949,141	762,837	25.0
San Diego–Carlsbad–San Marcos, CA	3,063,214	2,555,526	351,452	1,410,495	1,367,620	1,438,956	1,074,311	24.1
Sandusky, OH	76,106	67,153	5,672	34,324	24,194	35,491	28,350	19.8
San Francisco–Oakland–Fremont, CA	4,299,283	3,639,312	478,825	2,061,236	1,863,633	2,129,674	1,270,865	28.8
Oakland–Fremont–Hayward, CA	2,538,073	2,134,736	303,366	1,151,659	1,041,328	1,048,117	780,443	29.8
San Francisco–San Mateo–Redwood City, CA	1,761,210	1,504,576	175,459	909,577	822,305	1,081,557	490,422	27.6
San Jose–Sunnyvale–Santa Clara, CA	1,818,099	1,526,304	197,312	846,753	736,171	942,225	648,376	24.4
San Luis Obispo–Paso Robles, CA	267,786	210,769	33,817	117,760	104,942	114,634	87,759	20.5
Santa Barbara–Santa Maria–Goleta, CA	419,149	332,494	57,848	190,343	178,208	203,049	124,956	19.4
Santa Cruz–Watsonville, CA	259,653	216,625	25,303	122,501	95,378	111,726	87,913	25.1
Santa Fe, NM	142,962	119,579	13,515	68,995	58,476	72,411	50,007	21.8
Santa Rosa–Petaluma, CA	478,086	404,868	54,838	223,584	186,799	202,985	168,338	25.4
Savannah, GA	344,853	296,149	26,900	153,471	142,723	160,964	125,301	23.3
Scranton—Wilkes-Barre, PA	557,919	489,782	45,705	252,387	226,209	253,171	203,167	21.7
Seattle–Tacoma–Bellevue, WA	3,410,450	2,793,956	450,808	1,689,575	1,650,944	1,735,632	1,186,044	27.3
Seattle–Bellevue–Everett, WA	2,622,137	2,152,644	344,703	1,331,201	1,308,973	1,418,296	907,224	27.1
Tacoma, WA	788,313	641,312	106,105	358,374	341,971	317,336	278,820	28.3
Sebastian–Vero Beach, FL	137,111	115,629	12,035	50,623	42,487	51,702	42,488	20.8
Sheboygan, WI	114,041	99,072	10,409	57,124	48,448	56,875	47,948	18.9
Sherman–Denison, TX	119,581	96,754	16,298	51,361	38,245	47,070	41,347	24.7
Shreveport–Bossier City, LA	393,394	332,682	43,076	177,827	170,288	187,742	150,423	20.8
Sioux City, IA–NE–SD	141,362	118,436	15,329	70,372	64,221	72,056	55,807	17.6
Sioux Falls, SD	226,186	192,853	22,700	124,878	119,514	128,535	104,110	18.2
South Bend–Mishawaka, IN–MI	315,482	264,823	33,398	139,184	110,556	136,031	116,173	20.7
Spartanburg, SC	280,443	240,434	26,893	119,792	94,504	124,782	102,931	21.6
Spokane, WA	465,675	376,711	60,807	207,263	197,715	215,978	159,614	21.2
Springfield, IL	207,877	173,528	23,169	102,277	96,198	113,748	83,732	19.3
Springfield, MA	686,118	594,165	62,642	314,030	273,460	295,992	249,918	23.1
Springfield, MO	431,245	344,343	60,769	197,708	185,055	200,494	163,329	21.4
Springfield, OH	136,729	116,393	13,638	56,956	37,147	46,644	47,023	21.7
State College, PA	152,799	108,477	20,179	71,402	64,370	78,582	48,272	19.5
Steubenville–Weirton, OH–WV	123,037	110,583	7,826	51,074	36,376	43,978	42,089	24.6

[1] The portion of Sullivan city in Crawford County, MO, is legally part of the St. Louis, MO–IL MSA. That portion is not included in these figures for the St. Louis MSA.

Table B-4.   Migration and Commuting, 2009–2011—*Continued*

Metropolitan statistical area and division	Migration, 2009–2011			Commuting, 2009–2011				
	Total population age 1 year and older	Number who lived in the same house in prior year	Number who lived outside this metro area in prior year	Resident population age 16 and older	Lived and worked in this metro area	Total who worked in this metro area	Number who drove alone to work	Mean travel time to work
Stockton, CA	677,643	541,537	96,940	256,766	187,855	227,475	195,958	29.0
Sumter, SC	106,106	94,366	6,874	42,357	35,196	41,742	35,282	21.8
Syracuse, NY	654,660	555,883	67,523	297,161	278,182	305,830	239,295	20.6
Tallahassee, FL	363,816	277,797	55,284	165,493	160,356	170,255	133,628	21.6
Tampa–St. Petersburg–Clearwater, FL	2,764,483	2,307,559	326,880	1,193,766	1,147,980	1,189,887	961,646	25.4
Terre Haute, IN	170,433	148,366	14,489	72,563	64,328	74,941	60,714	22.3
Texarkana, TX–Texarkana, AR	134,139	111,955	14,636	54,387	49,936	57,546	44,764	18.2
Toledo, OH	643,888	538,596	78,554	285,250	259,983	298,320	239,557	20.1
Topeka, KS	230,675	195,688	24,746	110,503	98,879	108,220	90,385	20.2
Trenton–Ewing, NJ	363,178	317,219	23,504	171,556	115,452	219,891	121,027	27.0
Tucson, AZ	970,515	771,263	143,201	407,137	394,860	407,427	312,294	23.7
Tulsa, OK	927,119	775,135	113,745	429,158	411,012	436,638	355,764	21.0
Tuscaloosa, AL	217,425	180,433	23,155	90,247	81,147	93,749	76,510	21.8
Tyler, TX	207,645	167,446	23,704	91,321	79,516	98,998	73,904	21.5
Utica–Rome, NY	295,783	253,289	28,507	128,721	115,719	128,362	106,344	20.4
Valdosta, GA	137,924	110,107	16,076	56,954	51,885	59,970	46,731	18.7
Vallejo–Fairfield, CA	407,842	332,903	49,310	181,842	109,892	141,849	137,148	28.5
Victoria, TX	114,182	93,310	15,205	49,640	45,459	52,326	40,332	20.7
Vineland–Millville–Bridgeton, NJ	154,340	133,612	13,055	60,851	43,827	59,470	47,949	23.8
Virginia Beach–Norfolk–Newport News, VA–NC	1,649,715	1,360,212	190,359	823,011	798,535	832,560	667,197	23.4
Visalia–Porterville, CA	435,749	367,223	53,796	162,606	139,216	153,429	120,957	21.1
Waco, TX	232,190	186,234	29,789	102,859	95,935	108,865	82,672	19.0
Warner Robins, GA	138,657	113,995	13,672	63,833	49,974	66,714	52,929	20.8
Washington–Arlington–Alexandria, DC–VA–MD–WV	5,530,881	4,686,196	568,316	2,932,422	2,797,069	3,106,247	1,930,053	34.0
Bethesda–Rockville–Frederick, MD	1,194,440	1,029,279	110,219	633,479	594,914	581,148	428,652	34.3
Washington–Arlington–Alexandria, DC–VA–MD–WV	4,336,441	3,656,917	458,097	2,298,943	2,202,155	2,525,099	1,501,401	33.9
Waterloo–Cedar Falls, IA	165,377	135,909	19,279	82,378	77,028	89,303	67,284	17.1
Wausau, WI	132,316	116,574	10,538	67,607	57,885	69,457	55,821	18.4
Wenatchee–East Wenatchee, WA	109,490	96,420	7,874	48,793	45,846	47,796	38,271	17.8
Wheeling, WV–OH	146,540	130,616	10,570	61,563	53,831	63,805	51,281	22.1
Wichita, KS	614,158	514,817	76,325	289,741	281,798	292,987	246,063	18.5
Wichita Falls, TX	149,066	120,197	17,251	69,389	66,401	69,486	55,429	16.5
Williamsport, PA	115,295	101,132	8,646	52,795	45,329	54,549	42,513	19.4
Wilmington, NC	359,552	299,508	36,981	158,851	145,747	155,939	128,882	22.2
Winchester, VA–WV	127,057	107,577	11,245	58,045	40,758	57,667	47,683	30.5
Winston–Salem, NC	472,660	414,194	39,151	208,477	167,424	208,424	176,143	22.2
Worcester, MA	789,259	689,025	67,953	382,277	271,124	330,066	312,086	27.5
Yakima, WA	239,859	201,339	27,684	95,995	91,182	95,749	76,178	19.8
York–Hanover, PA	430,579	377,039	34,621	209,242	142,793	174,748	177,692	26.2
Youngstown–Warren–Boardman, OH–PA	560,203	499,803	42,842	230,633	194,873	222,912	198,696	21.6
Yuba City, CA	164,466	129,171	25,226	60,268	41,882	49,205	45,859	28.7
Yuma, AZ	195,148	159,935	21,052	69,587	65,931	68,198	53,653	19.1

Table B-5.   Population Characteristics, 2009–2011

Metropolitan statistical area and division	Total	Households						With one or more persons 65 years and over	Foreign-born population (percent of total)	Speaking language other than English at home, persons 5 years and over (percent)
		Family				Nonfamily				
		Total	With own children under 18			Householder living alone				
			Total	Single parent headed (percent)		Total	Percent age 65 or older			
Abilene, TX	59,462	38,897	16,768	33.6		16,986	38.1	16,100	5.3	14.4
Akron, OH	281,202	179,530	75,917	33.9		84,508	34.3	71,244	3.8	5.4
Albany, GA	57,611	38,805	16,263	49.6		16,264	29.4	13,699	2.0	3.5
Albany–Schenectady–Troy, NY	346,680	211,866	92,084	32.1		108,312	34.6	85,717	6.7	8.6
Albuquerque, NM	342,519	219,471	99,711	39.7		99,347	29.8	78,591	9.8	31.4
Alexandria, LA	53,987	35,402	15,831	39.0		16,750	38.8	14,790	2.5	4.8
Allentown–Bethlehem–Easton, PA–NJ	312,118	215,326	92,976	29.4		80,615	42.2	86,778	7.8	15.6
Altoona, PA	51,949	34,230	13,233	33.6		14,889	45.0	15,448	1.3	3.3
Amarillo, TX	92,663	62,367	28,631	33.7		25,894	30.8	20,119	8.9	20.1
Ames, IA	34,970	18,570	7,551	22.6		10,189	24.1	5,966	7.8	8.6
Anchorage, AK	137,268	92,771	48,750	30.8		33,416	22.4	20,714	8.0	15.1
Anderson, IN	50,290	32,433	12,860	39.5		15,236	40.1	14,367	2.2	(D)
Anderson, SC	73,126	51,293	20,646	33.9		19,379	38.4	20,115	2.4	3.8
Ann Arbor, MI	133,602	76,164	35,561	26.6		43,207	24.5	25,491	11.6	14.2
Anniston–Oxford, AL	45,694	30,314	11,145	37.7		13,290	36.2	12,435	2.4	(D)
Appleton, WI	87,477	60,241	28,059	25.5		22,362	36.2	18,339	3.7	6.7
Asheville, NC	181,164	114,332	42,714	31.2		54,727	38.4	54,727	5.6	7.5
Athens–Clarke County, GA	65,946	40,268	18,038	34.1		18,277	26.0	13,246	7.8	9.9
Atlanta–Sandy Springs–Marietta, GA	1,886,767	1,289,900	641,853	32.1		495,027	23.3	336,975	13.5	17.3
Atlantic City–Hammonton, NJ	100,739	66,847	30,159	36.4		28,905	39.1	28,185	16.5	24.9
Auburn–Opelika, AL	55,459	32,799	14,780	27.4		16,454	20.0	9,163	5.0	6.9
Augusta–Richmond County, GA–SC	205,567	141,309	60,833	41.7		56,053	31.9	49,504	4.0	5.7
Austin–Round Rock–San Marcos, TX	649,827	407,274	207,563	28.9		180,165	18.6	99,280	14.6	27.7
Bakersfield–Delano, CA	252,086	189,535	102,278	37.0		49,949	37.2	54,776	20.5	41.3
Baltimore–Towson, MD	1,022,038	666,607	297,086	34.7		292,459	33.4	247,299	9.1	11.4
Bangor, ME	62,698	39,263	16,212	30.2		16,922	38.2	15,553	2.5	4.8
Barnstable Town, MA	96,726	59,427	19,345	34.1		31,764	46.2	37,570	6.7	8.4
Baton Rouge, LA	292,728	197,253	89,451	37.0		77,662	28.9	61,939	3.6	6.7
Battle Creek, MI	53,216	34,868	14,965	43.6		15,843	36.9	14,042	3.8	6.2
Bay City, MI	43,864	28,620	11,470	36.4		12,288	39.6	12,182	1.5	3.6
Beaumont–Port Arthur, TX	144,092	98,473	43,598	39.9		39,559	37.8	37,378	7.1	13.7
Bellingham, WA	80,052	48,805	20,785	28.5		22,649	32.1	18,801	11.4	12.0
Bend, OR	64,514	44,302	18,663	30.0		15,344	39.1	16,553	4.4	6.6
Billings, MT	65,262	41,408	18,110	34.4		19,327	37.3	16,395	1.8	4.2
Binghamton, NY	100,597	63,287	26,577	33.8		30,854	40.2	28,568	4.8	7.4
Birmingham–Hoover, AL	433,751	294,284	127,627	33.5		121,091	33.7	105,122	4.3	5.9
Bismarck, ND	45,153	29,327	13,066	27.5		12,976	33.5	10,066	1.0	5.3
Blacksburg–Christiansburg–Radford, VA	62,319	35,717	13,540	29.3		18,540	29.4	14,223	6.5	8.2
Bloomington, IN	74,988	42,709	17,198	32.6		23,488	28.1	16,001	5.9	7.0
Bloomington–Normal, IL	63,160	38,770	18,165	27.7		18,254	27.8	11,806	5.9	7.7
Boise City–Nampa, ID	225,105	157,283	77,146	26.6		53,630	32.1	47,235	7.0	11.8
Boston–Cambridge–Quincy, MA–NH	1,751,250	1,101,302	505,164	27.0		507,098	35.7	429,177	16.7	22.6
Boston–Quincy, MA	723,888	434,196	199,660	31.1		223,454	34.4	174,756	17.9	23.8
Cambridge–Newton–Framingham, MA	578,681	367,066	170,316	21.0		163,938	34.6	140,757	19.5	25.1
Peabody, MA	286,251	188,747	87,153	31.5		81,388	40.7	76,042	14.8	23.7
Rockingham County–Strafford County, NH	162,430	111,293	48,035	23.2		38,318	37.2	37,622	4.4	6.4
Boulder, CO	118,937	70,519	33,080	24.4		33,382	24.0	20,835	11.0	16.3
Bowling Green, KY	47,801	30,279	13,992	29.8		14,008	30.5	10,042	7.0	9.1
Bremerton–Silverdale, WA	97,837	66,743	28,926	29.9		24,796	33.3	23,045	6.8	9.8
Bridgeport–Stamford–Norwalk, CT	332,735	226,835	109,629	23.3		89,388	37.3	86,481	20.0	27.9
Brownsville–Harlingen, TX	115,136	92,696	48,053	35.1		19,355	43.2	30,475	24.4	71.6
Brunswick, GA	43,745	30,159	11,627	41.8		12,026	41.0	12,444	4.0	7.5
Buffalo–Niagara Falls, NY	466,224	286,105	123,883	38.6		151,462	38.3	127,308	6.0	9.1
Burlington, NC	60,118	40,411	17,732	37.3		17,077	41.8	16,161	7.3	11.7
Burlington–South Burlington, VT	84,220	53,241	24,073	27.2		22,112	31.7	17,208	5.9	7.3
Canton–Massillon, OH	160,442	106,373	42,798	35.4		46,858	39.5	45,365	1.7	3.4
Cape Coral–Fort Myers, FL	237,009	154,600	52,687	35.5		67,196	48.8	94,531	14.9	21.0
Cape Girardeau–Jackson, MO–IL	36,946	24,907	10,764	35.0		9,680	37.9	9,391	2.0	(D)
Carson City, NV	21,068	13,546	5,176	37.7		6,302	36.4	6,352	10.5	19.2
Casper, WY	30,449	20,435	8,400	33.2		7,843	32.3	6,724	2.0	(D)
Cedar Rapids, IA	104,197	67,888	31,561	30.6		29,687	35.4	24,598	2.5	4.4
Champaign–Urbana, IL	91,231	50,580	22,572	32.0		29,347	27.3	18,146	10.5	14.4
Charleston, WV	125,350	82,601	31,938	32.7		36,671	39.5	35,493	1.2	2.0
Charleston–North Charleston–Summerville, SC	253,690	163,734	72,375	35.2		72,177	28.3	55,742	5.5	7.2
Charlotte–Gastonia–Rock Hill, NC–SC	667,115	448,800	218,839	32.4		180,609	24.9	126,140	10.1	13.5
Charlottesville, VA	77,152	46,838	18,970	26.9		23,227	31.6	19,450	8.5	10.1
Chattanooga, TN–GA	208,890	140,824	57,345	31.5		59,358	35.7	55,709	3.7	5.2
Cheyenne, WY	37,694	24,843	10,727	33.2		10,772	34.7	8,327	2.9	7.4
Chicago–Joliet–Naperville, IL–IN–WI	3,415,379	2,267,822	1,076,269	29.3		958,074	32.0	777,512	17.6	28.6
Chicago–Joliet–Naperville, IL	2,853,466	1,869,610	883,489	29.4		817,597	31.4	646,499	18.9	30.5
Gary, IN	260,374	177,185	78,218	35.0		72,662	34.7	65,573	5.8	12.0
Lake County–Kenosha County, IL–WI	301,539	221,027	114,562	24.0		67,815	36.9	65,440	15.9	24.6

(D) = Data withheld due to disclosure or does not meet statistical standards.

Table B-5.   Population Characteristics, 2009–2011—*Continued*

Metropolitan statistical area and division	Households Total	Family Total	Family With own children under 18 Total	Family With own children under 18 Single parent headed (percent)	Nonfamily Householder living alone Total	Nonfamily Householder living alone Percent age 65 or older	With one or more persons 65 years and over	Foreign-born population (percent of total)	Speaking language other than English at home, persons 5 years and over (percent)
Chico, CA	84,146	51,040	20,437	37.1	24,771	39.0	23,986	7.4	13.8
Cincinnati–Middletown, OH–KY–IN	812,020	542,837	248,573	32.5	224,091	33.0	182,171	4.2	5.9
Clarksville, TN–KY	100,174	71,138	36,665	32.2	24,478	29.4	18,223	4.5	8.0
Cleveland, TN	43,797	30,186	11,666	28.5	11,662	41.3	12,409	3.7	5.5
Cleveland–Elyria–Mentor, OH	844,591	528,109	226,806	37.9	272,176	35.2	225,912	5.9	10.1
Coeur d'Alene, ID	55,941	38,628	17,345	31.3	12,577	36.4	14,396	2.3	3.3
College Station–Bryan, TX	81,169	47,086	23,006	36.5	21,547	24.2	13,981	11.5	21.6
Colorado Springs, CO	243,981	164,265	78,666	28.9	65,376	27.1	46,589	6.9	11.5
Columbia, MO	68,101	39,392	19,400	29.2	19,603	24.0	12,087	5.9	8.0
Columbia, SC	294,118	191,577	86,717	38.6	85,144	28.1	63,262	4.9	7.0
Columbus, GA–AL	109,630	73,606	33,619	45.8	31,762	34.3	25,774	4.1	8.1
Columbus, IN	30,169	21,221	9,311	27.6	7,693	41.5	7,464	6.7	8.3
Columbus, OH	709,639	452,158	220,225	32.7	205,196	27.4	141,195	7.0	9.0
Corpus Christi, TX	154,399	106,282	46,321	41.8	39,342	32.7	38,967	7.1	38.3
Corvallis, OR	33,428	19,004	7,864	26.8	9,468	28.0	7,019	9.1	11.3
Crestview–Fort Walton Beach–Destin, FL	71,002	47,687	19,902	34.1	18,959	30.7	17,515	6.9	9.6
Cumberland, MD–WV	40,084	24,488	9,193	36.0	13,310	45.9	12,871	1.2	3.3
Dallas–Fort Worth–Arlington, TX	2,275,581	1,579,063	810,489	30.0	572,516	24.0	403,051	17.5	29.8
Dallas–Plano–Irving, TX	1,510,273	1,039,333	539,087	29.5	383,104	22.7	258,918	19.2	32.2
Fort Worth–Arlington, TX	765,308	539,730	271,402	30.9	189,412	26.6	144,133	14.1	25.1
Dalton, GA	48,366	36,262	16,969	30.7	9,348	37.0	11,075	15.1	25.3
Danville, IL	31,502	20,140	7,861	45.7	9,692	44.7	9,331	2.0	(D)
Danville, VA	44,663	30,003	10,576	41.3	13,026	44.3	14,183	2.3	(D)
Davenport–Moline–Rock Island, IA–IL	154,477	99,162	42,406	35.5	46,758	37.5	40,205	4.5	7.3
Dayton, OH	343,639	218,970	93,086	38.8	106,351	35.1	89,867	3.4	5.0
Decatur, AL	59,367	41,621	16,728	34.6	15,761	38.0	15,325	4.7	(D)
Decatur, IL	44,719	27,809	10,781	39.9	14,736	38.2	12,552	1.8	3.1
Deltona–Daytona Beach–Ormond Beach, FL	193,393	121,274	40,906	36.0	60,440	44.1	69,351	7.0	12.8
Denver–Aurora–Broomfield, CO[1]	997,755	629,677	303,652	28.8	294,702	25.2	185,660	12.1	19.9
Des Moines–West Des Moines, IA	224,132	149,590	73,686	28.1	60,228	30.2	44,068	7.4	10.8
Detroit–Warren–Livonia, MI	1,646,308	1,082,462	486,302	34.4	489,628	35.2	413,644	8.7	12.1
Detroit–Livonia–Dearborn, MI	672,320	424,009	195,382	46.1	219,124	34.1	170,619	7.7	12.2
Warren–Troy–Farmington Hills, MI	973,988	658,453	290,920	26.5	270,504	36.1	243,025	9.4	12.0
Dothan, AL	57,248	39,927	16,424	38.7	15,439	40.6	15,732	2.5	4.6
Dover, DE	56,947	40,041	17,840	39.4	14,130	39.0	15,302	4.8	8.6
Dubuque, IA	37,167	24,320	10,380	27.6	10,421	36.2	9,169	1.8	3.2
Duluth, MN–WI	118,763	71,986	29,940	35.6	37,024	38.3	30,768	2.2	4.3
Durham–Chapel Hill, NC	200,997	124,158	56,535	36.8	59,968	25.1	39,893	12.7	16.8
Eau Claire, WI	63,881	39,524	17,491	28.7	18,350	38.3	15,457	2.5	5.2
El Centro, CA	48,831	38,651	20,166	36.0	8,907	45.9	12,762	32.0	73.6
Elizabethtown, KY	43,755	31,805	15,136	32.6	10,605	30.8	9,323	3.8	6.4
Elkhart–Goshen, IN	69,535	50,123	23,358	32.8	16,518	35.8	15,890	8.3	17.2
Elmira, NY	35,836	22,838	10,095	42.3	10,607	40.1	9,609	2.9	(D)
El Paso, TX	251,931	190,352	99,299	35.7	53,494	35.4	59,361	26.0	73.6
Erie, PA	109,142	69,042	29,025	37.7	33,996	35.9	28,520	4.0	6.4
Eugene–Springfield, OR	145,099	86,803	34,528	35.6	41,506	37.5	38,139	5.9	9.6
Evansville, IN–KY	142,634	94,598	39,808	32.0	40,609	36.4	35,665	2.2	3.7
Fairbanks, AK	36,123	24,636	12,248	29.0	8,681	17.7	4,670	5.7	10.5
Fargo, ND–MN	86,909	50,030	24,200	25.7	28,367	25.2	15,124	4.7	6.2
Farmington, NM	41,891	31,404	14,150	37.5	8,923	35.7	9,785	4.2	34.4
Fayetteville, NC	134,475	91,926	46,146	42.9	35,830	25.4	24,487	5.7	11.1
Fayetteville–Springdale–Rogers, AR–MO	173,321	119,425	58,460	27.2	43,211	30.9	36,520	10.6	16.2
Flagstaff, AZ	44,858	28,845	11,647	36.9	11,361	20.7	8,596	5.6	24.1
Flint, MI	165,073	106,721	47,280	41.7	50,252	35.0	41,649	2.2	3.4
Florence, SC	78,178	53,945	23,066	45.1	21,125	33.2	19,960	2.3	3.0
Florence–Muscle Shoals, AL	61,091	40,394	16,186	32.5	18,343	41.5	18,122	2.1	2.9
Fond du Lac, WI	41,195	27,494	12,162	27.0	11,400	40.4	10,482	3.1	5.4
Fort Collins–Loveland, CO	119,773	76,274	33,380	24.0	30,405	30.0	24,649	5.4	9.1
Fort Smith, AR–OK	113,211	78,884	33,494	32.1	29,844	37.9	29,558	5.7	9.0
Fort Wayne, IN	160,087	107,747	50,698	32.8	43,621	33.0	35,537	5.3	8.7
Fresno, CA	285,735	208,019	109,765	36.1	61,503	37.0	66,323	22.2	43.8
Gadsden, AL	40,186	27,943	10,711	36.0	11,380	40.7	11,656	2.1	0.0
Gainesville, FL	102,180	56,400	22,207	37.7	31,116	23.7	20,946	10.4	13.4
Gainesville, GA	61,457	45,916	21,658	25.9	12,963	34.1	14,545	15.6	25.6
Glens Falls, NY	53,265	35,846	13,957	30.0	14,000	42.0	15,064	2.5	4.1
Goldsboro, NC	47,641	32,342	14,475	40.4	12,725	36.8	11,641	7.1	10.4
Grand Forks, ND–MN	39,628	23,505	10,681	30.1	12,312	30.4	8,328	3.5	6.7
Grand Junction, CO	58,636	38,740	17,223	25.3	15,741	38.5	15,657	4.7	10.3
Grand Rapids–Wyoming, MI	290,856	199,180	92,894	31.2	74,601	34.2	63,704	6.0	9.6
Great Falls, MT	32,950	21,376	8,605	31.8	10,117	36.2	9,112	2.8	(D)

[1]The Denver–Aurora metropolitan statistical area includes Broomfield County. Broomfield County, CO, was formed from parts of Adams, Boulder, Jefferson, and Weld counties on November 15, 2001, and is coextensive with Broomfield city. For the purposes of defining and presenting data for the Denver–Aurora metropolitan statistical area, Broomfield city is treated as if it were a county when data are available to do so. In many cases, the data will not be available.

(D) = Data withheld due to disclosure or does not meet statistical standards.

Table B-5. Population Characteristics, 2009–2011—*Continued*

Metropolitan statistical area and division	Total	Households						With one or more persons 65 years and over	Foreign-born population (percent of total)	Speaking language other than English at home, persons 5 years and over (percent)
		Family				Nonfamily				
		Total	With own children under 18		Householder living alone					
			Total	Single parent headed (percent)	Total	Percent age 65 or older				
Greeley, CO	89,222	63,354	31,011	26.2	20,536	30.8	17,049	8.3	17.4
Green Bay, WI	122,309	80,948	37,395	29.8	33,700	31.3	26,183	4.5	8.5
Greensboro–High Point, NC	285,114	185,324	82,636	38.6	83,936	32.1	67,551	8.1	11.1
Greenville, NC	71,887	42,733	20,998	40.7	22,040	28.5	14,022	5.2	8.1
Greenville–Mauldin–Easley, SC	241,916	161,718	69,905	33.6	68,093	32.9	59,138	6.7	9.6
Gulfport–Biloxi, MS	94,104	64,387	27,445	39.2	24,391	31.2	22,710	4.3	6.0
Hagerstown–Martinsburg, MD–WV	103,024	68,838	29,752	33.9	28,660	35.3	25,630	4.0	5.9
Hanford–Corcoran, CA	40,538	31,560	17,340	28.6	7,348	36.9	7,859	20.7	42.8
Harrisburg–Carlisle, PA	222,064	142,433	59,536	33.3	66,198	35.1	56,417	5.0	8.7
Harrisonburg, VA	45,018	29,302	11,723	29.7	10,330	40.2	11,000	8.5	13.2
Hartford–West Hartford–East Hartford, CT	469,280	310,053	140,873	32.9	131,293	38.1	122,295	12.9	20.7
Hattiesburg, MS	54,398	35,317	16,822	37.2	14,922	30.3	12,067	2.1	3.6
Hickory–Lenoir–Morganton, NC	138,102	94,607	37,833	31.6	37,410	40.3	38,587	5.2	8.2
Hinesville–Fort Stewart, GA	28,157	21,618	12,199	36.5	5,413	21.3	3,740	6.4	11.0
Holland–Grand Haven, MI	93,675	69,531	32,419	19.0	18,763	39.9	21,244	5.8	9.7
Honolulu, HI	308,950	216,023	87,628	25.0	72,680	33.2	94,797	19.9	28.2
Hot Springs, AR	39,137	24,847	8,607	35.7	12,089	45.4	13,671	3.9	5.9
Houma–Bayou Cane–Thibodaux, LA	74,378	53,236	23,882	35.6	16,698	37.1	17,443	3.1	15.3
Houston–Sugar Land–Baytown, TX	2,036,252	1,445,413	735,922	30.7	484,784	24.6	368,183	22.2	37.2
Huntington–Ashland, WV–KY–OH	114,544	75,778	28,224	37.7	33,589	41.4	33,744	1.1	1.8
Huntsville, AL	162,405	110,016	47,043	30.6	45,928	28.7	36,255	5.0	6.8
Idaho Falls, ID	43,985	33,956	17,680	22.6	8,325	38.9	9,686	5.4	10.5
Indianapolis–Carmel, IN	669,827	443,445	215,165	33.9	188,065	29.6	136,147	6.5	9.2
Iowa City, IA	61,786	33,963	15,562	26.2	19,224	24.3	10,497	8.0	12.3
Ithaca, NY	38,685	20,212	8,633	27.5	12,782	26.9	7,927	13.7	16.1
Jackson, MI	59,800	40,390	16,839	36.5	15,912	35.8	15,455	1.8	3.9
Jackson, MS	196,246	133,756	61,606	41.5	54,046	30.7	43,657	2.4	3.8
Jackson, TN	40,826	27,554	11,804	40.7	12,151	30.7	9,830	3.0	(D)
Jacksonville, FL	505,800	337,059	147,734	35.0	136,311	30.7	115,481	8.1	11.3
Jacksonville, NC	59,291	42,733	21,790	30.0	13,502	27.8	9,648	4.3	8.8
Janesville, WI	62,983	42,791	19,372	34.6	15,967	39.6	15,183	4.3	8.3
Jefferson City, MO	56,840	39,237	17,758	32.9	15,024	34.9	13,299	2.4	4.1
Johnson City, TN	83,089	54,571	20,648	32.2	23,442	38.5	22,806	2.8	3.7
Johnstown, PA	58,383	37,414	13,981	31.3	18,190	48.1	19,223	1.4	3.4
Jonesboro, AR	46,717	31,594	14,269	36.5	12,083	40.1	11,284	2.9	(D)
Joplin, MO	66,130	45,488	20,079	35.8	16,466	38.4	17,107	3.5	6.6
Kalamazoo–Portage, MI	127,533	80,260	37,314	35.3	37,388	30.1	28,569	4.7	7.4
Kankakee–Bradley, IL	41,113	28,234	12,995	35.8	10,585	44.2	10,630	4.4	7.9
Kansas City, MO–KS	793,657	523,748	249,470	32.8	225,057	31.5	172,440	6.3	9.5
Kennewick–Pasco–Richland, WA	87,366	62,242	30,338	29.9	20,616	30.4	18,400	14.7	26.7
Killeen–Temple–Fort Hood, TX	129,460	94,029	51,263	35.8	29,432	28.6	24,031	7.4	16.4
Kingsport–Bristol–Bristol, TN–VA	130,516	89,922	34,165	31.9	35,486	41.4	40,389	1.3	2.4
Kingston, NY	69,806	45,441	19,536	31.8	19,493	39.0	19,125	7.2	11.8
Knoxville, TN	286,992	182,234	73,407	31.2	90,532	32.8	73,069	4.0	5.3
Kokomo, IN	41,185	27,615	11,603	31.7	11,669	37.7	11,375	1.9	4.4
La Crosse, WI–MN	53,371	33,396	14,805	28.7	15,125	36.1	12,622	3.1	5.7
Lafayette, IN	77,206	45,423	21,032	27.9	21,982	28.1	14,949	9.2	12.5
Lafayette, LA	103,689	65,644	30,462	37.7	31,382	24.5	20,072	4.0	16.6
Lake Charles, LA	74,188	51,360	23,354	35.4	19,026	34.5	17,864	2.4	7.8
Lake Havasu City–Kingman, AZ	80,801	52,733	15,697	37.8	22,518	48.1	32,443	6.2	9.7
Lakeland–Winter Haven, FL	219,743	152,010	59,407	36.6	55,778	44.5	73,387	10.6	18.9
Lancaster, PA	193,775	136,089	57,516	23.0	47,093	42.2	52,657	4.6	15.3
Lansing–East Lansing, MI	179,245	111,032	49,321	31.7	53,274	29.1	38,222	6.6	9.4
Laredo, TX	66,750	55,632	31,483	37.5	9,123	37.0	13,943	29.1	(D)
Las Cruces, NM	73,836	51,435	23,339	37.3	17,388	32.7	18,562	17.9	51.7
Las Vegas–Paradise, NV	701,868	456,390	219,706	35.7	186,759	29.1	159,912	21.9	32.9
Lawrence, KS	43,154	23,620	10,668	27.9	11,028	24.5	6,902	6.7	9.8
Lawton, OK	44,634	30,333	15,306	42.1	11,715	30.9	8,953	5.6	11.8
Lebanon, PA	51,780	36,924	15,512	29.0	12,258	45.7	15,045	3.2	9.4
Lewiston, ID–WA	24,813	15,691	5,607	34.6	7,741	41.9	7,793	1.9	4.6
Lewiston–Auburn, ME	44,113	28,063	12,142	41.8	12,162	37.0	10,717	3.7	12.5
Lexington–Fayette, KY	189,963	120,443	56,248	35.0	55,424	28.5	37,737	6.7	9.0
Lima, OH	40,679	27,754	12,300	44.0	11,397	41.7	10,839	1.6	(D)
Lincoln, NE	120,451	74,774	35,088	29.5	34,444	29.1	23,718	7.0	10.5
Little Rock–North Little Rock–Conway, AR	272,417	180,378	77,765	38.3	77,481	27.0	58,733	4.1	6.6
Logan, UT–ID	39,292	29,890	16,030	16.8	6,370	35.7	7,029	6.4	13.4
Longview, TX	78,147	54,402	23,809	34.7	20,779	41.4	21,289	7.7	13.3
Longview, WA	40,112	27,270	11,207	37.8	10,242	39.9	10,990	4.7	7.7
Los Angeles–Long Beach–Santa Ana, CA	4,195,162	2,861,179	1,380,266	31.4	1,033,708	32.0	1,005,277	34.4	54.3
Los Angeles–Long Beach–Glendale, CA	3,206,808	2,157,043	1,043,667	33.7	818,021	30.7	758,798	35.5	57.1
Santa Ana–Anaheim–Irvine, CA	988,354	704,136	336,599	24.6	215,687	37.0	246,479	30.7	45.4
Louisville/Jefferson County, KY–IN	503,889	332,610	146,061	36.7	145,260	33.0	118,200	4.7	6.3

(D) = Data withheld due to disclosure or does not meet statistical standards.

Table B-5. Population Characteristics, 2009–2011—*Continued*

Metropolitan statistical area and division	Households Total	Family Total	Family With own children under 18 Total	Family With own children under 18 Single parent headed (percent)	Nonfamily Householder living alone Total	Nonfamily Householder living alone Percent age 65 or older	With one or more persons 65 years and over	Foreign-born population (percent of total)	Speaking language other than English at home, persons 5 years and over (percent)
Lubbock, TX	106,390	66,205	30,522	35.1	29,879	29.7	22,685	5.7	21.9
Lynchburg, VA	98,204	66,601	27,024	34.7	25,970	38.8	27,378	2.5	3.6
Macon, GA	84,566	57,043	22,961	42.5	23,553	34.0	21,868	3.0	4.4
Madera–Chowchilla, CA	41,781	32,796	16,113	31.3	7,435	34.9	11,129	21.2	43.2
Madison, WI	237,548	140,944	65,176	29.6	71,879	25.4	43,813	7.0	10.6
Manchester–Nashua, NH	153,465	103,788	48,060	28.5	38,745	32.1	33,473	8.3	12.5
Manhattan, KS	45,473	27,236	14,173	25.6	12,256	27.7	7,364	6.0	9.6
Mankato–North Mankato, MN	36,434	22,311	9,916	27.6	9,698	34.7	7,745	3.3	6.3
Mansfield, OH	48,467	31,560	13,032	36.3	14,887	41.5	14,109	1.5	(D)
McAllen–Edinburg–Mission, TX	213,207	174,894	98,280	30.8	33,051	41.0	49,662	29.7	85.2
Medford, OR	83,645	53,776	21,393	36.1	24,048	42.3	25,494	5.6	8.9
Memphis, TN–MS–AR	478,385	323,276	146,749	44.0	133,907	27.7	101,613	5.1	7.4
Merced, CA	74,181	57,297	31,406	33.2	13,589	37.2	16,396	25.3	52.3
Miami–Fort Lauderdale–Pompano Beach, FL	1,998,159	1,294,874	559,550	36.9	578,332	39.5	609,189	38.3	51.0
Fort Lauderdale–Pompano Beach–Deerfield Beach, FL	661,113	414,873	191,471	36.3	201,792	37.1	179,847	31.5	37.5
Miami–Miami Beach–Kendall, FL	816,522	560,964	243,458	37.8	210,556	35.6	236,905	51.5	72.8
West Palm Beach–Boca Raton–Boynton Beach, FL	520,524	319,037	124,621	36.1	165,984	47.5	192,437	22.5	27.9
Michigan City–La Porte, IN	42,512	28,065	11,720	38.6	12,580	37.7	11,299	3.1	5.4
Midland, TX	49,660	35,764	17,215	34.1	11,939	34.7	10,345	8.4	29.8
Milwaukee–Waukesha–West Allis, WI	615,533	385,612	179,243	37.1	188,186	33.5	140,312	6.9	12.2
Minneapolis–St. Paul–Bloomington, MN–WI	1,274,390	824,347	400,017	27.2	357,795	29.1	247,021	9.6	13.3
Missoula, MT	45,229	26,155	11,182	33.3	13,364	26.2	8,893	3.1	5.3
Mobile, AL	156,371	105,800	45,876	41.1	43,833	32.3	39,191	3.3	4.9
Modesto, CA	166,136	124,619	63,045	32.6	33,096	41.4	39,430	20.8	41.6
Monroe, LA	65,747	44,074	20,134	44.3	19,343	35.3	16,218	1.9	2.9
Monroe, MI	58,772	42,714	17,712	27.1	13,830	39.4	14,612	1.8	3.9
Montgomery, AL	139,859	95,000	43,470	41.4	38,951	33.5	32,968	3.2	4.6
Morgantown, WV	49,046	27,852	11,095	27.1	16,002	22.4	10,158	3.6	5.1
Morristown, TN	53,753	37,114	15,141	28.5	14,364	45.3	15,788	4.0	(D)
Mount Vernon–Anacortes, WA	45,373	30,931	12,598	34.5	11,622	44.1	13,358	9.4	13.9
Muncie, IN	45,985	27,785	11,243	41.4	13,589	34.6	12,149	2.1	2.9
Muskegon–Norton Shores, MI	64,767	44,780	19,415	40.5	16,878	39.1	16,487	2.0	4.4
Myrtle Beach–North Myrtle Beach–Conway, SC	112,170	73,801	26,733	36.0	29,629	39.9	33,900	6.9	8.4
Napa, CA	50,083	34,362	15,010	27.4	12,063	44.3	14,292	22.4	34.8
Naples–Marco Island, FL	118,898	80,487	24,445	33.0	32,827	52.9	53,306	23.3	31.6
Nashville–Davidson—Murfreesboro—Franklin, TN	605,509	402,979	184,250	31.0	164,561	26.6	121,867	7.5	10.0
New Haven–Milford, CT	329,691	215,069	96,802	35.8	94,214	37.8	86,922	11.6	21.0
New Orleans–Metairie–Kenner, LA	454,532	291,752	126,062	41.8	134,203	29.1	105,579	7.3	11.2
New York–Northern New Jersey–Long Island, NY–NJ–PA	6,815,327	4,523,236	2,086,009	31.5	1,901,205	36.5	1,785,959	28.7	38.7
Edison–New Brunswick, NJ	848,291	597,004	273,395	21.5	212,655	45.4	246,000	19.4	26.1
Nassau–Suffolk, NY	939,313	714,122	321,331	20.4	187,073	48.0	282,685	17.5	23.9
Newark–Union, NJ–PA	764,451	533,906	257,372	30.5	196,510	37.1	191,507	21.9	29.7
New York–White Plains–Wayne, NY–NJ	4,263,272	2,678,204	1,233,911	36.9	1,304,967	33.3	1,065,767	34.6	46.6
Niles–Benton Harbor, MI	60,458	39,465	15,285	35.9	18,276	39.8	18,138	5.8	7.9
North Port–Bradenton–Sarasota, FL	298,561	186,500	56,788	34.8	93,243	54.1	130,414	12.3	14.7
Norwich–New London, CT	107,486	70,658	30,994	32.3	29,718	37.2	28,002	8.9	14.6
Ocala, FL	133,433	89,861	26,958	39.5	35,947	50.8	57,006	8.1	12.2
Ocean City, NJ	43,355	28,296	10,650	33.5	12,783	46.9	14,988	5.3	9.2
Odessa, TX	49,277	34,107	16,716	38.0	12,618	33.0	9,976	12.8	42.5
Ogden–Clearfield, UT	176,913	137,991	73,829	21.0	31,307	33.6	33,911	5.6	11.0
Oklahoma City, OK	479,789	314,224	145,733	33.6	136,665	31.0	105,063	7.8	12.2
Olympia, WA	100,507	66,016	28,474	32.6	27,332	32.1	22,960	7.2	10.0
Omaha–Council Bluffs, NE–IA	333,335	218,639	105,035	29.5	93,735	30.3	67,562	6.7	10.6
Orlando–Kissimmee–Sanford, FL	762,102	514,518	223,621	34.5	190,952	30.0	180,618	16.2	29.0
Oshkosh–Neenah, WI	68,059	41,408	18,437	33.9	20,497	35.1	15,202	3.5	5.6
Owensboro, KY	43,748	30,286	12,627	35.5	11,675	41.3	11,549	1.7	(D)
Oxnard–Thousand Oaks–Ventura, CA	266,259	196,644	94,602	26.4	53,794	41.3	67,677	22.9	37.4
Palm Bay–Melbourne–Titusville, FL	219,281	142,194	50,626	33.2	63,132	44.9	75,949	8.9	9.8
Palm Coast, FL	35,262	26,107	7,961	26.4	7,647	52.3	14,653	13.7	15.1
Panama City–Lynn Haven–Panama City Beach, FL	67,521	43,001	16,221	33.5	19,772	35.0	17,776	5.0	6.5
Parkersburg–Marietta–Vienna, WV–OH	65,079	42,770	16,002	25.2	19,091	41.0	19,280	0.9	(D)
Pascagoula, MS	58,391	42,049	18,490	35.1	14,220	34.2	14,105	3.5	5.9
Pensacola–Ferry Pass–Brent, FL	166,826	111,670	45,367	35.8	45,154	35.3	43,932	5.7	8.2
Peoria, IL	151,310	99,775	43,486	33.9	43,679	36.3	38,495	2.9	4.6
Philadelphia–Camden–Wilmington, PA–NJ–DE–MD	2,222,507	1,446,710	651,063	32.3	650,015	35.8	565,808	9.7	14.8
Camden, NJ	458,351	317,615	144,881	29.2	118,353	38.3	118,016	9.0	14.7
Philadelphia, PA	1,502,579	951,084	425,154	33.2	464,106	35.0	384,498	10.1	15.2
Wilmington, DE–MD–NJ	261,577	178,011	81,028	32.8	67,556	36.8	63,294	8.5	12.9

(D) = Data withheld due to disclosure or does not meet statistical standards.

Table B-5.   Population Characteristics, 2009–2011—*Continued*

Metropolitan statistical area and division	Total	Family Total	Family With own children under 18 Total	Family With own children under 18 Single parent headed (percent)	Nonfamily Householder living alone Total	Nonfamily Householder living alone Percent age 65 or older	With one or more persons 65 years and over	Foreign-born population (percent of total)	Speaking language other than English at home, persons 5 years and over (percent)
Phoenix–Mesa–Glendale, AZ	1,515,084	1,006,303	472,590	33.9	400,208	31.1	359,459	14.6	25.9
Pine Bluff, AR	35,923	24,181	10,340	44.5	10,668	35.7	9,357	1.1	(D)
Pittsburgh, PA	986,270	613,883	239,547	31.0	317,259	40.7	290,647	3.2	5.1
Pittsfield, MA	55,338	32,285	12,932	38.7	20,094	44.3	17,689	4.6	7.4
Pocatello, ID	32,691	22,144	10,578	27.4	8,533	28.5	6,830	4.0	8.0
Portland–South Portland–Biddeford, ME	212,339	134,071	55,296	30.4	60,806	38.0	54,694	4.5	7.3
Portland–Vancouver–Hillsboro, OR–WA	864,818	550,126	257,655	29.0	238,657	30.2	184,021	12.5	17.3
Port St. Lucie, FL	163,431	108,750	39,376	36.6	45,755	48.3	63,345	13.0	18.4
Poughkeepsie–Newburgh–Middletown, NY	233,466	163,738	77,716	24.8	57,257	38.0	57,428	11.5	19.5
Prescott, AZ	90,660	56,448	15,961	35.0	27,916	44.9	36,016	6.4	10.0
Providence–New Bedford–Fall River, RI–MA	619,939	393,861	173,669	35.7	184,694	38.1	162,282	12.6	21.0
Provo–Orem, UT	144,281	117,873	69,300	12.7	17,707	37.7	23,241	7.3	13.0
Pueblo, CO	62,142	39,672	16,717	39.8	18,740	37.5	17,042	3.9	14.1
Punta Gorda, FL	70,475	46,245	11,818	39.9	20,545	62.0	36,269	9.8	11.1
Racine, WI	75,679	49,759	21,787	32.6	21,555	36.1	18,161	4.8	9.2
Raleigh–Cary, NC	423,144	286,273	146,990	27.6	110,780	24.1	72,715	11.8	15.6
Rapid City, SD	50,241	33,413	15,328	33.0	13,641	35.3	11,540	1.8	4.6
Reading, PA	155,043	107,365	47,118	33.6	38,317	39.9	40,803	6.8	16.7
Redding, CA	68,614	45,423	18,017	38.0	18,992	43.3	21,613	5.5	8.8
Reno–Sparks, NV	163,362	103,052	46,405	33.0	46,246	29.0	37,331	14.7	22.5
Richmond, VA	476,077	316,380	142,438	34.9	130,311	32.1	110,278	7.0	9.1
Riverside–San Bernardino–Ontario, CA	1,276,036	957,019	487,771	30.8	251,273	40.2	311,894	21.6	40.7
Roanoke, VA	127,682	83,430	32,556	32.9	38,270	37.0	35,367	4.4	5.7
Rochester, MN	72,848	48,876	23,394	24.5	19,819	33.8	16,313	7.5	10.3
Rochester, NY	416,727	265,556	118,741	36.2	122,734	34.9	104,583	6.8	10.6
Rockford, IL	131,197	87,359	39,598	35.5	36,400	36.0	32,864	8.1	12.9
Rocky Mount, NC	59,393	40,128	17,155	47.1	17,174	40.3	15,879	3.9	(D)
Rome, GA	35,180	24,300	10,484	28.3	9,249	46.7	9,916	6.3	(D)
Sacramento–Arden-Arcade–Roseville, CA	781,039	518,596	247,105	31.9	202,563	34.1	187,016	17.5	27.1
Saginaw–Saginaw Township North, MI	76,825	49,766	20,794	37.1	23,213	38.7	21,147	2.3	5.3
St. Cloud, MN	72,102	46,844	21,529	26.4	17,631	38.9	15,730	3.9	6.7
St. George, UT	46,473	36,279	15,739	21.2	8,419	47.7	15,278	5.7	7.7
St. Joseph, MO–KS	46,951	30,495	12,634	35.3	13,963	38.8	12,377	2.9	4.9
St. Louis, MO–IL[2]	1,111,725	728,839	323,010	34.4	321,575	34.3	265,678	4.4	6.4
Salem, OR	140,850	97,063	44,816	32.3	35,518	40.1	36,247	12.5	22.9
Salinas, CA	125,329	90,736	46,949	31.4	26,774	36.1	30,468	30.6	52.2
Salisbury, MD	44,453	29,658	13,235	45.2	11,317	37.1	11,465	6.6	9.3
Salt Lake City, UT	372,260	264,023	134,072	22.7	84,498	29.1	69,551	11.4	18.7
San Angelo, TX	42,507	28,852	11,722	35.1	11,093	37.5	11,122	7.2	(D)
San Antonio–New Braunfels, TX	750,639	522,612	249,848	33.2	190,016	29.1	167,620	11.9	39.0
San Diego–Carlsbad–San Marcos, CA	1,063,605	701,873	330,804	28.1	270,342	31.4	245,674	23.4	37.5
Sandusky, OH	31,571	20,994	8,035	34.1	9,113	38.6	9,066	1.6	(D)
San Francisco–Oakland–Fremont, CA	1,606,837	1,001,393	458,281	26.0	462,009	32.1	393,821	29.9	40.5
Oakland–Fremont–Hayward, CA	908,724	609,142	291,871	27.4	234,300	33.4	214,625	27.8	39.0
San Francisco–San Mateo–Redwood City, CA	698,113	392,251	166,410	23.5	227,709	30.8	179,196	32.9	42.5
San Jose–Sunnyvale–Santa Clara, CA	617,875	439,187	219,068	20.9	136,127	32.2	141,675	36.4	50.4
San Luis Obispo–Paso Robles, CA	100,976	63,700	25,110	28.8	26,886	39.1	28,662	10.4	16.9
Santa Barbara–Santa Maria–Goleta, CA	140,940	91,835	42,341	31.0	34,987	40.9	37,455	23.8	40.2
Santa Cruz–Watsonville, CA	92,855	58,246	26,814	29.7	24,010	33.9	21,290	18.3	30.6
Santa Fe, NM	60,976	35,241	13,750	38.3	20,868	33.6	16,306	14.1	36.4
Santa Rosa–Petaluma, CA	184,079	116,146	51,728	29.6	51,608	37.7	48,651	16.2	24.4
Savannah, GA	129,587	83,816	37,294	37.1	37,356	30.8	28,787	5.7	7.0
Scranton—Wilkes-Barre, PA	228,629	146,933	57,900	36.2	70,273	44.9	71,128	4.6	7.9
Seattle–Tacoma–Bellevue, WA	1,359,493	849,089	398,323	27.2	394,812	27.3	269,190	16.6	21.4
Seattle–Bellevue–Everett, WA	1,060,558	648,465	304,291	25.6	316,690	26.5	206,193	18.6	23.5
Tacoma, WA	298,935	200,624	94,032	32.3	78,122	30.6	62,997	9.9	14.3
Sebastian–Vero Beach, FL	56,814	36,778	12,333	36.2	17,139	60.1	25,375	10.3	15.0
Sheboygan, WI	45,925	30,522	12,952	25.3	12,399	39.7	11,614	5.1	9.9
Sherman–Denison, TX	46,169	32,411	13,354	38.9	11,292	42.9	12,950	5.2	9.2
Shreveport–Bossier City, LA	153,627	97,291	40,616	44.5	50,060	30.3	37,442	2.6	4.6
Sioux City, IA–NE–SD	54,307	36,613	17,497	36.9	15,070	41.5	13,117	9.5	16.6
Sioux Falls, SD	89,076	59,630	29,684	28.7	23,791	29.7	17,070	5.3	8.3
South Bend–Mishawaka, IN–MI	120,854	79,433	35,201	34.2	34,783	36.3	30,840	4.8	8.6
Spartanburg, SC	105,852	74,694	31,268	33.6	27,380	37.2	27,333	6.0	8.7
Spokane, WA	187,157	119,282	54,069	31.2	54,040	34.8	44,346	5.7	7.8
Springfield, IL	87,760	55,492	25,056	39.1	27,402	35.5	21,338	3.2	4.7
Springfield, MA	268,518	169,365	75,591	41.1	79,618	38.7	70,085	8.2	19.0
Springfield, MO	174,504	115,252	50,599	29.8	48,151	35.2	42,882	2.4	5.0
Springfield, OH	55,123	36,243	15,485	39.2	15,707	41.5	15,467	2.4	4.0
State College, PA	57,157	31,779	12,527	20.9	16,138	29.5	11,751	7.4	10.3
Steubenville–Weirton, OH–WV	51,019	33,904	12,420	35.9	15,172	46.6	16,386	0.9	2.2

[2]The portion of Sullivan city in Crawford County, MO, is legally part of the St. Louis, MO–IL MSA. That portion is not included in these figures for the St. Louis MSA.
(D) = Data withheld due to disclosure or does not meet statistical standards.

Table B-5. Population Characteristics, 2009–2011—*Continued*

Metropolitan statistical area and division	Total	Households						With one or more persons 65 years and over	Foreign-born population (percent of total)	Speaking language other than English at home, persons 5 years and over (percent)
		Family			Nonfamily					
		Total	With own children under 18		Householder living alone					
			Total	Single parent headed (percent)	Total	Percent age 65 or older				
Stockton, CA	213,967	157,321	82,563	32.8	44,098	37.9		50,713	23.2	40.1
Sumter, SC	39,026	26,813	11,672	40.6	11,118	38.1		10,071	3.5	(D)
Syracuse, NY	255,493	161,731	71,620	36.0	74,737	36.3		64,354	5.7	8.3
Tallahassee, FL	141,858	82,620	35,161	41.5	41,562	24.9		27,498	6.1	8.8
Tampa–St. Petersburg–Clearwater, FL	1,109,897	678,968	270,250	36.7	352,036	38.4		335,422	12.3	18.6
Terre Haute, IN	63,787	41,698	17,072	34.8	18,585	40.4		16,794	2.3	3.8
Texarkana, TX–Texarkana, AR	50,163	34,686	14,715	43.2	14,095	39.3		13,598	2.4	(D)
Toledo, OH	260,053	165,589	71,915	39.8	78,158	32.9		62,002	3.2	5.4
Topeka, KS	95,054	62,939	26,814	34.5	27,228	34.0		23,932	3.4	6.8
Trenton–Ewing, NJ	129,884	87,112	40,082	30.7	35,357	36.9		33,096	20.3	27.5
Tucson, AZ	379,608	236,779	98,320	37.2	116,361	35.2		106,098	13.2	28.5
Tulsa, OK	366,058	244,941	111,520	33.6	102,589	34.0		86,144	5.6	8.8
Tuscaloosa, AL	76,804	49,782	21,093	39.2	22,219	29.5		16,949	3.3	5.8
Tyler, TX	78,437	53,678	23,065	32.1	20,495	39.2		21,347	9.0	16.1
Utica–Rome, NY	117,848	75,219	32,594	35.4	35,529	42.4		33,973	6.5	10.5
Valdosta, GA	49,917	32,938	15,562	41.1	13,283	29.5		10,405	4.1	(D)
Vallejo–Fairfield, CA	140,265	100,374	45,344	32.7	31,603	34.2		32,895	19.9	29.3
Victoria, TX	42,878	30,991	12,947	40.7	10,295	41.0		11,654	5.8	25.3
Vineland–Millville–Bridgeton, NJ	50,409	35,126	15,951	43.1	12,801	45.9		14,224	11.3	25.5
Virginia Beach–Norfolk–Newport News, VA–NC	617,894	418,033	188,056	35.9	159,762	31.5		138,868	6.2	8.7
Visalia–Porterville, CA	129,790	101,009	55,195	34.6	23,184	39.6		29,178	22.9	47.8
Waco, TX	83,712	56,147	25,500	37.7	21,746	36.8		20,070	8.5	19.5
Warner Robins, GA	51,833	36,874	17,964	35.2	13,049	27.7		9,992	5.4	8.5
Washington–Arlington–Alexandria, DC–VA–MD–WV	2,047,323	1,336,254	645,106	27.6	567,965	25.6		405,618	21.5	26.2
Bethesda–Rockville–Frederick, MD	442,974	304,473	146,397	23.5	112,730	33.9		103,784	27.6	33.6
Washington–Arlington–Alexandria, DC–VA–MD–WV	1,604,349	1,031,781	498,709	28.9	455,235	23.5		301,834	19.9	24.1
Waterloo–Cedar Falls, IA	66,562	41,729	17,873	30.8	19,600	38.9		17,018	3.9	6.5
Wausau, WI	52,784	35,967	15,314	22.9	13,418	36.6		12,874	3.9	8.4
Wenatchee–East Wenatchee, WA	40,804	29,032	12,517	30.6	9,317	40.5		10,979	12.5	24.6
Wheeling, WV–OH	60,618	38,964	14,214	32.7	19,167	43.4		18,682	0.9	2.2
Wichita, KS	238,469	155,749	74,767	33.1	70,202	32.7		53,381	7.1	11.7
Wichita Falls, TX	54,891	36,456	15,948	33.3	15,480	36.8		14,125	6.1	11.7
Williamsport, PA	46,382	30,140	11,975	37.1	12,748	42.2		13,246	1.5	3.0
Wilmington, NC	152,534	96,771	37,215	36.1	44,346	33.7		41,624	4.7	6.6
Winchester, VA–WV	49,833	32,102	14,528	30.6	14,122	34.6		12,081	5.4	8.4
Winston-Salem, NC	188,200	124,430	53,660	34.7	56,163	34.5		46,868	7.9	12.0
Worcester, MA	298,720	201,042	94,129	28.8	79,687	37.9		72,109	11.1	17.7
Yakima, WA	80,136	59,149	30,037	39.0	16,840	40.0		19,303	17.9	39.3
York–Hanover, PA	168,021	118,423	51,020	30.9	40,884	41.7		43,361	3.5	6.5
Youngstown–Warren–Boardman, OH–PA	231,298	148,307	56,990	37.8	72,394	43.1		72,265	2.2	5.6
Yuba City, CA	55,168	40,420	20,522	29.6	12,074	39.5		13,814	18.3	32.1
Yuma, AZ	70,037	54,641	25,801	36.7	12,174	41.0		20,969	24.6	51.8

(D) = Data withheld due to disclosure or does not meet statistical standards.

Table B-6. Enrollment, Teachers, and Educational Attainment

Metropolitan statistical area and division	Public school enrollment[1]				Number of public school teachers, 2010–2011[2,3]		Public high school completers, 2008–2009[2,4]		Educational attainment, 2009–2011		
	2010–2011			Total, 2001[5]	Elementary[7]	Secondary[8]	Total	Diploma recipients	Population 25 years and over (thousands)	High school graduate or higher[9] (percent)	Bachelor's degree or higher (percent)
	Total[5]	Pre-Kindergarten to grade 8[6]	Grades 9–12								
Abilene, TX	28,248	20,593	7,655	29,555	825.4	871.8	1,619	1,619	104,554	83.2	20.8
Akron, OH	100,540	67,958	32,582	111,348	2,703.7	3,174.6	7,460	7,460	471,336	90.3	28.0
Albany, GA	27,666	20,336	7,330	28,852	849.5	757.2	1,519	1,437	97,848	77.7	15.8
Albany–Schenectady–Troy, NY	119,125	81,188	37,511	128,086	3,519.2	3,530.5	8,983	8,680	589,401	91.1	33.5
Albuquerque, NM	138,865	97,502	41,363	119,613	3,148.6	3,417.5	7,189	6,986	583,131	87.0	29.5
Alexandria, LA	27,505	20,248	7,257	27,106	1,032.1	741.6	1,553	1,333	101,348	80.3	16.4
Allentown–Bethlehem–Easton, PA–NJ	125,418	83,295	41,668	114,021	4,132.6	3,897.1	9,317	9,317	561,577	87.0	26.3
Altoona, PA	18,011	12,376	5,634	19,812	574.8	588.5	1,343	1,343	88,638	90.7	17.6
Amarillo, TX	47,363	34,583	12,780	40,869	1,320.3	1,253.7	2,647	2,647	158,364	83.8	23.3
Ames, IA	10,915	7,672	3,243	10,847	445.8	219.8	777	776	47,299	95.8	46.1
Anchorage, AK	66,515	46,282	20,233	62,534	2,372.7	1,306.7	4,125	3,993	240,088	92.2	29.6
Anderson, IN	18,913	13,038	3,859	20,100	474.0	467.0	1,130	1,130	89,062	87.0	17.2
Anderson, SC	30,314	21,635	8,679	27,685	1,230.6	516.4	1,692	1,692	126,920	80.6	18.8
Ann Arbor, MI	45,818	31,411	14,294	47,911	878.9	1,036.9	3,256	3,249	213,026	93.8	50.5
Anniston–Oxford, AL	18,628	13,380	5,248	18,175	538.5	528.8	1,114	1,063	78,629	77.6	16.0
Appleton, WI	37,875	26,064	11,811	34,759	967.0	1,199.8	2,850	2,840	149,710	92.8	25.8
Asheville, NC	54,468	38,131	16,297	51,231	1,784.9	1,883.3	3,382	3,322	305,579	87.8	29.1
Athens–Clarke County, GA	26,071	18,762	7,309	23,560	1,078.9	709.9	1,532	1,398	110,090	83.2	34.2
Atlanta–Sandy Springs–Marietta, GA	936,161	665,938	270,223	740,842	33,497.7	23,712.1	52,185	49,154	3,404,711	87.4	34.4
Atlantic City–Hammonton, NJ	46,726	30,973	14,079	43,489	1,973.3	1,360.9	3,115	3,115	185,159	84.5	23.0
Auburn–Opelika, AL	20,689	14,346	6,343	17,929	628.9	639.3	1,193	1,174	79,611	86.0	31.0
Augusta–Richmond County, GA–SC	93,000	66,172	26,828	92,720	3,191.9	2,294.0	5,137	4,910	362,577	85.0	23.5
Austin–Round Rock–San Marcos, TX	303,316	222,243	81,073	215,440	8,853.3	7,970.8	15,268	15,268	1,094,853	87.6	39.9
Bakersfield–Delano, CA	172,803	119,167	48,360	147,988	4,471.8	2,316.4	NA	NA	493,624	71.9	14.7
Baltimore–Towson, MD	388,184	269,046	119,138	400,459	13,908.8	11,523.1	26,107	25,824	1,823,882	88.3	35.3
Bangor, ME	21,003	14,334	6,669	24,590	1,134.6	560.1	1,538	1,526	103,439	90.4	24.0
Barnstable Town, MA	26,573	17,732	8,814	32,505	1,172.1	772.8	2,184	2,162	164,204	94.5	39.2
Baton Rouge, LA	119,923	88,314	31,609	110,967	5,366.1	2,711.9	6,790	5,743	509,061	85.7	26.7
Battle Creek, MI	20,915	14,196	6,523	24,448	501.9	463.4	1,484	1,483	90,816	88.2	18.7
Bay City, MI	14,909	9,649	5,102	17,444	230.7	323.3	1,098	1,095	74,554	88.4	18.6
Beaumont–Port Arthur, TX	68,545	49,282	19,263	71,893	1,817.5	2,071.6	3,945	3,945	256,066	83.4	15.9
Bellingham, WA	27,075	18,384	8,691	25,749	629.0	602.6	1,648	1,643	130,144	91.7	32.2
Bend, OR	23,992	16,266	7,726	19,807	694.4	346.3	1,793	1,680	110,681	93.4	30.0
Billings, MT	23,343	16,568	6,775	23,498	1,107.1	449.9	1,508	1,508	108,025	91.9	29.4
Binghamton, NY	35,486	24,264	11,074	42,896	1,181.6	1,238.5	2,869	2,750	169,365	89.5	24.8
Birmingham–Hoover, AL	175,572	123,527	52,045	170,263	5,581.4	5,281.3	10,480	9,956	757,821	85.1	27.1
Bismarck, ND	15,525	10,665	4,860	15,876	686.2	386.0	1,044	1,044	73,510	92.2	30.3
Blacksburg–Christiansburg–Radford, VA	18,477	12,923	5,554	18,249	461.8	629.8	1,300	1,131	93,243	86.0	31.6
Bloomington, IN	22,075	15,266	6,809	22,277	618.0	566.0	1,439	1,439	112,530	89.2	32.1
Bloomington–Normal, IL	25,463	17,929	7,534	24,342	1,058.9	553.4	1,514	1,513	101,652	93.8	41.9
Boise City–Nampa, ID	112,670	79,824	32,846	85,360	2,686.9	3085.7	6,210	6,189	390,779	89.4	28.5
Boston–Cambridge–Quincy, MA–NH	655,141	457,643	196,930	652,675	28,721.9	15628.5	45,060	44,524	3,105,923	90.6	42.7
Boston–Quincy, MA	262,281	184,257	77,731	257,829	11,391.0	6124.9	17,118	16,954	1,270,234	89.5	41.1
Cambridge–Newton–Framingham, MA	215,485	150,224	65,103	210,488	9,277.8	5140.6	15,200	15,077	1,042,911	91.9	49.9
Peabody, MA	113,667	79,641	33,909	118,199	4,927.6	2637.4	7,784	7,642	507,199	88.8	36.3
Rockingham County–Strafford County, NH	63,708	43,521	20,187	66,159	3,125.5	1725.6	4,958	4,851	285,579	93.5	34.6
Boulder, CO	44,532	31,190	13,342	47,246	1,608.9	1357.7	3,631	3,528	189,745	93.8	58.3
Bowling Green, KY	19,859	14,076	5,778	16,088	624.3	314.9	1,193	1,182	77,463	84.8	26.7
Bremerton–Silverdale, WA	37,084	24,623	12,461	41,612	903.7	903.7	2,743	2,736	169,797	93.3	28.4
Bridgeport–Stamford–Norwalk, CT	148,314	103,603	44,711	139,717	6,868.7	3252.5	9,625	9,622	619,213	88.4	43.9
Brownsville–Harlingen, TX	104,009	76,151	27,858	83,738	2,754.2	2,745.9	5,162	5,162	232,643	63.4	14.4
Brunswick, GA	18,195	13,091	5,104	17,150	629.4	455.5	993	952	75,300	83.9	20.2
Buffalo–Niagara Falls, NY	163,270	111,804	50,725	180,510	4,730.8	5,051.0	11,813	11,521	773,739	89.2	28.5
Burlington, NC	23,888	16,807	7,081	21,058	793.2	743.4	1,460	1,421	100,230	82.2	21.6
Burlington–South Burlington, VT	30,611	20,816	9,795	33,114	876.8	1,104.9	NA	NA	138,718	92.5	39.8
Canton–Massillon, OH	62,142	42,102	20,040	69,127	1,532.2	1,776.6	4,880	4,880	277,389	88.4	20.0
Cape Coral–Fort Myers, FL	81,967	58,351	23,616	58,369	1,770.9	1,968.2	4,520	4,258	452,765	86.8	24.1
Cape Girardeau–Jackson, MO–IL	12,943	9,113	3,830	13,408	406.0	474.0	923	923	62,653	83.9	23.1
Carson City, NV	8,257	5,479	2,778	8,431	288.5	269.6	NA	NA	38,662	87.7	21.5
Casper, WY	12,153	8,605	3,548	12,042	0.0	0.0	716	705	50,410	91.7	21.8

[1]Data obtained from public schools.
[2]Data obtained from public school districts.
[3]Full-time equivalent.
[4]Includes all students who have received diplomas, as well as individuals who received a certificate of attendance or other certificate of completion in lieu of a diploma during the previous school year and subsequent summer school. Use caution when comparing different areas as the types of high school completion credentials vary by state policy.
[5]Including ungraded students, these are students who are assigned to programs or classes without standard grade designation.
[6]Data for prekindergarten not available in all areas.
[7]Elementary is a general level of instruction classified by state and local practice, composed of any span of grades not above grade 8; preschool or kindergarten included only if it is an integral part of an elementary school or a regularly established school system.
[8]Secondary is a general level of instruction classified by state and local practice and composed of any span of grades beginning with the next grade following the elementary grades and ending with or below grade 12.
[9]High school equivalency credentials are included.
[10]The Denver–Aurora metropolitan statistical area includes Broomfield County. Broomfield County, CO, was formed from parts of Adams, Boulder, Jefferson, and Weld counties on November 15, 2001, and is coextensive with Broomfield city. For the purposes of defining and presenting data for the Denver–Aurora metropolitan statistical area, Broomfield city is treated as if it were a county when data are available to do so. In many cases, the data will not be available.
[11]The portion of Sullivan city in Crawford County, MO, is legally part of the St. Louis, MO–IL MSA. That portion is not included in these figures for the St. Louis MSA.
NA = Not available

Table B-6.   Enrollment, Teachers, and Educational Attainment—*Continued*

Metropolitan statistical area and division	Public school enrollment[1]			Number of public school teachers, 2010–2011[2,3]			Public high school completers, 2008–2009[2,4]		Educational attainment, 2009–2011		
	2010–2011			Total, 2001[5]	Elementary[7]	Secondary[8]	Total	Diploma recipients	Population 25 years and over (thousands)	High school graduate or higher[9] (percent)	Bachelor's degree or higher (percent)
	Total[5]	Pre-Kindergarten to grade 8[6]	Grades 9–12								
Cedar Rapids, IA	42,374	29,678	12,696	40,658	1,758.2	899.5	2,835	2,825	171,371	93.2	28.5
Champaign–Urbana, IL	30,181	21,400	8,781	29,886	1,429.3	718.3	1,876	1,870	134,374	92.6	38.3
Charleston, WV	48,391	34,918	13,473	48,908	1,410.8	1,830.0	2,824	2,824	215,890	84.3	21.1
Charleston–North Charleston–Summerville, SC	98,269	70,893	25,787	90,644	3,868.5	1,888.8	4,842	4,842	439,940	87.4	30.9
Charlotte–Gastonia–Rock Hill, NC–SC	294,920	210,691	83,861	216,720	9,629.1	8,141.1	15,924	15,702	1,151,916	86.8	32.6
Charlottesville, VA	25,863	18,094	7,769	24,408	614.0	769.6	1,861	1,687	131,635	87.1	42.2
Chattanooga, TN–GA	73,716	52,965	20,751	69,343	2,953.8	1,652.5	4,215	4,045	361,389	83.5	22.8
Cheyenne, WY	14,096	9,904	4,192	14,293	0.0	0.0	806	782	60,624	92.7	24.1
Chicago–Joliet–Naperville, IL–IN–WI	1,582,341	1,098,906	483,435	1,499,057	62,239.1	31,823.1	97,925	97,608	6,208,587	86.4	34.0
Chicago–Joliet–Naperville, IL	1,296,355	903,803	392,552	1,229,447	51,901.3	25,082.1	78,987	78,727	5,185,895	85.9	34.8
Gary, IN	122,835	84,822	38,013	115,642	3,272.0	2,942.0	7,424	7,424	467,252	88.3	20.6
Lake County–Kenosha County, IL–WI	163,151	110,281	52,870	153,968	7,065.8	3,799.0	11,514	11,457	555,440	88.8	37.9
Chico, CA	31,194	20,772	10,348	34,433	764.5	483.1	NA	NA	140,658	87.2	23.6
Cincinnati–Middletown, OH–KY–IN	321,395	228,496	92,857	322,738	8,310.6	7,660.6	20,948	20,920	1,399,145	88.2	29.3
Clarksville, TN–KY	43,339	31,401	11,931	36,940	1,742.4	743.8	2,709	2,672	165,598	87.6	19.1
Cleveland, TN	18,377	13,062	5,315	15,718	666.2	373.4	1,161	1,112	77,965	80.0	17.3
Cleveland–Elyria–Mentor, OH	299,951	203,391	96,141	328,084	7,850.4	8,855.5	20,389	20,389	1,422,360	88.4	27.7
Coeur d'Alene, ID	21,125	14,303	6,822	18,272	500.2	576.6	1,265	1,249	92,981	92.0	23.3
College Station–Bryan, TX	32,863	24,151	8,712	27,557	971.7	955.7	1,748	1,748	116,500	83.7	33.3
Colorado Springs, CO	115,021	81,512	33,509	98,114	3,323.8	2,956.8	7,123	6,814	411,094	93.5	35.0
Columbia, MO	24,231	16,982	7,249	22,533	643.7	942.8	1,652	1,652	100,698	92.0	45.8
Columbia, SC	129,718	90,367	39,351	112,482	5,173.5	2,540.7	6,824	6,824	497,522	87.3	29.3
Columbus, GA–AL	49,447	34,738	14,709	48,229	1,620.5	1,427.8	2,965	2,819	186,281	84.1	21.3
Columbus, IN	12,394	8,465	3,929	11,617	259.0	306.0	754	754	51,753	88.9	26.9
Columbus, OH	299,324	207,989	91,335	272,006	7,584.9	8,382.8	19,540	19,540	1,196,637	90.0	33.0
Corpus Christi, TX	79,116	57,460	21,656	80,375	2,090.2	2,100.6	4,780	4,780	275,054	79.6	19.9
Corvallis, OR	9,985	6,996	2,989	9,713	257.0	138.6	675	664	50,416	94.3	48.1
Crestview–Fort Walton Beach–Destin, FL	27,874	18,995	8,879	30,335	663.9	905.1	2,117	2,089	122,703	90.6	27.0
Cumberland, MD–WV	13,411	9,423	3,988	15,026	438.4	485.0	1,046	1,026	71,348	86.6	15.4
Dallas–Fort Worth–Arlington, TX	1,238,760	901,687	337,073	960,095	34,843.2	31,456.0	66,110	66,110	4,024,466	83.3	31.2
Dallas–Plano–Irving, TX	830,510	603,724	226,786	639,438	19,910.0	17,994.8	44,668	44,668	2,674,997	82.9	33.3
Fort Worth–Arlington, TX	408,250	297,963	110,287	320,657	14,933.2	13,461.2	21,442	21,442	1,349,469	84.0	27.0
Dalton, GA	28,186	20,645	7,541	23,913	949.2	655.0	1,532	1,418	88,932	68.6	12.0
Danville, IL	13,549	9,533	4,016	14,272	582.3	279.9	789	788	54,471	85.8	13.8
Danville, VA	15,674	11,028	4,646	16,900	373.4	548.3	1,133	1,007	74,871	77.3	14.4
Davenport–Moline–Rock Island, IA–IL	60,479	42,628	17,851	63,203	2,478.5	1,195.9	3,843	3,834	257,351	89.5	25.2
Dayton, OH	123,100	87,189	35,911	136,498	3,226.4	3,634.8	8,552	8,552	564,633	88.8	24.8
Decatur, AL	16,644	11,799	4,845	25,491	844.0	880.3	1,573	1,530	104,126	79.9	17.5
Decatur, IL	16,524	11,810	4,714	18,571	603.0	277.3	1,015	1,015	75,303	87.8	21.9
Deltona–Daytona Beach–Ormond Beach, FL	61,559	42,581	18,978	61,340	1,460.0	1,565.1	3,790	3,633	357,162	86.8	20.3
Denver–Aurora–Broomfield, CO[10]	437,891	314,950	122,941	358,921	11,453.7	9,932.5	23,983	22,561	1,698,851	89.2	38.3
Des Moines–West Des Moines, IA	98,132	70,668	27,464	83,720	4,051.2	1,855.3	5,885	5,869	374,143	91.8	33.8
Detroit–Warren–Livonia, MI	694,241	463,613	227,187	738,899	13,693.2	14,937.3	50,467	50,383	2,885,103	87.9	27.3
Detroit–Livonia–Dearborn, MI	297,077	201,298	93,934	348,669	6,412.2	5,887.7	20,591	20,565	1,181,910	83.8	20.8
Warren–Troy–Farmington Hills, MI	397,164	262,315	133,253	390,230	7,281.0	9,049.6	29,876	29,818	1,703,193	90.8	31.9
Dothan, AL	22,516	16,190	6,326	21,780	627.0	558.0	1,331	1,208	98,953	81.2	16.8
Dover, DE	27,686	18,914	8,772	25,011	833.0	834.0	1,566	1,512	104,559	84.1	19.8
Dubuque, IA	13,625	9,257	4,368	12,484	569.1	278.1	990	990	61,662	90.7	26.4
Duluth, MN–WI	37,976	25,979	11,997	43,675	1,023.1	1,102.1	2,810	2,805	190,046	92.4	24.0
Durham–Chapel Hill, NC	69,607	49,094	20,444	61,576	2,363.5	2,362.7	4,050	3,997	330,706	87.1	43.1
Eau Claire, WI	22,943	16,049	6,894	23,217	604.3	730.7	1,758	1,728	103,638	92.0	26.0
El Centro, CA	37,351	25,566	11,449	33,216	944.6	506.2	NA	NA	104,199	63.7	13.4
Elizabethtown, KY	19,175	13,158	6,005	17,402	402.3	270.4	1,389	1,363	77,385	86.1	18.5
Elkhart–Goshen, IN	35,885	25,604	10,281	32,751	991.0	930.0	2,028	2,028	123,933	81.1	17.9
Elmira, NY	12,941	9,232	3,709	13,810	378.8	336.9	863	815	60,875	88.3	20.6
El Paso, TX	181,525	127,184	54,341	156,466	5,055.0	5,150.0	10,170	10,170	472,264	72.8	20.3
Erie, PA	40,328	27,019	13,193	42,492	1,403.5	1,356.4	2,968	2,968	184,209	89.6	23.9
Eugene–Springfield, OR	44,784	30,430	14,354	46,967	1,349.0	664.4	3,152	3,075	236,478	90.4	27.2
Evansville, IN–KY	51,563	35,449	16,105	50,930	1,466.0	1,340.0	3,464	3,460	240,862	88.4	20.2
Fairbanks, AK	19,133	13,731	5,402	16,509	511.8	317.6	955	938	59,496	92.7	27.3
Fargo, ND–MN	29,139	20,456	8,683	27,992	1,199.4	684.5	1,901	1,901	128,502	94.2	34.7
Farmington, NM	23,779	17,093	6,686	24,136	560.3	569.9	1,198	1,189	79,126	80.8	15.3

[1]Data obtained from public schools.
[2]Data obtained from public school districts.
[3]Full–time equivalent.
[4]Includes all students who have received diplomas, as well as individuals who received a certificate of attendance or other certificate of completion in lieu of a diploma during the previous school year and subsequent summer school. Use caution when comparing different areas as the types of high school completion credentials vary by state policy.
[5]Including ungraded students, these are students who are assigned to programs or classes without standard grade designation.
[6]Data for prekindergarten not available in all areas.
[7]Elementary is a general level of instruction classified by state and local practice, composed of any span of grades not above grade 8; preschool or kindergarten included only if it is an integral part of an elementary school or a regularly established school system.
[8]Secondary is a general level of instruction classified by state and local practice and composed of any span of grades beginning with the next grade following the elementary grades and ending with or below grade 12.
[9]High school equivalency credentials are included.
[10]The Denver–Aurora metropolitan statistical area includes Broomfield County. Broomfield County, CO, was formed from parts of Adams, Boulder, Jefferson, and Weld counties on November 15, 2001, and is coextensive with Broomfield city. For the purposes of defining and presenting data for the Denver–Aurora metropolitan statistical area, Broomfield city is treated as if it were a county when data are available to do so. In many cases, the data will not be available.
NA = Not available

Table B-6. Enrollment, Teachers, and Educational Attainment—*Continued*

Metropolitan statistical area and division	Public school enrollment[1]			Number of public school teachers, 2010–2011[2,3]			Public high school completers, 2008–2009[2,4]		Educational attainment, 2009–2011		
	2010–2011			Total, 2001[5]	Elementary[7]	Secondary[8]	Total	Diploma recipients	Population 25 years and over (thousands)	High school graduate or higher[9] (percent)	Bachelor's degree or higher (percent)
	Total[5]	Pre-Kindergarten to grade 8[6]	Grades 9–12								
Fayetteville, NC	61,864	43,822	18,042	57,276	2,019.2	2,095.5	3,736	3,661	222,660	88.0	21.5
Fayetteville–Springdale–Rogers, AR–MO	81,788	59,150	22,610	57,781	2,373.6	2,060.4	4,336	4,336	289,214	83.1	26.3
Flagstaff, AZ	18,384	12,432	5,943	20,433	666.3	383.2	1,298	1,298	78,056	86.6	30.1
Flint, MI	72,773	48,687	23,405	80,645	1,309.9	1,531.1	4,857	4,855	280,890	88.6	18.8
Florence, SC	33,907	24,293	9,614	33,798	1,316.9	641.0	1,836	1,836	135,787	80.6	18.9
Florence–Muscle Shoals, AL	21,571	15,098	6,473	21,665	626.5	667.0	1,386	1,333	100,508	83.1	20.1
Fond du Lac, WI	13,953	9,939	4,014	15,733	349.2	448.1	1,110	1,088	69,683	89.3	18.9
Fort Collins–Loveland, CO	43,704	30,358	13,346	40,084	1,175.4	1,072.6	3,137	3,008	193,573	94.3	43.5
Fort Smith, AR–OK	53,306	38,111	15,136	50,698	1,579.1	1,490.8	3,177	3,177	196,436	81.7	15.5
Fort Wayne, IN	67,626	46,812	20,814	61,988	1,863.0	1,532.0	4,197	4,197	267,739	89.3	24.7
Fresno, CA	193,961	134,325	57,859	181,110	4,894.9	2,587.7	NA	NA	546,511	72.8	19.7
Gadsden, AL	16,062	10,984	5,078	15,818	498.5	483.0	978	927	71,519	82.0	13.8
Gainesville, FL	31,230	21,888	9,342	33,417	772.2	791.0	2,208	2,145	155,164	89.9	38.1
Gainesville, GA	32,929	24,052	8,877	24,312	1,185.6	786.3	1,589	1,479	113,731	79.3	23.0
Glens Falls, NY	19,206	12,896	6,211	22,700	603.2	694.7	1,509	1,455	92,038	88.7	22.5
Goldsboro, NC	19,631	14,099	5,532	19,493	576.2	676.6	1,190	1,170	79,844	81.7	15.8
Grand Forks, ND–MN	13,547	9,246	4,301	16,373	603.7	386.9	1,051	1,051	59,321	91.2	28.6
Grand Junction, CO	23,166	16,305	6,861	20,468	632.1	594.9	1,562	1,416	97,971	89.3	26.1
Grand Rapids–Wyoming, MI	127,134	87,513	39,275	126,945	2,472.3	2,913.9	9,009	8,938	498,359	89.0	26.9
Great Falls, MT	11,598	8,001	3,597	13,793	585.6	291.2	867	867	54,477	90.0	23.0
Greeley, CO	46,024	33,873	12,151	30,409	1,076.7	908.5	2,116	1,962	155,465	85.4	24.8
Green Bay, WI	50,695	35,017	15,678	47,474	1,425.4	1,744.4	3,812	3,763	203,438	90.0	23.4
Greensboro–High Point, NC	112,885	79,202	33,584	100,600	3,550.4	3,732.6	6,947	6,793	479,770	84.2	26.1
Greenville, NC	26,978	18,930	8,001	23,269	918.4	838.8	1,513	1,480	113,599	83.5	26.5
Greenville–Mauldin–Easley, SC	97,458	69,475	27,983	85,893	3,613.2	1,624.6	5,119	5,119	418,751	84.3	27.4
Gulfport–Biloxi, MS	38,133	26,937	10,689	39,830	1,016.6	941.9	2,034	1,847	163,429	84.7	20.4
Hagerstown–Martinsburg, MD–WV	42,588	30,221	12,367	35,270	1,373.0	1,471.0	2,772	2,739	184,413	85.2	19.1
Hanford–Corcoran, CA	28,052	19,853	8,199	25,364	781.6	383.2	NA	NA	92,409	70.4	13.0
Harrisburg–Carlisle, PA	78,438	53,086	25,324	97,684	2,277.3	2,552.9	5,414	5,414	376,951	89.6	28.6
Harrisonburg, VA	16,542	11,642	4,900	14,446	428.8	545.4	1,185	1,046	72,960	79.9	26.5
Hartford–West Hartford–East Hartford, CT	191,193	131,773	59,420	202,564	8,826.5	5,635.3	12,630	12,276	825,652	89.1	34.9
Hattiesburg, MS	23,218	16,386	6,446	21,370	620.1	680.7	1,305	1,204	88,533	85.3	26.0
Hickory–Lenoir–Morganton, NC	57,022	39,502	17,519	56,562	1,749.8	1,864.3	3,755	3,722	250,366	78.8	16.9
Hinesville–Fort Stewart, GA	12,529	9,520	3,009	13,446	390.0	324.9	752	705	43,982	90.3	17.3
Holland–Grand Haven, MI	43,328	29,857	13,283	48,302	845.3	1,004.5	2,826	2,823	161,928	90.4	29.9
Honolulu, HI	122,371	87,317	34,915	184,360	5,930.7	5,127.3	11,764	11,508	645,722	90.2	31.2
Hot Springs, AR	14,387	10,258	4,128	12,785	421.7	420.6	771	771	68,508	85.4	20.6
Houma–Bayou Cane–Thibodaux, LA	33,251	24,427	8,824	34,939	1,392.0	678.2	2,085	1,826	134,349	73.5	14.0
Houston–Sugar Land–Baytown, TX	1,191,796	868,036	323,760	945,865	32,780.2	29,245.2	61,258	61,258	3,734,983	80.6	28.4
Huntington–Ashland, WV–KY–OH	43,627	31,414	12,205	45,146	1,187.0	1,311.5	2,844	2,839	198,701	83.2	17.4
Huntsville, AL	61,947	42,593	19,354	55,244	1,948.0	1,865.7	3,950	3,869	278,559	87.5	34.0
Idaho Falls, ID	26,716	19,292	7,424	23,889	654.2	688.0	1,670	1,667	77,460	90.6	25.4
Indianapolis–Carmel, IN	298,534	210,576	87,958	249,895	7,530.0	6,487.0	16,437	16,437	1,144,400	88.1	30.8
Iowa City, IA	19,195	13,649	5,546	16,702	793.4	350.1	1,175	1,172	91,184	94.1	45.8
Ithaca, NY	11,526	7,692	3,781	13,424	399.5	408.8	876	840	57,164	92.7	50.3
Jackson, MI	24,447	16,572	7,745	25,983	460.2	589.7	1,797	1,790	108,289	89.0	18.4
Jackson, MS	87,716	61,915	24,555	83,997	2,300.5	2,232.6	4,557	4,239	344,871	85.5	28.7
Jackson, TN	15,900	11,225	4,675	16,299	661.1	343.9	1,083	1,043	74,401	84.1	22.5
Jacksonville, FL	207,183	146,790	60,393	189,365	4,996.5	5,054.7	11,931	11,379	897,216	88.5	27.1
Jacksonville, NC	23,890	17,351	6,539	21,147	708.0	739.2	1,490	1,472	92,476	89.3	17.7
Janesville, WI	27,701	19,181	8,520	27,420	758.0	1,007.2	2,027	2,001	106,482	87.3	18.8
Jefferson City, MO	20,601	14,069	6,532	22,452	793.7	912.7	1,980	1,980	100,118	87.5	24.9
Johnson City, TN	27,563	19,327	8,236	25,662	1,118.0	542.1	1,991	1,918	137,826	83.1	23.5
Johnstown, PA	18,957	12,821	6,129	19,958	544.3	628.1	1,539	1,539	102,107	88.1	17.9
Jonesboro, AR	20,903	15,267	5,634	18,370	677.5	599.2	1,247	1,247	77,073	80.7	20.3
Joplin, MO	29,784	21,214	8,570	26,826	845.4	998.1	1,736	1,736	113,160	83.1	19.1
Kalamazoo–Portage, MI	50,779	34,282	16,160	51,688	1,117.4	1,193.9	3,379	3,375	206,130	90.3	29.6
Kankakee–Bradley, IL	19,452	13,959	5,493	18,768	813.1	405.5	1,209	1,209	73,184	86.0	17.7
Kansas City, MO–KS	340,471	241,439	98,147	313,109	9,620.9	11,057.4	21,422	21,398	1,349,566	90.1	32.7
Kennewick–Pasco–Richland, WA	50,525	35,080	15,445	39,702	1,201.2	1,125.1	2,772	2,769	156,626	82.9	25.2
Killeen–Temple–Fort Hood, TX	79,705	59,719	19,986	64,068	2,269.1	2,115.3	3,994	3,994	240,890	88.2	19.4

[1]Data obtained from public schools.
[2]Data obtained from public school districts.
[3]Full–time equivalent.
[4]Includes all students who have received diplomas, as well as individuals who received a certificate of attendance or other certificate of completion in lieu of a diploma during the previous school year and subsequent summer school. Use caution when comparing different areas as the types of high school completion credentials vary by state policy.
[5]Including ungraded students, these are students who are assigned to programs or classes without standard grade designation.
[6]Data for prekindergarten not available in all areas.
[7]Elementary is a general level of instruction classified by state and local practice, composed of any span of grades not above grade 8; preschool or kindergarten included only if it is an integral part of an elementary school or a regularly established school system.
[8]Secondary is a general level of instruction classified by state and local practice and composed of any span of grades beginning with the next grade following the elementary grades and ending with or below grade 12.
[9]High school equivalency credentials are included.
NA = Not available

Table B-6.   Enrollment, Teachers, and Educational Attainment—*Continued*

Metropolitan statistical area and division	Public school enrollment[1]			Number of public school teachers, 2010–2011[2,3]			Public high school completers, 2008–2009[2,4]		Educational attainment, 2009–2011		
	2010–2011			Total, 2001[5]	Elementary[7]	Secondary[8]	Total	Diploma recipients	Population 25 years and over (thousands)	High school graduate or higher[9] (percent)	Bachelor's degree or higher (percent)
	Total[5]	Pre-Kindergarten to grade 8[6]	Grades 9–12								
Kingsport–Bristol–Bristol, TN–VA	44,132	30,750	13,382	44,158	1,584.8	1,065.9	3,050	2,822	222,516	82.1	18.2
Kingston, NY	24,424	15,861	8,445	28,998	738.3	803.4	1,995	1,947	127,524	87.5	29.4
Knoxville, TN	99,840	70,272	29,568	90,238	3,932.7	1,989.9	6,575	6,313	474,810	87.5	28.9
Kokomo, IN	16,136	10,992	5,144	17,011	497.0	457.0	1,057	1,057	67,848	89.1	19.4
La Crosse, WI–MN	20,611	14,037	6,574	19,404	559.7	750.1	1,676	1,626	85,757	92.9	28.6
Lafayette, IN	25,855	17,921	7,934	24,030	678.0	683.0	1,689	1,689	113,511	90.4	32.3
Lafayette, LA	38,721	27,874	10,847	37,509	1,589.5	779.6	2,252	2,089	173,889	84.2	25.1
Lake Charles, LA	34,181	25,043	9,138	34,213	1,621.4	697.2	1,943	1,785	128,838	84.0	19.8
Lake Havasu City–Kingman, AZ	25,658	17,983	7,670	25,094	706.6	339.1	1,522	1,522	145,840	84.7	12.1
Lakeland–Winter Haven, FL	94,404	67,957	26,447	79,463	2,398.0	2,612.0	5,191	4,884	408,619	81.6	17.5
Lancaster, PA	67,896	46,394	21,489	68,373	2,233.5	2,268.7	5,222	5,222	340,529	83.6	23.2
Lansing–East Lansing, MI	67,878	45,403	22,023	73,313	1,392.9	1,596.5	5,077	5,068	288,261	91.5	31.2
Laredo, TX	68,228	49,976	18,252	50,803	1,767.4	1,718.0	3,460	3,460	135,593	63.5	16.7
Las Cruces, NM	39,936	27,815	12,121	36,818	1,012.7	1,015.1	2,301	2,276	126,209	76.2	25.4
Las Vegas–Paradise, NV	318,941	225,474	92,981	231,654	6,907.5	5,529.2	NA	NA	1,286,318	83.4	21.9
Lawrence, KS	14,453	10,472	3,981	12,966	447.8	475.4	911	902	61,463	94.7	48.6
Lawton, OK	22,300	16,299	5,933	22,284	615.4	706.0	1,319	1,319	76,092	89.0	19.9
Lebanon, PA	18,879	13,140	5,739	17,880	531.8	593.0	1,308	1,308	91,568	85.7	19.0
Lewiston, ID–WA	8,937	6,109	2,828	9,323	235.1	270.9	621	617	42,130	89.3	18.5
Lewiston–Auburn, ME	16,214	11,365	4,849	16,564	768.9	409.3	1,006	1,000	73,393	87.5	19.0
Lexington–Fayette, KY	67,436	48,660	18,755	56,997	2,105.2	935.2	3,828	3,803	308,956	86.8	33.6
Lima, OH	15,877	11,578	4,299	19,216	457.5	507.7	1,116	1,116	69,250	87.7	16.2
Lincoln, NE	43,103	30,415	12,688	38,605	1,907.9	899.8	2,526	2,525	188,068	93.4	35.0
Little Rock–North Little Rock–Conway, AR	110,832	80,321	30,495	97,153	3,329.3	2,920.6	5,862	5,862	460,738	88.1	26.6
Logan, UT–ID	27,016	19,623	7,393	21,916	471.2	543.1	1,647	1,594	64,399	91.8	34.0
Longview, TX	38,794	28,146	10,648	37,449	1,106.6	1,213.8	2,385	2,385	140,843	81.6	16.9
Longview, WA	17,322	11,632	5,690	17,711	384.7	382.6	1,126	1,109	69,673	86.5	14.9
Los Angeles–Long Beach–Santa Ana, CA	2,089,996	1,397,052	681,962	2,175,965	50,707.8	29,109.9	NA	NA	8,353,845	77.8	30.8
Los Angeles–Long Beach–Glendale, CA	1,585,956	1,061,070	516,385	1,681,787	39,710.0	23,116.2	NA	NA	6,375,541	76.1	29.2
Santa Ana–Anaheim–Irvine, CA	504,040	335,982	165,577	494,178	10,997.8	5,993.7	NA	NA	1,978,304	83.5	36.1
Louisville/Jefferson County, KY–IN	189,277	134,024	55,058	171,894	5,452.6	3,141.3	11,222	11,139	867,062	86.8	25.4
Lubbock, TX	48,479	35,820	12,659	43,823	1,566.0	1,416.7	2,549	2,549	167,043	83.7	27.4
Lynchburg, VA	34,648	23,819	10,829	35,590	778.6	1,106.3	2,616	2,316	168,105	83.9	22.1
Macon, GA	37,518	27,216	10,302	37,164	1,240.5	1,020.2	1,865	1,646	151,587	82.1	20.3
Madera–Chowchilla, CA	29,993	20,980	9,013	24,780	743.5	423.5	NA	NA	92,323	67.4	14.0
Madison, WI	83,882	58,389	25,493	79,314	2,375.3	3,079.0	6,069	5,933	374,586	94.2	42.3
Manchester–Nashua, NH	63,889	42,240	21,649	66,091	2,675.6	1,409.8	4,734	4,587	272,685	90.5	34.4
Manhattan, KS	18,505	13,507	4,929	16,601	611.0	614.2	1,134	1,128	66,877	94.2	35.3
Mankato–North Mankato, MN	11,966	8,296	3,670	12,602	362.2	326.0	881	881	57,398	93.5	31.0
Mansfield, OH	17,192	12,109	5,083	23,003	454.0	603.7	1,174	1,174	86,296	85.5	14.3
McAllen–Edinburg–Mission, TX	211,601	155,069	56,532	144,376	5,618.7	5,738.3	9,997	9,997	425,043	61.2	15.8
Medford, OR	27,888	18,908	8,980	28,544	802.9	410.4	1,874	1,811	141,885	89.5	24.3
Memphis, TN–MS–AR	230,021	161,558	67,520	218,028	8,289.9	4,780.0	13,774	13,078	839,490	85.2	25.0
Merced, CA	55,543	37,854	17,593	51,595	1,413.9	766.0	NA	NA	145,370	66.2	11.8
Miami–Fort Lauderdale–Pompano Beach, FL	779,326	543,995	235,331	773,779	17,934.0	18,325.3	48,305	45,542	3,876,958	83.0	28.2
Fort Lauderdale–Pompano Beach–Deerfield Beach, FL	257,129	178,430	78,699	251,129	5,362.2	6,507.2	16,365	15,663	1,215,771	87.3	29.4
Miami–Miami Beach–Kendall, FL	346,842	244,165	102,677	368,356	8,465.0	7,138.0	20,773	19,207	1,713,501	77.5	25.4
West Palm Beach–Boca Raton–Boynton Beach, FL	175,355	121,400	53,955	154,294	4,106.8	4,680.1	11,167	10,672	947,686	87.2	31.8
Michigan City–La Porte, IN	16,780	11,503	5,277	17,865	489.0	444.0	1,081	1,081	76,547	86.2	17.4
Midland, TX	24,312	17,363	6,949	23,048	733.6	590.3	1,315	1,315	86,073	81.2	22.6
Milwaukee–Waukesha–West Allis, WI	237,550	163,359	74,191	242,156	5,791.7	6,539.7	17,103	16,981	1,024,522	89.3	31.4

[1]Data obtained from public schools.
[2]Data obtained from public school districts.
[3]Full-time equivalent.
[4]Includes all students who have received diplomas, as well as individuals who received a certificate of attendance or other certificate of completion in lieu of a diploma during the previous school year and subsequent summer school. Use caution when comparing different areas as the types of high school completion credentials vary by state policy.
[5]Including ungraded students, these are students who are assigned to programs or classes without standard grade designation.
[6]Data for prekindergarten not available in all areas.
[7]Elementary is a general level of instruction classified by state and local practice, composed of any span of grades not above grade 8; preschool or kindergarten included only if it is an integral part of an elementary school or a regularly established school system.
[8]Secondary is a general level of instruction classified by state and local practice and composed of any span of grades beginning with the next grade following the elementary grades and ending with or below grade 12.
[9]High school equivalency credentials are included.
NA = Not available

Table B-6.   Enrollment, Teachers, and Educational Attainment—*Continued*

Metropolitan statistical area and division	Public school enrollment[1]				Number of public school teachers, 2010–2011[2,3]		Public high school completers, 2008–2009[2,4]		Educational attainment, 2009–2011		
	2010–2011			Total, 2001[5]	Elementary[7]	Secondary[8]	Total	Diploma recipients	Population 25 years and over (thousands)	High school graduate or higher[9] (percent)	Bachelor's degree or higher (percent)
	Total[5]	Pre-Kindergarten to grade 8[6]	Grades 9–12								
Minneapolis–St. Paul–Bloomington, MN–WI	537,720	366,246	171,474	514,513	14,381.8	14,525.9	36,901	36,895	2,170,562	92.7	38.0
Missoula, MT	13,201	9,177	4,024	13,903	586.8	268.2	912	912	71,066	94.4	38.0
Mobile, AL	63,209	44,153	19,056	64,894	1,899.0	1,692.0	3,517	3,369	268,138	83.4	20.1
Modesto, CA	104,644	72,031	32,573	97,297	2,589.5	1,387.9	NA	NA	313,689	75.4	16.4
Monroe, LA	31,922	23,707	8,215	31,826	1,278.2	691.6	1,807	1,568	112,242	83.5	21.1
Monroe, MI	24,764	15,963	8,673	24,944	474.5	567.4	1,767	1,767	102,573	88.6	17.2
Montgomery, AL	56,177	40,577	15,600	57,029	1,587.2	1,431.4	2,899	2,747	242,515	85.0	27.1
Morgantown, WV	15,187	10,666	4,521	15,109	421.3	562.6	950	950	79,562	88.1	29.4
Morristown, TN	21,237	15,147	6,090	19,161	808.8	381.3	1,330	1,289	94,085	77.9	13.5
Mount Vernon–Anacortes, WA	18,996	13,033	5,963	18,894	446.0	445.3	1,150	1,145	79,866	88.1	23.4
Muncie, IN	16,467	11,226	5,241	17,663	446.0	496.0	1,162	1,162	70,956	85.5	22.1
Muskegon–Norton Shores, MI	29,240	19,726	9,355	32,509	555.9	665.8	2,036	2,031	113,851	87.5	16.8
Myrtle Beach–North Myrtle Beach–Conway, SC	38,534	27,536	10,998	29,894	1,484.1	787.2	2,091	2,091	190,554	87.4	22.8
Napa, CA	20,557	13,958	6,591	19,341	515.9	313.5	NA	NA	93,082	82.9	31.5
Naples–Marco Island, FL	42,919	30,283	12,636	34,196	1,229.4	907.0	2,633	2,477	237,627	85.7	31.4
Nashville–Davidson—Murfreesboro–Franklin, TN....	248,634	178,376	70,258	197,197	10,304.9	4,603.5	14,949	14,494	1,050,796	86.8	30.4
New Haven–Milford, CT	132,202	91,605	40,597	129,637	6,038.0	3,012.1	7,495	7,491	583,893	87.9	32.4
New Orleans–Metairie–Kenner, LA	148,155	107,632	40,523	190,988	6,611.7	2,998.3	8,607	7,842	782,047	84.5	26.4
New York–Northern New Jersey–Long Island, NY–NJ–PA	2,699,220	1,825,459	816,651	2,672,897	91,905.5	63,889.8	178,228	174,961	12,833,478	84.6	36.0
Edison–New Brunswick, NJ	358,107	236,868	109,167	335,005	13,663.3	9,536.5	25,544	25,544	1,594,414	90.4	37.5
Nassau–Suffolk, NY	463,958	312,181	149,436	461,463	13,827.7	14,323.0	35,228	34,666	1,922,769	90.0	36.4
Newark–Union, NJ–PA	345,037	234,419	99,124	330,223	13,586.2	10,060.3	24,055	24,055	1,447,112	87.7	36.5
New York–White Plains–Wayne, NY–NJ	1,532,118	1,041,991	458,924	1,546,206	50,828.3	29,970.0	93,401	90,696	7,869,183	81.5	35.5
Niles–Benton Harbor, MI	25,051	16,558	8,308	28,475	499.9	635.3	1,883	1,883	107,112	86.8	23.9
North Port–Bradenton–Sarasota, FL	85,148	60,270	24,878	72,058	2,094.2	2,145.6	5,192	5,045	532,476	89.4	27.6
Norwich–New London, CT	42,177	28,498	13,679	42,897	1,942.0	1,036.7	2,844	2,841	187,622	90.2	31.5
Ocala, FL	41,955	29,227	12,728	38,545	1,040.0	1,032.0	2,484	2,421	243,736	84.3	16.3
Ocean City, NJ	13,279	8,528	4,176	15,419	576.5	428.3	1,133	1,133	71,313	88.9	27.1
Odessa, TX...	27,936	20,581	7,355	26,831	753.2	686.4	1,424	1,424	82,206	72.9	13.0
Ogden–Clearfield, UT	121,265	88,091	33,174	102,903	2,349.3	1,951.2	6,580	6,470	316,962	92.3	28.9
Oklahoma City, OK	211,875	155,186	55,426	185,744	5,430.4	5,951.2	11,343	11,343	808,524	87.4	27.6
Olympia, WA	40,071	26,815	13,256	37,764	948.9	945.8	2,541	2,532	171,372	93.3	32.7
Omaha–Council Bluffs, NE–IA............................	145,828	103,938	41,890	130,557	5,377.2	3,738.9	8,873	8,825	558,065	91.0	32.5
Orlando–Kissimmee–Sanford, FL	335,322	233,470	101,852	275,139	7,623.7	9,466.9	20,886	19,875	1,406,495	87.4	27.5
Oshkosh–Neenah, WI	22,971	15,768	7,203	23,884	586.2	780.7	1,789	1,786	111,590	90.4	23.8
Owensboro, KY	18,850	13,743	5,091	17,071	611.8	266.3	1,262	1,247	76,918	86.6	16.5
Oxnard–Thousand Oaks–Ventura, CA	152,904	103,939	48,942	140,156	3,418.5	1,909.7	NA	NA	531,147	82.4	31.0
Palm Bay–Melbourne–Titusville, FL	71,866	49,970	21,896	70,596	1,985.5	1,744.5	5,005	4,931	393,208	90.3	25.5
Palm Coast, FL	12,931	9,028	3,903	6,760	346.0	301.4	783	754	70,900	90.4	22.7
Panama City–Lynn Haven–Panama City Beach, FL.....	25,935	18,746	7,189	25,743	630.3	581.1	1,555	1,532	115,429	87.1	20.5
Parkersburg–Marietta–Vienna, WV–OH	24,339	17,194	7,145	27,504	686.2	835.0	1,697	1,697	115,280	88.6	16.4
Pascagoula, MS	28,556	19,839	8,310	29,670	860.2	805.9	1,687	1,573	106,189	86.1	17.6
Pensacola–Ferry Pass–Brent, FL.........................	65,861	46,682	19,179	67,555	1,600.5	1,756.4	3,872	3,780	298,082	87.8	24.0
Peoria, IL	58,577	41,012	17,565	59,495	2,555.3	1,232.8	3,799	3,797	254,989	90.8	25.6
Philadelphia–Camden–Wilmington, PA–NJ–DE–MD	859,353	584,413	264,232	839,309	28,908.9	25,759.5	58,589	58,514	3,984,594	88.5	32.9
Camden, NJ	202,356	133,334	59,560	203,593	8,159.7	5,244.4	14,675	14,675	841,856	89.4	30.5
Philadelphia, PA	554,788	380,317	173,518	540,075	17,352.3	17,055.9	37,376	37,376	2,674,986	88.2	34.1
Wilmington, DE–MD–NJ	102,209	70,762	31,154	95,641	3,396.9	3,459.2	6,538	6,463	467,752	88.2	30.2
Phoenix–Mesa–Glendale, AZ...............................	733,248	517,932	215,241	558,149	21,972.8	9,524.7	41,151	41,151	2,691,672	86.0	28.0
Pine Bluff, AR...	15,853	11,159	4,661	18,539	507.7	443.8	944	944	66,104	81.8	15.7
Pittsburgh, PA...	319,329	212,687	106,596	348,333	9,839.4	11,033.8	25,295	25,295	1,668,898	91.4	28.9
Pittsfield, MA..	17,409	11,642	5,745	20,689	716.6	610.0	1,327	1,318	93,374	90.3	29.3
Pocatello, ID...	15,872	11,289	4,583	15,774	395.2	382.7	1,070	1,061	54,558	90.3	25.4
Portland–South Portland–Biddeford, ME	71,857	49,622	22,235	79,757	3,647.0	1,856.7	5,200	5,146	363,099	92.8	35.2
Portland–Vancouver–Hillsboro, OR–WA	334,292	231,640	102,652	309,955	10,111.9	5,601.8	20,934	20,181	1,512,414	90.2	33.8
Port St. Lucie, FL	58,917	41,296	17,621	45,795	1,327.5	1,488.5	3,448	3,294	305,862	85.9	22.2
Poughkeepsie–Newburgh–Middletown, NY	108,848	72,974	35,637	110,775	3,033.8	3,186.8	8,180	7,945	435,025	88.0	30.7
Prescott, AZ..	26,219	18,281	7,935	24,124	755.6	320.7	1,533	1,533	156,361	90.1	23.3
Providence–New Bedford–Fall River, RI–MA..........	224,603	153,767	70,815	250,658	7,586.2	7,693.8	16,018	15,892	1,083,255	83.4	28.8

[1]Data obtained from public schools.
[2]Data obtained from public school districts.
[3]Full–time equivalent.
[4]Includes all students who have received diplomas, as well as individuals who received a certificate of attendance or other certificate of completion in lieu of a diploma during the previous school year and subsequent summer school. Use caution when comparing different areas as the types of high school completion credentials vary by state policy.
[5]Including ungraded students, these are students who are assigned to programs or classes without standard grade designation.
[6]Data for prekindergarten not available in all areas.
[7]Elementary is a general level of instruction classified by state and local practice, composed of any span of grades not above grade 8; preschool or kindergarten included only if it is an integral part of an elementary school or a regularly established school system.
[8]Secondary is a general level of instruction classified by state and local practice and composed of any span of grades beginning with the next grade following the elementary grades and ending with or below grade 12.
[9]High school equivalency credentials are included.
NA = Not available

Table B-6. Enrollment, Teachers, and Educational Attainment—*Continued*

Metropolitan statistical area and division	Public school enrollment[1]			Number of public school teachers, 2010–2011[2,3]			Public high school completers, 2008–2009[2,4]		Educational attainment, 2009–2011		
	2010–2011			Total, 2001[5]	Elementary[7]	Secondary[8]	Total	Diploma recipients	Population 25 years and over (thousands)	High school graduate or higher[9] (percent)	Bachelor's degree or higher (percent)
	Total[5]	Pre-Kindergarten to grade 8[6]	Grades 9–12								
Provo–Orem, UT	124,433	91,727	32,706	83,634	2,483.9	1,989.1	5,784	5,757	257,336	93.4	35.1
Pueblo, CO	27,279	19,405	7,874	24,793	742.7	601.1	1,740	1,526	105,463	86.0	21.8
Punta Gorda, FL	16,640	10,768	5,872	17,169	330.0	443.1	1,422	1,402	128,335	88.2	21.1
Racine, WI	31,439	21,565	9,874	29,648	861.6	1,012.3	2,030	1,973	131,003	88.0	22.7
Raleigh–Cary, NC	187,992	135,326	52,666	130,417	6,293.4	5,812.8	10,714	10,585	735,197	89.6	41.3
Rapid City, SD	19,619	13,806	5,813	20,102	808.4	334.2	1,211	1,211	82,990	91.7	26.2
Reading, PA	67,746	46,118	21,586	64,401	2,123.7	2,193.6	4,784	4,784	272,601	84.4	22.3
Redding, CA	27,319	18,036	9,283	30,440	722.0	424.6	NA	NA	121,882	88.0	19.6
Reno–Sparks, NV	66,682	46,168	20,437	56,713	1,557.6	1,234.5	NA	NA	282,344	86.5	26.8
Richmond, VA	201,674	139,951	61,723	185,595	4,376.8	5,649.4	14,363	12,745	842,195	85.9	31.7
Riverside–San Bernardino–Ontario, CA	837,962	568,136	268,599	700,740	19,868.4	10,682.1	NA	NA	2,562,881	78.6	19.4
Roanoke, VA	44,728	31,101	13,627	44,058	1,052.0	1,262.3	3,207	2,844	216,638	86.2	25.7
Rochester, MN	29,855	20,554	9,301	30,789	835.9	846.8	2,194	2,194	124,851	93.8	36.1
Rochester, NY	160,597	108,453	51,487	180,943	5,064.4	5,448.4	12,117	11,759	702,872	88.9	32.3
Rockford, IL	57,726	40,746	16,980	52,640	2,441.9	1,176.5	3,223	3,223	230,689	85.3	20.6
Rocky Mount, NC	26,550	18,980	7,570	26,859	768.6	816.3	1,564	1,530	102,490	81.2	15.3
Rome, GA	16,269	11,804	4,465	15,624	580.4	491.7	947	880	62,967	77.1	18.7
Sacramento–Arden-Arcade–Roseville, CA	362,948	245,722	104,936	335,196	8,136.7	4,762.3	NA	NA	1,396,791	87.3	29.8
Saginaw–Saginaw Township North, MI	30,878	20,286	10,366	37,863	586.6	664.9	2,202	2,201	132,221	86.8	18.3
St. Cloud, MN	27,648	18,412	9,236	29,807	795.2	807.5	2,060	2,060	117,003	90.4	22.7
St. George, UT	27,917	20,599	7,318	18,374	520.3	522.3	1,349	1,331	83,598	91.1	25.3
St. Joseph, MO–KS	18,553	13,074	5,432	19,899	608.1	660.8	1,191	1,191	84,731	86.9	18.5
St. Louis, MO–IL[11]	421,459	290,218	131,241	430,825	14,718.2	12,876.3	29,624	29,622	1,886,265	89.4	30.0
Salem, OR	65,550	45,343	20,207	55,515	2,229.7	1,038.8	4,213	4,090	249,828	84.2	22.2
Salinas, CA	73,222	52,681	20,540	72,529	1,837.6	901.9	NA	NA	258,459	70.1	22.3
Salisbury, MD	17,302	12,497	4,805	17,201	679.5	529.7	1,118	1,085	79,219	84.4	24.1
Salt Lake City, UT	220,764	158,892	61,872	191,738	4,234.8	3,843.4	11,841	11,489	681,192	88.8	29.9
San Angelo, TX	18,954	13,759	5,195	19,501	548.0	478.0	1,202	1,202	70,499	81.7	21.8
San Antonio–New Braunfels, TX	414,105	299,181	114,924	327,913	10,952.7	10,560.6	21,837	21,837	1,352,228	82.5	25.7
San Diego–Carlsbad–San Marcos, CA	494,657	332,987	159,789	488,377	12,195.2	5,981.6	NA	NA	2,011,405	85.1	33.9
Sandusky, OH	12,239	8,474	3,765	15,112	336.8	450.4	922	922	54,196	89.5	20.3
San Francisco–Oakland–Fremont, CA	560,400	385,604	172,891	560,380	14,812.1	8,016.8	NA	NA	3,043,179	87.2	43.7
Oakland–Fremont–Hayward, CA	382,604	262,642	118,157	378,706	9,825.4	5,317.7	NA	NA	1,728,494	86.9	39.8
San Francisco–San Mateo–Redwood City, CA	177,796	122,962	54,734	181,674	4,986.7	2,699.1	NA	NA	1,314,685	87.5	48.7
San Jose–Sunnyvale–Santa Clara, CA	276,199	193,775	81,954	265,505	7,138.2	3,592.8	NA	NA	1,233,734	86.2	44.8
San Luis Obispo–Paso Robles, CA	34,282	22,750	11,499	37,561	831.1	520.6	NA	NA	178,234	89.2	30.6
Santa Barbara–Santa Maria–Goleta, CA	66,049	45,354	20,694	66,012	1,680.6	904.6	NA	NA	260,685	79.2	30.9
Santa Cruz–Watsonville, CA	36,398	24,548	11,808	40,462	985.5	508.7	NA	NA	169,523	84.1	36.6
Santa Fe, NM	17,690	13,326	4,364	15,356	465.6	398.1	770	766	103,174	86.4	36.6
Santa Rosa–Petaluma, CA	69,553	47,723	21,637	73,689	1,898.0	997.9	NA	NA	331,565	86.7	32.4
Savannah, GA	54,372	40,332	14,040	49,110	2,069.7	1,449.3	2,773	2,544	223,818	87.6	27.7
Scranton—Wilkes-Barre, PA	75,000	51,136	23,806	72,617	2,317.2	2,511.3	5,996	5,996	395,152	88.3	22.3
Seattle–Tacoma–Bellevue, WA	500,856	343,861	156,995	484,613	11,807.4	10,577.4	29,996	29,785	2,346,728	91.3	37.3
Seattle–Bellevue–Everett, WA	372,287	254,228	118,059	357,453	8,826.7	7,870.6	22,700	22,579	1,826,004	91.5	41.2
Tacoma, WA	128,569	89,633	38,936	127,160	2,980.7	2,706.8	7,296	7,206	520,724	90.4	23.6
Sebastian–Vero Beach, FL	17,740	12,373	5,367	14,974	394.1	432.9	1,148	1,108	103,043	87.3	26.3
Sheboygan, WI	19,253	13,061	6,192	19,715	518.5	675.4	1,551	1,542	78,576	90.5	22.0
Sherman–Denison, TX	21,022	15,135	5,887	19,823	643.8	697.7	1,390	1,390	81,021	85.4	19.7
Shreveport–Bossier City, LA	68,189	50,201	17,988	69,047	2,644.8	1,874.5	4,185	3,414	260,558	86.2	21.6
Sioux City, IA–NE–SD	25,452	17,947	7,505	25,598	1,115.5	547.2	1,690	1,684	91,101	84.3	20.3
Sioux Falls, SD	36,783	25,799	10,984	31,469	1,488.5	671.7	2,198	2,198	149,579	91.4	30.2
South Bend–Mishawaka, IN–MI	47,319	32,852	14,442	47,244	1,225.8	1,125.4	2,861	2,861	206,744	88.3	24.2
Spartanburg, SC	47,762	33,887	13,875	42,877	2,061.3	849.4	2,648	2,648	187,397	81.8	20.1
Spokane, WA	72,035	49,355	22,680	72,588	1,741.6	1,761.0	4,847	4,841	308,430	92.7	28.8
Springfield, IL	32,793	23,466	9,327	44,646	1,486.2	805.5	1,898	1,893	143,203	91.7	30.4
Springfield, MA	104,736	72,162	32,423	110,697	4,647.5	2,914.3	6,998	6,824	453,943	86.1	28.6
Springfield, MO	66,021	46,778	19,243	58,016	1,890.8	2,168.0	4,190	4,190	284,490	88.6	25.3
Springfield, OH	21,281	15,037	6,244	25,343	562.3	624.9	1,546	1,546	93,135	85.3	17.0
State College, PA	15,069	9,930	5,107	14,440	414.6	523.4	1,136	1,136	84,198	93.1	40.5
Steubenville–Weirton, OH–WV	17,083	12,172	4,911	19,727	446.8	790.6	1,292	1,292	88,508	88.8	14.7

[1] Data obtained from public schools.
[2] Data obtained from public school districts.
[3] Full–time equivalent.
[4] Includes all students who have received diplomas, as well as individuals who received a certificate of attendance or other certificate of completion in lieu of a diploma during the previous school year and subsequent summer school. Use caution when comparing different areas as the types of high school completion credentials vary by state policy.
[5] Including ungraded students, these are students who are assigned to programs or classes without standard grade designation.
[6] Data for prekindergarten not available in all areas.
[7] Elementary is a general level of instruction classified by state and local practice, composed of any span of grades not above grade 8; preschool or kindergarten included only if it is an integral part of an elementary school or a regularly established school system.
[8] Secondary is a general level of instruction classified by state and local practice and composed of any span of grades beginning with the next grade following the elementary grades and ending with or below grade 12.
[9] High school equivalency credentials are included.
[11] The portion of Sullivan city in Crawford County, MO, is legally part of the St. Louis, MO–IL MSA. That portion is not included in these figures for the St. Louis MSA.
NA = Not available

Table B-6. Enrollment, Teachers, and Educational Attainment—*Continued*

Metropolitan statistical area and division	Public school enrollment[1]				Number of public school teachers, 2010–2011[2,3]		Public high school completers, 2008–2009[2,4]		Educational attainment, 2009–2011		
	2010–2011			Total, 2001[5]	Elementary[7]	Secondary[8]	Total	Diploma recipients	Population 25 years and over (thousands)	High school graduate or higher[9] (percent)	Bachelor's degree or higher (percent)
	Total[5]	Pre-Kindergarten to grade 8[6]	Grades 9–12								
Stockton, CA	136,082	94,243	40,709	122,349	3,349.4	1,814.2	NA	NA	414,901	76.1	17.9
Sumter, SC	17,060	12,323	4,737	19,063	668.4	258.5	1,010	1,010	68,587	81.7	17.4
Syracuse, NY	105,944	71,906	33,327	117,293	3,114.1	3,310.3	7,610	7,324	434,050	88.9	28.9
Tallahassee, FL	48,095	35,089	13,006	47,821	1,157.5	1,193.1	2,654	2,578	221,150	88.5	35.5
Tampa–St. Petersburg–Clearwater, FL	388,073	273,460	114,504	344,109	10,473.5	10,101.3	22,801	22,075	1,963,207	87.0	25.3
Terre Haute, IN	26,389	18,359	8,030	27,571	897.0	490.0	1,645	1,645	113,993	86.5	18.1
Texarkana, TX–Texarkana, AR	24,443	17,610	6,760	22,926	755.3	811.2	1,410	1,410	91,072	85.0	17.0
Toledo, OH	105,031	73,994	31,037	107,290	2,565.4	3,013.7	6,676	6,676	424,292	88.7	23.6
Topeka, KS	38,521	26,721	11,510	37,504	1,176.5	1,351.7	2,490	2,436	156,872	90.8	25.9
Trenton–Ewing, NJ	52,587	34,855	15,762	56,398	2,463.9	1,879.3	4,014	4,014	243,690	87.0	37.8
Tucson, AZ	146,416	101,252	45,128	131,404	4,172.5	2,358.9	8,991	8,991	649,837	86.6	29.2
Tulsa, OK	162,908	119,114	43,528	153,369	4,252.7	4,569.8	8,870	8,870	613,881	88.0	25.6
Tuscaloosa, AL	32,056	22,857	9,199	30,260	1,032.6	915.4	1,827	1,698	131,069	85.0	24.2
Tyler, TX	34,608	25,455	9,153	30,812	1,008.6	1,012.7	1,805	1,805	133,822	84.7	24.3
Utica–Rome, NY	45,023	30,845	13,961	50,442	1,428.9	1,515.6	3,439	3,317	204,342	86.8	21.6
Valdosta, GA	22,715	16,514	6,201	20,982	783.4	600.2	1,199	1,133	82,588	81.6	20.0
Vallejo–Fairfield, CA	64,880	43,841	21,007	73,061	1,624.7	987.0	NA	NA	271,808	86.6	23.8
Victoria, TX	20,933	15,479	5,454	21,047	580.9	591.9	1,100	1,100	75,762	80.2	16.0
Vineland–Millville–Bridgeton, NJ	26,590	18,196	7,257	25,493	1,184.4	741.0	1,634	1,634	104,135	77.2	14.5
Virginia Beach–Norfolk–Newport News, VA–NC	269,087	186,686	82,401	275,921	5,984.3	7,819.8	19,104	17,240	1,078,675	89.6	28.1
Visalia–Porterville, CA	97,891	69,753	26,630	85,664	2,522.6	1,158.2	NA	NA	251,873	68.3	12.8
Waco, TX	43,838	31,498	12,340	39,227	1,313.0	1,357.2	2,347	2,347	141,492	81.9	22.3
Warner Robins, GA	27,061	19,146	7,915	21,529	904.8	706.6	1,598	1,523	89,467	88.0	24.9
Washington–Arlington–Alexandria, DC–VA–MD–WV	869,786	605,477	264,044	761,904	24,794.8	24,229.3	58,629	56,550	3,751,533	89.9	47.3
Bethesda–Rockville–Frederick, MD	184,211	126,178	58,033	171,065	6,557.7	4,834.6	13,319	13,151	823,347	91.0	53.0
Washington–Arlington–Alexandria, DC–VA–MD–WV	685,575	479,299	206,011	590,839	18,237.1	19,394.7	45,310	43,399	2,928,186	89.6	45.7
Waterloo–Cedar Falls, IA	23,913	16,133	7,780	24,831	1,129.2	576.3	1,882	1,877	106,257	90.5	25.7
Wausau, WI	19,930	13,576	6,354	19,731	522.3	710.9	1,669	1,656	90,674	89.3	21.6
Wenatchee–East Wenatchee, WA	19,715	13,524	6,191	19,791	480.8	442.3	1,297	1,295	73,125	82.3	21.6
Wheeling, WV–OH	19,117	13,484	5,633	21,578	508.1	702.5	1,403	1,403	105,343	88.3	18.4
Wichita, KS	106,671	75,317	30,814	100,074	3,017.5	3,506.3	6,495	6,485	396,617	88.8	27.3
Wichita Falls, TX	25,004	18,107	6,897	26,522	795.8	799.7	1,614	1,614	96,250	84.2	18.9
Williamsport, PA	16,422	11,205	5,217	19,094	569.2	603.4	1,215	1,215	79,419	86.9	18.4
Wilmington, NC	45,806	32,144	13,662	38,738	1,500.0	1,436.2	2,738	2,687	254,894	88.6	30.3
Winchester, VA–WV	20,755	14,339	6,416	17,660	551.3	715.2	1,536	1,389	86,852	82.9	22.8
Winston–Salem, NC	75,760	54,196	21,559	65,215	2,569.6	2,507.1	4,502	4,429	319,506	85.8	26.4
Worcester, MA	129,599	90,571	38,942	132,081	5,089.1	3,162.2	9,222	9,116	535,308	88.8	33.5
Yakima, WA	51,367	36,507	14,860	47,813	1,231.7	1,098.8	2,594	2,590	145,353	70.4	15.5
York–Hanover, PA	64,905	44,537	20,333	57,701	2,105.1	2,228.2	4,971	4,971	297,397	88.1	21.7
Youngstown–Warren–Boardman, OH–PA	81,791	55,741	26,015	95,934	2,333.3	2,715.4	6,177	6,177	394,430	87.9	18.9
Yuba City, CA	33,964	23,726	10,238	29,638	919.4	537.6	NA	NA	103,548	77.1	16.0
Yuma, AZ	38,104	25,905	12,188	30,520	1,021.9	483.4	2,288	2,288	120,474	71.9	14.1

[1]Data obtained from public schools.
[2]Data obtained from public school districts.
[3]Full-time equivalent.
[4]Includes all students who have received diplomas, as well as individuals who received a certificate of attendance or other certificate of completion in lieu of a diploma during the previous school year and subsequent summer school. Use caution when comparing different areas as the types of high school completion credentials vary by state policy.
[5]Including ungraded students, these are students who are assigned to programs or classes without standard grade designation.
[6]Data for prekindergarten not available in all areas.
[7]Elementary is a general level of instruction classified by state and local practice, composed of any span of grades not above grade 8; preschool or kindergarten included only if it is an integral part of an elementary school or a regularly established school system.
[8]Secondary is a general level of instruction classified by state and local practice and composed of any span of grades beginning with the next grade following the elementary grades and ending with or below grade 12.
[9]High school equivalency credentials are included.
NA = Not available

Table B-7.   Median Income, Household Income Distribution, and Poverty Status, 2009–2011

Metropolitan statistical area division	Median family income (in 2011 inflation-adjusted dollars)	Median household income (in 2011 inflation-adjusted dollars)	Total number of households	Percent of households by income level						Number whose income in the past 12 months was below poverty level[1]		
				Under $25,000	$25,000–$49,999	$50,000–$74,999	$75,000–$99,999	$100,000–$199,999	$200,000 and over	Families	Individuals	Children under 18
Abilene, TX	53,749	42,283	59,462	28.5	28.4	18.7	11.1	11.5	1.8	4,506	25,203	7,818
Akron, OH	62,232	48,395	281,202	25.5	25.9	19.3	12.1	14.4	2.8	19,455	106,867	34,299
Albany, GA	43,155	35,173	57,611	36.6	26.9	16.5	9.7	8.6	1.6	8,073	40,270	15,370
Albany–Schenectady–Troy, NY	76,124	58,771	346,680	20.3	21.7	19.7	13.6	21.0	3.7	15,679	92,370	27,730
Albuquerque, NM	58,836	47,822	342,519	26.1	25.6	18.4	11.3	15.5	3.0	30,404	157,212	55,117
Alexandria, LA	48,826	39,156	53,987	33.3	28.1	15.2	10.8	11.1	1.4	5,216	27,488	10,120
Allentown–Bethlehem–Easton, PA–NJ	68,898	56,701	312,118	21.0	23.1	19.4	13.6	19.2	3.7	18,179	90,674	31,937
Altoona, PA	53,789	42,816	51,949	29.3	27.8	20.9	10.2	10.0	1.8	3,213	17,101	5,312
Amarillo, TX	59,850	46,902	92,663	26.3	26.4	19.5	12.2	13.0	2.6	7,400	38,226	13,975
Ames, IA	73,988	48,690	34,970	26.1	24.8	18.5	13.6	14.5	2.5	1,210	16,161	1,677
Anchorage, AK	84,593	73,595	137,268	13.2	19.2	18.6	15.9	26.7	6.4	5,559	32,434	11,973
Anderson, IN	52,685	42,007	50,290	27.8	30.2	21.0	10.3	9.4	1.2	4,233	21,740	7,945
Anderson, SC	53,541	40,632	73,126	31.4	25.4	19.1	10.9	11.8	1.4	7,007	31,638	11,609
Ann Arbor, MI	82,753	57,329	133,602	21.7	22.3	17.0	12.0	21.4	5.7	5,701	47,070	10,568
Anniston–Oxford, AL	50,578	38,909	45,694	34.7	26.1	17.5	10.5	9.5	1.7	4,972	25,150	8,289
Appleton, WI	69,569	57,874	87,477	18.2	23.4	23.1	15.2	17.6	2.4	3,286	17,855	5,950
Asheville, NC	53,943	42,665	181,164	27.1	29.6	19.4	10.1	11.5	2.2	12,531	66,630	20,394
Athens–Clarke County, GA	55,133	40,267	65,946	34.9	22.8	17.2	9.3	12.8	3.0	6,648	52,220	11,987
Atlanta–Sandy Springs–Marietta, GA	64,813	55,280	1,886,767	21.3	23.9	18.9	12.4	18.6	5.0	148,465	777,288	282,906
Atlantic City–Hammonton, NJ	65,575	53,288	100,739	22.2	25.4	17.0	13.6	18.1	3.7	6,771	33,938	11,233
Auburn–Opelika, AL	57,531	41,231	55,459	33.0	26.2	15.7	10.8	12.3	2.0	3,899	29,927	6,339
Augusta–Richmond County, GA–SC	54,986	45,148	205,567	29.0	25.0	19.5	10.9	13.2	2.5	21,103	103,350	38,099
Austin–Round Rock–San Marcos, TX	72,470	57,839	649,827	19.9	23.4	18.8	12.9	19.7	5.3	40,948	253,014	83,475
Bakersfield–Delano, CA	51,040	46,793	252,086	27.0	25.5	18.3	10.9	15.8	2.4	35,209	183,684	80,481
Baltimore–Towson, MD	82,847	67,030	1,022,038	17.8	19.4	17.8	13.3	24.5	7.1	50,038	288,770	89,830
Bangor, ME	55,344	42,489	62,698	29.7	26.9	19.4	10.7	11.7	1.6	4,153	24,945	5,961
Barnstable Town, MA	75,019	58,551	96,726	19.8	23.2	18.8	14.3	19.4	4.5	3,798	19,939	5,328
Baton Rouge, LA	63,976	50,154	292,728	26.1	23.7	17.2	12.9	16.9	3.2	22,334	125,774	43,811
Battle Creek, MI	49,923	40,815	53,216	30.2	28.8	18.5	9.7	11.0	1.9	4,828	23,855	8,627
Bay City, MI	54,409	45,527	43,864	26.3	29.1	19.9	11.9	11.6	1.2	2,606	14,538	4,398
Beaumont–Port Arthur, TX	54,617	44,246	144,092	29.6	25.1	18.1	11.1	13.8	2.3	14,977	65,869	23,906
Bellingham, WA	65,801	50,978	80,052	24.3	24.8	20.1	13.8	14.8	2.3	4,204	30,262	6,978
Bend, OR	60,377	50,417	64,514	22.4	27.2	21.1	12.3	14.3	2.7	4,039	20,646	7,044
Billings, MT	60,675	48,677	65,262	24.1	27.1	19.9	12.8	13.8	2.4	3,557	18,873	6,387
Binghamton, NY	58,189	46,472	100,597	27.5	25.7	19.9	10.9	13.9	2.2	7,039	38,335	11,774
Birmingham–Hoover, AL	58,688	46,656	433,751	26.9	25.8	17.6	11.3	15.1	3.3	34,992	174,352	61,361
Bismarck, ND	73,926	57,085	45,153	19.9	23.9	19.8	15.8	17.8	2.9	1,782	9,729	2,792
Blacksburg–Christiansburg–Radford, VA	57,886	42,452	62,319	32.1	25.5	17.7	10.6	11.7	2.3	3,215	31,904	4,470
Bloomington, IN	55,454	39,326	74,988	33.5	26.0	17.0	10.6	10.8	2.0	4,744	38,845	5,708
Bloomington–Normal, IL	81,790	59,299	63,160	20.8	21.9	17.6	13.7	22.1	3.8	2,371	22,312	4,194
Boise City–Nampa, ID	56,921	48,046	225,105	23.6	28.0	20.5	11.8	13.8	2.3	17,346	92,474	33,327
Boston–Cambridge–Quincy, MA–NH	89,080	70,454	1,751,250	18.7	17.9	16.1	13.0	25.6	8.7	76,775	450,759	118,692
Boston–Quincy, MA	85,406	66,675	723,888	21.0	18.0	15.9	12.6	24.1	8.4	36,789	226,596	58,401
Cambridge–Newton–Framingham, MA	99,453	78,528	578,681	15.9	16.3	15.9	13.0	28.4	10.5	18,993	115,804	26,356
Peabody, MA	82,044	64,239	286,251	21.0	19.5	15.9	12.7	23.7	7.2	15,821	79,988	25,832
Rockingham County–Strafford County, NH	84,663	69,787	162,430	14.9	20.5	18.1	14.9	25.9	5.8	5,172	28,371	8,103
Boulder, CO	90,197	65,571	118,937	19.0	21.2	15.4	12.1	23.7	8.6	5,019	39,871	8,463
Bowling Green, KY	56,260	40,890	47,801	31.0	26.4	16.9	12.6	10.8	2.3	3,839	22,027	6,440
Bremerton–Silverdale, WA	71,770	60,171	97,837	16.7	24.2	20.8	14.0	20.5	3.8	4,622	24,759	7,499
Bridgeport–Stamford–Norwalk, CT	101,295	79,408	332,735	16.2	16.7	14.8	11.8	24.8	15.7	13,983	80,897	24,305
Brownsville–Harlingen, TX	35,316	32,287	115,136	40.1	27.1	15.7	7.0	8.5	1.6	27,183	140,118	63,009
Brunswick, GA	52,320	42,014	43,745	29.1	27.1	17.4	10.9	12.7	2.8	4,539	21,103	8,100
Buffalo–Niagara Falls, NY	62,806	47,894	466,224	27.1	24.6	18.3	12.1	15.2	2.7	30,878	157,893	51,215
Burlington, NC	53,741	42,072	60,118	29.3	27.9	18.4	11.2	11.1	2.1	5,182	25,802	9,749
Burlington–South Burlington, VT	75,785	60,229	84,220	19.3	21.7	20.2	15.1	19.3	4.4	3,477	22,829	5,453
Canton–Massillon, OH	54,267	43,609	160,442	27.2	29.1	18.7	11.4	11.7	2.0	11,495	60,561	22,384
Cape Coral–Fort Myers, FL	55,895	46,144	237,009	24.1	29.7	18.3	10.8	13.4	3.6	15,370	92,065	27,771
Cape Girardeau–Jackson, MO–IL	53,187	41,897	36,946	28.5	29.2	18.7	11.5	10.1	1.9	3,028	15,741	5,469
Carson City, NV	64,104	54,927	21,068	23.1	23.3	19.6	15.0	16.8	2.3	1,395	7,918	2,451
Casper, WY	64,292	56,203	30,449	19.1	25.5	21.9	12.1	17.9	3.5	1,135	6,175	1,897
Cedar Rapids, IA	71,096	55,342	104,197	19.3	25.4	20.6	14.4	17.7	2.6	4,110	24,351	7,761
Champaign–Urbana, IL	66,494	44,639	91,231	29.8	24.1	17.1	11.1	14.8	3.2	4,806	44,658	9,795
Charleston, WV	54,321	43,869	125,350	28.4	27.4	18.4	11.0	11.9	3.0	10,215	47,347	15,088
Charleston–North Charleston–Summerville, SC	60,143	50,226	253,690	25.1	24.6	19.1	12.0	15.7	3.4	19,954	106,311	36,026
Charlotte–Gastonia–Rock Hill, NC–SC	63,248	51,920	667,115	22.7	25.3	18.7	11.8	16.9	4.6	50,086	254,524	91,051
Charlottesville, VA	76,395	57,117	77,152	22.0	21.8	18.2	13.3	19.1	5.6	3,197	25,941	3,982
Chattanooga, TN–GA	53,651	42,651	208,890	29.5	27.1	17.3	11.3	12.2	2.6	18,153	87,943	29,689
Cheyenne, WY	66,729	51,864	37,694	20.2	27.5	20.1	13.6	16.1	2.4	1,924	9,510	3,453
Chicago–Joliet–Naperville, IL–IN–WI	72,127	59,482	3,415,379	20.7	21.8	18.1	13.1	20.5	5.8	230,704	1,262,137	454,831
Chicago–Joliet–Naperville, IL	71,881	59,280	2,853,466	20.9	21.8	18.1	13.0	20.4	5.8	195,089	1,076,049	382,500
Gary, IN	61,943	50,825	260,374	24.5	24.6	19.4	13.6	15.9	2.1	19,674	104,362	40,262
Lake County–Kenosha County, IL–WI	84,890	71,126	301,539	15.8	19.5	17.2	13.5	24.9	9.2	15,941	81,726	32,069

[1]The poverty status was determined for all people except institutionalized people, people in military group quarters, people in college dormitories, and unrelated individuals under 15 years old.

Table B-7. Median Income, Household Income Distribution, and Poverty Status, 2009–2011—*Continued*

Metropolitan statistical area division	Median family income (in 2011 inflation-adjusted dollars)	Median household income (in 2011 inflation-adjusted dollars)	Total number of households	Percent of households by income level						Number whose income in the past 12 months was below poverty level[1]		
				Under $25,000	$25,000–$49,999	$50,000–$74,999	$75,000–$99,999	$100,000–$199,999	$200,000 and over	Families	Individuals	Children under 18
Chico, CA	54,518	42,608	84,146	29.7	26.6	17.8	11.5	12.5	1.9	6,440	43,608	10,619
Cincinnati–Middletown, OH–KY–IN	67,068	53,302	812,020	23.0	23.8	19.0	12.8	17.6	3.7	53,972	284,574	100,055
Clarksville, TN–KY	51,517	43,176	100,174	27.0	29.0	20.7	11.5	10.5	1.3	9,671	45,807	17,618
Cleveland, TN	48,962	38,334	43,797	32.5	28.4	18.7	10.5	8.6	1.4	4,313	21,151	6,448
Cleveland–Elyria–Mentor, OH	61,733	47,147	844,591	26.6	25.7	18.3	11.5	14.8	3.2	60,006	311,509	111,260
Coeur d'Alene, ID	53,361	46,504	55,941	23.9	29.7	21.2	12.5	10.3	2.4	4,179	20,790	6,234
College Station–Bryan, TX	55,324	37,143	81,169	37.8	21.8	15.8	9.0	12.2	3.4	7,765	62,312	12,901
Colorado Springs, CO	68,526	55,414	243,981	20.6	24.0	20.2	12.4	19.3	3.5	15,148	79,248	28,814
Columbia, MO	65,933	46,246	68,101	27.9	25.1	18.5	11.7	13.8	3.0	3,977	32,147	7,123
Columbia, SC	58,843	46,910	294,118	25.9	26.5	18.7	11.8	14.4	2.7	22,337	117,151	37,805
Columbus, GA–AL	49,434	40,658	109,630	30.9	27.9	16.4	10.8	11.7	2.3	11,023	49,872	18,305
Columbus, IN	62,791	51,987	30,169	21.0	27.1	20.5	11.9	16.2	3.3	1,721	8,482	3,527
Columbus, OH	66,715	52,657	709,639	23.1	24.3	18.8	12.4	17.7	3.8	50,489	278,020	94,591
Corpus Christi, TX	51,868	44,197	154,399	27.8	27.0	18.0	10.7	14.2	2.4	16,255	81,868	34,528
Corvallis, OR	71,783	45,999	33,428	29.9	22.7	15.9	10.6	17.8	3.1	1,780	17,770	2,440
Crestview–Fort Walton Beach–Destin, FL	61,701	51,890	71,002	20.5	27.9	20.5	11.4	15.9	3.9	4,852	24,092	9,098
Cumberland, MD–WV	52,522	36,313	40,084	34.1	27.6	16.5	10.1	10.7	1.0	2,605	15,605	4,316
Dallas–Fort Worth–Arlington, TX	66,560	56,560	2,275,581	20.2	23.9	18.7	12.2	19.6	5.3	178,235	935,692	376,460
Dallas–Plano–Irving, TX	67,497	57,369	1,510,273	20.0	23.7	18.3	12.1	20.1	5.8	117,144	622,414	247,902
Fort Worth–Arlington, TX	65,039	55,204	765,308	20.6	24.4	19.5	12.6	18.6	4.3	61,091	313,278	128,558
Dalton, GA	43,900	38,787	48,366	31.5	28.8	18.9	9.6	9.8	1.3	6,708	30,532	11,480
Danville, IL	50,435	39,756	31,502	32.0	28.0	19.8	10.1	9.2	0.8	3,225	16,766	7,007
Danville, VA	44,998	35,993	44,663	35.3	29.6	17.8	8.3	8.3	0.7	4,815	20,962	7,168
Davenport–Moline–Rock Island, IA–IL	62,533	48,904	154,477	23.5	27.3	19.8	12.7	13.9	2.8	8,680	44,579	15,410
Dayton, OH	58,520	45,765	343,639	26.8	26.8	18.9	12.0	13.4	2.1	25,544	129,234	44,807
Decatur, AL	52,081	42,045	59,367	28.8	28.5	17.7	10.1	13.2	1.7	4,602	23,529	8,895
Decatur, IL	59,802	45,048	44,719	27.3	27.2	18.4	11.2	13.1	2.7	2,835	16,603	6,037
Deltona–Daytona Beach–Ormond Beach, FL	53,562	41,766	193,393	29.1	29.1	18.8	10.7	10.3	2.1	13,221	78,126	23,480
Denver–Aurora–Broomfield, CO[2]	75,854	60,452	997,755	19.1	22.4	18.4	13.3	21.4	5.5	56,136	313,810	107,521
Des Moines–West Des Moines, IA	72,443	58,580	224,132	18.7	23.7	20.1	14.0	20.0	3.6	10,825	58,567	21,699
Detroit–Warren–Livonia, MI	63,228	50,206	1,646,308	25.5	24.3	18.0	12.1	16.6	3.5	135,169	709,359	248,077
Detroit–Livonia–Dearborn, MI	50,514	40,102	672,320	33.3	25.6	16.7	9.9	12.4	2.1	80,286	433,184	159,025
Warren–Troy–Farmington Hills, MI	71,837	57,429	973,988	20.1	23.4	18.8	13.7	19.5	4.5	54,883	276,175	89,052
Dothan, AL	48,210	39,311	57,248	32.1	28.6	16.7	10.7	10.4	1.6	5,882	25,588	9,448
Dover, DE	62,988	54,391	56,947	21.6	24.3	21.7	15.1	15.7	1.6	3,746	20,874	8,879
Dubuque, IA	63,493	49,556	37,167	20.3	30.2	20.8	15.1	11.7	2.1	1,542	8,537	2,763
Duluth, MN–WI	61,097	45,591	118,763	27.7	26.0	20.1	11.8	12.7	1.7	6,881	42,038	10,640
Durham–Chapel Hill, NC	65,204	50,251	200,997	25.0	24.7	16.6	11.9	16.8	4.9	14,351	85,426	25,853
Eau Claire, WI	62,066	47,353	63,881	25.7	26.7	20.4	12.5	13.3	1.5	3,373	21,980	5,725
El Centro, CA	44,033	40,304	48,831	34.4	23.1	16.8	10.1	13.5	2.1	8,269	39,057	15,782
Elizabethtown, KY	54,687	46,340	43,755	25.9	27.6	20.2	11.9	12.4	2.0	3,871	18,516	8,496
Elkhart–Goshen, IN	52,175	44,076	69,535	23.9	31.6	21.6	11.3	10.1	1.5	6,668	33,975	15,300
Elmira, NY	58,013	48,046	35,836	27.6	24.6	19.6	12.0	13.7	2.6	3,031	13,036	4,573
El Paso, TX	42,214	38,314	251,931	32.8	28.7	16.8	8.9	10.9	1.9	39,531	189,847	79,590
Erie, PA	55,575	43,493	109,142	28.9	26.8	19.0	11.0	12.1	2.1	8,138	44,239	15,115
Eugene–Springfield, OR	54,183	41,028	145,099	30.4	27.6	18.7	10.4	10.7	2.1	10,218	66,413	14,100
Evansville, IN–KY	59,849	47,400	142,634	24.7	27.5	20.1	12.6	13.1	2.1	8,963	47,219	15,509
Fairbanks, AK	77,357	66,865	36,123	15.2	21.1	20.1	15.5	25.2	2.8	1,486	7,909	2,557
Fargo, ND–MN	70,137	50,780	86,909	23.5	25.8	19.3	13.3	14.9	3.2	3,251	26,474	5,865
Farmington, NM	58,747	48,943	41,891	26.0	24.9	17.9	14.5	14.9	1.9	5,512	28,060	10,982
Fayetteville, NC	50,979	44,167	134,475	26.3	29.1	19.5	10.9	12.5	1.7	13,710	63,653	24,867
Fayetteville–Springdale–Rogers, AR–MO	54,836	45,841	173,321	26.4	27.3	19.0	9.7	14.8	2.8	13,941	74,433	27,846
Flagstaff, AZ	57,990	48,627	44,858	26.1	25.2	17.9	13.2	15.2	2.3	4,112	27,690	7,904
Flint, MI	51,843	41,272	165,073	30.4	27.8	18.7	9.9	11.9	1.3	17,069	85,911	32,474
Florence, SC	48,584	39,319	78,178	32.0	28.4	17.8	9.0	10.9	1.8	9,186	41,868	15,194
Florence–Muscle Shoals, AL	50,991	39,228	61,091	32.8	27.7	18.0	10.3	9.9	1.3	5,175	24,318	7,997
Fond du Lac, WI	63,882	51,450	41,195	22.0	26.6	22.0	15.4	12.0	2.1	2,072	10,479	3,551
Fort Collins–Loveland, CO	73,647	56,624	119,773	21.9	22.5	19.2	13.9	18.8	3.7	5,821	41,644	8,557
Fort Smith, AR–OK	47,195	38,704	113,211	31.8	29.7	18.6	9.1	9.0	1.9	11,487	56,746	21,970
Fort Wayne, IN	59,504	48,719	160,087	23.2	27.8	21.4	12.4	12.8	2.3	11,130	58,167	21,925
Fresno, CA	51,244	45,786	285,735	28.3	25.5	17.5	11.1	14.9	2.8	40,775	226,168	95,929
Gadsden, AL	43,989	36,658	40,186	34.3	29.3	16.4	9.5	9.5	1.0	4,141	19,325	6,692
Gainesville, FL	59,163	40,421	102,180	33.1	24.8	16.0	9.8	12.9	3.5	7,254	60,504	10,108
Gainesville, GA	57,113	49,916	61,457	22.0	28.1	19.7	12.0	15.1	3.2	6,022	30,433	12,600
Glens Falls, NY	62,918	53,025	53,265	21.7	25.4	20.6	15.2	14.7	2.3	3,318	14,832	4,587
Goldsboro, NC	50,584	41,424	47,641	30.0	28.1	21.6	'9.2	9.6	1.5	5,282	25,269	9,764
Grand Forks, ND–MN	66,081	46,519	39,628	26.5	26.4	19.2	12.3	13.2	2.5	1,548	13,196	2,638
Grand Junction, CO	61,627	50,358	58,636	23.7	25.9	19.5	11.6	16.6	2.7	3,302	18,943	5,418
Grand Rapids–Wyoming, MI	59,300	49,208	290,856	24.1	26.6	20.3	13.1	13.4	2.5	22,478	116,477	43,572
Great Falls, MT	55,713	43,366	32,950	26.8	29.5	20.1	11.4	10.5	1.7	2,213	11,008	4,084

[1]The poverty status was determined for all people except institutionalized people, people in military group quarters, people in college dormitories, and unrelated individuals under 15 years old.
[2]The Denver–Aurora metropolitan statistical area includes Broomfield County. Broomfield County, CO, was formed from parts of Adams, Boulder, Jefferson, and Weld counties on November 15, 2001, and is coextensive with Broomfield city. For the purposes of defining and presenting data for the Denver–Aurora metropolitan statistical area, Broomfield city is treated as if it were a county when data are available to do so. In many cases, the data will not be available.

Table B-7.   Median Income, Household Income Distribution, and Poverty Status, 2009–2011—*Continued*

Metropolitan statistical area division	Median family income (in 2011 inflation-adjusted dollars)	Median household income (in 2011 inflation-adjusted dollars)	Total number of households	Percent of households by income level						Number whose income in the past 12 months was below poverty level[1]		
				Under $25,000	$25,000–$49,999	$50,000–$74,999	$75,000–$99,999	$100,000–$199,999	$200,000 and over	Families	Individuals	Children under 18
Greeley, CO	64,272	54,229	89,222	22.3	23.3	19.6	12.8	19.0	3.1	6,960	37,946	14,379
Green Bay, WI	64,338	51,429	122,309	21.6	27.1	20.7	13.9	14.5	2.3	6,096	32,448	11,229
Greensboro–High Point, NC	53,696	42,071	285,114	28.3	28.6	17.9	10.3	12.5	2.4	23,973	123,649	41,361
Greenville, NC	54,171	39,421	71,887	34.0	26.0	16.4	9.7	11.5	2.5	6,741	43,820	11,972
Greenville–Mauldin–Easley, SC	56,078	44,661	241,916	27.9	26.8	18.2	10.7	13.6	2.7	19,317	101,996	35,188
Gulfport–Biloxi, MS	51,384	42,351	94,104	29.1	27.7	18.1	11.4	11.9	1.8	10,236	45,788	17,241
Hagerstown–Martinsburg, MD–WV	62,001	51,015	103,024	23.4	25.3	20.4	12.7	16.2	2.0	5,980	32,703	11,519
Hanford–Corcoran, CA	51,068	47,314	40,538	25.1	26.6	20.8	10.2	15.4	1.9	5,321	27,610	12,977
Harrisburg–Carlisle, PA	69,174	55,627	222,064	19.1	25.9	20.3	14.2	17.2	3.3	10,260	55,177	19,324
Harrisonburg, VA	56,964	46,430	45,018	25.3	28.3	19.1	13.0	11.7	2.6	2,704	21,188	4,096
Hartford–West Hartford–East Hartford, CT	83,569	66,254	469,280	18.5	19.7	17.1	14.0	24.2	6.5	22,475	118,837	35,349
Hattiesburg, MS	51,141	40,113	54,398	33.7	25.7	17.0	10.3	11.4	1.9	5,934	31,117	9,325
Hickory–Lenoir–Morganton, NC	48,685	39,536	138,102	31.1	30.0	18.5	10.0	8.7	1.7	11,876	60,599	20,326
Hinesville–Fort Stewart, GA	48,822	44,232	28,157	27.3	27.9	21.3	12.5	10.0	1.1	3,736	15,203	6,972
Holland–Grand Haven, MI	65,133	54,350	93,675	19.7	26.0	20.8	14.1	16.9	2.5	4,699	29,299	8,569
Honolulu, HI	82,792	70,166	308,950	15.3	19.9	18.0	14.7	26.4	5.7	14,959	89,388	26,235
Hot Springs, AR	46,784	37,398	39,137	33.2	29.7	16.9	8.9	8.8	2.4	3,597	18,462	6,018
Houma–Bayou Cane–Thibodaux, LA	58,040	48,114	74,378	27.3	24.5	17.4	12.5	15.7	2.6	6,668	33,432	12,384
Houston–Sugar Land–Baytown, TX	64,787	55,792	2,036,252	21.7	23.3	17.4	12.3	19.3	6.0	189,499	967,110	394,684
Huntington–Ashland, WV–KY–OH	49,079	37,462	114,544	34.7	27.4	17.8	9.3	9.5	1.4	11,420	57,010	16,976
Huntsville, AL	69,282	53,959	162,405	22.9	23.4	16.9	11.7	20.6	4.5	10,956	52,046	17,703
Idaho Falls, ID	56,086	50,093	43,985	21.6	28.3	20.2	12.9	14.7	2.4	3,036	14,960	5,709
Indianapolis–Carmel, IN	64,122	51,451	669,827	22.5	25.9	18.7	12.3	16.9	3.7	47,182	243,707	91,492
Iowa City, IA	73,788	51,414	61,786	25.2	23.4	17.9	14.2	15.6	3.7	2,286	25,187	4,764
Ithaca, NY	71,347	50,220	38,685	27.0	22.9	18.5	10.4	17.6	3.7	1,632	18,570	2,359
Jackson, MI	56,295	46,349	59,800	26.8	26.6	20.7	11.8	12.6	1.5	4,686	24,404	9,163
Jackson, MS	55,784	44,864	196,246	28.1	26.5	17.4	11.7	13.2	3.2	18,891	96,301	35,972
Jackson, TN	50,584	40,141	40,826	31.4	27.9	17.4	10.8	9.9	2.7	4,033	22,459	8,534
Jacksonville, FL	61,921	51,403	505,800	22.8	25.8	19.5	12.7	15.7	3.5	36,773	193,182	64,696
Jacksonville, NC	49,346	44,363	59,291	24.0	32.7	21.7	10.5	9.9	1.2	4,894	23,392	8,716
Janesville, WI	59,580	48,591	62,983	23.0	28.4	21.2	13.6	12.3	1.5	4,578	22,423	8,049
Jefferson City, MO	62,962	51,781	56,840	23.5	24.7	21.6	14.5	14.4	1.4	3,421	16,486	5,479
Johnson City, TN	47,381	36,898	83,089	33.6	28.7	15.7	9.8	10.0	2.2	8,215	38,736	10,846
Johnstown, PA	53,099	40,953	58,383	30.2	28.9	19.4	11.5	8.8	1.3	3,505	19,337	6,434
Jonesboro, AR	48,797	37,171	46,717	35.2	25.9	17.6	9.3	9.4	2.6	5,792	26,112	9,182
Joplin, MO	48,295	39,953	66,130	30.5	29.3	19.5	9.7	9.4	1.6	5,963	29,764	10,419
Kalamazoo–Portage, MI	57,645	44,291	127,533	28.6	26.4	17.9	11.0	13.6	2.6	10,589	63,333	18,440
Kankakee–Bradley, IL	59,580	48,208	41,113	24.8	26.5	18.5	13.5	15.0	1.8	3,402	16,918	6,074
Kansas City, MO–KS	69,523	55,540	793,657	21.0	24.0	19.3	13.4	18.5	3.9	46,403	249,504	92,079
Kennewick–Pasco–Richland, WA	65,747	58,183	87,366	19.6	23.3	19.6	14.7	20.1	2.6	6,897	38,428	16,699
Killeen–Temple–Fort Hood, TX	56,720	48,440	129,460	23.3	28.1	19.7	13.4	13.9	1.6	11,102	57,594	24,660
Kingsport–Bristol–Bristol, TN–VA	47,851	37,842	130,516	32.9	29.3	17.0	10.4	8.7	1.8	11,508	50,613	14,602
Kingston, NY	69,209	56,253	69,806	21.1	22.8	19.9	12.7	19.0	4.4	3,440	22,349	5,509
Knoxville, TN	59,455	45,503	286,992	26.7	27.1	18.6	11.8	13.0	2.8	18,625	98,954	30,133
Kokomo, IN	56,468	43,307	41,185	27.0	27.7	19.7	12.8	11.4	1.4	3,144	15,211	5,447
La Crosse, WI–MN	67,314	50,824	53,371	23.9	25.2	20.7	13.9	14.3	2.0	2,077	16,426	3,400
Lafayette, IN	60,458	42,972	77,206	30.3	25.5	18.4	10.9	12.5	2.4	5,043	38,128	8,317
Lafayette, LA	62,062	47,936	103,689	28.4	22.9	17.8	10.1	16.4	4.4	8,211	45,429	13,989
Lake Charles, LA	55,349	42,319	74,188	29.2	25.4	17.4	12.1	13.5	2.4	6,610	33,981	12,199
Lake Havasu City–Kingman, AZ	45,598	38,626	80,801	30.7	31.5	19.9	9.3	7.2	1.3	6,669	35,955	12,601
Lakeland–Winter Haven, FL	50,533	42,365	219,743	28.1	29.4	19.4	11.7	9.8	1.6	20,713	105,995	40,337
Lancaster, PA	64,938	54,875	193,775	20.4	24.7	21.8	14.0	16.4	2.7	10,110	53,042	19,265
Lansing–East Lansing, MI	63,625	48,524	179,245	25.4	25.8	19.3	12.4	14.7	2.3	11,430	74,974	19,442
Laredo, TX	38,999	37,688	66,750	34.7	28.7	15.7	8.9	10.4	1.6	15,295	80,127	38,706
Las Cruces, NM	42,706	36,278	73,836	36.7	25.4	15.5	10.6	10.0	1.8	11,524	56,785	21,423
Las Vegas–Paradise, NV	60,427	52,406	701,868	21.1	26.3	20.0	12.9	16.3	3.3	50,630	283,517	103,095
Lawrence, KS	67,709	46,758	43,154	26.8	26.5	17.9	10.8	15.5	2.5	1,823	19,770	2,655
Lawton, OK	52,657	46,850	44,634	25.8	26.8	23.1	11.4	10.7	2.2	3,807	18,456	7,078
Lebanon, PA	62,927	53,361	51,780	19.8	25.9	22.5	14.1	15.0	2.6	2,660	13,084	4,925
Lewiston, ID–WA	54,717	43,044	24,813	26.5	30.3	20.5	11.1	9.8	1.7	1,245	7,421	2,520
Lewiston–Auburn, ME	54,675	43,144	44,113	28.5	27.7	19.4	11.4	11.5	1.5	3,175	16,116	5,691
Lexington–Fayette, KY	63,232	47,733	189,963	26.8	25.0	17.9	11.5	15.3	3.4	14,755	79,092	24,187
Lima, OH	52,297	41,043	40,679	31.4	27.2	19.0	10.5	10.6	1.3	4,228	20,688	8,228
Lincoln, NE	66,812	50,440	120,451	23.2	26.3	19.3	13.1	15.3	2.8	6,833	43,697	12,965
Little Rock–North Little Rock–Conway, AR	59,733	47,315	272,417	25.7	26.5	18.8	11.8	14.5	2.6	18,641	101,856	35,432
Logan, UT–ID	55,333	47,629	39,292	22.6	29.6	21.6	13.0	11.6	1.6	3,492	19,940	6,681
Longview, TX	55,138	44,448	78,147	27.9	27.4	18.6	11.9	11.2	2.9	6,806	32,857	12,946
Longview, WA	54,112	44,134	40,112	28.3	27.4	18.7	11.1	12.8	1.6	3,857	20,353	7,453
Los Angeles–Long Beach–Santa Ana, CA	65,421	58,900	4,195,162	21.3	21.9	17.3	12.2	20.7	6.8	354,838	2,022,875	693,853
Los Angeles–Long Beach–Glendale, CA	60,684	54,630	3,206,808	23.2	22.8	17.4	11.8	18.9	6.0	295,519	1,666,126	575,449
Santa Ana–Anaheim–Irvine, CA	82,430	73,596	988,354	15.2	18.8	16.9	13.3	26.4	9.3	59,319	356,749	118,404
Louisville/Jefferson County, KY–IN	60,673	47,308	503,889	25.4	26.7	18.7	11.8	14.2	3.1	38,053	188,830	66,406

[1] The poverty status was determined for all people except institutionalized people, people in military group quarters, people in college dormitories, and unrelated individuals under 15 years old.

Table B-7. Median Income, Household Income Distribution, and Poverty Status, 2009–2011—*Continued*

Metropolitan statistical area division	Median family income (in 2011 inflation-adjusted dollars)	Median household income (in 2011 inflation-adjusted dollars)	Total number of households	Percent of households by income level						Number whose income in the past 12 months was below poverty level[1]		
				Under $25,000	$25,000–$49,999	$50,000–$74,999	$75,000–$99,999	$100,000–$199,999	$200,000 and over	Families	Individuals	Children under 18
Lubbock, TX	54,890	43,158	106,390	30.2	26.8	17.6	10.7	11.8	2.9	9,015	55,608	17,318
Lynchburg, VA	56,747	45,155	98,204	27.3	27.2	19.4	12.0	12.2	1.9	7,116	37,968	11,219
Macon, GA	51,513	39,485	84,566	33.6	25.4	17.1	9.4	12.5	2.0	9,926	48,343	16,949
Madera–Chowchilla, CA	51,110	46,035	41,781	25.6	27.2	21.1	8.6	15.3	2.3	5,700	32,372	14,057
Madison, WI	78,453	59,607	237,548	19.2	22.7	19.4	14.9	19.9	4.0	9,229	68,497	16,350
Manchester–Nashua, NH	82,076	68,848	153,465	16.2	19.9	18.0	14.8	25.2	5.9	5,635	31,242	10,006
Manhattan, KS	61,154	45,961	45,473	26.6	28.2	18.7	12.6	11.9	2.1	2,523	20,595	4,184
Mankato–North Mankato, MN	65,019	50,785	36,434	22.0	27.0	21.6	13.4	14.3	1.6	1,586	14,475	2,490
Mansfield, OH	52,420	41,251	48,467	27.5	31.1	18.4	11.7	10.2	1.1	3,701	17,052	5,921
McAllen–Edinburg–Mission, TX	35,318	32,533	213,207	40.1	27.4	14.4	7.7	8.8	1.6	55,165	274,312	126,643
Medford, OR	52,107	41,952	83,645	28.7	28.3	19.4	11.3	10.3	2.0	6,630	33,978	9,980
Memphis, TN–MS–AR	55,631	46,079	478,385	27.5	25.7	18.2	11.2	14.4	3.0	48,585	245,974	98,018
Merced, CA	45,986	41,588	74,181	29.3	28.8	17.7	10.3	11.4	2.6	11,871	64,115	28,514
Miami–Fort Lauderdale–Pompano Beach, FL	55,070	46,592	1,998,159	27.0	25.6	17.5	10.7	14.9	4.4	166,542	914,908	272,286
Fort Lauderdale–Pompano Beach–Deerfield Beach, FL	60,330	50,093	661,113	24.5	25.4	18.1	11.4	16.5	4.1	43,558	242,448	71,285
Miami–Miami Beach–Kendall, FL	47,846	41,644	816,522	31.1	25.9	16.7	9.8	12.7	3.9	89,295	480,034	139,325
West Palm Beach–Boca Raton–Boynton Beach, FL	62,277	50,783	520,524	23.6	25.6	17.9	11.1	16.3	5.6	33,689	192,426	61,676
Michigan City–La Porte, IN	59,251	46,852	42,512	27.0	26.0	21.1	12.3	12.0	1.6	3,557	17,074	6,647
Midland, TX	65,909	56,711	49,660	19.1	24.3	20.8	12.4	16.7	6.7	3,521	16,988	6,816
Milwaukee–Waukesha–West Allis, WI	68,431	51,858	615,533	24.0	24.3	18.1	12.4	17.4	3.8	42,558	229,621	85,841
Minneapolis–St. Paul–Bloomington, MN–WI	80,659	64,687	1,274,390	17.1	21.0	19.2	14.7	22.5	5.4	57,528	346,876	116,726
Missoula, MT	59,453	42,868	45,229	29.6	27.0	17.2	10.9	12.8	2.6	2,698	19,840	4,097
Mobile, AL	51,300	41,576	156,377	31.0	26.1	19.1	10.4	11.1	2.3	16,631	78,303	28,966
Modesto, CA	54,132	48,170	166,136	25.8	25.7	18.5	12.1	15.6	2.4	20,979	104,132	41,281
Monroe, LA	48,783	38,275	65,747	34.0	26.2	16.5	8.9	12.4	2.1	8,530	40,323	16,431
Monroe, MI	62,417	53,057	58,772	21.7	25.2	20.6	14.6	15.8	2.1	3,681	17,959	6,416
Montgomery, AL	58,613	46,709	139,859	26.7	26.1	18.1	11.8	14.9	2.5	13,583	65,904	24,678
Morgantown, WV	58,188	41,992	49,046	33.3	24.1	16.7	10.6	12.0	3.3	2,801	24,319	3,023
Morristown, TN	45,667	35,815	53,753	35.1	29.3	17.5	8.8	8.8	1.3	5,283	25,312	8,153
Mount Vernon–Anacortes, WA	64,422	54,965	45,373	20.3	25.3	22.0	13.5	17.1	2.0	2,428	13,614	4,515
Muncie, IN	50,718	36,224	45,985	35.3	27.4	18.0	8.7	8.8	1.7	3,685	24,783	5,750
Muskegon–Norton Shores, MI	48,177	39,428	64,767	32.5	28.1	18.8	10.2	9.0	1.3	7,007	32,608	11,748
Myrtle Beach–North Myrtle Beach–Conway, SC	50,212	41,231	112,170	28.7	30.4	19.0	10.4	9.8	1.8	9,874	49,519	15,796
Napa, CA	77,174	68,403	50,083	16.4	21.0	17.7	12.0	24.6	8.2	2,668	14,762	4,850
Naples–Marco Island, FL	62,889	53,037	118,898	19.8	26.9	18.9	11.4	15.6	7.5	7,940	49,740	16,414
Nashville–Davidson—Murfreesboro—Franklin, TN	62,532	51,112	605,509	22.6	26.2	19.1	12.6	15.5	4.0	42,325	226,121	79,915
New Haven–Milford, CT	76,311	60,581	329,691	21.3	20.7	17.3	12.8	22.1	5.7	20,307	103,149	33,887
New Orleans–Metairie–Kenner, LA	57,860	46,356	454,532	27.9	25.3	16.6	11.3	15.2	3.8	40,220	203,613	69,149
New York–Northern New Jersey–Long Island, NY–NJ–PA	77,029	63,973	6,815,327	21.2	19.3	15.9	11.9	22.8	8.9	486,665	2,547,636	812,430
Edison–New Brunswick, NJ	92,274	75,775	848,291	15.1	18.1	16.3	13.6	27.6	9.2	32,754	177,807	59,780
Nassau–Suffolk, NY	102,890	89,426	939,313	11.8	14.9	15.3	13.8	32.3	12.0	29,627	168,367	49,996
Newark–Union, NJ–PA	88,236	71,601	764,451	17.4	18.6	16.0	12.5	24.9	10.6	41,742	216,783	73,771
New York–White Plains–Wayne, NY–NJ	64,296	55,369	4,263,272	25.1	20.6	15.9	11.0	19.3	7.9	382,542	1,984,679	628,883
Niles–Benton Harbor, MI	54,044	41,542	60,458	30.5	26.8	17.2	11.4	11.8	2.2	4,631	25,677	9,359
North Port–Bradenton–Sarasota, FL	57,308	46,519	298,561	24.9	28.5	18.6	11.1	13.5	3.4	17,363	93,977	28,141
Norwich–New London, CT	80,702	65,564	107,486	16.2	22.1	18.4	13.9	24.2	5.3	4,145	22,588	7,135
Ocala, FL	44,959	38,258	133,433	29.5	34.7	17.9	9.2	7.3	1.4	11,149	56,640	17,460
Ocean City, NJ	69,749	54,079	43,355	20.4	24.8	18.5	13.2	18.8	4.3	2,043	10,151	3,034
Odessa, TX	55,535	48,442	49,277	26.4	24.6	22.1	10.9	13.5	2.4	4,946	23,153	9,288
Ogden–Clearfield, UT	69,039	61,586	176,913	15.2	23.8	22.3	15.7	19.8	3.2	10,185	53,554	20,956
Oklahoma City, OK	59,744	47,487	479,789	25.5	26.5	18.8	11.7	14.4	3.0	36,817	195,650	68,182
Olympia, WA	74,045	62,021	100,507	18.6	21.3	21.4	15.4	20.5	2.7	5,072	28,735	8,596
Omaha–Council Bluffs, NE–IA	70,757	55,827	333,335	20.5	24.4	19.6	13.9	18.1	3.5	17,644	100,189	37,442
Orlando–Kissimmee–Sanford, FL	55,643	47,851	762,102	23.3	28.6	19.6	11.1	14.2	3.2	57,020	310,718	101,544
Oshkosh–Neenah, WI	63,380	49,120	68,059	23.1	27.6	21.7	12.7	12.3	2.6	3,406	20,170	5,538
Owensboro, KY	55,211	43,790	43,748	28.5	26.8	21.0	11.7	10.6	1.4	3,601	17,633	6,962
Oxnard–Thousand Oaks–Ventura, CA	84,076	74,456	266,259	15.2	18.7	16.5	13.4	27.6	8.6	15,516	88,015	30,883
Palm Bay–Melbourne–Titusville, FL	58,557	47,010	219,281	24.0	28.5	18.9	11.4	14.5	2.8	12,296	69,042	20,357
Palm Coast, FL	54,065	49,159	35,262	23.1	27.6	22.1	13.1	11.7	2.4	2,464	14,013	4,635
Panama City–Lynn Haven–Panama City Beach, FL	57,013	46,462	67,521	23.9	29.5	22.5	10.8	11.7	1.7	4,524	22,567	6,872
Parkersburg–Marietta–Vienna, WV–OH	54,061	41,205	65,079	30.1	27.9	18.1	10.6	11.7	1.7	4,473	25,327	7,411
Pascagoula, MS	54,555	47,456	58,391	26.1	26.1	20.6	12.2	12.6	2.4	4,996	25,495	9,629
Pensacola–Ferry Pass–Brent, FL	56,419	46,323	166,826	25.3	28.2	18.4	12.7	12.7	2.7	13,433	69,087	23,973
Peoria, IL	65,647	51,807	151,310	22.2	25.6	19.7	13.2	16.1	3.2	9,487	48,292	17,361
Philadelphia–Camden–Wilmington, PA–NJ–DE–MD	78,083	60,625	2,222,507	21.1	21.0	17.1	12.8	21.8	6.2	129,635	740,413	234,581
Camden, NJ	84,274	69,238	458,351	16.3	19.5	17.9	14.7	25.8	5.8	20,740	106,418	37,411
Philadelphia, PA	75,604	57,487	1,502,579	23.0	21.4	16.6	12.1	20.3	6.5	95,561	558,959	172,357
Wilmington, DE–MD–NJ	77,273	62,798	261,577	18.7	21.2	18.2	13.6	23.4	4.9	13,334	75,036	24,813

[1]The poverty status was determined for all people except institutionalized people, people in military group quarters, people in college dormitories, and unrelated individuals under 15 years old.

Table B-7.　Median Income, Household Income Distribution, and Poverty Status, 2009–2011—*Continued*

Metropolitan statistical area division	Median family income (in 2011 inflation-adjusted dollars)	Median household income (in 2011 inflation-adjusted dollars)	Total number of households	Percent of households by income level						Number whose income in the past 12 months was below poverty level[1]		
				Under $25,000	$25,000–$49,999	$50,000–$74,999	$75,000–$99,999	$100,000–$199,999	$200,000 and over	Families	Individuals	Children under 18
Phoenix–Mesa–Glendale, AZ	61,669	51,946	1,515,084	22.1	25.9	19.0	12.4	16.8	3.8	118,610	666,592	249,559
Pine Bluff, AR	46,278	36,869	35,923	35.3	28.0	15.7	10.4	9.6	1.0	4,289	21,535	7,988
Pittsburgh, PA	63,668	48,830	986,270	25.7	25.2	18.8	12.0	14.9	3.4	52,596	281,511	80,471
Pittsfield, MA	62,554	45,498	55,338	28.1	25.5	18.2	11.1	13.9	3.1	3,068	16,121	4,796
Pocatello, ID	54,279	43,317	32,691	26.6	29.5	20.9	11.2	10.8	1.0	2,238	12,911	4,315
Portland–South Portland–Biddeford, ME	71,125	57,332	212,339	20.4	23.0	20.6	14.2	18.0	3.6	8,522	49,923	13,990
Portland–Vancouver–Hillsboro, OR–WA	67,696	55,598	864,818	20.6	24.3	19.6	13.4	18.2	4.0	52,572	298,072	92,957
Port St. Lucie, FL	53,741	45,112	163,431	25.6	29.6	17.7	10.6	13.1	3.3	12,570	67,702	23,132
Poughkeepsie–Newburgh–Middletown, NY	84,844	70,206	233,466	16.7	18.8	17.8	14.1	26.8	5.8	12,132	68,966	25,820
Prescott, AZ	50,716	41,424	90,660	28.7	30.2	18.3	10.0	10.8	2.0	6,568	36,536	10,004
Providence–New Bedford–Fall River, RI–MA	70,128	54,360	619,939	24.3	21.7	17.8	12.8	19.4	4.0	36,717	199,615	61,691
Provo–Orem, UT	62,491	57,786	144,281	18.3	23.9	23.0	13.9	17.7	3.2	11,539	72,009	21,075
Pueblo, CO	51,020	40,143	62,142	32.3	26.9	18.2	10.3	11.1	1.3	5,442	28,623	9,908
Punta Gorda, FL	51,882	42,338	70,475	27.5	30.3	20.4	10.8	9.5	1.5	4,185	20,175	5,232
Racine, WI	65,850	53,083	75,679	22.1	25.1	20.3	13.5	16.4	2.7	4,549	24,673	9,656
Raleigh–Cary, NC	74,245	59,945	423,144	18.4	23.2	18.8	13.2	21.3	5.1	25,850	136,643	48,189
Rapid City, SD	61,191	49,087	50,241	22.0	28.7	21.4	12.4	12.8	2.7	3,076	16,647	5,785
Reading, PA	65,050	53,868	155,043	21.4	25.2	20.6	12.9	17.1	2.8	10,538	53,669	19,871
Redding, CA	52,682	42,931	68,614	29.0	27.9	18.7	10.7	11.2	2.4	5,650	30,871	9,026
Reno–Sparks, NV	62,734	52,252	163,362	22.3	25.4	19.1	11.5	17.9	3.8	9,948	59,309	19,374
Richmond, VA	71,297	56,982	476,077	19.2	24.4	19.0	13.7	19.3	4.4	26,281	144,483	45,415
Riverside–San Bernardino–Ontario, CA	60,468	54,629	1,276,036	21.9	24.0	18.9	13.0	18.9	3.4	126,075	701,562	278,052
Roanoke, VA	60,805	48,862	127,682	23.0	28.1	19.9	12.9	13.4	2.8	7,317	38,281	12,198
Rochester, MN	80,114	63,558	72,848	16.7	22.0	19.7	15.2	21.6	4.7	2,121	13,935	3,971
Rochester, NY	65,804	51,729	416,727	23.1	25.1	19.0	13.7	16.1	3.1	25,838	140,445	46,306
Rockford, IL	58,616	47,183	131,197	26.9	25.5	18.9	12.9	13.0	2.9	11,227	60,443	23,235
Rocky Mount, NC	47,333	38,513	59,393	32.5	29.2	17.3	10.5	9.2	1.3	5,940	28,590	10,366
Rome, GA	50,623	40,313	35,180	31.7	26.7	19.1	9.8	10.4	2.3	3,590	17,443	5,801
Sacramento—Arden-Arcade—Roseville, CA	69,171	57,644	781,039	20.4	23.1	18.4	13.1	20.7	4.4	54,436	315,258	105,663
Saginaw–Saginaw Township North, MI	52,675	41,545	76,825	29.6	28.8	18.6	9.6	11.6	1.8	6,878	38,007	13,842
St. Cloud, MN	65,141	51,445	72,102	22.6	25.8	21.1	14.5	14.2	1.9	3,914	24,517	6,103
St. George, UT	53,428	48,501	46,473	21.6	30.2	23.9	11.9	10.4	2.0	3,804	19,998	8,624
St. Joseph, MO–KS	55,951	44,617	46,951	26.4	28.8	20.6	12.4	10.4	1.4	2,852	16,822	5,693
St. Louis, MO–IL[3]	66,877	52,388	1,111,725	22.9	24.6	18.7	12.8	17.2	3.8	71,417	361,916	125,162
Salem, OR	54,532	46,681	140,850	24.3	29.0	20.1	11.8	13.0	1.9	12,915	67,317	26,699
Salinas, CA	61,470	56,808	125,329	19.9	24.0	19.1	12.2	19.5	5.4	11,845	68,116	27,945
Salisbury, MD	56,218	47,805	44,453	26.4	25.7	20.0	12.3	12.7	2.9	3,037	18,846	5,148
Salt Lake City, UT	67,540	58,432	372,260	18.3	23.9	21.6	14.0	18.4	3.9	24,831	138,758	52,175
San Angelo, TX	55,146	42,357	42,507	29.8	27.1	18.5	10.1	11.9	2.5	3,768	18,268	6,134
San Antonio–New Braunfels, TX	59,033	50,349	750,639	24.2	25.4	19.2	12.0	15.8	3.4	65,565	345,106	133,623
San Diego–Carlsbad–San Marcos, CA	71,562	61,247	1,063,605	19.3	22.3	17.5	13.2	21.8	6.0	71,355	428,247	131,169
Sandusky, OH	58,802	44,806	31,571	26.4	27.5	18.2	12.7	12.8	2.5	1,965	10,827	3,645
San Francisco–Oakland–Fremont, CA	91,326	74,927	1,606,837	16.9	17.3	15.8	11.9	26.6	11.5	73,395	468,706	121,821
Oakland–Fremont–Hayward, CA	87,706	72,244	908,724	17.1	18.2	16.5	12.2	26.4	9.6	49,761	294,493	88,755
San Francisco–San Mateo–Redwood City, CA	98,078	79,372	698,113	16.7	16.2	14.9	11.6	26.8	13.9	23,634	174,213	33,066
San Jose–Sunnyvale–Santa Clara, CA	98,803	86,278	617,875	14.1	15.5	14.3	12.4	29.7	14.0	30,326	185,834	56,504
San Luis Obispo–Paso Robles, CA	71,688	55,842	100,976	21.6	23.2	18.2	12.6	20.0	4.4	4,688	36,551	7,053
Santa Barbara–Santa Maria–Goleta, CA	69,274	60,652	140,940	19.8	21.9	18.4	11.7	21.8	6.5	8,900	64,375	19,266
Santa Cruz–Watsonville, CA	76,859	63,304	92,855	20.2	19.9	16.9	13.0	23.0	6.9	5,057	37,027	8,423
Santa Fe, NM	63,693	51,674	60,976	24.9	23.6	18.6	11.9	15.7	5.3	4,112	23,079	7,243
Santa Rosa–Petaluma, CA	75,402	62,692	184,079	18.6	22.1	18.4	13.0	22.1	5.8	8,296	55,239	15,142
Savannah, GA	57,291	47,732	129,587	25.7	26.2	19.5	11.3	14.5	2.7	9,533	57,602	20,202
Scranton—Wilkes-Barre, PA	56,668	44,058	228,629	28.2	27.6	18.3	11.2	12.4	2.3	15,046	78,168	26,609
Seattle–Tacoma–Bellevue, WA	80,723	65,452	1,359,493	17.0	21.0	18.6	13.8	23.5	6.1	62,545	381,059	111,069
Seattle–Bellevue–Everett, WA	85,346	68,312	1,060,558	16.5	20.0	18.0	13.8	24.8	7.0	45,462	286,698	79,734
Tacoma, WA	67,837	57,605	298,935	18.5	24.5	21.0	14.0	19.2	2.9	17,083	94,361	31,335
Sebastian–Vero Beach, FL	54,725	44,288	56,814	27.6	27.5	18.3	9.6	12.5	4.5	3,743	20,230	6,355
Sheboygan, WI	65,149	51,442	45,925	20.6	27.7	21.5	14.3	14.3	1.6	1,910	10,117	3,558
Sherman–Denison, TX	56,680	46,000	46,169	26.3	27.4	18.7	13.0	12.1	2.4	3,385	17,381	5,619
Shreveport–Bossier City, LA	55,761	42,445	153,627	30.7	25.8	16.8	11.0	12.8	3.0	13,071	68,437	26,362
Sioux City, IA–NE–SD	56,794	46,705	54,307	25.7	27.6	20.4	11.8	12.3	2.1	4,065	20,181	8,666
Sioux Falls, SD	68,385	54,945	89,076	20.0	25.1	21.7	15.0	15.3	2.8	3,973	20,580	6,430
South Bend–Mishawaka, IN–MI	56,151	44,372	120,854	27.4	28.5	17.7	11.6	12.6	2.3	10,285	51,004	19,146
Spartanburg, SC	51,996	42,111	105,852	29.4	28.0	18.0	11.4	11.6	1.7	9,337	47,222	16,558
Spokane, WA	61,219	47,835	187,157	25.9	25.9	19.6	12.5	13.4	2.8	11,659	68,543	18,876
Springfield, IL	67,652	52,925	87,760	23.0	23.9	19.5	13.5	17.3	2.8	5,997	29,404	10,998
Springfield, MA	64,037	50,591	268,518	26.5	22.9	17.9	12.6	17.2	2.8	19,084	103,786	34,774
Springfield, MO	52,326	41,813	174,504	29.0	29.6	19.4	9.9	10.1	1.9	14,265	72,743	23,810
Springfield, OH	51,721	42,125	55,123	29.3	29.2	18.2	10.7	11.5	1.1	4,717	24,979	8,955
State College, PA	68,155	48,102	57,157	27.6	23.8	18.5	11.7	15.5	2.9	1,908	27,421	3,228
Steubenville–Weirton, OH–WV	50,204	39,943	51,019	31.6	28.9	18.7	10.2	9.2	1.4	3,988	19,400	6,673

[1]The poverty status was determined for all people except institutionalized people, people in military group quarters, people in college dormitories, and unrelated individuals under 15 years old.
[3]The portion of Sullivan city in Crawford County, MO, is legally part of the St. Louis, MO–IL MSA. That portion is not included in these figures for the St. Louis MSA.

Table B-7.   Median Income, Household Income Distribution, and Poverty Status, 2009–2011—*Continued*

Metropolitan statistical area division	Median family income (in 2011 inflation-adjusted dollars)	Median household income (in 2011 inflation-adjusted dollars)	Total number of households	Percent of households by income level						Number whose income in the past 12 months was below poverty level[1]		
				Under $25,000	$25,000– $49,999	$50,000– $74,999	$75,000– $99,999	$100,000– $199,999	$200,000 and over	Families	Individuals	Children under 18
Stockton, CA	58,369	52,269	213,967	22.1	25.5	18.7	12.5	18.2	3.1	21,705	118,465	47,142
Sumter, SC	46,659	40,449	39,026	29.0	32.3	19.7	8.9	8.8	1.4	3,788	18,180	6,695
Syracuse, NY	64,957	51,528	255,493	24.6	23.9	19.5	12.5	16.6	2.8	15,898	92,361	30,878
Tallahassee, FL	60,144	43,260	141,858	30.1	25.3	16.6	11.2	14.2	2.5	11,696	81,493	18,763
Tampa–St. Petersburg–Clearwater, FL	55,333	45,052	1,109,897	26.9	27.7	18.6	10.8	13.0	3.0	74,321	420,618	126,653
Terre Haute, IN	53,133	41,882	63,787	29.6	28.0	19.5	10.5	10.6	1.8	4,979	27,414	8,971
Texarkana, TX–Texarkana, AR	52,240	41,979	50,163	31.6	25.2	19.9	11.0	10.3	1.9	4,992	24,174	9,319
Toledo, OH	56,714	43,418	260,053	29.5	26.2	18.3	11.0	12.7	2.2	22,351	116,397	38,580
Topeka, KS	63,034	48,421	95,054	23.6	27.5	20.2	13.0	13.6	2.2	6,828	33,655	12,617
Trenton–Ewing, NJ	91,454	73,168	129,884	17.8	17.8	15.4	13.2	25.3	10.4	6,899	39,940	13,553
Tucson, AZ	55,881	44,679	379,608	28.0	26.7	17.9	11.0	13.6	2.7	32,088	185,596	59,700
Tulsa, OK	58,175	46,807	366,058	25.3	27.3	18.9	11.6	13.9	3.0	26,880	137,164	51,104
Tuscaloosa, AL	53,722	41,589	76,804	31.9	25.6	17.5	11.0	11.7	2.2	7,420	43,352	13,079
Tyler, TX	59,354	45,220	78,437	26.9	27.2	17.2	11.0	13.7	3.9	6,001	33,506	12,003
Utica–Rome, NY	58,689	47,132	117,848	26.4	26.1	19.4	12.1	13.9	2.0	8,286	44,004	15,633
Valdosta, GA	45,807	36,086	49,917	35.4	27.0	18.0	8.9	9.1	1.6	5,740	32,434	10,635
Vallejo–Fairfield, CA	76,764	66,794	140,265	16.3	20.0	19.8	14.5	24.3	5.1	9,252	47,946	17,478
Victoria, TX	53,691	46,868	42,878	26.6	25.5	19.9	11.4	14.4	2.1	4,150	19,318	7,700
Vineland–Millville–Bridgeton, NJ	62,036	51,813	50,409	24.6	23.4	19.2	13.2	17.0	2.6	4,440	24,689	9,604
Virginia Beach–Norfolk–Newport News, VA–NC	69,160	58,460	617,894	18.2	24.0	20.6	14.1	19.6	3.5	33,546	176,198	65,114
Visalia–Porterville, CA	45,884	42,597	129,790	27.9	28.8	17.6	10.6	12.9	2.2	20,125	106,012	46,993
Waco, TX	51,654	41,121	83,712	31.0	26.8	17.2	10.7	12.2	2.2	8,966	51,442	18,246
Warner Robins, GA	64,745	54,668	51,833	20.3	25.2	21.2	15.0	16.6	1.7	4,179	19,339	8,238
Washington–Arlington–Alexandria, DC–VA–MD–WV	104,324	87,653	2,047,323	11.7	15.0	16.1	13.4	31.1	12.7	72,768	445,100	135,243
Bethesda–Rockville–Frederick, MD	110,140	91,778	442,974	10.7	14.6	15.8	12.6	31.9	14.4	13,955	80,572	24,325
Washington–Arlington–Alexandria, DC–VA–MD–WV	103,002	86,424	1,604,349	11.9	15.1	16.2	13.7	30.9	12.2	58,813	364,528	110,918
Waterloo–Cedar Falls, IA	62,721	46,655	66,562	25.3	27.8	19.3	12.1	13.2	2.3	4,201	24,750	8,102
Wausau, WI	64,289	51,594	52,784	20.8	27.5	20.6	14.2	14.6	2.3	2,382	14,920	5,763
Wenatchee–East Wenatchee, WA	57,531	49,965	40,804	20.6	29.5	21.4	12.1	13.7	2.8	2,922	16,107	5,842
Wheeling, WV–OH	52,015	39,921	60,618	30.5	29.5	18.2	10.4	9.9	1.6	4,168	21,227	6,511
Wichita, KS	62,800	49,458	238,469	23.9	26.6	19.7	12.7	14.7	2.4	15,420	84,968	32,031
Wichita Falls, TX	53,583	44,114	54,891	26.9	29.5	19.1	11.3	11.1	2.1	3,951	20,553	7,046
Williamsport, PA	53,579	42,400	46,382	28.4	29.0	21.6	10.6	9.1	1.3	3,185	17,130	5,665
Wilmington, NC	58,213	45,350	152,534	27.0	27.2	17.7	10.9	14.1	3.1	11,233	60,288	16,961
Winchester, VA–WV	64,262	50,466	49,833	25.2	24.5	17.7	11.4	18.3	3.1	2,540	17,241	5,458
Winston–Salem, NC	56,537	44,615	188,200	26.7	28.2	18.6	11.2	12.3	3.0	14,712	77,094	28,201
Worcester, MA	79,645	63,935	298,720	20.1	20.1	17.4	13.7	23.6	5.1	15,223	81,125	26,049
Yakima, WA	47,312	42,707	80,136	28.7	27.4	18.5	11.1	12.5	1.7	10,623	54,861	23,902
York–Hanover, PA	68,442	57,330	168,021	18.4	24.0	21.7	14.5	18.7	2.6	8,621	42,690	14,379
Youngstown–Warren–Boardman, OH–PA	53,308	41,492	231,298	29.7	28.7	19.3	10.6	10.2	1.5	18,136	89,092	32,519
Yuba City, CA	52,139	47,162	55,168	24.2	28.8	19.3	12.1	13.7	1.9	5,537	28,989	11,595
Yuma, AZ	44,146	41,142	70,037	28.8	29.7	21.0	9.7	9.3	1.5	9,158	38,427	15,488

[1]The poverty status was determined for all people except institutionalized people, people in military group quarters, people in college dormitories, and unrelated individuals under 15 years old.

Table B-8. Health Insurance, Medicare, Social Security, and SSI

Metropolitan statistical area and division	Persons with no health insurance, 2009–2011[1]		Persons with a disability, 2009–2011		Medicare program enrollment, 2010[2]		Social security program beneficiaries, December 2011			Supplemental security income program recipients, 2011	
	Number	Percent	Total 5 years and over	18 to 64 years	Number	Rate per 100,000 persons[3]	Number	Rate per 100,000 persons[3]	Retired workers, number	Number	Rate per 100,000 persons[3]
Abilene, TX	28,573	18.6	24,859	13,466	26,191	15,849	29,895	17,964	18,740	4,458	2,679
Akron, OH	80,152	11.5	86,145	44,856	111,727	15,888	130,255	18,569	83,320	15,620	2,227
Albany, GA	30,705	20.0	23,236	13,898	23,478	14,925	28,775	18,248	17,130	7,055	4,474
Albany–Schenectady–Troy, NY	66,504	7.7	97,936	49,888	142,423	16,357	168,710	19,359	113,195	20,634	2,368
Albuquerque, NM	148,001	16.9	107,144	58,852	125,864	14,189	150,685	16,768	94,780	21,953	2,443
Alexandria, LA	26,308	17.8	29,015	16,743	27,176	17,656	31,015	20,074	15,675	7,895	5,110
Allentown–Bethlehem–Easton, PA–NJ	80,587	9.9	102,406	51,873	145,133	17,674	170,270	20,641	114,260	18,444	2,236
Altoona, PA	12,477	10.0	18,684	9,772	27,831	21,899	29,105	22,899	17,905	4,913	3,865
Amarillo, TX	54,112	22.0	26,235	13,759	33,886	13,561	38,590	15,204	24,300	4,564	1,798
Ames, IA	5,285	6.0	6,198	2,888	10,507	11,734	11,415	12,731	8,365	655	731
Anchorage, AK	64,875	17.6	37,919	23,305	34,687	9,108	42,450	10,954	26,430	7,283	1,879
Anderson, IN	21,204	16.7	20,651	10,937	25,787	19,590	30,720	23,408	19,555	3,159	2,407
Anderson, SC	29,909	16.1	30,506	16,601	34,362	18,363	44,645	23,686	27,760	4,170	2,212
Ann Arbor, MI	26,023	7.6	28,854	15,363	41,318	11,983	50,220	14,433	33,480	5,129	1,474
Anniston–Oxford, AL	17,032	14.6	21,652	12,379	24,551	20,706	28,520	24,211	15,375	4,689	3,981
Appleton, WI	16,549	7.4	19,420	9,811	30,948	13,714	37,810	16,627	25,730	2,523	1,109
Asheville, NC	70,440	16.8	61,992	31,056	89,893	21,158	106,065	24,723	71,490	9,853	2,297
Athens–Clarke County, GA	32,401	17.0	23,341	13,934	23,851	12,387	29,240	15,125	18,630	4,637	2,399
Atlanta–Sandy Springs–Marietta, GA	1,016,514	19.4	484,810	274,838	548,225	10,405	692,525	12,922	446,865	99,264	1,852
Atlantic City–Hammonton, NJ	34,696	12.8	33,987	18,687	45,173	16,454	52,965	19,306	35,440	6,512	2,374
Auburn–Opelika, AL	19,191	13.8	17,032	10,214	14,920	10,638	20,920	14,582	11,860	3,298	2,299
Augusta–Richmond County, GA–SC	85,843	15.9	76,518	43,037	82,998	14,904	104,665	18,628	64,180	16,247	2,892
Austin–Round Rock–San Marcos, TX	332,830	19.4	151,341	89,516	160,684	9,362	196,015	10,990	126,425	25,172	1,411
Bakersfield–Delano, CA	171,416	21.2	99,489	61,187	92,166	10,977	109,465	12,852	63,980	33,616	3,947
Baltimore–Towson, MD	258,184	9.7	290,874	153,277	382,772	14,122	438,960	16,084	291,635	64,615	2,368
Bangor, ME	16,158	10.6	25,854	15,121	30,024	19,506	34,310	22,310	19,150	5,359	3,485
Barnstable Town, MA	12,360	5.8	25,097	10,562	61,520	28,496	66,520	30,829	49,870	3,642	1,688
Baton Rouge, LA	116,317	14.8	103,334	59,652	103,154	12,854	125,755	15,559	66,960	25,740	3,185
Battle Creek, MI	17,788	13.2	20,280	11,017	25,409	18,663	30,980	22,865	18,645	4,863	3,589
Bay City, MI	11,506	10.8	16,027	8,342	21,260	19,727	26,970	25,180	15,980	3,099	2,893
Beaumont–Port Arthur, TX	83,745	22.5	62,009	33,805	61,659	15,861	73,400	18,795	40,330	12,777	3,272
Bellingham, WA	26,791	13.4	25,706	13,857	31,397	15,610	37,155	18,243	24,925	4,221	2,073
Bend, OR	26,750	17.0	19,908	10,483	27,333	17,329	34,545	21,545	24,995	2,010	1,254
Billings, MT	25,713	16.4	19,764	10,280	25,649	16,228	29,715	18,561	20,065	2,562	1,600
Binghamton, NY	23,218	9.4	33,421	17,101	49,275	19,575	58,070	23,221	37,295	8,152	3,260
Birmingham–Hoover, AL	143,496	12.9	164,221	92,418	186,562	16,538	230,620	20,368	126,355	37,181	3,284
Bismarck, ND	8,126	7.6	11,230	5,270	17,170	15,784	19,670	17,740	13,300	1,225	1,105
Blacksburg–Christiansburg–Radford, VA	17,635	10.9	19,687	11,336	24,845	15,246	29,575	18,201	17,970	3,004	1,849
Bloomington, IN	25,617	13.4	22,825	13,051	25,988	13,485	31,550	16,247	20,695	2,849	1,467
Bloomington–Normal, IL	13,471	8.0	15,508	8,379	20,079	11,841	23,450	13,749	15,865	1,729	1,014
Boise City–Nampa, ID	98,373	16.1	69,511	37,099	79,285	12,859	98,970	15,768	66,010	10,923	1,740
Boston–Cambridge–Quincy, MA–NH	214,411	4.8	453,124	226,997	681,491	14,970	745,470	16,237	491,945	114,214	2,488
Boston–Quincy, MA	80,656	4.3	199,320	102,179	274,442	14,538	299,680	15,740	193,240	58,641	3,080
Cambridge–Newton–Framingham, MA	58,922	4.0	129,228	61,202	221,143	14,713	232,645	15,324	159,265	27,571	1,816
Peabody, MA	33,580	4.6	81,923	41,107	122,678	16,508	135,885	18,144	88,200	23,712	3,166
Rockingham County–Strafford County, NH	41,253	9.9	42,653	22,509	63,228	15,113	77,260	18,392	51,240	4,290	1,021
Boulder, CO	34,973	11.9	21,588	12,524	39,212	13,312	37,330	12,469	26,565	2,445	817
Bowling Green, KY	18,543	14.8	17,615	10,849	18,840	14,958	22,085	17,307	13,170	3,976	3,116
Bremerton–Silverdale, WA	27,375	11.5	33,935	19,661	38,356	15,273	44,170	17,347	29,620	5,014	1,969
Bridgeport–Stamford–Norwalk, CT	103,066	11.3	81,783	38,812	131,606	14,354	143,870	15,538	105,010	11,577	1,250
Brownsville–Harlingen, TX	142,435	35.2	51,073	25,336	46,514	11,450	56,485	13,640	32,140	22,317	5,389
Brunswick, GA	27,076	24.4	17,455	9,651	18,353	16,333	22,940	20,315	14,395	2,864	2,536
Buffalo–Niagara Falls, NY	84,814	7.6	144,085	76,432	214,380	18,880	250,170	22,060	155,775	35,562	3,136
Burlington, NC	25,843	17.2	20,538	9,940	26,554	17,570	31,320	20,432	21,255	3,031	1,977
Burlington–South Burlington, VT	13,713	6.5	22,765	12,181	27,359	12,950	35,945	16,913	23,355	4,320	2,033
Canton–Massillon, OH	47,823	12.0	53,654	27,599	77,974	19,280	87,425	21,647	55,965	9,376	2,322
Cape Coral–Fort Myers, FL	132,962	21.6	78,775	33,278	127,416	20,592	153,955	24,386	114,175	10,863	1,721
Cape Girardeau–Jackson, MO–IL	12,036	12.7	14,919	8,615	16,846	17,498	20,040	20,655	12,270	2,586	2,665
Carson City, NV	11,296	21.0	7,555	3,573	12,036	21,775	11,605	20,933	8,380	820	1,479
Casper, WY	9,993	13.4	8,727	4,520	10,895	14,440	12,935	16,938	8,380	1,168	1,529

[1]Civilian noninstitutionalized population.
[2]Unduplicated count of persons enrolled in either hospital and/or supplemental medical insurance as of July 1.
[3]Based on resident population estimated as of July 1 of the year shown.

Table B-8. Health Insurance, Medicare, Social Security, and SSI—*Continued*

Metropolitan statistical area and division	Persons with no health insurance, 2009–2011[1]		Persons with a disability, 2009–2011		Medicare program enrollment, 2010[2]		Social security program beneficiaries, December 2011			Supplemental security income program recipients, 2011	
	Number	Percent	Total 5 years and over	18 to 64 years	Number	Rate per 100,000 persons[3]	Number	Rate per 100,000 persons[3]	Retired workers, number	Number	Rate per 100,000 persons[3]
Cedar Rapids, IA	18,955	7.4	27,595	14,171	39,607	15,355	46,910	18,002	32,855	3,679	1,412
Champaign–Urbana, IL	23,915	10.4	20,509	10,031	28,516	12,297	31,350	13,493	20,635	3,220	1,386
Charleston, WV	40,373	13.4	56,415	32,673	62,908	20,674	75,600	24,895	39,045	12,989	4,277
Charleston–North Charleston–Summerville, SC...	112,365	17.2	74,672	40,382	91,254	13,731	113,465	16,634	70,960	13,145	1,927
Charlotte–Gastonia–Rock Hill, NC–SC	288,207	16.4	171,719	93,792	217,633	12,379	264,235	14,717	173,435	30,527	1,700
Charlottesville, VA	21,422	10.8	21,204	10,785	30,903	15,332	34,705	17,022	24,625	2,628	1,289
Chattanooga, TN–GA	75,204	14.4	85,757	48,043	90,939	17,219	111,095	20,829	69,020	13,614	2,552
Cheyenne, WY	12,011	13.6	11,204	6,356	13,899	15,151	15,655	16,891	10,440	1,411	1,522
Chicago–Joliet–Naperville, IL–IN–WI	1,358,834	14.5	874,049	441,895	1,214,898	12,841	1,376,265	14,480	911,700	207,923	2,188
Chicago–Joliet–Naperville, IL	1,164,202	14.9	714,368	357,746	1,003,603	12,731	1,121,490	14,156	748,760	181,860	2,295
Gary, IN	98,069	14.0	91,099	49,752	108,235	15,286	132,920	18,756	80,550	15,176	2,141
Lake County–Kenosha County, IL–WI	96,563	11.3	68,582	34,397	103,060	11,848	121,855	13,950	82,390	10,887	1,246
Chico, CA	35,760	16.4	35,418	20,183	41,100	18,682	47,585	21,603	29,625	11,581	5,258
Cincinnati–Middletown, OH–KY–IN	240,986	11.4	253,212	139,865	308,868	14,500	363,850	17,018	224,760	46,023	2,153
Clarksville, TN–KY	33,893	13.4	34,711	21,196	32,236	11,767	41,305	14,874	23,415	6,529	2,351
Cleveland, TN	17,344	15.1	21,897	12,598	21,527	18,592	27,075	23,174	16,035	3,268	2,797
Cleveland–Elyria–Mentor, OH	231,749	11.3	269,265	139,599	352,546	16,972	398,230	19,254	259,330	60,068	2,904
Coeur d'Alene, ID	24,776	17.9	17,160	9,690	24,741	17,864	30,420	21,554	20,185	2,410	1,708
College Station–Bryan, TX	36,721	16.4	24,342	13,464	22,399	9,796	26,260	11,337	16,445	4,375	1,889
Colorado Springs, CO	86,358	14.0	67,739	40,345	75,141	11,639	91,725	13,891	58,810	7,962	1,206
Columbia, MO	15,959	9.3	17,771	10,399	20,721	11,992	24,800	14,104	15,485	2,919	1,660
Columbia, SC	106,059	14.3	88,199	50,514	104,030	13,553	130,835	16,836	84,310	15,491	1,993
Columbus, GA–AL	42,902	15.6	49,371	29,540	44,178	14,982	53,170	17,639	30,525	9,901	3,285
Columbus, IN	9,358	12.3	8,399	4,397	13,344	17,376	15,560	19,982	9,990	1,212	1,556
Columbus, OH	216,744	11.9	205,106	116,032	227,347	12,379	267,330	14,384	165,515	39,786	2,141
Corpus Christi, TX	93,046	22.0	74,872	42,206	62,902	14,690	75,415	17,482	42,825	16,109	3,734
Corvallis, OR	10,295	12.1	8,661	4,885	10,275	12,006	13,430	15,629	9,715	964	1,122
Crestview–Fort Walton Beach–Destin, FL	28,224	16.5	24,653	13,463	30,074	16,632	34,875	19,007	22,810	2,812	1,533
Cumberland, MD–WV	11,250	11.6	16,895	9,230	21,065	20,392	23,685	23,021	14,400	2,976	2,893
Dallas–Fort Worth–Arlington, TX	1,436,183	22.6	580,523	323,856	650,327	10,206	774,120	11,861	490,575	118,488	1,815
Dallas–Plano–Irving, TX	978,666	23.2	365,112	201,149	422,558	9,976	496,885	11,434	316,310	80,310	1,848
Fort Worth–Arlington, TX	457,517	21.6	215,411	122,707	227,769	10,663	277,235	12,713	174,265	38,178	1,751
Dalton, GA	34,156	24.2	20,865	12,424	19,503	13,713	24,490	17,157	14,585	3,388	2,374
Danville, IL	9,052	11.3	11,715	6,056	16,322	19,996	18,620	22,844	11,275	2,793	3,427
Danville, VA	15,378	14.8	18,998	10,258	23,410	21,969	29,030	27,466	18,010	4,582	4,335
Davenport–Moline–Rock Island, IA–IL	39,626	10.6	41,518	20,579	65,065	17,136	75,475	19,792	51,790	7,352	1,928
Dayton, OH	95,379	11.5	116,307	62,687	144,389	17,158	162,950	19,275	104,280	19,632	2,322
Decatur, AL	24,491	16.1	24,996	13,775	27,520	17,890	34,710	22,529	20,055	4,742	3,078
Decatur, IL	13,147	12.1	14,425	7,734	21,480	19,392	24,055	21,724	15,340	3,206	2,895
Deltona–Daytona Beach–Ormond Beach, FL	92,629	19.0	71,734	34,515	112,495	22,745	131,685	26,614	91,605	10,623	2,147
Denver–Aurora–Broomfield, CO[4]	389,394	15.4	225,869	121,503	284,867	11,200	333,080	12,813	227,425	34,581	1,330
Des Moines–West Des Moines, IA	46,139	8.2	57,353	32,278	74,197	13,025	88,545	15,260	61,440	8,308	1,432
Detroit–Warren–Livonia, MI	543,078	12.7	576,726	321,104	672,356	15,650	827,065	19,298	508,240	125,963	2,939
Detroit–Livonia–Dearborn, MI	274,020	15.2	284,867	167,580	288,600	15,852	349,745	19,408	195,970	81,910	4,545
Warren–Troy–Farmington Hills, MI	269,058	10.9	291,859	153,524	383,756	15,501	477,320	19,218	312,270	44,053	1,774
Dothan, AL	20,901	14.6	26,944	14,614	26,906	18,474	35,250	24,051	20,405	5,901	4,026
Dover, DE	14,051	8.9	20,876	11,975	25,378	15,636	31,990	19,407	20,565	3,686	2,236
Dubuque, IA	5,822	6.3	10,202	4,936	16,787	17,925	19,135	20,217	13,145	1,548	1,636
Duluth, MN–WI	25,957	9.5	35,780	18,981	53,777	19,222	60,735	21,705	38,545	7,119	2,544
Durham–Chapel Hill, NC	76,607	15.4	53,246	29,042	63,319	12,554	78,705	15,343	53,110	9,199	1,793
Eau Claire, WI	14,261	9.0	16,228	7,796	26,802	16,632	31,195	19,178	20,610	3,068	1,886
El Centro, CA	35,618	21.6	19,973	9,451	23,212	13,300	27,175	15,348	15,715	10,547	5,957
Elizabethtown, KY	14,647	13.2	16,873	9,342	18,649	15,575	21,300	17,492	11,755	3,426	2,813
Elkhart–Goshen, IN	38,210	19.5	23,590	12,687	27,525	13,933	33,115	16,646	22,205	3,089	1,553
Elmira, NY	6,929	8.2	11,776	6,110	17,442	19,635	20,950	23,582	12,800	3,549	3,995
El Paso, TX	224,571	28.8	92,035	48,265	97,036	12,120	112,490	13,705	60,990	29,302	3,570
Erie, PA	25,937	9.4	42,183	22,551	49,589	17,675	59,165	21,056	36,400	11,092	3,948
Eugene–Springfield, OR	60,993	17.4	50,102	27,321	61,671	17,534	73,565	20,815	49,365	8,092	2,290
Evansville, IN–KY	44,191	12.5	46,386	24,361	62,136	17,324	74,475	20,694	45,835	8,238	2,289
Fairbanks, AK	13,463	14.7	9,374	6,383	6,989	7,162	9,220	9,295	5,935	1,127	1,136
Fargo, ND–MN	18,786	9.1	17,197	9,177	25,005	11,977	29,035	13,685	19,025	2,645	1,247
Farmington, NM	38,528	30.1	12,291	6,689	15,840	12,180	19,345	15,090	11,030	4,067	3,172

[1]Civilian noninstitutionalized population.
[2]Unduplicated count of persons enrolled in either hospital and/or supplemental medical insurance as of July 1.
[3]Based on resident population estimated as of July 1 of the year shown.
[4]The Denver–Aurora metropolitan statistical area includes Broomfield County. Broomfield County, CO, was formed from parts of Adams, Boulder, Jefferson, and Weld Counties on November 15, 2001, and is coextensive with Broomfield city. For the purposes of defining and presenting data for the Denver–Aurora metropolitan statistical area, Broomfield city is treated as if it were a county when data are available to do so. In many cases, the data were not available.

Table B-8. Health Insurance, Medicare, Social Security, and SSI—*Continued*

Metropolitan statistical area and division	Persons with no health insurance, 2009–2011[1]		Persons with a disability, 2009–2011		Medicare program enrollment, 2010[2]		Social security program beneficiaries, December 2011			Supplemental security income program recipients, 2011	
	Number	Percent	Total 5 years and over	18 to 64 years	Number	Rate per 100,000 persons[3]	Number	Rate per 100,000 persons[3]	Retired workers, number	Number	Rate per 100,000 persons[3]
Fayetteville, NC	47,877	14.4	45,584	27,137	44,289	12,088	55,335	14,789	30,135	10,873	2,906
Fayetteville–Springdale–Rogers, AR–MO	80,912	17.5	53,581	29,294	62,394	13,470	77,345	16,323	47,975	8,362	1,765
Flagstaff, AZ	24,937	18.7	13,750	8,505	17,793	13,237	16,695	12,412	10,665	2,832	2,105
Flint, MI	43,446	10.3	65,134	36,716	76,254	17,909	94,095	22,293	54,195	16,331	3,869
Florence, SC	33,138	16.3	32,139	18,945	36,506	17,759	43,900	21,294	25,505	8,590	4,167
Florence–Muscle Shoals, AL	17,905	12.3	26,129	13,770	30,850	20,967	37,495	25,456	21,085	5,060	3,435
Fond du Lac, WI	7,754	7.8	10,498	4,981	18,088	17,797	20,080	19,671	14,005	1,366	1,338
Fort Collins–Loveland, CO	37,350	12.5	26,512	13,016	39,274	13,107	46,310	15,158	32,905	2,536	830
Fort Smith, AR–OK	58,923	20.0	52,503	30,587	53,976	18,077	67,290	22,423	36,085	10,862	3,620
Fort Wayne, IN	56,881	13.8	44,158	22,967	60,355	14,499	74,850	17,845	49,305	7,854	1,872
Fresno, CA	185,660	20.2	103,781	56,555	107,863	11,593	121,670	12,904	77,050	42,186	4,474
Gadsden, AL	16,337	15.9	20,728	12,681	21,647	20,729	27,415	26,284	13,995	4,729	4,534
Gainesville, FL	41,470	15.9	29,728	16,760	36,624	13,858	41,185	15,462	26,850	5,858	2,199
Gainesville, GA	38,079	21.5	18,077	9,122	23,599	13,134	30,295	16,550	20,685	2,812	1,536
Glens Falls, NY	12,356	9.9	16,309	8,237	25,770	19,989	30,575	23,702	19,585	3,343	2,592
Goldsboro, NC	19,848	17.0	16,028	8,313	20,253	16,516	24,185	19,552	13,995	4,673	3,778
Grand Forks, ND–MN	8,095	8.4	9,906	5,660	14,203	14,425	15,730	16,042	10,385	1,317	1,343
Grand Junction, CO	26,246	18.0	18,395	9,120	24,653	16,802	28,070	19,084	19,245	2,288	1,556
Grand Rapids–Wyoming, MI	86,376	11.3	86,139	46,067	108,725	14,044	136,205	17,471	86,550	18,232	2,339
Great Falls, MT	11,516	14.9	11,617	6,080	14,918	18,343	17,085	20,877	11,305	1,859	2,272
Greeley, CO	38,731	15.4	27,085	14,995	26,125	10,333	33,650	13,010	21,835	3,292	1,273
Green Bay, WI	27,844	9.2	32,238	17,387	44,757	14,615	55,135	17,816	36,235	5,264	1,701
Greensboro–High Point, NC	120,841	16.8	87,473	47,706	116,006	16,027	139,535	19,089	92,855	16,319	2,233
Greenville, NC	31,145	16.7	21,249	11,531	24,288	12,816	30,125	15,634	17,620	6,432	3,338
Greenville–Mauldin–Easley, SC	104,061	16.4	79,764	44,240	104,597	16,421	128,565	19,859	81,015	13,172	2,035
Gulfport–Biloxi, MS	49,982	20.7	35,608	19,544	39,601	15,916	47,185	18,613	27,075	7,372	2,908
Hagerstown–Martinsburg, MD–WV	32,231	12.3	39,139	22,534	42,812	15,907	51,850	19,098	32,695	5,534	2,038
Hanford–Corcoran, CA	25,971	19.6	13,109	7,016	13,463	8,800	16,130	10,490	9,445	4,711	3,064
Harrisburg–Carlisle, PA	49,649	9.2	64,188	32,019	93,251	16,971	107,055	19,362	73,700	10,243	1,853
Harrisonburg, VA	19,676	15.9	11,679	5,908	15,546	12,414	21,030	16,616	14,515	1,651	1,304
Hartford–West Hartford–East Hartford, CT	93,320	7.8	127,859	62,825	194,914	16,077	219,435	18,086	155,645	22,372	1,844
Hattiesburg, MS	23,641	16.8	22,837	13,451	21,593	15,117	25,920	17,823	14,375	4,681	3,219
Hickory–Lenoir–Morganton, NC	61,287	17.0	56,286	30,914	65,885	18,026	82,880	22,734	55,025	7,308	2,005
Hinesville–Fort Stewart, GA	11,173	15.8	8,051	4,984	5,451	6,996	7,460	9,257	4,175	1,380	1,712
Holland–Grand Haven, MI	23,084	8.8	24,223	11,755	37,006	14,028	44,880	16,853	31,225	2,650	995
Honolulu, HI	54,988	6.1	92,323	40,714	145,428	15,257	159,550	16,558	119,750	17,144	1,779
Hot Springs, AR	18,532	19.6	17,712	8,933	27,530	28,670	28,795	29,648	18,815	3,636	3,744
Houma–Bayou Cane–Thibodaux, LA	35,843	17.4	32,867	18,496	31,031	14,906	38,305	18,364	17,210	8,117	3,891
Houston–Sugar Land–Baytown, TX	1,461,990	24.7	545,600	302,075	574,908	9,668	693,750	11,398	419,940	132,214	2,172
Huntington–Ashland, WV–KY–OH	41,530	14.7	57,684	33,302	61,257	21,292	68,625	23,861	34,160	14,754	5,130
Huntsville, AL	52,502	12.8	50,711	27,095	60,564	14,503	71,970	16,915	45,010	8,715	2,048
Idaho Falls, ID	18,843	14.5	15,680	8,280	16,473	12,635	20,110	15,226	12,865	2,176	1,648
Indianapolis–Carmel, IN	241,032	13.9	189,791	106,746	224,272	12,770	279,495	15,715	179,425	31,048	1,746
Iowa City, IA	12,173	8.0	11,536	6,394	16,974	11,124	20,210	13,048	14,170	1,826	1,179
Ithaca, NY	6,207	6.2	10,170	5,901	12,638	12,443	14,545	14,299	10,030	1,747	1,717
Jackson, MI	18,092	11.8	22,462	12,019	27,833	17,369	34,465	21,575	21,695	4,288	2,684
Jackson, MS	84,901	16.0	68,742	37,523	76,897	14,265	95,320	17,477	56,105	18,722	3,433
Jackson, TN	16,654	14.6	18,015	10,829	18,575	16,093	23,340	20,226	14,115	3,617	3,134
Jacksonville, FL	214,535	16.2	156,950	85,455	191,372	14,222	235,230	17,293	150,110	29,020	2,133
Jacksonville, NC	20,142	13.8	20,752	12,540	16,308	9,174	20,805	11,576	12,345	2,650	1,475
Janesville, WI	17,558	11.1	21,526	12,157	26,341	16,429	32,180	20,101	21,130	3,582	2,237
Jefferson City, MO	13,742	9.6	19,773	11,172	22,834	15,242	28,730	19,092	17,945	2,737	1,819
Johnson City, TN	27,034	13.8	34,922	19,731	40,054	20,156	48,550	24,297	28,340	5,987	2,996
Johnstown, PA	12,583	9.0	23,922	12,237	32,440	22,578	37,310	25,959	22,135	5,123	3,564
Jonesboro, AR	21,180	17.6	17,747	9,623	20,849	17,227	25,345	20,634	13,585	5,504	4,481
Joplin, MO	29,921	17.2	28,068	16,506	30,485	17,369	35,915	20,308	21,320	4,446	2,514
Kalamazoo–Portage, MI	38,272	11.8	40,438	23,157	51,388	15,735	62,600	19,073	40,135	8,180	2,492
Kankakee–Bradley, IL	14,430	13.0	14,611	7,829	18,622	16,414	21,340	18,769	12,900	2,731	2,402
Kansas City, MO–KS	266,634	13.2	226,279	121,392	282,731	13,891	336,385	16,388	221,215	32,497	1,583
Kennewick–Pasco–Richland, WA	41,668	16.5	26,113	14,850	30,860	12,181	36,875	13,961	23,995	4,985	1,887
Killeen–Temple–Fort Hood, TX	56,154	15.4	43,605	24,735	42,539	10,496	54,210	13,171	29,640	8,408	2,043

[1]Civilian noninstitutionalized population.
[2]Unduplicated count of persons enrolled in either hospital and/or supplemental medical insurance as of July 1.
[3]Based on resident population estimated as of July 1 of the year shown.

Table B-8. Health Insurance, Medicare, Social Security, and SSI—*Continued*

Metropolitan statistical area and division	Persons with no health insurance, 2009–2011[1]		Persons with a disability, 2009–2011		Medicare program enrollment, 2010[2]		Social security program beneficiaries, December 2011			Supplemental security income program recipients, 2011	
	Number	Percent	Total 5 years and over	18 to 64 years	Number	Rate per 100,000 persons[3]	Number	Rate per 100,000 persons[3]	Retired workers, number	Number	Rate per 100,000 persons[3]
Kingsport–Bristol–Bristol, TN–VA	38,725	12.7	61,709	34,090	72,063	23,280	87,355	28,198	48,920	10,761	3,474
Kingston, NY	20,567	11.6	24,680	13,278	31,820	17,436	38,440	21,069	24,940	4,554	2,496
Knoxville, TN	81,671	11.8	92,856	49,947	121,699	17,435	146,470	20,791	92,380	16,627	2,360
Kokomo, IN	13,256	13.6	14,840	7,783	19,438	19,696	24,240	24,587	16,195	2,368	2,402
La Crosse, WI–MN	9,974	7.6	13,222	6,421	21,452	16,049	24,845	18,474	17,235	2,397	1,782
Lafayette, IN	26,174	13.1	21,332	11,699	23,844	11,816	29,460	14,469	19,160	2,297	1,128
Lafayette, LA	45,178	16.7	31,228	17,487	34,977	12,778	42,285	15,248	22,210	7,823	2,821
Lake Charles, LA	31,159	15.8	30,992	17,407	30,688	15,374	37,430	18,638	19,070	6,157	3,066
Lake Havasu City–Kingman, AZ	31,061	15.7	35,161	17,121	47,586	23,771	58,670	28,994	41,355	4,208	2,080
Lakeland–Winter Haven, FL	111,603	18.8	85,367	42,239	108,603	18,038	137,250	22,519	91,345	18,193	2,985
Lancaster, PA	68,713	13.4	54,884	25,988	86,487	16,650	101,500	19,385	70,520	9,551	1,824
Lansing–East Lansing, MI	45,598	9.9	54,302	29,860	66,068	14,238	80,910	17,395	52,595	9,506	2,044
Laredo, TX	90,081	36.1	32,895	16,131	23,924	9,558	28,850	11,248	15,735	12,046	4,696
Las Cruces, NM	43,899	21.3	21,345	10,040	29,728	14,208	34,360	16,086	21,675	7,422	3,475
Las Vegas–Paradise, NV	434,218	22.5	193,701	106,368	231,700	11,874	283,050	14,368	195,400	33,124	1,681
Lawrence, KS	14,844	13.4	11,052	6,469	12,728	11,485	14,085	12,552	9,340	1,242	1,107
Lawton, OK	17,639	16.2	16,288	9,459	15,410	12,418	18,415	14,637	10,500	3,077	2,446
Lebanon, PA	12,850	9.8	14,465	6,593	25,280	18,927	29,640	22,068	21,105	2,330	1,735
Lewiston, ID–WA	8,172	13.6	10,340	4,947	13,664	22,441	15,670	25,490	9,830	1,750	2,847
Lewiston–Auburn, ME	10,152	9.5	17,039	9,146	20,881	19,388	24,015	22,361	14,285	3,810	3,548
Lexington–Fayette, KY	67,795	14.5	58,829	33,895	63,140	13,374	75,740	15,804	46,450	11,596	2,420
Lima, OH	12,673	12.3	14,426	7,679	18,074	16,998	21,615	20,373	13,465	2,961	2,791
Lincoln, NE	30,380	10.2	27,127	14,159	38,462	12,729	43,825	14,298	30,250	4,529	1,478
Little Rock–North Little Rock–Conway, AR	102,280	14.8	98,540	56,418	104,250	14,888	133,455	18,799	76,945	23,677	3,335
Logan, UT–ID	15,830	12.7	9,341	4,830	11,368	9,062	13,705	10,745	9,250	940	737
Longview, TX	44,071	21.3	33,598	18,136	36,942	17,233	41,440	19,126	24,515	6,525	3,012
Longview, WA	14,392	14.2	19,931	11,294	18,464	18,029	24,305	23,717	14,965	3,433	3,350
Los Angeles–Long Beach–Santa Ana, CA	2,753,460	21.6	1,127,325	537,831	1,528,096	11,911	1,572,525	12,148	1,068,985	491,097	3,794
Los Angeles–Long Beach–Glendale, CA	2,222,942	22.8	906,011	439,805	1,157,071	11,784	1,181,910	11,952	790,895	418,384	4,231
Santa Ana–Anaheim–Irvine, CA	530,518	17.7	221,314	98,026	371,025	12,325	390,615	12,783	278,090	72,713	2,380
Louisville/Jefferson County, KY–IN	163,071	12.9	178,286	101,217	201,698	15,714	245,375	18,950	146,165	36,082	2,787
Lubbock, TX	54,582	19.4	38,758	21,797	36,888	12,948	42,940	14,807	26,200	6,655	2,295
Lynchburg, VA	30,862	12.4	33,442	16,940	50,520	19,997	57,675	22,691	36,970	6,383	2,511
Macon, GA	38,220	16.8	31,239	17,082	37,907	16,319	46,235	19,850	26,470	9,280	3,984
Madera–Chowchilla, CA	30,301	21.1	16,522	8,099	20,744	13,750	22,985	15,030	15,275	4,751	3,107
Madison, WI	39,359	7.0	51,087	28,728	72,954	12,831	87,210	15,128	61,260	8,059	1,398
Manchester–Nashua, NH	37,947	9.6	41,737	22,424	58,177	14,518	70,455	17,539	44,955	6,474	1,612
Manhattan, KS	9,521	8.2	8,977	4,402	12,142	9,555	14,515	11,145	9,310	1,308	1,004
Mankato–North Mankato, MN	7,896	8.2	9,112	4,714	13,731	14,194	15,365	15,807	10,380	1,320	1,358
Mansfield, OH	14,298	12.1	15,230	7,526	24,399	19,602	27,500	22,265	17,620	3,156	2,555
McAllen–Edinburg–Mission, TX	285,030	36.8	103,588	52,254	75,740	9,776	93,105	11,670	51,370	41,579	5,212
Medford, OR	39,965	19.8	32,616	16,668	41,140	20,245	48,955	23,901	33,880	4,158	2,030
Memphis, TN–MS–AR	209,507	16.1	162,925	93,199	169,865	12,907	210,525	15,881	123,680	45,340	3,420
Merced, CA	50,050	19.8	37,886	22,267	26,904	10,518	33,570	12,917	20,175	11,172	4,299
Miami–Fort Lauderdale–Pompano Beach, FL	1,440,739	26.1	597,911	255,817	872,210	15,674	953,030	16,808	675,930	205,725	3,628
Fort Lauderdale–Pompano Beach–Deerfield Beach, FL	407,914	23.4	194,902	90,257	245,734	14,057	284,245	15,967	197,355	39,670	2,228
Miami–Miami Beach–Kendall, FL	761,811	30.8	252,167	111,556	368,414	14,758	381,305	14,925	262,805	145,629	5,700
West Palm Beach–Boca Raton–Boynton Beach, FL	271,014	20.7	150,842	54,004	258,062	19,548	287,480	21,531	215,770	20,426	1,530
Michigan City–La Porte, IN	14,862	14.3	14,179	7,138	18,392	16,500	22,925	20,584	14,550	2,164	1,943
Midland, TX	29,490	21.6	18,773	10,165	16,103	11,765	18,855	13,438	11,530	2,335	1,664
Milwaukee–Waukesha–West Allis, WI	151,603	9.8	170,881	88,448	229,706	14,763	271,275	17,365	179,850	44,220	2,831
Minneapolis–St. Paul–Bloomington, MN–WI	292,924	9.0	285,856	154,277	399,288	12,174	471,950	14,222	326,720	55,077	1,660
Missoula, MT	19,710	18.1	12,667	7,642	15,079	13,796	18,020	16,361	11,620	2,039	1,851
Mobile, AL	66,502	16.3	61,720	35,484	67,313	16,299	84,270	20,425	45,110	14,844	3,598
Modesto, CA	91,901	18.0	66,192	35,929	66,916	13,007	77,895	15,023	47,360	21,600	4,166
Monroe, LA	40,987	23.8	22,150	11,489	27,227	15,431	31,930	17,973	18,025	7,407	4,169
Monroe, MI	13,972	9.3	19,970	10,564	23,948	15,753	30,795	20,319	18,890	2,577	1,700
Montgomery, AL	46,223	12.8	57,001	32,703	58,190	15,537	71,555	18,899	40,600	14,742	3,894
Morgantown, WV	15,271	12.1	16,896	9,961	16,919	13,044	20,530	15,524	12,220	3,028	2,290
Morristown, TN	20,377	15.1	26,284	15,546	28,997	21,226	34,690	25,230	20,045	4,388	3,191
Mount Vernon–Anacortes, WA	18,572	16.0	15,889	7,581	21,696	18,559	25,415	21,518	17,880	2,308	1,954

[1]Civilian noninstitutionalized population.
[2]Unduplicated count of persons enrolled in either hospital and/or supplemental medical insurance as of July 1.
[3]Based on resident population estimated as of July 1 of the year shown.

Table B-8. Health Insurance, Medicare, Social Security, and SSI—*Continued*

Metropolitan statistical area and division	Persons with no health insurance, 2009–2011[1]		Persons with a disability, 2009–2011		Medicare program enrollment, 2010[2]		Social security program beneficiaries, December 2011			Supplemental security income program recipients, 2011	
	Number	Percent	Total 5 years and over	18 to 64 years	Number	Rate per 100,000 persons[3]	Number	Rate per 100,000 persons[3]	Retired workers, number	Number	Rate per 100,000 persons[3]
Muncie, IN	16,450	14.2	20,046	11,988	20,844	17,714	25,105	21,337	15,545	2,858	2,429
Muskegon–Norton Shores, MI	20,253	12.1	24,780	13,992	31,657	18,385	39,145	22,851	22,230	6,221	3,632
Myrtle Beach–North Myrtle Beach–Conway, SC	63,457	23.5	36,491	19,916	51,843	19,252	69,015	24,975	47,400	5,422	1,962
Napa, CA	21,112	15.7	14,142	6,310	23,727	17,384	25,100	18,177	17,240	2,654	1,922
Naples–Marco Island, FL	77,107	24.0	35,130	12,168	69,160	21,510	77,900	23,740	60,620	3,314	1,010
Nashville–Davidson—Murfreesboro—Franklin, TN	219,237	13.9	173,947	99,433	202,925	12,763	251,455	15,549	160,350	29,129	1,801
New Haven–Milford, CT	72,519	8.5	97,578	48,504	139,059	16,123	155,530	18,062	106,775	18,536	2,153
New Orleans–Metairie–Kenner, LA	204,311	17.7	157,086	87,527	170,507	14,601	202,790	17,026	112,835	42,805	3,594
New York–Northern New Jersey–Long Island, NY–NJ–PA	2,485,381	13.3	1,785,925	850,312	2,691,288	14,242	2,952,500	15,526	2,017,640	611,681	3,217
Edison–New Brunswick, NJ	251,717	10.9	220,621	94,524	375,995	16,066	433,065	18,432	309,070	29,471	1,254
Nassau–Suffolk, NY	276,422	9.8	244,423	110,748	458,574	16,188	522,740	18,385	356,175	40,952	1,440
Newark–Union, NJ–PA	286,558	13.5	195,853	95,477	296,790	13,819	336,040	15,608	234,180	45,449	2,111
New York–White Plains–Wayne, NY–NJ	1,670,684	14.5	1,125,028	549,563	1,559,929	13,475	1,660,655	14,230	1,118,215	495,809	4,249
Niles–Benton Harbor, MI	20,892	13.4	21,668	11,409	32,880	20,968	36,210	23,072	23,660	4,993	3,181
North Port–Bradenton–Sarasota, FL	129,003	18.5	97,226	37,045	179,324	25,535	200,355	28,245	151,575	9,447	1,332
Norwich–New London, CT	20,130	7.7	31,133	17,049	44,672	16,300	50,970	18,636	34,750	3,686	1,348
Ocala, FL	61,388	18.9	55,251	23,732	89,914	27,140	104,990	31,573	75,405	8,314	2,500
Ocean City, NJ	10,143	10.8	11,971	5,327	23,168	23,819	27,115	28,069	19,440	1,831	1,895
Odessa, TX	38,673	28.3	19,095	11,016	17,145	12,503	19,435	13,871	10,570	3,809	2,719
Ogden–Clearfield, UT	67,682	12.5	47,730	26,110	56,169	10,265	64,535	11,609	42,300	5,665	1,019
Oklahoma City, OK	220,545	17.8	164,523	94,706	171,182	13,662	206,460	16,154	130,595	26,981	2,111
Olympia, WA	27,453	11.1	31,124	17,672	39,335	15,593	47,985	18,701	31,590	4,924	1,919
Omaha–Council Bluffs, NE–IA	99,298	11.6	87,319	48,517	113,086	13,068	131,085	14,945	86,570	13,645	1,556
Orlando–Kissimmee–Sanford, FL	445,309	21.0	228,337	117,999	329,088	15,418	358,420	16,507	234,575	51,688	2,380
Oshkosh–Neenah, WI	13,200	8.2	17,458	9,114	25,236	15,112	30,920	18,438	20,955	2,313	1,379
Owensboro, KY	13,536	12.0	16,080	8,977	21,920	19,102	26,695	23,146	15,190	4,242	3,678
Oxnard–Thousand Oaks–Ventura, CA	135,110	16.6	80,080	39,417	109,347	13,281	120,935	14,539	83,325	16,571	1,992
Palm Bay–Melbourne–Titusville, FL	90,361	16.9	80,320	37,396	117,400	21,606	138,755	25,527	95,785	10,439	1,920
Palm Coast, FL	16,141	16.9	13,272	5,716	23,990	25,069	30,310	31,127	22,260	1,567	1,609
Panama City–Lynn Haven–Panama City Beach, FL	32,556	20.0	24,627	13,424	29,822	17,662	35,190	20,718	21,850	4,463	2,628
Parkersburg–Marietta–Vienna, WV–OH	20,646	12.8	28,074	15,703	35,093	21,655	40,915	25,218	22,670	6,298	3,882
Pascagoula, MS	32,785	20.5	26,014	15,065	24,108	14,859	32,285	19,832	18,290	3,925	2,411
Pensacola–Ferry Pass–Brent, FL	73,860	17.3	63,049	33,539	76,805	17,106	93,540	20,639	57,670	11,981	2,644
Peoria, IL	36,567	9.8	39,997	18,857	63,651	16,786	74,180	19,544	50,175	7,018	1,849
Philadelphia–Camden–Wilmington, PA–NJ–DE–MD	589,443	10.0	686,095	361,283	909,129	15,240	1,043,910	17,421	681,835	176,916	2,952
Camden, NJ	122,500	10.0	142,285	73,131	188,584	15,079	225,625	18,022	146,610	25,315	2,022
Philadelphia, PA	400,750	10.1	464,060	244,282	618,197	15,420	695,485	17,254	456,130	138,787	3,443
Wilmington, DE–MD–NJ	66,193	9.5	79,750	43,870	102,348	14,504	122,800	17,306	79,095	12,814	1,806
Phoenix–Mesa–Glendale, AZ	710,733	17.1	410,202	211,206	528,883	12,614	647,090	15,178	442,170	62,384	1,463
Pine Bluff, AR	15,097	16.2	17,102	9,967	17,712	17,666	20,600	20,824	10,730	5,282	5,339
Pittsburgh, PA	193,253	8.3	327,510	162,694	465,725	19,765	537,735	22,788	339,530	69,684	2,953
Pittsfield, MA	4,720	3.7	19,687	9,631	28,676	21,854	32,465	24,885	21,020	4,231	3,243
Pocatello, ID	13,309	14.8	11,124	6,151	12,728	14,040	14,215	15,543	8,660	1,868	2,042
Portland–South Portland–Biddeford, ME	45,889	9.0	62,934	32,042	92,332	17,960	106,125	20,575	69,985	9,537	1,849
Portland–Vancouver–Hillsboro, OR–WA	328,711	14.8	251,042	138,150	292,659	13,147	347,575	15,362	237,895	40,869	1,806
Port St. Lucie, FL	85,630	20.4	60,505	26,183	89,462	21,094	107,550	25,136	77,325	7,530	1,760
Poughkeepsie–Newburgh–Middletown, NY	65,553	10.1	76,744	42,324	97,391	14,529	115,825	17,214	73,315	12,700	1,887
Prescott, AZ	30,752	14.7	34,839	18,125	52,382	24,822	66,330	31,304	48,710	3,456	1,631
Providence–New Bedford–Fall River, RI–MA	143,518	9.1	203,000	109,271	278,340	17,387	318,840	19,925	206,195	52,566	3,285
Provo–Orem, UT	70,237	13.4	37,454	19,909	38,802	7,365	48,965	9,054	30,150	4,375	809
Pueblo, CO	23,801	15.3	25,557	14,894	29,579	18,596	32,820	20,443	18,960	6,001	3,738
Punta Gorda, FL	26,119	16.6	30,229	11,262	44,246	27,658	57,175	35,621	43,365	2,399	1,495
Racine, WI	18,754	9.8	20,816	10,648	32,538	16,651	38,435	19,671	24,785	4,860	2,487
Raleigh–Cary, NC	163,981	14.6	93,149	50,881	123,137	10,892	150,820	12,962	98,700	16,908	1,453
Rapid City, SD	16,189	13.2	15,051	8,106	20,834	16,485	25,405	19,792	17,245	2,235	1,741
Reading, PA	41,448	10.2	51,540	26,073	68,433	16,632	80,995	19,622	55,745	9,957	2,412
Redding, CA	27,208	15.5	31,321	17,283	38,928	21,966	45,995	25,873	27,665	9,959	5,602
Reno–Sparks, NV	92,891	22.0	43,807	23,878	61,316	14,413	71,810	16,715	50,410	6,227	1,449
Richmond, VA	157,883	12.8	143,445	79,174	181,797	14,448	217,430	17,129	143,250	26,743	2,107

[1]Civilian noninstitutionalized population.
[2]Unduplicated count of persons enrolled in either hospital and/or supplemental medical insurance as of July 1.
[3]Based on resident population estimated as of July 1 of the year shown.

Table B-8. Health Insurance, Medicare, Social Security, and SSI—*Continued*

Metropolitan statistical area and division	Persons with no health insurance, 2009–2011[1]		Persons with a disability, 2009–2011		Medicare program enrollment, 2010[2]		Social security program beneficiaries, December 2011			Supplemental security income program recipients, 2011	
	Number	Percent	Total 5 years and over	18 to 64 years	Number	Rate per 100,000 persons[3]	Number	Rate per 100,000 persons[3]	Retired workers, number	Number	Rate per 100,000 persons[3]
Riverside–San Bernardino–Ontario, CA	863,695	20.7	441,881	236,437	481,888	11,406	568,170	13,198	366,000	129,015	2,997
Roanoke, VA	33,580	11.0	40,564	20,915	58,304	18,887	69,430	22,479	44,115	7,491	2,425
Rochester, MN	12,558	6.8	14,418	6,925	27,074	14,555	31,345	16,707	22,745	2,482	1,323
Rochester, NY	82,080	7.9	124,940	69,929	179,675	17,042	215,975	20,466	142,435	31,987	3,031
Rockford, IL	45,358	13.1	39,475	20,600	55,254	15,813	67,105	19,263	43,395	7,487	2,149
Rocky Mount, NC	26,752	17.9	23,571	13,108	27,497	18,044	32,845	21,586	19,455	6,250	4,108
Rome, GA	17,290	18.3	16,247	9,316	17,119	17,774	20,530	21,388	12,500	3,078	3,207
Sacramento—Arden-Arcade—Roseville, CA	270,691	12.7	256,178	138,000	299,824	13,951	336,980	15,485	217,185	78,677	3,615
Saginaw–Saginaw Township North, MI	22,303	11.3	28,938	15,765	38,428	19,198	46,925	23,570	27,555	8,388	4,213
St. Cloud, MN	16,536	8.8	19,579	10,552	29,106	15,392	30,570	16,088	20,010	2,611	1,374
St. George, UT	23,184	16.8	14,288	6,026	23,230	16,819	28,455	20,086	20,800	1,193	842
St. Joseph, MO–KS	15,751	13.1	17,701	9,650	20,719	16,272	24,445	19,161	15,480	2,831	2,219
St. Louis, MO–IL[5]	299,496	10.8	334,649	176,831	439,065	15,609	517,905	18,383	329,460	59,662	2,118
Salem, OR	70,118	18.2	52,008	28,853	60,731	15,543	72,350	18,323	49,500	8,606	2,179
Salinas, CA	87,003	21.9	31,256	15,030	48,256	11,626	55,480	13,150	36,740	9,314	2,208
Salisbury, MD	15,784	13.2	15,753	8,409	19,558	15,621	23,205	18,486	15,455	3,050	2,430
Salt Lake City, UT	180,018	16.1	94,632	53,201	111,251	9,896	132,090	11,527	86,380	13,352	1,165
San Angelo, TX	22,492	21.0	14,153	7,394	18,204	16,279	21,070	18,573	13,450	2,921	2,575
San Antonio–New Braunfels, TX	416,069	19.8	279,508	154,307	277,235	12,940	337,690	15,385	197,725	62,425	2,844
San Diego–Carlsbad–San Marcos, CA	520,798	17.4	273,644	131,172	390,838	12,627	427,485	13,614	291,785	83,160	2,648
Sandusky, OH	9,086	12.0	12,329	6,765	16,162	20,968	17,550	22,866	11,435	1,508	1,965
San Francisco–Oakland–Fremont, CA	517,616	12.0	398,639	190,446	600,624	13,854	618,015	14,074	430,190	141,614	3,225
Oakland–Fremont–Hayward, CA	320,768	12.6	237,343	117,680	329,495	12,874	351,750	13,550	236,855	79,463	3,061
San Francisco–San Mateo–Redwood City, CA	196,848	11.2	161,296	72,766	271,129	15,265	266,265	14,833	193,335	62,151	3,462
San Jose–Sunnyvale–Santa Clara, CA	219,836	12.0	139,794	63,628	216,876	11,807	218,640	11,720	153,685	49,304	2,643
San Luis Obispo–Paso Robles, CA	40,210	15.4	28,563	13,672	45,605	16,913	51,645	18,989	36,790	5,230	1,923
Santa Barbara–Santa Maria–Goleta, CA	76,650	18.4	43,702	21,484	61,076	14,408	66,610	15,604	45,190	9,642	2,259
Santa Cruz–Watsonville, CA	38,963	14.9	22,388	11,773	34,080	12,989	38,925	14,728	26,350	5,854	2,215
Santa Fe, NM	28,290	19.9	18,378	9,784	24,694	17,128	29,065	19,956	20,260	2,759	1,894
Santa Rosa–Petaluma, CA	67,737	14.1	50,181	24,171	74,997	15,499	85,465	17,509	59,540	9,784	2,004
Savannah, GA	65,499	19.2	38,542	21,058	46,601	13,406	56,430	15,870	35,815	7,781	2,188
Scranton—Wilkes-Barre, PA	52,564	9.5	84,278	42,711	116,310	20,636	136,755	24,281	87,915	17,188	3,052
Seattle–Tacoma–Bellevue, WA	430,883	12.7	352,769	194,585	428,919	12,469	488,490	13,957	330,195	66,629	1,904
Seattle–Bellevue–Everett, WA	325,911	12.4	256,166	139,492	322,607	12,199	361,235	13,418	250,440	48,166	1,789
Tacoma, WA	104,972	13.6	96,603	55,093	106,312	13,369	127,255	15,751	79,755	18,463	2,285
Sebastian–Vero Beach, FL	27,354	20.0	20,114	7,680	36,230	26,248	41,905	30,170	31,050	2,032	1,463
Sheboygan, WI	8,284	7.3	11,727	5,343	19,147	16,576	23,110	20,070	16,315	1,659	1,441
Sherman–Denison, TX	26,246	22.0	19,050	9,964	22,834	18,890	25,705	21,170	16,395	2,910	2,397
Shreveport–Bossier City, LA	69,556	17.9	56,279	30,637	61,857	15,518	72,120	17,869	41,930	17,288	4,284
Sioux City, IA–NE–SD	18,182	12.8	15,287	7,940	22,635	15,765	25,520	17,715	16,730	2,379	1,651
Sioux Falls, SD	21,291	9.4	19,322	10,137	31,682	13,880	37,465	16,119	26,000	2,879	1,239
South Bend–Mishawaka, IN–MI	43,923	13.9	40,217	20,039	49,248	15,427	60,895	19,108	40,730	6,551	2,056
Spartanburg, SC	50,657	18.0	41,199	22,720	52,955	18,626	62,070	21,637	36,915	7,049	2,457
Spokane, WA	61,396	13.3	61,900	32,999	75,316	15,983	86,990	18,362	55,175	13,051	2,755
Springfield, IL	19,788	9.5	27,759	14,008	35,029	16,667	41,545	19,639	27,005	5,108	2,415
Springfield, MA	29,927	4.4	97,489	52,519	120,012	17,319	137,750	19,871	81,975	36,103	5,208
Springfield, MO	67,128	15.6	58,210	31,778	74,461	17,050	88,645	20,140	54,305	9,553	2,170
Springfield, OH	16,658	12.2	23,112	12,924	26,342	19,042	29,770	21,621	18,660	3,777	2,743
State College, PA	11,469	7.6	13,346	7,093	19,020	12,351	21,940	14,180	15,330	1,574	1,017
Steubenville–Weirton, OH–WV	14,568	11.9	19,580	10,188	27,633	22,203	32,060	26,014	18,115	4,049	3,285
Stockton, CA	115,821	17.1	78,484	43,905	83,639	12,205	96,410	13,848	59,015	29,095	4,179
Sumter, SC	18,207	17.7	15,188	8,829	17,477	16,264	21,455	19,966	12,595	4,144	3,856
Syracuse, NY	57,548	8.8	74,146	39,986	111,624	16,847	132,735	20,034	84,370	19,449	2,935
Tallahassee, FL	51,120	14.3	38,112	21,986	44,348	12,070	53,805	14,551	36,225	9,208	2,490
Tampa–St. Petersburg–Clearwater, FL	508,384	18.4	371,176	182,185	509,593	18,309	601,695	21,301	403,300	69,496	2,460
Terre Haute, IN	25,833	15.6	26,862	14,894	30,335	17,593	36,035	20,870	21,840	4,453	2,579
Texarkana, TX–Texarkana, AR	25,896	19.8	20,913	11,681	23,604	17,352	27,475	20,121	15,445	6,027	4,414
Toledo, OH	75,756	11.8	86,872	48,097	103,275	15,854	119,725	18,412	73,485	19,312	2,970
Topeka, KS	28,413	12.4	33,209	18,788	41,116	17,581	47,535	20,258	30,600	5,536	2,359
Trenton–Ewing, NJ	41,483	11.5	36,136	18,311	56,959	15,541	63,800	17,381	41,485	8,983	2,447

[1]Civilian noninstitutionalized population.
[2]Unduplicated count of persons enrolled in either hospital and/or supplemental medical insurance as of July 1.
[3]Based on resident population estimated as of July 1 of the year shown.
[5]The portion of Sullivan city in Crawford County, MO is legally part of the St. Louis, MO–IL MSA. That portion is not included in these figures for the St. Louis, MSA.

Table B-8. Health Insurance, Medicare, Social Security, and SSI—*Continued*

Metropolitan statistical area and division	Persons with no health insurance, 2009–2011[1]		Persons with a disability, 2009–2011		Medicare program enrollment, 2010[2]		Social security program beneficiaries, December 2011			Supplemental security income program recipients, 2011	
	Number	Percent	Total 5 years and over	18 to 64 years	Number	Rate per 100,000 persons[3]	Number	Rate per 100,000 persons[3]	Retired workers, number	Number	Rate per 100,000 persons[3]
Tucson, AZ	143,013	14.8	127,384	65,810	164,754	16,807	187,530	18,951	127,765	19,295	1,950
Tulsa, OK	171,235	18.4	137,195	78,065	142,507	15,201	172,070	18,171	107,720	20,945	2,212
Tuscaloosa, AL	27,804	12.8	30,466	17,661	33,507	15,268	42,775	19,307	21,635	8,987	4,056
Tyler, TX	43,952	21.1	29,113	14,748	35,822	17,081	40,205	18,842	25,595	5,222	2,447
Utica–Rome, NY	22,600	7.8	42,611	22,655	58,750	19,623	69,345	23,235	43,270	10,524	3,526
Valdosta, GA	31,412	23.4	19,289	11,563	17,620	12,623	22,535	15,835	13,130	4,541	3,191
Vallejo–Fairfield, CA	49,154	12.4	41,680	21,550	53,341	12,905	63,110	15,154	40,005	12,361	2,968
Victoria, TX	24,437	21.4	18,802	10,462	18,901	16,381	22,445	19,311	13,240	3,410	2,934
Vineland–Millville–Bridgeton, NJ	24,232	16.5	23,449	12,837	25,017	15,945	29,120	18,537	17,880	5,362	3,413
Virginia Beach–Norfolk–Newport News, VA–NC	187,669	11.9	169,258	87,951	219,668	13,141	263,990	15,715	171,350	32,483	1,934
Visalia–Porterville, CA	98,330	22.4	45,099	23,872	48,807	11,038	58,550	13,033	36,070	18,887	4,204
Waco, TX	43,873	18.9	30,389	16,114	34,941	14,874	40,475	16,966	24,130	7,048	2,954
Warner Robins, GA	20,059	14.7	15,326	8,324	17,478	12,493	21,090	14,653	12,725	3,172	2,204
Washington–Arlington–Alexandria, DC–VA–MD–WV	649,448	11.8	426,865	221,727	591,770	10,601	551,715	9,673	390,825	56,082	983
Bethesda–Rockville–Frederick, MD	134,340	11.2	92,792	42,289	147,747	12,260	151,460	12,349	110,650	15,355	1,252
Washington–Arlington–Alexandria, DC–VA–MD–WV	515,108	11.9	334,073	179,438	444,023	10,144	400,255	8,939	280,175	40,727	910
Waterloo–Cedar Falls, IA	13,435	8.1	19,978	9,801	28,525	16,997	32,820	19,502	22,225	3,357	1,995
Wausau, WI	11,825	8.9	13,604	6,765	20,414	15,227	25,455	18,940	17,575	2,081	1,548
Wenatchee–East Wenatchee, WA	22,868	20.7	14,832	7,834	18,888	17,034	22,170	19,716	15,785	2,029	1,804
Wheeling, WV–OH	15,084	10.6	23,793	13,073	30,038	20,303	35,440	24,077	21,470	4,670	3,173
Wichita, KS	86,189	14.0	76,514	42,269	88,671	14,232	104,825	16,758	68,010	12,101	1,935
Wichita Falls, TX	26,601	19.2	20,789	10,820	24,218	16,006	28,090	18,694	16,820	4,177	2,780
Williamsport, PA	12,405	10.9	16,431	8,283	23,023	19,828	26,575	22,763	17,655	3,401	2,913
Wilmington, NC	58,649	16.3	50,361	27,388	67,049	18,506	83,300	22,533	57,540	7,448	2,015
Winchester, VA–WV	19,466	15.4	16,235	8,462	19,996	15,564	24,090	18,522	16,125	2,281	1,754
Winston–Salem, NC	71,531	15.1	52,064	27,089	80,629	16,878	94,165	19,535	63,460	9,439	1,958
Worcester, MA	28,499	3.6	87,364	44,374	122,117	15,292	139,380	17,396	87,230	22,887	2,856
Yakima, WA	62,001	25.7	30,341	15,929	33,848	13,916	39,930	16,157	25,910	7,311	2,958
York–Hanover, PA	39,002	9.1	51,843	27,255	71,204	16,370	85,795	19,643	58,735	8,197	1,877
Youngstown–Warren–Boardman, OH–PA	63,200	11.4	84,248	43,568	115,610	20,434	136,560	24,267	83,750	18,575	3,301
Yuba City, CA	29,951	18.4	23,858	13,817	23,446	14,049	27,450	16,388	15,860	8,027	4,792
Yuma, AZ	37,962	20.1	20,970	8,168	26,197	13,383	31,300	15,582	21,025	4,102	2,042

[1]Civilian noninstitutionalized population.
[2]Unduplicated count of persons enrolled in either hospital and/or supplemental medical insurance as of July 1.
[3]Based on resident population estimated as of July 1 of the year shown.

Table B-9.   Housing Units and Building Permits

Metropolitan statistical area and division	Housing units						New private housing units authorized by building permits[4]			
	2011 (July 1)	2010[1] (estimates base)	2000[2] (estimates base)	Change, 2010–2011		Units per square mile of land area, 2011[3]	2011	Percent single family, 2011	2010	Percent single family, 2010
				Number	Percent					
Abilene, TX	70,070	69,721	65,224	349	0.5	25.5	159	96.2	390	69.7
Akron, OH	313,028	312,581	290,987	447	0.1	347.8	1,122	56.8	736	89.3
Albany, GA	65,659	66,060	63,765	-401	-0.6	34.0	206	88.3	248	69.4
Albany–Schenectady–Troy, NY	395,179	393,298	363,736	1,881	0.5	140.6	1,764	50.5	1,429	76.9
Albuquerque, NM	376,662	374,405	305,881	2,257	0.6	40.6	1,634	82.9	1,764	88.0
Alexandria, LA	64,765	64,570	60,590	195	0.3	33.0	376	74.5	434	78.3
Allentown–Bethlehem–Easton, PA–NJ	343,955	342,200	307,274	1,755	0.5	236.7	1,133	93.5	1,388	84.8
Altoona, PA	56,194	56,271	55,043	-77	-0.1	106.9	75	92.0	159	70.4
Amarillo, TX	103,444	102,547	91,577	897	0.9	28.3	703	93.3	927	61.7
Ames, IA	37,089	36,789	30,634	300	0.8	64.8	457	21.7	167	55.7
Anchorage, AK	156,709	154,361	127,711	2,348	1.5	6.0	524	76.5	533	79.5
Anderson, IN	58,910	59,068	56,924	-158	-0.3	130.4	75	97.3	80	95.0
Anderson, SC	84,934	84,772	73,219	162	0.2	118.7	280	95.7	420	67.6
Ann Arbor, MI	147,510	147,573	130,994	-63	0.0	208.9	477	41.9	368	86.1
Anniston–Oxford, AL	53,347	53,289	51,177	58	0.1	88.0	83	88.0	107	92.5
Appleton, WI	93,369	92,844	78,389	525	0.6	97.7	648	46.0	587	70.4
Asheville, NC	215,719	213,638	175,340	2,081	1.0	106.1	1,001	93.1	2,038	51.3
Athens–Clarke County, GA	81,792	81,719	67,531	73	0.1	79.8	327	73.4	226	100.0
Atlanta–Sandy Springs–Marietta, GA	2,168,011	2,165,495	1,644,489	2,516	0.1	260.0	8,634	72.0	7,575	84.3
Atlantic City–Hammonton, NJ	126,782	126,647	114,103	135	0.1	228.1	390	86.4	512	81.8
Auburn–Opelika, AL	63,483	62,391	50,295	1,092	1.8	104.5	957	77.2	971	64.2
Augusta–Richmond County, GA–SC	239,715	236,949	204,609	2,766	1.2	73.3	2,385	93.0	2,474	97.2
Austin–Round Rock–San Marcos, TX	721,242	706,505	496,066	14,737	2.1	170.9	10,239	60.9	8,786	70.6
Bakersfield–Delano, CA	286,955	284,367	231,571	2,588	0.9	35.3	969	73.5	1,656	73.1
Baltimore–Towson, MD	1,138,020	1,132,251	1,048,105	5,769	0.5	437.4	6,153	53.3	5,594	63.5
Bangor, ME	74,382	73,859	66,820	523	0.7	21.9	369	57.7	272	91.5
Barnstable Town, MA	161,001	160,281	147,084	720	0.4	408.9	404	84.7	418	91.1
Baton Rouge, LA	332,601	329,726	282,587	2,875	0.9	82.6	3,135	83.9	2,962	95.6
Battle Creek, MI	60,922	61,042	58,697	-120	-0.2	86.3	49	67.3	33	100.0
Bay City, MI	48,125	48,220	46,431	-95	-0.2	108.8	91	73.6	54	100.0
Beaumont–Port Arthur, TX	164,050	162,335	156,763	1,715	1.1	78.1	1,179	72.5	1,424	88.2
Bellingham, WA	91,280	90,665	73,897	615	0.7	43.3	605	69.3	458	87.6
Bend, OR	80,599	80,139	54,584	460	0.6	26.7	459	99.6	377	96.8
Billings, MT	71,454	70,384	60,049	1,070	1.5	15.3	272	94.1	457	70.2
Binghamton, NY	112,908	112,766	110,228	142	0.1	92.2	117	96.6	108	94.4
Birmingham–Hoover, AL	500,322	500,026	454,350	296	0.1	94.8	2,362	76.0	1,924	81.2
Bismarck, ND	48,561	47,833	39,599	728	1.5	13.6	844	75.4	650	86.8
Blacksburg–Christiansburg–Radford, VA	70,992	70,550	62,751	442	0.6	66.2	330	87.0	268	75.7
Bloomington, IN	84,552	84,409	75,740	143	0.2	63.9	236	71.6	263	74.5
Bloomington–Normal, IL	70,183	69,656	59,951	527	0.8	59.3	620	38.9	427	74.7
Boise City–Nampa, ID	248,100	246,052	181,189	2,048	0.8	21.1	1,840	85.8	1,693	96.3
Boston–Cambridge–Quincy, MA–NH	1,891,016	1,883,206	1,751,740	7,810	0.4	542.2	6,139	55.3	6,672	56.2
Boston–Quincy, MA	790,248	786,042	729,374	4,206	0.5	709.8	2,727	42.2	2,842	41.1
Cambridge–Newton–Framingham, MA	614,036	612,004	576,603	2,032	0.3	750.8	1,823	65.1	2,109	63.3
Peabody, MA	307,559	306,754	287,193	805	0.3	624.4	725	60.0	872	63.4
Rockingham County–Strafford County, NH	179,173	178,406	158,570	767	0.4	168.4	864	71.9	849	81.4
Boulder, CO	127,489	127,071	111,446	418	0.3	175.5	661	59.0	657	42.0
Bowling Green, KY	54,125	53,690	44,455	435	0.8	64.1	843	34.5	573	63.2
Bremerton–Silverdale, WA	108,364	107,367	92,653	997	0.9	274.4	540	83.5	623	75.1
Bridgeport–Stamford–Norwalk, CT	362,739	361,221	339,499	1,518	0.4	580.5	937	62.2	926	59.0
Brownsville–Harlingen, TX	142,312	141,924	119,483	388	0.3	159.7	1,136	92.7	1,258	84.4
Brunswick, GA	59,035	58,021	44,859	1,014	1.7	45.9	396	100.0	404	100.0
Buffalo–Niagara Falls, NY	518,766	519,094	511,561	-328	-0.1	331.5	1,315	60.1	1,498	69.2
Burlington, NC	67,068	66,576	55,446	492	0.7	158.2	556	71.8	847	52.3
Burlington–South Burlington, VT	93,173	92,359	82,718	814	0.9	74.4	681	44.2	585	55.6
Canton–Massillon, OH	179,025	178,913	170,053	112	0.1	184.6	256	82.4	452	68.1
Cape Coral–Fort Myers, FL	372,117	371,099	245,425	1,018	0.3	474.3	1,587	79.5	1,276	92.1
Cape Girardeau–Jackson, MO–IL	42,684	42,501	39,534	183	0.4	29.8	122	77.0	99	73.7
Carson City, NV	23,566	23,534	21,290	32	0.1	162.9	13	69.2	71	15.5
Casper, WY	34,400	33,807	29,886	593	1.8	6.4	402	63.7	807	32.7

[1]The April 1, 2010, estimates base population may differ from the April 1, 2010, Census count due to legal boundary updates, other geographic program changes, and Count Question Resolution actions.
[2]The April 1, 2000, housing estimates base reflects modifications to the Census 2000 population as documented in the Count Question Resolution program and geographic program revisions.
[3]Units per square mile was calculated on the basis of land area data from the 2010 census.
[4]Sample selected from a universe of 20,000 permit–issuing places.

Table B-9. Housing Units and Building Permits—*Continued*

Metropolitan statistical area and division	Housing units						New private housing units authorized by building permits[4]			
	2011 (July 1)	2010[1] (estimates base)	2000[2] (estimates base)	Change, 2010–2011		Units per square mile of land area, 2011[3]	2011	Percent single family, 2011	2010	Percent single family, 2010
				Number	Percent					
Cedar Rapids, IA	113,216	112,257	99,070	959	0.9	56.4	731	78.9	855	80.8
Champaign–Urbana, IL	101,677	101,120	88,148	557	0.6	52.9	518	41.5	529	47.4
Charleston, WV	141,027	141,584	141,680	-557	-0.4	55.8	295	89.8	358	80.4
Charleston–North Charleston–Summerville, SC....	301,977	298,542	232,985	3,435	1.2	116.7	3,822	67.9	3,060	91.1
Charlotte–Gastonia–Rock Hill, NC–SC	743,294	737,775	546,515	5,519	0.7	240.9	6,446	76.2	5,288	82.0
Charlottesville, VA	89,760	89,134	73,853	626	0.7	54.6	1,008	61.4	1,105	54.9
Chattanooga, TN–GA	235,722	234,440	205,376	1,282	0.5	112.8	1,331	72.1	1,086	87.9
Cheyenne, WY	41,095	40,462	34,219	633	1.6	15.3	279	98.6	238	100.0
Chicago–Joliet–Naperville, IL–IN–WI	3,797,079	3,797,247	3,462,461	-168	0.0	527.6	7,593	54.6	7,267	58.4
Chicago–Joliet–Naperville, IL	3,172,234	3,173,522	2,906,837	-1,288	0.0	689.2	5,799	49.9	5,154	53.3
Gary, IN	294,217	294,127	269,586	90	0.0	156.6	939	76.5	1,167	78.1
Lake County–Kenosha County, IL–WI	330,628	329,598	286,038	1,030	0.3	462.0	855	62.2	946	61.9
Chico, CA	95,902	95,835	85,510	67	0.1	58.6	240	84.2	512	30.7
Cincinnati–Middletown, OH–KY–IN	919,064	917,396	833,086	1,668	0.2	209.3	3,369	74.8	3,206	88.1
Clarksville, TN–KY	115,894	114,145	92,067	1,749	1.5	53.7	2,001	71.3	1,921	56.8
Cleveland, TN	49,561	49,386	44,193	175	0.4	64.9	376	80.6	550	48.5
Cleveland–Elyria–Mentor, OH	956,773	955,756	911,366	1,017	0.1	479.0	1,767	89.7	1,941	95.5
Coeur d'Alene, ID	64,319	63,177	46,608	1,142	1.8	51.7	623	67.6	627	75.4
College Station–Bryan, TX	96,459	95,016	75,080	1,443	1.5	45.9	1,444	42.9	995	78.1
Colorado Springs, CO	267,267	265,495	212,793	1,772	0.7	99.6	2,275	71.0	1,760	95.2
Columbia, MO	74,548	74,133	61,029	415	0.6	64.9	1,052	45.4	607	90.1
Columbia, SC	336,003	331,471	269,236	4,532	1.4	90.7	2,897	82.5	2,942	85.9
Columbus, GA–AL	128,891	128,214	115,812	677	0.5	66.6	1,060	85.5	1,384	62.8
Columbus, IN	33,321	33,098	29,866	223	0.7	81.9	178	100.0	131	100.0
Columbus, OH	796,880	792,340	680,490	4,540	0.6	200.9	4,730	51.2	4,444	65.0
Corpus Christi, TX	184,419	182,909	160,730	1,510	0.8	103.4	1,142	77.4	1,225	75.5
Corvallis, OR	36,384	36,246	31,985	138	0.4	53.8	364	18.1	93	80.6
Crestview–Fort Walton Beach–Destin, FL	92,394	92,407	78,927	-13	0.0	99.3	749	99.7	547	100.0
Cumberland, MD–WV	46,419	46,350	45,076	69	0.1	61.7	118	94.9	161	59.0
Dallas–Fort Worth–Arlington, TX	2,531,936	2,502,078	1,998,239	29,858	1.2	283.6	24,827	56.5	19,558	73.7
Dallas–Plano–Irving, TX	1,678,763	1,660,146	1,331,750	18,617	1.1	303.5	18,686	50.7	13,463	71.4
Fort Worth–Arlington, TX	853,173	841,932	666,489	11,241	1.3	251.2	6,141	74.2	6,095	78.9
Dalton, GA	56,360	55,878	45,063	482	0.9	88.8	63	100.0	101	89.1
Danville, IL	36,190	36,318	36,351	-128	-0.4	40.3	12	83.3	13	76.9
Danville, VA	53,802	53,745	51,103	57	0.1	53.2	142	61.3	160	84.4
Davenport–Moline–Rock Island, IA–IL	167,577	167,110	158,538	467	0.3	73.8	635	90.9	702	60.1
Dayton, OH	385,457	385,160	364,486	297	0.1	225.9	752	98.0	758	88.9
Decatur, AL	66,475	66,422	62,410	53	0.1	52.3	103	100.0	165	87.9
Decatur, IL	50,197	50,475	50,237	-278	-0.6	86.4	84	83.3	101	94.1
Deltona–Daytona Beach–Ormond Beach, FL	254,981	254,228	211,986	753	0.3	231.6	1,024	50.1	715	89.4
Denver–Aurora–Broomfield, CO[5]	1,083,735	1,078,837	891,106	4,898	0.5	129.9	6,673	54.4	5,042	72.6
Des Moines–West Des Moines, IA	242,364	240,203	199,401	2,161	0.9	84.0	2,640	85.2	2,815	78.4
Detroit–Warren–Livonia, MI	1,881,623	1,886,536	1,797,335	-4,913	-0.3	483.9	3,366	85.0	3,210	75.7
Detroit–Livonia–Dearborn, MI	817,730	821,693	826,165	-3,963	-0.5	1335.9	705	67.5	735	63.9
Warren–Troy–Farmington Hills, MI	1,063,893	1,064,843	971,170	-950	-0.1	324.7	2,661	89.7	2,475	79.2
Dothan, AL	67,424	66,897	59,718	527	0.8	39.3	288	100.0	321	84.4
Dover, DE	66,241	65,338	50,510	903	1.4	113.0	680	79.4	813	82.9
Dubuque, IA	39,273	38,951	35,503	322	0.8	64.6	410	68.5	548	59.1
Duluth, MN–WI	142,158	141,539	129,928	619	0.4	16.9	444	75.0	486	82.1
Durham–Chapel Hill, NC	225,865	222,760	180,055	3,105	1.4	128.4	1,924	79.3	1,913	80.0
Eau Claire, WI	69,747	69,336	60,303	411	0.6	42.4	364	67.3	357	81.8
El Centro, CA	56,285	56,067	43,876	218	0.4	13.5	257	50.2	102	100.0
Elizabethtown, KY	49,660	49,435	42,745	225	0.5	56.1	714	37.8	1,242	56.9
Elkhart–Goshen, IN	77,695	77,768	69,792	-73	-0.1	167.7	146	100.0	234	74.4
Elmira, NY	38,362	38,369	37,769	-7	0.0	94.2	138	24.6	76	89.5
El Paso, TX	274,807	270,307	224,448	4,500	1.7	271.4	4,153	79.0	4,549	65.1
Erie, PA	119,391	119,138	114,361	253	0.2	149.4	311	45.0	586	63.0
Eugene–Springfield, OR	157,074	156,112	138,965	962	0.6	34.5	670	52.4	550	84.4
Evansville, IN–KY	159,460	159,314	147,768	146	0.1	69.8	559	91.4	644	84.9
Fairbanks, AK	42,740	41,783	33,295	957	2.3	5.8	39	89.7	42	100.0
Fargo, ND–MN	93,839	91,897	73,559	1,942	2.1	33.4	1,536	39.6	1,318	57.7
Farmington, NM	49,971	49,341	43,229	630	1.3	9.1	213	71.8	273	73.6

[1]The April 1, 2010, estimates base population may differ from the April 1, 2010, Census count due to legal boundary updates, other geographic program changes, and Count Question Resolution actions.
[2]The April 1, 2000, housing estimates base reflects modifications to the Census 2000 population as documented in the Count Question Resolution program and geographic program revisions.
[3]Units per square mile was calculated on the basis of land area data from the 2010 census.
[4]Sample selected from a universe of 20,000 permit–issuing places.
[5]The Denver–Aurora metropolitan statistical area includes Broomfield County. Broomfield County, CO, was formed from parts of Adams, Boulder, Jefferson, and Weld Counties on November 15, 2001, and is coextensive with Broomfield city. For the purposes of defining and presenting data for the Denver–Aurora metropolitan statistical area, Broomfield city is treated as if it were a county when data are available to do so. In many cases, the data were not available.

Table B-9. Housing Units and Building Permits—*Continued*

Metropolitan statistical area and division	Housing units					Units per square mile of land area, 2011³	New private housing units authorized by building permits⁴			
	2011 (July 1)	2010¹ (estimates base)	2000² (estimates base)	Change, 2010–2011			2011	Percent single family, 2011	2010	Percent single family, 2010
				Number	Percent					
Fayetteville, NC	156,019	153,735	130,978	2,284	1.5	149.6	2,807	52.2	3,609	44.6
Fayetteville–Springdale–Rogers, AR–MO	201,313	198,299	144,428	3,014	1.5	63.6	1,206	96.0	1,221	88.5
Flagstaff, AZ	64,021	63,318	53,440	703	1.1	3.4	100	98.0	315	59.0
Flint, MI	191,117	192,180	183,673	-1,063	-0.6	300.0	66	100.0	78	100.0
Florence, SC	89,494	88,963	80,784	531	0.6	65.8	389	85.3	476	74.2
Florence–Muscle Shoals, AL	69,756	69,549	65,399	207	0.3	55.3	240	57.1	232	66.8
Fond du Lac, WI	44,102	43,910	39,269	192	0.4	61.3	237	36.3	229	49.3
Fort Collins–Loveland, CO	133,247	132,722	105,386	525	0.4	51.3	1,192	58.9	1,153	41.4
Fort Smith, AR–OK	130,281	128,891	115,380	1,390	1.1	32.6	590	78.0	690	75.5
Fort Wayne, IN	178,509	178,124	162,407	385	0.2	131.2	743	97.0	885	91.4
Fresno, CA	318,064	315,531	270,585	2,533	0.8	53.4	1,622	79.5	2,248	85.3
Gadsden, AL	47,346	47,454	45,963	-108	-0.2	88.5	99	82.8	105	100.0
Gainesville, FL	120,738	120,073	101,031	665	0.6	98.6	464	63.8	490	74.9
Gainesville, GA	69,428	68,825	51,155	603	0.9	176.8	228	100.0	184	100.0
Glens Falls, NY	67,883	67,570	61,622	313	0.5	40.0	242	91.7	279	91.4
Goldsboro, NC	53,239	52,949	47,354	290	0.5	96.3	205	100.0	279	79.9
Grand Forks, ND–MN	44,136	43,954	41,381	182	0.4	13.0	391	36.3	200	77.0
Grand Junction, CO	63,202	62,644	48,720	558	0.9	19.0	359	80.5	408	85.3
Grand Rapids–Wyoming, MI	324,117	323,764	293,140	353	0.1	116.4	900	95.6	843	99.4
Great Falls, MT	37,470	37,277	35,234	193	0.5	13.9	144	73.6	150	89.3
Greeley, CO	97,031	96,281	66,137	750	0.8	24.3	889	89.1	863	91.4
Green Bay, WI	137,983	137,212	118,233	771	0.6	73.8	880	55.0	1,134	53.9
Greensboro–High Point, NC	324,700	322,753	275,044	1,947	0.6	162.9	2,047	51.5	1,903	64.8
Greenville, NC	83,651	83,203	65,743	448	0.5	91.1	345	88.4	678	52.9
Greenville–Mauldin–Easley, SC	278,591	277,416	238,973	1,175	0.4	139.6	1,749	93.7	1,542	95.5
Gulfport–Biloxi, MS	117,774	114,182	106,013	3,592	3.1	78.9	1,669	74.8	1,744	75.3
Hagerstown–Martinsburg, MD–WV	115,816	115,329	93,951	487	0.4	114.9	529	98.5	699	91.1
Hanford–Corcoran, CA	44,170	43,867	36,562	303	0.7	31.8	222	64.0	265	72.8
Harrisburg–Carlisle, PA	242,838	240,818	217,004	2,020	0.8	149.7	1,113	85.5	1,612	81.6
Harrisonburg, VA	52,024	51,104	41,030	920	1.8	60.0	248	100.0	462	84.8
Hartford–West Hartford–East Hartford, CT	508,997	507,049	471,912	1,948	0.4	336.1	1,123	67.6	1,279	83.4
Hattiesburg, MS	62,761	61,878	50,499	883	1.4	39.0	64	75.0	74	100.0
Hickory–Lenoir–Morganton, NC	163,144	162,613	144,886	531	0.3	99.6	380	88.4	448	88.8
Hinesville–Fort Stewart, GA	33,735	32,770	26,216	965	2.9	37.9	201	100.0	111	100.0
Holland–Grand Haven, MI	102,785	102,495	86,879	290	0.3	182.4	611	77.1	434	91.0
Honolulu, HI	337,522	336,899	315,994	623	0.2	561.9	1,724	42.6	1,891	46.5
Hot Springs, AR	50,994	50,547	44,910	447	0.9	75.2	37	100.0	38	100.0
Houma–Bayou Cane–Thibodaux, LA	82,954	82,469	74,986	485	0.6	36.1	390	97.9	365	98.4
Houston–Sugar Land–Baytown, TX	2,342,598	2,308,217	1,799,795	34,381	1.5	265.4	31,271	73.2	27,452	81.3
Huntington–Ashland, WV–KY–OH	130,799	131,131	129,890	-332	-0.3	75.0	269	46.8	248	58.1
Huntsville, AL	185,404	181,424	147,323	3,980	2.2	136.2	2,019	99.8	2,275	100.0
Idaho Falls, ID	48,916	48,453	36,770	463	1.0	16.5	272	97.4	390	79.5
Indianapolis–Carmel, IN	761,961	757,441	644,888	4,520	0.6	197.7	5,259	68.7	5,921	64.1
Iowa City, IA	66,177	65,483	54,375	694	1.1	55.9	762	58.3	553	79.6
Ithaca, NY	41,789	41,674	38,614	115	0.3	88.1	153	66.7	153	73.9
Jackson, MI	69,521	69,458	62,911	63	0.1	99.1	57	96.5	63	100.0
Jackson, MS	223,280	222,584	196,570	696	0.3	59.9	1,360	88.8	1,391	93.7
Jackson, TN	48,869	48,857	44,407	12	0.0	58.0	174	100.0	249	100.0
Jacksonville, FL	602,025	598,490	475,072	3,535	0.6	188.1	3,911	83.0	3,606	93.9
Jacksonville, NC	70,366	68,226	55,743	2,140	3.1	92.3	2,031	92.1	2,375	89.9
Janesville, WI	68,474	68,422	62,193	52	0.1	95.4	99	96.0	111	91.0
Jefferson City, MO	63,997	63,555	56,728	442	0.7	28.5	211	86.7	222	81.5
Johnson City, TN	94,640	93,830	81,906	810	0.9	110.8	399	89.5	741	53.7
Johnstown, PA	65,445	65,650	65,785	-205	-0.3	95.1	62	100.0	117	100.0
Jonesboro, AR	51,845	51,438	46,186	407	0.8	35.4	765	45.5	611	66.0
Joplin, MO	75,340	74,981	67,480	359	0.5	59.6	310	61.0	202	71.3
Kalamazoo–Portage, MI	146,959	146,792	133,228	167	0.1	125.7	351	96.0	367	95.6
Kankakee–Bradley, IL	45,321	45,246	40,611	75	0.2	67.0	62	87.1	71	83.1
Kansas City, MO–KS	886,709	883,100	767,843	3,609	0.4	113.3	3,287	71.9	2,714	79.4
Kennewick–Pasco–Richland, WA	94,700	93,041	72,074	1,659	1.8	32.2	1,697	78.9	2,022	77.8
Killeen–Temple–Fort Hood, TX	163,080	159,366	122,165	3,714	2.3	57.9	2,208	82.2	2,241	87.4

¹The April 1, 2010, estimates base population may differ from the April 1, 2010, Census count due to legal boundary updates, other geographic program changes, and Count Question Resolution actions.
²The April 1, 2000, housing estimates base reflects modifications to the Census 2000 population as documented in the Count Question Resolution program and geographic program revisions.
³Units per square mile was calculated on the basis of land area data from the 2010 census.
⁴Sample selected from a universe of 20,000 permit–issuing places.

Table B-9.   Housing Units and Building Permits—*Continued*

Metropolitan statistical area and division	Housing units						New private housing units authorized by building permits[4]			
	2011 (July 1)	2010[1] (estimates base)	2000[2] (estimates base)	Change, 2010–2011		Units per square mile of land area, 2011[3]	2011	Percent single family, 2011	2010	Percent single family, 2010
				Number	Percent					
Kingsport–Bristol–Bristol, TN–VA	147,282	146,978	136,312	304	0.2	73.3	385	88.3	464	93.5
Kingston, NY	83,854	83,639	77,646	215	0.3	74.6	230	55.7	334	46.1
Knoxville, TN	317,060	315,615	276,180	1,445	0.5	170.8	1,180	95.1	2,273	63.9
Kokomo, IN	45,522	45,677	44,463	-155	-0.3	82.2	39	92.3	18	100.0
La Crosse, WI–MN	57,283	57,003	51,663	280	0.5	57.1	300	84.0	327	76.1
Lafayette, IN	85,248	84,505	70,839	743	0.9	66.7	1,244	59.2	531	84.9
Lafayette, LA	116,781	115,597	98,233	1,184	1.0	116.0	859	89.3	849	91.6
Lake Charles, LA	86,509	85,651	81,332	858	1.0	36.8	1,195	54.3	975	88.7
Lake Havasu City–Kingman, AZ	111,845	110,912	80,028	933	0.8	8.4	196	99.0	262	81.7
Lakeland–Winter Haven, FL	281,004	281,214	226,154	-210	-0.1	156.3	1,156	92.9	1,200	92.7
Lancaster, PA	204,747	202,954	180,036	1,793	0.9	216.9	1,204	60.7	1,381	83.2
Lansing–East Lansing, MI	199,051	199,026	181,876	25	0.0	117.2	416	89.9	677	66.6
Laredo, TX	74,518	73,496	55,209	1,022	1.4	22.2	956	66.9	663	95.9
Las Cruces, NM	82,980	81,493	65,253	1,487	1.8	21.8	644	95.7	974	82.0
Las Vegas–Paradise, NV	848,118	840,343	559,793	7,775	0.9	107.5	5,147	74.2	5,474	84.5
Lawrence, KS	46,999	46,731	40,249	268	0.6	103.1	490	25.9	288	66.0
Lawton, OK	51,726	50,739	45,418	987	1.9	48.4	280	91.4	326	91.4
Lebanon, PA	56,041	55,594	49,289	447	0.8	154.9	175	90.9	240	100.0
Lewiston, ID–WA	27,420	27,310	25,323	110	0.4	18.5	65	93.8	75	94.7
Lewiston–Auburn, ME	49,186	49,091	45,970	95	0.2	105.1	148	98.6	206	78.6
Lexington–Fayette, KY	210,867	209,138	175,295	1,729	0.8	143.6	1,501	67.2	1,361	84.9
Lima, OH	44,896	44,999	44,240	-103	-0.2	111.5	51	68.6	116	37.9
Lincoln, NE	128,650	127,750	110,654	900	0.7	91.3	1,059	64.2	1,032	62.8
Little Rock–North Little Rock–Conway, AR	310,816	306,883	261,951	3,933	1.3	76.1	3,230	46.9	3,559	53.3
Logan, UT–ID	42,122	41,552	32,909	570	1.4	23.0	542	54.4	655	55.9
Longview, TX	87,707	87,322	81,149	385	0.4	49.3	477	50.1	491	43.4
Longview, WA	43,607	43,450	38,626	157	0.4	38.2	113	100.0	131	88.5
Los Angeles–Long Beach–Santa Ana, CA	4,500,162	4,493,983	4,240,430	6,179	0.1	928.2	14,247	28.8	10,394	38.6
Los Angeles–Long Beach–Glendale, CA	3,449,273	3,445,076	3,270,933	4,197	0.1	850.0	9,895	23.0	7,260	32.8
Santa Ana–Anaheim–Irvine, CA	1,050,889	1,048,907	969,497	1,982	0.2	1329.2	4,352	41.9	3,134	51.8
Louisville/Jefferson County, KY–IN	561,919	559,840	493,119	2,079	0.4	136.7	2,397	72.5	2,525	79.6
Lubbock, TX	118,607	117,966	103,807	641	0.5	66.0	1,507	45.9	1,451	61.8
Lynchburg, VA	113,369	112,516	98,026	853	0.8	53.5	529	79.2	700	84.9
Macon, GA	101,219	101,587	94,105	-368	-0.4	58.8	396	43.9	368	95.1
Madera–Chowchilla, CA	49,130	49,140	40,376	-10	0.0	23.0	291	38.5	192	58.3
Madison, WI	254,185	252,878	212,655	1,307	0.5	93.3	1,443	49.8	1,198	66.3
Manchester–Nashua, NH	166,630	166,053	149,968	577	0.3	190.2	702	47.6	682	53.8
Manhattan, KS	52,440	51,355	42,674	1,085	2.1	28.6	767	52.9	830	56.7
Mankato–North Mankato, MN	39,317	39,075	33,213	242	0.6	32.9	281	65.8	331	59.2
Mansfield, OH	54,459	54,599	53,090	-140	-0.3	110.0	42	100.0	45	100.0
McAllen–Edinburg–Mission, TX	250,235	248,287	192,453	1,948	0.8	159.3	3,105	94.1	3,552	87.2
Medford, OR	91,349	90,937	75,739	412	0.5	32.8	362	70.2	373	78.6
Memphis, TN–MS–AR	551,592	550,896	480,874	696	0.1	120.5	2,210	74.4	2,429	68.1
Merced, CA	83,573	83,698	68,567	-125	-0.1	43.2	157	55.4	106	98.1
Miami–Fort Lauderdale–Pompano Beach, FL	2,469,512	2,464,418	2,149,876	5,094	0.2	486.4	7,532	57.1	5,877	54.0
Fort Lauderdale–Pompano Beach– Deerfield Beach, FL	810,795	810,388	741,020	407	0.1	670.2	2,444	59.2	1,168	83.8
Miami–Miami Beach–Kendall, FL	990,558	989,436	852,424	1,122	0.1	522.0	2,618	36.7	3,203	29.4
West Palm Beach–Boca Raton– Boynton Beach, FL	668,159	664,594	556,432	3,565	0.5	339.2	2,470	76.7	1,506	83.1
Michigan City–La Porte, IN	48,446	48,448	45,619	-2	0.0	81.0	143	83.2	228	68.4
Midland, TX	55,104	54,351	48,076	753	1.4	61.2	539	100.0	394	100.0
Milwaukee–Waukesha–West Allis, WI	671,786	669,879	618,277	1,907	0.3	461.8	1,593	57.4	1,941	49.8
Minneapolis–St. Paul–Bloomington, MN–WI	1,359,125	1,354,973	1,170,034	4,152	0.3	225.5	5,148	73.0	5,726	66.5
Missoula, MT	50,680	50,105	41,322	575	1.1	19.5	563	23.4	368	51.6
Mobile, AL	180,045	178,195	165,121	1,850	1.0	146.4	1,541	45.8	1,026	87.2
Modesto, CA	180,085	179,503	150,782	582	0.3	120.5	164	68.9	292	54.5
Monroe, LA	75,948	75,827	71,025	121	0.2	51.1	405	77.0	441	75.5
Monroe, MI	62,749	62,971	56,475	-222	-0.4	114.2	110	100.0	117	96.6
Montgomery, AL	162,214	161,573	144,658	641	0.4	59.8	972	68.7	993	47.5
Morgantown, WV	59,120	58,335	50,138	785	1.3	58.6	399	9.3	301	7.0
Morristown, TN	61,685	61,357	53,730	328	0.5	86.2	134	94.0	206	96.6
Mount Vernon–Anacortes, WA	51,945	51,473	42,703	472	0.9	30.0	179	100.0	207	98.1
Muncie, IN	52,179	52,357	51,034	-178	-0.3	133.1	82	87.8	50	92.0
Muskegon–Norton Shores, MI	73,399	73,561	68,570	-162	-0.2	147.0	95	97.9	106	79.2
Myrtle Beach–North Myrtle Beach–Conway, SC	188,889	185,992	122,066	2,897	1.6	166.6	1,776	83.4	1,508	92.0
Napa, CA	54,916	54,759	48,575	157	0.3	73.4	154	83.1	110	100.0
Naples–Marco Island, FL	198,423	197,298	144,548	1,125	0.6	99.3	1,320	69.7	1,259	60.8
Nashville-Davidson—Murfreesboro— Franklin, TN	673,106	667,655	543,316	5,451	0.8	118.3	5,394	76.0	5,092	77.3
New Haven–Milford, CT	363,231	362,004	340,728	1,227	0.3	600.9	689	61.2	1,019	44.4
New Orleans–Metairie–Kenner, LA	544,150	538,239	548,627	5,911	1.1	183.8	2,328	83.5	2,171	86.4

[1]The April 1, 2010, estimates base population may differ from the April 1, 2010, Census count due to legal boundary updates, other geographic program changes, and Count Question Resolution actions.
[2]The April 1, 2000, housing estimates base reflects modifications to the Census 2000 population as documented in the Count Question Resolution program and geographic program revisions.
[3]Units per square mile was calculated on the basis of land area data from the 2010 census.
[4]Sample selected from a universe of 20,000 permit–issuing places.

Table B-9.   Housing Units and Building Permits—*Continued*

Metropolitan statistical area and division	Housing units						New private housing units authorized by building permits[4]			
	2011 (July 1)	2010[1] (estimates base)	2000[2] (estimates base)	Change, 2010–2011		Units per square mile of land area, 2011[3]	2011	Percent single family, 2011	2010	Percent single family, 2010
				Number	Percent					
New York–Northern New Jersey–Long Island, NY–NJ–PA	7,537,225	7,527,755	7,091,638	9,470	0.1	1127.2	21,539	27.9	18,668	37.6
Edison–New Brunswick, NJ	957,412	954,390	875,310	3,022	0.3	560.4	3,602	67.9	4,524	60.0
Nassau–Suffolk, NY	1,041,588	1,038,331	980,522	3,257	0.3	870.3	1,709	62.6	1,494	87.7
Newark–Union, NJ–PA	853,473	852,181	804,585	1,292	0.2	391.3	2,255	52.8	2,646	56.5
New York–White Plains–Wayne, NY–NJ	4,684,752	4,682,853	4,431,221	1,899	0.0	2926.5	13,973	9.3	10,004	14.9
Niles–Benton Harbor, MI	76,755	76,922	73,461	-167	-0.2	135.2	136	95.6	133	100.0
North Port–Bradenton–Sarasota, FL	403,006	401,103	320,598	1,903	0.5	310.3	2,385	77.1	1,955	87.2
Norwich–New London, CT	121,662	120,994	110,685	668	0.6	183.0	209	93.3	344	82.8
Ocala, FL	164,037	164,049	122,645	-12	0.0	103.5	361	98.6	481	100.0
Ocean City, NJ	98,017	98,309	91,054	-292	-0.3	389.9	452	70.1	434	65.4
Odessa, TX	53,287	53,027	49,504	260	0.5	59.4	740	45.4	708	37.9
Ogden–Clearfield, UT	188,926	186,763	146,726	2,163	1.2	127.3	1,849	64.6	1,509	92.1
Oklahoma City, OK	543,337	539,077	472,153	4,260	0.8	98.6	3,261	94.4	3,635	83.4
Olympia, WA	109,965	108,182	86,672	1,783	1.6	152.3	1,028	83.5	1,156	91.1
Omaha–Council Bluffs, NE–IA	365,898	362,327	311,601	3,571	1.0	84.1	3,133	68.8	3,223	71.5
Orlando–Kissimmee–Sanford, FL	949,967	942,312	683,449	7,655	0.8	273.1	6,505	69.7	5,254	80.3
Oshkosh–Neenah, WI	73,732	73,329	64,725	403	0.5	169.7	385	51.9	359	71.6
Owensboro, KY	49,367	49,452	46,420	-85	-0.2	54.9	278	79.1	338	81.7
Oxnard–Thousand Oaks–Ventura, CA	282,505	281,695	251,727	810	0.3	153.3	568	49.5	590	35.4
Palm Bay–Melbourne–Titusville, FL	270,512	269,862	222,083	650	0.2	266.3	882	96.9	1,144	80.9
Palm Coast, FL	49,068	48,595	24,445	473	1.0	101.1	152	100.0	278	61.9
Panama City–Lynn Haven–Panama City Beach, FL	99,828	99,650	78,437	178	0.2	131.6	343	78.1	309	65.7
Parkersburg–Marietta–Vienna, WV–OH	75,079	75,203	74,003	-124	-0.2	55.2	102	88.2	159	69.2
Pascagoula, MS	70,662	69,397	59,231	1,265	1.8	58.8	303	100.0	329	88.8
Pensacola–Ferry Pass–Brent, FL	202,279	201,463	173,776	816	0.4	121.3	1,205	99.8	1,754	76.2
Peoria, IL	164,517	164,283	153,294	234	0.1	66.6	470	94.9	793	71.9
Philadelphia–Camden–Wilmington, PA–NJ–DE–MD	2,439,911	2,433,611	2,281,852	6,300	0.3	530.2	6,979	63.8	7,053	73.5
Camden, NJ	491,835	490,354	456,033	1,481	0.3	366.5	1,859	55.0	1,885	62.5
Philadelphia, PA	1,660,906	1,657,226	1,565,666	3,680	0.2	770.4	4,039	61.9	3,994	74.2
Wilmington, DE–MD–NJ	287,170	286,031	260,153	1,139	0.4	260.0	1,081	86.1	1,174	88.9
Phoenix–Mesa–Glendale, AZ	1,813,061	1,798,501	1,331,406	14,560	0.8	124.5	9,081	80.4	8,300	86.9
Pine Bluff, AR	41,580	41,931	43,138	-351	-0.8	20.5	69	53.6	126	36.5
Pittsburgh, PA	1,101,261	1,102,048	1,078,569	-787	-0.1	208.5	2,914	91.1	3,615	94.0
Pittsfield, MA	68,497	68,509	66,267	-12	0.0	73.9	122	79.5	139	89.9
Pocatello, ID	36,332	36,135	31,946	197	0.5	14.4	83	97.6	149	98.0
Portland–South Portland–Biddeford, ME	264,072	262,719	233,295	1,353	0.5	127.0	1,112	86.0	1,260	97.2
Portland–Vancouver–Hillsboro, OR–WA	930,273	925,076	790,934	5,197	0.6	139.2	5,213	60.1	4,476	75.0
Port St. Lucie, FL	215,937	215,160	156,747	777	0.4	193.6	539	87.4	492	87.8
Poughkeepsie–Newburgh–Middletown, NY	257,013	255,663	228,852	1,350	0.5	159.9	1,190	54.4	1,343	60.1
Prescott, AZ	111,093	110,433	81,666	660	0.6	13.7	302	96.0	339	69.9
Providence–New Bedford–Fall River, RI–MA	695,811	693,923	656,755	1,888	0.3	438.5	1,178	81.7	1,439	83.7
Provo–Orem, UT	154,243	151,852	107,126	2,391	1.6	28.6	1,932	75.2	1,985	78.2
Pueblo, CO	69,966	69,526	58,936	440	0.6	29.3	118	96.6	234	89.3
Punta Gorda, FL	100,612	100,632	79,772	-20	0.0	147.9	312	96.8	425	68.9
Racine, WI	82,454	82,164	74,734	290	0.4	248.0	107	92.5	240	65.0
Raleigh–Cary, NC	472,697	466,095	329,528	6,602	1.4	223.2	6,366	74.7	5,213	89.3
Rapid City, SD	56,443	55,949	47,415	494	0.9	9.0	412	75.2	642	68.2
Reading, PA	165,269	164,826	150,252	443	0.3	193.0	306	87.3	415	84.3
Redding, CA	77,343	77,313	68,802	30	0.0	20.5	138	70.3	253	66.0
Reno–Sparks, NV	187,834	186,832	145,503	1,002	0.5	28.6	556	96.0	606	77.9
Richmond, VA	535,873	531,648	452,758	4,225	0.8	94.3	2,709	86.8	3,456	71.5
Riverside–San Bernardino–Ontario, CA	1,509,205	1,500,344	1,186,087	8,861	0.6	55.4	4,736	71.3	6,336	83.4
Roanoke, VA	145,695	144,987	129,652	708	0.5	78.0	510	92.5	436	92.7
Rochester, MN	78,910	78,439	65,135	471	0.6	48.8	332	92.8	477	70.2
Rochester, NY	457,532	455,397	427,212	2,135	0.5	156.3	1,523	68.9	1,449	77.9
Rockford, IL	146,007	145,935	129,837	72	0.0	183.9	168	64.9	299	98.0
Rocky Mount, NC	67,199	67,124	61,058	75	0.1	64.3	192	86.5	212	99.1
Rome, GA	40,586	40,551	36,640	35	0.1	79.6	109	29.4	55	100.0
Sacramento–Arden-Arcade–Roseville, CA	875,022	871,793	714,950	3,229	0.4	171.8	2,491	75.2	2,702	80.2
Saginaw–Saginaw Township North, MI	86,482	86,844	85,519	-362	-0.4	108.1	177	51.4	137	82.5
St. Cloud, MN	78,652	78,114	63,773	538	0.7	44.9	368	66.8	314	100.0

[1]The April 1, 2010, estimates base population may differ from the April 1, 2010, Census count due to legal boundary updates, other geographic program changes, and Count Question Resolution actions.
[2]The April 1, 2000, housing estimates base reflects modifications to the Census 2000 population as documented in the Count Question Resolution program and geographic program revisions.
[3]Units per square mile was calculated on the basis of land area data from the 2010 census.
[4]Sample selected from a universe of 20,000 permit–issuing places.

Table B-9.   Housing Units and Building Permits—*Continued*

Metropolitan statistical area and division	Housing units						New private housing units authorized by building permits[4]			
	2011 (July 1)	2010[1] (estimates base)	2000[2] (estimates base)	Change, 2010–2011		Units per square mile of land area, 2011[3]	2011	Percent single family, 2011	2010	Percent single family, 2010
				Number	Percent					
St. George, UT	58,386	57,734	36,469	652	1.1	24.1	893	95.6	893	97.8
St. Joseph, MO–KS	53,808	53,638	50,575	170	0.3	32.5	118	72.9	131	73.3
St. Louis, MO–IL[6]	1,239,927	1,236,221	1,133,358	3,706	0.3	143.8	4,407	74.7	5,660	75.1
Salem, OR	152,173	151,250	132,641	923	0.6	79.1	431	74.0	699	67.0
Salinas, CA	138,788	139,048	131,701	-260	-0.2	42.3	156	83.3	279	40.1
Salisbury, MD	52,569	52,322	44,493	247	0.5	75.7	169	98.8	194	97.9
Salt Lake City, UT	415,871	410,030	342,309	5,841	1.4	43.5	3,457	61.9	2,989	63.0
San Angelo, TX	47,943	47,427	44,838	516	1.1	18.6	145	100.0	177	100.0
San Antonio–New Braunfels, TX	851,611	837,999	648,560	13,612	1.6	116.5	7,127	61.9	6,865	74.9
San Diego–Carlsbad–San Marcos, CA	1,168,679	1,164,786	1,040,151	3,893	0.3	277.8	5,370	41.8	3,494	65.0
Sandusky, OH	37,818	37,845	35,935	-27	-0.1	150.3	48	100.0	47	100.0
San Francisco–Oakland–Fremont, CA	1,747,071	1,741,999	1,606,855	5,072	0.3	707.2	5,783	33.3	4,621	45.8
Oakland–Fremont–Hayward, CA	985,950	982,812	894,766	3,138	0.3	677.7	3,033	51.1	3,403	52.0
San Francisco–San Mateo–Redwood City, CA	761,121	759,187	712,089	1,934	0.3	749.4	2,750	13.6	1,218	28.7
San Jose–Sunnyvale–Santa Clara, CA	651,162	649,790	595,867	1,372	0.2	243.1	3,097	32.4	4,179	20.6
San Luis Obispo–Paso Robles, CA	117,463	117,315	102,304	148	0.1	35.6	306	86.9	468	65.8
Santa Barbara–Santa Maria–Goleta, CA	152,839	152,834	142,878	5	0.0	55.9	231	58.0	400	57.3
Santa Cruz–Watsonville, CA	104,466	104,476	98,868	-10	0.0	234.6	208	47.6	158	75.3
Santa Fe, NM	72,218	71,266	57,703	952	1.3	37.8	94	100.0	96	100.0
Santa Rosa–Petaluma, CA	205,354	204,572	183,160	782	0.4	130.3	632	71.0	477	60.2
Savannah, GA	152,571	151,050	122,632	1,521	1.0	113.9	1,625	64.6	1,301	78.4
Scranton—Wilkes-Barre, PA	258,765	258,833	252,775	-68	0.0	148.1	439	93.6	687	96.8
Seattle–Tacoma–Bellevue, WA	1,471,082	1,463,295	1,255,539	7,787	0.5	250.5	11,230	54.1	10,040	61.1
Seattle–Bellevue–Everett, WA	1,143,854	1,137,920	978,499	5,934	0.5	272.2	8,664	52.9	8,140	54.4
Tacoma, WA	327,228	325,375	277,040	1,853	0.6	196.0	2,566	58.2	1,900	89.9
Sebastian–Vero Beach, FL	76,251	76,346	57,871	-95	-0.1	151.6	372	86.0	307	100.0
Sheboygan, WI	50,838	50,766	45,956	72	0.1	99.4	73	69.9	69	94.2
Sherman–Denison, TX	53,970	53,727	48,306	243	0.5	57.9	76	81.6	327	22.9
Shreveport–Bossier City, LA	174,728	173,669	159,774	1,059	0.6	67.4	1,401	81.2	1,300	86.3
Sioux City, IA–NE–SD	58,043	58,083	56,929	-40	-0.1	28.0	176	92.0	275	76.0
Sioux Falls, SD	97,551	95,862	75,635	1,689	1.8	37.9	1,129	63.4	1,081	69.8
South Bend–Mishawaka, IN–MI	140,717	140,735	130,885	-18	0.0	148.5	467	51.0	383	62.1
Spartanburg, SC	122,926	122,628	107,068	298	0.2	152.2	532	100.0	562	100.0
Spokane, WA	203,159	201,434	175,045	1,725	0.9	115.2	1,785	41.5	1,609	58.4
Springfield, IL	95,549	95,555	90,752	-6	0.0	80.8	391	68.8	399	71.7
Springfield, MA	288,769	288,535	276,488	234	0.1	156.6	512	83.2	633	89.3
Springfield, MO	193,801	192,346	156,517	1,455	0.8	64.5	1,304	53.7	1,338	67.6
Springfield, OH	61,201	61,419	61,054	-218	-0.4	154.0	142	36.6	57	93.0
State College, PA	64,115	63,295	53,125	820	1.3	57.8	259	79.9	426	81.5
Steubenville–Weirton, OH–WV	58,067	58,334	59,166	-267	-0.5	100.1	19	100.0	25	100.0
Stockton, CA	234,777	233,755	189,161	1,022	0.4	168.7	933	83.7	813	98.5
Sumter, SC	46,299	46,011	41,763	288	0.6	69.6	345	100.0	353	81.9
Syracuse, NY	288,152	287,712	278,105	440	0.2	120.8	1,220	57.1	1,139	72.5
Tallahassee, FL	163,710	163,078	136,761	632	0.4	68.6	1,039	55.3	625	92.3
Tampa–St. Petersburg–Clearwater, FL	1,360,231	1,353,159	1,144,023	7,072	0.5	541.2	6,342	71.1	6,501	67.6
Terre Haute, IN	73,807	74,135	72,517	-328	-0.4	50.4	423	27.0	189	85.2
Texarkana, TX–Texarkana, AR	58,005	57,774	54,189	231	0.4	38.4	361	22.4	237	41.4
Toledo, OH	301,190	301,322	285,496	-132	0.0	186.1	603	73.3	775	65.4
Topeka, KS	104,034	103,809	96,414	225	0.2	32.2	264	95.5	381	92.7
Trenton–Ewing, NJ	143,390	143,168	133,287	222	0.2	638.4	400	33.8	655	27.5
Tucson, AZ	442,484	440,909	366,725	1,575	0.4	48.2	2,242	61.9	1,938	89.1
Tulsa, OK	413,446	409,820	366,250	3,626	0.9	65.9	3,565	57.0	2,616	86.7
Tuscaloosa, AL	98,116	97,534	84,309	582	0.6	37.6	743	43.9	623	56.5
Tyler, TX	88,716	87,309	71,710	1,407	1.6	96.3	262	70.6	266	75.6
Utica–Rome, NY	137,696	137,561	134,867	135	0.1	52.5	254	92.9	314	89.8
Valdosta, GA	57,794	57,433	48,172	361	0.6	36.4	660	57.7	852	58.6
Vallejo–Fairfield, CA	153,308	152,698	134,493	610	0.4	186.6	387	100.0	467	100.0
Victoria, TX	50,757	50,537	46,606	220	0.4	22.6	148	100.0	103	100.0
Vineland–Millville–Bridgeton, NJ	55,921	55,834	52,872	87	0.2	115.6	182	100.0	246	93.9
Virginia Beach–Norfolk–Newport News, VA–NC	690,208	686,300	622,872	3,908	0.6	262.5	5,559	53.1	3,966	79.4

[1]The April 1, 2010, estimates base population may differ from the April 1, 2010, Census count due to legal boundary updates, other geographic program changes, and Count Question Resolution actions.
[2]The April 1, 2000, housing estimates base reflects modifications to the Census 2000 population as documented in the Count Question Resolution program and geographic program revisions.
[3]Units per square mile was calculated on the basis of land area data from the 2010 census.
[4]Sample selected from a universe of 20,000 permit–issuing places.
[6]The portion of Sullivan city in Crawford County, MO is legally part of the St. Louis, MO–IL MSA. That portion is not included in these figures for the St. Louis, MSA.

Table B-9. Housing Units and Building Permits—*Continued*

Metropolitan statistical area and division	Housing units						New private housing units authorized by building permits[4]			
	2011 (July 1)	2010[1] (estimates base)	2000[2] (estimates base)	Change, 2010–2011		Units per square mile of land area, 2011[3]	2011	Percent single family, 2011	2010	Percent single family, 2010
				Number	Percent					
Visalia–Porterville, CA	142,931	141,696	119,640	1,235	0.9	29.6	922	77.9	1,367	79.4
Waco, TX	95,934	95,124	84,804	810	0.9	92.5	523	84.3	602	73.4
Warner Robins, GA	58,841	58,329	44,492	512	0.9	156.7	653	81.6	646	100.0
Washington–Arlington–Alexandria, DC–VA–MD–WV	2,231,441	2,213,693	1,890,126	17,748	0.8	398.6	19,657	49.1	13,065	72.6
Bethesda–Rockville–Frederick, MD	468,833	466,041	407,872	2,792	0.6	407.1	3,156	51.5	2,838	61.8
Washington–Arlington–Alexandria, DC–VA–MD–WV	1,762,608	1,747,652	1,482,254	14,956	0.9	396.4	16,501	48.6	10,227	75.6
Waterloo–Cedar Falls, IA	71,575	71,332	66,409	243	0.3	47.6	410	84.4	391	94.4
Wausau, WI	57,874	57,734	50,390	140	0.2	37.5	276	72.5	262	95.4
Wenatchee–East Wenatchee, WA	52,057	51,469	43,340	588	1.1	11.0	246	100.0	320	97.8
Wheeling, WV–OH	69,366	69,542	69,229	-176	-0.3	73.5	27	70.4	38	86.8
Wichita, KS	264,562	263,043	238,588	1,519	0.6	63.8	1,062	83.9	1,259	83.1
Wichita Falls, TX	64,843	64,823	62,161	20	0.0	24.8	170	71.2	187	84.0
Williamsport, PA	52,266	52,499	52,460	-233	-0.4	42.5	156	48.7	207	96.1
Wilmington, NC	207,145	205,642	151,843	1,503	0.7	108.5	1,831	84.4	1,830	81.7
Winchester, VA–WV	57,522	56,906	45,088	616	1.1	54.1	452	64.8	346	100.0
Winston–Salem, NC	215,474	214,375	183,146	1,099	0.5	148.0	1,412	65.2	1,201	75.9
Worcester, MA	328,586	326,788	298,180	1,798	0.6	217.5	791	91.8	1,391	76.7
Yakima, WA	85,904	85,474	79,175	430	0.5	20.0	438	68.0	624	55.0
York–Hanover, PA	179,769	178,671	156,740	1,098	0.6	198.8	638	91.2	1,059	81.0
Youngstown–Warren–Boardman, OH–PA	258,932	259,729	256,786	-797	-0.3	152.1	256	100.0	325	89.8
Yuba City, CA	61,413	61,493	50,970	-80	-0.1	49.8	146	53.4	150	100.0
Yuma, AZ	88,146	87,849	74,123	297	0.3	16.0	360	99.4	455	100.0

[1]The April 1, 2010, estimates base population may differ from the April 1, 2010, Census count due to legal boundary updates, other geographic program changes, and Count Question Resolution actions.
[2]The April 1, 2000, housing estimates base reflects modifications to the Census 2000 population as documented in the Count Question Resolution program and geographic program revisions.
[3]Units per square mile was calculated on the basis of land area data from the 2010 census.
[4]Sample selected from a universe of 20,000 permit–issuing places.

Table B-10. Housing Units, 2009–2011

Metropolitan statistical area and division	Total housing units	1 unit detached (percent)	With 2 or more vehicles available (percent)	Owner-occupied Ownership rate	Housing units with a mortgage Number	Median monthly owner costs (dollars)	Units with costs 30 percent or more of household income (percent)	Renter-occupied Number	Median monthly rent (dollars)	Units with rent 30 percent or more of household income (percent)
Abilene, TX	69,797	74.3	58.8	65.6	19,815	1,058	23.3	20,484	734	52.4
Akron, OH	312,697	69.3	57.8	68.6	134,763	1,310	31.0	88,398	733	53.2
Albany, GA	65,406	62.8	52.9	57.6	20,882	1,144	35.9	24,454	692	57.8
Albany–Schenectady–Troy, NY	393,696	57.2	54.4	65.8	151,281	1,634	30.8	118,702	866	48.3
Albuquerque, NM	374,457	66.1	59.1	67.1	161,387	1,326	36.3	112,530	760	50.4
Alexandria, LA	64,891	69.2	54.1	68.5	18,818	1,080	27.3	17,000	677	54.9
Allentown–Bethlehem–Easton, PA–NJ	342,505	56.8	60.2	72.0	151,795	1,685	37.7	87,420	883	53.2
Altoona, PA	56,237	70.4	55.7	72.8	20,643	1,004	26.0	14,138	596	46.7
Amarillo, TX	102,701	69.4	59.6	64.5	36,552	1,181	25.6	32,914	699	51.3
Ames, IA	36,861	52.2	61.1	54.8	12,599	1,315	22.2	15,818	702	54.0
Anchorage, AK	154,854	56.9	63.7	64.7	66,595	1,891	32.9	48,516	1,066	46.4
Anderson, IN	59,062	77.7	57.5	71.6	23,354	1,020	26.8	14,302	667	51.4
Anderson, SC	84,809	67.7	62.2	71.8	32,466	1,070	27.9	20,603	643	55.4
Ann Arbor, MI	147,546	56.3	54.8	61.3	60,019	1,798	34.0	51,721	873	54.3
Anniston–Oxford, AL	53,310	70.0	60.2	68.8	17,475	1,034	29.7	14,271	606	52.0
Appleton, WI	92,959	73.0	67.0	75.0	45,815	1,388	28.3	21,889	695	39.7
Asheville, NC	214,069	66.0	61.1	69.5	75,036	1,244	36.1	55,315	742	51.6
Athens–Clarke County, GA	81,725	57.8	61.7	58.7	26,690	1,296	31.9	27,212	749	60.7
Atlanta–Sandy Springs–Marietta, GA	2,166,002	67.0	59.8	66.4	990,464	1,579	37.7	634,089	936	54.0
Atlantic City–Hammonton, NJ	126,664	56.9	51.8	70.2	48,744	1,937	53.3	30,021	1,007	58.6
Auburn–Opelika, AL	62,601	51.9	62.8	62.4	22,331	1,216	33.5	20,850	728	59.9
Augusta–Richmond County, GA–SC	237,484	65.6	60.1	67.7	90,092	1,175	31.4	66,478	729	51.2
Austin–Round Rock–San Marcos, TX	709,474	59.1	59.2	57.7	275,835	1,662	32.8	274,674	947	51.6
Bakersfield–Delano, CA	284,897	71.1	60.5	58.6	107,832	1,538	42.9	104,374	852	55.9
Baltimore–Towson, MD	1,133,447	45.3	55.4	67.0	514,933	1,942	36.5	336,904	1,086	53.6
Bangor, ME	73,981	63.4	59.4	68.0	28,082	1,192	29.8	20,071	693	57.2
Barnstable Town, MA	160,402	81.7	57.3	78.3	48,668	1,897	49.4	20,975	1,111	60.4
Baton Rouge, LA	330,382	66.5	58.4	69.2	126,723	1,245	26.6	90,155	776	53.7
Battle Creek, MI	61,024	73.4	55.7	70.3	24,257	1,112	35.9	15,793	645	53.2
Bay City, MI	48,205	76.2	58.8	79.2	19,508	1,127	32.5	9,143	593	54.8
Beaumont–Port Arthur, TX	162,719	71.4	57.2	68.0	46,033	1,162	26.5	46,074	724	48.1
Bellingham, WA	90,804	63.1	62.6	62.7	34,384	1,635	43.1	29,881	865	54.5
Bend, OR	80,253	72.6	67.4	66.0	30,827	1,638	48.0	21,942	910	54.7
Billings, MT	70,603	67.0	65.0	70.5	30,166	1,241	30.6	19,232	678	43.4
Binghamton, NY	112,799	62.7	55.1	68.8	40,424	1,156	26.1	31,390	650	51.9
Birmingham–Hoover, AL	500,064	69.3	61.0	70.7	202,870	1,282	32.2	126,999	775	54.0
Bismarck, ND	48,010	58.6	67.7	73.6	21,212	1,294	22.3	11,914	619	42.7
Blacksburg–Christiansburg–Radford, VA	70,884	59.0	62.7	61.2	22,969	1,209	28.8	24,176	738	60.0
Bloomington, IN	84,409	60.9	57.4	61.3	30,643	1,090	29.5	29,010	730	63.4
Bloomington–Normal, IL	69,753	61.9	59.5	66.9	29,858	1,418	19.5	20,879	713	44.6
Boise City–Nampa, ID	246,480	74.7	65.9	68.9	116,510	1,324	38.1	69,967	773	52.0
Boston–Cambridge–Quincy, MA–NH	1,884,815	47.8	51.1	61.9	795,366	2,292	39.8	666,812	1,167	50.4
Boston–Quincy, MA	786,934	42.9	44.6	57.6	309,063	2,291	40.4	306,899	1,209	52.5
Cambridge–Newton–Framingham, MA	612,381	48.5	53.5	62.7	263,400	2,407	37.8	215,779	1,247	46.4
Peabody, MA	306,954	50.3	53.4	64.0	135,312	2,217	41.6	103,000	992	52.9
Rockingham County–Strafford County, NH	178,546	62.1	67.9	74.7	87,591	2,089	40.5	41,134	996	49.9
Boulder, CO	127,205	60.6	62.2	64.1	57,047	1,872	33.8	42,711	1,048	59.3
Bowling Green, KY	53,773	66.0	59.4	61.7	19,755	1,129	30.0	18,319	636	53.5
Bremerton–Silverdale, WA	107,560	68.9	65.6	66.4	47,653	1,766	38.4	32,855	990	51.5
Bridgeport–Stamford–Norwalk, CT	361,567	57.4	59.8	69.2	168,839	2,814	46.8	102,579	1,253	55.8
Brownsville–Harlingen, TX	142,004	63.9	53.0	67.4	35,245	1,081	40.9	37,588	636	53.4
Brunswick, GA	58,226	59.5	60.2	68.0	17,949	1,233	37.0	14,016	744	50.8
Buffalo–Niagara Falls, NY	519,018	59.1	48.5	66.4	194,661	1,265	27.4	156,739	690	52.4
Burlington, NC	66,658	65.8	61.8	68.1	26,535	1,193	33.1	19,204	704	51.2
Burlington–South Burlington, VT	92,527	59.8	61.3	68.2	41,972	1,743	35.8	26,778	964	57.8
Canton–Massillon, OH	178,940	74.9	59.9	70.9	74,924	1,155	30.5	46,723	646	49.8
Cape Coral–Fort Myers, FL	371,291	52.6	47.9	72.2	101,766	1,524	48.8	65,815	921	58.4
Cape Girardeau–Jackson, MO–IL	42,522	70.1	61.5	68.2	15,481	1,047	27.8	11,764	617	47.3
Carson City, NV	23,546	58.3	60.6	60.7	8,094	1,700	33.9	8,279	883	49.4
Casper, WY	33,928	71.8	69.0	70.7	13,601	1,256	22.6	8,930	776	39.9

Table B-10. Housing Units, 2009–2011—*Continued*

Metropolitan statistical area and division	Total housing units	1 unit detached (percent)	With 2 or more vehicles available (percent)	Owner-occupied Ownership rate	Owner-occupied Housing units with a mortgage Number	Median monthly owner costs (dollars)	Units with costs 30 percent or more of household income (percent)	Renter-occupied Number	Median monthly rent (dollars)	Units with rent 30 percent or more of household income (percent)
Cedar Rapids, IA	112,439	70.9	64.4	74.8	53,415	1,235	21.7	26,274	635	41.3
Champaign–Urbana, IL	101,258	58.1	51.9	57.3	34,611	1,285	24.8	38,949	775	59.4
Charleston, WV	141,501	70.2	55.1	74.9	49,100	974	22.6	31,445	638	44.2
Charleston–North Charleston–Summerville, SC..	299,264	60.2	57.4	65.8	116,906	1,486	39.6	86,710	918	55.7
Charlotte–Gastonia–Rock Hill, NC–SC	738,811	67.0	60.1	66.8	344,478	1,405	33.2	221,487	820	51.3
Charlottesville, VA	89,182	66.6	61.6	64.8	33,939	1,620	32.6	27,158	1,041	54.4
Chattanooga, TN–GA	235,024	70.1	60.9	68.5	89,375	1,164	31.3	65,851	691	51.4
Cheyenne, WY	40,572	64.4	65.8	68.4	17,628	1,333	28.2	11,895	714	38.7
Chicago–Joliet–Naperville, IL–IN–WI	3,797,596	51.9	52.3	66.5	1,667,835	1,911	43.6	1,144,589	937	53.5
Chicago–Joliet–Naperville, IL	3,173,552	48.4	50.3	65.0	1,363,767	1,958	45.1	997,448	948	53.7
Gary, IN	294,225	72.5	57.5	72.0	130,947	1,265	30.5	72,818	781	52.0
Lake County–Kenosha County, IL–WI	329,819	67.4	66.3	75.4	173,121	2,070	42.0	74,323	943	52.3
Chico, CA	95,847	62.8	59.4	60.3	32,925	1,586	47.3	33,401	868	59.7
Cincinnati–Middletown, OH–KY–IN	917,554	65.0	60.0	68.5	410,499	1,406	29.8	255,438	719	50.8
Clarksville, TN–KY	114,510	69.9	63.2	61.9	42,986	1,133	29.5	38,165	767	48.1
Cleveland, TN	49,421	69.7	63.3	69.5	17,232	1,110	31.5	13,343	670	55.9
Cleveland–Elyria–Mentor, OH	956,106	65.0	52.4	66.8	387,269	1,399	34.9	280,132	726	52.0
Coeur d'Alene, ID	63,398	70.8	68.6	69.7	28,226	1,360	40.8	16,958	792	51.6
College Station–Bryan, TX	95,332	52.9	58.6	50.9	23,808	1,289	28.8	39,852	819	65.4
Colorado Springs, CO	265,856	66.4	63.5	64.6	123,182	1,532	35.3	86,398	852	49.3
Columbia, MO	74,233	61.0	61.0	59.1	28,733	1,245	24.1	27,870	759	53.7
Columbia, SC	332,404	64.6	59.9	67.9	138,614	1,206	29.8	94,478	798	52.5
Columbus, GA–AL	128,167	66.8	56.5	59.1	43,727	1,205	34.9	44,819	769	53.6
Columbus, IN	33,139	75.6	67.3	71.6	14,585	1,155	22.8	8,582	764	38.2
Columbus, OH	793,224	61.6	58.7	62.6	340,479	1,470	31.0	265,659	784	49.6
Corpus Christi, TX	183,230	66.8	53.6	61.4	51,115	1,352	34.1	59,582	806	53.4
Corvallis, OR	36,271	60.0	59.1	57.6	11,991	1,616	35.5	14,167	769	61.4
Crestview–Fort Walton Beach–Destin, FL	92,384	60.2	60.5	67.9	31,680	1,488	39.6	22,766	965	56.3
Cumberland, MD–WV	46,357	72.8	54.5	69.5	15,484	1,087	31.1	12,223	568	53.1
Dallas–Fort Worth–Arlington, TX	2,508,595	63.6	60.7	61.9	1,017,129	1,586	32.0	867,180	877	48.7
Dallas–Plano–Irving, TX	1,664,339	61.9	59.8	60.5	669,692	1,642	32.9	596,435	886	48.3
Fort Worth–Arlington, TX	844,256	67.0	62.4	64.6	347,437	1,478	30.2	270,745	858	49.5
Dalton, GA	55,971	59.6	61.2	67.9	19,663	1,066	38.6	15,508	670	44.3
Danville, IL	36,292	79.2	54.4	69.9	12,374	969	25.2	9,491	606	49.6
Danville, VA	53,742	70.6	59.6	69.6	17,152	1,004	34.1	13,589	600	55.3
Davenport–Moline–Rock Island, IA–IL	167,187	72.6	60.1	71.5	70,728	1,167	25.5	44,056	639	45.0
Dayton, OH	385,233	70.0	57.1	65.4	155,268	1,255	31.1	118,940	716	53.1
Decatur, AL	66,435	70.8	65.0	74.2	25,531	1,060	26.4	15,345	577	44.8
Decatur, IL	50,432	78.1	56.0	69.1	18,113	1,057	22.0	13,836	639	48.2
Deltona–Daytona Beach–Ormond Beach, FL	254,397	64.6	51.8	73.6	86,678	1,381	46.8	51,140	876	60.1
Denver–Aurora–Broomfield, CO[1]	1,079,841	59.3	59.9	64.2	509,142	1,717	35.1	356,748	914	51.3
Des Moines–West Des Moines, IA	240,644	67.5	64.1	71.7	119,045	1,369	25.2	63,324	742	45.6
Detroit–Warren–Livonia, MI	1,885,676	69.9	54.4	71.2	802,929	1,485	37.4	474,138	813	56.2
Detroit–Livonia–Dearborn, MI	820,903	69.1	45.2	65.4	280,476	1,342	40.3	232,385	776	61.5
Warren–Troy–Farmington Hills, MI	1,064,773	70.6	60.7	75.2	522,453	1,574	35.8	241,753	849	51.2
Dothan, AL	67,021	69.6	59.9	67.6	21,793	1,027	27.9	18,555	618	46.7
Dover, DE	65,536	65.0	63.1	73.3	28,235	1,517	38.5	15,223	952	56.8
Dubuque, IA	38,996	71.4	61.4	73.6	17,550	1,179	23.7	9,822	639	45.1
Duluth, MN–WI	141,671	73.6	60.6	71.5	52,790	1,188	30.3	33,837	642	54.1
Durham–Chapel Hill, NC	223,399	60.7	57.2	61.3	89,120	1,464	30.5	77,790	807	52.8
Eau Claire, WI	69,371	68.0	62.3	67.4	27,946	1,275	29.9	20,857	666	49.9
El Centro, CA	56,130	63.1	58.2	57.4	19,373	1,533	47.2	20,805	717	56.8
Elizabethtown, KY	49,492	67.0	63.7	64.6	19,726	1,110	26.8	15,474	714	42.8
Elkhart–Goshen, IN	77,745	71.8	59.7	73.2	36,490	1,074	30.6	18,639	702	50.5
Elmira, NY	38,379	67.1	51.0	66.2	13,992	1,077	21.8	12,127	688	48.0
El Paso, TX	271,247	67.4	57.6	61.9	94,860	1,106	35.7	95,909	688	51.4
Erie, PA	119,190	64.9	50.5	67.7	46,201	1,124	28.7	35,223	634	51.1
Eugene–Springfield, OR	156,338	61.9	58.2	59.0	56,466	1,497	41.9	59,527	809	58.5
Evansville, IN–KY	159,358	73.6	61.1	70.8	66,312	1,083	23.4	41,614	669	49.8
Fairbanks, AK	41,962	60.2	62.1	59.3	14,712	1,878	33.4	14,688	1,134	48.7
Fargo, ND–MN	92,319	49.8	61.9	58.2	35,285	1,351	23.4	36,331	640	46.0
Farmington, NM	49,462	58.9	65.3	74.8	16,283	1,223	26.5	10,548	728	41.2

[1]The Denver–Aurora metropolitan statistical area includes Broomfield County. Broomfield County, CO, was formed from parts of Adams, Boulder, Jefferson, and Weld Counties on November 15, 2001, and is coextensive with Broomfield city. For the purposes of defining and presenting data for the Denver–Aurora metropolitan statistical area, Broomfield city is treated as if it were a county when data are available to do so. In many cases, the data were not available.

Table B-10. Housing Units, 2009–2011—*Continued*

Metropolitan statistical area and division	Total housing units	1 unit detached (percent)	With 2 or more vehicles available (percent)	Owner-occupied Ownership rate	Housing units with a mortgage Number	Median monthly owner costs (dollars)	Units with costs 30 percent or more of household income (percent)	Renter-occupied Number	Median monthly rent (dollars)	Units with rent 30 percent or more of household income (percent)
Fayetteville, NC	154,180	64.5	59.0	58.0	57,304	1,233	33.1	56,495	827	48.5
Fayetteville–Springdale–Rogers, AR–MO	198,908	68.4	62.8	63.6	75,765	1,191	27.6	63,075	691	46.2
Flagstaff, AZ	63,454	59.4	57.9	60.0	16,390	1,487	36.7	17,941	945	56.0
Flint, MI	191,995	72.6	52.7	69.9	74,919	1,244	37.0	49,606	694	61.0
Florence, SC	89,077	62.1	55.8	68.4	31,208	1,021	28.2	24,733	625	50.4
Florence–Muscle Shoals, AL	69,617	75.4	62.4	71.4	24,201	1,019	29.6	17,465	587	53.0
Fond du Lac, WI	43,959	68.5	65.6	71.0	19,462	1,325	32.2	11,939	657	40.6
Fort Collins–Loveland, CO	132,854	67.4	68.3	65.8	59,316	1,573	35.6	40,921	925	57.6
Fort Smith, AR–OK	129,194	74.1	61.1	69.4	45,754	916	26.7	34,692	581	46.9
Fort Wayne, IN	178,218	74.6	60.4	71.5	80,197	1,052	22.8	45,703	639	44.0
Fresno, CA	316,029	67.5	56.2	54.6	115,670	1,621	43.7	129,799	858	57.4
Gadsden, AL	47,439	75.5	60.9	74.4	16,365	1,082	35.9	10,294	622	51.3
Gainesville, FL	120,215	50.0	52.7	55.4	35,284	1,428	37.8	45,583	883	62.6
Gainesville, GA	68,939	73.0	65.7	69.0	29,858	1,409	39.4	19,078	807	50.9
Glens Falls, NY	67,625	72.6	60.9	72.7	24,756	1,404	34.0	14,552	796	50.7
Goldsboro, NC	52,991	57.6	59.7	61.9	18,348	1,138	32.8	18,159	660	47.9
Grand Forks, ND–MN	43,989	55.2	59.4	59.2	14,231	1,254	25.1	16,185	653	47.9
Grand Junction, CO	62,755	71.9	66.0	72.9	29,899	1,423	38.8	15,880	827	54.9
Grand Rapids–Wyoming, MI	323,865	68.6	61.6	73.2	146,430	1,290	32.8	77,892	715	52.2
Great Falls, MT	37,310	63.5	64.5	67.5	13,613	1,147	31.0	10,713	590	39.0
Greeley, CO	96,445	71.9	69.0	70.2	47,843	1,531	34.8	26,628	799	56.7
Green Bay, WI	137,373	68.3	63.7	70.0	59,825	1,368	30.8	36,745	660	43.1
Greensboro–High Point, NC	323,125	66.1	58.4	65.7	129,749	1,207	34.2	97,848	704	52.4
Greenville, NC	83,299	49.6	56.1	56.9	27,898	1,236	32.6	30,977	693	54.7
Greenville–Mauldin–Easley, SC	277,668	64.8	59.6	68.3	108,353	1,180	29.5	76,605	709	51.4
Gulfport–Biloxi, MS	114,907	66.3	60.5	68.0	37,054	1,256	38.8	30,143	835	55.4
Hagerstown–Martinsburg, MD–WV	115,438	65.4	60.4	69.3	48,643	1,457	34.8	31,620	782	49.8
Hanford–Corcoran, CA	43,936	71.7	64.4	52.8	15,818	1,511	40.3	19,137	870	49.7
Harrisburg–Carlisle, PA	241,212	55.9	58.2	68.9	100,683	1,426	29.2	68,982	815	43.0
Harrisonburg, VA	51,279	58.4	67.4	62.1	17,749	1,264	34.3	17,070	801	50.3
Hartford–West Hartford–East Hartford, CT	507,490	59.6	57.9	68.7	228,148	1,947	35.8	146,651	953	51.9
Hattiesburg, MS	62,071	64.3	58.3	63.8	20,532	1,166	29.0	19,685	694	58.2
Hickory–Lenoir–Morganton, NC	162,677	66.6	65.8	73.1	61,216	1,023	30.2	37,109	624	50.2
Hinesville–Fort Stewart, GA	32,664	53.5	63.3	54.8	11,184	1,220	34.8	12,723	844	49.7
Holland–Grand Haven, MI	102,561	69.4	69.2	78.8	50,526	1,323	29.7	19,845	750	49.3
Honolulu, HI	337,046	46.8	55.0	56.0	120,416	2,430	47.7	135,894	1,391	57.2
Hot Springs, AR	50,626	65.4	57.0	70.0	15,009	1,029	36.5	11,730	718	52.0
Houma–Bayou Cane–Thibodaux, LA	82,559	70.4	60.3	75.1	28,078	1,150	23.3	18,544	701	47.3
Houston–Sugar Land–Baytown, TX	2,315,153	62.1	59.3	62.4	861,364	1,578	33.2	766,248	870	49.7
Huntington–Ashland, WV–KY–OH	131,069	71.7	55.1	69.0	40,708	960	24.7	35,556	603	52.7
Huntsville, AL	182,206	71.2	64.6	71.2	80,080	1,209	22.3	46,747	703	46.9
Idaho Falls, ID	48,551	72.5	71.7	75.1	22,577	1,211	30.0	10,949	685	49.4
Indianapolis–Carmel, IN	758,339	68.4	60.0	66.9	344,954	1,279	27.3	221,660	771	51.8
Iowa City, IA	65,621	52.3	59.1	62.3	26,568	1,393	25.5	23,319	783	56.3
Ithaca, NY	41,703	49.6	48.0	54.3	12,717	1,475	27.7	17,678	925	58.5
Jackson, MI	69,470	76.1	59.1	74.4	29,407	1,218	33.8	15,306	710	51.0
Jackson, MS	222,690	70.5	59.8	67.6	83,901	1,170	29.5	63,556	781	54.4
Jackson, TN	48,840	73.3	56.5	68.4	17,662	1,130	33.5	12,912	697	58.6
Jacksonville, FL	599,167	62.4	57.5	67.5	245,013	1,501	40.8	164,283	939	54.1
Jacksonville, NC	68,654	59.7	63.4	56.7	24,195	1,264	37.0	25,653	916	53.2
Janesville, WI	68,461	73.5	62.7	72.2	32,259	1,294	35.3	17,512	733	56.1
Jefferson City, MO	63,643	73.4	64.1	72.3	25,738	1,098	22.7	15,753	594	41.6
Johnson City, TN	93,974	66.7	63.0	68.8	30,638	1,039	32.4	25,932	609	50.2
Johnstown, PA	65,592	72.5	55.6	73.2	21,264	968	24.4	15,632	543	43.6
Jonesboro, AR	51,546	69.8	58.3	59.4	16,415	958	20.9	18,957	612	49.9
Joplin, MO	75,067	76.4	62.1	69.2	29,375	973	28.9	20,356	639	47.6
Kalamazoo–Portage, MI	146,799	66.9	57.1	67.8	58,747	1,249	31.6	41,106	688	59.5
Kankakee–Bradley, IL	45,273	71.6	58.0	69.4	18,344	1,414	37.5	12,564	774	51.4
Kansas City, MO–KS	883,811	69.9	60.8	67.5	387,310	1,434	28.2	257,571	798	47.8
Kennewick–Pasco–Richland, WA	93,372	64.9	68.7	67.7	40,966	1,326	23.0	28,179	745	44.2
Killeen–Temple–Fort Hood, TX	160,113	63.7	60.4	57.4	47,393	1,240	29.0	55,165	847	45.9

Table B-10. Housing Units, 2009–2011—*Continued*

Metropolitan statistical area and division	Total housing units	1 unit detached (percent)	With 2 or more vehicles available (percent)	Owner-occupied				Renter-occupied		
				Ownership rate	Housing units with a mortgage			Number	Median monthly rent (dollars)	Units with rent 30 percent or more of household income (percent)
					Number	Median monthly owner costs (dollars)	Units with costs 30 percent or more of household income (percent)			
Kingsport–Bristol–Bristol, TN–VA	147,067	68.8	63.4	73.6	50,664	997	29.1	34,477	583	46.8
Kingston, NY	83,664	68.9	58.8	69.4	31,775	1,884	43.9	21,382	986	57.6
Knoxville, TN	315,962	68.4	58.8	69.0	125,776	1,203	30.1	89,108	717	50.4
Kokomo, IN	45,640	76.3	60.3	72.1	20,086	1,037	22.4	11,503	634	52.8
La Crosse, WI–MN	57,042	65.0	62.9	67.8	23,727	1,341	27.2	17,197	692	50.7
Lafayette, IN	84,630	64.1	58.9	57.5	31,478	1,129	24.0	32,850	752	58.5
Lafayette, LA	115,825	65.0	56.8	68.3	42,052	1,217	27.7	32,858	731	46.5
Lake Charles, LA	85,517	69.4	56.2	71.9	27,968	1,063	26.8	20,810	720	50.3
Lake Havasu City–Kingman, AZ	111,123	60.6	57.1	71.1	33,521	1,138	45.2	23,312	805	52.5
Lakeland–Winter Haven, FL	281,173	59.3	51.3	71.3	90,879	1,292	41.2	63,148	846	58.8
Lancaster, PA	203,314	56.2	60.8	69.6	87,659	1,477	34.0	58,927	838	50.1
Lansing–East Lansing, MI	199,050	66.5	57.9	66.3	83,038	1,358	31.4	60,428	742	56.3
Laredo, TX	73,699	66.2	57.8	62.5	24,470	1,348	45.9	25,001	734	60.2
Las Cruces, NM	81,818	56.0	62.7	64.7	27,702	1,135	36.1	26,036	655	58.6
Las Vegas–Paradise, NV	841,950	58.0	53.3	55.4	305,322	1,700	46.9	313,332	1,014	53.1
Lawrence, KS	46,763	53.6	63.9	50.6	16,263	1,459	29.4	21,316	849	55.7
Lawton, OK	50,935	70.4	58.1	56.5	16,905	1,091	25.5	19,437	731	42.7
Lebanon, PA	55,695	59.0	64.1	72.7	23,477	1,363	29.4	14,128	689	46.2
Lewiston, ID–WA	27,330	68.1	65.8	70.0	10,682	1,187	30.5	7,447	643	46.5
Lewiston–Auburn, ME	49,112	56.6	56.4	65.9	20,342	1,350	36.3	15,030	679	49.5
Lexington–Fayette, KY	209,438	64.9	57.2	59.9	82,598	1,271	26.3	76,111	711	49.6
Lima, OH	44,970	73.6	58.2	69.5	17,397	1,067	26.7	12,423	620	55.6
Lincoln, NE	127,967	61.4	62.2	61.1	51,784	1,338	25.4	46,839	692	45.7
Little Rock–North Little Rock–Conway, AR	307,699	66.8	59.1	65.2	119,585	1,156	25.3	94,752	738	49.1
Logan, UT–ID	41,671	70.4	72.1	65.4	17,959	1,249	34.1	13,599	652	46.4
Longview, TX	87,415	69.2	60.6	69.4	27,908	1,110	26.4	23,876	711	43.6
Longview, WA	43,483	67.5	63.1	65.6	17,340	1,401	38.4	13,805	701	59.7
Los Angeles–Long Beach–Santa Ana, CA	4,495,216	49.8	57.8	50.0	1,607,388	2,485	53.7	2,098,003	1,228	58.4
Los Angeles–Long Beach–Glendale, CA	3,445,921	49.6	55.2	47.1	1,161,575	2,419	54.9	1,695,132	1,174	58.8
Santa Ana–Anaheim–Irvine, CA	1,049,295	50.7	66.3	59.2	445,813	2,668	50.5	402,871	1,457	56.8
Louisville/Jefferson County, KY–IN	560,298	69.5	58.0	68.5	241,804	1,214	28.8	158,943	698	48.1
Lubbock, TX	118,107	66.9	58.9	58.5	38,000	1,161	26.7	44,165	746	53.6
Lynchburg, VA	112,916	69.5	63.8	71.7	44,241	1,180	32.4	27,835	697	53.5
Macon, GA	101,991	67.5	55.2	63.4	34,205	1,239	37.1	30,969	720	60.9
Madera–Chowchilla, CA	49,145	81.6	65.9	61.2	18,107	1,689	55.3	16,201	849	50.7
Madison, WI	253,160	56.6	57.8	62.1	109,814	1,685	33.8	89,995	859	50.9
Manchester–Nashua, NH	166,174	56.7	63.3	67.9	78,524	2,064	39.1	49,272	1,011	50.1
Manhattan, KS	51,573	54.4	65.3	49.6	14,797	1,296	27.7	22,904	844	48.1
Mankato–North Mankato, MN	39,139	65.0	66.0	69.1	16,650	1,325	29.6	11,248	684	52.2
Mansfield, OH	54,550	72.3	57.8	69.6	20,272	1,104	29.4	14,712	600	39.4
McAllen–Edinburg–Mission, TX	248,689	65.6	54.7	69.1	73,632	1,076	39.6	65,836	615	57.1
Medford, OR	91,024	64.4	59.7	60.7	32,144	1,522	48.2	32,867	850	63.2
Memphis, TN–MS–AR	551,323	68.8	54.9	63.4	218,093	1,346	35.3	175,324	808	57.8
Merced, CA	83,693	72.8	61.4	53.7	29,162	1,507	45.8	34,378	826	56.1
Miami–Fort Lauderdale–Pompano Beach, FL	2,465,506	42.3	49.0	63.8	860,927	1,840	55.8	723,503	1,100	64.3
Fort Lauderdale–Pompano Beach–Deerfield Beach, FL	810,427	40.9	50.0	66.4	310,837	1,857	54.3	222,279	1,151	63.5
Miami–Miami Beach–Kendall, FL	989,772	40.9	48.3	56.6	323,357	1,835	59.1	354,197	1,050	65.7
West Palm Beach–Boca Raton–Boynton Beach, FL	665,307	46.2	48.8	71.8	226,733	1,821	53.0	147,027	1,127	62.1
Michigan City–La Porte, IN	48,447	78.1	61.3	74.8	21,340	1,094	29.0	10,699	682	54.4
Midland, TX	54,510	66.0	62.8	68.5	19,019	1,341	26.2	15,655	896	45.0
Milwaukee–Waukesha–West Allis, WI	670,319	54.5	53.4	61.5	269,752	1,632	35.6	236,776	790	52.2
Minneapolis–St. Paul–Bloomington, MN–WI	1,355,786	60.7	61.0	71.3	700,898	1,718	33.7	365,478	869	50.6
Missoula, MT	50,246	60.1	63.3	58.8	17,161	1,482	40.0	18,648	727	59.4
Mobile, AL	178,550	72.9	57.6	67.0	66,638	1,199	33.1	51,563	736	58.8
Modesto, CA	179,633	73.9	62.3	59.0	71,894	1,748	49.5	68,197	968	59.6
Monroe, LA	75,860	66.2	49.4	62.0	22,037	1,025	26.8	24,964	641	53.7
Monroe, MI	62,902	75.2	65.3	79.8	31,561	1,399	36.7	11,859	773	54.1
Montgomery, AL	161,693	70.8	59.8	67.9	65,021	1,193	31.6	44,846	793	55.5
Morgantown, WV	58,516	55.9	55.5	63.4	16,071	1,098	21.0	17,964	678	53.7
Morristown, TN	61,465	67.6	64.4	73.7	21,266	968	33.4	14,154	613	49.6
Mount Vernon–Anacortes, WA	51,566	69.5	66.5	67.2	20,465	1,743	46.3	14,900	917	51.2

Table B-10. Housing Units, 2009–2011—*Continued*

Metropolitan statistical area and division	Total housing units	1 unit detached (percent)	With 2 or more vehicles available (percent)	Owner-occupied Ownership rate	Housing units with a mortgage Number	Median monthly owner costs (dollars)	Units with costs 30 percent or more of household income (percent)	Renter-occupied Number	Median monthly rent (dollars)	Units with rent 30 percent or more of household income (percent)
Muncie, IN	52,318	71.6	56.7	64.3	19,130	950	26.8	16,396	651	60.1
Muskegon–Norton Shores, MI	73,510	75.7	56.4	73.8	29,767	1,090	34.4	16,950	655	58.4
Myrtle Beach–North Myrtle Beach–Conway, SC	186,555	45.5	58.5	70.4	47,728	1,274	43.7	33,169	808	59.8
Napa, CA	54,792	68.2	64.0	60.9	21,462	2,531	47.5	19,607	1,291	56.4
Naples–Marco Island, FL	197,519	40.0	51.4	74.8	48,895	1,840	54.6	29,933	966	58.8
Nashville–Davidson—Murfreesboro—Franklin, TN	668,800	65.4	62.6	66.8	291,841	1,379	32.8	201,112	810	51.2
New Haven–Milford, CT	362,299	53.5	54.2	63.7	149,373	2,059	42.6	119,644	1,040	57.8
New Orleans–Metairie–Kenner, LA	539,478	60.8	50.7	63.0	174,898	1,461	36.9	168,247	909	58.3
New York–Northern New Jersey–Long Island, NY–NJ–PA	7,530,183	36.3	36.7	51.9	2,408,262	2,715	49.3	3,275,765	1,179	53.6
Edison–New Brunswick, NJ	955,064	63.7	59.0	74.3	437,334	2,455	46.4	218,182	1,245	54.4
Nassau–Suffolk, NY	1,038,928	78.0	66.4	80.1	514,367	2,932	50.9	187,111	1,460	57.1
Newark–Union, NJ–PA	852,449	53.8	52.8	63.1	353,190	2,704	47.5	282,295	1,116	54.1
New York–White Plains–Wayne, NY–NJ	4,683,742	18.3	22.8	39.3	1,103,371	2,722	50.2	2,588,177	1,164	53.3
Niles–Benton Harbor, MI	76,879	76.3	55.9	72.7	27,785	1,128	30.6	16,516	620	54.4
North Port–Bradenton–Sarasota, FL	401,496	55.2	49.0	73.4	122,215	1,575	49.8	79,305	953	58.0
Norwich–New London, CT	121,121	66.1	61.4	68.8	51,430	1,915	38.5	33,552	994	48.5
Ocala, FL	164,044	65.1	49.9	77.6	56,840	1,156	47.0	29,918	819	60.7
Ocean City, NJ	98,225	51.3	53.3	74.2	20,020	1,958	50.9	11,191	988	59.8
Odessa, TX	53,067	60.2	58.2	64.6	14,222	1,104	26.5	17,430	710	42.9
Ogden–Clearfield, UT	187,274	73.0	72.5	75.0	100,755	1,436	30.5	44,274	809	44.6
Oklahoma City, OK	540,003	71.9	60.6	65.6	209,386	1,212	28.1	164,850	726	50.5
Olympia, WA	108,566	69.0	65.0	67.5	49,591	1,735	38.8	32,655	979	49.0
Omaha–Council Bluffs, NE–IA	363,093	70.9	61.6	67.4	164,092	1,394	26.5	108,646	764	46.7
Orlando–Kissimmee–Sanford, FL	943,949	59.6	56.6	64.6	357,390	1,622	47.9	269,923	1,000	62.0
Oshkosh–Neenah, WI	73,418	65.9	61.3	66.5	30,281	1,297	28.4	22,795	644	44.5
Owensboro, KY	49,440	73.2	63.2	71.0	18,259	970	24.9	12,673	602	43.7
Oxnard–Thousand Oaks–Ventura, CA	281,818	63.3	68.9	64.6	134,623	2,543	48.9	94,198	1,422	56.9
Palm Bay–Melbourne–Titusville, FL	270,038	64.1	54.4	73.8	105,876	1,387	41.8	57,471	888	57.2
Palm Coast, FL	48,701	77.7	59.9	80.0	18,116	1,443	49.6	7,051	1,070	60.7
Panama City–Lynn Haven–Panama City Beach, FL	99,694	52.5	58.6	63.9	25,824	1,391	42.1	24,350	929	52.6
Parkersburg–Marietta–Vienna, WV–OH	75,179	73.9	59.7	76.3	27,277	984	26.9	15,408	581	50.0
Pascagoula, MS	69,649	73.0	64.7	72.4	24,205	1,242	36.1	16,099	842	54.3
Pensacola–Ferry Pass–Brent, FL	201,664	68.6	57.7	69.0	75,337	1,339	40.5	51,740	871	56.9
Peoria, IL	164,336	77.2	60.1	72.8	70,074	1,193	23.3	41,096	670	45.6
Philadelphia–Camden–Wilmington, PA–NJ–DE–MD	2,435,028	44.6	51.2	68.7	1,070,717	1,856	38.0	694,927	960	54.3
Camden, NJ	490,701	62.6	59.7	74.5	250,803	2,043	42.1	117,012	1,023	55.3
Philadelphia, PA	1,658,042	36.9	47.3	66.7	683,935	1,814	37.2	500,365	942	54.1
Wilmington, DE–MD–NJ	286,285	58.3	58.7	70.4	135,979	1,708	34.5	77,550	983	54.0
Phoenix–Mesa–Glendale, AZ	1,801,538	64.2	55.0	64.3	726,338	1,546	40.3	541,565	916	52.4
Pine Bluff, AR	41,866	69.8	54.6	66.1	12,544	916	27.4	12,169	620	52.4
Pittsburgh, PA	1,101,964	67.1	52.5	70.2	417,033	1,242	27.1	293,654	679	47.0
Pittsfield, MA	68,519	64.0	48.7	68.4	24,097	1,454	38.3	17,486	744	51.7
Pocatello, ID	36,229	65.7	67.0	70.3	15,532	1,096	30.2	9,712	591	48.6
Portland–South Portland–Biddeford, ME	263,005	66.3	60.2	70.8	107,567	1,607	36.6	61,965	882	51.4
Portland–Vancouver–Hillsboro, OR–WA	926,114	61.9	58.6	61.4	402,974	1,782	41.3	334,000	899	52.4
Port St. Lucie, FL	215,284	61.8	52.4	76.0	74,467	1,520	52.1	39,276	978	61.7
Poughkeepsie–Newburgh–Middletown, NY	255,923	63.0	60.5	69.5	117,803	2,267	45.7	71,208	1,103	54.9
Prescott, AZ	110,571	64.7	58.0	70.8	38,517	1,309	47.5	26,495	788	54.6
Providence–New Bedford–Fall River, RI–MA	694,298	53.9	54.2	62.0	276,816	1,904	42.3	235,445	863	50.8
Provo–Orem, UT	152,359	66.9	75.1	68.4	77,123	1,530	36.2	45,627	826	51.3
Pueblo, CO	69,638	75.2	58.3	66.9	27,042	1,171	37.3	20,552	698	57.1
Punta Gorda, FL	100,624	68.5	47.6	77.7	28,338	1,372	52.8	15,687	898	55.3
Racine, WI	82,195	67.8	59.3	68.4	36,638	1,489	37.0	23,885	739	51.6
Raleigh–Cary, NC	467,429	63.2	63.3	67.9	228,491	1,499	29.8	135,745	858	48.1
Rapid City, SD	56,065	62.8	66.3	66.7	22,855	1,289	31.9	16,710	712	46.4
Reading, PA	164,972	54.5	60.4	72.2	76,394	1,479	34.6	43,080	808	53.7
Redding, CA	77,310	67.9	59.8	65.0	28,569	1,592	50.6	24,038	885	61.5
Reno–Sparks, NV	187,078	59.5	59.9	59.0	71,869	1,770	44.1	67,027	901	54.0
Richmond, VA	532,432	70.7	62.4	68.4	240,174	1,599	35.1	150,402	936	51.7

Table B-10. Housing Units, 2009–2011—*Continued*

Metropolitan statistical area and division	Total housing units	1 unit detached (percent)	With 2 or more vehicles available (percent)	Owner-occupied				Renter-occupied		
				Ownership rate	Housing units with a mortgage			Number	Median monthly rent (dollars)	Units with rent 30 percent or more of household income (percent)
					Number	Median monthly owner costs (dollars)	Units with costs 30 percent or more of household income (percent)			
Riverside–San Bernardino–Ontario, CA..............	1,502,164	69.0	65.0	65.4	636,646	1,950	52.4	441,019	1,106	60.8
Roanoke, VA	144,875	72.4	61.9	70.9	59,930	1,283	33.5	37,182	714	45.9
Rochester, MN	78,546	72.3	65.0	77.7	39,854	1,436	27.2	16,227	768	47.4
Rochester, NY	455,902	65.3	54.6	68.7	197,609	1,336	29.0	130,342	766	54.7
Rockford, IL	145,943	69.8	58.6	69.7	65,420	1,326	35.0	39,804	712	54.7
Rocky Mount, NC..	67,152	64.1	57.7	63.0	22,927	1,143	33.7	21,947	716	50.1
Rome, GA..	40,553	72.7	60.7	65.3	14,026	1,204	35.9	12,191	707	55.6
Sacramento—Arden-Arcade—Roseville, CA......	872,477	67.6	59.8	60.7	359,727	2,060	47.3	306,910	1,036	57.8
Saginaw–Saginaw Township North, MI..............	86,781	76.5	56.4	72.9	34,098	1,137	35.3	20,797	695	56.5
St. Cloud, MN..	78,195	70.5	66.5	72.0	34,900	1,360	29.9	20,198	700	51.7
St. George, UT	57,868	71.1	66.8	69.7	20,648	1,546	49.8	14,088	912	53.2
St. Joseph, MO–KS.......................................	53,652	73.5	59.7	68.7	19,807	1,061	24.5	14,716	637	46.1
St. Louis, MO–IL²	1,236,978	69.2	58.4	70.6	547,548	1,366	30.2	326,885	765	50.6
Salem, OR...	151,419	64.2	60.5	61.3	60,744	1,504	41.9	54,491	770	52.9
Salinas, CA...	139,007	62.9	63.1	50.0	45,122	2,316	52.9	62,686	1,167	57.2
Salisbury, MD	52,376	69.4	59.8	65.2	19,682	1,451	39.8	15,466	928	60.5
Salt Lake City, UT	411,267	64.6	65.3	67.9	192,886	1,544	36.3	119,432	861	51.7
San Angelo, TX	47,539	71.9	58.0	66.7	15,292	1,085	27.4	14,175	695	52.2
San Antonio–New Braunfels, TX	840,750	68.1	58.3	63.9	313,421	1,334	30.2	271,090	805	49.0
San Diego–Carlsbad–San Marcos, CA...............	1,165,610	51.4	61.0	54.1	438,635	2,431	51.8	488,029	1,267	58.8
Sandusky, OH..	37,849	73.4	59.6	68.8	13,905	1,238	30.7	9,853	695	47.1
San Francisco–Oakland–Fremont, CA	1,743,042	49.5	53.8	54.4	662,052	2,868	49.4	733,159	1,354	50.8
Oakland–Fremont–Hayward, CA...................	983,477	58.3	59.5	58.6	412,777	2,671	48.8	376,072	1,260	52.9
San Francisco–San Mateo–Redwood City, CA ...	759,565	38.2	46.3	48.8	249,275	3,279	50.3	357,087	1,469	48.5
San Jose–Sunnyvale–Santa Clara, CA..............	650,066	54.3	66.5	57.7	268,696	3,056	48.4	261,352	1,460	47.0
San Luis Obispo–Paso Robles, CA..................	117,340	68.2	65.0	59.2	40,837	2,239	52.3	41,170	1,175	60.7
Santa Barbara–Santa Maria–Goleta, CA	152,824	57.7	60.9	52.5	51,359	2,351	49.3	66,929	1,305	57.1
Santa Cruz–Watsonville, CA...........................	104,491	64.1	65.4	59.1	39,580	2,655	55.1	37,933	1,330	61.1
Santa Fe, NM...	71,482	62.4	60.5	68.8	27,262	1,622	46.8	19,010	890	52.4
Santa Rosa–Petaluma, CA.............................	204,735	67.7	62.8	60.0	79,939	2,389	51.7	73,721	1,216	56.3
Savannah, GA..	151,340	63.2	55.8	62.4	55,781	1,382	37.8	48,711	907	55.1
Scranton—Wilkes-Barre, PA	258,883	64.2	53.0	68.1	90,483	1,246	32.2	72,938	655	45.5
Seattle–Tacoma–Bellevue, WA	1,464,902	59.4	59.6	60.9	637,944	2,098	42.5	531,582	1,053	49.5
Seattle–Bellevue–Everett, WA	1,139,124	57.8	58.3	60.6	496,400	2,190	42.1	417,586	1,077	48.8
Tacoma, WA...	325,778	64.9	64.2	61.9	141,544	1,833	43.7	113,996	968	52.2
Sebastian–Vero Beach, FL.............................	76,332	63.9	49.3	75.3	22,251	1,370	46.5	14,044	861	60.1
Sheboygan, WI...	50,769	66.1	62.6	72.4	21,952	1,373	29.9	12,686	652	42.0
Sherman–Denison, TX....................................	53,786	73.6	60.7	67.3	16,324	1,250	32.0	15,107	746	45.7
Shreveport–Bossier City, LA	173,896	65.2	53.2	65.2	60,367	1,118	27.6	53,535	718	54.4
Sioux City, IA–NE–SD	58,057	73.8	60.8	67.6	22,867	1,075	22.3	17,610	626	49.0
Sioux Falls, SD..	96,189	66.9	67.4	68.1	43,994	1,272	24.0	28,392	686	42.3
South Bend–Mishawaka, IN–MI	140,747	77.8	57.1	72.2	59,735	1,065	28.1	33,606	695	52.2
Spartanburg, SC...	122,700	68.3	62.2	70.4	48,225	1,110	30.4	31,282	661	51.3
Spokane, WA...	201,819	65.9	61.5	64.0	82,586	1,368	35.1	67,347	742	53.8
Springfield, IL..	95,564	70.3	55.7	70.3	41,657	1,199	23.7	26,032	709	49.8
Springfield, MA..	288,594	57.5	50.8	63.3	115,723	1,608	35.3	98,465	790	53.3
Springfield, MO..	192,636	73.7	60.6	64.9	76,603	1,047	28.5	61,218	662	50.0
Springfield, OH..	61,368	73.2	57.3	67.1	23,943	1,109	29.2	18,116	651	51.2
State College, PA...	63,451	56.7	56.2	57.8	21,005	1,394	25.5	24,123	834	58.0
Steubenville–Weirton, OH–WV.........................	58,276	79.1	57.4	76.2	19,412	909	26.6	12,118	546	47.7
Stockton, CA..	234,003	72.7	63.9	59.3	96,653	1,939	50.5	87,169	1,005	58.5
Sumter, SC..	46,075	60.4	57.4	66.0	15,037	1,038	24.2	13,250	684	44.7
Syracuse, NY...	287,775	64.4	52.7	67.8	113,603	1,315	28.5	82,148	731	50.8
Tallahassee, FL..	162,963	55.1	55.5	58.9	55,917	1,393	36.5	58,297	897	65.3
Tampa–St. Petersburg–Clearwater, FL	1,354,587	55.5	49.4	67.5	474,290	1,502	45.6	361,247	926	57.8
Terre Haute, IN..	74,071	75.7	59.6	69.8	28,668	947	23.4	19,280	633	51.3
Texarkana, TX–Texarkana, AR	57,819	69.1	57.6	68.1	17,800	1,033	28.3	16,015	673	49.7
Toledo, OH..	301,279	67.8	55.3	66.0	116,275	1,240	31.6	88,540	657	52.5
Topeka, KS..	103,848	73.8	62.4	68.7	41,304	1,184	25.9	29,758	689	47.3
Trenton–Ewing, NJ..	143,207	48.5	55.1	66.5	62,691	2,270	39.7	43,541	1,105	51.6

²The portion of Sullivan city in Crawford County, MO is legally part of the St. Louis, MO–IL MSA. That portion is not included in these figures for the St. Louis, MSA.

Table B-10. Housing Units, 2009–2011—*Continued*

Metropolitan statistical area and division	Total housing units	1 unit detached (percent)	With 2 or more vehicles available (percent)	Owner-occupied				Renter-occupied		
				Ownership rate	Housing units with a mortgage			Number	Median monthly rent (dollars)	Units with rent 30 percent or more of household income (percent)
					Number	Median monthly owner costs (dollars)	Units with costs 30 percent or more of household income (percent)			
Tucson, AZ	441,245	58.6	52.7	63.2	162,093	1,406	39.2	139,514	770	54.0
Tulsa, OK	410,530	72.0	61.2	67.2	159,372	1,201	27.6	120,054	707	47.2
Tuscaloosa, AL	97,641	59.1	58.8	65.6	31,985	1,195	32.1	26,452	738	56.1
Tyler, TX	87,580	66.0	59.5	67.7	30,499	1,235	29.2	25,359	798	56.4
Utica–Rome, NY	137,589	63.1	52.2	69.0	46,664	1,190	26.0	36,548	652	48.3
Valdosta, GA	57,346	64.9	58.4	58.2	18,648	1,138	37.7	20,884	729	56.0
Vallejo–Fairfield, CA	152,793	71.6	66.1	63.2	69,627	2,210	49.9	51,549	1,229	55.0
Victoria, TX	50,657	71.2	59.7	68.9	13,884	1,198	28.2	13,331	710	49.8
Vineland–Millville–Bridgeton, NJ	55,860	65.6	54.7	67.7	22,188	1,652	41.6	16,291	936	60.5
Virginia Beach–Norfolk–Newport News, VA–NC	687,066	61.6	62.0	63.9	301,875	1,719	41.1	223,332	1,052	53.7
Visalia–Porterville, CA	141,922	75.5	61.6	58.3	55,561	1,436	46.0	54,071	798	54.7
Waco, TX	95,306	69.0	57.2	60.0	27,566	1,261	30.6	33,450	742	56.2
Warner Robins, GA	58,433	72.3	61.8	67.9	25,939	1,216	24.6	16,613	785	46.6
Washington–Arlington–Alexandria, DC–VA–MD–WV	2,217,179	46.5	56.6	64.5	1,082,932	2,390	36.1	727,546	1,382	48.8
Bethesda–Rockville–Frederick, MD	466,612	50.8	60.4	68.8	240,781	2,456	35.9	138,006	1,457	51.2
Washington–Arlington–Alexandria, DC–VA–MD–WV	1,750,567	45.4	55.5	63.3	842,151	2,371	36.2	589,540	1,361	48.3
Waterloo–Cedar Falls, IA	71,375	71.8	62.1	70.4	29,540	1,088	22.0	19,672	634	51.0
Wausau, WI	57,772	73.9	66.9	74.3	24,234	1,284	28.9	13,578	671	44.4
Wenatchee–East Wenatchee, WA	51,590	67.3	69.3	67.4	18,304	1,361	36.6	13,294	731	43.1
Wheeling, WV–OH	69,488	73.3	54.3	74.8	22,994	918	23.4	15,296	506	43.1
Wichita, KS	263,330	73.1	62.4	67.9	110,973	1,209	25.9	76,647	673	47.2
Wichita Falls, TX	64,829	73.7	59.5	66.9	19,980	1,109	25.4	18,177	687	46.6
Williamsport, PA	52,453	68.8	58.0	68.8	18,583	1,163	32.0	14,451	635	50.6
Wilmington, NC	205,942	61.4	59.9	66.9	68,936	1,416	40.6	50,516	847	57.9
Winchester, VA–WV	57,023	72.7	64.2	67.6	23,043	1,570	34.4	16,126	888	51.7
Winston–Salem, NC	214,623	67.5	60.6	69.1	88,379	1,174	30.3	58,164	681	50.9
Worcester, MA	327,232	56.3	57.4	66.2	147,311	1,912	35.8	101,100	881	47.9
Yakima, WA	85,571	67.5	66.2	62.0	32,692	1,266	33.6	30,423	722	55.9
York–Hanover, PA	178,898	64.2	65.2	75.7	88,198	1,517	34.6	40,888	793	48.4
Youngstown–Warren–Boardman, OH–PA	259,666	75.6	55.0	72.3	99,024	1,074	30.7	63,977	599	52.5
Yuba City, CA	61,465	69.3	63.9	60.4	24,211	1,637	46.8	21,827	829	53.3
Yuma, AZ	87,881	52.5	56.8	69.7	28,427	1,198	44.8	21,190	800	51.9

Table B-11. Personal Income and Earnings, by Place of Work

Metropolitan statistical area and division	Personal income											
	Total (million dollars)				Percent change, 2005–2011	Per capita[1] (dollars)			Earnings (million dollars)			
	2011	2010	2005	2001		2011	2010	2005	2011	2010	2005	2001
Abilene, TX	5,920	5,625	4,470	3,720	32.4	35,571	33,953	27,808	3,941	3,791	3,202	2,615
Akron, OH	28,066	26,693	23,714	20,945	18.4	40,011	37,978	33,757	19,282	18,650	17,228	14,548
Albany, GA	5,018	4,815	4,198	3,698	19.5	31,821	30,553	26,760	3,407	3,335	3,199	2,800
Albany–Schenectady–Troy, NY	39,168	37,601	30,672	26,423	27.7	44,944	43,172	35,890	28,955	28,284	24,481	21,031
Albuquerque, NM	31,459	30,293	25,338	21,193	24.2	35,007	34,039	31,299	22,632	22,157	19,817	16,544
Alexandria, LA	5,679	5,483	4,542	3,675	25.0	36,758	35,579	30,702	3,734	3,648	3,034	2,398
Allentown–Bethlehem–Easton, PA–NJ	33,075	31,677	26,609	23,076	24.3	40,095	38,522	33,779	21,020	20,231	18,141	15,326
Altoona, PA	4,386	4,186	3,542	3,137	23.8	34,511	32,951	27,949	3,094	2,976	2,708	2,364
Amarillo, TX	9,383	8,918	7,020	5,766	33.7	36,968	35,563	29,451	7,012	6,739	5,412	4,398
Ames, IA	3,356	3,161	2,558	2,146	31.2	37,429	35,292	30,866	2,724	2,604	2,138	1,773
Anchorage, AK	18,914	17,936	14,129	11,518	33.9	48,810	46,815	40,265	15,034	14,496	11,832	9,164
Anderson, IN	3,992	3,860	3,652	3,406	9.3	30,421	29,322	27,905	2,024	1,951	2,087	1,996
Anderson, SC	5,854	5,604	4,777	4,276	22.5	31,059	29,923	27,227	3,142	2,977	2,861	2,631
Ann Arbor, MI	14,204	13,297	12,745	11,629	11.5	40,821	38,515	37,241	12,689	12,305	12,137	10,851
Anniston–Oxford, AL	3,741	3,645	3,087	2,498	21.2	31,758	30,775	26,963	2,641	2,625	2,314	1,785
Appleton, WI	8,983	8,473	7,395	6,257	21.5	39,504	37,495	34,247	6,687	6,368	5,994	4,998
Asheville, NC	14,639	14,013	11,944	10,138	22.6	34,122	32,928	30,131	8,942	8,709	7,912	6,759
Athens–Clarke County, GA	6,051	5,831	4,884	4,069	23.9	31,302	30,238	27,290	4,382	4,322	3,825	3,152
Atlanta–Sandy Springs–Marietta, GA	212,830	201,632	179,145	150,564	18.8	39,713	38,142	37,683	171,979	165,213	153,413	130,779
Atlantic City–Hammonton, NJ	11,046	10,669	9,611	8,240	14.9	40,262	38,843	35,552	8,485	8,330	8,660	7,264
Auburn–Opelika, AL	4,190	3,968	3,109	2,465	34.8	29,208	28,188	24,646	2,567	2,465	2,071	1,539
Augusta–Richmond County, GA–SC	19,463	18,548	15,262	12,879	27.5	34,640	33,216	29,180	13,765	13,329	11,542	9,581
Austin–Round Rock–San Marcos, TX	72,152	67,321	51,047	42,617	41.3	40,455	38,953	35,124	58,481	54,979	43,735	37,762
Bakersfield–Delano, CA	26,744	25,092	19,806	15,283	35.0	31,400	29,772	26,036	20,245	18,855	15,522	11,392
Baltimore–Towson, MD	139,528	132,286	111,453	92,001	25.2	51,126	48,732	42,150	101,298	97,139	84,312	67,801
Bangor, ME	5,220	5,012	4,328	3,738	20.6	33,940	32,581	28,904	3,765	3,702	3,424	2,967
Barnstable Town, MA	11,968	11,403	9,849	8,850	21.5	55,465	52,796	44,365	5,612	5,469	5,336	4,413
Baton Rouge, LA	31,510	30,088	23,119	18,428	36.3	38,985	37,397	31,432	23,539	22,794	17,702	14,533
Battle Creek, MI	4,544	4,425	3,915	3,521	16.1	33,541	32,520	28,174	3,383	3,350	3,211	2,866
Bay City, MI	3,614	3,431	3,037	2,873	19.0	33,737	31,852	27,823	2,001	1,916	1,857	1,726
Beaumont–Port Arthur, TX	15,082	14,275	11,107	9,546	35.8	38,620	36,683	28,812	10,904	10,300	8,204	7,120
Bellingham, WA	7,759	7,361	5,609	4,481	38.3	38,098	36,511	30,248	5,007	4,797	4,023	3,061
Bend, OR	5,946	5,666	4,664	3,473	27.5	37,084	35,874	33,176	3,674	3,552	3,329	2,380
Billings, MT	6,309	5,965	4,963	4,039	27.1	39,405	37,629	33,636	4,630	4,400	3,834	3,068
Binghamton, NY	9,000	8,687	6,973	6,429	29.1	35,990	34,545	27,662	5,893	5,839	5,166	4,782
Birmingham–Hoover, AL	46,215	44,156	39,199	31,802	17.9	40,816	39,108	36,084	33,472	32,496	30,312	25,014
Bismarck, ND	4,709	4,363	3,326	2,660	41.6	42,468	39,916	33,273	3,591	3,329	2,636	2,071
Blacksburg–Christiansburg–Radford, VA	4,831	4,586	3,847	3,255	25.6	29,733	28,125	24,596	3,446	3,295	3,093	2,555
Bloomington, IN	6,004	5,743	4,809	4,121	24.8	30,915	29,719	26,217	3,978	3,870	3,405	2,841
Bloomington–Normal, IL	7,132	6,798	5,377	4,732	32.6	41,816	40,026	33,544	6,195	5,967	4,921	4,257
Boise City–Nampa, ID	21,512	20,560	17,985	14,311	19.6	34,274	33,265	32,881	16,178	15,662	14,174	11,563
Boston–Cambridge–Quincy, MA–NH	265,794	252,553	212,251	191,075	25.2	57,893	55,392	48,042	220,095	211,134	183,098	165,186
Boston–Quincy, MA	111,030	105,513	88,245	77,759	25.8	58,316	55,810	48,368	104,537	100,753	87,739	77,969
Cambridge–Newton–Framingham, MA	94,619	89,856	75,718	69,946	25.0	62,324	59,676	52,045	80,292	76,472	64,746	60,519
Peabody, MA	39,850	37,833	31,612	28,733	26.1	53,209	50,817	43,370	22,235	21,323	19,062	16,964
Rockingham County–Strafford County, NH..	20,295	19,352	16,676	14,637	21.7	48,315	46,230	40,687	13,030	12,585	11,552	9,734
Boulder, CO	15,536	14,768	13,289	12,280	16.9	51,893	50,031	47,419	12,907	12,300	11,097	11,286
Bowling Green, KY	4,010	3,813	3,121	2,498	28.5	31,422	30,182	27,351	2,996	2,874	2,552	1,960
Bremerton–Silverdale, WA	10,842	10,355	8,905	7,328	21.8	42,580	41,135	37,133	6,708	6,547	5,688	4,393
Bridgeport–Stamford–Norwalk, CT	72,687	69,692	61,073	54,761	19.0	78,504	75,890	68,036	52,411	50,261	45,348	41,111
Brownsville–Harlingen, TX	9,623	9,202	6,872	5,445	40.0	23,236	22,557	18,403	5,902	5,711	4,614	3,696
Brunswick, GA	3,693	3,550	3,155	2,546	17.1	32,708	31,551	31,078	2,146	2,115	1,991	1,576
Buffalo–Niagara Falls, NY	45,499	43,571	36,232	32,412	25.6	40,121	38,379	31,546	31,644	30,496	26,897	23,562
Burlington, NC	4,808	4,590	3,968	3,589	21.2	31,363	30,289	28,483	2,980	2,846	2,783	2,546
Burlington–South Burlington, VT	9,320	8,875	7,366	6,443	26.5	43,853	41,960	35,648	7,527	7,249	6,374	5,508
Canton–Massillon, OH	14,030	13,261	12,094	11,117	16.0	34,739	32,809	29,849	8,883	8,365	8,359	7,684
Cape Coral–Fort Myers, FL	27,161	25,779	21,184	14,415	28.2	43,022	41,548	38,167	12,027	11,503	12,009	7,850
Cape Girardeau–Jackson, MO–IL	3,290	3,171	2,593	2,234	26.9	33,907	32,877	27,832	2,383	2,335	2,031	1,703
Carson City, NV	2,208	2,150	2,168	1,732	1.9	39,833	38,948	38,718	1,837	1,815	1,787	1,451
Casper, WY	4,132	3,837	2,997	2,306	37.9	54,108	50,838	42,864	2,984	2,763	2,227	1,715
Cedar Rapids, IA	11,075	10,356	8,316	7,313	33.2	42,503	40,092	33,633	8,834	8,334	6,925	6,053
Champaign–Urbana, IL	8,654	8,371	6,478	5,887	33.6	37,246	36,058	29,261	6,417	6,268	5,110	4,477
Charleston, WV	11,949	11,378	9,492	8,549	25.9	39,348	37,392	31,140	9,293	8,890	7,754	6,828
Charleston–North Charleston–Summerville, SC.	25,706	24,141	19,124	14,850	34.4	37,685	36,155	31,964	19,424	18,331	14,826	11,382
Charlotte–Gastonia–Rock Hill, NC–SC	72,220	67,899	57,216	46,149	26.2	40,223	38,492	37,678	61,192	57,950	51,010	41,501
Charlottesville, VA	9,042	8,552	7,020	5,669	28.8	44,350	42,344	37,225	6,623	6,378	5,304	4,209
Chattanooga, TN–GA	19,236	18,355	15,671	13,524	22.8	36,066	34,684	31,369	13,990	13,496	12,430	10,616
Cheyenne, WY	4,345	4,080	3,208	2,490	35.4	46,882	44,285	37,420	3,120	2,943	2,348	1,838
Chicago–Joliet–Naperville, IL–IN–WI	436,998	419,999	375,515	328,417	16.4	45,977	44,338	40,481	340,490	327,754	304,142	264,711
Chicago–Joliet–Naperville, IL	365,651	351,607	314,133	274,772	16.4	46,153	44,547	40,586	291,401	280,196	262,236	229,310
Gary, IN	26,058	24,878	21,677	18,978	20.2	36,770	35,116	31,334	16,441	15,518	14,060	12,009
Lake County–Kenosha County, IL–WI	45,289	43,514	39,705	34,666	14.1	51,847	49,949	47,016	32,648	32,041	27,846	23,391

[1]Based on resident population estimated as of July 1 of the year shown.

Table B-11. Personal Income and Earnings, by Place of Work—*Continued*

Metropolitan statistical area and division	Personal income								Earnings (million dollars)			
	Total (million dollars)				Percent change, 2005–2011	Per capita[1] (dollars)						
	2011	2010	2005	2001		2011	2010	2005	2011	2010	2005	2001
Chico, CA	7,347	7,047	6,011	4,977	22.2	33,356	32,033	27,990	4,189	4,033	3,852	3,017
Cincinnati–Middletown, OH–KY–IN	87,485	83,388	75,148	64,886	16.4	40,918	39,105	36,294	65,650	63,457	58,989	50,326
Clarksville, TN–KY	11,015	10,022	7,569	5,595	45.5	39,666	36,425	30,219	8,736	7,973	6,139	4,246
Cleveland, TN	3,630	3,448	2,996	2,570	21.2	31,073	29,730	27,382	2,331	2,191	2,138	1,807
Cleveland–Elyria–Mentor, OH	87,622	83,241	76,110	69,347	15.1	42,365	40,106	36,042	67,582	64,638	61,633	55,521
Coeur d'Alene, ID	4,647	4,412	3,638	2,744	27.7	32,923	31,761	28,880	2,704	2,640	2,325	1,763
College Station–Bryan, TX	6,932	6,628	4,806	3,905	44.2	29,928	28,883	23,616	4,937	4,803	3,738	3,010
Colorado Springs, CO	26,409	24,722	20,148	17,210	31.1	39,994	37,999	34,278	19,948	18,959	16,359	13,700
Columbia, MO	6,567	6,218	5,031	4,083	30.5	37,350	35,875	31,665	4,987	4,761	4,115	3,276
Columbia, SC	27,471	26,334	21,991	18,372	24.9	35,350	34,202	31,454	20,896	20,305	17,870	14,777
Columbus, GA–AL	11,651	10,827	8,950	7,320	30.2	38,653	36,621	31,254	8,889	8,367	6,923	5,805
Columbus, IN	3,087	2,847	2,428	2,112	27.2	39,645	37,023	32,956	2,903	2,614	2,326	1,938
Columbus, OH	74,688	70,531	60,968	52,936	22.5	40,188	38,320	35,307	61,030	58,225	52,450	45,289
Corpus Christi, TX	16,655	15,693	12,201	9,895	36.5	38,609	36,654	29,307	12,028	11,405	9,211	7,442
Corvallis, OR	3,323	3,182	2,707	2,368	22.8	38,677	37,201	33,444	2,341	2,270	2,071	1,787
Crestview–Fort Walton Beach–Destin, FL	7,914	7,433	6,661	4,922	18.8	43,132	41,109	36,190	6,216	5,925	5,505	3,740
Cumberland, MD–WV	3,349	3,216	2,584	2,253	29.6	32,547	31,134	25,539	2,029	1,977	1,690	1,418
Dallas–Fort Worth–Arlington, TX	285,260	268,492	220,482	183,612	29.4	43,708	41,948	38,494	237,126	225,170	193,760	164,719
Dallas–Plano–Irving, TX	197,316	185,682	154,614	129,250	27.6	45,404	43,630	40,501	174,608	165,424	143,410	122,948
Fort Worth–Arlington, TX	87,944	82,809	65,868	54,362	33.5	40,327	38,613	34,481	62,518	59,746	50,350	41,771
Dalton, GA	3,890	3,766	3,571	3,042	8.9	27,249	26,463	26,674	3,334	3,311	3,543	2,966
Danville, IL	2,659	2,544	2,128	1,916	24.9	32,619	31,187	25,726	1,751	1,642	1,516	1,296
Danville, VA	3,308	3,178	2,888	2,476	14.5	31,297	29,881	26,855	1,865	1,812	1,883	1,595
Davenport–Moline–Rock Island, IA–IL	16,070	15,201	12,304	10,598	30.6	42,141	39,978	32,997	11,824	11,198	9,629	8,009
Dayton, OH	31,626	30,092	27,069	25,057	16.8	37,410	35,733	31,945	23,404	22,519	22,116	20,030
Decatur, AL	4,941	4,806	4,186	3,577	18.0	32,071	31,219	28,208	3,045	2,967	2,803	2,456
Decatur, IL	4,495	4,308	3,679	3,279	22.2	40,591	38,896	33,118	3,470	3,301	3,069	2,646
Deltona–Daytona Beach–Ormond Beach, FL	16,544	15,997	14,260	11,262	16.0	33,436	32,339	29,324	7,575	7,479	7,375	5,650
Denver–Aurora–Broomfield, CO[2]	127,324	119,986	101,788	89,048	25.1	48,980	46,969	43,634	103,112	98,393	87,019	75,682
Des Moines–West Des Moines, IA	26,092	24,463	20,043	16,067	30.2	44,966	42,772	38,427	22,105	20,952	17,642	13,839
Detroit–Warren–Livonia, MI	171,473	161,676	164,087	153,327	4.5	40,009	37,680	37,031	128,083	119,946	134,888	126,069
Detroit–Livonia–Dearborn, MI	61,293	59,207	59,624	57,411	2.8	34,012	32,617	30,416	50,804	47,801	53,779	51,783
Warren–Troy–Farmington Hills, MI	110,179	102,469	104,463	95,916	5.5	44,360	41,394	42,279	77,279	72,144	81,108	74,286
Dothan, AL	5,079	4,900	4,010	3,285	26.7	34,654	33,585	29,343	2,975	2,958	2,775	2,262
Dover, DE	5,489	5,225	4,118	3,237	33.3	33,302	32,078	28,484	3,954	3,856	3,310	2,508
Dubuque, IA	3,680	3,408	2,804	2,385	31.3	38,886	36,303	30,889	3,033	2,792	2,414	1,935
Duluth, MN–WI	10,141	9,664	8,266	7,287	22.7	36,242	34,547	29,876	6,925	6,635	6,058	5,190
Durham–Chapel Hill, NC	21,435	20,518	16,647	13,919	28.8	41,785	40,561	36,324	21,918	21,243	17,079	14,850
Eau Claire, WI	5,874	5,660	4,594	4,046	27.9	36,111	35,070	29,672	4,340	4,192	3,628	3,067
El Centro, CA	5,020	4,817	3,720	2,929	34.9	28,351	27,503	23,831	3,406	3,256	2,779	2,135
Elizabethtown, KY	4,700	4,301	3,297	2,748	42.6	38,597	35,484	29,851	4,201	3,789	2,798	2,245
Elkhart–Goshen, IN	6,392	6,087	6,092	4,928	4.9	32,131	30,815	31,688	5,911	5,634	6,486	4,917
Elmira, NY	3,155	3,040	2,469	2,227	27.8	35,517	34,227	27,787	2,199	2,111	1,779	1,584
El Paso, TX	24,696	23,047	17,100	13,858	44.4	30,088	28,665	23,486	18,515	17,330	13,635	11,119
Erie, PA	9,756	9,170	7,753	7,030	25.8	34,721	32,627	27,967	6,843	6,380	5,975	5,324
Eugene–Springfield, OR	12,214	11,680	10,096	8,653	21.0	34,561	33,193	30,064	7,707	7,451	7,143	5,954
Evansville, IN–KY	13,639	12,980	11,339	9,729	20.3	37,899	36,156	32,294	10,236	9,853	9,094	7,544
Fairbanks, AK	4,228	3,921	3,049	2,428	38.7	42,626	39,898	33,719	3,692	3,449	2,780	2,051
Fargo, ND–MN	9,068	8,421	6,325	5,124	43.4	42,740	40,216	33,414	7,377	6,903	5,326	4,255
Farmington, NM	4,022	3,804	3,044	2,438	32.1	31,373	29,218	24,388	3,061	2,893	2,427	1,966
Fayetteville, NC	16,184	15,038	11,122	8,379	45.5	43,254	40,900	32,379	14,031	13,258	9,784	7,096
Fayetteville–Springdale–Rogers, AR–MO	16,172	15,337	12,024	8,947	34.5	34,130	32,928	29,470	12,385	11,938	9,949	7,376
Flagstaff, AZ	4,621	4,447	3,680	2,897	25.6	34,353	33,035	28,972	3,253	3,160	2,709	2,058
Flint, MI	13,108	12,537	11,983	11,473	9.4	31,057	29,492	27,080	7,606	7,278	8,344	8,200
Florence, SC	6,754	6,557	5,601	4,808	20.6	32,762	31,878	28,121	4,638	4,550	4,216	3,682
Florence–Muscle Shoals, AL	4,719	4,576	3,739	3,243	26.2	32,038	31,082	26,015	2,798	2,736	2,366	2,018
Fond du Lac, WI	3,766	3,604	3,198	2,839	17.8	36,897	35,445	32,201	2,542	2,419	2,360	2,042
Fort Collins–Loveland, CO	12,150	11,454	9,631	8,508	26.2	39,767	38,109	35,008	8,227	7,829	7,129	6,227
Fort Smith, AR–OK	9,537	9,195	7,641	6,435	24.8	31,782	30,758	26,832	6,190	6,097	5,706	4,826
Fort Wayne, IN	14,698	13,929	12,585	11,562	16.8	35,042	33,419	31,210	11,539	11,037	10,549	9,692
Fresno, CA	29,741	28,539	24,078	19,745	23.5	31,542	30,583	27,598	20,492	19,710	18,355	14,555
Gadsden, AL	3,321	3,232	2,704	2,321	22.8	31,844	30,949	26,212	1,776	1,751	1,616	1,390
Gainesville, FL	9,455	9,123	7,709	5,928	22.7	35,497	34,505	30,890	7,093	6,958	6,194	4,716
Gainesville, GA	5,858	5,493	4,789	3,781	22.3	32,001	30,491	29,750	4,234	3,978	3,691	2,898
Glens Falls, NY	4,801	4,585	3,661	3,095	31.1	37,216	35,530	28,678	2,908	2,809	2,460	1,982
Goldsboro, NC	3,865	3,651	3,081	2,652	25.4	31,245	29,722	26,332	2,570	2,454	2,170	1,872
Grand Forks, ND–MN	3,862	3,646	2,885	2,428	33.8	39,382	36,988	29,507	2,983	2,860	2,347	1,901
Grand Junction, CO	5,173	4,923	3,898	3,158	32.7	35,169	33,647	29,939	3,428	3,292	2,743	2,144
Grand Rapids–Wyoming, MI	27,305	25,625	24,098	21,541	13.3	35,024	33,090	31,458	22,247	21,041	21,076	18,608
Great Falls, MT	3,228	3,105	2,500	2,135	29.1	39,448	38,090	31,240	2,264	2,214	1,838	1,513

[1]Based on resident population estimated as of July 1 of the year shown.
[2]The Denver–Aurora metropolitan statistical area includes Broomfield County. Broomfield County, CO, was formed from parts of Adams, Boulder, Jefferson, and Weld Counties on November 15, 2001, and is coextensive with Broomfield city. For the purposes of defining and presenting data for the Denver–Aurora metropolitan statistical area, Broomfield city is treated as if it were a county when data are available to do so. In many cases, the data were not available.

Table B-11. Personal Income and Earnings, by Place of Work—*Continued*

Metropolitan statistical area and division	Personal income											
	Total (million dollars)				Percent change, 2005–2011	Per capita[1] (dollars)			Earnings (million dollars)			
	2011	2010	2005	2001		2011	2010	2005	2011	2010	2005	2001
Greeley, CO	7,756	7,232	6,004	5,140	29.2	29,986	28,447	26,939	5,299	4,918	4,374	3,617
Green Bay, WI	12,084	11,587	9,914	8,623	21.9	39,046	37,730	33,403	10,000	9,590	8,591	7,228
Greensboro–High Point, NC	25,880	24,746	21,983	19,156	17.7	35,405	34,123	32,468	19,869	19,179	18,342	16,243
Greenville, NC	6,188	5,889	4,741	3,886	30.5	32,111	30,970	28,208	4,161	4,050	3,365	2,801
Greenville–Mauldin–Easley, SC	22,684	21,527	17,971	15,687	26.2	35,038	33,691	30,586	17,348	16,477	14,717	12,974
Gulfport–Biloxi, MS	8,853	8,697	7,492	6,122	18.2	34,922	34,821	28,741	6,850	6,722	5,854	4,995
Hagerstown–Martinsburg, MD–WV	9,395	8,944	7,332	5,861	28.1	34,604	33,156	29,249	5,571	5,322	4,957	3,977
Hanford–Corcoran, CA	4,522	4,121	3,398	2,510	33.1	29,407	26,905	23,413	3,380	3,050	2,700	1,859
Harrisburg–Carlisle, PA	22,751	21,706	18,364	15,973	23.9	41,148	39,388	34,928	20,165	19,452	17,508	14,817
Harrisonburg, VA	3,964	3,778	3,166	2,684	25.2	31,324	30,123	27,149	3,183	3,080	2,737	2,310
Hartford–West Hartford–East Hartford, CT	64,401	61,302	51,428	45,026	25.2	53,081	50,559	43,292	51,575	49,467	44,902	38,357
Hattiesburg, MS	4,544	4,355	3,445	2,846	31.9	31,248	30,377	26,338	3,161	3,086	2,545	2,076
Hickory–Lenoir–Morganton, NC	11,249	10,763	9,968	9,067	12.9	30,857	29,459	28,145	7,380	7,104	7,363	7,011
Hinesville–Fort Stewart, GA	2,154	2,011	1,676	1,278	28.5	26,726	25,987	21,941	3,227	2,952	2,072	1,385
Holland–Grand Haven, MI	8,995	8,514	7,785	6,770	15.5	33,777	32,242	30,497	5,918	5,456	5,894	5,248
Honolulu, HI	44,927	42,397	34,264	27,459	31.1	46,624	44,365	37,317	34,196	32,738	27,856	21,538
Hot Springs, AR	3,434	3,275	2,691	2,253	27.6	35,355	34,038	29,217	1,744	1,684	1,514	1,288
Houma–Bayou Cane–Thibodaux, LA	8,843	8,495	5,757	4,749	53.6	42,393	40,790	28,717	6,687	6,497	4,220	3,450
Houston–Sugar Land–Baytown, TX	289,790	268,695	209,655	170,599	38.2	47,612	44,959	39,868	240,196	223,846	180,993	150,379
Huntington–Ashland, WV–KY–OH	9,437	9,081	7,370	6,529	28.0	32,811	31,559	25,762	6,222	6,094	5,227	4,447
Huntsville, AL	17,073	16,278	12,415	9,868	37.5	40,126	38,814	33,303	15,217	14,775	11,693	9,264
Idaho Falls, ID	4,427	4,213	3,397	2,559	30.3	33,520	32,198	29,957	2,768	2,681	2,148	1,643
Indianapolis–Carmel, IN	72,161	68,429	60,018	51,772	20.2	40,572	38,862	36,550	58,912	56,458	51,401	43,747
Iowa City, IA	6,393	5,950	4,703	4,003	35.9	41,277	38,900	33,204	5,332	5,017	4,060	3,348
Ithaca, NY	3,689	3,539	2,819	2,417	30.9	36,263	34,810	28,347	3,083	3,004	2,532	2,083
Jackson, MI	5,015	4,760	4,380	4,009	14.5	31,396	29,717	26,863	3,177	2,990	3,046	2,718
Jackson, MS	20,476	19,565	16,657	13,599	22.9	37,544	36,227	32,073	15,519	15,035	13,218	10,781
Jackson, TN	3,951	3,774	3,233	2,755	22.2	34,237	32,683	28,933	3,189	3,070	2,910	2,464
Jacksonville, FL	55,375	52,940	45,618	34,845	21.4	40,709	39,253	36,521	39,028	37,974	34,879	27,059
Jacksonville, NC	8,296	7,892	5,043	3,698	64.5	46,163	43,972	32,077	7,280	7,103	4,318	3,064
Janesville, WI	5,332	5,113	4,566	4,090	16.8	33,305	31,897	29,125	3,350	3,203	3,345	2,941
Jefferson City, MO	5,335	5,154	4,355	3,740	22.5	35,453	34,355	30,149	4,203	4,140	3,675	3,077
Johnson City, TN	6,543	6,213	5,049	4,234	29.6	32,745	31,224	26,689	4,063	3,902	3,499	2,847
Johnstown, PA	4,716	4,531	3,913	3,555	20.5	32,810	31,336	26,622	2,930	2,858	2,549	2,192
Jonesboro, AR	3,948	3,742	2,988	2,470	32.1	32,141	30,857	26,548	2,746	2,611	2,253	1,828
Joplin, MO	5,555	5,313	4,406	3,764	26.1	31,408	30,215	26,516	4,023	3,901	3,436	2,920
Kalamazoo–Portage, MI	11,419	10,911	9,712	8,646	17.6	34,792	33,381	30,325	7,840	7,560	7,335	6,527
Kankakee–Bradley, IL	3,771	3,656	3,004	2,702	25.6	33,171	32,204	27,832	2,256	2,164	1,941	1,717
Kansas City, MO–KS	88,392	84,533	70,738	61,879	25.0	43,062	41,443	36,558	69,320	67,264	59,390	51,249
Kennewick–Pasco–Richland, WA	9,652	9,105	6,424	5,297	50.3	36,544	35,611	29,323	7,490	7,130	5,263	4,138
Killeen–Temple–Fort Hood, TX	16,476	15,348	10,680	7,919	54.3	40,029	37,593	29,870	13,028	12,297	8,708	6,273
Kingsport–Bristol–Bristol, TN–VA	10,234	9,728	8,191	7,286	24.9	33,035	31,419	27,077	6,795	6,411	5,893	5,184
Kingston, NY	7,223	6,964	5,562	4,774	29.9	39,589	38,166	30,488	3,382	3,345	2,862	2,410
Knoxville, TN	26,037	24,801	20,628	17,598	26.2	36,958	35,468	31,528	20,362	19,530	17,220	14,211
Kokomo, IN	3,266	3,067	3,059	2,813	6.7	33,126	31,087	30,354	2,482	2,297	2,868	2,665
La Crosse, WI–MN	5,135	4,943	4,041	3,536	27.1	38,184	36,917	31,194	3,919	3,789	3,276	2,826
Lafayette, IN	6,464	6,026	5,162	4,620	25.2	31,747	29,842	27,456	5,282	4,913	4,474	3,882
Lafayette, LA	12,253	11,555	8,232	6,578	48.8	44,184	42,117	32,676	10,316	9,797	7,004	5,745
Lake Charles, LA	7,295	6,913	5,614	4,756	29.9	36,324	34,550	28,605	5,427	5,165	4,442	3,763
Lake Havasu City–Kingman, AZ	5,291	5,073	4,377	3,198	20.9	26,145	25,165	23,187	2,355	2,300	2,292	1,644
Lakeland–Winter Haven, FL	20,385	19,530	16,330	12,273	24.8	33,447	32,392	29,833	10,799	10,621	10,255	7,848
Lancaster, PA	19,653	18,877	16,154	14,004	21.7	37,535	36,280	32,654	13,284	12,938	12,188	10,400
Lansing–East Lansing, MI	16,049	15,532	13,763	12,552	16.6	34,505	33,470	29,743	12,555	12,344	11,586	10,539
Laredo, TX	6,409	5,961	4,455	3,343	43.9	24,985	23,700	19,914	4,656	4,309	3,550	2,648
Las Cruces, NM	6,400	6,195	4,544	3,545	40.8	29,963	29,431	24,017	3,974	3,930	3,042	2,261
Las Vegas–Paradise, NV	70,289	67,738	64,181	44,007	9.5	35,680	34,668	37,109	51,822	50,543	49,817	35,360
Lawrence, KS	3,746	3,586	3,075	2,657	21.8	33,379	32,244	29,092	2,351	2,317	2,120	1,822
Lawton, OK	4,653	4,447	3,198	2,639	45.5	36,985	35,460	27,784	3,761	3,684	2,627	2,097
Lebanon, PA	5,169	4,919	3,959	3,337	30.6	38,489	36,784	31,368	2,744	2,601	2,191	1,846
Lewiston, ID–WA	2,201	2,120	1,737	1,542	26.7	35,796	34,751	29,453	1,426	1,398	1,222	1,096
Lewiston–Auburn, ME	3,887	3,741	3,272	2,802	18.8	36,192	34,746	30,479	2,587	2,526	2,293	1,948
Lexington–Fayette, KY	18,098	17,122	14,614	12,732	23.8	37,763	36,154	33,450	14,901	14,277	12,949	11,191
Lima, OH	3,369	3,202	2,937	2,777	14.7	31,750	30,143	27,480	2,921	2,801	2,721	2,439
Lincoln, NE	11,959	11,279	9,604	8,281	24.5	39,018	37,231	33,644	9,423	9,025	8,018	6,833
Little Rock–North Little Rock–Conway, AR	28,324	26,914	21,957	17,788	29.0	39,899	38,325	33,844	21,092	20,268	17,649	14,625
Logan, UT–ID	3,520	3,382	2,635	2,115	33.6	27,594	26,818	23,407	2,501	2,415	1,934	1,502
Longview, TX	8,397	7,822	5,945	5,011	41.2	38,756	36,437	29,278	6,465	5,986	4,541	3,686
Longview, WA	3,341	3,241	2,580	2,391	29.5	32,607	31,630	26,730	2,136	2,106	1,900	1,754
Los Angeles–Long Beach–Santa Ana, CA	575,045	550,283	496,595	415,686	15.8	44,423	42,842	39,021	444,484	428,632	412,501	344,666
Los Angeles–Long Beach–Glendale, CA	420,913	403,144	357,186	303,440	17.8	42,564	41,025	36,498	329,102	317,660	299,603	256,557
Santa Ana–Anaheim–Irvine, CA	154,132	147,138	139,409	112,247	10.6	50,440	48,760	47,417	115,382	110,972	112,898	88,108
Louisville/Jefferson County, KY–IN	50,546	48,093	41,228	36,052	22.6	39,037	37,400	33,820	36,972	35,734	32,309	27,957

[1]Based on resident population estimated as of July 1 of the year shown.

Table B-11. Personal Income and Earnings, by Place of Work—*Continued*

Metropolitan statistical area and division	Personal income								Earnings (million dollars)			
	Total (million dollars)				Percent change, 2005–2011	Per capita[1] (dollars)						
	2011	2010	2005	2001		2011	2010	2005	2011	2010	2005	2001
Lubbock, TX..............................	10,026	9,710	7,506	6,177	33.6	34,573	33,916	28,400	6,934	6,844	5,653	4,644
Lynchburg, VA............................	8,556	8,212	6,960	5,979	22.9	33,664	32,456	29,181	5,379	5,284	4,847	4,119
Macon, GA................................	8,281	7,944	6,952	6,060	19.1	35,554	34,184	30,473	5,244	5,117	4,944	4,382
Madera–Chowchilla, CA	4,378	4,071	3,333	2,520	31.4	28,631	26,874	23,755	2,904	2,656	2,338	1,604
Madison, WI..............................	26,497	25,019	21,294	17,616	24.4	45,964	43,908	39,591	21,915	20,771	18,542	14,839
Manchester–Nashua, NH	19,274	18,434	16,105	14,292	19.7	47,981	45,974	40,629	14,650	14,004	13,084	11,015
Manhattan, KS...........................	5,678	5,265	3,307	2,722	71.7	43,593	40,971	29,712	4,981	4,689	2,825	2,233
Mankato–North Mankato, MN	3,638	3,394	2,839	2,405	28.2	37,424	35,063	31,155	2,810	2,624	2,354	1,870
Mansfield, OH............................	3,794	3,640	3,455	3,175	9.8	30,714	29,290	27,049	2,528	2,462	2,697	2,465
McAllen–Edinburg–Mission, TX	17,248	16,511	11,668	8,744	47.8	21,620	21,167	17,286	11,212	10,821	8,168	6,049
Medford, OR..............................	7,087	6,814	6,072	4,994	16.7	34,602	33,494	31,188	4,291	4,214	4,214	3,348
Memphis, TN–MS–AR	51,198	49,138	44,057	37,668	16.2	38,622	37,280	34,865	40,964	39,790	37,821	32,108
Merced, CA...............................	7,406	6,956	5,803	4,642	27.6	28,497	27,092	23,923	4,453	4,133	3,826	2,820
Miami–Fort Lauderdale–Pompano Beach, FL.....	244,224	233,377	210,605	166,903	16.0	43,072	41,838	38,921	154,631	149,331	141,624	112,605
Fort Lauderdale–Pompano Beach–Deerfield Beach, FL....................	76,134	72,731	67,946	53,898	12.1	42,768	41,511	38,895	47,024	45,497	43,732	33,437
Miami–Miami Beach–Kendall, FL	96,658	92,227	77,373	62,048	24.9	37,834	36,846	32,429	71,598	68,757	63,284	51,462
West Palm Beach–Boca Raton–Boynton Beach, FL....................	71,432	68,418	65,286	50,957	9.4	53,500	51,717	51,070	36,009	35,078	34,608	27,706
Michigan City–La Porte, IN	3,525	3,346	2,993	2,728	17.8	31,650	30,010	27,324	2,258	2,161	2,094	1,875
Midland, TX...............................	9,144	7,982	5,186	4,032	76.3	65,173	58,262	42,331	7,553	6,519	4,039	3,036
Milwaukee–Waukesha–West Allis, WI..............	69,691	66,928	58,251	51,718	19.6	44,610	42,986	38,263	54,697	52,514	47,939	42,073
Minneapolis–St. Paul–Bloomington, MN–WI	161,468	152,789	133,840	114,625	20.6	48,657	46,498	42,740	129,028	123,322	111,893	96,397
Missoula, MT.............................	3,876	3,723	3,204	2,655	20.9	35,190	34,014	31,325	2,949	2,861	2,660	2,208
Mobile, AL................................	13,524	13,019	10,547	9,003	28.2	32,779	31,515	26,438	10,569	10,137	8,373	7,216
Modesto, CA..............................	16,652	15,981	14,233	11,528	17.0	32,115	31,006	28,465	10,350	9,966	9,911	7,642
Monroe, LA...............................	6,013	5,794	4,878	4,134	23.3	33,846	32,779	28,319	4,101	4,018	3,635	3,073
Monroe, MI...............................	5,403	5,082	4,792	4,339	12.7	35,647	33,443	31,448	2,371	2,288	2,499	2,206
Montgomery, AL..........................	13,800	13,300	11,520	9,449	19.8	36,450	35,449	32,121	10,342	10,150	9,163	7,469
Morgantown, WV.........................	4,659	4,434	3,278	2,758	42.1	35,226	34,026	27,331	3,878	3,764	2,700	2,172
Morristown, TN...........................	4,029	3,879	3,231	2,865	24.7	29,306	28,360	24,938	2,344	2,297	2,264	2,010
Mount Vernon–Anacortes, WA..........	4,552	4,359	3,622	3,070	25.7	38,543	37,230	32,724	2,690	2,628	2,479	2,033
Muncie, IN................................	3,549	3,410	3,152	2,988	12.6	30,164	28,981	26,673	2,344	2,267	2,277	2,177
Muskegon–Norton Shores, MI...........	5,099	4,865	4,475	4,150	14.0	29,766	28,271	25,774	3,154	2,987	3,121	2,858
Myrtle Beach–North Myrtle Beach–Conway, SC...	8,055	7,722	6,433	5,085	25.2	29,148	28,531	27,983	5,062	4,916	4,721	3,635
Napa, CA..................................	7,077	6,673	5,932	4,915	19.3	51,253	48,765	45,494	4,681	4,522	4,323	3,425
Naples–Marco Island, FL.................	19,447	18,500	16,771	11,225	16.0	59,264	57,321	54,549	7,639	7,370	7,741	5,451
Nashville–Davidson—Murfreesboro—Franklin, TN ...	68,129	64,674	52,294	42,777	30.3	42,129	40,551	36,382	55,923	53,509	45,429	36,341
New Haven–Milford, CT	42,606	40,636	33,857	30,051	25.8	49,478	47,118	39,965	26,975	26,193	24,064	21,010
New Orleans–Metairie–Kenner, LA	51,935	49,946	43,498	38,012	19.4	43,603	42,559	31,866	38,587	37,467	32,725	29,553
New York–Northern New Jersey–Long Island, NY–NJ–PA..........	1,079,532	1,032,838	863,632	749,499	25.0	56,770	54,591	46,510	827,577	799,576	685,170	599,205
Edison–New Brunswick, NJ	124,200	119,460	101,798	90,308	22.0	52,862	50,978	44,574	79,404	77,708	69,720	61,627
Nassau–Suffolk, NY	169,583	163,840	139,036	119,987	22.0	59,644	57,783	49,479	97,936	95,300	79,917	67,584
Newark–Union, NJ–PA	123,143	118,262	103,407	92,075	19.1	57,196	55,028	48,543	87,390	85,315	78,763	68,008
New York–White Plains–Wayne, NY–NJ	662,607	631,277	519,391	447,129	27.6	56,778	54,459	45,782	562,846	541,254	456,770	401,985
Niles–Benton Harbor, MI................	5,623	5,444	4,735	4,394	18.8	35,830	34,722	29,871	3,611	3,539	3,356	3,098
North Port–Bradenton–Sarasota, FL ...	33,859	32,421	29,790	22,309	13.7	47,732	46,086	44,149	14,575	14,151	15,083	10,893
Norwich–New London, CT	12,978	12,521	10,641	9,173	22.0	47,452	45,696	39,461	9,597	9,417	8,606	7,177
Ocala, FL.................................	10,877	10,431	8,611	6,290	26.3	32,709	31,475	28,366	4,580	4,492	4,445	3,228
Ocean City, NJ...........................	4,704	4,573	3,972	3,563	18.4	48,694	47,027	40,016	2,264	2,245	2,125	1,705
Odessa, TX...............................	5,378	4,686	3,287	2,667	63.6	38,385	34,163	26,215	4,452	3,727	2,573	2,056
Ogden–Clearfield, UT	18,976	17,942	14,202	11,607	33.6	34,134	32,649	29,141	11,904	11,381	9,534	7,645
Oklahoma City, OK	51,124	47,508	38,462	31,477	32.9	40,002	37,761	33,120	39,817	37,066	30,742	25,252
Olympia, WA..............................	10,585	10,098	7,998	6,624	32.3	41,251	39,912	35,230	6,152	6,051	5,080	4,142
Omaha–Council Bluffs, NE–IA...........	39,005	36,987	31,077	25,905	25.5	44,470	42,606	38,164	30,230	29,237	24,993	20,892
Orlando–Kissimmee–Sanford, FL.......	77,159	73,619	64,007	47,885	20.5	35,535	34,408	32,727	58,613	56,612	53,660	39,727
Oshkosh–Neenah, WI....................	6,447	6,198	5,270	4,612	22.3	38,444	37,095	32,641	5,648	5,447	4,807	4,159
Owensboro, KY...........................	3,999	3,773	3,140	2,704	27.4	34,677	32,845	28,166	2,721	2,570	2,301	1,977
Oxnard–Thousand Oaks–Ventura, CA	38,141	36,506	33,151	26,624	15.1	45,855	44,226	41,742	23,091	22,314	21,977	16,869
Palm Bay–Melbourne–Titusville, FL....	20,671	19,945	17,578	13,685	17.6	38,028	36,675	33,172	12,524	12,388	11,945	9,035
Palm Coast, FL...........................	3,230	3,034	2,190	1,299	47.5	33,170	31,595	28,440	824	813	752	445
Panama City–Lynn Haven–Panama City Beach, FL..	6,296	6,103	5,135	3,817	22.6	37,068	36,050	31,519	4,186	4,150	3,796	2,700
Parkersburg–Marietta–Vienna, WV–OH	5,304	5,059	4,329	3,971	22.5	32,694	31,220	26,580	3,612	3,471	3,247	2,957
Pascagoula, MS..........................	5,584	5,460	4,322	3,551	29.2	34,304	33,631	27,248	3,666	3,786	2,908	2,458
Pensacola–Ferry Pass–Brent, FL.......	16,352	15,523	13,017	10,419	25.6	36,079	34,496	29,619	9,966	9,595	8,672	6,980
Peoria, IL.................................	16,580	15,262	12,617	10,731	31.4	43,684	40,273	34,120	12,551	11,306	10,064	8,074
Philadelphia–Camden–Wilmington, PA–NJ–DE–MD ...	291,970	279,708	236,491	201,728	23.5	48,723	46,840	40,571	213,069	206,631	184,158	153,428
Camden, NJ	56,051	54,166	46,273	39,654	21.1	44,772	43,288	37,487	34,691	34,214	31,399	25,529
Philadelphia, PA	204,090	195,634	163,356	139,412	24.9	50,631	48,737	41,787	153,029	148,283	129,708	108,665
Wilmington, DE–MD–NJ................	31,829	29,908	26,862	22,662	18.5	44,857	42,350	39,183	25,350	24,135	23,050	19,233

[1]Based on resident population estimated as of July 1 of the year shown.

Table B-11. Personal Income and Earnings, by Place of Work—*Continued*

Metropolitan statistical area and division	Personal income								Earnings (million dollars)			
	Total (million dollars)				Percent change, 2005–2011	Per capita[1] (dollars)						
	2011	2010	2005	2001		2011	2010	2005	2011	2010	2005	2001
Phoenix–Mesa–Glendale, AZ	157,026	149,094	131,597	99,952	19.3	36,833	35,422	34,863	116,671	111,630	104,208	80,912
Pine Bluff, AR	3,053	2,984	2,575	2,219	18.6	30,866	29,801	24,776	2,046	2,044	1,912	1,628
Pittsburgh, PA	106,146	100,489	84,956	76,823	24.9	44,982	42,617	35,779	77,443	73,439	64,688	57,523
Pittsfield, MA	5,803	5,558	4,892	4,356	18.6	44,483	42,384	36,902	3,514	3,406	3,377	2,896
Pocatello, ID	2,652	2,540	2,210	1,854	20.0	28,998	27,951	26,049	1,819	1,741	1,666	1,375
Portland–South Portland–Biddeford, ME	22,675	21,571	18,631	15,882	21.7	43,960	41,987	36,510	16,398	15,962	14,314	12,004
Portland–Vancouver–Hillsboro, OR–WA	93,449	87,940	74,750	65,340	25.0	41,302	39,384	36,158	70,589	66,810	59,951	52,579
Port St. Lucie, FL	16,414	15,679	13,864	10,288	18.4	38,362	36,872	36,117	6,866	6,664	6,495	4,356
Poughkeepsie–Newburgh–Middletown, NY	28,585	27,416	22,773	19,488	25.5	42,482	40,841	34,563	16,136	15,778	13,903	11,600
Prescott, AZ	6,248	6,015	5,279	3,815	18.4	29,490	28,488	27,013	2,754	2,728	2,633	1,920
Providence–New Bedford–Fall River, RI–MA	69,116	66,193	57,418	49,432	20.4	43,192	41,343	35,589	43,964	42,523	39,328	32,673
Provo–Orem, UT	13,975	13,112	10,250	8,039	36.3	25,841	24,734	23,315	10,363	9,783	7,919	6,224
Pueblo, CO	5,099	4,832	4,010	3,597	27.1	31,760	30,302	26,766	3,178	3,021	2,569	2,297
Punta Gorda, FL	5,644	5,390	4,894	3,853	15.3	35,161	33,662	31,522	2,116	2,049	2,087	1,548
Racine, WI	7,508	7,239	6,533	5,778	14.9	38,425	37,026	33,803	4,566	4,353	4,242	3,647
Raleigh–Cary, NC	47,275	44,557	35,209	29,174	34.3	40,631	39,178	37,269	34,287	32,744	26,802	22,463
Rapid City, SD	5,299	4,944	3,943	3,148	34.4	41,286	38,986	33,366	3,552	3,363	2,841	2,292
Reading, PA	15,552	14,883	12,609	11,138	23.3	37,675	36,081	31,846	10,250	9,852	8,932	7,773
Redding, CA	6,305	6,105	5,478	4,480	15.1	35,466	34,431	31,195	3,574	3,493	3,708	2,904
Reno–Sparks, NV	17,922	17,160	16,970	13,224	5.6	41,718	40,252	42,795	11,921	11,598	11,871	9,775
Richmond, VA	54,641	51,643	44,587	36,484	22.5	43,046	40,974	37,749	41,849	40,189	35,977	29,360
Riverside–San Bernardino–Ontario, CA	128,982	123,561	108,598	83,537	18.8	29,961	29,107	28,020	74,124	71,656	71,711	50,663
Roanoke, VA	12,081	11,521	9,840	8,463	22.8	39,115	37,329	33,199	8,812	8,541	7,817	6,675
Rochester, MN	8,288	8,204	6,645	5,611	24.7	44,174	44,030	37,744	6,844	6,978	5,925	4,820
Rochester, NY	43,987	42,157	35,256	31,542	24.8	41,683	39,970	33,728	31,205	30,284	27,315	24,146
Rockford, IL	11,914	11,498	9,943	8,879	19.8	34,201	32,915	29,601	8,463	8,044	7,767	6,886
Rocky Mount, NC	4,775	4,629	4,042	3,669	18.1	31,380	30,371	27,494	3,113	3,066	3,022	2,776
Rome, GA	3,183	3,072	2,686	2,312	18.5	33,159	31,903	28,469	2,098	2,079	1,923	1,709
Sacramento—Arden-Arcade—Roseville, CA	88,670	85,088	75,029	59,784	18.2	40,745	39,492	36,872	64,484	62,483	60,356	46,312
Saginaw–Saginaw Township North, MI	6,372	6,070	5,639	5,440	13.0	32,007	30,356	27,191	4,644	4,387	4,632	4,613
St. Cloud, MN	6,699	6,363	5,434	4,550	23.3	35,253	33,622	30,323	5,337	5,076	4,562	3,684
St. George, UT	3,848	3,666	2,882	1,998	33.5	27,159	26,468	24,219	2,253	2,175	1,935	1,285
St. Joseph, MO–KS	4,362	4,153	3,335	2,954	30.8	34,189	32,632	27,010	3,098	2,971	2,456	2,089
St. Louis, MO–IL[3]	120,763	115,355	101,082	87,548	19.5	42,864	40,983	36,697	88,453	85,276	78,314	67,142
Salem, OR	13,180	12,659	10,512	8,944	25.4	33,378	32,315	28,563	8,483	8,364	7,432	6,079
Salinas, CA	17,356	16,678	15,095	12,995	15.0	41,138	40,055	37,259	11,904	11,641	11,249	9,309
Salisbury, MD	4,218	4,081	3,400	2,760	24.1	33,601	32,563	28,737	2,866	2,820	2,558	1,999
Salt Lake City, UT	45,373	42,882	35,347	29,605	28.4	39,595	38,007	34,273	40,788	38,928	32,179	27,548
San Angelo, TX	4,258	3,995	3,165	2,661	34.5	37,532	35,583	29,697	2,762	2,610	2,244	1,863
San Antonio–New Braunfels, TX	80,732	75,810	58,670	47,463	37.6	36,781	35,197	30,939	58,891	55,891	45,262	37,001
San Diego–Carlsbad–San Marcos, CA	146,956	139,578	122,030	99,443	20.4	46,800	44,951	41,530	110,042	105,620	97,200	77,153
Sandusky, OH	2,929	2,787	2,603	2,389	12.5	38,161	36,177	33,339	1,961	1,877	1,966	1,784
San Francisco–Oakland–Fremont, CA	269,588	254,377	227,850	203,812	18.3	61,395	58,567	55,065	202,200	192,303	179,929	164,244
Oakland–Fremont–Hayward, CA	136,687	129,725	115,292	102,171	18.6	52,653	50,562	47,240	88,002	85,114	82,802	70,244
San Francisco–San Mateo–Redwood City, CA	132,901	124,652	112,558	101,640	18.1	74,037	70,118	66,316	114,198	107,189	97,126	94,000
San Jose–Sunnyvale–Santa Clara, CA	113,844	104,472	89,629	85,810	27.0	61,028	56,723	51,810	111,688	102,648	88,369	90,061
San Luis Obispo–Paso Robles, CA	10,966	10,436	9,170	7,498	19.6	40,322	38,636	35,457	6,611	6,347	6,154	4,712
Santa Barbara–Santa Maria–Goleta, CA	19,303	18,310	16,702	13,371	15.6	45,219	43,120	40,928	13,065	12,508	11,901	9,340
Santa Cruz–Watsonville, CA	12,920	12,247	10,966	10,089	17.8	48,883	46,586	43,625	6,496	6,277	6,388	5,848
Santa Fe, NM	6,310	6,057	5,462	4,285	15.5	43,325	41,916	39,660	3,887	3,828	3,676	2,822
Santa Rosa–Petaluma, CA	22,127	20,975	19,537	17,542	13.3	45,331	43,274	41,931	12,840	12,387	12,686	11,028
Savannah, GA	14,337	13,471	10,583	8,404	35.5	40,321	38,652	33,646	9,426	9,087	7,727	6,140
Scranton—Wilkes-Barre, PA	20,777	19,989	16,965	15,162	22.5	36,889	35,460	30,476	13,314	12,946	12,057	10,573
Seattle–Tacoma–Bellevue, WA	178,307	167,885	138,212	119,033	29.0	50,944	48,692	43,215	145,917	138,307	116,035	102,962
Seattle–Bellevue–Everett, WA	145,189	136,260	112,633	97,818	28.9	53,931	51,370	45,970	124,484	117,408	99,231	90,160
Tacoma, WA	33,118	31,625	25,579	21,215	29.5	40,992	39,761	34,190	21,434	20,900	16,804	12,802
Sebastian–Vero Beach, FL	7,080	6,737	6,374	4,524	11.1	50,977	48,726	49,814	2,547	2,491	2,471	1,764
Sheboygan, WI	4,596	4,447	3,945	3,441	16.5	39,910	38,516	34,467	3,488	3,408	3,260	2,747
Sherman–Denison, TX	4,056	3,850	3,069	2,632	32.2	33,404	31,793	26,532	2,363	2,255	2,018	1,797
Shreveport–Bossier City, LA	15,700	14,870	11,986	9,755	31.0	38,899	37,185	31,287	11,484	10,939	9,270	7,404
Sioux City, IA–NE–SD	5,334	5,082	4,219	3,841	26.4	37,025	35,325	30,168	4,078	3,962	3,365	3,094
Sioux Falls, SD	10,480	9,715	7,845	6,095	33.6	45,087	42,399	37,969	8,235	7,717	6,417	5,061
South Bend–Mishawaka, IN–MI	11,499	10,976	9,945	8,656	15.6	36,083	34,401	31,350	7,960	7,626	7,331	6,216
Spartanburg, SC	9,085	8,722	7,407	6,482	22.7	31,670	30,625	28,005	7,082	6,810	6,108	5,373
Spokane, WA	17,027	16,329	13,025	11,394	30.7	35,940	34,590	29,574	12,128	11,721	10,198	8,708
Springfield, IL	9,130	8,759	7,053	6,417	29.4	43,158	41,605	34,408	7,281	7,012	5,870	5,233
Springfield, MA	27,711	26,695	22,758	19,839	21.8	39,975	38,521	33,059	16,817	16,398	15,266	13,122
Springfield, MO	14,658	13,997	11,506	9,589	27.4	33,302	31,998	28,559	10,329	9,997	8,983	7,290
Springfield, OH	4,788	4,572	4,107	3,872	16.6	34,777	33,082	29,051	2,535	2,425	2,355	2,392
State College, PA	5,469	5,192	4,101	3,453	33.4	35,347	33,602	28,175	4,536	4,324	3,582	2,921
Steubenville–Weirton, OH–WV	3,862	3,714	3,283	3,066	17.6	31,339	29,887	25,758	2,192	2,117	2,146	1,987

[1]Based on resident population estimated as of July 1 of the year shown.
[3]The portion of Sullivan city in Crawford County, MO is legally part of the St. Louis, MO–IL MSA. That portion is not included in these figures for the St. Louis, MSA.

Table B-11. Personal Income and Earnings, by Place of Work—*Continued*

Metropolitan statistical area and division	Personal income											
	Total (million dollars)				Percent change, 2005–2011	Per capita[1] (dollars)			Earnings (million dollars)			
	2011	2010	2005	2001		2011	2010	2005	2011	2010	2005	2001
Stockton, CA	21,592	20,802	18,300	14,998	18.0	31,013	30,251	27,855	13,106	12,726	12,695	9,734
Sumter, SC	3,215	3,102	2,679	2,228	20.0	29,915	28,839	25,252	2,330	2,185	2,061	1,700
Syracuse, NY	25,619	24,721	20,336	17,798	26.0	38,668	37,293	31,047	18,504	18,153	15,913	13,771
Tallahassee, FL	12,845	12,466	10,563	8,543	21.6	34,740	33,884	30,684	9,284	9,201	8,368	6,991
Tampa–St. Petersburg–Clearwater, FL	110,901	106,083	91,393	72,087	21.3	39,261	38,048	34,467	72,256	69,819	65,875	51,667
Terre Haute, IN	5,428	5,238	4,428	3,930	22.6	31,439	30,378	25,951	3,726	3,643	3,248	2,736
Texarkana, TX–Texarkana, AR	4,749	4,548	3,686	3,071	28.8	34,776	33,392	28,049	3,205	3,101	2,639	2,112
Toledo, OH	23,629	22,504	20,529	18,787	15.1	36,338	34,560	31,177	18,089	17,301	16,842	15,068
Topeka, KS	8,861	8,406	7,018	6,421	26.3	37,765	35,887	30,752	6,335	6,106	5,378	4,912
Trenton–Ewing, NJ	19,985	19,113	16,605	14,443	20.4	54,445	52,088	45,869	19,483	18,767	15,388	12,605
Tucson, AZ	34,596	33,278	28,574	21,929	21.1	34,961	33,884	31,048	21,775	21,218	19,027	14,974
Tulsa, OK	39,996	37,162	30,734	26,629	30.1	42,236	39,529	34,812	29,943	27,802	23,970	21,286
Tuscaloosa, AL	7,600	7,284	5,864	4,774	29.6	34,305	33,148	29,028	5,509	5,316	4,530	3,600
Tyler, TX	8,218	7,811	6,182	4,952	32.9	38,515	37,109	32,305	5,947	5,722	4,819	3,850
Utica–Rome, NY	10,567	10,225	8,236	7,285	28.3	35,406	34,159	27,584	6,821	6,721	5,742	4,965
Valdosta, GA	4,323	4,134	3,263	2,687	32.5	30,377	29,507	25,810	2,999	2,924	2,455	1,947
Vallejo–Fairfield, CA	15,859	15,293	14,105	12,033	12.4	38,078	36,929	34,557	9,226	9,081	8,220	6,427
Victoria, TX	4,627	4,298	3,402	2,913	36.0	39,808	37,232	30,313	3,386	3,134	2,613	2,198
Vineland–Millville–Bridgeton, NJ	5,541	5,325	4,237	3,686	30.8	35,272	33,947	27,871	3,704	3,636	3,221	2,687
Virginia Beach–Norfolk–Newport News, VA–NC	70,516	67,182	56,595	45,334	24.6	41,976	40,121	34,413	54,080	52,744	46,435	36,392
Visalia–Porterville, CA	13,316	12,410	10,230	8,044	30.2	29,640	27,982	25,077	8,724	7,994	7,307	5,454
Waco, TX	8,098	7,799	6,105	4,983	32.6	33,943	33,052	27,401	5,886	5,767	4,750	3,823
Warner Robins, GA	4,990	4,738	3,708	2,954	34.6	34,674	33,648	29,385	4,293	4,179	3,373	2,502
Washington–Arlington–Alexandria, DC–VA–MD–WV	338,498	321,521	262,193	211,329	29.1	59,345	57,321	50,187	299,187	288,872	237,901	189,012
Bethesda–Rockville–Frederick, MD	80,085	76,447	64,506	52,268	24.2	65,293	63,199	56,449	54,969	52,720	43,770	34,685
Washington–Arlington–Alexandria, DC–VA–MD–WV	258,413	245,074	197,688	159,061	30.7	57,715	55,705	48,434	244,219	236,152	194,132	154,327
Waterloo–Cedar Falls, IA	6,596	6,090	5,007	4,324	31.7	39,195	36,264	30,670	5,155	4,765	4,077	3,400
Wausau, WI	5,002	4,846	4,255	3,698	17.5	37,214	36,141	32,998	3,781	3,673	3,544	2,981
Wenatchee–East Wenatchee, WA	3,953	3,764	2,916	2,537	35.5	35,152	33,802	28,213	2,496	2,389	2,054	1,715
Wheeling, WV–OH	5,064	4,795	4,085	3,729	24.0	34,406	32,423	27,335	3,391	3,277	2,828	2,379
Wichita, KS	24,125	23,053	19,835	17,581	21.6	38,568	36,939	33,731	18,772	18,127	16,174	14,311
Wichita Falls, TX	5,510	5,295	4,497	3,957	22.5	36,671	34,953	29,753	3,834	3,739	3,377	2,926
Williamsport, PA	4,119	3,813	3,224	2,930	27.8	35,283	32,824	27,430	2,913	2,627	2,399	2,157
Wilmington, NC	12,770	12,090	9,790	7,735	30.4	34,543	33,236	30,713	8,015	7,701	6,540	5,276
Winchester, VA–WV	4,559	4,316	3,572	2,865	27.6	35,048	33,528	30,313	3,179	3,044	2,731	2,099
Winston–Salem, NC	17,554	16,670	15,185	12,936	15.6	36,416	34,840	33,942	12,754	12,343	11,501	10,042
Worcester, MA	36,494	34,756	29,016	25,904	25.8	45,548	43,483	37,140	22,003	21,138	19,151	16,880
Yakima, WA	8,247	7,829	5,924	5,227	39.2	33,371	32,029	25,916	5,395	5,137	4,212	3,571
York–Hanover, PA	16,326	15,559	13,207	11,086	23.6	37,380	35,708	32,286	10,382	9,934	9,219	7,513
Youngstown–Warren–Boardman, OH–PA	18,818	17,938	16,559	15,125	13.6	33,440	31,750	28,343	11,730	11,144	11,374	10,196
Yuba City, CA	5,428	5,200	4,229	3,427	28.3	32,404	31,097	27,276	3,308	3,168	2,763	2,153
Yuma, AZ	5,442	5,187	4,116	3,011	32.2	27,091	26,351	23,020	3,783	3,590	3,088	2,221

[1]Based on resident population estimated as of July 1 of the year shown.

Table B-12. Employees and Earnings, by Selected Major Industries, 2011

| | Employees | | | | | | Earnings | | | | | |
| | | Percent by selected major industries | | | | | | Percent by selected major industries | | | | |
Metropolitan statistical area and division	Total[1]	Manufacturing	Finance and insurance	Professional and technical services	Health care and social services	Government and government enterprises	Total[1] (million dollars)	Manufacturing	Finance and insurance	Professional and technical services	Health care and social services	Government and government enterprises
Abilene, TX	98,765	3.0	6.0	3.5	10.5	18.4	3,941	3.5	5.0	4.0	13.8	28.8
Akron, OH	403,347	10.0	4.1	5.8	12.9	12.6	19,282	15.0	4.4	6.8	13.6	14.9
Albany, GA	78,804	5.6	3.2	4.6	(D)	18.6	3,407	(D)	2.7	5.2	14.3	27.2
Albany–Schenectady–Troy, NY	537,845	4.2	6.1	7.9	12.7	19.1	28,955	6.9	7.1	11.0	11.9	26.0
Albuquerque, NM	482,523	4.1	4.0	8.9	11.5	18.3	22,632	6.3	4.0	12.5	11.8	26.6
Alexandria, LA	81,458	4.9	3.5	4.1	16.2	18.6	3,734	10.0	2.7	5.0	18.0	24.9
Allentown–Bethlehem–Easton, PA–NJ	426,161	8.6	4.7	4.9	14.6	10.2	21,020	13.3	4.2	5.1	16.6	12.2
Altoona, PA	73,355	10.4	3.4	3.9	15.7	12.7	3,094	13.2	3.4	4.6	19.5	16.0
Amarillo, TX	156,549	(D)	6.7	4.1	10.9	13.2	7,012	(D)	5.3	6.7	13.5	16.1
Ames, IA	56,087	7.2	2.4	4.2	7.3	35.3	2,724	15.7	1.9	4.0	7.6	40.1
Anchorage, AK	235,296	1.3	3.5	7.3	12.2	20.9	15,034	0.9	4.4	9.5	11.7	28.6
Anderson, IN	50,998	7.7	3.2	3.1	14.1	12.7	2,024	15.5	3.2	2.6	16.3	16.7
Anderson, SC	85,297	14.3	3.1	3.0	6.9	14.5	3,142	24.2	3.0	3.0	8.1	21.6
Ann Arbor, MI	243,300	6.2	2.6	9.1	10.8	30.8	12,689	9.7	2.9	11.9	11.1	35.5
Anniston–Oxford, AL	60,844	9.6	2.4	3.9	8.7	22.9	2,641	13.1	2.0	4.0	9.2	36.4
Appleton, WI	147,720	15.2	6.8	4.4	(D)	8.7	6,687	21.9	7.4	4.8	10.2	11.2
Asheville, NC	237,417	7.9	3.3	4.9	13.0	12.1	8,942	13.3	4.1	4.8	18.1	17.9
Athens–Clarke County, GA	109,941	6.7	3.2	4.5	10.8	25.6	4,382	12.0	4.0	3.7	15.4	33.5
Atlanta–Sandy Springs–Marietta, GA	3,115,980	5.0	5.3	8.5	8.6	10.8	171,979	7.3	7.6	12.2	8.5	12.7
Atlantic City–Hammonton, NJ	174,213	1.5	3.2	4.2	11.2	13.8	8,485	1.9	2.7	5.2	14.1	21.7
Auburn–Opelika, AL	68,979	8.4	2.8	4.3	5.9	24.1	2,567	11.7	2.5	4.2	7.2	37.1
Augusta–Richmond County, GA–SC	300,066	6.9	3.2	4.8	9.4	19.9	13,765	10.2	2.7	6.6	10.1	30.8
Austin–Round Rock–San Marcos, TX	1,104,889	4.9	6.0	9.7	8.1	15.5	58,481	9.7	6.1	13.5	9.0	17.6
Bakersfield–Delano, CA	366,018	4.0	3.0	4.8	9.3	16.8	20,245	5.1	2.2	4.8	8.0	23.3
Baltimore–Towson, MD	1,682,859	3.9	5.1	9.2	13.1	16.7	101,298	5.7	6.0	12.7	12.4	24.6
Bangor, ME	90,104	4.5	2.8	3.8	16.8	16.6	3,765	6.3	3.0	4.1	21.9	21.2
Barnstable Town, MA	138,000	1.6	4.1	7.0	13.2	11.1	5,612	2.4	3.9	8.5	18.2	19.1
Baton Rouge, LA	489,723	5.5	4.2	(D)	9.8	16.1	23,539	11.9	4.4	7.2	10.1	19.4
Battle Creek, MI	66,039	16.8	2.2	(D)	14.0	16.1	3,383	23.0	1.6	(D)	12.9	21.9
Bay City, MI	46,863	8.0	4.1	6.2	15.1	12.9	2,001	12.8	3.3	11.7	17.3	17.2
Beaumont–Port Arthur, TX	209,405	10.3	4.0	4.8	11.2	12.5	10,904	23.3	2.6	6.5	10.5	13.6
Bellingham, WA	110,012	8.4	3.3	5.9	10.7	14.6	5,007	13.7	3.5	5.8	11.5	19.0
Bend, OR	92,351	5.1	4.5	7.0	12.0	9.5	3,674	6.2	4.5	8.3	18.8	14.2
Billings, MT	107,113	3.3	4.7	6.2	13.0	9.6	4,630	6.5	5.0	7.4	17.2	14.1
Binghamton, NY	131,722	10.8	4.0	4.4	13.5	17.6	5,893	18.8	3.7	4.6	15.1	22.7
Birmingham–Hoover, AL	646,459	5.7	6.8	6.2	10.3	13.2	33,472	7.3	8.7	8.8	12.7	15.5
Bismarck, ND	82,131	2.3	5.3	5.3	(D)	16.4	3,591	3.4	5.2	6.6	16.6	21.1
Blacksburg–Christiansburg–Radford, VA	81,615	12.9	2.5	(D)	(D)	25.2	3,446	21.3	1.7	(D)	(D)	32.8
Bloomington, IN	102,200	8.9	2.5	4.2	10.0	25.1	3,978	14.3	2.1	4.6	12.9	32.0
Bloomington–Normal, IL	111,366	3.8	13.3	(D)	10.1	14.0	6,195	4.3	21.2	(D)	10.0	14.2
Boise City–Nampa, ID	354,568	7.0	5.1	6.1	11.6	12.7	16,178	11.7	6.3	8.4	12.9	15.7
Boston–Cambridge–Quincy, MA–NH	3,124,251	6.0	7.0	11.0	13.3	10.0	220,095	8.8	12.5	16.5	12.4	10.5
Boston–Quincy, MA	1,384,193	3.2	9.7	9.8	15.4	10.9	104,537	3.8	20.2	14.7	15.0	11.2
Cambridge–Newton–Framingham, MA	1,079,520	7.6	4.9	14.6	10.7	8.5	80,292	11.9	5.2	21.9	8.6	8.8
Peabody, MA	407,685	10.6	4.8	8.2	14.8	10.2	22,235	20.0	5.2	9.9	15.5	12.4
Rockingham County–Strafford County, NH	252,853	7.6	5.7	7.3	9.8	11.1	13,030	11.2	7.9	8.8	10.6	12.5
Boulder, CO	236,350	7.3	5.2	15.6	9.8	13.5	12,907	12.5	4.5	21.6	9.4	15.2
Bowling Green, KY	73,950	11.2	3.2	3.1	11.3	15.9	2,996	16.9	4.3	3.5	13.5	18.6
Bremerton–Silverdale, WA	121,486	1.6	3.0	6.6	11.2	33.2	6,708	1.6	2.2	5.9	9.9	56.2
Bridgeport–Stamford–Norwalk, CT	612,943	6.4	12.7	9.1	11.4	7.9	52,411	9.7	25.4	10.5	8.4	7.1
Brownsville–Harlingen, TX	174,174	3.5	3.8	2.7	19.8	18.2	5,902	5.2	3.3	2.7	20.7	29.6
Brunswick, GA	53,410	4.9	3.5	3.7	7.4	19.8	2,146	8.3	3.0	3.7	8.6	33.8
Buffalo–Niagara Falls, NY	645,173	8.2	6.3	6.1	12.7	14.1	31,644	12.8	6.3	7.7	13.3	20.2
Burlington, NC	78,721	11.7	3.6	3.8	11.9	9.4	2,980	16.6	4.3	3.9	16.4	11.7
Burlington–South Burlington, VT	154,681	9.1	3.6	7.4	13.6	14.0	7,527	14.4	4.7	9.8	14.4	19.0
Canton–Massillon, OH	213,558	12.5	4.9	4.1	13.9	10.1	8,883	20.6	4.5	4.0	16.7	13.1
Cape Coral–Fort Myers, FL	290,205	1.8	5.1	6.4	8.6	13.1	12,027	2.8	4.2	8.3	12.2	20.6
Cape Girardeau–Jackson, MO–IL	60,557	7.0	3.7	3.2	16.7	12.5	2,383	10.8	3.5	3.3	25.7	15.2
Carson City, NV	37,901	7.3	8.3	4.8	11.0	25.5	1,837	9.3	6.6	4.9	15.3	36.0
Casper, WY	54,254	3.6	4.3	4.6	12.1	11.4	2,984	4.4	2.9	4.7	13.1	13.1
Cedar Rapids, IA	173,712	12.4	6.3	4.2	(D)	10.4	8,834	22.0	7.2	4.6	9.7	11.0
Champaign–Urbana, IL	136,084	6.0	4.0	5.3	10.2	28.1	6,417	7.2	3.1	5.7	12.0	36.0
Charleston, WV	176,361	3.2	4.5	5.5	13.5	16.6	9,293	5.1	4.7	8.0	14.2	17.9
Charleston–North Charleston–Summerville, SC	411,272	5.7	3.5	7.0	8.3	17.6	19,424	10.0	5.7	9.8	9.5	26.5
Charlotte–Gastonia–Rock Hill, NC–SC	1,089,621	6.5	7.6	6.8	7.8	11.3	61,192	8.7	13.6	9.0	7.6	11.9
Charlottesville, VA	135,484	2.8	3.4	8.6	8.5	24.7	6,623	3.7	4.4	10.7	9.9	34.4
Chattanooga, TN–GA	299,554	10.5	6.9	4.7	9.9	12.9	13,990	14.0	9.0	5.9	11.6	17.4
Cheyenne, WY	63,105	2.7	5.6	4.4	7.8	27.8	3,120	4.4	4.2	4.4	8.3	41.2
Chicago–Joliet–Naperville, IL–IN–WI	5,544,983	7.7	6.9	8.0	11.2	10.8	340,490	10.9	9.8	12.5	9.7	12.9
Chicago–Joliet–Naperville, IL	4,703,282	7.1	7.2	8.3	11.3	10.4	291,401	9.3	10.6	13.4	9.7	12.6
Gary, IN	336,491	10.7	3.1	4.0	13.4	11.8	16,441	21.7	2.3	3.7	13.9	12.4
Lake County–Kenosha County, IL–WI	505,210	11.1	6.6	7.1	9.3	13.2	32,648	20.1	6.3	8.5	8.0	15.4

[1]Includes other industry categories not shown separately.
(D) = Data withheld to avoid disclosure or does not meet statistical standards.

Table B-12. Employees and Earnings, by Selected Major Industries, 2011—*Continued*

Metropolitan statistical area and division	Employees						Earnings					
	Total[1]	Percent by selected major industries					Total[1] (million dollars)	Percent by selected major industries				
		Manufacturing	Finance and insurance	Professional and technical services	Health care and social services	Government and government enterprises		Manufacturing	Finance and insurance	Professional and technical services	Health care and social services	Government and government enterprises
Chico, CA	99,654	4.4	3.7	5.2	15.2	15.4	4,189	4.9	3.3	5.3	19.2	21.3
Cincinnati–Middletown, OH–KY–IN	1,252,833	8.6	5.8	6.6	11.6	10.9	65,650	13.0	7.1	8.2	12.0	12.5
Clarksville, TN–KY	147,978	7.1	2.1	3.6	7.3	37.4	8,736	7.8	1.4	3.4	5.2	60.7
Cleveland, TN	52,829	15.9	3.4	3.0	(D)	11.6	2,331	23.2	3.3	3.0	(D)	12.8
Cleveland–Elyria–Mentor, OH	1,256,980	9.9	5.8	6.5	14.1	11.2	67,582	15.2	6.9	9.1	13.6	14.1
Coeur d'Alene, ID	74,621	6.4	5.1	5.5	9.8	14.1	2,704	8.5	5.0	6.9	12.1	20.9
College Station–Bryan, TX	124,455	4.4	3.3	5.4	8.2	27.6	4,937	5.9	2.5	5.8	10.4	35.7
Colorado Springs, CO	376,852	3.7	5.8	8.3	8.4	24.1	19,948	4.8	4.6	11.1	7.9	38.7
Columbia, MO	117,297	3.5	5.0	5.1	9.4	27.2	4,987	4.3	6.2	5.4	11.2	37.5
Columbia, SC	456,764	6.3	5.7	5.3	8.6	19.8	20,896	8.9	7.1	7.4	9.6	28.2
Columbus, GA–AL	177,753	6.1	7.6	4.5	9.8	26.8	8,889	7.1	9.1	5.1	9.2	43.9
Columbus, IN	54,657	28.7	2.8	3.8	7.6	12.1	2,903	44.3	4.2	3.8	7.0	11.3
Columbus, OH	1,184,132	5.7	6.6	7.7	11.2	14.4	61,030	8.5	8.4	11.1	10.6	17.5
Corpus Christi, TX	241,843	4.2	4.2	4.3	13.3	15.9	12,028	8.2	2.8	5.0	12.2	21.2
Corvallis, OR	55,141	6.9	2.4	7.2	11.9	26.8	2,341	14.1	1.9	7.4	15.1	30.2
Crestview–Fort Walton Beach–Destin, FL	121,301	3.0	4.1	7.1	7.7	25.8	6,216	4.0	3.1	9.3	6.8	47.3
Cumberland, MD–WV	48,908	9.3	2.8	(D)	(D)	17.9	2,029	14.4	2.3	(D)	17.0	25.3
Dallas–Fort Worth–Arlington, TX	4,022,102	6.7	7.9	7.7	8.8	10.0	237,126	10.1	8.9	10.5	9.7	10.9
Dallas–Plano–Irving, TX	2,816,119	6.3	8.5	8.7	8.7	9.8	174,608	9.2	9.9	11.8	9.6	10.1
Fort Worth–Arlington, TX	1,205,983	7.7	6.6	5.5	9.0	10.6	62,518	12.8	6.2	6.9	9.9	12.9
Dalton, GA	76,765	29.7	2.2	5.4	(D)	9.5	3,334	36.9	1.6	7.2	(D)	11.1
Danville, IL	37,921	14.0	4.7	(D)	9.9	16.3	1,751	20.9	3.7	(D)	9.2	22.1
Danville, VA	50,206	13.9	3.0	2.8	13.0	14.3	1,865	23.4	2.3	2.4	13.8	18.6
Davenport–Moline–Rock Island, IA–IL	226,828	10.6	4.9	4.1	11.5	12.8	11,824	15.1	4.4	6.1	10.6	17.4
Dayton, OH	469,323	8.8	4.1	6.0	13.4	15.6	23,404	12.1	4.0	8.3	14.4	24.6
Decatur, AL	72,447	17.1	3.3	3.0	(D)	12.8	3,045	32.5	2.9	3.0	(D)	15.7
Decatur, IL	64,830	16.5	4.0	4.5	13.3	9.6	3,470	28.7	2.8	4.4	12.8	10.5
Deltona–Daytona Beach–Ormond Beach, FL	198,853	4.4	3.9	5.0	14.8	11.2	7,575	6.7	3.7	5.2	19.5	17.3
Denver–Aurora–Broomfield, CO[2]	1,670,014	4.1	7.5	9.8	8.9	11.7	103,112	5.4	8.9	12.9	8.1	13.2
Des Moines–West Des Moines, IA	406,242	4.8	14.5	5.2	10.6	11.1	22,105	5.8	23.3	6.0	10.0	13.1
Detroit–Warren–Livonia, MI	2,300,015	9.4	5.0	9.2	13.4	9.2	128,083	15.2	5.5	13.5	12.6	11.8
Detroit–Livonia–Dearborn, MI	887,308	8.7	3.6	7.4	15.5	11.7	50,804	14.2	3.8	11.6	13.6	14.9
Warren–Troy–Farmington Hills, MI	1,412,707	9.8	5.8	10.3	12.1	7.6	77,279	15.8	6.6	14.8	11.9	9.8
Dothan, AL	76,407	6.7	3.2	2.8	(D)	14.7	2,975	8.4	3.1	3.5	14.9	19.4
Dover, DE	86,475	(D)	3.7	3.1	10.7	27.3	3,954	(D)	6.8	3.1	11.3	39.6
Dubuque, IA	68,281	12.3	6.1	5.5	12.5	7.3	3,033	19.0	7.1	7.2	14.1	8.4
Duluth, MN–WI	157,527	5.0	4.2	3.6	18.7	16.6	6,925	7.6	5.0	3.7	20.2	21.0
Durham–Chapel Hill, NC	365,895	9.5	4.4	10.1	13.5	17.2	21,918	21.1	5.9	12.1	13.0	19.4
Eau Claire, WI	105,783	10.5	5.4	3.8	13.5	11.5	4,340	15.0	5.3	3.8	17.4	14.5
El Centro, CA	69,931	4.2	2.2	2.4	7.6	26.1	3,406	3.9	1.8	1.8	4.4	39.3
Elizabethtown, KY	73,878	7.5	3.1	3.4	7.0	35.4	4,201	9.2	2.1	2.9	5.1	58.9
Elkhart–Goshen, IN	132,986	36.3	2.7	2.7	8.3	6.8	5,911	45.3	2.2	2.6	9.1	8.0
Elmira, NY	47,944	12.8	3.3	3.1	15.2	14.6	2,199	18.5	3.2	2.6	16.0	20.9
El Paso, TX	397,184	4.8	3.8	3.6	10.0	23.8	18,515	6.5	2.5	3.3	9.6	38.7
Erie, PA	160,353	13.7	4.9	3.5	16.2	11.5	6,843	23.4	6.3	3.6	17.7	15.2
Eugene–Springfield, OR	190,508	6.5	3.6	5.5	13.4	16.1	7,707	9.9	3.9	5.5	16.8	20.8
Evansville, IN–KY	208,589	13.4	2.7	3.6	12.8	9.6	10,236	21.3	2.3	4.2	13.5	10.1
Fairbanks, AK	59,014	1.4	1.8	4.7	9.5	36.1	3,692	1.4	1.6	3.2	8.0	51.6
Fargo, ND–MN	153,631	6.3	6.5	5.0	12.7	12.5	7,377	7.9	7.0	6.1	13.3	14.8
Farmington, NM	63,122	3.0	2.2	2.6	10.9	17.7	3,061	2.6	1.6	2.2	11.5	21.0
Fayetteville, NC	220,936	4.3	2.0	3.4	7.1	42.3	14,031	4.3	1.1	3.1	4.4	67.8
Fayetteville–Springdale–Rogers, AR–MO	263,813	10.8	3.1	5.4	8.7	11.4	12,385	10.9	3.2	6.6	9.0	13.9
Flagstaff, AZ	81,813	5.3	2.5	4.2	11.5	20.4	3,253	10.2	1.3	3.0	16.2	32.3
Flint, MI	185,014	6.1	4.5	4.7	15.4	12.7	7,606	12.3	5.2	6.1	18.6	18.6
Florence, SC	113,768	9.1	7.5	4.1	11.0	14.9	4,638	17.1	10.8	5.0	12.5	19.2
Florence–Muscle Shoals, AL	73,306	11.0	3.7	2.8	9.9	15.1	2,798	15.4	3.2	2.9	12.7	23.1
Fond du Lac, WI	58,096	16.9	4.8	2.9	11.0	10.4	2,542	25.0	4.1	2.5	13.2	12.8
Fort Collins–Loveland, CO	191,480	6.3	4.8	8.9	10.5	15.6	8,227	13.6	3.3	11.2	13.0	20.0
Fort Smith, AR–OK	151,393	13.6	3.1	(D)	(D)	13.8	6,190	17.9	2.6	(D)	(D)	17.6
Fort Wayne, IN	249,993	13.4	5.2	4.2	13.3	9.3	11,539	20.4	6.2	5.1	15.6	11.0
Fresno, CA	428,951	6.0	4.5	4.4	10.6	15.6	20,492	7.1	4.1	4.6	12.8	21.9
Gadsden, AL	47,567	10.9	3.6	3.0	(D)	12.5	1,776	16.4	3.5	2.9	(D)	16.8
Gainesville, FL	159,369	3.0	3.9	6.2	14.0	27.3	7,093	4.3	4.0	6.1	17.2	39.5
Gainesville, GA	97,488	16.3	5.6	3.5	11.7	11.0	4,234	19.3	6.6	3.1	15.1	12.9
Glens Falls, NY	68,725	9.7	4.0	(D)	12.7	15.0	2,908	15.5	3.8	(D)	14.1	21.1
Goldsboro, NC	58,380	9.2	3.0	2.3	11.9	25.1	2,570	10.8	2.8	2.1	11.5	37.4
Grand Forks, ND–MN	68,551	5.0	3.1	3.2	14.9	21.6	2,983	6.2	2.8	3.5	15.6	28.1
Grand Junction, CO	83,565	3.6	4.7	5.1	12.1	11.9	3,428	4.1	4.0	5.2	15.1	17.4
Grand Rapids–Wyoming, MI	471,748	13.6	5.3	5.1	12.4	7.3	22,247	19.7	7.6	7.0	13.8	10.0
Great Falls, MT	50,143	2.1	6.5	4.0	14.1	18.9	2,264	2.8	6.6	4.8	16.3	30.2

[1]Includes other industry categories not shown separately.

[2]The Denver–Aurora metropolitan statistical area includes Broomfield County. Broomfield County, CO, was formed from parts of Adams, Boulder, Jefferson, and Weld Counties on November 15, 2001, and is coextensive with Broomfield city. For the purposes of defining and presenting data for the Denver–Aurora metropolitan statistical area, Broomfield city is treated as if it were a county when data are available to do so. In many cases, the data were not available.

(D) = Data withheld to avoid disclosure or does not meet statistical standards.

Table B-12. Employees and Earnings, by Selected Major Industries, 2011—*Continued*

Metropolitan statistical area and division	Employees						Earnings					
	Total[1]	Percent by selected major industries					Total[1] (million dollars)	Percent by selected major industries				
		Manufacturing	Finance and insurance	Professional and technical services	Health care and social services	Government and government enterprises		Manufacturing	Finance and insurance	Professional and technical services	Health care and social services	Government and government enterprises
Greeley, CO	120,143	9.9	5.2	4.1	8.2	13.4	5,299	11.7	4.7	3.5	8.6	14.5
Green Bay, WI	204,277	14.0	7.1	4.5	10.2	10.7	10,000	18.0	7.5	5.2	12.5	11.8
Greensboro–High Point, NC	431,493	12.4	5.4	4.7	10.5	10.8	19,869	17.2	7.6	6.0	11.7	12.9
Greenville, NC	99,167	6.7	3.4	3.1	11.5	26.4	4,161	10.9	3.6	3.1	12.4	37.3
Greenville–Mauldin–Easley, SC	383,324	10.6	3.9	5.8	7.1	11.5	17,348	15.5	4.9	8.0	9.1	14.8
Gulfport–Biloxi, MS	145,670	4.0	3.0	4.4	6.1	23.9	6,850	6.2	2.5	5.3	6.5	38.3
Hagerstown–Martinsburg, MD–WV	125,323	6.7	6.3	4.1	12.2	15.9	5,571	10.8	7.4	4.8	14.0	24.0
Hanford–Corcoran, CA	55,008	8.2	2.1	2.3	10.1	33.5	3,380	8.3	1.3	1.6	8.2	42.3
Harrisburg–Carlisle, PA	388,850	5.5	6.7	5.6	11.6	16.8	20,165	7.6	7.9	7.4	14.0	21.6
Harrisonburg, VA	76,948	14.1	2.7	3.4	9.6	14.0	3,183	19.7	2.4	4.0	11.8	17.5
Hartford–West Hartford–East Hartford, CT	789,250	8.7	10.8	6.7	13.2	12.8	51,575	12.6	18.3	8.1	12.0	15.2
Hattiesburg, MS	79,488	4.4	3.8	(D)	11.1	20.2	3,161	6.7	3.3	(D)	18.0	27.2
Hickory–Lenoir–Morganton, NC	189,949	20.4	2.9	(D)	9.9	13.1	7,380	26.0	2.8	(D)	12.2	16.4
Hinesville–Fort Stewart, GA	44,848	3.9	(D)	2.2	2.7	61.1	3,227	3.8	0.7	1.1	1.2	83.0
Holland–Grand Haven, MI	135,364	23.6	3.3	4.2	7.8	11.4	5,918	34.8	2.8	4.3	6.9	15.3
Honolulu, HI	610,988	2.1	4.0	5.7	9.1	25.1	34,196	1.9	3.4	6.3	9.5	39.2
Hot Springs, AR	51,493	4.5	4.0	5.3	16.1	10.4	1,744	6.3	3.5	5.0	22.7	16.9
Houma–Bayou Cane–Thibodaux, LA	121,265	8.3	2.9	3.6	8.0	12.0	6,687	12.1	1.9	3.6	7.8	11.6
Houston–Sugar Land–Baytown, TX	3,538,942	6.9	5.2	8.1	8.9	10.7	240,196	10.7	5.4	11.5	7.2	10.0
Huntington–Ashland, WV–KY–OH	139,630	6.1	2.7	3.5	17.5	15.3	6,222	11.8	2.3	3.9	21.4	19.3
Huntsville, AL	264,993	8.7	2.5	14.3	6.5	20.1	15,217	11.3	1.8	22.6	6.3	32.4
Idaho Falls, ID	70,062	4.8	4.6	5.1	12.4	10.8	2,768	5.8	3.4	8.3	15.0	13.7
Indianapolis–Carmel, IN	1,108,725	7.6	5.6	6.3	11.0	11.7	58,912	14.2	6.7	8.7	12.6	13.7
Iowa City, IA	116,625	5.6	3.4	3.5	8.3	30.6	5,332	7.4	2.9	2.9	7.4	41.8
Ithaca, NY	66,194	5.1	2.6	6.7	(D)	10.2	3,083	8.0	2.6	6.4	(D)	13.3
Jackson, MI	72,426	11.8	2.9	3.9	12.6	12.8	3,177	18.2	2.4	3.9	14.7	17.8
Jackson, MS	338,780	5.0	5.7	5.3	10.8	18.4	15,519	6.6	7.2	7.0	12.6	23.1
Jackson, TN	73,654	11.4	3.2	(D)	10.0	18.0	3,189	16.5	2.7	(D)	12.7	22.0
Jacksonville, FL	791,320	3.7	8.6	6.6	11.2	12.0	39,028	5.4	11.5	8.1	12.4	18.5
Jacksonville, NC	113,229	0.9	1.5	2.2	3.9	58.2	7,280	0.6	0.8	1.6	2.3	81.1
Janesville, WI	76,227	11.5	3.1	2.9	13.2	12.2	3,350	17.5	2.7	2.8	16.5	15.5
Jefferson City, MO	98,527	6.1	4.0	3.6	(D)	27.4	4,203	7.4	4.1	4.3	(D)	33.2
Johnson City, TN	104,099	8.0	4.3	3.3	(D)	17.7	4,063	12.0	4.0	3.6	(D)	22.7
Johnstown, PA	74,399	6.2	5.1	5.2	18.6	13.0	2,930	8.4	4.9	6.9	21.6	18.6
Jonesboro, AR	66,584	10.5	3.2	2.6	15.3	14.4	2,746	13.6	3.1	2.8	19.4	17.6
Joplin, MO	100,382	13.0	3.0	2.5	12.7	10.4	4,023	17.8	3.1	2.3	15.3	12.5
Kalamazoo–Portage, MI	168,111	11.3	5.1	5.1	13.2	12.0	7,840	20.6	5.5	5.2	15.0	15.7
Kankakee–Bradley, IL	53,472	9.3	4.7	(D)	16.1	12.4	2,256	16.2	3.9	(D)	18.1	17.5
Kansas City, MO–KS	1,264,998	6.0	6.8	7.8	10.1	13.2	69,320	9.0	8.4	11.2	10.3	15.8
Kennewick–Pasco–Richland, WA	135,422	5.5	2.7	11.0	9.0	14.1	7,490	5.6	2.0	17.2	8.3	17.0
Killeen–Temple–Fort Hood, TX	220,698	3.5	3.5	3.6	8.6	39.5	13,028	2.9	1.6	3.6	8.4	61.2
Kingsport–Bristol–Bristol, TN–VA	156,210	14.1	3.0	2.9	(D)	11.1	6,795	26.3	2.5	3.1	(D)	12.5
Kingston, NY	84,247	4.9	3.6	4.8	12.9	16.9	3,382	6.9	3.1	4.1	13.4	30.8
Knoxville, TN	434,892	7.3	4.7	6.9	11.1	12.5	20,362	11.0	4.6	10.2	13.7	15.0
Kokomo, IN	51,529	19.3	3.2	3.1	(D)	14.9	2,482	41.6	2.6	2.8	(D)	15.8
La Crosse, WI–MN	92,427	9.3	5.0	3.2	16.8	12.3	3,919	13.6	5.5	3.3	21.7	14.8
Lafayette, IN	115,185	13.5	3.3	4.6	9.8	22.2	5,282	22.3	3.1	4.1	12.8	26.9
Lafayette, LA	196,462	5.8	3.5	6.3	12.3	9.3	10,316	7.4	2.9	7.9	13.4	10.1
Lake Charles, LA	111,910	8.1	3.0	4.4	11.1	14.7	5,427	19.8	2.4	5.9	12.0	15.7
Lake Havasu City–Kingman, AZ	62,316	4.9	3.1	3.3	13.8	13.6	2,355	6.3	2.3	2.6	21.9	19.6
Lakeland–Winter Haven, FL	257,420	5.8	5.5	4.0	11.3	11.7	10,799	9.0	6.7	4.9	14.4	15.0
Lancaster, PA	295,844	13.1	3.7	4.7	12.6	7.6	13,284	17.5	4.0	5.4	14.0	9.6
Lansing–East Lansing, MI	269,130	6.9	5.7	(D)	11.8	21.3	12,555	11.3	7.1	(D)	12.3	30.4
Laredo, TX	117,946	1.0	3.9	3.3	13.2	18.8	4,656	0.7	2.6	3.2	10.7	29.2
Las Cruces, NM	92,253	3.7	2.6	5.2	14.8	23.5	3,974	4.5	2.6	7.1	13.7	34.6
Las Vegas–Paradise, NV	1,067,839	2.0	5.9	5.3	7.2	10.2	51,822	2.7	5.0	7.3	8.7	16.2
Lawrence, KS	63,310	5.5	3.2	6.9	7.8	24.0	2,351	8.8	3.3	7.6	7.4	34.8
Lawton, OK	67,665	5.4	3.8	2.4	6.2	40.7	3,761	7.8	2.3	1.9	4.4	62.4
Lebanon, PA	64,489	14.3	2.7	3.3	11.5	13.0	2,744	18.5	2.0	3.2	13.7	20.1
Lewiston, ID–WA	34,382	9.6	6.1	3.6	14.5	15.8	1,426	13.8	6.2	3.6	16.8	19.0
Lewiston–Auburn, ME	63,102	8.4	5.3	5.2	16.7	9.1	2,587	12.0	6.1	5.7	21.2	11.4
Lexington–Fayette, KY	317,704	9.2	3.5	6.0	(D)	16.5	14,901	15.1	3.5	7.9	9.6	20.9
Lima, OH	63,609	12.6	3.3	2.9	17.0	10.6	2,921	24.8	2.2	2.5	19.8	13.3
Lincoln, NE	210,862	6.3	6.9	5.9	11.4	16.6	9,423	9.0	8.2	7.3	13.3	22.5
Little Rock–North Little Rock–Conway, AR	427,591	4.8	5.2	5.9	11.4	18.8	21,092	6.0	6.2	7.8	11.9	25.2
Logan, UT–ID	75,542	14.7	7.6	6.2	7.9	16.1	2,501	23.2	2.8	5.8	8.9	23.6
Longview, TX	134,785	9.0	4.1	(D)	11.0	9.1	6,465	12.8	2.9	4.6	11.1	9.2
Longview, WA	44,650	14.0	3.1	3.3	12.7	13.4	2,136	21.4	2.4	2.7	13.7	15.4
Los Angeles–Long Beach–Santa Ana, CA	7,374,060	7.6	5.5	8.7	9.6	10.0	444,484	9.9	7.3	12.0	9.5	13.0
Los Angeles–Long Beach–Glendale, CA	5,476,450	7.2	5.0	8.4	9.9	10.7	329,102	9.1	6.5	11.9	9.8	14.1
Santa Ana–Anaheim–Irvine, CA	1,897,610	8.6	7.0	9.7	8.6	8.0	115,382	12.0	9.8	12.5	8.9	10.0
Louisville/Jefferson County, KY–IN	751,994	8.8	6.2	5.6	10.7	11.2	36,972	13.2	8.7	6.9	13.7	13.9

[1]Includes other industry categories not shown separately.
(D) = Data withheld to avoid disclosure or does not meet statistical standards.

Table B-12. Employees and Earnings, by Selected Major Industries, 2011—Continued

Metropolitan statistical area and division	Employees						Earnings					
		Percent by selected major industries						Percent by selected major industries				
	Total[1]	Manufacturing	Finance and insurance	Professional and technical services	Health care and social services	Government and government enterprises	Total[1] (million dollars)	Manufacturing	Finance and insurance	Professional and technical services	Health care and social services	Government and government enterprises
Lubbock, TX	171,448	3.2	6.5	4.2	12.4	16.2	6,934	3.7	5.7	4.4	16.6	23.4
Lynchburg, VA	133,675	11.4	4.5	5.5	(D)	11.4	5,379	19.6	4.7	9.3	12.4	13.8
Macon, GA	131,151	4.5	8.2	3.9	14.2	12.1	5,244	7.3	9.5	5.3	19.5	15.6
Madera–Chowchilla, CA	56,658	5.8	2.1	2.6	12.0	19.0	2,904	7.1	1.1	1.9	14.5	22.4
Madison, WI	440,219	6.9	6.9	7.0	8.9	20.0	21,915	9.8	9.0	8.6	9.4	23.8
Manchester–Nashua, NH	251,231	11.0	5.8	8.1	11.9	9.3	14,650	16.7	8.9	10.5	11.7	10.8
Manhattan, KS	89,020	4.0	2.9	(D)	(D)	43.3	4,981	3.6	1.7	(D)	(D)	66.6
Mankato–North Mankato, MN	67,079	11.5	4.4	(D)	(D)	13.0	2,810	15.3	3.2	(D)	13.8	17.6
Mansfield, OH	64,066	14.3	2.9	2.7	13.6	13.1	2,528	21.5	2.6	2.8	15.1	18.9
McAllen–Edinburg–Mission, TX	318,332	2.3	3.9	3.0	19.8	17.3	11,212	2.4	3.4	3.2	20.6	26.4
Medford, OR	110,145	6.6	3.9	5.0	14.4	10.7	4,291	8.2	3.7	4.5	18.4	16.1
Memphis, TN–MS–AR	788,786	5.9	4.0	3.9	10.5	12.3	40,964	9.8	6.0	4.5	11.0	15.3
Merced, CA	90,378	8.4	2.8	3.1	9.1	19.0	4,453	9.1	1.6	2.2	9.5	23.7
Miami–Fort Lauderdale–Pompano Beach, FL	3,200,060	2.7	6.3	7.6	11.0	10.0	154,631	3.5	8.0	10.3	11.7	15.0
Fort Lauderdale–Pompano Beach–Deerfield Beach, FL	1,001,984	2.8	6.6	8.2	9.9	10.3	47,024	3.9	7.5	10.4	10.3	15.5
Miami–Miami Beach–Kendall, FL	1,455,592	2.8	5.5	6.9	11.1	10.4	71,598	3.2	7.9	10.1	11.7	15.8
West Palm Beach–Boca Raton–Boynton Beach, FL	742,484	2.3	7.6	8.0	12.1	8.8	36,009	3.5	9.1	10.8	13.7	12.5
Michigan City–La Porte, IN	55,092	14.6	2.6	3.0	11.4	13.8	2,258	22.3	2.3	2.5	14.0	16.8
Midland, TX	114,177	3.0	4.7	5.7	6.1	7.8	7,553	3.6	2.5	5.4	4.8	6.8
Milwaukee–Waukesha–West Allis, WI	977,360	12.3	6.2	5.8	13.2	9.6	54,697	17.7	8.9	7.9	13.0	11.1
Minneapolis–St. Paul–Bloomington, MN–WI	2,227,861	8.3	7.1	7.5	11.6	11.0	129,028	12.2	10.4	10.1	10.3	12.4
Missoula, MT	75,726	2.8	3.4	6.6	13.5	14.7	2,949	3.2	4.7	7.0	17.9	20.7
Mobile, AL	228,904	7.3	4.5	5.4	10.4	13.2	10,569	12.3	7.3	6.9	11.2	17.3
Modesto, CA	209,089	10.0	3.4	3.9	12.2	12.8	10,350	14.2	2.7	3.4	16.5	16.8
Monroe, LA	98,880	(D)	6.4	4.5	13.8	14.4	4,101	(D)	6.0	6.7	15.6	18.5
Monroe, MI	53,641	9.2	3.5	(D)	10.4	10.7	2,371	17.2	2.1	(D)	10.1	13.8
Montgomery, AL	220,730	8.1	4.5	5.2	8.9	20.5	10,342	11.1	5.2	7.2	9.7	30.8
Morgantown, WV	78,425	5.4	1.9	5.3	13.4	25.0	3,878	9.0	2.9	6.3	17.3	30.1
Morristown, TN	63,164	17.1	2.7	(D)	(D)	12.3	2,344	26.9	2.1	2.0	(D)	14.7
Mount Vernon–Anacortes, WA	62,526	8.7	3.9	4.5	9.0	18.1	2,690	16.3	4.3	4.2	8.5	24.2
Muncie, IN	58,319	6.5	4.5	4.5	16.8	19.2	2,344	9.6	4.2	6.2	20.5	23.7
Muskegon–Norton Shores, MI	78,964	14.4	3.2	3.1	15.3	10.8	3,154	25.4	2.4	2.5	17.5	16.1
Myrtle Beach–North Myrtle Beach–Conway, SC	143,387	2.4	4.0	3.3	6.9	11.4	5,062	3.5	6.7	4.2	11.1	18.0
Napa, CA	89,453	12.8	3.4	5.5	9.5	11.3	4,681	19.5	4.0	5.6	11.6	15.9
Naples–Marco Island, FL	177,410	1.7	6.3	5.8	10.5	7.6	7,639	2.5	7.5	6.6	15.3	11.6
Nashville–Davidson—Murfreesboro—Franklin, TN	1,014,230	6.5	5.4	6.2	10.9	10.5	55,923	7.9	6.8	8.7	19.9	11.1
New Haven–Milford, CT	483,731	7.3	5.1	6.3	15.9	10.8	26,975	11.0	5.9	8.3	16.2	14.8
New Orleans–Metairie–Kenner, LA	731,496	4.5	4.4	6.5	9.1	13.1	38,587	8.2	4.7	9.8	9.4	16.6
New York–Northern New Jersey–Long Island, NY–NJ–PA	11,034,883	3.5	8.3	9.0	13.5	11.5	827,577	4.3	18.7	12.6	10.4	12.7
Edison–New Brunswick, NJ	1,292,816	4.9	6.3	9.6	11.3	11.2	79,404	8.4	7.1	13.4	10.8	13.7
Nassau–Suffolk, NY	1,645,517	4.6	8.0	7.6	14.2	11.8	97,936	6.0	8.9	8.8	15.2	18.0
Newark–Union, NJ–PA	1,274,722	5.6	7.0	9.5	11.3	12.9	87,390	10.2	9.1	13.8	10.1	15.2
New York–White Plains–Wayne, NY–NJ	6,821,828	2.5	9.0	9.1	14.1	11.3	562,846	2.6	23.5	13.0	9.5	11.2
Niles–Benton Harbor, MI	81,625	14.9	3.4	4.0	11.4	11.4	3,611	29.1	3.1	3.8	11.9	13.8
North Port–Bradenton–Sarasota, FL	370,527	4.0	6.6	7.1	12.7	7.4	14,575	6.1	6.4	9.4	16.7	12.1
Norwich–New London, CT	168,357	8.8	2.9	5.7	11.4	25.8	9,597	17.0	2.0	8.0	11.0	31.1
Ocala, FL	130,504	5.2	4.6	4.3	11.4	13.8	4,580	8.6	4.1	4.6	15.9	22.3
Ocean City, NJ	62,394	1.3	4.0	3.9	9.0	16.3	2,264	1.4	3.2	4.2	12.1	28.5
Odessa, TX	84,504	6.4	3.3	3.5	7.1	11.7	4,452	8.2	2.0	4.0	6.6	11.8
Ogden–Clearfield, UT	280,960	8.3	6.1	6.2	9.0	19.2	11,904	12.7	3.5	6.9	9.4	30.8
Oklahoma City, OK	783,256	4.4	5.1	5.8	9.6	17.1	39,817	6.5	4.7	6.4	11.0	22.6
Olympia, WA	129,295	2.9	3.3	5.5	11.0	28.2	6,152	3.2	3.3	5.1	13.2	40.0
Omaha–Council Bluffs, NE–IA	571,142	5.7	7.6	6.6	11.0	12.7	30,230	6.4	9.4	8.6	10.8	16.0
Orlando–Kissimmee–Sanford, FL	1,268,308	3.2	4.7	6.9	9.6	9.3	58,613	4.9	6.0	10.1	11.4	12.4
Oshkosh–Neenah, WI	108,925	23.3	4.2	3.9	11.2	11.7	5,648	34.6	3.9	4.0	10.7	11.8
Owensboro, KY	64,454	12.7	5.0	2.7	8.9	16.3	2,721	20.8	4.8	2.7	8.8	20.4
Oxnard–Thousand Oaks–Ventura, CA	419,395	7.9	6.8	7.4	8.7	11.6	23,091	15.7	8.0	7.6	8.9	17.3
Palm Bay–Melbourne–Titusville, FL	261,646	8.2	4.1	7.1	12.6	12.2	12,524	15.3	3.5	9.6	13.4	18.4
Palm Coast, FL	22,525	3.3	2.5	3.6	10.6	17.2	824	4.5	2.5	4.8	15.7	25.5
Panama City–Lynn Haven–Panama City Beach, FL	98,513	3.2	3.4	5.7	9.2	18.6	4,186	4.7	3.2	8.0	11.0	31.6
Parkersburg–Marietta–Vienna, WV–OH	86,865	7.9	3.7	3.1	14.8	13.1	3,612	15.3	4.1	3.2	16.3	18.7
Pascagoula, MS	70,427	20.1	2.7	3.9	6.2	18.5	3,666	35.7	1.9	4.7	6.2	21.3
Pensacola–Ferry Pass–Brent, FL	221,870	2.7	4.6	5.6	12.3	18.9	9,966	4.1	4.4	6.7	15.1	33.2
Peoria, IL	221,642	12.4	4.4	6.2	14.7	9.9	12,551	26.4	3.6	9.5	13.7	10.3
Philadelphia–Camden–Wilmington, PA–NJ–DE–MD	3,433,182	5.3	7.2	8.6	14.2	10.7	213,069	7.5	9.4	12.9	13.7	12.5
Camden, NJ	642,366	6.0	5.8	7.2	12.8	13.8	34,691	9.5	6.4	8.7	13.8	18.9
Philadelphia, PA	2,372,725	5.8	6.9	9.2	14.9	9.6	153,029	7.8	9.3	13.9	14.0	11.0
Wilmington, DE–MD–NJ	418,091	(D)	11.2	7.5	12.3	12.0	25,350	(D)	14.6	12.8	12.0	13.3

[1]Includes other industry categories not shown separately.
(D) = Data withheld to avoid disclosure or does not meet statistical standards.

Table B-12. Employees and Earnings, by Selected Major Industries, 2011—*Continued*

Metropolitan statistical area and division	Employees						Earnings					
		Percent by selected major industries						Percent by selected major industries				
	Total[1]	Manufacturing	Finance and insurance	Professional and technical services	Health care and social services	Government and government enterprises	Total[1] (million dollars)	Manufacturing	Finance and insurance	Professional and technical services	Health care and social services	Government and government enterprises
Phoenix–Mesa–Glendale, AZ	2,255,342	5.3	7.4	6.8	10.4	10.9	116,671	8.6	8.1	8.7	12.0	13.5
Pine Bluff, AR	46,665	12.8	2.9	(D)	12.3	24.3	2,046	16.0	2.8	(D)	11.6	31.7
Pittsburgh, PA	1,422,971	6.6	6.0	7.3	14.2	9.2	77,443	9.4	6.8	10.4	14.0	10.9
Pittsfield, MA	82,164	5.8	4.0	6.0	15.8	10.8	3,514	11.4	5.1	7.5	19.6	13.6
Pocatello, ID	48,372	7.0	4.5	(D)	12.4	18.8	1,819	11.9	4.7	(D)	14.2	24.3
Portland–South Portland–Biddeford, ME	342,905	0.0	5.8	6.7	13.6	12.0	16,398	(D)	8.6	8.4	14.8	17.2
Portland–Vancouver–Hillsboro, OR–WA	1,339,443	8.8	5.0	7.5	11.0	11.0	70,589	14.4	5.5	8.9	11.4	14.1
Port St. Lucie, FL	183,630	3.0	5.9	5.8	13.2	10.7	6,866	4.4	4.7	6.7	16.8	17.4
Poughkeepsie–Newburgh–Middletown, NY	332,059	5.8	4.2	5.1	13.3	16.9	16,136	11.3	3.2	5.8	14.7	27.3
Prescott, AZ	79,564	4.2	3.4	4.6	12.0	13.9	2,754	5.4	2.5	3.9	15.7	23.1
Providence–New Bedford–Fall River, RI–MA	856,135	7.9	5.1	5.7	14.9	11.7	43,964	11.2	7.0	6.6	15.3	17.3
Provo–Orem, UT	263,914	6.9	6.1	8.1	8.8	11.7	10,363	10.5	3.7	10.6	9.9	13.7
Pueblo, CO	75,876	5.8	3.6	3.2	15.7	17.5	3,178	10.8	2.6	2.9	19.2	22.8
Punta Gorda, FL	65,410	1.2	4.8	5.0	15.0	9.7	2,116	1.3	4.2	5.1	24.8	17.9
Racine, WI	90,168	19.9	3.6	3.6	13.2	10.8	4,566	34.9	3.7	4.8	12.5	13.2
Raleigh–Cary, NC	670,971	4.4	4.7	9.5	9.0	14.2	34,287	7.4	6.9	13.4	9.4	16.6
Rapid City, SD	84,768	3.2	5.5	4.4	12.2	17.5	3,552	3.7	4.9	4.7	16.8	27.8
Reading, PA	221,419	12.8	4.1	5.3	12.7	11.2	10,250	19.9	3.9	6.5	13.7	13.7
Redding, CA	84,963	3.3	4.3	5.2	14.2	15.5	3,574	3.9	3.6	5.2	19.3	22.6
Reno–Sparks, NV	248,763	4.9	5.8	6.8	9.3	11.5	11,921	6.8	7.2	7.9	11.4	17.0
Richmond, VA	767,954	4.4	6.1	6.6	(D)	16.7	41,849	6.6	(D)	10.4	9.9	20.4
Riverside–San Bernardino–Ontario, CA	1,650,403	5.7	3.8	4.7	9.9	15.6	74,124	7.8	2.9	4.5	11.4	24.9
Roanoke, VA	191,859	8.9	5.3	5.4	(D)	11.6	8,812	13.8	5.5	6.0	(D)	15.1
Rochester, MN	129,162	8.4	3.0	3.4	32.5	8.4	6,844	12.9	2.0	2.3	47.0	9.5
Rochester, NY	621,096	10.2	4.6	6.1	13.4	12.4	31,205	15.3	4.5	7.4	12.5	16.2
Rockford, IL	180,624	16.1	4.9	3.8	13.9	9.6	8,463	25.4	4.8	3.7	16.0	12.6
Rocky Mount, NC	74,808	13.5	3.3	3.4	(D)	15.6	3,113	21.2	3.7	3.0	(D)	18.4
Rome, GA	50,069	11.3	3.7	3.4	16.6	13.5	2,098	16.8	3.5	3.0	25.9	16.0
Sacramento—Arden-Arcade—Roseville, CA	1,142,061	3.2	5.6	7.8	9.8	21.8	64,484	4.8	6.0	9.8	11.5	31.8
Saginaw–Saginaw Township North, MI	104,354	11.0	4.3	3.6	16.2	11.3	4,644	19.9	4.7	4.5	17.4	15.6
St. Cloud, MN	126,795	12.1	4.2	(D)	13.0	11.5	5,337	15.7	4.0	(D)	15.9	16.1
St. George, UT	70,578	3.9	6.3	5.0	12.1	11.1	2,253	4.9	3.7	4.9	18.1	16.8
St. Joseph, MO–KS	71,550	14.2	4.7	(D)	(D)	14.5	3,098	22.6	4.6	3.1	13.2	16.0
St. Louis, MO–IL[3]	1,663,175	6.7	6.0	6.3	12.4	11.3	88,453	10.7	6.6	8.8	12.2	13.8
Salem, OR	195,134	6.1	3.8	3.7	12.3	20.9	8,483	6.5	3.5	4.0	16.7	29.6
Salinas, CA	223,024	2.9	2.7	5.1	7.1	16.8	11,904	3.4	2.5	5.1	7.7	27.4
Salisbury, MD	66,474	6.5	3.1	4.2	15.0	16.7	2,866	8.0	2.8	4.2	19.0	22.1
Salt Lake City, UT	803,266	7.0	8.1	7.2	8.1	13.2	40,788	9.7	8.8	9.1	8.0	16.4
San Angelo, TX	68,453	5.8	4.8	3.6	12.5	18.6	2,762	9.4	3.6	3.5	14.7	28.6
San Antonio–New Braunfels, TX	1,200,208	4.1	7.4	5.6	10.4	16.4	58,891	5.1	8.9	6.8	10.6	24.6
San Diego–Carlsbad–San Marcos, CA	1,832,553	5.5	4.7	10.4	8.4	18.2	110,042	8.5	4.8	14.6	8.4	26.4
Sandusky, OH	47,835	12.4	3.1	2.8	12.1	11.9	1,961	22.5	2.2	2.4	14.5	16.5
San Francisco–Oakland–Fremont, CA	2,728,163	4.7	6.3	13.3	9.4	11.3	202,200	7.4	10.0	18.6	9.1	13.3
Oakland–Fremont–Hayward, CA	1,338,160	6.4	5.0	10.9	10.9	11.7	88,002	11.4	4.8	13.4	12.4	14.7
San Francisco–San Mateo–Redwood City, CA	1,390,003	3.0	7.4	15.6	7.9	10.9	114,198	4.4	13.9	22.7	6.6	12.3
San Jose–Sunnyvale–Santa Clara, CA	1,164,663	14.2	4.0	14.1	8.3	7.9	111,688	26.5	3.1	18.0	6.8	7.1
San Luis Obispo–Paso Robles, CA	150,755	4.1	3.9	7.2	9.2	13.9	6,611	6.3	3.2	7.3	11.7	21.5
Santa Barbara–Santa Maria–Goleta, CA	251,774	5.3	3.4	8.5	9.3	15.0	13,065	8.4	3.7	10.6	10.7	21.2
Santa Cruz–Watsonville, CA	138,323	4.6	3.4	8.2	11.0	13.3	6,496	7.2	3.1	8.0	13.8	18.8
Santa Fe, NM	86,749	1.5	3.6	7.9	11.9	20.9	3,887	1.4	6.6	8.5	13.9	29.5
Santa Rosa–Petaluma, CA	264,544	8.7	4.0	9.5	10.7	10.5	12,840	14.3	4.2	9.7	13.8	14.5
Savannah, GA	202,900	7.3	3.4	4.2	10.2	15.1	9,426	15.1	2.9	4.2	12.3	23.5
Scranton—Wilkes-Barre, PA	314,065	8.9	4.9	4.4	14.5	10.4	13,314	12.2	5.4	4.9	16.3	14.6
Seattle–Tacoma–Bellevue, WA	2,195,974	8.4	4.5	8.7	9.7	14.4	145,917	12.3	5.0	10.4	9.2	16.7
Seattle–Bellevue–Everett, WA	1,817,224	9.2	4.8	9.6	9.4	12.1	124,484	13.3	5.4	11.5	8.4	12.9
Tacoma, WA	378,750	4.7	3.4	4.3	11.5	25.4	21,434	6.1	3.0	4.1	13.7	39.1
Sebastian–Vero Beach, FL	66,248	3.0	5.5	6.0	13.9	8.6	2,547	4.3	5.1	7.4	18.6	13.6
Sheboygan, WI	72,977	26.0	5.4	3.4	10.4	8.4	3,488	39.9	5.0	2.7	12.4	9.7
Sherman–Denison, TX	58,246	9.4	6.1	2.9	15.3	11.5	2,363	19.8	5.6	3.2	17.8	14.2
Shreveport–Bossier City, LA	242,825	4.4	3.8	3.7	11.5	17.3	11,484	6.8	3.2	4.3	13.4	25.1
Sioux City, IA–NE–SD	90,966	12.3	4.6	2.4	11.2	11.2	4,078	14.6	4.6	3.1	13.0	13.5
Sioux Falls, SD	174,000	7.4	10.4	4.3	14.8	8.1	8,235	8.2	11.4	4.8	18.3	10.0
South Bend–Mishawaka, IN–MI	165,673	10.6	4.2	4.6	12.9	10.9	7,960	19.0	4.7	7.0	14.0	11.6
Spartanburg, SC	148,778	16.5	3.7	3.9	6.9	13.8	7,082	25.5	5.0	4.6	8.8	17.2
Spokane, WA	264,706	5.6	5.8	5.8	14.4	14.9	12,128	8.0	6.6	6.3	17.4	20.6
Springfield, IL	135,605	2.4	7.0	5.6	14.6	21.3	7,281	2.8	6.5	5.6	19.0	33.1
Springfield, MA	367,413	7.6	4.8	4.8	15.0	15.7	16,817	10.8	6.8	4.7	17.2	20.9
Springfield, MO	256,083	5.7	5.5	3.9	13.2	11.4	10,329	9.5	5.3	5.6	17.0	14.7
Springfield, OH	63,742	10.6	5.7	3.2	14.4	11.7	2,535	16.8	5.2	3.1	15.7	15.8
State College, PA	110,773	4.1	2.5	5.6	7.7	41.5	4,536	5.7	2.5	7.0	9.6	45.9
Steubenville–Weirton, OH–WV	52,603	12.3	2.6	2.8	(D)	12.3	2,192	21.2	2.1	2.7	(D)	14.1

[1]Includes other industry categories not shown separately.
[3]The portion of Sullivan city in Crawford County, MO is legally part of the St. Louis, MO–IL MSA. That portion is not included in these figures for the St. Louis, MSA.
(D) = Data withheld to avoided disclosure or does not meet statistical standards.

Table B-12. Employees and Earnings, by Selected Major Industries, 2011—*Continued*

Metropolitan statistical area and division	Employees						Earnings					
		Percent by selected major industries						Percent by selected major industries				
	Total[1]	Manufacturing	Finance and insurance	Professional and technical services	Health care and social services	Government and government enterprises	Total[1] (million dollars)	Manufacturing	Finance and insurance	Professional and technical services	Health care and social services	Government and government enterprises
Stockton, CA	269,053	7.1	3.9	3.5	11.1	13.6	13,106	9.0	3.2	3.1	13.1	20.0
Sumter, SC	53,429	11.4	2.2	3.1	11.1	23.4	2,330	13.8	2.3	3.4	10.7	39.6
Syracuse, NY	373,521	7.4	5.9	6.2	12.2	14.8	18,504	11.4	6.3	7.7	12.9	19.4
Tallahassee, FL	212,505	1.8	4.1	7.8	9.5	29.3	9,284	2.4	5.3	10.7	11.9	38.7
Tampa–St. Petersburg–Clearwater, FL	1,474,015	4.3	7.4	7.8	12.3	10.8	72,256	5.9	9.3	10.6	14.3	15.0
Terre Haute, IN	86,886	13.2	3.1	2.7	11.1	15.3	3,726	20.4	2.9	2.5	14.4	18.7
Texarkana, TX–Texarkana, AR	73,526	6.0	4.6	(D)	13.3	19.1	3,205	8.4	4.6	(D)	15.3	29.2
Toledo, OH	375,577	10.8	3.9	4.8	13.3	13.4	18,089	18.1	3.8	5.6	14.5	16.0
Topeka, KS	139,905	5.5	6.2	4.8	12.2	21.2	6,335	7.4	8.0	5.3	14.0	26.0
Trenton–Ewing, NJ	267,671	3.4	8.0	11.6	11.1	18.3	19,483	5.1	12.1	16.5	9.5	22.4
Tucson, AZ	479,306	5.3	4.9	7.0	13.2	17.3	21,775	10.5	4.6	8.3	15.1	25.7
Tulsa, OK	559,456	8.7	5.1	5.2	10.3	10.3	29,943	12.5	5.1	5.9	10.6	10.4
Tuscaloosa, AL	117,426	11.2	2.9	4.1	6.3	22.5	5,509	18.0	2.3	4.6	8.8	27.9
Tyler, TX	130,747	4.9	5.6	5.1	16.5	10.3	5,947	7.5	4.8	6.5	22.7	12.2
Utica–Rome, NY	157,689	7.4	6.2	4.1	16.0	20.6	6,821	9.9	6.6	4.8	15.7	29.9
Valdosta, GA	72,647	5.4	(D)	3.0	9.2	24.6	2,999	(D)	(D)	3.3	11.2	37.3
Vallejo–Fairfield, CA	165,827	5.7	4.2	4.3	12.2	18.9	9,226	11.0	3.8	3.4	15.7	27.8
Victoria, TX	68,931	8.6	4.2	(D)	10.8	12.7	3,386	17.5	2.7	(D)	11.6	12.8
Vineland–Millville–Bridgeton, NJ	73,019	11.5	2.6	2.4	12.7	20.0	3,704	15.3	2.2	2.0	13.5	28.0
Virginia Beach–Norfolk–Newport News, VA–NC	993,289	4.9	3.7	6.0	8.7	25.5	54,080	6.5	3.6	7.2	8.3	40.1
Visalia–Porterville, CA	187,073	6.4	3.0	2.5	7.5	17.1	8,724	7.6	2.4	2.4	7.0	22.2
Waco, TX	134,757	10.9	6.4	3.8	10.5	13.3	5,886	17.9	9.3	4.1	11.1	17.0
Warner Robins, GA	79,623	6.5	2.5	6.0	6.2	38.2	4,293	6.5	1.4	6.9	5.1	61.0
Washington–Arlington–Alexandria, DC–VA–MD–WV	3,914,861	1.4	3.7	15.5	8.0	19.9	299,187	1.6	4.1	23.3	6.2	29.7
Bethesda–Rockville–Frederick, MD	785,144	2.3	5.8	14.9	10.7	14.5	54,969	3.5	6.8	19.6	8.9	23.4
Washington–Arlington–Alexandria, DC–VA–MD–WV	3,129,717	1.1	3.1	15.6	7.3	21.2	244,219	1.2	3.5	24.1	5.6	31.1
Waterloo–Cedar Falls, IA	112,408	15.1	5.5	3.3	(D)	14.0	5,155	24.8	5.4	3.3	(D)	15.4
Wausau, WI	86,264	17.7	7.9	3.7	10.7	9.3	3,781	23.1	9.6	5.2	13.4	11.4
Wenatchee–East Wenatchee, WA	64,944	4.1	2.9	3.8	10.2	14.0	2,496	5.8	2.4	3.8	15.8	22.4
Wheeling, WV–OH	81,830	4.9	3.8	(D)	(D)	13.2	3,391	10.7	3.6	(D)	(D)	15.7
Wichita, KS	373,009	14.3	3.9	4.3	(D)	12.6	18,772	25.3	2.9	4.5	(D)	14.3
Wichita Falls, TX	88,386	6.3	5.1	(D)	10.5	20.8	3,834	9.4	3.7	(D)	12.3	28.3
Williamsport, PA	69,426	13.7	3.4	3.7	12.8	14.7	2,913	20.0	3.1	4.2	14.3	17.8
Wilmington, NC	192,310	4.2	3.8	6.5	8.5	14.4	8,015	8.7	4.5	8.6	11.1	19.3
Winchester, VA–WV	72,697	10.1	3.4	4.1	12.1	12.9	3,179	14.8	3.1	4.1	17.6	19.7
Winston-Salem, NC	263,188	8.8	5.4	5.3	13.9	10.1	12,754	14.1	8.3	7.2	15.9	10.8
Worcester, MA	417,112	8.5	5.4	6.4	14.8	12.7	22,003	13.5	7.7	7.7	15.7	15.4
Yakima, WA	120,952	7.0	2.7	2.9	12.5	14.9	5,395	7.7	2.4	2.7	14.2	19.1
York-Hanover, PA	220,677	14.8	3.1	4.4	11.5	10.3	10,382	21.0	2.6	4.5	13.5	14.4
Youngstown–Warren–Boardman, OH–PA	283,544	11.2	3.8	3.5	15.5	11.4	11,730	19.9	3.3	3.6	16.5	15.3
Yuba City, CA	67,821	3.6	3.2	3.9	9.9	22.5	3,308	4.1	1.7	2.9	11.6	33.7
Yuma, AZ	80,403	2.6	2.1	4.7	9.8	23.8	3,783	2.7	1.2	5.2	10.5	36.0

[1]Includes other industry categories not shown separately.
(D) = Data withheld to avoid disclosure or does not meet statistical standards.

Table B-13. Civilian Labor Force and Banking

Metropolitan statistical area and division	Civilian labor force										Banking 2012[2]	
	Total					Number of unemployed		Unemployment rate[1]			Number of offices	Deposits (million dollars)
	2011	2010	2005	2000	Change, 2005–2011	2011	2010	2011	2010	2005		
Abilene, TX	83,772	84,501	80,276	75,131	4.4	5,368	5,452	6.4	6.5	4.2	54	2,499
Akron, OH	374,097	380,423	378,862	365,082	-1.3	31,605	37,537	8.4	9.9	5.7	223	11,747
Albany, GA	73,504	74,838	74,828	71,643	-1.8	7,630	8,087	10.4	10.8	5.6	46	2,124
Albany–Schenectady–Troy, NY	440,416	448,212	454,737	434,539	-3.1	31,527	33,036	7.2	7.4	4.0	317	20,865
Albuquerque, NM	397,485	400,384	392,202	370,872	1.3	31,147	33,167	7.8	8.3	4.9	179	11,821
Alexandria, LA	67,806	68,982	67,958	63,519	-0.2	4,860	4,891	7.2	7.1	5.8	71	2,202
Allentown–Bethlehem–Easton, PA–NJ	422,220	422,501	408,548	385,305	3.3	36,827	38,840	8.7	9.2	4.9	296	14,577
Altoona, PA	64,967	64,894	64,984	62,375	0.0	4,530	4,920	7.0	7.6	5.2	59	2,182
Amarillo, TX	134,960	133,228	126,845	117,511	6.4	7,305	7,421	5.4	5.6	4.0	72	4,793
Ames, IA	48,571	48,862	46,855	46,543	3.7	2,191	2,328	4.5	4.8	3.1	39	2,050
Anchorage, AK	200,289	199,456	185,631	169,276	7.9	13,446	14,532	6.7	7.3	5.9	45	5,542
Anderson, IN	61,156	61,853	63,171	63,804	-3.2	6,432	7,024	10.5	11.4	6.5	46	1,271
Anderson, SC	84,118	84,546	83,693	84,358	0.5	8,342	9,680	9.9	11.4	7.4	61	2,309
Ann Arbor, MI	179,685	180,347	189,873	185,202	-5.4	11,618	14,534	6.5	8.1	4.4	100	6,706
Anniston–Oxford, AL	53,790	53,973	53,629	53,392	0.3	4,944	5,239	9.2	9.7	3.8	34	1,647
Appleton, WI	124,418	124,910	120,527	117,756	3.2	8,409	9,750	6.8	7.8	4.5	77	3,822
Asheville, NC	215,308	213,206	199,904	185,077	7.7	18,351	19,065	8.5	8.9	4.4	139	6,988
Athens–Clarke County, GA	108,418	108,533	99,871	89,410	8.6	7,955	8,203	7.3	7.6	4.2	58	3,006
Atlanta–Sandy Springs–Marietta, GA	2,686,993	2,658,658	2,592,383	2,377,185	3.6	258,997	270,475	9.6	10.2	5.3	1,354	120,990
Atlantic City–Hammonton, NJ	135,813	137,168	136,705	128,989	-0.7	17,467	17,453	12.9	12.7	5.3	87	5,098
Auburn–Opelika, AL	67,892	66,231	63,227	58,646	7.4	5,033	5,336	7.4	8.1	3.2	40	2,105
Augusta–Richmond County, GA–SC	259,101	257,690	253,568	234,389	2.2	23,808	23,884	9.2	9.3	6.0	132	7,451
Austin–Round Rock–San Marcos, TX	940,043	921,127	800,248	736,703	17.5	63,501	65,222	6.8	7.1	4.5	468	27,384
Bakersfield–Delano, CA	382,029	373,333	327,452	293,635	16.7	56,934	59,249	14.9	15.9	8.4	95	6,408
Baltimore–Towson, MD	1,440,848	1,432,015	1,376,739	1,330,644	4.7	107,554	118,961	7.5	8.3	4.4	812	63,645
Bangor, ME	78,770	78,340	76,752	74,854	2.6	6,393	6,803	8.1	8.7	5.1	55	2,216
Barnstable Town, MA	120,515	121,416	122,112	113,483	-1.3	9,880	10,934	8.2	9.0	4.9	113	6,476
Baton Rouge, LA	376,683	377,113	363,516	339,543	3.6	27,898	28,133	7.4	7.5	6.5	247	17,273
Battle Creek, MI	64,509	66,098	71,672	70,370	-10.0	5,728	7,322	8.9	11.1	6.6	33	957
Bay City, MI	51,715	52,850	55,517	56,823	-6.8	5,004	6,198	9.7	11.7	7.0	32	1,047
Beaumont–Port Arthur, TX	189,502	188,883	177,351	176,389	6.9	20,863	20,267	11.0	10.7	7.6	88	5,086
Bellingham, WA	106,230	106,414	102,044	88,022	4.1	8,843	9,544	8.3	9.0	5.0	68	2,997
Bend, OR	80,216	80,904	74,947	61,802	7.0	9,917	11,448	12.4	14.1	5.8	62	2,351
Billings, MT	87,612	86,949	83,158	76,480	5.4	4,498	4,602	5.1	5.3	3.0	48	4,101
Binghamton, NY	118,770	121,119	122,726	124,890	-3.2	9,950	10,628	8.4	8.8	4.9	64	2,667
Birmingham–Hoover, AL	530,139	528,138	527,690	533,010	0.5	43,796	47,236	8.3	8.9	3.5	356	29,406
Bismarck, ND	62,656	62,878	58,863	54,499	6.4	2,099	2,367	3.4	3.8	3.1	53	3,053
Blacksburg–Christiansburg–Radford, VA	83,919	81,532	77,176	73,034	8.7	5,692	6,701	6.8	8.2	4.0	65	2,665
Bloomington, IN	96,594	97,365	95,145	91,024	1.5	7,484	7,783	7.7	8.0	5.2	59	2,628
Bloomington–Normal, IL	91,405	92,253	86,919	85,458	5.2	6,575	7,177	7.2	7.8	4.3	64	12,111
Boise City–Nampa, ID	301,165	297,138	277,973	252,169	8.3	26,593	26,932	8.8	9.1	3.4	194	8,212
Boston–Cambridge–Quincy, MA–NH	2,444,959	2,450,901	2,368,264	2,378,742	3.2	161,173	185,133	6.6	7.6	4.5	1,516	233,760
Boston–Quincy, MA	989,622	993,850	946,155	959,590	4.6	69,384	79,830	7.0	8.0	4.8	631	165,784
Cambridge–Newton–Framingham, MA	828,752	831,159	809,917	821,797	2.3	48,516	56,635	5.9	6.8	4.1	513	44,245
Peabody, MA	381,493	381,902	375,677	372,932	1.5	29,660	33,505	7.8	8.8	5.2	253	17,098
Rockingham County–Strafford County, NH	245,092	243,990	236,515	224,423	3.6	13,613	15,163	5.6	6.2	4.0	119	6,633
Boulder, CO	175,874	175,420	169,617	160,390	3.7	10,883	12,134	6.2	6.9	4.5	108	6,826
Bowling Green, KY	64,224	63,919	60,556	55,029	6.1	5,468	6,018	8.5	9.4	5.3	59	2,044
Bremerton–Silverdale, WA	122,726	124,304	120,427	105,983	1.9	9,719	10,181	7.9	8.2	5.1	64	2,314
Bridgeport–Stamford–Norwalk, CT	481,769	480,412	454,312	445,342	6.0	38,574	40,380	8.0	8.4	4.4	409	33,662
Brownsville–Harlingen, TX	163,010	160,033	140,539	127,011	16.0	19,171	18,090	11.8	11.3	7.6	84	4,160
Brunswick, GA	50,060	50,757	52,049	46,688	-3.8	5,349	5,275	10.7	10.4	4.6	47	1,929
Buffalo–Niagara Falls, NY	570,521	577,613	584,616	578,523	-2.4	45,482	48,902	8.0	8.5	5.3	314	32,256
Burlington, NC	72,415	71,969	69,277	69,342	4.5	7,726	8,431	10.7	11.7	6.0	47	2,116
Burlington–South Burlington, VT	122,727	122,226	116,769	113,558	5.1	5,842	6,749	4.8	5.5	3.3	73	4,505
Canton–Massillon, OH	199,715	201,967	203,571	207,120	-1.9	18,493	22,766	9.3	11.3	6.3	137	5,956
Cape Coral–Fort Myers, FL	282,699	278,148	270,561	207,750	4.5	31,401	35,034	11.1	12.6	3.2	229	11,726
Cape Girardeau–Jackson, MO–IL	47,566	47,771	47,239	50,157	0.7	3,660	3,834	7.7	8.0	5.0	46	1,801
Carson City, NV	28,761	29,203	27,316	26,472	5.3	3,760	3,798	13.1	13.0	5.0	16	1,092
Casper, WY	42,907	42,060	39,354	36,536	9.0	2,537	3,029	5.9	7.2	3.5	21	1,961
Cedar Rapids, IA	146,448	147,986	137,915	135,913	6.2	8,767	9,195	6.0	6.2	4.4	106	5,141
Champaign–Urbana, IL	115,771	119,966	117,167	115,433	-1.2	9,775	10,906	8.4	9.1	4.3	109	4,843
Charleston, WV	137,235	138,285	139,820	145,084	-1.8	10,028	10,473	7.3	7.6	4.7	101	6,077
Charleston–North Charleston–Summerville, SC	328,687	321,936	294,751	268,196	11.5	27,773	29,892	8.4	9.3	5.4	209	9,699
Charlotte–Gastonia–Rock Hill, NC–SC	895,986	883,975	794,301	734,689	12.8	98,020	104,927	10.9	11.9	5.3	443	201,080
Charlottesville, VA	112,047	110,022	97,708	88,071	14.7	5,868	6,454	5.2	5.9	3.1	69	3,610
Chattanooga, TN–GA	262,178	258,813	253,990	247,294	3.2	21,817	22,808	8.3	8.8	4.8	173	8,661
Cheyenne, WY	45,064	44,436	41,611	40,237	8.3	3,015	3,349	6.7	7.5	4.2	31	1,350
Chicago–Joliet–Naperville, IL–IN–WI	4,831,445	4,848,872	4,710,186	4,760,792	2.6	475,845	506,293	9.8	10.4	5.9	3,183	313,859
Chicago–Joliet–Naperville, IL	4,058,732	4,073,417	3,944,150	4,014,703	2.9	403,636	425,005	9.9	10.4	6.0	2,635	282,999
Gary, IN	328,547	326,920	328,667	326,617	0.0	30,636	33,907	9.3	10.4	5.7	265	11,018
Lake County–Kenosha County, IL–WI	444,166	448,535	437,369	419,472	1.6	41,573	47,381	9.4	10.6	5.0	283	19,843

[1] Civilian unemployed as percent of total civilian labor force.
[2] As of June 30. Covers all FDIC–insured commercial banks and savings institutions; does not include U.S. branches of foreign banks.

Table B-13.   Civilian Labor Force and Banking—*Continued*

Metropolitan statistical area and division	Civilian labor force										Banking 2012[2]	
	Total					Number of unemployed		Unemployment rate[1]			Number of offices	Deposits (million dollars)
	2011	2010	2005	2000	Change, 2005–2011	2011	2010	2011	2010	2005		
Chico, CA	101,686	103,632	98,511	93,147	3.2	13,794	14,384	13.6	13.9	6.8	49	2,926
Cincinnati–Middletown, OH–KY–IN	1,099,561	1,107,565	1,093,094	1,045,789	0.6	94,558	106,340	8.6	9.6	5.3	805	66,283
Clarksville, TN–KY	115,380	114,368	104,825	97,639	10.1	11,456	11,496	9.9	10.1	5.8	86	3,374
Cleveland, TN	55,382	55,075	54,150	53,211	2.3	5,196	5,231	9.4	9.5	5.4	41	1,571
Cleveland–Elyria–Mentor, OH	1,082,818	1,080,862	1,091,575	1,105,888	-0.8	83,332	94,423	7.7	8.7	5.7	731	50,275
Coeur d'Alene, ID	72,048	71,742	66,283	56,530	8.7	7,414	7,432	10.3	10.4	4.2	48	1,817
College Station–Bryan, TX	116,045	116,670	103,114	93,157	12.5	7,593	7,666	6.5	6.6	4.2	72	3,811
Colorado Springs, CO	313,199	314,780	304,805	277,206	2.8	28,825	30,677	9.2	9.7	5.4	161	6,282
Columbia, MO	96,993	95,157	91,211	84,549	6.3	5,735	6,157	5.9	6.5	3.6	85	3,174
Columbia, SC	369,365	368,696	354,215	337,429	4.3	32,711	34,501	8.9	9.4	5.8	199	15,255
Columbus, GA–AL	130,956	129,119	128,044	125,172	2.3	12,215	12,404	9.3	9.6	5.7	72	7,008
Columbus, IN	39,998	38,149	37,377	37,522	7.0	2,972	3,551	7.4	9.3	4.8	26	1,201
Columbus, OH	956,643	960,392	921,915	881,927	3.8	72,222	83,419	7.5	8.7	5.2	564	47,373
Corpus Christi, TX	217,128	213,961	197,537	184,880	9.9	17,108	17,351	7.9	8.1	5.6	122	4,860
Corvallis, OR	44,859	44,175	42,154	41,224	6.4	2,948	3,260	6.6	7.4	4.9	15	890
Crestview–Fort Walton Beach–Destin, FL	99,218	96,038	95,801	80,410	3.6	7,313	7,563	7.4	7.9	2.8	79	3,470
Cumberland, MD–WV	50,779	50,497	49,168	45,973	3.3	4,167	4,520	8.2	9.0	5.8	27	885
Dallas–Fort Worth–Arlington, TX	3,286,655	3,242,289	3,007,967	2,844,220	9.3	256,531	265,611	7.8	8.2	5.2	1,706	178,849
Dallas–Plano–Irving, TX	2,193,376	2,164,858	2,011,373	1,913,740	9.0	171,765	176,989	7.8	8.2	5.2	1,169	147,656
Fort Worth–Arlington, TX	1,093,279	1,077,431	996,594	930,480	9.7	84,766	88,622	7.8	8.2	5.1	537	31,193
Dalton, GA	61,492	62,109	66,944	63,538	-8.1	7,625	7,778	12.4	12.5	4.6	38	2,005
Danville, IL	36,594	37,116	37,752	38,878	-3.1	3,891	4,599	10.6	12.4	6.6	32	1,081
Danville, VA	52,945	52,622	53,005	53,016	-0.1	5,123	6,049	9.7	11.5	7.8	39	1,709
Davenport–Moline–Rock Island, IA–IL	201,736	203,242	201,853	199,904	-0.1	15,396	17,203	7.6	8.5	4.7	157	7,468
Dayton, OH	411,593	415,234	424,310	431,838	-3.0	37,672	44,598	9.2	10.7	6.0	255	10,695
Decatur, AL	73,569	72,913	71,220	73,564	3.3	6,606	7,221	9.0	9.9	4.0	44	1,846
Decatur, IL	54,585	54,732	52,730	55,872	3.5	5,767	6,563	10.6	12.0	6.3	41	1,800
Deltona–Daytona Beach–Ormond Beach, FL	254,098	251,228	242,699	209,694	4.7	27,428	29,011	10.8	11.5	3.6	155	7,906
Denver–Aurora–Broomfield, CO[3]	1,399,772	1,401,417	1,326,889	1,243,637	5.5	116,747	126,293	8.3	9.0	5.2	715	59,304
Des Moines–West Des Moines, IA	313,206	316,067	295,862	277,021	5.9	18,525	19,531	5.9	6.2	4.0	225	15,567
Detroit–Warren–Livonia, MI	2,017,828	2,058,462	2,191,006	2,284,799	-7.9	232,078	285,218	11.5	13.9	7.3	1,133	97,088
Detroit–Livonia–Dearborn, MI	822,523	844,184	903,895	952,300	-9.0	103,348	124,794	12.6	14.8	8.7	379	38,711
Warren–Troy–Farmington Hills, MI	1,195,305	1,214,278	1,287,111	1,332,499	-7.1	128,730	160,424	10.8	13.2	6.3	754	58,377
Dothan, AL	65,141	64,488	64,869	65,635	0.4	5,343	5,544	8.2	8.6	3.3	54	2,800
Dover, DE	75,580	74,820	72,360	63,919	4.4	5,559	5,980	7.4	8.0	3.5	41	1,804
Dubuque, IA	53,259	53,577	50,725	48,732	5.0	2,933	3,296	5.5	6.2	4.4	41	2,486
Duluth, MN–WI	145,795	146,819	141,089	142,017	3.3	10,657	11,841	7.3	8.1	5.3	98	3,942
Durham–Chapel Hill, NC	265,003	262,476	246,491	231,882	7.5	21,505	21,469	8.1	8.2	4.3	127	9,498
Eau Claire, WI	89,888	90,626	86,823	83,467	3.5	6,064	6,592	6.7	7.3	4.6	64	2,444
El Centro, CA	77,561	77,232	60,763	56,067	27.6	23,011	23,082	29.7	29.9	16.1	20	1,651
Elizabethtown, KY	56,676	55,660	53,006	49,253	6.9	5,052	5,263	8.9	9.5	6.0	53	1,808
Elkhart–Goshen, IN	91,753	90,600	101,892	97,342	-10.0	10,247	12,241	11.2	13.5	4.5	66	2,302
Elmira, NY	40,015	40,780	40,640	42,801	-1.5	3,163	3,475	7.9	8.5	5.4	23	1,021
El Paso, TX	326,472	322,152	290,674	274,796	12.3	33,682	31,512	10.3	9.8	7.0	96	6,603
Erie, PA	140,259	139,332	141,034	140,269	-0.5	11,277	12,713	8.0	9.1	5.4	87	4,083
Eugene–Springfield, OR	181,183	182,675	174,568	169,694	3.8	17,158	20,007	9.5	11.0	6.2	97	4,128
Evansville, IN–KY	184,375	183,383	182,960	179,045	0.8	14,308	15,678	7.8	8.5	5.1	121	5,405
Fairbanks, AK	46,859	46,939	45,214	40,952	3.6	3,122	3,262	6.7	6.9	5.8	22	1,242
Fargo, ND–MN	121,229	120,760	113,111	104,117	7.2	4,693	4,928	3.9	4.1	2.9	91	5,506
Farmington, NM	55,307	55,401	54,181	49,680	2.1	4,319	5,015	7.8	9.1	5.4	28	1,303
Fayetteville, NC	164,543	160,608	146,755	133,687	12.1	16,708	15,495	10.2	9.6	5.5	73	2,928
Fayetteville–Springdale–Rogers, AR–MO	231,461	227,938	219,939	176,778	5.2	14,444	14,782	6.2	6.5	3.3	210	8,869
Flagstaff, AZ	72,898	74,921	67,298	62,496	8.3	6,738	7,286	9.2	9.7	4.9	24	1,190
Flint, MI	184,435	189,268	212,489	215,024	-13.2	20,133	26,181	10.9	13.8	7.7	89	3,735
Florence, SC	92,903	93,470	92,124	92,527	0.8	10,566	11,134	11.4	11.9	8.9	68	2,646
Florence–Muscle Shoals, AL	70,105	69,849	66,543	70,038	5.4	5,998	6,390	8.6	9.1	4.4	54	2,277
Fond du Lac, WI	55,301	55,824	56,138	55,970	-1.5	3,962	4,691	7.2	8.4	4.7	39	1,796
Fort Collins–Loveland, CO	178,043	178,171	167,508	146,659	6.3	12,042	13,224	6.8	7.4	4.5	107	5,324
Fort Smith, AR–OK	132,164	136,005	134,616	127,313	-1.8	11,412	11,156	8.6	8.2	4.5	127	4,327
Fort Wayne, IN	210,734	208,886	211,373	208,914	-0.3	18,971	21,663	9.0	10.4	5.1	130	6,250
Fresno, CA	442,054	440,128	408,052	388,267	8.3	73,118	74,091	16.5	16.8	9.0	151	10,233
Gadsden, AL	45,824	45,393	46,461	48,595	-1.4	4,162	4,299	9.1	9.5	4.0	27	1,050
Gainesville, FL	138,256	138,219	129,996	122,625	6.4	10,806	11,010	7.8	8.0	2.9	72	3,411
Gainesville, GA	89,960	87,979	83,358	73,894	7.9	7,330	8,084	8.1	9.2	4.4	53	2,584
Glens Falls, NY	67,690	68,097	67,683	63,520	0.0	5,321	5,543	7.9	8.1	4.6	51	2,089
Goldsboro, NC	54,656	54,128	51,555	50,900	6.0	5,144	5,118	9.4	9.5	5.2	34	1,409
Grand Forks, ND–MN	54,933	55,274	55,004	52,100	-0.1	2,544	2,412	4.6	4.4	3.7	48	2,360
Grand Junction, CO	79,048	79,996	71,483	59,016	10.6	7,607	8,563	9.6	10.7	5.0	43	2,278
Grand Rapids–Wyoming, MI	380,852	382,233	406,673	402,535	-6.3	31,438	40,157	8.3	10.5	5.9	242	13,801
Great Falls, MT	40,672	40,915	38,526	38,328	5.6	2,460	2,342	6.0	5.7	3.6	24	1,277

[1]Civilian unemployed as percent of total civilian labor force.
[2]As of June 30. Covers all FDIC–insured commercial banks and savings institutions; does not include U.S. branches of foreign banks.
[3]The Denver–Aurora metropolitan statistical area includes Broomfield County. Broomfield County, CO, was formed from parts of Adams, Boulder, Jefferson, and Weld Counties on November 15, 2001, and is coextensive with Broomfield city. For the purposes of defining and presenting data for the Denver–Aurora metropolitan statistical area, Broomfield city is treated as if it were a county when data are available to do so. In many cases, the data were not available.

Table B-13. Civilian Labor Force and Banking—*Continued*

Metropolitan statistical area and division	Civilian labor force										Banking 2012[2]	
	Total					Number of unemployed		Unemployment rate[1]			Number of offices	Deposits (million dollars)
	2011	2010	2005	2000	Change, 2005–2011	2011	2010	2011	2010	2005		
Greeley, CO	122,877	121,765	112,158	93,728	9.6	11,443	12,378	9.3	10.2	5.6	77	2,981
Green Bay, WI	173,095	173,876	168,507	162,787	2.7	12,212	13,637	7.1	7.8	4.7	123	5,925
Greensboro–High Point, NC	372,145	371,631	363,945	351,381	2.3	40,824	42,707	11.0	11.5	5.2	219	10,512
Greenville, NC	93,456	93,357	83,101	78,470	12.5	10,061	9,866	10.8	10.6	5.8	52	1,964
Greenville–Mauldin–Easley, SC	315,052	311,603	299,343	297,435	5.2	26,666	30,186	8.5	9.7	5.9	214	11,159
Gulfport–Biloxi, MS	118,055	114,900	120,858	116,945	-2.3	11,526	10,556	9.8	9.2	10.8	94	3,430
Hagerstown–Martinsburg, MD–WV	122,039	122,345	119,686	113,224	2.0	10,990	12,188	9.0	10.0	4.2	90	3,337
Hanford–Corcoran, CA	61,099	61,418	53,960	49,214	13.2	9,854	10,145	16.1	16.5	9.5	14	1,014
Harrisburg–Carlisle, PA	284,676	285,272	278,703	268,358	2.1	20,569	21,893	7.2	7.7	4.0	210	11,537
Harrisonburg, VA	69,093	67,553	61,590	55,446	12.2	4,248	4,617	6.1	6.8	3.2	54	1,909
Hartford–West Hartford–East Hartford, CT	655,192	654,151	611,385	589,340	7.2	57,194	60,726	8.7	9.3	5.0	393	38,822
Hattiesburg, MS	68,012	67,244	63,279	60,327	7.5	6,495	5,999	9.5	8.9	6.3	63	2,511
Hickory–Lenoir–Morganton, NC	170,616	172,244	177,676	188,253	-4.0	21,592	23,982	12.7	13.9	6.6	102	4,363
Hinesville–Fort Stewart, GA	33,337	32,875	28,849	24,045	15.6	3,044	2,956	9.1	9.0	5.4	13	569
Holland–Grand Haven, MI	128,202	127,233	136,175	136,058	-5.9	10,596	14,290	8.3	11.2	5.1	89	3,552
Honolulu, HI	460,643	452,745	439,390	433,110	4.8	26,432	26,388	5.7	5.8	2.7	189	27,516
Hot Springs, AR	42,968	42,317	41,735	38,466	3.0	3,557	3,428	8.3	8.1	5.5	54	1,727
Houma–Bayou Cane–Thibodaux, LA	102,003	103,082	96,727	86,817	5.5	5,461	5,614	5.4	5.4	5.9	89	3,863
Houston–Sugar Land–Baytown, TX	2,982,933	2,925,989	2,609,223	2,386,595	14.3	241,965	247,470	8.1	8.5	5.6	1,534	179,234
Huntington–Ashland, WV–KY–OH	128,298	129,836	131,221	125,778	-2.2	10,581	10,939	8.2	8.4	5.4	110	4,366
Huntsville, AL	213,874	211,887	192,955	183,533	10.8	16,182	15,933	7.6	7.5	3.2	116	6,607
Idaho Falls, ID	62,947	62,676	59,043	50,667	6.6	4,478	4,237	7.1	6.8	2.8	34	1,494
Indianapolis–Carmel, IN	902,936	897,387	877,729	820,765	2.9	76,072	81,540	8.4	9.1	4.8	590	33,287
Iowa City, IA	91,992	92,349	85,941	78,931	7.0	4,010	4,169	4.4	4.5	3.2	60	3,052
Ithaca, NY	55,331	56,884	54,648	50,848	1.2	3,233	3,379	5.8	5.9	3.6	32	1,761
Jackson, MI	71,149	72,612	78,249	79,088	-9.1	7,074	9,239	9.9	12.7	6.7	46	1,568
Jackson, MS	271,496	264,747	263,024	249,204	3.2	22,883	22,317	8.4	8.4	6.0	218	11,522
Jackson, TN	57,554	56,828	54,630	54,707	5.4	5,539	5,742	9.6	10.1	5.6	49	1,821
Jacksonville, FL	692,529	685,119	630,362	589,349	9.9	69,694	74,520	10.1	10.9	3.7	311	45,900
Jacksonville, NC	67,410	67,548	56,456	53,185	19.4	6,148	5,778	9.1	8.6	5.3	30	1,074
Janesville, WI	78,687	80,965	83,608	82,911	-5.9	7,464	9,074	9.5	11.2	5.9	46	2,115
Jefferson City, MO	78,402	78,339	77,869	76,569	0.7	5,376	5,709	6.9	7.3	4.4	63	3,858
Johnson City, TN	102,813	101,349	95,857	91,558	7.3	8,609	9,169	8.4	9.0	5.3	71	2,812
Johnstown, PA	68,352	68,788	67,327	66,652	1.5	5,885	6,340	8.6	9.2	6.1	79	2,777
Jonesboro, AR	59,169	58,226	56,299	54,229	5.1	4,519	4,423	7.6	7.6	5.0	58	2,731
Joplin, MO	87,774	87,102	82,371	81,844	6.6	6,801	7,298	7.7	8.4	4.9	80	2,633
Kalamazoo–Portage, MI	160,211	165,587	173,366	172,467	-7.6	14,136	17,770	8.8	10.7	5.6	94	3,341
Kankakee–Bradley, IL	55,889	56,643	52,577	52,406	6.3	6,806	7,524	12.2	13.3	6.6	43	1,898
Kansas City, MO–KS	1,055,723	1,050,668	1,027,710	999,659	2.7	85,663	93,284	8.1	8.9	5.7	782	42,826
Kennewick–Pasco–Richland, WA	134,627	134,095	113,697	99,026	18.4	10,649	10,408	7.9	7.8	6.1	55	2,349
Killeen–Temple–Fort Hood, TX	171,298	169,604	149,737	133,702	14.4	13,966	13,095	8.2	7.7	5.1	92	3,752
Kingsport–Bristol–Bristol, TN–VA	149,821	148,575	141,778	140,195	5.7	12,101	13,147	8.1	8.8	5.3	124	4,433
Kingston, NY	87,658	88,853	91,906	88,599	-4.6	7,147	7,292	8.2	8.2	4.4	62	3,180
Knoxville, TN	374,650	366,198	341,952	318,562	9.6	27,424	28,938	7.3	7.9	4.5	255	13,774
Kokomo, IN	42,826	42,489	47,225	50,452	-9.3	4,473	5,179	10.4	12.2	6.3	36	1,220
La Crosse, WI–MN	76,711	77,124	72,798	72,536	5.4	4,540	5,083	5.9	6.6	4.1	50	2,208
Lafayette, IN	97,908	97,209	94,466	93,802	3.6	7,636	8,849	7.8	9.1	4.8	70	2,555
Lafayette, LA	137,374	136,354	127,287	118,612	7.9	7,911	8,313	5.8	6.1	5.0	122	5,909
Lake Charles, LA	92,685	94,300	95,794	90,894	-3.2	6,352	6,715	6.9	7.1	7.1	79	3,242
Lake Havasu City–Kingman, AZ	88,006	91,056	88,319	68,673	-0.4	9,649	10,886	11.0	12.0	4.3	45	2,191
Lakeland–Winter Haven, FL	274,561	276,088	256,045	231,280	7.2	31,758	33,630	11.6	12.2	4.0	136	5,570
Lancaster, PA	266,366	269,272	268,382	250,543	-0.8	18,227	20,005	6.8	7.4	3.7	191	9,857
Lansing–East Lansing, MI	235,385	238,611	247,929	247,567	-5.1	19,107	23,833	8.1	10.0	5.9	124	5,150
Laredo, TX	100,246	97,324	85,825	70,828	16.8	8,111	8,677	8.1	8.9	6.0	58	5,828
Las Cruces, NM	92,186	91,783	84,661	76,503	8.9	6,886	7,094	7.5	7.7	5.7	45	1,647
Las Vegas–Paradise, NV	994,152	994,210	872,410	727,521	14.0	137,978	140,241	13.9	14.1	4.4	379	37,419
Lawrence, KS	61,838	62,745	63,150	58,476	-2.1	3,705	3,860	6.0	6.2	4.0	55	1,922
Lawton, OK	48,139	49,108	45,331	43,323	6.2	3,212	3,184	6.7	6.5	4.5	42	1,387
Lebanon, PA	73,400	73,515	70,330	64,143	4.4	4,819	5,212	6.6	7.1	3.6	45	1,903
Lewiston, ID–WA	29,354	29,421	29,559	28,622	-0.7	2,239	2,262	7.6	7.7	4.7	25	752
Lewiston–Auburn, ME	58,281	58,022	56,638	55,241	2.9	4,392	4,877	7.5	8.4	5.0	29	1,308
Lexington–Fayette, KY	239,092	238,500	228,571	228,020	4.6	18,788	20,128	7.9	8.4	4.7	191	8,573
Lima, OH	49,954	50,619	52,467	51,604	-4.8	4,804	5,447	9.6	10.8	6.0	35	1,749
Lincoln, NE	172,266	168,680	165,284	158,276	4.2	6,848	7,140	4.0	4.2	3.6	140	6,361
Little Rock–North Little Rock–Conway, AR	347,204	344,303	332,821	311,965	4.3	24,451	24,199	7.0	7.0	4.6	347	14,034
Logan, UT–ID	67,203	68,070	63,861	53,210	5.2	3,297	3,874	4.9	5.7	3.3	28	1,197
Longview, TX	113,790	113,080	102,246	92,647	11.3	7,858	8,467	6.9	7.5	5.0	83	4,135
Longview, WA	43,269	44,503	42,724	43,153	1.3	5,226	5,802	12.1	13.0	7.2	16	530
Los Angeles–Long Beach–Santa Ana, CA	6,528,034	6,501,576	6,360,244	6,158,469	2.6	744,792	769,811	11.4	11.8	5.0	2,481	343,441
Los Angeles–Long Beach–Glendale, CA	4,924,364	4,910,534	4,771,417	4,677,326	3.2	605,494	619,137	12.3	12.6	5.4	1,787	266,064
Santa Ana–Anaheim–Irvine, CA	1,603,670	1,591,042	1,588,827	1,481,143	0.9	139,298	150,674	8.7	9.5	3.8	694	77,378
Louisville/Jefferson County, KY–IN	633,716	630,783	610,683	610,053	3.8	61,432	64,220	9.7	10.2	5.9	467	23,628

[1]Civilian unemployed as percent of total civilian labor force.
[2]As of June 30. Covers all FDIC–insured commercial banks and savings institutions; does not include U.S. branches of foreign banks.

Table B-13. Civilian Labor Force and Banking—*Continued*

Metropolitan statistical area and division	Civilian labor force										Banking 2012[2]	
	Total					Number of unemployed		Unemployment rate[1]			Number of offices	Deposits (million dollars)
	2011	2010	2005	2000	Change, 2005–2011	2011	2010	2011	2010	2005		
Lubbock, TX	147,982	145,239	140,581	130,798	5.3	9,159	9,214	6.2	6.3	4.1	110	6,331
Lynchburg, VA	125,438	125,759	117,274	113,516	7.0	8,909	9,905	7.1	7.9	4.0	95	4,445
Macon, GA	111,919	111,470	110,825	104,415	1.0	11,323	11,615	10.1	10.4	5.5	65	3,057
Madera–Chowchilla, CA	66,369	67,260	62,012	54,910	7.0	10,134	10,487	15.3	15.6	7.9	21	959
Madison, WI	345,024	346,430	332,980	310,071	3.6	18,321	20,622	5.3	6.0	3.3	226	15,995
Manchester–Nashua, NH	228,370	228,756	225,339	214,534	1.3	12,669	14,522	5.5	6.3	3.7	103	10,893
Manhattan, KS	62,297	64,222	55,923	51,382	11.4	3,597	3,755	5.8	5.8	4.3	59	2,454
Mankato–North Mankato, MN	58,556	57,974	54,257	51,982	7.9	3,081	3,612	5.3	6.2	3.4	44	1,882
Mansfield, OH	59,341	60,103	62,466	63,272	-5.0	6,122	7,064	10.3	11.8	6.5	50	1,742
McAllen–Edinburg–Mission, TX	317,612	309,872	261,157	210,984	21.6	38,095	37,347	12.0	12.1	7.9	153	9,367
Medford, OR	102,261	102,498	99,278	90,558	3.0	11,806	12,796	11.5	12.5	6.2	76	2,779
Memphis, TN–MS–AR	625,230	614,516	603,342	593,697	3.6	62,142	61,792	9.9	10.1	6.2	407	22,967
Merced, CA	110,167	109,338	98,959	90,295	11.3	20,121	20,561	18.3	18.8	10.0	33	1,647
Miami–Fort Lauderdale–Pompano Beach, FL	2,875,403	2,823,480	2,673,194	2,500,458	7.6	300,640	317,974	10.5	11.3	4.2	1,655	168,186
Fort Lauderdale–Pompano Beach–Deerfield Beach, FL	990,714	977,632	949,838	855,214	4.3	91,103	93,913	9.2	9.6	3.6	485	40,131
Miami–Miami Beach–Kendall, FL	1,264,608	1,231,368	1,123,472	1,103,485	12.6	142,836	153,926	11.3	12.5	4.6	678	91,040
West Palm Beach–Boca Raton–Boynton Beach, FL	620,081	614,480	599,884	541,759	3.4	66,701	70,135	10.8	11.4	4.2	492	37,015
Michigan City–La Porte, IN	51,040	51,404	53,043	54,097	-3.8	5,331	6,097	10.4	11.9	6.0	32	1,638
Midland, TX	83,714	78,359	66,480	58,122	25.9	3,689	4,185	4.4	5.3	3.7	46	5,084
Milwaukee–Waukesha–West Allis, WI	797,439	798,039	786,657	807,509	1.4	63,362	70,940	7.9	8.9	5.0	577	58,238
Minneapolis–St. Paul–Bloomington, MN–WI	1,852,208	1,831,259	1,808,876	1,752,907	2.4	116,091	133,501	6.3	7.3	3.9	823	158,658
Missoula, MT	59,394	59,047	57,307	54,211	3.6	3,917	4,046	6.6	6.9	3.3	38	1,942
Mobile, AL	192,780	190,905	179,174	186,720	7.6	19,413	19,421	10.1	10.2	4.2	123	5,980
Modesto, CA	236,573	239,576	227,117	207,769	4.2	39,791	41,425	16.8	17.3	8.5	97	5,769
Monroe, LA	80,560	81,583	83,100	79,949	-3.1	6,236	6,399	7.7	7.8	5.7	63	2,799
Monroe, MI	68,733	70,724	77,808	77,194	-11.7	6,701	8,803	9.7	12.4	6.1	40	1,733
Montgomery, AL	171,414	171,750	167,513	165,208	2.3	15,343	15,551	9.0	9.1	3.7	116	7,909
Morgantown, WV	65,553	65,531	59,413	54,631	10.3	3,758	3,829	5.7	5.8	3.8	48	2,433
Morristown, TN	63,493	63,978	63,762	62,111	-0.4	7,014	7,469	11.0	11.7	5.9	45	1,635
Mount Vernon–Anacortes, WA	56,997	58,293	55,991	51,918	1.8	5,775	6,231	10.1	10.7	5.9	48	2,000
Muncie, IN	53,755	54,392	56,075	58,968	-4.1	5,458	6,136	10.2	11.3	6.7	41	1,631
Muskegon–Norton Shores, MI	82,113	83,335	89,985	85,583	-8.7	8,357	11,224	10.2	13.5	6.9	40	1,371
Myrtle Beach–North Myrtle Beach–Conway, SC	129,085	129,520	120,996	106,429	6.7	14,899	15,794	11.5	12.2	5.8	123	5,081
Napa, CA	76,460	75,734	71,460	66,625	7.0	6,888	7,317	9.0	9.7	4.4	48	2,702
Naples–Marco Island, FL	148,485	144,627	143,967	116,109	3.1	15,269	16,751	10.3	11.6	3.4	153	10,789
Nashville–Davidson—Murfreesboro—Franklin, TN	841,401	822,072	753,854	717,214	11.6	67,351	71,241	8.0	8.7	4.5	567	38,788
New Haven–Milford, CT	457,666	457,238	432,366	413,770	5.9	44,593	47,035	9.7	10.3	5.3	279	20,230
New Orleans–Metairie–Kenner, LA	540,770	540,813	NA	625,846	NA	39,069	39,585	7.2	7.3	NA	360	29,426
New York–Northern New Jersey–Long Island, NY–NJ–PA	9,439,624	9,467,954	9,147,469	8,922,073	3.2	805,625	849,332	8.5	9.0	4.9	5,783	1,163,425
Edison–New Brunswick, NJ	1,212,876	1,212,957	1,164,725	1,117,691	4.1	104,652	107,776	8.6	8.9	4.1	886	68,662
Nassau–Suffolk, NY	1,460,215	1,471,686	1,468,717	1,413,900	-0.6	103,049	108,412	7.1	7.4	4.2	972	98,343
Newark–Union, NJ–PA	1,100,450	1,099,952	1,075,765	1,060,497	2.3	101,167	103,447	9.2	9.4	4.5	846	74,786
New York–White Plains–Wayne, NY–NJ	5,666,083	5,683,359	5,438,262	5,329,985	4.2	496,757	529,697	8.8	9.3	5.3	3,079	921,634
Niles–Benton Harbor, MI	73,088	74,901	79,013	82,529	-7.5	7,415	9,350	10.1	12.5	6.8	60	1,828
North Port–Bradenton–Sarasota, FL	301,311	300,472	311,388	272,084	-3.2	32,479	35,954	10.8	12.0	3.4	305	16,390
Norwich–New London, CT	151,676	152,897	144,936	131,618	4.7	13,119	13,547	8.6	8.9	4.5	95	4,251
Ocala, FL	133,997	134,320	126,821	109,216	5.7	16,515	18,048	12.3	13.4	3.7	90	4,977
Ocean City, NJ	58,268	58,469	57,854	55,540	0.7	7,260	7,145	12.5	12.2	6.6	60	2,726
Odessa, TX	78,567	73,422	62,435	56,486	25.8	4,568	5,691	5.8	7.8	4.5	40	2,599
Ogden–Clearfield, UT	258,551	263,724	250,085	222,975	3.4	17,773	20,985	6.9	8.0	4.3	94	18,804
Oklahoma City, OK	579,785	574,952	574,611	552,592	0.9	32,953	37,185	5.7	6.5	4.4	417	25,727
Olympia, WA	129,026	130,457	121,377	108,262	6.3	10,661	11,033	8.3	8.5	5.0	68	2,890
Omaha–Council Bluffs, NE–IA	458,081	451,791	440,304	426,202	4.0	22,860	23,696	5.0	5.2	4.3	333	23,639
Orlando–Kissimmee–Sanford, FL	1,122,472	1,113,527	1,007,542	895,172	11.4	116,937	125,202	10.4	11.2	3.5	612	36,440
Oshkosh–Neenah, WI	96,133	96,268	91,625	89,983	4.9	6,322	7,085	6.6	7.4	4.5	43	2,148
Owensboro, KY	58,298	57,311	55,042	55,550	5.9	4,808	5,265	8.2	9.2	6.1	55	2,627
Oxnard–Thousand Oaks–Ventura, CA	437,011	434,750	416,751	392,665	4.9	43,922	46,907	10.1	10.8	4.8	183	14,897
Palm Bay–Melbourne–Titusville, FL	267,597	266,892	258,323	232,007	3.6	29,662	29,701	11.1	11.1	3.6	135	7,331
Palm Coast, FL	34,022	33,637	29,733	21,008	14.4	4,813	5,079	14.1	15.1	4.3	22	1,425
Panama City–Lynn Haven–Panama City Beach, FL	91,028	89,646	81,736	71,998	11.4	9,142	8,987	10.0	10.0	3.5	64	2,465
Parkersburg–Marietta–Vienna, WV–OH	76,499	77,314	79,786	79,392	-4.1	6,458	7,114	8.4	9.2	5.6	68	2,888
Pascagoula, MS	73,653	73,781	70,986	71,910	3.8	8,412	7,234	11.4	9.8	10.0	49	1,753
Pensacola–Ferry Pass–Brent, FL	213,691	210,796	201,472	187,472	6.1	20,837	20,990	9.8	10.0	3.7	106	4,686
Peoria, IL	202,717	201,548	190,577	187,201	6.4	17,765	20,921	8.8	10.4	4.9	165	6,656
Philadelphia–Camden–Wilmington, PA–NJ–DE–MD	2,975,724	2,984,343	2,925,792	2,846,067	1.7	254,905	265,305	8.6	8.9	4.7	1,890	447,649
Camden, NJ	667,424	670,897	650,647	610,472	2.6	65,320	67,387	9.8	10.0	4.3	336	22,241
Philadelphia, PA	1,954,911	1,961,480	1,922,370	1,885,606	1.7	161,744	167,260	8.3	8.5	4.9	1,323	106,247
Wilmington, DE–MD–NJ	353,389	351,966	352,775	349,989	0.2	27,841	30,658	7.9	8.7	4.3	231	319,161

[1]Civilian unemployed as percent of total civilian labor force.
[2]As of June 30. Covers all FDIC–insured commercial banks and savings institutions; does not include U.S. branches of foreign banks.
NA = Not available

Table B-13. Civilian Labor Force and Banking—*Continued*

Metropolitan statistical area and division	Civilian labor force										Banking 2012[2]	
	Total					Number of unemployed		Unemployment rate[1]			Number of offices	Deposits (million dollars)
	2011	2010	2005	2000	Change, 2005–2011	2011	2010	2011	2010	2005		
Phoenix–Mesa–Glendale, AZ	2,034,992	2,074,050	1,926,885	1,664,524	5.6	174,225	202,468	8.6	9.8	4.1	928	63,127
Pine Bluff, AR	44,344	44,325	46,316	44,884	-4.3	4,516	4,278	10.2	9.7	7.3	29	1,309
Pittsburgh, PA	1,231,920	1,222,273	1,200,458	1,191,585	2.6	89,154	95,684	7.2	7.8	5.2	873	96,657
Pittsfield, MA	72,397	72,663	72,646	70,160	-0.3	5,251	5,900	7.3	8.1	4.4	59	3,081
Pocatello, ID	44,269	43,866	43,772	41,979	1.1	3,575	3,519	8.1	8.0	3.6	32	827
Portland–South Portland–Biddeford, ME	289,671	288,500	283,960	270,116	2.0	18,381	20,298	6.3	7.0	3.9	196	20,748
Portland–Vancouver–Hillsboro, OR–WA	1,197,795	1,188,480	1,097,592	1,075,854	9.1	109,317	124,553	9.1	10.5	5.9	590	45,878
Port St. Lucie, FL	189,448	188,380	176,131	143,812	7.6	23,255	24,686	12.3	13.1	4.4	135	6,816
Poughkeepsie–Newburgh–Middletown, NY	319,135	322,256	324,911	301,587	-1.8	24,401	25,925	7.6	8.0	4.1	216	9,969
Prescott, AZ	91,959	95,773	90,659	75,667	1.4	9,175	10,490	10.0	11.0	4.4	58	2,924
Providence–New Bedford–Fall River, RI–MA	853,585	861,739	849,194	821,474	0.5	92,559	98,676	10.8	11.5	5.4	413	52,882
Provo–Orem, UT	222,864	225,371	210,888	183,907	5.7	14,600	17,933	6.6	8.0	4.0	89	4,366
Pueblo, CO	76,538	75,966	70,012	64,099	9.3	7,841	7,944	10.2	10.5	6.9	44	1,498
Punta Gorda, FL	70,507	70,376	65,546	55,163	7.6	7,587	8,408	10.8	11.9	3.9	62	3,076
Racine, WI	98,241	98,743	99,006	99,858	-0.8	8,784	9,957	8.9	10.1	6.0	66	3,025
Raleigh–Cary, NC	582,685	573,809	504,815	454,465	15.4	50,023	51,406	8.6	9.0	4.2	312	23,814
Rapid City, SD	67,399	66,713	65,167	61,102	3.4	3,205	3,524	4.8	5.3	3.5	39	2,109
Reading, PA	204,817	204,290	199,318	194,605	2.8	16,829	18,309	8.2	9.0	4.9	144	8,614
Redding, CA	83,452	84,437	81,918	74,838	1.9	12,272	13,285	14.7	15.7	7.3	48	2,415
Reno–Sparks, NV	226,515	228,344	211,526	196,686	7.1	29,608	29,880	13.1	13.1	4.3	89	71,831
Richmond, VA	675,378	668,241	619,645	564,833	9.0	46,864	51,890	6.9	7.8	3.7	375	73,803
Riverside–San Bernardino–Ontario, CA	1,799,005	1,798,152	1,707,382	1,420,114	5.4	241,248	257,677	13.4	14.3	5.3	601	36,368
Roanoke, VA	161,691	160,946	150,388	148,145	7.5	10,721	11,977	6.6	7.4	3.5	129	7,131
Rochester, MN	103,734	104,137	101,939	95,141	1.8	5,654	6,438	5.5	6.2	3.7	69	4,296
Rochester, NY	521,338	526,495	535,551	534,458	-2.7	39,917	42,913	7.7	8.2	4.7	271	14,473
Rockford, IL	168,067	170,905	164,702	168,515	2.0	21,600	26,377	12.9	15.4	6.7	104	5,361
Rocky Mount, NC	72,199	72,480	68,975	68,555	4.7	10,133	10,116	14.0	14.0	6.9	46	1,690
Rome, GA	47,590	48,352	50,469	44,900	-5.7	5,189	5,201	10.9	10.8	5.1	24	1,334
Sacramento—Arden-Arcade—Roseville, CA	1,039,429	1,048,855	1,013,921	909,228	2.5	123,238	130,898	11.9	12.5	4.9	427	34,141
Saginaw–Saginaw Township North, MI	90,082	91,185	98,275	100,214	-8.3	8,689	10,852	9.6	11.9	7.8	64	2,009
St. Cloud, MN	107,920	107,503	102,711	98,795	5.1	6,948	8,010	6.4	7.5	4.5	67	3,969
St. George, UT	56,873	58,635	57,443	39,148	-1.0	4,907	6,094	8.6	10.4	4.1	37	1,618
St. Joseph, MO–KS	72,089	71,476	64,885	60,474	11.1	5,316	5,874	7.4	8.2	5.7	53	2,133
St. Louis, MO–IL[4]	1,449,770	1,448,329	1,436,530	1,423,748	0.9	129,043	142,252	8.9	9.8	5.6	952	81,155
Salem, OR	197,534	198,774	184,403	177,751	7.1	19,533	21,170	9.9	10.7	6.3	97	4,247
Salinas, CA	222,857	220,933	206,975	203,188	7.7	27,648	27,974	12.4	12.7	7.3	82	7,411
Salisbury, MD	64,243	64,340	63,618	56,838	1.0	5,905	6,323	9.2	9.8	4.6	52	1,731
Salt Lake City, UT	595,346	605,220	569,029	522,137	4.6	38,968	47,218	6.5	7.8	4.1	270	310,959
San Angelo, TX	56,119	55,415	52,927	51,564	6.0	3,510	3,560	6.3	6.4	4.3	33	2,043
San Antonio–New Braunfels, TX	1,012,444	1,002,240	896,888	817,912	12.9	75,319	74,263	7.4	7.4	5.0	453	74,606
San Diego–Carlsbad–San Marcos, CA	1,583,807	1,572,611	1,492,594	1,376,008	6.1	157,704	165,550	10.0	10.5	4.3	637	60,886
Sandusky, OH	42,202	42,198	42,645	42,168	-1.0	3,665	4,382	8.7	10.4	6.3	26	1,016
San Francisco–Oakland–Fremont, CA	2,263,171	2,249,205	2,150,963	2,282,740	5.2	213,284	231,037	9.4	10.3	4.8	1,069	290,752
Oakland–Fremont–Hayward, CA	1,284,987	1,284,579	1,246,524	1,270,001	3.1	133,354	143,941	10.4	11.2	5.0	527	59,133
San Francisco–San Mateo– Redwood City, CA	978,184	964,626	904,439	1,012,739	8.2	79,930	87,096	8.2	9.0	4.6	542	231,619
San Jose–Sunnyvale–Santa Clara, CA	922,617	906,847	841,504	968,181	9.6	91,040	101,229	9.9	11.2	5.4	364	74,081
San Luis Obispo–Paso Robles, CA	138,650	138,182	131,725	122,463	5.3	12,854	13,668	9.3	9.9	4.3	80	5,181
Santa Barbara–Santa Maria–Goleta, CA	225,635	222,380	213,600	202,387	5.6	19,851	20,814	8.8	9.4	4.4	103	9,825
Santa Cruz–Watsonville, CA	150,740	149,934	143,273	148,350	5.2	18,226	18,914	12.1	12.6	6.3	51	4,308
Santa Fe, NM	74,644	75,805	76,305	70,781	-2.2	4,489	4,926	6.0	6.5	4.1	40	2,549
Santa Rosa–Petaluma, CA	257,279	256,053	253,887	253,260	1.3	25,136	26,767	9.8	10.5	4.5	132	9,993
Savannah, GA	175,569	174,889	166,572	142,860	5.4	15,779	15,956	9.0	9.1	4.3	112	5,613
Scranton–Wilkes-Barre, PA	281,504	281,780	277,870	272,967	1.3	26,175	26,889	9.3	9.5	5.6	228	10,995
Seattle–Tacoma–Bellevue, WA	1,878,163	1,886,638	1,726,969	1,647,399	8.8	163,248	182,170	8.7	9.7	5.0	939	74,260
Seattle–Bellevue–Everett, WA	1,490,919	1,494,197	1,359,706	1,307,433	9.7	125,312	141,987	8.4	9.5	4.8	739	65,529
Tacoma, WA	387,244	392,441	367,263	339,966	5.4	37,936	40,183	9.8	10.2	5.9	200	8,731
Sebastian–Vero Beach, FL	63,290	62,474	58,988	51,057	7.3	7,977	8,476	12.6	13.6	4.7	57	3,365
Sheboygan, WI	62,208	63,622	64,857	64,613	-4.1	4,724	5,657	7.6	8.9	4.0	45	1,873
Sherman–Denison, TX	58,711	57,955	56,552	56,260	3.8	4,871	4,884	8.3	8.4	5.4	46	1,846
Shreveport–Bossier City, LA	183,763	184,347	180,920	172,577	1.6	12,430	12,887	6.8	7.0	5.5	127	6,858
Sioux City, IA–NE–SD	77,457	78,583	74,466	77,273	4.0	4,512	5,288	5.8	6.7	4.7	75	2,880
Sioux Falls, SD	130,242	128,421	120,283	111,199	8.3	5,778	6,502	4.4	5.1	3.3	135	300,565
South Bend–Mishawaka, IN–MI	154,254	153,043	161,757	162,038	-4.6	15,276	17,270	9.9	11.3	5.2	87	4,809
Spartanburg, SC	132,077	133,290	131,300	130,780	0.6	13,768	15,374	10.4	11.5	7.5	75	3,570
Spokane, WA	230,985	235,966	223,009	211,201	3.6	21,784	23,274	9.4	9.9	5.6	124	6,114
Springfield, IL	116,567	116,591	111,802	112,377	4.3	8,983	9,490	7.7	8.1	4.7	93	5,224
Springfield, MA	350,151	352,004	351,472	344,243	-0.4	28,348	31,447	8.1	8.9	5.2	234	13,194
Springfield, MO	223,531	222,815	212,649	198,896	5.1	17,240	18,925	7.7	8.5	4.3	192	7,947
Springfield, OH	68,988	69,556	70,204	72,387	-1.7	6,152	7,221	8.9	10.4	6.2	41	1,506
State College, PA	75,959	75,799	72,608	68,414	4.6	4,293	4,674	5.7	6.2	4.0	70	2,531
Steubenville–Weirton, OH–WV	55,247	57,035	57,721	59,245	-4.3	6,325	7,464	11.4	13.1	7.2	47	1,769

[1]Civilian unemployed as percent of total civilian labor force.
[2]As of June 30. Covers all FDIC–insured commercial banks and savings institutions; does not include U.S. branches of foreign banks.
[4]The portion of Sullivan city in Crawford County, MO is legally part of the St. Louis, MO–IL MSA. That portion is not included in these figures for the St. Louis, MSA.

Table B-13.   Civilian Labor Force and Banking—*Continued*

Metropolitan statistical area and division	Civilian labor force										Banking 2012[2]	
	Total					Number of unemployed		Unemployment rate[1]			Number of offices	Deposits (million dollars)
	2011	2010	2005	2000	Change, 2005–2011	2011	2010	2011	2010	2005		
Stockton, CA	297,572	300,812	284,188	258,920	4.7	50,126	51,944	16.8	17.3	7.9	117	7,364
Sumter, SC	44,811	45,046	46,312	45,139	-3.2	5,118	5,457	11.4	12.1	8.5	18	797
Syracuse, NY	320,603	325,414	330,386	324,760	-3.0	26,304	28,051	8.2	8.6	4.9	197	10,728
Tallahassee, FL	192,390	191,936	177,970	172,551	8.1	15,991	15,905	8.3	8.3	3.1	106	5,339
Tampa–St. Petersburg–Clearwater, FL	1,308,379	1,289,095	1,248,334	1,200,045	4.8	142,058	152,187	10.9	11.8	3.9	786	60,279
Terre Haute, IN	79,701	80,717	80,580	81,386	-1.1	8,324	8,982	10.4	11.1	6.9	63	2,538
Texarkana, TX–Texarkana, AR	66,479	65,901	61,900	58,608	7.4	4,978	4,893	7.5	7.4	5.2	54	2,146
Toledo, OH	320,475	325,040	336,002	337,749	-4.6	30,425	36,123	9.5	11.1	6.5	211	9,959
Topeka, KS	122,277	123,548	123,501	120,404	-1.0	8,712	8,948	7.1	7.2	5.6	118	4,910
Trenton–Ewing, NJ	208,203	206,868	194,292	180,174	7.2	16,060	16,332	7.7	7.9	3.9	152	12,767
Tucson, AZ	465,613	479,054	437,823	409,019	6.3	39,207	45,259	8.4	9.4	4.5	193	12,152
Tulsa, OK	437,230	441,719	443,384	440,318	-1.4	30,100	34,154	6.9	7.7	4.4	310	21,606
Tuscaloosa, AL	101,206	100,721	94,826	93,105	6.7	8,679	9,103	8.6	9.0	3.4	63	3,142
Tyler, TX	104,089	102,729	95,590	86,261	8.9	8,126	8,109	7.8	7.9	5.0	92	4,551
Utica–Rome, NY	138,633	140,611	143,055	142,815	-3.1	11,351	11,280	8.2	8.0	4.9	82	3,698
Valdosta, GA	65,389	65,873	65,271	56,449	0.2	6,018	6,021	9.2	9.1	3.9	46	2,122
Vallejo–Fairfield, CA	215,472	214,620	208,894	194,209	3.1	24,646	25,809	11.4	12.0	5.4	68	3,301
Victoria, TX	60,920	59,600	56,782	55,698	7.3	4,170	4,480	6.8	7.5	4.7	34	2,598
Vineland–Millville–Bridgeton, NJ	70,761	71,266	69,280	65,539	2.1	9,467	9,689	13.4	13.6	6.4	42	2,626
Virginia Beach–Norfolk–Newport News, VA–NC	847,075	841,977	795,987	721,983	6.4	59,126	61,814	7.0	7.3	3.9	367	21,315
Visalia–Porterville, CA	208,098	208,491	183,709	171,834	13.3	34,578	35,205	16.6	16.9	9.5	66	3,865
Waco, TX	116,392	116,516	112,273	103,656	3.7	8,601	8,368	7.4	7.2	5.0	59	3,977
Warner Robins, GA	70,292	70,434	63,010	53,848	11.6	5,468	5,486	7.8	7.8	4.7	29	1,255
Washington–Arlington–Alexandria, DC–VA–MD–WV	3,172,533	3,133,387	2,903,240	2,670,068	9.3	183,939	198,460	5.8	6.3	3.4	1,763	190,707
Bethesda–Rockville–Frederick, MD	652,901	650,306	629,514	598,962	3.7	34,921	39,130	5.3	6.0	3.1	404	35,045
Washington–Arlington–Alexandria, DC–VA–MD–WV	2,519,632	2,483,081	2,273,726	2,071,106	10.8	149,018	159,330	5.9	6.4	3.5	1,359	155,662
Waterloo–Cedar Falls, IA	95,725	95,305	91,986	88,337	4.1	5,403	5,703	5.6	6.0	4.2	67	2,784
Wausau, WI	72,495	73,900	74,720	72,351	-3.0	5,494	6,652	7.6	9.0	4.2	63	2,871
Wenatchee–East Wenatchee, WA	62,226	63,020	59,110	54,536	5.3	5,156	5,518	8.3	8.8	5.7	36	1,943
Wheeling, WV–OH	68,514	69,776	68,891	69,391	-0.5	5,923	6,681	8.6	9.6	5.6	70	3,248
Wichita, KS	307,650	311,535	307,190	299,138	0.1	24,768	27,612	8.1	8.9	5.5	244	13,032
Wichita Falls, TX	73,153	73,912	74,435	71,647	-1.7	5,188	5,662	7.1	7.7	4.5	54	2,474
Williamsport, PA	61,373	60,536	59,477	59,251	3.2	4,705	5,310	7.7	8.8	5.4	52	1,987
Wilmington, NC	182,053	181,812	163,961	142,532	11.0	19,395	19,364	10.7	10.7	4.5	131	5,875
Winchester, VA–WV	68,094	66,780	61,907	54,907	10.0	4,480	5,002	6.6	7.5	3.0	58	2,293
Winston-Salem, NC	243,054	242,725	232,918	223,086	4.4	24,244	24,936	10.0	10.3	4.7	133	35,002
Worcester, MA	404,098	405,517	398,457	387,940	1.4	32,627	36,922	8.1	9.1	5.2	230	12,554
Yakima, WA	124,749	125,675	116,847	113,000	6.8	12,556	12,631	10.1	10.1	7.4	59	2,762
York–Hanover, PA	224,969	225,348	219,580	208,916	2.5	17,462	19,427	7.8	8.6	4.2	151	6,445
Youngstown–Warren–Boardman, OH–PA	267,833	272,149	280,338	284,494	-4.5	25,260	30,937	9.4	11.4	6.7	196	9,227
Yuba City, CA	71,300	70,962	65,828	62,152	8.3	13,241	13,732	18.6	19.4	9.5	27	1,576
Yuma, AZ	89,500	90,156	75,478	64,345	18.6	24,270	23,713	27.1	26.3	15.9	31	1,507

[1]Civilian unemployed as percent of total civilian labor force.
[2]As of June 30. Covers all FDIC–insured commercial banks and savings institutions; does not include U.S. branches of foreign banks.

Table B-14. Federal Government Expenditures and Private Business Establishments and Employment

Metropolitan statistical area and division	Federal government expenditures								Private nonfarm business				
	2010							2005 (million dollars)	Establishments		Employment[2]		Annual payroll per employee, 2010 (dollars)
	Total (million dollars)	Percent change, 2005–2010	Per capita[1] (dollars)	Direct payments to individuals		Salaries and wages (million dollars)	Total defense contracts (million dollars)		2010	Change, 2000–2010	2010	Change, 2000–2010	
				Amount (million dollars)	Percent of total expenditures								
Abilene, TX	1,522.1	23.9	9,211	871.8	57.3	319.2	74.7	1,228.3	3,899	-2.9	55,831	4.7	30,207
Akron, OH	5,424.2	33.1	7,714	3,629.1	66.9	239.3	443.7	4,075.0	16,572	-5.6	270,260	-10.6	40,521
Albany, GA	1,593.7	18.3	10,131	875.4	54.9	176.9	112.3	1,347.2	3,332	1.2	44,686	-15.5	31,912
Albany–Schenectady–Troy, NY	15,440.0	46.6	17,733	4,445.5	28.8	728.8	383.8	10,528.8	21,061	9.2	323,328	1.2	40,676
Albuquerque, NM	10,866.1	28.6	12,249	4,036.5	37.1	1,275.3	770.5	8,447.5	18,688	4.0	279,882	-0.3	36,467
Alexandria, LA	1,612.5	34.1	10,476	906.2	56.2	276.2	11.0	1,202.8	3,449	4.9	48,883	-1.7	32,133
Allentown–Bethlehem–Easton, PA–NJ	6,417.2	45.8	7,815	4,498.6	70.1	290.1	129.3	4,400.6	18,299	3.3	284,193	-1.1	42,739
Altoona, PA	1,300.8	39.1	10,235	913.3	70.2	83.3	1.9	934.9	3,217	-2.2	50,470	-2.7	31,406
Amarillo, TX	4,532.8	150.8	18,140	1,071.8	23.6	143.6	2,428.8	1,807.0	5,998	3.7	88,609	5.2	35,453
Ames, IA	1,268.6	133.3	14,168	315.9	24.9	85.6	15.0	543.8	2,031	5.1	28,112	-1.4	32,555
Anchorage, AK	5,174.2	36.5	13,587	1,164.5	22.5	1,152.4	964.8	3,790.1	10,425	12.0	160,120	30.8	54,380
Anderson, IN	1,214.0	36.7	9,222	878.7	72.4	33.7	4.5	888.2	2,342	-15.5	34,123	-19.4	29,486
Anderson, SC	1,233.9	44.6	6,594	927.7	75.2	86.7	14.6	853.6	3,681	-1.2	50,507	-14.4	31,124
Ann Arbor, MI	3,527.0	67.5	10,229	1,294.0	36.7	231.6	107.4	2,106.2	7,905	-4.2	132,543	-15.8	47,843
Anniston–Oxford, AL	1,726.3	31.5	14,559	874.2	50.6	233.1	415.3	1,312.3	2,427	-5.4	36,951	-9.0	31,674
Appleton, WI	1,113.3	37.4	4,933	779.1	70.0	72.0	50.5	810.1	5,818	6.1	101,841	-6.9	38,514
Asheville, NC	3,486.0	32.3	8,205	2,441.8	70.0	257.4	34.7	2,635.3	11,502	11.6	141,838	-3.7	32,818
Athens–Clarke County, GA	1,291.2	38.1	6,706	727.9	56.4	130.5	5.7	935.2	4,390	14.7	53,718	-1.3	31,561
Atlanta–Sandy Springs–Marietta, GA	40,616.0	56.7	7,709	17,533.3	43.2	5,338.8	4,883.8	25,919.2	129,166	11.6	2,003,047	-6.3	47,516
Atlantic City–Hammonton, NJ	2,365.5	28.6	8,616	1,503.7	63.6	301.1	40.6	1,839.7	6,482	1.6	113,533	-5.8	35,143
Auburn–Opelika, AL	762.5	38.1	5,437	493.2	64.7	70.4	22.7	552.1	2,352	18.1	34,910	8.2	28,109
Augusta–Richmond County, GA–SC	8,423.1	58.6	15,126	2,919.5	34.7	1,841.2	308.0	5,309.3	10,335	3.3	170,333	-3.9	38,028
Austin–Round Rock–San Marcos, TX	19,767.6	91.2	11,518	4,782.0	24.2	1,062.5	924.6	10,341.4	41,216	29.5	640,563	16.4	46,969
Bakersfield–Delano, CA	5,744.5	30.1	6,842	3,111.3	54.2	772.0	484.6	4,415.5	11,925	9.5	174,924	16.4	38,918
Baltimore–Towson, MD	42,393.2	69.4	15,640	18,546.0	43.7	5,294.7	5,598.5	25,030.7	65,169	4.7	1,059,610	1.4	47,495
Bangor, ME	1,644.1	53.0	10,681	856.7	52.1	173.7	131.4	1,074.6	4,193	0.5	57,599	1.3	34,059
Barnstable Town, MA	2,650.7	34.0	12,278	1,760.8	66.4	250.1	84.7	1,978.6	8,214	-1.5	68,819	-4.7	39,195
Baton Rouge, LA	11,347.0	38.5	14,140	3,355.7	29.6	395.4	326.2	8,194.6	17,751	10.4	309,320	10.0	40,642
Battle Creek, MI	1,481.8	33.9	10,884	849.0	57.3	156.6	156.0	1,106.4	2,681	-11.5	47,280	-22.1	41,272
Bay City, MI	897.4	45.2	8,327	693.5	77.3	40.3	1.8	618.0	2,291	-10.4	29,340	-17.0	36,232
Beaumont–Port Arthur, TX	3,258.9	24.7	8,383	2,286.3	70.2	214.5	49.8	2,612.7	7,926	-2.2	126,414	-2.1	42,834
Bellingham, WA	1,279.8	-14.0	6,363	820.6	64.1	120.9	22.1	1,487.4	6,244	15.9	67,421	13.1	35,649
Bend, OR	950.9	55.5	6,029	715.8	75.3	84.9	4.7	611.7	5,807	29.3	51,489	20.1	33,332
Billings, MT	1,203.6	36.2	7,615	712.9	59.2	162.4	3.5	883.4	5,898	13.5	69,312	14.0	35,702
Binghamton, NY	2,815.9	10.3	11,186	1,371.6	48.7	78.3	902.7	2,552.3	5,115	0.3	84,260	-7.8	36,754
Birmingham–Hoover, AL	10,252.3	45.2	9,089	6,487.2	63.3	970.2	291.3	7,059.2	25,686	0.2	434,225	-6.7	41,625
Bismarck, ND	1,625.9	82.3	14,947	481.5	29.6	185.3	6.7	891.9	3,426	15.3	51,589	22.5	35,363
Blacksburg–Christiansburg–Radford, VA	1,292.2	34.5	7,930	728.9	56.4	56.6	148.9	961.0	3,271	4.1	44,312	-9.9	33,377
Bloomington, IN	1,461.9	40.3	7,586	757.3	51.8	94.9	9.1	1,041.9	3,881	-0.1	56,353	-0.9	32,249
Bloomington–Normal, IL	758.0	28.1	4,470	548.2	72.3	67.4	0.3	591.7	3,702	4.5	76,070	-8.0	46,748
Boise City–Nampa, ID	4,516.3	58.8	7,325	2,197.5	48.7	524.3	45.0	2,844.5	16,456	20.2	209,672	6.1	36,444
Boston–Cambridge–Quincy, MA–NH	57,692.9	47.7	12,673	22,224.4	38.5	3,497.6	10,905.4	39,049.4	122,191	-2.5	2,224,822	-5.4	58,663
Boston–Quincy, MA	25,223.8	48.3	13,362	9,582.2	38.0	1,700.4	924.2	17,005.3	50,344	-3.0	1,009,509	-4.4	60,113
Cambridge–Newton–Framingham, MA	20,144.1	40.7	13,402	7,009.2	34.8	1,248.1	5,847.4	14,314.6	42,001	-2.5	791,554	-7.2	64,270
Peabody, MA	9,423.9	68.1	12,681	3,859.3	41.0	269.8	3,843.8	5,604.7	17,877	-3.8	263,022	-6.9	46,675
Rockingham County–Strafford County, NH	2,901.1	36.5	6,934	1,773.8	61.1	279.4	290.0	2,124.8	11,969	1.4	160,737	0.0	41,568
Boulder, CO	3,118.2	54.7	10,586	1,042.5	33.4	317.0	183.9	2,015.8	11,443	2.8	133,260	-15.6	52,636
Bowling Green, KY	960.1	69.8	7,623	660.7	68.8	64.9	1.9	565.4	2,830	8.8	47,111	6.1	33,855
Bremerton–Silverdale, WA	4,004.4	39.5	15,945	1,427.2	35.6	969.1	598.8	2,870.2	5,656	7.9	56,258	12.8	34,510
Bridgeport–Stamford–Norwalk, CT	13,539.9	99.8	14,768	7,462.3	55.1	303.9	4,045.9	6,777.6	27,027	-5.5	393,952	-11.5	76,725
Brownsville–Harlingen, TX	2,895.6	52.4	7,128	1,494.1	51.6	234.8	17.6	1,899.8	6,327	9.2	98,784	14.2	24,630
Brunswick, GA	1,113.1	25.7	9,906	624.4	56.1	209.9	12.0	885.2	2,860	3.1	32,228	-5.3	31,015
Buffalo–Niagara Falls, NY	10,696.4	28.6	9,420	6,827.0	63.8	753.4	285.9	8,320.1	26,899	0.2	455,704	-4.6	36,947
Burlington, NC	925.3	38.1	6,123	707.6	76.5	28.0	5.2	670.1	3,206	-4.2	48,238	-19.6	30,892
Burlington–South Burlington, VT	2,414.8	46.9	11,430	810.8	33.6	419.8	503.0	1,643.4	6,719	1.6	97,940	2.6	42,295
Canton–Massillon, OH	3,022.6	24.0	7,474	2,274.2	75.2	168.2	9.2	2,437.6	8,908	-10.6	137,639	-18.9	32,546
Cape Coral–Fort Myers, FL	4,275.2	34.8	6,909	3,683.2	86.2	190.7	4.9	3,172.4	15,569	25.6	167,156	16.8	33,556
Cape Girardeau–Jackson, MO–IL	771.9	45.3	8,018	478.9	62.0	61.4	11.5	531.4	3,126	16.0	40,784	2.7	30,415
Carson City, NV	1,497.0	109.5	27,083	315.5	21.1	66.8	14.4	714.7	2,041	-8.9	21,103	-14.9	39,017
Casper, WY	499.4	34.2	6,619	311.2	62.3	60.4	6.7	372.0	2,913	11.0	32,650	18.5	41,241
Cedar Rapids, IA	2,861.1	50.6	11,092	1,103.2	38.6	107.1	1,128.7	1,899.7	6,453	0.1	121,486	-1.9	41,199
Champaign–Urbana, IL	1,707.6	42.7	7,364	776.0	45.4	140.1	32.8	1,196.4	4,914	1.1	75,073	-3.3	35,799
Charleston, WV	4,374.4	51.4	14,376	1,963.7	44.9	298.8	24.7	2,889.3	7,318	-6.7	116,521	-1.4	38,714
Charleston–North Charleston–Summerville, SC	8,341.7	44.3	12,551	3,188.8	38.2	920.9	2,492.1	5,782.7	16,399	16.6	228,622	4.2	36,847
Charlotte–Gastonia–Rock Hill, NC–SC	9,160.6	39.3	5,211	6,179.9	67.5	766.7	113.0	6,574.3	44,513	14.7	727,384	0.6	45,592
Charlottesville, VA	1,876.0	51.8	9,307	894.4	47.7	178.2	199.2	1,235.9	5,636	12.5	74,628	5.4	40,955
Chattanooga, TN–GA	4,819.9	24.8	9,126	3,225.0	66.9	210.2	42.3	3,861.2	11,139	-1.7	194,365	-8.5	35,882
Cheyenne, WY	1,699.6	53.0	18,527	471.1	27.7	342.8	87.9	1,110.7	2,701	18.1	30,763	14.4	34,999
Chicago–Joliet–Naperville, IL–IN–WI	70,771.9	35.9	7,480	40,506.1	57.2	5,222.5	5,106.0	52,063.4	236,704	4.0	3,797,772	-10.5	50,795
Chicago–Joliet–Naperville, IL	60,361.8	38.7	7,657	33,702.4	55.8	4,436.8	4,317.4	43,517.7	199,826	4.2	3,219,892	-11.6	50,884
Gary, IN	5,168.5	33.1	7,299	3,759.9	72.7	210.2	36.9	3,884.0	14,472	0.5	224,323	-7.6	38,075
Lake County–Kenosha County, IL–WI	5,241.6	12.4	6,026	3,043.9	58.1	575.4	751.7	4,661.7	22,406	4.4	353,557	-1.4	58,060

[1]Based on resident population estimated as of July 1, 2010.
[2]For pay period as of March 12 of the year shown.

Table B-14. Federal Government Expenditures and Private Business Establishments and Employment—*Continued*

Metropolitan statistical area and division	Federal government expenditures								Private nonfarm business				
	2010							2005 (million dollars)	Establishments		Employment[2]		Annual payroll per employee, 2010 (dollars)
	Total (million dollars)	Percent change, 2005–2010	Per capita[1] (dollars)	Direct payments to individuals		Salaries and wages (million dollars)	Total defense contracts (million dollars)		2010	Change, 2000–2010	2010	Change, 2000–2010	
				Amount (million dollars)	Percent of total expenditures								
Chico, CA	1,788.2	24.4	8,128	1,310.9	73.3	47.0	0.5	1,437.8	4,712	2.5	53,911	0.3	32,388
Cincinnati–Middletown, OH–KY–IN	17,400.1	31.5	8,168	9,974.5	57.3	1,308.5	2,211.5	13,236.1	46,143	-2.9	874,547	-8.8	43,402
Clarksville, TN–KY	7,603.2	148.9	27,754	1,393.5	18.3	5,297.1	557.0	3,054.8	4,305	8.7	66,551	10.9	30,298
Cleveland, TN	850.6	47.1	7,346	677.5	79.6	21.2	0.1	578.2	2,103	-1.3	36,431	-13.6	32,791
Cleveland–Elyria–Mentor, OH	19,049.7	35.7	9,171	12,088.6	63.5	1,434.0	251.6	14,041.8	52,149	-8.4	870,158	-17.7	43,655
Coeur d'Alene, ID	1,486.4	109.3	10,773	661.4	44.5	61.7	13.4	710.2	4,430	20.9	43,432	17.3	31,652
College Station–Bryan, TX	1,505.2	43.5	6,583	697.0	46.3	130.1	58.8	1,049.2	4,346	16.8	59,051	14.1	30,271
Colorado Springs, CO	11,194.6	82.9	17,339	2,945.7	26.3	4,748.0	2,889.0	6,119.0	16,546	15.7	217,914	1.2	41,112
Columbia, MO	1,272.5	33.4	7,365	688.2	54.1	113.9	8.9	954.2	4,529	12.9	68,723	6.8	32,350
Columbia, SC	8,993.9	61.1	11,717	3,430.4	38.1	2,012.5	557.6	5,583.7	17,097	6.1	270,700	-0.5	35,917
Columbus, GA–AL	6,317.7	109.3	21,426	1,695.0	26.8	3,054.4	1,079.5	3,019.0	5,719	1.1	94,187	-10.7	34,287
Columbus, IN	709.5	65.7	9,239	360.8	50.9	185.4	19.5	428.3	1,855	-5.9	38,665	0.3	41,064
Columbus, OH	18,219.0	54.6	9,920	6,953.1	38.2	1,350.1	1,251.1	11,787.5	39,286	1.7	750,329	-6.2	42,820
Corpus Christi, TX	3,990.3	34.4	9,319	2,206.5	55.3	348.3	487.8	2,969.4	9,260	-1.1	141,978	7.0	34,775
Corvallis, OR	706.7	45.3	8,258	318.9	45.1	57.7	49.4	486.4	2,059	6.9	24,526	-10.0	39,496
Crestview–Fort Walton Beach–Destin, FL	3,812.1	25.3	21,082	1,348.5	35.4	868.9	1,397.5	3,042.8	4,995	4.1	56,733	-2.7	33,472
Cumberland, MD–WV	1,263.2	44.6	12,229	893.9	70.8	58.3	67.2	873.5	2,140	-8.0	30,127	0.0	30,512
Dallas–Fort Worth–Arlington, TX	46,644.0	46.2	7,320	20,031.4	42.9	4,049.8	15,187.7	31,895.1	140,481	10.8	2,510,280	-1.4	48,132
Dallas–Plano–Irving, TX	26,771.0	53.1	6,320	12,924.1	48.3	2,726.7	5,814.2	17,485.4	97,562	9.8	1,768,758	-4.5	50,383
Fort Worth–Arlington, TX	19,873.0	37.9	9,304	7,107.4	35.8	1,323.1	9,373.6	14,409.7	42,919	13.0	741,522	6.8	42,762
Dalton, GA	696.4	39.8	4,896	529.5	76.0	31.9	13.1	498.3	2,694	-11.4	56,109	-16.3	33,960
Danville, IL	774.1	23.8	9,484	505.7	65.3	56.9	14.7	625.5	1,538	-12.3	24,295	-16.2	35,038
Danville, VA	899.5	35.5	8,441	637.7	70.9	23.4	0.9	664.0	2,237	-8.1	30,668	-21.3	29,796
Davenport–Moline–Rock Island, IA–IL	3,590.3	51.2	9,456	2,309.9	64.3	452.5	363.7	2,375.0	9,180	-4.3	154,297	-8.4	39,709
Dayton, OH	9,572.2	25.8	11,375	4,833.1	50.5	1,488.9	1,546.3	7,606.1	17,408	-8.9	307,393	-19.7	39,638
Decatur, AL	1,109.8	23.3	7,215	838.0	75.5	50.4	16.5	900.1	3,108	-1.3	45,965	-11.7	36,588
Decatur, IL	1,043.4	51.4	9,420	631.9	60.6	63.7	2.0	689.1	2,510	-7.8	46,364	-18.9	38,830
Deltona–Daytona Beach–Ormond Beach, FL	4,310.1	33.0	8,714	3,619.1	84.0	119.4	115.2	3,240.9	11,779	9.0	127,546	-2.8	30,118
Denver–Aurora–Broomfield, CO[3]	22,522.1	58.0	8,855	8,742.4	38.8	2,642.9	2,410.9	14,255.0	73,663	9.3	1,038,146	-2.2	49,746
Des Moines–West Des Moines, IA	5,273.3	57.1	9,257	2,274.3	43.1	643.9	83.3	3,357.1	14,881	8.1	276,948	4.1	43,027
Detroit–Warren–Livonia, MI	38,663.6	34.4	8,999	24,782.8	64.1	2,388.3	2,718.6	28,777.6	97,211	-8.2	1,500,978	-24.9	47,939
Detroit–Livonia–Dearborn, MI	19,605.8	32.4	10,769	12,413.5	63.3	1,265.6	104.6	14,813.4	32,556	-9.6	567,799	-25.0	46,805
Warren–Troy–Farmington Hills, MI	19,057.8	36.5	7,698	12,369.4	64.9	1,122.7	2,614.0	13,964.2	64,655	-7.5	933,179	-24.8	48,629
Dothan, AL	1,173.3	26.7	8,056	871.5	74.3	45.3	12.9	925.9	3,486	-2.1	49,665	-9.4	33,322
Dover, DE	2,016.4	68.6	12,423	793.5	39.4	309.0	144.0	1,196.3	3,200	8.1	46,405	4.5	34,673
Dubuque, IA	640.7	34.7	6,841	462.5	72.2	35.9	3.8	475.8	2,738	3.0	50,579	1.2	35,676
Duluth, MN–WI	2,734.6	37.3	9,774	1,746.6	63.9	188.0	28.5	1,991.9	7,296	-0.5	105,453	3.1	34,085
Durham–Chapel Hill, NC	6,636.7	74.0	13,159	1,905.9	28.7	417.5	142.6	3,813.3	11,686	11.1	216,588	-2.9	51,110
Eau Claire, WI	1,101.3	38.7	6,834	731.2	66.4	85.0	21.9	793.9	4,166	6.2	67,629	6.4	33,324
El Centro, CA	1,240.1	35.2	7,105	646.8	52.2	178.5	47.7	917.4	2,368	4.2	29,223	15.3	29,712
Elizabethtown, KY	2,914.9	158.3	24,344	772.6	26.5	1,614.7	316.7	1,128.3	2,469	13.4	34,470	-0.5	30,505
Elkhart–Goshen, IN	913.7	-23.9	4,625	718.9	78.7	27.9	21.1	1,200.1	4,890	-2.4	94,310	-20.3	36,689
Elmira, NY	754.7	20.9	8,496	509.5	67.5	36.0	2.0	624.2	1,856	-3.2	32,630	-7.2	34,412
El Paso, TX	9,449.6	76.3	11,802	3,184.9	33.7	3,576.5	958.0	5,361.4	13,356	8.5	206,981	3.6	28,779
Erie, PA	2,238.2	36.7	7,977	1,634.9	73.0	120.8	41.5	1,637.8	6,287	-9.7	111,677	-8.8	34,012
Eugene–Springfield, OR	2,802.5	41.4	7,968	1,842.0	65.7	163.3	29.0	1,981.8	9,601	-0.9	111,667	-6.6	33,542
Evansville, IN–KY	2,764.7	26.1	7,708	1,910.4	69.1	147.1	145.7	2,191.9	8,559	-3.9	161,473	-2.3	37,299
Fairbanks, AK	1,546.6	2.9	15,849	269.6	17.4	343.6	493.1	1,503.7	2,443	12.3	27,160	25.7	44,072
Fargo, ND–MN	1,566.4	45.8	7,503	727.6	46.5	211.1	72.0	1,074.1	6,297	18.4	108,416	23.1	35,999
Farmington, NM	995.9	53.1	7,658	466.6	46.9	106.8	1.2	650.3	2,823	13.5	37,908	10.4	39,643
Fayetteville, NC	13,186.5	155.9	35,991	1,888.2	14.3	9,438.9	1,230.5	5,153.1	6,110	9.3	98,538	5.0	31,357
Fayetteville–Springdale–Rogers, AR–MO	2,474.5	42.4	5,342	1,627.7	65.8	208.5	159.6	1,737.5	10,646	26.4	176,303	21.1	42,543
Flagstaff, AZ	1,357.4	47.3	10,098	557.4	41.1	171.0	6.3	921.3	3,574	3.4	43,418	11.6	33,655
Flint, MI	3,751.3	45.4	8,810	2,834.3	75.6	129.6	8.1	2,580.2	7,904	-13.3	110,395	-27.2	36,671
Florence, SC	1,741.4	37.4	8,471	1,132.0	65.0	91.3	5.2	1,267.1	4,308	-5.0	70,246	-9.8	34,846
Florence–Muscle Shoals, AL	1,276.6	20.5	8,676	994.1	77.9	49.8	8.0	1,059.2	3,277	-2.6	44,185	-12.8	28,715
Fond du Lac, WI	626.2	35.5	6,161	474.8	75.8	23.2	7.1	462.1	2,440	-3.0	38,715	-14.2	34,081
Fort Collins–Loveland, CO	1,879.7	44.7	6,273	1,032.3	54.9	212.8	26.2	1,299.0	9,378	17.0	101,994	9.0	37,821
Fort Smith, AR–OK	2,326.1	38.6	7,790	1,604.7	69.0	189.4	42.1	1,677.7	6,274	7.7	103,366	-3.8	32,138
Fort Wayne, IN	3,457.0	14.2	8,305	1,747.6	50.6	220.6	905.2	3,026.4	10,451	1.9	176,058	-12.9	37,629
Fresno, CA	5,953.8	35.2	6,399	3,352.0	56.3	601.7	72.9	4,404.0	15,782	3.3	225,079	5.7	36,525
Gadsden, AL	966.6	37.0	9,256	741.7	76.7	42.2	4.3	705.5	2,032	-5.7	29,476	-14.2	30,118
Gainesville, FL	2,490.7	44.8	9,425	1,370.7	55.0	225.4	16.6	1,719.6	5,996	12.3	82,928	0.5	33,815
Gainesville, GA	1,157.9	69.3	6,444	658.1	56.8	62.2	264.1	684.0	3,950	17.5	57,810	-0.1	37,089
Glens Falls, NY	927.4	32.0	7,193	678.5	73.2	34.9	1.6	702.4	3,452	1.7	40,636	-10.2	35,549
Goldsboro, NC	1,332.9	24.4	10,870	657.7	49.3	302.7	74.2	1,071.3	2,221	-5.1	33,819	-10.3	29,949
Grand Forks, ND–MN	1,009.3	13.2	10,251	422.0	41.8	172.8	69.5	891.6	2,611	1.6	40,796	12.1	31,686
Grand Junction, CO	1,064.5	40.4	7,255	679.0	63.8	89.3	38.4	758.0	4,646	19.3	49,484	14.1	35,840
Grand Rapids–Wyoming, MI	4,504.9	36.4	5,819	3,109.6	69.0	327.2	89.0	3,302.0	17,943	-0.8	318,367	-13.6	39,743
Great Falls, MT	1,022.7	18.6	12,575	482.4	47.2	238.8	90.2	862.4	2,454	-4.3	30,287	9.1	29,813

[1]Based on resident population estimated as of July 1, 2010.
[2]For pay period as of March 12 of the year shown.
[3]The Denver–Aurora metropolitan statistical area includes Broomfield County. Broomfield County, CO, was formed from parts of Adams, Boulder, Jefferson, and Weld Counties on November 15, 2001, and is coextensive with Broomfield city. For the purposes of defining and presenting data for the Denver–Aurora metropolitan statistical area, Broomfield city is treated as if it were a county when data are available to do so. In many cases, the data were not available.

Table B-14. Federal Government Expenditures and Private Business Establishments and Employment—*Continued*

Metropolitan statistical area and division	Federal government expenditures								Private nonfarm business				
	2010							2005 (million dollars)	Establishments		Employment[2]		Annual payroll per employee, 2010 (dollars)
	Total (million dollars)	Percent change, 2005–2010	Per capita[1] (dollars)	Direct payments to individuals		Salaries and wages (million dollars)	Total defense contracts (million dollars)		2010	Change, 2000–2010	2010	Change, 2000–2010	
				Amount (million dollars)	Percent of total expenditures								
Greeley, CO	1,076.8	39.6	4,259	700.0	65.0	57.0	27.5	771.3	5,163	27.0	64,621	13.7	41,806
Green Bay, WI	1,805.7	37.0	5,896	1,200.8	66.5	122.1	51.1	1,317.8	7,621	-0.2	143,630	-1.7	39,631
Greensboro–High Point, NC	5,119.3	41.0	7,073	3,300.2	64.5	447.9	216.2	3,630.6	17,566	-3.6	296,342	-13.4	37,388
Greenville, NC	1,235.2	42.7	6,518	771.9	62.5	55.1	13.8	865.8	3,811	11.2	58,192	5.7	32,077
Greenville–Mauldin–Easley, SC	4,289.6	42.7	6,734	2,846.7	66.4	270.1	338.4	3,005.5	15,042	2.2	246,807	-15.1	36,855
Gulfport–Biloxi, MS	3,461.0	10.1	13,910	1,460.0	42.2	787.5	344.6	3,142.6	5,195	-5.6	82,104	-11.0	33,336
Hagerstown–Martinsburg, MD–WV	2,296.6	45.7	8,533	1,426.4	62.1	278.7	36.5	1,576.1	5,326	6.1	78,054	-3.4	33,520
Hanford–Corcoran, CA	994.5	32.7	6,501	463.5	46.6	195.1	28.9	749.7	1,614	4.9	22,572	21.7	32,635
Harrisburg–Carlisle, PA	12,034.5	88.5	21,902	3,182.4	26.4	713.5	993.0	6,382.7	13,410	4.0	259,399	0.8	39,747
Harrisonburg, VA	576.5	30.9	4,604	417.7	72.5	35.3	23.2	440.5	2,990	10.9	50,563	4.8	31,668
Hartford–West Hartford–East Hartford, CT	19,348.8	72.8	15,959	10,995.9	56.8	703.2	3,420.8	11,198.7	29,549	-1.4	529,323	-1.4	50,070
Hattiesburg, MS	1,387.3	43.3	9,712	712.3	51.3	317.7	88.2	967.9	3,316	10.4	48,817	12.7	31,684
Hickory–Lenoir–Morganton, NC	2,224.3	36.0	6,086	1,712.4	77.0	104.1	8.7	1,635.5	7,635	-6.1	120,569	-28.3	32,952
Hinesville–Fort Stewart, GA	526.0	-50.3	6,751	279.9	53.2	121.4	34.9	1,058.0	886	13.3	11,796	21.5	32,448
Holland–Grand Haven, MI	1,266.2	28.0	4,800	922.2	72.8	41.7	105.5	989.1	5,686	-3.5	86,972	-19.3	37,034
Honolulu, HI	17,392.9	70.7	18,247	4,616.1	26.5	7,676.7	2,218.2	10,192.1	21,592	4.6	335,934	6.4	38,329
Hot Springs, AR	1,017.6	40.1	10,597	801.6	78.8	42.3	22.1	726.1	2,702	5.1	30,557	-1.2	27,875
Houma–Bayou Cane–Thibodaux, LA	1,780.1	73.7	8,551	978.1	54.9	50.7	123.7	1,024.7	4,833	6.6	76,321	20.1	42,029
Houston–Sugar Land–Baytown, TX	36,145.6	36.1	6,078	18,383.6	50.9	2,793.3	3,886.9	26,561.1	122,517	13.6	2,176,567	10.6	53,512
Huntington–Ashland, WV–KY–OH	3,042.9	36.0	10,577	2,058.5	67.6	231.9	16.5	2,237.7	5,849	-7.6	92,663	-1.0	35,775
Huntsville, AL	10,321.0	29.8	24,715	2,138.2	20.7	1,360.8	5,254.2	7,951.7	9,355	12.6	165,379	14.8	44,846
Idaho Falls, ID	2,103.3	30.3	16,133	456.3	21.7	69.2	66.5	1,614.7	3,649	23.7	46,063	12.1	37,476
Indianapolis–Carmel, IN	16,770.2	63.1	9,549	7,739.5	46.2	1,921.8	1,374.2	10,282.6	42,317	4.9	742,919	-4.8	43,096
Iowa City, IA	1,203.5	19.3	7,887	470.8	39.1	133.2	11.9	1,008.4	3,746	11.0	64,260	12.8	33,342
Ithaca, NY	939.3	39.9	9,248	355.9	37.9	39.8	18.9	671.2	2,320	9.2	45,452	8.7	36,107
Jackson, MI	1,149.7	39.5	7,175	854.0	74.3	65.1	17.2	824.2	3,018	-11.5	44,688	-18.3	39,761
Jackson, MS	6,208.0	22.3	11,516	2,524.5	40.7	552.5	355.4	5,075.2	12,846	6.6	198,793	-7.0	36,804
Jackson, TN	1,011.8	47.1	8,766	694.2	68.6	85.2	0.1	687.7	2,810	-1.9	51,727	-8.7	33,758
Jacksonville, FL	12,558.3	36.3	9,333	7,837.1	62.4	1,747.8	970.7	9,215.9	34,085	19.1	482,315	0.5	40,228
Jacksonville, NC	2,938.6	10.2	16,530	740.6	25.2	1,099.6	920.0	2,667.5	2,692	3.5	33,244	13.9	25,309
Janesville, WI	1,258.0	40.3	7,846	747.8	59.4	40.5	204.4	896.6	3,292	-2.0	51,167	-15.8	35,653
Jefferson City, MO	3,845.0	112.4	25,666	695.4	18.1	214.4	10.2	1,810.5	3,599	3.9	50,030	-7.0	34,384
Johnson City, TN	1,862.8	37.7	9,374	1,311.9	70.4	138.1	11.9	1,353.0	3,835	2.3	62,347	-4.6	30,318
Johnstown, PA	2,819.4	100.1	19,623	1,176.4	41.7	158.9	1,180.9	1,408.9	3,437	-3.1	50,550	-1.7	31,565
Jonesboro, AR	953.8	33.4	7,881	604.2	63.3	64.8	11.5	715.1	2,766	3.8	39,555	1.4	31,120
Joplin, MO	1,283.1	35.5	7,310	859.6	67.0	87.9	37.8	946.6	4,245	4.0	73,093	2.4	32,732
Kalamazoo–Portage, MI	2,745.9	74.0	8,408	1,536.0	55.9	163.3	39.0	1,578.0	6,954	-6.7	118,831	-7.1	40,010
Kankakee–Bradley, IL	794.0	34.5	6,999	580.4	73.1	53.7	0.2	590.4	2,357	3.0	35,226	-41.0	32,886
Kansas City, MO–KS	18,387.4	34.1	9,034	9,341.9	50.8	2,972.4	1,385.0	13,708.6	50,129	0.2	860,640	-5.0	42,900
Kennewick–Pasco–Richland, WA	4,614.1	51.3	18,213	955.6	20.7	122.9	36.1	3,050.5	5,251	18.7	74,876	16.1	44,767
Killeen–Temple–Fort Hood, TX	12,413.6	183.9	30,628	1,861.1	15.0	8,731.2	1,306.7	4,372.6	5,915	14.4	94,773	9.7	33,739
Kingsport–Bristol–Bristol, TN–VA	3,110.1	54.1	10,047	2,135.4	68.7	108.5	205.9	2,018.6	6,092	-5.7	102,878	-6.3	36,756
Kingston, NY	1,284.7	30.2	7,040	875.5	68.1	54.7	6.1	986.8	4,708	8.0	45,087	-1.4	32,033
Knoxville, TN	9,945.5	28.0	14,248	4,165.2	41.9	421.6	195.2	7,772.5	16,062	0.4	287,528	3.6	39,578
Kokomo, IN	797.8	38.1	8,084	623.5	78.2	36.6	0.5	577.8	2,111	-7.8	31,429	-35.3	38,564
La Crosse, WI–MN	912.4	38.2	6,826	594.5	65.2	57.8	39.6	660.0	3,379	1.6	61,117	0.1	33,656
Lafayette, IN	1,245.0	40.1	6,170	680.3	54.6	72.0	17.6	888.4	3,954	2.6	64,411	-11.3	35,132
Lafayette, LA	1,650.0	41.9	6,028	1,060.3	64.3	152.3	32.3	1,162.9	8,804	20.3	127,331	14.8	40,001
Lake Charles, LA	1,486.8	18.1	7,449	994.8	66.9	101.2	45.8	1,259.0	4,389	-0.6	68,638	-3.5	36,564
Lake Havasu City–Kingman, AZ	1,474.8	32.3	7,367	1,258.7	85.3	36.4	6.0	1,114.4	3,713	7.7	39,714	14.0	29,491
Lakeland–Winter Haven, FL	4,156.6	39.9	6,904	3,363.3	80.9	153.2	49.3	2,971.6	10,943	13.9	159,201	-1.4	34,712
Lancaster, PA	2,993.7	36.1	5,763	2,290.4	76.5	177.0	44.0	2,200.0	12,043	5.3	207,278	-3.4	36,644
Lansing–East Lansing, MI	7,633.8	70.3	16,451	2,099.8	27.5	337.4	520.7	4,481.9	9,555	-7.1	151,434	-12.4	38,346
Laredo, TX	1,613.9	55.8	6,448	740.9	45.9	205.4	2.8	1,035.9	4,707	15.4	63,526	19.4	25,881
Las Cruces, NM	2,062.5	48.7	9,857	921.9	44.7	218.7	309.3	1,387.2	3,610	12.4	50,117	35.3	28,293
Las Vegas–Paradise, NV	11,254.2	25.6	5,768	6,884.9	61.2	1,452.3	443.1	8,963.1	39,597	33.6	731,876	14.5	37,191
Lawrence, KS	689.9	57.4	6,225	368.3	53.4	52.4	12.5	438.2	2,628	0.2	37,409	-0.2	28,499
Lawton, OK	3,180.5	113.1	25,629	666.7	21.0	1,851.8	466.2	1,492.5	2,219	0.9	32,704	18.5	30,847
Lebanon, PA	1,398.6	52.5	10,471	722.9	51.7	423.9	36.7	916.9	2,641	2.8	43,427	15.4	32,528
Lewiston, ID–WA	601.9	26.5	9,885	390.9	64.9	23.1	2.1	475.9	1,574	-5.2	20,901	1.1	32,652
Lewiston–Auburn, ME	874.9	28.5	8,123	593.2	67.8	46.5	1.1	680.6	2,767	-0.7	43,808	-4.5	34,369
Lexington–Fayette, KY	4,087.5	49.2	8,658	2,272.8	55.6	282.5	463.2	2,738.7	11,809	6.4	199,943	-4.5	38,075
Lima, OH	1,079.7	34.4	10,154	782.9	72.5	41.1	87.4	803.2	2,548	-10.3	46,523	-10.3	33,977
Lincoln, NE	2,912.4	34.6	9,639	1,103.9	37.9	331.7	19.0	2,163.9	8,222	8.9	130,287	-1.4	34,835
Little Rock–North Little Rock–Conway, AR	8,126.7	62.1	11,614	3,434.7	42.3	1,183.4	450.3	5,013.8	17,601	6.5	275,781	-2.0	37,689
Logan, UT–ID	747.8	78.5	5,961	369.9	49.5	42.2	52.6	419.0	3,352	28.9	39,056	18.8	28,825
Longview, TX	1,537.7	39.4	7,173	1,129.6	73.5	53.5	1.4	1,103.2	5,291	4.2	78,127	10.1	36,796
Longview, WA	779.0	47.3	7,607	558.9	71.7	46.3	17.2	529.0	2,206	-5.5	29,103	-10.5	40,179
Los Angeles–Long Beach–Santa Ana, CA	100,586.1	32.4	7,841	50,537.3	50.2	5,900.3	12,663.2	75,947.5	330,969	8.6	4,852,354	-7.4	49,462
Los Angeles–Long Beach–Glendale, CA	82,544.3	34.6	8,407	39,537.8	47.9	4,489.4	10,637.0	61,345.9	244,447	8.0	3,580,067	-7.3	49,180
Santa Ana–Anaheim–Irvine, CA	18,041.8	23.6	5,993	10,999.5	61.0	1,410.9	2,026.2	14,601.6	86,522	10.1	1,272,287	-7.7	50,256
Louisville/Jefferson County, KY–IN	12,859.1	34.2	10,018	6,818.2	53.0	879.2	3,130.3	9,580.3	29,859	1.4	515,000	-6.5	38,712

[1]Based on resident population estimated as of July 1, 2010.
[2]For pay period as of March 12 of the year shown.

Table B-14.　Federal Government Expenditures and Private Business Establishments and Employment—*Continued*

Metropolitan statistical area and division	Federal government expenditures									Private nonfarm business				
	2010								2005 (million dollars)	Establishments		Employment[2]		Annual payroll per employee, 2010 (dollars)
	Total (million dollars)	Percent change, 2005–2010	Per capita[1] (dollars)	Direct payments to individuals		Salaries and wages (million dollars)	Total defense contracts (million dollars)			2010	Change, 2000–2010	2010	Change, 2000–2010	
				Amount (million dollars)	Percent of total expenditures									
Lubbock, TX	1,967.8	35.6	6,907	1,296.3	65.9	156.8	13.8	1,451.2	6,960	5.0	104,164	10.3	30,078
Lynchburg, VA	2,163.5	26.6	8,564	1,389.2	64.2	93.9	115.4	1,708.9	6,006	3.4	94,003	-2.6	35,511
Macon, GA	2,105.7	36.3	9,065	1,408.0	66.9	193.1	12.5	1,544.6	5,286	-2.0	80,237	-12.1	34,791
Madera–Chowchilla, CA	847.3	30.9	5,616	564.7	66.6	44.6	0.9	647.1	1,910	2.4	24,501	5.8	34,637
Madison, WI	6,991.6	68.6	12,296	2,058.1	29.4	475.5	166.8	4,146.1	15,132	5.0	271,806	8.7	41,803
Manchester–Nashua, NH	3,353.3	24.4	8,368	1,688.0	50.3	369.5	700.2	2,695.2	10,827	-0.7	177,473	0.3	50,988
Manhattan, KS	3,855.4	197.0	30,338	443.4	11.5	2,861.5	324.0	1,298.2	2,709	9.2	36,731	8.4	27,275
Mankato–North Mankato, MN	594.8	33.7	6,148	385.9	64.9	62.3	6.1	444.8	2,547	8.3	45,315	10.3	32,423
Mansfield, OH	950.7	31.3	7,638	690.5	72.6	57.7	7.8	723.9	2,735	-9.4	42,532	-17.9	30,285
McAllen–Edinburg–Mission, TX	4,297.2	49.0	5,546	2,351.5	54.7	296.2	-35.5	2,884.6	11,045	32.8	167,097	45.5	25,454
Medford, OR	1,624.4	46.3	7,994	1,119.8	68.9	132.1	13.7	1,110.1	5,786	7.9	63,965	2.7	32,946
Memphis, TN–MS–AR	12,902.4	36.2	9,804	6,839.7	53.0	1,028.2	1,645.7	9,472.2	25,751	-2.3	509,166	-10.6	41,269
Merced, CA	1,519.8	43.2	5,942	902.7	59.4	54.0	54.7	1,061.2	2,884	-2.5	38,840	-1.8	33,991
Miami–Fort Lauderdale–Pompano Beach, FL	50,255.7	48.5	9,031	35,313.3	70.3	2,948.1	1,045.7	33,839.5	170,661	96.5	1,820,909	70.5	41,542
Fort Lauderdale–Pompano Beach–Deerfield Beach, FL	12,480.1	35.3	7,139	9,985.7	80.0	672.6	202.1	9,221.0	55,541	10.4	593,373	-4.2	41,206
Miami–Miami Beach–Kendall, FL	27,110.5	64.0	10,860	16,801.1	62.0	1,812.5	396.7	16,526.3	73,410	NA	802,109	NA	41,497
West Palm Beach–Boca Raton–Boynton Beach, FL	10,665.1	31.8	8,079	8,526.5	79.9	463.0	446.9	8,092.2	41,710	14.2	425,427	-5.2	42,094
Michigan City–La Porte, IN	756.1	32.1	6,783	587.0	77.6	37.9	4.2	572.5	2,478	-6.0	34,054	-15.5	32,171
Midland, TX	638.5	34.8	4,665	486.3	76.2	57.0	0.2	473.6	4,568	13.1	59,770	29.9	49,520
Milwaukee–Waukesha–West Allis, WI	12,331.2	41.7	7,925	7,587.0	61.5	782.7	292.8	8,701.1	38,424	-3.6	737,279	-6.7	44,922
Minneapolis–St. Paul–Bloomington, MN–WI	24,336.5	47.4	7,420	12,763.4	52.4	2,228.8	1,360.4	16,513.5	89,831	6.3	1,572,381	-3.5	50,388
Missoula, MT	818.8	29.7	7,491	444.6	54.3	103.8	5.5	631.5	4,171	15.1	46,219	11.9	29,657
Mobile, AL	3,934.1	27.0	9,526	2,439.0	62.0	317.4	507.9	3,097.2	8,826	-4.4	148,500	-5.1	37,193
Modesto, CA	3,048.2	35.9	5,925	2,056.7	67.5	93.7	18.4	2,243.2	8,366	1.3	121,595	0.8	38,543
Monroe, LA	1,379.0	34.9	7,816	927.5	67.3	77.4	10.1	1,022.6	4,538	2.2	65,464	-7.7	30,691
Monroe, MI	885.2	35.8	5,823	731.4	82.6	23.8	1.1	651.8	2,383	-4.1	34,678	-12.3	37,867
Montgomery, AL	5,924.7	37.2	15,819	2,125.1	35.9	832.7	422.8	4,318.2	7,741	-3.7	126,990	-6.6	35,428
Morgantown, WV	1,418.0	61.2	10,932	560.7	39.5	205.4	23.4	879.8	2,743	4.7	44,404	24.8	35,592
Morristown, TN	1,201.5	44.1	8,795	914.7	76.1	33.1	25.4	833.6	2,204	-4.1	38,916	-15.3	31,326
Mount Vernon–Anacortes, WA	846.6	35.4	7,242	624.4	73.8	29.4	19.2	625.1	3,432	5.4	38,013	6.6	36,265
Muncie, IN	932.8	40.9	7,927	638.6	68.5	56.0	0.4	662.2	2,440	-9.6	35,890	-28.9	30,100
Muskegon–Norton Shores, MI	1,299.3	30.4	7,546	934.7	71.9	41.1	37.2	996.2	3,378	-5.8	47,700	-17.0	35,224
Myrtle Beach–North Myrtle Beach–Conway, SC	1,722.0	43.5	6,395	1,381.3	80.2	64.1	6.7	1,200.2	8,246	14.7	92,343	7.0	26,661
Napa, CA	1,011.6	32.8	7,412	755.3	74.7	22.6	24.8	761.7	3,945	5.3	54,945	10.9	43,577
Naples–Marco Island, FL	2,069.4	42.1	6,436	1,768.4	85.5	53.2	61.7	1,456.0	9,856	16.3	101,450	10.0	36,682
Nashville-Davidson—Murfreesboro—Franklin, TN	15,209.1	65.3	9,566	7,004.5	46.1	1,180.6	181.3	9,199.6	37,619	8.8	652,935	0.5	43,536
New Haven–Milford, CT	11,538.3	102.0	13,378	8,447.3	73.2	480.1	79.2	5,713.1	19,607	-5.6	321,031	-5.3	46,908
New Orleans–Metairie–Kenner, LA	15,844.0	27.5	13,568	6,768.8	42.7	1,168.6	4,493.1	12,429.3	29,095	-7.7	446,087	-16.1	42,796
New York–Northern New Jersey–Long Island, NY–NJ–PA	169,410.6	36.5	8,965	93,556.7	55.2	10,184.2	8,653.9	124,095.4	533,395	3.6	7,273,295	-3.9	63,446
Edison–New Brunswick, NJ	19,043.9	37.3	8,138	11,739.4	61.6	1,218.1	3,237.4	13,865.9	61,568	2.6	873,339	-2.2	53,375
Nassau–Suffolk, NY	23,918.0	33.3	8,443	14,804.0	61.9	1,557.6	2,458.4	17,939.9	94,855	4.6	1,043,243	-3.9	47,955
Newark–Union, NJ–PA	17,359.5	40.4	8,083	10,189.5	58.7	1,319.5	1,240.5	12,365.3	57,679	-4.3	854,757	-9.2	58,577
New York–White Plains–Wayne, NY–NJ	109,089.3	36.5	9,424	56,823.8	52.1	6,089.0	1,717.5	79,924.3	319,293	5.0	4,501,956	-3.2	69,913
Niles–Benton Harbor, MI	1,365.2	40.8	8,706	965.8	70.7	31.8	2.9	969.5	3,675	-7.9	49,517	-18.2	37,526
North Port–Bradenton–Sarasota, FL	6,387.1	40.4	9,095	5,440.9	85.2	228.4	224.2	4,548.8	19,878	17.8	198,020	-18.3	33,987
Norwich–New London, CT	6,569.1	46.9	23,970	2,302.2	35.0	342.9	3,520.5	4,472.1	5,791	1.1	107,017	1.2	44,281
Ocala, FL	2,844.7	42.3	8,587	2,495.8	87.7	57.6	15.9	1,998.6	6,774	23.5	73,940	1.1	30,705
Ocean City, NJ	961.9	21.1	9,889	762.8	79.3	75.3	7.4	794.4	3,855	-4.1	24,464	-5.7	36,934
Odessa, TX	749.5	36.9	5,466	568.2	75.8	28.1	0.0	547.3	3,235	7.4	48,988	26.8	41,244
Ogden–Clearfield, UT	5,122.2	16.9	9,361	2,387.6	46.6	1,158.6	916.1	4,383.5	11,358	25.7	142,046	6.5	32,748
Oklahoma City, OK	12,811.2	37.7	10,225	5,909.5	46.1	2,251.8	987.1	9,302.9	32,997	11.0	452,754	3.6	38,358
Olympia, WA	4,306.4	76.4	17,071	1,252.4	29.1	122.2	119.1	2,441.9	5,826	15.4	63,625	20.1	34,544
Omaha–Council Bluffs, NE–IA	7,087.1	37.3	8,190	3,695.8	52.1	1,043.8	735.9	5,160.0	22,291	9.1	398,865	4.6	40,846
Orlando–Kissimmee–Sanford, FL	16,831.3	48.3	7,886	10,206.5	60.6	1,040.0	3,485.6	11,352.1	55,075	22.6	855,864	5.1	37,838
Oshkosh–Neenah, WI	8,060.3	277.1	48,267	703.2	8.7	82.1	7,100.1	2,137.4	3,602	-3.1	83,434	2.0	42,788
Owensboro, KY	952.5	52.4	8,301	731.6	76.8	39.5	2.2	624.8	2,566	-5.6	44,551	-2.7	33,564
Oxnard–Thousand Oaks–Ventura, CA	5,559.1	27.2	6,752	3,249.2	58.4	602.1	681.1	4,371.5	19,606	13.9	235,526	-1.0	45,848
Palm Bay–Melbourne–Titusville, FL	8,154.8	20.0	15,008	3,860.3	47.3	617.8	2,092.1	6,798.4	12,983	14.3	163,923	3.9	40,596
Palm Coast, FL	631.4	42.6	6,598	590.0	93.4	13.8	0.4	442.7	1,743	66.8	14,790	47.6	27,436
Panama City–Lynn Haven–Panama City Beach, FL	2,261.4	30.1	13,393	1,166.1	51.6	420.0	425.6	1,738.0	4,478	6.4	54,427	0.9	32,668
Parkersburg–Marietta–Vienna, WV–OH	1,521.5	10.1	9,389	1,044.5	68.6	180.8	16.5	1,382.2	3,770	-8.2	56,456	-9.8	32,261
Pascagoula, MS	1,226.4	-58.5	7,559	804.3	65.6	113.9	118.1	2,957.1	2,603	-2.9	51,421	12.8	41,759
Pensacola–Ferry Pass–Brent, FL	4,928.0	-12.7	10,976	3,137.9	63.7	514.0	532.2	5,642.8	9,083	6.5	115,893	-6.8	33,880
Peoria, IL	2,779.0	22.0	7,329	1,856.4	66.8	231.5	253.7	2,278.8	8,767	-0.7	161,610	-1.2	44,324
Philadelphia–Camden–Wilmington, PA–NJ–DE–MD	62,636.7	46.9	10,500	34,142.5	54.5	4,899.5	6,849.6	42,634.8	144,728	1.5	2,421,591	-3.8	50,025
Camden, NJ	11,837.1	35.9	9,465	6,405.9	54.1	1,268.2	2,149.8	8,711.2	27,986	-2.0	425,649	-2.3	43,832
Philadelphia, PA	45,563.0	50.8	11,365	24,424.0	53.6	3,218.2	4,616.2	30,219.8	98,111	3.4	1,699,017	-3.4	51,180
Wilmington, DE–MD–NJ	5,236.6	41.4	7,421	3,312.4	63.3	413.1	83.5	3,703.8	18,631	-2.6	296,925	-7.8	52,294

[1]Based on resident population estimated as of July 1, 2010.
[2]For pay period as of March 12 of the year shown.
NA = Not available

Table B-14. Federal Government Expenditures and Private Business Establishments and Employment—*Continued*

Metropolitan statistical area and division	Federal government expenditures 2010 Total (million dollars)	Percent change, 2005–2010	Per capita[1] (dollars)	Direct payments to individuals Amount (million dollars)	Direct payments to individuals Percent of total expenditures	Salaries and wages (million dollars)	Total defense contracts (million dollars)	2005 (million dollars)	Establishments 2010	Establishments Change, 2000–2010	Employment[2] 2010	Employment[2] Change, 2000–2010	Annual payroll per employee, 2010 (dollars)
Phoenix–Mesa–Glendale, AZ	33,532.2	40.0	7,997	17,516.4	52.2	1,920.1	4,444.2	23,946.1	87,723	18.5	1,453,359	5.4	43,299
Pine Bluff, AR	1,329.6	33.9	13,262	630.2	47.4	97.1	256.5	992.7	1,701	-9.2	25,697	-17.2	32,725
Pittsburgh, PA	28,473.6	36.4	12,084	17,765.8	62.4	1,614.9	2,023.4	20,876.7	59,240	-2.5	1,030,938	-2.5	42,185
Pittsfield, MA	1,352.8	33.8	10,309	876.0	64.8	54.6	111.3	1,011.4	4,029	-8.1	53,706	-8.9	37,546
Pocatello, ID	652.9	38.8	7,202	404.0	61.9	60.4	0.4	470.5	2,179	6.7	27,036	3.7	29,943
Portland–South Portland–Biddeford, ME	5,091.1	9.6	9,903	2,564.8	50.4	543.2	1,094.4	4,646.4	17,331	6.8	218,155	1.2	39,231
Portland–Vancouver–Hillsboro, OR–WA	15,688.0	50.6	7,048	8,868.8	56.5	1,546.5	563.3	10,413.7	62,467	10.1	870,794	0.4	45,500
Port St. Lucie, FL	3,198.9	13.6	7,543	2,848.6	89.0	83.6	5.7	2,814.9	9,862	22.1	98,963	9.7	32,018
Poughkeepsie–Newburgh–Middletown, NY	5,175.0	38.1	7,720	2,941.0	56.8	954.9	199.0	3,747.7	16,653	12.2	199,476	7.8	40,292
Prescott, AZ	1,624.2	38.8	7,696	1,305.4	80.4	70.5	1.1	1,170.5	5,639	13.1	50,830	10.3	30,036
Providence–New Bedford–Fall River, RI–MA	17,257.8	43.6	10,780	8,641.6	50.1	1,149.9	2,362.0	12,016.7	41,236	-1.2	590,501	-2.1	41,415
Provo–Orem, UT	2,575.7	110.5	4,889	1,428.0	55.4	166.8	497.2	1,223.4	10,807	48.5	155,079	7.6	33,856
Pueblo, CO	1,440.6	44.4	9,057	932.5	64.7	85.8	42.0	997.4	3,155	-1.0	46,849	-3.1	34,337
Punta Gorda, FL	1,438.9	23.8	8,994	1,353.3	94.1	26.1	0.8	1,162.2	3,525	14.7	36,934	16.6	27,429
Racine, WI	1,319.4	37.2	6,752	930.5	70.5	53.3	54.5	961.7	4,049	-2.4	64,177	-12.6	39,180
Raleigh–Cary, NC	9,618.5	70.9	8,508	3,535.8	36.8	704.4	186.1	5,628.6	28,933	21.7	410,617	10.8	43,539
Rapid City, SD	1,394.5	38.4	11,034	664.5	47.7	350.4	134.8	1,007.6	4,228	13.3	48,551	3.7	32,851
Reading, PA	2,648.7	39.8	6,438	2,019.6	76.2	146.1	65.2	1,894.3	8,285	1.6	142,598	-4.2	40,078
Redding, CA	1,678.2	33.0	9,469	1,190.6	70.9	96.8	3.9	1,262.1	4,323	-3.2	46,780	1.4	33,535
Reno–Sparks, NV	3,495.6	68.1	8,217	1,685.2	48.2	274.7	674.8	2,079.1	11,799	5.2	165,777	-2.4	39,414
Richmond, VA	13,630.3	54.8	10,833	5,932.1	43.5	2,084.2	1,096.7	8,807.3	31,037	8.3	477,439	-3.9	44,152
Riverside–San Bernardino–Ontario, CA	24,553.0	45.5	5,812	15,125.8	61.6	2,362.5	2,713.9	16,878.0	65,024	21.2	957,326	11.5	35,002
Roanoke, VA	2,553.1	14.1	8,270	1,707.7	66.9	228.5	129.4	2,237.5	8,189	0.4	132,266	-5.0	37,360
Rochester, MN	1,037.0	5.3	5,575	700.7	67.6	107.6	3.4	984.4	4,400	8.7	85,832	-0.9	41,035
Rochester, NY	10,403.0	57.3	9,867	5,443.1	52.3	460.4	1,939.3	6,613.4	23,539	2.4	415,085	-6.4	39,622
Rockford, IL	2,108.5	28.8	6,034	1,487.3	70.5	124.3	153.5	1,637.2	7,507	-3.1	126,265	-14.3	37,852
Rocky Mount, NC	1,296.2	39.5	8,506	832.7	64.2	61.0	16.0	929.5	3,001	-7.9	49,574	-14.5	33,349
Rome, GA	705.5	38.8	7,325	535.3	75.9	35.5	0.0	508.2	1,981	-1.7	33,956	-10.5	33,002
Sacramento—Arden-Arcade—Roseville, CA	32,388.0	64.3	15,070	9,359.7	28.9	1,258.0	4,694.0	19,712.9	44,514	10.2	621,068	1.2	43,038
Saginaw–Saginaw Township North, MI	1,822.0	43.6	9,102	1,264.2	69.4	102.1	16.2	1,268.9	4,494	-10.5	74,032	-20.1	35,195
St. Cloud, MN	1,217.3	54.0	6,438	805.5	66.2	128.5	1.0	790.3	5,236	11.6	89,360	7.2	35,617
St. George, UT	1,063.0	97.5	7,696	594.1	55.9	377.3	0.4	538.3	3,816	52.0	35,996	35.1	28,485
St. Joseph, MO–KS	959.9	32.3	7,539	661.5	68.9	55.1	15.2	725.4	3,259	10.5	48,746	13.6	33,203
St. Louis, MO–IL[4]	34,277.1	43.8	12,186	14,856.3	43.3	3,503.0	9,200.0	23,831.2	70,361	3.1	1,169,641	-4.5	42,923
Salem, OR	4,403.2	55.0	11,269	1,759.9	40.0	264.8	29.4	2,841.5	8,994	4.7	107,154	-0.2	31,491
Salinas, CA	3,298.5	45.1	7,947	1,611.2	48.8	588.4	385.9	2,273.3	8,336	-2.8	96,387	-8.3	40,580
Salisbury, MD	1,054.9	64.8	8,426	758.5	71.9	45.6	14.1	640.3	2,911	-1.0	39,241	-3.1	34,976
Salt Lake City, UT	9,696.7	73.2	8,625	4,143.6	42.7	1,280.0	944.9	5,599.9	31,549	13.1	526,157	4.6	41,090
San Angelo, TX	1,016.3	40.2	9,088	564.6	55.6	205.4	64.0	724.9	2,637	0.1	36,370	3.8	30,511
San Antonio–New Braunfels, TX	23,110.7	55.2	10,787	10,435.8	45.2	4,647.3	4,014.7	14,892.0	40,324	12.7	718,175	12.6	37,353
San Diego–Carlsbad–San Marcos, CA	37,302.9	33.5	12,051	13,557.1	36.3	4,765.8	11,593.0	27,937.3	75,794	11.6	1,101,324	4.7	47,193
Sandusky, OH	666.7	39.9	8,650	477.2	71.6	33.6	25.3	476.5	1,891	-7.3	28,166	-14.8	34,717
San Francisco–Oakland–Fremont, CA	40,303.3	35.1	9,296	18,832.6	46.7	3,330.8	1,586.8	29,824.0	117,723	-2.3	1,767,793	-11.9	64,785
Oakland–Fremont–Hayward, CA	21,436.0	30.4	8,376	10,564.0	49.3	1,581.8	604.4	16,440.8	57,937	-0.9	855,987	-11.9	56,936
San Francisco–San Mateo–Redwood City, CA	18,867.3	41.0	10,623	8,268.6	43.8	1,749.0	982.4	13,383.2	59,786	-3.7	911,806	-11.9	72,155
San Jose–Sunnyvale–Santa Clara, CA	16,250.0	26.9	8,846	6,101.7	37.5	965.3	4,727.3	12,804.2	45,032	-3.4	857,032	-15.2	85,079
San Luis Obispo–Paso Robles, CA	1,783.4	38.7	6,614	1,257.6	70.5	126.0	56.0	1,285.7	7,778	12.0	80,564	9.4	35,490
Santa Barbara–Santa Maria–Goleta, CA	3,677.4	21.0	8,675	1,810.4	49.2	416.1	701.1	3,038.7	11,207	3.0	134,494	-4.1	44,565
Santa Cruz–Watsonville, CA	1,598.2	39.5	6,091	1,035.4	64.8	53.2	9.7	1,145.6	6,781	-2.7	68,106	-14.1	41,937
Santa Fe, NM	2,153.9	81.9	14,940	627.1	29.1	136.2	45.2	1,184.4	4,778	2.3	44,097	-1.3	37,180
Santa Rosa–Petaluma, CA	3,142.9	31.4	6,495	2,215.7	70.5	203.3	47.1	2,392.6	13,186	-1.7	143,053	-12.2	43,501
Savannah, GA	7,185.6	167.5	20,671	1,812.9	25.2	4,120.0	735.9	2,686.1	8,380	11.5	125,822	8.8	35,846
Scranton—Wilkes-Barre, PA	5,883.8	31.7	10,439	4,128.8	70.2	378.7	374.1	4,467.5	13,345	-2.7	226,262	-1.2	32,816
Seattle–Tacoma–Bellevue, WA	33,849.9	58.5	9,841	13,251.6	39.1	8,503.9	3,712.7	21,359.7	96,771	6.7	1,435,764	-0.7	55,035
Seattle–Bellevue–Everett, WA	21,905.7	41.5	8,283	9,642.7	44.0	2,219.0	3,067.7	15,478.2	80,182	6.7	1,212,145	-2.1	58,070
Tacoma, WA	11,944.2	103.1	15,020	3,609.0	30.2	6,284.9	644.9	5,881.5	16,589	6.7	223,619	7.4	38,587
Sebastian–Vero Beach, FL	1,224.1	13.4	8,868	1,105.2	90.3	33.2	0.1	1,079.6	3,868	12.1	37,302	-3.4	32,989
Sheboygan, WI	765.1	45.3	6,624	498.7	65.2	28.1	38.1	526.6	2,681	3.0	50,582	-11.6	37,091
Sherman–Denison, TX	868.6	42.9	7,186	666.2	76.7	25.3	6.5	607.9	2,521	-2.3	38,858	-1.7	33,093
Shreveport–Bossier City, LA	3,640.2	25.4	9,132	2,103.8	57.8	623.1	159.8	2,903.7	9,161	6.9	146,359	2.2	34,683
Sioux City, IA–NE–SD	1,304.1	27.2	9,083	668.7	51.3	97.2	282.0	1,025.2	3,776	-3.2	65,889	-8.7	32,251
Sioux Falls, SD	1,894.1	12.9	8,289	1,180.4	62.3	219.2	43.2	1,677.4	7,026	13.4	122,755	14.9	37,637
South Bend–Mishawaka, IN–MI	3,311.7	7.7	10,374	1,530.2	46.2	153.0	1,124.3	3,076.2	6,721	-8.9	117,316	-12.6	35,607
Spartanburg, SC	1,826.7	42.4	6,425	1,398.5	76.6	85.6	4.8	1,282.5	6,338	0.9	108,393	-11.1	38,303
Spokane, WA	4,074.6	42.5	8,647	2,433.2	59.7	486.6	237.7	2,858.7	12,363	5.8	172,951	2.8	36,984
Springfield, IL	5,593.0	71.3	26,612	1,044.2	18.7	273.0	25.2	3,264.9	5,365	-4.4	83,181	-2.6	36,854
Springfield, MA	5,994.5	30.3	8,651	3,764.0	62.8	504.7	106.5	4,601.7	14,840	-12.6	238,379	-5.4	37,004
Springfield, MO	2,936.9	39.5	6,725	2,068.7	70.4	266.1	8.9	2,105.1	11,219	8.4	163,422	-0.4	31,970
Springfield, OH	1,247.9	30.1	9,021	879.0	70.4	72.3	22.3	959.5	2,449	-9.6	40,682	-20.3	30,820
State College, PA	1,405.5	56.7	9,127	610.2	43.4	72.0	236.8	896.9	3,189	2.0	43,058	-7.9	32,460
Steubenville–Weirton, OH–WV	1,287.0	21.7	10,341	1,036.3	80.5	31.6	5.3	1,057.2	2,361	-12.0	37,150	-15.6	30,100

[1]Based on resident population estimated as of July 1, 2010.
[2]For pay period as of March 12 of the year shown.
[3]The Denver–Aurora metropolitan statistical area includes Broomfield County. Broomfield County, CO, was formed from parts of Adams, Boulder, Jefferson, and Weld Counties on November 15, 2001, and is coextensive with Broomfield city. For the purposes of defining and presenting data for the Denver–Aurora metropolitan statistical area, Broomfield city is treated as if it were a county when data are available to do so. In many cases, the data were not available.
[4]The portion of Sullivan city in Crawford County, MO is legally part of the St. Louis, MO–IL MSA. That portion is not included in these figures for the St. Louis, MSA.

Table B-14. Federal Government Expenditures and Private Business Establishments and Employment—*Continued*

Metropolitan statistical area and division	Federal government expenditures								Private nonfarm business				
	2010								Establishments		Employment[2]		Annual payroll per employee, 2010 (dollars)
	Total (million dollars)	Percent change, 2005–2010	Per capita[1] (dollars)	Direct payments to individuals		Salaries and wages (million dollars)	Total defense contracts (million dollars)	2005 (million dollars)	2010	Change, 2000–2010	2010	Change, 2000–2010	
				Amount (million dollars)	Percent of total expenditures								
Stockton, CA	4,164.3	37.1	6,077	2,629.9	63.2	285.9	93.9	3,037.5	10,825	6.3	160,629	4.0	36,579
Sumter, SC	1,422.2	35.3	13,235	623.3	43.8	294.5	176.0	1,051.2	1,821	-2.3	27,620	-25.4	29,650
Syracuse, NY	6,233.8	43.8	9,408	3,257.6	52.3	396.9	1,191.0	4,335.4	15,278	1.8	252,257	-7.7	39,168
Tallahassee, FL	9,141.2	36.5	24,880	1,722.8	18.8	208.5	42.3	6,698.9	8,688	14.4	103,604	0.0	34,884
Tampa–St. Petersburg–Clearwater, FL	26,756.0	41.2	9,613	18,415.9	68.8	2,400.1	2,146.8	18,946.5	69,363	12.8	932,231	-9.7	39,829
Terre Haute, IN	1,548.2	23.3	8,979	988.2	63.8	146.0	25.6	1,255.7	3,742	-2.7	58,470	-6.7	34,362
Texarkana, TX–Texarkana, AR	1,482.9	2.6	10,902	864.7	58.3	172.1	133.4	1,444.7	2,897	0.9	41,839	-3.7	31,326
Toledo, OH	5,031.9	34.0	7,724	3,527.6	70.1	291.9	38.5	3,754.6	14,668	-8.3	259,247	-14.0	37,923
Topeka, KS	3,278.0	49.7	14,016	1,289.3	39.3	316.1	24.9	2,189.2	5,399	-5.9	86,080	-8.7	35,444
Trenton–Ewing, NJ	6,657.9	71.1	18,166	1,961.7	29.5	320.8	177.4	3,890.2	9,756	1.1	175,798	1.0	58,313
Tucson, AZ	14,248.6	49.0	14,535	5,158.2	36.2	1,074.4	5,268.8	9,560.1	20,319	9.1	301,151	2.6	36,919
Tulsa, OK	6,426.0	32.4	6,855	4,389.9	68.3	462.0	251.7	4,852.2	24,072	4.0	367,884	-2.5	41,144
Tuscaloosa, AL	1,920.5	45.6	8,751	1,138.7	59.3	113.4	122.9	1,318.9	4,312	-0.2	73,293	-1.1	35,936
Tyler, TX	1,498.6	45.1	7,146	1,048.1	69.9	80.8	56.3	1,032.9	5,442	12.0	85,222	15.3	36,537
Utica–Rome, NY	2,843.0	30.7	9,496	1,765.5	62.1	236.6	162.1	2,174.6	6,069	-1.3	99,758	-1.9	33,029
Valdosta, GA	1,241.8	26.9	8,896	646.4	52.1	286.4	89.1	978.4	3,018	9.9	40,176	1.6	27,987
Vallejo–Fairfield, CA	3,454.6	26.6	8,358	1,805.2	52.3	689.1	363.8	2,728.8	6,744	3.7	98,014	3.7	42,098
Victoria, TX	846.5	40.5	7,336	575.9	68.0	41.5	16.9	602.7	2,777	1.7	40,123	4.9	37,705
Vineland–Millville–Bridgeton, NJ	1,295.5	33.2	8,257	865.2	66.8	61.2	42.0	972.9	2,969	-1.9	45,030	-1.7	36,136
Virginia Beach–Norfolk–Newport News, VA–NC	27,891.6	30.6	16,685	9,209.1	33.0	6,402.6	9,027.1	21,360.4	37,589	9.0	592,401	2.0	36,987
Visalia–Porterville, CA	2,559.9	44.0	5,789	1,538.0	60.1	77.9	12.8	1,777.2	6,134	3.5	85,429	10.7	33,549
Waco, TX	2,019.0	35.1	8,595	1,131.9	56.1	190.6	256.7	1,494.5	4,919	1.6	95,173	5.0	31,672
Warner Robins, GA	2,499.9	22.8	17,869	773.4	30.9	982.5	572.7	2,036.1	2,301	17.0	33,656	26.0	30,489
Washington–Arlington–Alexandria, DC–VA–MD–WV	169,492.6	51.0	30,363	26,507.9	15.6	42,792.8	37,778.4	112,227.6	141,020	33.5	2,370,531	33.3	58,132
Bethesda–Rockville–Frederick, MD	23,309.8	31.5	19,342	5,458.3	23.4	5,396.8	3,125.5	17,729.3	32,226	5.4	481,197	1.0	54,887
Washington–Arlington–Alexandria, DC–VA–MD–WV	146,182.8	54.7	33,398	21,049.6	14.4	37,396.1	34,652.9	94,498.3	108,794	45.0	1,889,334	45.1	58,959
Waterloo–Cedar Falls, IA	1,272.3	37.5	7,581	862.0	67.8	89.6	15.3	925.0	4,132	0.3	75,209	5.6	34,691
Wausau, WI	828.7	40.3	6,181	543.6	65.6	72.1	2.2	590.5	3,397	-1.2	58,876	-7.5	36,954
Wenatchee–East Wenatchee, WA	800.5	45.0	7,219	515.7	64.4	53.0	15.3	552.1	3,106	9.9	32,097	13.0	33,626
Wheeling, WV–OH	1,326.9	14.8	8,969	977.7	73.7	77.3	9.4	1,156.1	3,459	-8.2	54,134	1.8	31,284
Wichita, KS	5,408.5	28.1	8,681	2,776.2	51.3	704.2	1,077.6	4,221.9	14,712	1.2	255,616	-1.5	39,728
Wichita Falls, TX	1,642.4	26.5	10,855	855.3	52.1	380.1	181.1	1,298.0	3,532	-2.2	47,344	-2.7	31,004
Williamsport, PA	969.5	32.9	8,350	703.5	72.6	64.5	20.3	729.3	2,853	-0.9	44,361	-10.3	32,187
Wilmington, NC	2,725.5	40.1	7,522	1,925.1	70.6	138.8	124.3	1,945.8	9,889	17.9	111,863	11.1	33,819
Winchester, VA–WV	805.7	52.9	6,271	557.0	69.1	128.5	9.2	527.0	3,070	11.1	44,437	-1.7	36,895
Winston–Salem, NC	3,416.7	45.9	7,152	2,257.4	66.1	153.7	53.4	2,341.5	10,336	-1.2	177,530	-10.1	40,379
Worcester, MA	6,321.4	41.3	7,916	3,944.3	62.4	313.7	165.3	4,475.3	17,625	-1.6	267,175	-8.9	42,890
Yakima, WA	1,822.9	44.5	7,495	1,004.1	55.1	134.0	62.6	1,261.9	4,684	-1.6	62,406	3.6	32,981
York–Hanover, PA	3,882.1	6.0	8,925	1,982.2	51.1	216.5	1,323.7	3,663.1	8,580	4.7	152,211	-0.6	38,424
Youngstown–Warren–Boardman, OH–PA	5,279.6	31.3	9,332	3,982.5	75.4	231.8	53.1	4,020.5	12,851	-9.0	197,193	-15.8	32,504
Yuba City, CA	1,364.9	28.8	8,178	780.1	57.2	244.2	12.9	1,059.4	2,524	1.4	28,931	10.3	33,397
Yuma, AZ	1,761.7	49.3	9,000	829.0	47.1	235.1	324.8	1,180.1	2,946	16.1	40,626	30.1	28,315

[1]Based on resident population estimated as of July 1, 2010.
[2]For pay period as of March 12 of the year shown.

PART C

METROPOLITAN COUNTIES

Note: Part C covers 366 metropolitan statistical areas, including 11 metropolitan statistical areas with 29 metropolitan divisions, and 1,100 county components defined by the Office of Management and Budget as of December 2009. For more information, see OMB Bulletin 10-02 at http://www.whitehouse.gov/sites/default/files/omb/assets/bulletins/b10-02.pdf .

For additional information, see Appendix C, Geographic Concepts.

Table C-1. Population and Population Characteristics

Metropolitan statistical area, division, and component county	Population				Net change		Percent change		Percent			
	2011 (July 1)	2010 Census (April 1)	2000[1] (estimates base)	1990[2] (April 1)	2010–2011[3]	2000–2010[4]	2010–2011[3]	2000–2010[4]	Under 15 years, 2011	15 to 44 years, 2011	45 to 64 years, 2011	65 years and over, 2011
Abilene, TX	166,416	165,252	160,245	148,004	1,164	5,007	0.7	3.1	19.8	42.1	24.5	13.6
Callahan County, TX	13,515	13,544	12,905	11,859	-29	639	-0.2	5.0	19.2	32.8	29.7	18.3
Jones County, TX	20,146	20,202	20,785	16,490	-56	-583	-0.3	-2.8	14.9	44.0	27.4	13.7
Taylor County, TX	132,755	131,506	126,555	119,655	1,249	4,951	0.9	3.9	20.7	42.7	23.5	13.2
Akron, OH	701,456	703,200	694,960	657,575	-1,744	8,240	-0.2	1.2	17.9	38.9	28.8	14.4
Portage County, OH	161,624	161,419	152,061	142,585	205	9,358	0.1	6.2	16.4	42.7	27.7	13.2
Summit County, OH	539,832	541,781	542,899	514,990	-1,949	-1,118	-0.4	-0.2	18.3	37.8	29.1	14.7
Albany, GA	157,688	157,308	157,833	146,583	380	-525	0.2	-0.3	21.4	40.6	25.8	12.2
Baker County, GA	3,085	3,451	4,074	3,615	-366	-623	-10.6	-15.3	20.7	35.8	32.8	10.6
Dougherty County, GA	94,788	94,565	96,065	96,321	223	-1,500	0.2	-1.6	21.7	41.7	24.2	12.4
Lee County, GA	28,575	28,298	24,757	16,250	277	3,541	1.0	14.3	22.5	41.6	27.3	8.7
Terrell County, GA	9,319	9,315	10,970	10,653	4	-1,655	0.0	-15.1	20.0	36.0	28.8	15.2
Worth County, GA	21,921	21,679	21,967	19,744	242	-288	1.1	-1.3	19.3	37.2	28.4	15.1
Albany–Schenectady–Troy, NY	871,478	870,716	825,875	809,642	762	44,841	0.1	5.4	17.0	39.9	28.8	14.2
Albany County, NYv	303,565	304,204	294,565	292,812	-639	9,639	-0.2	3.3	15.8	42.4	27.8	14.1
Rensselaer County, NY	159,395	159,429	152,538	154,429	-34	6,891	0.0	4.5	17.1	40.4	28.9	13.7
Saratoga County, NY	220,882	219,607	200,635	181,276	1,275	18,972	0.6	9.5	18.1	37.5	30.4	14.1
Schenectady County, NY	155,058	154,727	146,555	149,285	331	8,172	0.2	5.6	18.3	38.3	28.3	15.1
Schoharie County, NY	32,578	32,749	31,582	31,840	-171	1,167	-0.5	3.7	15.7	37.5	30.6	16.2
Albuquerque, NM	898,642	887,077	729,649	599,416	11,565	157,428	1.3	21.6	20.3	40.3	26.8	12.6
Bernalillo County, NM	670,968	662,564	556,678	480,577	8,404	105,886	1.3	19.0	20.0	41.3	26.3	12.5
Sandoval County, NM	134,259	131,561	89,908	63,319	2,698	41,653	2.1	46.3	21.6	37.6	28.2	12.7
Torrance County, NM	16,345	16,383	16,911	10,285	-38	-528	-0.2	-3.1	19.0	35.2	31.0	14.8
Valencia County, NM	77,070	76,569	66,152	45,235	501	10,417	0.7	15.7	21.4	37.2	28.0	13.4
Alexandria, LA	154,505	153,922	145,035	149,082	583	8,887	0.4	6.1	21.0	39.0	26.4	13.6
Grant Parish, LA	22,131	22,309	18,698	17,526	-178	3,611	-0.8	19.3	18.8	42.7	25.9	12.6
Rapides Parish, LA	132,374	131,613	126,337	131,556	761	5,276	0.6	4.2	21.3	38.4	26.5	13.8
Allentown–Bethlehem–Easton, PA–NJ	824,916	821,173	740,395	686,718	3,743	80,778	0.5	10.9	18.2	37.5	28.9	15.4
Warren County, NJ	108,339	108,692	102,437	91,675	-353	6,255	-0.3	6.1	18.6	36.0	30.9	14.4
Carbon County, PA	65,154	65,249	58,802	56,803	-95	6,447	-0.1	11.0	16.7	34.2	31.1	18.0
Lehigh County, PA	352,947	349,497	312,090	291,130	3,450	37,407	1.0	12.0	19.1	38.4	27.7	14.8
Northampton County, PA	298,476	297,735	267,066	247,110	741	30,669	0.2	11.5	17.4	37.7	29.0	15.9
Altoona, PA	127,099	127,089	129,144	130,542	10	-2,055	0.0	-1.6	17.3	36.1	28.8	17.8
Blair County, PA	127,099	127,089	129,144	130,542	10	-2,055	0.0	-1.6	17.3	36.1	28.8	17.8
Amarillo, TX	253,823	249,881	226,522	196,111	3,942	23,359	1.6	10.3	22.1	41.3	24.7	11.9
Armstrong County, TX	1,928	1,901	2,148	2,021	27	-247	1.4	-11.5	17.6	31.6	30.4	20.4
Carson County, TX	6,259	6,182	6,516	6,576	77	-334	1.2	-5.1	20.6	32.6	29.8	17.0
Potter County, TX	122,285	121,073	113,546	97,841	1,212	7,527	1.0	6.6	23.8	41.6	23.7	10.9
Randall County, TX	123,351	120,725	104,312	89,673	2,626	16,413	2.2	15.7	20.5	41.7	25.4	12.5
Ames, IA	89,663	89,542	79,981	74,252	121	9,561	0.1	12.0	14.6	55.7	19.5	10.2
Story County, IA	89,663	89,542	79,981	74,252	121	9,561	0.1	12.0	14.6	55.7	19.5	10.2
Anchorage, AK	387,516	380,821	319,605	266,021	6,695	61,216	1.8	19.2	21.9	43.3	27.0	7.7
Anchorage Municipality, AK	295,570	291,826	260,283	226,338	3,744	31,543	1.3	12.1	21.5	44.4	26.6	7.6
Matanuska–Susitna Borough, AK	91,946	88,995	59,322	39,683	2,951	29,673	3.3	50.0	23.4	40.0	28.4	8.3
Anderson, IN	131,235	131,636	133,358	130,669	-401	-1,722	-0.3	-1.3	18.7	38.3	27.2	15.7
Madison County, IN	131,235	131,636	133,358	130,669	-401	-1,722	-0.3	-1.3	18.7	38.3	27.2	15.7
Anderson, SC	188,488	187,126	165,740	145,177	1,362	21,386	0.7	12.9	19.6	37.2	27.8	15.4
Anderson County, SC	188,488	187,126	165,740	145,177	1,362	21,386	0.7	12.9	19.6	37.2	27.8	15.4
Ann Arbor, MI	347,962	344,791	322,895	282,937	3,171	21,896	0.9	6.8	16.6	48.1	24.8	10.5
Washtenaw County, MI	347,962	344,791	322,895	282,937	3,171	21,896	0.9	6.8	16.6	48.1	24.8	10.5
Anniston–Oxford, AL	117,797	118,572	112,249	116,032	-775	6,323	-0.7	5.6	18.9	39.2	27.3	14.6
Calhoun County, AL	117,797	118,572	112,249	116,032	-775	6,323	-0.7	5.6	18.9	39.2	27.3	14.6
Appleton, WI	227,403	225,666	201,602	174,801	1,737	24,064	0.8	11.9	20.7	39.5	27.8	11.9
Calumet County, WI	49,490	48,971	40,631	34,291	519	8,340	1.1	20.5	22.0	37.7	28.6	11.6
Outagamie County, WI	177,913	176,695	160,971	140,510	1,218	15,724	0.7	9.8	20.4	40.0	27.6	12.0
Asheville, NC	429,017	424,858	369,171	308,005	4,159	55,687	1.0	15.1	16.7	36.0	28.6	18.7
Buncombe County, NC	241,419	238,314	206,330	174,357	3,101	31,988	1.3	15.5	16.8	38.6	28.3	16.2
Haywood County, NC	58,855	59,036	54,033	46,948	-181	5,003	-0.3	9.3	15.5	32.8	30.1	21.7
Henderson County, NC	107,927	106,740	89,173	69,747	1,187	17,567	1.1	19.7	17.0	32.1	28.1	22.8
Madison County, NC	20,816	20,764	19,635	16,953	52	1,129	0.3	5.7	15.9	35.7	30.3	18.1
Athens–Clarke County, GA	193,317	192,541	166,079	136,025	776	26,462	0.4	15.9	17.2	50.9	21.5	10.4
Clarke County, GA	117,344	116,714	101,489	87,594	630	15,225	0.5	15.0	14.9	59.9	16.4	8.8
Madison County, GA	27,921	28,120	25,730	21,050	-199	2,390	-0.7	9.3	19.6	37.6	29.1	13.8
Oconee County, GA	33,366	32,808	26,225	17,618	558	6,583	1.7	25.1	22.2	36.5	29.7	11.6
Oglethorpe County, GA	14,686	14,899	12,635	9,763	-213	2,264	-1.4	17.9	18.9	37.2	29.2	14.7
Atlanta–Sandy Springs–Marietta, GA	5,359,205	5,268,860	4,247,981	3,068,975	90,345	1,020,879	1.7	24.0	21.8	43.4	25.5	9.3
Barrow County, GA	69,912	69,367	46,144	29,721	545	23,223	0.8	50.3	23.7	42.6	23.9	9.8
Bartow County, GA	100,421	100,157	76,019	55,915	264	24,138	0.3	31.8	21.8	40.7	26.4	11.1
Butts County, GA	23,504	23,655	19,522	15,326	-151	4,133	-0.6	21.2	18.6	40.8	27.4	13.2
Carroll County, GA	111,159	110,527	87,268	71,422	632	23,259	0.6	26.7	21.0	43.6	24.1	11.3
Cherokee County, GA	218,286	214,346	141,903	90,204	3,940	72,443	1.8	51.1	22.7	40.9	26.6	9.8
Clayton County, GA	261,532	259,424	236,517	181,436	2,108	22,907	0.8	9.7	24.5	45.3	23.2	6.9
Cobb County, GA	697,553	688,078	607,751	447,745	9,475	80,327	1.4	13.2	21.0	43.5	26.4	9.1
Coweta County, GA	129,629	127,317	89,215	53,853	2,312	38,102	1.8	42.7	22.1	40.4	26.7	10.8
Dawson County, GA	22,459	22,330	15,999	9,429	129	6,331	0.6	39.6	18.2	36.6	30.1	15.1

[1] The April 1, 2000, Population Estimates base reflects modifications to the Census 2000 population as documented in the Count Question Resolution program and geographic program revisions.
[2] The April 1, 1990, census counts include corrections processed through August 1997, results of special censuses and test censuses, and do not include adjustments for census coverage errors.
[3] Based on the April 1, 2010, estimates base and the July 1, 2011, estimates.
[4] Based on the April 1, 2010, complete count and the April 1, 2000 estimates base.
0 = Represents zero or amounts to zero.

Table C-1.   Population and Population Characteristics—*Continued*

Metropolitan statistical area, division, and component county	Population 2011 (July 1)	Population 2010 Census (April 1)	Population 2000¹ (estimates base)	Population 1990² (April 1)	Net change 2010–2011³	Net change 2000–2010⁴	Percent change 2010–2011³	Percent change 2000–2010⁴	Percent Under 15 years, 2011	Percent 15 to 44 years, 2011	Percent 45 to 64 years, 2011	Percent 65 years and over, 2011
Atlanta–Sandy Springs–Marietta, GA—*Continued*												
DeKalb County, GA	699,893	691,893	665,865	546,174	8,000	26,028	1.2	3.9	20.2	45.7	24.7	9.4
Douglas County, GA	133,355	132,403	92,174	71,120	952	40,229	0.7	43.6	23.0	42.5	25.5	9.0
Fayette County, GA	107,784	106,567	91,263	62,415	1,217	15,304	1.1	16.8	19.3	33.6	33.2	13.9
Forsyth County, GA	181,840	175,511	98,407	44,083	6,329	77,104	3.6	78.4	25.4	39.3	26.1	9.3
Fulton County, GA	949,599	920,581	816,006	648,776	29,018	104,575	3.2	12.8	19.8	46.5	24.5	9.2
Gwinnett County, GA	824,941	805,321	588,448	352,910	19,620	216,873	2.4	36.9	23.9	43.9	25.1	7.2
Haralson County, GA	28,638	28,780	25,690	21,966	-142	3,090	-0.5	12.0	20.5	38.0	26.8	14.7
Heard County, GA	11,744	11,834	11,012	8,628	-90	822	-0.8	7.5	20.1	37.7	28.4	13.9
Henry County, GA	207,360	203,922	119,341	58,741	3,438	84,581	1.7	70.9	23.1	42.4	25.8	8.8
Jasper County, GA	13,885	13,900	11,426	8,453	-15	2,474	-0.1	21.7	20.6	37.1	28.9	13.4
Lamar County, GA	18,194	18,317	15,912	13,038	-123	2,405	-0.7	15.1	17.7	40.5	27.3	14.5
Meriwether County, GA	21,617	21,992	22,534	22,411	-375	-542	-1.7	-2.4	19.3	35.1	29.3	16.4
Newton County, GA	100,814	99,958	62,001	41,808	856	37,957	0.9	61.2	23.4	41.6	24.7	10.3
Paulding County, GA	143,542	142,324	81,678	41,611	1,218	60,646	0.9	74.3	24.5	43.9	24.0	7.6
Pickens County, GA	29,415	29,431	22,983	14,432	-16	6,448	-0.1	28.1	18.2	34.6	29.8	17.4
Pike County, GA	17,751	17,869	13,688	10,224	-118	4,181	-0.7	30.5	21.6	37.7	27.9	12.8
Rockdale County, GA	85,765	85,215	70,111	54,091	550	15,104	0.6	21.5	21.4	39.6	27.8	11.2
Spalding County, GA	64,033	64,073	58,417	54,457	-40	5,656	-0.1	9.7	21.1	38.7	26.3	13.9
Walton County, GA	84,580	83,768	60,687	38,586	812	23,081	1.0	38.0	21.7	38.8	26.7	12.8
Atlantic City–Hammonton, NJ	274,338	274,549	252,552	224,327	-211	21,997	-0.1	8.7	18.7	37.9	28.9	14.4
Atlantic County, NJ	274,338	274,549	252,552	224,327	-211	21,997	-0.1	8.7	18.7	37.9	28.9	14.4
Auburn–Opelika, AL	143,468	140,247	115,092	87,146	3,221	25,155	2.3	21.9	18.1	51.1	21.6	9.2
Lee County, AL	143,468	140,247	115,092	87,146	3,221	25,155	2.3	21.9	18.1	51.1	21.6	9.2
Augusta–Richmond County, GA–SC	561,858	556,877	499,684	435,799	4,981	57,193	0.9	11.4	20.2	40.0	27.0	12.8
Burke County, GA	23,504	23,316	22,243	20,579	188	1,073	0.8	4.8	22.8	38.1	27.1	12.0
Columbia County, GA	128,112	124,053	89,288	66,031	4,059	34,765	3.3	38.9	21.9	39.9	27.7	10.5
McDuffie County, GA	21,673	21,875	21,231	20,119	-202	644	-0.9	3.0	21.7	36.5	27.8	14.1
Richmond County, GA	201,217	200,549	199,775	189,719	668	774	0.3	0.4	20.7	42.9	24.8	11.6
Aiken County, SC	160,682	160,099	142,552	120,991	583	17,547	0.4	12.3	18.3	37.2	28.6	15.9
Edgefield County, SC	26,670	26,985	24,595	18,360	-315	2,390	-1.2	9.7	16.7	39.4	30.1	13.8
Austin–Round Rock–San Marcos, TX	1,783,519	1,716,289	1,249,763	846,227	67,230	466,526	3.9	37.3	21.4	47.2	23.1	8.3
Bastrop County, TX	75,115	74,171	57,733	38,263	944	16,438	1.3	28.5	21.6	37.0	29.5	11.9
Caldwell County, TX	38,442	38,066	32,194	26,392	376	5,872	1.0	18.2	21.2	41.7	25.2	11.9
Hays County, TX	164,050	157,107	97,589	65,614	6,943	59,518	4.4	61.0	20.3	48.1	22.7	8.8
Travis County, TX	1,063,130	1,024,266	812,280	576,407	38,864	211,986	3.8	26.1	20.5	49.6	22.4	7.5
Williamson County, TX	442,782	422,679	249,967	139,551	20,103	172,712	4.8	69.1	23.9	43.3	23.4	9.3
Bakersfield–Delano, CA	851,710	839,631	661,645	544,981	12,079	177,986	1.4	26.9	24.9	43.8	22.2	9.1
Kern County, CA	851,710	839,631	661,645	544,981	12,079	177,986	1.4	26.9	24.9	43.8	22.2	9.1
Baltimore–Towson, MD	2,729,110	2,710,489	2,552,994	2,382,172	18,621	157,495	0.7	6.2	18.7	40.4	28.0	12.8
Anne Arundel County, MD	544,403	537,656	489,656	427,239	6,747	48,000	1.3	9.8	19.1	40.1	28.6	12.1
Baltimore County, MD	809,941	805,029	754,292	692,134	4,912	50,737	0.6	6.7	17.9	39.6	27.8	14.7
Carroll County, MD	167,288	167,134	150,897	123,372	154	16,237	0.1	10.8	19.1	36.2	31.1	13.5
Harford County, MD	246,489	244,826	218,590	182,132	1,663	26,236	0.7	12.0	19.6	38.0	29.6	12.8
Howard County, MD	293,142	287,085	247,842	187,328	6,057	39,243	2.1	15.8	20.5	39.4	29.5	10.6
Queen Anne's County, MD	48,354	47,798	40,563	33,953	556	7,235	1.2	17.8	18.9	34.0	31.5	15.5
Baltimore city, MD	619,493	620,961	651,154	736,014	-1,468	-30,193	-0.2	-4.6	18.2	44.7	25.3	11.8
Bangor, ME	153,786	153,923	144,919	146,601	-137	9,004	-0.1	6.2	16.0	40.0	29.3	14.7
Penobscot County, ME	153,786	153,923	144,919	146,601	-137	9,004	-0.1	6.2	16.0	40.0	29.3	14.7
Barnstable Town, MA	215,769	215,888	222,230	186,605	-119	-6,342	-0.1	-2.9	13.5	28.6	32.5	25.4
Barnstable County, MA	215,769	215,888	222,230	186,605	-119	-6,342	-0.1	-2.9	13.5	28.6	32.5	25.4
Baton Rouge, LA	808,242	802,484	705,973	623,850	5,758	96,511	0.7	13.7	20.3	43.3	25.5	11.0
Ascension Parish, LA	109,985	107,215	76,627	58,214	2,770	30,588	2.6	39.9	23.7	42.0	25.3	9.1
East Baton Rouge Parish, LA	441,438	440,171	412,852	380,105	1,267	27,319	0.3	6.6	19.2	45.2	24.4	11.2
East Feliciana Parish, LA	20,117	20,267	21,360	19,211	-150	-1,093	-0.7	-5.1	17.0	38.2	31.5	13.3
Iberville Parish, LA	33,230	33,387	33,320	31,049	-157	67	-0.5	0.2	18.3	41.0	28.5	12.3
Livingston Parish, LA	130,251	128,026	91,814	70,523	2,225	36,212	1.7	39.4	22.8	41.8	25.2	10.3
Pointe Coupee Parish, LA	22,703	22,802	22,763	22,540	-99	39	-0.4	0.2	19.9	34.3	30.1	15.7
St. Helena Parish, LA	10,949	11,203	10,525	9,874	-254	678	-2.3	6.4	20.8	35.9	28.9	14.4
West Baton Rouge Parish, LA	24,109	23,788	21,601	19,419	321	2,187	1.3	10.1	20.7	40.8	27.3	11.3
West Feliciana Parish, LA	15,460	15,625	15,111	12,915	-165	514	-1.1	3.4	13.7	41.7	33.8	10.7
Battle Creek, MI	135,490	136,146	137,985	135,982	-656	-1,839	-0.5	-1.3	19.6	37.4	28.1	15.0
Calhoun County, MI	135,490	136,146	137,985	135,982	-656	-1,839	-0.5	-1.3	19.6	37.4	28.1	15.0
Bay City, MI	107,110	107,771	110,157	111,723	-661	-2,386	-0.6	-2.2	17.9	35.8	29.7	16.6
Bay County, MI	107,110	107,771	110,157	111,723	-661	-2,386	-0.6	-2.2	17.9	35.8	29.7	16.6
Beaumont–Port Arthur, TX	390,535	388,745	385,090	361,218	1,790	3,655	0.5	0.9	20.2	40.0	26.6	13.1
Hardin County, TX	55,246	54,635	48,073	41,320	611	6,562	1.1	13.7	21.4	37.4	27.4	13.8
Jefferson County, TX	252,802	252,273	252,051	239,389	529	222	0.2	0.1	19.9	41.3	26.1	12.7
Orange County, TX	82,487	81,837	84,966	80,509	650	-3,129	0.8	-3.7	20.4	37.8	27.7	14.1
Bellingham, WA	203,663	201,140	166,814	127,780	2,523	34,326	1.3	20.6	16.9	43.1	26.3	13.8
Whatcom County, WA	203,663	201,140	166,814	127,780	2,523	34,326	1.3	20.6	16.9	43.1	26.3	13.8

¹ The April 1, 2000, Population Estimates base reflects modifications to the Census 2000 population as documented in the Count Question Resolution program and geographic program revisions.
² The April 1, 1990, census counts include corrections processed through August 1997, results of special censuses and test censuses, and do not include adjustments for census coverage errors.
³ Based on the April 1, 2010, estimates base and the July 1, 2011, estimates.
⁴ Based on the April 1, 2010, complete count and the April 1, 2000 estimates base.

Table C-1. Population and Population Characteristics—*Continued*

Metropolitan statistical area, division, and component county	Population				Net change		Percent change		Percent			
	2011 (July 1)	2010 Census (April 1)	2000[1] (estimates base)	1990[2] (April 1)	2010– 2011[3]	2000– 2010[4]	2010– 2011[3]	2000– 2010[4]	Under 15 years, 2011	15 to 44 years, 2011	45 to 64 years, 2011	65 years and over, 2011
Bend, OR..	160,338	157,733	115,367	74,976	2,605	42,366	1.7	36.7	18.8	36.8	28.8	15.6
Deschutes County, OR	160,338	157,733	115,367	74,976	2,605	42,366	1.7	36.7	18.8	36.8	28.8	15.6
Billings, MT...................................	160,097	158,050	138,904	121,499	2,047	19,146	1.3	13.8	19.3	37.8	28.2	14.7
Carbon County, MT.....................	10,028	10,078	9,552	8,080	-50	526	-0.5	5.5	15.4	29.4	35.9	19.3
Yellowstone County, MT.............	150,069	147,972	129,352	113,419	2,097	18,620	1.4	14.4	19.6	38.3	27.7	14.3
Binghamton, NY............................	250,074	251,725	252,320	264,497	-1,651	-595	-0.7	-0.2	16.7	38.0	28.9	16.5
Broome County, NY....................	199,031	200,600	200,536	212,160	-1,569	64	-0.8	0.0	16.2	39.0	28.2	16.6
Tioga County, NY........................	51,043	51,125	51,784	52,337	-82	-659	-0.2	-1.3	18.6	34.0	31.4	16.0
Birmingham–Hoover, AL................	1,132,264	1,128,047	1,052,238	956,668	4,217	75,809	0.4	7.2	19.8	39.9	27.1	13.2
Bibb County, AL..........................	22,766	22,915	20,826	16,598	-149	2,089	-0.7	10.0	18.1	41.6	27.1	13.3
Blount County, AL.......................	57,677	57,322	51,024	39,248	355	6,298	0.6	12.3	20.0	38.0	26.9	15.0
Chilton County, AL......................	43,895	43,643	39,593	32,458	252	4,050	0.6	10.2	20.6	38.7	26.5	14.1
Jefferson County, AL..................	658,931	658,466	662,047	651,520	465	-3,581	0.1	-0.5	19.6	40.3	26.9	13.3
St. Clair County, AL....................	84,398	83,593	64,742	49,811	805	18,851	1.0	29.1	19.6	39.0	27.7	13.6
Shelby County, AL......................	197,936	195,085	143,293	99,363	2,851	51,792	1.5	36.1	21.0	40.7	27.2	11.1
Walker County, AL......................	66,661	67,023	70,713	67,670	-362	-3,690	-0.5	-5.2	18.4	36.1	28.9	16.7
Bismarck, ND................................	110,879	108,779	94,719	83,831	2,100	14,060	1.9	14.8	18.9	39.6	27.5	13.9
Burleigh County, ND...................	83,145	81,308	69,416	60,131	1,837	11,892	2.3	17.1	18.7	40.4	27.3	13.7
Morton County, ND.....................	27,734	27,471	25,303	23,700	263	2,168	1.0	8.6	19.5	37.4	28.3	14.8
Blacksburg–Christiansburg–Radford, VA......	162,487	162,958	151,272	140,715	-471	11,686	-0.3	7.7	13.6	51.6	22.2	12.6
Giles County, VA........................	17,124	17,286	16,657	16,366	-162	629	-0.9	3.8	17.3	34.3	29.8	18.5
Montgomery County, VA.............	94,342	94,392	83,629	73,913	-50	10,763	-0.1	12.9	12.7	58.0	19.2	10.1
Pulaski County, VA.....................	34,607	34,872	35,127	34,496	-265	-255	-0.8	-0.7	15.7	35.1	30.8	18.4
Radford city, VA.........................	16,414	16,408	15,859	15,940	6	549	0.0	3.5	10.5	67.2	13.6	8.7
Bloomington, IN............................	194,193	192,714	175,506	156,669	1,479	17,208	0.8	9.8	14.9	50.3	22.9	11.9
Greene County, IN......................	32,895	33,165	33,157	30,410	-270	8	-0.8	0.0	19.2	35.5	29.2	16.1
Monroe County, IN......................	139,799	137,974	120,563	108,978	1,825	17,411	1.3	14.4	13.4	56.1	20.1	10.4
Owen County, IN.........................	21,499	21,575	21,786	17,281	-76	-211	-0.4	-1.0	18.3	34.9	31.6	15.2
Bloomington–Normal, IL................	170,556	169,572	150,433	129,180	984	19,139	0.6	12.7	18.6	47.3	23.7	10.4
McLean County, IL......................	170,556	169,572	150,433	129,180	984	19,139	0.6	12.7	18.6	47.3	23.7	10.4
Boise City–Nampa, ID...................	627,664	616,561	464,840	319,596	11,103	151,721	1.8	32.6	23.1	41.0	24.6	11.3
Ada County, ID...........................	400,842	392,365	300,904	205,775	8,477	91,461	2.2	30.4	21.8	41.9	25.4	10.9
Boise County, ID........................	7,025	7,028	6,670	3,509	-3	358	0.0	5.4	16.8	27.2	39.0	17.0
Canyon County, ID.....................	191,694	188,923	131,441	90,076	2,771	57,482	1.5	43.7	26.3	40.6	21.8	11.2
Gem County, ID..........................	16,665	16,719	15,181	11,844	-54	1,538	-0.3	10.1	19.6	32.2	29.2	18.9
Owyhee County, ID.....................	11,438	11,526	10,644	8,392	-88	882	-0.8	8.3	23.6	36.6	25.6	14.2
Boston–Cambridge–Quincy, MA–NH	4,591,112	4,552,402	4,391,344	4,133,895	38,710	161,058	0.9	3.7	17.5	41.4	27.8	13.3
Boston–Quincy, MA	1,903,947	1,887,792	1,812,937	1,715,269	16,155	74,855	0.9	4.1	17.1	43.3	26.5	13.0
Norfolk County, MA....................	675,436	670,850	650,308	616,087	4,586	20,542	0.7	3.2	18.2	37.8	29.3	14.7
Plymouth County, MA..................	497,579	494,919	472,822	435,276	2,660	22,097	0.5	4.7	19.2	36.1	30.3	14.4
Suffolk County, MA.....................	730,932	722,023	689,807	663,906	8,909	32,216	1.2	4.7	14.7	53.5	21.3	10.6
Cambridge–Newton–Framingham, MA	1,518,171	1,503,085	1,465,396	1,398,468	15,086	37,689	1.0	2.6	17.3	41.7	27.7	13.3
Middlesex County, MA	1,518,171	1,503,085	1,465,396	1,398,468	15,086	37,689	1.0	2.6	17.3	41.7	27.7	13.3
Peabody, MA	748,930	743,159	723,419	670,080	5,771	19,740	0.8	2.7	18.6	37.6	29.5	14.4
Essex County, MA	748,930	743,159	723,419	670,080	5,771	19,740	0.8	2.7	18.6	37.6	29.5	14.4
Rockingham County–Strafford County, NH....	420,064	418,366	389,592	350,078	1,698	28,774	0.4	7.4	17.3	38.3	31.5	12.9
Rockingham County, NH.............	296,207	295,223	277,359	245,845	984	17,864	0.3	6.4	17.6	36.0	33.2	13.2
Strafford County, NH..................	123,857	123,143	112,233	104,233	714	10,910	0.6	9.7	16.6	43.8	27.4	12.2
Boulder, CO[5]................................	299,378	294,567	269,814	225,339	4,811	24,753	1.6	9.2	17.3	45.2	27.0	10.5
Boulder County, CO[5].................	299,378	294,567	269,814	225,339	4,811	24,753	1.6	9.2	17.3	45.2	27.0	10.5
Bowling Green, KY........................	127,607	125,953	104,166	88,077	1,654	21,787	1.3	20.9	18.7	45.2	24.3	11.7
Edmonson County, KY................	12,090	12,161	11,644	10,357	-71	517	-0.6	4.4	17.4	37.2	28.8	16.7
Warren County, KY.....................	115,517	113,792	92,522	77,720	1,725	21,270	1.5	23.0	18.9	46.1	23.8	11.2
Bremerton–Silverdale, WA............	254,633	251,133	231,969	189,731	3,500	19,164	1.4	8.3	17.8	39.3	29.2	13.7
Kitsap County, WA......................	254,633	251,133	231,969	189,731	3,500	19,164	1.4	8.3	17.8	39.3	29.2	13.7
Bridgeport–Stamford–Norwalk, CT..............	925,899	916,829	882,567	827,645	9,070	34,262	1.0	3.9	20.0	38.0	28.4	13.7
Fairfield County, CT....................	925,899	916,829	882,567	827,645	9,070	34,262	1.0	3.9	20.0	38.0	28.4	13.7
Brownsville–Harlingen, TX............	414,123	406,220	335,227	260,120	7,903	70,993	1.9	21.2	27.3	40.8	20.6	11.3
Cameron County, TX...................	414,123	406,220	335,227	260,120	7,903	70,993	1.9	21.2	27.3	40.8	20.6	11.3
Brunswick, GA..............................	112,923	112,370	93,044	82,207	553	19,326	0.5	20.8	19.8	36.5	28.4	15.3
Brantley County, GA...................	18,367	18,411	14,629	11,077	-44	3,782	-0.2	25.9	21.6	38.3	28.4	11.7
Glynn County, GA.......................	80,386	79,626	67,568	62,496	760	12,058	1.0	17.8	19.9	36.7	27.8	15.6
McIntosh County, GA..................	14,170	14,333	10,847	8,634	-163	3,486	-1.1	32.1	16.4	33.0	32.0	18.6
Buffalo–Niagara Falls, NY............	1,134,039	1,135,509	1,170,111	1,189,340	-1,470	-34,602	-0.1	-3.0	17.2	38.2	28.8	15.8
Erie County, NY..........................	918,028	919,040	950,265	968,584	-1,012	-31,225	-0.1	-3.3	17.2	38.6	28.4	15.8
Niagara County, NY....................	216,011	216,469	219,846	220,756	-458	-3,377	-0.2	-1.5	17.1	36.6	30.2	16.1

[1] The April 1, 2000, Population Estimates base reflects modifications to the Census 2000 population as documented in the Count Question Resolution program and geographic program revisions.
[2] The April 1, 1990, census counts include corrections processed through August 1997, results of special censuses and test censuses, and do not include adjustments for census coverage errors.
[3] Based on the April 1, 2010, estimates base and the July 1, 2011, estimates.
[4] Based on the April 1, 2010, complete count and the April 1, 2000 estimates base.
0 = Represents zero or amounts to zero.

Table C-1.   Population and Population Characteristics—*Continued*

Metropolitan statistical area, division, and component county	Population				Net change		Percent change		Percent			
	2011 (July 1)	2010 Census (April 1)	2000[1] (estimates base)	1990[2] (April 1)	2010– 2011[3]	2000– 2010[4]	2010– 2011[3]	2000– 2010[4]	Under 15 years, 2011	15 to 44 years, 2011	45 to 64 years, 2011	65 years and over, 2011
Burlington, NC	153,291	151,131	130,800	108,213	2,160	20,331	1.4	15.5	19.4	39.1	26.7	14.8
Alamance County, NC	153,291	151,131	130,800	108,213	2,160	20,331	1.4	15.5	19.4	39.1	26.7	14.8
Burlington–South Burlington, VT	212,535	211,261	198,889	177,059	1,274	12,372	0.6	6.2	16.6	43.1	28.4	11.9
Chittenden County, VT	157,491	156,545	146,571	131,761	946	9,974	0.6	6.8	15.7	45.2	27.4	11.7
Franklin County, VT	48,113	47,746	45,417	39,980	367	2,329	0.8	5.1	19.7	37.8	30.2	12.4
Grand Isle County, VT	6,931	6,970	6,901	5,318	-39	69	-0.6	1.0	15.5	32.7	37.4	14.4
Canton–Massillon, OH	403,869	404,422	406,934	394,106	-553	-2,512	-0.1	-0.6	18.4	35.8	29.2	16.6
Carroll County, OH	28,782	28,836	28,836	26,521	-54	0	-0.2	0.0	18.3	33.4	31.4	16.9
Stark County, OH	375,087	375,586	378,098	367,585	-499	-2,512	-0.1	-0.7	18.4	36.0	29.0	16.5
Cape Coral–Fort Myers, FL	631,330	618,754	440,888	335,113	12,576	177,866	2.0	40.3	16.0	32.6	27.3	24.1
Lee County, FL	631,330	618,754	440,888	335,113	12,576	177,866	2.0	40.3	16.0	32.6	27.3	24.1
Cape Girardeau–Jackson, MO–IL	97,024	96,275	90,312	82,878	749	5,963	0.8	6.6	18.2	40.5	26.3	15.0
Alexander County, IL	8,036	8,238	9,590	10,626	-202	-1,352	-2.5	-14.1	19.0	34.8	28.8	17.4
Bollinger County, MO	12,356	12,363	12,029	10,619	-7	334	-0.1	2.8	18.9	34.7	29.8	16.6
Cape Girardeau County, MO	76,632	75,674	68,693	61,633	958	6,981	1.3	10.2	18.1	42.0	25.5	14.4
Carson City, NV	55,439	55,274	52,457	40,443	165	2,817	0.3	5.4	17.5	36.4	29.0	17.0
Carson City, NV	55,439	55,274	52,457	40,443	165	2,817	0.3	5.4	17.5	36.4	29.0	17.0
Casper, WY	76,366	75,450	66,533	61,226	916	8,917	1.2	13.4	19.9	40.0	27.6	12.5
Natrona County, WY	76,366	75,450	66,533	61,226	916	8,917	1.2	13.4	19.9	40.0	27.6	12.5
Cedar Rapids, IA	260,575	257,940	237,230	210,640	2,635	20,710	1.0	8.7	20.1	39.4	26.8	13.7
Benton County, IA	26,092	26,076	25,308	22,429	16	768	0.1	3.0	20.2	35.0	29.2	15.5
Jones County, IA	20,608	20,638	20,221	19,444	-30	417	-0.1	2.1	18.0	34.8	29.8	17.4
Linn County, IA	213,875	211,226	191,701	168,767	2,649	19,525	1.3	10.2	20.3	40.3	26.2	13.2
Champaign–Urbana, IL	232,336	231,891	210,275	202,848	445	21,616	0.2	10.3	16.3	50.5	22.1	11.2
Champaign County, IL	201,685	201,081	179,669	173,025	604	21,412	0.3	11.9	15.9	53.0	20.9	10.2
Ford County, IL	13,976	14,081	14,241	14,275	-105	-160	-0.7	-1.1	19.1	34.0	28.1	18.9
Piatt County, IL	16,675	16,729	16,365	15,548	-54	364	-0.3	2.2	18.9	33.6	30.8	16.7
Charleston, WV	303,674	304,284	309,635	307,689	-610	-5,351	-0.2	-1.7	17.8	36.1	30.1	16.1
Boone County, WV	24,444	24,629	25,535	25,870	-185	-906	-0.8	-3.5	18.9	36.5	30.3	14.3
Clay County, WV	9,357	9,386	10,330	9,983	-29	-944	-0.3	-9.1	19.8	34.7	29.3	16.1
Kanawha County, WV	192,315	193,063	200,073	207,619	-748	-7,010	-0.4	-3.5	17.0	36.1	30.1	16.8
Lincoln County, WV	21,550	21,720	22,108	21,382	-170	-388	-0.8	-1.8	18.6	36.1	30.0	15.3
Putnam County, WV	56,008	55,486	51,589	42,835	522	3,897	0.9	7.6	19.3	36.1	29.9	14.7
Charleston–North Charleston– Summerville, SC	682,121	664,607	549,033	506,877	17,514	115,574	2.6	21.1	19.4	42.6	26.1	11.8
Berkeley County, SC	183,525	177,843	142,651	128,658	5,682	35,192	3.2	24.7	21.0	42.9	25.9	10.2
Charleston County, SC	357,704	350,209	309,969	295,159	7,495	40,240	2.1	13.0	17.6	43.2	26.1	13.0
Dorchester County, SC	140,892	136,555	96,413	83,060	4,337	40,142	3.2	41.6	22.0	40.9	26.4	10.7
Charlotte–Gastonia–Rock Hill, NC–SC	1,795,472	1,758,038	1,330,448	1,024,096	37,434	427,590	2.1	32.1	21.6	42.9	25.2	10.4
Anson County, NC	26,609	26,948	25,275	23,474	-339	1,673	-1.3	6.6	17.5	39.7	27.9	14.8
Cabarrus County, NC	181,468	178,011	131,063	98,935	3,457	46,948	1.9	35.8	22.5	40.4	25.6	11.5
Gaston County, NC	207,031	206,086	190,365	174,769	945	15,721	0.5	8.3	19.6	39.1	27.8	13.6
Mecklenburg County, NC	944,373	919,628	695,454	511,211	24,745	224,174	2.7	32.2	21.4	45.7	23.9	9.1
Union County, NC	205,463	201,292	123,677	84,210	4,171	77,615	2.1	62.8	24.8	39.3	25.8	10.1
York County, SC	230,528	226,073	164,614	131,497	4,455	61,459	2.0	37.3	21.0	40.2	27.2	11.7
Charlottesville, VA	203,882	201,559	174,021	144,151	2,323	27,538	1.2	15.8	16.8	43.0	26.3	13.9
Albemarle County, VA	100,553	98,970	79,236	68,177	1,583	19,734	1.6	24.9	17.7	40.5	27.3	14.5
Fluvanna County, VA	26,061	25,691	20,047	12,429	370	5,644	1.4	28.2	18.5	36.9	28.5	16.1
Greene County, VA	18,660	18,403	15,244	10,297	257	3,159	1.4	20.7	21.0	36.4	29.3	13.3
Nelson County, VA	15,097	15,020	14,445	12,778	77	575	0.5	4.0	15.7	29.8	34.1	20.5
Charlottesville city, VA	43,511	43,475	45,049	40,470	36	-1,574	0.1	-3.5	12.4	59.6	18.5	9.4
Chattanooga, TN–GA	533,372	528,143	476,531	433,039	5,229	51,612	1.0	10.8	18.2	38.9	28.0	14.9
Catoosa County, GA	64,530	63,942	53,282	42,464	588	10,660	0.9	20.0	20.1	39.3	27.0	13.6
Dade County, GA	16,570	16,633	15,154	13,183	-63	1,479	-0.4	9.8	16.9	40.1	28.2	14.8
Walker County, GA	68,848	68,756	61,053	58,310	92	7,703	0.1	12.6	18.9	37.5	28.0	15.5
Hamilton County, TN	340,855	336,463	307,896	285,536	4,392	28,567	1.3	9.3	17.8	39.4	27.9	14.9
Marion County, TN	28,223	28,237	27,776	24,683	-14	461	0.0	1.7	17.6	35.3	30.5	16.5
Sequatchie County, TN	14,346	14,112	11,370	8,863	234	2,742	1.7	24.1	18.9	35.8	28.5	16.7
Cheyenne, WY	92,680	91,738	81,607	73,142	942	10,131	1.0	12.4	20.3	39.2	27.6	12.9
Laramie County, WY	92,680	91,738	81,607	73,142	942	10,131	1.0	12.4	20.3	39.2	27.6	12.9
Chicago–Joliet–Naperville, IL–IN–WI	9,504,753	9,461,105	9,098,316	8,181,939	43,648	362,789	0.5	4.0	20.4	41.9	26.0	11.6
Chicago–Joliet–Naperville, IL	7,922,566	7,883,147	7,628,412	6,894,440	39,419	254,735	0.5	3.3	20.3	42.5	25.6	11.6
Cook County, IL	5,217,080	5,194,675	5,376,741	5,105,044	22,405	-182,066	0.4	-3.4	19.4	43.5	25.0	12.1
DeKalb County, IL	104,743	105,160	88,969	77,932	-417	16,191	-0.4	18.2	18.3	49.9	21.7	10.1
DuPage County, IL	923,222	916,924	904,161	781,689	6,298	12,763	0.7	1.4	19.9	39.4	28.8	11.9
Grundy County, IL	50,130	50,063	37,535	32,337	67	12,528	0.1	33.4	22.2	40.3	26.2	11.3
Kane County, IL	520,271	515,269	404,119	317,471	5,002	111,150	1.0	27.5	23.8	40.9	25.3	10.0
Kendall County, IL	116,631	114,736	54,544	39,413	1,895	60,192	1.7	110.4	26.1	44.1	22.2	7.6
McHenry County, IL	308,944	308,760	260,077	183,241	184	48,683	0.1	18.7	21.7	38.6	29.1	10.6
Will County, IL	681,545	677,560	502,266	357,313	3,985	175,294	0.6	34.9	23.4	40.9	26.0	9.7

[1] The April 1, 2000, Population Estimates base reflects modifications to the Census 2000 population as documented in the Count Question Resolution program and geographic program revisions.
[2] The April 1, 1990, census counts include corrections processed through August 1997, results of special censuses and test censuses, and do not include adjustments for census coverage errors.
[3] Based on the April 1, 2010, estimates base and the July 1, 2011, estimates.
[4] Based on the April 1, 2010, complete count and the April 1, 2000 estimates base.
0 = Represents zero or amounts to zero.

Table C-1. Population and Population Characteristics—*Continued*

Metropolitan statistical area, division, and component county	Population				Net change		Percent change		Percent			
	2011 (July 1)	2010 Census (April 1)	2000[1] (estimates base)	1990[2] (April 1)	2010–2011[3]	2000–2010[4]	2010–2011[3]	2000–2010[4]	Under 15 years, 2011	15 to 44 years, 2011	45 to 64 years, 2011	65 years and over, 2011
Gary, IN.............................	708,672	708,070	675,971	642,900	602	32,099	0.1	4.7	20.5	38.5	27.7	13.4
Jasper County, IN	33,416	33,478	30,043	24,823	-62	3,435	-0.2	11.4	20.6	37.6	27.3	14.5
Lake County, IN......................	495,558	496,005	484,564	475,594	-447	11,441	-0.1	2.4	20.8	38.4	27.3	13.4
Newton County, IN	14,161	14,244	14,566	13,551	-83	-322	-0.6	-2.2	18.2	34.1	30.6	17.1
Porter County, IN	165,537	164,343	146,798	128,932	1,194	17,545	0.7	12.0	19.4	39.2	28.7	12.7
Lake County–Kenosha County, IL–WI........	873,515	869,888	793,933	644,599	3,627	75,955	0.4	9.6	21.7	39.6	27.8	10.9
Lake County, IL......................	706,222	703,462	644,356	516,418	2,760	59,106	0.4	9.2	21.9	39.4	28.0	10.8
Kenosha County, WI.................	167,293	166,426	149,577	128,181	867	16,849	0.5	11.3	20.9	40.5	27.2	11.4
Chico, CA	220,266	220,000	203,171	182,120	266	16,829	0.1	8.3	16.7	41.8	25.9	15.6
Butte County, CA	220,266	220,000	203,171	182,120	266	16,829	0.1	8.3	16.7	41.8	25.9	15.6
Cincinnati–Middletown, OH–KY–IN..............	2,138,038	2,130,151	2,009,632	1,844,888	7,887	120,519	0.4	6.0	20.5	39.6	27.5	12.4
Dearborn County, IN	50,113	50,047	46,109	38,835	66	3,938	0.1	8.5	20.2	36.2	30.1	13.5
Franklin County, IN	23,041	23,087	22,151	19,580	-46	936	-0.2	4.2	20.8	35.3	29.3	14.6
OH County, IN	6,065	6,128	5,623	5,315	-63	505	-1.0	9.0	17.8	33.4	31.6	17.2
Boone County, KY	121,737	118,811	85,991	57,589	2,926	32,820	2.5	38.2	23.5	40.4	26.3	9.9
Bracken County, KY	8,513	8,488	8,279	7,766	25	209	0.3	2.5	21.1	36.7	28.3	14.0
Campbell County, KY...............	90,940	90,336	88,616	83,866	604	1,720	0.7	1.9	18.8	41.0	27.5	12.7
Gallatin County, KY	8,612	8,589	7,870	5,393	23	719	0.3	9.1	21.9	38.1	28.0	11.9
Grant County, KY	24,816	24,662	22,384	15,737	154	2,278	0.6	10.2	23.0	40.1	25.6	11.3
Kenton County, KY	160,406	159,720	151,464	142,005	686	8,256	0.4	5.5	20.9	40.8	27.1	11.3
Pendleton County, KY	14,698	14,877	14,390	12,062	-179	487	-1.2	3.4	19.5	37.8	30.1	12.6
Brown County, OH..................	44,687	44,846	42,285	34,966	-159	2,561	-0.4	6.1	19.7	36.4	29.0	14.8
Butler County, OH	369,999	368,130	332,807	291,479	1,869	35,323	0.5	10.6	20.7	40.6	26.8	11.8
Clermont County, OH	199,139	197,363	177,977	150,094	1,776	19,386	0.9	10.9	20.9	37.7	29.1	12.3
Hamilton County, OH...............	800,362	802,374	845,303	866,228	-2,012	-42,929	-0.3	-5.1	19.5	40.0	27.2	13.3
Warren County, OH	214,910	212,693	158,383	113,973	2,217	54,310	1.0	34.3	22.4	38.6	27.9	11.1
Clarksville, TN–KY..................	277,701	273,949	232,000	189,279	3,752	41,949	1.4	18.1	23.3	45.3	21.7	9.7
Christian County, KY	73,591	73,955	72,265	68,941	-364	1,690	-0.5	2.3	24.7	45.0	19.7	10.6
Trigg County, KY	14,305	14,339	12,597	10,361	-34	1,742	-0.2	13.8	18.0	32.3	30.1	19.6
Montgomery County, TN..........	176,619	172,331	134,768	100,498	4,288	37,563	2.5	27.9	23.6	47.3	21.1	8.0
Stewart County, TN	13,186	13,324	12,370	9,479	-138	954	-1.0	7.7	18.0	34.4	30.6	17.0
Cleveland, TN	116,834	115,788	104,015	87,355	1,046	11,773	0.9	11.3	18.8	39.2	27.1	14.9
Bradley County, TN	100,055	98,963	87,965	73,712	1,092	10,998	1.1	12.5	19.0	39.9	26.7	14.4
Polk County, TN	16,779	16,825	16,050	13,643	-46	775	-0.3	4.8	18.0	35.2	29.4	17.5
Cleveland–Elyria–Mentor, OH.....................	2,068,283	2,077,240	2,148,143	2,102,207	-8,957	-70,903	-0.4	-3.3	18.5	37.0	29.1	15.4
Cuyahoga County, OH	1,270,294	1,280,122	1,393,978	1,412,140	-9,828	-113,856	-0.8	-8.2	18.1	37.7	28.5	15.6
Geauga County, OH	93,228	93,389	90,895	81,087	-161	2,494	-0.2	2.7	20.0	31.7	32.1	16.1
Lake County, OH	229,885	230,041	227,511	215,500	-156	2,530	-0.1	1.1	17.8	35.5	30.4	16.3
Lorain County, OH	301,614	301,356	284,664	271,126	258	16,692	0.1	5.9	19.1	37.1	29.2	14.6
Medina County, OH	173,262	172,332	151,095	122,354	930	21,237	0.5	14.1	20.1	36.2	30.1	13.5
Coeur d'Alene, ID	141,132	138,494	108,685	69,795	2,638	29,809	1.9	27.4	20.1	37.3	27.7	14.9
Kootenai County, ID	141,132	138,494	108,685	69,795	2,638	29,809	1.9	27.4	20.1	37.3	27.7	14.9
College Station–Bryan, TX	231,623	228,660	184,885	150,998	2,963	43,775	1.3	23.7	17.6	55.5	18.1	8.9
Brazos County, TX	197,632	194,851	152,415	121,862	2,781	42,436	1.4	27.8	17.2	59.2	16.2	7.4
Burleson County, TX	17,251	17,187	16,470	13,625	64	717	0.4	4.4	19.4	33.1	29.9	17.7
Robertson County, TX	16,740	16,622	16,000	15,511	118	622	0.7	3.9	20.9	35.1	27.3	16.7
Colorado Springs, CO	660,319	645,613	537,484	409,482	14,706	108,129	2.3	20.1	21.2	42.2	26.2	10.3
El Paso County, CO	636,963	622,263	516,929	397,014	14,700	105,334	2.4	20.4	21.4	42.7	25.7	10.2
Teller County, CO...................	23,356	23,350	20,555	12,468	6	2,795	0.0	13.6	15.8	29.7	40.5	14.0
Columbia, MO	175,831	172,786	145,666	122,010	3,045	27,120	1.8	18.6	17.5	50.3	22.5	9.7
Boone County, MO	165,627	162,642	135,454	112,379	2,985	27,188	1.8	20.1	17.4	51.1	22.1	9.4
Howard County, MO................	10,204	10,144	10,212	9,631	60	-68	0.6	-0.7	18.0	38.1	28.3	15.6
Columbia, SC	777,116	767,598	647,158	548,935	9,518	120,440	1.2	18.6	19.3	42.5	26.4	11.7
Calhoun County, SC	15,145	15,175	15,185	12,753	-30	-10	-0.2	-0.1	17.8	33.8	31.6	16.8
Fairfield County, SC................	23,571	23,956	23,454	22,295	-385	502	-1.6	2.1	18.1	34.2	32.0	15.6
Kershaw County, SC................	62,273	61,697	52,647	43,599	576	9,050	0.9	17.2	20.2	35.9	29.4	14.5
Lexington County, SC..............	267,129	262,391	216,014	167,526	4,738	46,377	1.8	21.5	20.1	39.6	27.7	12.6
Richland County, SC	389,116	384,504	320,677	286,321	4,612	63,827	1.2	19.9	18.8	46.8	24.4	10.0
Saluda County, SC..................	19,882	19,875	19,181	16,441	7	694	0.0	3.6	19.3	37.2	27.0	16.6
Columbus, GA–AL...................	301,439	294,865	281,768	266,452	6,574	13,097	2.2	4.6	20.9	42.5	24.9	11.8
Russell County, AL	54,572	52,947	49,756	46,860	1,625	3,191	3.1	6.4	20.5	41.1	25.9	12.6
Chattahoochee County, GA.......	11,749	11,267	14,882	16,934	482	-3,615	4.3	-24.3	23.1	63.4	9.8	3.7
Harris County, GA	32,265	32,024	23,695	17,788	241	8,329	0.8	35.2	18.5	35.1	32.6	13.7
Marion County, GA	8,746	8,742	7,144	5,590	4	1,598	0.0	22.4	19.6	34.5	30.9	15.0
Muscogee County, GA..............	194,107	189,885	186,291	179,280	4,222	3,594	2.2	1.9	21.3	43.2	24.0	11.5
Columbus, IN	77,870	76,794	71,435	63,657	1,076	5,359	1.4	7.5	20.5	38.7	26.6	14.2
Bartholomew County, IN	77,870	76,794	71,435	63,657	1,076	5,359	1.4	7.5	20.5	38.7	26.6	14.2

[1] The April 1, 2000, Population Estimates base reflects modifications to the Census 2000 population as documented in the Count Question Resolution program and geographic program revisions.
[2] The April 1, 1990, census counts include corrections processed through August 1997, results of special censuses and test censuses, and do not include adjustments for census coverage errors.
[3] Based on the April 1, 2010, estimates base and the July 1, 2011, estimates.
[4] Based on the April 1, 2010, complete count and the April 1, 2000 estimates base.
0 = Represents zero or amounts to zero.

Table C-1.   Population and Population Characteristics—*Continued*

Metropolitan statistical area, division, and component county	Population				Net change		Percent change		Percent			
	2011 (July 1)	2010 Census (April 1)	2000[1] (estimates base)	1990[2] (April 1)	2010–2011[3]	2000–2010[4]	2010–2011[3]	2000–2010[4]	Under 15 years, 2011	15 to 44 years, 2011	45 to 64 years, 2011	65 years and over, 2011
Columbus, OH	1,858,464	1,836,536	1,612,694	1,405,178	21,928	223,842	1.2	13.9	20.5	43.0	25.7	10.8
Delaware County, OH	178,341	174,214	109,989	66,929	4,127	64,225	2.4	58.4	24.1	38.5	27.5	9.9
Fairfield County, OH	147,066	146,156	122,759	103,468	910	23,397	0.6	19.1	21.0	38.5	27.9	12.6
Franklin County, OH	1,178,799	1,163,414	1,068,978	961,437	15,385	94,436	1.3	8.8	20.1	45.5	24.4	10.1
Licking County, OH	167,248	166,492	145,491	128,300	756	21,001	0.5	14.4	20.1	37.6	28.7	13.6
Madison County, OH	43,401	43,435	40,213	37,078	-34	3,222	-0.1	8.0	18.0	41.1	28.3	12.6
Morrow County, OH	34,855	34,827	31,628	27,749	28	3,199	0.1	10.1	20.5	36.3	29.3	13.8
Pickaway County, OH	55,990	55,698	52,727	48,248	292	2,971	0.5	5.6	18.8	40.4	27.6	13.1
Union County, OH	52,764	52,300	40,909	31,969	464	11,391	0.9	27.8	22.3	41.6	26.5	9.7
Corpus Christi, TX	431,381	428,185	403,280	367,786	3,196	24,905	0.7	6.2	21.3	39.5	26.0	13.1
Aransas County, TX	23,374	23,158	22,497	17,892	216	661	0.9	2.9	15.8	29.0	30.3	24.9
Nueces County, TX	343,281	340,223	313,645	291,145	3,058	26,578	0.9	8.5	21.4	40.5	25.8	12.3
San Patricio County, TX	64,726	64,804	67,138	58,749	-78	-2,334	-0.1	-3.5	23.0	37.9	25.7	13.4
Corvallis, OR	85,928	85,579	78,153	70,811	349	7,426	0.4	9.5	13.9	49.2	24.6	12.3
Benton County, OR	85,928	85,579	78,153	70,811	349	7,426	0.4	9.5	13.9	49.2	24.6	12.3
Crestview–Fort Walton Beach–Destin, FL	183,482	180,822	170,498	143,777	2,660	10,324	1.5	6.1	18.3	39.9	27.6	14.2
Okaloosa County, FL	183,482	180,822	170,498	143,777	2,660	10,324	1.5	6.1	18.3	39.9	27.6	14.2
Cumberland, MD–WV	102,884	103,299	102,008	101,643	-415	1,291	-0.4	1.3	15.1	39.4	27.6	18.0
Allegany County, MD	74,692	75,087	74,930	74,946	-395	157	-0.5	0.2	14.5	40.6	26.9	18.0
Mineral County, WV	28,192	28,212	27,078	26,697	-20	1,134	-0.1	4.2	16.8	36.2	29.3	17.7
Dallas–Fort Worth–Arlington, TX	6,526,548	6,371,773	5,161,544	3,989,294	154,775	1,210,229	2.4	23.4	23.2	43.4	24.3	9.0
Dallas–Plano–Irving, TX	4,345,790	4,235,751	3,451,226	2,622,562	110,039	784,525	2.6	22.7	23.3	44.0	24.0	8.7
Collin County, TX	812,226	782,341	491,675	264,036	29,885	290,666	3.8	59.1	23.8	42.9	25.3	8.1
Dallas County, TX	2,416,014	2,368,139	2,218,899	1,852,691	47,875	149,240	2.0	6.7	23.3	44.7	23.1	8.9
Delta County, TX	5,212	5,231	5,327	4,857	-19	-96	-0.4	-1.8	17.7	32.8	28.9	20.6
Denton County, TX	686,406	662,614	432,976	273,644	23,792	229,638	3.6	53.0	23.0	45.7	24.0	7.4
Ellis County, TX	152,753	149,610	111,360	85,167	3,143	38,250	2.1	34.3	23.4	40.1	26.1	10.4
Hunt County, TX	86,531	86,129	76,596	64,343	402	9,533	0.5	12.4	20.6	38.2	27.1	14.1
Kaufman County, TX	105,358	103,350	71,313	52,220	2,008	32,037	1.9	44.9	23.8	39.8	25.9	10.5
Rockwall County, TX	81,290	78,337	43,080	25,604	2,953	35,257	3.8	81.8	24.0	39.6	26.3	10.0
Fort Worth–Arlington, TX	2,180,758	2,136,022	1,710,318	1,366,732	44,736	425,704	2.1	24.9	23.1	42.3	25.0	9.6
Johnson County, TX	152,734	150,934	126,811	97,165	1,800	24,123	1.2	19.0	22.4	39.1	26.6	11.9
Parker County, TX	118,376	116,927	88,495	64,785	1,449	28,432	1.2	32.1	20.3	37.5	29.5	12.7
Tarrant County, TX	1,849,815	1,809,034	1,446,219	1,170,103	40,781	362,815	2.3	25.1	23.4	43.0	24.5	9.1
Wise County, TX	59,833	59,127	48,793	34,679	706	10,334	1.2	21.2	21.4	37.6	28.3	12.7
Dalton, GA	142,741	142,227	120,031	98,609	514	22,196	0.4	18.5	23.2	41.0	24.3	11.5
Murray County, GA	39,557	39,628	36,506	26,147	-71	3,122	-0.2	8.6	22.0	40.5	26.1	11.4
Whitfield County, GA	103,184	102,599	83,525	72,462	585	19,074	0.6	22.8	23.7	41.2	23.6	11.5
Danville, IL	81,509	81,625	83,919	88,257	-116	-2,294	-0.1	-2.7	20.1	35.9	27.6	16.4
Vermilion County, IL	81,509	81,625	83,919	88,257	-116	-2,294	-0.1	-2.7	20.1	35.9	27.6	16.4
Danville, VA	105,696	106,561	110,156	108,728	-865	-3,595	-0.8	-3.3	17.5	33.8	30.4	18.3
Pittsylvania County, VA	62,844	63,506	61,745	55,672	-662	1,761	-1.0	2.9	17.0	33.3	32.0	17.7
Danville city, VA	42,852	43,055	48,411	53,056	-203	-5,356	-0.5	-11.1	18.2	34.7	28.0	19.2
Davenport–Moline–Rock Island, IA–IL	381,342	379,690	376,019	368,145	1,652	3,671	0.4	1.0	19.4	37.3	28.0	15.2
Henry County, IL	50,328	50,486	51,020	51,159	-158	-534	-0.3	-1.0	19.0	34.5	29.2	17.4
Mercer County, IL	16,363	16,434	16,957	17,290	-71	-523	-0.4	-3.1	18.5	32.7	30.3	18.5
Rock Island County, IL	147,556	147,546	149,374	148,723	10	-1,828	0.0	-1.2	18.7	37.0	27.9	16.4
Scott County, IA	167,095	165,224	158,668	150,973	1,871	6,556	1.1	4.1	20.3	39.0	27.5	13.2
Dayton, OH	845,388	841,502	848,153	843,837	3,886	-6,651	0.5	-0.8	18.6	38.3	27.7	15.4
Greene County, OH	162,846	161,573	147,886	136,731	1,273	13,687	0.8	9.3	17.3	41.9	27.0	13.9
Miami County, OH	102,857	102,506	98,868	93,184	351	3,638	0.3	3.7	19.5	35.9	28.9	15.7
Montgomery County, OH	537,602	535,153	559,062	573,809	2,449	-23,909	0.5	-4.3	18.8	37.9	27.5	15.8
Preble County, OH	42,083	42,270	42,337	40,113	-187	-67	-0.4	-0.2	19.7	35.2	29.6	15.5
Decatur, AL	154,070	153,829	145,867	131,556	241	7,962	0.2	5.5	19.4	37.9	28.1	14.5
Lawrence County, AL	34,117	34,339	34,803	31,513	-222	-464	-0.6	-1.3	18.6	37.0	29.3	15.2
Morgan County, AL	119,953	119,490	111,064	100,043	463	8,426	0.4	7.6	19.7	38.2	27.8	14.3
Decatur, IL	110,730	110,768	114,706	117,206	-38	-3,938	0.0	-3.4	18.8	36.4	28.3	16.5
Macon County, IL	110,730	110,768	114,706	117,206	-38	-3,938	0.0	-3.4	18.8	36.4	28.3	16.5
Deltona–Daytona Beach–Ormond Beach, FL	494,804	494,593	443,343	370,737	211	51,250	0.0	11.6	15.2	33.8	29.5	21.5
Volusia County, FL	494,804	494,593	443,343	370,737	211	51,250	0.0	11.6	15.2	33.8	29.5	21.5
Denver–Aurora–Broomfield, CO[5]	2,599,504	2,543,482	2,179,240	1,650,489	56,022	364,242	2.2	16.7	20.8	42.6	26.3	10.3
Adams County, CO[5]	451,443	441,603	348,618	265,038	9,840	92,985	2.2	26.7	24.3	44.2	22.9	8.5
Arapahoe County, CO	584,948	572,003	487,967	391,572	12,945	84,036	2.3	17.2	21.0	42.0	26.7	10.4
Broomfield County, CO[5]	57,352	55,889	38,272	0	1,463	17,617	2.6	46.0	20.9	43.2	25.5	10.4
Clear Creek County, CO	9,012	9,088	9,322	7,619	-76	-234	-0.8	-2.5	13.7	32.6	40.4	13.3
Denver County, CO	619,968	600,158	554,636	467,549	19,810	45,522	3.3	8.2	18.9	48.6	22.3	10.3
Douglas County, CO	292,167	285,465	175,766	60,391	6,702	109,699	2.3	62.4	25.0	39.5	27.8	7.8
Elbert County, CO	23,174	23,086	19,872	9,646	88	3,214	0.4	16.2	19.0	31.9	38.6	10.4
Gilpin County, CO	5,467	5,441	4,757	3,070	26	684	0.5	14.4	14.6	33.7	41.5	10.2
Jefferson County, CO[5]	539,884	534,543	525,507	438,430	5,341	9,036	1.0	1.7	17.9	38.0	31.0	13.1
Park County, CO	16,089	16,206	14,523	7,174	-117	1,683	-0.7	11.6	14.7	30.0	42.5	12.8

[1] The April 1, 2000, Population Estimates base reflects modifications to the Census 2000 population as documented in the Count Question Resolution program and geographic program revisions.
[2] The April 1, 1990, census counts include corrections processed through August 1997, results of special censuses and test censuses, and do not include adjustments for census coverage errors.
[3] Based on the April 1, 2010, estimates base and the July 1, 2011, estimates.
[4] Based on the April 1, 2010, complete count and the April 1, 2000 estimates base.
[5] The Denver–Aurora metropolitan statistical area includes Broomfield County. Broomfield County, CO, was formed from parts of Adams, Boulder, Jefferson, and Weld Counties on November 15, 2001, and is coextensive with Broomfield city. For the purposes of defining and presenting data for the Denver–Aurora metropolitan statistical area, Broomfield city is treated as if it were a county when data are available to do so. In many cases, the data were not available.
0 = Represents zero or amounts to zero.

Table C-1. Population and Population Characteristics—*Continued*

Metropolitan statistical area, division, and component county	Population				Net change		Percent change		Percent			
	2011 (July 1)	2010 Census (April 1)	2000¹ (estimates base)	1990² (April 1)	2010–2011³	2000–2010⁴	2010–2011³	2000–2010⁴	Under 15 years, 2011	15 to 44 years, 2011	45 to 64 years, 2011	65 years and over, 2011
Des Moines–West Des Moines, IA	580,255	569,633	481,394	416,346	10,622	88,239	1.9	18.3	21.9	41.5	25.3	11.3
Dallas County, IA	69,444	66,135	40,750	29,755	3,309	25,385	5.0	62.3	24.9	41.8	23.5	9.8
Guthrie County, IA	10,901	10,954	11,353	10,935	-53	-399	-0.5	-3.5	19.0	30.5	30.5	20.0
Madison County, IA	15,779	15,679	14,019	12,483	100	1,660	0.6	11.8	22.6	34.3	28.3	14.8
Polk County, IA	437,399	430,640	374,601	327,140	6,759	56,039	1.6	15.0	21.5	42.4	25.1	11.0
Warren County, IA	46,732	46,225	40,671	36,033	507	5,554	1.1	13.7	21.0	37.9	27.4	13.7
Detroit–Warren–Livonia, MI	4,285,832	4,296,250	4,452,557	4,248,699	-10,418	-156,307	-0.2	-3.5	19.4	38.5	28.7	13.5
Detroit–Livonia–Dearborn, MI	1,802,096	1,820,584	2,061,162	2,111,687	-18,488	-240,578	-1.0	-11.7	20.3	39.7	27.2	12.8
Wayne County, MI	1,802,096	1,820,584	2,061,162	2,111,687	-18,488	-240,578	-1.0	-11.7	20.3	39.7	27.2	12.8
Warren–Troy–Farmington Hills, MI	2,483,736	2,475,666	2,391,395	2,137,012	8,070	84,271	0.3	3.5	18.7	37.6	29.7	13.9
Lapeer County, MI	88,082	88,319	87,904	74,768	-237	415	-0.3	0.5	18.7	35.5	31.9	13.9
Livingston County, MI	181,722	180,967	156,951	115,645	755	24,016	0.4	15.3	19.8	35.7	31.9	12.5
Macomb County, MI	842,145	840,978	788,149	717,400	1,167	52,829	0.1	6.7	18.5	38.3	28.7	14.5
Oakland County, MI	1,210,145	1,202,362	1,194,156	1,083,592	7,783	8,206	0.6	0.7	18.7	37.8	29.9	13.6
St. Clair County, MI	161,642	163,040	164,235	145,607	-1,398	-1,195	-0.9	-0.7	18.7	35.7	30.6	15.0
Dothan, AL	146,562	145,639	130,861	120,352	923	14,778	0.6	11.3	19.7	36.9	27.6	15.8
Geneva County, AL	26,781	26,790	25,764	23,647	-9	1,026	0.0	4.0	18.0	35.2	28.9	17.8
Henry County, AL	17,412	17,302	16,310	15,374	110	992	0.6	6.1	18.5	34.3	29.2	18.1
Houston County, AL	102,369	101,547	88,787	81,331	822	12,760	0.8	14.4	20.3	37.8	27.0	14.8
Dover, DE	164,834	162,310	126,697	110,993	2,524	35,613	1.6	28.1	20.4	39.8	25.9	13.9
Kent County, DE	164,834	162,310	126,697	110,993	2,524	35,613	1.6	28.1	20.4	39.8	25.9	13.9
Dubuque, IA	94,648	93,653	89,143	86,403	995	4,510	1.1	5.1	19.4	38.0	27.3	15.3
Dubuque County, IA	94,648	93,653	89,143	86,403	995	4,510	1.1	5.1	19.4	38.0	27.3	15.3
Duluth, MN–WI	279,815	279,771	275,486	269,249	44	4,285	0.0	1.6	16.6	38.3	29.4	15.7
Carlton County, MN	35,455	35,386	31,671	29,259	69	3,715	0.2	11.7	19.1	36.4	29.4	15.0
St. Louis County, MN	200,255	200,226	200,528	198,232	29	-302	0.0	-0.2	16.0	38.6	29.4	16.0
Douglas County, WI	44,105	44,159	43,287	41,758	-54	872	-0.1	2.0	17.6	38.1	29.7	14.6
Durham–Chapel Hill, NC	512,979	504,357	426,493	344,665	8,622	77,864	1.7	18.3	18.5	44.5	25.4	11.6
Chatham County, NC	64,195	63,505	49,329	38,979	690	14,176	1.1	28.7	18.1	32.8	30.1	18.9
Durham County, NC	273,392	267,587	223,314	181,844	5,805	44,273	2.2	19.8	19.4	47.1	23.5	10.0
Orange County, NC	135,755	133,801	118,227	93,662	1,954	15,574	1.5	13.2	16.8	47.5	25.6	10.1
Person County, NC	39,637	39,464	35,623	30,180	173	3,841	0.4	10.8	18.7	35.5	30.2	15.6
Eau Claire, WI	162,657	161,151	148,337	137,543	1,506	12,814	0.9	8.6	17.9	42.2	26.4	13.5
Chippewa County, WI	62,778	62,415	55,195	52,360	363	7,220	0.6	13.1	19.3	36.9	29.3	14.5
Eau Claire County, WI	99,879	98,736	93,142	85,183	1,143	5,594	1.2	6.0	17.1	45.5	24.6	12.9
El Centro, CA	177,057	174,528	142,361	109,303	2,529	32,167	1.4	22.6	23.8	43.1	22.5	10.6
Imperial County, CA	177,057	174,528	142,361	109,303	2,529	32,167	1.4	22.6	23.8	43.1	22.5	10.6
Elizabethtown, KY	121,771	119,736	107,547	100,919	2,035	12,189	1.7	11.3	21.0	40.7	26.7	11.7
Hardin County, KY	107,456	105,543	94,174	89,240	1,913	11,369	1.8	12.1	21.2	41.2	26.5	11.1
Larue County, KY	14,315	14,193	13,373	11,679	122	820	0.9	6.1	19.4	36.6	28.2	15.9
Elkhart–Goshen, IN	198,941	197,559	182,791	156,198	1,382	14,768	0.7	8.1	23.8	39.1	24.7	12.4
Elkhart County, IN	198,941	197,559	182,791	156,198	1,382	14,768	0.7	8.1	23.8	39.1	24.7	12.4
Elmira, NY	88,840	88,830	91,070	95,195	10	-2,240	0.0	-2.5	18.2	37.1	29.0	15.7
Chemung County, NY	88,840	88,830	91,070	95,195	10	-2,240	0.0	-2.5	18.2	37.1	29.0	15.7
El Paso, TX	820,790	800,647	679,622	591,610	20,143	121,025	2.5	17.8	24.6	43.1	22.0	10.3
El Paso County, TX	820,790	800,647	679,622	591,610	20,143	121,025	2.5	17.8	24.6	43.1	22.0	10.3
Erie, PA	280,985	280,566	280,843	275,575	419	-277	0.1	-0.1	18.3	39.4	27.7	14.6
Erie County, PA	280,985	280,566	280,843	275,575	419	-277	0.1	-0.1	18.3	39.4	27.7	14.6
Eugene–Springfield, OR	353,416	351,715	322,959	282,912	1,701	28,756	0.5	8.9	15.9	41.0	27.6	15.4
Lane County, OR	353,416	351,715	322,959	282,912	1,701	28,756	0.5	8.9	15.9	41.0	27.6	15.4
Evansville, IN–KY	359,879	358,676	342,815	324,858	1,203	15,861	0.3	4.6	19.2	38.1	28.2	14.5
Gibson County, IN	33,505	33,503	32,500	31,913	2	1,003	0.0	3.1	19.5	36.6	28.4	15.5
Posey County, IN	25,720	25,910	27,061	25,968	-190	-1,151	-0.7	-4.3	18.6	35.0	31.7	14.7
Vanderburgh County, IN	180,305	179,703	171,922	165,058	602	7,781	0.3	4.5	18.5	40.0	27.1	14.4
Warrick County, IN	60,275	59,689	52,383	44,920	586	7,306	1.0	13.9	20.9	35.8	29.4	13.9
Henderson County, KY	46,406	46,250	44,829	43,044	156	1,421	0.3	3.2	19.6	37.2	29.0	14.3
Webster County, KY	13,668	13,621	14,120	13,955	47	-499	0.3	-3.5	19.5	36.8	28.4	15.3
Fairbanks, AK	99,192	97,581	82,840	77,720	1,611	14,741	1.7	17.8	21.5	46.8	24.9	6.8
Fairbanks North Star Borough, AK	99,192	97,581	82,840	77,720	1,611	14,741	1.7	17.8	21.5	46.8	24.9	6.8
Fargo, ND–MN	212,171	208,777	174,367	153,296	3,394	34,410	1.6	19.7	18.5	48.0	23.0	10.5
Clay County, MN	59,803	58,999	51,229	50,422	804	7,770	1.4	15.2	19.3	45.9	22.8	11.9
Cass County, ND	152,368	149,778	123,138	102,874	2,590	26,640	1.7	21.6	18.2	48.9	23.0	9.9
Farmington, NM	128,200	130,044	113,801	91,605	-1,844	16,243	-1.4	14.3	24.2	39.6	25.0	11.3
San Juan County, NM	128,200	130,044	113,801	91,605	-1,844	16,243	-1.4	14.3	24.2	39.6	25.0	11.3
Fayetteville, NC	374,157	366,383	336,609	297,569	7,774	29,774	2.1	8.8	23.0	45.3	22.4	9.3
Cumberland County, NC	324,885	319,431	302,963	274,713	5,454	16,468	1.7	5.4	22.5	45.4	22.5	9.6
Hoke County, NC	49,272	46,952	33,646	22,856	2,320	13,306	4.9	39.5	26.0	45.1	21.5	7.3
Fayetteville–Springdale–Rogers, AR–MO	473,830	463,204	347,045	239,495	10,626	116,159	2.3	33.5	22.4	43.2	22.9	11.4
Benton County, AR	227,556	221,339	153,406	97,530	6,217	67,933	2.8	44.3	23.4	41.0	23.2	12.3
Madison County, AR	15,776	15,717	14,243	11,618	59	1,474	0.4	10.3	19.4	35.0	29.5	16.1
Washington County, AR	207,521	203,065	157,715	113,409	4,456	45,350	2.2	28.8	21.5	46.9	21.7	9.9
McDonald County, MO	22,977	23,083	21,681	16,938	-106	1,402	-0.5	6.5	22.9	37.6	26.4	13.1
Flagstaff, AZ	134,511	134,421	116,320	96,591	90	18,101	0.1	15.6	19.2	47.1	24.4	9.3
Coconino County, AZ	134,511	134,421	116,320	96,591	90	18,101	0.1	15.6	19.2	47.1	24.4	9.3

¹ The April 1, 2000, Population Estimates base reflects modifications to the Census 2000 population as documented in the Count Question Resolution program and geographic program revisions.
² The April 1, 1990, census counts include corrections processed through August 1997, results of special censuses and test censuses, and do not include adjustments for census coverage errors.
³ Based on the April 1, 2010, estimates base and the July 1, 2011, estimates.
⁴ Based on the April 1, 2010, complete count and the April 1, 2000 estimates base.
0 = Represents zero or amounts to zero.

Table C-1. Population and Population Characteristics—_Continued_

Metropolitan statistical area, division, and component county	Population				Net change		Percent change		Percent			
	2011 (July 1)	2010 Census (April 1)	2000[1] (estimates base)	1990[2] (April 1)	2010–2011[3]	2000–2010[4]	2010–2011[3]	2000–2010[4]	Under 15 years, 2011	15 to 44 years, 2011	45 to 64 years, 2011	65 years and over, 2011
Flint, MI	422,080	425,790	436,141	430,459	-3,710	-10,351	-0.9	-2.4	20.1	37.9	27.9	14.1
Genesee County, MI	422,080	425,790	436,141	430,459	-3,710	-10,351	-0.9	-2.4	20.1	37.9	27.9	14.1
Florence, SC	206,161	205,566	193,155	176,195	595	12,411	0.3	6.4	20.2	38.2	27.6	14.0
Darlington County, SC	68,299	68,681	67,394	61,851	-382	1,287	-0.6	1.9	19.6	36.7	28.8	14.8
Florence County, SC	137,862	136,885	125,761	114,344	977	11,124	0.7	8.8	20.4	39.0	27.0	13.6
Florence–Muscle Shoals, AL	147,293	147,137	142,950	131,327	156	4,187	0.1	2.9	17.6	37.1	28.0	17.3
Colbert County, AL	54,512	54,428	54,984	51,666	84	-556	0.2	-1.0	17.9	35.9	28.6	17.6
Lauderdale County, AL	92,781	92,709	87,966	79,661	72	4,743	0.1	5.4	17.4	37.8	27.7	17.1
Fond du Lac, WI	102,079	101,633	97,296	90,083	446	4,337	0.4	4.5	18.5	37.5	28.7	15.4
Fond du Lac County, WI	102,079	101,633	97,296	90,083	446	4,337	0.4	4.5	18.5	37.5	28.7	15.4
Fort Collins–Loveland, CO	305,525	299,630	251,494	186,136	5,895	48,136	2.0	19.1	17.3	44.1	26.3	12.3
Larimer County, CO	305,525	299,630	251,494	186,136	5,895	48,136	2.0	19.1	17.3	44.1	26.3	12.3
Fort Smith, AR–OK	300,087	298,592	273,170	234,078	1,495	25,422	0.5	9.3	21.0	38.0	26.7	14.3
Crawford County, AR	61,944	61,948	53,247	42,493	-4	8,701	0.0	16.3	21.4	37.7	27.2	13.7
Franklin County, AR	18,047	18,125	17,771	14,897	-78	354	-0.4	2.0	19.9	36.0	27.1	17.0
Sebastian County, AR	127,127	125,744	115,071	99,590	1,383	10,673	1.1	9.3	21.1	39.4	26.2	13.3
Le Flore County, OK	50,628	50,384	48,109	43,270	244	2,275	0.5	4.7	20.6	36.9	26.9	15.7
Sequoyah County, OK	42,341	42,391	38,972	33,828	-50	3,419	-0.1	8.8	21.1	36.6	27.0	15.3
Fort Wayne, IN	419,453	416,257	390,156	354,435	3,196	26,101	0.8	6.7	21.9	39.3	26.3	12.5
Allen County, IN	358,327	355,329	331,849	300,836	2,998	23,480	0.8	7.1	22.3	39.9	25.8	12.0
Wells County, IN	27,734	27,636	27,600	25,948	98	36	0.4	0.1	20.0	35.4	28.7	16.0
Whitley County, IN	33,392	33,292	30,707	27,651	100	2,585	0.3	8.4	19.7	36.1	29.8	14.4
Fresno, CA	942,904	930,450	799,407	667,479	12,454	131,043	1.3	16.4	24.5	43.1	22.1	10.3
Fresno County, CA	942,904	930,450	799,407	667,479	12,454	131,043	1.3	16.4	24.5	43.1	22.1	10.3
Gadsden, AL	104,303	104,430	103,459	99,840	-127	971	-0.1	0.9	18.7	37.4	28.0	15.9
Etowah County, AL	104,303	104,430	103,459	99,840	-127	971	-0.1	0.9	18.7	37.4	28.0	15.9
Gainesville, FL	266,369	264,275	232,392	191,263	2,094	31,883	0.8	13.7	14.7	51.2	22.6	11.5
Alachua County, FL	249,365	247,336	217,955	181,596	2,029	29,381	0.8	13.5	14.5	52.1	22.2	11.1
Gilchrist County, FL	17,004	16,939	14,437	9,667	65	2,502	0.4	17.3	17.2	37.3	27.8	17.7
Gainesville, GA	183,052	179,684	139,277	95,434	3,368	40,407	1.9	29.0	23.3	41.2	24.0	11.5
Hall County, GA	183,052	179,684	139,277	95,434	3,368	40,407	1.9	29.0	23.3	41.2	24.0	11.5
Glens Falls, NY	128,996	128,923	124,345	118,539	73	4,578	0.1	3.7	16.4	36.0	30.9	16.7
Warren County, NY	65,831	65,707	63,303	59,209	124	2,404	0.2	3.8	16.1	34.6	31.8	17.5
Washington County, NY	63,165	63,216	61,042	59,330	-51	2,174	-0.1	3.6	16.7	37.6	30.0	15.8
Goldsboro, NC	123,697	122,623	113,329	104,666	1,074	9,294	0.9	8.2	20.6	39.7	26.3	13.3
Wayne County, NC	123,697	122,623	113,329	104,666	1,074	9,294	0.9	8.2	20.6	39.7	26.3	13.3
Grand Forks, ND–MN	98,054	98,461	97,478	103,272	-407	983	-0.4	1.0	17.3	45.8	24.5	12.5
Polk County, MN	31,456	31,600	31,369	32,589	-144	231	-0.5	0.7	19.1	36.7	27.8	16.4
Grand Forks County, ND	66,598	66,861	66,109	70,683	-263	752	-0.4	1.1	16.4	50.1	23.0	10.6
Grand Junction, CO	147,083	146,723	116,255	93,145	360	30,468	0.2	26.2	19.5	38.2	27.1	15.2
Mesa County, CO	147,083	146,723	116,255	93,145	360	30,468	0.2	26.2	19.5	38.2	27.1	15.2
Grand Rapids–Wyoming, MI	779,604	774,160	740,482	645,918	5,444	33,678	0.7	4.5	21.2	40.6	26.4	11.9
Barry County, MI	58,820	59,173	56,755	50,057	-353	2,418	-0.6	4.3	19.4	34.7	30.9	15.0
Ionia County, MI	63,979	63,905	61,518	57,024	74	2,387	0.1	3.9	19.8	41.2	27.4	11.7
Kent County, MI	608,453	602,622	574,335	500,631	5,831	28,287	1.0	4.9	21.6	41.5	25.6	11.3
Newaygo County, MI	48,352	48,460	47,874	38,206	-108	586	-0.2	1.2	19.8	34.7	29.6	15.9
Great Falls, MT	81,837	81,327	80,357	77,691	510	970	0.6	1.2	18.9	38.1	27.3	15.7
Cascade County, MT	81,837	81,327	80,357	77,691	510	970	0.6	1.2	18.9	38.1	27.3	15.7
Greeley, CO	258,638	252,825	180,926	131,821	5,813	71,899	2.3	39.7	23.3	42.5	24.2	9.9
Weld County, CO	258,638	252,825	180,926	131,821	5,813	71,899	2.3	39.7	23.3	42.5	24.2	9.9
Green Bay, WI	309,469	306,241	282,599	243,698	3,228	23,642	1.1	8.4	20.1	39.3	27.8	12.7
Brown County, WI	251,412	248,007	226,778	194,594	3,405	21,229	1.4	9.4	20.6	40.6	26.9	11.9
Kewaunee County, WI	20,589	20,574	20,187	18,878	15	387	0.1	1.9	18.9	34.3	29.9	17.0
Oconto County, WI	37,468	37,660	35,634	30,226	-192	2,026	-0.5	5.7	17.8	33.5	32.6	16.2
Greensboro–High Point, NC	730,966	723,801	643,430	540,041	7,165	80,371	1.0	12.5	19.2	40.5	26.8	13.4
Guilford County, NC	495,279	488,406	421,048	347,431	6,873	67,358	1.4	16.0	19.2	42.3	25.9	12.5
Randolph County, NC	142,358	141,752	130,454	106,546	606	11,298	0.4	8.7	20.2	37.5	27.9	14.5
Rockingham County, NC	93,329	93,643	91,928	86,064	-314	1,715	-0.3	1.9	17.8	35.4	30.2	16.7
Greenville, NC	192,690	189,510	152,772	123,864	3,180	36,738	1.7	24.0	18.8	47.6	23.3	10.3
Greene County, NC	21,556	21,362	18,974	15,384	194	2,388	0.9	12.6	19.3	40.4	27.8	12.4
Pitt County, NC	171,134	168,148	133,798	108,480	2,986	34,350	1.8	25.7	18.8	48.5	22.7	10.1
Greenville–Mauldin–Easley, SC	647,401	636,986	559,940	472,155	10,415	77,046	1.6	13.8	19.4	40.9	26.3	13.4
Greenville County, SC	461,299	451,225	379,616	320,127	10,074	71,609	2.2	18.9	20.3	40.4	26.3	13.0
Laurens County, SC	66,528	66,537	69,567	58,132	-9	-3,030	0.0	-4.4	19.0	37.2	28.4	15.4
Pickens County, SC	119,574	119,224	110,757	93,896	350	8,467	0.3	7.6	16.5	44.9	24.8	13.8
Gulfport–Biloxi, MS	253,511	248,820	246,190	207,875	4,691	2,630	1.9	1.1	20.2	40.5	26.7	12.5
Hancock County, MS	44,649	43,929	42,967	31,760	720	962	1.6	2.2	19.3	35.8	29.4	15.5
Harrison County, MS	191,040	187,105	189,601	165,365	3,935	-2,496	2.1	-1.3	20.5	41.5	26.1	11.8
Stone County, MS	17,822	17,786	13,622	10,750	36	4,164	0.2	30.6	19.7	41.0	26.7	12.6

[1] The April 1, 2000, Population Estimates base reflects modifications to the Census 2000 population as documented in the Count Question Resolution program and geographic program revisions.
[2] The April 1, 1990, census counts include corrections processed through August 1997, results of special censuses and test censuses, and do not include adjustments for census coverage errors.
[3] Based on the April 1, 2010, estimates base and the July 1, 2011, estimates.
[4] Based on the April 1, 2010, complete count and the April 1, 2000 estimates base.
0 = Represents zero or amounts to zero.

Table C-1.   Population and Population Characteristics—*Continued*

Metropolitan statistical area, division, and component county	Population 2011 (July 1)	Population 2010 Census (April 1)	Population 2000[1] (estimates base)	Population 1990[2] (April 1)	Net change 2010–2011[3]	Net change 2000–2010[4]	Percent change 2010–2011[3]	Percent change 2000–2010[4]	Percent Under 15 years, 2011	Percent 15 to 44 years, 2011	Percent 45 to 64 years, 2011	Percent 65 years and over, 2011
Hagerstown–Martinsburg, MD–WV	271,488	269,140	222,771	192,774	2,348	46,369	0.9	20.8	19.3	38.7	28.3	13.7
Washington County, MD	148,203	147,430	131,923	121,393	773	15,507	0.5	11.8	18.7	38.8	28.1	14.4
Berkeley County, WV	105,750	104,169	75,905	59,253	1,581	28,264	1.5	37.2	20.7	39.6	28.0	11.7
Morgan County, WV	17,535	17,541	14,943	12,128	-6	2,598	0.0	17.4	16.2	32.7	32.1	19.0
Hanford–Corcoran, CA	153,765	152,982	129,461	101,469	783	23,521	0.5	18.2	23.3	46.9	21.8	8.0
Kings County, CA	153,765	152,982	129,461	101,469	783	23,521	0.5	18.2	23.3	46.9	21.8	8.0
Harrisburg–Carlisle, PA	552,911	549,475	509,074	474,242	3,436	40,401	0.6	7.9	17.8	38.6	28.8	14.8
Cumberland County, PA	237,892	235,406	213,674	195,257	2,486	21,732	1.1	10.2	16.6	39.3	28.3	15.8
Dauphin County, PA	268,977	268,100	251,798	237,813	877	16,302	0.3	6.5	18.7	38.4	28.9	14.0
Perry County, PA	46,042	45,969	43,602	41,172	73	2,367	0.2	5.4	18.4	36.5	30.8	14.4
Harrisonburg, VA	126,562	125,228	108,193	88,189	1,334	17,035	1.1	15.7	16.7	47.5	22.8	12.9
Rockingham County, VA	76,589	76,314	67,725	57,482	275	8,589	0.4	12.7	19.2	36.4	28.5	15.8
Harrisonburg city, VA	49,973	48,914	40,468	30,707	1,059	8,446	2.2	20.9	12.9	64.5	14.1	8.5
Hartford–West Hartford–East Hartford, CT	1,213,255	1,212,381	1,148,618	1,123,678	874	63,763	0.1	5.6	17.8	38.7	29.0	14.6
Hartford County, CT	894,705	894,014	857,183	851,783	691	36,831	0.1	4.3	18.3	38.5	28.5	14.7
Middlesex County, CT	166,043	165,676	155,071	143,196	367	10,605	0.2	6.8	16.8	35.6	31.8	15.9
Tolland County, CT	152,507	152,691	136,364	128,699	-184	16,327	-0.1	12.0	15.8	43.1	28.9	12.3
Hattiesburg, MS	145,428	142,842	123,812	109,603	2,586	19,030	1.8	15.4	20.6	44.8	22.9	11.6
Forrest County, MS	75,842	74,934	72,604	68,314	908	2,330	1.2	3.2	19.8	46.8	21.8	11.6
Lamar County, MS	57,422	55,658	39,070	30,424	1,764	16,588	3.2	42.5	21.9	43.8	23.2	11.1
Perry County, MS	12,164	12,250	12,138	10,865	-86	112	-0.7	0.9	20.2	37.4	28.1	14.3
Hickory–Lenoir–Morganton, NC	364,567	365,497	341,851	292,405	-930	23,646	-0.3	6.9	18.5	37.2	28.8	15.5
Alexander County, NC	37,087	37,198	33,603	27,544	-111	3,595	-0.3	10.7	18.2	36.9	29.1	15.8
Burke County, NC	90,904	90,912	89,148	75,740	-8	1,764	0.0	2.0	17.7	37.0	28.8	16.4
Caldwell County, NC	82,395	83,029	77,415	70,709	-634	5,614	-0.8	7.3	18.0	36.6	29.4	16.0
Catawba County, NC	154,181	154,358	141,685	118,412	-177	12,673	-0.1	8.9	19.3	37.8	28.3	14.6
Hinesville–Fort Stewart, GA	80,587	77,917	71,914	58,947	2,670	6,003	3.4	8.3	26.1	47.2	20.3	6.5
Liberty County, GA	65,451	63,453	61,610	52,745	1,998	1,843	3.1	3.0	26.3	47.7	19.7	6.4
Long County, GA	15,136	14,464	10,304	6,202	672	4,160	4.6	40.4	25.3	45.0	22.7	7.0
Holland–Grand Haven, MI	266,300	263,801	238,314	187,768	2,499	25,487	0.9	10.7	21.1	41.3	25.5	12.1
Ottawa County, MI	266,300	263,801	238,314	187,768	2,499	25,487	0.9	10.7	21.1	41.3	25.5	12.1
Honolulu, HI	963,607	953,207	876,156	836,231	10,400	77,051	1.1	8.8	18.3	41.3	25.5	14.8
Honolulu County, Hawaii	963,607	953,207	876,156	836,231	10,400	77,051	1.1	8.8	18.3	41.3	25.5	14.8
Hot Springs, AR	97,124	96,024	88,068	73,397	1,100	7,956	1.1	9.0	17.1	33.5	28.3	21.1
Garland County, AR	97,124	96,024	88,068	73,397	1,100	7,956	1.1	9.0	17.1	33.5	28.3	21.1
Houma–Bayou Cane–Thibodaux, LA	208,583	208,178	194,477	182,842	405	13,701	0.2	7.0	20.9	40.6	26.5	12.1
Lafourche Parish, LA	96,666	96,318	89,974	85,860	348	6,344	0.4	7.1	20.2	40.5	26.6	12.7
Terrebonne Parish, LA	111,917	111,860	104,503	96,982	57	7,357	0.1	7.0	21.6	40.6	26.3	11.5
Houston–Sugar Land–Baytown, TX	6,086,538	5,946,800	4,715,407	3,767,218	139,738	1,231,393	2.3	26.1	23.3	43.4	24.5	8.9
Austin County, TX	28,665	28,417	23,590	19,832	248	4,827	0.9	20.5	20.2	34.7	29.2	15.8
Brazoria County, TX	319,973	313,166	241,767	191,707	6,807	71,399	2.2	29.5	23.1	41.4	25.6	9.9
Chambers County, TX	35,552	35,096	26,031	20,088	456	9,065	1.3	34.8	23.1	40.1	27.1	9.7
Fort Bend County, TX	606,953	585,375	354,452	225,421	21,578	230,923	3.7	65.1	24.0	41.2	27.0	7.7
Galveston County, TX	295,747	291,309	250,158	217,396	4,438	41,151	1.5	16.5	21.0	39.3	28.2	11.5
Harris County, TX	4,180,894	4,092,459	3,400,578	2,818,101	88,435	691,881	2.2	20.3	23.5	44.8	23.3	8.4
Liberty County, TX	76,206	75,643	70,154	52,726	563	5,489	0.7	7.8	21.0	40.6	26.9	11.5
Montgomery County, TX	471,734	455,746	293,768	182,201	15,988	161,978	3.5	55.1	22.7	39.7	26.8	10.8
San Jacinto County, TX	26,801	26,384	22,246	16,372	417	4,138	1.6	18.6	19.6	32.9	30.1	17.4
Waller County, TX	44,013	43,205	32,663	23,374	808	10,542	1.9	32.3	20.8	43.8	25.0	10.4
Huntington–Ashland, WV–KY–OH	287,599	287,702	288,649	288,189	-103	-947	0.0	-0.3	17.6	38.1	27.8	16.4
Boyd County, KY	49,466	49,542	49,752	51,096	-76	-210	-0.2	-0.4	17.6	36.5	29.1	16.8
Greenup County, KY	36,865	36,910	36,891	36,796	-45	19	-0.1	0.1	18.1	35.4	29.1	17.4
Lawrence County, OH	62,489	62,450	62,319	61,834	39	131	0.1	0.2	19.0	37.2	28.1	15.7
Cabell County, WV	96,653	96,319	96,784	96,827	334	-465	0.3	-0.5	16.5	41.4	26.2	15.9
Wayne County, WV	42,126	42,481	42,903	41,636	-355	-422	-0.8	-1.0	18.1	36.4	28.5	17.0
Huntsville, AL	425,480	417,593	342,376	293,047	7,887	75,217	1.9	22.0	19.2	40.5	27.9	12.4
Limestone County, AL	85,369	82,782	65,676	54,135	2,587	17,106	3.1	26.0	19.6	39.8	28.0	12.5
Madison County, AL	340,111	334,811	276,700	238,912	5,300	58,111	1.6	21.0	19.1	40.6	27.8	12.4
Idaho Falls, ID	132,073	130,374	101,677	88,750	1,699	28,697	1.3	28.2	27.3	38.9	22.9	10.9
Bonneville County, ID	105,772	104,234	82,522	72,207	1,538	21,712	1.5	26.3	26.7	39.1	23.1	11.1
Jefferson County, ID	26,301	26,140	19,155	16,543	161	6,985	0.6	36.5	30.0	38.3	22.0	9.8
Indianapolis–Carmel, IN	1,778,568	1,756,241	1,525,104	1,294,217	22,327	231,137	1.3	15.2	21.7	41.2	26.1	11.0
Boone County, IN	57,481	56,640	46,107	38,147	841	10,533	1.5	22.8	22.7	36.9	28.9	11.4
Brown County, IN	15,099	15,242	14,957	14,080	-143	285	-0.9	1.9	16.1	30.4	35.6	18.0
Hamilton County, IN	282,810	274,569	182,740	108,936	8,241	91,829	3.0	50.3	24.8	40.3	26.0	8.9
Hancock County, IN	70,529	70,002	55,391	45,527	527	14,611	0.8	26.4	21.0	37.0	29.0	13.1
Hendricks County, IN	147,979	145,448	104,093	75,717	2,531	41,355	1.7	39.7	22.3	39.9	26.8	11.0
Johnson County, IN	141,656	139,654	115,209	88,109	2,002	24,445	1.4	21.2	21.5	39.6	26.3	12.5
Marion County, IN	911,296	903,393	860,454	797,159	7,903	42,939	0.9	5.0	21.2	43.2	24.9	10.7
Morgan County, IN	69,464	68,894	66,689	55,920	570	2,205	0.8	3.3	20.0	36.7	29.8	13.5
Putnam County, IN	37,917	37,963	36,019	30,315	-46	1,944	-0.1	5.4	16.5	42.5	27.2	13.8
Shelby County, IN	44,337	44,436	43,445	40,307	-99	991	-0.2	2.3	19.7	36.7	29.6	14.1

[1] The April 1, 2000, Population Estimates base reflects modifications to the Census 2000 population as documented in the Count Question Resolution program and geographic program revisions.
[2] The April 1, 1990, census counts include corrections processed through August 1997, results of special censuses and test censuses, and do not include adjustments for census coverage errors.
[3] Based on the April 1, 2010, estimates base and the July 1, 2011, estimates.
[4] Based on the April 1, 2010, complete count and the April 1, 2000 estimates base.
0 = Represents zero or amounts to zero.

Table C-1. Population and Population Characteristics—*Continued*

Metropolitan statistical area, division, and component county	Population 2011 (July 1)	Population 2010 Census (April 1)	Population 2000¹ (estimates base)	Population 1990² (April 1)	Net change 2010–2011³	Net change 2000–2010⁴	Percent change 2010–2011³	Percent change 2000–2010⁴	Percent Under 15 years, 2011	Percent 15 to 44 years, 2011	Percent 45 to 64 years, 2011	Percent 65 years and over, 2011
Iowa City, IA	154,893	152,586	131,676	115,731	2,307	20,910	1.5	15.9	17.1	50.6	22.3	10.0
Johnson County, IA	133,038	130,882	111,006	96,119	2,156	19,876	1.6	17.9	16.6	53.3	21.3	8.8
Washington County, IA	21,855	21,704	20,670	19,612	151	1,034	0.7	5.0	20.4	33.7	28.4	17.5
Ithaca, NY	101,723	101,564	96,501	94,097	159	5,063	0.2	5.2	12.4	54.3	22.3	11.1
Tompkins County, NY	101,723	101,564	96,501	94,097	159	5,063	0.2	5.2	12.4	54.3	22.3	11.1
Jackson, MI	159,748	160,248	158,422	149,756	-500	1,826	-0.3	1.2	18.6	38.1	28.8	14.5
Jackson County, MI	159,748	160,248	158,422	149,756	-500	1,826	-0.3	1.2	18.6	38.1	28.8	14.5
Jackson, MS	545,394	539,057	497,197	446,941	6,337	41,860	1.2	8.4	21.4	41.5	25.7	11.4
Copiah County, MS	29,247	29,449	28,757	27,592	-202	692	-0.7	2.4	20.7	38.1	27.1	14.1
Hinds County, MS	248,184	245,285	250,800	254,441	2,899	-5,515	1.2	-2.2	21.5	42.9	24.8	10.9
Madison County, MS	96,941	95,203	74,674	53,794	1,738	20,529	1.8	27.5	22.1	40.2	27.0	10.7
Rankin County, MS	143,702	141,617	115,327	87,161	2,085	26,290	1.5	22.8	20.8	41.5	25.9	11.8
Simpson County, MS	27,320	27,503	27,639	23,953	-183	-136	-0.7	-0.5	21.7	36.7	27.2	14.3
Jackson, TN	115,396	115,425	107,377	90,801	-29	8,048	0.0	7.5	19.6	40.2	26.5	13.7
Chester County, TN	17,141	17,131	15,540	12,819	10	1,591	0.1	10.2	18.5	41.8	25.0	14.7
Madison County, TN	98,255	98,294	91,837	77,982	-39	6,457	0.0	7.0	19.8	40.0	26.8	13.5
Jacksonville, FL	1,360,251	1,345,596	1,122,750	925,213	14,655	222,846	1.1	19.8	19.5	40.4	27.6	12.5
Baker County, FL	27,154	27,115	22,259	18,486	39	4,856	0.1	21.8	21.5	40.6	26.4	11.5
Clay County, FL	192,370	190,865	140,814	105,986	1,505	50,051	0.8	35.5	20.7	38.9	28.2	12.3
Duval County, FL	870,709	864,263	778,879	672,971	6,446	85,384	0.7	11.0	19.6	42.4	26.6	11.4
Nassau County, FL	74,195	73,314	57,663	43,941	881	15,651	1.2	27.1	17.5	34.5	30.9	17.1
St. Johns County, FL	195,823	190,039	123,135	83,829	5,784	66,904	3.0	54.3	18.4	35.1	30.4	16.1
Jacksonville, NC	179,719	177,772	150,355	149,838	1,947	27,417	1.1	18.2	22.1	52.9	17.4	7.6
Onslow County, NC	179,719	177,772	150,355	149,838	1,947	27,417	1.1	18.2	22.1	52.9	17.4	7.6
Janesville, WI	160,092	160,331	152,307	139,510	-239	8,024	-0.1	5.3	20.2	38.6	27.3	13.8
Rock County, WI	160,092	160,331	152,307	139,510	-239	8,024	-0.1	5.3	20.2	38.6	27.3	13.8
Jefferson City, MO	150,480	149,807	140,052	120,704	673	9,755	0.4	7.0	19.3	39.9	27.9	12.9
Callaway County, MO	44,420	44,332	40,766	32,809	88	3,566	0.2	8.7	18.1	41.0	28.3	12.6
Cole County, MO	76,448	75,990	71,397	63,579	458	4,593	0.6	6.4	19.5	40.1	28.0	12.5
Moniteau County, MO	15,697	15,607	14,827	12,298	90	780	0.6	5.3	20.9	38.7	26.6	13.8
Osage County, MO	13,915	13,878	13,062	12,018	37	816	0.3	6.2	20.3	37.2	27.3	15.2
Johnson City, TN	199,818	198,716	181,607	160,390	1,102	17,109	0.6	9.4	16.5	38.8	28.2	16.6
Carter County, TN	57,185	57,424	56,742	51,505	-239	682	-0.4	1.2	16.4	36.9	29.3	17.4
Unicoi County, TN	18,280	18,313	17,667	16,549	-33	646	-0.2	3.7	16.6	33.3	30.1	19.9
Washington County, TN	124,353	122,979	107,198	92,336	1,374	15,781	1.1	14.7	16.5	40.4	27.4	15.7
Johnstown, PA	143,728	143,679	152,598	163,062	49	-8,919	0.0	-5.8	15.7	35.8	29.8	18.7
Cambria County, PA	143,728	143,679	152,598	163,062	49	-8,919	0.0	-5.8	15.7	35.8	29.8	18.7
Jonesboro, AR	122,829	121,026	107,762	93,620	1,803	13,264	1.5	12.3	20.8	42.2	24.0	13.0
Craighead County, AR	98,315	96,443	82,148	68,956	1,872	14,295	1.9	17.4	21.0	43.6	23.2	12.2
Poinsett County, AR	24,514	24,583	25,614	24,664	-69	-1,031	-0.3	-4.0	20.0	36.5	27.3	16.2
Joplin, MO	176,849	175,518	157,322	134,910	1,331	18,196	0.8	11.6	21.3	39.0	25.5	14.2
Jasper County, MO	118,435	117,404	104,686	90,465	1,031	12,718	0.9	12.1	21.6	40.3	24.6	13.6
Newton County, MO	58,414	58,114	52,636	44,445	300	5,478	0.5	10.4	20.8	36.5	27.3	15.4
Kalamazoo–Portage, MI	328,205	326,589	314,866	293,471	1,616	11,723	0.5	3.7	18.9	42.4	25.8	12.8
Kalamazoo County, MI	252,074	250,331	238,603	223,411	1,743	11,728	0.7	4.9	18.5	44.4	24.7	12.4
Van Buren County, MI	76,131	76,258	76,263	70,060	-127	-5	-0.2	0.0	20.4	35.9	29.5	14.2
Kankakee–Bradley, IL	113,698	113,449	103,833	96,255	249	9,616	0.2	9.3	20.7	39.4	26.2	13.7
Kankakee County, IL	113,698	113,449	103,833	96,255	249	9,616	0.2	9.3	20.7	39.4	26.2	13.7
Kansas City, MO–KS	2,052,676	2,035,334	1,836,038	1,636,527	17,342	199,296	0.9	10.9	21.2	39.8	26.8	12.2
Franklin County, KS	25,931	25,992	24,784	21,994	-61	1,208	-0.2	4.9	21.1	36.7	27.9	14.3
Johnson County, KS	552,991	544,179	451,086	355,021	8,812	93,093	1.6	20.6	21.7	40.1	26.9	11.2
Leavenworth County, KS	77,176	76,227	68,691	64,371	949	7,536	1.2	11.0	20.6	40.3	27.8	11.4
Linn County, KS	9,612	9,656	9,570	8,254	-44	86	-0.5	0.9	18.8	31.3	30.2	19.6
Miami County, KS	32,715	32,787	28,351	23,466	-72	4,436	-0.2	15.6	21.6	35.3	29.7	13.5
Wyandotte County, KS	158,224	157,505	157,882	162,026	719	-377	0.5	-0.2	24.0	41.2	24.1	10.7
Bates County, MO	17,008	17,049	16,653	15,025	-41	396	-0.2	2.4	20.2	33.9	28.1	17.8
Caldwell County, MO	9,315	9,424	8,969	8,380	-109	455	-1.2	5.1	20.2	33.6	28.9	17.3
Cass County, MO	100,052	99,478	82,092	63,808	574	17,386	0.6	21.2	21.5	37.3	27.2	14.0
Clay County, MO	225,161	221,939	184,006	153,411	3,222	37,933	1.5	20.6	21.3	40.8	26.4	11.5
Clinton County, MO	20,789	20,743	18,979	16,595	46	1,764	0.2	9.3	20.0	34.9	28.9	16.2
Jackson County, MO	676,360	674,158	654,880	633,234	2,202	19,278	0.3	2.9	20.6	40.4	26.4	12.6
Lafayette County, MO	33,209	33,381	32,960	31,107	-172	421	-0.5	1.3	19.6	35.5	28.3	16.7
Platte County, MO	90,903	89,322	73,781	57,867	1,581	15,541	1.8	21.1	19.9	39.4	29.1	11.6
Ray County, MO	23,230	23,494	23,354	21,968	-264	140	-1.1	0.6	20.1	35.4	29.6	14.9
Kennewick–Pasco–Richland, WA	264,133	253,340	191,822	150,033	10,793	61,518	4.3	32.1	24.5	40.9	24.2	10.5
Benton County, WA	180,678	175,177	142,475	112,560	5,501	32,702	3.1	23.0	22.2	39.3	26.6	11.9
Franklin County, WA	83,455	78,163	49,347	37,473	5,292	28,816	6.8	58.4	29.3	44.3	19.1	7.3

¹ The April 1, 2000, Population Estimates base reflects modifications to the Census 2000 population as documented in the Count Question Resolution program and geographic program revisions.
² The April 1, 1990, census counts include corrections processed through August 1997, results of special censuses and test censuses, and do not include adjustments for census coverage errors.
³ Based on the April 1, 2010, estimates base and the July 1, 2011, estimates.
⁴ Based on the April 1, 2010, complete count and the April 1, 2000 estimates base.
0 = Represents zero or amounts to zero.

Table C-1.   Population and Population Characteristics—*Continued*

Metropolitan statistical area, division, and component county	Population 2011 (July 1)	Population 2010 Census (April 1)	Population 2000¹ (estimates base)	Population 1990² (April 1)	Net change 2010–2011³	Net change 2000–2010⁴	Percent change 2010–2011³	Percent change 2000–2010⁴	Percent Under 15 years, 2011	Percent 15 to 44 years, 2011	Percent 45 to 64 years, 2011	Percent 65 years and over, 2011
Killeen–Temple–Fort Hood, TX	411,595	405,300	330,714	268,820	6,295	74,586	1.6	22.6	23.9	46.1	21.1	9.0
Bell County, TX	315,196	310,235	237,974	191,073	4,961	72,261	1.6	30.4	24.2	46.0	21.0	8.9
Coryell County, TX	76,508	75,388	74,978	64,226	1,120	410	1.5	0.5	23.7	49.2	19.5	7.7
Lampasas County, TX	19,891	19,677	17,762	13,521	214	1,915	1.1	10.8	19.6	35.5	28.8	16.1
Kingsport–Bristol–Bristol, TN–VA	309,793	309,544	298,484	275,678	249	11,060	0.1	3.7	16.6	35.1	29.7	18.6
Hawkins County, TN	56,671	56,833	53,563	44,565	-162	3,270	-0.3	6.1	17.9	35.4	29.6	17.1
Sullivan County, TN	157,419	156,823	153,048	143,596	596	3,775	0.4	2.5	16.5	34.8	29.6	19.0
Scott County, VA	23,126	23,177	23,403	23,204	-51	-226	-0.2	-1.0	15.5	34.0	29.6	20.8
Washington County, VA	54,827	54,876	51,103	45,887	-49	3,773	-0.1	7.4	15.9	35.3	30.7	18.1
Bristol city, VA	17,750	17,835	17,367	18,426	-85	468	-0.5	2.7	17.0	37.2	27.0	18.8
Kingston, NY	182,448	182,493	177,749	165,380	-45	4,744	0.0	2.7	15.7	37.9	31.1	15.3
Ulster County, NY	182,448	182,493	177,749	165,380	-45	4,744	0.0	2.7	15.7	37.9	31.1	15.3
Knoxville, TN	704,500	698,030	616,079	534,910	6,470	81,951	0.9	13.3	17.8	39.6	27.6	15.0
Anderson County, TN	75,233	75,129	71,330	68,250	104	3,799	0.1	5.3	17.6	35.1	29.7	17.6
Blount County, TN	123,901	123,010	105,823	85,962	891	17,187	0.7	16.2	17.8	36.4	29.2	16.6
Knox County, TN	436,929	432,226	382,032	335,749	4,703	50,194	1.1	13.1	18.0	42.3	26.5	13.3
Loudon County, TN	49,237	48,556	39,086	31,255	681	9,470	1.4	24.2	16.4	31.5	29.7	22.4
Union County, TN	19,200	19,109	17,808	13,694	91	1,301	0.5	7.3	19.6	36.8	29.4	14.3
Kokomo, IN	98,588	98,688	101,541	96,946	-100	-2,853	-0.1	-2.8	18.9	35.5	28.7	16.9
Howard County, IN	82,800	82,752	84,964	80,827	48	-2,212	0.1	-2.6	19.1	35.7	28.5	16.7
Tipton County, IN	15,788	15,936	16,577	16,119	-148	-641	-0.9	-3.9	17.9	34.8	29.7	17.6
La Crosse, WI–MN	134,488	133,665	126,838	116,401	823	6,827	0.6	5.4	17.4	42.1	26.4	14.1
Houston County, MN	18,916	19,027	19,718	18,497	-111	-691	-0.6	-3.5	17.9	33.0	31.2	17.9
La Crosse County, WI	115,572	114,638	107,120	97,904	934	7,518	0.8	7.0	17.4	43.6	25.6	13.5
Lafayette, IN	203,608	201,789	178,541	158,848	1,819	23,248	0.9	13.0	17.6	50.7	21.3	10.5
Benton County, IN	8,853	8,854	9,421	9,441	-1	-567	0.0	-6.0	20.9	35.5	28.0	15.6
Carroll County, IN	20,031	20,155	20,165	18,809	-124	-10	-0.6	0.0	19.3	35.1	29.5	16.1
Tippecanoe County, IN	174,724	172,780	148,955	130,598	1,944	23,825	1.1	16.0	17.2	53.2	20.0	9.6
Lafayette, LA	277,307	273,738	239,086	208,859	3,569	34,652	1.3	14.5	20.6	43.1	25.6	10.7
Lafayette Parish, LA	224,390	221,578	190,503	164,762	2,812	31,075	1.3	16.3	20.3	44.1	25.2	10.4
St. Martin Parish, LA	52,917	52,160	48,583	44,097	757	3,577	1.5	7.4	21.7	39.1	27.2	12.0
Lake Charles, LA	200,822	199,607	193,568	177,394	1,215	6,039	0.6	3.1	20.9	39.7	26.6	12.8
Calcasieu Parish, LA	194,092	192,768	183,577	168,134	1,324	9,191	0.7	5.0	20.9	39.7	26.5	12.9
Cameron Parish, LA	6,730	6,839	9,991	9,260	-109	-3,152	-1.6	-31.5	20.1	37.1	30.4	12.4
Lake Havasu City–Kingman, AZ	202,351	200,186	155,032	93,497	2,165	45,154	1.1	29.1	16.7	29.4	30.0	24.0
Mohave County, AZ	202,351	200,186	155,032	93,497	2,165	45,154	1.1	29.1	16.7	29.4	30.0	24.0
Lakeland–Winter Haven, FL	609,492	602,095	483,924	405,382	7,397	118,171	1.2	24.4	19.3	36.7	25.7	18.3
Polk County, FL	609,492	602,095	483,924	405,382	7,397	118,171	1.2	24.4	19.3	36.7	25.7	18.3
Lancaster, PA	523,594	519,445	470,658	422,822	4,149	48,787	0.8	10.4	20.3	37.7	26.7	15.2
Lancaster County, PA	523,594	519,445	470,658	422,822	4,149	48,787	0.8	10.4	20.3	37.7	26.7	15.2
Lansing–East Lansing, MI	465,138	464,036	447,728	432,684	1,102	16,308	0.2	3.6	17.6	44.3	26.0	12.1
Clinton County, MI	75,469	75,382	64,753	57,893	87	10,629	0.1	16.4	19.6	38.4	28.8	13.3
Eaton County, MI	108,056	107,759	103,655	92,879	297	4,104	0.3	4.0	18.3	37.3	29.8	14.6
Ingham County, MI	281,613	280,895	279,320	281,912	718	1,575	0.3	0.6	16.8	48.6	23.8	10.8
Laredo, TX	256,496	250,304	193,117	133,239	6,192	57,187	2.5	29.6	29.2	44.2	18.7	8.0
Webb County, TX	256,496	250,304	193,117	133,239	6,192	57,187	2.5	29.6	29.2	44.2	18.7	8.0
Las Cruces, NM	213,598	209,233	174,682	135,510	4,365	34,551	2.1	19.8	22.0	42.0	23.4	12.6
Doña Ana County, NM	213,598	209,233	174,682	135,510	4,365	34,551	2.1	19.8	22.0	42.0	23.4	12.6
Las Vegas–Paradise, NV	1,969,975	1,951,269	1,375,765	741,368	18,706	575,504	1.0	41.8	20.8	42.7	24.8	11.7
Clark County, NV	1,969,975	1,951,269	1,375,765	741,368	18,706	575,504	1.0	41.8	20.8	42.7	24.8	11.7
Lawrence, KS	112,211	110,826	99,962	81,798	1,385	10,864	1.2	10.9	15.5	54.9	20.5	9.1
Douglas County, KS	112,211	110,826	99,962	81,798	1,385	10,864	1.2	10.9	15.5	54.9	20.5	9.1
Lawton, OK	125,815	124,098	114,996	111,486	1,717	9,102	1.4	7.9	21.2	46.2	22.4	10.2
Comanche County, OK	125,815	124,098	114,996	111,486	1,717	9,102	1.4	7.9	21.2	46.2	22.4	10.2
Lebanon, PA	134,311	133,568	120,327	113,744	743	13,241	0.6	11.0	18.9	35.9	28.0	17.2
Lebanon County, PA	134,311	133,568	120,327	113,744	743	13,241	0.6	11.0	18.9	35.9	28.0	17.2
Lewiston, ID–WA	61,476	60,888	57,961	51,359	588	2,927	1.0	5.0	17.9	35.7	27.9	18.5
Nez Perce County, ID	39,543	39,265	37,410	33,754	278	1,855	0.7	5.0	18.0	36.8	27.2	18.1
Asotin County, WA	21,933	21,623	20,551	17,605	310	1,072	1.4	5.2	17.7	33.8	29.1	19.4
Lewiston–Auburn, ME	107,398	107,702	103,793	105,259	-304	3,909	-0.3	3.8	18.5	38.2	29.0	14.3
Androscoggin County, ME	107,398	107,702	103,793	105,259	-304	3,909	-0.3	3.8	18.5	38.2	29.0	14.3
Lexington–Fayette, KY	479,244	472,099	408,326	348,428	7,145	63,773	1.5	15.6	18.9	44.3	25.5	11.3
Bourbon County, KY	19,998	19,985	19,360	19,236	13	625	0.1	3.2	19.6	36.0	29.0	15.4
Clark County, KY	35,537	35,613	33,144	29,496	-76	2,469	-0.2	7.4	19.2	37.1	29.1	14.7
Fayette County, KY	301,569	295,803	260,512	225,366	5,766	35,291	1.9	13.5	17.9	47.3	24.2	10.6
Jessamine County, KY	49,046	48,586	39,041	30,508	460	9,545	0.9	24.4	21.4	40.6	26.2	11.8
Scott County, KY	48,149	47,173	33,061	23,867	976	14,112	2.1	42.7	22.3	42.4	25.7	9.6
Woodford County, KY	24,945	24,939	23,208	19,955	6	1,731	0.0	7.5	19.1	35.6	31.8	13.5
Lima, OH	106,094	106,331	108,473	109,755	-237	-2,142	-0.2	-2.0	19.6	38.1	27.4	15.0
Allen County, OH	106,094	106,331	108,473	109,755	-237	-2,142	-0.2	-2.0	19.6	38.1	27.4	15.0
Lincoln, NE	306,503	302,157	266,787	229,091	4,346	35,370	1.4	13.3	19.4	45.2	24.0	11.3
Lancaster County, NE	289,800	285,407	250,291	213,641	4,393	35,116	1.5	14.0	19.5	45.6	23.9	11.1
Seward County, NE	16,703	16,750	16,496	15,450	-47	254	-0.3	1.5	18.9	39.2	26.7	15.3

¹ The April 1, 2000, Population Estimates base reflects modifications to the Census 2000 population as documented in the Count Question Resolution program and geographic program revisions.
² The April 1, 1990, census counts include corrections processed through August 1997, results of special censuses and test censuses, and do not include adjustments for census coverage errors.
³ Based on the April 1, 2010, estimates base and the July 1, 2011, estimates.
⁴ Based on the April 1, 2010, complete count and the April 1, 2000 estimates base.
0 = Represents zero or amounts to zero.

Table C-1.   Population and Population Characteristics—*Continued*

Metropolitan statistical area, division, and component county	Population				Net change		Percent change		Percent			
	2011 (July 1)	2010 Census (April 1)	2000[1] (estimates base)	1990[2] (April 1)	2010– 2011[3]	2000– 2010[4]	2010– 2011[3]	2000– 2010[4]	Under 15 years, 2011	15 to 44 years, 2011	45 to 64 years, 2011	65 years and over, 2011
Little Rock–North Little Rock–Conway, AR.....	709,901	699,757	610,518	534,943	10,144	89,239	1.4	14.6	20.4	41.4	25.9	12.3
Faulkner County, AR	116,342	113,237	86,014	60,006	3,105	27,223	2.7	31.6	20.3	46.7	22.9	10.2
Grant County, AR	17,988	17,853	16,464	13,948	135	1,389	0.8	8.4	19.7	37.3	28.2	14.8
Lonoke County, AR	69,341	68,356	52,828	39,268	985	15,528	1.4	29.4	22.5	41.1	25.1	11.4
Perry County, AR	10,405	10,445	10,209	7,969	-40	236	-0.4	2.3	18.1	35.5	28.9	17.5
Pulaski County, AR	386,299	382,748	361,474	349,569	3,551	21,274	0.9	5.9	20.3	41.1	26.5	12.2
Saline County, AR	109,526	107,118	83,529	64,183	2,408	23,589	2.2	28.2	20.2	38.2	26.6	15.0
Logan, UT–ID	127,549	125,442	102,720	79,415	2,107	22,722	1.7	22.1	26.8	48.0	16.8	8.4
Franklin County, ID	12,850	12,786	11,329	9,232	64	1,457	0.5	12.9	29.4	36.3	21.3	13.0
Cache County, UT	114,699	112,656	91,391	70,183	2,043	21,265	1.8	23.3	26.5	49.3	16.3	7.9
Longview, TX	216,666	214,369	194,042	180,053	2,297	20,327	1.1	10.5	20.8	39.0	26.1	14.2
Gregg County, TX	123,081	121,730	111,379	104,948	1,351	10,351	1.1	9.3	21.5	40.1	24.7	13.6
Rusk County, TX	53,759	53,330	47,372	43,735	429	5,958	0.8	12.6	19.4	39.2	27.3	14.1
Upshur County, TX	39,826	39,309	35,291	31,370	517	4,018	1.3	11.4	20.5	35.0	28.7	15.8
Longview, WA	102,478	102,410	92,948	82,119	68	9,462	0.1	10.2	19.7	35.7	28.6	16.0
Cowlitz County, WA	102,478	102,410	92,948	82,119	68	9,462	0.1	10.2	19.7	35.7	28.6	16.0
Los Angeles–Long Beach–Santa Ana, CA	12,944,801	12,828,837	12,365,627	11,273,720	115,964	463,210	0.9	3.7	19.7	44.2	24.8	11.3
Los Angeles–Long Beach–Glendale, CA..	9,889,056	9,818,605	9,519,338	8,863,052	70,451	299,267	0.7	3.1	19.6	44.7	24.6	11.1
Los Angeles County, CA	9,889,056	9,818,605	9,519,338	8,863,052	70,451	299,267	0.7	3.1	19.6	44.7	24.6	11.1
Santa Ana–Anaheim–Irvine, CA	3,055,745	3,010,232	2,846,289	2,410,668	45,513	163,943	1.5	5.8	19.7	42.6	25.7	11.9
Orange County, CA	3,055,745	3,010,232	2,846,289	2,410,668	45,513	163,943	1.5	5.8	19.7	42.6	25.7	11.9
Louisville/Jefferson County, KY–IN	1,294,849	1,283,566	1,161,975	1,056,156	11,283	121,591	0.9	10.5	19.7	39.3	28.0	13.0
Clark County, IN	111,570	110,232	96,472	87,774	1,338	13,760	1.2	14.3	19.7	39.7	27.7	12.9
Floyd County, IN	74,989	74,578	70,823	64,404	411	3,755	0.6	5.3	19.3	38.2	29.3	13.2
Harrison County, IN	39,336	39,364	34,325	29,890	-28	5,039	-0.1	14.7	19.0	36.7	30.0	14.3
Washington County, IN	28,147	28,262	27,223	23,717	-115	1,039	-0.4	3.8	20.0	37.3	29.0	13.7
Bullitt County, KY	75,109	74,319	61,236	47,567	790	13,083	1.1	21.4	20.1	39.5	28.8	11.6
Henry County, KY	15,443	15,416	15,060	12,823	27	356	0.2	2.4	20.0	35.8	29.5	14.7
Jefferson County, KY	746,906	741,096	693,604	665,123	5,810	47,492	0.8	6.8	19.3	39.8	27.5	13.5
Meade County, KY	29,562	28,602	26,349	24,170	960	2,253	3.4	8.6	22.6	40.9	26.0	10.5
Nelson County, KY	43,974	43,437	37,477	29,710	537	5,960	1.2	15.9	21.2	38.5	28.4	11.8
Oldham County, KY	60,642	60,316	46,178	33,263	326	14,138	0.5	30.6	21.9	37.9	30.6	9.7
Shelby County, KY	43,068	42,074	33,337	24,824	994	8,737	2.4	26.2	20.6	38.8	28.3	12.4
Spencer County, KY	17,378	17,061	11,766	6,801	317	5,295	1.9	45.0	20.8	38.5	29.7	10.9
Trimble County, KY	8,725	8,809	8,125	6,090	-84	684	-1.0	8.4	20.1	37.8	28.7	13.3
Lubbock, TX	290,002	284,890	249,700	229,940	5,112	35,190	1.8	14.1	20.6	46.2	22.0	11.2
Crosby County, TX	6,092	6,059	7,072	7,304	33	-1,013	0.5	-14.3	23.8	34.3	24.6	17.3
Lubbock County, TX	283,910	278,831	242,628	222,636	5,079	36,203	1.8	14.9	20.5	46.5	22.0	11.0
Lynchburg, VA	254,171	252,634	228,616	206,226	1,537	24,018	0.6	10.5	17.0	39.1	27.9	16.1
Amherst County, VA	32,167	32,353	31,894	28,578	-186	459	-0.6	1.4	16.7	36.4	29.7	17.2
Appomattox County, VA	15,041	14,973	13,705	12,300	68	1,268	0.5	9.3	18.0	34.6	29.5	17.9
Bedford County, VA	69,246	68,676	60,371	45,553	570	8,305	0.8	13.8	17.4	32.9	32.9	16.8
Campbell County, VA	55,032	54,842	51,078	47,499	190	3,764	0.3	7.4	17.2	37.7	29.0	16.1
Bedford city, VA	6,181	6,222	6,299	6,176	-41	-77	-0.7	-1.2	16.6	34.5	27.1	21.9
Lynchburg city, VA	76,504	75,568	65,269	66,120	936	10,299	1.2	15.8	16.4	48.1	21.5	14.1
Macon, GA	232,920	232,293	222,368	206,786	627	9,925	0.3	4.5	20.5	39.0	27.3	13.2
Bibb County, GA	156,433	155,547	153,887	150,137	886	1,660	0.6	1.1	21.3	40.1	25.8	12.8
Crawford County, GA	12,567	12,630	12,495	8,991	-63	135	-0.5	1.1	18.4	36.7	31.3	13.6
Jones County, GA	28,516	28,669	23,639	20,739	-153	5,030	-0.5	21.3	20.8	37.8	28.4	13.0
Monroe County, GA	26,625	26,424	21,757	17,113	201	4,667	0.8	21.5	18.0	36.8	31.0	14.3
Twiggs County, GA	8,779	9,023	10,590	9,806	-244	-1,567	-2.7	-14.8	16.8	32.9	33.3	17.0
Madera–Chowchilla, CA	152,925	150,865	123,109	88,090	2,060	27,756	1.4	22.5	23.4	41.6	23.4	11.6
Madera County, CA	152,925	150,865	123,109	88,090	2,060	27,756	1.4	22.5	23.4	41.6	23.4	11.6
Madison, WI	576,467	568,593	501,774	432,323	7,874	66,819	1.4	13.3	18.1	44.5	26.2	11.1
Columbia County, WI	56,909	56,833	52,468	45,088	76	4,365	0.1	8.3	18.9	36.1	30.1	14.9
Dane County, WI	495,959	488,073	426,526	367,085	7,886	61,547	1.6	14.4	17.9	46.0	25.6	10.5
Iowa County, WI	23,599	23,687	22,780	20,150	-88	907	-0.4	4.0	20.1	34.4	31.3	14.2
Manchester–Nashua, NH	401,696	400,721	380,841	335,838	975	19,880	0.2	5.2	18.7	39.2	29.9	12.2
Hillsborough County, NH	401,696	400,721	380,841	335,838	975	19,880	0.2	5.2	18.7	39.2	29.9	12.2
Manhattan, KS	130,240	127,081	108,999	113,720	3,159	18,082	2.5	16.6	20.3	54.4	17.2	8.2
Geary County, KS	35,323	34,362	27,947	30,453	961	6,415	2.8	23.0	27.0	48.0	17.6	7.5
Pottawatomie County, KS	21,920	21,604	18,209	16,128	316	3,395	1.5	18.6	24.4	37.6	25.9	12.2
Riley County, KS	72,997	71,115	62,843	67,139	1,882	8,272	2.6	13.2	15.8	62.5	14.4	7.3
Mankato–North Mankato, MN	97,204	96,740	85,712	82,120	464	11,028	0.5	12.9	16.9	47.8	23.2	12.1
Blue Earth County, MN	64,384	64,013	55,941	54,044	371	8,072	0.6	14.4	16.1	50.0	21.9	12.0
Nicollet County, MN	32,820	32,727	29,771	28,076	93	2,956	0.3	9.9	18.6	43.6	25.6	12.2
Mansfield, OH	123,510	124,475	128,852	126,137	-965	-4,377	-0.8	-3.4	18.2	36.7	28.6	16.6
Richland County, OH	123,510	124,475	128,852	126,137	-965	-4,377	-0.8	-3.4	18.2	36.7	28.6	16.6
McAllen–Edinburg–Mission, TX	797,810	774,769	569,463	383,545	23,041	205,306	3.0	36.1	29.0	43.2	18.3	9.5
Hidalgo County, TX	797,810	774,769	569,463	383,545	23,041	205,306	3.0	36.1	29.0	43.2	18.3	9.5
Medford, OR	204,822	203,206	181,269	146,387	1,616	21,937	0.8	12.1	17.7	35.2	28.9	18.1
Jackson County, OR	204,822	203,206	181,269	146,387	1,616	21,937	0.8	12.1	17.7	35.2	28.9	18.1

[1] The April 1, 2000, Population Estimates base reflects modifications to the Census 2000 population as documented in the Count Question Resolution program and geographic program revisions.
[2] The April 1, 1990, census counts include corrections processed through August 1997, results of special censuses and test censuses, and do not include adjustments for census coverage errors.
[3] Based on the April 1, 2010, estimates base and the July 1, 2011, estimates.
[4] Based on the April 1, 2010, complete count and the April 1, 2000 estimates base.

Table C-1. Population and Population Characteristics—*Continued*

Metropolitan statistical area, division, and component county	Population 2011 (July 1)	Population 2010 Census (April 1)	Population 2000[1] (estimates base)	Population 1990[2] (April 1)	Net change 2010–2011[3]	Net change 2000–2010[4]	Percent change 2010–2011[3]	Percent change 2000–2010[4]	Percent Under 15 years, 2011	Percent 15 to 44 years, 2011	Percent 45 to 64 years, 2011	Percent 65 years and over, 2011
Memphis, TN–MS–AR	1,325,605	1,316,100	1,205,204	1,067,263	9,505	110,896	0.7	9.2	21.6	41.5	26.0	10.8
Crittenden County, AR	50,525	50,902	50,866	49,939	-377	36	-0.7	0.1	23.7	39.5	25.6	11.1
DeSoto County, MS	164,053	161,252	107,199	67,910	2,801	54,053	1.7	50.4	23.0	41.7	24.8	10.5
Marshall County, MS	36,786	37,144	34,993	30,361	-358	2,151	-1.0	6.1	19.1	38.6	29.0	13.3
Tate County, MS	28,719	28,886	25,370	21,432	-167	3,516	-0.6	13.9	21.2	39.4	26.4	13.1
Tunica County, MS	10,628	10,778	9,227	8,164	-150	1,551	-1.4	16.8	25.7	40.5	24.1	9.8
Fayette County, TN	38,513	38,413	28,806	25,559	100	9,607	0.3	33.4	18.9	34.2	31.3	15.5
Shelby County, TN	935,088	927,644	897,472	826,330	7,444	30,172	0.8	3.4	21.5	42.2	25.9	10.4
Tipton County, TN	61,293	61,081	51,271	37,568	212	9,810	0.3	19.1	21.9	39.6	27.1	11.4
Merced, CA	259,898	255,793	210,554	178,403	4,105	45,239	1.6	21.5	25.7	43.5	21.2	9.6
Merced County, CA	259,898	255,793	210,554	178,403	4,105	45,239	1.6	21.5	25.7	43.5	21.2	9.6
Miami–Fort Lauderdale–Pompano Beach, FL	5,670,125	5,564,635	5,007,564	4,056,228	105,490	557,071	1.9	11.1	17.5	39.7	26.8	16.0
Fort Lauderdale–Pompano Beach– Deerfield Beach, FL	1,780,172	1,748,066	1,623,018	1,255,531	32,106	125,048	1.8	7.7	18.1	39.7	28.0	14.3
Broward County, FL	1,780,172	1,748,066	1,623,018	1,255,531	32,106	125,048	1.8	7.7	18.1	39.7	28.0	14.3
Miami–Miami Beach–Kendall, FL	2,554,766	2,496,435	2,253,362	1,937,194	58,331	243,073	2.3	10.8	17.6	42.2	26.0	14.2
Miami–Dade County, FL	2,554,766	2,496,435	2,253,362	1,937,194	58,331	243,073	2.3	10.8	17.6	42.2	26.0	14.2
West Palm Beach–Boca Raton– Boynton Beach, FL	1,335,187	1,320,134	1,131,184	863,503	15,053	188,950	1.1	16.7	16.6	35.1	26.6	21.8
Palm Beach County, FL	1,335,187	1,320,134	1,131,184	863,503	15,053	188,950	1.1	16.7	16.6	35.1	26.6	21.8
Michigan City–La Porte, IN	111,374	111,467	110,106	107,066	-93	1,361	-0.1	1.2	18.5	38.3	28.7	14.5
LaPorte County, IN	111,374	111,467	110,106	107,066	-93	1,361	-0.1	1.2	18.5	38.3	28.7	14.5
Midland, TX	140,308	136,872	116,009	106,611	3,436	20,863	2.5	18.0	23.0	41.1	25.0	10.9
Midland County, TX	140,308	136,872	116,009	106,611	3,436	20,863	2.5	18.0	23.0	41.1	25.0	10.9
Milwaukee–Waukesha–West Allis, WI	1,562,216	1,555,908	1,500,741	1,432,149	6,308	55,167	0.4	3.7	20.2	40.1	27.1	12.7
Milwaukee County, WI	952,532	947,735	940,164	959,212	4,797	7,571	0.5	0.8	20.9	43.4	24.3	11.4
Ozaukee County, WI	86,568	86,395	82,317	72,894	173	4,078	0.2	5.0	18.4	33.9	32.0	15.7
Washington County, WI	132,386	131,887	117,493	95,328	499	14,394	0.4	12.3	19.8	35.7	30.6	13.9
Waukesha County, WI	390,730	389,891	360,767	304,715	839	29,124	0.2	8.1	19.0	34.8	31.5	14.7
Minneapolis–St. Paul–Bloomington, MN–WI	3,318,486	3,279,833	2,968,806	2,538,776	38,653	311,027	1.2	10.5	20.5	41.4	27.1	11.0
Anoka County, MN	333,140	330,844	298,084	243,641	2,296	32,760	0.7	11.0	20.9	40.0	28.9	10.2
Carver County, MN	92,638	91,042	70,205	47,915	1,596	20,837	1.8	29.7	24.4	38.9	28.1	8.7
Chisago County, MN	53,916	53,887	41,101	30,521	29	12,786	0.1	31.1	20.4	38.1	29.2	12.4
Dakota County, MN	402,006	398,552	355,904	275,210	3,454	42,648	0.9	12.0	21.3	39.8	28.4	10.4
Hennepin County, MN	1,168,431	1,152,425	1,116,200	1,032,431	16,006	36,225	1.4	3.2	18.9	42.9	26.6	11.5
Isanti County, MN	38,283	37,816	31,287	25,921	467	6,529	1.2	20.9	21.1	38.0	28.0	12.9
Ramsey County, MN	514,696	508,640	511,035	485,760	6,056	-2,395	1.2	-0.5	19.4	42.9	25.5	12.2
Scott County, MN	132,556	129,928	89,498	57,846	2,628	40,430	2.0	45.2	25.1	41.4	25.5	8.0
Sherburne County, MN	89,319	88,499	64,417	41,945	820	24,082	0.9	37.4	23.8	42.4	25.2	8.6
Washington County, MN	241,280	238,136	201,130	145,860	3,144	37,006	1.3	18.4	21.3	38.1	29.5	11.0
Wright County, MN	126,437	124,700	89,986	68,710	1,737	34,714	1.4	38.6	25.0	40.1	24.9	10.0
Pierce County, WI	40,862	41,019	36,804	32,765	-157	4,215	-0.4	11.5	17.8	44.2	27.1	10.9
St. Croix County, WI	84,922	84,345	63,155	50,251	577	21,190	0.7	33.6	22.6	39.2	27.8	10.4
Missoula, MT	110,138	109,299	95,802	78,687	839	13,497	0.8	14.1	16.3	46.1	25.9	11.8
Missoula County, MT	110,138	109,299	95,802	78,687	839	13,497	0.8	14.1	16.3	46.1	25.9	11.8
Mobile, AL	412,577	412,992	399,843	378,643	-415	13,149	-0.1	3.3	20.5	39.5	26.7	13.2
Mobile County, AL	412,577	412,992	399,843	378,643	-415	13,149	-0.1	3.3	20.5	39.5	26.7	13.2
Modesto, CA	518,522	514,453	446,997	370,522	4,069	67,456	0.8	15.1	23.3	42.0	23.8	10.9
Stanislaus County, CA	518,522	514,453	446,997	370,522	4,069	67,456	0.8	15.1	23.3	42.0	23.8	10.9
Monroe, LA	177,651	176,441	170,053	162,987	1,210	6,388	0.7	3.8	21.4	40.4	25.1	13.1
Ouachita Parish, LA	154,919	153,720	147,250	142,191	1,199	6,470	0.8	4.4	21.8	41.2	24.5	12.5
Union Parish, LA	22,732	22,721	22,803	20,796	11	-82	0.0	-0.4	19.1	34.9	29.1	16.9
Monroe, MI	151,560	152,021	145,945	133,600	-461	6,076	-0.3	4.2	19.2	36.6	30.4	13.8
Monroe County, MI	151,560	152,021	145,945	133,600	-461	6,076	-0.3	4.2	19.2	36.6	30.4	13.8
Montgomery, AL	378,608	374,536	346,528	305,175	4,072	28,008	1.1	8.1	20.1	42.1	25.6	12.2
Autauga County, AL	55,267	54,571	43,671	34,222	696	10,900	1.3	25.0	21.5	40.2	26.0	12.3
Elmore County, AL	80,162	79,303	65,874	49,210	859	13,429	1.1	20.4	19.2	41.1	27.4	12.3
Lowndes County, AL	11,147	11,299	13,473	12,658	-152	-2,174	-1.3	-16.1	20.1	36.1	28.7	15.2
Montgomery County, AL	232,032	229,363	223,510	209,085	2,669	5,853	1.2	2.6	20.1	43.2	24.7	12.0
Morgantown, WV	132,251	129,709	111,200	104,546	2,542	18,509	2.0	16.6	13.9	50.8	23.7	11.7
Monongalia County, WV	98,528	96,189	81,866	75,509	2,339	14,323	2.4	17.5	13.2	55.2	21.5	10.2
Preston County, WV	33,723	33,520	29,334	29,037	203	4,186	0.6	14.3	15.9	37.9	30.1	16.2
Morristown, TN	137,494	136,608	123,081	100,591	886	13,527	0.6	11.0	18.7	37.0	27.9	16.4
Grainger County, TN	22,766	22,657	20,659	17,095	109	1,998	0.5	9.7	17.8	35.8	29.9	16.4
Hamblen County, TN	63,062	62,544	58,128	50,480	518	4,416	0.8	7.6	19.6	37.4	26.8	16.2
Jefferson County, TN	51,666	51,407	44,294	33,016	259	7,113	0.5	16.1	17.9	37.1	28.4	16.7
Mount Vernon–Anacortes, WA	118,109	116,901	102,979	79,545	1,208	13,922	1.0	13.5	19.3	36.3	27.8	16.6
Skagit County, WA	118,109	116,901	102,979	79,545	1,208	13,922	1.0	13.5	19.3	36.3	27.8	16.6
Muncie, IN	117,660	117,671	118,769	119,659	-11	-1,098	0.0	-0.9	16.2	44.9	23.9	15.0
Delaware County, IN	117,660	117,671	118,769	119,659	-11	-1,098	0.0	-0.9	16.2	44.9	23.9	15.0
Muskegon–Norton Shores, MI	171,302	172,188	170,200	158,983	-886	1,988	-0.5	1.2	20.1	37.9	28.1	13.9
Muskegon County, MI	171,302	172,188	170,200	158,983	-886	1,988	-0.5	1.2	20.1	37.9	28.1	13.9

[1] The April 1, 2000, Population Estimates base reflects modifications to the Census 2000 population as documented in the Count Question Resolution program and geographic program revisions.
[2] The April 1, 1990, census counts include corrections processed through August 1997, results of special censuses and test censuses, and do not include adjustments for census coverage errors.
[3] Based on the April 1, 2010, estimates base and the July 1, 2011, estimates.
[4] Based on the April 1, 2010, complete count and the April 1, 2000 estimates base.
0 = Represents zero or amounts to zero.

Table C-1.　Population and Population Characteristics—*Continued*

Metropolitan statistical area, division, and component county	Population				Net change		Percent change		Percent			
	2011 (July 1)	2010 Census (April 1)	2000[1] (estimates base)	1990[2] (April 1)	2010– 2011[3]	2000– 2010[4]	2010– 2011[3]	2000– 2010[4]	Under 15 years, 2011	15 to 44 years, 2011	45 to 64 years, 2011	65 years and over, 2011
Myrtle Beach–North Myrtle Beach–												
Conway, SC	276,340	269,291	196,629	144,053	7,049	72,662	2.6	37.0	16.7	37.3	28.2	17.7
Horry County, SC	276,340	269,291	196,629	144,053	7,049	72,662	2.6	37.0	16.7	37.3	28.2	17.7
Napa, CA	138,088	136,484	124,279	110,765	1,604	12,205	1.2	9.8	18.7	38.3	27.7	15.3
Napa County, CA	138,088	136,484	124,279	110,765	1,604	12,205	1.2	9.8	18.7	38.3	27.7	15.3
Naples–Marco Island, FL..............	328,134	321,520	251,377	152,099	6,614	70,143	2.1	27.9	15.9	31.1	25.8	27.2
Collier County, FL	328,134	321,520	251,377	152,099	6,614	70,143	2.1	27.9	15.9	31.1	25.8	27.2
Nashville–Davidson—Murfreesboro—												
Franklin, TN	1,617,142	1,589,934	1,311,789	1,048,216	27,208	278,145	1.7	21.2	20.3	42.6	26.2	10.9
Cannon County, TN	13,761	13,801	12,826	10,467	-40	975	-0.3	7.6	17.7	36.2	29.2	16.9
Cheatham County, TN	39,078	39,105	35,912	27,140	-27	3,193	-0.1	8.9	20.0	38.1	30.4	11.5
Davidson County, TN..............	635,475	626,681	569,891	510,786	8,794	56,790	1.4	10.0	18.7	46.3	24.5	10.5
Dickson County, TN.................	50,081	49,666	43,156	35,061	415	6,510	0.8	15.1	20.2	38.2	28.0	13.6
Hickman County, TN	24,406	24,690	22,295	16,754	-284	2,395	-1.2	10.7	17.9	38.5	29.1	14.5
Macon County, TN...................	22,485	22,248	20,386	15,906	237	1,862	1.1	9.1	20.5	38.3	26.9	14.3
Robertson County, TN..............	67,106	66,283	54,433	41,492	823	11,850	1.2	21.8	21.5	38.4	28.0	12.1
Rutherford County, TN..............	268,921	262,604	182,023	118,570	6,317	80,581	2.4	44.3	21.6	46.5	23.4	8.5
Smith County, TN....................	19,150	19,166	17,712	14,143	-16	1,454	-0.1	8.2	19.8	36.9	29.4	13.9
Sumner County, TN..................	163,686	160,645	130,449	103,281	3,041	30,196	1.9	23.1	20.5	38.4	28.1	13.0
Trousdale County, TN...............	7,816	7,870	7,259	5,920	-54	611	-0.7	8.4	19.3	37.8	29.1	13.8
Williamson County, TN.............	188,560	183,182	126,638	81,021	5,378	56,544	2.9	44.7	23.7	36.6	29.5	10.1
Wilson County, TN...................	116,617	113,993	88,809	67,675	2,624	25,184	2.3	28.4	20.4	37.8	29.2	12.6
New Haven–Milford, CT	861,113	862,477	824,008	804,219	-1,364	38,469	-0.2	4.7	17.9	39.6	28.0	14.6
New Haven County, CT..............	861,113	862,477	824,008	804,219	-1,364	38,469	-0.2	4.7	17.9	39.6	28.0	14.6
New Orleans–Metairie–Kenner, LA	1,191,089	1,167,764	1,316,510	1,264,383	23,325	-148,746	2.0	-11.3	19.3	40.6	27.7	12.4
Jefferson Parish, LA..................	432,640	432,552	455,466	448,306	88	-22,914	0.0	-5.0	18.7	39.4	28.1	13.9
Orleans Parish, LA...................	360,740	343,829	484,674	496,938	16,911	-140,845	4.9	-29.1	18.0	44.6	26.2	11.2
Plaquemines Parish, LA.............	23,628	23,042	26,757	25,575	586	-3,715	2.5	-13.9	22.6	39.5	26.7	11.2
St. Bernard Parish, LA...............	39,558	35,897	67,229	66,631	3,661	-31,332	10.2	-46.6	21.9	43.6	25.4	9.1
St. Charles Parish, LA...............	52,517	52,780	48,072	42,437	-263	4,708	-0.5	9.8	21.7	39.4	28.7	10.2
St. John the Baptist Parish, LA	45,221	45,924	43,044	39,996	-703	2,880	-1.5	6.7	21.9	39.8	27.5	10.8
St. Tammany Parish, LA.............	236,785	233,740	191,268	144,500	3,045	42,472	1.3	22.2	20.9	36.6	29.4	13.1
New York–Northern New Jersey–												
Long Island, NY–NJ–PA	19,015,900	18,897,109	18,323,002	16,863,671	118,791	574,107	0.6	3.1	18.6	41.5	26.6	13.3
Edison–New Brunswick, NJ	2,349,499	2,340,249	2,173,869	1,898,329	9,250	166,380	0.4	7.7	19.1	37.7	28.2	15.1
Middlesex County, NJ	814,217	809,858	750,162	671,712	4,359	59,696	0.5	8.0	18.7	42.2	26.6	12.5
Monmouth County, NJ	631,020	630,380	615,301	553,192	640	15,079	0.1	2.5	18.8	36.0	31.0	14.1
Ocean County, NJ	579,369	576,567	510,916	433,203	2,802	65,651	0.5	12.8	19.5	33.2	26.2	21.1
Somerset County, NJ	324,893	323,444	297,490	240,222	1,449	25,954	0.4	8.7	20.0	37.1	30.3	12.6
Nassau–Suffolk, NY	2,843,252	2,832,882	2,753,913	2,609,212	10,370	78,969	0.4	2.9	18.7	37.5	29.1	14.6
Nassau County, NY	1,344,436	1,339,532	1,334,544	1,287,873	4,904	4,988	0.4	0.4	18.4	36.8	29.4	15.4
Suffolk County, NY	1,498,816	1,493,350	1,419,369	1,321,339	5,466	73,981	0.4	5.2	19.0	38.2	28.9	13.9
Newark–Union, NJ–PA	2,153,014	2,147,727	2,098,843	1,959,933	5,287	48,884	0.2	2.3	19.7	39.1	28.5	12.8
Essex County, NJ	785,137	783,969	793,633	777,964	1,168	-9,664	0.1	-1.2	20.5	42.0	25.9	11.7
Hunterdon County, NJ.............	128,038	128,349	121,989	107,852	-311	6,360	-0.2	5.2	18.1	33.5	35.1	13.4
Morris County, NJ	494,976	492,276	470,212	421,330	2,700	22,064	0.5	4.7	19.0	36.5	30.4	14.2
Sussex County, NJ	148,517	149,265	144,166	130,936	-748	5,099	-0.5	3.5	18.4	35.8	33.2	12.5
Union County, NJ	539,494	536,499	522,541	493,819	2,995	13,958	0.6	2.7	20.1	40.0	27.2	12.7
Pike County, PA	56,852	57,369	46,302	28,032	-517	11,067	-0.9	23.9	17.5	33.4	32.5	16.5
New York–White Plains–Wayne, NY–NJ	11,670,135	11,576,251	11,296,377	10,396,197	93,884	279,874	0.8	2.5	18.2	43.7	25.4	12.7
Bergen County, NJ	911,004	905,116	884,118	825,380	5,888	20,998	0.7	2.4	18.1	37.4	29.3	15.2
Hudson County, NJ	641,224	634,266	608,975	553,099	6,958	25,291	1.1	4.2	17.3	49.2	23.0	10.5
Passaic County, NJ	502,007	501,226	489,049	470,872	781	12,177	0.2	2.5	20.4	41.4	25.9	12.3
Bronx County, NY...................	1,392,002	1,385,108	1,332,650	1,203,789	6,894	52,458	0.5	3.9	21.9	44.2	23.2	10.7
Kings County, NY	2,532,645	2,504,700	2,465,326	2,300,664	27,945	39,374	1.1	1.6	19.7	45.1	23.7	11.5
New York County, NY..............	1,601,948	1,585,873	1,537,195	1,487,536	16,075	48,678	1.0	3.2	12.5	49.7	24.1	13.7
Putnam County, NY.................	99,933	99,710	95,745	83,941	223	3,965	0.2	4.1	18.3	36.0	32.7	13.0
Queens County, NY.................	2,247,848	2,230,722	2,229,379	1,951,598	17,126	1,343	0.8	0.1	17.1	43.8	26.2	12.9
Richmond County, NY..............	470,467	468,730	443,728	378,977	1,737	25,002	0.4	5.6	18.8	40.1	28.1	13.0
Rockland County, NY..............	315,158	311,687	286,753	265,475	3,471	24,934	1.1	8.7	23.1	37.0	26.2	13.7
Westchester County, NY..............	955,899	949,113	923,459	874,866	6,786	25,654	0.7	2.8	19.3	37.8	28.1	14.8
Niles–Benton Harbor, MI..............	156,941	156,813	162,453	161,378	128	-5,640	0.1	-3.5	19.0	35.6	28.8	16.7
Berrien County, MI	156,941	156,813	162,453	161,378	128	-5,640	0.1	-3.5	19.0	35.6	28.8	16.7
North Port–Bradenton–Sarasota, FL	709,355	702,281	589,959	489,483	7,074	112,322	1.0	19.0	14.6	29.1	28.3	28.0
Manatee County, FL..............	327,142	322,833	264,002	211,707	4,309	58,831	1.3	22.3	16.9	31.8	27.6	23.7
Sarasota County, FL.................	382,213	379,448	325,957	277,776	2,765	53,491	0.7	16.4	12.6	26.8	29.0	31.7
Norwich–New London, CT	273,502	274,055	259,088	254,957	-553	14,967	-0.2	5.8	17.2	38.7	29.5	14.6
New London County, CT..............	273,502	274,055	259,088	254,957	-553	14,967	-0.2	5.8	17.2	38.7	29.5	14.6
Ocala, FL	332,529	331,298	258,916	194,835	1,231	72,382	0.4	28.0	15.7	30.9	27.2	26.3
Marion County, FL..................	332,529	331,298	258,916	194,835	1,231	72,382	0.4	28.0	15.7	30.9	27.2	26.3

[1] The April 1, 2000, Population Estimates base reflects modifications to the Census 2000 population as documented in the Count Question Resolution program and geographic program revisions.
[2] The April 1, 1990, census counts include corrections processed through August 1997, results of special censuses and test censuses, and do not include adjustments for census coverage errors.
[3] Based on the April 1, 2010, estimates base and the July 1, 2011, estimates.
[4] Based on the April 1, 2010, complete count and the April 1, 2000 estimates base.
0 = Represents zero or amounts to zero.

Table C-1. Population and Population Characteristics—*Continued*

Metropolitan statistical area, division, and component county	Population 2011 (July 1)	Population 2010 Census (April 1)	Population 2000[1] (estimates base)	Population 1990[2] (April 1)	Net change 2010–2011[3]	Net change 2000–2010[4]	Percent change 2010–2011[3]	Percent change 2000–2010[4]	Percent Under 15 years, 2011	Percent 15 to 44 years, 2011	Percent 45 to 64 years, 2011	Percent 65 years and over, 2011
Ocean City, NJ	96,601	97,265	102,326	95,089	-664	-5,061	-0.7	-4.9	14.8	31.5	31.7	22.0
Cape May County, NJ	96,601	97,265	102,326	95,089	-664	-5,061	-0.7	-4.9	14.8	31.5	31.7	22.0
Odessa, TX	140,111	137,130	121,123	118,934	2,981	16,007	2.2	13.2	24.9	42.1	23.0	10.1
Ector County, TX	140,111	137,130	121,123	118,934	2,981	16,007	2.2	13.2	24.9	42.1	23.0	10.1
Ogden–Clearfield, UT	555,916	547,184	442,656	351,799	8,732	104,528	1.6	23.6	27.5	42.4	20.9	9.2
Davis County, UT	311,811	306,479	238,994	187,941	5,332	67,485	1.7	28.2	29.0	42.5	20.1	8.4
Morgan County, UT	9,685	9,469	7,129	5,528	216	2,340	2.3	32.8	29.2	36.6	23.3	10.9
Weber County, UT	234,420	231,236	196,533	158,330	3,184	34,703	1.4	17.7	25.4	42.5	21.8	10.2
Oklahoma City, OK	1,278,053	1,252,987	1,095,421	971,042	25,066	157,566	2.0	14.4	21.0	42.0	25.1	11.9
Canadian County, OK	119,492	115,541	87,697	74,409	3,951	27,844	3.4	31.8	22.3	40.7	26.0	11.0
Cleveland County, OK	261,281	255,755	208,016	174,253	5,526	47,739	2.2	22.9	18.9	46.6	23.9	10.5
Grady County, OK	53,020	52,431	45,516	41,747	589	6,915	1.1	15.2	20.4	37.6	27.8	14.2
Lincoln County, OK	34,155	34,273	32,080	29,216	-118	2,193	-0.3	6.8	20.5	35.0	29.0	15.5
Logan County, OK	42,499	41,848	33,924	29,011	651	7,924	1.6	23.4	20.3	39.1	27.8	12.7
McClain County, OK	35,235	34,506	27,740	22,795	729	6,766	2.1	24.4	22.0	36.9	27.7	13.4
Oklahoma County, OK	732,371	718,633	660,448	599,611	13,738	58,185	1.9	8.8	21.6	41.6	24.7	12.1
Olympia, WA	256,591	252,264	207,355	161,238	4,327	44,909	1.7	21.7	18.6	39.9	28.1	13.4
Thurston County, WA	256,591	252,264	207,355	161,238	4,327	44,909	1.7	21.7	18.6	39.9	28.1	13.4
Omaha–Council Bluffs, NE–IA	877,110	865,350	767,041	685,797	11,760	98,309	1.4	12.8	22.0	41.2	25.6	11.2
Harrison County, IA	14,828	14,928	15,666	14,730	-100	-738	-0.7	-4.7	18.7	33.3	30.2	17.8
Mills County, IA	14,992	15,059	14,547	13,202	-67	512	-0.4	3.5	20.4	34.1	31.7	13.8
Pottawattamie County, IA	93,518	93,158	87,704	82,628	360	5,454	0.4	6.2	20.0	37.6	27.9	14.5
Cass County, NE	25,188	25,241	24,334	21,318	-53	907	-0.2	3.7	20.3	34.4	30.8	14.5
Douglas County, NE	524,861	517,110	463,585	416,444	7,751	53,525	1.5	11.5	22.0	42.7	24.6	10.7
Sarpy County, NE	162,561	158,840	122,595	102,583	3,721	36,245	2.3	29.6	24.1	42.8	24.3	8.8
Saunders County, NE	20,867	20,780	19,830	18,285	87	950	0.4	4.8	20.8	33.1	30.1	15.9
Washington County, NE	20,295	20,234	18,780	16,607	61	1,454	0.3	7.7	19.9	34.9	30.7	14.5
Orlando–Kissimmee–Sanford, FL	2,171,360	2,134,411	1,644,561	1,224,844	36,949	489,850	1.7	29.8	19.0	42.8	25.6	12.6
Lake County, FL	301,019	297,052	210,528	152,104	3,967	86,524	1.3	41.1	17.0	31.7	26.6	24.7
Orange County, FL	1,169,107	1,145,956	896,344	677,491	23,151	249,612	2.0	27.8	19.3	46.4	24.3	9.9
Osceola County, FL	276,163	268,685	172,493	107,728	7,478	96,192	2.8	55.8	21.1	42.4	25.2	11.3
Seminole County, FL	425,071	422,718	365,196	287,521	2,353	57,522	0.6	15.8	18.0	41.2	28.4	12.4
Oshkosh–Neenah, WI	167,699	166,994	156,763	140,320	705	10,231	0.4	6.5	17.7	41.2	27.6	13.5
Winnebago County, WI	167,699	166,994	156,763	140,320	705	10,231	0.4	6.5	17.7	41.2	27.6	13.5
Owensboro, KY	115,333	114,752	109,875	104,681	581	4,877	0.5	4.4	20.3	37.1	27.7	14.9
Daviess County, KY	97,234	96,656	91,545	87,189	578	5,111	0.6	5.6	20.3	37.4	27.6	14.7
Hancock County, KY	8,572	8,565	8,392	7,864	7	173	0.1	2.1	21.2	36.1	28.6	14.1
McLean County, KY	9,527	9,531	9,938	9,628	-4	-407	0.0	-4.1	19.1	35.1	28.4	17.3
Oxnard–Thousand Oaks–Ventura, CA	831,771	823,318	753,197	669,016	8,453	70,121	1.0	9.3	20.7	40.7	26.6	12.0
Ventura County, CA	831,771	823,318	753,197	669,016	8,453	70,121	1.0	9.3	20.7	40.7	26.6	12.0
Palm Bay–Melbourne–Titusville, FL	543,566	543,376	476,230	398,978	190	67,146	0.0	14.1	15.7	32.8	30.7	20.8
Brevard County, FL	543,566	543,376	476,230	398,978	190	67,146	0.0	14.1	15.7	32.8	30.7	20.8
Palm Coast, FL	97,376	95,696	49,832	28,701	1,680	45,864	1.8	92.0	15.8	30.1	28.8	25.3
Flagler County, FL	97,376	95,696	49,832	28,701	1,680	45,864	1.8	92.0	15.8	30.1	28.8	25.3
Panama City–Lynn Haven–Panama City Beach, FL	169,856	168,852	148,217	126,994	1,004	20,635	0.6	13.9	18.0	38.8	28.3	14.8
Bay County, FL	169,856	168,852	148,217	126,994	1,004	20,635	0.6	13.9	18.0	38.8	28.3	14.8
Parkersburg–Marietta–Vienna, WV–OH	162,248	162,056	164,624	161,907	192	-2,568	0.1	-1.6	17.2	35.5	29.9	17.3
Washington County, OH	61,755	61,778	63,251	62,254	-23	-1,473	0.0	-2.3	16.7	35.4	30.0	17.9
Pleasants County, WV	7,611	7,605	7,514	7,546	6	91	0.1	1.2	16.0	37.4	30.2	16.4
Wirt County, WV	5,762	5,717	5,873	5,192	45	-156	0.8	-2.7	16.7	33.6	33.8	15.9
Wood County, WV	87,120	86,956	87,986	86,915	164	-1,030	0.2	-1.2	17.8	35.6	29.5	17.1
Pascagoula, MS	162,790	162,246	150,564	131,916	544	11,682	0.3	7.8	21.0	39.3	27.0	12.7
George County, MS	22,889	22,578	19,144	16,673	311	3,434	1.4	17.9	22.0	39.4	25.5	13.1
Jackson County, MS	139,901	139,668	131,420	115,243	233	8,248	0.2	6.3	20.8	39.3	27.2	12.6
Pensacola–Ferry Pass–Brent, FL	453,218	448,991	412,153	344,406	4,227	36,838	0.9	8.9	18.3	39.9	27.7	14.2
Escambia County, FL	299,114	297,619	294,410	262,445	1,495	3,209	0.5	1.1	17.8	40.5	27.0	14.7
Santa Rosa County, FL	154,104	151,372	117,743	81,961	2,732	33,629	1.8	28.6	19.2	38.7	29.0	13.2
Peoria, IL	379,556	379,186	366,899	358,552	370	12,287	0.1	3.3	19.7	38.1	27.2	15.0
Marshall County, IL	12,533	12,640	13,180	12,846	-107	-540	-0.8	-4.1	17.3	32.4	30.3	20.0
Peoria County, IL	186,834	186,494	183,433	182,827	340	3,061	0.2	1.7	20.0	39.9	26.1	14.0
Stark County, IL	5,667	5,994	6,332	6,534	-327	-338	-5.5	-5.3	18.6	33.5	30.0	17.9
Tazewell County, IL	135,661	135,394	128,485	123,692	267	6,909	0.2	5.4	19.3	37.2	27.8	15.7
Woodford County, IL	38,861	38,664	35,469	32,653	197	3,195	0.5	9.0	21.0	35.5	28.6	14.9
Philadelphia–Camden–Wilmington, PA–NJ–DE–MD	5,992,414	5,965,343	5,687,147	5,435,550	27,071	278,196	0.5	4.9	18.9	40.2	27.5	13.5
Camden, NJ	1,251,921	1,250,679	1,186,999	1,127,972	1,242	63,680	0.1	5.4	19.3	38.9	28.5	13.3
Burlington County, NJ	449,576	448,734	423,394	395,066	842	25,340	0.2	6.0	18.5	37.8	29.6	14.1
Camden County, NJ	513,241	513,657	508,932	502,824	-416	4,725	-0.1	0.9	19.8	39.7	27.5	13.0
Gloucester County, NJ	289,104	288,288	254,673	230,082	816	33,615	0.3	13.2	19.5	39.1	28.7	12.7
Philadelphia, PA	4,030,926	4,008,994	3,849,647	3,728,991	21,932	159,347	0.5	4.1	18.7	40.5	27.1	13.6
Bucks County, PA	626,854	625,249	597,635	541,174	1,605	27,614	0.3	4.6	18.2	35.6	31.3	14.9
Chester County, PA	503,897	498,886	433,501	376,389	5,011	65,385	1.0	15.1	20.0	37.8	29.0	13.1
Delaware County, PA	559,494	558,979	550,864	547,658	515	8,115	0.1	1.5	18.7	39.1	27.8	14.4
Montgomery County, PA	804,210	799,874	750,097	678,193	4,336	49,777	0.5	6.6	18.5	37.3	28.9	15.3
Philadelphia County, PA	1,536,471	1,526,006	1,517,550	1,585,577	10,465	8,456	0.7	0.6	18.7	45.5	23.7	12.1

[1] The April 1, 2000, Population Estimates base reflects modifications to the Census 2000 population as documented in the Count Question Resolution program and geographic program revisions.
[2] The April 1, 1990, census counts include corrections processed through August 1997, results of special censuses and test censuses, and do not include adjustments for census coverage errors.
[3] Based on the April 1, 2010, estimates base and the July 1, 2011, estimates.
[4] Based on the April 1, 2010, complete count and the April 1, 2000 estimates base.
0 = Represents zero or amounts to zero.

Table C-1. Population and Population Characteristics—*Continued*

Metropolitan statistical area, division, and component county	Population				Net change		Percent change		Percent			
	2011 (July 1)	2010 Census (April 1)	2000¹ (estimates base)	1990² (April 1)	2010–2011³	2000–2010⁴	2010–2011³	2000–2010⁴	Under 15 years, 2011	15 to 44 years, 2011	45 to 64 years, 2011	65 years and over, 2011
Philadelphia–Camden–Wilmington, PA–NJ–DE–MD—*Continued*												
Wilmington, DE–MD–NJ	709,567	705,670	650,501	578,587	3,897	55,169	0.6	8.5	19.0	40.6	27.7	12.7
New Castle County, DE	541,971	538,479	500,265	441,946	3,492	38,214	0.6	7.6	18.8	41.5	27.1	12.5
Cecil County, MD	101,694	101,108	85,951	71,347	586	15,157	0.6	17.6	20.1	38.3	29.5	12.1
Salem County, NJ	65,902	66,083	64,285	65,294	-181	1,798	-0.3	2.8	18.8	36.5	29.6	15.1
Phoenix–Mesa–Glendale, AZ	4,263,236	4,192,887	3,251,876	2,238,498	70,349	941,011	1.7	28.9	21.7	41.7	23.9	12.7
Maricopa County, AZ	3,880,244	3,817,117	3,072,149	2,122,101	63,127	744,968	1.7	24.2	21.7	42.0	23.9	12.5
Pinal County, AZ	382,992	375,770	179,727	116,397	7,222	196,043	1.9	109.1	22.3	39.4	23.6	14.8
Pine Bluff, AR	98,924	100,258	107,341	106,958	-1,334	-7,083	-1.3	-6.6	19.1	39.6	27.5	13.7
Cleveland County, AR	8,672	8,689	8,571	7,781	-17	118	-0.2	1.4	20.4	35.2	28.0	16.4
Jefferson County, AR	76,246	77,435	84,278	85,487	-1,189	-6,843	-1.5	-8.1	19.6	39.2	27.6	13.7
Lincoln County, AR	14,006	14,134	14,492	13,690	-128	-358	-0.9	-2.5	15.7	44.9	27.0	12.3
Pittsburgh, PA	2,359,746	2,356,285	2,431,087	2,468,289	3,461	-74,802	0.1	-3.1	16.1	36.7	29.9	17.2
Allegheny County, PA	1,227,066	1,223,348	1,281,666	1,336,449	3,718	-58,318	0.3	-4.6	15.9	38.6	28.8	16.6
Armstrong County, PA	68,568	68,941	72,392	73,478	-373	-3,451	-0.5	-4.8	16.2	33.8	31.4	18.5
Beaver County, PA	170,414	170,539	181,412	186,093	-125	-10,873	-0.1	-6.0	16.3	34.2	30.9	18.5
Butler County, PA	184,848	183,862	174,083	152,013	986	9,779	0.5	5.6	17.8	36.6	30.2	15.4
Fayette County, PA	136,097	136,606	148,644	145,351	-509	-12,038	-0.4	-8.1	16.1	35.4	30.4	18.0
Washington County, PA	208,282	207,820	202,897	204,584	462	4,923	0.2	2.4	16.5	35.1	30.8	17.6
Westmoreland County, PA	364,471	365,169	369,993	370,321	-698	-4,824	-0.2	-1.3	15.7	33.6	31.7	19.0
Pittsfield, MA	130,458	131,219	134,953	139,352	-761	-3,734	-0.6	-2.8	15.1	34.7	31.2	19.0
Berkshire County, MA	130,458	131,219	134,953	139,352	-761	-3,734	-0.6	-2.8	15.1	34.7	31.2	19.0
Pocatello, ID	91,457	90,656	83,103	73,112	801	7,553	0.9	9.1	23.3	42.3	23.0	11.5
Bannock County, ID	83,691	82,839	75,565	66,026	852	7,274	1.0	9.6	23.0	42.8	22.8	11.4
Power County, ID	7,766	7,817	7,538	7,086	-51	279	-0.7	3.7	26.1	36.6	24.8	12.4
Portland–South Portland–Biddeford, ME	515,807	514,098	487,568	441,257	1,709	26,530	0.3	5.4	16.8	36.9	31.1	15.2
Cumberland County, ME	282,401	281,674	265,612	243,135	727	16,062	0.3	6.0	16.7	38.4	30.3	14.6
Sagadahoc County, ME	35,207	35,293	35,214	33,535	-86	79	-0.2	0.2	16.6	33.7	32.5	17.2
York County, ME	198,199	197,131	186,742	164,587	1,068	10,389	0.5	5.6	16.9	35.4	31.9	15.7
Portland–Vancouver–Hillsboro, OR–WA	2,262,605	2,226,009	1,927,881	1,523,741	36,596	298,128	1.6	15.5	19.5	42.1	26.8	11.7
Clackamas County, OR	380,207	375,992	338,391	278,850	4,215	37,601	1.1	11.1	18.8	36.6	30.4	14.2
Columbia County, OR	49,402	49,351	43,560	37,557	51	5,791	0.1	13.3	18.8	35.4	31.1	14.6
Multnomah County, OR	748,031	735,334	660,486	583,887	12,697	74,848	1.7	11.3	17.3	46.5	25.5	10.7
Washington County, OR	540,410	529,710	445,342	311,554	10,700	84,368	2.0	18.9	21.2	43.1	25.3	10.4
Yamhill County, OR	100,000	99,193	84,992	65,551	807	14,201	0.8	16.7	20.3	39.7	26.2	13.8
Clark County, WA	433,418	425,363	345,238	238,053	8,055	80,125	1.9	23.2	21.5	39.5	27.0	12.0
Skamania County, WA	11,137	11,066	9,872	8,289	71	1,194	0.6	12.1	17.5	33.0	34.3	15.3
Port St. Lucie, FL	427,874	424,107	319,426	251,071	3,767	104,681	0.9	32.8	16.8	32.4	27.9	22.9
Martin County, FL	147,495	146,318	126,731	100,900	1,177	19,587	0.8	15.5	14.1	28.6	29.7	27.7
St. Lucie County, FL	280,379	277,789	192,695	150,171	2,590	85,094	0.9	44.2	18.2	34.5	26.9	20.4
Poughkeepsie–Newburgh–Middletown, NY	672,871	670,301	621,517	567,033	2,570	48,784	0.4	7.8	19.9	39.3	28.3	12.4
Dutchess County, NY	297,999	297,488	280,150	259,462	511	17,338	0.2	6.2	17.3	39.1	29.8	13.9
Orange County, NY	374,872	372,813	341,367	307,571	2,059	31,446	0.6	9.2	22.0	39.5	27.2	11.3
Prescott, AZ	211,888	211,033	167,517	107,714	855	43,516	0.4	26.0	15.1	28.5	31.1	25.2
Yavapai County, AZ	211,888	211,033	167,517	107,714	855	43,516	0.4	26.0	15.1	28.5	31.1	25.2
Providence–New Bedford–Fall River, RI–MA	1,600,224	1,600,852	1,582,997	1,509,789	-628	17,855	0.0	1.1	17.3	39.9	28.2	14.6
Bristol County, MA	548,922	548,285	534,678	506,325	637	13,607	0.1	2.5	17.8	39.3	28.4	14.5
Bristol County, RI	49,800	49,875	50,648	48,859	-75	-773	-0.2	-1.5	16.2	36.4	30.5	16.9
Kent County, RI	165,535	166,158	167,090	161,143	-623	-932	-0.4	-0.6	16.4	36.5	31.1	16.1
Newport County, RI	82,695	82,888	85,433	87,194	-193	-2,545	-0.2	-3.0	15.4	36.3	30.8	17.5
Providence County, RI	626,709	626,667	621,602	596,270	42	5,065	0.0	0.8	17.8	42.5	26.2	13.6
Washington County, RI	126,563	126,979	123,546	109,998	-416	3,433	-0.3	2.8	15.4	37.7	31.3	15.6
Provo–Orem, UT	540,834	526,810	376,774	269,407	14,024	150,036	2.7	39.8	30.0	48.6	14.7	6.7
Juab County, UT	10,335	10,246	8,238	5,817	89	2,008	0.9	24.4	30.8	38.6	20.4	10.3
UT County, UT	530,499	516,564	368,536	263,590	13,935	148,028	2.7	40.2	30.0	48.8	14.5	6.6
Pueblo, CO	160,545	159,063	141,472	123,051	1,482	17,591	0.9	12.4	20.1	37.4	27.0	15.6
Pueblo County, CO	160,545	159,063	141,472	123,051	1,482	17,591	0.9	12.4	20.1	37.4	27.0	15.6
Punta Gorda, FL	160,511	159,978	141,627	110,975	533	18,351	0.3	13.0	11.1	23.6	30.2	35.1
Charlotte County, FL	160,511	159,978	141,627	110,975	533	18,351	0.3	13.0	11.1	23.6	30.2	35.1
Racine, WI	195,388	195,408	188,831	175,034	-20	6,577	0.0	3.5	20.3	37.3	29.0	13.4
Racine County, WI	195,388	195,408	188,831	175,034	-20	6,577	0.0	3.5	20.3	37.3	29.0	13.4
Raleigh–Cary, NC	1,163,515	1,130,490	797,071	544,031	33,025	333,419	2.9	41.8	21.9	43.7	25.1	9.3
Franklin County, NC	61,140	60,619	47,260	36,414	521	13,359	0.9	28.3	20.1	37.8	28.9	13.3
Johnston County, NC	172,595	168,878	121,965	81,306	3,717	46,913	2.2	38.5	23.2	40.4	25.8	10.6
Wake County, NC	929,780	900,993	627,846	426,311	28,787	273,147	3.2	43.5	21.7	44.7	24.8	8.8
Rapid City, SD	128,361	126,382	112,818	103,221	1,979	13,564	1.6	12.0	20.6	38.7	27.1	13.6
Meade County, SD	25,546	25,434	24,253	21,878	112	1,181	0.4	4.9	20.8	38.9	27.9	12.4
Pennington County, SD	102,815	100,948	88,565	81,343	1,867	12,383	1.8	14.0	20.6	38.6	26.9	13.9
Reading, PA	412,778	411,442	373,638	336,523	1,336	37,804	0.3	10.1	19.2	38.4	27.7	14.7
Berks County, PA	412,778	411,442	373,638	336,523	1,336	37,804	0.3	10.1	19.2	38.4	27.7	14.7
Redding, CA	177,774	177,223	163,256	147,036	551	13,967	0.3	8.6	17.9	35.4	29.4	17.3
Shasta County, CA	177,774	177,223	163,256	147,036	551	13,967	0.3	8.6	17.9	35.4	29.4	17.3
Reno–Sparks, NV	429,606	425,417	342,885	257,193	4,189	82,532	1.0	24.1	19.3	40.7	27.4	12.6
Storey County, NV	3,896	4,010	3,399	2,526	-114	611	-2.8	18.0	12.7	26.3	41.3	19.8
Washoe County, NV	425,710	421,407	339,486	254,667	4,303	81,921	1.0	24.1	19.4	40.8	27.2	12.6

¹ The April 1, 2000, Population Estimates base reflects modifications to the Census 2000 population as documented in the Count Question Resolution program and geographic program revisions.
² The April 1, 1990, census counts include corrections processed through August 1997, results of special censuses and test censuses, and do not include adjustments for census coverage errors.
³ Based on the April 1, 2010, estimates base and the July 1, 2011, estimates.
⁴ Based on the April 1, 2010, complete count and the April 1, 2000 estimates base.
0 = Represents zero or amounts to zero.

Table C-1. Population and Population Characteristics—*Continued*

Metropolitan statistical area, division, and component county	Population				Net change		Percent change		Percent			
	2011 (July 1)	2010 Census (April 1)	2000[1] (estimates base)	1990[2] (April 1)	2010–2011[3]	2000–2010[4]	2010–2011[3]	2000–2010[4]	Under 15 years, 2011	15 to 44 years, 2011	45 to 64 years, 2011	65 years and over, 2011
Richmond, VA	1,269,380	1,258,251	1,096,957	949,244	11,129	161,294	0.9	14.7	19.0	40.5	28.1	12.5
Amelia County, VA	12,805	12,690	11,400	8,787	115	1,290	0.9	11.3	17.9	34.2	31.8	16.2
Caroline County, VA	28,674	28,545	22,121	19,217	129	6,424	0.5	29.0	19.9	38.1	28.4	13.7
Charles City County, VA	7,241	7,256	6,926	6,282	-15	330	-0.2	4.8	14.0	31.8	36.6	17.5
Chesterfield County, VA	320,277	316,236	259,903	209,599	4,041	56,333	1.3	21.7	20.7	39.7	28.8	10.9
Cumberland County, VA	9,969	10,052	9,017	7,825	-83	1,035	-0.8	11.5	18.4	35.4	29.4	16.8
Dinwiddie County, VA	27,918	28,001	24,533	22,279	-83	3,468	-0.3	14.1	17.7	37.6	30.7	14.1
Goochland County, VA	21,883	21,717	16,863	14,163	166	4,854	0.8	28.8	15.9	32.4	35.7	15.9
Hanover County, VA	100,342	99,863	86,320	63,306	479	13,543	0.5	15.7	19.5	35.8	31.0	13.7
Henrico County, VA	310,445	306,935	262,300	217,878	3,510	44,635	1.1	17.0	19.8	40.6	27.0	12.6
King and Queen County, VA	6,997	6,945	6,630	6,289	52	315	0.7	4.8	16.0	32.8	32.9	18.3
King William County, VA	15,981	15,935	13,146	10,913	46	2,789	0.3	21.2	20.1	37.8	29.5	12.5
Louisa County, VA	33,395	33,153	25,627	20,325	242	7,526	0.7	29.4	17.8	34.9	32.3	15.1
New Kent County, VA	18,822	18,429	13,462	10,466	393	4,967	2.1	36.9	17.6	35.4	34.0	12.9
Powhatan County, VA	28,110	28,046	22,377	15,328	64	5,669	0.2	25.3	17.0	37.7	32.3	13.0
Prince George County, VA	36,555	35,725	33,047	27,390	830	2,678	2.3	8.1	18.7	43.0	27.7	10.6
Sussex County, VA	12,087	12,087	12,504	10,248	0	-417	0.0	-3.3	13.8	42.9	28.8	14.6
Colonial Heights city, VA	17,440	17,411	16,897	16,064	29	514	0.2	3.0	18.3	35.5	26.2	20.1
Hopewell city, VA	22,580	22,591	22,354	23,101	-11	237	0.0	1.1	21.2	38.9	25.1	14.8
Petersburg city, VA	32,326	32,420	33,740	37,071	-94	-1,320	-0.3	-3.9	18.1	38.2	28.2	15.5
Richmond city, VA	205,533	204,214	197,790	202,713	1,319	6,424	0.6	3.2	16.4	48.8	23.8	10.9
Riverside–San Bernardino–Ontario, CA	4,304,997	4,224,851	3,254,821	2,588,793	80,146	970,030	1.9	29.8	23.1	42.8	23.5	10.6
Riverside County, CA	2,239,620	2,189,641	1,545,387	1,170,413	49,979	644,254	2.3	41.7	22.8	41.8	23.4	12.0
San Bernardino County, CA	2,065,377	2,035,210	1,709,434	1,418,380	30,167	325,776	1.5	19.1	23.5	43.8	23.5	9.1
Roanoke, VA	308,861	308,707	288,309	268,513	154	20,398	0.0	7.1	17.5	36.2	29.8	16.6
Botetourt County, VA	32,928	33,148	30,496	24,992	-220	2,652	-0.7	8.7	17.5	31.5	34.0	17.0
Craig County, VA	5,099	5,190	5,091	4,372	-91	99	-1.8	1.9	17.2	33.1	33.0	16.6
Franklin County, VA	56,419	56,159	47,286	39,549	260	8,873	0.5	18.8	16.8	33.8	31.1	18.3
Roanoke County, VA	92,740	92,376	85,778	79,278	364	6,598	0.4	7.7	17.1	34.9	30.4	17.6
Roanoke city, VA	96,714	97,032	94,911	96,487	-318	2,121	-0.3	2.2	18.6	39.7	27.4	14.3
Salem city, VA	24,961	24,802	24,747	23,835	159	55	0.6	0.2	15.9	39.0	27.6	17.5
Rochester, MN	187,612	186,011	163,618	141,945	1,601	22,393	0.9	13.7	21.1	38.4	27.0	13.5
Dodge County, MN	20,243	20,087	17,731	15,731	156	2,356	0.8	13.3	23.5	37.6	26.2	12.7
Olmsted County, MN	145,769	144,248	124,277	106,470	1,521	19,971	1.1	16.1	21.1	39.3	26.7	12.9
Wabasha County, MN	21,600	21,676	21,610	19,744	-76	66	-0.4	0.3	18.6	33.6	30.2	17.5
Rochester, NY	1,055,278	1,054,323	1,037,831	1,002,410	955	16,492	0.1	1.6	17.9	39.2	28.5	14.4
Livingston County, NY	65,070	65,393	64,328	62,372	-323	1,065	-0.5	1.7	15.8	40.7	29.5	14.1
Monroe County, NY	745,625	744,344	735,343	713,968	1,281	9,001	0.2	1.2	18.1	40.1	27.7	14.2
Ontario County, NY	108,525	107,931	100,224	95,101	594	7,707	0.6	7.7	17.8	35.7	30.7	15.8
Orleans County, NY	42,622	42,883	44,171	41,846	-261	-1,288	-0.6	-2.9	17.3	37.7	30.3	14.6
Wayne County, NY	93,436	93,772	93,765	89,123	-336	7	-0.4	0.0	18.7	35.6	30.9	14.8
Rockford, IL	348,360	349,431	320,204	283,719	-1,071	29,227	-0.3	9.1	20.7	38.1	27.3	13.9
Boone County, IL	54,367	54,165	41,786	30,806	202	12,379	0.4	29.6	23.0	38.8	26.0	12.2
Winnebago County, IL	293,993	295,266	278,418	252,913	-1,273	16,848	-0.4	6.1	20.3	38.0	27.5	14.2
Rocky Mount, NC	152,157	152,392	143,026	133,369	-235	9,366	-0.2	6.5	19.4	36.9	29.1	14.6
Edgecombe County, NC	56,041	56,552	55,606	56,692	-511	946	-0.9	1.7	19.7	36.4	29.0	14.9
Nash County, NC	96,116	95,840	87,420	76,677	276	8,420	0.3	9.6	19.3	37.2	29.1	14.4
Rome, GA	95,989	96,317	90,565	81,251	-328	5,752	-0.3	6.4	20.0	39.4	26.2	14.5
Floyd County, GA	95,989	96,317	90,565	81,251	-328	5,752	-0.3	6.4	20.0	39.4	26.2	14.5
Sacramento–Arden–Arcade–Roseville, CA	2,176,235	2,149,127	1,796,857	1,506,792	27,108	352,270	1.3	19.6	20.1	41.4	26.1	12.4
El Dorado County, CA	180,938	181,058	156,299	125,995	-120	24,759	-0.1	15.8	17.8	33.3	33.6	15.4
Placer County, CA	357,138	348,432	248,399	172,796	8,706	100,033	2.5	40.3	19.6	36.6	28.0	15.8
Sacramento County, CA	1,436,105	1,418,788	1,223,499	1,066,789	17,317	195,289	1.2	16.0	20.8	42.4	25.3	11.5
Yolo County, CA	202,054	200,849	168,660	141,212	1,205	32,189	0.6	19.1	18.0	49.8	22.1	10.2
Saginaw–Saginaw Township North, MI	199,088	200,169	210,039	211,946	-1,081	-9,870	-0.5	-4.7	18.7	37.6	28.0	15.6
Saginaw County, MI	199,088	200,169	210,039	211,946	-1,081	-9,870	-0.5	-4.7	18.7	37.6	28.0	15.6
St. Cloud, MN	190,014	189,093	167,392	149,509	921	21,701	0.5	13.0	19.3	43.8	24.6	12.3
Benton County, MN	38,671	38,451	34,226	30,185	220	4,225	0.6	12.3	20.9	42.7	24.6	11.9
Stearns County, MN	151,343	150,642	133,166	119,324	701	17,476	0.5	13.1	18.9	44.0	24.6	12.4
St. George, UT	141,666	138,115	90,354	48,560	3,551	47,761	2.6	52.9	25.5	37.1	19.9	17.6
Washington County, UT	141,666	138,115	90,354	48,560	3,551	47,761	2.6	52.9	25.5	37.1	19.9	17.6
St. Joseph, MO–KS	127,574	127,329	122,336	115,816	245	4,993	0.2	4.1	19.0	39.7	27.0	14.3
Doniphan County, KS	7,945	7,945	8,249	8,134	0	-304	0.0	-3.7	17.8	38.6	27.2	16.4
Andrew County, MO	17,196	17,291	16,492	14,632	-95	799	-0.5	4.8	19.2	35.0	30.0	15.8
Buchanan County, MO	89,666	89,201	85,998	83,083	465	3,203	0.5	3.7	19.6	40.1	26.3	14.0
DeKalb County, MO	12,767	12,892	11,597	9,967	-125	1,295	-1.0	11.2	14.7	43.6	28.3	13.5

[1] The April 1, 2000, Population Estimates base reflects modifications to the Census 2000 population as documented in the Count Question Resolution program and geographic program revisions.
[2] The April 1, 1990, census counts include corrections processed through August 1997, results of special censuses and test censuses, and do not include adjustments for census coverage errors.
[3] Based on the April 1, 2010, estimates base and the July 1, 2011, estimates.
[4] Based on the April 1, 2010, complete count and the April 1, 2000 estimates base.
0 = Represents zero or amounts to zero.

Table C-1. Population and Population Characteristics—*Continued*

Metropolitan statistical area, division, and component county	Population				Net change		Percent change		Percent			
	2011 (July 1)	2010 Census (April 1)	2000¹ (estimates base)	1990² (April 1)	2010–2011³	2000–2010⁴	2010–2011³	2000–2010⁴	Under 15 years, 2011	15 to 44 years, 2011	45 to 64 years, 2011	65 years and over, 2011
St. Louis, MO–IL⁶	2,817,355	2,812,896	2,698,687	2,580,720	4,459	114,209	0.2	4.2	19.3	39.2	27.9	13.5
Bond County, IL	17,727	17,768	17,633	14,991	-41	135	-0.2	0.8	16.7	40.2	28.1	14.9
Calhoun County, IL	5,048	5,089	5,084	5,322	-41	5	-0.8	0.1	17.3	32.4	29.7	20.6
Clinton County, IL	37,956	37,762	35,535	33,944	194	2,227	0.5	6.3	18.4	39.1	28.1	14.5
Jersey County, IL	22,916	22,985	21,668	20,539	-69	1,317	-0.3	6.1	18.2	36.8	28.8	16.2
Macoupin County, IL	47,687	47,765	49,019	47,679	-78	-1,254	-0.2	-2.6	18.3	35.5	29.1	17.1
Madison County, IL	268,459	269,282	258,941	249,238	-823	10,341	-0.3	4.0	18.6	39.1	27.8	14.5
Monroe County, IL	33,306	32,957	27,619	22,422	349	5,338	1.1	19.3	19.6	35.8	30.3	14.4
St. Clair County, IL	270,259	270,056	256,082	262,852	203	13,974	0.1	5.5	20.6	39.5	27.2	12.7
Franklin County, MO	101,938	101,492	93,807	80,603	446	7,685	0.4	8.2	20.0	36.9	28.9	14.2
Jefferson County, MO	219,480	218,733	198,099	171,380	747	20,634	0.3	10.4	20.5	38.9	29.0	11.5
Lincoln County, MO	53,076	52,566	38,944	28,892	510	13,622	1.0	35.0	22.8	39.0	27.1	11.1
St. Charles County, MO	365,151	360,485	283,883	212,751	4,666	76,602	1.3	27.0	20.9	39.8	27.6	11.7
St. Louis County, MO	998,692	998,954	1,016,315	993,508	-262	-17,361	0.0	-1.7	18.7	37.5	28.7	15.2
Warren County, MO	32,515	32,513	24,525	19,534	2	7,988	0.0	32.6	20.5	35.7	28.7	15.1
Washington County, MO	25,076	25,195	23,344	20,380	-119	1,851	-0.5	7.9	19.8	37.6	28.9	13.7
St. Louis city, MO	318,069	319,294	348,189	396,685	-1,225	-28,895	-0.4	-8.3	17.7	46.3	25.1	10.9
Salem, OR	394,865	390,738	347,214	278,024	4,127	43,524	1.1	12.5	21.5	40.0	25.0	13.5
Marion County, OR	318,872	315,335	284,834	228,483	3,537	30,501	1.1	10.7	21.9	40.2	24.8	13.1
Polk County, OR	75,993	75,403	62,380	49,541	590	13,023	0.8	20.9	19.5	39.5	25.8	15.1
Salinas, CA	421,898	415,057	401,762	355,660	6,841	13,295	1.6	3.3	22.4	43.6	23.2	10.8
Monterey County, CA	421,898	415,057	401,762	355,660	6,841	13,295	1.6	3.3	22.4	43.6	23.2	10.8
Salisbury, MD	125,529	125,203	109,391	97,779	326	15,812	0.3	14.5	17.6	42.6	26.3	13.5
Somerset County, MD	26,339	26,470	24,747	23,440	-131	1,723	-0.5	7.0	14.0	45.6	26.3	14.1
Wicomico County, MD	99,190	98,733	84,644	74,339	457	14,089	0.5	16.6	18.6	41.8	26.3	13.3
Salt Lake City, UT	1,145,905	1,124,197	968,858	768,075	21,708	155,339	1.9	16.0	24.8	44.8	21.6	8.8
Salt Lake County, UT	1,048,985	1,029,655	898,387	725,956	19,330	131,268	1.9	14.6	24.6	45.1	21.4	8.9
Summit County, UT	37,594	36,324	29,736	15,518	1,270	6,588	3.5	22.2	22.6	39.4	30.0	8.0
Tooele County, UT	59,326	58,218	40,735	26,601	1,108	17,483	1.9	42.9	30.4	42.1	19.9	7.6
San Angelo, TX	113,443	111,823	105,781	100,087	1,620	6,042	1.4	5.7	19.8	41.7	24.5	13.9
Irion County, TX	1,620	1,599	1,771	1,629	21	-172	1.3	-9.7	17.0	33.1	31.4	18.4
Tom Green County, TX	111,823	110,224	104,010	98,458	1,599	6,214	1.5	6.0	19.9	41.9	24.4	13.9
San Antonio–New Braunfels, TX	2,194,927	2,142,508	1,711,703	1,407,745	52,419	430,805	2.4	25.2	22.2	42.1	24.6	11.2
Atascosa County, TX	45,579	44,911	38,628	30,533	668	6,283	1.5	16.3	23.7	37.4	25.7	13.3
Bandera County, TX	20,538	20,485	17,645	10,562	53	2,840	0.3	16.1	14.8	27.7	36.4	21.1
Bexar County, TX	1,756,153	1,714,773	1,392,931	1,185,394	41,380	321,842	2.4	23.1	22.5	43.6	23.5	10.4
Comal County, TX	111,963	108,472	78,021	51,832	3,491	30,451	3.2	39.0	19.0	33.9	31.0	16.1
Guadalupe County, TX	135,757	131,533	89,023	64,873	4,224	42,510	3.2	47.8	22.3	40.0	26.0	11.8
Kendall County, TX	34,781	33,410	23,743	14,589	1,371	9,667	4.1	40.7	19.1	32.0	31.6	17.3
Medina County, TX	46,367	46,006	39,304	27,312	361	6,702	0.8	17.1	20.6	37.3	28.2	13.9
Wilson County, TX	43,789	42,918	32,408	22,650	871	10,510	2.0	32.4	21.0	35.7	30.1	13.1
San Diego–Carlsbad–San Marcos, CA	3,140,069	3,095,313	2,813,833	2,498,016	44,756	281,480	1.4	10.0	19.1	44.6	24.7	11.6
San Diego County, CA	3,140,069	3,095,313	2,813,833	2,498,016	44,756	281,480	1.4	10.0	19.1	44.6	24.7	11.6
Sandusky, OH	76,751	77,079	79,551	76,781	-328	-2,472	-0.4	-3.1	17.6	34.1	30.7	17.6
Erie County, OH	76,751	77,079	79,551	76,781	-328	-2,472	-0.4	-3.1	17.6	34.1	30.7	17.6
San Francisco–Oakland–Fremont, CA	4,391,037	4,335,391	4,123,740	3,711,756	55,646	211,651	1.3	5.1	17.5	42.2	27.4	12.9
Oakland–Fremont–Hayward, CA	2,595,971	2,559,296	2,392,557	2,108,078	36,675	166,739	1.4	7.0	19.2	41.7	27.1	12.0
Alameda County, CA	1,529,875	1,510,271	1,443,741	1,304,347	19,604	66,530	1.3	4.6	18.6	43.5	26.4	11.5
Contra Costa County, CA	1,066,096	1,049,025	948,816	803,731	17,071	100,209	1.6	10.6	20.0	39.1	28.1	12.8
San Francisco–San Mateo–Redwood City, CA	1,795,066	1,776,095	1,731,183	1,603,678	18,971	44,912	1.1	2.6	15.1	43.0	27.8	14.2
Marin County, CA	255,031	252,409	247,289	230,096	2,622	5,120	1.0	2.1	17.2	32.9	32.6	17.4
San Francisco County, CA	812,826	805,235	776,733	723,959	7,591	28,502	0.9	3.7	11.3	48.8	26.1	13.8
San Mateo County, CA	727,209	718,451	707,161	649,623	8,758	11,290	1.2	1.6	18.5	39.9	28.0	13.6
San Jose–Sunnyvale–Santa Clara, CA	1,865,450	1,836,911	1,735,819	1,534,274	28,539	101,092	1.6	5.8	20.2	43.0	25.5	11.3
San Benito County, CA	56,072	55,269	53,234	36,697	803	2,035	1.5	3.8	23.2	40.7	26.1	10.0
Santa Clara County, CA	1,809,378	1,781,642	1,682,585	1,497,577	27,736	99,057	1.6	5.9	20.1	43.1	25.5	11.3
San Luis Obispo–Paso Robles, CA	271,969	269,637	246,681	217,162	2,332	22,956	0.9	9.3	15.0	41.6	27.8	15.6
San Luis Obispo County, CA	271,969	269,637	246,681	217,162	2,332	22,956	0.9	9.3	15.0	41.6	27.8	15.6
Santa Barbara–Santa Maria–Goleta, CA	426,878	423,895	399,347	369,608	2,983	24,548	0.7	6.1	18.7	44.9	23.4	13.0
Santa Barbara County, CA	426,878	423,895	399,347	369,608	2,983	24,548	0.7	6.1	18.7	44.9	23.4	13.0
Santa Cruz–Watsonville, CA	264,298	262,382	255,602	229,734	1,916	6,780	0.7	2.7	17.1	43.1	28.2	11.6
Santa Cruz County, CA	264,298	262,382	255,602	229,734	1,916	6,780	0.7	2.7	17.1	43.1	28.2	11.6
Santa Fe, NM	145,648	144,170	129,292	98,928	1,478	14,878	1.0	11.5	17.1	34.8	32.1	16.0
Santa Fe County, NM	145,648	144,170	129,292	98,928	1,478	14,878	1.0	11.5	17.1	34.8	32.1	16.0
Santa Rosa–Petaluma, CA	488,116	483,878	458,614	388,222	4,238	25,264	0.9	5.5	17.9	38.3	29.5	14.4
Sonoma County, CA	488,116	483,878	458,614	388,222	4,238	25,264	0.9	5.5	17.9	38.3	29.5	14.4
Savannah, GA	355,576	347,611	293,000	257,899	7,965	54,611	2.3	18.6	20.1	43.4	24.7	11.8
Bryan County, GA	31,377	30,233	23,417	15,438	1,144	6,816	3.8	29.1	24.1	40.4	26.2	9.2
Chatham County, GA	271,544	265,128	232,048	216,774	6,416	33,080	2.4	14.3	19.1	44.3	24.2	12.5
Effingham County, GA	52,655	52,250	37,535	25,687	405	14,715	0.8	39.2	23.0	41.1	26.3	9.6
Scranton–Wilkes-Barre, PA	563,223	563,631	560,625	575,322	-408	3,006	-0.1	0.5	16.4	37.0	28.8	17.8
Lackawanna County, PA	214,166	214,437	213,295	219,097	-271	1,142	-0.1	0.5	16.6	37.3	28.5	17.6
Luzerne County, PA	320,651	320,918	319,250	328,149	-267	1,668	-0.1	0.5	16.2	37.0	28.9	17.9
Wyoming County, PA	28,406	28,276	28,080	28,076	130	196	0.5	0.7	16.9	35.5	30.4	17.2

¹ The April 1, 2000, Population Estimates base reflects modifications to the Census 2000 population as documented in the Count Question Resolution program and geographic program revisions.
² The April 1, 1990, census counts include corrections processed through August 1997, results of special censuses and test censuses, and do not include adjustments for census coverage errors.
³ Based on the April 1, 2010, estimates base and the July 1, 2011, estimates.
⁴ Based on the April 1, 2010, complete count and April 1, 2000 estimates base.
⁶ The portion of Sullivan city in Crawford County, MO is legally part of the St. Louis, MO–IL MSA. That portion is not included in these figures for the St. Louis, MSA.
0 = Represents zero or amounts to zero.

Table C-1.   Population and Population Characteristics—*Continued*

Metropolitan statistical area, division, and component county	Population — 2011 (July 1)	Population — 2010 Census (April 1)	Population — 2000¹ (estimates base)	Population — 1990² (April 1)	Net change 2010–2011³	Net change 2000–2010⁴	Percent change 2010–2011³	Percent change 2000–2010⁴	Percent Under 15 years, 2011	Percent 15 to 44 years, 2011	Percent 45 to 64 years, 2011	Percent 65 years and over, 2011
Seattle–Tacoma–Bellevue, WA	3,500,026	3,439,809	3,043,878	2,559,136	60,217	395,931	1.8	13.0	18.7	43.1	27.0	11.1
Seattle–Bellevue–Everett, WA	2,692,122	2,644,584	2,343,058	1,972,933	47,538	301,526	1.8	12.9	18.3	43.4	27.2	11.1
King County, WA	1,969,722	1,931,249	1,737,034	1,507,305	38,473	194,215	2.0	11.2	17.7	44.2	26.9	11.2
Snohomish County, WA	722,400	713,335	606,024	465,628	9,065	107,311	1.3	17.7	19.8	41.3	28.2	10.7
Tacoma, WA	807,904	795,225	700,820	586,203	12,679	94,405	1.6	13.5	20.3	42.1	26.3	11.3
Pierce County, WA	807,904	795,225	700,820	586,203	12,679	94,405	1.6	13.5	20.3	42.1	26.3	11.3
Sebastian–Vero Beach, FL	138,894	138,028	112,947	90,208	866	25,081	0.6	22.2	15.1	29.2	28.2	27.6
Indian River County, FL	138,894	138,028	112,947	90,208	866	25,081	0.6	22.2	15.1	29.2	28.2	27.6
Sheboygan, WI	115,149	115,507	112,646	103,877	-358	2,861	-0.3	2.5	19.3	36.5	29.5	14.7
Sheboygan County, WI	115,149	115,507	112,646	103,877	-358	2,861	-0.3	2.5	19.3	36.5	29.5	14.7
Sherman–Denison, TX	121,419	120,877	110,595	95,019	542	10,282	0.4	9.3	19.8	36.5	27.8	15.9
Grayson County, TX	121,419	120,877	110,595	95,019	542	10,282	0.4	9.3	19.8	36.5	27.8	15.9
Shreveport–Bossier City, LA	403,595	398,604	375,965	360,009	4,991	22,639	1.3	6.0	20.9	40.0	25.9	13.2
Bossier Parish, LA	119,732	116,979	98,310	86,088	2,753	18,669	2.4	19.0	21.6	41.7	24.6	12.0
Caddo Parish, LA	257,051	254,969	252,161	248,253	2,082	2,808	0.8	1.1	20.6	39.5	26.2	13.6
De Soto Parish, LA	26,812	26,656	25,494	25,668	156	1,162	0.6	4.6	20.2	36.3	28.8	14.7
Sioux City, IA–NE–SD	144,062	143,577	143,053	131,350	485	524	0.3	0.4	22.4	38.8	25.8	13.0
Woodbury County, IA	102,509	102,172	103,877	98,276	337	-1,705	0.3	-1.6	22.1	39.5	25.5	12.9
Dakota County, NE	20,913	21,006	20,253	16,742	-93	753	-0.4	3.7	25.1	39.3	24.0	11.5
Dixon County, NE	5,989	6,000	6,339	6,143	-11	-339	-0.2	-5.3	21.2	32.6	28.4	17.8
Union County, SD	14,651	14,399	12,584	10,189	252	1,815	1.8	14.4	21.1	35.1	29.3	14.4
Sioux Falls, SD	232,433	228,261	187,093	153,500	4,172	41,168	1.8	22.0	21.8	41.6	25.3	11.4
Lincoln County, SD	46,793	44,828	24,131	15,427	1,965	20,697	4.4	85.8	25.4	42.6	22.9	9.2
McCook County, SD	5,556	5,618	5,832	5,688	-62	-214	-1.1	-3.7	21.5	30.9	28.5	19.0
Minnehaha County, SD	171,752	169,468	148,281	123,809	2,284	21,187	1.3	14.3	20.9	42.1	25.6	11.3
Turner County, SD	8,332	8,347	8,849	8,576	-15	-502	-0.2	-5.7	19.3	32.6	29.2	18.8
South Bend–Mishawaka, IN–MI	318,688	319,224	316,663	296,529	-536	2,561	-0.2	0.8	20.0	39.3	26.9	13.8
St. Joseph County, IN	266,700	266,931	265,559	247,052	-231	1,372	-0.1	0.5	20.2	40.3	26.1	13.4
Cass County, MI	51,988	52,293	51,104	49,477	-305	1,189	-0.6	2.3	18.7	34.1	31.2	16.0
Spartanburg, SC	286,868	284,307	253,791	226,793	2,561	30,516	0.9	12.0	20.0	39.3	26.9	13.8
Spartanburg County, SC	286,868	284,307	253,791	226,793	2,561	30,516	0.9	12.0	20.0	39.3	26.9	13.8
Spokane, WA	473,761	471,221	417,939	361,333	2,540	53,282	0.5	12.7	19.0	40.7	27.1	13.3
Spokane County, WA	473,761	471,221	417,939	361,333	2,540	53,282	0.5	12.7	19.0	40.7	27.1	13.3
Springfield, IL	211,547	210,170	201,437	189,550	1,377	8,733	0.7	4.3	19.4	37.6	28.9	14.1
Menard County, IL	12,703	12,705	12,486	11,164	-2	219	0.0	1.8	18.5	34.2	31.4	15.9
Sangamon County, IL	198,844	197,465	188,951	178,386	1,379	8,514	0.7	4.5	19.4	37.8	28.8	14.0
Springfield, MA	693,204	692,942	680,014	672,964	262	12,928	0.0	1.9	17.2	40.4	28.2	14.2
Franklin County, MA	71,599	71,372	71,535	70,086	227	-163	0.3	-0.2	15.5	35.0	33.8	15.7
Hampden County, MA	463,783	463,490	456,228	456,310	293	7,262	0.1	1.6	18.9	39.2	27.5	14.3
Hampshire County, MA	157,822	158,080	152,251	146,568	-258	5,829	-0.2	3.8	13.0	46.4	27.6	13.0
Springfield, MO	440,142	436,712	368,374	298,818	3,430	68,338	0.8	18.6	19.1	41.4	25.4	14.1
Christian County, MO	78,570	77,422	54,285	32,644	1,148	23,137	1.5	42.6	22.5	39.0	26.0	12.6
Dallas County, MO	16,749	16,777	15,661	12,646	-28	1,116	-0.2	7.1	19.7	33.8	29.2	17.2
Greene County, MO	277,214	275,174	240,391	207,949	2,040	34,783	0.7	14.5	17.6	43.4	24.8	14.2
Polk County, MO	31,170	31,137	26,992	21,826	33	4,145	0.1	15.4	19.7	38.1	25.8	16.5
Webster County, MO	36,439	36,202	31,045	23,753	237	5,157	0.7	16.6	22.6	37.1	26.7	13.6
Springfield, OH	137,691	138,333	144,742	147,538	-642	-6,409	-0.5	-4.4	19.3	36.1	28.3	16.4
Clark County, OH	137,691	138,333	144,742	147,538	-642	-6,409	-0.5	-4.4	19.3	36.1	28.3	16.4
State College, PA	154,722	153,990	135,758	124,812	732	18,232	0.5	13.4	12.6	54.7	21.2	11.5
Centre County, PA	154,722	153,990	135,758	124,812	732	18,232	0.5	13.4	12.6	54.7	21.2	11.5
Steubenville–Weirton, OH–WV	123,243	124,454	132,008	142,523	-1,211	-7,554	-1.0	-5.7	15.9	34.4	31.0	18.6
Jefferson County, OH	68,828	69,709	73,894	80,298	-881	-4,185	-1.3	-5.7	16.1	34.9	30.6	18.4
Brooke County, WV	23,844	24,069	25,447	26,992	-225	-1,378	-0.9	-5.4	15.2	34.7	31.2	19.0
Hancock County, WV	30,571	30,676	32,667	35,233	-105	-1,991	-0.3	-6.1	16.2	33.1	31.8	18.9
Stockton, CA	696,214	685,306	563,598	480,628	10,908	121,708	1.6	21.6	23.9	41.9	23.6	10.6
San Joaquin County, CA	696,214	685,306	563,598	480,628	10,908	121,708	1.6	21.6	23.9	41.9	23.6	10.6
Sumter, SC	107,460	107,456	104,646	101,276	4	2,810	0.0	2.7	21.1	40.0	25.6	13.3
Sumter County, SC	107,460	107,456	104,646	101,276	4	2,810	0.0	2.7	21.1	40.0	25.6	13.3
Syracuse, NY	662,553	662,577	650,154	659,924	-24	12,423	0.0	1.9	18.2	39.6	28.3	14.0
Madison County, NY	73,365	73,442	69,441	69,166	-77	4,001	-0.1	5.8	17.0	39.3	29.4	14.3
Onondaga County, NY	466,960	467,026	458,336	468,973	-66	8,690	0.0	1.9	18.4	39.5	27.9	14.2
Oswego County, NY	122,228	122,109	122,377	121,785	119	-268	0.1	-0.2	18.2	40.0	28.9	12.9
Tallahassee, FL	369,758	367,413	320,304	259,107	2,345	47,109	0.6	14.7	16.5	48.4	24.3	10.8
Gadsden County, FL	46,151	46,389	45,087	41,116	-238	1,302	-0.5	2.9	20.1	37.3	28.5	14.1
Jefferson County, FL	14,658	14,761	12,902	11,296	-103	1,859	-0.7	14.4	15.4	35.0	32.1	17.5
Leon County, FL	277,971	275,487	239,452	192,493	2,484	36,035	0.9	15.0	15.7	51.8	22.6	9.8
Wakulla County, FL	30,978	30,776	22,863	14,202	202	7,913	0.7	34.6	18.1	41.0	29.6	11.3

¹ The April 1, 2000, Population Estimates base reflects modifications to the Census 2000 population as documented in the Count Question Resolution program and geographic program revisions.
² The April 1, 1990, census counts include corrections processed through August 1997, results of special censuses and test censuses, and do not include adjustments for census coverage errors.
³ Based on the April 1, 2010, estimates base and the July 1, 2011, estimates.
⁴ Based on the April 1, 2010, complete count and the April 1, 2000 estimates base.
0 = Represents zero or amounts to zero.

Table C-1. Population and Population Characteristics—*Continued*

Metropolitan statistical area, division, and component county	Population				Net change		Percent change		Percent			
	2011 (July 1)	2010 Census (April 1)	2000[1] (estimates base)	1990[2] (April 1)	2010– 2011[3]	2000– 2010[4]	2010– 2011[3]	2000– 2010[4]	Under 15 years, 2011	15 to 44 years, 2011	45 to 64 years, 2011	65 years and over, 2011
Tampa–St. Petersburg–Clearwater, FL	2,824,724	2,783,243	2,395,997	2,067,959	41,481	387,246	1.5	16.2	17.1	37.4	28.1	17.4
Hernando County, FL	173,094	172,778	130,802	101,115	316	41,976	0.2	32.1	15.9	30.1	27.9	26.1
Hillsborough County, FL	1,267,775	1,229,226	998,948	834,054	38,549	230,278	3.1	23.1	19.3	42.6	26.2	11.9
Pasco County, FL	466,457	464,697	344,765	281,131	1,760	119,932	0.4	34.8	17.2	34.2	27.6	21.0
Pinellas County, FL	917,398	916,542	921,482	851,659	856	-4,940	0.1	-0.5	14.3	33.3	31.0	21.4
Terre Haute, IN	172,663	172,425	170,943	166,578	238	1,482	0.1	0.9	17.8	41.3	26.6	14.3
Clay County, IN	26,894	26,890	26,556	24,705	4	334	0.0	1.3	19.1	37.2	28.4	15.4
Sullivan County, IN	21,356	21,475	21,751	18,993	-119	-276	-0.6	-1.3	17.0	39.5	28.2	15.3
Vermillion County, IN	16,231	16,212	16,788	16,773	19	-576	0.1	-3.4	18.9	34.6	29.2	17.3
Vigo County, IN	108,182	107,848	105,848	106,107	334	2,000	0.3	1.9	17.5	43.6	25.4	13.5
Texarkana, TX–Texarkana, AR	136,552	136,027	129,749	120,132	525	6,278	0.4	4.8	20.0	39.4	26.4	14.2
Miller County, AR	43,759	43,462	40,443	38,467	297	3,019	0.7	7.5	20.4	39.3	26.4	14.0
Bowie County, TX	92,793	92,565	89,306	81,665	228	3,259	0.2	3.6	19.8	39.4	26.4	14.3
Toledo, OH	650,266	651,429	659,188	654,157	-1,163	-7,759	-0.2	-1.2	19.0	39.9	27.5	13.7
Fulton County, OH	42,510	42,698	42,084	38,498	-188	614	-0.4	1.5	20.4	35.6	29.6	14.5
Lucas County, OH	440,005	441,815	455,054	462,361	-1,810	-13,239	-0.4	-2.9	19.6	39.9	27.1	13.4
Ottawa County, OH	41,396	41,428	40,985	40,029	-32	443	-0.1	1.1	16.4	30.9	33.3	19.5
Wood County, OH	126,355	125,488	121,065	113,269	867	4,423	0.7	3.7	17.3	44.2	26.0	12.5
Topeka, KS	234,647	233,870	224,551	210,257	777	9,319	0.3	4.2	20.5	36.3	28.2	15.0
Jackson County, KS	13,433	13,462	12,657	11,525	-29	805	-0.2	6.4	21.2	34.5	28.5	15.7
Jefferson County, KS	18,941	19,126	18,426	15,905	-185	700	-1.0	3.8	19.3	33.1	31.7	15.8
Osage County, KS	16,306	16,295	16,712	15,248	11	-417	0.1	-2.5	20.1	32.4	30.5	17.0
Shawnee County, KS	178,941	177,934	169,871	160,976	1,007	8,063	0.6	4.7	20.6	37.3	27.5	14.6
Wabaunsee County, KS	7,026	7,053	6,885	6,603	-27	168	-0.4	2.4	21.0	31.5	31.7	15.9
Trenton–Ewing, NJ	367,063	366,513	350,761	325,759	550	15,752	0.2	4.5	18.4	41.4	27.2	12.9
Mercer County, NJ	367,063	366,513	350,761	325,759	550	15,752	0.2	4.5	18.4	41.4	27.2	12.9
Tucson, AZ	989,569	980,263	843,746	666,957	9,306	136,517	0.9	16.2	18.8	39.4	25.9	15.9
Pima County, AZ	989,569	980,263	843,746	666,957	9,306	136,517	0.9	16.2	18.8	39.4	25.9	15.9
Tulsa, OK	946,962	937,478	859,532	761,019	9,484	77,946	1.0	9.1	21.2	39.5	26.2	13.1
Creek County, OK	70,467	69,967	67,367	60,915	500	2,600	0.7	3.9	20.3	35.8	28.5	15.3
Okmulgee County, OK	39,937	40,069	39,685	36,490	-132	384	-0.3	1.0	20.3	36.7	27.0	16.1
Osage County, OK	47,425	47,472	44,437	41,645	-47	3,035	-0.1	6.8	19.5	35.0	30.1	15.4
Pawnee County, OK	16,730	16,577	16,612	15,575	153	-35	0.9	-0.2	20.3	34.8	28.4	16.5
Rogers County, OK	87,706	86,905	70,641	55,170	801	16,264	0.9	23.0	20.8	38.0	27.5	13.8
Tulsa County, OK	610,599	603,403	563,299	503,341	7,196	40,104	1.2	7.1	21.5	41.0	25.2	12.3
Wagoner County, OK	74,098	73,085	57,491	47,883	1,013	15,594	1.4	27.1	21.7	38.1	27.2	13.0
Tuscaloosa, AL	221,553	219,461	192,034	176,151	2,092	27,427	1.0	14.3	17.9	46.9	23.7	11.5
Greene County, AL	8,921	9,045	9,974	10,153	-124	-929	-1.4	-9.3	19.7	33.4	30.6	16.4
Hale County, AL	15,421	15,760	17,185	15,498	-339	-1,425	-2.2	-8.3	19.4	35.4	29.3	15.9
Tuscaloosa County, AL	197,211	194,656	164,875	150,500	2,555	29,781	1.3	18.1	17.7	48.4	22.9	10.9
Tyler, TX	213,381	209,714	174,706	151,309	3,667	35,008	1.7	20.0	21.3	39.9	24.4	14.4
Smith County, TX	213,381	209,714	174,706	151,309	3,667	35,008	1.7	20.0	21.3	39.9	24.4	14.4
Utica–Rome, NY	298,447	299,397	299,896	316,645	-950	-499	-0.3	-0.2	17.5	37.2	28.7	16.5
Herkimer County, NY	64,160	64,519	64,427	65,809	-359	92	-0.6	0.1	17.6	35.7	29.9	16.7
Oneida County, NY	234,287	234,878	235,469	250,836	-591	-591	-0.3	-0.3	17.5	37.6	28.4	16.5
Valdosta, GA	142,307	139,588	119,560	99,244	2,719	20,028	1.9	16.8	20.6	46.3	22.5	10.6
Brooks County, GA	15,889	16,243	16,450	15,398	-354	-207	-2.2	-1.3	19.4	35.4	28.7	16.6
Echols County, GA	4,129	4,034	3,754	2,334	95	280	2.4	7.5	23.9	44.2	22.5	9.4
Lanier County, GA	10,404	10,078	7,241	5,531	326	2,837	3.2	39.2	22.6	43.1	24.1	10.2
Lowndes County, GA	111,885	109,233	92,115	75,981	2,652	17,118	2.4	18.6	20.5	48.2	21.5	9.8
Vallejo–Fairfield, CA	416,471	413,344	394,542	339,469	3,127	18,802	0.8	4.8	19.7	40.6	28.0	11.7
Solano County, CA	416,471	413,344	394,542	339,469	3,127	18,802	0.8	4.8	19.7	40.6	28.0	11.7
Victoria, TX	116,230	115,384	111,663	99,394	846	3,721	0.7	3.3	21.9	37.2	26.6	14.3
Calhoun County, TX	21,442	21,381	20,647	19,053	61	734	0.3	3.6	21.6	36.5	26.5	15.4
Goliad County, TX	7,243	7,210	6,928	5,980	33	282	0.5	4.1	17.9	30.5	32.1	19.6
Victoria County, TX	87,545	86,793	84,088	74,361	752	2,705	0.9	3.2	22.2	37.9	26.2	13.6
Vineland–Millville–Bridgeton, NJ	157,095	156,898	146,438	138,053	197	10,460	0.1	7.1	20.0	41.6	25.5	12.8
Cumberland County, NJ	157,095	156,898	146,438	138,053	197	10,460	0.1	7.1	20.0	41.6	25.5	12.8

[1] The April 1, 2000, Population Estimates base reflects modifications to the Census 2000 population as documented in the Count Question Resolution program and geographic program revisions.
[2] The April 1, 1990, census counts include corrections processed through August 1997, results of special censuses and test censuses, and do not include adjustments for census coverage errors.
[3] Based on the April 1, 2010, estimates base and the July 1, 2011, estimates.
[4] Based on the April 1, 2010, complete count and the April 1, 2000 estimates base.
0 = Represents zero or amounts to zero.

Table C-1.   Population and Population Characteristics—*Continued*

Metropolitan statistical area, division, and component county	Population				Net change		Percent change		Percent			
	2011 (July 1)	2010 Census (April 1)	2000[1] (estimates base)	1990[2] (April 1)	2010– 2011[3]	2000– 2010[4]	2010– 2011[3]	2000– 2010[4]	Under 15 years, 2011	15 to 44 years, 2011	45 to 64 years, 2011	65 years and over, 2011
Virginia Beach–Norfolk–Newport News, VA–NC	1,679,894	1,671,683	1,576,370	1,450,855	8,211	95,313	0.5	6.0	19.3	42.7	26.2	11.8
Currituck County, NC	23,955	23,547	18,190	13,736	408	5,357	1.7	29.5	18.7	36.1	31.9	13.3
Gloucester County, VA	36,901	36,858	34,780	30,131	43	2,078	0.1	6.0	17.0	35.5	32.2	15.3
Isle of Wight County, VA	35,356	35,270	29,728	25,053	86	5,542	0.2	18.6	17.7	33.3	33.6	15.4
James City County, VA	68,200	67,009	48,102	34,779	1,191	18,907	1.8	39.3	16.9	32.5	29.1	21.5
Mathews County, VA	8,962	8,978	9,207	8,348	-16	-229	-0.2	-2.5	13.9	27.7	32.3	26.1
Surry County, VA	6,931	7,058	6,829	6,145	-127	229	-1.8	3.4	15.9	32.9	35.0	16.2
York County, VA	66,134	65,464	56,297	42,434	670	9,167	1.0	16.3	20.2	37.7	29.7	12.4
Chesapeake city, VA	225,050	222,209	199,184	151,982	2,841	23,025	1.3	11.6	20.7	40.3	28.3	10.7
Hampton city, VA	136,401	137,436	146,437	133,773	-1,035	-9,001	-0.8	-6.1	18.5	42.1	26.8	12.6
Newport News city, VA	179,611	180,719	180,150	171,477	-1,108	569	-0.6	0.3	20.4	44.7	24.0	10.8
Norfolk city, VA	242,628	242,803	234,403	261,250	-175	8,400	-0.1	3.6	17.9	51.2	21.5	9.4
Poquoson city, VA	12,000	12,150	11,566	11,005	-150	584	-1.2	5.0	17.8	33.8	32.3	16.2
Portsmouth city, VA	95,684	95,535	100,565	103,910	149	-5,030	0.2	-5.0	20.1	41.3	25.5	13.1
Suffolk city, VA	84,930	84,585	63,677	52,143	345	20,908	0.4	32.8	21.3	39.0	27.9	11.8
Virginia Beach city, VA	442,707	437,994	425,257	393,089	4,713	12,737	1.1	3.0	19.6	43.9	25.7	10.9
Williamsburg city, VA	14,444	14,068	11,998	11,600	376	2,070	2.7	17.3	8.9	62.3	15.9	13.0
Visalia–Porterville, CA	449,253	442,179	368,021	311,932	7,074	74,158	1.6	20.2	27.0	42.4	20.9	9.6
Tulare County, CA	449,253	442,179	368,021	311,932	7,074	74,158	1.6	20.2	27.0	42.4	20.9	9.6
Waco, TX	238,564	234,906	213,517	189,123	3,658	21,389	1.6	10.0	20.8	43.2	23.4	12.5
McLennan County, TX	238,564	234,906	213,517	189,123	3,658	21,389	1.6	10.0	20.8	43.2	23.4	12.5
Warner Robins, GA	143,925	139,900	110,765	89,208	4,025	29,135	2.9	26.3	21.7	42.0	25.8	10.5
Houston County, GA	143,925	139,900	110,765	89,208	4,025	29,135	2.9	26.3	21.7	42.0	25.8	10.5
Washington–Arlington–Alexandria, DC–VA–MD–WV	5,703,948	5,582,170	4,796,183	4,122,259	121,778	785,987	2.2	16.4	19.7	43.4	26.7	10.2
Bethesda–Rockville–Frederick, MD	1,226,539	1,205,162	1,068,618	913,083	21,377	136,544	1.8	12.8	19.8	39.6	28.3	12.4
Frederick County, MD	236,745	233,385	195,277	150,208	3,360	38,108	1.4	19.5	20.3	39.3	29.0	11.4
Montgomery County, MD	989,794	971,777	873,341	762,875	18,017	98,436	1.9	11.3	19.7	39.7	28.1	12.6
Washington–Arlington–Alexandria, DC–VA–MD–WV	4,477,409	4,377,008	3,727,565	3,209,176	100,401	649,443	2.3	17.4	19.7	44.4	26.2	9.7
District of Columbia, DC	617,996	601,723	572,059	606,900	16,273	29,664	2.7	5.2	14.4	51.2	23.1	11.4
Calvert County, MD	89,256	88,737	74,563	51,372	519	14,174	0.6	19.0	20.2	37.0	31.4	11.4
Charles County, MD	149,130	146,551	120,546	101,154	2,579	26,005	1.8	21.6	20.7	41.1	28.3	9.8
Prince George's County, MD	871,233	863,420	801,515	722,705	7,813	61,905	0.9	7.7	19.5	44.3	26.4	9.8
Arlington County, VA	216,004	207,627	189,453	170,895	8,377	18,174	4.0	9.6	13.9	55.0	22.4	8.7
Clarke County, VA	14,258	14,034	12,652	12,101	224	1,382	1.6	10.9	17.7	31.9	33.8	16.6
Fairfax County, VA	1,100,692	1,081,726	969,749	818,310	18,966	111,977	1.8	11.5	20.1	41.4	28.3	10.2
Fauquier County, VA	66,071	65,203	55,139	48,700	868	10,064	1.3	18.3	20.1	35.1	31.6	13.2
Loudoun County, VA	325,405	312,311	169,599	86,185	13,094	142,712	4.2	84.1	25.8	42.6	24.8	6.9
Prince William County, VA	419,006	402,002	280,813	214,954	17,004	121,189	4.2	43.2	24.1	43.9	25.0	7.1
Spotsylvania County, VA	124,327	122,397	90,395	57,397	1,930	32,002	1.6	35.4	22.0	40.2	27.6	10.3
Stafford County, VA	132,133	128,961	92,446	62,255	3,172	36,515	2.5	39.5	22.6	42.6	27.2	7.6
Warren County, VA	37,749	37,575	31,584	26,142	174	5,991	0.5	19.0	19.3	37.5	30.0	13.2
Alexandria city, VA	144,301	139,966	128,283	111,183	4,335	11,683	3.1	9.1	15.4	51.1	24.3	9.3
Fairfax city, VA	22,549	22,565	21,498	19,945	-16	1,067	-0.1	5.0	17.2	42.3	27.0	13.5
Falls Church city, VA	12,751	12,332	10,377	9,464	419	1,955	3.4	18.8	20.2	39.4	30.2	10.2
Fredericksburg city, VA	25,691	24,286	19,279	19,033	1,405	5,007	5.8	26.0	18.0	52.0	20.4	9.6
Manassas city, VA	39,300	37,821	35,135	27,757	1,479	2,686	3.9	7.6	23.7	45.0	24.3	7.0
Manassas Park city, VA	15,332	14,273	10,290	6,798	1,059	3,983	7.4	38.7	24.8	49.4	20.6	5.1
Jefferson County, WV	54,225	53,498	42,190	35,926	727	11,308	1.4	26.8	19.5	39.2	29.0	12.2
Waterloo–Cedar Falls, IA	168,289	167,819	163,706	158,640	470	4,113	0.3	2.5	18.0	42.1	25.1	14.8
Black Hawk County, IA	131,549	131,090	128,012	123,798	459	3,078	0.4	2.4	17.9	43.6	24.6	13.9
Bremer County, IA	24,281	24,276	23,325	22,813	5	951	0.0	4.1	17.9	38.5	26.0	17.5
Grundy County, IA	12,459	12,453	12,369	12,029	6	84	0.0	0.7	19.5	33.2	28.7	18.7
Wausau, WI	134,400	134,063	125,834	115,400	337	8,229	0.3	6.5	19.8	37.2	28.6	14.4
Marathon County, WI	134,400	134,063	125,834	115,400	337	8,229	0.3	6.5	19.8	37.2	28.6	14.4
Wenatchee–East Wenatchee, WA	112,448	110,884	99,219	78,455	1,564	11,665	1.4	11.8	21.1	36.5	27.1	15.3
Chelan County, WA	73,477	72,453	66,616	52,250	1,024	5,837	1.4	8.8	20.7	36.0	27.6	15.7
Douglas County, WA	38,971	38,431	32,603	26,205	540	5,828	1.4	17.9	22.0	37.3	26.1	14.5
Wheeling, WV–OH	147,197	147,950	153,172	159,301	-753	-5,222	-0.5	-3.4	15.9	35.6	30.6	17.8
Belmont County, OH	70,151	70,400	70,226	71,074	-249	174	-0.4	0.2	15.8	36.0	30.5	17.6
Marshall County, WV	32,800	33,107	35,519	37,356	-307	-2,412	-0.9	-6.8	16.7	34.1	31.8	17.5
Ohio County, WV	44,246	44,443	47,427	50,871	-197	-2,984	-0.4	-6.3	15.5	36.1	30.0	18.4
Wichita, KS	625,526	623,061	571,166	511,111	2,465	51,895	0.4	9.1	22.4	39.5	25.9	12.3
Butler County, KS	65,817	65,880	59,482	50,580	-63	6,398	-0.1	10.8	21.8	37.7	27.8	12.7
Harvey County, KS	34,846	34,684	32,869	31,028	162	1,815	0.5	5.5	20.7	35.5	26.4	17.3
Sedgwick County, KS	501,076	498,365	452,869	403,662	2,711	45,496	0.5	10.0	22.6	40.2	25.4	11.7
Sumner County, KS	23,787	24,132	25,946	25,841	-345	-1,814	-1.4	-7.0	21.0	34.0	29.1	15.9

[1] The April 1, 2000, Population Estimates base reflects modifications to the Census 2000 population as documented in the Count Question Resolution program and geographic program revisions.
[2] The April 1, 1990, census counts include corrections processed through August 1997, results of special censuses and test censuses, and do not include adjustments for census coverage errors.
[3] Based on the April 1, 2010, estimates base and the July 1, 2011, estimates.
[4] Based on the April 1, 2010, complete count and the April 1, 2000 estimates base.
0 = Represents zero or amounts to zero.

Table C-1. Population and Population Characteristics—*Continued*

Metropolitan statistical area, division, and component county	Population				Net change		Percent change		Percent			
	2011 (July 1)	2010 Census (April 1)	2000[1] (estimates base)	1990[2] (April 1)	2010–2011[3]	2000–2010[4]	2010–2011[3]	2000–2010[4]	Under 15 years, 2011	15 to 44 years, 2011	45 to 64 years, 2011	65 years and over, 2011
Wichita Falls, TX	150,261	151,306	151,524	140,375	-1,045	-218	-0.7	-0.1	19.2	41.5	25.4	13.8
Archer County, TX	8,842	9,054	8,854	7,973	-212	200	-2.3	2.3	18.4	33.3	31.6	16.7
Clay County, TX	10,721	10,752	11,006	10,024	-31	-254	-0.3	-2.3	18.4	31.7	31.5	18.4
Wichita County, TX	130,698	131,500	131,664	122,378	-802	-164	-0.6	-0.1	19.4	42.9	24.5	13.2
Williamsport, PA	116,747	116,111	120,044	118,710	636	-3,933	0.5	-3.3	16.9	37.8	28.8	16.5
Lycoming County, PA	116,747	116,111	120,044	118,710	636	-3,933	0.5	-3.3	16.9	37.8	28.8	16.5
Wilmington, NC	369,685	362,315	274,532	200,124	7,370	87,783	2.0	32.0	16.5	38.6	28.0	16.9
Brunswick County, NC	110,097	107,431	73,143	50,985	2,666	34,288	2.5	46.9	15.4	30.7	31.4	22.5
New Hanover County, NC	206,189	202,667	160,307	120,284	3,522	42,360	1.7	26.4	16.5	43.4	25.9	14.2
Pender County, NC	53,399	52,217	41,082	28,855	1,182	11,135	2.3	27.1	18.6	36.6	29.4	15.4
Winchester, VA–WV	130,065	128,472	102,997	84,168	1,593	25,475	1.2	24.7	19.6	38.4	28.0	14.0
Frederick County, VA	79,666	78,305	59,209	45,723	1,361	19,096	1.7	32.3	20.3	38.2	28.4	13.1
Winchester city, VA	26,587	26,203	23,585	21,947	384	2,618	1.5	11.1	19.2	42.2	24.6	14.0
Hampshire County, WV	23,812	23,964	20,203	16,498	-152	3,761	-0.6	18.6	17.6	34.9	30.6	16.9
Winston–Salem, NC	482,025	477,717	421,961	361,426	4,308	55,756	0.9	13.2	19.7	38.6	27.5	14.2
Davie County, NC	41,552	41,240	34,835	27,859	312	6,405	0.8	18.4	18.8	34.0	30.0	17.2
Forsyth County, NC	354,952	350,670	306,067	265,855	4,282	44,603	1.2	14.6	20.3	39.9	26.6	13.2
Stokes County, NC	47,242	47,401	44,711	37,224	-159	2,690	-0.3	6.0	17.3	35.1	30.9	16.6
Yadkin County, NC	38,279	38,406	36,348	30,488	-127	2,058	-0.3	5.7	18.7	35.9	28.9	16.5
Worcester, MA	801,227	798,552	750,963	709,711	2,675	47,589	0.3	6.3	18.8	39.4	28.9	12.9
Worcester County, MA	801,227	798,552	750,963	709,711	2,675	47,589	0.3	6.3	18.8	39.4	28.9	12.9
Yakima, WA	247,141	243,231	222,581	188,823	3,910	20,650	1.6	9.3	25.6	40.0	22.7	11.7
Yakima County, WA	247,141	243,231	222,581	188,823	3,910	20,650	1.6	9.3	25.6	40.0	22.7	11.7
York–Hanover, PA	436,770	434,972	381,751	339,574	1,798	53,221	0.4	13.9	19.0	37.7	29.0	14.4
York County, PA	436,770	434,972	381,751	339,574	1,798	53,221	0.4	13.9	19.0	37.7	29.0	14.4
Youngstown–Warren–Boardman, OH–PA	562,739	565,773	602,964	613,604	-3,034	-37,191	-0.5	-6.2	17.3	35.1	29.7	17.9
Mahoning County, OH	237,270	238,823	257,555	264,806	-1,553	-18,732	-0.7	-7.3	17.2	35.2	29.8	17.8
Trumbull County, OH	209,264	210,312	225,116	227,795	-1,048	-14,804	-0.5	-6.6	17.7	34.7	30.0	17.6
Mercer County, PA	116,205	116,638	120,293	121,003	-433	-3,655	-0.4	-3.0	16.9	35.5	28.9	18.6
Yuba City, CA	167,497	166,892	139,149	122,643	605	27,743	0.4	19.9	23.3	40.8	24.2	11.8
Sutter County, CA	94,919	94,737	78,930	64,409	182	15,807	0.2	20.0	22.5	40.1	24.3	13.0
Yuba County, CA	72,578	72,155	60,219	58,234	423	11,936	0.6	19.8	24.2	41.6	24.0	10.2
Yuma, AZ	200,870	195,751	160,026	106,895	5,119	35,725	2.6	22.3	22.8	40.3	21.0	15.9
Yuma County, AZ	200,870	195,751	160,026	106,895	5,119	35,725	2.6	22.3	22.8	40.3	21.0	15.9

[1] The April 1, 2000, Population Estimates base reflects modifications to the Census 2000 population as documented in the Count Question Resolution program and geographic program revisions.
[2] The April 1, 1990, census counts include corrections processed through August 1997, results of special censuses and test censuses, and do not include adjustments for census coverage errors.
[3] Based on the April 1, 2010, estimates base and the July 1, 2011, estimates.
[4] Based on the April 1, 2010, complete count and the April 1, 2000 estimates base.

Table C-2. Population Characteristics and Housing Units

Metropolitan statistical area, division, and component county	Population characteristics, 2011						Housing units					
	One race (percent)					Hispanic or Latino origin[1] (percent)	2011 (July 1)	2010 (July 1)	2005 (July 1)	2000[2] (estimates base)	Change, 2010–2011	
	White alone	Black or African American alone	Asian alone	American Indian, Alaska Native alone	Native Hawaiian and Other Pacific Islander alone						Number	Percent
Abilene, TX	87.3	7.9	1.5	1.0	0.1	21.8	70,070	69,721	67,934	65,224	349	0.5
Callahan County, TX	95.4	1.6	0.5	0.7	0.1	8.5	6,607	6,549	6,279	5,908	58	0.9
Jones County, TX	84.0	12.7	0.7	1.2	0.0	25.5	7,415	7,422	7,377	7,241	-7	-0.1
Taylor County, TX	87.0	7.9	1.7	1.0	0.1	22.6	56,048	55,750	54,278	52,075	298	0.5
Akron, OH	83.5	12.2	2.1	0.2	0.0	1.6	313,028	312,581	306,332	290,987	447	0.1
Portage County, OH	92.3	4.4	1.5	0.2	0.0	1.4	67,707	67,472	65,105	60,113	235	0.3
Summit County, OH	80.8	14.6	2.3	0.2	0.0	1.7	245,321	245,109	241,227	230,874	212	0.1
Albany, GA	44.9	52.5	1.1	0.3	0.2	2.4	65,659	66,060	66,098	63,765	-401	-0.6
Baker County, GA	51.2	46.4	1.1	0.4	0.1	4.9	1,634	1,652	1,715	1,728	-18	-1.1
Dougherty County, GA	30.4	67.1	0.9	0.3	0.2	2.5	40,648	40,801	40,825	39,660	-153	-0.4
Lee County, GA	76.0	20.0	2.4	0.3	0.1	2.2	10,176	10,276	10,006	8,815	-100	-1.0
Terrell County, GA	37.4	60.6	0.4	0.4	0.2	2.1	4,005	4,080	4,298	4,457	-75	-1.8
Worth County, GA	69.0	29.2	0.5	0.3	0.1	1.9	9,196	9,251	9,254	9,105	-55	-0.6
Albany–Schenectady–Troy, NY	85.6	8.3	3.4	0.3	0.1	4.4	395,179	393,298	380,940	363,736	1,881	0.5
Albany County, NY	78.9	13.3	5.1	0.3	0.1	5.2	138,165	137,740	134,778	130,004	425	0.3
Rensselaer County, NY	88.1	6.9	2.4	0.3	0.0	4.1	71,833	71,475	69,173	66,129	358	0.5
Saratoga County, NY	94.5	1.7	2.0	0.2	0.0	2.6	99,514	98,656	93,716	86,697	858	0.9
Schenectady County, NY	81.3	10.8	3.9	0.6	0.2	6.0	68,364	68,196	66,682	65,071	168	0.2
Schoharie County, NY	96.0	1.6	0.7	0.3	0.0	2.9	17,303	17,231	16,591	15,835	72	0.4
Albuquerque, NM	85.1	3.1	2.2	6.7	0.2	47.1	376,662	374,405	345,258	305,881	2,257	0.6
Bernalillo County, NM	85.4	3.4	2.6	5.7	0.2	48.1	285,191	284,234	267,601	238,864	957	0.3
Sandoval County, NM	79.7	2.5	1.6	13.3	0.2	36.0	53,067	52,287	42,919	35,123	780	1.5
Torrance County, NM	91.1	2.0	0.5	3.6	0.2	39.9	7,871	7,798	7,624	7,245	73	0.9
Valencia County, NM	90.3	1.8	0.7	4.9	0.1	58.6	30,533	30,086	27,114	24,649	447	1.5
Alexandria, LA	66.6	29.8	1.1	0.9	0.0	2.9	64,765	64,570	62,425	60,590	195	0.3
Grant Parish, LA	80.8	16.2	0.3	1.1	0.0	4.4	8,908	8,886	8,664	8,531	22	0.2
Rapides Parish, LA	64.2	32.1	1.3	0.8	0.0	2.7	55,857	55,684	53,761	52,059	173	0.3
Allentown–Bethlehem–Easton, PA–NJ	88.8	6.1	2.7	0.5	0.1	13.5	343,955	342,200	328,836	307,274	1,755	0.5
Warren County, NJ	91.8	3.9	2.7	0.2	0.1	7.4	44,908	44,925	44,217	41,138	-17	0.0
Carbon County, PA	96.3	1.8	0.6	0.3	0.1	3.4	34,509	34,299	32,386	30,488	210	0.6
Lehigh County, PA	86.0	7.7	3.2	0.7	0.1	19.5	143,655	142,613	136,961	128,879	1,042	0.7
Northampton County, PA	89.4	5.8	2.6	0.3	0.1	10.8	120,883	120,363	115,272	106,769	520	0.4
Altoona, PA	96.2	1.8	0.6	0.1	0.0	1.0	56,194	56,271	56,145	55,043	-77	-0.1
Blair County, PA	96.2	1.8	0.6	0.1	0.0	1.0	56,194	56,271	56,145	55,043	-77	-0.1
Amarillo, TX	87.7	6.7	2.8	1.1	0.1	26.2	103,444	102,547	97,261	91,577	897	0.9
Armstrong County, TX	96.8	1.2	0.0	1.0	0.0	6.2	899	904	921	919	-5	-0.6
Carson County, TX	95.9	0.8	0.5	1.3	0.0	9.0	2,766	2,784	2,823	2,811	-18	-0.6
Potter County, TX	81.9	10.7	4.1	1.3	0.1	36.0	47,304	47,272	46,087	44,638	32	0.1
Randall County, TX	92.8	3.0	1.6	0.9	0.1	17.6	52,475	51,587	47,430	43,209	888	1.7
Ames, IA	89.2	2.8	6.2	0.2	0.0	3.1	37,089	36,789	34,306	30,634	300	0.8
Story County, IA	89.2	2.8	6.2	0.2	0.0	3.1	37,089	36,789	34,306	30,634	300	0.8
Anchorage, AK	71.8	4.8	6.8	7.6	1.7	6.9	156,709	154,361	143,236	127,711	2,348	1.5
Anchorage Municipality, AK	67.6	5.9	8.4	8.2	2.1	7.9	113,467	113,032	109,159	100,396	435	0.4
Matanuska–Susitna Borough, AK	85.1	1.2	1.4	5.8	0.3	3.9	43,242	41,329	34,077	27,315	1,913	4.6
Anderson, IN	89.1	8.4	0.4	0.4	0.0	3.4	58,910	59,068	58,719	56,924	-158	-0.3
Madison County, IN	89.1	8.4	0.4	0.4	0.0	3.4	58,910	59,068	58,719	56,924	-158	-0.3
Anderson, SC	80.9	16.6	0.8	0.3	0.0	3.1	84,934	84,772	79,997	73,219	162	0.2
Anderson County, SC	80.9	16.6	0.8	0.3	0.0	3.1	84,934	84,772	79,997	73,219	162	0.2
Ann Arbor, MI	75.2	12.9	8.3	0.4	0.1	4.2	147,510	147,573	144,845	130,994	-63	0.0
Washtenaw County, MI	75.2	12.9	8.3	0.4	0.1	4.2	147,510	147,573	144,845	130,994	-63	0.0
Anniston–Oxford, AL	76.2	20.9	0.8	0.5	0.1	3.4	53,347	53,289	52,620	51,177	58	0.1
Calhoun County, AL	76.2	20.9	0.8	0.5	0.1	3.4	53,347	53,289	52,620	51,177	58	0.1
Appleton, WI	93.3	1.0	2.9	1.5	0.0	3.7	93,369	92,844	88,627	78,389	525	0.6
Calumet County, WI	95.7	0.6	2.1	0.5	0.0	3.6	19,838	19,695	18,713	15,773	143	0.7
Outagamie County, WI	92.6	1.1	3.1	1.8	0.0	3.8	73,531	73,149	69,914	62,616	382	0.5
Asheville, NC	91.9	4.8	1.0	0.6	0.1	6.6	215,719	213,638	196,856	175,340	2,081	1.0
Buncombe County, NC	89.7	6.7	1.1	0.5	0.1	6.2	114,383	113,366	104,819	93,984	1,017	0.9
Haywood County, NC	96.6	1.3	0.4	0.6	0.0	3.4	35,361	34,954	32,119	28,641	407	1.2
Henderson County, NC	93.2	3.4	1.1	0.6	0.2	10.0	55,380	54,710	49,612	43,000	670	1.2
Madison County, NC	96.6	1.4	0.4	0.3	0.0	2.2	10,595	10,608	10,306	9,715	-13	-0.1
Athens–Clarke County, GA	74.8	19.8	3.4	0.3	0.1	8.1	81,792	81,719	77,157	67,531	73	0.1
Clarke County, GA	66.8	26.5	4.4	0.4	0.1	10.5	51,113	51,065	48,812	42,263	48	0.1
Madison County, GA	88.6	9.1	0.7	0.3	0.0	4.4	11,761	11,784	11,261	10,514	-23	-0.2
Oconee County, GA	89.3	5.8	3.3	0.3	0.0	4.5	12,386	12,386	11,147	9,396	0	0.0
Oglethorpe County, GA	79.2	18.0	0.6	0.3	0.0	4.0	6,532	6,484	5,937	5,358	48	0.7

[1] Persons of Hispanic origin may be any race.
[2] The April 1, 2000, housing estimates base reflects modifications to the Census 2000 population as documented in the Count Question Resolution program and geographic program revisions.

Table C-2. Population Characteristics and Housing Units—*Continued*

Metropolitan statistical area, division, and component county	Population characteristics, 2011						Housing units					
	One race (percent)					Hispanic or Latino origin[1] (percent)	2011 (July 1)	2010 (July 1)	2005 (July 1)	2000[2] (estimates base)	Change, 2010–2011	
	White alone	Black or African American alone	Asian alone	American Indian, Alaska Native alone	Native Hawaiian and Other Pacific Islander alone						Number	Percent
Atlanta–Sandy Springs–Marietta, GA	59.4	33.0	5.0	0.5	0.1	10.6	2,168,011	2,165,495	1,983,493	1,644,489	2,516	0.1
Barrow County, GA	82.0	12.0	3.5	0.5	0.1	9.1	26,390	26,400	23,094	17,319	-10	0.0
Bartow County, GA	85.9	10.8	0.9	0.6	0.1	7.9	40,111	39,823	36,116	28,760	288	0.7
Butts County, GA	70.4	27.5	0.5	0.3	0.0	2.8	9,337	9,357	8,813	7,362	-20	-0.2
Carroll County, GA	78.0	18.7	0.9	0.5	0.1	6.4	44,374	44,607	42,365	34,078	-233	-0.5
Cherokee County, GA	89.4	6.4	1.8	0.6	0.1	9.9	82,789	82,359	71,690	51,982	430	0.5
Clayton County, GA	26.1	66.0	5.0	0.7	0.1	13.5	104,309	104,704	100,665	86,500	-395	-0.4
Cobb County, GA	66.7	25.9	4.7	0.5	0.1	12.5	287,462	286,490	270,749	237,414	972	0.3
Coweta County, GA	78.2	17.9	1.6	0.4	0.1	7.0	50,774	50,171	43,384	33,198	603	1.2
Dawson County, GA	96.4	1.1	0.7	0.4	0.1	4.1	10,468	10,433	9,178	7,150	35	0.3
DeKalb County, GA	37.8	54.4	5.2	0.6	0.1	9.8	303,750	304,968	290,881	261,237	-1,218	-0.4
Douglas County, GA	55.7	40.1	1.6	0.4	0.1	8.6	51,980	51,672	45,596	34,874	308	0.6
Fayette County, GA	72.7	20.8	4.1	0.4	0.1	6.5	40,986	40,793	38,171	32,747	193	0.5
Forsyth County, GA	88.1	3.3	6.7	0.5	0.1	9.6	64,864	64,052	51,367	36,508	812	1.3
Fulton County, GA	47.5	44.5	5.8	0.4	0.1	8.1	435,891	437,106	399,595	348,589	-1,215	-0.3
Gwinnett County, GA	60.9	25.0	10.8	0.9	0.1	20.5	292,402	291,547	266,330	209,585	855	0.3
Haralson County, GA	92.4	5.4	0.6	0.3	0.0	1.4	12,277	12,287	11,737	10,716	-10	-0.1
Heard County, GA	86.6	10.6	0.5	0.5	0.0	2.1	5,166	5,148	4,964	4,501	18	0.3
Henry County, GA	56.5	37.8	3.1	0.3	0.1	6.0	77,027	76,534	65,629	43,223	493	0.6
Jasper County, GA	75.4	22.2	0.4	0.5	0.0	4.1	6,166	6,153	5,714	4,813	13	0.2
Lamar County, GA	66.5	31.1	0.5	0.3	0.0	2.2	7,477	7,474	7,051	6,165	3	0.0
Meriwether County, GA	58.5	39.4	0.7	0.4	0.0	1.7	9,884	9,957	9,895	9,211	-73	-0.7
Newton County, GA	55.4	41.3	1.0	0.3	0.0	4.8	38,394	38,342	33,560	22,995	52	0.1
Paulding County, GA	78.8	17.8	1.0	0.4	0.1	5.3	52,342	52,130	43,517	29,246	212	0.4
Pickens County, GA	96.4	1.6	0.4	0.4	0.0	2.9	13,607	13,684	12,852	10,702	-77	-0.6
Pike County, GA	86.9	11.0	0.4	0.3	0.0	1.2	6,863	6,820	6,108	4,978	43	0.6
Rockdale County, GA	48.9	46.7	1.9	0.5	0.1	9.9	33,484	33,272	29,960	25,143	212	0.6
Spalding County, GA	63.8	33.2	1.0	0.5	0.1	4.0	26,930	26,777	25,447	23,004	153	0.6
Walton County, GA	80.8	16.2	1.2	0.4	0.1	3.7	32,507	32,435	29,065	22,489	72	0.2
Atlantic City–Hammonton, NJ	71.8	17.3	7.9	0.7	0.1	17.3	126,782	126,647	122,432	114,103	135	0.1
Atlantic County, NJ	71.8	17.3	7.9	0.7	0.1	17.3	126,782	126,647	122,432	114,103	135	0.1
Auburn–Opelika, AL	72.3	23.0	2.7	0.4	0.1	3.4	63,483	62,391	56,323	50,295	1,092	1.8
Lee County, AL	72.3	23.0	2.7	0.4	0.1	3.4	63,483	62,391	56,323	50,295	1,092	1.8
Augusta–Richmond County, GA–SC	59.9	35.6	1.9	0.4	0.1	4.7	239,715	236,949	222,791	204,609	2,766	1.2
Burke County, GA	48.3	49.7	0.4	0.2	0.1	2.9	9,928	9,865	9,428	8,845	63	0.6
Columbia County, GA	77.1	15.8	4.0	0.4	0.2	5.3	50,331	48,626	41,448	33,410	1,705	3.5
McDuffie County, GA	57.6	40.3	0.4	0.3	0.1	2.4	9,304	9,319	9,237	8,925	-15	-0.2
Richmond County, GA	40.8	54.4	1.8	0.4	0.2	4.3	86,534	86,331	85,223	82,224	203	0.2
Aiken County, SC	72.0	24.8	0.9	0.5	0.1	5.1	72,976	72,253	67,477	61,988	723	1.0
Edgefield County, SC	60.7	37.4	0.4	0.4	0.1	5.5	10,642	10,555	9,978	9,217	87	0.8
Austin–Round Rock–San Marcos, TX	83.5	7.9	5.0	1.3	0.1	31.8	721,242	706,505	605,684	496,066	14,737	2.1
Bastrop County, TX	87.2	8.1	0.9	1.7	0.1	33.2	29,895	29,315	26,304	22,240	580	2.0
Caldwell County, TX	88.8	7.4	1.0	1.3	0.1	47.9	13,942	13,759	13,131	11,856	183	1.3
Hays County, TX	91.2	4.1	1.4	1.2	0.2	35.8	61,821	59,416	46,802	35,759	2,405	4.0
Travis County, TX	81.3	8.9	6.0	1.4	0.1	33.9	447,069	441,242	392,344	335,665	5,827	1.3
Williamson County, TX	84.8	6.8	5.1	0.9	0.1	23.6	168,515	162,773	127,103	90,546	5,742	3.5
Bakersfield–Delano, CA	83.0	6.3	4.7	2.7	0.3	50.0	286,955	284,367	258,904	231,571	2,588	0.9
Kern County, CA	83.0	6.3	4.7	2.7	0.3	50.0	286,955	284,367	258,904	231,571	2,588	0.9
Baltimore–Towson, MD	63.4	29.1	4.8	0.4	0.1	4.8	1,138,020	1,132,251	1,099,693	1,048,105	5,769	0.5
Anne Arundel County, MD	77.1	16.1	3.6	0.4	0.1	6.4	214,520	212,562	203,071	186,946	1,958	0.9
Baltimore County, MD	65.4	26.8	5.2	0.4	0.1	4.4	336,939	335,622	327,876	313,613	1,317	0.4
Carroll County, MD	93.2	3.5	1.5	0.2	0.0	2.8	62,584	62,406	60,711	54,255	178	0.3
Harford County, MD	81.6	13.2	2.6	0.3	0.1	3.7	96,024	95,554	91,207	83,254	470	0.5
Howard County, MD	63.2	18.2	14.9	0.4	0.1	6.0	111,200	109,282	102,180	92,830	1,918	1.8
Queen Anne's County, MD	89.8	7.1	1.1	0.4	0.0	3.2	20,303	20,140	18,883	16,682	163	0.8
Baltimore city, MD	31.5	63.6	2.5	0.4	0.1	4.3	296,450	296,685	295,765	300,525	-235	-0.1
Bangor, ME	95.5	0.8	1.0	1.2	0.0	1.1	74,382	73,859	70,673	66,820	523	0.7
Penobscot County, ME	95.5	0.8	1.0	1.2	0.0	1.1	74,382	73,859	70,673	66,820	523	0.7
Barnstable Town, MA	94.2	2.3	1.2	0.7	0.1	2.3	161,001	160,281	155,798	147,084	720	0.4
Barnstable County, MA	94.2	2.3	1.2	0.7	0.1	2.3	161,001	160,281	155,798	147,084	720	0.4
Baton Rouge, LA	60.8	35.8	1.9	0.3	0.0	3.6	332,601	329,726	303,788	282,587	2,875	0.9
Ascension Parish, LA	74.7	22.7	1.0	0.4	0.1	4.8	41,702	40,757	34,966	29,171	945	2.3
East Baton Rouge Parish, LA	50.0	45.5	3.0	0.3	0.0	3.8	187,711	187,358	177,044	169,094	353	0.2
East Feliciana Parish, LA	53.3	44.9	0.3	0.3	0.0	1.1	8,017	8,012	7,919	7,913	5	0.1
Iberville Parish, LA	49.4	49.1	0.4	0.2	0.0	2.2	12,730	12,707	12,333	11,951	23	0.2
Livingston Parish, LA	92.0	5.9	0.5	0.4	0.0	3.1	51,607	50,195	42,483	36,256	1,412	2.8
Pointe Coupee Parish, LA	62.1	36.5	0.3	0.2	0.0	2.4	11,188	11,126	10,745	10,296	62	0.6
St. Helena Parish, LA	45.2	53.1	0.2	0.4	0.0	1.3	5,130	5,150	4,958	5,051	-20	-0.4
West Baton Rouge Parish, LA	60.2	37.9	0.5	0.2	0.0	2.7	9,392	9,324	8,584	8,371	68	0.7
West Feliciana Parish, LA	52.5	46.4	0.3	0.2	0.0	1.7	5,124	5,097	4,756	4,484	27	0.5

[1] Persons of Hispanic origin may be any race.
[2] The April 1, 2000, housing estimates base reflects modifications to the Census 2000 population as documented in the Count Question Resolution program and geographic program revisions.

Table C-2.   Population Characteristics and Housing Units—*Continued*

Metropolitan statistical area, division, and component county	Population characteristics, 2011						Housing units				Change, 2010–2011	
	One race (percent)					Hispanic or Latino origin[1] (percent)	2011 (July 1)	2010 (July 1)	2005 (July 1)	2000[2] (estimates base)	Number	Percent
	White alone	Black or African American alone	Asian alone	American Indian, Alaska Native alone	Native Hawaiian and Other Pacific Islander alone							
Battle Creek, MI	83.6	11.1	1.6	0.7	0.1	4.6	60,922	61,042	60,740	58,697	-120	-0.2
Calhoun County, MI	83.6	11.1	1.6	0.7	0.1	4.6	60,922	61,042	60,740	58,697	-120	-0.2
Bay City, MI	95.2	1.7	0.6	0.6	0.0	4.7	48,125	48,220	47,988	46,431	-95	-0.2
Bay County, MI	95.2	1.7	0.6	0.6	0.0	4.7	48,125	48,220	47,988	46,431	-95	-0.2
Beaumont–Port Arthur, TX	70.3	24.8	2.6	0.8	0.1	13.5	164,050	162,335	160,095	156,763	1,715	1.1
Hardin County, TX	91.6	6.2	0.6	0.5	0.0	4.9	23,032	22,597	21,384	19,840	435	1.9
Jefferson County, TX	59.9	34.1	3.6	1.0	0.1	17.7	105,562	104,424	103,440	102,114	1,138	1.1
Orange County, TX	88.0	8.9	1.1	0.6	0.1	6.4	35,456	35,314	35,271	34,809	142	0.4
Bellingham, WA	88.0	1.2	3.9	3.1	0.3	8.2	91,280	90,665	84,216	73,897	615	0.7
Whatcom County, WA	88.0	1.2	3.9	3.1	0.3	8.2	91,280	90,665	84,216	73,897	615	0.7
Bend, OR	94.8	0.4	1.0	1.1	0.2	7.7	80,599	80,139	69,372	54,584	460	0.6
Deschutes County, OR	94.8	0.4	1.0	1.1	0.2	7.7	80,599	80,139	69,372	54,584	460	0.6
Billings, MT	92.0	0.7	0.7	4.1	0.1	4.6	71,454	70,384	65,806	60,049	1,070	1.5
Carbon County, MT	97.3	0.4	0.3	1.0	0.0	2.1	6,524	6,441	5,993	5,489	83	1.3
Yellowstone County, MT	91.6	0.8	0.7	4.3	0.1	4.8	64,930	63,943	59,813	54,560	987	1.5
Binghamton, NY	90.3	4.3	3.0	0.2	0.0	3.1	112,908	112,766	111,866	110,228	142	0.1
Broome County, NY	88.6	5.2	3.6	0.2	0.1	3.5	90,658	90,563	89,931	88,783	95	0.1
Tioga County, NY	97.0	0.9	0.8	0.2	0.0	1.5	22,250	22,203	21,935	21,445	47	0.2
Birmingham–Hoover, AL	68.5	28.6	1.3	0.4	0.1	4.4	500,322	500,026	481,883	454,350	296	0.1
Bibb County, AL	76.2	22.3	0.1	0.3	0.1	2.0	9,014	8,984	8,735	8,330	30	0.3
Blount County, AL	96.1	1.9	0.2	0.6	0.1	8.6	24,144	23,887	22,757	21,139	257	1.1
Chilton County, AL	87.7	10.3	0.3	0.5	0.2	7.8	19,339	19,276	18,683	17,654	63	0.3
Jefferson County, AL	54.7	42.3	1.5	0.4	0.1	4.0	299,482	300,552	296,036	288,162	-1,070	-0.4
St. Clair County, AL	88.6	9.1	0.7	0.4	0.1	2.2	36,188	35,543	31,655	27,296	645	1.8
Shelby County, AL	85.0	11.4	2.0	0.4	0.1	6.0	81,696	80,968	72,041	59,362	728	0.9
Walker County, AL	91.8	6.1	0.3	0.4	0.1	2.1	30,459	30,816	31,976	32,407	-357	-1.2
Bismarck, ND	93.4	0.7	0.5	4.0	0.1	1.4	48,561	47,833	43,844	39,599	728	1.5
Burleigh County, ND	93.2	0.7	0.5	4.1	0.0	1.4	36,409	35,754	32,560	29,014	655	1.8
Morton County, ND	93.9	0.5	0.3	3.6	0.1	1.5	12,152	12,079	11,284	10,585	73	0.6
Blacksburg–Christiansburg–Radford, VA	89.6	4.6	3.7	0.3	0.0	2.3	70,992	70,550	66,947	62,751	442	0.6
Giles County, VA	96.9	1.6	0.3	0.2	0.0	1.2	8,341	8,319	8,136	7,742	22	0.3
Montgomery County, VA	87.6	4.2	5.7	0.3	0.1	2.9	38,979	38,569	35,632	32,538	410	1.1
Pulaski County, VA	92.5	5.3	0.5	0.2	0.0	1.4	17,253	17,235	16,855	16,326	18	0.1
Radford city, VA	86.6	8.2	2.6	0.2	0.0	2.4	6,419	6,427	6,324	6,145	-8	-0.1
Bloomington, IN	91.1	2.6	4.1	0.3	0.0	2.5	84,552	84,409	81,849	75,740	143	0.2
Greene County, IN	98.1	0.4	0.3	0.3	0.0	1.1	15,098	15,210	15,604	15,050	-112	-0.7
Monroe County, IN	88.3	3.4	5.6	0.3	0.1	3.1	59,424	59,107	56,209	50,841	317	0.5
Owen County, IN	97.9	0.5	0.4	0.4	0.0	1.1	10,030	10,092	10,036	9,849	-62	-0.6
Bloomington–Normal, IL	85.5	7.6	4.5	0.3	0.0	4.6	70,183	69,656	66,879	59,951	527	0.8
McLean County, IL	85.5	7.6	4.5	0.3	0.0	4.6	70,183	69,656	66,879	59,951	527	0.8
Boise City–Nampa, ID	93.2	1.0	1.9	1.2	0.2	12.8	248,100	246,052	218,857	181,189	2,048	0.8
Ada County, ID	92.7	1.2	2.5	0.9	0.2	7.3	161,083	159,471	141,931	118,544	1,612	1.0
Boise County, ID	95.7	0.4	0.6	1.0	0.1	3.6	5,335	5,292	4,835	4,336	43	0.8
Canyon County, ID	94.0	0.7	0.9	1.6	0.3	24.1	69,774	69,409	60,884	47,970	365	0.5
Gem County, ID	96.2	0.2	0.6	0.8	0.1	8.2	7,132	7,099	6,557	5,886	33	0.5
Owyhee County, ID	91.5	0.8	0.8	5.0	0.2	25.9	4,776	4,781	4,650	4,453	-5	-0.1
Boston–Cambridge–Quincy, MA–NH	82.3	8.5	6.8	0.4	0.1	9.3	1,891,016	1,883,206	1,825,947	1,751,740	7,810	0.4
Boston–Quincy, MA	76.7	13.9	6.8	0.4	0.1	9.9	790,248	786,042	760,506	729,374	4,206	0.5
Norfolk County, MA	83.0	6.2	8.9	0.2	0.0	3.5	271,502	270,359	263,708	255,109	1,143	0.4
Plymouth County, MA	87.5	9.1	1.4	0.3	0.1	3.3	201,419	200,161	192,961	181,541	1,258	0.6
Suffolk County, MA	63.5	24.4	8.5	0.8	0.2	20.3	317,327	315,522	303,837	292,724	1,805	0.6
Cambridge–Newton–Framingham, MA	82.8	5.2	9.8	0.3	0.1	6.8	614,036	612,004	594,609	576,603	2,032	0.3
Middlesex County, MA	82.8	5.2	9.8	0.3	0.1	6.8	614,036	612,004	594,609	576,603	2,032	0.3
Peabody, MA	88.1	5.6	3.4	0.8	0.1	16.9	307,559	306,754	299,114	287,193	805	0.3
Essex County, MA	88.1	5.6	3.4	0.8	0.1	16.9	307,559	306,754	299,114	287,193	805	0.3
Rockingham County–Strafford County, NH	95.4	0.9	2.1	0.2	0.0	2.1	179,173	178,406	171,718	158,570	767	0.4
Rockingham County, NH	95.9	0.8	1.8	0.2	0.0	2.2	127,196	126,709	122,173	113,049	487	0.4
Strafford County, NH	94.1	1.1	2.7	0.3	0.0	1.9	51,977	51,697	49,545	45,521	280	0.5
Boulder, CO[3]	91.2	1.1	4.3	0.9	0.1	13.7	127,489	127,071	122,756	111,446	418	0.3
Boulder County, CO[3]	91.2	1.1	4.3	0.9	0.1	13.7	127,489	127,071	122,756	111,446	418	0.3
Bowling Green, KY	86.7	8.5	2.6	0.3	0.1	4.3	54,125	53,690	49,739	44,455	435	0.8
Edmonson County, KY	97.0	1.6	0.2	0.3	0.0	0.8	6,470	6,467	6,382	6,098	3	0.0
Warren County, KY	85.7	9.3	2.9	0.3	0.1	4.7	47,655	47,223	43,357	38,357	432	0.9
Bremerton–Silverdale, WA	83.8	3.0	5.1	1.7	1.0	6.6	108,364	107,367	100,774	92,653	997	0.9
Kitsap County, WA	83.8	3.0	5.1	1.7	1.0	6.6	108,364	107,367	100,774	92,653	997	0.9
Bridgeport–Stamford–Norwalk, CT	80.9	11.8	4.9	0.5	0.1	17.4	362,739	361,221	351,146	339,499	1,518	0.4
Fairfield County, CT	80.9	11.8	4.9	0.5	0.1	17.4	362,739	361,221	351,146	339,499	1,518	0.4
Brownsville–Harlingen, TX	97.4	0.8	0.8	0.6	0.1	88.1	142,312	141,924	134,625	119,483	388	0.3
Cameron County, TX	97.4	0.8	0.8	0.6	0.1	88.1	142,312	141,924	134,625	119,483	388	0.3

[1] Persons of Hispanic origin may be any race.
[2] The April 1, 2000, housing estimates base reflects modifications to the Census 2000 population as documented in the Count Question Resolution program and geographic program revisions.
[3] The Denver–Aurora metropolitan statistical area includes Broomfield County. Broomfield County, CO, was formed from parts of Adams, Boulder, Jefferson, and Weld Counties on November 15, 2001, and is coextensive with Broomfield city. For the purposes of defining and presenting data for the Denver–Aurora metropolitan statistical area, Broomfield city is treated as if it were a county when data are available to do so. In many cases, the data were not available.

Table C-2.   Population Characteristics and Housing Units—*Continued*

Metropolitan statistical area, division, and component county	Population characteristics, 2011						Housing units					
	One race (percent)					Hispanic or Latino origin[1] (percent)	2011 (July 1)	2010 (July 1)	2005 (July 1)	2000[2] (estimates base)	Change, 2010–2011	
	White alone	Black or African American alone	Asian alone	American Indian, Alaska Native alone	Native Hawaiian and Other Pacific Islander alone						Number	Percent
Brunswick, GA	72.8	24.0	1.0	0.5	0.2	5.2	59,035	58,021	51,904	44,859	1,014	1.7
Brantley County, GA	94.3	3.6	0.2	0.4	0.0	2.0	8,252	8,085	7,430	6,481	167	2.1
Glynn County, GA	69.9	26.5	1.3	0.5	0.2	6.5	41,168	40,716	37,113	32,644	452	1.1
McIntosh County, GA	61.9	35.9	0.4	0.5	0.1	1.6	9,615	9,220	7,361	5,734	395	4.3
Buffalo–Niagara Falls, NY	82.5	12.6	2.4	0.8	0.0	4.3	518,766	519,094	518,229	511,561	-328	-0.1
Erie County, NY	81.1	13.9	2.7	0.7	0.0	4.7	419,406	419,974	420,401	415,859	-568	-0.1
Niagara County, NY	88.9	7.0	0.9	1.1	0.0	2.3	99,360	99,120	97,828	95,702	240	0.2
Burlington, NC	76.2	19.2	1.3	1.4	0.1	11.4	67,068	66,576	61,417	55,446	492	0.7
Alamance County, NC	76.2	19.2	1.3	1.4	0.1	11.4	67,068	66,576	61,417	55,446	492	0.7
Burlington–South Burlington, VT	93.4	1.8	2.4	0.5	0.0	1.7	93,173	92,359	88,800	82,718	814	0.9
Chittenden County, VT	92.6	2.2	3.0	0.3	0.0	1.9	66,345	65,723	63,177	58,883	622	0.9
Franklin County, VT	95.8	0.6	0.5	1.0	0.0	1.3	21,763	21,588	20,699	19,178	175	0.8
Grand Isle County, VT	95.3	0.5	0.4	1.0	0.1	1.3	5,065	5,048	4,924	4,657	17	0.3
Canton–Massillon, OH	89.7	7.2	0.7	0.3	0.0	1.6	179,025	178,913	176,333	170,053	112	0.1
Carroll County, OH	97.8	0.6	0.2	0.3	0.0	0.9	13,740	13,698	13,499	13,001	42	0.3
Stark County, OH	89.1	7.7	0.8	0.3	0.0	1.7	165,285	165,215	162,834	157,052	70	0.0
Cape Coral–Fort Myers, FL	87.6	8.8	1.5	0.5	0.1	18.6	372,117	371,099	316,255	245,425	1,018	0.3
Lee County, FL	87.6	8.8	1.5	0.5	0.1	18.6	372,117	371,099	316,255	245,425	1,018	0.3
Cape Girardeau–Jackson, MO–IL	88.1	8.8	1.1	0.4	0.0	1.9	42,684	42,501	41,589	39,534	183	0.4
Alexander County, IL	61.6	35.8	0.3	0.4	0.1	2.0	3,924	4,006	4,318	4,587	-82	-2.0
Bollinger County, MO	97.7	0.5	0.3	0.6	0.0	0.8	5,895	5,878	5,806	5,514	17	0.3
Cape Girardeau County, MO	89.3	7.3	1.3	0.3	0.0	2.1	32,865	32,617	31,465	29,433	248	0.8
Carson City, NV	90.1	2.2	2.3	2.6	0.3	22.0	23,566	23,534	22,985	21,290	32	0.1
Carson City, NV	90.1	2.2	2.3	2.6	0.3	22.0	23,566	23,534	22,985	21,290	32	0.1
Casper, WY	94.9	1.1	0.7	1.3	0.1	7.1	34,400	33,807	31,421	29,886	593	1.8
Natrona County, WY	94.9	1.1	0.7	1.3	0.1	7.1	34,400	33,807	31,421	29,886	593	1.8
Cedar Rapids, IA	92.4	3.6	1.7	0.3	0.1	2.5	113,216	112,257	108,190	99,070	959	0.9
Benton County, IA	98.1	0.4	0.3	0.2	0.0	1.1	11,100	11,095	10,961	10,377	5	0.0
Jones County, IA	96.5	2.1	0.4	0.3	0.0	1.4	8,978	8,911	8,621	8,127	67	0.8
Linn County, IA	91.4	4.1	1.9	0.3	0.1	2.8	93,138	92,251	88,608	80,566	887	1.0
Champaign–Urbana, IL	77.9	11.1	8.2	0.4	0.1	5.0	101,677	101,120	94,633	88,148	557	0.6
Champaign County, IL	74.9	12.7	9.4	0.4	0.1	5.5	88,119	87,569	81,312	75,289	550	0.6
Ford County, IL	97.6	0.9	0.3	0.3	0.0	2.4	6,294	6,282	6,206	6,055	12	0.2
Piatt County, IL	97.9	0.6	0.4	0.2	0.0	1.2	7,264	7,269	7,115	6,804	-5	-0.1
Charleston, WV	92.4	5.0	0.9	0.2	0.0	0.9	141,027	141,584	142,435	141,680	-557	-0.4
Boone County, WV	98.6	0.6	0.1	0.1	0.0	0.4	10,972	11,069	11,458	11,578	-97	-0.9
Clay County, WV	98.6	0.3	0.1	0.2	0.0	0.4	4,542	4,572	4,737	4,839	-30	-0.7
Kanawha County, WV	89.2	7.4	1.1	0.2	0.0	1.1	92,196	92,618	93,521	93,811	-422	-0.5
Lincoln County, WV	99.0	0.2	0.1	0.1	0.0	0.5	9,849	9,887	9,979	9,845	-38	-0.4
Putnam County, WV	96.8	1.0	0.8	0.2	0.0	0.9	23,468	23,438	22,740	21,607	30	0.1
Charleston–North Charleston– Summerville, SC	67.8	27.8	1.7	0.6	0.1	5.4	301,977	298,542	266,273	232,985	3,435	1.2
Berkeley County, SC	68.9	25.5	2.4	0.7	0.1	6.1	75,194	73,372	63,298	54,756	1,822	2.5
Charleston County, SC	66.8	29.7	1.5	0.5	0.1	5.4	170,207	169,984	157,166	140,990	223	0.1
Dorchester County, SC	69.0	26.2	1.7	0.7	0.1	4.5	56,576	55,186	45,809	37,239	1,390	2.5
Charlotte–Gastonia–Rock Hill, NC–SC	69.4	24.6	3.3	0.7	0.1	10.1	743,294	737,775	653,755	546,515	5,519	0.7
Anson County, NC	48.2	48.6	1.1	0.8	0.1	3.2	11,693	11,576	11,021	10,216	117	1.0
Cabarrus County, NC	79.4	15.9	2.2	0.6	0.1	9.6	73,110	71,937	63,168	52,840	1,173	1.6
Gaston County, NC	80.9	15.7	1.3	0.6	0.0	6.1	89,136	88,686	84,559	78,881	450	0.5
Mecklenburg County, NC	60.7	31.5	4.8	0.8	0.1	12.4	399,407	398,510	352,974	292,745	897	0.2
Union County, NC	83.8	12.1	1.8	0.6	0.1	10.7	73,667	72,870	60,880	45,766	797	1.1
York County, SC	76.5	19.3	1.6	0.9	0.1	4.7	96,281	94,196	81,153	66,067	2,085	2.2
Charlottesville, VA	80.5	12.7	4.0	0.4	0.1	4.9	89,760	89,134	83,471	73,853	626	0.7
Albemarle County, VA	82.4	10.1	4.7	0.4	0.1	5.6	42,460	42,122	39,232	33,716	338	0.8
Fluvanna County, VA	81.6	15.5	0.7	0.2	0.0	3.0	10,464	10,384	9,765	8,003	80	0.8
Greene County, VA	89.2	6.8	1.5	0.3	0.0	4.5	7,601	7,508	6,906	5,984	93	1.2
Nelson County, VA	83.9	13.6	0.5	0.4	0.0	3.4	9,989	9,931	9,344	8,553	58	0.6
Charlottesville city, VA	70.7	19.1	6.8	0.4	0.1	4.4	19,246	19,189	18,224	17,597	57	0.3
Chattanooga, TN–GA	82.4	14.1	1.5	0.5	0.1	3.7	235,722	234,440	222,445	205,376	1,282	0.5
Catoosa County, GA	93.8	2.8	1.3	0.4	0.1	2.5	26,689	26,606	24,782	21,747	83	0.3
Dade County, GA	96.0	1.4	0.8	0.4	0.0	1.9	7,407	7,305	6,822	6,218	102	1.4
Walker County, GA	93.2	4.6	0.5	0.3	0.1	1.7	30,232	30,100	28,324	25,618	132	0.4
Hamilton County, TN	75.8	20.2	1.8	0.6	0.1	4.6	151,937	151,107	143,973	134,796	830	0.5
Marion County, TN	94.1	3.9	0.5	0.4	0.0	1.4	12,912	12,954	12,874	12,135	-42	-0.3
Sequatchie County, TN	97.5	0.6	0.3	0.5	0.0	3.3	6,545	6,368	5,670	4,862	177	2.8

[1] Persons of Hispanic origin may be any race.
[2] The April 1, 2000, housing estimates base reflects modifications to the Census 2000 population as documented in the Count Question Resolution program and geographic program revisions.

Table C-2.   Population Characteristics and Housing Units—*Continued*

Metropolitan statistical area, division, and component county	Population characteristics, 2011						Housing units					
	One race (percent)					Hispanic or Latino origin[1] (percent)	2011 (July 1)	2010 (July 1)	2005 (July 1)	2000[2] (estimates base)	Change, 2010–2011	
	White alone	Black or African American alone	Asian alone	American Indian, Alaska Native alone	Native Hawaiian and Other Pacific Islander alone						Number	Percent
Cheyenne, WY	92.3	2.7	1.2	1.2	0.2	13.3	41,095	40,462	37,744	34,219	633	1.6
Laramie County, WY	92.3	2.7	1.2	1.2	0.2	13.3	41,095	40,462	37,744	34,219	633	1.6
Chicago–Joliet–Naperville, IL–IN–WI	74.0	17.6	5.9	0.7	0.1	21.1	3,797,079	3,797,247	3,675,474	3,462,461	-168	0.0
Chicago–Joliet–Naperville, IL	72.5	18.7	6.3	0.7	0.1	22.0	3,172,234	3,173,522	3,073,805	2,906,837	-1,288	0.0
Cook County, IL	66.0	25.0	6.5	0.8	0.1	24.4	2,175,941	2,180,359	2,141,972	2,096,143	-4,418	-0.2
DeKalb County, IL	88.3	6.8	2.7	0.4	0.1	10.5	41,377	41,079	37,310	32,973	298	0.7
DuPage County, IL	82.4	5.1	10.4	0.4	0.0	13.6	355,617	356,179	351,272	335,818	-562	-0.2
Grundy County, IL	96.2	1.6	0.8	0.3	0.0	8.4	20,228	19,996	18,011	15,037	232	1.2
Kane County, IL	87.4	6.1	3.7	1.0	0.1	31.1	183,179	182,047	167,217	139,166	1,132	0.6
Kendall County, IL	88.4	6.1	3.3	0.4	0.0	15.9	41,308	40,321	30,246	19,499	987	2.4
McHenry County, IL	94.3	1.3	2.6	0.5	0.0	11.7	116,213	116,040	109,294	92,689	173	0.1
Will County, IL	81.6	11.5	4.8	0.4	0.0	15.9	238,371	237,501	218,483	175,512	870	0.4
Gary, IN	77.7	19.0	1.3	0.4	0.0	14.3	294,217	294,127	285,660	269,586	90	0.0
Jasper County, IN	97.5	0.8	0.4	0.3	0.0	5.5	13,225	13,168	12,467	11,220	57	0.4
Lake County, IN	70.5	25.9	1.4	0.5	0.1	17.0	208,673	208,750	204,050	195,006	-77	0.0
Newton County, IN	97.8	0.6	0.3	0.3	0.1	5.2	6,015	6,030	5,980	5,744	-15	-0.2
Porter County, IN	93.5	3.4	1.3	0.4	0.0	8.6	66,304	66,179	63,163	57,616	125	0.2
Lake County–Kenosha County, IL–WI	84.2	7.3	5.6	0.8	0.1	18.7	330,628	329,598	316,009	286,038	1,030	0.3
Lake County, IL	83.2	7.4	6.6	0.8	0.1	20.3	261,147	260,310	249,613	226,046	837	0.3
Kenosha County, WI	88.3	7.0	1.6	0.8	0.1	12.0	69,481	69,288	66,396	59,992	193	0.3
Chico, CA	87.0	1.8	4.4	2.3	0.3	14.7	95,902	95,835	92,258	85,510	67	0.1
Butte County, CA	87.0	1.8	4.4	2.3	0.3	14.7	95,902	95,835	92,258	85,510	67	0.1
Cincinnati–Middletown, OH–KY–IN	83.8	12.2	2.0	0.2	0.1	2.7	919,064	917,396	892,044	833,086	1,668	0.2
Dearborn County, IN	97.6	0.8	0.4	0.2	0.1	1.0	20,216	20,171	19,528	17,808	45	0.2
Franklin County, IN	98.4	0.4	0.2	0.2	0.0	1.1	9,570	9,538	9,257	8,614	32	0.3
OH County, IN	98.2	0.5	0.3	0.2	0.0	1.3	2,794	2,784	2,658	2,400	10	0.4
Boone County, KY	93.0	2.9	2.2	0.3	0.1	3.7	46,711	46,154	41,959	33,376	557	1.2
Bracken County, KY	98.1	0.5	0.1	0.2	0.0	1.2	3,833	3,840	3,825	3,712	-7	-0.2
Campbell County, KY	94.7	2.8	0.9	0.2	0.1	1.7	39,710	39,523	38,447	36,899	187	0.5
Gallatin County, KY	96.0	1.7	0.3	0.2	0.1	4.5	3,826	3,786	3,592	3,355	40	1.1
Grant County, KY	97.4	1.0	0.4	0.3	0.2	2.5	9,875	9,942	9,914	9,292	-67	-0.7
Kenton County, KY	91.9	4.8	1.0	0.3	0.1	2.8	68,863	68,976	67,181	63,569	-113	-0.2
Pendleton County, KY	98.1	0.5	0.2	0.3	0.0	1.0	6,378	6,338	6,125	5,758	40	0.6
Brown County, OH	97.5	1.0	0.3	0.2	0.0	0.7	19,396	19,301	17,657	17,172	95	0.5
Butler County, OH	87.5	7.7	2.5	0.3	0.1	4.1	149,076	148,273	141,665	129,594	803	0.5
Clermont County, OH	96.1	1.4	1.0	0.2	0.0	1.6	81,161	80,656	77,569	68,985	505	0.6
Hamilton County, OH	69.7	25.8	2.1	0.3	0.1	2.7	375,812	377,364	379,153	373,396	-1,552	-0.4
Warren County, OH	90.8	3.5	4.1	0.2	0.0	2.4	81,843	80,750	73,514	59,156	1,093	1.4
Clarksville, TN–KY	75.2	18.6	1.8	0.7	0.4	7.0	115,894	114,145	103,613	92,067	1,749	1.5
Christian County, KY	73.6	21.3	1.2	0.7	0.4	6.4	29,526	29,458	28,710	27,211	68	0.2
Trigg County, KY	89.4	8.1	0.4	0.3	0.0	1.3	7,915	7,810	7,337	6,699	105	1.3
Montgomery County, TN	73.2	19.6	2.2	0.7	0.4	8.1	71,622	70,099	61,117	52,181	1,523	2.2
Stewart County, TN	94.8	1.8	1.1	0.6	0.0	2.1	6,831	6,778	6,449	5,976	53	0.8
Cleveland, TN	92.9	4.1	0.9	0.5	0.1	4.4	49,561	49,386	47,200	44,193	175	0.4
Bradley County, TN	92.2	4.6	1.0	0.6	0.1	4.9	41,532	41,395	39,570	36,825	137	0.3
Polk County, TN	97.3	0.7	0.2	0.4	0.1	1.5	8,029	7,991	7,630	7,368	38	0.5
Cleveland–Elyria–Mentor, OH	75.6	20.3	2.0	0.2	0.0	4.8	956,773	955,756	941,938	911,366	1,017	0.1
Cuyahoga County, OH	65.1	30.0	2.7	0.2	0.0	4.9	620,830	621,763	622,194	616,906	-933	-0.2
Geauga County, OH	97.0	1.4	0.6	0.1	0.0	1.1	36,681	36,574	35,440	32,821	107	0.3
Lake County, OH	93.7	3.5	1.2	0.2	0.0	3.6	101,515	101,202	98,142	93,480	313	0.3
Lorain County, OH	87.1	8.9	1.0	0.3	0.1	8.4	127,748	127,036	121,471	111,363	712	0.6
Medina County, OH	96.3	1.4	1.0	0.1	0.0	1.7	69,999	69,181	64,691	56,796	818	1.2
Coeur d'Alene, ID	95.2	0.4	0.8	1.4	0.1	4.0	64,319	63,177	55,596	46,608	1,142	1.8
Kootenai County, ID	95.2	0.4	0.8	1.4	0.1	4.0	64,319	63,177	55,596	46,608	1,142	1.8
College Station–Bryan, TX	80.9	12.0	4.6	0.7	0.1	23.2	96,459	95,016	85,495	75,080	1,443	1.5
Brazos County, TX	81.1	11.1	5.3	0.7	0.1	23.9	79,068	77,700	68,619	59,036	1,368	1.8
Burleson County, TX	85.1	12.4	0.2	0.9	0.0	19.1	8,867	8,832	8,628	8,185	35	0.4
Robertson County, TX	74.6	22.1	0.8	1.0	0.0	19.4	8,524	8,484	8,248	7,859	40	0.5
Colorado Springs, CO	84.6	6.5	2.8	1.3	0.4	15.0	267,267	265,495	248,013	212,793	1,772	0.7
El Paso County, CO	84.3	6.7	2.9	1.3	0.4	15.4	254,559	252,852	236,071	202,435	1,707	0.7
Teller County, CO	95.0	0.7	0.8	1.1	0.1	5.6	12,708	12,643	11,942	10,358	65	0.5
Columbia, MO	84.0	9.2	3.7	0.5	0.1	3.1	74,548	74,133	69,203	61,029	415	0.6
Boone County, MO	83.6	9.4	3.9	0.5	0.1	3.2	69,961	69,551	64,653	56,685	410	0.6
Howard County, MO	91.9	5.4	0.3	0.5	0.1	1.4	4,587	4,582	4,550	4,344	5	0.1
Columbia, SC	62.3	33.6	1.8	0.5	0.1	5.2	336,003	331,471	301,929	269,236	4,532	1.4
Calhoun County, SC	55.0	43.2	0.3	0.5	0.1	3.2	7,328	7,341	7,249	6,843	-13	-0.2
Fairfield County, SC	39.5	58.9	0.3	0.2	0.0	1.8	11,768	11,681	11,157	10,361	87	0.7
Kershaw County, SC	72.4	25.2	0.6	0.4	0.1	3.9	27,908	27,478	25,183	22,690	430	1.6
Lexington County, SC	81.3	15.0	1.5	0.5	0.1	5.7	116,403	113,958	102,332	90,979	2,445	2.1
Richland County, SC	48.9	46.3	2.3	0.4	0.1	4.9	163,244	161,724	146,994	129,821	1,520	0.9
Saluda County, SC	69.6	26.7	0.2	1.3	1.0	14.8	9,352	9,289	9,014	8,542	63	0.7

[1] Persons of Hispanic origin may be any race.
[2] The April 1, 2000, housing estimates base reflects modifications to the Census 2000 population as documented in the Count Question Resolution program and geographic program revisions.

Table C-2. Population Characteristics and Housing Units—*Continued*

Metropolitan statistical area, division, and component county	Population characteristics, 2011						Housing units					
	One race (percent)					Hispanic or Latino origin[1] (percent)	2011 (July 1)	2010 (July 1)	2005 (July 1)	2000[2] (estimates base)	Change, 2010–2011	
	White alone	Black or African American alone	Asian alone	American Indian, Alaska Native alone	Native Hawaiian and Other Pacific Islander alone						Number	Percent
Columbus, GA–AL..........................	54.2	40.9	1.8	0.5	0.2	6.1	128,891	128,214	123,192	115,812	677	0.5
Russell County, AL	55.0	41.9	0.6	0.5	0.2	4.1	24,980	24,595	23,496	22,866	385	1.6
Chattahoochee County, GA......................	72.3	19.7	2.4	1.2	0.7	14.0	3,374	3,376	3,354	3,321	-2	-0.1
Harris County, GA	79.4	17.8	1.0	0.4	0.1	2.9	13,530	13,397	12,343	10,327	133	1.0
Marion County, GA....................	63.1	33.6	0.8	0.7	0.4	6.7	4,294	4,156	3,691	3,126	138	3.3
Muscogee County, GA....................	48.3	46.1	2.3	0.5	0.2	6.7	82,713	82,690	80,308	76,172	23	0.0
Columbus, IN..........................	92.0	2.2	3.7	0.5	0.1	6.3	33,321	33,098	31,697	29,866	223	0.7
Bartholomew County, IN	92.0	2.2	3.7	0.5	0.1	6.3	33,321	33,098	31,697	29,866	223	0.7
Columbus, OH..........................	78.8	15.2	3.3	0.3	0.1	3.7	796,880	792,340	760,376	680,490	4,540	0.6
Delaware County, OH	90.0	3.6	4.5	0.2	0.0	2.2	67,478	66,378	59,187	42,375	1,100	1.7
Fairfield County, OH	90.4	6.2	1.2	0.2	0.0	1.8	59,089	58,687	55,625	47,950	402	0.7
Franklin County, OH	71.2	21.5	4.0	0.3	0.1	4.9	529,336	527,186	512,279	470,967	2,150	0.4
Licking County, OH	93.5	3.6	0.8	0.3	0.0	1.5	69,744	69,291	65,871	58,829	453	0.7
Madison County, OH	90.9	6.8	0.6	0.3	0.0	1.5	15,989	15,939	15,493	14,400	50	0.3
Morrow County, OH	97.6	0.6	0.3	0.1	0.0	1.2	14,253	14,155	13,345	12,133	98	0.7
Pickaway County, OH	94.7	3.6	0.4	0.2	0.0	1.2	21,402	21,275	20,357	18,600	127	0.6
Union County, OH	93.0	2.7	2.7	0.3	0.0	1.3	19,589	19,429	18,219	15,236	160	0.8
Corpus Christi, TX........................	92.1	3.9	1.7	0.9	0.1	58.2	184,419	182,909	172,381	160,730	1,510	0.8
Aransas County, TX...................	93.4	1.7	2.1	1.1	0.1	25.5	15,507	15,354	14,167	12,816	153	1.0
Nueces County, TX....................	91.6	4.4	1.8	0.8	0.1	61.0	142,435	141,033	132,001	122,984	1,402	1.0
San Patricio County, TX	94.5	2.2	0.9	0.9	0.1	54.9	26,477	26,522	26,213	24,930	-45	-0.2
Corvallis, OR............................	88.7	1.1	5.5	0.9	0.3	6.7	36,384	36,246	34,767	31,985	138	0.4
Benton County, OR.....................	88.7	1.1	5.5	0.9	0.3	6.7	36,384	36,246	34,767	31,985	138	0.4
Crestview–Fort Walton Beach–Destin, FL.......	82.7	9.8	3.1	0.7	0.2	7.2	92,394	92,407	86,889	78,927	-13	0.0
Okaloosa County, FL...................	82.7	9.8	3.1	0.7	0.2	7.2	92,394	92,407	86,889	78,927	-13	0.0
Cumberland, MD–WV	90.7	6.9	0.7	0.2	0.0	1.3	46,419	46,350	45,887	45,076	69	0.1
Allegany County, MD....................	89.1	8.3	0.8	0.2	0.0	1.5	33,358	33,311	33,113	32,981	47	0.1
Mineral County, WV	95.2	3.0	0.4	0.1	0.0	0.8	13,061	13,039	12,774	12,095	22	0.2
Dallas–Fort Worth–Arlington, TX	75.9	15.5	5.6	1.0	0.1	28.1	2,531,936	2,502,078	2,278,949	1,998,239	29,858	1.2
Dallas–Plano–Irving, TX........................	74.2	16.5	6.3	1.0	0.1	29.3	1,678,763	1,660,146	1,516,444	1,331,750	18,617	1.1
Collin County, TX......................	76.2	9.1	11.5	0.8	0.1	15.2	307,353	300,960	252,918	194,599	6,393	2.1
Dallas County, TX.....................	69.3	22.5	5.3	1.2	0.1	38.9	943,980	943,258	905,350	853,417	722	0.1
Delta County, TX......................	87.3	8.0	0.7	1.4	0.0	6.1	2,456	2,458	2,446	2,407	-2	-0.1
Denton County, TX....................	81.0	8.9	6.8	0.9	0.1	18.7	264,071	256,139	218,461	168,245	7,932	3.1
Ellis County, TX......................	87.6	9.4	0.7	0.8	0.1	24.3	55,143	54,365	47,420	39,087	778	1.4
Hunt County, TX......................	86.8	8.7	1.1	1.2	0.2	14.5	37,134	36,704	34,801	32,476	430	1.2
Kaufman County, TX....................	85.6	10.8	1.0	0.9	0.0	18.0	39,320	38,323	32,650	26,187	997	2.6
Rockwall County, TX...................	88.7	6.2	2.6	0.8	0.1	16.6	29,306	27,939	22,398	15,332	1,367	4.9
Fort Worth–Arlington, TX......................	79.3	13.3	4.2	0.9	0.2	25.6	853,173	841,932	762,505	666,489	11,241	1.3
Johnson County, TX....................	93.2	3.1	0.8	1.0	0.4	18.9	57,502	56,720	51,461	46,201	782	1.4
Parker County, TX.....................	94.7	2.1	0.6	0.9	0.1	11.2	48,241	46,628	40,193	34,055	1,613	3.5
Tarrant County, TX....................	76.7	15.3	4.8	0.9	0.2	27.3	723,263	714,805	649,082	566,999	8,458	1.2
Wise County, TX.......................	95.4	1.5	0.5	1.0	0.0	17.9	24,167	23,779	21,769	19,234	388	1.6
Dalton, GA...............................	92.5	3.5	1.2	1.2	0.2	27.1	56,360	55,878	51,584	45,063	482	0.9
Murray County, GA.....................	95.9	1.4	0.4	0.9	0.3	13.6	15,909	15,979	15,437	14,316	-70	-0.4
Whitfield County, GA...................	91.2	4.3	1.4	1.4	0.2	32.3	40,451	39,899	36,147	30,747	552	1.4
Danville, IL..............................	83.6	13.3	0.8	0.3	0.0	4.4	36,190	36,318	36,701	36,351	-128	-0.4
Vermilion County, IL....................	83.6	13.3	0.8	0.3	0.0	4.4	36,190	36,318	36,701	36,351	-128	-0.4
Danville, VA.............................	65.1	32.8	0.6	0.3	0.0	2.6	53,802	53,745	52,941	51,103	57	0.1
Pittsylvania County, VA.................	76.1	22.1	0.3	0.3	0.0	2.2	31,494	31,307	30,133	28,032	187	0.6
Danville city, VA......................	48.8	48.6	1.0	0.3	0.0	3.0	22,308	22,438	22,808	23,071	-130	-0.6
Davenport–Moline–Rock Island, IA–IL..........	88.6	7.0	1.7	0.4	0.0	7.8	167,577	167,110	163,437	158,538	467	0.3
Henry County, IL......................	96.3	1.8	0.4	0.3	0.0	4.9	22,188	22,161	21,845	21,275	27	0.1
Mercer County, IL.....................	98.4	0.4	0.4	0.1	0.0	1.9	7,363	7,358	7,267	7,101	5	0.1
Rock Island County, IL..................	85.9	9.3	1.8	0.6	0.0	11.9	65,758	65,756	65,154	64,497	2	0.0
Scott County, IA	87.8	7.1	2.1	0.4	0.1	5.7	72,268	71,835	69,171	65,665	433	0.6
Dayton, OH..............................	80.5	15.1	1.9	0.3	0.0	2.2	385,457	385,160	378,565	364,486	297	0.1
Greene County, OH....................	86.5	7.6	3.0	0.3	0.1	2.4	68,523	68,241	64,390	58,243	282	0.4
Miami County, OH.....................	94.7	2.2	1.3	0.2	0.0	1.4	44,523	44,256	42,795	40,570	267	0.6
Montgomery County, OH	74.7	21.0	1.8	0.3	0.0	2.4	254,513	254,775	253,557	248,484	-262	-0.1
Preble County, OH....................	97.5	0.6	0.5	0.2	0.0	0.7	17,898	17,888	17,823	17,189	10	0.1
Decatur, AL..............................	82.7	12.3	0.5	2.1	0.1	6.5	66,475	66,422	65,227	62,410	53	0.1
Lawrence County, AL	78.1	11.8	0.2	5.7	0.0	1.9	15,184	15,229	15,368	15,018	-45	-0.3
Morgan County, AL....................	84.0	12.4	0.6	1.1	0.1	7.8	51,291	51,193	49,859	47,392	98	0.2
Decatur, IL..............................	79.8	16.4	1.1	0.3	0.0	2.0	50,197	50,475	50,641	50,237	-278	-0.6
Macon County, IL......................	79.8	16.4	1.1	0.3	0.0	2.0	50,197	50,475	50,641	50,237	-278	-0.6

[1] Persons of Hispanic origin may be any race.
[2] The April 1, 2000, housing estimates base reflects modifications to the Census 2000 population as documented in the Count Question Resolution program and geographic program revisions.

Table C-2.   Population Characteristics and Housing Units—*Continued*

Metropolitan statistical area, division, and component county	White alone	Black or African American alone	Asian alone	American Indian, Alaska Native alone	Native Hawaiian and Other Pacific Islander alone	Hispanic or Latino origin[1] (percent)	2011 (July 1)	2010 (July 1)	2005 (July 1)	2000[2] (estimates base)	Number	Percent
Deltona–Daytona Beach–Ormond Beach, FL	85.2	10.9	1.6	0.4	0.1	11.5	254,981	254,228	239,652	211,986	753	0.3
Volusia County, FL	85.2	10.9	1.6	0.4	0.1	11.5	254,981	254,228	239,652	211,986	753	0.3
Denver–Aurora–Broomfield, CO[3]..................	85.8	5.9	3.9	1.5	0.2	22.7	1,083,735	1,078,837	1,016,179	891,106	4,898	0.5
Adams County, CO[3]	87.6	3.5	3.8	2.1	0.2	38.2	163,419	163,136	154,554	127,125	283	0.2
Arapahoe County, CO	79.4	10.5	5.2	1.1	0.2	18.7	239,767	238,390	224,874	197,160	1,377	0.6
Broomfield County, CO[3].................	89.0	1.5	6.1	0.9	0.1	11.6	22,881	22,646	18,748	14,659	235	1.0
Clear Creek County, CO	95.9	0.8	0.6	1.0	0.0	5.4	5,710	5,685	5,510	5,097	25	0.4
Denver County, CO	80.8	10.3	3.6	2.1	0.2	31.8	286,790	285,708	271,670	251,132	1,082	0.4
Douglas County, CO	91.8	1.4	3.9	0.5	0.1	7.8	108,344	106,859	91,672	63,316	1,485	1.4
Elbert County, CO	95.5	0.8	0.9	0.8	0.1	5.7	8,961	8,939	8,326	7,111	22	0.2
Gilpin County, CO	95.0	0.7	1.4	0.9	0.2	5.6	3,580	3,560	3,303	2,932	20	0.6
Jefferson County, CO[3]	92.4	1.3	2.7	1.2	0.1	14.6	230,174	229,967	224,762	211,889	207	0.1
Park County, CO	95.5	0.5	0.7	1.1	0.0	4.9	14,109	13,947	12,760	10,685	162	1.2
Des Moines–West Des Moines, IA	89.6	4.9	3.2	0.4	0.1	6.8	242,364	240,203	223,789	199,401	2,161	0.9
Dallas County, IA.......................	94.0	1.6	2.7	0.3	0.1	6.2	28,065	27,260	21,788	16,765	805	3.0
Guthrie County, IA.......................	98.4	0.2	0.4	0.2	0.0	2.0	5,744	5,756	5,683	5,465	-12	-0.2
Madison County, IA......................	98.1	0.5	0.4	0.2	0.0	1.4	6,569	6,554	6,229	5,658	15	0.2
Polk County, IA.........................	87.5	6.2	3.7	0.5	0.1	7.8	183,277	182,262	173,190	156,222	1,015	0.6
Warren County, IA.......................	97.4	0.7	0.5	0.3	0.0	2.0	18,709	18,371	16,899	15,291	338	1.8
Detroit–Warren–Livonia, MI	71.2	22.9	3.5	0.4	0.0	4.0	1,881,623	1,886,536	1,875,314	1,797,335	-4,913	-0.3
Detroit–Livonia–Dearborn, MI..................	54.3	40.3	2.7	0.4	0.0	5.4	817,730	821,693	829,100	826,165	-3,963	-0.5
Wayne County, MI	54.3	40.3	2.7	0.4	0.0	5.4	817,730	821,693	829,100	826,165	-3,963	-0.5
Warren–Troy–Farmington Hills, MI.............	83.4	10.3	4.0	0.4	0.0	3.0	1,063,893	1,064,843	1,046,214	971,170	-950	-0.1
Lapeer County, MI.......................	96.7	1.2	0.4	0.5	0.0	4.2	36,329	36,331	35,598	32,748	-2	0.0
Livingston County, MI	96.9	0.6	0.8	0.4	0.0	2.0	72,749	72,809	70,496	58,921	-60	-0.1
Macomb County, MI.....................	85.2	9.3	3.1	0.3	0.0	2.4	356,501	356,626	348,371	320,292	-125	0.0
Oakland County, MI.....................	77.7	14.1	5.8	0.3	0.0	3.6	526,755	527,255	520,284	492,097	-500	-0.1
St. Clair County, MI.....................	94.5	2.6	0.5	0.5	0.0	2.9	71,559	71,822	71,465	67,112	-263	-0.4
Dothan, AL..................................	73.7	23.5	0.7	0.6	0.1	3.1	67,424	66,897	64,038	59,718	527	0.8
Geneva County, AL......................	87.2	10.0	0.3	0.9	0.1	3.4	12,720	12,687	12,523	12,091	33	0.3
Henry County, AL.......................	69.8	28.4	0.4	0.4	0.0	2.5	8,998	8,891	8,580	8,031	107	1.2
Houston County, AL.....................	70.8	26.2	0.9	0.5	0.1	3.1	45,706	45,319	42,935	39,596	387	0.9
Dover, DE..................................	69.2	24.6	2.2	0.7	0.1	6.0	66,241	65,338	58,841	50,510	903	1.4
Kent County, DE........................	69.2	24.6	2.2	0.7	0.1	6.0	66,241	65,338	58,841	50,510	903	1.4
Dubuque, IA................................	94.5	2.7	1.1	0.2	0.3	2.0	39,273	38,951	37,838	35,503	322	0.8
Dubuque County, IA.....................	94.5	2.7	1.1	0.2	0.3	2.0	39,273	38,951	37,838	35,503	322	0.8
Duluth, MN–WI..............................	92.7	1.4	0.9	2.7	0.0	1.3	142,158	141,539	136,906	129,928	619	0.4
Carlton County, MN......................	89.9	1.5	0.5	5.8	0.0	1.5	15,703	15,656	14,951	13,736	47	0.3
St. Louis County, MN	93.0	1.5	1.0	2.3	0.0	1.3	103,433	103,058	100,146	95,835	375	0.4
Douglas County, WI	93.4	1.2	0.9	2.0	0.0	1.2	23,022	22,825	21,809	20,357	197	0.9
Durham–Chapel Hill, NC	64.7	27.6	4.5	0.9	0.1	11.3	225,865	222,760	206,887	180,055	3,105	1.4
Chatham County, NC......................	82.4	13.5	1.2	1.3	0.1	13.2	29,246	28,753	25,453	21,399	493	1.7
Durham County, NC......................	53.5	38.5	4.7	1.0	0.1	13.5	122,012	120,217	110,995	95,432	1,795	1.5
Orange County, NC......................	77.5	12.4	7.1	0.7	0.1	8.1	56,239	55,597	53,290	47,732	642	1.2
Person County, NC......................	70.5	27.0	0.4	0.8	0.0	4.2	18,368	18,193	17,149	15,492	175	1.0
Eau Claire, WI..............................	94.2	1.2	2.6	0.6	0.0	1.7	69,747	69,336	66,336	60,303	411	0.6
Chippewa County, WI	95.5	1.6	1.3	0.5	0.0	1.3	27,433	27,185	25,594	22,835	248	0.9
Eau Claire County, WI	93.4	1.0	3.4	0.6	0.0	2.0	42,314	42,151	40,742	37,468	163	0.4
El Centro, CA...............................	89.3	3.8	2.4	2.6	0.2	80.6	56,285	56,067	50,138	43,876	218	0.4
Imperial County, CA	89.3	3.8	2.4	2.6	0.2	80.6	56,285	56,067	50,138	43,876	218	0.4
Elizabethtown, KY	83.1	11.3	1.9	0.5	0.3	4.9	49,660	49,435	46,359	42,745	225	0.5
Hardin County, KY......................	81.6	12.4	2.1	0.5	0.3	5.2	43,500	43,263	40,221	36,888	237	0.5
Larue County, KY.......................	94.7	3.2	0.2	0.3	0.0	2.9	6,160	6,172	6,138	5,857	-12	-0.2
Elkhart–Goshen, IN...........................	90.1	6.0	1.1	0.6	0.1	14.5	77,695	77,768	75,700	69,792	-73	-0.1
Elkhart County, IN	90.1	6.0	1.1	0.6	0.1	14.5	77,695	77,768	75,700	69,792	-73	-0.1
Elmira, NY.................................	88.9	6.9	1.3	0.3	0.0	2.7	38,362	38,369	38,287	37,769	-7	0.0
Chemung County, NY	88.9	6.9	1.3	0.3	0.0	2.7	38,362	38,369	38,287	37,769	-7	0.0
El Paso, TX.................................	92.8	3.6	1.2	1.0	0.2	81.4	274,807	270,307	248,113	224,448	4,500	1.7
El Paso County, TX......................	92.8	3.6	1.2	1.0	0.2	81.4	274,807	270,307	248,113	224,448	4,500	1.7
Erie, PA....................................	89.2	7.4	1.2	0.2	0.0	3.5	119,391	119,138	117,392	114,361	253	0.2
Erie County, PA	89.2	7.4	1.2	0.2	0.0	3.5	119,391	119,138	117,392	114,361	253	0.2
Eugene–Springfield, OR	90.6	1.1	2.7	1.3	0.3	7.6	157,074	156,112	148,578	138,965	962	0.6
Lane County, OR........................	90.6	1.1	2.7	1.3	0.3	7.6	157,074	156,112	148,578	138,965	962	0.6
Evansville, IN–KY...........................	90.6	6.3	1.0	0.3	0.0	2.1	159,460	159,314	155,733	147,768	146	0.1
Gibson County, IN.......................	95.7	2.0	0.5	0.2	0.0	1.4	14,598	14,645	14,636	14,118	-47	-0.3
Posey County, IN........................	97.3	1.1	0.3	0.2	0.0	1.0	11,144	11,207	11,302	11,081	-63	-0.6
Vanderburgh County, IN..................	87.2	9.2	1.1	0.3	0.1	2.3	83,205	83,003	80,985	76,308	202	0.2
Warrick County, IN	95.2	1.6	1.7	0.2	0.0	1.7	24,265	24,203	22,695	20,544	62	0.3
Henderson County, KY...................	89.7	8.0	0.5	0.3	0.0	1.9	20,377	20,320	19,980	19,471	57	0.3
Webster County, KY.....................	93.3	4.3	0.3	0.3	0.5	4.7	5,871	5,936	6,135	6,246	-65	-1.1
Fairbanks, AK...............................	78.2	5.0	2.8	7.2	0.4	6.3	42,740	41,783	37,677	33,295	957	2.3
Fairbanks North Star Borough, AK...........	78.2	5.0	2.8	7.2	0.4	6.3	42,740	41,783	37,677	33,295	957	2.3

[1] Persons of Hispanic origin may be any race.

[2] The April 1, 2000, housing estimates base reflects modifications to the Census 2000 population as documented in the Count Question Resolution program and geographic program revisions.

[3]The Denver–Aurora metropolitan statistical area includes Broomfield County. Broomfield County, CO, was formed from parts of Adams, Boulder, Jefferson, and Weld Counties on November 15, 2001, and is coextensive with Broomfield city. For the purposes of defining and presenting data for the Denver–Aurora metropolitan statistical area, Broomfield city is treated as if it were a county when data are available to do so. In many cases, the data were not available.

Table C-2.   Population Characteristics and Housing Units—_Continued_

| Metropolitan statistical area, division, and component county | Population characteristics, 2011 | | | | | | Housing units | | | | | |
| | One race (percent) | | | | | Hispanic or Latino origin[1] (percent) | 2011 (July 1) | 2010 (July 1) | 2005 (July 1) | 2000[2] (estimates base) | Change, 2010–2011 | |
	White alone	Black or African American alone	Asian alone	American Indian, Alaska Native alone	Native Hawaiian and Other Pacific Islander alone						Number	Percent
Fargo, ND–MN	92.5	2.2	2.1	1.4	0.1	2.6	93,839	91,897	83,587	73,559	1,942	2.1
Clay County, MN	93.5	1.5	1.5	1.4	0.1	3.6	24,279	23,959	21,858	19,746	320	1.3
Cass County, ND	92.1	2.4	2.4	1.4	0.1	2.2	69,560	67,938	61,729	53,813	1,622	2.4
Farmington, NM	58.6	0.9	0.5	37.2	0.1	19.6	49,971	49,341	46,668	43,229	630	1.3
San Juan County, NM	58.6	0.9	0.5	37.2	0.1	19.6	49,971	49,341	46,668	43,229	630	1.3
Fayetteville, NC	54.1	36.5	2.3	2.8	0.4	10.2	156,019	153,735	142,082	130,978	2,284	1.5
Cumberland County, NC	54.6	36.9	2.4	1.7	0.4	9.9	137,161	135,524	126,847	118,436	1,637	1.2
Hoke County, NC	51.1	33.8	1.3	9.6	0.4	12.6	18,858	18,211	15,235	12,542	647	3.6
Fayetteville–Springdale–Rogers, AR–MO	89.9	2.4	2.6	1.7	1.1	15.2	201,313	198,299	173,404	144,428	3,014	1.5
Benton County, AR	90.7	1.9	3.1	1.8	0.4	15.7	95,116	93,084	78,431	64,219	2,032	2.2
Madison County, AR	95.9	0.5	0.5	1.4	0.1	5.0	7,554	7,482	7,093	6,527	72	1.0
Washington County, AR	88.5	3.3	2.3	1.4	2.0	15.8	88,713	87,808	78,068	64,397	905	1.0
McDonald County, MO	90.7	1.2	1.1	3.0	1.3	11.5	9,930	9,925	9,812	9,285	5	0.1
Flagstaff, AZ	66.6	1.6	1.6	27.4	0.2	13.9	64,021	63,318	59,358	53,440	703	1.1
Coconino County, AZ	66.6	1.6	1.6	27.4	0.2	13.9	64,021	63,318	59,358	53,440	703	1.1
Flint, MI	75.2	20.9	0.9	0.6	0.0	3.1	191,117	192,180	193,310	183,673	-1,063	-0.6
Genesee County, MI	75.2	20.9	0.9	0.6	0.0	3.1	191,117	192,180	193,310	183,673	-1,063	-0.6
Florence, SC	55.9	41.7	1.0	0.4	0.0	2.2	89,494	88,963	84,925	80,784	531	0.6
Darlington County, SC	56.7	41.6	0.4	0.3	0.0	1.8	30,267	30,299	30,089	28,972	-32	-0.1
Florence County, SC	55.5	41.7	1.3	0.4	0.0	2.3	59,227	58,664	54,836	51,812	563	1.0
Florence–Muscle Shoals, AL	84.9	12.5	0.7	0.5	0.0	2.3	69,756	69,549	68,019	65,399	207	0.3
Colbert County, AL	81.2	16.3	0.5	0.5	0.0	2.2	25,723	25,758	25,459	24,979	-35	-0.1
Lauderdale County, AL	87.1	10.3	0.8	0.4	0.1	2.4	44,033	43,791	42,560	40,420	242	0.6
Fond du Lac, WI	95.7	1.4	1.2	0.5	0.0	4.5	44,102	43,910	42,193	39,269	192	0.4
Fond du Lac County, WI	95.7	1.4	1.2	0.5	0.0	4.5	44,102	43,910	42,193	39,269	192	0.4
Fort Collins–Loveland, CO	93.5	1.0	2.1	1.0	0.1	10.8	133,247	132,722	124,032	105,386	525	0.4
Larimer County, CO	93.5	1.0	2.1	1.0	0.1	10.8	133,247	132,722	124,032	105,386	525	0.4
Fort Smith, AR–OK	82.9	3.9	2.3	6.5	0.1	8.5	130,281	128,891	122,633	115,380	1,390	1.1
Crawford County, AR	91.9	1.6	1.5	2.3	0.1	6.3	26,535	26,115	23,783	21,317	420	1.6
Franklin County, AR	95.1	1.0	1.0	1.2	0.1	2.2	8,024	8,021	7,889	7,671	3	0.0
Sebastian County, AR	83.6	6.7	4.2	2.2	0.2	12.6	55,358	54,651	52,082	49,325	707	1.3
Le Flore County, OK	78.6	2.2	0.6	12.6	0.1	7.1	21,593	21,448	20,910	20,137	145	0.7
Sequoyah County, OK	67.4	2.1	0.5	20.6	0.1	3.8	18,771	18,656	17,969	16,930	115	0.6
Fort Wayne, IN	84.3	10.4	2.5	0.4	0.1	6.0	178,509	178,124	173,944	162,407	385	0.2
Allen County, IN	82.0	12.1	2.8	0.5	0.1	6.7	152,441	152,184	148,702	138,917	257	0.2
Wells County, IN	97.9	0.5	0.5	0.3	0.0	2.2	11,649	11,659	11,533	10,980	-10	-0.1
Whitley County, IN	97.8	0.4	0.4	0.3	0.0	1.7	14,419	14,281	13,709	12,510	138	1.0
Fresno, CA	77.7	5.9	10.3	3.0	0.3	50.9	318,064	315,531	294,828	270,585	2,533	0.8
Fresno County, CA	77.7	5.9	10.3	3.0	0.3	50.9	318,064	315,531	294,828	270,585	2,533	0.8
Gadsden, AL	81.5	15.5	0.7	0.6	0.3	3.5	47,346	47,454	47,079	45,963	-108	-0.2
Etowah County, AL	81.5	15.5	0.7	0.6	0.3	3.5	47,346	47,454	47,079	45,963	-108	-0.2
Gainesville, FL	72.6	19.3	5.2	0.4	0.1	8.6	120,738	120,073	112,571	101,031	665	0.6
Alachua County, FL	71.3	20.3	5.6	0.3	0.1	8.9	113,371	112,766	105,843	95,127	605	0.5
Gilchrist County, FL	92.0	5.7	0.4	0.6	0.1	5.2	7,367	7,307	6,728	5,904	60	0.8
Gainesville, GA	87.4	8.1	2.0	1.0	0.2	26.8	69,428	68,825	61,166	51,155	603	0.9
Hall County, GA	87.4	8.1	2.0	1.0	0.2	26.8	69,428	68,825	61,166	51,155	603	0.9
Glens Falls, NY	95.7	2.2	0.6	0.2	0.0	2.2	67,883	67,570	64,965	61,622	313	0.5
Warren County, NY	96.5	1.2	0.7	0.2	0.0	1.9	38,949	38,726	37,159	34,839	223	0.6
Washington County, NY	94.8	3.3	0.5	0.3	0.0	2.4	28,934	28,844	27,806	26,783	90	0.3
Goldsboro, NC	63.9	32.0	1.3	0.7	0.1	10.1	53,239	52,949	50,856	47,354	290	0.5
Wayne County, NC	63.9	32.0	1.3	0.7	0.1	10.1	53,239	52,949	50,856	47,354	290	0.5
Grand Forks, ND–MN	92.2	1.7	1.6	2.4	0.0	3.9	44,136	43,954	42,686	41,381	182	0.4
Polk County, MN	94.8	0.9	0.8	1.6	0.0	5.5	14,597	14,610	14,453	14,006	-13	-0.1
Grand Forks County, ND	90.9	2.1	1.9	2.8	0.1	3.1	29,539	29,344	28,233	27,375	195	0.7
Grand Junction, CO	94.5	0.9	0.9	1.5	0.1	13.6	63,202	62,644	56,947	48,720	558	0.9
Mesa County, CO	94.5	0.9	0.9	1.5	0.1	13.6	63,202	62,644	56,947	48,720	558	0.9
Grand Rapids–Wyoming, MI	86.3	8.5	2.0	0.7	0.1	8.6	324,117	323,764	315,759	293,140	353	0.1
Barry County, MI	97.3	0.5	0.4	0.5	0.0	2.4	27,090	27,010	26,028	23,890	80	0.3
Ionia County, MI	92.8	4.9	0.4	0.6	0.0	4.5	24,788	24,778	24,022	22,011	10	0.0
Kent County, MI	83.8	10.3	2.5	0.7	0.1	9.9	247,231	246,901	240,898	224,045	330	0.1
Newaygo County, MI	95.9	1.3	0.4	0.9	0.0	5.5	25,008	25,075	24,811	23,194	-67	-0.3
Great Falls, MT	89.9	1.4	0.8	4.5	0.1	3.6	37,470	37,277	36,117	35,234	193	0.5
Cascade County, MT	89.9	1.4	0.8	4.5	0.1	3.6	37,470	37,277	36,117	35,234	193	0.5
Greeley, CO	93.5	1.3	1.3	1.7	0.1	28.5	97,031	96,281	87,428	66,137	750	0.8
Weld County, CO	93.5	1.3	1.3	1.7	0.1	28.5	97,031	96,281	87,428	66,137	750	0.8

[1] Persons of Hispanic origin may be any race.

[2] The April 1, 2000, housing estimates base reflects modifications to the Census 2000 population as documented in the Count Question Resolution program and geographic program revisions.

Table C-2. Population Characteristics and Housing Units—*Continued*

Metropolitan statistical area, division, and component county	Population characteristics, 2011						Housing units					
	One race (percent)					Hispanic or Latino origin[1] (percent)	2011 (July 1)	2010 (July 1)	2005 (July 1)	2000[2] (estimates base)	Change, 2010–2011	
	White alone	Black or African American alone	Asian alone	American Indian, Alaska Native alone	Native Hawaiian and Other Pacific Islander alone						Number	Percent
Green Bay, WI	91.2	2.0	2.4	2.6	0.1	6.4	137,983	137,212	131,248	118,233	771	0.6
Brown County, WI	89.7	2.4	2.9	2.9	0.1	7.5	105,024	104,371	100,127	90,193	653	0.6
Kewaunee County, WI	97.8	0.5	0.4	0.4	0.0	2.4	9,327	9,304	9,009	8,225	23	0.2
Oconto County, WI	97.0	0.3	0.3	1.3	0.0	1.5	23,632	23,537	22,112	19,815	95	0.4
Greensboro–High Point, NC	68.2	26.1	3.1	0.8	0.1	7.8	324,700	322,753	302,820	275,044	1,947	0.6
Guilford County, NC	59.9	33.1	4.1	0.7	0.1	7.3	219,682	218,017	201,365	180,346	1,665	0.8
Randolph County, NC	90.2	6.2	1.0	1.1	0.1	10.7	61,276	61,041	58,903	54,442	235	0.4
Rockingham County, NC	78.2	19.1	0.5	0.5	0.1	5.7	43,742	43,695	42,552	40,256	47	0.1
Greenville, NC	61.1	34.7	1.6	0.7	0.2	6.6	83,651	83,203	75,204	65,743	448	0.5
Greene County, NC	58.9	37.1	0.4	2.2	0.2	14.6	8,283	8,213	7,907	7,368	70	0.9
Pitt County, NC	61.4	34.4	1.7	0.5	0.1	5.6	75,368	74,990	67,297	58,375	378	0.5
Greenville–Mauldin–Easley, SC	79.0	17.1	1.8	0.5	0.1	7.0	278,591	277,416	260,901	238,973	1,175	0.4
Greenville County, SC	77.2	18.4	2.1	0.5	0.1	8.3	196,668	195,461	180,361	162,802	1,207	0.6
Laurens County, SC	72.2	25.9	0.4	0.3	0.1	4.3	30,600	30,710	30,874	30,180	-110	-0.4
Pickens County, SC	89.6	7.0	1.7	0.2	0.0	3.3	51,323	51,245	49,666	45,991	78	0.2
Gulfport–Biloxi, MS	74.5	20.2	2.4	0.6	0.1	4.8	117,774	114,182	118,596	106,013	3,592	3.1
Hancock County, MS	88.3	8.0	1.0	0.5	0.1	3.5	22,658	21,840	24,179	21,059	818	3.7
Harrison County, MS	71.0	23.1	2.9	0.6	0.2	5.5	87,773	85,181	88,281	79,623	2,592	3.0
Stone County, MS	78.3	19.8	0.3	0.6	0.0	1.5	7,343	7,161	6,136	5,331	182	2.5
Hagerstown–Martinsburg, MD–WV	87.6	8.5	1.2	0.3	0.1	3.5	115,816	115,329	106,497	93,951	487	0.4
Washington County, MD	85.6	10.2	1.5	0.3	0.1	3.6	60,819	60,814	57,880	52,970	5	0.0
Berkeley County, WV	88.9	7.4	0.9	0.3	0.1	3.8	45,197	44,762	39,516	32,911	435	1.0
Morgan County, WV	97.0	0.9	0.3	0.3	0.0	1.2	9,800	9,753	9,101	8,070	47	0.5
Hanford–Corcoran, CA	81.2	7.9	4.2	2.9	0.3	51.4	44,170	43,867	40,678	36,562	303	0.7
Kings County, CA	81.2	7.9	4.2	2.9	0.3	51.4	44,170	43,867	40,678	36,562	303	0.7
Harrisburg–Carlisle, PA	83.9	10.6	3.0	0.3	0.1	4.9	242,838	240,818	230,395	217,004	2,020	0.8
Cumberland County, PA	91.5	3.5	3.1	0.2	0.0	2.8	101,122	99,989	93,911	86,931	1,133	1.1
Dauphin County, PA	74.9	18.6	3.3	0.3	0.1	7.3	121,188	120,406	116,565	111,129	782	0.6
Perry County, PA	97.5	0.8	0.4	0.2	0.1	1.4	20,528	20,423	19,919	18,944	105	0.5
Harrisonburg, VA	91.4	4.1	2.0	0.6	0.1	9.7	52,024	51,104	45,778	41,030	920	1.8
Rockingham County, VA	95.4	2.0	0.7	0.6	0.0	5.5	34,137	33,660	30,657	27,334	477	1.4
Harrisonburg city, VA	85.3	7.4	4.0	0.7	0.2	16.2	17,887	17,444	15,121	13,696	443	2.5
Hartford–West Hartford–East Hartford, CT	81.4	11.9	4.1	0.4	0.1	12.9	508,997	507,049	492,867	471,912	1,948	0.4
Hartford County, CT	78.2	14.6	4.5	0.5	0.1	15.7	375,454	374,249	365,392	353,035	1,205	0.3
Middlesex County, CT	90.3	5.0	2.6	0.2	0.1	5.0	75,270	74,837	72,046	67,290	433	0.6
Tolland County, CT	90.7	3.7	3.6	0.2	0.1	4.6	58,273	57,963	55,429	51,587	310	0.5
Hattiesburg, MS	68.7	28.7	1.0	0.3	0.1	2.9	62,761	61,878	55,119	50,499	883	1.4
Forrest County, MS	61.0	36.1	1.0	0.4	0.1	3.7	32,122	32,289	30,388	29,558	-167	-0.5
Lamar County, MS	76.8	20.5	1.2	0.3	0.0	2.2	25,083	24,070	19,382	15,843	1,013	4.2
Perry County, MS	77.9	20.6	0.2	0.3	0.0	1.1	5,556	5,519	5,359	5,098	37	0.7
Hickory–Lenoir–Morganton, NC	87.8	7.2	2.7	0.6	0.2	6.5	163,144	162,613	157,152	144,886	531	0.3
Alexander County, NC	91.5	5.8	1.1	0.4	0.0	4.4	16,341	16,189	15,302	14,086	152	0.9
Burke County, NC	86.5	7.0	3.6	0.8	0.6	5.5	41,040	40,880	39,710	37,442	160	0.4
Caldwell County, NC	92.2	5.2	0.6	0.6	0.1	4.7	37,841	37,659	36,238	33,439	182	0.5
Catawba County, NC	85.4	8.8	3.6	0.5	0.0	8.5	67,922	67,885	65,902	59,919	37	0.1
Hinesville–Fort Stewart, GA	54.2	38.6	2.0	0.7	0.6	10.7	33,735	32,770	29,389	26,216	965	2.9
Liberty County, GA	50.9	41.5	2.2	0.7	0.6	10.4	27,323	26,740	24,417	21,996	583	2.2
Long County, GA	68.4	26.2	1.0	0.8	0.4	12.0	6,412	6,030	4,972	4,220	382	6.3
Holland–Grand Haven, MI	93.3	1.8	2.7	0.6	0.0	8.8	102,785	102,495	98,099	86,879	290	0.3
Ottawa County, MI	93.3	1.8	2.7	0.6	0.0	8.8	102,785	102,495	98,099	86,879	290	0.3
Honolulu, HI	22.2	2.5	43.6	0.4	9.6	8.5	337,522	336,899	327,967	315,994	623	0.2
Honolulu County, Hawaii	22.2	2.5	43.6	0.4	9.6	8.5	337,522	336,899	327,967	315,994	623	0.2
Hot Springs, AR	88.1	8.3	0.8	0.7	0.1	5.0	50,994	50,547	48,028	44,910	447	0.9
Garland County, AR	88.1	8.3	0.8	0.7	0.1	5.0	50,994	50,547	48,028	44,910	447	0.9
Houma–Bayou Cane–Thibodaux, LA	76.3	16.6	1.0	4.3	0.1	4.1	82,954	82,469	78,659	74,986	485	0.6
Lafourche Parish, LA	81.1	13.6	0.8	2.8	0.1	4.0	38,894	38,582	36,478	34,962	312	0.8
Terrebonne Parish, LA	72.1	19.2	1.1	5.5	0.1	4.2	44,060	43,887	42,181	40,024	173	0.4
Houston–Sugar Land–Baytown, TX	72.8	17.6	6.8	1.0	0.1	35.9	2,342,598	2,308,217	2,053,210	1,799,795	34,381	1.5
Austin County, TX	87.6	9.8	0.5	0.8	0.0	24.6	13,233	12,928	11,681	10,202	305	2.4
Brazoria County, TX	79.2	12.6	5.6	0.8	0.1	28.3	120,579	118,336	105,146	90,646	2,243	1.9
Chambers County, TX	87.3	8.9	1.2	1.1	0.1	20.0	13,593	13,291	11,992	10,342	302	2.3
Fort Bend County, TX	58.3	21.5	17.5	0.6	0.1	24.2	208,696	197,031	148,758	116,019	11,665	5.9
Galveston County, TX	80.1	14.0	3.2	0.8	0.1	22.9	133,510	132,492	123,955	111,737	1,018	0.8
Harris County, TX	71.4	19.3	6.4	1.1	0.1	41.4	1,612,088	1,598,696	1,452,850	1,298,318	13,392	0.8
Liberty County, TX	85.6	11.3	0.6	1.0	0.1	19.1	28,957	28,759	27,829	26,370	198	0.7
Montgomery County, TX	90.2	4.8	2.3	1.0	0.1	21.4	182,513	177,650	144,297	112,769	4,863	2.7
San Jacinto County, TX	86.2	10.6	0.5	0.9	0.0	11.8	13,337	13,187	12,495	11,500	150	1.1
Waller County, TX	72.0	24.3	0.6	1.6	0.1	30.4	16,092	15,847	14,207	11,892	245	1.5

[1] Persons of Hispanic origin may be any race.
[2] The April 1, 2000, housing estimates base reflects modifications to the Census 2000 population as documented in the Count Question Resolution program and geographic program revisions.

Table C-2.   Population Characteristics and Housing Units—*Continued*

Metropolitan statistical area, division, and component county	Population characteristics, 2011						Housing units				Change, 2010–2011	
	One race (percent)					Hispanic or Latino origin[1] (percent)	2011 (July 1)	2010 (July 1)	2005 (July 1)	2000[2] (estimates base)	Number	Percent
	White alone	Black or African American alone	Asian alone	American Indian, Alaska Native alone	Native Hawaiian and Other Pacific Islander alone							
Huntington–Ashland, WV–KY–OH	94.8	2.9	0.6	0.2	0.0	1.0	130,799	131,131	130,930	129,890	-332	-0.3
Boyd County, KY	94.9	3.0	0.5	0.3	0.0	1.5	21,674	21,802	21,811	21,967	-128	-0.6
Greenup County, KY	97.3	0.9	0.5	0.3	0.0	0.9	16,294	16,331	16,267	15,991	-37	-0.2
Lawrence County, OH	95.9	2.2	0.4	0.2	0.0	0.8	27,538	27,603	27,718	27,199	-65	-0.2
Cabell County, WV	91.6	5.1	1.1	0.2	0.0	1.2	46,131	46,168	45,901	45,618	-37	-0.1
Wayne County, WV	98.5	0.3	0.2	0.2	0.0	0.6	19,162	19,227	19,233	19,115	-65	-0.3
Huntsville, AL	72.4	22.2	2.2	0.8	0.1	4.9	185,404	181,424	162,844	147,323	3,980	2.2
Limestone County, AL	82.8	13.3	1.2	0.9	0.2	5.7	36,019	34,977	30,919	26,893	1,042	3.0
Madison County, AL	69.8	24.5	2.5	0.8	0.1	4.7	149,385	146,447	131,925	120,430	2,938	2.0
Idaho Falls, ID	95.5	0.6	0.8	1.1	0.1	11.5	48,916	48,453	42,612	36,770	463	1.0
Bonneville County, ID	95.4	0.7	0.9	1.1	0.1	11.8	40,059	39,731	35,223	30,500	328	0.8
Jefferson County, ID	96.2	0.4	0.5	1.2	0.1	10.4	8,857	8,722	7,389	6,270	135	1.5
Indianapolis–Carmel, IN	79.9	15.3	2.4	0.4	0.1	6.4	761,961	757,441	721,017	644,888	4,520	0.6
Boone County, IN	95.5	1.2	1.8	0.2	0.0	2.4	23,046	22,754	20,707	17,946	292	1.3
Brown County, IN	97.5	0.6	0.3	0.4	0.0	1.3	8,460	8,285	7,782	7,167	175	2.1
Hamilton County, IN	89.3	3.8	5.0	0.2	0.0	3.6	109,440	106,772	92,165	69,487	2,668	2.5
Hancock County, IN	95.4	2.3	0.8	0.2	0.0	1.8	28,400	28,125	26,171	21,764	275	1.0
Hendricks County, IN	90.7	5.3	2.2	0.3	0.1	3.1	56,047	55,454	50,502	39,214	593	1.1
Johnson County, IN	94.7	1.5	2.1	0.3	0.0	3.2	57,319	56,649	52,135	45,082	670	1.2
Marion County, IN	67.8	27.0	2.1	0.5	0.1	9.6	417,800	417,862	411,073	387,181	-62	0.0
Morgan County, IN	97.8	0.5	0.4	0.3	0.0	1.3	27,627	27,754	27,672	25,911	-127	-0.5
Putnam County, IN	93.7	4.2	0.8	0.3	0.0	1.7	14,724	14,706	14,269	13,520	18	0.1
Shelby County, IN	96.8	1.3	0.6	0.3	0.1	3.7	19,098	19,080	18,541	17,616	18	0.1
Iowa City, IA	88.6	4.4	4.7	0.3	0.1	4.9	66,177	65,483	61,454	54,375	694	1.1
Johnson County, IA	87.2	5.0	5.4	0.3	0.1	4.9	56,579	55,967	52,329	45,832	612	1.1
Washington County, IA	97.3	0.9	0.4	0.3	0.1	5.1	9,598	9,516	9,125	8,543	82	0.9
Ithaca, NY	82.4	4.3	9.7	0.5	0.1	4.6	41,789	41,674	40,587	38,614	115	0.3
Tompkins County, NY	82.4	4.3	9.7	0.5	0.1	4.6	41,789	41,674	40,587	38,614	115	0.3
Jackson, MI	88.3	8.2	0.7	0.4	0.0	3.1	69,521	69,458	67,659	62,911	63	0.1
Jackson County, MI	88.3	8.2	0.7	0.4	0.0	3.1	69,521	69,458	67,659	62,911	63	0.1
Jackson, MS	49.7	48.0	1.1	0.3	0.1	2.2	223,280	222,584	211,677	196,570	696	0.3
Copiah County, MS	47.5	51.2	0.3	0.2	0.0	2.7	12,256	12,184	11,749	11,104	72	0.6
Hinds County, MS	29.0	69.1	0.8	0.2	0.0	1.6	103,036	103,421	102,652	100,298	-385	-0.4
Madison County, MS	58.0	38.4	2.2	0.4	0.1	3.0	39,088	38,558	34,325	28,791	530	1.4
Rankin County, MS	77.8	19.7	1.2	0.3	0.1	2.7	56,944	56,487	51,330	45,075	457	0.8
Simpson County, MS	63.0	35.5	0.4	0.3	0.1	1.6	11,956	11,934	11,621	11,302	22	0.2
Jackson, TN	65.0	32.4	0.9	0.3	0.0	3.3	48,869	48,857	47,425	44,407	12	0.0
Chester County, TN	88.1	9.4	0.4	0.4	0.0	2.2	7,027	6,980	6,649	6,176	47	0.7
Madison County, TN	61.0	36.4	1.0	0.3	0.0	3.5	41,842	41,877	40,776	38,231	-35	-0.1
Jacksonville, FL	71.5	22.1	3.6	0.4	0.1	7.2	602,025	598,490	544,478	475,072	3,535	0.6
Baker County, FL	83.8	13.9	0.5	0.3	0.0	2.2	9,782	9,687	8,683	7,586	95	1.0
Clay County, FL	83.2	10.5	3.1	0.5	0.1	8.0	76,175	75,478	66,648	53,731	697	0.9
Duval County, FL	62.8	29.8	4.3	0.4	0.1	7.9	389,434	388,486	362,194	329,806	948	0.2
Nassau County, FL	90.2	6.9	1.0	0.5	0.1	3.5	35,286	35,009	30,790	25,907	277	0.8
St. Johns County, FL	89.8	5.9	2.3	0.3	0.1	5.5	91,348	89,830	76,163	58,042	1,518	1.7
Jacksonville, NC	76.8	16.2	2.1	0.8	0.3	10.5	70,366	68,226	61,663	55,743	2,140	3.1
Onslow County, NC	76.8	16.2	2.1	0.8	0.3	10.5	70,366	68,226	61,663	55,743	2,140	3.1
Janesville, WI	91.2	5.1	1.1	0.5	0.1	7.8	68,474	68,422	66,336	62,193	52	0.1
Rock County, WI	91.2	5.1	1.1	0.5	0.1	7.8	68,474	68,422	66,336	62,193	52	0.1
Jefferson City, MO	89.4	7.7	0.9	0.4	0.1	2.3	63,997	63,555	61,533	56,728	442	0.7
Callaway County, MO	92.2	4.8	0.6	0.6	0.0	1.7	18,724	18,522	17,698	16,166	202	1.1
Cole County, MO	85.1	11.5	1.3	0.4	0.1	2.5	32,432	32,265	31,414	28,946	167	0.5
Moniteau County, MO	94.1	3.9	0.4	0.4	0.1	4.0	6,199	6,176	6,087	5,745	23	0.4
Osage County, MO	98.7	0.3	0.1	0.3	0.1	0.7	6,642	6,592	6,334	5,871	50	0.8
Johnson City, TN	94.3	3.1	0.9	0.3	0.0	2.7	94,640	93,830	88,035	81,906	810	0.9
Carter County, TN	96.7	1.6	0.3	0.2	0.0	1.6	27,821	27,746	27,017	25,910	75	0.3
Unicoi County, TN	98.1	0.4	0.2	0.4	0.0	4.1	8,857	8,830	8,667	8,216	27	0.3
Washington County, TN	92.6	4.2	1.2	0.4	0.0	3.0	57,962	57,254	52,351	47,780	708	1.2
Johnstown, PA	94.1	4.0	0.6	0.1	0.0	1.5	65,445	65,650	65,920	65,785	-205	-0.3
Cambria County, PA	94.1	4.0	0.6	0.1	0.0	1.5	65,445	65,650	65,920	65,785	-205	-0.3
Jonesboro, AR	84.7	12.3	1.0	0.5	0.0	4.2	51,845	51,438	48,891	46,186	407	0.8
Craighead County, AR	83.2	13.5	1.2	0.5	0.0	4.6	40,985	40,515	37,857	35,134	470	1.2
Poinsett County, AR	90.6	7.6	0.2	0.3	0.0	2.3	10,860	10,923	11,034	11,052	-63	-0.6
Joplin, MO	91.6	1.9	1.2	1.8	0.6	6.2	75,340	74,981	72,580	67,480	359	0.5
Jasper County, MO	91.7	2.4	1.0	1.6	0.5	7.0	50,855	50,668	48,970	45,570	187	0.4
Newton County, MO	91.3	1.0	1.5	2.3	0.9	4.7	24,485	24,313	23,610	21,910	172	0.7
Kalamazoo–Portage, MI	84.9	9.6	2.0	0.7	0.0	5.6	146,959	146,792	143,083	133,228	167	0.1
Kalamazoo County, MI	82.8	11.1	2.4	0.5	0.1	4.1	110,249	110,007	106,824	99,250	242	0.2
Van Buren County, MI	91.6	4.4	0.5	1.2	0.0	10.5	36,710	36,785	36,259	33,978	-75	-0.2
Kankakee–Bradley, IL	81.3	15.5	1.0	0.4	0.0	9.2	45,321	45,246	43,337	40,611	75	0.2
Kankakee County, IL	81.3	15.5	1.0	0.4	0.0	9.2	45,321	45,246	43,337	40,611	75	0.2

[1] Persons of Hispanic origin may be any race.
[2] The April 1, 2000, housing estimates base reflects modifications to the Census 2000 population as documented in the Count Question Resolution program and geographic program revisions.

Table C-2. Population Characteristics and Housing Units—*Continued*

| Metropolitan statistical area, division, and component county | Population characteristics, 2011 | | | | | | Housing units | | | | | |
| | One race (percent) | | | | | Hispanic or Latino origin[1] (percent) | 2011 (July 1) | 2010 (July 1) | 2005 (July 1) | 2000[2] (estimates base) | Change, 2010–2011 | |
	White alone	Black or African American alone	Asian alone	American Indian, Alaska Native alone	Native Hawaiian and Other Pacific Islander alone						Number	Percent
Kansas City, MO–KS	81.6	12.7	2.4	0.6	0.2	8.3	886,709	883,100	842,172	767,843	3,609	0.4
Franklin County, KS	94.8	1.4	0.5	0.9	0.0	3.5	11,132	11,147	10,880	10,230	-15	-0.1
Johnson County, KS	88.2	4.7	4.3	0.5	0.1	7.3	229,051	226,571	210,985	181,823	2,480	1.1
Leavenworth County, KS	84.9	9.7	1.4	0.9	0.1	6.0	28,845	28,697	27,010	24,401	148	0.5
Linn County, KS	96.8	0.6	0.3	0.7	0.1	2.1	5,499	5,446	5,149	4,705	53	1.0
Miami County, KS	95.7	1.5	0.4	0.6	0.0	2.7	13,268	13,190	12,311	10,987	78	0.6
Wyandotte County, KS	67.6	25.1	2.7	1.4	0.2	26.7	66,539	66,747	66,043	65,911	-208	-0.3
Bates County, MO	96.6	1.1	0.2	0.8	0.0	1.7	7,862	7,842	7,708	7,244	20	0.3
Caldwell County, MO	96.9	0.8	0.2	0.5	0.0	1.7	4,597	4,605	4,604	4,493	-8	-0.2
Cass County, MO	93.0	3.8	0.7	0.6	0.1	4.0	40,153	40,031	36,960	31,690	122	0.3
Clay County, MO	89.0	5.6	2.2	0.6	0.3	6.0	95,183	93,918	86,652	76,213	1,265	1.3
Clinton County, MO	95.7	1.6	0.4	0.8	0.0	1.6	8,868	8,876	8,653	7,884	-8	-0.1
Jackson County, MO	70.6	24.1	1.7	0.6	0.3	8.4	311,377	312,105	305,092	288,261	-728	-0.2
Lafayette County, MO	94.6	2.4	0.4	0.5	0.2	2.3	14,728	14,718	14,410	13,706	10	0.1
Platte County, MO	88.2	6.3	2.4	0.6	0.3	5.1	39,641	39,223	35,850	30,919	418	1.1
Ray County, MO	96.3	1.5	0.3	0.6	0.1	1.9	9,966	9,984	9,865	9,376	-18	-0.2
Kennewick–Pasco–Richland, WA	91.4	1.9	2.6	1.2	0.2	28.8	94,700	93,041	84,183	72,074	1,659	1.8
Benton County, WA	91.5	1.5	2.9	1.2	0.2	18.8	69,580	68,618	63,309	55,965	962	1.4
Franklin County, WA	91.3	2.5	2.1	1.4	0.4	50.5	25,120	24,423	20,874	16,109	697	2.9
Killeen–Temple–Fort Hood, TX	71.1	20.2	2.8	1.1	0.8	21.0	163,080	159,366	140,187	122,165	3,714	2.3
Bell County, TX	68.9	22.1	3.1	1.1	0.8	22.2	128,777	125,470	108,794	92,801	3,307	2.6
Coryell County, TX	74.9	16.8	2.2	1.1	0.9	16.6	25,490	25,183	23,209	21,748	307	1.2
Lampasas County, TX	90.9	3.8	1.2	1.2	0.2	18.2	8,813	8,713	8,184	7,616	100	1.1
Kingsport–Bristol–Bristol, TN–VA	95.9	2.2	0.5	0.3	0.0	1.4	147,282	146,978	143,100	136,312	304	0.2
Hawkins County, TN	96.6	1.6	0.5	0.3	0.0	1.3	26,973	26,870	26,032	24,417	103	0.4
Sullivan County, TN	95.4	2.4	0.6	0.3	0.0	1.6	73,868	73,760	71,954	69,079	108	0.1
Scott County, VA	98.2	0.8	0.2	0.2	0.1	1.1	11,933	11,916	11,806	11,349	17	0.1
Washington County, VA	97.1	1.5	0.4	0.2	0.0	1.4	25,699	25,601	24,643	23,008	98	0.4
Bristol city, VA	91.0	5.9	0.8	0.4	0.0	1.5	8,809	8,831	8,665	8,459	-22	-0.2
Kingston, NY	88.8	6.6	1.8	0.4	0.0	9.0	83,854	83,639	81,321	77,646	215	0.3
Ulster County, NY	88.8	6.6	1.8	0.4	0.0	9.0	83,854	83,639	81,321	77,646	215	0.3
Knoxville, TN	89.6	6.7	1.5	0.4	0.1	3.5	317,060	315,615	298,262	276,180	1,445	0.5
Anderson County, TN	92.6	4.1	1.1	0.4	0.0	2.3	34,769	34,714	33,908	32,516	55	0.2
Blount County, TN	94.3	3.1	0.8	0.4	0.0	2.9	55,624	55,266	51,615	47,066	358	0.6
Knox County, TN	86.7	9.0	2.0	0.4	0.1	3.6	195,694	194,952	184,933	171,389	742	0.4
Loudon County, TN	96.3	1.4	0.6	0.4	0.2	7.1	22,030	21,725	19,260	17,284	305	1.4
Union County, TN	97.7	0.4	0.2	0.4	0.1	1.5	8,943	8,958	8,546	7,925	-15	-0.2
Kokomo, IN	90.7	6.0	0.9	0.3	0.0	2.6	45,522	45,677	45,877	44,463	-155	-0.3
Howard County, IN	89.3	7.1	1.0	0.4	0.0	2.7	38,567	38,679	38,903	37,605	-112	-0.3
Tipton County, IN	98.1	0.4	0.4	0.2	0.0	2.3	6,955	6,998	6,974	6,858	-43	-0.6
La Crosse, WI–MN	93.0	1.4	3.7	0.4	0.0	1.5	57,283	57,003	54,725	51,663	280	0.5
Houston County, MN	97.5	0.6	0.5	0.2	0.0	0.8	8,591	8,601	8,500	8,171	-10	-0.1
La Crosse County, WI	92.2	1.5	4.2	0.5	0.0	1.6	48,692	48,402	46,225	43,492	290	0.6
Lafayette, IN	88.4	3.9	5.6	0.3	0.0	7.2	85,248	84,505	80,068	70,839	743	0.9
Benton County, IN	97.9	0.8	0.2	0.2	0.0	4.9	3,942	3,937	3,915	3,821	5	0.1
Carroll County, IN	98.1	0.5	0.1	0.3	0.0	3.8	9,482	9,472	9,222	8,674	10	0.1
Tippecanoe County, IN	86.8	4.4	6.5	0.4	0.1	7.7	71,824	71,096	66,931	58,344	728	1.0
Lafayette, LA	69.8	27.0	1.4	0.4	0.0	3.7	116,781	115,597	106,790	98,233	1,184	1.0
Lafayette Parish, LA	70.6	26.1	1.5	0.4	0.0	4.0	94,718	93,656	85,774	78,012	1,062	1.1
St. Martin Parish, LA	66.6	31.0	0.8	0.5	0.0	2.3	22,063	21,941	21,016	20,221	122	0.6
Lake Charles, LA	72.3	24.5	1.1	0.5	0.1	2.7	86,509	85,651	85,344	81,332	858	1.0
Calcasieu Parish, LA	71.5	25.3	1.1	0.5	0.1	2.7	82,976	82,058	80,569	76,006	918	1.1
Cameron Parish, LA	96.0	2.3	0.2	0.6	0.0	2.8	3,533	3,593	4,775	5,326	-60	-1.7
Lake Havasu City–Kingman, AZ	92.5	1.2	1.2	2.7	0.2	15.2	111,845	110,912	99,091	80,028	933	0.8
Mohave County, AZ	92.5	1.2	1.2	2.7	0.2	15.2	111,845	110,912	99,091	80,028	933	0.8
Lakeland–Winter Haven, FL	80.4	15.3	1.8	0.6	0.1	18.1	281,004	281,214	256,428	226,154	-210	-0.1
Polk County, FL	80.4	15.3	1.8	0.6	0.1	18.1	281,004	281,214	256,428	226,154	-210	-0.1
Lancaster, PA	91.5	4.4	2.0	0.4	0.1	8.9	204,747	202,954	194,015	180,036	1,793	0.9
Lancaster County, PA	91.5	4.4	2.0	0.4	0.1	8.9	204,747	202,954	194,015	180,036	1,793	0.9
Lansing–East Lansing, MI	83.2	9.3	3.9	0.6	0.1	6.2	199,051	199,026	195,433	181,876	25	0.0
Clinton County, MI	94.2	2.1	1.4	0.5	0.0	4.0	30,770	30,695	29,353	24,640	75	0.2
Eaton County, MI	88.7	6.8	1.8	0.5	0.0	4.8	47,163	47,050	45,798	42,139	113	0.2
Ingham County, MI	78.1	12.2	5.4	0.7	0.1	7.3	121,118	121,281	120,282	115,097	-163	-0.1
Laredo, TX	97.8	0.6	0.7	0.6	0.0	95.4	74,518	73,496	65,604	55,209	1,022	1.4
Webb County, TX	97.8	0.6	0.7	0.6	0.0	95.4	74,518	73,496	65,604	55,209	1,022	1.4
Las Cruces, NM	92.5	2.1	1.3	2.2	0.1	65.9	82,980	81,493	74,143	65,253	1,487	1.8
Doña Ana County, NM	92.5	2.1	1.3	2.2	0.1	65.9	82,980	81,493	74,143	65,253	1,487	1.8
Las Vegas–Paradise, NV	73.8	11.0	9.1	1.2	0.8	29.7	848,118	840,343	726,134	559,793	7,775	0.9
Clark County, NV	73.8	11.0	9.1	1.2	0.8	29.7	848,118	840,343	726,134	559,793	7,775	0.9

[1] Persons of Hispanic origin may be any race.
[2] The April 1, 2000, housing estimates base reflects modifications to the Census 2000 population as documented in the Count Question Resolution program and geographic program revisions.

Table C-2. Population Characteristics and Housing Units—*Continued*

Metropolitan statistical area, division, and component county	Population characteristics, 2011					Hispanic or Latino origin[1] (percent)	Housing units				Change, 2010–2011	
	One race (percent)						2011 (July 1)	2010 (July 1)	2005 (July 1)	2000[2] (estimates base)	Number	Percent
	White alone	Black or African American alone	Asian alone	American Indian, Alaska Native alone	Native Hawaiian and Other Pacific Islander alone							
Lawrence, KS	85.3	4.2	4.1	2.8	0.1	5.5	46,999	46,731	44,678	40,249	268	0.6
Douglas County, KS	85.3	4.2	4.1	2.8	0.1	5.5	46,999	46,731	44,678	40,249	268	0.6
Lawton, OK	67.2	17.7	2.4	6.2	0.6	11.5	51,726	50,739	47,174	45,418	987	1.9
Comanche County, OK	67.2	17.7	2.4	6.2	0.6	11.5	51,726	50,739	47,174	45,418	987	1.9
Lebanon, PA	94.3	2.8	1.3	0.3	0.0	9.7	56,041	55,594	53,053	49,289	447	0.8
Lebanon County, PA	94.3	2.8	1.3	0.3	0.0	9.7	56,041	55,594	53,053	49,289	447	0.8
Lewiston, ID–WA	92.2	0.5	0.8	4.1	0.1	3.1	27,420	27,310	26,401	25,323	110	0.4
Nez Perce County, ID	90.8	0.4	0.8	5.5	0.1	3.1	17,501	17,438	16,890	16,211	63	0.4
Asotin County, WA	94.8	0.5	0.7	1.5	0.2	3.1	9,919	9,872	9,511	9,112	47	0.5
Lewiston–Auburn, ME	93.1	3.8	0.8	0.4	0.0	1.6	49,186	49,091	47,996	45,970	95	0.2
Androscoggin County, ME	93.1	3.8	0.8	0.4	0.0	1.6	49,186	49,091	47,996	45,970	95	0.2
Lexington–Fayette, KY	84.1	11.0	2.4	0.3	0.1	5.9	210,867	209,138	195,267	175,295	1,729	0.8
Bourbon County, KY	91.5	6.2	0.4	0.4	0.0	7.1	8,927	8,927	8,768	8,348	0	0.0
Clark County, KY	93.1	5.0	0.4	0.2	0.0	2.6	15,686	15,706	15,258	13,763	-20	-0.1
Fayette County, KY	79.1	14.7	3.4	0.4	0.1	7.0	136,182	135,160	127,426	116,166	1,022	0.8
Jessamine County, KY	93.7	3.2	1.0	0.3	0.0	2.8	19,488	19,331	17,703	14,646	157	0.8
Scott County, KY	91.7	5.5	1.0	0.3	0.0	4.3	19,813	19,303	15,946	12,986	510	2.6
Woodford County, KY	92.8	5.0	0.6	0.2	0.1	6.8	10,771	10,711	10,166	9,386	60	0.6
Lima, OH	84.4	12.1	0.7	0.2	0.0	2.5	44,896	44,999	44,973	44,240	-103	-0.2
Allen County, OH	84.4	12.1	0.7	0.2	0.0	2.5	44,896	44,999	44,973	44,240	-103	-0.2
Lincoln, NE	89.7	3.5	3.5	0.9	0.1	5.8	128,650	127,750	121,957	110,654	900	0.7
Lancaster County, NE	89.3	3.6	3.6	0.9	0.1	6.0	121,765	120,875	115,226	104,228	890	0.7
Seward County, NE	97.6	0.5	0.5	0.4	0.0	1.9	6,885	6,875	6,731	6,426	10	0.1
Little Rock–North Little Rock–Conway, AR	73.6	22.4	1.6	0.6	0.1	5.0	310,816	306,883	286,130	261,951	3,933	1.3
Faulkner County, AR	85.5	10.6	1.2	0.7	0.1	4.0	48,325	46,612	40,221	34,562	1,713	3.7
Grant County, AR	95.3	2.6	0.3	0.5	0.0	2.3	7,808	7,758	7,394	6,953	50	0.6
Lonoke County, AR	90.4	6.4	0.9	0.7	0.1	3.5	27,715	27,237	24,239	20,767	478	1.8
Perry County, AR	95.4	2.2	0.2	0.7	0.0	2.5	4,907	4,907	4,831	4,697	0	0.0
Pulaski County, AR	60.2	35.1	2.1	0.6	0.1	6.0	176,324	175,557	169,648	161,075	767	0.4
Saline County, AR	91.7	5.4	0.9	0.6	0.0	3.9	45,737	44,812	39,797	33,897	925	2.1
Logan, UT–ID	94.1	0.8	2.0	0.9	0.5	9.7	42,122	41,552	37,817	32,909	570	1.4
Franklin County, ID	97.5	0.3	0.1	0.7	0.1	6.9	4,591	4,528	4,241	3,874	63	1.4
Cache County, UT	93.7	0.8	2.2	0.9	0.5	10.0	37,531	37,024	33,576	29,035	507	1.4
Longview, TX	78.7	17.6	0.9	0.9	0.1	14.9	87,707	87,322	84,660	81,149	385	0.4
Gregg County, TX	75.7	20.3	1.2	1.0	0.1	17.2	49,698	49,515	47,985	46,350	183	0.4
Rusk County, TX	79.0	17.9	0.5	0.9	0.1	15.2	21,258	21,191	20,752	19,875	67	0.3
Upshur County, TX	87.5	9.2	0.5	0.9	0.0	7.4	16,751	16,616	15,923	14,924	135	0.8
Longview, WA	92.2	0.8	1.6	1.8	0.3	8.1	43,607	43,450	41,178	38,626	157	0.4
Cowlitz County, WA	92.2	0.8	1.6	1.8	0.3	8.1	43,607	43,450	41,178	38,626	157	0.4
Los Angeles–Long Beach–Santa Ana, CA	72.5	7.6	15.2	1.4	0.4	44.8	4,500,162	4,493,983	4,394,076	4,240,430	6,179	0.1
Los Angeles–Long Beach–Glendale, CA	71.8	9.3	14.2	1.5	0.4	48.1	3,449,273	3,445,076	3,370,334	3,270,933	4,197	0.1
Los Angeles County, CA	71.8	9.3	14.2	1.5	0.4	48.1	3,449,273	3,445,076	3,370,334	3,270,933	4,197	0.1
Santa Ana–Anaheim–Irvine, CA	74.9	2.1	18.4	1.1	0.4	34.1	1,050,889	1,048,907	1,023,742	969,497	1,982	0.2
Orange County, CA	74.9	2.1	18.4	1.1	0.4	34.1	1,050,889	1,048,907	1,023,742	969,497	1,982	0.2
Louisville/Jefferson County, KY–IN	82.2	13.9	1.6	0.3	0.1	4.1	561,919	559,840	535,282	493,119	2,079	0.4
Clark County, IN	89.4	7.2	0.9	0.4	0.1	4.9	47,961	47,776	45,547	41,163	185	0.4
Floyd County, IN	91.5	5.3	1.0	0.3	0.0	2.8	32,068	31,968	31,038	29,096	100	0.3
Harrison County, IN	97.7	0.7	0.4	0.3	0.0	1.6	16,757	16,534	15,464	13,703	223	1.3
Washington County, IN	98.2	0.4	0.3	0.3	0.0	1.2	12,232	12,220	12,014	11,187	12	0.1
Bullitt County, KY	97.1	0.9	0.6	0.4	0.0	1.5	29,629	29,319	27,214	23,140	310	1.1
Henry County, KY	95.1	2.9	0.2	0.3	0.1	3.2	6,598	6,640	6,651	6,366	-42	-0.6
Jefferson County, KY	74.3	21.0	2.3	0.3	0.1	4.5	338,463	337,616	324,856	305,912	847	0.3
Meade County, KY	92.2	4.1	0.7	0.6	0.1	3.5	11,784	11,764	11,450	11,108	20	0.2
Nelson County, KY	92.8	5.1	0.5	0.2	0.0	2.0	18,188	18,075	17,086	14,945	113	0.6
Oldham County, KY	92.1	4.6	1.4	0.3	0.1	3.5	20,773	20,688	19,169	15,643	85	0.4
Shelby County, KY	89.0	7.7	0.7	0.5	0.2	9.1	16,731	16,606	15,223	12,871	125	0.8
Spencer County, KY	96.5	1.6	0.4	0.2	0.1	1.6	6,767	6,704	5,822	4,528	63	0.9
Trimble County, KY	97.1	0.8	0.5	0.6	0.1	2.6	3,968	3,930	3,748	3,457	38	1.0
Lubbock, TX	87.3	7.8	2.2	1.1	0.1	33.0	118,607	117,966	113,496	103,807	641	0.5
Crosby County, TX	93.1	4.3	0.2	0.8	0.1	52.3	2,855	2,902	3,039	3,202	-47	-1.6
Lubbock County, TX	87.2	7.8	2.2	1.1	0.1	32.6	115,752	115,064	110,457	100,605	688	0.6
Lynchburg, VA	78.9	17.7	1.4	0.4	0.0	2.2	113,369	112,516	105,869	98,026	853	0.8
Amherst County, VA	77.6	19.0	0.5	0.9	0.0	2.0	14,034	13,976	13,555	12,959	58	0.4
Appomattox County, VA	77.7	20.1	0.3	0.3	0.0	1.3	7,044	6,922	6,348	5,824	122	1.8
Bedford County, VA	91.4	6.0	1.1	0.3	0.0	1.8	32,167	31,937	29,762	26,811	230	0.7
Campbell County, VA	82.5	14.5	1.1	0.3	0.0	1.9	24,872	24,769	23,568	22,024	103	0.4
Bedford city, VA	77.0	20.4	0.6	0.2	0.0	2.3	2,995	2,920	2,808	2,702	75	2.6
Lynchburg city, VA	65.8	29.2	2.5	0.4	0.1	3.2	32,257	31,992	29,828	27,706	265	0.8

[1] Persons of Hispanic origin may be any race.
[2] The April 1, 2000, housing estimates base reflects modifications to the Census 2000 population as documented in the Count Question Resolution program and geographic program revisions.

Table C-2. Population Characteristics and Housing Units—*Continued*

Metropolitan statistical area, division, and component county	Population characteristics, 2011						Housing units				Change, 2010–2011	
	One race (percent)					Hispanic or Latino origin[1] (percent)	2011 (July 1)	2010 (July 1)	2005 (July 1)	2000[2] (estimates base)	Number	Percent
	White alone	Black or African American alone	Asian alone	American Indian, Alaska Native alone	Native Hawaiian and Other Pacific Islander alone							
Macon, GA	53.1	43.8	1.4	0.3	0.1	2.7	101,219	101,587	98,972	94,105	-368	-0.4
Bibb County, GA.............................	44.1	52.5	1.7	0.3	0.1	3.1	69,272	69,662	69,188	67,217	-390	-0.6
Crawford County, GA........................	74.9	22.8	0.4	0.6	0.1	2.8	5,212	5,292	5,279	4,870	-80	-1.5
Jones County, GA.............................	73.0	25.0	0.7	0.3	0.0	1.3	11,743	11,688	10,872	9,296	55	0.5
Monroe County, GA...........................	73.7	23.9	0.9	0.4	0.0	2.2	10,797	10,710	9,310	8,426	87	0.8
Twiggs County, GA...........................	56.6	41.5	0.2	0.4	0.0	1.5	4,195	4,235	4,323	4,296	-40	-0.9
Madera–Chowchilla, CA	86.3	4.4	2.2	4.5	0.2	54.5	49,130	49,140	45,362	40,376	-10	0.0
Madera County, CA	86.3	4.4	2.2	4.5	0.2	54.5	49,130	49,140	45,362	40,376	-10	0.0
Madison, WI	88.2	4.7	4.4	0.5	0.0	5.6	254,185	252,878	239,758	212,655	1,307	0.5
Columbia County, WI	96.5	1.4	0.5	0.5	0.1	2.6	26,220	26,137	24,965	22,688	83	0.3
Dane County, WI	86.8	5.3	5.0	0.5	0.0	6.1	217,244	216,022	204,406	180,385	1,222	0.6
Iowa County, WI	98.0	0.4	0.6	0.2	0.0	1.4	10,721	10,719	10,387	9,582	2	0.0
Manchester–Nashua, NH	92.2	2.4	3.4	0.3	0.1	5.5	166,630	166,053	160,727	149,968	577	0.3
Hillsborough County, NH....................	92.2	2.4	3.4	0.3	0.1	5.5	166,630	166,053	160,727	149,968	577	0.3
Manhattan, KS	82.6	8.9	3.4	0.9	0.3	8.3	52,440	51,355	45,161	42,674	1,085	2.1
Geary County, KS	70.2	18.4	3.4	1.2	0.8	13.1	14,837	14,517	11,774	11,926	320	2.2
Pottawatomie County, KS...................	94.6	1.3	0.8	0.9	0.1	4.7	8,783	8,626	7,875	7,309	157	1.8
Riley County, KS	85.0	6.6	4.2	0.7	0.2	7.0	28,820	28,212	25,512	23,439	608	2.2
Mankato–North Mankato, MN	93.5	2.6	2.0	0.4	0.0	3.0	39,317	39,075	37,241	33,213	242	0.6
Blue Earth County, MN	93.1	2.8	2.3	0.3	0.0	2.6	26,399	26,202	24,788	21,973	197	0.8
Nicollet County, MN	94.5	2.3	1.5	0.5	0.0	3.8	12,918	12,873	12,453	11,240	45	0.3
Mansfield, OH	87.9	9.4	0.7	0.2	0.0	1.5	54,459	54,599	54,701	53,090	-140	-0.3
Richland County, OH	87.9	9.4	0.7	0.2	0.0	1.5	54,459	54,599	54,701	53,090	-140	-0.3
McAllen–Edinburg–Mission, TX	97.2	0.8	1.0	0.5	0.0	90.7	250,235	248,287	226,956	192,453	1,948	0.8
Hidalgo County, TX	97.2	0.8	1.0	0.5	0.0	90.7	250,235	248,287	226,956	192,453	1,948	0.8
Medford, OR	93.0	0.8	1.3	1.5	0.3	11.2	91,349	90,937	85,608	75,739	412	0.5
Jackson County, OR	93.0	0.8	1.3	1.5	0.3	11.2	91,349	90,937	85,608	75,739	412	0.5
Memphis, TN–MS–AR	50.4	45.9	1.9	0.4	0.1	5.2	551,592	550,896	524,653	480,874	696	0.1
Crittenden County, AR.......................	47.0	50.9	0.7	0.4	0.0	2.1	21,296	21,489	21,051	20,505	-193	-0.9
DeSoto County, MS...........................	74.1	22.8	1.3	0.4	0.1	5.0	62,244	61,634	53,238	40,813	610	1.0
Marshall County, MS	51.4	47.3	0.3	0.3	0.0	3.3	14,956	14,881	13,925	13,235	75	0.5
Tate County, MS	67.7	30.6	0.3	0.3	0.0	2.4	10,970	10,947	10,250	9,362	23	0.2
Tunica County, MS	25.3	72.8	0.7	0.2	0.1	2.5	4,840	4,803	4,515	3,706	37	0.8
Fayette County, TN	70.3	28.0	0.6	0.3	0.0	2.4	15,874	15,669	13,085	11,214	205	1.3
Shelby County, TN	43.6	52.3	2.4	0.4	0.1	5.8	397,976	398,274	386,849	362,962	-298	-0.1
Tipton County, TN	78.3	18.9	0.6	0.5	0.1	2.3	23,436	23,199	21,740	19,077	237	1.0
Merced, CA	82.1	4.3	7.9	2.4	0.4	55.7	83,573	83,698	77,686	68,567	-125	-0.1
Merced County, CA...........................	82.1	4.3	7.9	2.4	0.4	55.7	83,573	83,698	77,686	68,567	-125	-0.1
Miami–Fort Lauderdale–Pompano Beach, FL	74.1	21.5	2.4	0.4	0.1	41.8	2,469,512	2,464,418	2,358,423	2,149,876	5,094	0.2
Fort Lauderdale–Pompano Beach– Deerfield Beach, FL.............................	66.7	27.4	3.5	0.4	0.1	25.8	810,795	810,388	793,132	741,020	407	0.1
Broward County, FL..........................	66.7	27.4	3.5	0.4	0.1	25.8	810,795	810,388	793,132	741,020	407	0.1
Miami–Miami Beach–Kendall, FL	77.5	19.3	1.7	0.3	0.1	64.5	990,558	989,436	934,527	852,424	1,122	0.1
Miami–Dade County, FL	77.5	19.3	1.7	0.3	0.1	64.5	990,558	989,436	934,527	852,424	1,122	0.1
West Palm Beach–Boca Raton– Boynton Beach, FL.............................	77.4	17.8	2.5	0.6	0.1	19.6	668,159	664,594	630,764	556,432	3,565	0.5
Palm Beach County, FL	77.4	17.8	2.5	0.6	0.1	19.6	668,159	664,594	630,764	556,432	3,565	0.5
Michigan City–La Porte, IN	86.2	10.9	0.6	0.4	0.0	5.6	48,446	48,448	47,552	45,619	-2	0.0
LaPorte County, IN...........................	86.2	10.9	0.6	0.4	0.0	5.6	48,446	48,448	47,552	45,619	-2	0.0
Midland, TX..	89.1	7.0	1.4	1.1	0.1	38.8	55,104	54,351	50,926	48,076	753	1.4
Midland County, TX..........................	89.1	7.0	1.4	1.1	0.1	38.8	55,104	54,351	50,926	48,076	753	1.4
Milwaukee–Waukesha–West Allis, WI...........	77.2	17.0	3.1	0.7	0.1	9.7	671,786	669,879	651,555	618,277	1,907	0.3
Milwaukee County, WI.......................	65.9	27.0	3.6	0.9	0.1	13.6	418,935	418,053	410,724	400,085	882	0.2
Ozaukee County, WI	95.2	1.5	1.9	0.3	0.0	2.4	36,412	36,267	35,082	32,037	145	0.4
Washington County, WI	96.5	1.0	1.2	0.4	0.0	2.7	54,940	54,695	51,330	45,818	245	0.4
Waukesha County, WI	94.2	1.4	2.9	0.3	0.0	4.3	161,499	160,864	154,419	140,337	635	0.4
Minneapolis–St. Paul–Bloomington, MN–WI	83.0	7.6	5.9	0.9	0.1	5.5	1,359,125	1,354,973	1,301,433	1,170,034	4,152	0.3
Anoka County, MN	88.3	4.5	4.0	0.8	0.0	3.8	127,170	126,688	121,366	108,126	482	0.4
Carver County, MN	94.0	1.4	2.8	0.3	0.0	4.0	34,866	34,536	31,848	24,896	330	1.0
Chisago County, MN	96.0	1.2	0.9	0.7	0.0	1.7	21,419	21,172	19,584	15,533	247	1.2
Dakota County, MN	87.4	4.9	4.6	0.5	0.1	6.1	160,275	159,598	152,797	133,769	677	0.4
Hennepin County, MN	77.3	12.0	6.5	1.2	0.1	6.9	510,206	509,469	496,739	468,925	737	0.1
Isanti County, MN	96.2	0.8	0.9	0.5	0.1	1.7	15,284	15,321	14,598	12,058	-37	-0.2
Ramsey County, MN	72.6	11.2	12.0	1.0	0.1	7.2	217,195	217,197	214,394	206,488	-2	0.0
Scott County, MN	88.3	2.8	5.9	1.0	0.1	4.6	47,691	47,124	43,072	31,614	567	1.2
Sherburne County, MN......................	94.5	2.0	1.3	0.5	0.0	2.2	32,481	32,379	30,009	22,850	102	0.3
Washington County, MN	88.5	3.8	5.1	0.5	0.0	3.5	93,077	92,374	85,547	73,677	703	0.8
Wright County, MN	95.7	1.1	1.2	0.4	0.0	2.6	49,178	49,000	44,694	34,365	178	0.4
Pierce County, WI............................	96.8	0.6	0.9	0.4	0.0	1.5	16,202	16,132	15,260	13,464	70	0.4
St. Croix County, WI	96.5	0.7	1.1	0.5	0.0	2.1	34,081	33,983	31,525	24,269	98	0.3

[1] Persons of Hispanic origin may be any race.
[2] The April 1, 2000, housing estimates base reflects modifications to the Census 2000 population as documented in the Count Question Resolution program and geographic program revisions.

Table C-2.   Population Characteristics and Housing Units—*Continued*

Metropolitan statistical area, division, and component county	Population characteristics, 2011						Housing units				Change, 2010–2011	
	One race (percent)					Hispanic or Latino origin[1] (percent)	2011 (July 1)	2010 (July 1)	2005 (July 1)	2000[2] (estimates base)		
	White alone	Black or African American alone	Asian alone	American Indian, Alaska Native alone	Native Hawaiian and Other Pacific Islander alone						Number	Percent
Missoula, MT	92.8	0.5	1.3	2.7	0.1	2.8	50,680	50,105	46,557	41,322	575	1.1
Missoula County, MT	92.8	0.5	1.3	2.7	0.1	2.8	50,680	50,105	46,557	41,322	575	1.1
Mobile, AL	60.8	34.9	1.9	0.9	0.1	2.5	180,045	178,195	171,626	165,121	1,850	1.0
Mobile County, AL	60.8	34.9	1.9	0.9	0.1	2.5	180,045	178,195	171,626	165,121	1,850	1.0
Modesto, CA	84.5	3.3	5.7	1.9	0.8	42.6	180,085	179,503	169,253	150,782	582	0.3
Stanislaus County, CA	84.5	3.3	5.7	1.9	0.8	42.6	180,085	179,503	169,253	150,782	582	0.3
Monroe, LA	62.1	35.6	0.9	0.3	0.0	2.2	75,948	75,827	73,282	71,025	121	0.2
Ouachita Parish, LA	60.8	36.8	1.0	0.3	0.0	1.9	64,689	64,481	62,175	60,158	208	0.3
Union Parish, LA	71.4	27.2	0.2	0.4	0.1	4.2	11,259	11,346	11,107	10,867	-87	-0.8
Monroe, MI	95.1	2.3	0.6	0.4	0.0	3.1	62,749	62,971	61,751	56,475	-222	-0.4
Monroe County, MI	95.1	2.3	0.6	0.4	0.0	3.1	62,749	62,971	61,751	56,475	-222	-0.4
Montgomery, AL	53.6	43.0	1.6	0.4	0.1	3.2	162,214	161,573	154,559	144,658	641	0.4
Autauga County, AL	78.6	18.5	0.9	0.5	0.1	2.6	22,460	22,135	20,275	17,733	325	1.5
Elmore County, AL	76.3	21.1	0.7	0.4	0.1	2.8	33,245	32,657	29,768	25,677	588	1.8
Lowndes County, AL	25.9	72.8	0.3	0.2	0.0	1.1	5,048	5,140	5,478	5,801	-92	-1.8
Montgomery County, AL	41.1	55.0	2.1	0.4	0.1	3.6	101,461	101,641	99,038	95,447	-180	-0.2
Morgantown, WV	92.8	3.1	2.3	0.2	0.1	1.7	59,120	58,335	54,511	50,138	785	1.3
Monongalia County, WV	91.1	3.8	3.1	0.2	0.1	2.0	43,875	43,238	40,124	36,699	637	1.5
Preston County, WV	97.6	1.2	0.2	0.2	0.1	0.8	15,245	15,097	14,387	13,439	148	1.0
Morristown, TN	94.2	3.2	0.6	0.6	0.1	6.7	61,685	61,357	58,370	53,730	328	0.5
Grainger County, TN	97.9	0.7	0.2	0.2	0.0	2.4	10,971	10,894	10,489	9,712	77	0.7
Hamblen County, TN	91.9	4.6	0.8	0.7	0.1	11.0	27,021	26,963	26,083	24,694	58	0.2
Jefferson County, TN	95.4	2.4	0.5	0.4	0.0	3.3	23,693	23,500	21,798	19,324	193	0.8
Mount Vernon–Anacortes, WA	91.4	0.9	2.0	2.6	0.3	17.3	51,945	51,473	47,554	42,703	472	0.9
Skagit County, WA	91.4	0.9	2.0	2.6	0.3	17.3	51,945	51,473	47,554	42,703	472	0.9
Muncie, IN	89.4	7.1	1.1	0.3	0.1	1.9	52,179	52,357	52,502	51,034	-178	-0.3
Delaware County, IN	89.4	7.1	1.1	0.3	0.1	1.9	52,179	52,357	52,502	51,034	-178	-0.3
Muskegon–Norton Shores, MI	81.3	14.6	0.6	0.9	0.0	4.9	73,399	73,561	72,793	68,570	-162	-0.2
Muskegon County, MI	81.3	14.6	0.6	0.9	0.0	4.9	73,399	73,561	72,793	68,570	-162	-0.2
Myrtle Beach–North Myrtle Beach–Conway, SC	82.5	13.9	1.1	0.6	0.1	6.3	188,889	185,992	151,809	122,066	2,897	1.6
Horry County, SC	82.5	13.9	1.1	0.6	0.1	6.3	188,889	185,992	151,809	122,066	2,897	1.6
Napa, CA	85.8	2.3	7.2	1.3	0.4	32.9	54,916	54,759	52,882	48,575	157	0.3
Napa County, CA	85.8	2.3	7.2	1.3	0.4	32.9	54,916	54,759	52,882	48,575	157	0.3
Naples–Marco Island, FL	90.2	6.9	1.2	0.5	0.1	26.3	198,423	197,298	182,515	144,548	1,125	0.6
Collier County, FL	90.2	6.9	1.2	0.5	0.1	26.3	198,423	197,298	182,515	144,548	1,125	0.6
Nashville–Davidson—Murfreesboro—Franklin, TN	79.8	15.5	2.4	0.4	0.1	6.8	673,106	667,655	612,336	543,316	5,451	0.8
Cannon County, TN	96.6	1.5	0.2	0.3	0.1	1.6	6,079	6,037	5,819	5,428	42	0.7
Cheatham County, TN	96.1	1.8	0.4	0.4	0.1	2.4	15,910	15,663	14,893	13,482	247	1.6
Davidson County, TN	66.2	27.9	3.2	0.5	0.1	9.9	285,020	283,978	269,181	252,994	1,042	0.4
Dickson County, TN	92.9	4.4	0.6	0.4	0.0	3.2	20,955	20,820	19,627	17,613	135	0.6
Hickman County, TN	93.1	4.9	0.3	0.5	0.0	1.9	10,429	10,311	9,773	8,915	118	1.1
Macon County, TN	97.2	0.8	0.3	0.6	0.0	4.6	9,913	9,861	9,495	8,901	52	0.5
Robertson County, TN	89.9	7.7	0.6	0.5	0.1	6.1	26,264	26,086	24,163	20,995	178	0.7
Rutherford County, TN	81.2	12.9	3.1	0.5	0.1	6.9	103,913	102,968	89,459	70,623	945	0.9
Smith County, TN	95.6	2.3	0.3	0.5	0.0	2.3	8,574	8,529	8,105	7,663	45	0.5
Sumner County, TN	90.3	6.7	1.1	0.3	0.1	4.0	66,771	65,968	59,263	51,688	803	1.2
Trousdale County, TN	87.8	9.8	0.2	0.6	0.0	2.7	3,375	3,368	3,239	3,092	7	0.2
Williamson County, TN	90.6	4.7	3.1	0.3	0.1	4.6	69,735	68,498	58,890	47,008	1,237	1.8
Wilson County, TN	90.2	6.7	1.2	0.4	0.1	3.4	46,168	45,568	40,429	34,914	600	1.3
New Haven–Milford, CT	79.9	13.7	3.7	0.4	0.1	15.4	363,231	362,004	353,296	340,728	1,227	0.3
New Haven County, CT	79.9	13.7	3.7	0.4	0.1	15.4	363,231	362,004	353,296	340,728	1,227	0.3
New Orleans–Metairie–Kenner, LA	60.4	34.7	2.8	0.5	0.1	8.0	544,150	538,239	584,884	548,627	5,911	1.1
Jefferson Parish, LA	66.9	27.0	4.0	0.6	0.1	12.7	190,182	189,135	196,381	187,887	1,047	0.6
Orleans Parish, LA	35.0	60.1	2.9	0.4	0.1	5.2	194,138	189,896	227,110	215,095	4,242	2.2
Plaquemines Parish, LA	71.3	21.3	3.4	1.7	0.2	5.3	9,771	9,596	11,650	10,475	175	1.8
St. Bernard Parish, LA	75.3	19.4	2.1	0.8	0.1	9.4	16,757	16,794	26,931	26,791	-37	-0.2
St. Charles Parish, LA	70.4	26.9	0.9	0.4	0.0	5.1	19,986	19,896	18,503	17,406	90	0.5
St. John the Baptist Parish, LA	44.0	53.6	0.8	0.4	0.1	4.9	17,582	17,510	16,826	15,584	72	0.4
St. Tammany Parish, LA	84.5	12.0	1.4	0.5	0.0	4.9	95,734	95,412	87,483	75,389	322	0.3
New York–Northern New Jersey–Long Island, NY–NJ–PA	66.7	19.6	10.5	1.0	0.1	23.3	7,537,225	7,527,755	7,326,538	7,091,638	9,470	0.1
Edison–New Brunswick, NJ	78.3	8.0	11.6	0.4	0.1	13.2	957,412	954,390	927,248	875,310	3,022	0.3
Middlesex County, NJ	64.5	10.7	22.2	0.6	0.1	18.9	296,076	294,801	285,760	273,690	1,275	0.4
Monmouth County, NJ	85.1	7.7	5.2	0.3	0.1	9.9	258,987	258,410	251,726	240,862	577	0.2
Ocean County, NJ	93.2	3.4	1.9	0.3	0.0	8.6	278,862	278,052	269,962	248,738	810	0.3
Somerset County, NJ	73.5	9.5	14.8	0.3	0.1	13.3	123,487	123,127	119,800	112,020	360	0.3
Nassau–Suffolk, NY	82.0	10.0	5.8	0.5	0.1	16.1	1,041,588	1,038,331	1,014,822	980,522	3,257	0.3
Nassau County, NY	77.7	12.0	8.2	0.5	0.1	15.0	468,593	468,346	463,425	458,196	247	0.1
Suffolk County, NY	85.9	8.1	3.6	0.6	0.1	17.0	572,995	569,985	551,397	522,326	3,010	0.5

[1] Persons of Hispanic origin may be any race.

[2] The April 1, 2000, housing estimates base reflects modifications to the Census 2000 population as documented in the Count Question Resolution program and geographic program revisions.

Table C-2.   Population Characteristics and Housing Units—*Continued*

Metropolitan statistical area, division, and component county	Population characteristics, 2011						Housing units					
	One race (percent)					Hispanic or Latino origin[1] (percent)	2011 (July 1)	2010 (July 1)	2005 (July 1)	2000[2] (estimates base)	Change, 2010–2011	
	White alone	Black or African American alone	Asian alone	American Indian, Alaska Native alone	Native Hawaiian and Other Pacific Islander alone						Number	Percent
New York–Northern New Jersey–Long Island, NY–NJ–PA—*Continued*												
Newark–Union, NJ–PA	69.6	22.4	5.6	0.5	0.1	18.4	853,473	852,181	832,533	804,585	1,292	0.2
Essex County, NJ	50.1	42.2	4.9	0.7	0.1	20.8	312,952	312,954	306,703	301,007	-2	0.0
Hunterdon County, NJ	92.1	3.0	3.5	0.2	0.0	5.5	49,724	49,487	48,276	45,084	237	0.5
Morris County, NJ	85.2	3.5	9.4	0.3	0.0	11.8	190,659	189,842	184,423	174,408	817	0.4
Sussex County, NJ	94.5	2.0	1.9	0.2	0.0	6.7	62,265	62,057	60,162	56,581	208	0.3
Union County, NJ	69.4	23.0	5.0	0.7	0.1	28.1	199,684	199,489	196,116	192,936	195	0.1
Pike County, PA	90.4	6.3	1.2	0.4	0.0	9.2	38,189	38,352	36,853	34,569	-163	-0.4
New York–White Plains–Wayne, NY–NJ	60.0	23.7	12.4	1.3	0.2	28.0	4,684,752	4,682,853	4,551,935	4,431,221	1,899	0.0
Bergen County, NJ	76.1	6.6	15.0	0.4	0.1	16.8	352,478	352,388	346,713	339,860	90	0.0
Hudson County, NJ	67.0	15.1	14.2	1.2	0.2	42.4	272,798	270,335	252,622	240,648	2,463	0.9
Passaic County, NJ	76.0	14.7	5.4	1.4	0.2	37.7	176,264	175,966	173,322	170,008	298	0.2
Bronx County, NY	45.9	43.3	4.2	2.9	0.4	53.8	512,311	511,896	501,921	490,455	415	0.1
Kings County, NY	49.5	36.1	11.0	1.0	0.1	20.0	1,001,210	1,000,293	959,666	930,934	917	0.1
New York County, NY	65.4	18.5	11.8	1.2	0.2	25.6	846,172	847,090	820,501	798,499	-918	-0.1
Putnam County, NY	93.2	2.8	2.1	0.3	0.1	12.0	38,421	38,224	37,225	35,021	197	0.5
Queens County, NY	50.4	21.0	24.3	1.3	0.2	27.8	832,132	835,127	823,437	817,285	-2,995	-0.4
Richmond County, NY	77.9	11.7	7.9	0.6	0.1	17.6	176,819	176,656	173,464	164,015	163	0.1
Rockland County, NY	78.2	12.8	6.5	0.5	0.1	16.1	104,559	104,057	99,753	94,993	502	0.5
Westchester County, NY	75.4	15.8	5.8	0.8	0.1	22.4	371,588	370,821	363,311	349,503	767	0.2
Niles–Benton Harbor, MI	79.9	15.6	1.7	0.6	0.1	4.7	76,755	76,922	75,885	73,461	-167	-0.2
Berrien County, MI	79.9	15.6	1.7	0.6	0.1	4.7	76,755	76,922	75,885	73,461	-167	-0.2
North Port–Bradenton–Sarasota, FL	89.6	7.0	1.6	0.4	0.1	11.4	403,006	401,103	374,109	320,598	1,903	0.5
Manatee County, FL	86.8	9.3	1.8	0.5	0.1	15.1	173,660	172,690	161,602	138,104	970	0.6
Sarasota County, FL	91.9	5.0	1.4	0.3	0.1	8.2	229,346	228,413	212,507	182,494	933	0.4
Norwich–New London, CT	84.8	6.5	4.3	1.0	0.1	8.8	121,662	120,994	116,755	110,685	668	0.6
New London County, CT	84.8	6.5	4.3	1.0	0.1	8.8	121,662	120,994	116,755	110,685	668	0.6
Ocala, FL	83.6	12.8	1.4	0.5	0.1	11.2	164,037	164,049	146,909	122,645	-12	0.0
Marion County, FL	83.6	12.8	1.4	0.5	0.1	11.2	164,037	164,049	146,909	122,645	-12	0.0
Ocean City, NJ	92.0	5.1	1.0	0.3	0.1	6.4	98,017	98,309	96,139	91,054	-292	-0.3
Cape May County, NJ	92.0	5.1	1.0	0.3	0.1	6.4	98,017	98,309	96,139	91,054	-292	-0.3
Odessa, TX	91.5	4.8	0.9	1.4	0.2	53.9	53,287	53,027	51,155	49,504	260	0.5
Ector County, TX	91.5	4.8	0.9	1.4	0.2	53.9	53,287	53,027	51,155	49,504	260	0.5
Ogden–Clearfield, UT	93.2	1.4	1.7	0.9	0.5	12.1	188,926	186,763	169,560	146,726	2,163	1.2
Davis County, UT	93.2	1.3	1.9	0.7	0.7	8.6	98,843	97,570	87,595	74,118	1,273	1.3
Morgan County, UT	97.9	0.3	0.5	0.2	0.1	2.6	3,039	3,006	2,522	2,159	33	1.1
Weber County, UT	93.1	1.6	1.4	1.3	0.3	17.1	87,044	86,187	79,443	70,449	857	1.0
Oklahoma City, OK	76.8	10.6	2.9	4.6	0.1	11.7	543,337	539,077	509,817	472,153	4,260	0.8
Canadian County, OK	85.2	2.8	3.0	5.0	0.1	7.2	46,715	45,810	40,060	33,965	905	2.0
Cleveland County, OK	81.0	4.6	4.0	5.0	0.1	7.2	106,399	104,822	95,962	84,856	1,577	1.5
Grady County, OK	86.8	2.6	0.4	5.8	0.1	4.8	22,477	22,219	20,953	19,428	258	1.2
Lincoln County, OK	86.1	2.0	0.2	6.7	0.0	2.7	15,325	15,208	14,571	13,705	117	0.8
Logan County, OK	82.6	9.5	0.5	3.4	0.1	5.4	17,598	17,195	15,612	13,905	403	2.3
McClain County, OK	87.1	1.0	0.4	6.5	0.1	7.2	14,219	13,996	12,619	11,189	223	1.6
Oklahoma County, OK	72.0	15.6	3.1	4.1	0.2	15.5	320,604	319,827	310,040	295,105	777	0.2
Olympia, WA	84.3	3.0	5.4	1.6	0.8	7.4	109,965	108,182	96,943	86,672	1,783	1.6
Thurston County, WA	84.3	3.0	5.4	1.6	0.8	7.4	109,965	108,182	96,943	86,672	1,783	1.6
Omaha–Council Bluffs, NE–IA	86.6	8.0	2.2	0.9	0.1	9.2	365,898	362,327	341,191	311,601	3,571	1.0
Harrison County, IA	98.3	0.2	0.3	0.4	0.0	1.2	6,699	6,731	6,773	6,606	-32	-0.5
Mills County, IA	97.7	0.4	0.4	0.4	0.1	2.6	6,129	6,109	5,986	5,668	20	0.3
Pottawattamie County, IA	95.6	1.6	0.7	0.6	0.0	6.7	39,342	39,330	38,386	35,814	12	0.0
Cass County, NE	97.5	0.4	0.4	0.4	0.1	2.6	11,125	11,117	10,888	10,173	8	0.1
Douglas County, NE	81.9	11.7	2.8	1.1	0.1	11.5	221,663	219,580	207,427	192,685	2,083	0.9
Sarpy County, NE	90.1	4.3	2.2	0.7	0.1	7.6	63,343	61,938	54,910	44,983	1,405	2.3
Saunders County, NE	97.9	0.4	0.4	0.3	0.0	2.2	9,261	9,221	8,830	8,260	40	0.4
Washington County, NE	97.7	0.7	0.3	0.3	0.1	2.2	8,336	8,301	7,991	7,412	35	0.4
Orlando–Kissimmee–Sanford, FL	75.8	17.0	4.2	0.6	0.2	25.9	949,967	942,312	835,957	683,449	7,655	0.8
Lake County, FL	85.2	10.3	2.0	0.6	0.1	12.6	145,303	144,996	127,874	102,688	307	0.2
Orange County, FL	70.0	21.7	5.2	0.5	0.2	27.5	492,209	487,839	434,446	361,359	4,370	0.9
Osceola County, FL	80.8	12.8	3.0	0.7	0.2	46.3	129,830	128,170	104,562	72,310	1,660	1.3
Seminole County, FL	81.6	11.7	3.9	0.4	0.1	17.7	182,625	181,307	169,075	147,092	1,318	0.7
Oshkosh–Neenah, WI	93.7	1.9	2.4	0.7	0.0	3.6	73,732	73,329	70,659	64,725	403	0.5
Winnebago County, WI	93.7	1.9	2.4	0.7	0.0	3.6	73,732	73,329	70,659	64,725	403	0.5
Owensboro, KY	93.2	4.4	0.6	0.2	0.1	2.4	49,367	49,452	49,191	46,420	-85	-0.2
Daviess County, KY	92.4	5.0	0.7	0.2	0.1	2.6	41,407	41,454	41,110	38,427	-47	-0.1
Hancock County, KY	97.2	1.2	0.3	0.3	0.0	1.2	3,736	3,734	3,704	3,603	2	0.1
McLean County, KY	98.1	0.8	0.1	0.3	0.0	1.2	4,224	4,264	4,377	4,390	-40	-0.9

[1] Persons of Hispanic origin may be any race.
[2] The April 1, 2000, housing estimates base reflects modifications to the Census 2000 population as documented in the Count Question Resolution program and geographic program revisions.

Table C-2. Population Characteristics and Housing Units—*Continued*

Metropolitan statistical area, division, and component county	White alone	Black or African American alone	Asian alone	American Indian, Alaska Native alone	Native Hawaiian and Other Pacific Islander alone	Hispanic or Latino origin[1] (percent)	2011 (July 1)	2010 (July 1)	2005 (July 1)	2000[2] (estimates base)	Number	Percent
Oxnard–Thousand Oaks–Ventura, CA	85.3	2.2	7.2	1.8	0.3	40.9	282,505	281,695	270,687	251,727	810	0.3
Ventura County, CA	85.3	2.2	7.2	1.8	0.3	40.9	282,505	281,695	270,687	251,727	810	0.3
Palm Bay–Melbourne–Titusville, FL	84.4	10.5	2.2	0.4	0.1	8.4	270,512	269,862	253,057	222,083	650	0.2
Brevard County, FL	84.4	10.5	2.2	0.4	0.1	8.4	270,512	269,862	253,057	222,083	650	0.2
Palm Coast, FL	83.8	11.7	2.3	0.3	0.1	9.0	49,068	48,595	40,479	24,445	473	1.0
Flagler County, FL	83.8	11.7	2.3	0.3	0.1	9.0	49,068	48,595	40,479	24,445	473	1.0
Panama City–Lynn Haven–Panama City Beach, FL	83.1	11.2	2.1	0.7	0.1	5.1	99,828	99,650	90,008	78,437	178	0.2
Bay County, FL	83.1	11.2	2.1	0.7	0.1	5.1	99,828	99,650	90,008	78,437	178	0.2
Parkersburg–Marietta–Vienna, WV–OH	96.7	1.2	0.5	0.2	0.0	0.8	75,079	75,203	75,148	74,003	-124	-0.2
Washington County, OH	96.5	1.2	0.6	0.2	0.0	0.8	28,329	28,367	28,373	27,758	-38	-0.1
Pleasants County, WV	97.2	1.4	0.1	0.2	0.0	0.8	3,402	3,390	3,335	3,213	12	0.4
Wirt County, WV	98.3	0.2	0.2	0.2	0.0	0.5	3,223	3,231	3,257	3,261	-8	-0.2
Wood County, WV	96.6	1.2	0.6	0.2	0.0	0.9	40,125	40,215	40,183	39,771	-90	-0.2
Pascagoula, MS	75.9	20.2	1.9	0.4	0.1	4.5	70,662	69,397	65,836	59,231	1,265	1.8
George County, MS	89.9	8.7	0.3	0.3	0.0	2.1	9,505	9,330	8,347	7,541	175	1.9
Jackson County, MS	73.6	22.1	2.2	0.5	0.1	4.9	61,157	60,067	57,489	51,690	1,090	1.8
Pensacola–Ferry Pass–Brent, FL	76.2	17.3	2.6	0.9	0.2	4.8	202,279	201,463	191,771	173,776	816	0.4
Escambia County, FL	70.1	23.1	2.9	0.9	0.2	4.9	136,551	136,703	132,685	124,651	-152	-0.1
Santa Rosa County, FL	88.2	6.0	2.0	0.9	0.2	4.6	65,728	64,760	59,086	49,125	968	1.5
Peoria, IL	86.4	9.4	2.0	0.3	0.0	3.0	164,517	164,283	159,910	153,294	234	0.1
Marshall County, IL	98.0	0.5	0.5	0.2	0.0	2.7	5,882	5,914	5,986	5,891	-32	-0.5
Peoria County, IL	75.7	17.9	3.3	0.4	0.0	4.0	83,067	83,034	81,088	78,225	33	0.0
Stark County, IL	97.7	0.7	0.4	0.3	0.0	1.2	2,654	2,674	2,747	2,720	-20	-0.7
Tazewell County, IL	96.4	1.3	0.8	0.3	0.0	2.0	57,701	57,516	55,544	52,960	185	0.3
Woodford County, IL	97.4	0.7	0.6	0.2	0.0	1.5	15,213	15,145	14,545	13,498	68	0.4
Philadelphia–Camden–Wilmington, PA–NJ–DE–MD	70.9	21.4	5.2	0.4	0.1	8.1	2,439,911	2,433,611	2,376,909	2,281,852	6,300	0.3
Camden, NJ	75.7	17.2	4.5	0.4	0.1	9.6	491,835	490,354	477,757	456,033	1,481	0.3
Burlington County, NJ	75.2	17.3	4.6	0.3	0.1	6.7	176,098	175,615	170,796	161,319	483	0.3
Camden County, NJ	71.0	20.9	5.4	0.6	0.1	14.7	204,923	204,943	202,463	199,164	-20	0.0
Gloucester County, NJ	84.6	10.5	2.8	0.2	0.1	5.0	110,814	109,796	104,498	95,550	1,018	0.9
Philadelphia, PA	69.1	22.9	5.6	0.4	0.1	7.6	1,660,906	1,657,226	1,621,771	1,565,666	3,680	0.2
Bucks County, PA	90.4	3.9	4.1	0.3	0.1	4.4	246,488	245,956	239,738	225,494	532	0.2
Chester County, PA	87.7	6.4	4.0	0.3	0.1	6.7	193,919	192,462	181,559	163,762	1,457	0.8
Delaware County, PA	73.0	20.1	4.9	0.2	0.0	3.1	223,105	222,902	221,255	216,921	203	0.1
Montgomery County, PA	82.4	9.0	6.6	0.2	0.1	4.4	327,140	325,735	313,825	297,520	1,405	0.4
Philadelphia County, PA	45.9	44.3	6.6	0.8	0.1	12.6	670,254	670,171	665,394	661,969	83	0.0
Wilmington, DE–MD–NJ	72.8	20.9	3.7	0.4	0.1	8.0	287,170	286,031	277,381	260,153	1,139	0.4
New Castle County, DE	68.5	24.3	4.5	0.4	0.1	9.0	218,418	217,511	211,385	199,538	907	0.4
Cecil County, MD	89.7	6.7	1.2	0.4	0.1	3.6	41,288	41,103	39,109	34,468	185	0.5
Salem County, NJ	81.8	14.8	0.9	0.5	0.0	7.1	27,464	27,417	26,887	26,147	47	0.2
Phoenix–Mesa–Glendale, AZ	85.2	5.4	3.6	3.0	0.3	29.9	1,813,061	1,798,501	1,591,299	1,331,406	14,560	0.8
Maricopa County, AZ	85.4	5.4	3.7	2.7	0.3	30.0	1,650,557	1,639,279	1,478,079	1,250,368	11,278	0.7
Pinal County, AZ	83.5	5.0	1.9	6.6	0.5	28.7	162,504	159,222	113,220	81,038	3,282	2.1
Pine Bluff, AR	50.1	47.6	0.7	0.4	0.0	2.0	41,580	41,931	42,688	43,138	-351	-0.8
Cleveland County, AR	86.6	12.1	0.2	0.4	0.0	1.8	4,069	4,064	3,978	3,831	5	0.1
Jefferson County, AR	42.7	54.8	0.9	0.4	0.0	1.7	32,693	33,006	33,790	34,355	-313	-0.9
Lincoln County, AR	68.2	29.9	0.3	0.4	0.0	3.4	4,818	4,861	4,920	4,952	-43	-0.9
Pittsburgh, PA	88.0	8.5	1.8	0.1	0.0	1.4	1,101,261	1,102,048	1,097,589	1,078,569	-787	-0.1
Allegheny County, PA	81.8	13.3	2.9	0.2	0.0	1.7	588,591	589,201	589,267	583,726	-610	-0.1
Armstrong County, PA	98.0	0.9	0.2	0.1	0.0	0.6	32,449	32,521	32,717	32,361	-72	-0.2
Beaver County, PA	91.3	6.4	0.5	0.1	0.0	1.3	77,963	78,211	78,600	77,777	-248	-0.3
Butler County, PA	96.7	1.2	1.0	0.1	0.0	1.1	78,387	78,167	74,913	69,882	220	0.3
Fayette County, PA	93.4	4.8	0.3	0.1	0.0	0.9	62,248	62,773	64,997	66,449	-525	-0.8
Washington County, PA	94.3	3.4	0.7	0.1	0.0	1.2	93,242	92,977	91,162	87,317	265	0.3
Westmoreland County, PA	95.4	2.5	0.8	0.1	0.0	1.0	168,381	168,198	165,933	161,057	183	0.1
Pittsfield, MA	93.4	3.0	1.3	0.3	0.0	3.5	68,497	68,509	67,755	66,267	-12	0.0
Berkshire County, MA	93.4	3.0	1.3	0.3	0.0	3.5	68,497	68,509	67,755	66,267	-12	0.0
Pocatello, ID	92.1	0.8	1.3	3.3	0.3	9.0	36,332	36,135	34,086	31,946	197	0.5
Bannock County, ID	91.9	0.8	1.4	3.3	0.3	7.0	33,401	33,191	31,184	29,101	210	0.6
Power County, ID	93.8	0.9	0.4	2.8	0.2	30.6	2,931	2,944	2,902	2,845	-13	-0.4
Portland–South Portland–Biddeford, ME	94.7	1.7	1.6	0.4	0.0	1.6	264,072	262,719	251,402	233,295	1,353	0.5
Cumberland County, ME	93.3	2.5	2.1	0.4	0.0	1.9	139,546	138,658	132,437	122,606	888	0.6
Sagadahoc County, ME	96.3	0.9	0.8	0.4	0.0	1.3	18,388	18,288	17,558	16,478	100	0.5
York County, ME	96.5	0.7	1.1	0.3	0.0	1.3	106,138	105,773	101,407	94,211	365	0.3

[1] Persons of Hispanic origin may be any race.
[2] The April 1, 2000, housing estimates base reflects modifications to the Census 2000 population as documented in the Count Question Resolution program and geographic program revisions.

Table C-2. Population Characteristics and Housing Units—*Continued*

Metropolitan statistical area, division, and component county	Population characteristics, 2011						Housing units					
	One race (percent)					Hispanic or Latino origin[1] (percent)	2011 (July 1)	2010 (July 1)	2005 (July 1)	2000[2] (estimates base)	Change, 2010–2011	
	White alone	Black or African American alone	Asian alone	American Indian, Alaska Native alone	Native Hawaiian and Other Pacific Islander alone						Number	Percent
Portland–Vancouver–Hillsboro, OR–WA.......	85.6	3.0	5.9	1.3	0.5	11.1	930,273	925,076	867,939	790,934	5,197	0.6
Clackamas County, OR..............................	91.1	1.0	3.8	1.1	0.3	8.0	157,798	156,945	148,262	136,970	853	0.5
Columbia County, OR..............................	93.6	0.5	1.0	1.4	0.2	4.2	20,811	20,698	19,532	17,563	113	0.5
Multnomah County, OR............................	81.2	5.7	6.7	1.5	0.6	11.1	326,227	324,832	307,389	288,624	1,395	0.4
Washington County, OR..........................	83.6	2.0	8.9	1.2	0.5	16.0	213,993	212,450	198,104	178,894	1,543	0.7
Yamhill County, OR.................................	92.2	1.1	1.6	2.0	0.2	15.1	37,345	37,110	34,064	30,268	235	0.6
Clark County, WA...................................	88.1	2.1	4.3	1.0	0.7	7.8	168,403	167,413	155,544	134,038	990	0.6
Skamania County, WA.............................	93.7	0.5	0.9	1.7	0.1	5.6	5,696	5,628	5,044	4,577	68	1.2
Port St. Lucie, FL......................................	81.2	14.7	1.6	0.7	0.1	15.3	215,937	215,160	193,096	156,747	777	0.4
Martin County, FL...................................	90.6	5.7	1.2	1.0	0.2	12.4	78,356	78,131	74,124	65,490	225	0.3
St. Lucie County, FL................................	76.2	19.5	1.8	0.6	0.1	16.8	137,581	137,029	118,972	91,257	552	0.4
Poughkeepsie–Newburgh–Middletown, NY.....	82.8	11.0	3.1	0.6	0.1	15.1	257,013	255,663	245,355	228,852	1,350	0.5
Dutchess County, NY	82.9	10.6	3.7	0.4	0.1	10.8	119,431	118,638	113,493	106,087	793	0.7
Orange County, NY	82.7	11.3	2.6	0.8	0.1	18.5	137,582	137,025	131,862	122,765	557	0.4
Prescott, AZ...	94.1	0.8	0.9	2.0	0.1	13.9	111,093	110,433	99,236	81,666	660	0.6
Yavapai County, AZ................................	94.1	0.8	0.9	2.0	0.1	13.9	111,093	110,433	99,236	81,666	660	0.6
Providence–New Bedford–Fall River, RI–MA.....	88.0	6.2	2.7	0.8	0.1	10.6	695,811	693,923	680,123	656,755	1,888	0.3
Bristol County, MA.................................	91.3	4.2	2.0	0.6	0.1	6.3	231,083	230,535	226,090	216,954	548	0.2
Bristol County, RI..................................	95.9	1.0	1.6	0.2	0.0	2.3	20,892	20,850	20,449	19,884	42	0.2
Kent County, RI.....................................	94.2	1.7	2.2	0.3	0.1	3.5	73,766	73,701	72,389	70,400	65	0.1
Newport County, RI...............................	91.2	3.9	1.7	0.5	0.1	4.5	41,956	41,796	40,957	39,566	160	0.4
Providence County, RI............................	81.2	10.7	3.9	1.1	0.2	19.3	265,668	264,835	260,032	253,133	833	0.3
Washington County, RI...........................	94.2	1.4	1.8	0.9	0.0	2.6	62,446	62,206	60,206	56,818	240	0.4
Provo–Orem, UT..	93.8	0.7	1.5	0.8	0.8	10.9	154,243	151,852	130,457	107,126	2,391	1.6
Juab County, UT.....................................	96.7	0.4	0.3	1.0	0.2	4.0	3,505	3,502	3,173	2,809	3	0.1
UT County, UT.......................................	93.8	0.7	1.6	0.8	0.8	11.0	150,738	148,350	127,284	104,317	2,388	1.6
Pueblo, CO..	91.1	2.4	1.0	2.9	0.1	41.6	69,966	69,526	65,843	58,936	440	0.6
Pueblo County, CO................................	91.1	2.4	1.0	2.9	0.1	41.6	69,966	69,526	65,843	58,936	440	0.6
Punta Gorda, FL..	91.0	6.0	1.3	0.3	0.1	5.9	100,612	100,632	91,271	79,772	-20	0.0
Charlotte County, FL..............................	91.0	6.0	1.3	0.3	0.1	5.9	100,612	100,632	91,271	79,772	-20	0.0
Racine, WI...	84.7	11.5	1.2	0.6	0.1	11.7	82,454	82,164	79,497	74,734	290	0.4
Racine County, WI.................................	84.7	11.5	1.2	0.6	0.1	11.7	82,454	82,164	79,497	74,734	290	0.4
Raleigh–Cary, NC	71.6	20.8	4.6	0.9	0.1	10.3	472,697	466,095	401,896	329,528	6,602	1.4
Franklin County, NC...............................	69.8	27.1	0.6	0.9	0.1	10.3	26,894	26,577	23,837	20,379	317	1.2
Johnston County, NC	80.9	15.8	0.7	0.9	0.1	13.0	68,539	67,682	60,047	50,177	857	1.3
Wake County, NC...................................	70.0	21.3	5.6	0.9	0.1	10.0	377,264	371,836	318,012	258,972	5,428	1.5
Rapid City, SD..	85.9	1.4	1.0	8.3	0.1	3.9	56,443	55,949	52,268	47,415	494	0.9
Meade County, SD..................................	92.2	1.7	0.8	2.5	0.1	3.5	11,022	11,000	10,788	10,139	22	0.2
Pennington County, SD...........................	84.3	1.3	1.1	9.7	0.1	4.0	45,421	44,949	41,480	37,276	472	1.1
Reading, PA..	89.5	6.3	1.5	0.7	0.1	16.8	165,269	164,826	160,323	150,252	443	0.3
Berks County, PA	89.5	6.3	1.5	0.7	0.1	16.8	165,269	164,826	160,323	150,252	443	0.3
Redding, CA..	89.1	1.0	2.7	3.0	0.2	8.8	77,343	77,313	74,271	68,802	30	0.0
Shasta County, CA.................................	89.1	1.0	2.7	3.0	0.2	8.8	77,343	77,313	74,271	68,802	30	0.0
Reno–Sparks, NV......................................	86.2	2.5	5.4	2.1	0.7	22.6	187,834	186,832	172,148	145,503	1,002	0.5
Storey County, NV.................................	93.2	1.1	1.6	1.8	0.4	6.0	2,005	1,990	1,833	1,600	15	0.8
Washoe County, NV................................	86.1	2.6	5.5	2.1	0.7	22.7	185,829	184,842	170,315	143,903	987	0.5
Richmond, VA..	63.9	30.1	3.3	0.6	0.1	5.2	535,873	531,648	499,343	452,758	4,225	0.8
Amelia County, VA..................................	74.3	23.5	0.3	0.6	0.1	2.5	5,367	5,359	5,012	4,601	8	0.1
Caroline County, VA	66.3	29.3	0.8	0.8	0.1	3.5	11,802	11,729	10,347	8,891	73	0.6
Charles City County, VA.........................	41.9	47.9	0.4	7.0	0.1	1.5	3,249	3,229	3,104	2,899	20	0.6
Chesterfield County, VA..........................	70.9	22.7	3.4	0.6	0.1	7.4	123,688	122,555	112,972	97,708	1,133	0.9
Cumberland County, VA	65.0	32.3	0.4	0.4	0.0	2.1	4,653	4,626	4,389	4,076	27	0.6
Dinwiddie County, VA.............................	64.6	33.0	0.5	0.5	0.0	2.7	11,559	11,422	10,725	9,709	137	1.2
Goochland County, VA	78.0	19.4	1.2	0.3	0.0	2.1	8,668	8,618	7,804	6,556	50	0.6
Hanover County, VA...............................	86.9	9.7	1.5	0.4	0.1	2.3	38,608	38,360	36,458	32,198	248	0.6
Henrico County, VA................................	60.7	29.9	6.8	0.4	0.1	5.1	133,770	132,778	125,353	112,657	992	0.7
King and Queen County, VA....................	68.3	27.8	0.3	1.7	0.0	2.9	3,426	3,414	3,205	3,006	12	0.4
King William County, VA.........................	77.4	18.0	0.8	1.5	0.0	2.2	6,585	6,522	5,849	5,193	63	1.0
Louisa County, VA	79.2	17.7	0.5	0.4	0.0	2.4	16,537	16,319	14,131	11,884	218	1.3
New Kent County, VA	82.0	13.8	1.0	1.1	0.0	2.2	7,423	7,295	6,248	5,202	128	1.8
Powhatan County, VA.............................	84.4	13.6	0.5	0.3	0.0	1.9	10,115	10,043	9,061	7,508	72	0.7
Prince George County, VA.......................	62.5	32.2	1.8	0.7	0.3	6.5	12,064	12,056	11,590	10,712	8	0.1
Sussex County, VA.................................	40.5	57.8	0.5	0.4	0.0	2.4	4,679	4,696	4,608	4,654	-17	-0.4
Colonial Heights city, VA........................	82.6	11.4	3.3	0.4	0.1	4.4	7,836	7,831	7,697	7,342	5	0.1
Hopewell city, VA	57.9	37.6	1.0	0.5	0.2	6.7	10,241	10,121	9,743	9,751	120	1.2
Petersburg city, VA................................	18.8	77.8	0.9	0.3	0.1	4.1	16,629	16,326	16,005	15,972	303	1.9
Richmond city, VA..................................	44.1	50.4	2.4	0.6	0.2	6.3	98,974	98,349	95,042	92,239	625	0.6

[1] Persons of Hispanic origin may be any race.
[2] The April 1, 2000, housing estimates base reflects modifications to the Census 2000 population as documented in the Count Question Resolution program and geographic program revisions.

Table C-2. Population Characteristics and Housing Units—*Continued*

Metropolitan statistical area, division, and component county	One race (percent) White alone	One race (percent) Black or African American alone	One race (percent) Asian alone	One race (percent) American Indian, Alaska Native alone	One race (percent) Native Hawaiian and Other Pacific Islander alone	Hispanic or Latino origin[1] (percent)	2011 (July 1)	2010 (July 1)	2005 (July 1)	2000[2] (estimates base)	Change, 2010–2011 Number	Change, 2010–2011 Percent
Riverside–San Bernardino–Ontario, CA.........	79.4	8.2	6.7	1.9	0.4	47.9	1,509,205	1,500,344	1,373,390	1,186,087	8,861	0.6
Riverside County, CA...............................	81.0	7.0	6.5	1.9	0.4	46.1	807,145	800,707	714,686	584,632	6,438	0.8
San Bernardino County, CA......................	77.7	9.6	6.9	2.0	0.5	49.9	702,060	699,637	658,704	601,455	2,423	0.3
Roanoke, VA	83.0	13.2	1.7	0.3	0.0	3.3	145,695	144,987	139,354	129,652	708	0.5
Botetourt County, VA...............................	94.8	3.3	0.6	0.3	0.0	1.2	14,627	14,562	13,864	12,589	65	0.4
Craig County, VA.....................................	98.5	0.3	0.2	0.3	0.0	0.9	2,819	2,809	2,726	2,549	10	0.4
Franklin County, VA.................................	89.5	8.4	0.5	0.5	0.1	2.7	29,730	29,315	26,458	22,731	415	1.4
Roanoke County, VA.................................	90.0	5.5	2.8	0.2	0.0	2.3	40,113	40,016	38,754	36,090	97	0.2
Roanoke city, VA.....................................	66.3	28.8	1.8	0.4	0.1	5.6	47,556	47,453	46,862	45,299	103	0.2
Salem city, VA...	89.1	7.4	1.7	0.3	0.0	2.6	10,850	10,832	10,690	10,394	18	0.2
Rochester, MN	89.4	4.0	4.5	0.3	0.1	4.2	78,910	78,439	74,855	65,135	471	0.6
Dodge County, MN...................................	97.5	0.5	0.5	0.4	0.0	4.7	7,980	7,947	7,625	6,645	33	0.4
Olmsted County, MN................................	87.0	5.0	5.6	0.3	0.1	4.3	60,958	60,495	57,412	49,428	463	0.8
Wabasha County, MN...............................	97.8	0.5	0.5	0.2	0.0	2.7	9,972	9,997	9,818	9,062	-25	-0.3
Rochester, NY	82.6	12.3	2.6	0.4	0.1	6.4	457,532	455,397	444,928	427,212	2,135	0.5
Livingston County, NY.............................	94.2	2.7	1.3	0.3	0.0	2.9	27,353	27,123	25,965	24,146	230	0.8
Monroe County, NY..................................	78.0	16.0	3.4	0.4	0.1	7.5	321,813	320,593	315,019	304,391	1,220	0.4
Ontario County, NY..................................	94.4	2.6	1.1	0.3	0.0	3.7	48,653	48,193	45,737	42,550	460	1.0
Orleans County, NY.................................	90.8	6.2	0.5	0.7	0.0	4.3	18,518	18,431	18,023	17,352	87	0.5
Wayne County, NY...................................	93.9	3.3	0.6	0.3	0.0	3.9	41,195	41,057	40,184	38,773	138	0.3
Rockford, IL	83.9	10.9	2.3	0.5	0.1	12.7	146,007	145,935	140,190	129,837	72	0.0
Boone County, IL.....................................	93.2	2.5	1.4	0.7	0.1	20.3	20,123	19,971	18,293	15,415	152	0.8
Winnebago County, IL..............................	82.1	12.5	2.4	0.5	0.0	11.2	125,884	125,964	121,897	114,422	-80	-0.1
Rocky Mount, NC......................................	52.0	45.1	0.7	0.8	0.0	5.5	67,199	67,124	65,224	61,058	75	0.1
Edgecombe County, NC............................	40.7	57.3	0.3	0.6	0.1	3.9	24,730	24,838	24,845	24,011	-108	-0.4
Nash County, NC......................................	58.7	37.9	1.0	0.9	0.0	6.5	42,469	42,286	40,379	37,047	183	0.4
Rome, GA...	81.2	14.8	1.4	0.8	0.3	9.7	40,586	40,551	39,200	36,640	35	0.1
Floyd County, GA.....................................	81.2	14.8	1.4	0.8	0.3	9.7	40,586	40,551	39,200	36,640	35	0.1
Sacramento—Arden–Arcade—Roseville, CA....	72.2	7.8	12.6	1.5	0.9	20.5	875,022	871,793	825,979	714,950	3,229	0.4
El Dorado County, CA..............................	90.4	0.9	3.7	1.4	0.2	12.3	88,774	88,157	82,697	71,278	617	0.7
Placer County, CA...................................	87.0	1.6	6.3	1.1	0.3	13.3	154,365	152,648	138,611	107,239	1,717	1.1
Sacramento County, CA	65.7	10.9	15.0	1.6	1.1	22.0	556,332	555,934	534,429	474,843	398	0.1
Yolo County, CA......................................	75.6	3.0	14.1	1.9	0.6	30.5	75,551	75,054	70,242	61,590	497	0.7
Saginaw–Saginaw Township North, MI.........	76.9	19.4	1.1	0.5	0.1	7.8	86,482	86,844	87,482	85,519	-362	-0.4
Saginaw County, MI	76.9	19.4	1.1	0.5	0.1	7.8	86,482	86,844	87,482	85,519	-362	-0.4
St. Cloud, MN...	93.1	3.0	1.9	0.4	0.1	2.7	78,652	78,114	73,901	63,773	538	0.7
Benton County, MN.................................	94.7	2.1	1.1	0.5	0.0	1.8	16,133	16,140	15,587	13,465	-7	0.0
Stearns County, MN................................	92.7	3.2	2.1	0.4	0.1	2.9	62,519	61,974	58,314	50,308	545	0.9
St. George, UT	93.9	0.8	0.8	1.7	0.8	10.0	58,386	57,734	48,914	36,469	652	1.1
Washington County, UT	93.9	0.8	0.8	1.7	0.8	10.0	58,386	57,734	48,914	36,469	652	1.1
St. Joseph, MO–KS	91.2	5.4	0.8	0.6	0.2	4.4	53,808	53,638	52,698	50,575	170	0.3
Doniphan County, KS	93.0	3.4	0.3	1.2	0.0	2.3	3,574	3,576	3,573	3,487	-2	-0.1
Andrew County, MO................................	97.2	0.8	0.5	0.3	0.0	1.8	7,353	7,306	7,095	6,662	47	0.6
Buchanan County, MO..............................	90.5	5.6	0.9	0.6	0.2	5.4	38,534	38,427	37,873	36,583	107	0.3
DeKalb County, MO.................................	86.6	11.7	0.3	0.5	0.1	1.9	4,347	4,329	4,157	3,843	18	0.4
St. Louis, MO–IL[4]...................................	77.4	18.3	2.2	0.3	0.0	2.7	1,239,927	1,236,221	1,199,716	1,133,358	3,706	0.3
Bond County, IL......................................	91.3	6.5	0.4	0.6	0.0	3.2	7,077	7,089	6,978	6,690	-12	-0.2
Calhoun County, IL..................................	99.0	0.1	0.3	0.2	0.0	1.1	2,852	2,835	2,791	2,679	17	0.6
Clinton County, IL...................................	94.3	3.8	0.5	0.3	0.1	2.9	15,421	15,311	14,681	13,801	110	0.7
Jersey County, IL....................................	97.5	0.5	0.4	0.3	0.0	1.1	9,876	9,848	9,456	8,908	28	0.3
Macoupin County, IL................................	97.5	1.0	0.3	0.3	0.0	1.0	21,499	21,584	21,713	21,093	-85	-0.4
Madison County, IL..................................	89.0	8.0	0.9	0.3	0.0	2.9	117,246	117,106	114,604	108,968	140	0.1
Monroe County, IL...................................	98.1	0.4	0.5	0.2	0.0	1.4	13,539	13,392	12,390	10,752	147	1.1
St. Clair County, IL..................................	65.8	30.5	1.3	0.3	0.1	3.4	117,006	116,249	111,506	104,442	757	0.7
Franklin County, MO................................	97.0	1.0	0.4	0.3	0.0	1.5	43,535	43,420	41,536	38,301	115	0.3
Jefferson County, MO..............................	96.7	1.0	0.7	0.3	0.0	1.7	87,937	87,625	83,387	75,714	312	0.4
Lincoln County, MO.................................	95.5	2.1	0.4	0.4	0.0	2.1	21,513	21,011	18,549	15,502	502	2.4
St. Charles County, MO	91.3	4.4	2.3	0.3	0.1	2.9	142,766	141,016	128,187	105,535	1,750	1.2
St. Louis County, MO...............................	71.0	23.4	3.6	0.2	0.0	2.6	438,119	438,032	433,709	423,697	87	0.0
Warren County, MO.................................	95.1	2.2	0.5	0.5	0.0	3.0	14,823	14,685	13,254	11,047	138	0.9
Washington County, MO	95.8	2.4	0.2	0.4	0.0	1.1	11,079	11,016	10,745	9,882	63	0.6
St. Louis city, MO...................................	46.2	48.3	2.9	0.3	0.0	3.6	175,639	176,002	176,230	176,347	-363	-0.2
Salem, OR...	90.3	1.2	2.1	2.5	0.7	22.4	152,173	151,250	143,341	132,641	923	0.6
Marion County, OR..................................	90.1	1.4	2.1	2.5	0.8	24.8	121,413	120,948	115,585	108,170	465	0.4
Polk County, OR......................................	91.1	0.7	2.0	2.5	0.3	12.4	30,760	30,302	27,756	24,471	458	1.5
Salinas, CA..	82.5	3.7	6.9	2.7	0.6	56.1	138,788	139,048	136,963	131,701	-260	-0.2
Monterey County, CA...............................	82.5	3.7	6.9	2.7	0.6	56.1	138,788	139,048	136,963	131,701	-260	-0.2
Salisbury, MD..	66.6	28.6	2.3	0.3	0.1	4.4	52,569	52,322	49,109	44,493	247	0.5
Somerset County, MD..............................	54.7	42.5	0.8	0.3	0.0	3.3	11,237	11,130	10,606	10,093	107	1.0
Wicomico County, MD..............................	69.7	24.9	2.7	0.3	0.1	4.7	41,332	41,192	38,503	34,400	140	0.3

[1] Persons of Hispanic origin may be any race.
[2] The April 1, 2000, housing estimates base reflects modifications to the Census 2000 population as documented in the Count Question Resolution program and geographic program revisions.
[4] The portion of Sullivan city in Crawford County, MO is legally part of the St. Louis, MO–IL MSA. That portion is not included in these figures for the St. Louis, MSA.

Table C-2. Population Characteristics and Housing Units—*Continued*

Metropolitan statistical area, division, and component county	Population characteristics, 2011						Housing units					
	One race (percent)					Hispanic or Latino origin[1] (percent)	2011 (July 1)	2010 (July 1)	2005 (July 1)	2000[2] (estimates base)	Change, 2010–2011	
	White alone	Black or African American alone	Asian alone	American Indian, Alaska Native alone	Native Hawaiian and Other Pacific Islander alone						Number	Percent
Salt Lake City, UT	89.9	1.8	3.3	1.3	1.5	17.0	415,871	410,030	379,192	342,309	5,841	1.4
Salt Lake County, UT	89.4	1.8	3.5	1.3	1.6	17.4	368,781	364,031	340,244	311,006	4,750	1.3
Summit County, UT	95.8	0.7	1.4	0.5	0.1	11.8	27,407	26,544	21,775	17,490	863	3.3
Tooele County, UT	94.7	0.8	0.8	1.2	0.4	11.7	19,683	19,455	17,173	13,813	228	1.2
San Angelo, TX	91.1	4.6	1.1	1.1	0.1	36.1	47,943	47,427	46,041	44,838	516	1.1
Irion County, TX	96.3	1.5	0.2	0.5	0.0	25.5	844	856	889	909	-12	-1.4
Tom Green County, TX	91.0	4.7	1.2	1.1	0.1	36.3	47,099	46,571	45,152	43,929	528	1.1
San Antonio–New Braunfels, TX	87.3	7.1	2.3	1.2	0.2	54.2	851,611	837,999	744,861	648,560	13,612	1.6
Atascosa County, TX	95.9	1.3	0.6	1.0	0.1	62.3	17,879	17,631	16,446	14,853	248	1.4
Bandera County, TX	96.6	0.8	0.4	1.0	0.0	17.0	11,768	11,560	10,632	9,480	208	1.8
Bexar County, TX	85.9	8.0	2.6	1.3	0.2	58.9	672,307	662,874	593,569	521,415	9,433	1.4
Comal County, TX	94.6	2.1	0.9	0.8	0.1	25.6	47,901	47,108	39,939	32,720	793	1.7
Guadalupe County, TX	88.0	7.2	1.6	1.0	0.2	36.0	51,815	50,015	41,087	33,538	1,800	3.6
Kendall County, TX	96.0	1.0	0.8	0.7	0.1	21.2	14,245	14,055	11,986	9,624	190	1.4
Medina County, TX	94.1	2.7	0.8	1.0	0.1	50.1	18,319	17,991	16,657	14,824	328	1.8
Wilson County, TX	95.2	2.0	0.5	0.9	0.0	38.5	17,377	16,765	14,545	12,106	612	3.7
San Diego–Carlsbad–San Marcos, CA	77.0	5.6	11.4	1.4	0.6	32.5	1,168,679	1,164,786	1,125,143	1,040,151	3,893	0.3
San Diego County, CA	77.0	5.6	11.4	1.4	0.6	32.5	1,168,679	1,164,786	1,125,143	1,040,151	3,893	0.3
Sandusky, OH	87.8	8.7	0.6	0.3	0.0	3.5	37,818	37,845	37,301	35,935	-27	-0.1
Erie County, OH	87.8	8.7	0.6	0.3	0.0	3.5	37,818	37,845	37,301	35,935	-27	-0.1
San Francisco–Oakland–Fremont, CA	60.9	8.8	24.0	1.0	0.8	22.0	1,747,071	1,741,999	1,690,008	1,606,855	5,072	0.3
Oakland–Fremont–Hayward, CA	59.4	11.6	22.1	1.1	0.8	23.6	985,950	982,812	949,417	894,766	3,138	0.3
Alameda County, CA	52.8	13.0	27.0	1.2	1.0	22.8	584,622	582,549	564,447	540,165	2,073	0.4
Contra Costa County, CA	68.8	9.7	15.2	1.0	0.6	24.8	401,328	400,263	384,970	354,601	1,065	0.3
San Francisco–San Mateo–Redwood City, CA	63.0	4.6	26.6	0.9	0.9	19.6	761,121	759,187	740,591	712,089	1,934	0.3
Marin County, CA	86.2	3.0	5.8	1.2	0.3	15.7	111,541	111,214	108,773	104,989	327	0.3
San Francisco County, CA	54.5	6.3	33.9	0.9	0.5	15.4	378,247	376,942	363,667	346,533	1,305	0.3
San Mateo County, CA	64.4	3.2	25.8	0.9	1.6	25.6	271,333	271,031	268,151	260,567	302	0.1
San Jose–Sunnyvale–Santa Clara, CA	59.3	2.9	32.0	1.5	0.5	28.0	651,162	649,790	629,350	595,867	1,372	0.2
San Benito County, CA	88.8	1.2	3.2	3.1	0.3	56.9	17,887	17,870	17,747	16,490	17	0.1
Santa Clara County, CA	58.4	3.0	32.9	1.4	0.5	27.2	633,275	631,920	611,603	579,377	1,355	0.2
San Luis Obispo–Paso Robles, CA	89.1	2.4	3.7	1.4	0.2	21.3	117,463	117,315	112,226	102,304	148	0.1
San Luis Obispo County, CA	89.1	2.4	3.7	1.4	0.2	21.3	117,463	117,315	112,226	102,304	148	0.1
Santa Barbara–Santa Maria–Goleta, CA	86.1	2.4	5.5	2.2	0.3	43.4	152,839	152,834	150,576	142,878	5	0.0
Santa Barbara County, CA	86.1	2.4	5.5	2.2	0.3	43.4	152,839	152,834	150,576	142,878	5	0.0
Santa Cruz–Watsonville, CA	88.0	1.4	4.8	1.7	0.2	32.7	104,466	104,476	102,268	98,868	-10	0.0
Santa Cruz County, CA	88.0	1.4	4.8	1.7	0.2	32.7	104,466	104,476	102,268	98,868	-10	0.0
Santa Fe, NM	91.5	1.1	1.3	4.0	0.2	50.9	72,218	71,266	65,282	57,703	952	1.3
Santa Fe County, NM	91.5	1.1	1.3	4.0	0.2	50.9	72,218	71,266	65,282	57,703	952	1.3
Santa Rosa–Petaluma, CA	87.9	1.9	4.1	2.2	0.4	25.4	205,354	204,572	196,459	183,160	782	0.4
Sonoma County, CA	87.9	1.9	4.1	2.2	0.4	25.4	205,354	204,572	196,459	183,160	782	0.4
Savannah, GA	61.2	34.1	2.2	0.4	0.1	5.3	152,571	151,050	136,781	122,632	1,521	1.0
Bryan County, GA	80.0	15.2	1.8	0.4	0.1	5.2	11,961	11,843	10,427	8,680	118	1.0
Chatham County, GA	54.9	40.2	2.5	0.4	0.1	5.7	120,476	119,323	109,063	99,786	1,153	1.0
Effingham County, GA	82.9	14.0	0.9	0.3	0.1	3.1	20,134	19,884	17,291	14,166	250	1.3
Scranton–Wilkes-Barre, PA	93.5	3.5	1.3	0.3	0.0	6.2	258,765	258,833	256,976	252,775	-68	0.0
Lackawanna County, PA	93.6	2.9	1.8	0.3	0.0	5.2	96,798	96,831	96,429	95,355	-33	0.0
Luzerne County, PA	93.0	4.1	1.1	0.4	0.1	7.2	148,716	148,748	147,386	144,718	-32	0.0
Wyoming County, PA	97.5	1.0	0.4	0.2	0.0	1.7	13,251	13,254	13,161	12,702	-3	0.0
Seattle–Tacoma–Bellevue, WA	75.2	5.9	11.8	1.3	0.9	9.2	1,471,082	1,463,295	1,372,178	1,255,539	7,787	0.5
Seattle–Bellevue–Everett, WA	74.6	5.5	13.5	1.2	0.7	9.2	1,143,854	1,137,920	1,067,086	978,499	5,934	0.5
King County, WA	71.9	6.5	15.0	1.1	0.8	9.2	854,703	851,261	800,953	742,281	3,442	0.4
Snohomish County, WA	81.7	2.8	9.2	1.6	0.5	9.2	289,151	286,659	266,133	236,218	2,492	0.9
Tacoma, WA	77.3	7.1	6.2	1.6	1.4	9.4	327,228	325,375	305,092	277,040	1,853	0.6
Pierce County, WA	77.3	7.1	6.2	1.6	1.4	9.4	327,228	325,375	305,092	277,040	1,853	0.6
Sebastian–Vero Beach, FL	87.6	9.3	1.3	0.4	0.1	11.6	76,251	76,346	69,401	57,871	-95	-0.1
Indian River County, FL	87.6	9.3	1.3	0.4	0.1	11.6	76,251	76,346	69,401	57,871	-95	-0.1
Sheboygan, WI	92.0	1.6	4.7	0.4	0.0	5.6	50,838	50,766	49,291	45,956	72	0.1
Sheboygan County, WI	92.0	1.6	4.7	0.4	0.0	5.6	50,838	50,766	49,291	45,956	72	0.1
Sherman–Denison, TX	88.9	6.1	1.0	1.7	0.1	11.8	53,970	53,727	51,213	48,306	243	0.5
Grayson County, TX	88.9	6.1	1.0	1.7	0.1	11.8	53,970	53,727	51,213	48,306	243	0.5
Shreveport–Bossier City, LA	57.5	39.1	1.3	0.6	0.1	3.6	174,728	173,669	166,663	159,774	1,059	0.6
Bossier Parish, LA	74.1	21.3	1.8	0.7	0.2	6.1	50,369	49,351	44,946	40,821	1,018	2.1
Caddo Parish, LA	49.7	47.3	1.1	0.5	0.1	2.6	111,981	112,028	109,950	107,752	-47	0.0
De Soto Parish, LA	58.6	39.1	0.2	0.9	0.1	2.9	12,378	12,290	11,767	11,201	88	0.7

[1] Persons of Hispanic origin may be any race.
[2] The April 1, 2000, housing estimates base reflects modifications to the Census 2000 population as documented in the Count Question Resolution program and geographic program revisions.
[4] The portion of Sullivan city in Crawford County, MO is legally part of the St. Louis, MO–IL MSA. That portion is not included in these figures for the St. Louis, MSA.

Table C-2.   Population Characteristics and Housing Units—*Continued*

Metropolitan statistical area, division, and component county	Population characteristics, 2011						Housing units					
	One race (percent)					Hispanic or Latino origin[1] (percent)	2011 (July 1)	2010 (July 1)	2005 (July 1)	2000[2] (estimates base)	Change, 2010–2011	
	White alone	Black or African American alone	Asian alone	American Indian, Alaska Native alone	Native Hawaiian and Other Pacific Islander alone						Number	Percent
Sioux City, IA–NE–SD	90.6	2.4	2.3	2.3	0.2	15.9	58,043	58,083	57,967	56,929	-40	-0.1
Woodbury County, IA	89.8	2.6	2.5	2.4	0.2	14.0	41,387	41,484	41,639	41,396	-97	-0.2
Dakota County, NE	88.3	3.4	3.2	3.4	0.3	35.9	7,614	7,631	7,681	7,533	-17	-0.2
Dixon County, NE	97.6	0.6	0.2	0.5	0.2	11.1	2,680	2,688	2,716	2,654	-8	-0.3
Union County, SD	96.2	0.8	1.0	0.7	0.1	2.3	6,362	6,280	5,931	5,346	82	1.3
Sioux Falls, SD	91.4	3.0	1.4	2.2	0.1	3.6	97,551	95,862	86,956	75,635	1,689	1.8
Lincoln County, SD	96.0	0.8	1.1	0.7	0.0	1.4	18,665	17,875	14,165	9,136	790	4.4
McCook County, SD	98.2	0.3	0.2	0.6	0.1	2.0	2,493	2,491	2,469	2,379	2	0.1
Minnehaha County, SD	89.7	3.8	1.5	2.8	0.1	4.3	72,442	71,557	66,416	60,269	885	1.2
Turner County, SD	97.5	0.3	0.2	1.1	0.0	1.5	3,951	3,939	3,906	3,851	12	0.3
South Bend–Mishawaka, IN–MI	83.2	11.8	1.8	0.6	0.1	6.8	140,717	140,735	137,497	130,885	-18	0.0
St. Joseph County, IN	81.9	13.0	2.0	0.5	0.1	7.5	114,833	114,848	112,250	107,018	-15	0.0
Cass County, MI	90.1	5.5	0.7	1.0	0.0	3.1	25,884	25,887	25,247	23,867	-3	0.0
Spartanburg, SC	75.1	20.9	2.1	0.4	0.0	6.1	122,926	122,628	116,644	107,068	298	0.2
Spartanburg County, SC	75.1	20.9	2.1	0.4	0.0	6.1	122,926	122,628	116,644	107,068	298	0.2
Spokane, WA	90.3	1.8	2.2	1.7	0.4	4.7	203,159	201,434	188,703	175,045	1,725	0.9
Spokane County, WA	90.3	1.8	2.2	1.7	0.4	4.7	203,159	201,434	188,703	175,045	1,725	0.9
Springfield, IL	84.7	11.3	1.6	0.2	0.0	1.9	95,549	95,555	94,139	90,752	-6	0.0
Menard County, IL	97.6	0.9	0.3	0.3	0.0	1.1	5,656	5,654	5,574	5,282	2	0.0
Sangamon County, IL	83.9	12.0	1.7	0.2	0.0	1.9	89,893	89,901	88,565	85,470	-8	0.0
Springfield, MA	86.5	7.9	2.7	0.6	0.1	15.8	288,769	288,535	284,214	276,488	234	0.1
Franklin County, MA	94.9	1.3	1.4	0.4	0.0	3.3	33,806	33,758	33,022	31,938	48	0.1
Hampden County, MA	84.1	10.5	2.1	0.8	0.2	21.4	192,197	192,174	189,959	185,900	23	0.0
Hampshire County, MA	89.6	3.0	4.8	0.3	0.1	4.9	62,766	62,603	61,233	58,650	163	0.3
Springfield, MO	93.5	2.3	1.2	0.7	0.1	2.8	193,801	192,346	176,295	156,517	1,455	0.8
Christian County, MO	96.1	0.8	0.6	0.7	0.1	2.7	31,896	31,576	26,914	21,831	320	1.0
Dallas County, MO	96.6	0.4	0.3	0.9	0.1	1.7	7,700	7,662	7,460	6,909	38	0.5
Greene County, MO	91.8	3.1	1.7	0.7	0.1	3.2	126,220	125,387	115,828	104,544	833	0.7
Polk County, MO	96.5	1.0	0.4	0.6	0.0	2.1	13,441	13,304	12,552	11,185	137	1.0
Webster County, MO	96.3	1.1	0.2	0.7	0.0	1.9	14,544	14,417	13,541	12,048	127	0.9
Springfield, OH	87.6	8.9	0.7	0.3	0.1	2.8	61,201	61,419	61,536	61,054	-218	-0.4
Clark County, OH	87.6	8.9	0.7	0.3	0.1	2.8	61,201	61,419	61,536	61,054	-218	-0.4
State College, PA	89.5	3.3	5.4	0.1	0.1	2.7	64,115	63,295	59,101	53,125	820	1.3
Centre County, PA	89.5	3.3	5.4	0.1	0.1	2.7	64,115	63,295	59,101	53,125	820	1.3
Steubenville–Weirton, OH–WV	94.0	4.0	0.4	0.1	0.0	1.1	58,067	58,334	59,064	59,166	-267	-0.5
Jefferson County, OH	92.1	5.7	0.4	0.1	0.0	1.1	32,651	32,826	33,324	33,288	-175	-0.5
Brooke County, WV	97.0	1.3	0.4	0.1	0.0	0.7	10,930	10,967	11,068	11,128	-37	-0.3
Hancock County, WV	95.9	2.4	0.3	0.1	0.0	1.1	14,486	14,541	14,672	14,750	-55	-0.4
Stockton, CA	68.7	8.2	15.5	2.0	0.7	39.4	234,777	233,755	220,356	189,161	1,022	0.4
San Joaquin County, CA	68.7	8.2	15.5	2.0	0.7	39.4	234,777	233,755	220,356	189,161	1,022	0.4
Sumter, SC	49.5	46.9	1.2	0.5	0.1	3.5	46,299	46,011	43,996	41,763	288	0.6
Sumter County, SC	49.5	46.9	1.2	0.5	0.1	3.5	46,299	46,011	43,996	41,763	288	0.6
Syracuse, NY	86.0	8.5	2.5	0.8	0.0	3.6	288,152	287,712	284,290	278,105	440	0.2
Madison County, NY	95.0	2.1	0.9	0.7	0.0	2.0	32,042	31,757	30,303	28,634	285	0.9
Onondaga County, NY	81.8	11.4	3.2	0.9	0.0	4.3	202,513	202,356	200,372	196,627	157	0.1
Oswego County, NY	96.6	1.0	0.7	0.5	0.0	2.2	53,597	53,599	53,615	52,844	-2	0.0
Tallahassee, FL	62.5	32.8	2.4	0.4	0.1	6.2	163,710	163,078	152,781	136,761	632	0.4
Gadsden County, FL	42.1	55.5	0.6	0.6	0.1	10.1	19,561	19,506	18,444	17,702	55	0.3
Jefferson County, FL	62.1	35.8	0.6	0.3	0.0	3.9	6,727	6,632	5,966	5,245	95	1.4
Leon County, FL	63.7	30.8	3.0	0.3	0.1	5.9	124,701	124,136	116,751	103,996	565	0.5
Wakulla County, FL	82.0	14.9	0.5	0.6	0.1	3.6	12,721	12,804	11,620	9,818	-83	-0.6
Tampa–St. Petersburg–Clearwater, FL	81.8	12.5	3.1	0.5	0.1	16.6	1,360,231	1,353,159	1,274,106	1,144,023	7,072	0.5
Hernando County, FL	91.1	5.6	1.2	0.4	0.1	10.6	84,887	84,504	74,662	62,729	383	0.5
Hillsborough County, FL	75.8	17.6	3.6	0.5	0.1	25.1	540,190	536,093	494,675	425,987	4,097	0.8
Pasco County, FL	90.4	5.1	2.3	0.4	0.1	12.1	231,008	228,928	206,879	173,708	2,080	0.9
Pinellas County, FL	83.8	10.7	3.1	0.4	0.1	8.3	504,146	503,634	497,890	481,599	512	0.1
Terre Haute, IN	91.6	5.2	1.2	0.3	0.0	2.0	73,807	74,135	74,265	72,517	-328	-0.4
Clay County, IN	98.0	0.5	0.3	0.2	0.0	1.2	11,679	11,702	11,664	11,104	-23	-0.2
Sullivan County, IN	93.8	4.6	0.2	0.3	0.0	1.5	8,891	8,939	9,087	8,801	-48	-0.5
Vermillion County, IN	98.3	0.4	0.2	0.3	0.0	1.0	7,463	7,488	7,558	7,406	-25	-0.3
Vigo County, IN	88.6	7.1	1.8	0.4	0.0	2.4	45,774	46,006	45,956	45,206	-232	-0.5
Texarkana, TX–Texarkana, AR	72.0	24.4	0.8	0.9	0.1	5.8	58,005	57,774	56,706	54,189	231	0.4
Miller County, AR	72.8	24.2	0.5	0.8	0.1	3.0	19,369	19,281	18,794	17,729	88	0.5
Bowie County, TX	71.6	24.4	0.9	1.0	0.1	7.1	38,636	38,493	37,912	36,460	143	0.4
Toledo, OH	82.2	13.7	1.4	0.4	0.0	5.9	301,190	301,322	296,737	285,496	-132	0.0
Fulton County, OH	97.5	0.6	0.5	0.4	0.0	7.7	17,490	17,407	17,113	16,223	83	0.5
Lucas County, OH	76.0	19.4	1.6	0.4	0.0	5.9	202,272	202,630	201,352	196,273	-358	-0.2
Ottawa County, OH	97.4	1.0	0.3	0.2	0.0	4.3	28,009	27,909	26,939	25,531	100	0.4
Wood County, OH	94.0	2.7	1.6	0.3	0.0	4.6	53,419	53,376	51,333	47,469	43	0.1

[1] Persons of Hispanic origin may be any race.
[2] The April 1, 2000, housing estimates base reflects modifications to the Census 2000 population as documented in the Count Question Resolution program and geographic program revisions.

Table C-2. Population Characteristics and Housing Units—*Continued*

Metropolitan statistical area, division, and component county	White alone	Black or African American alone	Asian alone	American Indian, Alaska Native alone	Native Hawaiian and Other Pacific Islander alone	Hispanic or Latino origin[1] (percent)	2011 (July 1)	2010 (July 1)	2005 (July 1)	2000[2] (estimates base)	Number	Percent
Topeka, KS	87.0	6.9	1.0	1.7	0.1	9.0	104,034	103,809	101,281	96,414	225	0.2
Jackson County, KS	87.7	0.7	0.4	8.1	0.0	3.6	5,817	5,779	5,513	5,092	38	0.7
Jefferson County, KS	96.4	0.6	0.2	0.9	0.0	1.9	8,157	8,160	7,957	7,502	-3	0.0
Osage County, KS	96.9	0.5	0.2	0.7	0.0	2.3	7,508	7,503	7,380	7,018	5	0.1
Shawnee County, KS	84.6	8.8	1.2	1.4	0.1	11.1	79,330	79,140	77,248	73,772	190	0.2
Wabaunsee County, KS	96.4	0.7	0.2	0.6	0.0	3.0	3,222	3,227	3,183	3,030	-5	-0.2
Trenton–Ewing, NJ	66.9	21.0	9.3	0.6	0.2	15.5	143,390	143,168	140,004	133,287	222	0.2
Mercer County, NJ	66.9	21.0	9.3	0.6	0.2	15.5	143,390	143,168	140,004	133,287	222	0.2
Tucson, AZ	86.2	4.0	2.8	4.2	0.2	35.1	442,484	440,909	413,357	366,725	1,575	0.4
Pima County, AZ	86.2	4.0	2.8	4.2	0.2	35.1	442,484	440,909	413,357	366,725	1,575	0.4
Tulsa, OK	74.8	8.6	1.8	8.5	0.1	8.7	413,446	409,820	388,954	366,250	3,626	0.9
Creek County, OK	80.5	2.4	0.4	10.1	0.1	3.5	29,884	29,761	28,957	27,977	123	0.4
Okmulgee County, OK	66.7	8.9	0.4	16.3	0.0	3.6	17,891	17,891	17,751	17,314	0	0.0
Osage County, OK	66.4	11.6	0.3	14.5	0.0	3.2	21,349	21,139	20,032	18,809	210	1.0
Pawnee County, OK	80.8	1.0	0.3	12.0	0.0	2.5	7,747	7,745	7,635	7,464	2	0.0
Rogers County, OK	76.6	1.2	1.1	13.0	0.1	4.1	35,843	35,160	31,264	27,479	683	1.9
Tulsa County, OK	74.5	10.9	2.4	6.5	0.1	11.3	270,673	268,430	256,526	244,043	2,243	0.8
Wagoner County, OK	77.5	3.9	1.4	10.0	0.0	5.0	30,059	29,694	26,789	23,164	365	1.2
Tuscaloosa, AL	63.5	34.0	1.2	0.3	0.1	2.9	98,116	97,534	90,678	84,309	582	0.6
Greene County, AL	18.7	80.4	0.2	0.2	0.0	0.9	4,969	5,007	5,117	5,105	-38	-0.8
Hale County, AL	40.6	58.3	0.3	0.2	0.0	1.1	7,588	7,656	7,774	7,750	-68	-0.9
Tuscaloosa County, AL	67.3	30.0	1.3	0.3	0.1	3.1	85,559	84,871	77,787	71,454	688	0.8
Tyler, TX	78.2	18.1	1.4	0.8	0.1	17.9	88,716	87,309	80,345	71,710	1,407	1.6
Smith County, TX	78.2	18.1	1.4	0.8	0.1	17.9	88,716	87,309	80,345	71,710	1,407	1.6
Utica–Rome, NY	90.0	5.5	2.4	0.3	0.0	4.1	137,696	137,561	136,438	134,867	135	0.1
Herkimer County, NY	96.7	1.3	0.6	0.3	0.0	1.7	33,461	33,381	32,826	32,017	80	0.2
Oneida County, NY	88.2	6.7	2.9	0.3	0.1	4.8	104,235	104,180	103,612	102,850	55	0.1
Valdosta, GA	61.4	34.6	1.4	0.6	0.1	5.9	57,794	57,433	51,657	48,172	361	0.6
Brooks County, GA	62.7	35.3	0.4	0.3	0.1	5.2	7,738	7,706	7,311	7,122	32	0.4
Echols County, GA	89.5	5.3	0.3	3.0	0.4	29.4	1,560	1,558	1,544	1,479	2	0.1
Lanier County, GA	71.8	24.2	1.1	0.7	0.0	4.9	4,358	4,248	3,445	3,014	110	2.6
Lowndes County, GA	59.2	36.6	1.6	0.5	0.2	5.2	44,138	43,921	39,357	36,557	217	0.5
Vallejo–Fairfield, CA	60.8	15.2	15.2	1.2	1.0	24.6	153,308	152,698	147,570	134,493	610	0.4
Solano County, CA	60.8	15.2	15.2	1.2	1.0	24.6	153,308	152,698	147,570	134,493	610	0.4
Victoria, TX	90.1	6.0	1.7	0.8	0.1	44.4	50,757	50,537	49,192	46,606	220	0.4
Calhoun County, TX	90.4	3.3	4.5	0.7	0.0	47.1	11,495	11,410	10,941	10,236	85	0.7
Goliad County, TX	92.1	5.4	0.3	1.0	0.1	35.1	3,727	3,710	3,611	3,426	17	0.5
Victoria County, TX	89.9	6.7	1.2	0.9	0.1	44.5	35,535	35,417	34,640	32,944	118	0.3
Vineland–Millville–Bridgeton, NJ	72.9	21.5	1.4	1.5	0.1	27.6	55,921	55,834	54,114	52,872	87	0.2
Cumberland County, NJ	72.9	21.5	1.4	1.5	0.1	27.6	55,921	55,834	54,114	52,872	87	0.2
Virginia Beach–Norfolk–Newport News, VA–NC	61.2	31.4	3.6	0.5	0.1	5.6	690,208	686,300	662,366	622,872	3,908	0.6
Currituck County, NC	90.7	6.3	0.7	0.5	0.1	3.2	14,583	14,453	13,287	10,682	130	0.9
Gloucester County, VA	87.7	8.8	0.8	0.5	0.0	2.7	15,832	15,852	15,258	14,493	-20	-0.1
Isle of Wight County, VA	72.3	24.7	0.9	0.4	0.1	2.0	14,710	14,633	13,534	12,066	77	0.5
James City County, VA	81.4	13.6	2.3	0.3	0.1	4.8	30,282	29,797	26,108	20,770	485	1.6
Mathews County, VA	88.2	9.2	0.4	0.3	0.1	1.5	5,672	5,669	5,540	5,310	3	0.1
Surry County, VA	52.2	45.4	0.3	0.4	0.0	1.4	3,429	3,444	3,394	3,290	-15	-0.4
York County, VA	77.1	13.9	5.2	0.4	0.2	4.8	27,334	26,849	24,703	20,785	485	1.8
Chesapeake city, VA	63.4	30.1	3.0	0.5	0.1	4.6	83,961	83,196	78,992	72,663	765	0.9
Hampton city, VA	44.0	49.7	2.4	0.5	0.1	4.7	60,118	59,566	58,254	57,312	552	0.9
Newport News city, VA	51.5	41.0	2.9	0.5	0.2	7.6	76,140	76,198	75,849	74,297	-58	-0.1
Norfolk city, VA	49.3	43.1	3.4	0.6	0.2	6.9	95,011	95,018	94,495	94,433	-7	0.0
Poquoson city, VA	94.9	1.0	2.2	0.4	0.0	1.9	4,726	4,726	4,538	4,300	0	0.0
Portsmouth city, VA	42.7	52.9	1.2	0.5	0.1	3.3	40,494	40,806	41,250	41,609	-312	-0.8
Suffolk city, VA	53.0	42.7	1.7	0.4	0.1	3.2	33,393	33,038	30,412	24,711	355	1.1
Virginia Beach city, VA	69.3	20.1	6.3	0.4	0.2	7.0	179,257	177,879	172,019	162,272	1,378	0.8
Williamsburg city, VA	75.9	14.9	5.7	0.4	0.0	6.9	5,266	5,176	4,733	3,879	90	1.7
Visalia–Porterville, CA	88.5	2.2	3.9	2.8	0.2	61.3	142,931	141,696	130,319	119,640	1,235	0.9
Tulare County, CA	88.5	2.2	3.9	2.8	0.2	61.3	142,931	141,696	130,319	119,640	1,235	0.9
Waco, TX	80.3	15.1	1.6	1.1	0.1	24.2	95,934	95,124	90,427	84,804	810	0.9
McLennan County, TX	80.3	15.1	1.6	1.1	0.1	24.2	95,934	95,124	90,427	84,804	810	0.9
Warner Robins, GA	65.1	29.2	2.6	0.4	0.2	6.2	58,841	58,329	52,894	44,492	512	0.9
Houston County, GA	65.1	29.2	2.6	0.4	0.2	6.2	58,841	58,329	52,894	44,492	512	0.9
Washington–Arlington–Alexandria, DC–VA–MD–WV	60.1	26.4	9.6	0.7	0.1	14.1	2,231,441	2,213,693	2,095,443	1,890,126	17,748	0.8
Bethesda–Rockville–Frederick, MD	67.5	16.5	12.4	0.7	0.1	15.6	468,833	466,041	445,791	407,872	2,792	0.6
Frederick County, MD	83.8	9.2	4.1	0.5	0.1	7.6	91,258	90,136	84,121	73,020	1,122	1.2
Montgomery County, MD	63.6	18.2	14.4	0.7	0.1	17.5	377,575	375,905	361,670	334,852	1,670	0.4

[1] Persons of Hispanic origin may be any race.
[2] The April 1, 2000, housing estimates base reflects modifications to the Census 2000 population as documented in the Count Question Resolution program and geographic program revisions.

Table C-2. Population Characteristics and Housing Units—*Continued*

Metropolitan statistical area, division, and component county	Population characteristics, 2011						Housing units				Change, 2010–2011	
	One race (percent)					Hispanic or Latino origin[1] (percent)	2011 (July 1)	2010 (July 1)	2005 (July 1)	2000[2] (estimates base)	Number	Percent
	White alone	Black or African American alone	Asian alone	American Indian, Alaska Native alone	Native Hawaiian and Other Pacific Islander alone							
Washington–Arlington–Alexandria,												
DC–VA–MD–WV	58.1	29.1	8.8	0.7	0.1	13.7	1,762,608	1,747,652	1,649,652	1,482,254	14,956	0.9
District of Columbia, DC......................	42.4	50.7	3.7	0.6	0.1	9.5	298,902	296,719	284,844	274,861	2,183	0.7
Calvert County, MD	81.7	13.8	1.5	0.4	0.1	2.9	34,148	33,780	32,035	27,570	368	1.1
Charles County, MD	51.0	41.6	3.1	0.7	0.1	4.5	55,810	54,963	50,380	43,891	847	1.5
Prince George's County, MD	26.6	65.4	4.3	1.0	0.2	15.2	329,794	328,182	317,264	302,208	1,612	0.5
Arlington County, VA............................	77.3	9.1	9.7	0.8	0.1	15.2	106,717	105,405	95,478	90,255	1,312	1.2
Clarke County, VA...............................	91.0	5.5	1.1	0.3	0.1	3.6	6,238	6,235	5,928	5,382	3	0.0
Fairfax County, VA..............................	68.1	9.9	18.0	0.6	0.1	15.8	410,075	407,997	393,974	359,606	2,078	0.5
Fauquier County, VA............................	87.2	8.6	1.4	0.5	0.1	6.5	25,605	25,600	24,254	21,053	5	0.0
Loudoun County, VA............................	72.8	8.0	15.3	0.5	0.1	12.6	112,189	109,442	94,045	62,166	2,747	2.5
Prince William County, VA....................	65.6	21.3	7.9	1.1	0.2	20.5	139,175	137,115	124,598	98,060	2,060	1.5
Spotsylvania County, VA	78.4	15.8	2.4	0.4	0.1	7.8	45,407	45,185	41,815	33,288	222	0.5
Stafford County, VA.............................	75.1	17.7	3.0	0.6	0.2	9.5	44,480	43,978	40,243	31,408	502	1.1
Warren County, VA..............................	91.5	4.9	1.1	0.4	0.0	3.7	16,057	15,975	14,899	13,287	82	0.5
Alexandria city, VA..............................	67.4	22.4	6.4	0.8	0.2	16.4	72,709	72,376	69,226	64,255	333	0.5
Fairfax city, VA...................................	73.6	5.9	15.7	0.9	0.2	16.2	8,683	8,680	8,631	8,206	3	0.0
Falls Church city, VA...........................	81.5	4.7	9.5	0.4	0.0	9.1	5,589	5,489	5,093	4,749	100	1.8
Fredericksburg city, VA........................	69.1	23.6	3.1	0.8	0.1	11.0	10,777	10,467	9,398	8,923	310	3.0
Manassas city, VA	74.9	15.5	5.3	1.1	0.2	31.5	13,158	13,123	12,719	12,127	35	0.3
Manassas Park city, VA	70.9	14.8	9.2	1.2	0.3	33.5	4,976	4,904	4,444	3,344	72	1.5
Jefferson County, WV	89.1	6.8	1.4	0.3	0.1	4.8	22,119	22,037	20,384	17,615	82	0.4
Waterloo–Cedar Falls, IA........................	89.4	7.0	1.3	0.3	0.2	3.3	71,575	71,332	69,615	66,409	243	0.3
Black Hawk County, IA	87.1	8.8	1.5	0.4	0.2	3.9	56,125	55,887	54,338	51,757	238	0.4
Bremer County, IA...............................	97.3	0.8	0.8	0.1	0.0	1.2	9,942	9,915	9,771	9,348	27	0.3
Grundy County, IA...............................	98.7	0.2	0.2	0.1	0.1	1.1	5,508	5,530	5,506	5,304	-22	-0.4
Wausau, WI...	92.0	0.7	5.5	0.5	0.0	2.3	57,874	57,734	54,997	50,390	140	0.2
Marathon County, WI	92.0	0.7	5.5	0.5	0.0	2.3	57,874	57,734	54,997	50,390	140	0.2
Wenatchee–East Wenatchee, WA..............	94.4	0.6	1.0	1.7	0.2	27.4	52,057	51,469	47,065	43,340	588	1.1
Chelan County, WA..............................	94.6	0.5	1.0	1.6	0.2	26.5	35,870	35,465	32,738	30,400	405	1.1
Douglas County, WA	94.1	0.7	1.0	1.8	0.2	28.9	16,187	16,004	14,327	12,940	183	1.1
Wheeling, WV–OH	94.7	3.2	0.5	0.1	0.0	0.8	69,366	69,542	69,747	69,229	-176	-0.3
Belmont County, OH.............................	94.0	4.1	0.4	0.1	0.0	0.7	32,487	32,452	32,158	31,243	35	0.1
Marshall County, WV............................	98.0	0.6	0.4	0.2	0.0	0.9	15,880	15,918	15,933	15,820	-38	-0.2
Ohio County, WV.................................	93.3	3.8	0.8	0.2	0.0	0.9	20,999	21,172	21,656	22,166	-173	-0.8
Wichita, KS	84.0	7.9	3.5	1.3	0.1	11.8	264,562	263,043	252,636	238,588	1,519	0.6
Butler County, KS................................	94.1	1.9	0.8	1.1	0.1	4.1	26,131	26,058	25,148	23,165	73	0.3
Harvey County, KS	94.4	1.8	0.8	0.9	0.0	10.9	14,590	14,527	14,109	13,386	63	0.4
Sedgwick County, KS	81.4	9.5	4.2	1.4	0.1	13.2	213,023	211,593	202,407	191,159	1,430	0.7
Sumner County, KS..............................	94.9	1.2	0.3	1.3	0.0	4.6	10,818	10,865	10,972	10,878	-47	-0.4
Wichita Falls, TX	85.0	9.6	1.9	1.3	0.1	15.8	64,843	64,823	63,688	62,161	20	0.0
Archer County, TX	96.6	0.8	0.2	1.1	0.1	8.0	4,129	4,107	3,983	3,837	22	0.5
Clay County, TX..................................	95.5	1.1	0.3	1.5	0.0	5.1	5,143	5,150	5,113	4,990	-7	-0.1
Wichita County, TX..............................	83.4	10.9	2.1	1.3	0.1	17.2	55,571	55,566	54,592	53,334	5	0.0
Williamsport, PA	92.9	4.7	0.6	0.2	0.0	1.5	52,266	52,499	52,862	52,460	-233	-0.4
Lycoming County, PA............................	92.9	4.7	0.6	0.2	0.0	1.5	52,266	52,499	52,862	52,460	-233	-0.4
Wilmington, NC....................................	82.1	14.4	1.0	0.7	0.1	5.5	207,145	205,642	181,503	151,843	1,503	0.7
Brunswick County, NC..........................	85.4	11.6	0.6	0.8	0.1	5.1	78,410	77,482	64,429	51,418	928	1.2
New Hanover County, NC......................	81.1	15.0	1.3	0.6	0.1	5.4	101,828	101,436	93,062	79,630	392	0.4
Pender County, NC..............................	78.9	18.0	0.5	0.9	0.1	6.4	26,907	26,724	24,012	20,795	183	0.7
Winchester, VA–WV	90.9	5.4	1.4	0.5	0.1	7.6	57,522	56,906	51,616	45,088	616	1.1
Frederick County, VA...........................	91.8	4.6	1.3	0.4	0.1	6.9	31,774	31,346	27,774	23,331	428	1.4
Winchester city, VA.............................	82.4	11.5	2.6	0.9	0.1	15.8	11,905	11,872	11,430	10,588	33	0.3
Hampshire County, WV	97.3	1.2	0.2	0.2	0.1	1.1	13,843	13,688	12,412	11,169	155	1.1
Winston–Salem, NC...............................	74.7	21.2	1.6	0.7	0.1	10.6	215,474	214,375	201,612	183,146	1,099	0.5
Davie County, NC	90.5	6.7	0.7	0.6	0.0	6.4	18,298	18,238	16,965	14,955	60	0.3
Forsyth County, NC.............................	68.1	27.1	2.0	0.8	0.1	12.2	157,710	156,872	146,998	133,141	838	0.5
Stokes County, NC..............................	93.8	4.4	0.3	0.4	0.0	2.7	22,082	21,924	20,851	19,229	158	0.7
Yadkin County, NC...............................	94.5	3.5	0.3	0.6	0.1	10.0	17,384	17,341	16,798	15,821	43	0.2
Worcester, MA	88.8	4.8	4.2	0.3	0.1	9.6	328,586	326,788	316,426	298,180	1,798	0.6
Worcester County, MA	88.8	4.8	4.2	0.3	0.1	9.6	328,586	326,788	316,426	298,180	1,798	0.6
Yakima, WA...	88.6	1.4	1.4	5.6	0.2	45.8	85,904	85,474	82,261	79,175	430	0.5
Yakima County, WA	88.6	1.4	1.4	5.6	0.2	45.8	85,904	85,474	82,261	79,175	430	0.5
York–Hanover, PA	90.4	6.2	1.3	0.3	0.1	5.8	179,769	178,671	169,786	156,740	1,098	0.6
York County, PA..................................	90.4	6.2	1.3	0.3	0.1	5.8	179,769	178,671	169,786	156,740	1,098	0.6
Youngstown–Warren–Boardman, OH–PA	86.3	11.1	0.6	0.2	0.0	2.8	258,932	259,729	260,443	256,786	-797	-0.3
Mahoning County, OH...........................	81.1	16.1	0.8	0.2	0.0	4.8	111,363	111,833	112,640	111,786	-470	-0.4
Trumbull County, OH............................	89.2	8.4	0.5	0.2	0.0	1.4	95,821	96,163	96,354	95,105	-342	-0.4
Mercer County, PA	91.9	5.8	0.7	0.2	0.0	1.1	51,748	51,733	51,449	49,895	15	0.0
Yuba City, CA	77.1	3.1	11.9	2.6	0.4	27.9	61,413	61,493	56,927	50,970	-80	-0.1
Sutter County, CA................................	75.3	2.4	15.5	2.3	0.4	29.4	33,886	33,858	31,950	28,324	28	0.1
Yuba County, CA.................................	79.5	3.9	7.2	3.1	0.5	25.9	27,527	27,635	24,977	22,646	-108	-0.4
Yuma, AZ	91.6	2.6	1.5	2.2	0.2	60.1	88,146	87,849	83,150	74,123	297	0.3
Yuma County, AZ	91.6	2.6	1.5	2.2	0.2	60.1	88,146	87,849	83,150	74,123	297	0.3

[1] Persons of Hispanic origin may be any race.
[2] The April 1, 2000, housing estimates base reflects modifications to the Census 2000 population as documented in the Count Question Resolution program and geographic program revisions.

Table C-3.   Personal Income and Earnings, by Industry

Metropolitan statistical area, division, and component county	Personal income Total (million dollars) 2011	2010	2005	Per capita[1] (dollars) 2011	2005	Percent change, 2005–2011	Earnings, 2011 Total[2] (million dollars)	Manufacturing	Retail trade	Finance and insurance	Professional and technical services	Health care and social services	Government and government enterprises
Abilene, TX	5,920	5,625	4,470	35,571	27,808	32.4	3,941	3.5	7.2	5.0	4.0	13.8	28.8
Callahan County, TX	452	430	339	33,412	25,550	33.1	125	5.5	9.7	4.0	(D)	(D)	26.7
Jones County, TX	539	525	422	26,734	20,848	27.7	212	5.9	6.3	5.2	(D)	(D)	28.2
Taylor County, TX	4,929	4,670	3,709	37,132	29,150	32.9	3,604	3.3	7.2	5.0	4.4	15.1	28.9
Akron, OH	28,066	26,693	23,714	40,011	33,757	18.4	19,282	15.0	6.5	4.4	6.8	13.6	14.9
Portage County, OH	5,860	5,533	4,736	36,260	30,074	23.8	3,091	23.0	6.9	1.7	4.0	5.4	28.2
Summit County, OH	22,206	21,161	18,979	41,135	34,822	17.0	16,191	13.4	6.4	5.0	7.3	15.2	12.4
Albany, GA	5,018	4,815	4,198	31,821	26,760	19.5	3,407	(D)	6.9	2.7	5.2	14.3	27.2
Baker County, GA	122	113	104	39,650	26,147	17.9	60	(D)	1.2	(D)	(D)	2.1	10.1
Dougherty County, GA	2,719	2,644	2,495	28,689	26,366	9.0	2,714	9.8	6.7	2.8	5.9	17.9	28.5
Lee County, GA	1,177	1,109	791	41,198	29,829	48.9	275	2.9	9.9	2.4	4.1	(D)	25.6
Terrell County, GA	299	284	245	32,048	24,154	22.0	137	11.9	6.4	4.3	1.9	(D)	21.7
Worth County, GA	700	666	565	31,944	26,053	24.0	222	7.6	7.1	2.4	1.5	(D)	20.6
Albany–Schenectady–Troy, NY	39,168	37,601	30,672	44,944	35,890	27.7	28,955	6.9	6.2	7.1	11.0	11.9	26.0
Albany County, NY	14,657	14,168	11,780	48,284	38,905	24.4	15,834	3.6	5.7	8.1	10.3	11.5	31.4
Rensselaer County, NY	6,331	6,086	4,968	39,716	31,826	27.4	3,211	6.5	6.4	4.8	6.4	13.9	23.2
Saratoga County, NY	10,301	9,838	7,864	46,637	36,923	31.0	5,091	12.0	8.0	8.9	8.5	9.6	18.1
Schenectady County, NY	6,721	6,407	5,198	43,348	34,604	29.3	4,363	13.8	5.5	3.6	20.5	14.4	17.2
Schoharie County, NY	1,157	1,102	862	35,530	26,499	34.3	457	(D)	8.0	5.4	4.1	10.0	33.8
Albuquerque, NM	31,459	30,293	25,338	35,007	31,299	24.2	22,632	6.3	6.8	4.0	12.5	11.8	26.6
Bernalillo County, NM	24,311	23,473	20,224	36,233	32,867	20.2	19,863	4.3	6.7	4.2	13.8	12.5	26.9
Sandoval County, NM	4,421	4,188	2,991	32,931	27,841	47.8	1,858	28.9	6.2	2.4	4.1	4.1	21.8
Torrance County, NM	498	480	407	30,439	24,390	22.1	164	3.3	9.2	1.2	(D)	5.4	33.8
Valencia County, NM	2,229	2,153	1,716	28,921	24,481	29.9	747	4.6	9.4	1.9	2.6	12.5	29.1
Alexandria, LA	5,679	5,483	4,542	36,758	30,702	25.0	3,734	10.0	7.5	2.7	5.0	18.0	24.9
Grant Parish, LA	566	558	440	25,596	21,580	28.8	226	(D)	3.9	(D)	1.6	(D)	50.1
Rapides Parish, LA	5,113	4,925	4,102	38,624	32,160	24.6	3,508	10.6	7.8	2.9	5.3	19.1	23.3
Allentown–Bethlehem–Easton, PA–NJ	33,075	31,677	26,609	40,095	33,779	24.3	21,020	13.3	6.5	4.2	5.1	16.6	12.2
Warren County, NJ	4,868	4,682	4,021	44,938	36,943	21.1	2,341	24.7	9.2	1.7	4.7	13.0	16.7
Carbon County, PA	2,111	2,013	1,699	32,394	27,251	24.2	891	11.2	7.6	2.3	2.2	15.6	16.4
Lehigh County, PA	14,432	13,793	11,602	40,890	35,017	24.4	11,663	9.9	5.6	4.0	5.2	20.7	9.5
Northampton County, PA	11,664	11,189	9,286	39,078	32,562	25.6	6,126	15.8	7.1	5.8	5.7	10.4	15.0
Altoona, PA	4,386	4,186	3,542	34,511	27,949	23.8	3,094	13.2	9.1	3.4	4.6	19.5	16.0
Blair County, PA	4,386	4,186	3,542	34,511	27,949	23.8	3,094	13.2	9.1	3.4	4.6	19.5	16.0
Amarillo, TX	9,383	8,918	7,020	36,968	29,451	33.7	7,012	(D)	7.4	5.3	6.7	13.5	16.1
Armstrong County, TX	83	80	75	43,129	36,717	11.2	25	(D)	1.9	(D)	4.4	(D)	23.4
Carson County, TX	243	248	199	38,854	30,931	21.9	469	(D)	1.5	0.5	(D)	(D)	11.7
Potter County, TX	4,123	3,965	3,318	33,714	27,938	24.2	4,970	8.9	7.1	5.5	7.8	16.4	16.3
Randall County, TX	4,934	4,625	3,428	40,001	30,849	43.9	1,548	6.1	10.5	6.2	5.0	8.6	16.4
Ames, IA	3,356	3,161	2,558	37,429	30,866	31.2	2,724	15.7	5.0	1.9	4.0	7.6	40.1
Story County, IA	3,356	3,161	2,558	37,429	30,866	31.2	2,724	15.7	5.0	1.9	4.0	7.6	40.1
Anchorage, AK	18,914	17,936	14,129	48,810	40,265	33.9	15,034	0.9	5.9	4.4	9.5	11.7	28.6
Anchorage Municipality, AK	15,062	14,322	11,714	50,958	42,366	28.6	13,672	0.9	5.4	4.6	9.9	11.2	29.1
Matanuska–Susitna Borough, AK	3,853	3,615	2,415	41,905	32,459	59.5	1,362	0.8	10.7	2.7	5.1	16.6	23.9
Anderson, IN	3,992	3,860	3,652	30,421	27,905	9.3	2,024	15.5	6.8	3.2	2.6	16.3	16.7
Madison County, IN	3,992	3,860	3,652	30,421	27,905	9.3	2,024	15.5	6.8	3.2	2.6	16.3	16.7
Anderson, SC	5,854	5,604	4,777	31,059	27,227	22.5	3,142	24.2	9.6	3.0	3.0	8.1	21.6
Anderson County, SC	5,854	5,604	4,777	31,059	27,227	22.5	3,142	24.2	9.6	3.0	3.0	8.1	21.6
Ann Arbor, MI	14,204	13,297	12,745	40,821	37,241	11.5	12,689	9.7	4.7	2.9	11.9	11.1	35.5
Washtenaw County, MI	14,204	13,297	12,745	40,821	37,241	11.5	12,689	9.7	4.7	2.9	11.9	11.1	35.5
Anniston–Oxford, AL	3,741	3,645	3,087	31,758	26,963	21.2	2,641	13.1	7.2	2.0	4.0	9.2	36.4
Calhoun County, AL	3,741	3,645	3,087	31,758	26,963	21.2	2,641	13.1	7.2	2.0	4.0	9.2	36.4
Appleton, WI	8,983	8,473	7,395	39,504	34,247	21.5	6,687	21.9	6.7	7.4	4.8	10.2	11.2
Calumet County, WI	2,152	1,993	1,606	43,473	34,772	34.0	741	29.8	5.2	5.1	5.5	(D)	10.1
Outagamie County, WI	6,832	6,480	5,789	38,400	34,104	18.0	5,947	20.9	6.9	7.7	4.7	11.5	11.3
Asheville, NC	14,639	14,013	11,944	34,122	30,131	22.6	8,942	13.3	8.6	4.1	4.8	18.1	17.9
Buncombe County, NC	8,321	7,966	6,815	34,467	30,750	22.1	6,084	11.1	8.3	4.1	5.4	20.6	17.4
Haywood County, NC	1,854	1,796	1,552	31,496	27,193	19.4	862	17.7	10.9	4.4	4.4	10.5	24.1
Henderson County, NC	3,869	3,675	3,083	35,853	31,591	25.5	1,797	18.8	8.8	4.2	3.4	15.3	16.2
Madison County, NC	595	576	494	28,579	24,569	20.5	200	9.9	5.7	2.1	(D)	(D)	22.4
Athens–Clarke County, GA	6,051	5,831	4,884	31,302	27,290	23.9	4,382	12.0	6.5	4.0	3.7	15.4	33.5
Clarke County, GA	3,003	2,927	2,627	25,587	23,987	14.3	3,672	13.3	6.3	3.6	3.4	17.1	35.3
Madison County, GA	819	800	743	29,317	27,407	10.1	177	7.0	6.4	3.3	3.2	(D)	34.0
Oconee County, GA	1,780	1,662	1,149	53,361	40,145	55.0	430	5.1	7.9	7.3	6.6	10.4	19.9
Oglethorpe County, GA	450	441	365	30,618	26,622	23.3	103	3.2	4.8	2.4	1.7	(D)	25.8

[1] Based on resident population estimated as of July 1.
[2] Includes other industry categories not shown separately.
(D) = Data withheld to avoid disclosure or does not meet statistical standards.

Table C-3.   Personal Income and Earnings, by Industry—*Continued*

Metropolitan statistical area, division, and component county	Total (million dollars)			Per capita[1] (dollars)		Percent change, 2005–2011	Total[2] (million dollars)	Percentage by selected major industries					
	2011	2010	2005	2011	2005			Manufacturing	Retail trade	Finance and insurance	Professional and technical services	Health care and social services	Government and government enterprises
Atlanta–Sandy Springs–Marietta, GA	212,830	201,632	179,145	39,713	37,683	18.8	171,979	7.3	5.8	7.6	12.2	8.5	12.7
Barrow County, GA	2,136	2,029	1,549	30,556	26,751	37.9	794	12.9	10.0	2.4	0.0	7.8	20.2
Bartow County, GA	2,788	2,706	2,498	27,762	27,650	11.6	1,874	28.1	6.4	2.6	5.2	7.7	15.0
Butts County, GA	596	583	542	25,336	24,596	9.8	283	12.4	7.3	3.0	(D)	(D)	28.4
Carroll County, GA	3,220	3,093	2,639	28,964	25,742	22.0	1,997	19.8	7.9	2.4	(D)	15.4	20.0
Cherokee County, GA	8,054	7,486	6,189	36,898	33,981	30.1	2,592	8.8	9.8	4.5	7.5	9.2	18.4
Clayton County, GA	6,997	6,673	6,296	26,755	24,565	11.1	6,339	5.0	5.9	1.3	1.9	7.0	13.9
Cobb County, GA	32,034	30,644	27,744	45,923	42,898	15.5	23,069	8.8	6.5	5.9	14.1	9.3	9.1
Coweta County, GA	4,387	4,135	3,216	33,842	29,678	36.4	1,656	14.4	10.4	2.7	4.6	11.2	18.3
Dawson County, GA	728	702	621	32,395	31,679	17.1	330	10.0	21.4	5.0	3.7	5.4	17.4
DeKalb County, GA	28,179	27,162	25,404	40,262	37,974	10.9	22,481	4.2	5.4	5.4	9.0	10.7	18.3
Douglas County, GA	3,969	3,789	3,124	29,761	27,558	27.1	1,798	9.1	12.3	3.1	3.5	11.1	18.3
Fayette County, GA	4,792	4,596	4,190	44,460	41,098	14.4	2,314	8.2	8.5	3.7	7.9	13.1	15.3
Forsyth County, GA	7,520	6,847	4,879	41,354	35,448	54.1	3,328	14.1	6.1	2.7	10.7	8.9	11.7
Fulton County, GA	54,556	51,035	47,394	57,451	57,887	15.1	72,434	4.5	3.5	11.4	16.5	7.7	10.5
Gwinnett County, GA	27,108	25,717	23,470	32,861	33,011	15.5	20,637	10.4	9.1	6.8	11.0	6.5	10.3
Haralson County, GA	812	793	712	28,347	25,428	14.1	360	26.5	9.7	2.8	(D)	(D)	22.4
Heard County, GA	309	307	246	26,289	21,707	25.3	154	15.7	1.6	0.0	4.7	1.8	19.3
Henry County, GA	6,250	5,911	4,649	30,143	27,411	34.4	2,620	7.2	10.7	3.5	3.3	11.8	23.4
Jasper County, GA	414	396	326	29,818	25,122	26.9	103	20.3	5.8	2.8	1.9	0.0	27.6
Lamar County, GA	485	472	427	26,630	25,155	13.6	181	16.8	7.9	(D)	(D)	4.3	32.5
Meriwether County, GA	604	576	514	27,952	22,769	17.5	236	14.8	7.2	3.7	0.9	(D)	33.6
Newton County, GA	2,604	2,474	2,024	25,830	23,629	28.7	1,098	30.0	7.1	2.0	2.6	9.4	22.4
Paulding County, GA	5,237	4,850	3,049	36,485	26,948	71.8	1,036	5.6	11.5	2.3	5.2	8.2	26.4
Pickens County, GA	1,071	1,021	894	36,407	32,775	19.8	359	12.1	9.6	4.5	4.6	15.6	20.1
Pike County, GA	543	519	428	30,608	26,935	26.8	126	13.5	4.6	2.7	(D)	(D)	26.9
Rockdale County, GA	2,731	2,634	2,405	31,840	30,802	13.5	1,752	14.3	8.7	3.2	4.6	11.5	13.8
Spalding County, GA	1,812	1,753	1,619	28,305	26,506	11.9	1,070	19.0	8.3	2.7	3.2	14.3	21.7
Walton County, GA	2,896	2,730	2,095	34,236	28,426	38.2	958	13.2	13.9	2.0	3.0	7.5	21.6
Atlantic City–Hammonton, NJ	11,046	10,669	9,611	40,262	35,552	14.9	8,485	1.9	6.9	2.7	5.2	14.1	21.7
Atlantic County, NJ	11,046	10,669	9,611	40,262	35,552	14.9	8,485	1.9	6.9	2.7	5.2	14.1	21.7
Auburn–Opelika, AL	4,190	3,968	3,109	29,208	24,646	34.8	2,567	11.7	7.5	2.5	4.2	7.2	37.1
Lee County, AL	4,190	3,968	3,109	29,208	24,646	34.8	2,567	11.7	7.5	2.5	4.2	7.2	37.1
Augusta–Richmond County, GA–SC	19,463	18,548	15,262	34,640	29,180	27.5	13,765	10.2	6.1	2.7	6.6	10.1	30.8
Burke County, GA	671	635	484	28,549	21,091	38.7	462	5.6	4.8	1.4	(D)	(D)	16.7
Columbia County, GA	5,473	5,123	3,701	42,717	34,756	47.9	1,553	11.4	13.4	4.3	6.3	10.1	18.4
McDuffie County, GA	676	649	604	31,174	28,189	11.9	328	23.8	8.7	2.3	2.1	7.7	23.8
Richmond County, GA	6,101	5,904	5,314	30,320	27,133	14.8	7,068	8.0	4.2	2.1	5.2	13.1	45.3
Aiken County, SC	5,646	5,393	4,524	35,141	30,130	24.8	4,057	12.6	6.2	3.3	10.6	7.0	12.3
Edgefield County, SC	897	844	636	33,615	24,267	41.0	298	15.1	12.5	1.4	(D)	(D)	36.2
Austin–Round Rock–San Marcos, TX	72,152	67,321	51,047	40,455	35,124	41.3	58,481	9.7	6.1	6.1	13.5	9.0	17.6
Bastrop County, TX	2,139	2,050	1,687	28,473	24,720	26.8	810	7.3	10.2	2.6	4.0	6.5	29.4
Caldwell County, TX	983	958	827	25,577	22,727	18.9	396	6.1	9.3	2.9	2.8	13.3	22.1
Hays County, TX	5,364	4,933	3,373	32,700	26,923	59.0	2,679	8.8	11.5	2.8	6.4	10.1	23.8
Travis County, TX	45,925	43,259	34,486	49,329	38,693	33.2	45,271	9.7	5.4	6.6	15.8	9.2	17.9
Williamson County, TX	17,741	16,122	10,674	40,067	32,136	66.2	9,324	10.1	7.5	5.4	5.7	7.9	13.2
Bakersfield–Delano, CA	26,744	25,092	19,806	31,400	26,036	35.0	20,245	5.1	5.7	2.2	4.8	8.0	23.3
Kern County, CA	26,744	25,092	19,806	31,400	26,036	35.0	20,245	5.1	5.7	2.2	4.8	8.0	23.3
Baltimore–Towson, MD	139,528	132,286	111,453	51,126	42,150	25.2	101,298	5.7	5.2	6.0	12.7	12.4	24.6
Anne Arundel County, MD	30,634	29,129	24,685	56,270	47,823	24.1	24,203	7.1	5.1	2.2	10.7	7.1	38.4
Baltimore County, MD	41,247	39,310	34,389	50,926	43,580	19.9	27,165	6.7	7.1	9.2	11.0	13.7	18.5
Carroll County, MD	7,613	7,313	6,361	45,507	38,431	19.7	3,302	9.3	8.1	2.9	9.6	14.0	15.6
Harford County, MD	12,159	11,516	9,371	49,329	39,308	29.8	6,387	5.5	7.3	2.5	9.7	9.0	41.1
Howard County, MD	19,435	18,257	14,731	66,300	54,844	31.9	12,981	4.2	5.3	5.4	28.9	6.3	10.1
Queen Anne's County, MD	2,399	2,258	1,858	49,605	41,401	29.1	810	8.7	8.8	2.6	9.3	6.7	19.6
Baltimore city, MD	26,041	24,503	20,058	42,036	32,270	29.8	26,449	3.7	2.3	7.7	9.5	19.7	22.6
Bangor, ME	5,220	5,012	4,328	33,940	28,904	20.6	3,765	6.3	10.0	3.0	4.1	21.9	21.2
Penobscot County, ME	5,220	5,012	4,328	33,940	28,904	20.6	3,765	6.3	10.0	3.0	4.1	21.9	21.2
Barnstable Town, MA	11,968	11,403	9,849	55,465	44,365	21.5	5,612	2.4	10.2	3.9	8.5	18.2	19.1
Barnstable County, MA	11,968	11,403	9,849	55,465	44,365	21.5	5,612	2.4	10.2	3.9	8.5	18.2	19.1
Baton Rouge, LA	31,510	30,088	23,119	38,985	31,432	36.3	23,539	11.9	6.1	4.4	7.2	10.1	19.4
Ascension Parish, LA	4,552	4,256	2,803	41,388	31,238	62.4	2,893	22.2	7.8	2.7	4.1	7.7	9.8
East Baton Rouge Parish, LA	18,529	17,783	14,333	41,974	34,636	29.3	16,231	7.9	5.8	5.3	9.5	12.5	20.5
East Feliciana Parish, LA	683	661	555	33,974	27,631	23.1	288	6.5	4.9	3.0	1.4	(D)	51.0
Iberville Parish, LA	1,065	1,024	825	32,040	25,221	29.1	1,153	43.3	3.2	1.7	2.1	(D)	15.7
Livingston Parish, LA	4,146	3,936	2,793	31,832	25,571	48.5	1,316	8.8	10.2	2.8	(D)	6.9	22.5
Pointe Coupee Parish, LA	832	797	597	36,650	27,054	39.3	381	6.6	7.6	3.6	(D)	5.5	16.8
St. Helena Parish, LA	382	369	258	34,856	24,509	48.0	113	13.8	6.6	0.0	(D)	(D)	26.5
West Baton Rouge Parish, LA	896	854	635	37,160	28,965	41.0	774	23.1	4.8	0.5	(D)	(D)	11.3
West Feliciana Parish, LA	425	409	320	27,474	20,745	32.7	389	6.1	2.6	1.2	(D)	4.7	35.7

[1] Based on resident population estimated as of July 1.
[2] Includes other industry categories not shown separately.
(D) = Data withheld to avoid disclosure or does not meet statistical standards.

Table C-3. Personal Income and Earnings, by Industry—*Continued*

Metropolitan statistical area, division, and component county	Personal income Total (million dollars) 2011	2010	2005	Per capita[1] (dollars) 2011	2005	Percent change, 2005–2011	Earnings, 2011 Total[2] (million dollars)	Manufacturing	Retail trade	Finance and insurance	Professional and technical services	Health care and social services	Government and government enterprises
Battle Creek, MI	4,544	4,425	3,915	33,541	28,174	16.1	3,383	23.0	5.5	1.6	(D)	12.9	21.9
Calhoun County, MI	4,544	4,425	3,915	33,541	28,174	16.1	3,383	23.0	5.5	1.6	(D)	12.9	21.9
Bay City, MI	3,614	3,431	3,037	33,737	27,823	19.0	2,001	12.8	8.5	3.3	11.7	17.3	17.2
Bay County, MI	3,614	3,431	3,037	33,737	27,823	19.0	2,001	12.8	8.5	3.3	11.7	17.3	17.2
Beaumont–Port Arthur, TX	15,082	14,275	11,107	38,620	28,812	35.8	10,904	23.3	6.7	2.6	6.5	10.5	13.6
Hardin County, TX	2,148	2,022	1,450	38,882	28,354	48.1	770	7.4	9.6	2.3	4.9	14.8	14.7
Jefferson County, TX	9,786	9,275	7,362	38,712	29,348	32.9	8,723	23.0	6.4	2.5	7.3	10.8	13.2
Orange County, TX	3,148	2,978	2,295	38,163	27,480	37.2	1,411	33.8	7.2	3.1	3.1	5.9	15.7
Bellingham, WA	7,759	7,361	5,609	38,098	30,248	38.3	5,007	13.7	8.4	3.5	5.8	11.5	19.0
Whatcom County, WA	7,759	7,361	5,609	38,098	30,248	38.3	5,007	13.7	8.4	3.5	5.8	11.5	19.0
Bend, OR	5,946	5,666	4,664	37,084	33,176	27.5	3,674	6.2	9.3	4.5	8.3	18.8	14.2
Deschutes County, OR	5,946	5,666	4,664	37,084	33,176	27.5	3,674	6.2	9.3	4.5	8.3	18.8	14.2
Billings, MT	6,309	5,965	4,963	39,405	33,636	27.1	4,630	6.5	8.3	5.0	7.4	17.2	14.1
Carbon County, MT	360	343	326	35,892	32,877	10.3	125	1.7	7.7	3.1	5.8	8.3	25.4
Yellowstone County, MT	5,949	5,623	4,637	39,640	33,690	28.3	4,504	6.6	8.3	5.1	7.4	17.4	13.8
Binghamton, NY	9,000	8,687	6,973	35,990	27,662	29.1	5,893	18.8	7.0	3.7	4.6	15.1	22.7
Broome County, NY	7,158	6,913	5,553	35,963	27,701	28.9	5,014	14.4	7.2	4.1	5.1	16.9	23.6
Tioga County, NY	1,842	1,774	1,420	36,097	27,508	29.8	878	44.2	5.9	1.6	2.1	5.3	17.5
Birmingham–Hoover, AL	46,215	44,156	39,199	40,816	36,084	17.9	33,472	7.3	6.2	8.7	8.8	12.7	15.5
Bibb County, AL	550	535	453	24,180	20,538	21.6	236	7.4	6.8	1.6	1.4	(D)	29.9
Blount County, AL	1,570	1,524	1,309	27,220	23,959	20.0	447	12.8	9.6	2.6	3.8	(D)	24.7
Chilton County, AL	1,266	1,209	995	28,844	23,716	27.3	429	15.5	11.1	2.8	1.7	(D)	22.9
Jefferson County, AL	29,042	27,821	25,733	44,074	39,291	12.9	25,847	6.8	5.5	8.4	9.4	14.3	15.8
St. Clair County, AL	2,721	2,571	1,958	32,240	26,969	39.0	835	15.9	9.5	3.0	3.3	7.9	19.9
Shelby County, AL	8,855	8,340	6,871	44,734	40,017	28.9	4,673	7.0	7.4	14.2	9.1	7.1	10.3
Walker County, AL	2,211	2,156	1,881	33,167	27,464	17.5	1,004	9.0	11.9	3.3	4.2	16.2	17.8
Bismarck, ND	4,709	4,363	3,326	42,468	33,273	41.6	3,591	3.4	7.5	5.2	6.6	16.6	21.1
Burleigh County, ND	3,636	3,390	2,605	43,731	35,025	39.6	3,006	1.7	7.5	5.5	6.7	19.8	22.3
Morton County, ND	1,073	973	721	38,680	28,177	48.9	584	12.4	7.2	3.7	6.3	(D)	14.5
Blacksburg–Christiansburg–Radford, VA[3]	4,831	4,586	3,847	29,733	24,596	25.6	3,446	21.3	6.4	1.7	0.0	(D)	32.8
Giles County, VA	516	493	420	30,123	24,752	22.9	267	31.9	7.7	1.8	7.5	(D)	14.8
Montgomery County, VA[3]	3,175	3,010	2,426	28,668	23,177	30.9	2,553	15.8	6.0	1.8	0.0	(D)	38.2
Pulaski County, VA	1,140	1,082	1,001	32,947	28,794	14.0	626	39.0	7.8	1.3	1.9	(D)	18.4
Radford city, VA[3]	NA	NA	NA	NA	NA	NA	NA	NA	NA	NA	NA	NA	NA
Bloomington, IN	6,004	5,743	4,809	30,915	26,217	24.8	3,978	14.3	5.9	2.1	4.6	12.9	32.0
Greene County, IN	1,022	995	859	31,059	25,777	19.0	339	6.2	8.6	3.1	6.0	(D)	28.6
Monroe County, IN	4,337	4,114	3,385	31,021	26,417	28.1	3,370	12.4	5.8	2.0	4.8	14.7	33.8
Owen County, IN	645	635	565	30,009	25,721	14.1	268	48.2	4.6	2.3	1.3	6.9	14.2
Bloomington–Normal, IL	7,132	6,798	5,377	41,816	33,544	32.6	6,195	4.3	4.8	21.2	0.0	10.0	14.2
McLean County, IL	7,132	6,798	5,377	41,816	33,544	32.6	6,195	4.3	4.8	21.2	0.0	10.0	14.2
Boise City–Nampa, ID	21,512	20,560	17,985	34,274	32,881	19.6	16,178	11.7	7.5	6.3	8.4	12.9	15.7
Ada County, ID	15,927	15,201	13,616	39,734	39,042	17.0	13,173	11.2	7.3	7.2	9.6	13.7	15.2
Boise County, ID	257	245	200	36,633	28,700	28.4	63	1.2	4.4	(D)	(D)	3.1	41.5
Canyon County, ID	4,519	4,336	3,528	23,575	21,516	28.1	2,593	15.5	9.2	2.6	3.7	11.0	16.9
Gem County, ID	448	443	375	26,895	22,987	19.6	150	5.0	7.3	2.4	2.7	(D)	26.3
Owyhee County, ID	361	335	266	31,541	24,224	35.5	199	3.9	3.2	(D)	(D)	(D)	15.2
Boston–Cambridge–Quincy, MA–NH	265,794	252,553	212,251	57,893	48,042	25.2	220,095	8.8	4.3	12.5	16.5	12.4	10.5
Boston–Quincy, MA	111,030	105,513	88,245	58,316	48,368	25.8	104,537	3.8	3.8	20.2	14.7	15.0	11.2
Norfolk County, MA	45,123	42,880	35,776	66,806	54,911	26.1	27,102	7.8	6.3	15.5	11.5	12.7	9.0
Plymouth County, MA	25,360	24,106	20,168	50,968	41,473	25.7	12,243	6.6	8.0	6.0	8.7	14.4	18.0
Suffolk County, MA	40,546	38,527	32,300	55,472	47,044	25.5	65,193	1.6	2.0	24.8	17.2	16.0	10.9
Cambridge–Newton–Framingham, MA	94,619	89,856	75,718	62,324	52,045	25.0	80,292	11.9	3.6	5.2	21.9	8.6	8.8
Middlesex County, MA	94,619	89,856	75,718	62,324	52,045	25.0	80,292	11.9	3.6	5.2	21.9	8.6	8.8
Peabody, MA	39,850	37,833	31,612	53,209	43,370	26.1	22,235	20.0	6.5	5.2	9.9	15.5	12.4
Essex County, MA	39,850	37,833	31,612	53,209	43,370	26.1	22,235	20.0	6.5	5.2	9.9	15.5	12.4
Rockingham County–Strafford County, NH	20,295	19,352	16,676	48,315	40,687	21.7	13,030	11.2	9.5	7.9	8.8	10.6	12.5
Rockingham County, NH	15,658	14,917	12,920	52,861	44,371	21.2	9,969	10.7	10.0	6.4	9.9	9.6	9.5
Strafford County, NH	4,637	4,435	3,756	37,442	31,648	23.5	3,061	12.8	7.6	12.9	5.0	13.8	22.0
Boulder, CO[4]	15,536	14,768	13,289	51,893	47,419	16.9	12,907	12.5	4.8	4.5	21.6	9.4	15.2
Boulder County, CO[4]	15,536	14,768	13,289	51,893	47,419	16.9	12,907	12.5	4.8	4.5	21.6	9.4	15.2
Bowling Green, KY	4,010	3,813	3,121	31,422	27,351	28.5	2,996	16.9	7.2	4.3	3.5	13.5	18.6
Edmonson County, KY	310	296	238	25,668	19,859	30.4	78	(D)	5.9	(D)	1.1	(D)	51.7
Warren County, KY	3,699	3,517	2,883	32,025	28,231	28.3	2,918	17.4	7.3	4.5	3.5	13.9	17.8
Bremerton–Silverdale, WA	10,842	10,355	8,905	42,580	37,133	21.8	6,708	1.6	6.0	2.2	5.9	9.9	56.2
Kitsap County, WA	10,842	10,355	8,905	42,580	37,133	21.8	6,708	1.6	6.0	2.2	5.9	9.9	56.2
Bridgeport–Stamford–Norwalk, CT	72,687	69,692	61,073	78,504	68,036	19.0	52,411	9.7	5.2	25.4	10.5	8.4	7.1
Fairfield County, CT	72,687	69,692	61,073	78,504	68,036	19.0	52,411	9.7	5.2	25.4	10.5	8.4	7.1
Brownsville–Harlingen, TX	9,623	9,202	6,872	23,236	18,403	40.0	5,902	5.2	8.8	3.3	2.7	20.7	29.6
Cameron County, TX	9,623	9,202	6,872	23,236	18,403	40.0	5,902	5.2	8.8	3.3	2.7	20.7	29.6

[1] Based on resident population estimated as of July 1.
[2] Includes other industry categories not shown separately.
[3] Radford city included with Montgomery County, VA, in the Blacksburg–Christiansburg–Radford, VA MSA.
[4] The Denver–Aurora metropolitan statistical area includes Broomfield County. Broomfield County, CO, was formed from parts of Adams, Boulder, Jefferson, and Weld Counties on November 15, 2001, and is coextensive with Broomfield city. For the purposes of defining and presenting data for the Denver–Aurora metropolitan statistical area, Broomfield city is treated as if it were a county when data are available to do so. In many cases, the data were not available.
(D) = Data withheld to avoid disclosure or does not meet statistical standards.

Table C-3. Personal Income and Earnings, by Industry—*Continued*

Metropolitan statistical area, division, and component county	Personal income Total (million dollars) 2011	2010	2005	Per capita[1] (dollars) 2011	2005	Percent change, 2005–2011	Earnings, 2011 Total[2] (million dollars)	Manufacturing	Retail trade	Finance and insurance	Professional and technical services	Health care and social services	Government and government enterprises
Brunswick, GA	3,693	3,550	3,155	32,708	31,078	17.1	2,146	8.3	7.8	3.0	3.7	8.6	33.8
Brantley County, GA	421	405	333	22,900	20,142	26.3	102	5.3	5.3	1.4	(D)	4.4	38.3
Glynn County, GA	2,944	2,827	2,570	36,619	35,407	14.5	1,952	8.8	7.9	3.1	3.9	9.2	33.4
McIntosh County, GA	329	318	252	23,235	20,326	30.5	93	1.1	8.8	1.6	2.5	1.2	36.2
Buffalo–Niagara Falls, NY	45,499	43,571	36,232	40,121	31,546	25.6	31,644	12.8	6.5	6.3	7.7	13.3	20.2
Erie County, NY	37,864	36,286	30,145	41,245	32,354	25.6	27,864	12.2	6.3	6.9	8.2	13.4	19.4
Niagara County, NY	7,635	7,285	6,087	35,345	28,074	25.4	3,781	17.2	8.1	2.0	3.9	13.1	26.2
Burlington, NC	4,808	4,590	3,968	31,363	28,483	21.2	2,980	16.6	7.9	4.3	3.9	16.4	11.7
Alamance County, NC	4,808	4,590	3,968	31,363	28,483	21.2	2,980	16.6	7.9	4.3	3.9	16.4	11.7
Burlington–South Burlington, VT	9,320	8,875	7,366	43,853	35,648	26.5	7,527	14.4	7.7	4.7	9.8	14.4	19.0
Chittenden County, VT	7,042	6,729	5,687	44,715	37,375	23.8	6,401	14.1	7.3	5.2	11.4	14.9	17.7
Franklin County, VT	1,977	1,847	1,440	41,088	30,513	37.3	1,053	17.0	9.6	1.6	(D)	11.9	26.7
Grand Isle County, VT	301	299	239	43,433	32,842	25.9	72	(D)	8.6	1.1	7.5	(D)	21.4
Canton–Massillon, OH	14,030	13,261	12,094	34,739	29,849	16.0	8,883	20.6	7.9	4.5	4.0	16.7	13.1
Carroll County, OH	778	756	722	27,044	24,800	7.8	335	20.0	10.2	1.8	2.1	0.0	14.8
Stark County, OH	13,252	12,506	11,372	35,330	30,240	16.5	8,548	20.6	7.8	4.6	4.1	17.3	13.1
Cape Coral–Fort Myers, FL	27,161	25,779	21,184	43,022	38,167	28.2	12,027	2.8	10.1	4.2	8.3	12.2	20.6
Lee County, FL	27,161	25,779	21,184	43,022	38,167	28.2	12,027	2.8	10.1	4.2	8.3	12.2	20.6
Cape Girardeau–Jackson, MO–IL	3,290	3,171	2,593	33,907	27,832	26.9	2,383	10.8	8.2	3.5	3.3	25.7	15.2
Alexander County, IL	217	214	174	26,943	19,533	24.4	97	7.0	3.3	1.2	0.8	(D)	35.7
Bollinger County, MO	330	327	273	26,746	21,916	21.0	96	5.6	9.5	(D)	2.7	10.0	22.2
Cape Girardeau County, MO	2,743	2,630	2,146	35,792	29,890	27.8	2,190	11.2	8.4	3.7	3.4	27.5	14.0
Carson City, NV	2,208	2,150	2,168	39,833	38,718	1.9	1,837	9.3	6.6	6.6	4.9	15.3	36.0
Carson City, NV	2,208	2,150	2,168	39,833	38,718	1.9	1,837	9.3	6.6	6.6	4.9	15.3	36.0
Casper, WY	4,132	3,837	2,997	54,108	42,864	37.9	2,984	4.4	6.4	2.9	4.7	13.1	13.1
Natrona County, WY	4,132	3,837	2,997	54,108	42,864	37.9	2,984	4.4	6.4	2.9	4.7	13.1	13.1
Cedar Rapids, IA	11,075	10,356	8,316	42,503	33,633	33.2	8,834	22.0	7.5	7.2	4.6	9.7	11.0
Benton County, IA	1,107	1,009	798	42,432	30,372	38.8	444	10.7	7.1	3.3	2.2	(D)	17.8
Jones County, IA	691	630	505	33,518	24,530	36.7	373	12.0	9.3	2.9	2.4	(D)	19.4
Linn County, IA	9,277	8,717	7,013	43,378	34,996	32.3	8,017	23.0	7.5	7.7	4.9	10.7	10.3
Champaign–Urbana, IL	8,654	8,371	6,478	37,246	29,261	33.6	6,417	7.2	5.1	3.1	5.7	12.0	36.0
Champaign County, IL	7,223	7,024	5,448	35,815	28,576	32.6	5,783	7.3	5.0	3.1	6.2	12.8	38.4
Ford County, IL	622	589	464	44,484	32,904	34.1	373	8.3	8.2	1.9	1.5	(D)	11.8
Piatt County, IL	808	759	566	48,481	34,022	42.7	262	3.8	4.8	4.2	2.8	9.6	17.4
Charleston, WV	11,949	11,378	9,492	39,348	31,140	25.9	9,293	5.1	5.7	4.7	8.0	14.2	17.9
Boone County, WV	707	682	558	28,912	22,044	26.7	702	0.3	3.5	0.8	0.0	2.8	13.3
Clay County, WV	222	213	174	23,708	17,708	27.2	116	2.9	4.2	0.0	0.4	7.8	24.2
Kanawha County, WV	8,213	7,836	6,727	42,704	34,698	22.1	6,958	4.5	6.0	5.6	9.5	17.1	19.4
Lincoln County, WV	533	519	425	24,722	19,181	25.3	191	0.3	4.6	1.0	2.4	(D)	27.1
Putnam County, WV	2,275	2,127	1,607	40,617	29,978	41.5	1,327	11.5	6.0	2.6	5.5	7.9	10.9
Charleston–North Charleston–Summerville, SC	25,706	24,141	19,124	37,685	31,964	34.4	19,424	10.0	6.9	5.7	9.8	9.5	26.5
Berkeley County, SC	6,090	5,685	4,182	33,184	27,249	45.6	2,866	17.6	6.0	3.9	16.8	3.9	18.9
Charleston County, SC	14,900	14,158	11,915	41,656	35,934	25.1	15,129	7.6	6.8	6.3	9.1	10.6	28.4
Dorchester County, SC	4,715	4,298	3,026	33,468	26,728	55.8	1,428	20.7	10.2	2.5	4.3	8.1	21.7
Charlotte–Gastonia–Rock Hill, NC–SC	72,220	67,899	57,216	40,223	37,678	26.2	61,192	8.7	6.2	13.6	9.0	7.6	11.9
Anson County, NC	650	653	630	24,417	23,695	3.1	388	18.7	5.8	2.2	(D)	(D)	30.6
Cabarrus County, NC	6,453	6,155	4,932	35,561	32,705	30.8	3,350	9.1	10.4	3.4	5.8	7.8	21.3
Gaston County, NC	6,889	6,655	6,009	33,275	31,051	14.6	3,548	20.8	8.7	3.2	3.5	17.6	14.7
Mecklenburg County, NC	43,073	40,142	34,798	45,610	43,569	23.8	46,478	6.2	5.3	16.4	10.3	6.9	10.3
Union County, NC	7,305	6,857	4,988	35,552	31,013	46.4	2,966	20.3	7.9	3.3	4.5	5.0	17.6
York County, SC	7,850	7,436	5,859	34,053	31,146	34.0	4,461	15.8	9.7	8.1	5.7	9.5	14.8
Charlottesville, VA[5]	9,042	8,552	7,020	44,350	37,225	28.8	6,623	3.7	5.4	4.4	10.7	9.9	34.4
Albemarle County, VA[5]	6,779	6,421	5,322	47,052	40,239	27.4	6,032	3.7	5.2	4.6	10.8	10.7	35.2
Fluvanna County, VA	951	894	698	36,507	28,705	36.3	232	1.8	4.0	1.6	4.0	(D)	32.0
Greene County, VA	710	666	529	38,073	30,822	34.4	192	2.7	11.0	1.2	18.1	(D)	23.2
Nelson County, VA	602	571	470	39,862	31,719	28.0	166	6.4	4.9	2.3	7.3	7.7	21.6
Charlottesville city, VA[5]	NA	NA	NA	NA	NA	NA	NA	NA	NA	NA	NA	NA	NA
Chattanooga, TN–GA	19,236	18,355	15,671	36,066	31,369	22.8	13,990	14.0	7.8	9.0	5.9	11.6	17.4
Catoosa County, GA	1,916	1,817	1,545	29,685	25,862	24.0	723	9.4	12.2	2.8	2.6	15.1	19.1
Dade County, GA	446	430	387	26,906	23,924	15.1	156	18.6	7.8	3.4	3.3	6.2	18.4
Walker County, GA	1,876	1,800	1,551	27,250	23,796	21.0	621	31.0	7.0	4.1	(D)	6.3	25.9
Hamilton County, TN	13,637	13,007	11,150	40,007	35,073	22.3	12,024	13.2	7.5	9.9	6.7	12.1	16.8
Marion County, TN	906	873	727	32,107	26,211	24.6	358	23.5	10.6	3.5	(D)	(D)	16.5
Sequatchie County, TN	456	428	311	31,791	24,233	46.8	109	3.1	11.5	5.8	(D)	8.2	26.4

[1] Based on resident population estimated as of July 1.
[2] Includes other industry categories not shown separately.
[3]Radford city included with Montgomery County, VA, in the Blacksburg–Christiansburg–Radford, VA MSA.
[5] Charlottesville city included with Albemarle County, VA, in the Charlottesville, VA MSA.
(D) = Data withheld to avoid disclosure or does not meet statistical standards.
NA = Not available

Table C-3.   Personal Income and Earnings, by Industry—*Continued*

Metropolitan statistical area, division, and component county	Total (million dollars) 2011	Total (million dollars) 2010	Total (million dollars) 2005	Per capita[1] (dollars) 2011	Per capita[1] (dollars) 2005	Percent change, 2005–2011	Total[2] (million dollars)	Manufacturing	Retail trade	Finance and insurance	Professional and technical services	Health care and social services	Government and government enterprises
Cheyenne, WY	4,345	4,080	3,208	46,882	37,420	35.4	3,120	4.4	6.8	4.2	4.4	8.3	41.2
Laramie County, WY	4,345	4,080	3,208	46,882	37,420	35.4	3,120	4.4	6.8	4.2	4.4	8.3	41.2
Chicago–Joliet–Naperville, IL–IN–WI	436,998	419,999	375,515	45,977	40,481	16.4	340,490	10.9	5.0	9.8	12.5	9.7	12.9
Chicago–Joliet–Naperville, IL	365,651	351,607	314,133	46,153	40,586	16.4	291,401	9.3	4.7	10.6	13.4	9.7	12.6
Cook County, IL	244,872	236,610	213,634	46,937	41,023	14.6	209,873	7.9	4.1	12.4	14.8	9.7	12.8
DeKalb County, IL	3,311	3,129	2,724	31,612	27,671	21.6	2,155	11.8	7.1	2.7	2.3	12.1	33.5
DuPage County, IL	50,324	48,464	45,749	54,509	50,197	10.0	46,214	9.7	5.6	7.5	13.1	8.5	7.9
Grundy County, IL	1,746	1,661	1,357	34,829	30,715	28.7	1,280	10.8	5.5	1.9	(D)	8.7	11.4
Kane County, IL	19,403	18,461	15,935	37,293	33,520	21.8	12,364	18.2	6.2	4.8	7.7	11.6	17.1
Kendall County, IL	4,450	4,075	2,489	38,151	30,685	78.8	1,424	23.5	9.0	2.5	4.3	5.8	20.7
McHenry County, IL	12,608	11,976	10,912	40,811	37,081	15.5	5,487	20.2	7.7	3.0	4.5	11.3	16.3
Will County, IL	28,938	27,231	21,333	42,459	33,992	35.6	12,604	13.5	8.4	3.5	4.6	10.5	17.2
Gary, IN	26,058	24,878	21,677	36,770	31,334	20.2	16,441	21.7	7.2	2.3	3.7	13.9	12.4
Jasper County, IN	1,203	1,119	919	36,012	28,947	30.9	697	13.6	6.6	2.0	1.9	5.7	13.9
Lake County, IN	17,269	16,618	14,743	34,847	30,116	17.1	12,168	21.7	7.4	2.3	3.5	15.1	12.5
Newton County, IN	468	430	380	33,054	26,265	23.0	229	15.1	3.0	2.9	1.6	(D)	16.6
Porter County, IN	7,118	6,712	5,635	42,999	36,113	26.3	3,346	24.1	6.5	2.4	4.7	12.2	11.5
Lake County–Kenosha County, IL–WI	45,289	43,514	39,705	51,847	47,016	14.1	32,648	20.1	6.9	6.3	8.5	8.0	15.4
Lake County, IL	39,306	37,785	34,704	55,656	50,705	13.3	29,548	20.6	6.9	6.7	8.9	7.3	15.0
Kenosha County, WI	5,983	5,729	5,001	35,766	31,242	19.6	3,101	15.0	7.3	2.1	3.9	14.4	18.9
Chico, CA	7,347	7,047	6,011	33,356	27,990	22.2	4,189	4.9	9.1	3.3	5.3	19.2	21.3
Butte County, CA	7,347	7,047	6,011	33,356	27,990	22.2	4,189	4.9	9.1	3.3	5.3	19.2	21.3
Cincinnati–Middletown, OH–KY–IN	87,485	83,388	75,148	40,918	36,294	16.4	65,650	13.0	5.6	7.1	8.2	12.0	12.5
Dearborn County, IN	1,773	1,702	1,522	35,376	31,426	16.5	849	13.7	8.0	2.5	2.8	7.1	20.2
Franklin County, IN	842	799	669	36,561	29,027	25.9	210	15.8	9.3	3.9	2.9	(D)	23.1
OH County, IN	220	209	156	36,241	26,261	40.8	72	(D)	2.4	(D)	1.6	4.1	23.4
Boone County, KY	4,346	4,073	3,378	35,704	32,033	28.7	4,289	17.0	6.5	4.1	3.7	5.9	9.7
Bracken County, KY	260	248	212	30,499	24,864	22.4	68	(D)	4.8	2.9	3.0	5.8	28.6
Campbell County, KY	3,413	3,256	2,817	37,531	31,990	21.2	1,477	12.2	7.9	2.5	6.0	11.7	25.4
Gallatin County, KY	229	222	193	26,547	23,458	18.5	126	(D)	5.1	(D)	1.4	(D)	17.8
Grant County, KY	738	704	588	29,743	24,496	25.6	235	13.1	13.4	2.9	3.0	(D)	26.3
Kenton County, KY	6,451	6,138	5,545	40,219	36,063	16.3	4,017	8.2	4.8	8.0	7.8	15.7	19.1
Pendleton County, KY	411	399	334	27,961	22,469	22.9	116	15.2	4.9	2.1	0.0	(D)	28.8
Brown County, OH	1,363	1,298	1,162	30,492	26,305	17.3	524	7.3	7.0	1.8	3.0	(D)	21.5
Butler County, OH	13,538	12,960	11,491	36,590	32,764	17.8	8,910	17.8	7.2	8.1	3.2	10.9	13.8
Clermont County, OH	7,177	6,872	6,358	36,038	33,556	12.9	3,347	11.2	9.4	8.8	6.7	9.2	13.8
Hamilton County, OH	37,522	35,888	33,873	46,881	41,801	10.8	36,885	11.8	4.3	7.2	10.7	13.9	10.5
Warren County, OH	9,202	8,620	6,850	42,818	35,036	34.3	4,526	16.4	7.9	9.5	6.5	7.5	12.7
Clarksville, TN–KY	11,015	10,022	7,569	39,666	30,219	45.5	8,736	7.8	4.2	1.4	3.4	5.2	60.7
Christian County, KY	2,359	2,258	2,067	32,061	28,354	14.2	5,783	4.6	1.7	0.6	2.5	2.6	79.7
Trigg County, KY	534	499	419	37,352	30,746	27.6	165	10.4	7.6	2.4	11.8	(D)	24.9
Montgomery County, TN	7,680	6,849	4,770	43,485	31,566	61.0	2,594	14.4	9.7	3.0	5.3	11.1	21.3
Stewart County, TN	441	415	313	33,477	24,390	40.9	195	12.7	4.5	1.3	0.0	5.0	49.5
Cleveland, TN	3,630	3,448	2,996	31,073	27,382	21.2	2,331	23.2	7.5	3.3	3.0	(D)	12.8
Bradley County, TN	3,170	3,001	2,607	31,687	28,029	21.6	2,216	24.1	7.4	3.5	3.1	(D)	11.6
Polk County, TN	460	446	388	27,412	23,708	18.4	115	7.4	10.3	(D)	1.5	(D)	36.4
Cleveland–Elyria–Mentor, OH	87,622	83,241	76,110	42,365	36,042	15.1	67,582	15.2	5.3	6.9	9.1	13.6	14.1
Cuyahoga County, OH	55,556	52,989	49,520	43,735	37,216	12.2	51,130	11.9	4.5	8.2	10.6	14.6	13.9
Geauga County, OH	4,770	4,506	4,080	51,165	43,578	16.9	1,932	23.7	7.8	3.0	4.8	9.5	12.4
Lake County, OH	9,276	8,800	7,926	40,351	34,819	17.0	5,734	31.1	7.2	2.4	4.5	10.1	12.6
Lorain County, OH	10,943	10,304	8,858	36,283	30,041	23.5	5,559	24.6	7.9	2.6	3.4	12.1	18.5
Medina County, OH	7,077	6,642	5,726	40,843	34,712	23.6	3,227	17.4	9.0	2.6	5.7	9.8	13.0
Coeur d'Alene, ID	4,647	4,412	3,638	32,923	28,880	27.7	2,704	8.5	10.6	5.0	6.9	12.1	20.9
Kootenai County, ID	4,647	4,412	3,638	32,923	28,880	27.7	2,704	8.5	10.6	5.0	6.9	12.1	20.9
College Station–Bryan, TX	6,932	6,628	4,806	29,928	23,616	44.2	4,937	5.9	7.7	2.5	5.8	10.4	35.7
Brazos County, TX	5,740	5,484	3,931	29,045	23,146	46.0	4,381	5.9	7.4	2.4	6.3	11.4	38.2
Burleson County, TX	592	575	447	34,291	26,010	32.5	276	5.5	13.0	2.7	2.8	(D)	14.6
Robertson County, TX	600	569	429	35,859	25,960	40.1	280	7.0	6.1	4.1	1.9	4.7	18.0
Colorado Springs, CO	26,409	24,722	20,148	39,994	34,278	31.1	19,948	4.8	5.8	4.6	11.1	7.9	38.7
El Paso County, CO	25,421	23,779	19,389	39,909	34,269	31.1	19,598	4.9	5.8	4.7	11.1	8.0	39.1
Teller County, CO	988	944	759	42,297	34,522	30.2	350	0.9	8.0	2.8	9.3	5.2	18.5
Columbia, MO	6,567	6,218	5,031	37,350	31,665	30.5	4,987	4.3	7.6	6.2	5.4	11.2	37.5
Boone County, MO	6,196	5,871	4,756	37,409	31,963	30.3	4,862	4.1	7.6	6.4	5.4	11.5	38.1
Howard County, MO	371	347	275	36,385	27,257	35.0	125	11.5	7.0	(D)	2.5	(D)	17.2
Columbia, SC	27,471	26,334	21,991	35,350	31,454	24.9	20,896	8.9	6.5	7.1	7.4	9.6	28.2
Calhoun County, SC	521	501	457	34,431	30,064	14.0	279	32.3	3.2	1.7	2.2	(D)	13.7
Fairfield County, SC	638	638	581	27,062	24,073	9.8	461	19.9	3.8	0.6	8.5	5.8	17.7
Kershaw County, SC	2,076	1,992	1,653	33,331	29,253	25.6	934	22.2	9.8	6.7	3.5	6.4	20.2
Lexington County, SC	9,406	9,040	7,670	35,211	32,615	22.6	5,504	11.5	9.3	4.4	6.2	8.2	20.4
Richland County, SC	14,143	13,506	11,117	36,347	31,855	27.2	13,523	5.7	5.3	8.7	8.4	10.8	32.7
Saluda County, SC	687	657	512	34,544	26,772	34.1	194	36.8	5.2	3.4	1.2	3.8	24.4

[1] Based on resident population estimated as of July 1.
[2] Includes other industry categories not shown separately.
(D) = Data withheld to avoid disclosure or does not meet statistical standards.

Table C-3.   Personal Income and Earnings, by Industry—_Continued_

Metropolitan statistical area, division, and component county	Personal income												
	Total (million dollars)			Per capita[1] (dollars)		Percent change, 2005–2011	Earnings, 2011						
							Total[2] (million dollars)	Percentage by selected major industries					
	2011	2010	2005	2011	2005			Manufacturing	Retail trade	Finance and insurance	Professional and technical services	Health care and social services	Government and government enterprises
Columbus, GA–AL	11,651	10,827	8,950	38,653	31,254	30.2	8,889	7.1	4.8	9.1	5.1	9.2	43.9
Russell County, AL	1,742	1,627	1,221	31,920	24,550	42.7	648	26.8	10.0	3.5	1.8	8.8	22.2
Chattahoochee County, GA	401	378	336	34,166	23,847	19.4	2,006	(D)	0.2	(D)	3.1	(D)	93.3
Harris County, GA	1,585	1,455	1,024	49,114	36,352	54.7	274	4.8	4.2	6.8	(D)	(D)	20.9
Marion County, GA	235	222	191	26,821	24,389	23.0	69	27.9	6.5	(D)	0.6	5.0	26.4
Muscogee County, GA	7,689	7,144	6,178	39,611	33,119	24.5	5,892	7.2	5.7	13.0	6.5	12.9	30.7
Columbus, IN	3,087	2,847	2,428	39,645	32,956	27.2	2,903	44.3	4.7	4.2	3.8	7.0	11.3
Bartholomew County, IN	3,087	2,847	2,428	39,645	32,956	27.2	2,903	44.3	4.7	4.2	3.8	7.0	11.3
Columbus, OH	74,688	70,531	60,968	40,188	35,307	22.5	61,030	8.5	6.3	8.4	11.1	10.6	17.5
Delaware County, OH	10,428	9,556	6,238	58,470	41,821	67.2	5,482	7.5	6.8	10.8	28.2	6.9	8.9
Fairfield County, OH	4,937	4,728	4,284	33,569	30,875	15.2	2,150	13.5	8.9	2.3	4.0	16.3	18.3
Franklin County, OH	46,735	44,564	40,713	39,646	36,828	14.8	46,418	6.1	5.9	9.1	10.6	11.3	18.5
Licking County, OH	6,270	5,781	4,846	37,491	30,679	29.4	2,882	12.8	11.3	6.7	6.0	11.5	17.0
Madison County, OH	1,533	1,436	1,239	35,311	30,008	23.7	908	20.9	7.5	1.2	4.7	0.0	21.1
Morrow County, OH	1,068	997	869	30,646	25,356	22.9	332	14.5	6.4	1.5	(D)	(D)	24.8
Pickaway County, OH	1,826	1,704	1,385	32,617	26,161	31.8	907	21.0	5.7	1.8	(D)	8.9	27.5
Union County, OH	1,892	1,764	1,394	35,851	29,684	35.7	1,950	43.6	3.7	1.2	(D)	3.3	10.6
Corpus Christi, TX	16,655	15,693	12,201	38,609	29,307	36.5	12,028	8.2	6.1	2.8	5.0	12.2	21.2
Aransas County, TX	994	936	726	42,512	30,813	36.9	304	0.9	13.7	4.3	5.5	(D)	17.5
Nueces County, TX	13,196	12,439	9,712	38,441	29,835	35.9	10,486	7.9	5.9	2.9	5.2	13.5	20.7
San Patricio County, TX	2,465	2,319	1,763	38,087	26,226	39.8	1,238	12.8	5.5	1.5	3.1	4.3	26.3
Corvallis, OR	3,323	3,182	2,707	38,677	33,444	22.8	2,341	14.1	4.8	1.9	7.4	15.1	30.2
Benton County, OR	3,323	3,182	2,707	38,677	33,444	22.8	2,341	14.1	4.8	1.9	7.4	15.1	30.2
Crestview–Fort Walton Beach–Destin, FL	7,914	7,433	6,661	43,132	36,190	18.8	6,216	4.0	6.0	3.1	9.3	6.8	47.3
Okaloosa County, FL	7,914	7,433	6,661	43,132	36,190	18.8	6,216	4.0	6.0	3.1	9.3	6.8	47.3
Cumberland, MD–WV	3,349	3,216	2,584	32,547	25,539	29.6	2,029	14.4	7.3	2.3	(D)	17.0	25.3
Allegany County, MD	2,454	2,352	1,896	32,855	25,633	29.4	1,604	9.3	7.2	2.6	(D)	21.5	26.5
Mineral County, WV	895	863	688	31,733	25,283	30.1	425	33.6	7.6	1.3	2.0	(D)	20.7
Dallas–Fort Worth–Arlington, TX	285,260	268,492	220,482	43,708	38,494	29.4	237,126	10.1	5.7	8.9	10.5	9.7	10.9
Dallas–Plano–Irving, TX	197,316	185,682	154,614	45,404	40,501	27.6	174,608	9.2	5.4	9.9	11.8	9.6	10.1
Collin County, TX	42,576	39,133	29,603	52,419	45,741	43.8	25,867	8.6	6.9	9.5	11.0	9.8	9.2
Dallas County, TX	109,692	104,548	94,240	45,402	41,869	16.4	130,542	8.6	4.7	10.8	12.5	9.5	9.2
Delta County, TX	163	147	112	31,187	21,092	45.0	60	(D)	2.0	2.0	0.0	18.5	23.6
Denton County, TX	29,084	27,035	19,889	42,371	35,922	46.2	11,366	9.0	8.1	5.3	9.2	10.2	17.8
Ellis County, TX	5,329	5,020	3,723	34,885	28,646	43.1	2,220	25.5	8.1	2.3	2.8	7.2	16.3
Hunt County, TX	2,746	2,638	2,227	31,736	26,888	23.3	1,753	37.3	7.5	2.3	3.4	7.7	20.0
Kaufman County, TX	3,572	3,356	2,435	33,901	27,864	46.7	1,512	13.9	8.2	3.2	4.0	7.2	21.3
Rockwall County, TX	4,155	3,804	2,386	51,116	39,534	74.2	1,289	6.2	9.5	4.6	8.7	16.5	15.1
Fort Worth–Arlington, TX	87,944	82,809	65,868	40,327	34,481	33.5	62,518	12.8	6.7	6.2	6.9	9.9	12.9
Johnson County, TX	5,081	4,871	3,918	33,269	27,846	29.7	2,465	14.0	7.7	2.4	3.2	8.1	15.3
Parker County, TX	4,962	4,382	3,187	41,914	31,282	55.7	1,895	7.0	9.6	2.6	5.3	8.5	13.9
Tarrant County, TX	75,777	71,524	57,180	40,965	35,471	32.5	56,770	13.0	6.5	6.6	7.2	10.1	12.8
Wise County, TX	2,124	2,032	1,582	35,494	28,455	34.2	1,389	7.9	7.4	2.0	2.5	6.8	13.3
Dalton, GA	3,890	3,766	3,571	27,249	26,674	8.9	3,334	36.9	7.4	1.6	7.2	(D)	11.1
Murray County, GA	996	976	943	25,177	23,744	5.6	456	44.2	7.0	2.4	(D)	(D)	17.4
Whitfield County, GA	2,894	2,790	2,628	28,044	27,910	10.1	2,878	35.7	7.4	1.4	8.3	8.5	10.1
Danville, IL	2,659	2,544	2,128	32,619	25,726	24.9	1,751	20.9	5.8	3.7	(D)	9.2	22.1
Vermilion County, IL	2,659	2,544	2,128	32,619	25,726	24.9	1,751	20.9	5.8	3.7	(D)	9.2	22.1
Danville, VA[6]	3,308	3,178	2,888	31,297	26,855	14.5	1,865	23.4	8.3	2.3	2.4	13.8	18.6
Pittsylvania County, VA[6]	3,308	3,178	2,888	31,297	26,855	14.5	1,865	23.4	8.3	2.3	2.4	13.8	18.6
Danville city, VA[6]	NA	NA	NA	NA	NA	NA	NA	NA	NA	NA	NA	NA	NA
Davenport–Moline–Rock Island, IA–IL	16,070	15,201	12,304	42,141	32,997	30.6	11,824	15.1	6.6	4.4	6.1	10.6	17.4
Henry County, IL	1,882	1,772	1,484	37,404	29,336	26.9	790	11.7	7.5	5.0	2.2	6.2	20.7
Mercer County, IL	665	619	493	40,639	29,507	35.0	222	13.0	5.2	3.1	1.2	3.5	25.8
Rock Island County, IL	5,774	5,565	4,652	39,132	31,630	24.1	5,770	14.0	4.6	4.7	4.4	9.1	22.7
Scott County, IA	7,749	7,244	5,676	46,372	35,800	36.5	5,041	16.9	8.9	4.0	8.9	13.3	10.4
Dayton, OH	31,626	30,092	27,069	37,410	31,945	16.8	23,404	12.1	5.5	4.0	8.3	14.4	24.6
Greene County, OH	6,162	5,844	5,063	37,842	32,407	21.7	5,487	4.6	5.5	1.7	14.4	5.5	50.2
Miami County, OH	3,808	3,593	3,136	37,021	30,877	21.4	2,114	30.3	7.2	2.2	(D)	9.9	13.5
Montgomery County, OH	20,259	19,348	17,718	37,684	32,392	14.3	15,251	11.7	5.2	5.1	7.5	18.7	17.2
Preble County, OH	1,397	1,308	1,152	33,188	27,051	21.2	552	30.7	7.0	2.2	(D)	(D)	17.5
Decatur, AL	4,941	4,806	4,186	32,071	28,208	18.0	3,045	32.5	7.1	2.9	3.0	(D)	15.7
Lawrence County, AL	994	971	833	29,144	24,200	19.3	412	31.4	7.3	1.9	1.6	(D)	19.0
Morgan County, AL	3,947	3,834	3,353	32,904	29,420	17.7	2,633	32.7	7.0	3.1	3.2	8.0	15.2
Decatur, IL	4,495	4,308	3,679	40,591	33,118	22.2	3,470	28.7	5.3	2.8	4.4	12.8	10.5
Macon County, IL	4,495	4,308	3,679	40,591	33,118	22.2	3,470	28.7	5.3	2.8	4.4	12.8	10.5
Deltona–Daytona Beach–Ormond Beach, FL	16,544	15,997	14,260	33,436	29,324	16.0	7,575	6.7	10.3	3.7	5.2	19.5	17.3
Volusia County, FL	16,544	15,997	14,260	33,436	29,324	16.0	7,575	6.7	10.3	3.7	5.2	19.5	17.3

[1] Based on resident population estimated as of July 1.
[2] Includes other industry categories not shown separately.
[6] Danville city included with Pittsylvania County, VA, in the Danville, VA MSA.
(D) = Data withheld to avoid disclosure or does not meet statistical standards.
NA = Not available

Table C-3.   Personal Income and Earnings, by Industry—*Continued*

Metropolitan statistical area, division, and component county	Personal income												
	Total (million dollars)			Per capita[1] (dollars)		Percent change, 2005–2011	Earnings, 2011						
							Total[2] (million dollars)	Percentage by selected major industries					
	2011	2010	2005	2011	2005			Manufacturing	Retail trade	Finance and insurance	Professional and technical services	Health care and social services	Government and government enterprises
Denver–Aurora–Broomfield, CO[4]	127,324	119,986	101,788	48,980	43,634	25.1	103,112	5.4	5.0	8.9	12.9	8.1	13.2
Adams County, CO[4]	14,925	14,130	12,045	33,061	30,482	23.9	10,274	8.9	7.2	2.5	5.5	9.5	16.9
Arapahoe County, CO	28,656	27,380	24,879	48,989	47,437	15.2	26,729	2.1	5.3	11.5	13.6	9.0	9.1
Broomfield County, CO[4]	2,345	2,184	1,652	40,892	35,675	41.9	2,836	19.4	6.5	3.9	18.8	3.0	2.8
Clear Creek County, CO	499	488	461	55,335	50,410	8.1	298	0.3	3.2	5.3	9.6	(D)	12.8
Denver County, CO	33,811	31,599	26,593	54,537	48,203	27.1	40,565	3.4	3.0	10.2	13.1	7.1	14.6
Douglas County, CO	20,879	18,905	11,771	71,463	48,416	77.4	6,823	2.5	7.5	10.6	16.5	7.2	9.6
Elbert County, CO	1,034	972	847	44,606	38,187	22.0	196	3.6	7.9	4.2	10.1	2.2	22.5
Gilpin County, CO	238	224	194	43,444	40,333	22.4	283	(D)	0.3	0.2	1.6	(D)	9.7
Jefferson County, CO[4]	24,391	23,569	22,818	45,179	43,908	6.9	14,977	12.9	6.7	5.8	14.0	10.3	17.8
Park County, CO	546	533	528	33,936	32,614	3.3	131	2.0	6.4	3.0	10.8	3.2	30.9
Des Moines–West Des Moines, IA	26,092	24,463	20,043	44,966	38,427	30.2	22,105	5.8	5.5	23.3	6.0	10.0	13.1
Dallas County, IA	3,315	2,970	1,904	47,740	35,892	74.1	2,249	4.6	6.3	42.6	3.5	7.9	8.1
Guthrie County, IA	458	401	358	41,971	31,792	27.9	245	5.8	3.1	7.2	1.5	5.1	17.6
Madison County, IA	597	555	463	37,816	31,023	28.9	236	8.4	6.8	4.0	3.1	6.2	22.6
Polk County, IA	19,830	18,762	15,919	45,336	39,894	24.6	18,869	5.9	5.3	22.0	6.4	10.3	13.2
Warren County, IA	1,892	1,774	1,400	40,496	32,297	35.2	508	4.7	10.0	3.8	4.6	11.4	23.4
Detroit–Warren–Livonia, MI	171,473	161,676	164,087	40,009	37,031	4.5	128,083	15.2	5.7	5.5	13.5	12.6	11.8
Detroit–Livonia–Dearborn, MI	61,293	59,207	59,624	34,012	30,416	2.8	50,804	14.2	4.7	3.8	11.6	13.6	14.9
Wayne County, MI	61,293	59,207	59,624	34,012	30,416	2.8	50,804	14.2	4.7	3.8	11.6	13.6	14.9
Warren–Troy–Farmington Hills, MI	110,179	102,469	104,463	44,360	42,279	5.5	77,279	15.8	6.5	6.6	14.8	11.9	9.8
Lapeer County, MI	2,803	2,669	2,676	31,825	29,165	4.8	1,041	23.1	9.0	3.6	(D)	7.0	23.2
Livingston County, MI	7,392	6,915	6,556	40,677	36,665	12.7	2,798	19.7	9.2	6.4	8.2	9.1	12.8
Macomb County, MI	30,079	28,608	28,613	35,717	34,525	5.1	19,808	28.4	7.3	2.1	6.5	10.9	15.4
Oakland County, MI	64,497	59,091	61,485	53,297	51,099	4.9	51,078	10.6	5.9	8.6	19.4	12.3	6.8
St. Clair County, MI	5,408	5,185	5,133	33,459	30,518	5.4	2,554	14.5	7.7	4.5	(D)	16.6	17.5
Dothan, AL	5,079	4,900	4,010	34,654	29,343	26.7	2,975	8.4	9.9	3.1	3.5	14.9	19.4
Geneva County, AL	805	793	678	30,047	26,076	18.7	258	10.5	8.2	3.5	(D)	(D)	27.8
Henry County, AL	555	528	416	31,888	24,831	33.5	202	15.0	5.6	2.4	5.5	(D)	18.6
Houston County, AL	3,719	3,579	2,916	36,330	31,053	27.5	2,516	7.6	10.4	3.1	3.7	17.6	18.6
Dover, DE	5,489	5,225	4,118	33,302	28,484	33.3	3,954	(D)	7.8	6.8	3.1	11.3	39.6
Kent County, DE	5,489	5,225	4,118	33,302	28,484	33.3	3,954	(D)	7.8	6.8	3.1	11.3	39.6
Dubuque, IA	3,680	3,408	2,804	38,886	30,889	31.3	3,033	19.0	6.9	7.1	7.2	14.1	8.4
Dubuque County, IA	3,680	3,408	2,804	38,886	30,889	31.3	3,033	19.0	6.9	7.1	7.2	14.1	8.4
Duluth, MN–WI	10,141	9,664	8,266	36,242	29,876	22.7	6,925	7.6	6.8	5.0	3.7	20.2	21.0
Carlton County, MN	1,131	1,091	893	31,902	25,995	26.6	673	15.9	6.1	3.4	1.6	10.8	37.6
St. Louis County, MN	7,622	7,213	6,242	38,059	31,457	22.1	5,360	5.7	6.9	5.7	4.2	23.3	19.1
Douglas County, WI	1,388	1,360	1,130	31,478	25,764	22.8	891	12.9	7.0	2.3	2.2	8.1	20.0
Durham–Chapel Hill, NC	21,435	20,518	16,647	41,785	36,324	28.8	21,918	21.1	3.6	5.9	12.1	13.0	19.4
Chatham County, NC	3,094	2,937	2,246	48,191	39,380	37.7	943	16.6	6.8	6.3	8.7	12.1	14.0
Durham County, NC	10,568	10,177	8,592	38,654	35,535	23.0	16,205	26.5	2.7	6.1	14.1	15.1	9.4
Orange County, NC	6,609	6,267	4,807	48,683	39,558	37.5	4,268	2.1	5.4	5.2	6.2	5.6	58.8
Person County, NC	1,165	1,137	1,001	29,386	26,398	16.3	501	16.6	9.6	3.3	2.1	9.7	19.7
Eau Claire, WI	5,874	5,660	4,594	36,111	29,672	27.9	4,340	15.0	8.2	5.3	3.8	17.4	14.5
Chippewa County, WI	2,158	2,077	1,666	34,375	27,853	29.6	1,293	26.4	9.9	2.4	2.3	9.5	14.5
Eau Claire County, WI	3,716	3,583	2,928	37,203	30,817	26.9	3,046	10.2	7.5	6.5	4.5	20.7	14.5
El Centro, CA	5,020	4,817	3,720	28,351	23,831	34.9	3,406	3.9	7.1	1.8	1.8	4.4	39.3
Imperial County, CA	5,020	4,817	3,720	28,351	23,831	34.9	3,406	3.9	7.1	1.8	1.8	4.4	39.3
Elizabethtown, KY	4,700	4,301	3,297	38,597	29,851	42.6	4,201	9.2	4.8	2.1	2.9	5.1	58.9
Hardin County, KY	4,178	3,814	2,912	38,880	30,132	43.5	4,075	9.1	4.8	2.0	2.9	5.0	60.0
Larue County, KY	522	487	384	36,474	27,876	35.8	126	13.4	5.7	4.7	1.5	9.3	24.5
Elkhart–Goshen, IN	6,392	6,087	6,092	32,131	31,688	4.9	5,911	45.3	5.0	2.2	2.6	9.1	8.0
Elkhart County, IN	6,392	6,087	6,092	32,131	31,688	4.9	5,911	45.3	5.0	2.2	2.6	9.1	8.0
Elmira, NY	3,155	3,040	2,469	35,517	27,787	27.8	2,199	18.5	7.4	3.2	2.6	16.0	20.9
Chemung County, NY	3,155	3,040	2,469	35,517	27,787	27.8	2,199	18.5	7.4	3.2	2.6	16.0	20.9
El Paso, TX	24,696	23,047	17,100	30,088	23,486	44.4	18,515	6.5	6.9	2.5	3.3	9.6	38.7
El Paso County, TX	24,696	23,047	17,100	30,088	23,486	44.4	18,515	6.5	6.9	2.5	3.3	9.6	38.7
Erie, PA	9,756	9,170	7,753	34,721	27,967	25.8	6,843	23.4	7.0	6.3	3.6	17.7	15.2
Erie County, PA	9,756	9,170	7,753	34,721	27,967	25.8	6,843	23.4	7.0	6.3	3.6	17.7	15.2
Eugene–Springfield, OR	12,214	11,680	10,096	34,561	30,064	21.0	7,707	9.9	8.9	3.9	5.5	16.8	20.8
Lane County, OR	12,214	11,680	10,096	34,561	30,064	21.0	7,707	9.9	8.9	3.9	5.5	16.8	20.8

[1] Based on resident population estimated as of July 1.
[2] Includes other industry categories not shown separately.
[4]The Denver–Aurora metropolitan statistical area includes Broomfield County. Broomfield County, CO, was formed from parts of Adams, Boulder, Jefferson, and Weld Counties on November 15, 2001, and is coextensive with Broomfield city. For the purposes of defining and presenting data for the Denver–Aurora metropolitan statistical area, Broomfield city is treated as if it were a county when data are available to do so. In many cases, the data were not available.
(D) = Data withheld to avoid disclosure or does not meet statistical standards.

Table C-3. Personal Income and Earnings, by Industry—*Continued*

Metropolitan statistical area, division, and component county	Personal income												
	Total (million dollars)			Per capita[1] (dollars)		Percent change, 2005–2011	Earnings, 2011						
							Total[2] (million dollars)	Percentage by selected major industries					
	2011	2010	2005	2011	2005			Manufacturing	Retail trade	Finance and insurance	Professional and technical services	Health care and social services	Government and government enterprises
Evansville, IN–KY	13,639	12,980	11,339	37,899	32,294	20.3	10,236	21.3	6.0	2.3	4.2	13.5	10.1
Gibson County, IN	1,175	1,105	982	35,066	29,529	19.6	1,110	44.6	4.4	0.8	2.1	5.0	6.4
Posey County, IN	1,048	986	865	40,731	32,643	21.2	720	44.8	5.5	1.4	(D)	(D)	8.6
Vanderburgh County, IN	6,961	6,678	5,895	38,608	33,539	18.1	6,234	14.3	6.4	2.6	5.3	16.6	9.7
Warrick County, IN	2,515	2,384	1,913	41,726	34,125	31.5	916	23.1	5.2	4.0	5.5	19.3	12.5
Henderson County, KY	1,499	1,414	1,295	32,311	28,447	15.8	994	25.2	6.8	2.0	2.3	11.7	14.3
Webster County, KY	441	413	389	32,258	27,768	13.4	263	3.9	3.3	(D)	(D)	(D)	12.7
Fairbanks, AK	4,228	3,921	3,049	42,626	33,719	38.7	3,692	1.4	5.4	1.6	3.2	8.0	51.6
Fairbanks North Star Borough, AK	4,228	3,921	3,049	42,626	33,719	38.7	3,692	1.4	5.4	1.6	3.2	8.0	51.6
Fargo, ND–MN	9,068	8,421	6,325	42,740	33,414	43.4	7,377	7.9	7.0	7.0	6.1	13.3	14.8
Clay County, MN	2,120	2,017	1,523	35,448	28,132	39.2	1,000	5.6	7.3	2.5	3.0	9.9	24.1
Cass County, ND	6,948	6,404	4,803	45,602	35,528	44.7	6,377	8.3	6.9	7.7	6.6	13.9	13.4
Farmington, NM	4,022	3,804	3,044	31,373	24,388	32.1	3,061	2.6	7.2	1.6	2.2	11.5	21.0
San Juan County, NM	4,022	3,804	3,044	31,373	24,388	32.1	3,061	2.6	7.2	1.6	2.2	11.5	21.0
Fayetteville, NC	16,184	15,038	11,122	43,254	32,379	45.5	14,031	4.3	3.8	1.1	3.1	4.4	67.8
Cumberland County, NC	14,515	13,560	10,226	44,678	33,672	41.9	13,658	3.8	3.7	1.1	3.2	4.2	68.9
Hoke County, NC	1,669	1,478	896	33,868	22,515	86.2	373	20.8	5.7	1.4	(D)	8.4	28.9
Fayetteville–Springdale–Rogers, AR–MO	16,172	15,337	12,024	34,130	29,470	34.5	12,385	10.9	6.2	3.2	6.6	9.0	13.9
Benton County, AR	8,361	7,831	5,822	36,744	31,175	43.6	6,516	8.8	5.3	3.4	9.2	6.3	8.3
Madison County, AR	346	352	340	21,921	23,123	1.6	159	25.9	8.6	1.9	2.0	5.3	21.6
Washington County, AR	6,894	6,585	5,341	33,220	29,060	29.1	5,412	11.6	6.7	3.2	4.1	12.9	20.1
McDonald County, MO	571	569	520	24,849	22,891	9.8	298	35.4	11.9	2.1	(D)	(D)	17.2
Flagstaff, AZ	4,621	4,447	3,680	34,353	28,972	25.6	3,253	10.2	7.2	1.3	3.0	16.2	32.3
Coconino County, AZ	4,621	4,447	3,680	34,353	28,972	25.6	3,253	10.2	7.2	1.3	3.0	16.2	32.3
Flint, MI	13,108	12,537	11,983	31,057	27,080	9.4	7,606	12.3	8.4	5.2	6.1	18.6	18.6
Genesee County, MI	13,108	12,537	11,983	31,057	27,080	9.4	7,606	12.3	8.4	5.2	6.1	18.6	18.6
Florence, SC	6,754	6,557	5,601	32,762	28,121	20.6	4,638	17.1	7.8	10.8	5.0	12.5	19.2
Darlington County, SC	2,005	1,969	1,793	29,355	26,294	11.8	1,130	32.4	6.7	2.3	1.8	9.5	14.1
Florence County, SC	4,749	4,588	3,808	34,450	29,072	24.7	3,508	12.1	8.2	13.5	6.0	13.4	20.8
Florence–Muscle Shoals, AL	4,719	4,576	3,739	32,038	26,015	26.2	2,798	15.4	10.0	3.2	2.9	12.7	23.1
Colbert County, AL	1,730	1,689	1,379	31,743	25,364	25.5	1,321	20.3	7.9	2.8	1.4	9.7	26.9
Lauderdale County, AL	2,989	2,887	2,360	32,211	26,411	26.6	1,477	10.9	11.9	3.7	4.2	15.4	19.7
Fond du Lac, WI	3,766	3,604	3,198	36,897	32,201	17.8	2,542	25.0	6.7	4.1	2.5	13.2	12.8
Fond du Lac County, WI	3,766	3,604	3,198	36,897	32,201	17.8	2,542	25.0	6.7	4.1	2.5	13.2	12.8
Fort Collins–Loveland, CO	12,150	11,454	9,631	39,767	35,008	26.2	8,227	13.6	6.8	3.3	11.2	13.0	20.0
Larimer County, CO	12,150	11,454	9,631	39,767	35,008	26.2	8,227	13.6	6.8	3.3	11.2	13.0	20.0
Fort Smith, AR–OK	9,537	9,195	7,641	31,782	26,832	24.8	6,190	17.9	7.1	2.6	(D)	(D)	17.6
Crawford County, AR	1,716	1,661	1,350	27,699	23,373	27.1	987	20.2	6.3	2.0	(D)	7.1	13.3
Franklin County, AR	552	540	460	30,593	25,444	20.1	237	19.6	8.0	3.7	1.7	0.0	24.9
Sebastian County, AR	4,710	4,495	3,783	37,052	31,678	24.5	3,843	20.7	6.5	2.6	6.2	15.8	12.8
Le Flore County, OK	1,388	1,357	1,125	27,423	23,025	23.4	685	8.7	7.6	2.8	(D)	(D)	36.2
Sequoyah County, OK	1,171	1,142	923	27,649	22,705	26.9	438	1.4	12.3	3.0	5.5	(D)	35.9
Fort Wayne, IN	14,698	13,929	12,585	35,042	31,210	16.8	11,539	20.4	6.0	6.2	5.1	15.6	11.0
Allen County, IN	12,613	11,982	10,888	35,199	31,722	15.8	10,423	18.6	6.0	6.7	5.6	16.6	10.8
Wells County, IN	952	897	775	34,321	27,856	22.8	539	28.3	5.4	1.9	(D)	12.9	12.6
Whitley County, IN	1,134	1,050	922	33,958	28,649	23.0	577	44.6	5.5	1.7	1.4	(D)	13.4
Fresno, CA	29,741	28,539	24,078	31,542	27,598	23.5	20,492	7.1	6.8	4.1	4.6	12.8	21.9
Fresno County, CA	29,741	28,539	24,078	31,542	27,598	23.5	20,492	7.1	6.8	4.1	4.6	12.8	21.9
Gadsden, AL	3,321	3,232	2,704	31,844	26,212	22.8	1,776	16.4	8.4	3.5	2.9	(D)	16.8
Etowah County, AL	3,321	3,232	2,704	31,844	26,212	22.8	1,776	16.4	8.4	3.5	2.9	(D)	16.8
Gainesville, FL	9,455	9,123	7,709	35,497	30,890	22.7	7,093	4.3	6.2	4.0	6.1	17.2	39.5
Alachua County, FL	8,931	8,617	7,296	35,816	31,212	22.4	6,927	4.4	6.2	4.0	6.2	17.6	39.6
Gilchrist County, FL	524	506	413	30,828	26,127	27.0	165	1.5	4.9	1.5	(D)	(D)	34.4
Gainesville, GA	5,858	5,493	4,789	32,001	29,750	22.3	4,234	19.3	6.9	6.6	3.1	15.1	12.9
Hall County, GA	5,858	5,493	4,789	32,001	29,750	22.3	4,234	19.3	6.9	6.6	3.1	15.1	12.9
Glens Falls, NY	4,801	4,585	3,661	37,216	28,678	31.1	2,908	15.5	8.3	3.8	(D)	14.1	21.1
Warren County, NY	2,676	2,567	2,046	40,649	31,382	30.8	1,998	13.5	9.1	4.8	4.6	17.3	14.4
Washington County, NY	2,125	2,018	1,615	33,639	25,855	31.6	909	19.8	6.7	1.6	(D)	7.1	35.9
Goldsboro, NC	3,865	3,651	3,081	31,245	26,332	25.4	2,570	10.8	6.4	2.8	2.1	11.5	37.4
Wayne County, NC	3,865	3,651	3,081	31,245	26,332	25.4	2,570	10.8	6.4	2.8	2.1	11.5	37.4
Grand Forks, ND–MN	3,862	3,646	2,885	39,382	29,507	33.8	2,983	6.2	8.0	2.8	3.5	15.6	28.1
Polk County, MN	1,221	1,159	897	38,824	28,805	36.1	661	13.9	5.9	2.3	1.9	13.6	20.6
Grand Forks County, ND	2,640	2,487	1,988	39,646	29,836	32.8	2,322	4.0	8.6	2.9	3.9	16.2	30.2

[1] Based on resident population estimated as of July 1.
[2] Includes other industry categories not shown separately.
(D) = Data withheld to avoid disclosure or does not meet statistical standards.

Table C-3. Personal Income and Earnings, by Industry—*Continued*

Metropolitan statistical area, division, and component county	Personal income												
	Total (million dollars)			Per capita[1] (dollars)		Percent change, 2005–2011	Earnings, 2011						
							Total[2] (million dollars)	Percentage by selected major industries					
	2011	2010	2005	2011	2005			Manufacturing	Retail trade	Finance and insurance	Professional and technical services	Health care and social services	Government and government enterprises
Grand Junction, CO	5,173	4,923	3,898	35,169	29,939	32.7	3,428	4.1	8.0	4.0	5.2	15.1	17.4
Mesa County, CO	5,173	4,923	3,898	35,169	29,939	32.7	3,428	4.1	8.0	4.0	5.2	15.1	17.4
Grand Rapids–Wyoming, MI	27,305	25,625	24,098	35,024	31,458	13.3	22,247	19.7	6.7	7.6	7.0	13.8	10.0
Barry County, MI	1,957	1,863	1,783	33,268	29,907	9.7	736	23.6	5.2	6.8	0.0	10.6	15.9
Ionia County, MI	1,713	1,597	1,489	26,781	22,991	15.1	963	21.6	6.8	3.7	1.4	(D)	24.7
Kent County, MI	22,263	20,858	19,645	36,589	33,173	13.3	19,952	19.5	6.6	7.8	7.6	14.7	8.7
Newaygo County, MI	1,372	1,308	1,181	28,371	23,878	16.2	596	17.4	10.2	8.2	3.2	10.4	21.7
Great Falls, MT	3,228	3,105	2,500	39,448	31,240	29.1	2,264	2.8	7.8	6.6	4.8	16.3	30.2
Cascade County, MT	3,228	3,105	2,500	39,448	31,240	29.1	2,264	2.8	7.8	6.6	4.8	16.3	30.2
Greeley, CO	7,756	7,232	6,004	29,986	26,939	29.2	5,299	11.7	6.0	4.7	3.5	8.6	14.5
Weld County, CO	7,756	7,232	6,004	29,986	26,939	29.2	5,299	11.7	6.0	4.7	3.5	8.6	14.5
Green Bay, WI	12,084	11,587	9,914	39,046	33,403	21.9	10,000	18.0	5.5	7.5	5.2	12.5	11.8
Brown County, WI	9,929	9,536	8,209	39,493	34,406	21.0	9,082	17.7	5.5	8.1	5.5	13.6	11.3
Kewaunee County, WI	787	739	629	38,207	30,467	25.0	459	21.0	3.6	2.4	3.3	3.0	14.2
Oconto County, WI	1,368	1,312	1,076	36,508	28,642	27.1	460	20.5	7.4	2.2	2.0	(D)	20.2
Greensboro–High Point, NC	25,880	24,746	21,983	35,405	32,468	17.7	19,869	17.2	6.6	7.6	6.0	11.7	12.9
Guilford County, NC	18,816	17,915	15,954	37,990	35,596	17.9	16,370	14.2	6.6	8.7	7.0	12.0	12.3
Randolph County, NC	4,183	4,054	3,588	29,385	26,325	16.6	2,180	33.2	6.2	2.5	2.1	9.3	14.8
Rockingham County, NC	2,881	2,777	2,441	30,868	26,367	18.0	1,319	27.0	7.9	2.6	(D)	11.9	16.4
Greenville, NC	6,188	5,889	4,741	32,111	28,208	30.5	4,161	10.9	7.1	3.6	3.1	12.4	37.3
Greene County, NC	567	560	501	26,317	24,885	13.2	255	5.7	4.1	2.0	2.4	10.2	35.2
Pitt County, NC.	5,620	5,329	4,240	32,841	28,661	32.6	3,906	11.2	7.3	3.7	3.2	12.6	37.4
Greenville–Mauldin–Easley, SC	22,684	21,527	17,971	35,038	30,586	26.2	17,348	15.5	7.0	4.9	8.0	9.1	14.8
Greenville County, SC	17,386	16,412	13,464	37,689	33,196	29.1	14,653	14.4	6.8	5.3	9.2	9.6	12.1
Laurens County, SC	1,970	1,893	1,704	29,609	25,199	15.6	878	30.9	5.9	1.8	(D)	(D)	22.3
Pickens County, SC	3,328	3,222	2,803	27,833	24,512	18.7	1,817	17.0	8.9	3.3	2.7	9.1	32.4
Gulfport–Biloxi, MS	8,853	8,697	7,492	34,922	28,741	18.2	6,850	6.2	6.5	2.5	5.3	6.5	38.3
Hancock County, MS	1,496	1,545	1,308	33,515	27,402	14.4	1,104	7.8	4.4	1.5	11.3	(D)	38.4
Harrison County, MS	6,854	6,660	5,811	35,878	29,378	18.0	5,547	5.4	6.8	2.6	4.2	7.6	38.5
Stone County, MS	503	491	374	28,199	24,646	34.2	199	18.9	9.1	2.5	4.1	11.0	30.4
Hagerstown–Martinsburg, MD–WV	9,395	8,944	7,332	34,604	29,249	28.1	5,571	10.8	8.9	7.4	4.8	14.0	24.0
Washington County, MD	5,485	5,230	4,350	37,008	30,615	26.1	3,609	13.8	10.2	10.2	4.3	15.8	15.8
Berkeley County, WV	3,352	3,178	2,498	31,696	27,120	34.2	1,819	4.8	6.3	2.2	5.9	11.7	40.2
Morgan County, WV	558	536	483	31,830	29,366	15.5	143	10.5	8.7	3.4	2.5	(D)	27.3
Hanford–Corcoran, CA	4,522	4,121	3,398	29,407	23,413	33.1	3,380	8.3	4.4	1.3	1.6	8.2	42.3
Kings County, CA	4,522	4,121	3,398	29,407	23,413	33.1	3,380	8.3	4.4	1.3	1.6	8.2	42.3
Harrisburg–Carlisle, PA	22,751	21,706	18,364	41,148	34,928	23.9	20,165	7.6	5.2	7.9	7.4	14.0	21.6
Cumberland County, PA	10,123	9,644	8,069	42,552	36,124	25.5	8,043	6.3	6.3	9.1	8.8	12.9	18.2
Dauphin County, PA	11,046	10,544	9,007	41,067	34,955	22.6	11,710	8.5	4.2	7.3	6.6	14.9	23.7
Perry County, PA	1,582	1,518	1,289	34,367	28,810	22.8	411	4.5	9.4	3.1	3.2	8.8	26.3
Harrisonburg, VA[7]	3,964	3,778	3,166	31,324	27,149	25.2	3,183	19.7	7.9	2.4	4.0	11.8	17.5
Rockingham County, VA[7]	3,964	3,778	3,166	31,324	27,149	25.2	3,183	19.7	7.9	2.4	4.0	11.8	17.5
Harrisonburg city, VA[7]	NA	NA	NA	NA	NA	NA	NA	NA	NA	NA	NA	NA	NA
Hartford–West Hartford–East Hartford, CT	64,401	61,302	51,428	53,081	43,292	25.2	51,575	12.6	5.0	18.3	8.1	12.0	15.2
Hartford County, CT	48,291	45,816	38,593	53,974	43,951	25.1	43,734	12.5	4.7	20.9	8.3	11.6	13.5
Middlesex County, CT	8,999	8,638	7,212	54,198	44,468	24.8	4,955	17.2	6.6	4.5	7.0	15.5	17.6
Tolland County, CT	7,110	6,848	5,623	46,624	38,080	26.5	2,886	7.2	6.5	2.9	6.1	11.8	36.2
Hattiesburg, MS	4,544	4,355	3,445	31,248	26,338	31.9	3,161	6.7	9.4	3.3	(D)	18.0	27.2
Forrest County, MS	2,290	2,229	1,956	30,198	27,149	17.1	2,270	5.9	7.8	2.8	4.0	17.5	31.8
Lamar County, MS	1,974	1,852	1,247	34,386	26,719	58.3	762	3.8	15.0	5.3	(D)	21.0	14.8
Perry County, MS	280	274	242	22,981	20,034	15.4	129	38.6	4.8	1.9	1.7	9.0	19.3
Hickory–Lenoir–Morganton, NC	11,249	10,763	9,968	30,857	28,145	12.9	7,380	26.0	7.3	2.8	(D)	12.2	16.4
Alexander County, NC	1,131	1,086	974	30,499	27,231	16.7	474	29.3	4.7	3.8	4.5	(D)	20.1
Burke County, NC	2,735	2,636	2,421	30,084	27,048	12.9	1,596	24.5	6.6	3.7	3.3	17.3	22.9
Caldwell County, NC	2,246	2,175	2,119	27,261	26,417	6.0	1,181	21.6	7.8	2.7	(D)	11.8	17.7
Catawba County, NC	5,137	4,866	4,453	33,320	29,958	15.4	4,128	27.4	7.7	2.5	3.5	11.7	13.1
Hinesville–Fort Stewart, GA	2,154	2,011	1,676	26,726	21,941	28.5	3,227	3.8	1.9	0.7	1.1	1.2	83.0
Liberty County, GA	1,829	1,711	1,460	27,940	22,558	25.3	3,180	3.9	1.9	0.7	1.1	1.2	83.3
Long County, GA	325	300	216	21,473	18,519	50.3	47	0.0	2.6	(D)	(D)	2.0	58.6
Holland–Grand Haven, MI	8,995	8,514	7,785	33,777	30,497	15.5	5,918	34.8	5.1	2.8	4.3	6.9	15.3
Ottawa County, MI	8,995	8,514	7,785	33,777	30,497	15.5	5,918	34.8	5.1	2.8	4.3	6.9	15.3

[1] Based on resident population estimated as of July 1.
[2] Includes other industry categories not shown separately.
[7] Harrisonburg city included with Rockingham County, VA, in the Harrisonburg, VA MSA.
(D) = Data withheld to avoid disclosure or does not meet statistical standards.
NA = Not available

Table C-3. Personal Income and Earnings, by Industry—*Continued*

	Personal income												
	Total (million dollars)			Per capita[1] (dollars)		Percent change, 2005–2011	Earnings, 2011						
Metropolitan statistical area, division, and component county							Total[2] (million dollars)	Percentage by selected major industries					
	2011	2010	2005	2011	2005			Manufacturing	Retail trade	Finance and insurance	Professional and technical services	Health care and social services	Government and government enterprises
Honolulu, HI	44,927	42,397	34,264	46,624	37,317	31.1	34,196	1.9	5.2	3.4	6.3	9.5	39.2
Honolulu County, Hawaii	44,927	42,397	34,264	46,624	37,317	31.1	34,196	1.9	5.2	3.4	6.3	9.5	39.2
Hot Springs, AR	3,434	3,275	2,691	35,355	29,217	27.6	1,744	6.3	11.7	3.5	5.0	22.7	16.9
Garland County, AR	3,434	3,275	2,691	35,355	29,217	27.6	1,744	6.3	11.7	3.5	5.0	22.7	16.9
Houma–Bayou Cane–Thibodaux, LA	8,843	8,495	5,757	42,393	28,717	53.6	6,687	12.1	5.7	1.9	3.6	7.8	11.6
Lafourche Parish, LA	4,392	4,194	2,779	45,437	29,997	58.0	3,274	6.6	4.8	1.7	3.1	6.0	12.3
Terrebonne Parish, LA	4,450	4,301	2,977	39,764	27,616	49.5	3,414	17.4	6.6	2.2	4.1	9.5	11.0
Houston–Sugar Land–Baytown, TX	289,790	268,695	209,655	47,612	39,868	38.2	240,196	10.7	4.7	5.4	11.5	7.2	10.0
Austin County, TX	1,129	1,085	791	39,374	30,056	42.6	708	23.5	10.0	3.7	7.5	6.0	13.2
Brazoria County, TX	12,376	11,667	8,526	38,677	31,078	45.2	6,250	23.8	6.9	2.4	5.0	5.9	14.8
Chambers County, TX	1,741	1,613	959	48,969	32,630	81.5	716	26.6	4.1	1.4	4.7	(D)	14.5
Fort Bend County, TX	29,465	27,236	17,457	48,545	37,708	68.8	11,148	12.7	7.0	5.5	7.8	8.7	11.8
Galveston County, TX	12,849	12,257	9,414	43,444	34,256	36.5	6,474	16.5	6.7	5.5	5.7	7.1	27.2
Harris County, TX	204,593	188,994	154,973	48,935	42,091	32.0	203,376	9.9	4.3	5.7	12.3	7.1	8.8
Liberty County, TX	2,618	2,510	2,019	34,353	27,175	29.7	1,063	12.2	10.3	2.0	(D)	(D)	20.3
Montgomery County, TX	22,883	21,299	13,921	48,508	37,368	64.4	9,454	9.0	8.1	4.1	9.5	9.2	13.4
San Jacinto County, TX	847	801	615	31,607	24,598	37.7	134	4.3	6.4	2.5	6.2	4.4	32.1
Waller County, TX	1,290	1,232	979	29,320	26,286	31.8	873	25.3	6.7	1.2	6.3	2.7	22.5
Huntington–Ashland, WV–KY–OH	9,437	9,081	7,370	32,811	25,762	28.0	6,222	11.8	7.5	2.3	3.9	21.4	19.3
Boyd County, KY	1,652	1,608	1,370	33,405	27,722	20.7	1,698	18.2	6.5	1.9	5.0	24.5	11.9
Greenup County, KY	1,342	1,279	965	36,391	26,422	39.0	440	7.9	7.8	2.3	(D)	25.2	17.9
Lawrence County, OH	1,912	1,826	1,462	30,595	23,398	30.8	583	(D)	10.6	2.5	2.3	15.2	26.8
Cabell County, WV	3,294	3,175	2,649	34,079	27,933	24.4	2,909	12.1	8.1	2.9	4.5	24.6	18.2
Wayne County, WV	1,237	1,192	925	29,361	21,584	33.7	592	6.5	4.9	0.8	1.8	(D)	39.6
Huntsville, AL	17,073	16,278	12,415	40,126	33,303	37.5	15,217	11.3	5.3	1.8	22.6	6.3	32.4
Limestone County, AL	2,924	2,739	1,970	34,250	27,633	48.4	1,511	9.8	10.1	1.4	6.7	4.9	32.9
Madison County, AL	14,149	13,539	10,444	41,601	34,644	35.5	13,705	11.5	4.7	1.9	24.3	6.5	32.4
Idaho Falls, ID	4,427	4,213	3,397	33,520	29,957	30.3	2,768	5.8	9.4	3.4	8.3	15.0	13.7
Bonneville County, ID	3,701	3,543	2,918	34,989	31,822	26.8	2,420	5.0	10.0	3.6	9.5	17.1	13.5
Jefferson County, ID	726	669	478	27,612	22,070	51.8	348	11.3	4.7	1.8	(D)	(D)	15.3
Indianapolis–Carmel, IN	72,161	68,429	60,018	40,572	36,550	20.2	58,912	14.2	5.8	6.7	8.7	12.6	13.7
Boone County, IN	3,045	2,847	2,376	52,975	46,341	28.2	1,528	10.2	11.9	2.4	6.6	7.4	12.2
Brown County, IN	541	511	480	35,863	31,383	12.9	150	7.2	7.3	2.0	(D)	(D)	24.6
Hamilton County, IN	14,656	13,620	10,760	51,824	45,779	36.2	8,206	5.0	7.1	13.2	12.2	10.7	8.9
Hancock County, IN	3,083	2,838	2,385	43,714	37,834	29.3	1,275	15.0	6.0	2.1	13.9	8.4	16.6
Hendricks County, IN	5,355	5,062	4,092	36,188	31,951	30.9	2,905	8.1	10.7	1.9	5.0	8.2	16.3
Johnson County, IN	5,180	4,916	4,230	36,570	33,364	22.5	2,305	12.8	10.7	3.4	4.9	11.9	16.8
Marion County, IN	34,910	33,484	31,175	38,309	35,697	12.0	40,335	16.2	4.6	6.5	8.9	14.2	13.9
Morgan County, IN	2,614	2,495	2,176	37,634	31,989	20.1	722	16.0	9.0	3.4	(D)	11.5	20.9
Putnam County, IN	1,206	1,151	982	31,817	25,989	22.9	595	23.5	5.4	2.5	(D)	(D)	21.2
Shelby County, IN	1,568	1,506	1,362	35,376	31,332	15.1	890	30.7	6.8	1.3	2.3	(D)	16.0
Iowa City, IA	6,393	5,950	4,703	41,277	33,204	35.9	5,332	7.4	5.5	2.9	2.9	7.4	41.8
Johnson County, IA	5,501	5,132	4,020	41,349	33,420	36.8	4,885	7.0	5.4	2.8	3.0	7.4	44.2
Washington County, IA	893	818	683	40,837	31,982	30.7	446	11.7	6.9	4.2	1.7	7.2	16.3
Ithaca, NY	3,689	3,539	2,819	36,263	28,347	30.9	3,083	8.0	5.2	2.6	6.4	(D)	13.3
Tompkins County, NY	3,689	3,539	2,819	36,263	28,347	30.9	3,083	8.0	5.2	2.6	6.4	(D)	13.3
Jackson, MI	5,015	4,760	4,380	31,396	26,863	14.5	3,177	18.2	6.9	2.4	3.9	14.7	17.8
Jackson County, MI	5,015	4,760	4,380	31,396	26,863	14.5	3,177	18.2	6.9	2.4	3.9	14.7	17.8
Jackson, MS	20,476	19,565	16,657	37,544	32,073	22.9	15,519	6.6	6.8	7.2	7.0	12.6	23.1
Copiah County, MS	718	708	610	24,552	20,943	17.7	385	31.9	7.8	1.8	(D)	(D)	21.1
Hinds County, MS	8,804	8,507	7,807	35,473	31,562	12.8	8,587	2.7	5.1	7.0	7.5	15.2	30.8
Madison County, MS	4,870	4,511	3,444	50,233	40,586	41.4	2,991	14.0	8.4	9.7	10.6	8.5	8.3
Rankin County, MS	5,219	4,978	4,072	36,317	31,234	28.2	3,201	7.3	9.4	6.4	4.1	12.3	16.6
Simpson County, MS	866	860	724	31,689	26,206	19.6	355	2.1	8.9	3.9	(D)	(D)	23.0
Jackson, TN	3,951	3,774	3,233	34,237	28,933	22.2	3,189	16.5	7.8	2.7	(D)	12.7	22.0
Chester County, TN	481	456	380	28,057	23,255	26.4	193	10.1	9.1	2.7	(D)	0.0	22.6
Madison County, TN	3,470	3,318	2,853	35,315	29,906	21.6	2,996	17.0	7.7	2.7	(D)	13.5	22.0
Jacksonville, FL	55,375	52,940	45,618	40,709	36,521	21.4	39,028	5.4	6.9	11.5	8.1	12.4	18.5
Baker County, FL	690	670	595	25,426	23,975	16.0	313	3.6	8.3	1.8	1.9	(D)	44.7
Clay County, FL	6,440	6,172	5,352	33,476	31,590	20.3	2,121	3.3	12.0	3.4	6.2	17.7	21.1
Duval County, FL	34,705	33,428	29,848	39,858	36,005	16.3	32,453	5.4	6.3	12.9	8.5	12.2	18.0
Nassau County, FL	3,420	3,248	2,561	46,099	39,055	33.6	1,053	9.2	7.8	2.9	4.9	9.5	24.6
St. Johns County, FL	10,120	9,422	7,262	51,677	45,312	39.3	3,087	5.7	9.2	6.5	6.2	13.1	16.9
Jacksonville, NC	8,296	7,892	5,043	46,163	32,077	64.5	7,280	0.6	3.2	0.8	1.6	2.3	81.1
Onslow County, NC	8,296	7,892	5,043	46,163	32,077	64.5	7,280	0.6	3.2	0.8	1.6	2.3	81.1

[1] Based on resident population estimated as of July 1.
[2] Includes other industry categories not shown separately.
(D) = Data withheld to avoid disclosure or does not meet statistical standards.

Table C-3.   Personal Income and Earnings, by Industry—*Continued*

Metropolitan statistical area, division, and component county	Personal income Total (million dollars) 2011	Total (million dollars) 2010	Total (million dollars) 2005	Per capita[1] (dollars) 2011	Per capita[1] (dollars) 2005	Percent change, 2005–2011	Earnings, 2011 Total[2] (million dollars)	Manufacturing	Retail trade	Finance and insurance	Professional and technical services	Health care and social services	Government and government enterprises
Janesville, WI....................................	5,332	5,113	4,566	33,305	29,125	16.8	3,350	17.5	9.2	2.7	2.8	16.5	15.5
Rock County, WI	5,332	5,113	4,566	33,305	29,125	16.8	3,350	17.5	9.2	2.7	2.8	16.5	15.5
Jefferson City, MO................................	5,335	5,154	4,355	35,453	30,149	22.5	4,203	7.4	6.2	4.1	4.3	(D)	33.2
Callaway County, MO	1,275	1,238	1,042	28,697	24,421	22.3	825	11.7	4.2	1.9	2.7	(D)	22.4
Cole County, MO	3,069	2,967	2,517	40,147	34,506	21.9	2,973	4.6	6.6	4.7	5.3	11.5	37.9
Moniteau County, MO	503	480	396	32,019	25,834	27.1	219	15.3	6.7	3.6	1.4	(D)	22.4
Osage County, MO	488	468	400	35,100	29,606	22.1	187	24.0	8.2	3.5	0.0	6.2	18.8
Johnson City, TN..................................	6,543	6,213	5,049	32,745	26,689	29.6	4,063	12.0	8.0	4.0	3.6	(D)	22.7
Carter County, TN................................	1,599	1,544	1,339	27,962	23,211	19.4	564	8.9	11.9	3.5	3.6	(D)	20.9
Unicoi County, TN................................	565	544	473	30,910	26,344	19.6	313	38.3	4.7	1.2	0.0	5.6	17.3
Washington County, TN	4,379	4,125	3,237	35,215	28,511	35.3	3,186	10.0	7.6	4.4	4.0	22.2	23.6
Johnstown, PA.....................................	4,716	4,531	3,913	32,810	26,622	20.5	2,930	8.4	7.9	4.9	6.9	21.6	18.6
Cambria County, PA	4,716	4,531	3,913	32,810	26,622	20.5	2,930	8.4	7.9	4.9	6.9	21.6	18.6
Jonesboro, AR	3,948	3,742	2,988	32,141	26,548	32.1	2,746	13.6	7.7	3.1	2.8	19.4	17.6
Craighead County, AR	3,204	3,033	2,397	32,588	27,393	33.6	2,422	14.2	7.8	3.2	3.2	21.1	17.3
Poinsett County, AR	744	709	591	30,350	23,594	25.8	324	9.1	6.6	2.5	(D)	6.5	20.2
Joplin, MO	5,555	5,313	4,406	31,408	26,516	26.1	4,023	17.8	8.6	3.1	2.3	15.3	12.5
Jasper County, MO	3,519	3,410	2,887	29,709	26,196	21.9	2,988	18.6	8.9	3.3	2.8	10.8	12.4
Newton County, MO	2,036	1,903	1,519	34,854	27,147	34.1	1,035	15.3	7.8	2.6	1.0	28.2	12.7
Kalamazoo–Portage, MI	11,419	10,911	9,712	34,792	30,325	17.6	7,840	20.6	6.0	5.5	5.2	15.0	15.7
Kalamazoo County, MI	9,058	8,663	7,736	35,933	31,802	17.1	6,676	21.9	6.1	5.8	4.8	16.6	14.2
Van Buren County, MI	2,361	2,248	1,976	31,013	25,657	19.5	1,163	12.6	5.8	4.1	7.2	5.6	24.5
Kankakee–Bradley, IL	3,771	3,656	3,004	33,171	27,832	25.6	2,256	16.2	7.6	3.9	(D)	18.1	17.5
Kankakee County, IL............................	3,771	3,656	3,004	33,171	27,832	25.6	2,256	16.2	7.6	3.9	(D)	18.1	17.5
Kansas City, MO–KS	88,392	84,533	70,738	43,062	36,558	25.0	69,320	9.0	5.8	8.4	11.2	10.3	15.8
Franklin County, KS	879	851	715	33,885	28,002	22.9	479	9.9	6.4	1.9	2.7	0.0	20.2
Johnson County, KS.............................	31,271	29,372	24,191	56,550	47,956	29.3	22,980	8.6	5.8	11.9	13.7	10.6	7.9
Leavenworth County, KS	2,652	2,555	2,113	34,360	29,431	25.5	2,173	2.9	3.2	3.0	5.4	4.6	67.1
Linn County, KS	302	292	249	31,382	24,834	21.1	129	6.9	4.8	(D)	(D)	1.5	24.2
Miami County, KS	1,378	1,311	977	42,131	31,768	41.1	382	7.9	12.1	4.0	3.7	12.2	27.2
Wyandotte County, KS	4,562	4,420	3,743	28,836	24,246	21.9	5,324	18.3	5.2	1.3	2.2	15.3	21.3
Bates County, MO	552	537	463	32,429	27,020	19.3	228	6.0	12.3	5.2	5.8	7.0	26.8
Caldwell County, MO	339	319	266	36,370	28,698	27.3	131	0.9	6.6	(D)	1.3	(D)	20.3
Cass County, MO	3,526	3,404	2,783	35,244	30,081	26.7	1,207	3.5	12.1	3.9	3.3	9.6	22.7
Clay County, MO	8,604	8,294	6,953	38,213	34,650	23.7	6,292	14.8	7.4	2.8	13.1	7.6	14.5
Clinton County, MO	741	704	583	35,628	28,593	27.0	227	2.4	5.5	4.1	0.0	17.2	30.3
Jackson County, MO	27,436	26,600	22,878	40,564	34,738	19.9	26,568	6.9	4.9	9.6	12.4	11.0	17.0
Lafayette County, MO	1,256	1,196	1,001	37,831	30,067	25.6	483	8.2	8.0	3.3	5.3	0.0	21.6
Platte County, MO	4,051	3,864	3,119	44,561	37,749	29.9	2,435	8.3	7.9	4.9	4.7	6.5	10.6
Ray County, MO	843	814	706	36,311	29,896	19.5	284	8.3	11.6	4.3	3.8	(D)	23.4
Kennewick–Pasco–Richland, WA...............	9,652	9,105	6,424	36,544	29,323	50.3	7,490	5.6	5.8	2.0	17.2	8.3	17.0
Benton County, WA	7,173	6,832	5,036	39,700	31,926	42.4	5,830	4.7	5.5	2.2	21.4	8.8	15.9
Franklin County, WA	2,479	2,273	1,389	29,711	22,630	78.6	1,660	8.5	6.9	1.3	2.7	6.8	21.0
Killeen–Temple–Fort Hood, TX	16,476	15,348	10,680	40,029	29,870	54.3	13,028	2.9	4.3	1.6	3.6	8.4	61.2
Bell County, TX	12,678	11,802	8,090	40,222	30,413	56.7	11,959	2.8	4.0	1.5	2.9	8.9	63.7
Coryell County, TX	2,826	2,646	1,992	36,932	27,439	41.8	828	1.6	6.4	3.2	13.2	(D)	37.1
Lampasas County, TX	973	900	597	48,898	31,570	63.0	241	11.0	16.2	2.7	2.5	10.3	20.8
Kingsport–Bristol–Bristol, TN–VA[8]...........	10,234	9,728	8,191	33,035	27,077	24.9	6,795	26.3	7.5	2.5	3.1	(D)	12.5
Hawkins County, TN............................	1,621	1,550	1,310	28,610	23,590	23.8	665	33.4	5.9	1.6	0.0	(D)	19.4
Sullivan County, TN............................	5,510	5,244	4,444	35,000	28,956	24.0	4,256	28.6	7.0	2.6	3.7	17.8	9.4
Scott County, VA	646	618	527	27,942	22,825	22.6	226	21.9	9.6	2.0	1.8	14.4	27.0
Washington County, VA[8]	2,457	2,316	1,910	33,851	27,123	28.6	1,647	18.0	8.9	3.0	2.9	(D)	15.9
Bristol city, VA[8].................................	NA	NA	NA	NA	NA	NA	NA	NA	NA	NA	NA	NA	NA
Kingston, NY	7,223	6,964	5,562	39,589	30,488	29.9	3,382	6.9	10.0	3.1	4.1	13.4	30.8
Ulster County, NY...............................	7,223	6,964	5,562	39,589	30,488	29.9	3,382	6.9	10.0	3.1	4.1	13.4	30.8
Knoxville, TN.......................................	26,037	24,801	20,628	36,958	31,528	26.2	20,362	11.0	7.6	4.6	10.2	13.7	15.0
Anderson County, TN	2,730	2,646	2,163	36,289	30,018	26.2	2,981	27.4	4.2	2.8	22.4	8.2	12.1
Blount County, TN	3,964	3,827	3,274	31,995	28,389	21.1	2,584	17.5	9.1	4.4	3.2	8.4	15.1
Knox County, TN	16,994	16,088	13,451	38,894	33,275	26.3	13,896	5.4	8.0	5.2	9.2	16.3	15.6
Loudon County, TN	1,856	1,764	1,343	37,698	30,579	38.2	759	22.9	7.9	3.4	5.6	7.5	14.9
Union County, TN	493	476	397	25,662	21,182	24.2	141	32.5	7.8	1.4	0.0	6.4	26.3
Kokomo, IN	3,266	3,067	3,059	33,126	30,354	6.7	2,482	41.6	6.3	2.6	2.8	(D)	15.8
Howard County, IN..............................	2,672	2,515	2,538	32,267	30,082	5.3	2,243	44.0	6.1	2.7	2.7	8.8	15.7
Tipton County, IN	594	552	521	37,631	31,753	14.0	239	19.4	7.9	2.6	3.6	(D)	16.1

[1] Based on resident population estimated as of July 1.
[2] Includes other industry categories not shown separately.
[8] Bristol city included with Washington County, VA, in the Kingsport–Bristol–Bristol, TN–VA MSA.
[9] Bedford city included with Bedford County, VA, in the Lynchburg, VA MSA.
(D) = Data withheld to avoid disclosure or does not meet statistical standards.
NA = Not available

Table C-3.　Personal Income and Earnings, by Industry—*Continued*

Metropolitan statistical area, division, and component county	Personal income Total (million dollars) 2011	2010	2005	Per capita[1] (dollars) 2011	2005	Percent change, 2005–2011	Earnings, 2011 Total[2] (million dollars)	Manufacturing	Retail trade	Finance and insurance	Professional and technical services	Health care and social services	Government and government enterprises
La Crosse, WI–MN	5,135	4,943	4,041	38,184	31,194	27.1	3,919	13.6	6.5	5.5	3.3	21.7	14.8
Houston County, MN	767	734	636	40,554	32,510	20.6	258	8.3	5.0	2.4	(D)	11.1	21.5
La Crosse County, WI	4,368	4,209	3,405	37,796	30,959	28.3	3,662	14.0	6.6	5.8	3.5	22.4	14.4
Lafayette, IN	6,464	6,026	5,162	31,747	27,456	25.2	5,282	22.3	5.5	3.1	4.1	12.8	26.9
Benton County, IN	355	315	258	40,109	28,924	37.7	213	8.2	4.1	2.9	1.4	(D)	13.9
Carroll County, IN	662	629	599	33,062	29,536	10.6	321	29.3	4.9	2.0	2.4	(D)	12.6
Tippecanoe County, IN	5,447	5,083	4,306	31,172	27,108	26.5	4,748	22.4	5.6	3.2	4.3	14.2	28.4
Lafayette, LA	12,253	11,555	8,232	44,184	32,676	48.8	10,316	7.4	6.3	2.9	7.9	13.4	10.1
Lafayette Parish, LA	10,560	9,950	7,084	47,060	35,062	49.1	9,668	7.1	6.2	2.9	8.2	13.8	9.6
St. Martin Parish, LA	1,693	1,606	1,148	31,989	23,014	47.4	648	13.2	8.8	2.2	3.4	8.3	18.4
Lake Charles, LA	7,295	6,913	5,614	36,324	28,605	29.9	5,427	19.8	6.0	2.4	5.9	12.0	15.7
Calcasieu Parish, LA	7,058	6,683	5,410	36,366	29,021	30.5	5,245	19.9	6.2	2.5	6.1	12.3	15.5
Cameron Parish, LA	236	230	204	35,114	20,739	15.7	182	16.1	(D)	(D)	(D)	2.2	22.8
Lake Havasu City–Kingman, AZ	5,291	5,073	4,377	26,145	23,187	20.9	2,355	6.3	13.1	2.3	2.6	21.9	19.6
Mohave County, AZ	5,291	5,073	4,377	26,145	23,187	20.9	2,355	6.3	13.1	2.3	2.6	21.9	19.6
Lakeland–Winter Haven, FL	20,385	19,530	16,330	33,447	29,833	24.8	10,799	9.0	8.6	6.7	4.9	14.4	15.0
Polk County, FL	20,385	19,530	16,330	33,447	29,833	24.8	10,799	9.0	8.6	6.7	4.9	14.4	15.0
Lancaster, PA	19,653	18,877	16,154	37,535	32,654	21.7	13,284	17.5	7.4	4.0	5.4	14.0	9.6
Lancaster County, PA	19,653	18,877	16,154	37,535	32,654	21.7	13,284	17.5	7.4	4.0	5.4	14.0	9.6
Lansing–East Lansing, MI	16,049	15,532	13,763	34,505	29,743	16.6	12,555	11.3	5.4	7.1	(D)	12.3	30.4
Clinton County, MI	2,711	2,583	2,167	35,926	30,225	25.1	975	15.5	7.1	3.9	(D)	7.2	14.7
Eaton County, MI	3,637	3,538	3,116	33,655	28,833	16.7	1,756	10.1	7.6	18.3	(D)	6.1	20.1
Ingham County, MI	9,701	9,412	8,480	34,450	29,969	14.4	9,824	11.1	4.9	5.4	6.1	13.9	33.8
Laredo, TX	6,409	5,961	4,455	24,985	19,914	43.9	4,656	0.7	8.7	2.6	3.2	10.7	29.2
Webb County, TX	6,409	5,961	4,455	24,985	19,914	43.9	4,656	0.7	8.7	2.6	3.2	10.7	29.2
Las Cruces, NM	6,400	6,195	4,544	29,963	24,017	40.8	3,974	4.5	5.9	2.6	7.1	13.7	34.6
Doña Ana County, NM	6,400	6,195	4,544	29,963	24,017	40.8	3,974	4.5	5.9	2.6	7.1	13.7	34.6
Las Vegas–Paradise, NV	70,289	67,738	64,181	35,680	37,109	9.5	51,822	2.7	7.4	5.0	7.3	8.7	16.2
Clark County, NV	70,289	67,738	64,181	35,680	37,109	9.5	51,822	2.7	7.4	5.0	7.3	8.7	16.2
Lawrence, KS	3,746	3,586	3,075	33,379	29,092	21.8	2,351	8.8	7.0	3.3	7.6	7.4	34.8
Douglas County, KS	3,746	3,586	3,075	33,379	29,092	21.8	2,351	8.8	7.0	3.3	7.6	7.4	34.8
Lawton, OK	4,653	4,447	3,198	36,985	27,784	45.5	3,761	7.8	4.6	2.3	1.9	4.4	62.4
Comanche County, OK	4,653	4,447	3,198	36,985	27,784	45.5	3,761	7.8	4.6	2.3	1.9	4.4	62.4
Lebanon, PA	5,169	4,919	3,959	38,489	31,368	30.6	2,744	18.5	7.7	2.0	3.2	13.7	20.1
Lebanon County, PA	5,169	4,919	3,959	38,489	31,368	30.6	2,744	18.5	7.7	2.0	3.2	13.7	20.1
Lewiston, ID–WA	2,201	2,120	1,737	35,796	29,453	26.7	1,426	13.8	8.8	6.2	3.6	16.8	19.0
Nez Perce County, ID	1,428	1,375	1,130	36,109	29,673	26.4	1,126	16.3	7.4	6.8	3.4	16.8	18.8
Asotin County, WA	773	746	607	35,230	29,053	27.2	299	4.5	13.8	3.9	4.1	16.6	19.6
Lewiston–Auburn, ME	3,887	3,741	3,272	36,192	30,479	18.8	2,587	12.0	8.3	6.1	5.7	21.2	11.4
Androscoggin County, ME	3,887	3,741	3,272	36,192	30,479	18.8	2,587	12.0	8.3	6.1	5.7	21.2	11.4
Lexington–Fayette, KY	18,098	17,122	14,614	37,763	33,450	23.8	14,901	15.1	6.8	3.5	7.9	9.6	20.9
Bourbon County, KY	610	593	577	30,504	28,976	5.7	367	23.8	6.7	3.3	(D)	(D)	14.4
Clark County, KY	1,196	1,162	1,026	33,660	29,832	16.6	746	21.1	7.9	2.5	4.9	10.5	11.5
Fayette County, KY	12,048	11,344	9,714	39,950	35,254	24.0	11,059	9.3	6.6	4.1	9.2	12.0	24.1
Jessamine County, KY	1,547	1,479	1,203	31,544	27,651	28.6	800	19.9	15.5	1.8	3.9	4.2	15.6
Scott County, KY	1,655	1,551	1,171	34,376	29,543	41.4	1,378	50.3	3.6	1.3	3.3	(D)	7.8
Woodford County, KY	1,042	995	924	41,755	38,613	12.7	551	22.9	5.2	2.1	8.3	(D)	14.9
Lima, OH	3,369	3,202	2,937	31,750	27,480	14.7	2,921	24.8	7.1	2.2	2.5	19.8	13.3
Allen County, OH	3,369	3,202	2,937	31,750	27,480	14.7	2,921	24.8	7.1	2.2	2.5	19.8	13.3
Lincoln, NE	11,959	11,279	9,604	39,018	33,644	24.5	9,423	9.0	6.1	8.2	7.3	13.3	22.5
Lancaster County, NE	11,254	10,631	9,090	38,833	33,810	23.8	9,029	8.6	6.1	8.4	7.5	13.9	22.8
Seward County, NE	705	649	514	42,216	30,958	37.2	394	17.6	4.0	3.4	3.1	(D)	16.1
Little Rock–North Little Rock–Conway, AR	28,324	26,914	21,957	39,899	33,844	29.0	21,092	6.0	7.0	6.2	7.8	11.9	25.2
Faulkner County, AR	3,869	3,610	2,664	33,255	26,854	45.2	2,248	9.3	7.6	2.7	11.9	11.1	18.2
Grant County, AR	586	564	477	32,601	27,658	23.0	194	18.8	7.8	2.0	2.9	(D)	23.7
Lonoke County, AR	2,286	2,160	1,628	32,972	27,037	40.4	688	10.8	9.5	3.8	2.9	9.0	22.1
Perry County, AR	333	323	262	32,041	25,303	27.2	83	(D)	5.9	2.5	1.8	(D)	25.8
Pulaski County, AR	16,973	16,278	14,184	43,938	38,515	19.7	16,792	5.1	6.2	7.0	7.8	12.2	26.3
Saline County, AR	4,276	3,980	2,742	39,040	29,332	55.9	1,087	7.0	15.8	2.7	3.2	13.1	24.3

[1] Based on resident population estimated as of July 1.
[2] Includes other industry categories not shown separately.
(D) = Data withheld to avoid disclosure or does not meet statistical standards.

Table C-3. Personal Income and Earnings, by Industry—*Continued*

Metropolitan statistical area, division, and component county	Total (million dollars)			Per capita¹ (dollars)		Percent change, 2005–2011	Earnings, 2011						
							Total² (million dollars)	Percentage by selected major industries					
	2011	2010	2005	2011	2005			Manufacturing	Retail trade	Finance and insurance	Professional and technical services	Health care and social services	Government and government enterprises
Logan, UT–ID	3,520	3,382	2,635	27,594	23,407	33.6	2,501	23.2	7.1	2.8	5.8	8.9	23.6
Franklin County, ID	350	340	281	27,265	23,234	24.8	156	3.9	8.7	2.3	2.2	(D)	23.2
Cache County, UT	3,169	3,042	2,355	27,631	23,428	34.6	2,345	24.5	7.0	2.8	6.1	9.5	23.6
Longview, TX	8,397	7,822	5,945	38,756	29,278	41.2	6,465	12.8	7.7	2.9	4.6	11.1	9.2
Gregg County, TX	5,320	4,965	3,837	43,222	33,247	38.7	5,204	14.3	8.0	2.7	5.4	12.1	7.5
Rusk County, TX	1,657	1,550	1,171	30,821	23,565	41.5	859	7.4	5.9	3.5	(D)	6.4	14.0
Upshur County, TX	1,420	1,307	937	35,663	24,692	51.5	401	4.3	7.4	4.4	4.8	8.5	21.1
Longview, WA	3,341	3,241	2,580	32,607	26,730	29.5	2,136	21.4	7.2	2.4	2.7	13.7	15.4
Cowlitz County, WA	3,341	3,241	2,580	32,607	26,730	29.5	2,136	21.4	7.2	2.4	2.7	13.7	15.4
Los Angeles–Long Beach–Santa Ana, CA	575,045	550,283	496,595	44,423	39,021	15.8	444,484	9.9	5.9	7.3	12.0	9.5	13.0
Los Angeles–Long Beach–Glendale, CA	420,913	403,144	357,186	42,564	36,498	17.8	329,102	9.1	5.7	6.5	11.9	9.8	14.1
Los Angeles County, CA	420,913	403,144	357,186	42,564	36,498	17.8	329,102	9.1	5.7	6.5	11.9	9.8	14.1
Santa Ana–Anaheim–Irvine, CA	154,132	147,138	139,409	50,440	47,417	10.6	115,382	12.0	6.3	9.8	12.5	8.9	10.0
Orange County, CA	154,132	147,138	139,409	50,440	47,417	10.6	115,382	12.0	6.3	9.8	12.5	8.9	10.0
Louisville/Jefferson County, KY–IN	50,546	48,093	41,228	39,037	33,820	22.6	36,972	13.2	5.7	8.7	6.9	13.7	13.9
Clark County, IN	3,782	3,614	3,047	33,898	29,940	24.1	2,506	16.2	8.3	4.8	2.5	9.3	19.7
Floyd County, IN	3,016	2,890	2,503	40,219	34,810	20.5	1,603	22.2	6.2	4.7	5.4	11.2	21.2
Harrison County, IN	1,264	1,203	1,020	32,122	27,300	23.9	525	13.1	7.8	3.0	(D)	(D)	20.6
Washington County, IN	832	792	693	29,544	24,856	19.9	287	26.5	7.1	3.1	2.3	(D)	21.1
Bullitt County, KY	2,293	2,185	1,818	30,533	26,487	26.2	906	14.4	5.8	2.3	7.7	5.7	15.9
Henry County, KY	477	459	406	30,890	26,431	17.4	158	18.5	5.9	2.5	(D)	(D)	27.2
Jefferson County, KY	31,241	29,832	26,314	41,828	37,062	18.7	28,457	11.8	5.2	10.0	7.9	15.3	12.1
Meade County, KY	1,155	1,042	695	39,065	23,364	66.2	233	12.4	9.2	2.6	3.6	(D)	24.0
Nelson County, KY	1,454	1,377	1,140	33,071	28,091	27.6	712	29.2	8.4	2.4	(D)	11.1	13.9
Oldham County, KY	2,708	2,533	1,945	44,660	35,849	39.2	764	5.9	6.7	9.3	6.8	13.3	25.2
Shelby County, KY	1,515	1,414	1,117	35,173	29,546	35.6	677	27.2	8.4	3.1	4.7	8.8	15.3
Spencer County, KY	605	555	361	34,806	24,212	67.3	81	(D)	8.9	3.8	(D)	(D)	37.9
Trimble County, KY	205	199	168	23,461	19,160	21.6	63	(D)	3.1	4.5	1.8	(D)	28.1
Lubbock, TX	10,026	9,710	7,506	34,573	28,400	33.6	6,934	3.7	9.0	5.7	4.4	16.6	23.4
Crosby County, TX	191	232	214	31,281	32,825	-11.0	68	1.5	25.8	(D)	1.5	(D)	31.7
Lubbock County, TX	9,836	9,477	7,292	34,644	28,288	34.9	6,866	3.8	8.9	5.7	4.4	16.7	23.3
Lynchburg, VA⁹,¹⁰	8,556	8,212	6,960	33,664	29,181	22.9	5,379	19.6	7.0	4.7	9.3	12.4	13.8
Amherst County, VA	969	941	823	30,120	25,765	17.7	450	19.8	6.9	1.6	(D)	(D)	30.0
Appomattox County, VA	466	449	374	30,992	26,732	24.7	157	5.6	11.9	1.8	3.6	(D)	28.2
Bedford County, VA⁹	2,911	2,790	2,348	38,595	33,068	24.0	1,000	13.6	7.1	3.5	7.7	10.3	15.2
Campbell County, VA¹⁰	4,210	4,032	3,415	32,008	28,091	23.3	3,773	21.7	6.8	5.6	11.1	15.0	10.8
Bedford city, VA⁹	NA	NA	NA	NA	NA	NA	NA	NA	NA	NA	NA	NA	NA
Lynchburg city, VA¹⁰	NA	NA	NA	NA	NA	NA	NA	NA	NA	NA	NA	NA	NA
Macon, GA	8,281	7,944	6,952	35,554	30,473	19.1	5,244	7.3	7.9	9.5	5.3	19.5	15.6
Bibb County, GA	5,581	5,368	4,927	35,676	31,994	13.3	4,564	8.1	8.3	10.5	5.7	21.9	13.4
Crawford County, GA	394	377	327	31,327	25,373	20.5	93	2.0	7.0	2.2	1.8	5.6	22.1
Jones County, GA	974	932	739	34,168	27,180	31.8	188	1.4	6.1	4.4	(D)	(D)	30.1
Monroe County, GA	1,049	992	725	39,397	30,105	44.7	347	2.7	5.5	1.4	4.7	5.4	32.3
Twiggs County, GA	283	274	234	32,267	23,431	21.2	53	(D)	3.1	(D)	(D)	(D)	27.4
Madera–Chowchilla, CA	4,378	4,071	3,333	28,631	23,755	31.4	2,904	7.1	5.7	1.1	1.9	14.5	22.4
Madera County, CA	4,378	4,071	3,333	28,631	23,755	31.4	2,904	7.1	5.7	1.1	1.9	14.5	22.4
Madison, WI	26,497	25,019	21,294	45,964	39,591	24.4	21,915	9.8	6.2	9.0	8.6	9.4	23.8
Columbia County, WI	2,309	2,230	1,914	40,580	34,552	20.6	1,204	26.1	6.9	2.5	2.3	10.5	16.7
Dane County, WI	23,269	21,911	18,619	46,916	40,559	25.0	20,123	8.9	5.3	9.6	9.2	9.6	24.6
Iowa County, WI	919	878	761	38,940	32,523	20.7	588	8.4	35.1	2.1	1.8	0.0	12.3
Manchester–Nashua, NH	19,274	18,434	16,105	47,981	40,629	19.7	14,650	16.7	8.2	8.9	10.5	11.7	10.8
Hillsborough County, NH	19,274	18,434	16,105	47,981	40,629	19.7	14,650	16.7	8.2	8.9	10.5	11.7	10.8
Manhattan, KS	5,678	5,265	3,307	43,593	29,712	71.7	4,981	3.6	4.0	1.7	(D)	(D)	66.6
Geary County, KS	1,463	1,393	875	41,409	32,290	67.2	3,003	1.3	1.6	0.5	(D)	0.9	86.6
Pottawatomie County, KS	792	735	558	36,131	28,713	41.9	506	22.5	8.1	2.8	(D)	(D)	11.4
Riley County, KS	3,423	3,137	1,874	46,890	28,934	82.7	1,471	1.8	7.6	3.8	4.0	11.0	44.8
Mankato–North Mankato, MN	3,638	3,394	2,839	37,424	31,155	28.2	2,810	15.3	6.9	3.2	(D)	13.8	17.6
Blue Earth County, MN	2,370	2,197	1,835	36,808	30,632	29.1	2,075	11.2	8.2	3.6	3.7	18.7	15.8
Nicollet County, MN	1,268	1,198	1,003	38,630	32,158	26.4	736	26.8	3.2	2.1	(D)	(D)	22.5
Mansfield, OH	3,794	3,640	3,455	30,714	27,049	9.8	2,528	21.5	8.9	2.6	2.8	15.1	18.9
Richland County, OH	3,794	3,640	3,455	30,714	27,049	9.8	2,528	21.5	8.9	2.6	2.8	15.1	18.9

¹ Based on resident population estimated as of July 1.
² Includes other industry categories not shown separately.
³ Radford city included with Montgomery County, VA, in the Blacksburg–Christiansburg–Radford, VA MSA.
⁹ Bedford city included with Bedford County, VA, in the Lynchburg, VA MSA.
¹⁰ Lynchburg city included with Campbell County, VA, in the Lynchburg, VA MSA.
(D) = Data withheld to avoid disclosure or does not meet statistical standards.
NA = Not available

Table C-3. Personal Income and Earnings, by Industry—*Continued*

Metropolitan statistical area, division, and component county	Personal income Total (million dollars) 2011	2010	2005	Per capita[1] (dollars) 2011	2005	Percent change, 2005–2011	Earnings, 2011 Total[2] (million dollars)	Manufacturing	Retail trade	Finance and insurance	Professional and technical services	Health care and social services	Government and government enterprises
McAllen–Edinburg–Mission, TX	17,248	16,511	11,668	21,620	17,286	47.8	11,212	2.4	10.3	3.4	3.2	20.6	26.4
Hidalgo County, TX	17,248	16,511	11,668	21,620	17,286	47.8	11,212	2.4	10.3	3.4	3.2	20.6	26.4
Medford, OR	7,087	6,814	6,072	34,602	31,188	16.7	4,291	8.2	10.9	3.7	4.5	18.4	16.1
Jackson County, OR	7,087	6,814	6,072	34,602	31,188	16.7	4,291	8.2	10.9	3.7	4.5	18.4	16.1
Memphis, TN–MS–AR	51,198	49,138	44,057	38,622	34,865	16.2	40,964	9.8	6.6	6.0	4.5	11.0	15.3
Crittenden County, AR	1,609	1,558	1,300	31,850	25,873	23.8	879	11.3	7.1	2.0	2.0	10.9	18.1
DeSoto County, MS	5,535	5,173	4,308	33,737	31,468	28.5	2,579	9.1	10.4	2.3	2.8	12.1	13.6
Marshall County, MS	965	934	798	26,236	22,130	21.0	319	12.0	9.3	4.6	1.5	(D)	22.0
Tate County, MS	823	791	682	28,643	25,293	20.6	310	9.8	9.2	3.0	2.1	(D)	28.3
Tunica County, MS	329	306	236	30,943	22,597	39.6	516	1.8	2.2	0.7	0.0	(D)	8.7
Fayette County, TN	1,678	1,542	1,065	43,579	31,470	57.6	639	23.4	10.0	5.0	0.0	(D)	12.2
Shelby County, TN	38,117	36,814	34,129	40,763	37,373	11.7	35,150	9.6	6.2	6.5	4.9	11.7	15.2
Tipton County, TN	2,143	2,021	1,540	34,959	27,482	39.2	572	13.5	9.3	2.5	(D)	(D)	23.4
Merced, CA	7,406	6,956	5,803	28,497	23,923	27.6	4,453	9.1	6.6	1.6	2.2	9.5	23.7
Merced County, CA	7,406	6,956	5,803	28,497	23,923	27.6	4,453	9.1	6.6	1.6	2.2	9.5	23.7
Miami–Fort Lauderdale–Pompano Beach, FL	244,224	233,377	210,605	43,072	38,921	16.0	154,631	3.5	7.9	8.0	10.3	11.7	15.0
Fort Lauderdale–Pompano Beach– Deerfield Beach, FL	76,134	72,731	67,946	42,768	38,895	12.1	47,024	3.9	8.8	7.5	10.4	10.3	15.5
Broward County, FL	76,134	72,731	67,946	42,768	38,895	12.1	47,024	3.9	8.8	7.5	10.4	10.3	15.5
Miami–Miami Beach–Kendall, FL	96,658	92,227	77,373	37,834	32,429	24.9	71,598	3.2	7.3	7.9	10.1	11.7	15.8
Miami–Dade County, FL	96,658	92,227	77,373	37,834	32,429	24.9	71,598	3.2	7.3	7.9	10.1	11.7	15.8
West Palm Beach–Boca Raton– Boynton Beach, FL	71,432	68,418	65,286	53,500	51,070	9.4	36,009	3.5	7.7	9.1	10.8	13.7	12.5
Palm Beach County, FL	71,432	68,418	65,286	53,500	51,070	9.4	36,009	3.5	7.7	9.1	10.8	13.7	12.5
Michigan City–La Porte, IN	3,525	3,346	2,993	31,650	27,324	17.8	2,258	22.3	6.9	2.3	2.5	14.0	16.8
LaPorte County, IN	3,525	3,346	2,993	31,650	27,324	17.8	2,258	22.3	6.9	2.3	2.5	14.0	16.8
Midland, TX	9,144	7,982	5,186	65,173	42,331	76.3	7,553	3.6	4.3	2.5	5.4	4.8	6.8
Midland County, TX	9,144	7,982	5,186	65,173	42,331	76.3	7,553	3.6	4.3	2.5	5.4	4.8	6.8
Milwaukee–Waukesha–West Allis, WI	69,691	66,928	58,251	44,610	38,263	19.6	54,697	17.7	5.1	8.9	7.9	13.0	11.1
Milwaukee County, WI	37,035	36,000	31,393	38,881	33,664	18.0	33,870	14.5	4.2	9.6	8.2	14.5	13.1
Ozaukee County, WI	5,247	4,987	4,530	60,615	53,179	15.8	2,516	24.9	5.9	9.6	8.7	13.1	9.3
Washington County, WI	5,978	5,577	4,805	45,159	38,196	24.4	2,926	29.0	7.5	6.1	3.1	11.3	10.9
Waukesha County, WI	21,430	20,364	17,524	54,847	46,252	22.3	15,385	21.5	6.4	7.9	7.9	10.2	7.2
Minneapolis–St. Paul–Bloomington, MN–WI	161,468	152,789	133,840	48,657	42,740	20.6	129,028	12.2	4.9	10.4	10.1	10.3	12.4
Anoka County, MN	13,276	12,670	11,323	39,850	35,404	17.2	6,913	26.2	6.9	2.9	4.8	12.7	14.1
Carver County, MN	5,357	4,968	3,879	57,830	46,587	38.1	2,412	29.1	4.5	2.6	5.7	10.5	11.3
Chisago County, MN	1,896	1,785	1,478	35,160	29,394	28.3	728	15.8	6.3	2.1	2.0	27.0	18.9
Dakota County, MN	18,612	17,744	16,105	46,299	42,177	15.6	11,449	13.0	6.7	8.5	8.0	7.4	12.1
Hennepin County, MN	67,157	63,614	56,374	57,476	50,469	19.1	70,877	9.6	4.3	13.9	13.4	9.3	9.7
Isanti County, MN	1,399	1,325	1,138	36,544	31,253	23.0	609	13.2	9.9	3.4	(D)	21.3	17.5
Ramsey County, MN	23,349	22,299	20,371	45,365	40,941	14.6	23,802	12.2	4.1	7.4	5.9	12.8	17.3
Scott County, MN	6,018	5,581	4,343	45,400	37,085	38.6	2,603	16.2	5.6	1.6	8.6	8.3	21.0
Sherburne County, MN	2,990	2,782	2,288	33,474	28,187	30.7	1,308	14.3	7.2	2.3	3.1	13.8	18.8
Washington County, MN	11,949	11,240	9,367	49,523	42,581	27.6	4,177	14.7	8.5	8.7	6.4	13.2	15.9
Wright County, MN	4,703	4,286	3,417	37,196	30,874	37.6	2,031	13.5	8.4	2.1	2.9	8.5	17.4
Pierce County, WI	1,389	1,327	1,165	33,989	29,624	19.2	580	12.0	4.4	2.9	(D)	8.1	32.0
St. Croix County, WI	3,374	3,168	2,594	39,734	33,660	30.1	1,540	22.9	8.2	3.8	5.3	12.1	14.4
Missoula, MT	3,876	3,723	3,204	35,190	31,325	20.9	2,949	3.2	9.0	4.7	7.0	17.9	20.7
Missoula County, MT	3,876	3,723	3,204	35,190	31,325	20.9	2,949	3.2	9.0	4.7	7.0	17.9	20.7
Mobile, AL	13,524	13,019	10,547	32,779	26,438	28.2	10,569	12.3	6.6	7.3	6.9	11.2	17.3
Mobile County, AL	13,524	13,019	10,547	32,779	26,438	28.2	10,569	12.3	6.6	7.3	6.9	11.2	17.3
Modesto, CA	16,652	15,981	14,233	32,115	28,465	17.0	10,350	14.2	7.7	2.7	3.4	16.5	16.8
Stanislaus County, CA	16,652	15,981	14,233	32,115	28,465	17.0	10,350	14.2	7.7	2.7	3.4	16.5	16.8
Monroe, LA	6,013	5,794	4,878	33,846	28,319	23.3	4,101	(D)	8.4	6.0	6.7	15.6	18.5
Ouachita Parish, LA	5,307	5,110	4,301	34,256	28,772	23.4	3,848	9.4	8.4	6.2	7.0	16.6	18.3
Union Parish, LA	706	684	577	31,051	25,344	22.3	253	(D)	9.4	2.3	3.0	(D)	21.9
Monroe, MI	5,403	5,082	4,792	35,647	31,448	12.7	2,371	17.2	6.6	2.1	(D)	10.1	13.8
Monroe County, MI	5,403	5,082	4,792	35,647	31,448	12.7	2,371	17.2	6.6	2.1	(D)	10.1	13.8
Montgomery, AL	13,800	13,300	11,520	36,450	32,121	19.8	10,342	11.1	6.2	5.2	7.2	9.7	30.8
Autauga County, AL	1,805	1,714	1,371	32,657	27,601	31.6	609	14.1	11.1	3.3	3.0	(D)	20.4
Elmore County, AL	2,723	2,616	1,993	33,975	27,306	36.7	934	16.5	11.5	2.6	3.8	9.4	23.7
Lowndes County, AL	359	355	300	32,176	24,171	19.7	192	38.1	3.5	1.3	1.3	2.3	16.3
Montgomery County, AL	8,913	8,615	7,857	38,414	35,137	13.4	8,607	9.7	5.4	5.7	8.0	10.6	32.6
Morgantown, WV	4,659	4,434	3,278	35,226	27,331	42.1	3,878	9.0	5.4	2.9	6.3	17.3	30.1
Monongalia County, WV	3,708	3,523	2,580	37,632	29,178	43.7	3,457	9.2	5.1	3.0	6.9	18.6	29.5
Preston County, WV	951	912	698	28,197	22,146	36.3	421	6.7	7.4	1.8	2.0	6.9	35.2
Morristown, TN	4,029	3,879	3,231	29,306	24,938	24.7	2,344	26.9	8.5	2.1	2.0	(D)	14.7
Grainger County, TN	650	624	496	28,567	22,661	31.2	173	22.3	8.6	1.8	0.0	4.5	24.1
Hamblen County, TN	1,894	1,824	1,559	30,034	26,020	21.5	1,537	28.9	8.3	2.1	1.9	13.2	12.4
Jefferson County, TN	1,485	1,431	1,177	28,742	24,624	26.2	635	23.5	8.7	2.1	2.6	(D)	17.8

[1] Based on resident population estimated as of July 1.
[2] Includes other industry categories not shown separately.
(D) = Data withheld to avoid disclosure or does not meet statistical standards.

Table C-3. Personal Income and Earnings, by Industry—*Continued*

Metropolitan statistical area, division, and component county	Personal income												
	Total (million dollars)			Per capita[1] (dollars)		Percent change, 2005–2011	Earnings, 2011						
							Total[2] (million dollars)	Percentage by selected major industries					
	2011	2010	2005	2011	2005			Manufacturing	Retail trade	Finance and insurance	Professional and technical services	Health care and social services	Government and government enterprises
Mount Vernon–Anacortes, WA	4,552	4,359	3,622	38,543	32,724	25.7	2,690	16.3	10.1	4.3	4.2	8.5	24.2
Skagit County, WA	4,552	4,359	3,622	38,543	32,724	25.7	2,690	16.3	10.1	4.3	4.2	8.5	24.2
Muncie, IN	3,549	3,410	3,152	30,164	26,673	12.6	2,344	9.6	8.0	4.2	6.2	20.5	23.7
Delaware County, IN	3,549	3,410	3,152	30,164	26,673	12.6	2,344	9.6	8.0	4.2	6.2	20.5	23.7
Muskegon–Norton Shores, MI	5,099	4,865	4,475	29,766	25,774	14.0	3,154	25.4	10.5	2.4	2.5	17.5	16.1
Muskegon County, MI	5,099	4,865	4,475	29,766	25,774	14.0	3,154	25.4	10.5	2.4	2.5	17.5	16.1
Myrtle Beach–North Myrtle Beach–Conway, SC	8,055	7,722	6,433	29,148	27,983	25.2	5,062	3.5	12.0	6.7	4.2	11.1	18.0
Horry County, SC	8,055	7,722	6,433	29,148	27,983	25.2	5,062	3.5	12.0	6.7	4.2	11.1	18.0
Napa, CA	7,077	6,673	5,932	51,253	45,494	19.3	4,681	19.5	5.6	4.0	5.6	11.6	15.9
Napa County, CA	7,077	6,673	5,932	51,253	45,494	19.3	4,681	19.5	5.6	4.0	5.6	11.6	15.9
Naples–Marco Island, FL	19,447	18,500	16,771	59,264	54,549	16.0	7,639	2.5	9.3	7.5	6.6	15.3	11.6
Collier County, FL	19,447	18,500	16,771	59,264	54,549	16.0	7,639	2.5	9.3	7.5	6.6	15.3	11.6
Nashville–Davidson––Murfreesboro––Franklin, TN	68,129	64,674	52,294	42,129	36,382	30.3	55,923	7.9	6.8	6.8	8.7	19.9	11.1
Cannon County, TN	416	405	363	30,217	27,635	14.4	120	6.4	8.0	0.0	(D)	14.0	21.0
Cheatham County, TN	1,300	1,252	1,130	33,268	29,999	15.0	541	23.6	6.5	1.6	(D)	0.0	13.9
Davidson County, TN	30,069	28,757	24,153	47,318	40,953	24.5	34,097	3.9	5.9	6.6	10.0	25.1	10.0
Dickson County, TN	1,547	1,484	1,245	30,887	26,850	24.3	772	19.9	10.4	3.2	(D)	14.3	16.4
Hickman County, TN	587	572	489	24,065	20,406	20.2	173	15.1	6.1	1.8	(D)	7.4	32.4
Macon County, TN	638	606	526	28,353	24,766	21.1	245	8.5	12.5	5.4	3.6	(D)	19.4
Robertson County, TN	2,261	2,123	1,786	33,699	29,911	26.6	989	26.0	9.1	2.2	(D)	5.2	17.9
Rutherford County, TN	8,714	8,229	6,525	32,404	29,483	33.5	6,394	24.7	6.6	4.3	3.1	11.6	16.0
Smith County, TN	610	570	477	31,878	25,774	27.9	270	22.7	7.2	3.5	1.5	(D)	18.2
Sumner County, TN	6,007	5,678	4,527	36,698	31,412	32.7	2,401	13.9	7.8	4.3	5.5	12.1	16.8
Trousdale County, TN	294	280	177	37,583	23,840	65.6	155	7.4	11.1	0.0	12.6	13.2	15.5
Williamson County, TN	11,200	10,469	7,483	59,399	48,559	49.7	7,641	2.7	7.9	13.7	14.5	15.0	6.8
Wilson County, TN	4,485	4,248	3,411	38,461	34,124	31.5	2,125	14.5	14.4	2.9	(D)	8.8	11.4
New Haven–Milford, CT	42,606	40,636	33,857	49,478	39,965	25.8	26,975	11.0	6.1	5.9	8.3	16.2	14.8
New Haven County, CT	42,606	40,636	33,857	49,478	39,965	25.8	26,975	11.0	6.1	5.9	8.3	16.2	14.8
New Orleans–Metairie–Kenner, LA	51,935	49,946	43,498	43,603	31,866	19.4	38,587	8.2	5.8	4.7	9.8	9.4	16.6
Jefferson Parish, LA	19,391	18,737	15,695	44,821	34,378	23.5	13,692	7.2	8.0	6.0	9.0	12.8	11.0
Orleans Parish, LA	15,347	14,655	14,887	42,542	30,118	3.1	14,289	3.3	3.4	4.7	13.6	7.3	22.8
Plaquemines Parish, LA	943	923	788	39,919	26,667	19.7	1,346	19.3	(D)	0.6	(D)	(D)	15.9
St. Bernard Parish, LA	1,383	1,334	1,421	34,958	19,925	-2.7	797	24.9	6.2	0.8	2.1	(D)	16.2
St. Charles Parish, LA	1,969	1,928	1,532	37,441	30,235	28.5	2,039	32.4	3.4	0.9	4.4	2.5	11.1
St. John the Baptist Parish, LA	1,653	1,618	1,290	36,548	28,484	28.1	1,170	30.5	5.1	3.8	3.3	5.9	11.6
St. Tammany Parish, LA	11,249	10,751	7,884	47,508	36,273	42.7	5,254	4.5	9.0	4.6	8.7	13.4	17.5
New York–Northern New Jersey–Long Island, NY–NJ–PA	1,079,532	1,032,838	863,632	56,770	46,510	25.0	827,577	4.3	5.0	18.7	12.6	10.4	12.7
Edison–New Brunswick, NJ	124,200	119,460	101,798	52,862	44,574	22.0	79,404	8.4	6.9	7.1	13.4	10.8	13.7
Middlesex County, NJ	40,062	38,336	32,143	49,203	40,826	24.6	32,391	9.8	5.6	6.0	14.4	8.2	14.1
Monmouth County, NJ	36,823	35,595	30,870	58,355	49,169	19.3	18,673	3.9	8.2	8.0	13.6	14.7	15.6
Ocean County, NJ	23,594	22,796	19,181	40,724	34,497	23.0	9,204	3.2	11.3	2.8	5.8	20.5	21.9
Somerset County, NJ	23,721	22,733	19,604	73,011	62,710	21.0	19,137	12.8	5.5	9.9	15.3	6.5	7.2
Nassau–Suffolk, NY	169,583	163,840	139,036	59,644	49,479	22.0	97,936	6.0	7.2	8.9	8.8	15.2	18.0
Nassau County, NY	91,120	88,059	75,462	67,776	56,639	20.8	51,153	3.3	7.5	8.5	9.0	18.0	15.9
Suffolk County, NY	78,463	75,780	63,574	52,350	43,023	23.4	46,783	8.9	6.9	9.3	8.5	12.2	20.3
Newark–Union, NJ–PA	123,143	118,262	103,407	57,196	48,543	19.1	87,390	10.2	5.7	9.1	13.8	10.1	15.2
Essex County, NJ	41,578	40,012	33,995	52,956	43,231	22.3	31,459	7.5	4.1	11.1	12.9	10.7	21.2
Hunterdon County, NJ	8,669	8,359	7,669	67,710	59,880	13.0	4,192	4.9	11.1	10.0	15.0	11.0	15.6
Morris County, NJ	35,504	34,180	30,551	71,730	62,930	16.2	29,175	11.7	6.0	10.2	16.2	8.6	9.2
Sussex County, NJ	7,393	7,154	6,370	49,782	42,409	16.1	2,428	5.9	10.2	2.7	8.2	15.2	21.9
Union County, NJ	27,978	26,626	23,279	51,860	44,243	20.2	19,597	14.3	6.1	5.2	12.5	10.4	13.2
Pike County, PA	2,020	1,930	1,544	35,523	28,593	30.8	540	(D)	11.1	2.3	5.4	9.0	31.0
New York–White Plains–Wayne, NY–NJ	662,607	631,277	519,391	56,778	45,782	27.6	562,846	2.6	4.2	23.5	13.0	9.5	11.2
Bergen County, NJ	60,214	57,439	50,550	66,096	56,706	19.1	39,011	7.9	6.9	5.3	11.6	14.8	9.3
Hudson County, NJ	30,379	28,753	21,152	47,377	34,412	43.6	23,303	2.5	4.7	30.5	8.6	6.4	14.9
Passaic County, NJ	21,691	20,640	17,409	43,209	35,269	24.6	12,339	12.3	8.5	4.4	6.3	12.7	18.3
Bronx County, NY	44,249	42,595	33,034	31,788	24,438	34.0	17,247	2.3	6.2	3.3	3.5	29.5	13.2
Kings County, NY	99,662	95,051	72,234	39,351	29,534	38.0	31,488	3.2	7.6	6.5	5.8	27.7	9.7
New York County, NY	194,317	183,660	155,775	121,301	98,994	24.7	347,122	0.9	2.7	32.4	16.4	4.8	10.4
Putnam County, NY	5,374	5,192	4,450	53,781	44,687	20.8	1,801	5.9	5.9	4.0	7.3	18.6	23.4
Queens County, NY	94,447	89,935	72,381	42,017	33,123	30.5	34,685	4.0	6.6	5.6	3.1	16.6	10.2
Richmond County, NY	22,811	22,053	18,169	48,486	39,755	25.5	5,906	(D)	8.6	3.8	5.1	28.5	10.5
Rockland County, NY	16,951	16,109	13,748	53,787	46,022	23.3	9,169	11.4	6.1	8.0	8.1	13.8	18.8
Westchester County, NY	72,509	69,849	60,489	75,855	64,805	19.9	40,776	5.0	5.5	11.8	10.5	13.2	15.1

[1] Based on resident population estimated as of July 1.
[2] Includes other industry categories not shown separately.
(D) = Data withheld to avoid disclosure or does not meet statistical standards.

Table C-3. Personal Income and Earnings, by Industry—*Continued*

Metropolitan statistical area, division, and component county	Personal income Total (million dollars) 2011	2010	2005	Per capita[1] (dollars) 2011	2005	Percent change, 2005-2011	Earnings, 2011 Total[2] (million dollars)	Manufacturing	Retail trade	Finance and insurance	Professional and technical services	Health care and social services	Government and government enterprises
Niles–Benton Harbor, MI	5,623	5,444	4,735	35,830	29,871	18.8	3,611	29.1	5.9	3.1	3.8	11.9	13.8
Berrien County, MI	5,623	5,444	4,735	35,830	29,871	18.8	3,611	29.1	5.9	3.1	3.8	11.9	13.8
North Port–Bradenton–Sarasota, FL	33,859	32,421	29,790	47,732	44,149	13.7	14,575	6.1	9.3	6.4	9.4	16.7	12.1
Manatee County, FL	13,308	12,750	11,621	40,678	37,871	14.5	6,256	9.0	8.9	3.9	9.6	13.4	12.9
Sarasota County, FL	20,551	19,671	18,169	53,769	49,385	13.1	8,320	4.0	9.6	8.3	9.2	19.3	11.5
Norwich–New London, CT	12,978	12,521	10,641	47,452	39,461	22.0	9,597	17.0	5.5	2.0	8.0	11.0	31.1
New London County, CT	12,978	12,521	10,641	47,452	39,461	22.0	9,597	17.0	5.5	2.0	8.0	11.0	31.1
Ocala, FL	10,877	10,431	8,611	32,709	28,366	26.3	4,580	8.6	10.8	4.1	4.6	15.9	22.3
Marion County, FL	10,877	10,431	8,611	32,709	28,366	26.3	4,580	8.6	10.8	4.1	4.6	15.9	22.3
Ocean City, NJ	4,704	4,573	3,972	48,694	40,016	18.4	2,264	1.4	11.1	3.2	4.2	12.1	28.5
Cape May County, NJ	4,704	4,573	3,972	48,694	40,016	18.4	2,264	1.4	11.1	3.2	4.2	12.1	28.5
Odessa, TX	5,378	4,686	3,287	38,385	26,215	63.6	4,452	8.2	6.1	2.0	4.0	6.6	11.8
Ector County, TX	5,378	4,686	3,287	38,385	26,215	63.6	4,452	8.2	6.1	2.0	4.0	6.6	11.8
Ogden–Clearfield, UT	18,976	17,942	14,202	34,134	29,141	33.6	11,904	12.7	7.1	3.5	6.9	9.4	30.8
Davis County, UT	10,837	10,240	8,020	34,755	29,792	35.1	6,932	10.2	6.3	2.9	8.7	7.4	35.0
Morgan County, UT	322	301	207	33,278	26,007	55.4	113	12.1	5.8	2.7	6.2	0.0	16.8
Weber County, UT	7,817	7,401	5,974	33,344	28,427	30.8	4,859	16.1	8.3	4.4	4.4	12.5	25.2
Oklahoma City, OK	51,124	47,508	38,462	40,002	33,120	32.9	39,817	6.5	6.4	4.7	6.4	11.0	22.6
Canadian County, OK	4,720	4,284	2,980	39,501	30,049	58.4	1,670	12.4	7.5	3.1	3.8	5.8	20.9
Cleveland County, OK	9,478	8,852	7,050	36,275	30,685	34.4	4,270	5.4	8.9	3.0	7.6	9.6	32.1
Grady County, OK	1,642	1,536	1,223	30,979	24,831	34.3	732	10.7	9.6	3.2	3.7	7.1	19.5
Lincoln County, OK	1,014	963	774	29,695	23,435	31.1	394	9.2	8.3	8.2	3.3	(D)	22.1
Logan County, OK	1,635	1,476	1,112	38,467	30,469	47.0	575	4.1	7.3	4.4	0.0	(D)	18.8
McClain County, OK	1,524	1,387	875	43,239	28,865	74.1	421	2.3	14.1	3.4	4.3	(D)	21.4
Oklahoma County, OK	31,111	29,010	24,448	42,480	35,780	27.3	31,754	6.4	5.8	5.0	6.7	12.0	21.6
Olympia, WA	10,585	10,098	7,998	41,251	35,230	32.3	6,152	3.2	7.2	3.3	5.1	13.2	40.0
Thurston County, WA	10,585	10,098	7,998	41,251	35,230	32.3	6,152	3.2	7.2	3.3	5.1	13.2	40.0
Omaha–Council Bluffs, NE–IA	39,005	36,987	31,077	44,470	38,164	25.5	30,230	6.4	5.6	9.4	8.6	10.8	16.0
Harrison County, IA	621	550	460	41,885	29,913	35.2	302	4.5	5.8	2.9	1.5	(D)	15.2
Mills County, IA	670	635	558	44,674	37,470	19.9	258	4.0	3.7	2.9	(D)	(D)	36.6
Pottawattamie County, IA	3,426	3,272	2,839	36,640	31,473	20.7	1,974	13.0	8.7	2.7	3.0	13.6	16.4
Cass County, NE	1,058	976	857	41,991	34,036	23.5	340	8.0	5.6	4.6	2.6	(D)	20.6
Douglas County, NE	24,673	23,584	20,400	47,008	41,793	20.9	22,449	6.0	5.3	10.8	9.7	12.4	12.2
Sarpy County, NE	6,806	6,327	4,621	41,865	32,950	47.3	4,017	4.0	5.4	7.0	8.1	4.7	33.5
Saunders County, NE	878	807	654	42,072	31,945	34.3	324	4.2	5.6	3.7	2.6	(D)	21.9
Washington County, NE	874	834	690	43,059	34,717	26.7	565	17.1	8.6	3.4	2.3	7.2	24.9
Orlando–Kissimmee–Sanford, FL	77,159	73,619	64,007	35,535	32,727	20.5	58,613	4.9	7.4	6.0	10.1	11.4	12.4
Lake County, FL	10,188	9,697	8,109	33,846	30,303	25.6	3,954	4.6	11.6	3.2	4.3	19.8	18.8
Orange County, FL	42,076	40,111	34,473	35,990	32,727	22.1	41,510	5.4	6.3	5.9	10.7	10.6	11.4
Osceola County, FL	7,504	7,054	5,410	27,171	23,726	38.7	3,595	1.7	9.9	2.5	3.1	14.7	20.2
Seminole County, FL	17,391	16,757	16,015	40,914	39,365	8.6	9,555	3.9	9.6	8.7	12.0	10.3	11.2
Oshkosh–Neenah, WI	6,447	6,198	5,270	38,444	32,641	22.3	5,648	34.6	4.4	3.9	4.0	10.7	11.8
Winnebago County, WI	6,447	6,198	5,270	38,444	32,641	22.3	5,648	34.6	4.4	3.9	4.0	10.7	11.8
Owensboro, KY	3,999	3,773	3,140	34,677	28,166	27.4	2,721	20.8	7.2	4.8	2.7	8.8	20.4
Daviess County, KY	3,427	3,237	2,667	35,246	28,629	28.5	2,267	14.6	8.1	5.5	3.2	10.2	22.4
Hancock County, KY	261	245	195	30,440	22,938	33.7	326	70.0	1.4	1.9	(D)	1.7	6.9
McLean County, KY	311	290	278	32,674	28,310	12.1	129	5.4	7.3	(D)	(D)	3.6	18.5
Oxnard–Thousand Oaks–Ventura, CA	38,141	36,506	33,151	45,855	41,742	15.1	23,091	15.7	6.7	8.0	7.6	8.9	17.3
Ventura County, CA	38,141	36,506	33,151	45,855	41,742	15.1	23,091	15.7	6.7	8.0	7.6	8.9	17.3
Palm Bay–Melbourne–Titusville, FL	20,671	19,945	17,578	38,028	33,172	17.6	12,524	15.3	6.7	3.5	9.6	13.4	18.4
Brevard County, FL	20,671	19,945	17,578	38,028	33,172	17.6	12,524	15.3	6.7	3.5	9.6	13.4	18.4
Palm Coast, FL	3,230	3,034	2,190	33,170	28,440	47.5	824	4.5	11.2	2.5	4.8	15.7	25.5
Flagler County, FL	3,230	3,034	2,190	33,170	28,440	47.5	824	4.5	11.2	2.5	4.8	15.7	25.5
Panama City–Lynn Haven–Panama City Beach, FL	6,296	6,103	5,135	37,068	31,519	22.6	4,186	4.7	8.1	3.2	8.0	11.0	31.6
Bay County, FL	6,296	6,103	5,135	37,068	31,519	22.6	4,186	4.7	8.1	3.2	8.0	11.0	31.6
Parkersburg–Marietta–Vienna, WV–OH	5,304	5,059	4,329	32,694	26,580	22.5	3,612	15.3	8.5	4.1	3.2	16.3	18.7
Washington County, OH	2,086	1,983	1,670	33,785	26,692	25.0	1,340	21.1	7.1	3.7	3.8	17.6	12.0
Pleasants County, WV	241	228	196	31,718	25,516	23.2	179	(D)	4.0	(D)	2.3	6.1	18.4
Wirt County, WV	131	124	104	22,699	17,743	26.3	34	(D)	7.2	(D)	(D)	9.8	40.5
Wood County, WV	2,846	2,725	2,360	32,666	27,187	20.6	2,059	13.0	9.7	4.8	2.9	16.4	22.8
Pascagoula, MS	5,584	5,460	4,322	34,304	27,248	29.2	3,666	35.7	5.2	1.9	4.7	6.2	21.3
George County, MS	583	577	477	25,477	23,034	22.3	226	8.3	12.5	3.1	3.8	5.7	32.9
Jackson County, MS	5,001	4,882	3,845	35,748	27,881	30.1	3,440	37.5	4.7	1.8	4.7	6.3	20.6
Pensacola–Ferry Pass–Brent, FL	16,352	15,523	13,017	36,079	29,619	25.6	9,966	4.1	7.0	4.4	6.7	15.1	33.2
Escambia County, FL	10,782	10,300	8,845	36,047	29,647	21.9	8,135	4.6	6.6	5.0	6.3	16.0	33.7
Santa Rosa County, FL	5,569	5,223	4,172	36,141	29,560	33.5	1,831	1.7	8.7	2.2	8.4	11.2	30.6

[1] Based on resident population estimated as of July 1.
[2] Includes other industry categories not shown separately.
(D) = Data withheld to avoid disclosure or does not meet statistical standards.

Table C-3.   Personal Income and Earnings, by Industry—*Continued*

| Metropolitan statistical area, division, and component county | Personal income | | | | | | Earnings, 2011 | | | | | | |
| | Total (million dollars) | | | Per capita[1] (dollars) | | Percent change, 2005–2011 | Total[2] (million dollars) | Percentage by selected major industries | | | | | |
	2011	2010	2005	2011	2005			Manufacturing	Retail trade	Finance and insurance	Professional and technical services	Health care and social services	Government and government enterprises
Peoria, IL	16,580	15,262	12,617	43,684	34,120	31.4	12,551	26.4	4.8	3.6	9.5	13.7	10.3
Marshall County, IL	516	480	395	41,192	30,504	30.7	221	25.0	3.1	3.1	1.6	6.8	12.2
Peoria County, IL	8,478	7,857	6,416	45,375	35,087	32.1	6,854	12.2	5.0	4.6	15.9	20.9	11.0
Stark County, IL	237	208	178	41,870	29,053	33.1	108	11.1	6.1	(D)	2.7	3.6	13.5
Tazewell County, IL	5,685	5,160	4,413	41,909	33,740	28.8	4,756	47.9	4.4	2.6	2.0	4.5	8.5
Woodford County, IL	1,664	1,556	1,214	42,811	32,789	37.0	612	21.9	6.1	2.2	(D)	7.9	15.9
Philadelphia–Camden–Wilmington, PA–NJ–DE–MD	291,970	279,708	236,491	48,723	40,571	23.5	213,069	7.5	5.4	9.4	12.9	13.7	12.5
Camden, NJ	56,051	54,166	46,273	44,772	37,487	21.1	34,691	9.5	8.0	6.4	8.7	13.8	18.9
Burlington County, NJ	21,722	21,017	18,197	48,318	40,686	19.4	15,085	9.7	7.4	10.0	9.3	11.1	18.7
Camden County, NJ	22,120	21,433	18,584	43,099	36,299	19.0	13,661	8.5	7.1	4.3	9.2	18.0	18.7
Gloucester County, NJ	12,208	11,716	9,492	42,228	34,499	28.6	5,945	11.5	11.5	1.9	5.8	11.0	19.9
Philadelphia, PA	204,090	195,634	163,356	50,631	41,787	24.9	153,029	7.8	4.8	9.3	13.9	14.0	11.0
Bucks County, PA	34,232	33,137	28,167	54,609	45,703	21.5	18,125	12.1	7.7	4.4	9.9	13.1	9.7
Chester County, PA	29,965	28,689	24,228	59,467	51,494	23.7	22,825	8.7	5.6	13.5	16.4	9.1	7.3
Delaware County, PA	27,860	26,827	23,775	49,795	43,060	17.2	15,744	11.0	5.7	7.9	9.1	14.4	11.0
Montgomery County, PA	52,047	49,849	42,242	64,718	54,198	23.2	41,926	10.2	5.2	10.9	16.7	13.0	6.4
Philadelphia County, PA	59,986	57,133	44,944	39,041	30,146	33.5	54,409	3.3	3.1	8.2	13.3	16.8	16.4
Wilmington, DE–MD–NJ	31,829	29,908	26,862	44,857	39,183	18.5	25,350	(D)	4.9	14.6	12.8	12.0	13.3
New Castle County, DE	25,101	23,480	21,510	46,315	41,101	16.7	21,893	(D)	4.8	16.7	14.5	12.3	12.2
Cecil County, MD	4,036	3,838	3,194	39,689	32,984	26.4	1,797	22.2	6.6	1.7	(D)	10.4	23.0
Salem County, NJ	2,692	2,590	2,158	40,847	33,010	24.7	1,660	16.0	4.6	1.6	4.5	9.8	17.2
Phoenix–Mesa–Glendale, AZ	157,026	149,094	131,597	36,833	34,863	19.3	116,671	8.6	8.1	8.1	8.7	12.0	13.5
Maricopa County, AZ	147,724	140,352	126,011	38,071	35,606	17.2	113,411	8.7	8.1	8.2	8.9	12.1	12.8
Pinal County, AZ	9,302	8,742	5,586	24,287	23,698	66.5	3,260	5.8	7.3	1.8	2.3	7.8	38.6
Pine Bluff, AR	3,053	2,984	2,575	30,866	24,776	18.6	2,046	16.0	6.0	2.8	(D)	11.6	31.7
Cleveland County, AR	278	276	245	32,051	27,670	13.4	47	7.7	(D)	0.0	(D)	7.9	37.9
Jefferson County, AR	2,411	2,352	2,040	31,627	25,328	18.2	1,841	16.8	6.3	3.0	(D)	12.7	30.6
Lincoln County, AR	364	356	289	25,991	19,942	25.9	158	9.0	3.4	1.7	0.8	(D)	43.2
Pittsburgh, PA	106,146	100,489	84,956	44,982	35,779	24.9	77,443	9.4	6.0	6.8	10.4	14.0	10.9
Allegheny County, PA	59,895	56,967	49,067	48,812	39,738	22.1	52,639	6.8	5.3	8.7	12.6	14.5	9.7
Armstrong County, PA	2,338	2,216	2,018	34,094	28,577	15.9	1,171	12.3	7.8	3.3	2.7	14.8	14.6
Beaver County, PA	6,480	6,182	5,175	38,025	29,602	25.2	3,162	17.0	7.6	2.4	8.1	14.9	14.5
Butler County, PA	8,110	7,652	6,079	43,876	33,860	33.4	5,149	18.3	7.3	2.4	5.2	10.4	13.8
Fayette County, PA	4,563	4,415	3,784	33,527	26,565	20.6	2,178	10.2	9.4	1.7	3.7	16.6	17.6
Washington County, PA	9,630	8,695	6,937	46,237	33,782	38.8	5,560	11.0	5.9	3.2	5.5	12.0	10.7
Westmoreland County, PA	15,129	14,362	11,896	41,510	32,418	27.2	7,583	15.8	8.0	2.8	6.0	13.2	13.3
Pittsfield, MA	5,803	5,558	4,892	44,483	36,902	18.6	3,514	11.4	8.2	5.1	7.5	19.6	13.6
Berkshire County, MA	5,803	5,558	4,892	44,483	36,902	18.6	3,514	11.4	8.2	5.1	7.5	19.6	13.6
Pocatello, ID	2,652	2,540	2,210	28,998	26,049	20.0	1,819	11.9	7.0	4.7	(D)	14.2	24.3
Bannock County, ID	2,412	2,330	2,047	28,818	26,440	17.8	1,630	8.9	7.8	5.2	(D)	15.7	25.4
Power County, ID	240	210	163	30,936	21,973	47.2	189	37.4	(D)	(D)	1.1	1.1	15.0
Portland–South Portland–Biddeford, ME	22,675	21,571	18,631	43,960	36,510	21.7	16,398	(D)	7.2	8.6	8.4	14.8	17.2
Cumberland County, ME	13,277	12,553	10,822	47,015	39,172	22.7	11,216	6.7	6.7	11.4	9.9	16.6	12.9
Sagadahoc County, ME	1,445	1,388	1,180	41,044	32,955	22.4	1,005	(D)	6.0	2.3	6.9	5.3	13.9
York County, ME	7,953	7,630	6,628	40,124	33,442	20.0	4,177	11.9	8.9	2.7	4.9	12.2	29.6
Portland–Vancouver–Hillsboro, OR–WA	93,449	87,940	74,750	41,302	36,158	25.0	70,589	14.4	5.8	5.5	8.9	11.4	14.1
Clackamas County, OR	17,457	16,538	14,601	45,915	40,637	19.6	9,402	13.1	7.3	5.2	9.1	13.4	10.8
Columbia County, OR	1,675	1,597	1,385	33,907	29,503	20.9	506	16.9	8.8	3.2	3.7	8.2	22.6
Multnomah County, OR	31,161	29,424	25,012	41,658	37,062	24.6	31,753	7.8	5.0	6.7	11.2	11.5	17.4
Washington County, OR	23,043	21,522	17,885	42,639	36,443	28.8	18,788	27.6	5.8	4.8	5.7	8.4	7.4
Yamhill County, OR	3,398	3,202	2,751	33,980	30,287	23.5	1,678	22.9	6.9	3.2	3.6	13.4	15.8
Clark County, WA	16,338	15,301	12,833	37,665	32,548	27.3	8,354	9.7	7.0	3.9	8.7	15.0	19.0
Skamania County, WA	377	358	282	33,877	27,389	33.7	107	10.5	6.4	1.8	6.8	(D)	41.9
Port St. Lucie, FL	16,414	15,679	13,864	38,362	36,117	18.4	6,866	4.4	10.1	4.7	6.7	16.8	17.4
Martin County, FL	7,787	7,435	7,271	52,798	51,237	7.1	3,433	5.5	10.2	5.6	8.6	17.0	10.9
St. Lucie County, FL	8,627	8,243	6,593	30,768	27,249	30.8	3,433	3.4	10.1	3.9	4.8	16.7	24.0
Poughkeepsie–Newburgh–Middletown, NY	28,585	27,416	22,773	42,482	34,563	25.5	16,136	11.3	8.2	3.2	5.8	14.7	27.3
Dutchess County, NY	13,565	12,962	10,829	45,521	36,788	25.3	7,674	17.9	6.5	3.3	5.7	14.8	21.9
Orange County, NY	15,019	14,454	11,944	40,066	32,766	25.7	8,462	5.4	9.6	3.1	5.9	14.6	32.2
Prescott, AZ	6,248	6,015	5,279	29,490	27,013	18.4	2,754	5.4	10.6	2.5	3.9	15.7	23.1
Yavapai County, AZ	6,248	6,015	5,279	29,490	27,013	18.4	2,754	5.4	10.6	2.5	3.9	15.7	23.1
Providence–New Bedford–Fall River, RI–MA	69,116	66,193	57,418	43,192	35,589	20.4	43,964	11.2	6.6	7.0	6.6	15.3	17.3
Bristol County, MA	22,991	21,986	18,847	41,884	34,555	22.0	12,867	16.2	8.6	3.0	4.6	16.4	14.5
Bristol County, RI	2,735	2,605	2,354	54,919	45,569	16.2	861	11.7	5.1	4.9	6.3	12.9	16.9
Kent County, RI	7,642	7,341	6,549	46,167	38,564	16.7	4,601	11.8	9.3	8.2	6.9	15.1	14.0
Newport County, RI	4,303	4,115	3,692	52,038	43,971	16.6	2,999	7.5	5.2	2.9	10.3	7.2	40.4
Providence County, RI	25,236	24,192	20,682	40,268	32,567	22.0	19,445	7.4	4.5	10.7	7.4	16.4	15.5
Washington County, RI	6,209	5,955	5,293	49,057	41,544	17.3	3,190	15.9	8.7	3.3	5.9	12.1	23.5

[1] Based on resident population estimated as of July 1.
[2] Includes other industry categories not shown separately.
(D) = Data withheld to avoid disclosure or does not meet statistical standards.

Table C-3. Personal Income and Earnings, by Industry—*Continued*

Metropolitan statistical area, division, and component county	Total (million dollars) 2011	Total 2010	Total 2005	Per capita[1] (dollars) 2011	Per capita 2005	Percent change, 2005–2011	Earnings, 2011 Total[2] (million dollars)	Manufacturing	Retail trade	Finance and insurance	Professional and technical services	Health care and social services	Government and government enterprises
Provo–Orem, UT	13,975	13,112	10,250	25,841	23,315	36.3	10,363	10.5	8.0	3.7	10.6	9.9	13.7
Juab County, UT	252	242	202	24,351	22,605	24.7	147	22.3	4.1	1.8	5.8	(D)	20.4
UT County, UT	13,724	12,870	10,048	25,870	23,330	36.6	10,216	10.3	8.0	3.8	10.7	10.1	13.6
Pueblo, CO	5,099	4,832	4,010	31,760	26,766	27.1	3,178	10.8	7.9	2.6	2.9	19.2	22.8
Pueblo County, CO	5,099	4,832	4,010	31,760	26,766	27.1	3,178	10.8	7.9	2.6	2.9	19.2	22.8
Punta Gorda, FL	5,644	5,390	4,894	35,161	31,522	15.3	2,116	1.3	13.0	4.2	5.1	24.8	17.9
Charlotte County, FL	5,644	5,390	4,894	35,161	31,522	15.3	2,116	1.3	13.0	4.2	5.1	24.8	17.9
Racine, WI	7,508	7,239	6,533	38,425	33,803	14.9	4,566	34.9	5.6	3.7	4.8	12.5	13.2
Racine County, WI	7,508	7,239	6,533	38,425	33,803	14.9	4,566	34.9	5.6	3.7	4.8	12.5	13.2
Raleigh–Cary, NC	47,275	44,557	35,209	40,631	37,269	34.3	34,287	7.4	6.2	6.9	13.4	9.4	16.6
Franklin County, NC	1,814	1,760	1,443	29,670	26,602	25.7	719	22.1	5.8	2.7	4.6	8.7	17.4
Johnston County, NC	5,894	5,515	4,294	34,149	29,736	37.2	2,465	22.7	9.0	3.1	3.6	7.0	18.9
Wake County, NC	39,567	37,283	29,471	42,555	39,503	34.3	31,103	5.9	6.0	7.3	14.3	9.6	16.4
Rapid City, SD	5,299	4,944	3,943	41,286	33,366	34.4	3,552	3.7	8.0	4.9	4.7	16.8	27.8
Meade County, SD	1,017	940	843	39,801	33,601	20.6	600	1.6	5.4	3.5	5.4	7.0	31.8
Pennington County, SD	4,283	4,004	3,100	41,655	33,302	38.1	2,952	4.1	8.5	5.1	4.6	18.8	27.0
Reading, PA	15,552	14,883	12,609	37,675	31,846	23.3	10,250	19.9	7.5	3.9	6.5	13.7	13.7
Berks County, PA	15,552	14,883	12,609	37,675	31,846	23.3	10,250	19.9	7.5	3.9	6.5	13.7	13.7
Redding, CA	6,305	6,105	5,478	35,466	31,195	15.1	3,574	3.9	10.2	3.6	5.2	19.3	22.6
Shasta County, CA	6,305	6,105	5,478	35,466	31,195	15.1	3,574	3.9	10.2	3.6	5.2	19.3	22.6
Reno–Sparks, NV	17,922	17,160	16,970	41,718	42,795	5.6	11,921	6.8	6.8	7.2	7.9	11.4	17.0
Storey County, NV	132	131	138	33,924	35,920	-3.9	182	18.7	(D)	(D)	1.7	(D)	8.3
Washoe County, NV	17,790	17,029	16,833	41,790	42,862	5.7	11,739	6.6	6.9	7.3	8.0	11.6	17.2
Richmond, VA[11,12]	54,641	51,643	44,587	43,046	37,749	22.5	41,849	6.6	5.3	(D)	10.4	9.9	20.4
Amelia County, VA	447	425	385	34,892	32,212	16.1	143	7.2	7.8	1.5	2.5	(D)	18.5
Caroline County, VA	1,037	971	765	36,160	30,046	35.5	341	4.2	4.1	1.3	(D)	(D)	31.6
Charles City County, VA	237	230	229	32,755	32,377	3.8	93	13.4	3.3	(D)	(D)	1.9	18.0
Chesterfield County, VA	14,156	13,324	11,287	44,198	38,922	25.4	7,611	10.6	7.6	7.7	8.7	10.3	17.4
Cumberland County, VA	304	292	241	30,459	25,414	26.2	66	8.1	6.6	1.5	(D)	(D)	33.7
Dinwiddie County, VA[11]	2,952	2,774	2,243	37,994	29,740	31.6	1,618	12.8	9.8	2.3	(D)	(D)	25.9
Goochland County, VA	1,390	1,310	1,059	63,540	54,721	31.3	1,106	2.5	2.1	0.0	4.8	2.8	6.5
Hanover County, VA	4,599	4,383	3,759	45,832	38,971	22.3	2,619	7.0	9.0	2.7	5.9	13.1	11.4
Henrico County, VA	13,824	13,137	11,954	44,529	41,733	15.6	12,221	3.8	6.1	17.2	12.3	13.3	9.6
King and Queen County, VA	231	216	195	33,018	28,724	18.4	87	8.3	4.1	0.6	(D)	(D)	27.0
King William County, VA	621	582	492	38,882	34,467	26.3	194	33.3	5.6	2.8	3.7	(D)	20.6
Louisa County, VA	1,372	1,293	985	41,096	32,999	39.4	709	14.3	5.3	2.2	(D)	3.0	11.4
New Kent County, VA	691	648	518	36,705	32,448	33.5	196	3.6	6.7	1.3	3.4	(D)	26.0
Powhatan County, VA	1,233	1,162	923	43,860	34,999	33.6	413	2.2	3.5	13.7	7.2	3.6	31.7
Prince George County, VA[12]	2,302	2,121	1,630	38,924	28,632	41.2	2,513	10.4	2.0	0.6	(D)	(D)	66.3
Sussex County, VA	359	338	293	29,736	24,566	22.6	171	(D)	8.2	1.2	(D)	(D)	44.4
Colonial Heights city, VA[11]	NA	NA	NA	NA	NA	NA	NA	NA	NA	NA	NA	NA	NA
Hopewell city, VA[12]	NA	NA	NA	NA	NA	NA	NA	NA	NA	NA	NA	NA	NA
Petersburg city, VA[11]	NA	NA	NA	NA	NA	NA	NA	NA	NA	NA	NA	NA	NA
Richmond city, VA	8,887	8,437	7,631	43,239	38,643	16.5	11,751	4.8	2.4	6.9	16.3	11.3	25.7
Riverside–San Bernardino–Ontario, CA	128,982	123,561	108,598	29,961	28,020	18.8	74,124	7.8	9.1	2.9	4.5	11.4	24.9
Riverside County, CA	67,025	63,950	55,177	29,927	28,563	21.5	34,811	7.9	9.9	2.9	4.6	10.6	23.9
San Bernardino County, CA	61,958	59,611	53,421	29,998	27,481	16.0	39,313	7.8	8.3	3.0	4.5	12.1	25.8
Roanoke, VA[13]	12,081	11,521	9,840	39,115	33,199	22.8	8,812	13.8	6.4	5.5	6.0	(D)	15.1
Botetourt County, VA	1,401	1,337	1,129	42,560	35,491	24.2	528	22.6	(D)	1.9	3.9	5.9	14.1
Craig County, VA	161	155	140	31,500	27,255	14.7	37	(D)	8.0	3.9	(D)	8.5	31.7
Franklin County, VA	1,841	1,748	1,438	32,626	27,675	28.0	614	17.9	9.7	2.3	2.7	(D)	18.6
Roanoke County, VA[13]	4,789	4,590	4,157	40,688	36,611	15.2	3,681	19.9	6.3	5.9	6.4	(D)	15.8
Roanoke city, VA	3,889	3,691	2,976	40,215	31,681	30.7	3,953	6.4	6.7	6.0	6.4	22.2	13.9
Salem city, VA[13]	NA	NA	NA	NA	NA	NA	NA	NA	NA	NA	NA	NA	NA
Rochester, MN	8,288	8,204	6,645	44,174	37,744	24.7	6,844	12.9	4.8	2.0	2.3	47.0	9.5
Dodge County, MN	771	744	636	38,067	32,821	21.1	385	18.4	2.7	2.0	2.2	(D)	15.9
Olmsted County, MN	6,665	6,640	5,302	45,721	39,288	25.7	6,104	11.8	4.8	1.9	2.3	52.1	8.8
Wabasha County, MN	852	819	706	39,457	32,545	20.6	355	25.9	6.0	3.4	1.1	8.8	15.7
Rochester, NY	43,987	42,157	35,256	41,683	33,728	24.8	31,205	15.3	6.1	4.5	7.4	12.5	16.2
Livingston County, NY	2,106	2,043	1,704	32,361	26,084	23.6	1,125	8.7	8.5	1.8	2.5	8.8	36.0
Monroe County, NY	32,728	31,283	26,433	43,894	35,792	23.8	24,827	15.1	5.4	5.1	8.3	13.4	13.4
Ontario County, NY	4,540	4,350	3,376	41,834	32,378	34.5	2,907	14.4	10.4	2.2	5.1	12.7	18.7
Orleans County, NY	1,265	1,235	1,039	29,691	23,893	21.8	712	19.9	4.6	6.9	2.5	(D)	38.4
Wayne County, NY	3,348	3,246	2,705	35,832	28,856	23.8	1,634	21.2	6.5	1.8	3.5	7.2	30.5

[1] Based on resident population estimated as of July 1.
[2] Includes other industry categories not shown separately.
[11] Colonial Heights and Petersburg cities included with Dinwiddie County, VA, in the Richmond, VA MSA.
[12] Hopewell city included with Prince George County, VA, in the Richmond, VA MSA.
[13] Salem city included with Roanoke County, VA, in the Roanoke, VA MSA.
(D) = Data withheld due to avoid disclosure or does not meet statistical standards.
NA = Not available

Table C-3. Personal Income and Earnings, by Industry—*Continued*

Metropolitan statistical area, division, and component county	Total (million dollars)			Per capita[1] (dollars)		Percent change, 2005–2011	Total[2] (million dollars)	Manufacturing	Retail trade	Finance and insurance	Professional and technical services	Health care and social services	Government and government enterprises
	2011	2010	2005	2011	2005								
Rockford, IL	11,914	11,498	9,943	34,201	29,601	19.8	8,463	25.4	6.6	4.8	3.7	16.0	12.6
Boone County, IL	1,808	1,713	1,420	33,252	28,561	27.3	890	41.6	5.2	2.9	1.8	4.2	14.9
Winnebago County, IL	10,107	9,784	8,523	34,377	29,782	18.6	7,573	23.5	6.8	5.0	3.9	17.4	12.4
Rocky Mount, NC	4,775	4,629	4,042	31,380	27,494	18.1	3,113	21.2	7.6	3.7	3.0	(D)	18.4
Edgecombe County, NC	1,525	1,494	1,373	27,218	24,457	11.1	974	18.1	8.0	2.0	1.2	(D)	24.8
Nash County, NC	3,249	3,134	2,669	33,807	29,371	21.7	2,138	22.6	7.5	4.4	3.8	9.6	15.5
Rome, GA	3,183	3,072	2,686	33,159	28,469	18.5	2,098	16.8	5.8	3.5	3.0	25.9	16.0
Floyd County, GA	3,183	3,072	2,686	33,159	28,469	18.5	2,098	16.8	5.8	3.5	3.0	25.9	16.0
Sacramento—Arden-Arcade—Roseville, CA	88,670	85,088	75,029	40,745	36,872	18.2	64,484	4.8	6.4	6.0	9.8	11.5	31.8
El Dorado County, CA	9,041	8,739	7,688	49,967	43,931	17.6	3,481	3.1	7.5	9.8	11.0	12.6	19.9
Placer County, CA	17,313	16,327	13,836	48,476	44,238	25.1	9,386	7.4	11.1	8.8	7.5	16.0	12.8
Sacramento County, CA	54,862	52,812	47,563	38,202	34,952	15.3	45,009	4.3	5.5	5.7	10.7	11.1	35.3
Yolo County, CA	7,455	7,211	5,942	36,896	31,898	25.5	6,607	5.4	5.0	2.0	6.2	6.7	41.5
Saginaw–Saginaw Township North, MI	6,372	6,070	5,639	32,007	27,191	13.0	4,644	19.9	7.5	4.7	4.5	17.4	15.6
Saginaw County, MI	6,372	6,070	5,639	32,007	27,191	13.0	4,644	19.9	7.5	4.7	4.5	17.4	15.6
St. Cloud, MN	6,699	6,363	5,434	35,253	30,323	23.3	5,337	15.7	7.2	4.0	(D)	15.9	16.1
Benton County, MN	1,325	1,275	1,148	34,270	30,692	15.4	935	25.0	5.8	2.2	(D)	7.8	9.4
Stearns County, MN	5,373	5,088	4,286	35,504	30,225	25.4	4,403	13.7	7.5	4.3	3.1	17.6	17.5
St. George, UT	3,848	3,666	2,882	27,159	24,219	33.5	2,253	4.9	10.6	3.7	4.9	18.1	16.8
Washington County, UT	3,848	3,666	2,882	27,159	24,219	33.5	2,253	4.9	10.6	3.7	4.9	18.1	16.8
St. Joseph, MO–KS	4,362	4,153	3,335	34,189	27,010	30.8	3,098	22.6	7.3	4.6	3.1	13.2	16.0
Doniphan County, KS	257	240	196	32,364	24,951	31.0	133	19.1	3.5	3.3	1.1	(D)	29.8
Andrew County, MO	765	724	526	44,465	31,882	45.3	165	1.0	12.1	2.8	(D)	(D)	20.4
Buchanan County, MO	3,025	2,897	2,389	33,732	27,652	26.6	2,627	25.6	7.0	4.5	3.6	15.5	13.8
DeKalb County, MO	315	292	224	24,697	17,610	40.7	173	1.6	9.0	9.1	0.6	(D)	34.3
St. Louis, MO–IL[14]	120,763	115,355	101,082	42,864	36,697	19.5	88,453	10.7	5.7	6.6	8.8	12.2	13.8
Bond County, IL	614	586	493	34,642	27,401	24.6	278	15.4	3.0	1.7	1.4	(D)	25.0
Calhoun County, IL	170	161	135	33,613	26,193	25.5	46	(D)	7.9	(D)	(D)	(D)	25.7
Clinton County, IL	1,489	1,408	1,147	39,241	31,271	29.8	629	7.0	8.0	3.0	3.1	10.3	23.0
Jersey County, IL	882	835	669	38,503	29,723	31.9	269	1.3	9.8	2.4	6.1	(D)	24.4
Macoupin County, IL	1,741	1,648	1,365	36,510	28,193	27.5	603	8.7	6.7	3.7	2.6	(D)	19.3
Madison County, IL	10,237	9,898	8,337	38,133	31,490	22.8	5,772	19.5	7.2	3.7	6.6	11.1	17.3
Monroe County, IL	1,489	1,400	1,074	44,712	34,622	38.7	457	4.7	9.9	5.2	11.6	6.9	17.1
St. Clair County, IL	9,913	9,562	7,922	36,680	30,322	25.1	6,824	5.3	5.9	3.1	7.6	11.5	32.0
Franklin County, MO	3,651	3,483	3,005	35,811	30,535	21.5	1,918	24.7	7.7	3.6	2.8	11.1	12.4
Jefferson County, MO	7,612	7,254	6,164	34,681	29,330	23.5	2,621	10.7	8.2	3.6	3.2	11.5	18.5
Lincoln County, MO	1,609	1,523	1,233	30,310	26,263	30.5	586	13.5	9.9	4.8	1.7	4.7	22.1
St. Charles County, MO	15,065	14,165	11,397	41,257	34,653	32.2	7,237	10.7	8.3	8.5	5.5	10.4	12.9
St. Louis County, MO	52,714	50,414	46,971	52,783	46,779	12.2	43,243	9.9	6.0	7.4	9.7	12.5	8.6
Warren County, MO	1,096	1,039	821	33,708	28,220	33.5	340	27.0	8.5	2.7	(D)	5.4	18.5
Washington County, MO	639	609	495	25,481	20,434	29.2	214	19.9	6.6	2.7	0.8	6.1	37.7
St. Louis city, MO	11,842	11,370	9,855	37,232	30,327	20.2	17,416	10.2	2.0	7.5	11.7	14.6	16.4
Salem, OR	13,180	12,659	10,512	33,378	28,563	25.4	8,483	6.5	6.7	3.5	4.0	16.7	29.6
Marion County, OR	10,791	10,371	8,635	33,841	28,837	25.0	7,617	6.1	6.9	3.7	4.5	17.3	29.1
Polk County, OR	2,389	2,288	1,877	31,437	27,368	27.3	866	10.3	5.2	1.6	(D)	11.0	34.1
Salinas, CA	17,356	16,678	15,095	41,138	37,259	15.0	11,904	3.4	6.0	2.5	5.1	7.7	27.4
Monterey County, CA	17,356	16,678	15,095	41,138	37,259	15.0	11,904	3.4	6.0	2.5	5.1	7.7	27.4
Salisbury, MD	4,218	4,081	3,400	33,601	28,737	24.1	2,866	8.0	8.1	2.8	4.2	19.0	22.1
Somerset County, MD	748	727	603	28,387	23,386	24.0	413	5.8	3.5	1.2	2.4	11.0	45.6
Wicomico County, MD	3,470	3,354	2,796	34,985	30,230	24.1	2,452	8.4	8.9	3.0	4.5	20.3	18.2
Salt Lake City, UT	45,373	42,882	35,347	39,595	34,273	28.4	40,788	9.7	7.3	8.8	9.1	8.0	16.4
Salt Lake County, UT	40,995	38,786	32,326	39,081	34,100	26.8	38,438	9.8	7.3	9.1	9.4	8.2	16.1
Summit County, UT	2,731	2,540	1,862	72,643	54,531	46.7	1,340	4.7	9.0	5.4	7.6	6.2	10.6
Tooele County, UT	1,646	1,557	1,160	27,748	23,546	41.9	1,009	11.0	4.6	1.1	(D)	5.7	33.4
San Angelo, TX	4,258	3,995	3,165	37,532	29,697	34.5	2,762	9.4	6.9	3.6	3.5	14.7	28.6
Irion County, TX	89	80	54	54,975	33,717	63.8	45	(D)	1.6	(D)	(D)	2.3	12.5
Tom Green County, TX	4,169	3,915	3,111	37,279	29,635	34.0	2,717	9.6	7.0	3.7	3.6	14.9	28.8
San Antonio–New Braunfels, TX	80,732	75,810	58,670	36,781	30,939	37.6	58,891	5.1	6.9	8.9	6.8	10.6	24.6
Atascosa County, TX	1,378	1,306	989	30,238	23,272	39.4	597	3.1	10.1	3.1	2.7	(D)	19.3
Bandera County, TX	747	714	574	36,390	29,530	30.3	189	0.7	6.7	3.4	5.1	(D)	20.8
Bexar County, TX	63,533	59,912	47,759	36,177	31,230	33.0	52,708	4.5	6.5	9.5	7.2	11.1	25.4
Comal County, TX	4,984	4,594	3,177	44,519	34,908	56.9	2,306	7.8	10.2	3.1	4.5	10.2	13.4
Guadalupe County, TX	5,044	4,635	3,032	37,157	28,712	66.4	1,620	21.5	8.4	2.6	(D)	6.9	20.1
Kendall County, TX	2,007	1,821	1,121	57,707	40,251	79.1	691	6.5	13.2	6.2	9.8	10.5	14.6
Medina County, TX	1,513	1,429	1,038	32,638	24,149	45.8	445	1.6	9.5	4.6	3.9	(D)	31.5
Wilson County, TX	1,524	1,400	980	34,810	26,003	55.5	335	4.6	13.7	2.7	6.9	(D)	30.7

[1] Based on resident population estimated as of July 1.
[2] Includes other industry categories not shown separately.
[14] The portion of Sullivan city in Crawford County, MO is legally part of the St. Louis, MO–IL MSA. That portion is not included in these figures for the St. Louis, MSA.
(D) = Data withheld due to avoid disclosure or does not meet statistical standards.

Table C-3.   Personal Income and Earnings, by Industry—*Continued*

Metropolitan statistical area, division, and component county	Personal income						Earnings, 2011						
	Total (million dollars)			Per capita[1] (dollars)		Percent change, 2005–2011	Total[2] (million dollars)	Percentage by selected major industries					
	2011	2010	2005	2011	2005			Manufacturing	Retail trade	Finance and insurance	Professional and technical services	Health care and social services	Government and government enterprises
San Diego–Carlsbad–San Marcos, CA..................	146,956	139,578	122,030	46,800	41,530	20.4	110,042	8.5	5.4	4.8	14.6	8.4	26.4
San Diego County, CA	146,956	139,578	122,030	46,800	41,530	20.4	110,042	8.5	5.4	4.8	14.6	8.4	26.4
Sandusky, OH..	2,929	2,787	2,603	38,161	33,339	12.5	1,961	22.5	7.1	2.2	2.4	14.5	16.5
Erie County, OH	2,929	2,787	2,603	38,161	33,339	12.5	1,961	22.5	7.1	2.2	2.4	14.5	16.5
San Francisco–Oakland–Fremont, CA	269,588	254,377	227,850	61,395	55,065	18.3	202,200	7.4	5.1	10.0	18.6	9.1	13.3
Oakland–Fremont–Hayward, CA..........................	136,687	129,725	115,292	52,653	47,240	18.6	88,002	11.4	5.8	4.8	13.4	12.4	14.7
Alameda County, CA	75,908	72,025	63,757	49,617	44,228	19.1	57,402	11.2	5.5	2.8	14.7	11.6	16.2
Contra Costa County, CA	60,779	57,700	51,534	57,011	51,585	17.9	30,601	11.7	6.2	8.6	11.1	13.8	11.9
San Francisco–San Mateo–Redwood City, CA.....	132,901	124,652	112,558	74,037	66,316	18.1	114,198	4.4	4.7	13.9	22.7	6.6	12.3
Marin County, CA	21,872	20,854	19,919	85,761	81,567	9.8	10,249	1.5	7.4	11.1	18.5	11.7	12.4
San Francisco County, CA	60,433	55,851	49,085	74,349	64,330	23.1	67,018	1.3	3.9	16.6	24.4	5.3	15.0
San Mateo County, CA	50,597	47,947	43,554	69,577	63,115	16.2	36,931	10.8	5.2	9.9	20.6	7.6	7.2
San Jose–Sunnyvale–Santa Clara, CA..................	113,844	104,472	89,629	61,028	51,810	27.0	111,688	26.5	4.3	3.1	18.0	6.8	7.1
San Benito County, CA	1,964	1,882	1,748	35,029	31,988	12.4	865	20.6	13.0	2.3	(D)	4.9	22.3
Santa Clara County, CA	111,880	102,590	87,881	61,833	52,457	27.3	110,823	26.5	4.2	3.1	18.1	6.8	7.0
San Luis Obispo–Paso Robles, CA......................	10,966	10,436	9,170	40,322	35,457	19.6	6,611	6.3	8.7	3.2	7.3	11.7	21.5
San Luis Obispo County, CA	10,966	10,436	9,170	40,322	35,457	19.6	6,611	6.3	8.7	3.2	7.3	11.7	21.5
Santa Barbara–Santa Maria–Goleta, CA	19,303	18,310	16,702	45,219	40,928	15.6	13,065	8.4	6.4	3.7	10.6	10.7	21.2
Santa Barbara County, CA	19,303	18,310	16,702	45,219	40,928	15.6	13,065	8.4	6.4	3.7	10.6	10.7	21.2
Santa Cruz–Watsonville, CA...............................	12,920	12,247	10,966	48,883	43,625	17.8	6,496	7.2	7.5	3.1	8.0	13.8	18.8
Santa Cruz County, CA	12,920	12,247	10,966	48,883	43,625	17.8	6,496	7.2	7.5	3.1	8.0	13.8	18.8
Santa Fe, NM..	6,310	6,057	5,462	43,325	39,690	15.5	3,887	1.4	9.2	6.6	8.5	13.9	29.5
Santa Fe County, NM	6,310	6,057	5,462	43,325	39,690	15.5	3,887	1.4	9.2	6.6	8.5	13.9	29.5
Santa Rosa–Petaluma, CA...................................	22,127	20,975	19,537	45,331	41,931	13.3	12,840	14.3	7.6	4.2	9.7	13.8	14.5
Sonoma County, CA	22,127	20,975	19,537	45,331	41,931	13.3	12,840	14.3	7.6	4.2	9.7	13.8	14.5
Savannah, GA..	14,337	13,471	10,583	40,321	33,646	35.5	9,426	15.1	6.6	2.9	4.2	12.3	23.5
Bryan County, GA...	1,258	1,167	884	40,085	33,281	42.3	328	6.6	10.0	2.8	5.0	(D)	28.6
Chatham County, GA	11,264	10,588	8,436	41,480	34,826	33.5	8,580	14.7	6.4	3.0	4.2	13.3	23.0
Effingham County, GA	1,816	1,715	1,262	34,485	27,607	43.8	518	26.8	7.2	1.7	4.4	3.8	28.2
Scranton–Wilkes-Barre, PA	20,777	19,989	16,965	36,889	30,476	22.5	13,314	12.2	8.0	5.4	4.9	16.3	14.6
Lackawanna County, PA	8,175	7,878	6,638	38,171	31,268	23.2	5,194	11.0	8.5	6.7	5.9	19.5	13.4
Luzerne County, PA	11,685	11,230	9,583	36,441	30,309	21.9	7,541	11.5	7.8	4.8	4.5	15.4	15.7
Wyoming County, PA	917	880	743	32,275	26,385	23.4	578	32.5	6.5	1.5	2.2	(D)	11.8
Seattle–Tacoma–Bellevue, WA	178,307	167,885	138,212	50,944	43,215	29.0	145,917	12.3	6.0	5.0	10.4	9.2	16.7
Seattle–Bellevue–Everett, WA	145,189	136,260	112,633	53,931	45,970	28.9	124,484	13.3	6.0	5.4	11.5	8.4	12.9
King County, WA	113,922	106,402	89,432	57,837	49,815	27.4	106,060	9.8	5.9	5.6	12.6	8.4	12.2
Snohomish County, WA	31,266	29,859	23,201	43,281	35,429	34.8	18,423	33.5	6.6	4.2	5.2	8.5	16.5
Tacoma, WA	33,118	31,625	25,579	40,992	34,190	29.5	21,434	6.1	5.9	3.0	4.1	13.7	39.1
Pierce County, WA	33,118	31,625	25,579	40,992	34,190	29.5	21,434	6.1	5.9	3.0	4.1	13.7	39.1
Sebastian–Vero Beach, FL...................................	7,080	6,737	6,374	50,977	49,814	11.1	2,547	4.3	10.9	5.1	7.4	18.6	13.6
Indian River County, FL	7,080	6,737	6,374	50,977	49,814	11.1	2,547	4.3	10.9	5.1	7.4	18.6	13.6
Sheboygan, WI..	4,596	4,447	3,945	39,910	34,467	16.5	3,488	39.9	5.6	5.0	2.7	12.4	9.7
Sheboygan County, WI	4,596	4,447	3,945	39,910	34,467	16.5	3,488	39.9	5.6	5.0	2.7	12.4	9.7
Sherman–Denison, TX..	4,056	3,850	3,069	33,404	26,532	32.2	2,363	19.8	8.7	5.6	3.2	17.8	14.2
Grayson County, TX	4,056	3,850	3,069	33,404	26,532	32.2	2,363	19.8	8.7	5.6	3.2	17.8	14.2
Shreveport–Bossier City, LA	15,700	14,870	11,986	38,899	31,287	31.0	11,484	6.8	7.3	3.2	4.3	13.4	25.1
Bossier Parish, LA..	4,394	4,071	3,045	36,697	28,336	44.3	3,183	4.7	8.6	1.8	2.7	6.6	37.3
Caddo Parish, LA	10,490	10,015	8,289	40,810	33,212	26.5	7,825	7.1	6.7	3.8	5.1	17.0	20.2
De Soto Parish, LA	816	784	651	30,417	25,017	25.2	475	15.5	7.8	1.7	1.9	(D)	24.4
Sioux City, IA–NE–SD	5,334	5,082	4,219	37,025	30,168	26.4	4,078	14.6	6.8	4.6	3.1	13.0	13.5
Woodbury County, IA	3,560	3,429	2,975	34,726	29,572	19.7	2,663	10.1	8.6	3.7	3.2	16.6	15.9
Dakota County, NE	613	600	488	29,320	24,165	25.7	620	38.6	4.8	7.9	(D)	(D)	11.2
Dixon County, NE	215	210	168	35,926	28,103	28.4	121	(D)	1.6	0.0	(D)	2.4	16.2
Union County, SD...	946	843	589	64,557	44,915	60.5	673	13.2	2.7	6.3	6.1	12.6	5.5
Sioux Falls, SD...	10,480	9,715	7,845	45,087	37,969	33.6	8,235	8.2	7.3	11.4	4.8	18.3	10.0
Lincoln County, SD	2,600	2,301	1,261	55,556	36,442	106.2	1,027	9.8	7.2	13.0	4.9	12.0	6.3
McCook County, SD	277	232	167	49,806	28,893	65.3	176	0.0	3.1	2.4	1.6	5.1	7.6
Minnehaha County, SD....................................	7,166	6,812	6,129	41,724	38,847	16.9	6,793	8.3	7.7	11.8	5.0	20.2	10.7
Turner County, SD	437	369	287	52,458	34,048	52.2	239	6.8	2.1	(D)	1.3	(D)	7.7
South Bend–Mishawaka, IN–MI	11,499	10,976	9,945	36,083	31,350	15.6	7,960	19.0	5.9	4.7	7.0	14.0	11.6
St. Joseph County, IN	9,678	9,288	8,434	36,289	31,842	14.8	7,415	19.0	5.9	4.8	7.5	14.6	10.9
Cass County, MI...	1,821	1,688	1,511	35,027	28,860	20.5	545	18.6	5.3	3.4	(D)	6.7	20.9
Spartanburg, SC...	9,085	8,722	7,407	31,670	28,005	22.7	7,082	25.5	6.2	5.0	4.6	8.8	17.2
Spartanburg County, SC..................................	9,085	8,722	7,407	31,670	28,005	22.7	7,082	25.5	6.2	5.0	4.6	8.8	17.2

[1] Based on resident population estimated as of July 1.
[2] Includes other industry categories not shown separately.
(D) = Data withheld to avoid disclosure or does not meet statistical standards.

Table C-3. Personal Income and Earnings, by Industry—*Continued*

Metropolitan statistical area, division, and component county	Personal income												
	Total (million dollars)			Per capita[1] (dollars)		Percent change, 2005–2011	Earnings, 2011						
							Total[2] (million dollars)	Percentage by selected major industries					
	2011	2010	2005	2011	2005			Manufacturing	Retail trade	Finance and insurance	Professional and technical services	Health care and social services	Government and government enterprises
Spokane, WA	17,027	16,329	13,025	35,940	29,574	30.7	12,128	8.0	8.0	6.6	6.3	17.4	20.6
Spokane County, WA	17,027	16,329	13,025	35,940	29,574	30.7	12,128	8.0	8.0	6.6	6.3	17.4	20.6
Springfield, IL	9,130	8,759	7,053	43,158	34,408	29.4	7,281	2.8	5.5	6.5	5.6	19.0	33.1
Menard County, IL	528	494	388	41,543	30,928	35.9	157	0.6	4.7	4.8	3.7	(D)	22.1
Sangamon County, IL	8,602	8,265	6,665	43,261	34,635	29.1	7,124	2.9	5.5	6.6	5.6	19.4	33.3
Springfield, MA	27,711	26,695	22,758	39,975	33,059	21.8	16,817	10.8	6.9	6.8	4.7	17.2	20.9
Franklin County, MA	3,049	2,929	2,522	42,588	35,083	20.9	1,413	14.3	8.4	2.9	3.9	12.9	18.4
Hampden County, MA	18,401	17,742	15,165	39,677	32,884	21.3	11,890	11.6	6.6	8.6	4.7	19.1	18.5
Hampshire County, MA	6,260	6,024	5,072	39,664	32,643	23.4	3,513	6.6	7.0	2.6	5.0	12.5	30.4
Springfield, MO	14,658	13,997	11,506	33,302	28,559	27.4	10,329	9.5	8.4	5.3	5.6	17.0	14.7
Christian County, MO	2,515	2,363	1,763	32,014	26,734	42.6	822	6.4	10.1	5.9	4.7	6.9	17.8
Dallas County, MO	481	462	417	28,709	25,562	15.2	149	3.7	10.8	4.0	2.1	(D)	21.7
Greene County, MO	9,822	9,426	7,892	35,429	30,674	24.5	8,652	10.1	8.0	5.4	6.2	19.5	13.3
Polk County, MO	846	798	662	27,154	22,572	27.9	384	2.4	9.5	3.8	(D)	(D)	30.8
Webster County, MO	994	947	772	27,266	22,700	28.7	322	12.8	11.1	3.8	0.0	5.2	23.3
Springfield, OH	4,788	4,572	4,107	34,777	29,051	16.6	2,535	16.8	7.0	5.2	3.1	15.7	15.8
Clark County, OH	4,788	4,572	4,107	34,777	29,051	16.6	2,535	16.8	7.0	5.2	3.1	15.7	15.8
State College, PA	5,469	5,192	4,101	35,347	28,175	33.4	4,536	5.7	5.9	2.5	7.0	9.6	45.9
Centre County, PA	5,469	5,192	4,101	35,347	28,175	33.4	4,536	5.7	5.9	2.5	7.0	9.6	45.9
Steubenville–Weirton, OH–WV	3,862	3,714	3,283	31,339	25,758	17.6	2,192	21.2	6.8	2.1	2.7	(D)	14.1
Jefferson County, OH	2,185	2,099	1,835	31,742	25,753	19.1	1,212	9.4	7.4	1.7	2.7	(D)	14.8
Brooke County, WV	740	714	632	31,037	25,591	17.1	461	34.4	5.0	2.5	1.8	(D)	11.2
Hancock County, WV	938	901	816	30,670	25,899	14.9	519	37.2	7.0	2.7	3.6	7.1	14.8
Stockton, CA	21,592	20,802	18,300	31,013	27,855	18.0	13,106	9.0	7.6	3.2	3.1	13.1	20.0
San Joaquin County, CA	21,592	20,802	18,300	31,013	27,855	18.0	13,106	9.0	7.6	3.2	3.1	13.1	20.0
Sumter, SC	3,215	3,102	2,679	29,915	25,252	20.0	2,330	13.8	5.6	2.3	3.4	10.7	39.6
Sumter County, SC	3,215	3,102	2,679	29,915	25,252	20.0	2,330	13.8	5.6	2.3	3.4	10.7	39.6
Syracuse, NY	25,619	24,721	20,336	38,668	31,047	26.0	18,504	11.4	6.5	6.3	7.7	12.9	19.4
Madison County, NY	2,470	2,394	2,004	33,663	28,044	23.2	1,190	12.5	7.5	3.7	5.4	12.9	21.2
Onondaga County, NY	19,327	18,603	15,293	41,389	33,181	26.4	15,456	11.1	6.2	7.0	8.6	13.1	18.4
Oswego County, NY	3,823	3,723	3,039	31,275	24,776	25.8	1,858	13.2	7.7	2.1	2.0	11.3	27.3
Tallahassee, FL	12,845	12,466	10,563	34,740	30,684	21.6	9,284	2.4	6.1	5.3	10.7	11.9	38.7
Gadsden County, FL	1,282	1,261	1,138	27,778	25,149	12.6	624	8.6	6.0	1.5	0.0	4.0	39.8
Jefferson County, FL	424	415	366	28,954	25,766	15.9	122	0.4	6.9	3.0	3.8	(D)	33.7
Leon County, FL	10,236	9,920	8,374	36,823	32,446	22.2	8,274	1.5	6.0	5.7	11.8	13.0	38.8
Wakulla County, FL	903	871	685	29,157	25,655	31.8	265	16.5	8.2	2.2	5.4	(D)	37.7
Tampa–St. Petersburg–Clearwater, FL	110,901	106,083	91,393	39,261	34,467	21.3	72,256	5.9	7.8	9.3	10.6	14.3	15.0
Hernando County, FL	5,319	5,146	4,230	30,729	26,919	25.7	1,811	4.3	11.9	3.4	4.3	25.2	19.4
Hillsborough County, FL	49,671	47,340	39,260	39,180	34,343	26.5	41,126	4.2	6.9	10.3	12.2	11.8	15.4
Pasco County, FL	14,974	14,213	11,286	32,102	26,754	32.7	4,849	4.0	12.1	3.7	4.7	21.6	19.9
Pinellas County, FL	40,936	39,385	36,617	44,622	39,397	11.8	24,470	9.4	8.1	9.2	9.7	16.2	12.8
Terre Haute, IN	5,428	5,238	4,428	31,439	25,951	22.6	3,726	20.4	6.7	2.9	2.5	14.4	18.7
Clay County, IN	833	802	673	30,977	24,844	23.8	396	28.3	7.1	1.9	1.6	(D)	15.6
Sullivan County, IN	623	599	493	29,175	22,721	26.4	334	11.8	6.3	2.0	1.3	4.3	27.5
Vermillion County, IN	546	523	459	33,665	27,625	19.1	301	25.7	6.0	(D)	1.8	8.9	11.4
Vigo County, IN	3,426	3,315	2,803	31,666	26,637	22.2	2,695	19.7	6.8	3.5	2.9	18.3	18.9
Texarkana, TX–Texarkana, AR	4,749	4,548	3,686	34,776	28,049	28.8	3,205	8.4	8.0	4.6	(D)	15.3	29.2
Miller County, AR	1,468	1,385	1,163	33,539	27,578	26.2	813	22.2	6.8	2.0	(D)	4.9	14.9
Bowie County, TX	3,281	3,163	2,523	35,360	28,272	30.1	2,392	3.7	8.5	5.5	2.8	18.8	34.1
Toledo, OH	23,629	22,504	20,529	36,338	31,177	15.1	18,089	18.1	6.9	3.8	5.6	14.5	16.0
Fulton County, OH	1,497	1,412	1,336	35,211	31,143	12.0	1,003	35.0	5.5	2.0	1.6	(D)	13.5
Lucas County, OH	15,796	15,119	13,989	35,900	31,140	12.9	12,797	13.9	7.4	4.3	6.8	17.9	15.3
Ottawa County, OH	1,637	1,549	1,361	39,553	32,689	20.3	814	19.2	6.9	2.3	0.0	8.7	16.8
Wood County, OH	4,699	4,423	3,843	37,190	30,817	22.3	3,474	28.1	5.3	2.4	3.4	7.2	19.4
Topeka, KS	8,861	8,406	7,018	37,765	30,752	26.3	6,335	7.4	5.3	8.0	5.3	14.0	26.0
Jackson County, KS	479	442	387	35,661	28,985	23.7	244	3.8	7.6	3.5	2.0	(D)	39.7
Jefferson County, KS	659	618	507	34,779	26,473	29.9	178	5.1	5.8	(D)	3.0	(D)	28.2
Osage County, KS	519	495	418	31,807	24,770	24.1	124	3.2	8.6	(D)	2.3	(D)	41.5
Shawnee County, KS	6,963	6,621	5,515	38,913	32,082	26.3	5,726	7.7	5.2	8.6	5.6	15.5	25.0
Wabaunsee County, KS	242	230	191	34,429	27,552	26.8	63	11.4	3.4	4.9	1.3	(D)	31.1

[1] Based on resident population estimated as of July 1.
[2] Includes other industry categories not shown separately.
(D) = Data withheld to avoid disclosure or does not meet statistical standards.

Table C-3.   Personal Income and Earnings, by Industry—*Continued*

Metropolitan statistical area, division, and component county	Personal income						Earnings, 2011						
	Total (million dollars)			Per capita[1] (dollars)		Percent change, 2005–2011	Total[2] (million dollars)	Percentage by selected major industries					
	2011	2010	2005	2011	2005			Manufacturing	Retail trade	Finance and insurance	Professional and technical services	Health care and social services	Government and government enterprises
Trenton–Ewing, NJ	19,985	19,113	16,605	54,445	45,869	20.4	19,483	5.1	3.9	12.1	16.5	9.5	22.4
Mercer County, NJ	19,985	19,113	16,605	54,445	45,869	20.4	19,483	5.1	3.9	12.1	16.5	9.5	22.4
Tucson, AZ	34,596	33,278	28,574	34,961	31,048	21.1	21,775	10.5	6.6	4.6	8.3	15.1	25.7
Pima County, AZ	34,596	33,278	28,574	34,961	31,048	21.1	21,775	10.5	6.6	4.6	8.3	15.1	25.7
Tulsa, OK	39,996	37,162	30,734	42,236	34,812	30.1	29,943	12.5	6.2	5.1	5.9	10.6	10.4
Creek County, OK	2,310	2,210	1,746	32,787	25,788	32.3	1,052	22.5	6.9	3.2	(D)	8.7	15.8
Okmulgee County, OK	1,181	1,140	905	29,574	22,869	30.5	502	18.9	8.7	3.2	2.0	(D)	36.1
Osage County, OK	1,684	1,586	1,224	35,513	26,410	37.6	511	4.6	6.7	2.3	4.1	(D)	25.0
Pawnee County, OK	516	493	404	30,823	24,393	27.6	215	3.6	7.9	2.8	(D)	10.7	30.6
Rogers County, OK	3,230	3,063	2,246	36,826	27,969	43.8	1,627	21.8	5.5	2.4	(D)	7.5	21.7
Tulsa County, OK	28,579	26,339	22,561	46,804	39,706	26.7	25,636	11.5	6.1	5.4	6.7	11.5	8.3
Wagoner County, OK	2,496	2,330	1,648	33,686	25,685	51.5	401	19.0	10.6	2.6	2.3	(D)	23.9
Tuscaloosa, AL	7,600	7,284	5,864	34,305	29,028	29.6	5,509	18.0	6.3	2.3	4.6	8.8	27.9
Greene County, AL	283	272	257	31,678	26,528	10.1	121	17.5	4.0	1.4	(D)	(D)	25.2
Hale County, AL	470	461	394	30,458	23,692	19.3	184	15.6	6.1	2.0	1.2	(D)	25.1
Tuscaloosa County, AL	6,848	6,552	5,214	34,724	29,670	31.3	5,204	18.0	6.3	2.3	4.8	9.3	28.1
Tyler, TX	8,218	7,811	6,182	38,515	32,305	32.9	5,947	7.5	8.6	4.8	6.5	22.7	12.2
Smith County, TX	8,218	7,811	6,182	38,515	32,305	32.9	5,947	7.5	8.6	4.8	6.5	22.7	12.2
Utica–Rome, NY	10,567	10,225	8,236	35,406	27,584	28.3	6,821	9.9	8.4	6.6	4.8	15.7	29.9
Herkimer County, NY	2,121	2,049	1,637	33,060	25,459	29.6	854	16.8	9.4	2.0	2.2	10.4	27.5
Oneida County, NY	8,446	8,177	6,599	36,049	28,168	28.0	5,966	8.9	8.3	7.2	5.2	16.5	30.3
Valdosta, GA	4,323	4,134	3,263	30,377	25,810	32.5	2,999	(D)	7.9	0.0	3.3	11.2	37.3
Brooks County, GA	501	477	401	31,531	24,859	25.0	171	7.0	4.9	2.7	1.3	7.6	18.8
Echols County, GA	96	93	80	23,181	20,229	19.9	39	(D)	(D)	(D)	0.9	(D)	21.4
Lanier County, GA	265	250	176	25,434	21,761	50.7	73	5.9	6.2	0.0	1.1	9.6	28.1
Lowndes County, GA	3,462	3,313	2,606	30,938	26,523	32.8	2,715	7.0	8.3	2.2	3.5	11.6	39.0
Vallejo–Fairfield, CA	15,859	15,293	14,105	38,078	34,557	12.4	9,226	11.0	7.2	3.8	3.4	15.7	27.8
Solano County, CA	15,859	15,293	14,105	38,078	34,557	12.4	9,226	11.0	7.2	3.8	3.4	15.7	27.8
Victoria, TX	4,627	4,298	3,402	39,808	30,313	36.0	3,386	17.5	10.0	2.7	(D)	11.6	12.8
Calhoun County, TX	695	661	515	32,413	24,864	34.9	818	45.0	4.6	1.1	(D)	2.1	9.1
Goliad County, TX	215	207	169	29,735	23,869	27.6	75	(D)	6.9	2.1	(D)	(D)	29.4
Victoria County, TX	3,716	3,429	2,718	42,452	32,189	36.7	2,493	9.0	11.8	3.2	3.0	15.1	13.5
Vineland–Millville–Bridgeton, NJ	5,541	5,325	4,237	35,272	27,871	30.8	3,704	15.3	7.3	2.2	2.0	13.5	28.0
Cumberland County, NJ	5,541	5,325	4,237	35,272	27,871	30.8	3,704	15.3	7.3	2.2	2.0	13.5	28.0
Virginia Beach–Norfolk–Newport News, VA–NC[15,16]	70,516	67,182	56,595	41,976	34,413	24.6	54,080	6.5	5.0	3.6	7.2	8.3	40.1
Currituck County, NC	957	899	709	39,949	31,641	34.9	297	0.9	11.1	7.7	(D)	(D)	20.7
Gloucester County, VA	1,435	1,370	1,135	38,886	31,517	26.4	442	2.3	12.6	3.4	3.9	13.7	28.5
Isle of Wight County, VA	1,516	1,434	1,112	42,883	34,136	36.4	581	(D)	5.4	2.4	6.3	(D)	15.0
James City County, VA[15]	4,316	4,021	2,953	52,228	41,692	46.2	2,176	(D)	6.7	3.3	6.9	(D)	25.0
Mathews County, VA	473	452	382	52,738	42,602	23.8	97	3.3	8.3	4.7	8.3	(D)	22.0
Surry County, VA	242	231	181	34,860	26,341	33.6	253	1.8	0.5	0.3	1.8	0.2	10.0
York County, VA[16]	3,716	3,507	2,925	47,564	39,017	27.1	1,376	1.8	8.1	1.6	(D)	5.6	33.6
Chesapeake city, VA	9,566	9,116	7,542	42,504	35,058	26.8	5,373	5.8	8.9	3.3	10.8	6.9	19.8
Hampton city, VA	5,456	5,259	4,531	40,001	32,062	20.4	4,430	3.5	4.7	1.2	10.6	7.8	52.9
Newport News city, VA	6,242	5,997	5,170	34,752	28,154	20.7	6,826	28.8	4.3	1.8	6.3	8.7	29.4
Norfolk city, VA	8,947	8,568	7,399	36,873	30,875	20.9	14,896	2.8	2.7	3.4	6.0	9.0	55.4
Poquoson city, VA[16]	NA	NA	NA	NA	NA	NA	NA	NA	NA	NA	NA	NA	NA
Portsmouth city, VA	3,596	3,413	2,946	37,583	30,036	22.1	3,828	3.7	2.3	0.8	3.0	8.0	62.0
Suffolk city, VA	3,336	3,169	2,404	39,279	30,832	38.8	1,544	10.2	6.9	2.0	6.8	13.9	28.2
Virginia Beach city, VA	20,718	19,745	17,207	46,799	39,446	20.4	11,961	2.8	6.1	7.3	9.1	9.7	32.6
Williamsburg city, VA[15]	NA	NA	NA	NA	NA	NA	NA	NA	NA	NA	NA	NA	NA
Visalia–Porterville, CA	13,316	12,410	10,230	29,640	25,077	30.2	8,724	7.6	7.1	2.4	2.4	7.0	22.2
Tulare County, CA	13,316	12,410	10,230	29,640	25,077	30.2	8,724	7.6	7.1	2.4	2.4	7.0	22.2
Waco, TX	8,098	7,799	6,105	33,943	27,401	32.6	5,886	17.9	6.0	9.3	4.1	11.1	17.0
McLennan County, TX	8,098	7,799	6,105	33,943	27,401	32.6	5,886	17.9	6.0	9.3	4.1	11.1	17.0
Warner Robins, GA	4,990	4,738	3,708	34,674	29,385	34.6	4,293	6.5	5.0	1.4	6.9	5.1	61.0
Houston County, GA	4,990	4,738	3,708	34,674	29,385	34.6	4,293	6.5	5.0	1.4	6.9	5.1	61.0
Washington–Arlington–Alexandria, DC–VA–MD–WV[17,18,19]	338,498	321,521	262,193	59,345	50,187	29.1	299,187	1.6	3.3	4.1	23.3	6.2	29.7
Bethesda–Rockville–Frederick, MD	80,085	76,447	64,506	65,293	56,449	24.2	54,969	3.5	4.5	6.8	19.6	8.9	23.4
Frederick County, MD	11,035	10,542	8,659	46,610	39,147	27.4	6,609	5.7	6.5	7.1	17.2	9.5	22.1
Montgomery County, MD	69,050	65,904	55,846	69,762	60,602	23.6	48,360	3.2	4.2	6.7	19.9	8.9	23.6

[1] Based on resident population estimated as of July 1.
[2] Includes other industry categories not shown separately.
[15] Williamsburg city included with James City County, VA, in the Virginia Beach–Norfolk–Newport News, VA–NC MSA.
[16] Poquoson city included with York County, VA, in the Virginia Beach–Norfolk–Newport News, VA–NC MSA.
[17] Fairfax and Falls Church cities included with Fairfax County, VA, in the Washington–Arlington–Alexandria, DC–VA–MD–WV MSA.
[18] Manassas and Manassas Park cities included with Prince William County, VA, in the Washington–Arlington–Alexandria, DC–VA–MD–WV MSA.
[19] Fredericksburg city included with Spotsylvania County, VA, in the Washington–Arlington–Alexandria, DC–VA–MD–WV MSA.
(D) = Data withheld to avoid disclosure or does not meet statistical standards.
NA = Not available

Table C-3. Personal Income and Earnings, by Industry—*Continued*

Metropolitan statistical area, division, and component county	Personal income Total (million dollars) 2011	2010	2005	Per capita[1] (dollars) 2011	2005	Percent change, 2005–2011	Earnings, 2011 Total[2] (million dollars)	Manufacturing	Retail trade	Finance and insurance	Professional and technical services	Health care and social services	Government and government enterprises
Washington–Arlington–Alexandria, DC–VA–MD–WV[17,18,19]	258,413	245,074	197,688	57,715	48,434	30.7	244,219	1.2	(D)	3.5	24.1	5.6	31.1
District of Columbia, DC	45,598	43,082	31,965	73,783	56,362	42.6	84,518	0.2	0.9	3.2	22.6	5.3	42.8
Calvert County, MD	4,238	4,060	3,286	47,483	38,081	29.0	1,412	2.7	7.0	1.7	6.7	14.9	22.4
Charles County, MD	6,678	6,350	5,138	44,778	37,078	30.0	2,612	1.7	12.0	2.3	7.4	10.7	32.7
Prince George's County, MD	35,037	33,889	29,435	40,215	34,496	19.0	23,725	2.7	6.5	2.0	10.1	7.6	38.1
Arlington County, VA	17,818	16,655	12,697	82,491	67,622	40.3	21,663	0.4	1.8	3.6	25.2	2.9	38.7
Clarke County, VA	590	568	504	41,366	36,764	17.0	232	14.3	4.6	2.8	12.0	6.4	16.9
Fairfax County, VA[17]	78,392	75,161	65,599	69,008	62,404	19.5	70,297	1.1	3.7	5.3	36.8	5.9	15.6
Fauquier County, VA	3,594	3,426	3,038	54,400	48,458	18.3	1,467	3.3	7.6	3.8	15.3	10.5	21.5
Loudoun County, VA	18,627	16,971	10,855	57,242	42,582	71.6	11,311	4.2	5.4	2.9	20.9	5.8	14.8
Prince William County, VA[18]	21,307	19,840	15,013	44,986	37,577	41.9	9,903	4.0	(D)	(D)	(D)	(D)	31.3
Spotsylvania County, VA[19]	6,135	5,790	4,699	40,893	34,382	30.5	3,086	(D)	11.9	3.0	8.8	22.0	17.5
Stafford County, VA	5,539	5,253	4,039	41,917	34,340	37.1	3,001	1.5	4.9	0.0	11.8	4.3	40.7
Warren County, VA	1,483	1,413	1,178	39,289	33,264	25.9	594	11.2	8.5	2.8	4.1	11.1	18.4
Alexandria city, VA	11,311	10,648	8,662	78,383	67,573	30.6	9,568	(D)	3.7	3.6	24.7	4.5	31.4
Fairfax city, VA[17]	NA	NA	NA	NA	NA	NA	NA	NA	NA	NA	NA	NA	NA
Falls Church city, VA[17]	NA	NA	NA	NA	NA	NA	NA	NA	NA	NA	NA	NA	NA
Fredericksburg city, VA[19]	NA	NA	NA	NA	NA	NA	NA	NA	NA	NA	NA	NA	NA
Manassas city, VA[18]	NA	NA	NA	NA	NA	NA	NA	NA	NA	NA	NA	NA	NA
Manassas Park city, VA[18]	NA	NA	NA	NA	NA	NA	NA	NA	NA	NA	NA	NA	NA
Jefferson County, WV	2,067	1,967	1,583	38,127	32,521	30.6	830	5.5	6.4	2.2	4.8	7.9	30.8
Waterloo–Cedar Falls, IA	6,596	6,090	5,007	39,195	30,670	31.7	5,155	24.8	6.0	5.4	3.3	(D)	15.4
Black Hawk County, IA	4,928	4,605	3,844	37,461	30,265	28.2	4,251	27.0	6.3	4.8	3.6	12.5	15.7
Bremer County, IA	1,048	940	750	43,157	31,458	39.8	575	18.9	5.9	10.8	2.0	(D)	16.7
Grundy County, IA	620	545	413	49,783	33,307	50.1	329	6.5	3.7	3.6	1.5	(D)	9.7
Wausau, WI	5,002	4,846	4,255	37,214	32,998	17.5	3,781	23.1	7.1	9.6	5.2	13.4	11.4
Marathon County, WI	5,002	4,846	4,255	37,214	32,998	17.5	3,781	23.1	7.1	9.6	5.2	13.4	11.4
Wenatchee–East Wenatchee, WA	3,953	3,764	2,916	35,152	28,213	35.5	2,496	5.8	8.3	2.4	3.8	15.8	22.4
Chelan County, WA	2,764	2,637	2,074	37,619	30,163	33.3	2,015	6.1	7.9	2.7	3.7	18.0	20.6
Douglas County, WA	1,189	1,126	843	30,500	24,340	41.0	482	4.8	10.0	1.5	3.9	6.7	29.5
Wheeling, WV–OH	5,064	4,795	4,085	34,406	27,335	24.0	3,391	10.7	8.3	3.6	(D)	(D)	15.7
Belmont County, OH	2,195	2,063	1,771	31,286	25,221	24.0	1,156	5.4	10.9	3.6	(D)	14.6	17.9
Marshall County, WV	1,190	1,120	876	36,275	25,678	35.8	873	26.3	5.0	1.2	(D)	(D)	11.7
Ohio County, WV	1,680	1,612	1,438	37,969	31,878	16.8	1,362	5.1	8.1	5.0	7.6	22.5	16.4
Wichita, KS	24,125	23,053	19,835	38,568	33,731	21.6	18,772	25.3	6.2	2.9	4.5	(D)	14.3
Butler County, KS	2,481	2,401	1,954	37,697	31,237	27.0	1,177	16.5	9.2	3.3	3.2	(D)	22.1
Harvey County, KS	1,333	1,278	1,052	38,254	31,330	26.8	943	21.5	6.5	2.8	3.9	(D)	10.0
Sedgwick County, KS	19,368	18,495	16,099	38,653	34,464	20.3	16,243	26.4	5.9	2.9	4.6	12.1	13.8
Sumner County, KS	943	879	731	39,651	29,464	29.1	410	15.6	6.3	3.3	2.2	(D)	20.3
Wichita Falls, TX	5,510	5,295	4,497	36,671	29,753	22.5	3,834	9.4	6.8	3.7	(D)	12.3	28.3
Archer County, TX	404	379	284	45,689	31,360	42.1	163	2.1	6.1	1.4	3.6	1.4	15.4
Clay County, TX	470	442	313	43,795	27,630	50.2	162	4.5	7.4	3.7	3.3	(D)	15.8
Wichita County, TX	4,637	4,474	3,900	35,477	29,826	18.9	3,508	10.0	6.8	3.8	(D)	13.4	29.5
Williamsport, PA	4,119	3,813	3,224	35,283	27,430	27.8	2,913	20.0	6.8	3.1	4.2	14.3	17.8
Lycoming County, PA	4,119	3,813	3,224	35,283	27,430	27.8	2,913	20.0	6.8	3.1	4.2	14.3	17.8
Wilmington, NC	12,770	12,090	9,790	34,543	30,713	30.4	8,015	8.7	8.5	4.5	8.6	11.1	19.3
Brunswick County, NC	3,674	3,465	2,528	33,375	28,780	45.3	1,546	4.8	8.7	4.1	5.5	8.8	18.8
New Hanover County, NC	7,445	7,052	6,061	36,108	32,690	22.8	5,951	9.8	8.6	4.8	9.8	12.7	19.0
Pender County, NC	1,650	1,573	1,200	30,907	26,388	37.5	519	8.4	7.2	2.3	3.4	(D)	24.6
Winchester, VA–WV[20]	4,559	4,316	3,572	35,048	30,313	27.6	3,179	14.8	9.1	3.1	4.1	17.6	19.7
Frederick County, VA[20]	3,972	3,752	3,090	37,382	32,361	28.5	2,972	15.5	9.2	3.1	4.3	18.8	18.7
Winchester city, VA[20]	NA	NA	NA	NA	NA	NA	NA	NA	NA	NA	NA	NA	NA
Hampshire County, WV	587	564	482	24,634	21,570	21.6	206	4.1	7.6	4.1	2.1	(D)	33.9
Winston–Salem, NC	17,554	16,670	15,185	36,416	33,942	15.6	12,754	14.1	7.4	8.3	7.2	15.9	10.8
Davie County, NC	1,490	1,423	1,277	35,863	33,123	16.7	500	16.0	10.8	4.1	3.8	9.2	16.2
Forsyth County, NC	13,489	12,760	11,707	38,003	36,014	15.2	11,405	13.7	7.3	8.8	7.6	16.7	9.9
Stokes County, NC	1,420	1,366	1,194	30,062	25,858	19.0	374	17.0	7.4	3.0	4.7	12.4	24.1
Yadkin County, NC	1,154	1,122	1,007	30,142	26,791	14.6	475	20.1	6.1	4.0	1.9	6.7	16.0
Worcester, MA	36,494	34,756	29,016	45,548	37,140	25.8	22,003	13.5	6.0	7.7	7.7	15.7	15.4
Worcester County, MA	36,494	34,756	29,016	45,548	37,140	25.8	22,003	13.5	6.0	7.7	7.7	15.7	15.4
Yakima, WA	8,247	7,829	5,924	33,371	25,916	39.2	5,395	7.7	7.0	2.4	2.7	14.2	19.1
Yakima County, WA	8,247	7,829	5,924	33,371	25,916	39.2	5,395	7.7	7.0	2.4	2.7	14.2	19.1
York–Hanover, PA	16,326	15,559	13,207	37,380	32,286	23.6	10,382	21.0	6.5	2.6	4.5	13.5	14.4
York County, PA	16,326	15,559	13,207	37,380	32,286	23.6	10,382	21.0	6.5	2.6	4.5	13.5	14.4
Youngstown–Warren–Boardman, OH–PA	18,818	17,938	16,559	33,440	28,343	13.6	11,730	19.9	8.5	3.3	3.6	16.5	15.3
Mahoning County, OH	8,307	7,906	7,246	35,012	29,254	14.6	5,274	10.3	8.8	3.7	5.1	17.2	17.2
Trumbull County, OH	6,660	6,350	6,075	31,826	27,879	9.6	4,026	30.7	8.0	2.3	2.4	13.9	14.2
Mercer County, PA	3,851	3,682	3,237	33,136	27,293	19.0	2,431	22.6	8.5	4.2	2.2	19.3	12.9
Yuba City, CA	5,428	5,200	4,229	32,404	27,276	28.3	3,308	4.1	7.0	1.7	2.9	11.6	33.7
Sutter County, CA	3,219	3,092	2,597	33,908	29,259	23.9	1,822	5.5	9.8	2.3	3.3	13.0	15.1
Yuba County, CA	2,209	2,108	1,632	30,437	24,621	35.4	1,486	2.4	3.6	1.0	2.4	9.9	56.5
Yuma, AZ	5,442	5,187	4,116	27,091	23,020	32.2	3,783	2.7	6.6	1.2	5.2	10.5	36.0
Yuma County, AZ	5,442	5,187	4,116	27,091	23,020	32.2	3,783	2.7	6.6	1.2	5.2	10.5	36.0

[1] Based on resident population estimated as of July 1.
[2] Includes other industry categories not shown separately.
[17] Fairfax and Falls Church cities included with Fairfax County, VA, in the Washington–Arlington–Alexandria, DC–VA–MD–WV MSA.
[18] Manassas and Manassas Park cities included with Prince William County, VA, in the Washington–Arlington–Alexandria, DC–VA–MD–WV MSA.
[19] Fredericksburg city included with Spotsylvania County, VA, in the Washington–Arlington–Alexandria, DC–VA–MD–WV MSA.
[20] Winchester city included with Frederick County, VA, in the Winchester, VA–WV MSA.
(D) = Data withheld due to avoid disclosure or does not meet statistical standards.
NA = Not available

Table C-4.   Labor Force and Private Business Establishments and Employment

Metropolitan statistical area, division, and component county	Civilian labor force								Private nonfarm businesses				
	Total				Number of unemployed		Unemployment rate[1]		Establishments		Employment[2]		Annual payroll per employee 2010 (dollars)
	2011	2010	2005	Change, 2005–2011	2011	2010	2011	2010	2010	Change, 2000–2010	2010	Change, 2000–2010	
Abilene, TX...	83,772	84,501	80,276	4.4	5,368	5,452	6.4	6.5	3,899	-2.9	55,831	4.7	30,207
Callahan County, TX.............................	7,014	7,053	7,010	0.1	437	422	6.2	6.0	230	16.2	1,517	52.0	33,366
Jones County, TX.................................	8,065	8,133	7,888	2.2	607	613	7.5	7.5	300	-5.7	2,547	-19.1	27,260
Taylor County, TX.................................	68,693	69,315	65,378	5.1	4,324	4,417	6.3	6.4	3,369	-3.8	51,767	5.3	30,259
Akron, OH...	374,097	380,423	378,862	-1.3	31,605	37,537	8.4	9.9	16,572	-5.6	270,260	-10.6	40,521
Portage County, OH.............................	91,043	92,463	89,083	2.2	7,569	8,893	8.3	9.6	2,967	-4.5	40,739	-12.9	34,652
Summit County, OH.............................	283,054	287,960	289,779	-2.3	24,036	28,644	8.5	9.9	13,605	-5.8	229,521	-10.1	41,563
Albany, GA...	73,504	74,838	74,828	-1.8	7,630	8,087	10.4	10.8	3,332	1.2	44,686	-15.5	31,912
Baker County, GA.................................	1,509	1,539	1,803	-16.3	134	146	8.9	9.5	24	14.3	235	9.8	33,043
Dougherty County, GA.........................	42,318	43,006	41,476	2.0	4,804	4,992	11.4	11.6	2,455	-5.0	37,187	-18.5	32,887
Lee County, GA...................................	15,180	15,489	16,515	-8.1	1,213	1,336	8.0	8.6	373	79.3	3,220	30.2	28,027
Terrell County, GA..............................	4,071	4,131	4,614	-11.8	451	463	11.1	11.2	180	-5.8	1,601	-24.1	25,408
Worth County, GA...............................	10,426	10,673	10,420	0.1	1,028	1,150	9.9	10.8	300	4.2	2,443	0.4	26,357
Albany–Schenectady–Troy, NY...............	440,416	448,212	454,737	-3.1	31,527	33,036	7.2	7.4	21,061	9.2	323,328	1.2	40,676
Albany County, NY..............................	153,850	156,360	159,405	-3.5	10,802	11,113	7.0	7.1	9,465	6.6	167,941	-0.3	42,300
Rensselaer County, NY.........................	81,504	83,040	83,893	-2.8	6,138	6,515	7.5	7.8	2,979	9.1	41,409	-1.3	37,167
Saratoga County, NY............................	115,570	117,696	120,088	-3.8	7,592	8,058	6.6	6.8	4,961	19.9	61,076	13.5	38,946
Schenectady County, NY.......................	74,090	75,485	75,478	-1.8	5,553	5,893	7.5	7.8	3,100	4.7	47,433	-4.4	41,379
Schoharie County, NY..........................	15,402	15,631	15,873	-3.0	1,442	1,457	9.4	9.3	556	-3.0	5,469	-3.9	30,582
Albuquerque, NM...................................	397,485	400,384	392,202	1.3	31,147	33,167	7.8	8.3	18,688	4.0	279,882	-0.3	36,467
Bernalillo County, NM.........................	304,106	306,461	304,176	0.0	23,011	24,691	7.6	8.1	15,943	1.7	242,996	-2.9	36,639
Sandoval County, NM..........................	55,982	56,174	49,915	12.2	4,826	4,895	8.6	8.7	1,612	32.0	24,395	23.5	41,235
Torrance County, NM..........................	6,531	6,576	7,567	-13.7	618	649	9.5	9.9	233	4.5	1,797	-2.7	23,724
Valencia County, NM...........................	30,866	31,173	30,544	1.1	2,692	2,932	8.7	9.4	900	5.8	10,694	19.4	23,823
Alexandria, LA.......................................	67,806	68,982	67,958	-0.2	4,860	4,891	7.2	7.1	3,449	4.9	48,883	-1.7	32,133
Grant Parish, LA.................................	9,418	9,599	8,578	9.8	687	709	7.3	7.4	188	-6.9	1,663	14.4	25,820
Rapides Parish, LA..............................	58,388	59,383	59,380	-1.7	4,173	4,182	7.1	7.0	3,261	5.7	47,220	-2.2	32,356
Allentown–Bethlehem–Easton, PA–NJ.......	422,220	422,501	408,548	3.3	36,827	38,840	8.7	9.2	18,299	3.3	284,193	-1.1	42,739
Warren County, NJ..............................	59,440	59,319	58,741	1.2	5,016	5,520	8.4	9.3	2,533	-6.9	28,027	-10.1	44,300
Carbon County, PA..............................	31,785	31,781	30,317	4.8	3,231	3,322	10.2	10.5	1,128	-0.9	13,323	-7.6	26,945
Lehigh County, PA..............................	179,433	179,685	171,281	4.8	15,598	16,398	8.7	9.1	8,410	2.8	153,146	-5.1	46,305
Northampton County, PA......................	151,562	151,716	148,209	2.3	12,982	13,600	8.6	9.0	6,228	9.8	89,697	11.6	38,510
Altoona, PA...	64,967	64,894	64,984	0.0	4,530	4,920	7.0	7.6	3,217	-2.2	50,470	-2.7	31,406
Blair County, PA.................................	64,967	64,894	64,984	0.0	4,530	4,920	7.0	7.6	3,217	-2.2	50,470	-2.7	31,406
Amarillo, TX...	134,960	133,228	126,845	6.4	7,305	7,421	5.4	5.6	5,998	3.7	88,609	5.2	35,453
Armstrong County, TX..........................	992	977	1,126	-11.9	49	48	4.9	4.9	31	-3.1	184	0.0	20,005
Carson County, TX..............................	3,306	3,262	3,498	-5.5	164	165	5.0	5.1	109	-14.2	4,071	385.8	72,969
Potter County, TX...............................	58,103	57,405	56,683	2.5	3,674	3,764	6.3	6.6	3,571	-1.7	58,798	-5.1	35,293
Randall County, TX.............................	72,559	71,584	65,538	10.7	3,418	3,444	4.7	4.8	2,287	14.9	25,556	19.2	29,956
Ames, IA...	48,571	48,862	46,855	3.7	2,191	2,328	4.5	4.8	2,031	5.1	28,112	-1.4	32,555
Story County, IA.................................	48,571	48,862	46,855	3.7	2,191	2,328	4.5	4.8	2,031	5.1	28,112	-1.4	32,555
Anchorage, AK.......................................	200,289	199,456	185,631	7.9	13,446	14,532	6.7	7.3	10,425	12.0	160,120	30.8	54,380
Anchorage Municipality, AK..................	157,210	156,732	148,927	5.6	9,606	10,644	6.1	6.8	8,470	7.4	145,065	28.6	55,588
Matanuska–Susitna Borough, AK...........	43,079	42,724	36,704	17.4	3,840	3,888	8.9	9.1	1,955	37.6	15,055	56.1	42,743
Anderson, IN..	61,156	61,853	63,171	-3.2	6,432	7,024	10.5	11.4	2,342	-15.5	34,123	-19.4	29,486
Madison County, IN.............................	61,156	61,853	63,171	-3.2	6,432	7,024	10.5	11.4	2,342	-15.5	34,123	-19.4	29,486
Anderson, SC..	84,118	84,546	83,693	0.5	8,342	9,680	9.9	11.4	3,681	-1.2	50,507	-14.4	31,124
Anderson County, SC...........................	84,118	84,546	83,693	0.5	8,342	9,680	9.9	11.4	3,681	-1.2	50,507	-14.4	31,124
Ann Arbor, MI...	179,685	180,347	189,873	-5.4	11,618	14,534	6.5	8.1	7,905	-4.2	132,543	-15.8	47,843
Washtenaw County, MI........................	179,685	180,347	189,873	-5.4	11,618	14,534	6.5	8.1	7,905	-4.2	132,543	-15.8	47,843
Anniston–Oxford, AL...............................	53,790	53,973	53,629	0.3	4,944	5,239	9.2	9.7	2,427	-5.4	36,951	-9.0	31,674
Calhoun County, AL.............................	53,790	53,973	53,629	0.3	4,944	5,239	9.2	9.7	2,427	-5.4	36,951	-9.0	31,674
Appleton, WI..	124,418	124,910	120,527	3.2	8,409	9,750	6.8	7.8	5,818	6.1	101,841	-6.9	38,514
Calumet County, WI............................	27,317	27,363	25,211	8.4	1,565	1,800	5.7	6.6	860	11.8	11,591	-6.7	33,654
Outagamie County, WI.........................	97,101	97,547	95,316	1.9	6,844	7,950	7.0	8.1	4,958	5.2	90,250	-6.9	39,138
Asheville, NC..	215,308	213,206	199,904	7.7	18,351	19,065	8.5	8.9	11,502	11.6	141,838	-3.7	32,818
Buncombe County, NC..........................	125,456	124,306	116,067	8.1	10,345	10,841	8.2	8.7	7,199	12.8	95,736	-3.3	33,456
Haywood County, NC..........................	28,845	28,473	27,347	5.5	2,842	2,842	9.9	10.0	1,413	0.8	13,974	-7.1	29,867
Henderson County, NC.........................	50,897	50,448	46,645	9.1	4,171	4,390	8.2	8.7	2,576	16.8	29,284	-2.4	32,924
Madison County, NC............................	10,110	9,979	9,845	2.7	993	992	9.8	9.9	314	-0.3	2,844	-10.2	24,767
Athens–Clarke County, GA.......................	108,418	108,533	99,871	8.6	7,955	8,203	7.3	7.6	4,390	14.7	53,718	-1.3	31,561
Clarke County, GA..............................	65,606	65,611	59,464	10.3	4,929	5,015	7.5	7.6	2,897	11.6	42,608	3.2	32,302
Madison County, GA............................	15,911	15,956	15,572	2.2	1,251	1,315	7.9	8.2	365	-28.6	2,123	-69.4	24,120
Oconee County, GA..............................	18,671	18,705	17,229	8.4	1,143	1,200	6.1	6.4	943	62.9	7,897	47.4	30,500
Oglethorpe County, GA.........................	8,230	8,261	7,606	8.2	632	673	7.7	8.1	185	30.3	1,090	29.6	24,768

[1] Civilian unemployed as percent of total civilian labor force.
[2] For pay period including March 12 of the year shown.

Table C-4. Labor Force and Private Business Establishments and Employment—*Continued*

Metropolitan statistical area, division, and component county	Civilian labor force								Private nonfarm businesses				
	Total				Number of unemployed		Unemployment rate[1]		Establishments		Employment[2]		Annual payroll per employee 2010 (dollars)
	2011	2010	2005	Change, 2005–2011	2011	2010	2011	2010	2010	Change, 2000–2010	2010	Change, 2000–2010	
Atlanta–Sandy Springs–Marietta, GA	2,686,993	2,658,658	2,592,383	3.6	258,997	270,475	9.6	10.2	129,166	11.6	2,003,047	-6.3	47,516
Barrow County, GA	34,424	34,205	30,708	12.1	3,200	3,493	9.3	10.2	1,020	25.8	12,762	33.6	32,322
Bartow County, GA	48,802	48,531	44,895	8.7	4,971	5,419	10.2	11.2	1,835	14.8	26,454	-0.4	34,478
Butts County, GA	10,120	9,951	9,164	10.4	1,192	1,169	11.8	11.7	351	3.2	3,787	-11.9	27,506
Carroll County, GA	52,170	51,546	51,007	2.3	5,562	5,703	10.7	11.1	1,981	7.3	29,435	6.1	35,611
Cherokee County, GA	112,406	111,334	100,416	11.9	9,102	9,724	8.1	8.7	4,528	39.5	37,340	27.5	30,485
Clayton County, GA	129,784	128,181	136,952	-5.2	15,776	16,043	12.2	12.5	3,930	-10.2	70,758	-20.1	32,669
Cobb County, GA	371,429	368,205	371,734	-0.1	33,060	35,384	8.9	9.6	18,950	5.6	301,709	-3.6	48,407
Coweta County, GA	62,717	62,159	56,194	11.6	5,573	5,952	8.9	9.6	2,037	22.3	25,959	9.5	30,712
Dawson County, GA	11,358	11,298	10,357	9.7	1,006	1,116	8.9	9.9	606	22.4	5,826	38.0	23,907
DeKalb County, GA	364,638	360,578	370,600	-1.6	36,846	38,161	10.1	10.6	16,067	-5.3	252,597	-23.1	44,321
Douglas County, GA	68,214	67,435	59,880	13.9	6,982	7,207	10.2	10.7	2,484	18.0	33,317	14.0	30,983
Fayette County, GA	52,392	51,666	53,527	-2.1	4,230	4,294	8.1	8.3	3,126	29.7	36,182	22.3	36,579
Forsyth County, GA	90,431	89,584	75,601	19.6	6,575	7,103	7.3	7.9	5,060	113.7	55,589	87.3	41,746
Fulton County, GA	449,190	444,262	460,241	-2.4	46,980	48,648	10.5	11.0	32,989	6.6	681,304	-11.3	59,956
Gwinnett County, GA	427,058	422,563	400,947	6.5	36,266	38,179	8.5	9.0	21,126	18.8	281,534	-2.1	43,650
Haralson County, GA	12,783	12,716	12,918	-1.0	1,331	1,452	10.4	11.4	427	-3.8	4,885	-12.7	34,062
Heard County, GA	5,058	5,038	4,967	1.8	551	604	10.9	12.0	120	0.8	1,036	-28.2	34,482
Henry County, GA	104,821	103,330	89,168	17.6	10,175	10,236	9.7	9.9	3,253	43.2	40,613	42.8	29,859
Jasper County, GA	6,498	6,446	6,272	3.6	690	733	10.6	11.4	163	1.9	1,350	-26.7	26,856
Lamar County, GA	8,584	8,486	7,813	9.9	1,013	1,039	11.8	12.2	239	0.8	2,351	-24.8	26,791
Meriwether County, GA	9,311	9,173	9,875	-5.7	1,196	1,191	12.8	13.0	310	-9.4	3,201	-36.2	33,204
Newton County, GA	48,196	47,602	42,637	13.0	5,543	5,648	11.5	11.9	1,352	14.5	16,148	3.6	35,463
Paulding County, GA	72,416	71,831	58,954	22.8	6,797	7,288	9.4	10.1	1,599	62.5	14,444	57.3	26,297
Pickens County, GA	14,519	14,298	14,328	1.3	1,409	1,403	9.7	9.8	652	34.7	5,422	8.3	30,656
Pike County, GA	8,292	8,189	7,756	6.9	810	830	9.8	10.1	242	24.1	1,463	19.8	26,544
Rockdale County, GA	41,592	41,087	39,338	5.7	4,497	4,600	10.8	11.2	2,037	2.8	26,497	-16.0	37,351
Spalding County, GA	28,965	28,649	28,308	2.3	3,630	3,729	12.5	13.0	1,166	-1.4	16,317	-15.4	29,195
Walton County, GA	40,825	40,315	37,826	7.9	4,034	4,127	9.9	10.2	1,516	24.0	14,767	29.8	30,889
Atlantic City–Hammonton, NJ	135,813	137,168	136,705	-0.7	17,467	17,453	12.9	12.7	6,482	1.6	113,533	-5.8	35,143
Atlantic County, NJ	135,813	137,168	136,705	-0.7	17,467	17,453	12.9	12.7	6,482	1.6	113,533	-5.8	35,143
Auburn–Opelika, AL	67,892	66,231	63,227	7.4	5,033	5,336	7.4	8.1	2,352	18.1	34,910	8.2	28,109
Lee County, AL	67,892	66,231	63,227	7.4	5,033	5,336	7.4	8.1	2,352	18.1	34,910	8.2	28,109
Augusta–Richmond County, GA–SC	259,101	257,690	253,568	2.2	23,808	23,884	9.2	9.3	10,335	3.3	170,333	-3.9	38,028
Burke County, GA	9,645	9,584	10,138	-4.9	1,101	1,095	11.4	11.4	303	-5.0	4,838	-10.1	41,973
Columbia County, GA	63,896	63,442	57,208	11.7	4,537	4,464	7.1	7.0	2,132	18.2	26,284	13.0	31,740
McDuffie County, GA	10,262	10,164	10,701	-4.1	1,138	1,099	11.1	10.8	444	-5.5	6,172	-16.9	29,404
Richmond County, GA	87,830	87,505	90,352	-2.8	9,290	9,469	10.6	10.8	4,360	-2.1	80,515	-3.9	36,904
Aiken County, SC	76,200	75,731	74,035	2.9	6,694	6,650	8.8	8.8	2,759	5.3	48,205	-8.1	44,902
Edgefield County, SC	11,268	11,264	11,134	1.2	1,048	1,107	9.3	9.8	337	-0.9	4,319	-13.4	28,427
Austin–Round Rock–San Marcos, TX	940,043	921,127	800,248	17.5	63,501	65,222	6.8	7.1	41,216	29.5	640,563	16.4	46,969
Bastrop County, TX	35,777	35,113	33,734	6.1	2,801	2,914	7.8	8.3	1,010	27.8	10,931	50.9	27,685
Caldwell County, TX	16,759	16,411	16,005	4.7	1,425	1,438	8.5	8.8	533	7.9	5,361	26.9	25,872
Hays County, TX	84,267	82,481	67,201	25.4	5,633	5,698	6.7	6.9	3,187	45.8	37,501	56.0	29,250
Travis County, TX	576,384	564,661	503,342	14.5	38,150	39,099	6.6	6.9	28,431	20.7	470,425	5.5	49,343
Williamson County, TX	226,856	222,461	179,966	26.1	15,492	16,073	6.8	7.2	8,055	67.7	116,345	69.1	45,865
Bakersfield–Delano, CA	382,029	373,333	327,452	16.7	56,934	59,249	14.9	15.9	11,925	9.5	174,924	16.4	38,918
Kern County, CA	382,029	373,333	327,452	16.7	56,934	59,249	14.9	15.9	11,925	9.5	174,924	16.4	38,918
Baltimore–Towson, MD	1,440,848	1,432,015	1,376,739	4.7	107,554	118,961	7.5	8.3	65,169	4.7	1,059,610	1.4	47,495
Anne Arundel County, MD	296,863	294,513	276,546	7.3	18,934	20,803	6.4	7.1	13,523	11.1	200,134	8.3	46,054
Baltimore County, MD	443,127	440,274	422,440	4.9	33,246	36,615	7.5	8.3	19,805	4.3	310,646	-1.2	43,762
Carroll County, MD	93,855	93,250	92,599	1.4	5,976	6,705	6.4	7.2	4,258	4.6	47,373	8.8	34,029
Harford County, MD	136,434	135,513	130,172	4.8	9,792	10,793	7.2	8.0	5,318	10.0	65,678	11.6	36,640
Howard County, MD	167,369	165,719	155,344	7.7	8,614	9,374	5.1	5.7	8,581	16.9	150,997	11.9	57,135
Queen Anne's County, MD	27,128	26,842	25,228	7.5	1,877	1,975	6.9	7.4	1,365	14.0	10,705	11.8	32,688
Baltimore city, MD	276,072	275,904	274,410	0.6	29,115	32,696	10.5	11.9	12,319	-9.7	274,077	-8.1	52,973
Bangor, ME	78,770	78,340	76,752	2.6	6,393	6,803	8.1	8.7	4,193	0.5	57,599	1.3	34,059
Penobscot County, ME	78,770	78,340	76,752	2.6	6,393	6,803	8.1	8.7	4,193	0.5	57,599	1.3	34,059
Barnstable Town, MA	120,515	121,416	122,112	-1.3	9,880	10,934	8.2	9.0	8,214	-1.5	68,819	-4.7	39,195
Barnstable County, MA	120,515	121,416	122,112	-1.3	9,880	10,934	8.2	9.0	8,214	-1.5	68,819	-4.7	39,195
Baton Rouge, LA	376,683	377,113	363,516	3.6	27,898	28,133	7.4	7.5	17,751	10.4	309,320	10.0	40,642
Ascension Parish, LA	51,388	51,603	45,952	11.8	3,488	3,676	6.8	7.1	1,972	29.9	30,367	19.9	42,393
East Baton Rouge Parish, LA	215,626	215,724	213,498	1.0	15,518	15,505	7.2	7.2	12,185	6.0	230,086	7.8	40,978
East Feliciana Parish, LA	7,696	7,709	8,223	-6.4	672	681	8.7	8.8	265	5.2	3,700	6.9	31,546
Iberville Parish, LA	12,523	12,481	12,618	-0.8	1,356	1,308	10.8	10.5	531	-2.0	9,276	-12.8	55,296
Livingston Parish, LA	59,711	59,860	53,504	11.6	4,181	4,299	7.0	7.2	1,601	30.4	17,393	42.2	27,720
Pointe Coupee Parish, LA	9,554	9,513	9,930	-3.8	861	815	9.0	8.6	383	5.9	4,287	13.5	35,622
St. Helena Parish, LA	4,439	4,438	4,369	1.6	567	563	12.8	12.7	120	33.3	1,134	52.0	29,706
West Baton Rouge Parish, LA	10,947	10,983	10,481	4.4	856	887	7.8	8.1	500	16.3	10,588	19.6	40,598
West Feliciana Parish, LA	4,799	4,802	4,941	-2.9	399	399	8.3	8.3	194	12.8	2,489	-7.6	51,281

[1] Civilian unemployed as percent of total civilian labor force.
[2] For pay period including March 12 of the year shown.

Table C-4.   Labor Force and Private Business Establishments and Employment—*Continued*

Metropolitan statistical area, division, and component county	Civilian labor force								Private nonfarm businesses				
	Total				Number of unemployed		Unemployment rate[1]		Establishments		Employment[2]		Annual payroll per employee 2010 (dollars)
	2011	2010	2005	Change, 2005–2011	2011	2010	2011	2010	2010	Change, 2000–2010	2010	Change, 2000–2010	
Battle Creek, MI.............................	64,509	66,098	71,672	-10.0	5,728	7,322	8.9	11.1	2,681	-11.5	47,280	-22.1	41,272
Calhoun County, MI..........................	64,509	66,098	71,672	-10.0	5,728	7,322	8.9	11.1	2,681	-11.5	47,280	-22.1	41,272
Bay City, MI..................................	51,715	52,850	55,517	-6.8	5,004	6,198	9.7	11.7	2,291	-10.4	29,340	-17.0	36,232
Bay County, MI...............................	51,715	52,850	55,517	-6.8	5,004	6,198	9.7	11.7	2,291	-10.4	29,340	-17.0	36,232
Beaumont–Port Arthur, TX.................	189,502	188,883	177,351	6.9	20,863	20,267	11.0	10.7	7,926	-2.2	126,414	-2.1	42,834
Hardin County, TX...........................	27,705	27,687	24,677	12.3	2,608	2,594	9.4	9.4	779	5.7	8,317	-5.6	33,155
Jefferson County, TX........................	120,358	119,853	111,802	7.7	13,614	13,123	11.3	10.9	5,763	-2.5	98,789	-1.6	43,957
Orange County, TX..........................	41,439	41,343	40,872	1.4	4,641	4,550	11.2	11.0	1,384	-5.3	19,308	-3.1	41,256
Bellingham, WA..............................	106,230	106,414	102,044	4.1	8,843	9,544	8.3	9.0	6,244	15.9	67,421	13.1	35,649
Whatcom County, WA.......................	106,230	106,414	102,044	4.1	8,843	9,544	8.3	9.0	6,244	15.9	67,421	13.1	35,649
Bend, OR.....................................	80,216	80,940	74,947	7.0	9,917	11,448	12.4	14.1	5,807	29.3	51,489	20.1	33,332
Deschutes County, OR	80,216	80,940	74,947	7.0	9,917	11,448	12.4	14.1	5,807	29.3	51,489	20.1	33,332
Billings, MT..................................	87,612	86,949	83,158	5.4	4,498	4,602	5.1	5.3	5,898	13.5	69,312	14.0	35,702
Carbon County, MT..........................	5,321	5,281	5,334	-0.2	301	308	5.7	5.8	391	27.8	2,129	8.8	22,778
Yellowstone County, MT....................	82,291	81,668	77,824	5.7	4,197	4,294	5.1	5.3	5,507	12.6	67,183	14.1	36,111
Binghamton, NY..............................	118,770	121,119	122,726	-3.2	9,950	10,628	8.4	8.8	5,115	0.3	84,260	-7.8	36,754
Broome County, NY.........................	93,831	95,760	96,389	-2.7	7,937	8,547	8.5	8.9	4,308	0.2	72,363	-12.8	35,165
Tioga County, NY............................	24,939	25,359	26,337	-5.3	2,013	2,081	8.1	8.2	807	0.9	11,897	42.6	46,420
Birmingham–Hoover, AL	530,139	528,138	527,690	0.5	43,796	47,236	8.3	8.9	25,686	0.2	434,225	-6.7	41,625
Bibb County, AL	9,216	9,155	8,808	4.6	913	945	9.9	10.3	293	-11.5	2,926	-14.0	32,141
Blount County, AL	26,347	26,235	26,323	0.1	2,191	2,349	8.3	9.0	701	-5.5	6,433	-18.2	26,789
Chilton County, AL	19,913	19,830	19,574	1.7	1,707	1,828	8.6	9.2	735	-5.2	6,756	-0.9	27,012
Jefferson County, AL........................	306,677	305,452	315,476	-2.8	26,766	28,673	8.7	9.4	16,614	-4.9	315,652	-12.8	43,295
St. Clair County, AL.........................	37,634	37,548	33,574	12.1	3,130	3,430	8.3	9.1	1,211	7.9	12,868	2.9	29,291
Shelby County, AL...........................	102,675	102,167	94,338	8.8	6,470	7,038	6.3	6.9	4,817	28.3	74,152	29.9	42,012
Walker County, AL...........................	27,677	27,751	29,597	-6.5	2,619	2,973	9.5	10.7	1,315	-8.9	15,438	-2.5	30,267
Bismarck, ND................................	62,656	62,878	58,863	6.4	2,099	2,367	3.4	3.8	3,426	15.3	51,589	22.5	35,363
Burleigh County, ND........................	47,427	47,579	44,323	7.0	1,484	1,671	3.1	3.5	2,691	15.8	42,964	22.4	35,304
Morton County, ND..........................	15,229	15,299	14,540	4.7	615	696	4.0	4.5	735	13.4	8,625	22.8	35,660
Blacksburg–Christiansburg–													
Radford, VA..................................	83,919	81,532	77,176	8.7	5,692	6,701	6.8	8.2	3,271	4.1	44,312	-9.9	33,377
Giles County, VA............................	8,518	8,328	8,402	1.4	632	784	7.4	9.4	305	-6.7	3,750	-18.8	38,267
Montgomery County, VA.....................	48,996	47,342	43,395	12.9	3,120	3,458	6.4	7.3	1,989	10.9	26,032	7.8	31,081
Pulaski County, VA..........................	18,077	17,783	18,107	-0.2	1,263	1,699	7.0	9.6	654	-1.7	10,400	-21.8	37,331
Radford city, VA.............................	8,328	8,079	7,272	14.5	677	760	8.1	9.4	323	-9.3	4,130	-41.9	33,452
Bloomington, IN..............................	96,594	97,365	95,145	1.5	7,484	7,783	7.7	8.0	3,881	-0.1	56,353	-0.9	32,249
Greene County, IN..........................	15,475	15,581	16,726	-7.5	1,406	1,437	9.1	9.2	591	-8.1	5,540	-7.1	26,832
Monroe County, IN..........................	70,592	71,108	66,661	5.9	5,028	5,197	7.1	7.3	2,990	2.2	46,907	-0.9	32,988
Owen County, IN............................	10,527	10,676	11,758	-10.5	1,050	1,149	10.0	10.8	300	-4.8	3,906	10.7	31,056
Bloomington–Normal, IL.....................	91,405	92,253	86,919	5.2	6,575	7,177	7.2	7.8	3,702	4.5	76,070	-8.0	46,748
McLean County, IL..........................	91,405	92,253	86,919	5.2	6,575	7,177	7.2	7.8	3,702	4.5	76,070	-8.0	46,748
Boise City–Nampa, ID.......................	301,165	297,138	277,973	8.3	26,593	26,932	8.8	9.1	16,456	20.2	209,672	6.1	36,444
Ada County, ID	199,770	197,470	184,794	8.1	15,894	16,517	8.0	8.4	12,217	20.5	164,035	7.1	38,716
Boise County, ID	3,240	3,192	3,635	-10.9	310	309	9.6	9.7	144	16.1	527	2.5	19,321
Canyon County, ID	86,516	85,057	77,740	11.3	9,351	9,119	10.8	10.7	3,564	20.9	41,278	2.7	28,745
Gem County, ID	7,133	6,995	7,140	-0.1	811	774	11.4	11.1	354	13.1	2,228	-3.3	23,449
Owyhee County, ID..........................	4,506	4,424	4,664	-3.4	227	213	5.0	4.8	177	10.6	1,604	9.7	25,898
Boston–Cambridge–Quincy, MA–NH	2,444,959	2,450,901	2,368,264	3.2	161,173	185,133	6.6	7.6	122,191	-2.5	2,224,822	-5.4	58,663
Boston–Quincy, MA	989,622	993,850	946,155	4.6	69,384	79,830	7.0	8.0	50,344	-3.0	1,009,509	-4.4	60,113
Norfolk County, MA..........................	363,147	364,734	355,805	2.1	22,630	26,632	6.2	7.3	19,033	-3.3	307,860	-8.8	49,509
Plymouth County, MA.......................	262,513	264,139	258,355	1.6	20,401	23,381	7.8	8.9	11,786	1.3	145,545	-1.5	41,367
Suffolk County, MA..........................	363,962	364,977	331,995	9.6	26,353	29,817	7.2	8.2	19,525	-5.2	556,104	-2.6	70,890
Cambridge–Newton–Framingham, MA	828,752	831,159	809,917	2.3	48,516	56,635	5.9	6.8	42,001	-2.5	791,554	-7.2	64,270
Middlesex County, MA	828,752	831,159	809,917	2.3	48,516	56,635	5.9	6.8	42,001	-2.5	791,554	-7.2	64,270
Peabody, MA	381,493	381,902	375,677	1.5	29,660	33,505	7.8	8.8	17,877	-3.8	263,022	-6.9	46,675
Essex County, MA	381,493	381,902	375,677	1.5	29,660	33,505	7.8	8.8	17,877	-3.8	263,022	-6.9	46,675
Rockingham County–Strafford													
County, NH..................................	245,092	243,990	236,515	3.6	13,613	15,163	5.6	6.2	11,969	1.4	160,737	0.0	41,568
Rockingham County, NH....................	174,943	174,446	170,256	2.8	9,916	11,058	5.7	6.3	9,453	1.2	125,033	-0.2	41,802
Strafford County, NH........................	70,149	69,544	66,259	5.9	3,697	4,105	5.3	5.9	2,516	2.2	35,704	0.8	40,746
Boulder, CO[3]................................	175,874	175,420	169,617	3.7	10,883	12,134	6.2	6.9	11,443	2.8	133,260	-15.6	52,636
Boulder County, CO [3]......................	175,874	175,420	169,617	3.7	10,883	12,134	6.2	6.9	11,443	2.8	133,260	-15.6	52,636
Bowling Green, KY...........................	64,224	63,919	60,556	6.1	5,468	6,018	8.5	9.4	2,830	8.8	47,111	6.1	33,855
Edmonson County, KY	5,148	5,186	5,401	-4.7	592	696	11.5	13.4	132	29.4	786	3.6	22,789
Warren County, KY..........................	59,076	58,733	55,155	7.1	4,876	5,322	8.3	9.1	2,698	7.9	46,325	6.1	34,042
Bremerton–Silverdale, WA..................	122,726	124,304	120,427	1.9	9,719	10,181	7.9	8.2	5,656	7.9	56,258	12.8	34,510
Kitsap County, WA...........................	122,726	124,304	120,427	1.9	9,719	10,181	7.9	8.2	5,656	7.9	56,258	12.8	34,510
Bridgeport–Stamford–Norwalk, CT...........	481,769	480,412	454,312	6.0	38,574	40,380	8.0	8.4	27,027	-5.5	393,952	-11.5	76,725
Fairfield County, CT.........................	481,769	480,412	454,312	6.0	38,574	40,380	8.0	8.4	27,027	-5.5	393,952	-11.5	76,725
Brownsville–Harlingen, TX..................	163,010	160,033	140,539	16.0	19,171	18,090	11.8	11.3	6,327	9.2	98,784	14.2	24,630
Cameron County, TX.........................	163,010	160,033	140,539	16.0	19,171	18,090	11.8	11.3	6,327	9.2	98,784	14.2	24,630

[1] Civilian unemployed as percent of total civilian labor force.
[2] For pay period including March 12 of the year shown.
[3] The Denver–Aurora metropolitan statistical area includes Broomfield County. Broomfield County, CO, was formed from parts of Adams, Boulder, Jefferson, and Weld Counties on November 15, 2001, and is coextensive with Broomfield city. For the purposes of defining and presenting data for the Denver–Aurora metropolitan statistical area, Broomfield city is treated as if it were a county when data are available to do so. In many cases, the data were not available.

Table C-4. Labor Force and Private Business Establishments and Employment—*Continued*

Metropolitan statistical area, division, and component county	Civilian labor force								Private nonfarm businesses				
	Total				Number of unemployed		Unemployment rate[1]		Establishments		Employment[2]		Annual payroll per employee 2010 (dollars)
	2011	2010	2005	Change, 2005–2011	2011	2010	2011	2010	2010	Change, 2000–2010	2010	Change, 2000–2010	
Brunswick, GA	50,060	50,757	52,049	-3.8	5,349	5,275	10.7	10.4	2,860	3.1	32,228	-5.3	31,015
Brantley County, GA	7,651	7,775	7,607	0.6	879	886	11.5	11.4	177	-1.1	1,308	-10.5	24,510
Glynn County, GA	36,684	37,134	39,177	-6.4	3,857	3,741	10.5	10.1	2,489	5.2	29,675	-2.9	31,609
McIntosh County, GA	5,725	5,848	5,265	8.7	613	648	10.7	11.1	194	-14.9	1,245	-38.5	23,680
Buffalo–Niagara Falls, NY	570,521	577,613	584,616	-2.4	45,482	48,902	8.0	8.5	26,899	0.2	455,704	-4.6	36,947
Erie County, NY	460,282	465,641	472,772	-2.6	36,191	38,584	7.9	8.3	22,393	0.2	397,398	-3.7	37,742
Niagara County, NY	110,239	111,972	111,844	-1.4	9,291	10,318	8.4	9.2	4,506	0.3	58,306	-10.5	31,529
Burlington, NC	72,415	71,969	69,277	4.5	7,726	8,431	10.7	11.7	3,206	-4.2	48,238	-19.6	30,892
Alamance County, NC	72,415	71,969	69,277	4.5	7,726	8,431	10.7	11.7	3,206	-4.2	48,238	-19.6	30,892
Burlington–South Burlington, VT	122,727	122,226	116,769	5.1	5,842	6,749	4.8	5.5	6,719	1.6	97,940	2.6	42,295
Chittenden County, VT	92,489	92,091	86,749	6.6	4,103	4,770	4.4	5.2	5,503	3.7	85,348	1.9	43,619
Franklin County, VT	26,327	26,234	25,794	2.1	1,468	1,675	5.6	6.4	1,023	-8.8	11,964	2.8	33,438
Grand Isle County, VT	3,911	3,901	4,226	-7.5	271	304	6.9	7.8	193	4.9	628	0.0	31,061
Canton–Massillon, OH	199,715	201,967	203,571	-1.9	18,493	22,766	9.3	11.3	8,908	-10.6	137,639	-18.9	32,546
Carroll County, OH	13,792	14,057	14,084	-2.1	1,357	1,761	9.8	12.5	470	-2.9	4,849	-5.7	26,290
Stark County, OH	185,923	187,910	189,487	-1.9	17,136	21,005	9.2	11.2	8,438	-11.0	132,790	-19.3	32,775
Cape Coral–Fort Myers, FL	282,699	278,148	270,561	4.5	31,401	35,034	11.1	12.6	15,569	25.6	167,156	16.8	33,556
Lee County, FL	282,699	278,148	270,561	4.5	31,401	35,034	11.1	12.6	15,569	25.6	167,156	16.8	33,556
Cape Girardeau–Jackson, MO–IL	47,566	47,771	47,239	0.7	3,660	3,834	7.7	8.0	3,126	16.0	40,784	2.7	30,415
Alexander County, IL	3,035	3,002	3,317	-8.5	398	357	13.1	11.9	123	-24.1	1,259	-27.1	32,066
Bollinger County, MO	5,652	5,699	5,860	-3.5	501	545	8.9	9.6	206	-2.4	1,391	1.3	21,163
Cape Girardeau County, MO	38,879	39,070	38,062	2.1	2,761	2,932	7.1	7.5	2,797	20.5	38,134	4.2	30,698
Carson City, NV	28,761	29,203	27,316	5.3	3,760	3,798	13.1	13.0	2,141	-8.9	21,103	-14.9	39,017
Carson City, NV	28,761	29,203	27,316	5.3	3,760	3,798	13.1	13.0	2,141	-8.9	21,103	-14.9	39,017
Casper, WY	42,907	42,060	39,354	9.0	2,537	3,029	5.9	7.2	2,913	11.0	32,650	18.5	41,241
Natrona County, WY	42,907	42,060	39,354	9.0	2,537	3,029	5.9	7.2	2,913	11.0	32,650	18.5	41,241
Cedar Rapids, IA	146,448	147,986	137,915	6.2	8,767	9,195	6.0	6.2	6,453	0.1	121,486	-1.9	41,199
Benton County, IA	14,066	14,264	14,412	-2.4	857	948	6.1	6.6	572	-9.9	4,331	-6.6	29,136
Jones County, IA	10,599	10,722	10,410	1.8	660	703	6.2	6.6	511	2.0	4,514	-0.7	28,117
Linn County, IA	121,783	123,000	113,093	7.7	7,250	7,544	6.0	6.1	5,370	1.2	112,641	-1.7	42,187
Champaign–Urbana, IL	115,771	119,966	117,167	-1.2	9,775	10,906	8.4	9.1	4,914	1.1	75,073	-3.3	35,799
Champaign County, IL	100,761	104,379	100,832	-0.1	8,472	9,422	8.4	9.0	4,180	3.2	68,378	-3.3	36,262
Ford County, IL	6,646	6,915	7,243	-8.2	626	721	9.4	10.4	380	-10.2	4,112	0.6	31,856
Piatt County, IL	8,364	8,672	9,092	-8.0	677	763	8.1	8.8	354	-8.5	2,583	-9.7	29,809
Charleston, WV	137,235	138,285	139,820	-1.8	10,028	10,473	7.3	7.6	7,318	-6.7	116,521	-1.4	38,714
Boone County, WV	8,951	9,016	9,435	-5.1	660	685	7.4	7.6	316	-19.8	7,247	31.2	51,435
Clay County, WV	3,229	3,350	3,532	-8.6	385	493	11.9	14.7	111	-18.4	1,445	18.3	36,336
Kanawha County, WV	90,347	90,918	92,037	-1.8	6,353	6,525	7.0	7.2	5,481	-8.5	89,768	-7.2	37,990
Lincoln County, WV	7,703	7,824	7,948	-3.1	754	842	9.8	10.8	214	-7.8	2,080	16.8	36,044
Putnam County, WV	27,005	27,177	26,868	0.5	1,876	1,928	6.9	7.1	1,196	9.5	15,981	23.6	37,574
Charleston–North Charleston–Summerville, SC	328,687	321,936	294,751	11.5	27,773	29,892	8.4	9.3	16,399	16.6	228,622	4.2	36,847
Berkeley County, SC	84,280	82,439	71,404	18.0	7,651	8,068	9.1	9.8	2,623	45.3	37,369	40.5	37,489
Charleston County, SC	176,222	172,671	166,789	5.7	14,593	15,807	8.3	9.2	11,621	10.8	168,876	-0.5	37,598
Dorchester County, SC	68,185	66,826	56,558	20.6	5,529	6,017	8.1	9.0	2,155	21.1	22,377	-3.2	30,100
Charlotte–Gastonia–Rock Hill, NC–SC	895,986	883,975	794,301	12.8	98,020	104,927	10.9	11.9	44,513	14.7	727,384	0.6	45,592
Anson County, NC	10,869	10,845	10,649	2.1	1,330	1,529	12.2	14.1	417	-9.2	4,243	-31.8	28,461
Cabarrus County, NC	89,557	88,704	77,785	15.1	9,058	10,085	10.1	11.4	3,907	23.1	55,864	5.8	32,635
Gaston County, NC	98,998	97,937	96,872	2.2	11,473	12,456	11.6	12.7	3,935	-6.3	57,599	-18.6	32,855
Mecklenburg County, NC	483,667	475,540	430,027	12.5	51,515	53,478	10.7	11.2	27,886	15.0	502,944	0.9	50,871
Union County, NC	98,873	97,417	82,975	19.2	9,192	9,830	9.3	10.1	3,919	34.9	42,518	8.5	33,161
York County, SC	114,022	113,532	95,993	18.8	15,452	17,549	13.6	15.5	4,449	16.7	64,216	15.3	36,298
Charlottesville, VA	112,047	110,022	97,708	14.7	5,868	6,454	5.2	5.9	5,636	12.5	74,628	5.4	40,955
Albemarle County, VA	55,747	54,682	47,720	16.8	2,712	2,951	4.9	5.4	2,514	44.0	36,318	58.8	44,384
Fluvanna County, VA	14,329	14,070	12,875	11.3	745	820	5.2	5.8	400	23.1	2,610	23.6	29,154
Greene County, VA	11,006	10,826	9,720	13.2	564	641	5.1	5.9	324	24.6	2,181	23.9	32,482
Nelson County, VA	7,958	7,841	7,471	6.5	430	498	5.4	6.4	386	0.0	3,029	17.4	24,501
Charlottesville city, VA	23,007	22,603	19,922	15.5	1,417	1,544	6.2	6.8	2,012	-12.3	30,490	-26.5	40,122
Chattanooga, TN–GA	262,178	258,813	253,990	3.2	21,817	22,808	8.3	8.8	11,139	-1.7	194,365	-8.5	35,882
Catoosa County, GA	34,216	33,841	35,050	-2.4	2,654	2,748	7.8	8.1	925	22.2	12,250	13.3	28,865
Dade County, GA	8,168	8,105	8,489	-3.8	664	712	8.1	8.8	216	-2.7	2,310	-8.4	31,442
Walker County, GA	33,160	32,969	33,046	0.3	2,888	3,147	8.7	9.5	715	-21.3	10,079	-39.3	28,010
Hamilton County, TN	167,419	164,878	158,655	5.5	13,731	14,179	8.2	8.6	8,656	-2.1	162,622	-7.0	37,337
Marion County, TN	12,868	12,674	12,884	-0.1	1,313	1,343	10.2	10.6	442	1.8	5,267	-2.4	28,336
Sequatchie County, TN	6,347	6,346	5,866	8.2	567	679	8.9	10.7	185	10.1	1,837	-23.5	24,263

[1] Civilian unemployed as percent of total civilian labor force.
[2] For pay period including March 12 of the year shown.

Table C-4. Labor Force and Private Business Establishments and Employment—*Continued*

Metropolitan statistical area, division, and component county	Civilian labor force								Private nonfarm businesses				
	Total				Number of unemployed		Unemployment rate[1]		Establishments		Employment[2]		Annual payroll per employee 2010 (dollars)
	2011	2010	2005	Change, 2005–2011	2011	2010	2011	2010	2010	Change, 2000–2010	2010	Change, 2000–2010	
Cheyenne, WY....................	45,064	44,436	41,611	8.3	3,015	3,349	6.7	7.5	2,701	18.1	30,763	14.4	34,999
Laramie County, WY	45,064	44,436	41,611	8.3	3,015	3,349	6.7	7.5	2,701	18.1	30,763	14.4	34,999
Chicago–Joliet–Naperville, IL–IN–WI.........	4,831,445	4,848,872	4,710,186	2.6	475,845	506,293	9.8	10.4	236,704	4.0	3,797,772	-10.5	50,795
Chicago–Joliet–Naperville, IL.........	4,058,732	4,073,417	3,944,150	2.9	403,636	425,005	9.9	10.4	199,826	4.2	3,219,892	-11.6	50,884
Cook County, IL....................	2,575,226	2,582,931	2,557,156	0.7	267,475	279,399	10.4	10.8	127,875	-0.2	2,169,587	-15.1	53,369
DeKalb County, IL	58,924	59,257	53,335	10.5	5,392	5,823	9.2	9.8	1,965	0.9	25,328	-2.8	32,362
DuPage County, IL	517,675	519,907	514,513	0.6	41,293	44,396	8.0	8.5	33,124	2.3	554,348	-10.7	51,941
Grundy County, IL	27,700	27,830	23,385	18.5	3,270	3,445	11.8	12.4	1,074	17.2	14,980	37.1	51,381
Kane County, IL....................	273,903	275,207	248,964	10.0	27,133	28,889	9.9	10.5	12,199	18.5	170,329	-6.2	38,737
Kendall County, IL................	65,541	65,984	44,362	47.7	5,688	6,241	8.7	9.5	1,926	67.5	20,131	56.8	30,179
McHenry County, IL	174,781	175,705	166,951	4.7	16,357	17,570	9.4	10.0	7,823	14.3	81,205	-11.9	38,772
Will County, IL.....................	364,982	366,596	335,484	8.8	37,028	39,242	10.1	10.7	13,840	37.6	183,984	28.8	39,761
Gary, IN............................	328,547	326,920	328,667	0.0	30,636	33,907	9.3	10.4	14,472	0.5	224,323	-7.6	38,075
Jasper County, IN.................	15,652	15,614	15,217	2.9	1,381	1,578	8.8	10.1	741	-5.2	8,588	-14.4	31,132
Lake County, IN...................	223,334	222,311	225,290	-0.9	22,084	24,369	9.9	11.0	9,995	-0.5	164,664	-8.1	38,992
Newton County, IN...............	6,908	6,876	7,080	-2.4	659	730	9.5	10.6	285	-1.4	2,517	-21.5	30,723
Porter County, IN	82,653	82,119	81,080	1.9	6,512	7,230	7.9	8.8	3,451	5.0	48,554	-3.2	36,575
Lake County–Kenosha County, IL–WI...	444,166	448,535	437,369	1.6	41,573	47,381	9.4	10.6	22,406	4.4	353,557	-1.4	58,060
Lake County, IL....................	358,515	361,430	354,595	1.1	33,857	38,037	9.4	10.5	19,392	5.9	307,578	-0.6	61,763
Kenosha County, WI..............	85,651	87,105	82,774	3.5	7,716	9,344	9.0	10.7	3,014	-3.9	45,979	-6.7	33,287
Chico, CA...........................	101,686	103,632	98,511	3.2	13,794	14,384	13.6	13.9	4,712	2.5	53,911	0.3	32,388
Butte County, CA	101,686	103,632	98,511	3.2	13,794	14,384	13.6	13.9	4,712	2.5	53,911	0.3	32,388
Cincinnati–Middletown, OH–KY–IN..........	1,099,561	1,107,565	1,093,094	0.6	94,558	106,340	8.6	9.6	46,143	-2.9	874,547	-8.8	43,402
Dearborn County, IN	25,903	26,055	26,416	-1.9	2,309	2,733	8.9	10.5	968	-0.5	13,690	2.8	30,339
Franklin County, IN...............	11,529	11,598	12,045	-4.3	1,054	1,244	9.1	10.7	439	21.9	4,579	14.8	29,077
OH County, IN	3,171	3,191	3,152	0.6	280	333	8.8	10.4	83	7.8	1,269	-29.3	28,671
Boone County, KY.................	64,737	65,030	59,766	8.3	5,218	5,960	8.1	9.2	2,820	17.4	61,688	5.5	35,598
Bracken County, KY..............	4,243	4,224	4,414	-3.9	457	467	10.8	11.1	98	-15.5	853	-23.4	29,142
Campbell County, KY.............	46,317	46,479	45,859	1.0	4,294	4,773	9.3	10.3	1,618	0.2	23,908	2.3	32,735
Gallatin County, KY...............	4,154	4,193	4,046	2.7	394	461	9.5	11.0	89	-6.3	778	-45.6	22,924
Grant County, KY..................	12,380	12,473	12,569	-1.5	1,244	1,421	10.0	11.4	393	-12.1	4,007	-17.0	26,804
Kenton County, KY................	85,017	85,455	83,843	1.4	7,594	8,616	8.9	10.1	3,118	-3.4	68,711	7.6	40,145
Pendleton County, KY	7,278	7,360	7,480	-2.7	786	917	10.8	12.5	185	-9.3	1,598	-6.5	29,782
Brown County, OH................	21,863	22,053	21,940	-0.4	2,317	2,553	10.6	11.6	541	-9.4	6,184	-6.8	28,411
Butler County, OH................	191,310	192,410	185,719	3.0	16,431	17,946	8.6	9.3	6,945	10.2	120,242	5.1	39,306
Clermont County, OH............	105,587	106,679	104,133	1.4	9,030	10,351	8.6	9.7	3,554	8.5	44,640	-7.2	34,657
Hamilton County, OH.............	406,861	410,075	418,151	-2.7	34,879	38,976	8.6	9.5	21,382	-14.1	450,229	-19.1	48,764
Warren County, OH...............	109,211	110,290	103,561	5.5	8,271	9,589	7.6	8.7	3,910	33.1	72,171	22.2	42,025
Clarksville, TN–KY.................	115,380	114,368	104,825	10.1	11,456	11,496	9.9	10.1	4,305	8.7	66,551	10.9	30,298
Christian County, KY.............	26,470	26,487	26,421	0.2	3,091	3,183	11.7	12.0	1,348	2.0	24,184	7.0	32,173
Trigg County, KY..................	6,504	6,602	6,459	0.7	656	773	10.1	11.7	244	-2.8	2,349	-14.3	24,450
Montgomery County, TN.........	76,363	75,281	66,003	15.7	7,004	6,811	9.2	9.0	2,550	13.7	38,658	15.4	29,617
Stewart County, TN...............	6,043	5,998	5,942	1.7	705	729	11.7	12.2	163	11.6	1,360	16.7	26,400
Cleveland, TN.....................	55,382	55,075	54,150	2.3	5,196	5,231	9.4	9.5	2,103	-1.3	36,431	-13.6	32,791
Bradley County, TN...............	47,867	47,641	46,838	2.2	4,311	4,382	9.0	9.2	1,881	0.5	34,930	-13.0	33,032
Polk County, TN...................	7,515	7,434	7,312	2.8	885	849	11.8	11.4	222	-14.6	1,501	-26.2	27,181
Cleveland–Elyria–Mentor, OH....................	1,082,818	1,080,862	1,091,575	-0.8	83,332	94,423	7.7	8.7	52,149	-8.4	870,158	-17.7	43,655
Cuyahoga County, OH...........	644,854	643,453	663,028	-2.7	51,474	57,819	8.0	9.0	33,667	-11.9	629,692	-19.2	46,283
Geauga County, OH..............	50,487	50,306	50,937	-0.9	3,267	3,703	6.5	7.4	2,741	4.8	29,824	2.2	38,280
Lake County, OH..................	131,619	131,350	131,175	0.3	9,328	10,655	7.1	8.1	6,139	-3.8	82,878	-14.7	39,020
Lorain County, OH................	158,978	158,977	153,676	3.5	12,791	14,698	8.0	9.2	5,627	-3.4	78,424	-20.6	34,778
Medina County, OH..............	96,880	96,776	92,759	4.4	6,472	7,548	6.7	7.8	3,975	1.2	49,340	-7.3	35,253
Coeur d'Alene, ID.................	72,048	71,742	66,283	8.7	7,414	7,432	10.3	10.4	4,430	20.9	43,432	17.3	31,652
Kootenai County, ID..............	72,048	71,742	66,283	8.7	7,414	7,432	10.3	10.4	4,430	20.9	43,432	17.3	31,652
College Station–Bryan, TX	116,045	116,670	103,114	12.5	7,593	7,666	6.5	6.6	4,346	16.8	59,051	14.1	30,271
Brazos County, TX................	100,643	101,148	86,902	15.8	6,398	6,423	6.4	6.4	3,765	17.1	53,932	13.8	29,922
Burleson County, TX.............	8,044	8,114	8,636	-6.9	549	581	6.8	7.2	306	9.7	2,511	9.6	32,299
Robertson County, TX...........	7,358	7,408	7,576	-2.9	646	662	8.8	8.9	275	22.2	2,608	24.0	35,543
Colorado Springs, CO............	313,199	314,780	304,805	2.8	28,825	30,677	9.2	9.7	16,546	15.7	217,914	1.2	41,112
El Paso County, CO	300,553	302,033	292,088	2.9	27,722	29,462	9.2	9.8	15,850	16.0	212,715	1.3	41,414
Teller County, CO.................	12,646	12,747	12,717	-0.6	1,103	1,215	8.7	9.5	696	8.9	5,199	-1.9	28,767
Columbia, MO......................	96,993	95,157	91,211	6.3	5,735	6,157	5.9	6.5	4,529	12.9	68,723	6.8	32,350
Boone County, MO................	91,749	90,020	85,796	6.9	5,339	5,748	5.8	6.4	4,336	14.0	66,916	7.1	32,591
Howard County, MO..............	5,244	5,137	5,415	-3.2	396	409	7.6	8.0	193	-7.7	1,807	-0.8	23,417

[1] Civilian unemployed as percent of total civilian labor force.
[2] For pay period including March 12 of the year shown.

Table C-4. Labor Force and Private Business Establishments and Employment—*Continued*

Metropolitan statistical area, division, and component county	Civilian labor force								Private nonfarm businesses				
	Total				Number of unemployed		Unemployment rate[1]		Establishments		Employment[2]		Annual payroll per employee 2010 (dollars)
	2011	2010	2005	Change, 2005–2011	2011	2010	2011	2010	2010	Change, 2000–2010	2010	Change, 2000–2010	
Columbia, SC............................	369,365	368,696	354,215	4.3	32,711	34,501	8.9	9.4	17,097	6.1	270,700	-0.5	35,917
Calhoun County, SC..................	6,781	6,701	7,070	-4.1	818	782	12.1	11.7	243	20.3	3,032	45.2	31,920
Fairfield County, SC..................	10,714	10,763	11,283	-5.0	1,332	1,450	12.4	13.5	318	-1.5	4,554	-33.7	43,643
Kershaw County, SC.................	29,519	29,621	28,906	2.1	2,803	3,100	9.5	10.5	1,141	-3.8	13,176	-13.4	31,844
Lexington County, SC...............	132,547	132,124	127,197	4.2	10,362	10,831	7.8	8.2	6,068	22.1	87,222	28.1	32,763
Richland County, SC.................	180,783	180,491	170,517	6.0	16,593	17,500	9.2	9.7	9,066	-1.4	159,117	-9.4	38,072
Saluda County, SC...................	9,021	8,996	9,242	-2.4	803	838	8.9	9.3	261	6.5	3,599	-14.2	25,603
Columbus, GA–AL.....................	130,956	129,119	128,044	2.3	12,215	12,404	9.3	9.6	5,719	1.1	94,187	-10.7	34,287
Russell County, AL...................	23,088	22,554	21,319	8.3	2,343	2,322	10.1	10.3	838	-7.4	10,619	-4.9	30,099
Chattahoochee County, GA.......	2,090	2,024	2,671	-21.8	373	334	17.8	16.5	67	17.5	627	-53.5	29,671
Harris County, GA....................	17,080	16,882	15,385	11.0	1,190	1,237	7.0	7.3	398	-4.3	3,360	-21.8	26,266
Marion County, GA...................	4,018	3,972	3,432	17.1	349	360	8.7	9.1	76	-1.3	1,182	-45.6	25,321
Muscogee County, GA...............	84,680	83,687	85,237	-0.7	7,960	8,151	9.4	9.7	4,340	3.2	78,399	-9.4	35,370
Columbus, IN...........................	39,998	38,149	37,377	7.0	2,972	3,551	7.4	9.3	1,855	-5.9	38,665	0.3	41,064
Bartholomew County, IN	39,998	38,149	37,377	7.0	2,972	3,551	7.4	9.3	1,855	-5.9	38,665	0.3	41,064
Columbus, OH..........................	956,643	960,392	921,915	3.8	72,222	83,419	7.5	8.7	39,286	1.7	750,329	-6.2	42,820
Delaware County, OH...............	92,550	92,793	83,197	11.2	5,628	6,603	6.1	7.1	3,802	50.9	66,214	54.4	45,005
Fairfield County, OH................	74,248	74,620	72,862	1.9	5,681	6,630	7.7	8.9	2,562	0.8	32,416	4.2	30,028
Franklin County, OH................	616,711	618,786	598,790	3.0	46,646	53,522	7.6	8.6	27,122	-3.0	560,399	-10.6	44,171
Licking County, OH..................	84,426	85,008	81,348	3.8	6,788	8,024	8.0	9.4	2,923	2.1	46,241	-4.9	33,157
Madison County, OH................	20,079	20,168	19,741	1.7	1,658	1,902	8.3	9.4	699	-3.6	10,160	-9.8	32,350
Morrow County, OH..................	17,424	17,512	17,657	-1.3	1,607	1,828	9.2	10.4	380	-7.1	3,664	-28.3	27,299
Pickaway County, OH...............	24,341	24,567	23,937	1.7	2,292	2,704	9.4	11.0	796	-2.2	10,406	-14.2	33,644
Union County, OH....................	26,864	26,938	24,383	10.2	1,922	2,206	7.2	8.2	1,002	25.1	20,829	-3.3	53,294
Corpus Christi, TX....................	217,128	213,961	197,537	9.9	17,108	17,351	7.9	8.1	9,260	-1.1	141,978	7.0	34,775
Aransas County, TX.................	10,969	10,837	10,990	-0.2	881	921	8.0	8.5	471	-1.3	3,972	10.6	24,065
Nueces County, TX..................	176,671	173,685	156,921	12.6	13,438	13,235	7.6	7.6	7,763	-1.4	125,354	7.3	35,224
San Patricio County, TX...........	29,488	29,439	29,626	-0.5	2,789	3,195	9.5	10.9	1,026	1.4	12,652	2.7	33,687
Corvallis, OR...........................	44,859	44,175	42,154	6.4	2,948	3,260	6.6	7.4	2,059	6.9	24,526	-10.0	39,496
Benton County, OR..................	44,859	44,175	42,154	6.4	2,948	3,260	6.6	7.4	2,059	6.9	24,526	-10.0	39,496
Crestview–Fort Walton Beach–Destin, FL....	99,218	96,038	95,801	3.6	7,313	7,563	7.4	7.9	4,995	4.1	56,733	-2.7	33,472
Okaloosa County, FL................	99,218	96,038	95,801	3.6	7,313	7,563	7.4	7.9	4,995	4.1	56,733	-2.7	33,472
Cumberland, MD–WV	50,779	50,497	49,168	3.3	4,167	4,520	8.2	9.0	2,140	-8.0	30,127	0.0	30,512
Allegany County, MD...............	36,996	36,751	35,585	4.0	3,134	3,400	8.5	9.3	1,671	-9.5	23,745	-5.5	29,798
Mineral County, WV.................	13,783	13,746	13,583	1.5	1,033	1,120	7.5	8.1	469	-2.3	6,382	27.6	33,168
Dallas–Fort Worth–Arlington, TX	3,286,655	3,242,289	3,007,967	9.3	256,531	265,611	7.8	8.2	140,481	10.8	2,510,280	-1.4	48,132
Dallas–Plano–Irving, TX..............	2,193,376	2,164,858	2,011,373	9.0	171,765	176,989	7.8	8.2	97,562	9.8	1,768,758	-4.5	50,383
Collin County, TX....................	435,101	429,236	368,326	18.1	30,552	31,439	7.0	7.3	17,719	59.9	288,674	57.5	53,961
Dallas County, TX...................	1,176,200	1,161,562	1,145,146	2.7	98,479	101,828	8.4	8.8	61,295	-3.9	1,231,305	-16.7	52,340
Delta County, TX.....................	2,325	2,285	2,418	-3.8	207	203	8.9	8.9	60	-16.7	617	31.0	14,104
Denton County, TX...................	374,542	369,501	314,857	19.0	26,031	26,806	7.0	7.3	11,343	41.4	155,931	41.0	38,111
Ellis County, TX......................	74,518	73,453	66,454	12.1	6,039	6,117	8.1	8.3	2,445	19.4	31,486	10.5	33,283
Hunt County, TX......................	40,392	39,708	38,608	4.6	3,409	3,343	8.4	8.4	1,385	7.4	21,671	5.7	41,556
Kaufman County, TX................	50,043	49,414	43,108	16.1	4,168	4,305	8.3	8.7	1,654	13.1	20,306	0.0	30,039
Rockwall County, TX................	40,255	39,699	32,456	24.0	2,880	2,948	7.2	7.4	1,661	59.6	18,768	71.6	31,024
Fort Worth–Arlington, TX..........................	1,093,279	1,077,431	996,594	9.7	84,766	88,622	7.8	8.2	42,919	13.0	741,522	6.8	42,762
Johnson County, TX.................	73,705	72,939	72,282	2.0	5,599	6,163	7.6	8.4	2,544	16.9	31,577	18.9	34,770
Parker County, TX...................	56,913	56,132	50,776	12.1	4,038	4,290	7.1	7.6	2,195	41.3	22,513	43.8	33,072
Tarrant County, TX	934,168	920,160	845,872	10.4	73,065	75,882	7.8	8.2	37,001	10.9	671,984	4.8	43,507
Wise County, TX......................	28,493	28,200	27,664	3.0	2,064	2,287	7.2	8.1	1,179	31.6	15,448	41.4	40,799
Dalton, GA..............................	61,492	62,109	66,944	-8.1	7,625	7,778	12.4	12.5	2,694	-11.4	56,109	-16.3	33,960
Murray County, GA..................	17,614	17,758	21,122	-16.6	2,297	2,309	13.0	13.0	417	-10.5	8,262	-23.7	31,994
Whitfield County, GA................	43,878	44,351	45,822	-4.2	5,328	5,469	12.1	12.3	2,277	-11.6	47,847	-14.9	34,300
Danville, IL..............................	36,594	37,116	37,752	-3.1	3,891	4,599	10.6	12.4	1,538	-12.3	24,295	-16.2	35,038
Vermilion County, IL................	36,594	37,116	37,752	-3.1	3,891	4,599	10.6	12.4	1,538	-12.3	24,295	-16.2	35,038
Danville, VA............................	52,945	52,622	53,005	-0.1	5,123	6,049	9.7	11.5	2,237	-8.1	30,668	-21.3	29,796
Pittsylvania County, VA	33,162	32,966	31,976	3.7	2,759	3,357	8.3	10.2	857	-8.6	8,385	-28.7	26,498
Danville city, VA......................	19,783	19,656	21,029	-5.9	2,364	2,692	11.9	13.7	1,380	-7.7	22,283	-18.1	31,038
Davenport–Moline–Rock Island, IA–IL.......	201,736	203,242	201,853	-0.1	15,396	17,203	7.6	8.5	9,180	-4.3	154,297	-8.4	39,709
Henry County, IL.....................	27,073	27,277	27,235	-0.6	2,074	2,495	7.7	9.1	1,130	-2.8	13,074	-11.8	30,621
Mercer County, IL....................	8,637	8,745	8,892	-2.9	771	948	8.9	10.8	301	-14.0	2,337	-2.7	28,995
Rock Island County, IL.............	77,750	78,171	77,712	0.0	6,431	7,471	8.3	9.6	3,350	-8.1	61,270	-11.8	47,073
Scott County, IA.....................	88,276	89,049	88,014	0.3	6,120	6,289	6.9	7.1	4,399	-0.7	77,616	-5.1	35,749
Dayton, OH.............................	411,593	415,234	424,310	-3.0	37,672	44,598	9.2	10.7	17,408	-8.9	307,393	-19.7	39,638
Greene County, OH..................	79,329	79,877	77,041	3.0	6,639	7,826	8.4	9.8	2,983	3.3	48,446	7.3	37,891
Miami County, OH....................	53,518	54,120	54,617	-2.0	4,638	5,669	8.7	10.5	2,129	-4.4	33,021	-14.2	34,225
Montgomery County, OH	257,589	260,040	270,973	-4.9	24,311	28,812	9.4	11.1	11,638	-12.3	217,779	-24.8	41,073
Preble County, OH...................	21,157	21,197	21,679	-2.4	2,084	2,291	9.9	10.8	658	-8.7	8,147	-13.0	33,606

[1] Civilian unemployed as percent of total civilian labor force.
[2] For pay period including March 12 of the year shown.

Table C-4. Labor Force and Private Business Establishments and Employment—*Continued*

Metropolitan statistical area, division, and component county	Civilian labor force								Private nonfarm businesses				Annual payroll per employee 2010 (dollars)
	Total				Number of unemployed		Unemployment rate[1]		Establishments		Employment[2]		
	2011	2010	2005	Change, 2005–2011	2011	2010	2011	2010	2010	Change, 2000–2010	2010	Change, 2000–2010	
Decatur, AL	73,569	72,913	71,220	3.3	6,606	7,221	9.0	9.9	3,108	-1.3	45,965	-11.7	36,588
Lawrence County, AL	15,740	15,606	15,856	-0.7	1,590	1,724	10.1	11.0	414	-0.2	4,395	-18.4	38,847
Morgan County, AL	57,829	57,307	55,364	4.5	5,016	5,497	8.7	9.6	2,694	-1.5	41,570	-10.9	36,350
Decatur, IL	54,585	54,732	52,730	3.5	5,767	6,563	10.6	12.0	2,510	-7.8	46,364	-18.9	38,830
Macon County, IL	54,585	54,732	52,730	3.5	5,767	6,563	10.6	12.0	2,510	-7.8	46,364	-18.9	38,830
Deltona–Daytona Beach–Ormond Beach, FL	254,098	251,228	242,699	4.7	27,428	29,011	10.8	11.5	11,779	9.0	127,546	-2.8	30,118
Volusia County, FL	254,098	251,228	242,699	4.7	27,428	29,011	10.8	11.5	11,779	9.0	127,546	-2.8	30,118
Denver–Aurora–Broomfield, CO[3]	1,399,772	1,401,417	1,326,889	5.5	116,747	126,293	8.3	9.0	73,663	9.3	1,038,146	-2.2	49,746
Adams County, CO[3]	231,640	231,479	211,960	9.3	22,535	23,662	9.7	10.2	8,169	13.1	129,834	1.8	40,579
Arapahoe County, CO	319,084	319,054	301,597	5.8	26,106	27,880	8.2	8.7	16,768	2.2	235,955	-19.3	52,059
Broomfield County, CO[3]	30,912	30,887	24,738	25.0	2,267	2,418	7.3	7.8	1,717	NA	32,234	NA	61,403
Clear Creek County, CO	5,666	5,692	5,892	-3.8	414	472	7.3	8.3	343	2.7	2,535	-8.3	32,157
Denver County, CO	322,078	323,088	304,927	5.6	29,272	32,085	9.1	9.9	22,055	-1.6	368,327	-10.4	53,794
Douglas County, CO	160,069	160,223	144,245	11.0	10,254	11,331	6.4	7.1	7,450	82.7	77,902	105.5	49,808
Elbert County, CO	12,851	12,908	13,017	-1.3	936	1,066	7.3	8.3	506	11.7	2,009	-13.4	30,182
Gilpin County, CO	3,582	3,609	3,369	6.3	233	281	6.5	7.8	109	31.3	4,415	18.8	35,623
Jefferson County, CO[3]	304,791	305,316	307,415	-0.9	24,023	26,277	7.9	8.6	16,097	0.7	183,719	0.7	44,020
Park County, CO	9,099	9,161	9,729	-6.5	707	821	7.8	9.0	449	12.8	1,216	-9.0	26,340
Des Moines–West Des Moines, IA	313,206	316,067	295,862	5.9	18,525	19,531	5.9	6.2	14,881	8.1	276,948	4.1	43,027
Dallas County, IA	36,220	36,541	29,397	23.2	1,725	1,829	4.8	5.0	1,520	86.0	29,040	196.4	42,022
Guthrie County, IA	5,630	5,702	6,107	-7.8	354	392	6.3	6.9	323	7.7	2,678	43.4	31,814
Madison County, IA	8,153	8,263	8,129	0.3	523	586	6.4	7.1	364	5.5	2,631	-5.2	28,035
Polk County, IA	237,599	239,657	227,664	4.4	14,511	15,164	6.1	6.3	11,899	3.3	234,631	-3.9	44,023
Warren County, IA	25,604	25,904	24,565	4.2	1,412	1,560	5.5	6.0	775	-0.5	7,968	5.1	26,092
Detroit–Warren–Livonia, MI	2,017,828	2,058,462	2,191,006	-7.9	232,078	285,218	11.5	13.9	97,211	-8.2	1,500,978	-24.9	47,939
Detroit–Livonia–Dearborn, MI	822,523	844,184	903,895	-9.0	103,348	124,794	12.6	14.8	32,556	-9.6	567,799	-25.0	46,805
Wayne County, MI	822,523	844,184	903,895	-9.0	103,348	124,794	12.6	14.8	32,556	-9.6	567,799	-25.0	46,805
Warren–Troy–Farmington Hills, MI	1,195,305	1,214,278	1,287,111	-7.1	128,730	160,424	10.8	13.2	64,655	-7.5	933,179	-24.8	48,629
Lapeer County, MI	40,542	41,382	45,426	-10.8	5,317	6,577	13.1	15.9	1,577	-13.4	14,670	-32.4	31,790
Livingston County, MI	88,278	89,248	95,277	-7.3	8,354	10,278	9.5	11.5	4,028	6.0	43,503	-2.3	34,038
Macomb County, MI	402,745	409,536	424,463	-5.1	46,288	57,330	11.5	14.0	17,753	-5.8	252,508	-24.7	43,291
Oakland County, MI	587,577	596,620	636,891	-7.7	58,772	74,122	10.0	12.4	38,128	-9.0	584,159	-26.2	53,356
St. Clair County, MI	76,163	77,492	85,054	-10.5	9,999	12,117	13.1	15.6	3,169	-10.3	38,339	-20.9	34,747
Dothan, AL	65,141	64,488	64,869	0.4	5,343	5,544	8.2	8.6	3,486	-2.1	49,665	-9.4	33,322
Geneva County, AL	11,347	11,262	11,569	-1.9	941	1,005	8.3	8.9	422	-7.5	3,961	-10.2	27,505
Henry County, AL	7,273	7,243	7,427	-2.1	614	679	8.4	9.4	299	-8.0	2,761	-34.0	30,039
Houston County, AL	46,521	45,983	45,873	1.4	3,788	3,860	8.1	8.4	2,765	-0.5	42,943	-7.1	34,070
Dover, DE	75,580	74,820	72,360	4.4	5,559	5,980	7.4	8.0	3,200	8.1	46,405	4.5	34,673
Kent County, DE	75,580	74,820	72,360	4.4	5,559	5,980	7.4	8.0	3,200	8.1	46,405	4.5	34,673
Dubuque, IA	53,259	53,577	50,725	5.0	2,933	3,296	5.5	6.2	2,738	3.0	50,579	1.2	35,676
Dubuque County, IA	53,259	53,577	50,725	5.0	2,933	3,296	5.5	6.2	2,738	3.0	50,579	1.2	35,676
Duluth, MN–WI	145,795	146,819	141,089	3.3	10,657	11,841	7.3	8.1	7,296	-0.5	105,453	3.1	34,085
Carlton County, MN	17,981	18,101	17,012	5.7	1,395	1,555	7.8	8.6	715	4.7	8,022	-11.5	32,935
St. Louis County, MN	104,859	105,360	101,280	3.5	7,638	8,370	7.3	7.9	5,509	-0.5	83,692	5.7	34,358
Douglas County, WI	22,955	23,358	22,797	0.7	1,624	1,916	7.1	8.2	1,072	-3.3	13,739	-2.0	33,096
Durham–Chapel Hill, NC	265,003	262,476	246,491	7.5	21,505	21,469	8.1	8.2	11,686	11.1	216,588	-2.9	51,110
Chatham County, NC	33,055	32,677	31,010	6.6	2,645	2,578	8.0	7.9	1,264	35.2	13,319	1.4	29,131
Durham County, NC	140,993	139,626	131,002	7.6	11,990	11,943	8.5	8.6	6,634	11.5	155,943	-4.4	57,161
Orange County, NC	71,395	70,636	65,591	8.8	4,806	4,728	6.7	6.7	3,087	6.9	39,220	8.9	38,880
Person County, NC	19,560	19,537	18,888	3.6	2,064	2,220	10.6	11.4	701	-6.2	8,106	-24.9	29,998
Eau Claire, WI	89,888	90,626	86,823	3.5	6,064	6,592	6.7	7.3	4,166	6.2	67,629	6.4	33,324
Chippewa County, WI	33,750	34,017	32,802	2.9	2,509	2,698	7.4	7.9	1,512	22.3	19,593	11.3	34,593
Eau Claire County, WI	56,138	56,609	54,021	3.9	3,555	3,894	6.3	6.9	2,654	-1.2	48,036	4.6	32,807
El Centro, CA	77,561	77,232	60,763	27.6	23,011	23,082	29.7	29.9	2,368	4.2	29,223	15.3	29,712
Imperial County, CA	77,561	77,232	60,763	27.6	23,011	23,082	29.7	29.9	2,368	4.2	29,223	15.3	29,712
Elizabethtown, KY	56,676	55,660	53,006	6.9	5,052	5,263	8.9	9.5	2,469	13.4	34,470	-0.5	30,505
Hardin County, KY	49,693	48,756	46,133	7.7	4,451	4,589	9.0	9.4	2,238	14.4	32,318	-1.2	31,029
Larue County, KY	6,983	6,904	6,873	1.6	601	674	8.6	9.8	231	4.5	2,152	11.6	22,636
Elkhart–Goshen, IN	91,753	90,600	101,892	-10.0	10,247	12,241	11.2	13.5	4,890	-2.4	94,310	-20.3	36,689
Elkhart County, IN	91,753	90,600	101,892	-10.0	10,247	12,241	11.2	13.5	4,890	-2.4	94,310	-20.3	36,689
Elmira, NY	40,015	40,780	40,640	-1.5	3,163	3,475	7.9	8.5	1,856	-3.2	32,630	-7.2	34,412
Chemung County, NY	40,015	40,780	40,640	-1.5	3,163	3,475	7.9	8.5	1,856	-3.2	32,630	-7.2	34,412
El Paso, TX	326,472	322,152	290,674	12.3	33,682	31,512	10.3	9.8	13,356	8.5	206,981	3.6	28,779
El Paso County, TX	326,472	322,152	290,674	12.3	33,682	31,512	10.3	9.8	13,356	8.5	206,981	3.6	28,779
Erie, PA	140,259	139,332	141,034	-0.5	11,277	12,713	8.0	9.1	6,287	-9.7	111,677	-8.8	34,012
Erie County, PA	140,259	139,332	141,034	-0.5	11,277	12,713	8.0	9.1	6,287	-9.7	111,677	-8.8	34,012
Eugene–Springfield, OR	181,183	182,675	174,568	3.8	17,158	20,007	9.5	11.0	9,601	-0.9	111,667	-6.6	33,542
Lane County, OR	181,183	182,675	174,568	3.8	17,158	20,007	9.5	11.0	9,601	-0.9	111,667	-6.6	33,542

[1] Civilian unemployed as percent of total civilian labor force.
[2] For pay period including March 12 of the year shown.
[3] The Denver–Aurora metropolitan statistical area includes Broomfield County. Broomfield County, CO, was formed from parts of Adams, Boulder, Jefferson, and Weld Counties on November 15, 2001, and is coextensive with Broomfield city. For the purposes of defining and presenting data for the Denver–Aurora metropolitan statistical area, Broomfield city is treated as if it were a county when data are available to do so. In many cases, the data were not available.
NA = Not available

Table C-4.   Labor Force and Private Business Establishments and Employment—*Continued*

Metropolitan statistical area, division, and component county	Civilian labor force								Private nonfarm businesses				Annual payroll per employee 2010 (dollars)
	Total				Number of unemployed		Unemployment rate[1]		Establishments		Employment[2]		
	2011	2010	2005	Change, 2005–2011	2011	2010	2011	2010	2010	Change, 2000–2010	2010	Change, 2000–2010	
Evansville, IN–KY	184,375	183,383	182,960	0.8	14,308	15,678	7.8	8.5	8,559	-3.9	161,473	-2.3	37,299
Gibson County, IN	17,078	16,793	17,302	-1.3	1,367	1,310	8.0	7.8	725	-3.2	16,089	33.4	43,090
Posey County, IN	13,064	12,956	13,867	-5.8	939	1,007	7.2	7.8	510	-4.0	8,381	10.9	48,344
Vanderburgh County, IN	92,879	92,408	91,414	1.6	7,234	8,006	7.8	8.7	4,970	-5.4	105,690	-4.9	36,015
Warrick County, IN	31,648	31,413	30,594	3.4	2,222	2,414	7.0	7.7	1,080	4.1	12,587	7.9	36,954
Henderson County, KY	23,348	23,446	23,125	1.0	2,029	2,353	8.7	10.0	1,037	-4.4	16,255	-18.7	34,260
Webster County, KY	6,358	6,367	6,658	-4.5	517	588	8.1	9.2	237	-7.4	2,471	-12.3	38,793
Fairbanks, AK	46,859	46,939	45,214	3.6	3,122	3,262	6.7	6.9	2,443	12.3	27,160	25.7	44,072
Fairbanks North Star Borough, AK	46,859	46,939	45,214	3.6	3,122	3,262	6.7	6.9	2,443	12.3	27,160	25.7	44,072
Fargo, ND–MN	121,229	120,760	113,111	7.2	4,693	4,928	3.9	4.1	6,297	18.4	108,416	23.1	35,999
Clay County, MN	34,004	32,979	30,815	10.3	1,686	1,594	5.0	4.8	1,275	11.2	16,773	14.0	24,886
Cass County, ND	87,225	87,781	82,296	6.0	3,007	3,334	3.4	3.8	5,022	20.3	91,643	25.0	38,033
Farmington, NM	55,307	55,401	54,181	2.1	4,319	5,015	7.8	9.1	2,823	13.5	37,908	10.4	39,643
San Juan County, NM	55,307	55,401	54,181	2.1	4,319	5,015	7.8	9.1	2,823	13.5	37,908	10.4	39,643
Fayetteville, NC	164,543	160,608	146,755	12.1	16,708	15,495	10.2	9.6	6,110	9.3	98,538	5.0	31,357
Cumberland County, NC	142,251	138,907	128,201	11.0	14,512	13,520	10.2	9.7	5,704	7.5	92,996	4.3	31,797
Hoke County, NC	22,292	21,701	18,554	20.1	2,196	1,975	9.9	9.1	406	43.5	5,542	17.3	23,983
Fayetteville–Springdale–Rogers, AR–MO	231,461	227,938	219,939	5.2	14,444	14,782	6.2	6.5	10,646	26.4	176,303	21.1	42,543
Benton County, AR	108,995	107,131	99,771	9.2	6,873	6,859	6.3	6.4	5,315	45.3	91,062	35.0	50,369
Madison County, AR	7,517	7,422	7,800	-3.6	468	500	6.2	6.7	184	-7.1	2,283	17.4	26,018
Washington County, AR	103,897	102,311	100,453	3.4	6,254	6,436	6.0	6.3	4,832	14.3	77,716	9.0	35,041
McDonald County, MO	11,052	11,074	11,915	-7.2	849	987	7.7	8.9	315	-7.1	5,242	8.2	25,006
Flagstaff, AZ	72,898	74,921	67,298	8.3	6,738	7,286	9.2	9.7	3,574	3.4	43,418	11.6	33,655
Coconino County, AZ	72,898	74,921	67,298	8.3	6,738	7,286	9.2	9.7	3,574	3.4	43,418	11.6	33,655
Flint, MI	184,435	189,268	212,489	-13.2	20,133	26,181	10.9	13.8	7,904	-13.3	110,395	-27.2	36,671
Genesee County, MI	184,435	189,268	212,489	-13.2	20,133	26,181	10.9	13.8	7,904	-13.3	110,395	-27.2	36,671
Florence, SC	92,903	93,470	92,124	0.8	10,566	11,134	11.4	11.9	4,308	-5.0	70,246	-9.8	34,846
Darlington County, SC	30,561	30,790	30,498	0.2	3,690	3,919	12.1	12.7	1,130	-11.4	18,188	-15.7	40,055
Florence County, SC	62,342	62,680	61,626	1.2	6,876	7,215	11.0	11.5	3,178	-2.5	52,058	-7.6	33,026
Florence–Muscle Shoals, AL	70,105	69,849	66,543	5.4	5,998	6,390	8.6	9.1	3,277	-2.6	44,185	-12.8	28,715
Colbert County, AL	25,208	25,163	24,775	1.7	2,268	2,455	9.0	9.8	1,284	-5.6	18,700	-3.5	32,728
Lauderdale County, AL	44,897	44,686	41,768	7.5	3,730	3,935	8.3	8.8	1,993	-0.5	25,485	-18.5	25,771
Fond du Lac, WI	55,301	55,824	56,138	-1.5	3,962	4,691	7.2	8.4	2,440	-3.0	38,715	-14.2	34,081
Fond du Lac County, WI	55,301	55,824	56,138	-1.5	3,962	4,691	7.2	8.4	2,440	-3.0	38,715	-14.2	34,081
Fort Collins–Loveland, CO	178,043	178,171	167,508	6.3	12,042	13,224	6.8	7.4	9,378	17.0	101,994	9.0	37,821
Larimer County, CO	178,043	178,171	167,508	6.3	12,042	13,224	6.8	7.4	9,378	17.0	101,994	9.0	37,821
Fort Smith, AR–OK	132,164	136,005	134,616	-1.8	11,412	11,156	8.6	8.2	6,274	7.7	103,366	-3.8	32,138
Crawford County, AR	27,814	28,439	27,313	1.8	2,363	2,218	8.5	7.8	1,104	20.7	21,636	29.0	27,403
Franklin County, AR	7,910	8,111	8,483	-6.8	590	569	7.5	7.0	276	-1.8	3,266	3.9	29,400
Sebastian County, AR	59,513	60,696	59,394	0.2	4,945	4,478	8.3	7.4	3,516	6.4	64,096	-12.1	35,328
Le Flore County, OK	19,828	20,799	21,350	-7.1	1,864	2,053	9.4	9.9	790	9.3	7,976	1.4	27,622
Sequoyah County, OK	17,099	17,960	18,076	-5.4	1,650	1,838	9.6	10.2	588	-2.5	6,392	-4.4	23,214
Fort Wayne, IN	210,734	208,886	211,373	-0.3	18,971	21,663	9.0	10.4	10,451	1.9	176,058	-12.9	37,629
Allen County, IN	179,007	177,435	178,841	0.1	16,254	18,536	9.1	10.4	9,137	2.1	156,788	-12.4	38,183
Wells County, IN	14,120	13,951	14,857	-5.0	1,177	1,314	8.3	9.4	634	4.3	9,387	-17.8	31,137
Whitley County, IN	17,607	17,500	17,675	-0.4	1,540	1,813	8.7	10.4	680	-2.3	9,883	-15.1	35,019
Fresno, CA	442,054	440,128	408,052	8.3	73,118	74,091	16.5	16.8	15,782	3.3	225,079	5.7	36,525
Fresno County, CA	442,054	440,128	408,052	8.3	73,118	74,091	16.5	16.8	15,782	3.3	225,079	5.7	36,525
Gadsden, AL	45,824	45,393	46,461	-1.4	4,162	4,299	9.1	9.5	2,032	-5.7	29,476	-14.2	30,118
Etowah County, AL	45,824	45,393	46,461	-1.4	4,162	4,299	9.1	9.5	2,032	-5.7	29,476	-14.2	30,118
Gainesville, FL	138,256	138,219	129,996	6.4	10,806	11,010	7.8	8.0	5,996	12.3	82,928	0.5	33,815
Alachua County, FL	130,699	130,662	122,566	6.6	10,068	10,259	7.7	7.9	5,786	11.9	81,509	0.1	33,925
Gilchrist County, FL	7,557	7,557	7,430	1.7	738	751	9.8	9.9	210	23.5	1,419	32.2	27,524
Gainesville, GA	89,960	87,979	83,358	7.9	7,330	8,084	8.1	9.2	3,950	17.5	57,810	-0.1	37,089
Hall County, GA	89,960	87,979	83,358	7.9	7,330	8,084	8.1	9.2	3,950	17.5	57,810	-0.1	37,089
Glens Falls, NY	67,690	68,097	67,683	0.0	5,321	5,543	7.9	8.1	3,452	1.7	40,636	-10.2	35,549
Warren County, NY	35,604	35,824	35,508	0.3	2,910	3,033	8.2	8.5	2,372	2.3	31,125	-11.4	36,067
Washington County, NY	32,086	32,273	32,175	-0.3	2,411	2,510	7.5	7.8	1,080	0.6	9,511	-6.0	33,853
Goldsboro, NC	54,656	54,128	51,555	6.0	5,144	5,118	9.4	9.5	2,221	-5.1	33,819	-10.3	29,949
Wayne County, NC	54,656	54,128	51,555	6.0	5,144	5,118	9.4	9.5	2,221	-5.1	33,819	-10.3	29,949
Grand Forks, ND–MN	54,933	55,274	55,004	-0.1	2,544	2,412	4.6	4.4	2,611	1.6	40,796	12.1	31,686
Polk County, MN	17,865	17,561	16,884	5.8	1,090	999	6.1	5.7	771	-7.2	9,735	11.4	30,397
Grand Forks County, ND	37,068	37,713	38,120	-2.8	1,454	1,413	3.9	3.7	1,840	5.8	31,061	12.3	32,090

[1] Civilian unemployed as percent of total civilian labor force.
[2] For pay period including March 12 of the year shown.

Table C-4.   Labor Force and Private Business Establishments and Employment—*Continued*

Metropolitan statistical area, division, and component county	Civilian labor force								Private nonfarm businesses				
	Total				Number of unemployed		Unemployment rate[1]		Establishments		Employment[2]		Annual payroll per employee 2010 (dollars)
	2011	2010	2005	Change, 2005–2011	2011	2010	2011	2010	2010	Change, 2000–2010	2010	Change, 2000–2010	
Grand Junction, CO	79,048	79,996	71,483	10.6	7,607	8,563	9.6	10.7	4,646	19.3	49,484	14.1	35,840
Mesa County, CO	79,048	79,996	71,483	10.6	7,607	8,563	9.6	10.7	4,646	19.3	49,484	14.1	35,840
Grand Rapids–Wyoming, MI	380,852	382,233	406,673	-6.3	31,438	40,157	8.3	10.5	17,943	-0.8	318,367	-13.6	39,743
Barry County, MI	28,415	28,550	30,881	-8.0	2,088	2,775	7.3	9.7	892	-11.5	8,970	-23.5	32,324
Ionia County, MI	28,634	28,814	30,898	-7.3	2,853	3,574	10.0	12.4	882	-14.9	9,737	-18.6	27,916
Kent County, MI	302,511	303,458	321,487	-5.9	24,298	31,089	8.0	10.2	15,353	0.5	290,955	-13.4	40,569
Newaygo County, MI	21,292	21,411	23,407	-9.0	2,199	2,719	10.3	12.7	816	5.4	8,705	-2.5	33,018
Great Falls, MT	40,672	40,915	38,526	5.6	2,460	2,342	6.0	5.7	2,454	-4.3	30,287	9.1	29,813
Cascade County, MT	40,672	40,915	38,526	5.6	2,460	2,342	6.0	5.7	2,454	-4.3	30,287	9.1	29,813
Greeley, CO	122,877	121,765	112,158	9.6	11,443	12,378	9.3	10.2	5,163	27.0	64,621	13.7	41,806
Weld County, CO	122,877	121,765	112,158	9.6	11,443	12,378	9.3	10.2	5,163	27.0	64,621	13.7	41,806
Green Bay, WI	173,095	173,876	168,507	2.7	12,212	13,637	7.1	7.8	7,621	-0.2	143,630	-1.7	39,631
Brown County, WI	141,012	141,509	136,324	3.4	9,626	10,649	6.8	7.5	6,375	1.3	131,408	-0.4	40,276
Kewaunee County, WI	11,687	11,784	11,858	-1.4	814	955	7.0	8.1	478	-2.8	5,481	-1.3	38,401
Oconto County, WI	20,396	20,583	20,325	0.3	1,772	2,033	8.7	9.9	768	-9.8	6,741	-22.6	28,059
Greensboro–High Point, NC	372,145	371,631	363,945	2.3	40,824	42,707	11.0	11.5	17,566	-3.6	296,342	-13.4	37,388
Guilford County, NC	254,303	253,634	242,582	4.8	27,571	28,543	10.8	11.3	13,266	-2.9	236,853	-11.0	39,038
Randolph County, NC	73,516	73,458	75,300	-2.4	7,824	8,241	10.6	11.2	2,588	-6.8	36,865	-21.8	30,661
Rockingham County, NC	44,326	44,539	46,063	-3.8	5,429	5,923	12.2	13.3	1,712	-4.1	22,624	-21.6	31,076
Greenville, NC	93,456	93,357	83,101	12.5	10,061	9,866	10.8	10.6	3,811	11.2	58,192	5.7	32,077
Greene County, NC	9,218	9,228	9,007	2.3	987	987	10.7	10.7	242	16.9	1,852	-8.4	24,206
Pitt County, NC	84,238	84,129	74,094	13.7	9,074	8,879	10.8	10.6	3,569	10.9	56,340	6.2	32,336
Greenville–Mauldin–Easley, SC	315,052	311,603	299,343	5.2	26,666	30,186	8.5	9.7	15,042	2.2	246,807	-15.1	36,855
Greenville County, SC	225,947	223,426	209,177	8.0	18,366	20,862	8.1	9.3	12,072	3.8	206,754	-14.5	38,388
Laurens County, SC	30,922	30,628	33,101	-6.6	3,204	3,580	10.4	11.7	944	3.2	15,782	-8.0	30,871
Pickens County, SC	58,183	57,549	57,065	2.0	5,096	5,744	8.8	10.0	2,026	-7.2	24,271	-23.6	27,696
Gulfport–Biloxi, MS	118,055	114,900	120,858	-2.3	11,526	10,556	9.8	9.2	5,195	-5.6	82,104	-11.0	33,336
Hancock County, MS	19,904	19,306	21,074	-5.6	2,014	1,783	10.1	9.2	708	-6.0	10,083	1.1	38,002
Harrison County, MS	89,680	87,350	92,934	-3.5	8,697	8,028	9.7	9.2	4,205	-5.7	69,211	-13.4	32,853
Stone County, MS	8,471	8,244	6,850	23.7	815	745	9.6	9.0	282	-3.4	2,810	18.7	28,489
Hagerstown–Martinsburg, MD–WV	122,039	122,345	119,686	2.0	10,990	12,188	9.0	10.0	5,326	6.1	78,054	-3.4	33,520
Washington County, MD	69,463	69,567	68,311	1.7	6,795	7,550	9.8	10.9	3,489	4.8	55,216	-5.8	33,726
Berkeley County, WV	45,409	45,568	44,240	2.6	3,601	3,968	7.9	8.7	1,588	10.0	20,661	4.3	33,519
Morgan County, WV	7,167	7,210	7,135	0.4	594	670	8.3	9.3	249	0.4	2,177	-9.5	28,331
Hanford–Corcoran, CA	61,099	61,418	53,960	13.2	9,854	10,145	16.1	16.5	1,614	4.9	22,572	21.7	32,635
Kings County, CA	61,099	61,418	53,960	13.2	9,854	10,145	16.1	16.5	1,614	4.9	22,572	21.7	32,635
Harrisburg–Carlisle, PA	284,676	285,272	278,703	2.1	20,569	21,893	7.2	7.7	13,410	4.0	259,399	0.8	39,747
Cumberland County, PA	122,628	122,743	120,172	2.0	8,156	8,586	6.7	7.0	5,725	2.8	111,674	-3.2	38,586
Dauphin County, PA	137,838	138,227	134,353	2.6	10,520	11,261	7.6	8.1	6,889	4.7	141,587	4.0	41,371
Perry County, PA	24,210	24,302	24,178	0.1	1,893	2,046	7.8	8.4	796	6.3	6,138	4.0	23,391
Harrisonburg, VA	69,093	67,553	61,590	12.2	4,248	4,617	6.1	6.8	2,990	10.9	50,563	4.8	31,668
Rockingham County, VA	43,270	42,339	40,504	6.8	2,363	2,636	5.5	6.2	1,408	22.4	24,261	4.7	33,335
Harrisonburg city, VA	25,823	25,214	21,086	22.5	1,885	1,981	7.3	7.9	1,582	2.4	26,302	5.0	30,131
Hartford–West Hartford–													
East Hartford, CT	655,192	654,151	611,385	7.2	57,194	60,726	8.7	9.3	29,549	-1.4	529,323	(D)	50,070
Hartford County, CT	472,551	472,107	440,336	7.3	43,526	46,319	9.2	9.8	22,843	-1.5	442,369	-7.2	52,180
Middlesex County, CT	95,001	94,613	89,784	5.8	7,201	7,516	7.6	7.9	4,220	-0.4	57,798	-4.4	41,629
Tolland County, CT	87,640	87,431	81,265	7.8	6,467	6,891	7.4	7.9	2,486	-1.8	29,156	(D)	34,791
Hattiesburg, MS	68,012	67,244	63,279	7.5	6,495	5,999	9.5	8.9	3,316	10.4	48,817	12.7	31,684
Forrest County, MS	35,533	35,041	35,750	-0.6	3,709	3,358	10.4	9.6	1,850	-13.3	31,123	-7.6	33,923
Lamar County, MS	27,345	27,077	22,378	22.2	2,182	2,025	8.0	7.5	1,307	81.5	16,015	107.8	26,357
Perry County, MS	5,134	5,126	5,151	-0.3	604	616	11.8	12.0	159	5.3	1,679	-14.0	40,982
Hickory–Lenoir–Morganton, NC	170,616	172,244	177,676	-4.0	21,592	23,982	12.7	13.9	7,635	-6.1	120,569	-28.3	32,952
Alexander County, NC	17,964	18,269	18,383	-2.3	2,044	2,430	11.4	13.3	588	1.9	6,674	-23.7	26,340
Burke County, NC	39,821	40,111	41,775	-4.7	5,058	5,526	12.7	13.8	1,457	-7.0	20,843	-38.0	31,636
Caldwell County, NC	38,814	39,226	40,019	-3.0	5,121	5,706	13.2	14.5	1,410	-10.1	18,547	-40.3	29,429
Catawba County, NC	74,017	74,638	77,499	-4.5	9,369	10,320	12.7	13.8	4,180	-5.3	74,505	-21.3	34,790
Hinesville–Fort Stewart, GA	33,337	32,875	28,849	15.6	3,044	2,956	9.1	9.0	886	13.3	11,796	21.5	32,448
Liberty County, GA	25,750	25,406	23,060	11.7	2,499	2,442	9.7	9.6	814	10.7	11,464	20.8	32,761
Long County, GA	7,587	7,469	5,789	31.1	545	514	7.2	6.9	72	53.2	332	50.9	21,627
Holland–Grand Haven, MI	128,202	127,233	136,175	-5.9	10,596	14,290	8.3	11.2	5,686	-3.5	86,972	-19.3	37,034
Ottawa County, MI	128,202	127,233	136,175	-5.9	10,596	14,290	8.3	11.2	5,686	-3.5	86,972	-19.3	37,034
Honolulu, HI	460,643	452,745	439,390	4.8	26,432	26,388	5.7	5.8	21,592	4.6	335,934	6.4	38,329
Honolulu County, Hawaii	460,643	452,745	439,390	4.8	26,432	26,388	5.7	5.8	21,592	4.6	335,934	6.4	38,329
Hot Springs, AR	42,968	42,317	41,735	3.0	3,557	3,428	8.3	8.1	2,702	5.1	30,557	-1.2	27,875
Garland County, AR	42,968	42,317	41,735	3.0	3,557	3,428	8.3	8.1	2,702	5.1	30,557	-1.2	27,875
Houma–Bayou Cane–Thibodaux, LA	102,003	103,082	96,727	5.5	5,461	5,614	5.4	5.4	4,833	6.6	76,321	20.1	42,029
Lafourche Parish, LA	48,254	48,675	45,543	6.0	2,559	2,542	5.3	5.2	1,923	4.7	27,330	12.6	43,589
Terrebonne Parish, LA	53,749	54,407	51,184	5.0	2,902	3,072	5.4	5.6	2,910	7.9	48,991	24.8	41,158

[1] Civilian unemployed as percent of total civilian labor force.
[2] For pay period including March 12 of the year shown.

Table C-4. Labor Force and Private Business Establishments and Employment—*Continued*

Metropolitan statistical area, division, and component county	Civilian labor force								Private nonfarm businesses				
	Total				Number of unemployed		Unemployment rate[1]		Establishments		Employment[2]		Annual payroll per employee 2010 (dollars)
	2011	2010	2005	Change, 2005–2011	2011	2010	2011	2010	2010	Change, 2000–2010	2010	Change, 2000–2010	
Houston–Sugar Land–Baytown, TX	2,982,933	2,925,989	2,609,223	14.3	241,965	247,470	8.1	8.5	122,517	13.6	2,176,567	10.6	53,512
Austin County, TX	14,321	13,948	12,829	11.6	1,170	1,097	8.2	7.9	575	4.9	9,439	62.8	39,082
Brazoria County, TX	153,299	150,327	133,855	14.5	13,221	13,441	8.6	8.9	4,817	25.5	70,292	15.5	41,443
Chambers County, TX	17,618	17,283	14,016	25.7	1,576	1,606	8.9	9.3	493	31.1	8,176	28.2	52,336
Fort Bend County, TX	300,276	294,933	235,559	27.5	22,039	23,035	7.3	7.8	9,223	53.5	114,920	46.1	40,595
Galveston County, TX	148,320	145,100	138,058	7.4	13,466	13,318	9.1	9.2	5,115	6.5	77,680	12.3	37,583
Harris County, TX	2,054,025	2,014,856	1,827,969	12.4	167,760	171,568	8.2	8.5	91,528	7.9	1,754,182	6.9	56,210
Liberty County, TX	32,490	31,940	31,343	3.7	3,440	3,552	10.6	11.1	1,049	0.9	11,405	-2.3	35,113
Montgomery County, TX	231,457	227,074	189,539	22.1	16,571	17,084	7.2	7.5	8,883	53.1	120,627	41.0	48,123
San Jacinto County, TX	11,105	10,902	10,184	9.0	1,071	1,096	9.6	10.1	181	24.8	1,026	-1.6	27,610
Waller County, TX	20,022	19,626	15,871	26.2	1,651	1,673	8.2	8.5	653	25.3	8,820	19.9	38,754
Huntington–Ashland, WV–KY–OH	128,298	129,836	131,221	-2.2	10,581	10,939	8.2	8.4	5,849	-7.6	92,663	-1.0	35,775
Boyd County, KY	22,808	22,921	22,948	-0.6	2,048	2,012	9.0	8.8	1,403	-5.0	24,229	-4.9	41,050
Greenup County, KY	16,984	17,167	17,175	-1.1	1,625	1,698	9.6	9.9	498	-2.7	4,947	1.1	30,035
Lawrence County, OH	28,206	28,621	28,555	-1.2	2,371	2,466	8.4	8.6	835	-9.1	10,177	-1.0	27,752
Cabell County, WV	43,275	43,788	44,706	-3.2	3,166	3,247	7.3	7.4	2,540	-9.0	45,719	1.5	35,092
Wayne County, WV	17,025	17,339	17,837	-4.6	1,371	1,516	8.1	8.7	573	-8.8	7,591	-4.1	37,555
Huntsville, AL	213,874	211,887	192,955	10.8	16,182	15,933	7.6	7.5	9,355	12.6	165,379	14.8	44,846
Limestone County, AL	39,912	39,830	34,915	14.3	3,026	3,268	7.6	8.2	1,262	15.7	13,849	-20.0	31,700
Madison County, AL	173,962	172,057	158,040	10.1	13,156	12,665	7.6	7.4	8,093	12.1	151,530	19.5	46,048
Idaho Falls, ID	62,947	62,676	59,043	6.6	4,478	4,237	7.1	6.8	3,649	23.7	46,063	12.1	37,476
Bonneville County, ID	51,005	50,735	48,412	5.4	3,615	3,369	7.1	6.6	3,216	23.5	42,671	12.4	38,428
Jefferson County, ID	11,942	11,941	10,631	12.3	863	868	7.2	7.3	433	24.8	3,392	7.7	25,506
Indianapolis–Carmel, IN	902,936	897,387	877,729	2.9	76,072	81,540	8.4	9.1	42,317	4.9	742,919	-4.8	43,096
Boone County, IN	28,272	28,040	27,174	4.0	2,059	2,176	7.3	7.8	1,336	5.7	16,878	32.5	33,785
Brown County, IN	7,663	7,664	7,998	-4.2	642	737	8.4	9.6	363	-5.2	2,197	-3.3	22,799
Hamilton County, IN	141,952	141,094	130,720	8.6	8,901	9,816	6.3	7.0	7,394	39.0	99,612	24.7	43,032
Hancock County, IN	36,661	36,607	34,420	6.5	2,886	3,282	7.9	9.0	1,371	8.4	15,786	11.7	36,091
Hendricks County, IN	75,739	75,272	69,425	9.1	5,466	5,935	7.2	7.9	2,851	32.8	45,819	72.8	31,066
Johnson County, IN	72,965	72,585	70,035	4.2	5,609	6,127	7.7	8.4	2,936	11.5	37,376	-5.9	29,979
Marion County, IN	463,504	460,173	459,301	0.9	43,502	45,767	9.4	9.9	23,255	-4.6	489,364	-13.3	46,732
Morgan County, IN	35,449	35,349	37,194	-4.7	3,172	3,502	8.9	9.9	1,203	-8.0	11,192	-18.9	29,908
Putnam County, IN	17,600	17,471	17,793	-1.1	1,817	1,898	10.3	10.9	695	1.8	10,316	-6.1	28,092
Shelby County, IN	23,131	23,132	23,669	-2.3	2,018	2,300	8.7	9.9	913	-4.9	14,379	-6.9	34,974
Iowa City, IA	91,992	92,349	85,941	7.0	4,010	4,169	4.4	4.5	3,746	11.0	64,260	12.8	33,342
Johnson County, IA	79,970	80,255	73,707	8.5	3,412	3,525	4.3	4.4	3,043	14.1	57,673	12.9	34,042
Washington County, IA	12,022	12,094	12,234	-1.7	598	644	5.0	5.3	703	-0.8	6,587	11.8	27,213
Ithaca, NY	55,331	56,884	54,648	1.2	3,233	3,379	5.8	5.9	2,320	9.2	45,452	8.7	36,107
Tompkins County, NY	55,331	56,884	54,648	1.2	3,233	3,379	5.8	5.9	2,320	9.2	45,452	8.7	36,107
Jackson, MI	71,149	72,612	78,249	-9.1	7,074	9,239	9.9	12.7	3,018	-11.5	44,688	-18.3	39,761
Jackson County, MI	71,149	72,612	78,249	-9.1	7,074	9,239	9.9	12.7	3,018	-11.5	44,688	-18.3	39,761
Jackson, MS	271,496	264,747	263,024	3.2	22,883	22,317	8.4	8.4	12,846	6.6	198,793	-7.0	36,804
Copiah County, MS	12,801	12,372	12,536	2.1	1,520	1,371	11.9	11.1	421	-8.1	5,858	-2.5	25,216
Hinds County, MS	120,650	117,706	122,474	-1.5	11,440	11,212	9.5	9.5	5,769	-13.9	95,129	-29.8	39,197
Madison County, MS	49,578	48,365	44,160	12.3	3,693	3,621	7.4	7.5	2,821	44.1	42,557	54.6	38,693
Rankin County, MS	76,567	74,721	71,851	6.6	5,091	5,023	6.6	6.7	3,422	36.3	49,637	24.6	33,473
Simpson County, MS	11,900	11,583	12,003	-0.9	1,139	1,090	9.6	9.4	413	-1.9	5,612	17.7	23,462
Jackson, TN	57,554	56,828	54,630	5.4	5,539	5,742	9.6	10.1	2,810	-1.9	51,727	-8.7	33,758
Chester County, TN	8,274	8,168	7,630	8.4	802	830	9.7	10.2	242	-0.8	2,809	-17.3	23,838
Madison County, TN	49,280	48,660	47,000	4.9	4,737	4,912	9.6	10.1	2,568	-2.0	48,918	-8.1	34,328
Jacksonville, FL	692,529	685,119	630,362	9.9	69,694	74,520	10.1	10.9	34,085	19.1	482,315	0.5	40,228
Baker County, FL	12,494	12,327	11,022	13.4	1,239	1,293	9.9	10.5	359	29.1	5,261	37.6	29,529
Clay County, FL	97,148	96,159	85,943	13.0	9,010	9,752	9.3	10.1	3,517	24.9	36,348	16.2	28,367
Duval County, FL	447,217	442,507	418,101	7.0	47,548	50,690	10.6	11.5	23,681	13.2	382,646	-2.9	42,763
Nassau County, FL	37,412	37,016	32,457	15.3	3,586	3,855	9.6	10.4	1,595	32.7	14,466	13.5	31,500
St. Johns County, FL	98,258	97,110	82,839	18.6	8,311	8,930	8.5	9.2	4,933	44.7	43,594	15.0	32,060
Jacksonville, NC	67,410	67,548	56,456	19.4	6,148	5,778	9.1	8.6	2,692	3.5	33,244	13.9	25,309
Onslow County, NC	67,410	67,548	56,456	19.4	6,148	5,778	9.1	8.6	2,692	3.5	33,244	13.9	25,309
Janesville, WI	78,687	80,965	83,608	-5.9	7,464	9,074	9.5	11.2	3,292	-2.0	51,167	-15.8	35,653
Rock County, WI	78,687	80,965	83,608	-5.9	7,464	9,074	9.5	11.2	3,292	-2.0	51,167	-15.8	35,653
Jefferson City, MO	78,402	78,339	77,869	0.7	5,376	5,709	6.9	7.3	3,599	3.9	50,030	-7.0	34,384
Callaway County, MO	22,877	22,861	22,613	1.2	1,722	1,821	7.5	8.0	761	12.1	11,195	4.1	35,438
Cole County, MO	40,532	40,492	40,179	0.9	2,606	2,772	6.4	6.8	2,236	2.2	33,408	-10.3	35,156
Moniteau County, MO	7,584	7,581	7,569	0.2	578	613	7.6	8.1	333	-1.2	2,622	-16.0	27,456
Osage County, MO	7,409	7,405	7,508	-1.3	470	503	6.3	6.8	269	3.5	2,805	4.5	27,457
Johnson City, TN	102,813	101,349	95,857	7.3	8,609	9,169	8.4	9.0	3,835	2.3	62,347	-4.6	30,318
Carter County, TN	29,021	28,708	29,111	-0.3	2,655	2,909	9.1	10.1	731	-1.6	9,036	-9.6	25,781
Unicoi County, TN	8,801	8,666	8,249	6.7	858	893	9.7	10.3	256	-1.2	4,062	8.8	35,035
Washington County, TN	64,991	63,975	58,497	11.1	5,096	5,367	7.8	8.4	2,848	3.6	49,249	-4.6	30,762

[1] Civilian unemployed as percent of total civilian labor force.
[2] For pay period including March 12 of the year shown.

Table C-4. Labor Force and Private Business Establishments and Employment—*Continued*

Metropolitan statistical area, division, and component county	Civilian labor force								Private nonfarm businesses				
	Total				Number of unemployed		Unemployment rate[1]		Establishments		Employment[2]		Annual payroll per employee 2010 (dollars)
	2011	2010	2005	Change, 2005–2011	2011	2010	2011	2010	2010	Change, 2000–2010	2010	Change, 2000–2010	
Johnstown, PA	68,352	68,788	67,327	1.5	5,885	6,340	8.6	9.2	3,437	-3.1	50,550	-1.7	31,565
Cambria County, PA	68,352	68,788	67,327	1.5	5,885	6,340	8.6	9.2	3,437	-3.1	50,550	-1.7	31,565
Jonesboro, AR	59,169	58,226	56,299	5.1	4,519	4,423	7.6	7.6	2,766	3.8	39,555	1.4	31,120
Craighead County, AR	48,428	47,641	44,874	7.9	3,551	3,460	7.3	7.3	2,403	7.0	36,024	5.4	31,636
Poinsett County, AR	10,741	10,585	11,425	-6.0	968	963	9.0	9.1	363	-13.6	3,531	-27.0	25,852
Joplin, MO	87,774	87,102	82,371	6.6	6,801	7,298	7.7	8.4	4,245	4.0	73,093	2.4	32,732
Jasper County, MO	58,462	57,975	54,607	7.1	4,484	4,776	7.7	8.2	2,971	-3.5	54,436	-1.5	33,142
Newton County, MO	29,312	29,127	27,764	5.6	2,317	2,522	7.9	8.7	1,274	27.1	18,657	16.1	31,535
Kalamazoo–Portage, MI	160,211	165,587	173,366	-7.6	14,136	17,770	8.8	10.7	6,954	-6.7	118,831	-7.1	40,010
Kalamazoo County, MI	124,194	128,340	132,520	-6.3	10,181	12,968	8.2	10.1	5,627	-4.7	102,770	-7.3	40,789
Van Buren County, MI	36,017	37,247	40,846	-11.8	3,955	4,802	11.0	12.9	1,327	-14.2	16,061	-5.7	35,029
Kankakee–Bradley, IL	55,889	56,643	52,577	6.3	6,806	7,524	12.2	13.3	2,357	3.0	35,226	-41.0	32,886
Kankakee County, IL	55,889	56,643	52,577	6.3	6,806	7,524	12.2	13.3	2,357	3.0	35,226	-41.0	32,886
Kansas City, MO–KS	1,055,723	1,050,668	1,027,710	2.7	85,663	93,284	8.1	8.9	50,129	0.2	860,640	-5.0	42,900
Franklin County, KS	13,447	13,376	13,863	-3.0	1,148	1,205	8.5	9.0	566	-2.9	9,433	22.3	33,828
Johnson County, KS	301,113	299,658	290,841	3.5	17,890	19,383	5.9	6.5	16,873	6.2	294,278	4.1	46,613
Leavenworth County, KS	33,526	33,191	33,097	1.3	2,771	2,756	8.3	8.3	1,186	5.6	13,312	-11.5	33,214
Linn County, KS	4,703	4,634	4,896	-3.9	504	478	10.7	10.3	179	-7.3	1,152	-16.6	42,662
Miami County, KS	17,131	16,940	16,328	4.9	1,309	1,283	7.6	7.6	718	16.2	6,529	-4.9	29,355
Wyandotte County, KS	71,625	71,234	73,578	-2.7	7,110	7,391	9.9	10.4	2,995	-2.8	63,326	2.8	42,280
Bates County, MO	7,971	7,905	7,941	0.4	830	871	10.4	11.0	351	-10.0	2,834	-7.2	25,118
Caldwell County, MO	4,419	4,376	4,409	0.2	393	411	8.9	9.4	165	-10.3	786	-21.7	29,627
Cass County, MO	51,229	51,042	48,755	5.1	4,396	4,913	8.6	9.6	1,856	4.2	17,788	14.9	27,722
Clay County, MO	121,143	120,334	111,293	8.9	9,354	10,224	7.7	8.5	4,751	1.3	82,696	-2.2	41,432
Clinton County, MO	10,422	10,316	10,336	0.8	1,038	1,073	10.0	10.4	381	-9.7	3,086	-10.1	25,989
Jackson County, MO	339,642	338,985	336,508	0.9	32,466	36,422	9.6	10.7	16,800	-6.7	317,355	-15.6	43,574
Lafayette County, MO	16,947	16,773	16,722	1.3	1,666	1,721	9.8	10.3	730	-8.5	6,254	-11.8	24,528
Platte County, MO	50,837	50,401	47,347	7.4	3,646	3,919	7.2	7.8	2,191	17.8	38,897	8.8	35,262
Ray County, MO	11,568	11,503	11,796	-1.9	1,142	1,234	9.9	10.7	387	-4.7	2,914	-21.7	26,582
Kennewick–Pasco–Richland, WA	134,627	134,095	113,697	18.4	10,649	10,408	7.9	7.8	5,251	18.7	74,876	16.1	44,767
Benton County, WA	97,225	96,809	84,590	14.9	7,356	7,151	7.6	7.4	3,906	18.4	58,282	15.3	47,820
Franklin County, WA	37,402	37,286	29,107	28.5	3,293	3,257	8.8	8.7	1,345	19.6	16,594	19.0	34,045
Killeen–Temple–Fort Hood, TX	171,298	169,604	149,737	14.4	13,966	13,095	8.2	7.7	5,915	14.4	94,773	9.7	33,739
Bell County, TX	136,597	135,296	114,370	19.4	10,982	10,338	8.0	7.6	4,770	17.1	81,289	8.0	34,949
Coryell County, TX	24,912	24,632	25,421	-2.0	2,280	2,118	9.2	8.6	755	4.1	9,938	31.5	26,166
Lampasas County, TX	9,789	9,676	9,946	-1.6	704	639	7.2	6.6	390	5.1	3,546	-0.7	27,222
Kingsport–Bristol–Bristol, TN–VA	149,821	148,575	141,778	5.7	12,101	13,147	8.1	8.8	6,092	-5.7	102,878	-6.3	36,756
Hawkins County, TN	26,617	26,345	25,674	3.7	2,378	2,514	8.9	9.5	615	-2.4	8,596	-28.9	31,521
Sullivan County, TN	76,009	75,352	72,399	5.0	5,875	6,397	7.7	8.5	3,360	-7.8	63,307	-1.7	38,481
Scott County, VA	10,256	10,244	9,827	4.4	830	972	8.1	9.5	299	-8.8	3,398	4.6	30,324
Washington County, VA	28,577	28,369	26,094	9.5	2,249	2,469	7.9	8.7	1,203	3.4	16,897	16.7	38,726
Bristol city, VA	8,362	8,265	7,784	7.4	769	795	9.2	9.6	615	-11.1	10,680	-31.3	29,674
Kingston, NY	87,658	88,853	91,906	-4.6	7,147	7,292	8.2	8.2	4,708	8.0	45,087	-1.4	32,033
Ulster County, NY	87,658	88,853	91,906	-4.6	7,147	7,292	8.2	8.2	4,708	8.0	45,087	-1.4	32,033
Knoxville, TN	374,650	366,198	341,952	9.6	27,424	28,938	7.3	7.9	16,062	0.4	287,528	3.6	39,578
Anderson County, TN	37,413	36,588	34,933	7.1	3,132	3,291	8.4	9.0	1,613	-6.2	41,637	5.2	53,465
Blount County, TN	65,513	64,115	59,769	9.6	5,016	5,354	7.7	8.4	2,274	4.6	38,015	-1.1	35,209
Knox County, TN	237,269	231,885	216,490	9.6	16,490	17,443	6.9	7.5	11,092	-0.7	194,398	3.8	37,940
Loudon County, TN	25,283	24,691	21,930	15.3	1,944	2,022	7.7	8.2	880	18.4	11,782	13.7	33,565
Union County, TN	9,172	8,919	8,830	3.9	842	828	9.2	9.3	203	7.4	1,696	-17.7	26,014
Kokomo, IN	42,826	42,489	47,225	-9.3	4,473	5,179	10.4	12.2	2,111	-7.8	31,429	-35.3	38,564
Howard County, IN	35,470	35,261	39,151	-9.4	3,713	4,368	10.5	12.4	1,813	-8.0	28,412	-36.6	39,032
Tipton County, IN	7,356	7,228	8,074	-8.9	760	811	10.3	11.2	298	-6.9	3,017	-20.5	34,159
La Crosse, WI–MN	76,711	77,124	72,798	5.4	4,540	5,083	5.9	6.6	3,379	1.6	61,117	0.1	33,656
Houston County, MN	10,869	10,882	11,072	-1.8	764	861	7.0	7.9	451	15.6	4,027	-0.1	25,206
La Crosse County, WI	65,842	66,242	61,726	6.7	3,776	4,222	5.7	6.4	2,928	-0.2	57,090	0.1	34,253
Lafayette, IN	97,908	97,209	94,466	3.6	7,636	8,849	7.8	9.1	3,954	2.6	64,411	-11.3	35,132
Benton County, IN	4,267	4,249	4,598	-7.2	372	436	8.7	10.3	205	-18.7	1,543	-26.7	27,994
Carroll County, IN	9,781	9,715	10,511	-6.9	805	929	8.2	9.6	398	-2.7	4,240	-16.5	29,558
Tippecanoe County, IN	83,860	83,245	79,357	5.7	6,459	7,484	7.7	9.0	3,351	5.0	58,628	-10.4	35,723
Lafayette, LA	137,374	136,354	127,287	7.9	7,911	8,313	5.8	6.1	8,804	20.3	127,331	14.8	40,001
Lafayette Parish, LA	114,282	113,352	104,531	9.3	6,315	6,571	5.5	5.8	7,920	18.9	116,362	13.5	40,443
St. Martin Parish, LA	23,092	23,002	22,756	1.5	1,596	1,742	6.9	7.6	884	34.8	10,969	29.9	35,302
Lake Charles, LA	92,685	94,300	95,794	-3.2	6,352	6,715	6.9	7.1	4,389	-0.6	68,638	-3.5	36,564
Calcasieu Parish, LA	89,641	91,201	91,316	-1.8	6,175	6,525	6.9	7.2	4,240	0.0	67,061	-3.1	36,414
Cameron Parish, LA	3,044	3,099	4,478	-32.0	177	190	5.8	6.1	149	-15.3	1,577	-15.9	42,948
Lake Havasu City–Kingman, AZ	88,006	91,056	88,319	-0.4	9,649	10,886	11.0	12.0	3,713	7.7	39,714	14.0	29,491
Mohave County, AZ	88,006	91,056	88,319	-0.4	9,649	10,886	11.0	12.0	3,713	7.7	39,714	14.0	29,491
Lakeland–Winter Haven, FL	274,561	276,088	256,045	7.2	31,758	33,630	11.6	12.2	10,943	13.9	159,201	-1.4	34,712
Polk County, FL	274,561	276,088	256,045	7.2	31,758	33,630	11.6	12.2	10,943	13.9	159,201	-1.4	34,712
Lancaster, PA	266,366	269,272	268,382	-0.8	18,227	20,005	6.8	7.4	12,043	5.3	207,278	-3.4	36,644
Lancaster County, PA	266,366	269,272	268,382	-0.8	18,227	20,005	6.8	7.4	12,043	5.3	207,278	-3.4	36,644

[1] Civilian unemployed as percent of total civilian labor force.
[2] For pay period including March 12 of the year shown.

Table C-4. Labor Force and Private Business Establishments and Employment—*Continued*

Metropolitan statistical area, division, and component county	Civilian labor force								Private nonfarm businesses				Annual payroll per employee 2010 (dollars)
	Total				Number of unemployed		Unemployment rate[1]		Establishments		Employment[2]		
	2011	2010	2005	Change, 2005–2011	2011	2010	2011	2010	2010	Change, 2000–2010	2010	Change, 2000–2010	
Lansing–East Lansing, MI	235,385	238,611	247,929	-5.1	19,107	23,833	8.1	10.0	9,555	-7.1	151,434	-12.4	38,346
Clinton County, MI	37,511	37,954	37,248	0.7	2,591	3,276	6.9	8.6	1,245	6.5	14,995	9.6	32,318
Eaton County, MI	54,634	55,359	58,623	-6.8	4,011	5,087	7.3	9.2	2,062	3.8	37,482	19.9	37,579
Ingham County, MI	143,240	145,298	152,058	-5.8	12,505	15,470	8.7	10.6	6,248	-12.4	98,957	-22.6	39,550
Laredo, TX	100,246	97,324	85,825	16.8	8,111	8,677	8.1	8.9	4,707	15.4	63,526	19.4	25,881
Webb County, TX	100,246	97,324	85,825	16.8	8,111	8,677	8.1	8.9	4,707	15.4	63,526	19.4	25,881
Las Cruces, NM	92,186	91,783	84,661	8.9	6,886	7,094	7.5	7.7	3,610	12.4	50,117	35.3	28,293
Doña Ana County, NM	92,186	91,783	84,661	8.9	6,886	7,094	7.5	7.7	3,610	12.4	50,117	35.3	28,293
Las Vegas–Paradise, NV	994,152	994,210	872,410	14.0	137,978	140,241	13.9	14.1	39,597	33.6	731,876	14.5	37,191
Clark County, NV	994,152	994,210	872,410	14.0	137,978	140,241	13.9	14.1	39,597	33.6	731,876	14.5	37,191
Lawrence, KS	61,838	62,745	63,150	-2.1	3,705	3,860	6.0	6.2	2,628	0.2	37,409	-0.2	28,499
Douglas County, KS	61,838	62,745	63,150	-2.1	3,705	3,860	6.0	6.2	2,628	0.2	37,409	-0.2	28,499
Lawton, OK	48,139	49,108	45,331	6.2	3,212	3,184	6.7	6.5	2,219	0.9	32,704	18.5	30,847
Comanche County, OK	48,139	49,108	45,331	6.2	3,212	3,184	6.7	6.5	2,219	0.9	32,704	18.5	30,847
Lebanon, PA	73,400	73,515	70,330	4.4	4,819	5,212	6.6	7.1	2,641	2.8	43,427	15.4	32,528
Lebanon County, PA	73,400	73,515	70,330	4.4	4,819	5,212	6.6	7.1	2,641	2.8	43,427	15.4	32,528
Lewiston, ID–WA	29,354	29,421	29,559	-0.7	2,239	2,262	7.6	7.7	1,574	-5.2	20,901	1.1	32,652
Nez Perce County, ID	19,120	19,006	19,096	0.1	1,323	1,311	6.9	6.9	1,142	-6.2	16,374	-1.1	33,807
Asotin County, WA	10,234	10,415	10,463	-2.2	916	951	9.0	9.1	432	-2.5	4,527	9.6	28,475
Lewiston–Auburn, ME	58,281	58,022	56,638	2.9	4,392	4,877	7.5	8.4	2,767	-0.7	43,808	-4.5	34,369
Androscoggin County, ME	58,281	58,022	56,638	2.9	4,392	4,877	7.5	8.4	2,767	-0.7	43,808	-4.5	34,369
Lexington–Fayette, KY	239,092	238,500	228,571	4.6	18,788	20,128	7.9	8.4	11,809	6.4	199,943	-4.5	38,075
Bourbon County, KY	9,422	9,410	9,791	-3.8	845	908	9.0	9.6	390	-1.5	6,013	10.7	35,565
Clark County, KY	16,765	16,782	17,029	-1.6	1,654	1,803	9.9	10.7	762	-0.3	10,675	-14.4	33,974
Fayette County, KY	152,998	152,490	146,049	4.8	11,397	12,131	7.4	8.0	8,247	4.5	143,310	-5.2	38,960
Jessamine County, KY	23,352	23,300	21,843	6.9	1,950	2,086	8.4	9.0	1,031	16.0	13,927	11.8	30,075
Scott County, KY	23,580	23,563	20,589	14.5	1,999	2,172	8.5	9.2	841	28.6	19,059	-2.1	41,777
Woodford County, KY	12,975	12,955	13,270	-2.2	943	1,028	7.3	7.9	538	5.5	6,959	-16.2	34,162
Lima, OH	49,954	50,619	52,467	-4.8	4,804	5,447	9.6	10.8	2,548	-10.3	46,523	-10.3	33,977
Allen County, OH	49,954	50,619	52,467	-4.8	4,804	5,447	9.6	10.8	2,548	-10.3	46,523	-10.3	33,977
Lincoln, NE	172,266	168,680	165,284	4.2	6,848	7,140	4.0	4.2	8,222	8.9	130,287	-1.4	34,835
Lancaster County, NE	163,271	159,872	156,033	4.6	6,516	6,792	4.0	4.2	7,780	9.2	125,217	-0.9	35,097
Seward County, NE	8,995	8,808	9,251	-2.8	332	348	3.7	4.0	442	4.7	5,070	-12.8	28,356
Little Rock–North Little Rock–Conway, AR	347,204	344,303	332,821	4.3	24,451	24,199	7.0	7.0	17,601	6.5	275,781	-2.0	37,689
Faulkner County, AR	57,970	57,609	51,782	12.0	4,071	4,153	7.0	7.2	2,327	30.5	34,054	16.4	35,991
Grant County, AR	8,499	8,414	8,623	-1.4	608	588	7.2	7.0	266	-2.2	2,991	-0.9	29,127
Lonoke County, AR	33,083	32,798	30,648	7.9	2,246	2,214	6.8	6.8	1,001	6.2	10,561	19.3	25,574
Perry County, AR	4,788	4,729	4,943	-3.1	414	391	8.6	8.3	113	-6.6	933	51.2	27,609
Pulaski County, AR	189,904	188,184	189,704	0.1	13,647	13,373	7.2	7.1	12,125	0.7	208,999	-6.7	39,651
Saline County, AR	52,960	52,569	47,121	12.4	3,465	3,480	6.5	6.6	1,769	30.3	18,243	16.5	27,319
Logan, UT–ID	67,203	68,070	63,861	5.2	3,297	3,874	4.9	5.7	3,352	28.9	39,056	18.8	28,825
Franklin County, ID	6,223	6,052	6,142	1.3	353	325	5.7	5.4	292	19.7	1,932	14.8	25,232
Cache County, UT	60,980	62,018	57,719	5.6	2,944	3,549	4.8	5.7	3,060	29.8	37,124	19.0	29,012
Longview, TX	113,790	113,080	102,246	11.3	7,858	8,467	6.9	7.5	5,291	4.2	78,127	10.1	36,796
Gregg County, TX	66,811	66,417	60,673	10.1	4,514	4,895	6.8	7.4	4,010	3.7	63,330	10.2	36,973
Rusk County, TX	26,473	26,268	22,767	16.3	1,864	1,966	7.0	7.5	811	3.7	10,580	11.2	38,416
Upshur County, TX	20,506	20,395	18,806	9.0	1,480	1,606	7.2	7.9	470	9.6	4,217	6.8	30,067
Longview, WA	43,269	44,503	42,724	1.3	5,226	5,802	12.1	13.0	2,206	-5.5	29,103	-10.5	40,179
Cowlitz County, WA	43,269	44,503	42,724	1.3	5,226	5,802	12.1	13.0	2,206	-5.5	29,103	-10.5	40,179
Los Angeles–Long Beach–Santa Ana, CA	6,528,034	6,501,576	6,360,244	2.6	744,792	769,811	11.4	11.8	330,969	8.6	4,852,354	-7.4	49,462
Los Angeles–Long Beach–Glendale, CA	4,924,364	4,910,534	4,771,417	3.2	605,494	619,137	12.3	12.6	244,447	8.0	3,580,067	-7.3	49,180
Los Angeles County, CA	4,924,364	4,910,534	4,771,417	3.2	605,494	619,137	12.3	12.6	244,447	8.0	3,580,067	-7.3	49,180
Santa Ana–Anaheim–Irvine, CA	1,603,670	1,591,042	1,588,827	0.9	139,298	150,674	8.7	9.5	86,522	10.1	1,272,287	-7.7	50,256
Orange County, CA	1,603,670	1,591,042	1,588,827	0.9	139,298	150,674	8.7	9.5	86,522	10.1	1,272,287	-7.7	50,256
Louisville/Jefferson County, KY–IN	633,716	630,783	610,683	3.8	61,432	64,220	9.7	10.2	29,859	1.4	515,000	-6.5	38,712
Clark County, IN	55,899	55,576	53,351	4.8	4,867	5,216	8.7	9.4	2,393	-2.4	40,729	-3.0	32,892
Floyd County, IN	37,209	37,055	37,472	-0.7	2,983	3,279	8.0	8.8	1,753	1.9	25,727	-3.9	32,667
Harrison County, IN	19,930	19,830	19,617	1.6	1,655	1,796	8.3	9.1	670	2.9	9,100	7.5	28,633
Washington County, IN	13,679	13,648	14,006	-2.3	1,289	1,421	9.4	10.4	456	-2.6	4,344	-25.8	25,958
Bullitt County, KY	38,439	38,189	35,806	7.4	4,074	4,140	10.6	10.8	1,065	15.3	13,948	30.4	27,546
Henry County, KY	7,447	7,464	7,889	-5.6	686	765	9.2	10.2	218	-12.4	1,844	-31.3	31,773
Jefferson County, KY	364,514	362,777	351,115	3.8	36,588	37,865	10.0	10.4	19,628	-1.0	380,915	-8.5	41,286
Meade County, KY	12,208	12,045	12,162	0.4	1,552	1,487	12.7	12.3	338	10.8	3,161	4.6	30,390
Nelson County, KY	21,570	21,401	20,547	5.0	2,495	2,501	11.6	11.7	919	4.7	11,916	-4.1	33,231
Oldham County, KY	28,511	28,436	26,173	8.9	2,176	2,343	7.6	8.2	1,231	23.7	10,262	10.4	31,475
Shelby County, KY	21,406	21,361	20,020	6.9	1,800	1,936	8.4	9.1	895	23.8	11,335	-3.8	30,839
Spencer County, KY	8,758	8,758	8,174	7.1	849	922	9.7	10.5	209	22.2	1,104	16.5	21,155
Trimble County, KY	4,146	4,243	4,351	-4.7	418	549	10.1	12.9	84	15.1	615	16.3	41,995

[1] Civilian unemployed as percent of total civilian labor force.
[2] For pay period including March 12 of the year shown.

Table C-4. Labor Force and Private Business Establishments and Employment—*Continued*

Metropolitan statistical area, division, and component county	Civilian labor force								Private nonfarm businesses				
	Total				Number of unemployed		Unemployment rate[1]		Establishments		Employment[2]		Annual payroll per employee 2010 (dollars)
	2011	2010	2005	Change, 2005–2011	2011	2010	2011	2010	2010	Change, 2000–2010	2010	Change, 2000–2010	
Lubbock, TX	147,982	145,239	140,581	5.3	9,159	9,214	6.2	6.3	6,960	5.0	104,164	10.3	30,078
Crosby County, TX	2,591	2,511	2,931	-11.6	241	208	9.3	8.3	107	-15.7	828	-10.4	38,627
Lubbock County, TX	145,391	142,728	137,650	5.6	8,918	9,006	6.1	6.3	6,853	5.4	103,336	10.5	30,010
Lynchburg, VA	125,438	125,759	117,274	7.0	8,909	9,905	7.1	7.9	6,006	3.4	94,003	-2.6	35,511
Amherst County, VA	15,567	15,704	15,416	1.0	1,117	1,338	7.2	8.5	601	0.5	6,697	-7.2	28,935
Appomattox County, VA	7,354	7,438	6,866	7.1	543	666	7.4	9.0	297	6.8	2,408	-23.3	24,251
Bedford County, VA	35,899	35,935	34,162	5.1	2,208	2,440	6.2	6.8	1,436	52.4	12,682	47.1	30,585
Campbell County, VA	28,126	28,148	26,845	4.8	1,889	2,063	6.7	7.3	1,148	18.6	13,531	-3.7	38,567
Bedford city, VA	2,592	2,611	2,543	1.9	225	257	8.7	9.8	308	-36.5	3,732	-37.4	27,700
Lynchburg city, VA	35,900	35,923	31,442	14.2	2,927	3,141	8.2	8.7	2,216	-12.7	54,953	-4.5	37,721
Macon, GA	111,919	111,470	110,825	1.0	11,323	11,615	10.1	10.4	5,286	-2.0	80,237	-12.1	34,791
Bibb County, GA	73,237	72,904	73,312	-0.1	7,686	7,835	10.5	10.7	4,277	-6.8	70,570	-15.6	35,122
Crawford County, GA	6,108	6,111	6,309	-3.2	604	648	9.9	10.6	98	28.9	517	-20.1	27,263
Jones County, GA	14,496	14,466	13,755	5.4	1,287	1,355	8.9	9.4	338	41.4	2,490	18.0	28,706
Monroe County, GA	13,959	13,907	12,773	9.3	1,232	1,273	8.8	9.2	496	24.6	5,953	66.6	33,259
Twiggs County, GA	4,119	4,082	4,676	-11.9	514	504	12.5	12.3	77	-17.2	707	-46.2	41,648
Madera–Chowchilla, CA	66,369	67,260	62,012	7.0	10,134	10,487	15.3	15.6	1,910	2.4	24,501	5.8	34,637
Madera County, CA	66,369	67,260	62,012	7.0	10,134	10,487	15.3	15.6	1,910	2.4	24,501	5.8	34,637
Madison, WI	345,024	346,430	332,980	3.6	18,321	20,622	5.3	6.0	15,132	5.0	271,806	8.7	41,803
Columbia County, WI	32,184	32,331	31,732	1.4	2,367	2,595	7.4	8.0	1,394	-3.3	18,998	4.2	30,744
Dane County, WI	298,714	299,832	286,918	4.1	15,046	16,941	5.0	5.7	13,185	6.5	244,080	10.2	42,882
Iowa County, WI	14,126	14,267	14,330	-1.4	908	1,086	6.4	7.6	553	-7.1	8,728	-15.9	35,699
Manchester–Nashua, NH	228,370	228,756	225,339	1.3	12,669	14,522	5.5	6.3	10,827	-0.7	177,473	0.3	50,988
Hillsborough County, NH	228,370	228,756	225,339	1.3	12,669	14,522	5.5	6.3	10,827	-0.7	177,473	0.3	50,988
Manhattan, KS	62,297	64,222	55,923	11.4	3,597	3,755	5.8	5.8	2,709	9.2	36,731	8.4	27,275
Geary County, KS	14,754	15,181	11,142	32.4	1,189	1,208	8.1	8.0	595	1.4	7,917	-5.0	27,471
Pottawatomie County, KS	11,451	11,787	10,807	6.0	606	616	5.3	5.2	571	15.4	7,458	26.5	33,092
Riley County, KS	36,092	37,254	33,974	6.2	1,802	1,931	5.0	5.2	1,543	10.3	21,356	8.6	25,171
Mankato–North Mankato, MN	58,556	57,974	54,257	7.9	3,081	3,612	5.3	6.2	2,547	8.3	45,315	10.3	32,423
Blue Earth County, MN	38,765	38,378	35,437	9.4	2,065	2,414	5.3	6.3	1,903	13.1	34,040	23.6	31,380
Nicollet County, MN	19,791	19,596	18,820	5.2	1,016	1,198	5.1	6.1	644	-3.9	11,275	-16.6	35,574
Mansfield, OH	59,341	60,103	62,466	-5.0	6,122	7,064	10.3	11.8	2,735	-9.4	42,532	-17.9	30,285
Richland County, OH	59,341	60,103	62,466	-5.0	6,122	7,064	10.3	11.8	2,735	-9.4	42,532	-17.9	30,285
McAllen–Edinburg–Mission, TX	317,612	309,872	261,157	21.6	38,095	37,347	12.0	12.1	11,045	32.8	167,097	45.5	25,454
Hidalgo County, TX	317,612	309,872	261,157	21.6	38,095	37,347	12.0	12.1	11,045	32.8	167,097	45.5	25,454
Medford, OR	102,261	102,498	99,278	3.0	11,806	12,796	11.5	12.5	5,786	7.9	63,965	2.7	32,946
Jackson County, OR	102,261	102,498	99,278	3.0	11,806	12,796	11.5	12.5	5,786	7.9	63,965	2.7	32,946
Memphis, TN–MS–AR	625,230	614,516	603,342	3.6	62,142	61,792	9.9	10.1	25,751	-2.3	509,166	-10.6	41,269
Crittenden County, AR	21,564	20,875	22,400	-3.7	2,712	2,388	12.6	11.4	872	-8.0	13,295	-15.8	30,245
DeSoto County, MS	80,735	78,644	71,650	12.7	6,440	6,180	8.0	7.9	2,521	36.9	40,717	31.2	29,474
Marshall County, MS	15,486	15,118	15,414	0.5	2,017	1,981	13.0	13.1	427	-1.8	6,214	-13.4	25,743
Tate County, MS	12,551	12,250	11,933	5.2	1,408	1,382	11.2	11.3	375	-9.4	3,882	-30.4	27,202
Tunica County, MS	4,807	4,586	4,525	6.2	915	790	19.0	17.2	218	9.5	11,306	-39.1	26,424
Fayette County, TN	18,023	17,758	16,164	11.5	1,901	1,908	10.5	10.7	550	23.3	6,094	44.7	37,140
Shelby County, TN	442,972	436,369	434,479	2.0	43,888	44,035	9.9	10.1	20,038	-6.1	419,469	-12.1	43,862
Tipton County, TN	29,092	28,916	26,777	8.6	2,861	3,128	9.8	10.8	750	1.9	8,189	-15.7	27,021
Merced, CA	110,167	109,338	98,959	11.3	20,121	20,561	18.3	18.8	2,884	-2.5	38,840	-1.8	33,991
Merced County, CA	110,167	109,338	98,959	11.3	20,121	20,561	18.3	18.8	2,884	-2.5	38,840	-1.8	33,991
Miami–Fort Lauderdale–Pompano Beach, FL	2,875,403	2,823,480	2,673,194	7.6	300,640	317,974	10.5	11.3	170,661	11.3	1,820,909	-5.3	41,542
Fort Lauderdale–Pompano Beach–Deerfield Beach, FL	990,714	977,632	949,838	4.3	91,103	93,913	9.2	9.6	55,541	10.4	593,373	-4.2	41,206
Broward County, FL	990,714	977,632	949,838	4.3	91,103	93,913	9.2	9.6	55,541	10.4	593,373	-4.2	41,206
Miami–Miami Beach–Kendall, FL	1,264,608	1,231,368	1,123,472	12.6	142,836	153,926	11.3	12.5	73,410	10.4	802,109	-6.1	41,497
Miami–Dade County, FL	1,264,608	1,231,368	1,123,472	12.6	142,836	153,926	11.3	12.5	73,410	10.4	802,109	-6.1	41,497
West Palm Beach–Boca Raton–Boynton Beach, FL	620,081	614,480	599,884	3.4	66,701	70,135	10.8	11.4	41,710	14.2	425,427	-5.2	42,094
Palm Beach County, FL	620,081	614,480	599,884	3.4	66,701	70,135	10.8	11.4	41,710	14.2	425,427	-5.2	42,094
Michigan City–La Porte, IN	51,040	51,404	53,043	-3.8	5,331	6,097	10.4	11.9	2,478	-6.0	34,054	-15.5	32,171
LaPorte County, IN	51,040	51,404	53,043	-3.8	5,331	6,097	10.4	11.9	2,478	-6.0	34,054	-15.5	32,171
Midland, TX	83,714	78,359	66,480	25.9	3,689	4,185	4.4	5.3	4,568	13.1	59,770	29.9	49,520
Midland County, TX	83,714	78,359	66,480	25.9	3,689	4,185	4.4	5.3	4,568	13.1	59,770	29.9	49,520
Milwaukee–Waukesha–West Allis, WI	797,439	798,039	786,657	1.4	63,362	70,940	7.9	8.9	38,424	-3.6	737,279	-6.7	44,922
Milwaukee County, WI	461,017	461,268	453,562	1.6	41,416	45,655	9.0	9.9	20,015	-6.1	444,142	-7.6	45,341
Ozaukee County, WI	47,022	47,043	47,895	-1.8	2,819	3,261	6.0	6.9	2,747	-4.7	34,606	-7.3	38,903
Washington County, WI	74,331	74,507	72,329	2.8	5,147	5,981	6.9	8.0	3,142	1.2	45,364	-4.2	36,924
Waukesha County, WI	215,069	215,221	212,871	1.0	13,980	16,043	6.5	7.5	12,520	-0.4	213,147	-5.4	46,729

[1] Civilian unemployed as percent of total civilian labor force.
[2] For pay period including March 12 of the year shown.

Table C-4.   Labor Force and Private Business Establishments and Employment—*Continued*

Metropolitan statistical area, division, and component county	Civilian labor force								Private nonfarm businesses				
	Total				Number of unemployed		Unemployment rate[1]		Establishments		Employment[2]		Annual payroll per employee 2010 (dollars)
	2011	2010	2005	Change, 2005–2011	2011	2010	2011	2010	2010	Change, 2000–2010	2010	Change, 2000–2010	
Minneapolis–St. Paul–													
Bloomington, MN–WI	1,852,208	1,831,259	1,808,876	2.4	116,091	133,501	6.3	7.3	89,831	6.3	1,572,381	-3.5	50,388
Anoka County, MN	190,498	188,785	189,505	0.5	12,601	14,870	6.6	7.9	7,309	10.4	102,847	1.6	47,558
Carver County, MN	50,425	49,985	48,012	5.0	2,842	3,467	5.6	6.9	2,333	33.3	33,298	20.9	45,165
Chisago County, MN	29,087	28,893	27,024	7.6	2,251	2,657	7.7	9.2	1,242	13.0	12,921	21.1	32,302
Dakota County, MN	232,031	229,428	227,693	1.9	13,938	16,216	6.0	7.1	9,885	14.9	160,483	4.1	43,645
Hennepin County, MN	657,760	649,497	651,868	0.9	39,604	45,176	6.0	7.0	38,946	-0.5	786,394	-9.1	56,936
Isanti County, MN	20,924	20,759	21,028	-0.5	1,716	1,981	8.2	9.5	770	2.7	8,238	12.5	33,097
Ramsey County, MN	274,023	270,291	271,083	1.1	18,048	20,045	6.6	7.4	13,216	-3.5	284,332	-6.8	48,334
Scott County, MN	74,145	73,378	69,743	6.3	4,394	5,188	5.9	7.1	3,074	39.0	37,580	21.0	40,345
Sherburne County, MN	49,573	49,179	46,486	6.6	3,547	4,183	7.2	8.5	1,898	44.7	19,341	34.6	33,041
Washington County, MN	133,172	131,328	125,448	6.2	8,089	9,045	6.1	6.9	5,315	18.1	65,736	13.3	37,027
Wright County, MN	69,526	68,822	62,697	10.9	4,890	5,633	7.0	8.2	2,995	26.6	30,974	20.7	34,010
Pierce County, WI	23,796	23,693	23,448	1.5	1,376	1,608	5.8	6.8	780	-2.0	5,923	-13.3	30,761
St. Croix County, WI	47,248	47,221	44,841	5.4	2,795	3,432	5.9	7.3	2,068	22.9	24,314	9.6	32,828
Missoula, MT	59,394	59,047	57,307	3.6	3,917	4,046	6.6	6.9	4,171	15.1	46,219	11.9	29,657
Missoula County, MT	59,394	59,047	57,307	3.6	3,917	4,046	6.6	6.9	4,171	15.1	46,219	11.9	29,657
Mobile, AL	192,780	190,905	179,174	7.6	19,413	19,421	10.1	10.2	8,826	-4.4	148,500	-5.1	37,193
Mobile County, AL	192,780	190,905	179,174	7.6	19,413	19,421	10.1	10.2	8,826	-4.4	148,500	-5.1	37,193
Modesto, CA	236,573	239,576	227,117	4.2	39,791	41,425	16.8	17.3	8,366	1.3	121,595	0.8	38,543
Stanislaus County, CA	236,573	239,576	227,117	4.2	39,791	41,425	16.8	17.3	8,366	1.3	121,595	0.8	38,543
Monroe, LA	80,560	81,583	83,100	-3.1	6,236	6,399	7.7	7.8	4,538	2.2	65,464	-7.7	30,691
Ouachita Parish, LA	70,769	71,610	72,619	-2.5	5,457	5,542	7.7	7.7	4,200	2.3	61,434	-6.6	31,004
Union Parish, LA	9,791	9,973	10,481	-6.6	779	857	8.0	8.6	338	0.6	4,030	-21.7	25,915
Monroe, MI	68,733	70,724	77,808	-11.7	6,701	8,803	9.7	12.4	2,383	-4.1	34,678	-12.3	37,867
Monroe County, MI	68,733	70,724	77,808	-11.7	6,701	8,803	9.7	12.4	2,383	-4.1	34,678	-12.3	37,867
Montgomery, AL	171,414	171,750	167,513	2.3	15,343	15,551	9.0	9.1	7,741	-3.7	126,990	-6.6	35,428
Autauga County, AL	25,930	25,907	23,831	8.8	2,076	2,033	8.0	7.8	871	13.3	10,167	11.5	26,857
Elmore County, AL	35,777	35,892	34,282	4.4	2,974	3,062	8.3	8.5	1,111	1.8	13,768	46.9	28,733
Lowndes County, AL	4,352	4,341	4,896	-11.1	722	708	16.6	16.3	125	-16.7	2,112	-1.8	49,895
Montgomery County, AL	105,355	105,610	104,504	0.8	9,571	9,748	9.1	9.2	5,634	-6.6	100,943	-12.5	36,901
Morgantown, WV	65,553	65,531	59,413	10.3	3,758	3,829	5.7	5.8	2,743	4.7	44,404	24.8	35,592
Monongalia County, WV	49,759	49,650	44,904	10.8	2,660	2,622	5.3	5.3	2,180	9.3	39,846	32.3	36,378
Preston County, WV	15,794	15,881	14,509	8.9	1,098	1,207	7.0	7.6	563	-9.9	4,558	-16.5	28,720
Morristown, TN	63,493	63,978	63,762	-0.4	7,014	7,469	11.0	11.7	2,204	-4.1	38,916	-15.3	31,326
Grainger County, TN	9,945	10,050	10,171	-2.2	1,200	1,300	12.1	12.9	221	-10.2	2,015	-30.8	26,743
Hamblen County, TN	29,458	29,565	29,782	-1.1	3,123	3,216	10.6	10.9	1,314	-6.4	26,881	-17.0	32,334
Jefferson County, TN	24,090	24,363	23,809	1.2	2,691	2,953	11.2	12.1	669	3.1	10,020	-5.8	29,543
Mount Vernon–Anacortes, WA	56,997	58,293	55,991	1.8	5,775	6,231	10.1	10.7	3,432	5.4	38,013	6.6	36,265
Skagit County, WA	56,997	58,293	55,991	1.8	5,775	6,231	10.1	10.7	3,432	5.4	38,013	6.6	36,265
Muncie, IN	53,755	54,392	56,075	-4.1	5,458	6,136	10.2	11.3	2,440	-9.6	35,890	-28.9	30,100
Delaware County, IN	53,755	54,392	56,075	-4.1	5,458	6,136	10.2	11.3	2,440	-9.6	35,890	-28.9	30,100
Muskegon–Norton Shores, MI	82,113	83,335	89,985	-8.7	8,357	11,224	10.2	13.5	3,378	-5.8	47,700	-17.0	35,224
Muskegon County, MI	82,113	83,335	89,985	-8.7	8,357	11,224	10.2	13.5	3,378	-5.8	47,700	-17.0	35,224
Myrtle Beach–North Myrtle Beach–													
Conway, SC	129,085	129,520	120,996	6.7	14,899	15,794	11.5	12.2	8,246	14.7	92,343	7.0	26,661
Horry County, SC	129,085	129,520	120,996	6.7	14,899	15,794	11.5	12.2	8,246	14.7	92,343	7.0	26,661
Napa, CA	76,460	75,734	71,460	7.0	6,888	7,317	9.0	9.7	3,945	5.3	54,945	10.9	43,577
Napa County, CA	76,460	75,734	71,460	7.0	6,888	7,317	9.0	9.7	3,945	5.3	54,945	10.9	43,577
Naples–Marco Island, FL	148,485	144,627	143,967	3.1	15,269	16,751	10.3	11.6	9,856	16.3	101,450	10.0	36,682
Collier County, FL	148,485	144,627	143,967	3.1	15,269	16,751	10.3	11.6	9,856	16.3	101,450	10.0	36,682
Nashville–Davidson—Murfreesboro—													
Franklin, TN	841,401	822,072	753,854	11.6	67,351	71,241	8.0	8.7	37,619	8.8	652,935	0.5	43,536
Cannon County, TN	6,679	6,526	6,459	3.4	593	623	8.9	9.5	164	-2.4	1,378	1.9	26,438
Cheatham County, TN	20,854	20,352	20,489	1.8	1,782	1,852	8.5	9.1	541	3.2	5,558	-17.2	32,940
Davidson County, TN	332,843	325,381	305,809	8.8	27,213	28,918	8.2	8.9	18,124	-2.6	370,484	-7.0	46,025
Dickson County, TN	25,096	24,393	22,961	9.3	2,405	2,383	9.6	9.8	923	4.2	11,863	-11.5	30,804
Hickman County, TN	10,728	10,521	10,252	4.6	1,139	1,219	10.6	11.6	268	-12.7	2,305	-1.4	27,961
Macon County, TN	10,980	10,668	10,587	3.7	1,077	1,062	9.8	10.0	343	11.4	3,282	-19.5	27,325
Robertson County, TN	34,888	34,000	31,878	9.4	2,896	2,968	8.3	8.7	1,060	10.0	15,638	12.5	29,612
Rutherford County, TN	143,619	140,369	119,257	20.4	11,511	12,224	8.0	8.7	4,497	30.3	82,514	15.1	37,782
Smith County, TN	9,387	9,210	9,163	2.4	883	961	9.4	10.4	283	-7.5	3,402	-30.9	32,334
Sumner County, TN	84,228	82,337	76,287	10.4	6,763	7,195	8.0	8.7	2,876	13.0	35,839	2.2	31,834
Trousdale County, TN	3,822	3,704	3,718	2.8	402	387	10.5	10.4	126	5.0	1,079	-12.5	24,511
Williamson County, TN	96,464	94,269	82,099	17.5	5,974	6,494	6.2	6.9	6,065	39.0	90,432	29.4	52,877
Wilson County, TN	61,813	60,342	54,895	12.6	4,713	4,955	7.6	8.2	2,349	15.0	29,161	9.7	34,142

[1] Civilian unemployed as percent of total civilian labor force.
[2] For pay period including March 12 of the year shown.

Table C-4.   Labor Force and Private Business Establishments and Employment—*Continued*

Metropolitan statistical area, division, and component county	Civilian labor force								Private nonfarm businesses				Annual payroll per employee 2010 (dollars)
	Total				Number of unemployed		Unemployment rate[1]		Establishments		Employment[2]		
	2011	2010	2005	Change, 2005–2011	2011	2010	2011	2010	2010	Change, 2000–2010	2010	Change, 2000–2010	
New Haven–Milford, CT	457,666	457,238	432,366	5.9	44,593	47,035	9.7	10.3	19,607	-5.6	321,031	-5.3	46,908
New Haven County, CT	457,666	457,238	432,366	5.9	44,593	47,035	9.7	10.3	19,607	-5.6	321,031	-5.3	46,908
New Orleans–Metairie–Kenner, LA [4]	540,770	540,813	NA	NA	39,069	39,585	7.2	7.3	29,095	-7.7	446,087	-16.1	42,796
Jefferson Parish, LA	211,904	212,054	NA	NA	14,334	14,670	6.8	6.9	11,805	-8.1	178,959	-17.4	40,158
Orleans Parish, LA	146,037	146,021	NA	NA	12,860	12,970	8.8	8.9	8,436	-20.6	149,038	-28.5	45,824
Plaquemines Parish, LA	9,019	8,946	NA	NA	621	556	6.9	6.2	697	-4.9	10,074	-13.0	58,734
St. Bernard Parish, LA	16,620	16,540	NA	NA	1,301	1,235	7.8	7.5	638	-46.4	6,736	-51.6	40,831
St. Charles Parish, LA	24,899	24,934	NA	NA	1,669	1,726	6.7	6.9	953	8.0	20,015	13.0	57,487
St. John the Baptist Parish, LA	20,567	20,741	NA	NA	1,906	2,098	9.3	10.1	733	17.1	14,065	25.2	43,362
St. Tammany Parish, LA	111,724	111,577	NA	NA	6,378	6,330	5.7	5.7	5,833	25.8	67,200	29.8	36,423
New York–Northern New Jersey– Long Island, NY–NJ–PA	9,439,624	9,467,954	9,147,469	3.2	805,625	849,332	8.5	9.0	533,395	3.6	7,273,295	-3.9	63,446
Edison–New Brunswick, NJ	1,212,876	1,212,957	1,164,725	4.1	104,652	107,776	8.6	8.9	61,568	2.6	873,339	-2.2	53,375
Middlesex County, NJ	436,228	436,381	415,943	4.9	36,682	37,932	8.4	8.7	21,160	2.7	359,401	-7.9	56,398
Monmouth County, NJ	329,571	329,433	324,105	1.7	28,317	29,006	8.6	8.8	18,842	0.9	216,744	0.7	44,946
Ocean County, NJ	267,070	266,859	249,615	7.0	26,790	27,239	10.0	10.2	11,830	7.7	124,361	11.2	33,675
Somerset County, NJ	180,007	180,284	175,062	2.8	12,863	13,599	7.1	7.5	9,736	-0.5	172,833	-1.7	71,834
Nassau–Suffolk, NY	1,460,215	1,471,686	1,468,717	-0.6	103,049	108,412	7.1	7.4	94,855	4.6	1,043,243	-3.9	47,955
Nassau County, NY	681,544	687,378	690,300	-1.3	45,676	48,648	6.7	7.1	47,113	-0.2	511,467	-9.0	47,961
Suffolk County, NY	778,671	784,308	778,417	0.0	57,373	59,764	7.4	7.6	47,742	9.8	531,776	1.7	47,950
Newark–Union, NJ–PA	1,100,450	1,099,952	1,075,765	2.3	101,167	103,447	9.2	9.4	57,679	-4.3	854,757	-9.2	58,577
Essex County, NJ	370,417	370,372	361,843	2.4	40,080	41,017	10.8	11.1	19,129	-3.2	294,720	-9.9	55,137
Hunterdon County, NJ	71,262	71,278	71,314	-0.1	4,899	5,112	6.9	7.2	3,895	-0.2	43,969	3.3	56,452
Morris County, NJ	272,849	272,994	267,813	1.9	19,130	20,029	7.0	7.3	16,776	-4.5	275,054	-9.0	69,412
Sussex County, NJ	83,728	83,859	83,224	0.6	7,652	8,009	9.1	9.6	3,367	-5.0	31,228	2.3	35,009
Union County, NJ	275,886	275,137	265,654	3.9	26,642	26,635	9.7	9.7	13,625	-7.7	202,217	-13.3	54,221
Pike County, PA	26,308	26,312	25,917	1.5	2,764	2,645	10.5	10.1	887	23.4	7,569	39.0	24,721
New York–White Plains–Wayne, NY–NJ	5,666,083	5,683,359	5,438,262	4.2	496,757	529,697	8.8	9.3	319,293	5.0	4,501,956	-3.2	69,913
Bergen County, NJ	479,131	476,243	467,206	2.6	37,854	39,721	7.9	8.3	31,322	-5.6	407,968	-13.0	55,655
Hudson County, NJ	312,467	310,845	288,312	8.4	32,165	33,564	10.3	10.8	12,618	-4.9	204,105	-6.3	64,194
Passaic County, NJ	246,012	244,764	235,518	4.5	27,288	28,397	11.1	11.6	11,648	-2.0	143,593	-15.5	43,895
Bronx County, NY	545,178	547,387	501,171	8.8	66,797	69,768	12.3	12.7	16,355	16.0	228,150	10.6	41,717
Kings County, NY	1,119,975	1,125,040	1,057,799	5.9	108,686	115,363	9.7	10.3	48,212	26.4	489,378	13.3	37,219
New York County, NY	921,593	926,586	892,020	3.3	68,317	74,670	7.4	8.1	103,667	-3.8	1,968,327	-5.4	98,386
Putnam County, NY	54,048	54,251	56,117	-3.7	3,545	3,733	6.6	6.9	2,907	10.8	20,698	8.4	41,796
Queens County, NY	1,118,132	1,123,718	1,077,108	3.8	90,174	97,399	8.1	8.7	43,305	19.3	484,123	1.8	42,874
Richmond County, NY	241,002	242,162	228,713	5.4	19,740	21,253	8.2	8.8	8,495	13.8	91,227	7.7	37,114
Rockland County, NY	155,845	156,791	151,364	3.0	10,136	11,037	6.5	7.0	9,212	7.2	96,968	-3.5	43,318
Westchester County, NY	472,700	475,572	482,934	-2.1	32,055	34,792	6.8	7.3	31,552	2.5	367,419	-6.4	59,987
Niles–Benton Harbor, MI	73,088	74,901	79,013	-7.5	7,415	9,350	10.1	12.5	3,675	-7.9	49,517	-18.2	37,526
Berrien County, MI	73,088	74,901	79,013	-7.5	7,415	9,350	10.1	12.5	3,675	-7.9	49,517	-18.2	37,526
North Port–Bradenton–Sarasota, FL	301,311	300,472	311,388	-3.2	32,479	35,954	10.8	12.0	19,878	17.8	198,020	-18.3	33,987
Manatee County, FL	140,040	139,704	143,449	-2.4	15,185	16,853	10.8	12.1	7,501	33.9	79,439	-2.5	33,002
Sarasota County, FL	161,271	160,768	167,939	-4.0	17,294	19,101	10.7	11.9	12,377	9.8	118,581	-26.4	34,647
Norwich–New London, CT	151,676	152,897	144,936	4.7	13,119	13,547	8.6	8.9	5,791	1.1	107,017	1.2	44,281
New London County, CT	151,676	152,897	144,936	4.7	13,119	13,547	8.6	8.9	5,791	1.1	107,017	1.2	44,281
Ocala, FL	133,997	134,320	126,821	5.7	16,515	18,048	12.3	13.4	6,774	23.5	73,940	1.1	30,705
Marion County, FL	133,997	134,320	126,821	5.7	16,515	18,048	12.3	13.4	6,774	23.5	73,940	1.1	30,705
Ocean City, NJ	58,268	58,469	57,854	0.7	7,260	7,145	12.5	12.2	3,855	-4.1	24,464	-5.7	36,934
Cape May County, NJ	58,268	58,469	57,854	0.7	7,260	7,145	12.5	12.2	3,855	-4.1	24,464	-5.7	36,934
Odessa, TX	78,567	73,422	62,435	25.8	4,568	5,691	5.8	7.8	3,235	7.4	48,988	26.8	41,244
Ector County, TX	78,567	73,422	62,435	25.8	4,568	5,691	5.8	7.8	3,235	7.4	48,988	26.8	41,244
Ogden–Clearfield, UT	258,551	263,724	250,085	3.4	17,773	20,985	6.9	8.0	11,358	25.7	142,046	6.5	32,748
Davis County, UT	143,526	146,347	137,062	4.7	8,943	10,668	6.2	7.3	6,194	34.5	71,439	15.2	33,052
Morgan County, UT	4,193	4,299	3,852	8.9	238	312	5.7	7.3	224	50.3	1,424	34.2	34,702
Weber County, UT	110,832	113,078	109,171	1.5	8,592	10,005	7.8	8.8	4,940	15.5	69,183	-1.6	32,394
Oklahoma City, OK	579,785	574,952	574,611	0.9	32,953	37,185	5.7	6.5	32,997	11.0	452,754	3.6	38,358
Canadian County, OK	55,793	55,256	51,241	8.9	2,786	3,128	5.0	5.7	2,262	32.9	22,546	18.4	34,079
Cleveland County, OK	125,178	124,008	118,453	5.7	6,332	7,132	5.1	5.8	5,323	24.7	64,856	36.1	31,373
Grady County, OK	23,180	23,046	23,477	-1.3	1,347	1,575	5.8	6.8	1,056	13.8	10,306	-3.5	30,343
Lincoln County, OK	14,556	14,468	14,794	-1.6	856	995	5.9	6.9	571	12.8	5,301	5.5	29,435
Logan County, OK	19,160	19,024	18,172	5.4	993	1,158	5.2	6.1	717	36.1	5,779	18.6	26,544
McClain County, OK	15,691	15,574	14,754	6.4	824	953	5.3	6.1	756	31.9	6,910	36.8	28,953
Oklahoma County, OK	326,227	323,576	333,720	-2.2	19,815	22,244	6.1	6.9	22,312	5.1	337,056	-2.3	40,769

[1] Civilian unemployed as percent of total civilian labor force.
[2] For pay period including March 12 of the year shown.
[4] Because of Hurricane Katrina, no annual average Local Area Unemployment Statistics were produced in 2005 for the counties in the New Orleans the New Orleans–Metairie–Kenner, LA metropolitan area.

Table C-4. Labor Force and Private Business Establishments and Employment—*Continued*

Metropolitan statistical area, division, and component county	Civilian labor force								Private nonfarm businesses				Annual payroll per employee 2010 (dollars)
	Total				Number of unemployed		Unemployment rate[1]		Establishments		Employment[2]		
	2011	2010	2005	Change, 2005–2011	2011	2010	2011	2010	2010	Change, 2000–2010	2010	Change, 2000–2010	
Olympia, WA	129,026	130,457	121,377	6.3	10,661	11,033	8.3	8.5	5,826	15.4	63,625	20.1	34,544
Thurston County, WA	129,026	130,457	121,377	6.3	10,661	11,033	8.3	8.5	5,826	15.4	63,625	20.1	34,544
Omaha–Council Bluffs, NE–IA	458,081	451,791	440,304	4.0	22,860	23,696	5.0	5.2	22,291	9.1	398,865	4.6	40,846
Harrison County, IA	7,252	7,335	8,056	-10.0	375	392	5.2	5.3	348	-4.9	2,956	-8.8	29,381
Mills County, IA	7,696	7,780	8,166	-5.8	340	353	4.4	4.5	290	20.8	2,123	-21.4	27,364
Pottawattamie County, IA	48,223	48,751	48,596	-0.8	2,507	2,598	5.2	5.3	1,998	4.7	30,824	6.0	30,041
Cass County, NE	13,553	13,352	14,019	-3.3	717	779	5.3	5.8	532	2.5	3,316	-17.1	29,385
Douglas County, NE	276,984	272,045	266,163	4.1	14,136	14,591	5.1	5.4	14,962	5.7	310,438	1.5	43,046
Sarpy County, NE	82,002	80,530	72,979	12.4	3,772	3,905	4.6	4.8	3,125	36.1	39,612	43.9	36,143
Saunders County, NE	11,112	10,922	11,156	-0.4	514	541	4.6	5.0	499	9.4	3,483	5.2	27,591
Washington County, NE	11,259	11,076	11,169	0.8	499	537	4.4	4.8	537	11.9	6,113	4.0	38,038
Orlando–Kissimmee–Sanford, FL	1,122,472	1,113,527	1,007,542	11.4	116,937	125,202	10.4	11.2	55,075	22.6	855,864	5.1	37,838
Lake County, FL	127,861	127,182	117,375	8.9	14,319	15,583	11.2	12.3	6,273	35.9	65,657	20.5	30,352
Orange County, FL	620,155	614,953	549,459	12.9	63,812	68,132	10.3	11.1	31,531	19.5	590,962	2.8	40,043
Osceola County, FL	136,698	135,544	115,507	18.3	15,832	16,747	11.6	12.4	4,821	44.0	59,493	23.8	28,785
Seminole County, FL	237,758	235,848	225,201	5.6	22,974	24,740	9.7	10.5	12,450	17.7	139,752	1.9	35,886
Oshkosh–Neenah, WI	96,133	96,268	91,625	4.9	6,322	7,085	6.6	7.4	3,602	-3.1	83,434	2.0	42,788
Winnebago County, WI	96,133	96,268	91,625	4.9	6,322	7,085	6.6	7.4	3,602	-3.1	83,434	2.0	42,788
Owensboro, KY	58,298	57,311	55,042	5.9	4,808	5,265	8.2	9.2	2,566	-5.6	44,551	-2.7	33,564
Daviess County, KY	49,493	48,630	46,259	7.0	4,035	4,399	8.2	9.0	2,269	-5.8	40,223	-2.5	32,166
Hancock County, KY	4,232	4,181	4,148	2.0	348	402	8.2	9.6	132	2.3	3,225	5.2	52,567
McLean County, KY	4,573	4,500	4,635	-1.3	425	464	9.3	10.3	165	-7.8	1,103	-24.6	28,971
Oxnard–Thousand Oaks–Ventura, CA	437,011	434,750	416,751	4.9	43,922	46,907	10.1	10.8	19,606	13.9	235,526	-1.0	45,848
Ventura County, CA	437,011	434,750	416,751	4.9	43,922	46,907	10.1	10.8	19,606	13.9	235,526	-1.0	45,848
Palm Bay–Melbourne–Titusville, FL	267,597	266,892	258,323	3.6	29,662	29,701	11.1	11.1	12,983	14.3	163,923	3.9	40,596
Brevard County, FL	267,597	266,892	258,323	3.6	29,662	29,701	11.1	11.1	12,983	14.3	163,923	3.9	40,596
Palm Coast, FL	34,022	33,637	29,733	14.4	4,813	5,079	14.1	15.1	1,743	66.8	14,790	47.6	27,436
Flagler County, FL	34,022	33,637	29,733	14.4	4,813	5,079	14.1	15.1	1,743	66.8	14,790	47.6	27,436
Panama City–Lynn Haven–Panama City Beach, FL	91,028	89,646	81,736	11.4	9,142	8,987	10.0	10.0	4,478	6.4	54,427	0.9	32,668
Bay County, FL	91,028	89,646	81,736	11.4	9,142	8,987	10.0	10.0	4,478	6.4	54,427	0.9	32,668
Parkersburg–Marietta–Vienna, WV–OH	76,499	77,314	79,786	-4.1	6,458	7,114	8.4	9.2	3,770	-8.2	56,456	-9.8	32,261
Washington County, OH	31,934	32,317	32,468	-1.6	2,615	2,903	8.2	9.0	1,459	-7.3	21,284	-8.5	34,382
Pleasants County, WV	3,151	3,182	3,234	-2.6	299	326	9.5	10.2	122	-10.3	2,107	16.3	40,075
Wirt County, WV	2,339	2,357	2,539	-7.9	257	272	11.0	11.5	70	-5.4	386	26.1	21,534
Wood County, WV	39,075	39,458	41,545	-5.9	3,287	3,613	8.4	9.2	2,119	-8.7	32,679	-12.1	30,503
Pascagoula, MS	73,653	73,781	70,986	3.8	8,412	7,234	11.4	9.8	2,603	-2.9	51,421	12.8	41,759
George County, MS	9,425	9,376	8,598	9.6	1,217	1,003	12.9	10.7	318	4.6	3,115	5.7	31,609
Jackson County, MS	64,228	64,405	62,388	2.9	7,195	6,231	11.2	9.7	2,285	-3.9	48,306	13.3	42,414
Pensacola–Ferry Pass–Brent, FL	213,691	210,796	201,472	6.1	20,837	20,990	9.8	10.0	9,083	6.5	115,893	-6.8	33,880
Escambia County, FL	140,603	138,714	134,568	4.5	14,194	14,303	10.1	10.3	6,618	0.5	95,298	-10.6	34,350
Santa Rosa County, FL	73,088	72,082	66,904	9.2	6,643	6,687	9.1	9.3	2,465	26.7	20,595	15.7	31,707
Peoria, IL	202,717	201,548	190,577	6.4	17,765	20,921	8.8	10.4	8,767	-0.7	161,610	-1.2	44,324
Marshall County, IL	7,046	6,968	7,096	-0.7	617	689	8.8	9.9	280	-5.7	2,965	2.3	27,382
Peoria County, IL	97,714	97,056	91,853	6.4	9,244	10,655	9.5	11.0	4,725	-2.4	106,050	-2.1	49,786
Stark County, IL	2,844	2,823	2,826	0.6	276	315	9.7	11.2	121	-8.3	906	-9.9	32,254
Tazewell County, IL	73,955	73,755	68,826	7.5	6,142	7,528	8.3	10.2	2,849	0.5	43,610	2.4	34,603
Woodford County, IL	21,158	20,946	19,976	5.9	1,486	1,734	7.0	8.3	792	9.1	8,079	-7.2	32,668
Philadelphia–Camden–Wilmington, PA–NJ–DE–MD	2,975,724	2,984,343	2,925,792	1.7	254,905	265,305	8.6	8.9	144,728	1.5	2,421,591	-3.8	50,025
Camden, NJ	667,424	670,897	650,647	2.6	65,320	67,387	9.8	10.0	27,986	-2.0	425,649	-2.3	43,832
Burlington County, NJ	241,524	242,714	238,628	1.2	21,452	22,128	8.9	9.1	10,395	0.7	173,658	-0.1	47,910
Camden County, NJ	267,945	269,200	263,493	1.7	28,376	29,072	10.6	10.8	11,750	-6.6	167,916	-8.7	42,833
Gloucester County, NJ	157,955	158,983	148,526	6.3	15,492	16,187	9.8	10.2	5,841	3.5	84,075	8.1	37,404
Philadelphia, PA	1,954,911	1,961,480	1,922,370	1.7	161,744	167,260	8.3	8.5	98,111	3.4	1,699,017	-3.4	51,180
Bucks County, PA	339,394	340,939	342,318	-0.9	24,767	26,127	7.3	7.7	18,821	5.7	241,568	-2.4	40,799
Chester County, PA	264,539	265,802	257,078	2.9	16,147	17,264	6.1	6.5	13,787	13.2	224,631	18.1	58,319
Delaware County, PA	278,454	279,474	280,099	-0.6	22,290	23,160	8.0	8.3	12,772	-4.0	201,536	-7.2	51,383
Montgomery County, PA	429,051	431,269	423,851	1.2	28,880	30,863	6.7	7.2	25,798	0.0	460,670	-7.3	53,973
Philadelphia County, PA	643,473	643,996	619,024	3.9	69,660	69,846	10.8	10.8	26,933	4.5	570,612	-5.9	50,438
Wilmington, DE–MD–NJ	353,389	351,966	352,775	0.2	27,841	30,658	7.9	8.7	18,631	-2.6	296,925	-7.8	52,294
New Castle County, DE	271,024	269,241	271,356	-0.1	19,913	21,774	7.3	8.1	15,655	-3.3	255,149	-9.6	53,706
Cecil County, MD	50,711	51,082	50,094	1.2	4,523	5,232	8.9	10.2	1,783	8.5	23,573	13.2	39,284
Salem County, NJ	31,654	31,643	31,325	1.1	3,405	3,652	10.8	11.5	1,193	-8.0	18,203	-4.3	49,355
Phoenix–Mesa–Glendale, AZ	2,034,992	2,074,050	1,926,885	5.6	174,225	202,468	8.6	9.8	87,723	18.5	1,453,359	5.4	43,299
Maricopa County, AZ	1,895,128	1,931,210	1,840,207	3.0	159,759	185,755	8.4	9.6	84,520	17.4	1,411,836	4.3	43,662
Pinal County, AZ	139,864	142,840	86,678	61.4	14,466	16,713	10.3	11.7	3,203	56.9	41,523	65.2	30,945
Pine Bluff, AR	44,344	44,325	46,316	-4.3	4,516	4,278	10.2	9.7	1,701	-9.2	25,697	-17.2	32,725
Cleveland County, AR	4,125	4,153	4,253	-3.0	327	334	7.9	8.0	81	-27.7	461	-41.6	24,907
Jefferson County, AR	35,085	35,018	36,839	-4.8	3,708	3,468	10.6	9.9	1,460	-8.9	23,682	-17.1	33,044
Lincoln County, AR	5,134	5,154	5,224	-1.7	481	476	9.4	9.2	160	0.0	1,554	-7.3	30,180

[1] Civilian unemployed as percent of total civilian labor force.
[2] For pay period including March 12 of the year shown.

Table C-4. Labor Force and Private Business Establishments and Employment—*Continued*

Metropolitan statistical area, division, and component county	Civilian labor force								Private nonfarm businesses				
	Total				Number of unemployed		Unemployment rate[1]		Establishments		Employment[2]		Annual payroll per employee 2010 (dollars)
	2011	2010	2005	Change, 2005–2011	2011	2010	2011	2010	2010	Change, 2000–2010	2010	Change, 2000–2010	
Pittsburgh, PA	1,231,920	1,222,273	1,200,458	2.6	89,154	95,684	7.2	7.8	59,240	-2.5	1,030,938	-2.5	42,185
Allegheny County, PA	647,620	642,263	629,960	2.8	45,084	48,256	7.0	7.5	33,347	-4.3	662,099	-4.2	45,277
Armstrong County, PA	33,588	33,404	33,002	1.8	2,806	3,058	8.4	9.2	1,273	-14.6	13,304	-20.2	31,316
Beaver County, PA	89,345	88,589	89,605	-0.3	6,640	7,055	7.4	8.0	3,458	-0.5	47,953	-3.3	33,818
Butler County, PA	99,627	98,817	95,137	4.7	6,661	7,167	6.7	7.3	4,642	9.1	73,914	16.7	37,309
Fayette County, PA	63,799	63,429	65,426	-2.5	5,956	6,405	9.3	10.1	2,742	-1.7	36,226	6.5	29,370
Washington County, PA	107,048	106,319	102,586	4.3	7,794	8,470	7.3	8.0	5,028	2.5	78,848	6.2	44,197
Westmoreland County, PA	190,893	189,452	184,742	3.3	14,213	15,273	7.4	8.1	8,750	-3.0	118,594	-7.7	35,138
Pittsfield, MA	72,397	72,663	72,646	-0.3	5,251	5,900	7.3	8.1	4,029	-8.1	53,706	-8.9	37,546
Berkshire County, MA	72,397	72,663	72,646	-0.3	5,251	5,900	7.3	8.1	4,029	-8.1	53,706	-8.9	37,546
Pocatello, ID	44,269	43,866	43,772	1.1	3,575	3,519	8.1	8.0	2,179	6.7	27,036	3.7	29,943
Bannock County, ID	40,635	40,259	40,029	1.5	3,241	3,184	8.0	7.9	2,018	6.5	24,888	3.2	29,758
Power County, ID	3,634	3,607	3,743	-2.9	334	335	9.2	9.3	161	8.1	2,148	9.2	32,085
Portland–South Portland–Biddeford, ME	289,671	288,500	283,960	2.0	18,381	20,298	6.3	7.0	17,331	6.8	218,155	1.2	39,231
Cumberland County, ME	159,436	158,498	154,545	3.2	9,566	10,313	6.0	6.5	10,900	5.7	154,313	2.8	41,034
Sagadahoc County, ME	19,114	19,144	18,407	3.8	1,256	1,301	6.6	6.8	949	21.0	13,362	-4.0	41,810
York County, ME	111,121	110,858	111,008	0.1	7,559	8,684	6.8	7.8	5,482	6.7	50,480	-2.1	33,039
Portland–Vancouver–Hillsboro, OR–WA	1,197,795	1,188,480	1,097,592	9.1	109,317	124,553	9.1	10.5	62,467	10.1	870,794	0.4	45,500
Clackamas County, OR	202,378	199,859	191,232	5.8	17,582	20,032	8.7	10.0	10,747	11.7	137,534	18.9	38,379
Columbia County, OR	24,818	24,603	23,340	6.3	2,567	2,950	10.3	12.0	952	12.5	6,915	-23.5	29,272
Multnomah County, OR	407,497	402,077	362,362	12.5	34,741	39,345	8.5	9.8	24,645	4.6	370,175	-8.6	46,328
Washington County, OR	294,403	290,348	269,807	9.1	22,600	25,854	7.7	8.9	14,150	13.7	219,441	2.3	53,433
Yamhill County, OR	49,399	48,779	44,285	11.5	4,552	5,138	9.2	10.5	2,286	12.1	27,728	15.1	32,534
Clark County, WA	214,130	217,611	201,564	6.2	26,630	30,545	12.4	14.0	9,497	18.2	107,740	10.0	40,170
Skamania County, WA	5,170	5,203	5,002	3.4	645	689	12.5	13.2	190	15.9	1,261	2.9	28,327
Port St. Lucie, FL	189,448	188,380	176,131	7.6	23,255	24,686	12.3	13.1	9,862	22.1	98,963	9.7	32,018
Martin County, FL	64,157	63,714	64,123	0.1	6,923	7,341	10.8	11.5	4,981	16.7	47,045	-3.3	33,804
St. Lucie County, FL	125,291	124,666	112,008	11.9	16,332	17,345	13.0	13.9	4,881	28.2	51,918	24.9	30,399
Poughkeepsie–Newburgh–Middletown, NY	319,135	322,256	324,911	-1.8	24,401	25,925	7.6	8.0	16,653	12.2	199,476	7.8	40,292
Dutchess County, NY	145,180	146,520	147,143	-1.3	10,795	11,407	7.4	7.8	7,440	10.0	96,409	5.9	45,247
Orange County, NY	173,955	175,736	177,768	-2.1	13,606	14,518	7.8	8.3	9,213	14.1	103,067	9.7	35,656
Prescott, AZ	91,959	95,773	90,659	1.4	9,175	10,490	10.0	11.0	5,639	13.1	50,830	10.3	30,036
Yavapai County, AZ	91,959	95,773	90,659	1.4	9,175	10,490	10.0	11.0	5,639	13.1	50,830	10.3	30,036
Providence–New Bedford–Fall River, RI–MA	853,585	861,739	849,194	0.5	92,559	98,676	10.8	11.5	41,236	-1.2	590,501	(D)	41,415
Bristol County, MA	290,171	291,438	287,754	0.8	29,160	31,952	10.0	11.0	12,804	-3.1	192,766	-5.1	39,871
Bristol County, RI	26,966	27,270	28,038	-3.8	2,607	2,744	9.7	10.1	1,230	8.8	13,144	(D)	28,503
Kent County, RI	94,995	96,468	95,739	-0.8	10,180	11,070	10.7	11.5	4,817	-2.2	68,851	-4.0	39,654
Newport County, RI	44,817	45,251	44,291	1.2	4,612	4,769	10.3	10.5	2,758	2.1	28,719	0.6	38,389
Providence County, RI	324,175	327,918	320,833	1.0	39,124	40,907	12.1	12.5	15,836	-2.7	247,734	-6.0	44,187
Washington County, RI	72,461	73,394	72,539	-0.1	6,876	7,234	9.5	9.9	3,791	8.4	39,287	9.5	41,131
Provo–Orem, UT	222,864	225,371	210,888	5.7	14,600	17,933	6.6	8.0	10,807	48.5	155,079	7.6	33,856
Juab County, UT	4,101	4,136	3,951	3.8	363	413	8.9	10.0	182	23.0	2,110	20.7	26,991
UT County, UT	218,763	221,235	206,937	5.7	14,237	17,520	6.5	7.9	10,625	49.1	152,969	7.5	33,951
Pueblo, CO	76,538	75,966	70,012	9.3	7,841	7,944	10.2	10.5	3,155	-1.0	46,849	-3.1	34,337
Pueblo County, CO	76,538	75,966	70,012	9.3	7,841	7,944	10.2	10.5	3,155	-1.0	46,849	-3.1	34,337
Punta Gorda, FL	70,507	70,376	65,546	7.6	7,587	8,408	10.8	11.9	3,525	14.7	36,934	16.6	27,429
Charlotte County, FL	70,507	70,376	65,546	7.6	7,587	8,408	10.8	11.9	3,525	14.7	36,934	16.6	27,429
Racine, WI	98,241	98,743	99,006	-0.8	8,784	9,957	8.9	10.1	4,049	-2.4	64,177	-12.6	39,180
Racine County, WI	98,241	98,743	99,006	-0.8	8,784	9,957	8.9	10.1	4,049	-2.4	64,177	-12.6	39,180
Raleigh–Cary, NC	582,685	573,809	504,815	15.4	50,023	51,406	8.6	9.0	28,933	21.7	410,617	10.8	43,539
Franklin County, NC	28,622	28,151	26,200	9.2	2,939	2,963	10.3	10.5	921	21.8	9,288	14.0	36,660
Johnston County, NC	80,490	79,363	71,455	12.6	7,730	8,004	9.6	10.1	3,094	20.8	35,795	20.8	31,081
Wake County, NC	473,573	466,295	407,160	16.3	39,354	40,439	8.3	8.7	24,918	21.8	365,534	9.9	44,933
Rapid City, SD	67,399	66,713	65,167	3.4	3,205	3,524	4.8	5.3	4,228	13.3	48,551	3.7	32,851
Meade County, SD	12,713	12,597	12,706	0.1	642	715	5.0	5.7	671	29.3	5,011	7.7	38,932
Pennington County, SD	54,686	54,116	52,461	4.2	2,563	2,809	4.7	5.2	3,557	10.7	43,540	3.2	32,151
Reading, PA	204,817	204,290	199,318	2.8	16,829	18,309	8.2	9.0	8,285	1.6	142,598	-4.2	40,078
Berks County, PA	204,817	204,290	199,318	2.8	16,829	18,309	8.2	9.0	8,285	1.6	142,598	-4.2	40,078
Redding, CA	83,452	84,437	81,918	1.9	12,272	13,285	14.7	15.7	4,323	-3.2	46,780	1.4	33,535
Shasta County, CA	83,452	84,437	81,918	1.9	12,272	13,285	14.7	15.7	4,323	-3.2	46,780	1.4	33,535
Reno–Sparks, NV	226,515	228,344	211,526	7.1	29,608	29,880	13.1	13.1	11,799	5.2	165,777	-2.4	39,414
Storey County, NV	2,237	2,263	2,275	-1.7	314	325	14.0	14.4	86	10.3	371	-20.0	21,229
Washoe County, NV	224,278	226,081	209,251	7.2	29,294	29,555	13.1	13.1	11,713	5.2	165,406	-2.3	39,455

[1] Civilian unemployed as percent of total civilian labor force.
[2] For pay period including March 12 of the year shown.

Table C-4.   Labor Force and Private Business Establishments and Employment—*Continued*

Metropolitan statistical area, division, and component county	Civilian labor force								Private nonfarm businesses				Annual payroll per employee 2010 (dollars)
	Total				Number of unemployed		Unemployment rate[1]		Establishments		Employment[2]		
	2011	2010	2005	Change, 2005–2011	2011	2010	2011	2010	2010	Change, 2000–2010	2010	Change, 2000–2010	
Richmond, VA	675,378	668,241	619,645	9.0	46,864	51,890	6.9	7.8	31,037	8.3	477,439	-3.9	44,152
Amelia County, VA	6,697	6,633	6,357	5.3	463	519	6.9	7.8	286	12.6	1,866	7.1	28,032
Caroline County, VA	14,863	14,747	12,942	14.8	1,176	1,325	7.9	9.0	384	5.5	3,780	27.1	35,846
Charles City County, VA	3,944	3,927	3,781	4.3	325	378	8.2	9.6	139	7.8	1,184	-18.2	34,425
Chesterfield County, VA	177,154	175,114	159,633	11.0	10,855	12,034	6.1	6.9	6,794	23.6	96,097	17.3	38,641
Cumberland County, VA	4,880	4,820	4,480	8.9	348	375	7.1	7.8	147	11.4	844	6.0	27,831
Dinwiddie County, VA	14,162	14,014	12,673	11.7	952	1,060	6.7	7.6	367	46.8	4,123	-15.1	37,975
Goochland County, VA	11,837	11,728	10,410	13.7	630	738	5.3	6.3	624	45.1	10,999	232.1	70,223
Hanover County, VA	55,837	55,174	53,857	3.7	3,225	3,580	5.8	6.5	3,014	12.6	39,376	15.2	34,532
Henrico County, VA	174,249	172,187	157,494	10.6	10,629	11,733	6.1	6.8	8,700	20.6	155,199	4.6	48,281
King and Queen County, VA	3,418	3,398	3,284	4.1	252	293	7.4	8.6	107	3.9	899	58.0	38,860
King William County, VA	8,752	8,636	7,962	9.9	588	630	6.7	7.3	334	7.7	2,853	-10.4	38,372
Louisa County, VA	17,080	16,945	15,197	12.4	1,195	1,367	7.0	8.1	550	11.8	6,381	52.4	44,631
New Kent County, VA	10,312	10,217	8,846	16.6	661	753	6.4	7.4	335	26.9	2,561	16.1	29,201
Powhatan County, VA	14,584	14,454	13,594	7.3	841	977	5.8	6.8	645	38.7	3,917	-24.2	31,354
Prince George County, VA	14,823	14,566	15,121	-2.0	1,015	1,026	6.8	7.0	439	23.3	6,354	44.4	34,031
Sussex County, VA	4,515	4,507	4,434	1.8	409	480	9.1	10.7	193	-1.5	2,208	-24.6	27,795
Colonial Heights city, VA	9,205	9,102	9,116	1.0	700	762	7.6	8.4	702	7.2	9,564	-6.1	23,131
Hopewell city, VA	10,657	10,515	10,338	3.1	1,130	1,172	10.6	11.1	464	-2.7	6,562	-19.1	41,852
Petersburg city, VA	14,473	14,366	14,044	3.1	1,767	1,906	12.2	13.3	740	-15.8	12,125	-13.7	34,399
Richmond city, VA	103,936	103,191	96,082	8.2	9,703	10,782	9.3	10.4	6,073	-19.1	110,547	-31.9	49,891
Riverside–San Bernardino–Ontario, CA......	1,799,005	1,798,152	1,707,382	5.4	241,248	257,677	13.4	14.3	65,024	21.2	957,326	11.5	35,002
Riverside County, CA	938,434	937,496	854,252	9.9	127,818	135,873	13.6	14.5	33,546	26.3	456,308	16.2	34,121
San Bernardino County, CA..........	860,571	860,656	853,130	0.9	113,430	121,804	13.2	14.2	31,478	16.2	501,018	7.6	35,805
Roanoke, VA	161,691	160,946	150,388	7.5	10,721	11,977	6.6	7.4	8,189	0.4	132,266	-5.0	37,360
Botetourt County, VA	17,967	17,875	17,126	4.9	997	1,130	5.5	6.3	743	27.2	8,763	38.0	36,400
Craig County, VA	2,598	2,569	2,516	3.3	196	199	7.5	7.7	59	0.0	387	12.8	23,948
Franklin County, VA	28,987	28,955	25,498	13.7	1,918	2,245	6.6	7.8	1,131	18.6	11,088	-1.1	28,089
Roanoke County, VA	49,882	49,621	46,937	6.3	2,771	3,134	5.6	6.3	2,102	47.0	30,386	29.6	35,891
Roanoke city, VA	49,136	48,848	45,508	8.0	4,026	4,336	8.2	8.9	3,190	-23.6	63,018	-16.3	38,908
Salem city, VA	13,121	13,078	12,803	2.5	813	933	6.2	7.1	964	0.4	18,624	-17.7	40,770
Rochester, MN	103,734	104,137	101,939	1.8	5,654	6,438	5.5	6.2	4,400	8.7	85,832	-0.9	41,035
Dodge County, MN......................	11,116	11,174	11,159	-0.4	677	776	6.1	6.9	421	1.9	4,059	0.4	37,130
Olmsted County, MN...................	80,730	81,003	78,200	3.2	4,272	4,842	5.3	6.0	3,397	13.5	76,039	1.0	42,106
Wabasha County, MN...................	11,888	11,960	12,580	-5.5	705	820	5.9	6.9	582	-9.6	5,734	-21.6	29,597
Rochester, NY	521,338	526,495	535,551	-2.7	39,917	42,913	7.7	8.2	23,539	2.4	415,085	-6.4	39,622
Livingston County, NY	32,087	32,469	32,909	-2.5	2,505	2,755	7.8	8.5	1,254	1.2	12,688	1.2	29,363
Monroe County, NY	366,795	370,245	376,737	-2.6	27,783	29,710	7.6	8.0	17,088	1.5	331,991	-8.5	41,151
Ontario County, NY	56,182	56,672	56,883	-1.2	4,050	4,306	7.2	7.6	2,793	9.3	42,510	7.5	35,192
Orleans County, NY	19,056	19,316	19,983	-4.6	1,747	1,929	9.2	10.0	671	-1.9	8,202	11.3	29,499
Wayne County, NY	47,218	47,793	49,039	-3.7	3,832	4,213	8.1	8.8	1,733	3.6	19,694	-6.6	34,226
Rockford, IL	168,067	170,905	164,702	2.0	21,600	26,377	12.9	15.4	7,507	-3.1	126,265	-14.3	37,852
Boone County, IL........................	26,123	26,520	24,474	6.7	3,519	4,215	13.5	15.9	855	21.8	11,363	-2.4	38,413
Winnebago County, IL..................	141,944	144,385	140,228	1.2	18,081	22,162	12.7	15.3	6,652	-5.6	114,902	-15.3	37,797
Rocky Mount, NC	72,199	72,480	68,975	4.7	10,133	10,116	14.0	14.0	3,001	-7.9	49,574	-14.5	33,349
Edgecombe County, NC	25,620	25,686	24,425	4.9	4,064	4,026	15.9	15.7	805	-15.6	14,184	-17.4	33,459
Nash County, NC	46,579	46,794	44,550	4.6	6,069	6,090	13.0	13.0	2,196	-4.8	35,390	-13.2	33,305
Rome, GA..................................	47,590	48,352	50,469	-5.7	5,189	5,201	10.9	10.8	1,981	-1.7	33,956	-10.5	33,002
Floyd County, GA........................	47,590	48,352	50,469	-5.7	5,189	5,201	10.9	10.8	1,981	-1.7	33,956	-10.5	33,002
Sacramento—Arden-Arcade—													
Roseville, CA	1,039,429	1,048,855	1,013,921	2.5	123,238	130,898	11.9	12.5	44,514	10.2	621,068	1.2	43,038
El Dorado County, CA..................	90,962	91,841	91,224	-0.3	10,710	11,435	11.8	12.5	4,261	7.7	41,027	7.4	36,759
Placer County, CA	175,078	176,733	164,557	6.4	18,895	20,248	10.8	11.5	9,309	27.6	118,322	26.0	44,469
Sacramento County, CA	675,639	681,970	665,605	1.5	81,541	86,727	12.1	12.7	27,140	5.5	404,195	-4.6	43,586
Yolo County, CA	97,750	98,311	92,535	5.6	12,092	12,488	12.4	12.7	3,804	11.1	57,524	0.2	40,718
Saginaw–Saginaw Township North, MI.......	90,082	91,185	98,275	-8.3	8,689	10,852	9.6	11.9	4,494	-10.5	74,032	-20.1	35,195
Saginaw County, MI	90,082	91,185	98,275	-8.3	8,689	10,852	9.6	11.9	4,494	-10.5	74,032	-20.1	35,195
St. Cloud, MN.............................	107,920	107,503	102,711	5.1	6,948	8,010	6.4	7.5	5,236	11.6	89,360	7.2	35,617
Benton County, MN	22,363	22,327	22,146	1.0	1,596	1,864	7.1	8.3	905	20.5	13,981	22.7	32,095
Stearns County, MN	85,557	85,176	80,565	6.2	5,352	6,146	6.3	7.2	4,331	9.9	75,379	4.8	36,270
St. George, UT	56,873	58,635	57,443	-1.0	4,907	6,094	8.6	10.4	3,816	52.0	35,996	35.1	28,485
Washington County, UT	56,873	58,635	57,443	-1.0	4,907	6,094	8.6	10.4	3,816	52.0	35,996	35.1	28,485
St. Joseph, MO–KS......................	72,089	71,476	64,885	11.1	5,316	5,874	7.4	8.2	3,259	10.5	48,746	13.6	33,203
Doniphan County, KS	4,765	4,751	4,436	7.4	383	427	8.0	9.0	163	-9.9	1,162	-43.2	34,772
Andrew County, MO	10,633	10,562	9,812	8.4	665	772	6.3	7.3	342	41.3	1,759	-23.0	27,443
Buchanan County, MO	51,005	50,541	45,572	11.9	3,797	4,175	7.4	8.3	2,524	8.1	43,945	18.5	33,652
DeKalb County, MO	5,686	5,622	5,065	12.3	471	500	8.3	8.9	230	19.8	1,880	26.0	27,131

[1] Civilian unemployed as percent of total civilian labor force.
[2] For pay period including March 12 of the year shown.

Table C-4.   Labor Force and Private Business Establishments and Employment—*Continued*

Metropolitan statistical area, division, and component county	Civilian labor force								Private nonfarm businesses				Annual payroll per employee 2010 (dollars)
	Total				Number of unemployed		Unemployment rate[1]		Establishments		Employment[2]		
	2011	2010	2005	Change, 2005–2011	2011	2010	2011	2010	2010	Change, 2000–2010	2010	Change, 2000–2010	
St. Louis, MO–IL[5]	1,449,770	1,448,329	1,436,530	0.9	129,043	142,252	8.9	9.8	70,361	3.1	1,169,641	-4.5	42,923
Bond County, IL	8,435	8,436	8,441	-0.1	780	852	9.2	10.1	325	-7.7	3,855	-7.8	28,058
Calhoun County, IL	2,548	2,540	2,547	0.0	264	277	10.4	10.9	97	-11.0	604	-13.3	22,104
Clinton County, IL	19,416	19,279	18,460	5.2	1,550	1,578	8.0	8.2	870	5.8	8,854	9.2	27,516
Jersey County, IL	11,846	11,740	11,438	3.6	1,105	1,098	9.3	9.4	454	8.9	4,742	2.2	24,489
Macoupin County, IL	24,013	23,969	24,331	-1.3	2,396	2,552	10.0	10.6	953	-11.0	8,865	-14.8	29,538
Madison County, IL	138,131	138,104	134,600	2.6	12,494	13,627	9.0	9.9	5,970	2.8	83,947	-1.6	37,144
Monroe County, IL	18,315	18,238	17,203	6.5	1,355	1,434	7.4	7.9	785	19.1	7,345	17.7	34,429
St. Clair County, IL	127,085	126,769	120,914	5.1	13,056	13,793	10.3	10.9	5,455	0.4	78,526	4.3	33,827
Franklin County, MO	53,501	53,698	52,527	1.9	4,999	5,762	9.3	10.7	2,625	8.5	30,761	-3.3	31,054
Jefferson County, MO	117,808	117,978	115,913	1.6	10,440	11,864	8.9	10.1	4,065	16.4	39,509	10.7	30,061
Lincoln County, MO	27,224	27,239	24,546	10.9	2,771	3,072	10.2	11.3	900	18.4	7,831	13.1	30,595
St. Charles County, MO	201,263	201,160	186,396	8.0	14,709	16,785	7.3	8.3	7,960	27.3	112,751	18.0	34,551
St. Louis County, MO	526,916	525,700	536,250	-1.7	43,217	47,651	8.2	9.1	29,730	-1.4	544,168	-7.3	47,746
Warren County, MO	17,269	17,360	15,356	12.5	1,555	1,829	9.0	10.5	567	2.0	5,810	-2.6	29,823
Washington County, MO	10,424	10,468	10,013	4.1	1,256	1,407	12.0	13.4	370	16.0	2,923	-0.1	25,328
St. Louis city, MO	145,576	145,651	157,595	-7.6	17,096	18,671	11.7	12.8	9,235	-4.2	229,150	-13.1	47,684
Salem, OR	197,534	198,774	184,403	7.1	19,533	21,170	9.9	10.7	8,994	4.7	107,154	-0.2	31,491
Marion County, OR	158,269	159,378	148,651	6.5	16,104	17,530	10.2	11.0	7,668	2.9	96,142	1.6	32,012
Polk County, OR	39,265	39,396	35,752	9.8	3,429	3,640	8.7	9.2	1,326	16.0	11,012	-13.9	26,937
Salinas, CA	222,857	220,933	206,975	7.7	27,648	27,974	12.4	12.7	8,336	-2.8	96,387	-8.3	40,580
Monterey County, CA	222,857	220,933	206,975	7.7	27,648	27,974	12.4	12.7	8,336	-2.8	96,387	-8.3	40,580
Salisbury, MD	64,243	64,340	63,618	1.0	5,905	6,323	9.2	9.8	2,911	-1.0	39,241	-3.1	34,976
Somerset County, MD	11,004	11,092	11,522	-4.5	1,139	1,282	10.4	11.6	383	-5.4	3,757	18.5	36,540
Wicomico County, MD	53,239	53,248	52,096	2.2	4,766	5,041	9.0	9.5	2,528	-0.2	35,484	-4.9	34,810
Salt Lake City, UT	595,346	605,220	569,029	4.6	38,968	47,218	6.5	7.8	31,549	13.1	526,157	4.6	41,090
Salt Lake County, UT	546,055	555,071	521,997	4.6	35,745	43,272	6.5	7.8	28,784	11.0	492,702	2.5	41,777
Summit County, UT	21,537	21,926	21,645	-0.5	1,306	1,636	6.1	7.5	2,021	35.6	23,039	49.2	27,315
Tooele County, UT	27,754	28,223	25,387	9.3	1,917	2,310	6.9	8.2	744	59.7	10,416	60.7	39,064
San Angelo, TX	56,119	55,415	52,927	6.0	3,510	3,560	6.3	6.4	2,637	0.1	36,370	3.8	30,511
Irion County, TX	873	856	960	-9.1	48	42	5.5	4.9	47	11.9	278	9.4	36,849
Tom Green County, TX	55,246	54,559	51,967	6.3	3,462	3,518	6.3	6.4	2,590	-0.1	36,092	3.8	30,462
San Antonio–New Braunfels, TX	1,012,444	1,002,240	896,888	12.9	75,319	74,263	7.4	7.4	40,324	12.7	718,175	12.6	37,353
Atascosa County, TX	19,758	19,572	19,057	3.7	1,567	1,558	7.9	8.0	629	15.4	6,478	9.5	28,731
Bandera County, TX	9,870	9,808	9,689	1.9	676	703	6.8	7.2	360	12.1	2,010	21.0	22,095
Bexar County, TX	804,768	796,464	715,837	12.4	60,889	59,847	7.6	7.5	32,493	9.0	628,964	10.0	38,131
Comal County, TX	55,012	54,479	48,948	12.4	3,810	3,777	6.9	6.9	2,806	36.9	35,340	41.5	32,743
Guadalupe County, TX	65,583	64,993	51,826	26.5	4,388	4,396	6.7	6.8	1,780	31.0	25,211	31.9	32,617
Kendall County, TX	16,590	16,408	14,334	15.7	1,034	1,004	6.2	6.1	1,090	50.1	10,099	62.9	37,403
Medina County, TX	20,725	20,526	19,467	6.5	1,535	1,523	7.4	7.4	639	11.3	5,298	8.0	25,498
Wilson County, TX	20,138	19,990	17,730	13.6	1,420	1,455	7.1	7.3	527	34.8	4,775	53.1	25,165
San Diego–Carlsbad–San Marcos, CA	1,583,807	1,572,611	1,492,594	6.1	157,704	165,550	10.0	10.5	75,794	11.6	1,101,324	4.7	47,193
San Diego County, CA	1,583,807	1,572,611	1,492,594	6.1	157,704	165,550	10.0	10.5	75,794	11.6	1,101,324	4.7	47,193
Sandusky, OH	42,202	42,198	42,645	-1.0	3,665	4,382	8.7	10.4	1,891	-7.3	28,166	-14.8	34,717
Erie County, OH	42,202	42,198	42,645	-1.0	3,665	4,382	8.7	10.4	1,891	-7.3	28,166	-14.8	34,717
San Francisco–Oakland–Fremont, CA	2,263,171	2,249,025	2,150,963	5.2	213,284	231,037	9.4	10.3	117,723	-2.3	1,767,793	-11.9	64,785
Oakland–Fremont–Hayward, CA	1,284,987	1,284,579	1,246,524	3.1	133,354	143,941	10.4	11.2	57,937	-0.9	855,987	-11.9	56,936
Alameda County, CA	760,931	761,264	735,682	3.4	78,903	85,747	10.4	11.3	36,036	-1.0	562,649	-14.2	56,889
Contra Costa County, CA	524,056	523,315	510,842	2.6	54,451	58,194	10.4	11.1	21,901	-0.7	293,338	-7.1	57,025
San Francisco–San Mateo– Redwood City, CA	978,184	964,626	904,439	8.2	79,930	87,096	8.2	9.0	59,786	-3.7	911,806	-11.9	72,155
Marin County, CA	135,339	133,128	129,333	4.6	9,985	10,666	7.4	8.0	9,528	-7.1	92,752	-12.7	53,606
San Francisco County, CA	462,530	456,589	414,134	11.7	39,811	43,623	8.6	9.6	30,589	-2.6	490,701	-11.7	74,190
San Mateo County, CA	380,315	374,909	360,972	5.4	30,134	32,807	7.9	8.8	19,669	-3.6	328,353	-11.9	74,353
San Jose–Sunnyvale–Santa Clara, CA	922,617	906,847	841,504	9.6	91,040	101,229	9.9	11.2	45,032	-3.4	857,032	-15.2	85,079
San Benito County, CA	26,391	26,044	24,550	7.5	4,140	4,487	15.7	17.2	912	-5.5	9,980	-7.4	35,227
Santa Clara County, CA	896,226	880,803	816,954	9.7	86,900	96,742	9.7	11.0	44,120	-3.4	847,052	-15.3	85,666
San Luis Obispo–Paso Robles, CA	138,650	138,182	131,725	5.3	12,854	13,668	9.3	9.9	7,778	12.0	80,564	9.4	35,490
San Luis Obispo County, CA	138,650	138,182	131,725	5.3	12,854	13,668	9.3	9.9	7,778	12.0	80,564	9.4	35,490
Santa Barbara–Santa Maria–Goleta, CA	225,635	222,380	213,600	5.6	19,851	20,814	8.8	9.4	11,207	3.0	134,494	-4.1	44,565
Santa Barbara County, CA	225,635	222,380	213,600	5.6	19,851	20,814	8.8	9.4	11,207	3.0	134,494	-4.1	44,565
Santa Cruz–Watsonville, CA	150,740	149,934	143,273	5.2	18,226	18,914	12.1	12.6	6,781	-2.7	68,106	-14.1	41,937
Santa Cruz County, CA	150,740	149,934	143,273	5.2	18,226	18,914	12.1	12.6	6,781	-2.7	68,106	-14.1	41,937
Santa Fe, NM	74,644	75,805	76,305	-2.2	4,489	4,926	6.0	6.5	4,778	2.3	44,097	-1.3	37,180
Santa Fe County, NM	74,644	75,805	76,305	-2.2	4,489	4,926	6.0	6.5	4,778	2.3	44,097	-1.3	37,180

[1] Civilian unemployed as percent of total civilian labor force.
[2] For pay period including March 12 of the year shown.
[5] The portion of Sullivan city in Crawford County, MO is legally part of the St. Louis, MO–IL MSA. That portion is not included in these figures for the St. Louis, MSA.

Table C-4. Labor Force and Private Business Establishments and Employment—*Continued*

Metropolitan statistical area, division, and component county	Civilian labor force								Private nonfarm businesses				
	Total				Number of unemployed		Unemployment rate[1]		Establishments		Employment[2]		Annual payroll per employee 2010 (dollars)
	2011	2010	2005	Change, 2005–2011	2011	2010	2011	2010	2010	Change, 2000–2010	2010	Change, 2000–2010	
Santa Rosa–Petaluma, CA	257,279	256,053	253,887	1.3	25,136	26,767	9.8	10.5	13,186	-1.7	143,053	-12.2	43,501
Sonoma County, CA	257,279	256,053	253,887	1.3	25,136	26,767	9.8	10.5	13,186	-1.7	143,053	-12.2	43,501
Savannah, GA	175,569	174,889	166,572	5.4	15,779	15,956	9.0	9.1	8,380	11.5	125,822	8.8	35,846
Bryan County, GA	15,459	15,478	15,384	0.5	1,278	1,373	8.3	8.9	584	46.7	5,469	73.5	25,523
Chatham County, GA	132,848	132,099	125,404	5.9	12,231	12,129	9.2	9.2	7,099	7.2	113,589	6.0	36,338
Effingham County, GA	27,262	27,312	25,784	5.7	2,270	2,454	8.3	9.0	697	39.7	6,764	26.4	35,935
Scranton–Wilkes–Barre, PA	281,504	281,780	277,870	1.3	26,175	26,889	9.3	9.5	13,345	-2.7	226,262	-1.2	32,816
Lackawanna County, PA	107,096	106,900	105,644	1.4	9,755	9,726	9.1	9.1	5,372	-0.9	95,796	2.6	31,420
Luzerne County, PA	160,117	160,670	157,917	1.4	15,077	15,879	9.4	9.9	7,326	-4.4	122,286	-4.0	33,609
Wyoming County, PA	14,291	14,210	14,309	-0.1	1,343	1,284	9.4	9.0	647	2.5	8,180	-0.2	37,311
Seattle–Tacoma–Bellevue, WA	1,878,163	1,886,638	1,726,969	8.8	163,248	182,170	8.7	9.7	96,771	6.7	1,435,764	-0.7	55,035
Seattle–Bellevue–Everett, WA	1,490,919	1,494,197	1,359,706	9.7	125,312	141,987	8.4	9.5	80,182	6.7	1,212,145	-2.1	58,070
King County, WA	1,105,546	1,107,058	1,012,944	9.1	89,579	101,058	8.1	9.1	63,149	5.6	999,263	-3.3	60,803
Snohomish County, WA	385,373	387,139	346,762	11.1	35,733	40,929	9.3	10.6	17,033	11.2	212,882	4.0	45,243
Tacoma, WA	387,244	392,441	367,263	5.4	37,936	40,183	9.8	10.2	16,589	6.7	223,619	7.4	38,587
Pierce County, WA	387,244	392,441	367,263	5.4	37,936	40,183	9.8	10.2	16,589	6.7	223,619	7.4	38,587
Sebastian–Vero Beach, FL	63,290	62,474	58,988	7.3	7,977	8,476	12.6	13.6	3,868	12.1	37,302	-3.4	32,989
Indian River County, FL	63,290	62,474	58,988	7.3	7,977	8,476	12.6	13.6	3,868	12.1	37,302	-3.4	32,989
Sheboygan, WI	62,208	63,622	64,857	-4.1	4,724	5,657	7.6	8.9	2,681	3.0	50,582	-11.6	37,091
Sheboygan County, WI	62,208	63,622	64,857	-4.1	4,724	5,657	7.6	8.9	2,681	3.0	50,582	-11.6	37,091
Sherman–Denison, TX	58,711	57,955	56,552	3.8	4,871	4,884	8.3	8.4	2,521	-2.3	38,858	-1.7	33,093
Grayson County, TX	58,711	57,955	56,552	3.8	4,871	4,884	8.3	8.4	2,521	-2.3	38,858	-1.7	33,093
Shreveport–Bossier City, LA	183,763	184,347	180,920	1.6	12,430	12,887	6.8	7.0	9,161	6.9	146,359	2.2	34,683
Bossier Parish, LA	55,494	55,559	51,661	7.4	3,149	3,175	5.7	5.7	2,405	22.2	35,239	14.6	29,476
Caddo Parish, LA	116,978	117,442	117,823	-0.7	8,404	8,787	7.2	7.5	6,357	1.6	106,704	-1.3	36,055
De Soto Parish, LA	11,291	11,346	11,436	-1.3	877	925	7.8	8.2	399	15.3	4,416	2.3	43,091
Sioux City, IA–NE–SD	77,457	78,583	74,466	4.0	4,512	5,288	5.8	6.7	3,776	-3.2	65,859	-8.7	32,251
Woodbury County, IA	54,539	55,705	53,260	2.4	3,240	3,764	5.9	6.8	2,756	-6.0	46,488	-2.2	30,863
Dakota County, NE	11,470	11,467	10,534	8.9	726	913	6.3	8.0	431	-2.5	10,078	-7.4	34,422
Dixon County, NE	3,207	3,156	3,145	2.0	153	155	4.8	4.9	113	-10.3	1,053	49.6	30,556
Union County, SD	8,241	8,255	7,527	9.5	393	456	4.8	5.5	476	19.0	8,240	-36.4	37,641
Sioux Falls, SD	130,242	128,421	120,283	8.3	5,778	6,502	4.4	5.1	7,026	13.4	122,755	14.9	37,637
Lincoln County, SD	25,427	25,030	19,262	32.0	960	1,063	3.8	4.2	1,122	85.1	10,954	110.4	36,058
McCook County, SD	2,761	2,728	2,955	-6.6	126	147	4.6	5.4	175	-1.7	891	-30.0	24,481
Minnehaha County, SD	97,733	96,401	93,563	4.5	4,511	5,085	4.6	5.3	5,477	6.6	109,168	10.6	38,050
Turner County, SD	4,321	4,262	4,503	-4.0	181	207	4.2	4.9	252	-8.0	1,742	6.2	28,428
South Bend–Mishawaka, IN–MI	154,254	153,043	161,757	-4.6	15,276	17,270	9.9	11.3	6,721	-8.9	117,316	-12.6	35,607
St. Joseph County, IN	128,868	127,611	134,110	-3.9	13,053	14,550	10.1	11.4	5,959	-9.1	110,434	-11.7	35,903
Cass County, MI	25,386	25,432	27,647	-8.2	2,223	2,720	8.8	10.7	762	-7.1	6,882	-24.5	30,870
Spartanburg, SC	132,077	133,290	131,300	0.6	13,768	15,374	10.4	11.5	6,338	0.9	108,393	-11.1	38,303
Spartanburg County, SC	132,077	133,290	131,300	0.6	13,768	15,374	10.4	11.5	6,338	0.9	108,393	-11.1	38,303
Spokane, WA	230,985	235,966	223,009	3.6	21,784	23,274	9.4	9.9	12,363	5.8	172,951	2.8	36,984
Spokane County, WA	230,985	235,966	223,009	3.6	21,784	23,274	9.4	9.9	12,363	5.8	172,951	2.8	36,984
Springfield, IL	116,567	116,591	111,802	4.3	8,983	9,490	7.7	8.1	5,365	-4.4	83,181	-2.6	36,854
Menard County, IL	7,076	7,074	6,963	1.6	533	560	7.5	7.9	225	-8.9	1,425	1.7	28,909
Sangamon County, IL	109,491	109,517	104,839	4.4	8,450	8,930	7.7	8.2	5,140	-4.2	81,756	-2.7	36,992
Springfield, MA	350,151	352,004	351,472	-0.4	28,348	31,447	8.1	8.9	14,840	-12.6	238,379	-5.4	37,004
Franklin County, MA	38,558	38,865	39,568	-2.6	2,598	3,026	6.7	7.8	1,590	-11.6	19,387	-21.7	35,789
Hampden County, MA	223,728	224,959	224,100	-0.2	20,558	22,546	9.2	10.0	9,709	-16.3	163,812	-9.6	39,322
Hampshire County, MA	87,865	88,180	87,804	0.1	5,192	5,875	5.9	6.7	3,541	-1.3	55,180	19.9	30,549
Springfield, MO	223,531	222,815	212,649	5.1	17,240	18,925	7.7	8.5	11,219	8.4	163,422	-0.4	31,970
Christian County, MO	41,095	40,935	37,365	10.0	3,086	3,368	7.5	8.2	1,605	33.2	12,388	10.9	25,225
Dallas County, MO	7,395	7,412	7,454	-0.8	753	847	10.2	11.4	253	-7.3	2,466	-11.5	17,519
Greene County, MO	143,790	143,200	137,138	4.9	10,704	11,664	7.4	8.1	8,141	6.4	136,859	-0.2	33,390
Polk County, MO	14,525	14,467	13,974	3.9	1,298	1,394	8.9	9.6	575	-3.0	6,836	-10.9	25,781
Webster County, MO	16,726	16,801	16,718	0.0	1,399	1,652	8.4	9.8	645	3.7	4,873	-8.8	25,257
Springfield, OH	68,988	69,556	70,204	-1.7	6,152	7,221	8.9	10.4	2,449	-9.6	40,682	-20.3	30,820
Clark County, OH	68,988	69,556	70,204	-1.7	6,152	7,221	8.9	10.4	2,449	-9.6	40,682	-20.3	30,820
State College, PA	75,959	75,799	72,608	4.6	4,293	4,674	5.7	6.2	3,189	2.0	43,058	-7.9	32,460
Centre County, PA	75,959	75,799	72,608	4.6	4,293	4,674	5.7	6.2	3,189	2.0	43,058	-7.9	32,460
Steubenville–Weirton, OH–WV	55,247	57,035	57,721	-4.3	6,325	7,464	11.4	13.1	2,361	-12.0	37,150	-15.6	30,100
Jefferson County, OH	31,022	32,232	31,585	-1.8	3,489	4,313	11.2	13.4	1,344	-14.0	19,328	-13.4	31,078
Brooke County, WV	10,410	10,661	11,245	-7.4	1,183	1,321	11.4	12.4	401	-10.3	7,886	4.8	29,825
Hancock County, WV	13,815	14,142	14,891	-7.2	1,653	1,830	12.0	12.9	616	-8.6	9,936	-29.9	28,414
Stockton, CA	297,572	300,812	284,188	4.7	50,126	51,944	16.8	17.3	10,825	6.3	160,629	4.0	36,579
San Joaquin County, CA	297,572	300,812	284,188	4.7	50,126	51,944	16.8	17.3	10,825	6.3	160,629	4.0	36,579
Sumter, SC	44,811	45,046	46,312	-3.2	5,118	5,457	11.4	12.1	1,821	-2.3	27,620	-25.4	29,650
Sumter County, SC	44,811	45,046	46,312	-3.2	5,118	5,457	11.4	12.1	1,821	-2.3	27,620	-25.4	29,650

[1] Civilian unemployed as percent of total civilian labor force.
[2] For pay period including March 12 of the year shown.

Table C-4. Labor Force and Private Business Establishments and Employment—*Continued*

Metropolitan statistical area, division, and component county	Civilian labor force								Private nonfarm businesses				
	Total				Number of unemployed		Unemployment rate[1]		Establishments		Employment[2]		Annual payroll per employee 2010 (dollars)
	2011	2010	2005	Change, 2005–2011	2011	2010	2011	2010	2010	Change, 2000–2010	2010	Change, 2000–2010	
Syracuse, NY	320,603	325,414	330,386	-3.0	26,304	28,051	8.2	8.6	15,278	1.8	252,257	-7.7	39,168
Madison County, NY	35,890	36,327	36,149	-0.7	2,921	3,015	8.1	8.3	1,417	2.9	17,233	-14.0	30,625
Onondaga County, NY	227,249	230,691	233,921	-2.9	17,474	18,732	7.7	8.1	11,750	1.3	211,654	-7.5	40,214
Oswego County, NY	57,464	58,396	60,316	-4.7	5,909	6,304	10.3	10.8	2,111	4.3	23,370	-5.2	35,996
Tallahassee, FL	192,390	191,936	177,970	8.1	15,991	15,905	8.3	8.3	8,688	14.4	103,604	0.0	34,884
Gadsden County, FL	20,240	20,276	20,321	-0.4	2,092	2,166	10.3	10.7	646	12.3	8,870	-5.5	30,231
Jefferson County, FL	6,816	6,801	6,759	0.8	606	604	8.9	8.9	259	8.4	1,673	3.2	23,908
Leon County, FL	149,905	149,469	136,604	9.7	12,006	11,857	8.0	7.9	7,366	14.4	89,906	-0.2	35,784
Wakulla County, FL	15,429	15,390	14,286	8.0	1,287	1,278	8.3	8.3	417	20.5	3,155	26.6	28,129
Tampa–St. Petersburg–Clearwater, FL	1,308,379	1,289,095	1,248,334	4.8	142,058	152,187	10.9	11.8	69,363	12.8	932,231	-9.7	39,829
Hernando County, FL	62,857	61,814	56,616	11.0	8,449	8,778	13.4	14.2	2,931	23.7	28,487	20.7	28,150
Hillsborough County, FL......................	611,769	602,552	565,617	8.2	64,306	68,895	10.5	11.4	31,840	18.7	489,503	-2.7	43,067
Pasco County, FL	192,126	189,326	176,269	9.0	23,088	24,551	12.0	13.0	8,326	34.4	75,326	15.5	29,579
Pinellas County, FL	441,627	435,403	449,832	-1.8	46,215	49,963	10.5	11.5	26,266	0.7	338,915	-23.2	38,411
Terre Haute, IN	79,701	80,717	80,580	-1.1	8,324	8,982	10.4	11.1	3,742	-2.7	58,470	-6.7	34,362
Clay County, IN	12,736	12,784	13,305	-4.3	1,368	1,359	10.7	10.6	500	-5.5	5,009	-16.5	28,805
Sullivan County, IN..............................	8,744	8,838	9,286	-5.8	879	933	10.1	10.6	353	-8.8	3,496	-9.7	34,274
Vermillion County, IN	7,738	7,874	8,124	-4.8	908	1,010	11.7	12.8	287	-0.3	3,961	-18.7	49,586
Vigo County, IN	50,483	51,221	49,865	1.2	5,169	5,680	10.2	11.1	2,602	-1.5	46,004	-4.0	33,663
Texarkana, TX–Texarkana, AR	66,479	65,901	61,900	7.4	4,978	4,893	7.5	7.4	2,897	0.9	41,839	-3.7	31,326
Miller County, AR	20,864	20,223	19,631	6.3	1,466	1,143	7.0	5.7	717	-3.0	11,229	-0.8	32,929
Bowie County, TX	45,615	45,678	42,269	7.9	3,512	3,750	7.7	8.2	2,180	2.3	30,610	-4.8	30,737
Toledo, OH	320,475	325,040	336,002	-4.6	30,425	36,123	9.5	11.1	14,668	-8.3	259,247	-14.0	37,923
Fulton County, OH...............................	22,104	22,531	23,046	-4.1	2,079	2,585	9.4	11.5	972	-11.5	14,826	-27.4	33,408
Lucas County, OH	211,690	214,733	223,616	-5.3	20,429	24,219	9.7	11.3	9,947	-10.5	188,403	-14.6	38,157
Ottawa County, OH	21,132	21,449	21,743	-2.8	2,509	2,898	11.9	13.5	1,020	-11.8	9,962	-18.6	38,420
Wood County, OH................................	65,549	66,327	67,597	-3.0	5,408	6,421	8.3	9.7	2,729	3.6	46,056	-4.3	38,313
Topeka, KS	122,277	123,548	123,501	-1.0	8,712	8,948	7.1	7.2	5,399	-5.9	86,080	-8.7	35,444
Jackson County, KS	6,856	6,912	7,154	-4.2	468	465	6.8	6.7	270	-5.3	2,956	-10.4	25,775
Jefferson County, KS...........................	9,915	10,079	10,143	-2.2	740	821	7.5	8.1	321	-14.4	2,365	7.3	29,425
Osage County, KS	8,466	8,537	9,120	-7.2	722	722	8.5	8.5	270	-22.6	3,289	-5.4	17,154
Shawnee County, KS	93,298	94,241	93,310	0.0	6,539	6,692	7.0	7.1	4,413	-4.1	76,520	-9.5	36,935
Wabaunsee County, KS	3,742	3,779	3,774	-0.8	243	248	6.5	6.6	125	-2.3	950	35.5	23,805
Trenton–Ewing, NJ	208,203	206,868	194,292	7.2	16,060	16,332	7.7	7.9	9,756	1.1	175,798	1.0	58,313
Mercer County, NJ	208,203	206,868	194,292	7.2	16,060	16,332	7.7	7.9	9,756	1.1	175,798	1.0	58,313
Tucson, AZ	465,613	479,054	437,823	6.3	39,207	45,259	8.4	9.4	20,319	9.1	301,151	2.6	36,919
Pima County, AZ	465,613	479,054	437,823	6.3	39,207	45,259	8.4	9.4	20,319	9.1	301,151	2.6	36,919
Tulsa, OK	437,230	441,719	443,384	-1.4	30,100	34,154	6.9	7.7	24,072	4.0	367,884	-2.5	41,144
Creek County, OK................................	30,199	30,721	32,107	-5.9	2,180	2,672	7.2	8.7	1,409	10.5	14,647	-7.5	34,422
Okmulgee County, OK	16,005	16,109	16,840	-5.0	1,557	1,645	9.7	10.2	700	4.9	7,518	15.0	28,631
Osage County, OK	20,308	20,473	20,800	-2.4	1,506	1,651	7.4	8.1	613	15.2	5,704	34.8	28,650
Pawnee County, OK.............................	7,217	7,331	7,808	-7.6	590	697	8.2	9.5	289	-6.8	2,463	-9.1	27,966
Rogers County, OK..............................	40,030	40,488	39,900	0.3	2,583	3,001	6.5	7.4	1,643	25.7	23,260	49.4	39,955
Tulsa County, OK.................................	289,483	292,314	293,889	-1.5	19,487	22,030	6.7	7.5	18,510	1.2	306,457	-5.7	42,492
Wagoner County, OK...........................	33,988	34,283	32,040	6.1	2,197	2,458	6.5	7.2	908	18.5	7,835	3.3	29,769
Tuscaloosa, AL......................................	101,206	100,721	94,826	6.7	8,679	9,103	8.6	9.0	4,312	-0.2	73,293	-1.1	35,936
Greene County, AL	3,167	3,254	3,424	-7.5	450	564	14.2	17.3	107	-20.1	1,376	4.5	28,091
Hale County, AL..................................	5,866	5,904	7,000	-16.2	702	791	12.0	13.4	192	-16.5	2,130	-33.6	28,838
Tuscaloosa County, AL.........................	92,173	91,563	84,402	9.2	7,527	7,748	8.2	8.5	4,013	1.5	69,787	0.3	36,308
Tyler, TX...	104,089	102,729	95,590	8.9	8,126	8,109	7.8	7.9	5,442	12.0	85,222	15.3	36,537
Smith County, TX................................	104,089	102,729	95,590	8.9	8,126	8,109	7.8	7.9	5,442	12.0	85,222	15.3	36,537
Utica–Rome, NY	138,633	140,611	143,055	-3.1	11,351	11,280	8.2	8.0	6,069	-1.3	99,758	-1.9	33,029
Herkimer County, NY...........................	30,880	31,398	31,706	-2.6	2,607	2,670	8.4	8.5	1,168	-1.3	11,984	-13.7	29,674
Oneida County, NY..............................	107,753	109,213	111,349	-3.2	8,744	8,610	8.1	7.9	4,901	-1.3	87,774	0.0	33,487
Valdosta, GA	65,389	65,873	65,271	0.2	6,018	6,021	9.2	9.1	3,018	9.9	40,176	1.6	27,987
Brooks County, GA..............................	7,436	7,496	8,345	-10.9	700	705	9.4	9.4	199	-4.3	1,995	-16.5	26,795
Echols County, GA..............................	1,954	1,975	2,330	-16.1	143	149	7.3	7.5	18	50.0	(D)	(D)	(D)
Lanier County, GA...............................	4,553	4,608	3,835	18.7	388	409	8.5	8.9	111	-5.9	924	-5.9	23,249
Lowndes County, GA............................	51,446	51,794	50,761	1.3	4,787	4,758	9.3	9.2	2,690	11.7	37,257	3.1	28,109
Vallejo–Fairfield, CA	215,472	214,620	208,894	3.1	24,646	25,809	11.4	12.0	6,744	3.7	98,014	3.7	42,098
Solano County, CA	215,472	214,620	208,894	3.1	24,646	25,809	11.4	12.0	6,744	3.7	98,014	3.7	42,098
Victoria, TX	60,920	59,600	56,782	7.3	4,170	4,480	6.8	7.5	2,777	1.7	40,123	4.9	37,705
Calhoun County, TX.............................	10,395	10,057	9,369	11.0	950	884	9.1	8.8	411	(D)	8,742	8.5	46,249
Goliad County, TX...............................	3,615	3,549	3,406	6.1	221	252	6.1	7.1	110	-1.8	791	11.1	28,799
Victoria County, TX	46,910	45,994	44,007	6.6	2,999	3,344	6.4	7.3	2,256	2.2	30,590	3.7	35,493
Vineland–Millville–Bridgeton, NJ	70,761	71,266	69,280	2.1	9,467	9,689	13.4	13.6	2,969	-1.9	45,030	-1.7	36,136
Cumberland County, NJ	70,761	71,266	69,280	2.1	9,467	9,689	13.4	13.6	2,969	-1.9	45,030	-1.7	36,136

[1] Civilian unemployed as percent of total civilian labor force.
[2] For pay period including March 12 of the year shown.

Table C-4. Labor Force and Private Business Establishments and Employment—*Continued*

Metropolitan statistical area, division, and component county	Civilian labor force								Private nonfarm businesses				
	Total				Number of unemployed		Unemployment rate[1]		Establishments		Employment[2]		Annual payroll per employee 2010 (dollars)
	2011	2010	2005	Change, 2005–2011	2011	2010	2011	2010	2010	Change, 2000–2010	2010	Change, 2000–2010	
Virginia Beach–Norfolk–Newport News, VA–NC	847,075	841,977	795,987	6.4	59,126	61,814	7.0	7.3	37,589	9.0	592,401	2.0	36,987
Currituck County, NC	12,542	12,504	12,163	3.1	883	874	7.0	7.0	584	29.5	3,869	23.3	33,711
Gloucester County, VA	20,316	20,253	19,926	2.0	1,192	1,320	5.9	6.5	895	10.8	7,310	16.3	24,773
Isle of Wight County, VA	19,318	19,247	17,479	10.5	1,259	1,368	6.5	7.1	641	21.2	9,716	1.5	29,831
James City County, VA	35,170	34,888	28,974	21.4	1,851	1,902	5.3	5.5	1,638	58.1	22,841	85.0	33,166
Mathews County, VA	4,528	4,479	4,425	2.3	272	266	6.0	5.9	179	-16.7	971	-19.9	21,601
Surry County, VA	3,864	3,832	3,660	5.6	301	305	7.8	8.0	82	-2.4	(D)	(D)	(D)
York County, VA	34,049	33,720	30,751	10.7	1,829	1,822	5.4	5.4	1,451	22.8	17,357	24.5	29,866
Chesapeake city, VA	119,508	118,778	112,386	6.3	7,737	8,124	6.5	6.8	5,384	19.7	82,824	8.3	35,854
Hampton city, VA	66,713	66,184	67,176	-0.7	5,625	5,707	8.4	8.6	2,411	-1.6	41,878	-14.1	35,077
Newport News city, VA	91,864	91,283	86,823	5.8	7,203	7,468	7.8	8.2	3,759	1.8	85,647	0.9	41,847
Norfolk city, VA	107,278	106,876	96,697	10.9	8,987	9,567	8.4	9.0	5,840	7.0	114,921	-1.7	43,345
Poquoson city, VA	6,658	6,621	6,201	7.4	361	386	5.4	5.8	222	25.4	1,454	2.9	23,047
Portsmouth city, VA	45,125	44,942	45,091	0.1	3,904	4,133	8.7	9.2	1,768	5.3	28,414	10.8	33,682
Suffolk city, VA	42,867	42,639	38,029	12.7	3,059	3,229	7.1	7.6	1,498	29.7	20,698	26.9	35,314
Virginia Beach city, VA	230,961	229,456	221,406	4.3	13,782	14,447	6.0	6.3	10,757	4.9	144,704	-0.3	34,682
Williamsburg city, VA	6,314	6,275	4,800	31.5	881	896	14.0	14.3	480	-39.8	9,797	-42.8	27,429
Visalia–Porterville, CA	208,098	208,491	183,709	13.3	34,578	35,205	16.6	16.9	6,134	3.5	85,429	10.7	33,549
Tulare County, CA	208,098	208,491	183,709	13.3	34,578	35,205	16.6	16.9	6,134	3.5	85,429	10.7	33,549
Waco, TX	116,392	116,516	112,273	3.7	8,601	8,368	7.4	7.2	4,919	1.6	95,173	5.0	31,672
McLennan County, TX	116,392	116,516	112,273	3.7	8,601	8,368	7.4	7.2	4,919	1.6	95,173	5.0	31,672
Warner Robins, GA	70,292	70,434	63,010	11.6	5,468	5,486	7.8	7.8	2,301	17.0	33,656	26.0	30,489
Houston County, GA	70,292	70,434	63,010	11.6	5,468	5,486	7.8	7.8	2,301	17.0	33,656	26.0	30,489
Washington–Arlington–Alexandria, DC–VA–MD–WV	3,172,533	3,133,387	2,903,240	9.3	183,939	198,460	5.8	6.3	141,020	33.5	2,370,531	33.3	58,132
Bethesda–Rockville–Frederick, MD	652,901	650,306	629,514	3.7	34,921	39,130	5.3	6.0	32,226	5.4	481,197	1.0	54,887
Frederick County, MD	127,744	127,393	121,263	5.3	7,821	8,791	6.1	6.9	5,796	17.4	80,958	11.9	39,861
Montgomery County, MD	525,157	522,913	508,251	3.3	27,100	30,339	5.2	5.8	26,430	3.1	400,239	-1.0	57,926
Washington–Arlington–Alexandria, DC–VA–MD–WV	2,519,632	2,483,081	2,273,726	10.8	149,018	159,330	5.9	6.4	108,794	45.0	1,889,334	45.1	58,959
District of Columbia, DC	344,333	343,379	319,303	7.8	35,273	34,690	10.2	10.1	21,502	9.4	463,076	11.6	66,915
Calvert County, MD	47,773	47,522	46,363	3.0	2,820	3,153	5.9	6.6	1,720	15.4	17,161	15.0	38,781
Charles County, MD	79,036	78,540	73,256	7.9	4,743	5,213	6.0	6.6	2,668	10.8	31,435	6.8	34,351
Prince George's County, MD	464,524	462,138	445,698	4.2	32,391	35,620	7.0	7.7	14,250	3.1	237,908	-5.1	43,362
Arlington County, VA	136,359	133,537	124,137	9.8	5,174	5,785	3.8	4.3	6,019	15.2	126,195	10.0	70,507
Clarke County, VA	8,040	7,902	7,788	3.2	399	460	5.0	5.8	396	31.6	3,237	-1.2	35,962
Fairfax County, VA	638,882	625,828	571,893	11.7	27,405	30,354	4.3	4.9	28,782	12.5	558,906	9.8	68,526
Fauquier County, VA	37,311	36,684	35,643	4.7	1,820	2,122	4.9	5.8	1,785	17.8	16,150	19.3	38,896
Loudoun County, VA	188,286	184,487	148,244	27.0	7,861	8,784	4.2	4.8	8,072	79.0	117,300	72.4	54,506
Prince William County, VA	230,911	226,191	190,880	21.0	11,816	12,830	5.1	5.7	6,971	59.0	83,363	34.5	38,058
Spotsylvania County, VA	68,606	67,178	62,281	10.2	3,684	3,955	5.4	5.9	2,294	71.1	25,691	41.5	31,919
Stafford County, VA	71,111	69,690	61,957	14.8	3,671	4,015	5.2	5.8	2,061	42.6	28,223	57.9	36,830
Warren County, VA	20,904	20,531	18,724	11.6	1,332	1,471	6.4	7.2	800	5.3	9,141	13.5	31,302
Alexandria city, VA	92,159	90,013	85,299	8.0	4,463	4,612	4.8	5.1	4,490	-3.3	78,808	-3.3	56,661
Fairfax city, VA	14,022	13,589	12,859	9.0	901	811	6.4	6.0	2,301	6.1	27,783	-18.8	46,126
Falls Church city, VA	7,864	7,583	6,468	21.6	563	473	7.2	6.2	803	-7.4	9,368	-39.1	45,116
Fredericksburg city, VA	14,263	13,877	11,294	26.3	1,352	1,304	9.5	9.4	1,328	-20.4	20,562	-13.6	37,977
Manassas city, VA	22,031	21,683	20,654	6.7	1,433	1,624	6.5	7.5	1,409	-27.7	22,248	-8.5	60,172
Manassas Park city, VA	8,452	8,289	6,562	28.8	437	484	5.2	5.8	282	74.1	2,979	18.2	43,167
Jefferson County, WV	24,765	24,440	24,423	1.4	1,480	1,570	6.0	6.4	861	6.8	9,800	-8.7	27,872
Waterloo–Cedar Falls, IA	95,725	95,305	91,986	4.1	5,403	5,703	5.6	6.0	4,132	0.3	75,209	5.6	34,691
Black Hawk County, IA	74,736	74,347	71,408	4.7	4,406	4,577	5.9	6.2	3,228	1.9	64,244	6.5	34,651
Bremer County, IA	14,034	13,995	13,713	2.3	642	710	4.6	5.1	608	-5.1	8,237	2.6	33,502
Grundy County, IA	6,955	6,963	6,865	1.3	355	416	5.1	6.0	296	-3.9	2,728	-4.9	39,224
Wausau, WI	72,495	73,900	74,720	-3.0	5,494	6,652	7.6	9.0	3,397	-1.2	58,876	-7.5	36,954
Marathon County, WI	72,495	73,900	74,720	-3.0	5,494	6,652	7.6	9.0	3,397	-1.2	58,876	-7.5	36,954
Wenatchee–East Wenatchee, WA	62,226	63,020	59,110	5.3	5,156	5,518	8.3	8.8	3,106	9.9	32,097	13.0	33,626
Chelan County, WA	40,518	41,056	39,244	3.2	3,418	3,675	8.4	9.0	2,424	6.1	26,063	7.6	34,935
Douglas County, WA	21,708	21,964	19,866	9.3	1,738	1,843	8.0	8.4	682	26.3	6,034	43.9	27,971
Wheeling, WV–OH	68,514	69,776	68,891	-0.5	5,923	6,681	8.6	9.6	3,459	-8.2	54,134	1.8	31,284
Belmont County, OH	33,650	34,367	32,343	4.0	2,908	3,351	8.6	9.8	1,493	-8.2	18,574	-4.6	29,018
Marshall County, WV	14,439	14,659	15,268	-5.4	1,374	1,500	9.5	10.2	493	-11.0	8,157	21.3	39,541
Ohio County, WV	20,425	20,750	21,280	-4.0	1,641	1,830	8.0	8.8	1,473	-7.1	27,403	1.5	30,362
Wichita, KS	307,650	311,535	307,190	0.1	24,768	27,612	8.1	8.9	14,712	1.2	255,616	-1.5	39,728
Butler County, KS	31,763	32,191	32,029	-0.8	2,432	2,752	7.7	8.5	1,286	0.4	13,277	10.7	29,668
Harvey County, KS	17,311	17,579	18,021	-3.9	1,128	1,337	6.5	7.6	815	-0.4	12,517	6.8	31,974
Sedgwick County, KS	247,445	250,384	244,871	1.1	20,384	22,486	8.2	9.0	12,119	1.9	225,261	-2.5	40,990
Sumner County, KS	11,131	11,381	12,269	-9.3	824	1,037	7.4	9.1	492	-9.7	4,561	-6.2	27,994

[1] Civilian unemployed as percent of total civilian labor force.
[2] For pay period including March 12 of the year shown.

Table C-4.   Labor Force and Private Business Establishments and Employment—*Continued*

Metropolitan statistical area, division, and component county	Civilian labor force								Private nonfarm businesses				
	Total				Number of unemployed		Unemployment rate[1]		Establishments		Employment[2]		Annual payroll per employee 2010 (dollars)
	2011	2010	2005	Change, 2005–2011	2011	2010	2011	2010	2010	Change, 2000–2010	2010	Change, 2000–2010	
Wichita Falls, TX	73,153	73,912	74,435	-1.7	5,188	5,662	7.1	7.7	3,532	-2.2	47,344	-2.7	31,004
Archer County, TX	5,013	5,042	5,303	-5.5	295	304	5.9	6.0	184	21.9	1,251	75.0	34,576
Clay County, TX	5,869	5,928	6,492	-9.6	358	394	6.1	6.6	128	0.0	970	-3.5	26,148
Wichita County, TX	62,271	62,942	62,640	-0.6	4,535	4,964	7.3	7.9	3,220	-3.4	45,123	-3.9	31,009
Williamsport, PA	61,373	60,536	59,477	3.2	4,705	5,310	7.7	8.8	2,853	-0.9	44,361	-10.3	32,187
Lycoming County, PA	61,373	60,536	59,477	3.2	4,705	5,310	7.7	8.8	2,853	-0.9	44,361	-10.3	32,187
Wilmington, NC	182,053	181,812	163,961	11.0	19,395	19,364	10.7	10.7	9,889	17.9	111,863	11.1	33,819
Brunswick County, NC	50,489	50,563	43,177	16.9	5,801	5,933	11.5	11.7	2,287	35.9	22,950	29.8	29,421
New Hanover County, NC	107,246	107,137	98,690	8.7	10,666	10,682	9.9	10.0	6,697	11.4	81,712	5.5	35,595
Pender County, NC	24,318	24,112	22,094	10.1	2,928	2,749	12.0	11.4	905	29.8	7,201	29.2	27,679
Winchester, VA–WV	68,094	66,780	61,907	10.0	4,480	5,002	6.6	7.5	3,070	11.1	44,437	-1.7	36,895
Frederick County, VA	43,881	43,068	38,532	13.9	2,607	3,056	5.9	7.1	1,428	20.5	20,447	8.7	36,181
Winchester city, VA	14,715	14,235	13,827	6.4	1,129	1,064	7.7	7.5	1,306	4.9	21,339	-9.6	39,105
Hampshire County, WV	9,498	9,477	9,548	-0.5	744	882	7.8	9.3	336	0.9	2,651	-4.4	24,623
Winston–Salem, NC	243,054	242,725	232,918	4.4	24,244	24,936	10.0	10.3	10,336	-1.2	177,530	-10.1	40,379
Davie County, NC	20,793	20,855	19,987	4.0	2,123	2,272	10.2	10.9	792	14.5	7,998	-9.6	27,928
Forsyth County, NC	178,667	178,116	169,471	5.4	17,857	18,056	10.0	10.1	8,312	-2.1	156,137	-10.5	42,218
Stokes County, NC	24,309	24,456	24,140	0.7	2,369	2,619	9.7	10.7	609	0.2	5,490	-1.5	26,782
Yadkin County, NC	19,285	19,298	19,320	-0.2	1,895	1,989	9.8	10.3	623	-6.6	7,905	-8.8	26,116
Worcester, MA	404,098	405,517	398,457	1.4	32,627	36,922	8.1	9.1	17,625	-1.6	267,175	-8.9	42,890
Worcester County, MA	404,098	405,517	398,457	1.4	32,627	36,922	8.1	9.1	17,625	-1.6	267,175	-8.9	42,890
Yakima, WA	124,749	125,675	116,847	6.8	12,556	12,631	10.1	10.1	4,684	-1.6	62,406	3.6	32,981
Yakima County, WA	124,749	125,675	116,847	6.8	12,556	12,631	10.1	10.1	4,684	-1.6	62,406	3.6	32,981
York–Hanover, PA	224,969	225,348	219,580	2.5	17,462	19,427	7.8	8.6	8,580	4.7	152,211	-0.6	38,424
York County, PA	224,969	225,348	219,580	2.5	17,462	19,427	7.8	8.6	8,580	4.7	152,211	-0.6	38,424
Youngstown–Warren–Boardman, OH–PA	267,833	272,149	280,338	-4.5	25,260	30,937	9.4	11.4	12,851	-9.0	197,193	-15.8	32,504
Mahoning County, OH	112,938	114,525	119,363	-5.4	10,832	12,979	9.6	11.3	5,796	-10.0	83,327	-16.5	31,854
Trumbull County, OH	101,706	103,738	105,140	-3.3	9,758	12,294	9.6	11.9	4,271	-9.7	70,556	-19.8	34,459
Mercer County, PA	53,189	53,886	55,835	-4.7	4,670	5,664	8.8	10.5	2,784	-5.7	43,310	-6.7	30,570
Yuba City, CA	71,300	70,962	65,828	8.3	13,241	13,732	18.6	19.4	2,524	1.4	28,931	10.3	33,397
Sutter County, CA	43,305	43,018	40,087	8.0	8,153	8,368	18.8	19.5	1,705	3.3	19,735	14.3	34,372
Yuba County, CA	27,995	27,944	25,741	8.8	5,088	5,364	18.2	19.2	819	-2.3	9,196	2.5	31,303
Yuma, AZ	89,500	90,156	75,478	18.6	24,270	23,713	27.1	26.3	2,946	16.1	40,626	30.1	28,315
Yuma County, AZ	89,500	90,156	75,478	18.6	24,270	23,713	27.1	26.3	2,946	16.1	40,626	30.1	28,315

[1] Civilian unemployed as percent of total civilian labor force.
[2] For pay period including March 12 of the year shown.

PART D
MICROPOLITAN AREAS

Note: Part D presents data for the 576 micropolitan areas and their 688 component counties, defined by the Office of Management and Budget as of December 2009. For more information, see OMB Bulletin 10-02 at http://www.whitehouse .gov/sites/default/files/omb/assets/bulletins/b10-02.pdf .

For additional information, see Appendix C, Geographic Concepts.

Table D-1. Population and Personal Income

Micropolitan statistical area component counties	2011 estimate (July 1)	2010 census count (April 1)	2000 estimates base (April 1)[1]	1990 estimates base (April 1)[2]	Net change 2010–2011[3]	Net change 2000–2010[4]	Percent change 2010–2011[3]	Percent change 2000–2010[4]	Total (million dollars) 2011	Total (million dollars) 2010	Percentage change, 2010–2011	Per capita[5] 2011	Per capita[5] 2010
Abbeville, LA	58,276	57,999	53,807	50,055	277	4,192	0.5	7.8	1,806	1,735	4.1	30,998	29,873
Vermilion Parish, LA	58,276	57,999	53,807	50,055	277	4,192	0.5	7.8	1,806	1,735	4.1	30,998	29,873
Aberdeen, SD	40,878	40,602	39,827	39,936	276	775	0.7	1.9	2,112	1,785	18.3	51,660	43,842
Brown County, SD	36,822	36,531	35,460	35,580	291	1,071	0.8	3.0	1,851	1,611	14.9	50,274	43,964
Edmunds County, SD	4,056	4,071	4,367	4,356	-15	-296	-0.4	-6.8	261	174	49.5	64,239	42,737
Aberdeen, WA	72,546	72,797	67,194	64,175	-251	5,603	-0.3	8.3	2,202	2,109	4.4	30,355	28,938
Grays Harbor County, WA	72,546	72,797	67,194	64,175	-251	5,603	-0.3	8.3	2,202	2,109	4.4	30,355	28,938
Ada, OK	37,799	37,492	35,143	34,119	307	2,349	0.8	6.7	1,302	1,218	6.9	34,445	32,394
Pontotoc County, OK	37,799	37,492	35,143	34,119	307	2,349	0.8	6.7	1,302	1,218	6.9	34,445	32,394
Adrian, MI	99,440	99,892	98,890	91,476	-452	1,002	-0.5	1.0	3,243	3,016	7.5	32,611	30,235
Lenawee County, MI	99,440	99,892	98,890	91,476	-452	1,002	-0.5	1.0	3,243	3,016	7.5	32,611	30,235
Alamogordo, NM	65,703	63,797	62,298	51,928	1,906	1,499	3.0	2.4	1,981	1,869	6.0	30,154	29,054
Otero County, NM	65,703	63,797	62,298	51,928	1,906	1,499	3.0	2.4	1,981	1,869	6.0	30,154	29,054
Albany–Lebanon, OR	118,122	116,672	103,069	91,227	1,450	13,603	1.2	13.2	3,553	3,397	4.6	30,083	29,070
Linn County, OR	118,122	116,672	103,069	91,227	1,450	13,603	1.2	13.2	3,553	3,397	4.6	30,083	29,070
Albemarle, NC	60,626	60,585	58,100	51,765	41	2,485	0.1	4.3	1,833	1,768	3.6	30,227	29,189
Stanly County, NC	60,626	60,585	58,100	51,765	41	2,485	0.1	4.3	1,833	1,768	3.6	30,227	29,189
Albert Lea, MN	31,172	31,255	32,584	33,060	-83	-1,329	-0.3	-4.1	1,217	1,139	6.9	39,052	36,454
Freeborn County, MN	31,172	31,255	32,584	33,060	-83	-1,329	-0.3	-4.1	1,217	1,139	6.9	39,052	36,454
Albertville, AL	94,166	93,019	82,231	70,832	1,147	10,788	1.2	13.1	2,876	2,824	1.8	30,543	30,303
Marshall County, AL	94,166	93,019	82,231	70,832	1,147	10,788	1.2	13.1	2,876	2,824	1.8	30,543	30,303
Alexander City, AL	52,336	53,155	53,677	49,889	-819	-522	-1.5	-1.0	1,540	1,507	2.2	29,421	28,429
Coosa County, AL	10,713	11,539	12,202	11,063	-826	-663	-7.2	-5.4	254	259	-1.9	23,678	22,576
Tallapoosa County, AL	41,623	41,616	41,475	38,826	7	141	0.0	0.3	1,286	1,248	3.1	30,899	30,044
Alexandria, MN	36,172	36,009	32,821	28,674	163	3,188	0.5	9.7	1,364	1,301	4.8	37,703	36,146
Douglas County, MN	36,172	36,009	32,821	28,674	163	3,188	0.5	9.7	1,364	1,301	4.8	37,703	36,146
Alice, TX	41,339	40,838	39,326	37,679	501	1,512	1.2	3.8	1,645	1,434	14.7	39,800	35,047
Jim Wells County, TX	41,339	40,838	39,326	37,679	501	1,512	1.2	3.8	1,645	1,434	14.7	39,800	35,047
Allegan, MI	111,234	111,408	105,665	90,509	-174	5,743	-0.2	5.4	3,734	3,549	5.2	33,565	31,823
Allegan County, MI	111,234	111,408	105,665	90,509	-174	5,743	-0.2	5.4	3,734	3,549	5.2	33,565	31,823
Alma, MI	42,145	42,476	42,285	38,982	-331	191	-0.8	0.5	1,292	1,204	7.3	30,647	28,360
Gratiot County, MI	42,145	42,476	42,285	38,982	-331	191	-0.8	0.5	1,292	1,204	7.3	30,647	28,360
Alpena, MI	29,386	29,598	31,314	30,605	-212	-1,716	-0.7	-5.5	988	950	4.0	33,612	32,149
Alpena County, MI	29,386	29,598	31,314	30,605	-212	-1,716	-0.7	-5.5	988	950	4.0	33,612	32,149
Altus, OK	26,447	26,446	28,439	28,764	1	-1,993	0.0	-7.0	855	852	0.3	32,331	32,189
Jackson County, OK	26,447	26,446	28,439	28,764	1	-1,993	0.0	-7.0	855	852	0.3	32,331	32,189
Americus, GA	37,531	37,829	36,966	33,822	-298	863	-0.8	2.3	1,036	995	4.1	27,599	26,263
Schley County, GA	5,020	5,010	3,766	3,590	10	1,244	0.2	33.0	103	102	1.5	20,566	20,288
Sumter County, GA	32,511	32,819	33,200	30,232	-308	-381	-0.9	-1.1	933	894	4.3	28,685	27,173
Amsterdam, NY	49,916	50,219	49,708	51,981	-303	511	-0.6	1.0	1,641	1,593	3.1	32,882	31,688
Montgomery County, NY	49,916	50,219	49,708	51,981	-303	511	-0.6	1.0	1,641	1,593	3.1	32,882	31,688
Andrews, TX	15,445	14,786	13,004	14,338	659	1,782	4.5	13.7	609	533	14.3	39,435	35,914
Andrews County, TX	15,445	14,786	13,004	14,338	659	1,782	4.5	13.7	609	533	14.3	39,435	35,914
Angola, IN	34,028	34,185	33,214	27,446	-157	971	-0.5	2.9	1,065	1,000	6.5	31,284	29,282
Steuben County, IN	34,028	34,185	33,214	27,446	-157	971	-0.5	2.9	1,065	1,000	6.5	31,284	29,282
Arcadia, FL	34,894	34,862	32,209	23,865	32	2,653	0.1	8.2	857	829	3.5	24,574	23,712
DeSoto County, FL	34,894	34,862	32,209	23,865	32	2,653	0.1	8.2	857	829	3.5	24,574	23,712
Ardmore, OK	57,482	56,980	54,452	50,707	502	2,528	0.9	4.6	2,171	2,045	6.1	37,764	35,835
Carter County, OK	48,096	47,557	45,621	42,919	539	1,936	1.1	4.2	1,802	1,696	6.2	37,462	35,620
Love County, OK	9,386	9,423	8,831	7,788	-37	592	-0.4	6.7	369	349	5.8	39,308	36,920
Arkadelphia, AR	22,858	22,995	23,546	21,437	-137	-551	-0.6	-2.3	695	672	3.4	30,386	29,254
Clark County, AR	22,858	22,995	23,546	21,437	-137	-551	-0.6	-2.3	695	672	3.4	30,386	29,254
Ashland, OH	53,153	53,139	52,523	47,507	14	616	0.0	1.2	1,564	1,490	4.9	29,422	28,036
Ashland County, OH	53,153	53,139	52,523	47,507	14	616	0.0	1.2	1,564	1,490	4.9	29,422	28,036
Ashtabula, OH	101,345	101,497	102,728	99,880	-152	-1,231	-0.1	-1.2	3,176	2,967	7.0	31,339	29,245
Ashtabula County, OH	101,345	101,497	102,728	99,880	-152	-1,231	-0.1	-1.2	3,176	2,967	7.0	31,339	29,245
Astoria, OR	37,153	37,039	35,630	33,301	114	1,409	0.3	4.0	1,301	1,223	6.4	35,021	32,985
Clatsop County, OR	37,153	37,039	35,630	33,301	114	1,409	0.3	4.0	1,301	1,223	6.4	35,021	32,985
Atchison, KS	16,793	16,924	16,774	16,932	-131	150	-0.8	0.9	529	479	10.4	31,499	28,375
Atchison County, KS	16,793	16,924	16,774	16,932	-131	150	-0.8	0.9	529	479	10.4	31,499	28,375
Athens, OH	64,769	64,757	62,223	59,549	12	2,534	0.0	4.1	1,768	1,703	3.8	27,296	26,296
Athens County, OH	64,769	64,757	62,223	59,549	12	2,534	0.0	4.1	1,768	1,703	3.8	27,296	26,296
Athens, TN	52,508	52,266	49,015	42,383	242	3,251	0.5	6.6	1,502	1,441	4.2	28,598	27,592
McMinn County, TN	52,508	52,266	49,015	42,383	242	3,251	0.5	6.6	1,502	1,441	4.2	28,598	27,592

[1]The April 1, 2000, Population Estimates base reflects modifications to the Census 2000 population as documented in the Count Question Resolution program and geographic program revisions.
[2]The April 1, 1990, census counts include corrections processed through August 1997, results of special censuses and test censuses, and do not include adjustments for census coverage errors.
[3]Based on the April 1, 2010, census counts and the July 1, 2011, estimates.
[4]Based on the April 1, 2010, census counts and the April 1, 2000, estimates base.
[5]Based on resident population estimated as of April 1, 2010 and July 1, 2011 of the year shown.

Table D-1. Population and Personal Income—*Continued*

| Micropolitan statistical area component counties | Population | | | | | | | | Personal Income | | | | |
| | 2011 estimate (July 1) | 2010 census count (April 1) | 2000 estimates base (April 1)[1] | 1990 estimates base (April 1)[2] | Net change | | Percent change | | Total (million dollars) | | Percentage change, 2010–2011 | Per capita[5] | |
					2010–2011[3]	2000–2010[4]	2010–2011[3]	2000–2010[4]	2011	2010		2011	2010
Athens, TX	78,826	78,532	73,277	58,543	294	5,255	0.4	7.2	2,514	2,432	3.4	31,891	30,898
Henderson County, TX	78,826	78,532	73,277	58,543	294	5,255	0.4	7.2	2,514	2,432	3.4	31,891	30,898
Auburn, IN	42,462	42,223	40,285	35,324	239	1,938	0.6	4.8	1,353	1,280	5.7	31,863	30,282
DeKalb County, IN	42,462	42,223	40,285	35,324	239	1,938	0.6	4.8	1,353	1,280	5.7	31,863	30,282
Auburn, NY	79,738	80,026	81,963	82,313	-288	-1,937	-0.4	-2.4	2,716	2,612	4.0	34,061	32,648
Cayuga County, NY	79,738	80,026	81,963	82,313	-288	-1,937	-0.4	-2.4	2,716	2,612	4.0	34,061	32,648
Augusta–Waterville, ME	121,935	122,151	117,114	115,904	-216	5,037	-0.2	4.3	4,506	4,323	4.2	36,958	35,400
Kennebec County, ME	121,935	122,151	117,114	115,904	-216	5,037	-0.2	4.3	4,506	4,323	4.2	36,958	35,400
Austin, MN	39,349	39,163	38,603	37,385	186	560	0.5	1.5	1,584	1,502	5.5	40,268	38,340
Mower County, MN	39,349	39,163	38,603	37,385	186	560	0.5	1.5	1,584	1,502	5.5	40,268	38,340
Bainbridge, GA	27,694	27,842	28,240	25,517	-148	-398	-0.5	-1.4	795	766	3.8	28,718	27,543
Decatur County, GA	27,694	27,842	28,240	25,517	-148	-398	-0.5	-1.4	795	766	3.8	28,718	27,543
Baraboo, WI	62,290	61,976	55,225	46,975	314	6,751	0.5	12.2	2,291	2,181	5.0	36,782	35,157
Sauk County, WI	62,290	61,976	55,225	46,975	314	6,751	0.5	12.2	2,291	2,181	5.0	36,782	35,157
Barre, VT	59,626	59,534	58,039	54,928	92	1,495	0.2	2.6	2,635	2,521	4.5	44,190	42,300
Washington County, VT	59,626	59,534	58,039	54,928	92	1,495	0.2	2.6	2,635	2,521	4.5	44,190	42,300
Bartlesville, OK	51,476	50,976	48,996	48,066	500	1,980	1.0	4.0	2,272	2,116	7.4	44,131	41,445
Washington County, OK	51,476	50,976	48,996	48,066	500	1,980	1.0	4.0	2,272	2,116	7.4	44,131	41,445
Bastrop, LA	27,608	27,979	31,021	31,938	-371	-3,042	-1.3	-9.8	822	780	5.4	29,775	27,923
Morehouse Parish, LA	27,608	27,979	31,021	31,938	-371	-3,042	-1.3	-9.8	822	780	5.4	29,775	27,923
Batavia, NY	59,993	60,079	60,370	60,060	-86	-291	-0.1	-0.5	2,029	1,971	3.0	33,826	32,808
Genesee County, NY	59,993	60,079	60,370	60,060	-86	-291	-0.1	-0.5	2,029	1,971	3.0	33,826	32,808
Batesville, AR	36,861	36,647	34,233	31,192	214	2,414	0.6	7.1	1,146	1,106	3.6	31,088	30,109
Independence County, AR	36,861	36,647	34,233	31,192	214	2,414	0.6	7.1	1,146	1,106	3.6	31,088	30,109
Bay City, TX	36,809	36,702	37,957	36,928	107	-1,255	0.3	-3.3	1,225	1,160	5.6	33,287	31,564
Matagorda County, TX	36,809	36,702	37,957	36,928	107	-1,255	0.3	-3.3	1,225	1,160	5.6	33,287	31,564
Beatrice, NE	22,031	22,311	22,993	22,794	-280	-682	-1.3	-3.0	902	825	9.4	40,942	36,988
Gage County, NE	22,031	22,311	22,993	22,794	-280	-682	-1.3	-3.0	902	825	9.4	40,942	36,988
Beaver Dam, WI	88,661	88,759	85,897	76,559	-98	2,862	-0.1	3.3	3,111	2,959	5.1	35,086	33,342
Dodge County, WI	88,661	88,759	85,897	76,559	-98	2,862	-0.1	3.3	3,111	2,959	5.1	35,086	33,342
Beckley, WV	79,127	78,859	79,220	76,819	268	-361	0.3	-0.5	2,916	2,729	6.8	36,852	34,593
Raleigh County, WV	79,127	78,859	79,220	76,819	268	-361	0.3	-0.5	2,916	2,729	6.8	36,852	34,593
Bedford, IN	46,195	46,134	45,922	42,836	61	212	0.1	0.5	1,442	1,380	4.5	31,205	29,899
Lawrence County, IN	46,195	46,134	45,922	42,836	61	212	0.1	0.5	1,442	1,380	4.5	31,205	29,899
Beeville, TX	32,095	31,861	32,359	25,135	234	-498	0.7	-1.5	857	794	8.0	26,697	24,900
Bee County, TX	32,095	31,861	32,359	25,135	234	-498	0.7	-1.5	857	794	8.0	26,697	24,900
Bellefontaine, OH	45,688	45,858	46,005	42,310	-170	-147	-0.4	-0.3	1,574	1,505	4.6	34,452	32,852
Logan County, OH	45,688	45,858	46,005	42,310	-170	-147	-0.4	-0.3	1,574	1,505	4.6	34,452	32,852
Bemidji, MN	45,264	44,442	39,650	34,384	822	4,792	1.8	12.1	1,441	1,392	3.5	31,834	31,229
Beltrami County, MN	45,264	44,442	39,650	34,384	822	4,792	1.8	12.1	1,441	1,392	3.5	31,834	31,229
Bennettsville, SC	28,509	28,933	28,818	29,716	-424	115	-1.5	0.4	689	674	2.1	24,156	23,344
Marlboro County, SC	28,509	28,933	28,818	29,716	-424	115	-1.5	0.4	689	674	2.1	24,156	23,344
Bennington, VT	36,970	37,125	36,994	35,845	-155	131	-0.4	0.4	1,534	1,478	3.8	41,502	39,828
Bennington County, VT	36,970	37,125	36,994	35,845	-155	131	-0.4	0.4	1,534	1,478	3.8	41,502	39,828
Berlin, NH–VT	38,979	39,361	39,570	41,233	-382	-209	-1.0	-0.5	1,311	1,277	2.7	33,633	32,511
Coos County, NH	32,688	33,055	33,111	34,828	-367	-56	-1.1	-0.2	1,145	1,116	2.5	35,019	33,867
Essex County, VT	6,291	6,306	6,459	6,405	-15	-153	-0.2	-2.4	166	160	3.8	26,433	25,420
Big Rapids, MI	43,300	42,798	40,553	37,308	502	2,245	1.2	5.5	1,183	1,131	4.6	27,328	26,396
Mecosta County, MI	43,300	42,798	40,553	37,308	502	2,245	1.2	5.5	1,183	1,131	4.6	27,328	26,396
Big Spring, TX	35,122	35,012	33,627	32,343	110	1,385	0.3	4.1	1,116	1,073	4.1	31,781	30,634
Howard County, TX	35,122	35,012	33,627	32,343	110	1,385	0.3	4.1	1,116	1,073	4.1	31,781	30,634
Bishop, CA	18,478	18,546	17,945	18,281	-68	601	-0.4	3.3	700	668	4.8	37,905	36,074
Inyo County, CA	18,478	18,546	17,945	18,281	-68	601	-0.4	3.3	700	668	4.8	37,905	36,074
Blackfoot, ID	45,952	45,607	41,735	37,583	345	3,872	0.8	9.3	1,264	1,190	6.2	27,500	26,009
Bingham County, ID	45,952	45,607	41,735	37,583	345	3,872	0.8	9.3	1,264	1,190	6.2	27,500	26,009
Bloomsburg–Berwick, PA	85,772	85,562	82,387	80,937	210	3,175	0.2	3.9	2,855	2,743	4.1	33,288	31,949
Columbia County, PA	67,476	67,295	64,151	63,202	181	3,144	0.3	4.9	2,093	2,005	4.4	31,025	29,670
Montour County, PA	18,296	18,267	18,236	17,735	29	31	0.2	0.2	762	739	3.1	41,632	40,361
Bluefield, WV–VA	107,180	107,342	107,578	110,940	-162	-236	-0.2	-0.2	3,525	3,365	4.7	32,884	31,348
Tazewell County, VA	44,715	45,078	44,598	45,960	-363	480	-0.8	1.1	1,485	1,413	5.1	33,203	31,352
Mercer County, WV	62,465	62,264	62,980	64,980	201	-716	0.3	-1.1	2,040	1,952	4.5	32,656	31,346
Blytheville, AR	45,966	46,480	51,979	57,525	-514	-5,499	-1.1	-10.6	1,505	1,403	7.3	32,741	30,283
Mississippi County, AR	45,966	46,480	51,979	57,525	-514	-5,499	-1.1	-10.6	1,505	1,403	7.3	32,741	30,283
Bogalusa, LA	47,139	47,168	43,926	43,185	-29	3,242	-0.1	7.4	1,298	1,267	2.4	27,527	26,928
Washington Parish, LA	47,139	47,168	43,926	43,185	-29	3,242	-0.1	7.4	1,298	1,267	2.4	27,527	26,928
Bonham, TX	33,958	33,915	31,242	24,804	43	2,673	0.1	8.6	1,009	963	4.7	29,708	28,390
Fannin County, TX	33,958	33,915	31,242	24,804	43	2,673	0.1	8.6	1,009	963	4.7	29,708	28,390

[1]The April 1, 2000, Population Estimates base reflects modifications to the Census 2000 population as documented in the Count Question Resolution program and geographic program revisions.
[2]The April 1, 1990, census counts include corrections processed through August 1997, results of special censuses and test censuses, and do not include adjustments for census coverage errors.
[3]Based on the April 1, 2010, census counts and the July 1, 2011, estimates.
[4]Based on the April 1, 2010, census counts and the April 1, 2000, estimates base.
[5]Based on resident population estimated as of April 1, 2010 and July 1, 2011 of the year shown.

Table D-1. Population and Personal Income—*Continued*

Micropolitan statistical area component counties	2011 estimate (July 1)	2010 census count (April 1)	2000 estimates base (April 1)[1]	1990 estimates base (April 1)[2]	Net change 2010–2011[3]	Net change 2000–2010[4]	Percent change 2010–2011[3]	Percent change 2000–2010[4]	Total (million dollars) 2011	Total (million dollars) 2010	Percentage change, 2010–2011	Per capita[5] 2011	Per capita[5] 2010
Boone, IA	26,255	26,306	26,224	25,186	-51	82	-0.2	0.3	1,074	995	7.9	40,920	37,879
Boone County, IA	26,255	26,306	26,224	25,186	-51	82	-0.2	0.3	1,074	995	7.9	40,920	37,879
Boone, NC	51,333	51,079	42,695	36,952	254	8,384	0.5	19.6	1,522	1,461	4.2	29,648	28,633
Watauga County, NC	51,333	51,079	42,695	36,952	254	8,384	0.5	19.6	1,522	1,461	4.2	29,648	28,633
Borger, TX	22,132	22,150	23,857	25,689	-18	-1,707	-0.1	-7.2	825	790	4.5	37,298	35,705
Hutchinson County, TX	22,132	22,150	23,857	25,689	-18	-1,707	-0.1	-7.2	825	790	4.5	37,298	35,705
Bozeman, MT	91,377	89,513	67,831	50,484	1,864	21,682	2.1	32.0	3,357	3,152	6.5	36,735	35,174
Gallatin County, MT	91,377	89,513	67,831	50,484	1,864	21,682	2.1	32.0	3,357	3,152	6.5	36,735	35,174
Bradford, PA	43,222	43,450	45,936	47,131	-228	-2,486	-0.5	-5.4	1,477	1,382	6.9	34,171	31,854
McKean County, PA	43,222	43,450	45,936	47,131	-228	-2,486	-0.5	-5.4	1,477	1,382	6.9	34,171	31,854
Brainerd, MN	91,153	91,067	82,249	66,040	86	8,818	0.1	10.7	3,180	3,043	4.5	34,888	33,348
Cass County, MN	28,390	28,567	27,150	21,791	-177	1,417	-0.6	5.2	1,069	1,025	4.3	37,649	35,796
Crow Wing County, MN	62,763	62,500	55,099	44,249	263	7,401	0.4	13.4	2,111	2,018	4.6	33,640	32,229
Branson, MO	84,999	83,877	68,361	44,639	1,122	15,516	1.3	22.7	2,507	2,399	4.5	29,498	28,530
Stone County, MO	32,263	32,202	28,658	19,078	61	3,544	0.2	12.4	1,072	1,022	4.9	33,231	31,737
Taney County, MO	52,736	51,675	39,703	25,561	1,061	11,972	2.1	30.2	1,435	1,377	4.2	27,214	26,539
Brenham, TX	33,791	33,718	30,373	26,154	73	3,345	0.2	11.0	1,495	1,409	6.0	44,229	41,755
Washington County, TX	33,791	33,718	30,373	26,154	73	3,345	0.2	11.0	1,495	1,409	6.0	44,229	41,755
Brevard, NC	32,820	33,090	29,334	25,520	-270	3,756	-0.8	12.8	1,008	977	3.1	30,703	29,540
Transylvania County, NC	32,820	33,090	29,334	25,520	-270	3,756	-0.8	12.8	1,008	977	3.1	30,703	29,540
Brigham City, UT	50,290	49,975	42,745	36,485	315	7,230	0.6	16.9	1,516	1,431	6.0	30,148	28,514
Box Elder County, UT	50,290	49,975	42,745	36,485	315	7,230	0.6	16.9	1,516	1,431	6.0	30,148	28,514
Brookhaven, MS	34,889	34,869	33,166	30,278	20	1,703	0.1	5.1	960	930	3.3	27,516	26,658
Lincoln County, MS	34,889	34,869	33,166	30,278	20	1,703	0.1	5.1	960	930	3.3	27,516	26,658
Brookings, OR	22,426	22,364	21,137	19,327	62	1,227	0.3	5.8	716	684	4.6	31,907	30,603
Curry County, OR	22,426	22,364	21,137	19,327	62	1,227	0.3	5.8	716	684	4.6	31,907	30,603
Brookings, SD	32,226	31,965	28,220	25,207	261	3,745	0.8	13.3	1,313	1,169	12.3	40,730	36,480
Brookings County, SD	32,226	31,965	28,220	25,207	261	3,745	0.8	13.3	1,313	1,169	12.3	40,730	36,480
Brownsville, TN	18,470	18,787	19,797	19,437	-317	-1,010	-1.7	-5.1	586	578	1.3	31,710	30,815
Haywood County, TN	18,470	18,787	19,797	19,437	-317	-1,010	-1.7	-5.1	586	578	1.3	31,710	30,815
Brownwood, TX	38,186	38,106	37,674	34,371	80	432	0.2	1.1	1,227	1,175	4.5	32,136	30,804
Brown County, TX	38,186	38,106	37,674	34,371	80	432	0.2	1.1	1,227	1,175	4.5	32,136	30,804
Bucyrus, OH	43,389	43,784	46,966	47,870	-395	-3,182	-0.9	-6.8	1,357	1,265	7.3	31,286	28,920
Crawford County, OH	43,389	43,784	46,966	47,870	-395	-3,182	-0.9	-6.8	1,357	1,265	7.3	31,286	28,920
Burley, ID	43,341	43,021	41,590	38,893	320	1,431	0.7	3.4	1,435	1,303	10.1	33,106	30,184
Cassia County, ID	23,186	22,952	21,416	19,532	234	1,536	1.0	7.2	800	740	8.1	34,515	32,066
Minidoka County, ID	20,155	20,069	20,174	19,361	86	-105	0.4	-0.5	635	563	12.8	31,486	28,019
Burlington, IA–IL	47,365	47,656	50,564	50,710	-291	-2,908	-0.6	-5.8	1,827	1,696	7.7	38,566	35,619
Henderson County, IL	7,196	7,331	8,213	8,096	-135	-882	-1.8	-10.7	265	243	9.3	36,872	33,101
Des Moines County, IA	40,169	40,325	42,351	42,614	-156	-2,026	-0.4	-4.8	1,561	1,453	7.4	38,869	36,077
Butte–Silver Bow, MT	34,383	34,200	34,606	33,941	183	-406	0.5	-1.2	1,329	1,264	5.2	38,666	36,928
Silver Bow County, MT	34,383	34,200	34,606	33,941	183	-406	0.5	-1.2	1,329	1,264	5.2	38,666	36,928
Cadillac, MI	47,629	47,584	44,962	38,507	45	2,622	0.1	5.8	1,302	1,229	5.9	27,326	25,819
Missaukee County, MI	14,911	14,849	14,478	12,147	62	371	0.4	2.6	397	369	7.5	26,591	24,854
Wexford County, MI	32,718	32,735	30,484	26,360	-17	2,251	-0.1	7.4	905	860	5.2	27,661	26,256
Calhoun, GA	55,621	55,186	44,104	35,067	435	11,082	0.8	25.1	1,467	1,412	3.9	26,382	25,577
Gordon County, GA	55,621	55,186	44,104	35,067	435	11,082	0.8	25.1	1,467	1,412	3.9	26,382	25,577
Cambridge, MD	32,640	32,618	30,674	30,236	22	1,944	0.1	6.3	1,135	1,090	4.1	34,771	33,390
Dorchester County, MD	32,640	32,618	30,674	30,236	22	1,944	0.1	6.3	1,135	1,090	4.1	34,771	33,390
Cambridge, OH	39,927	40,087	40,792	39,024	-160	-705	-0.4	-1.7	1,196	1,129	6.0	29,955	28,186
Guernsey County, OH	39,927	40,087	40,792	39,024	-160	-705	-0.4	-1.7	1,196	1,129	6.0	29,955	28,186
Camden, AR	31,024	31,488	34,534	36,400	-464	-3,046	-1.5	-8.8	948	925	2.5	30,566	29,408
Calhoun County, AR	5,144	5,368	5,744	5,826	-224	-376	-4.2	-6.5	146	145	0.3	28,356	27,272
Ouachita County, AR	25,880	26,120	28,790	30,574	-240	-2,670	-0.9	-9.3	802	780	2.9	31,006	29,844
Campbellsville, KY	24,731	24,512	22,927	21,146	219	1,585	0.9	6.9	713	679	5.0	28,837	27,649
Taylor County, KY	24,731	24,512	22,927	21,146	219	1,585	0.9	6.9	713	679	5.0	28,837	27,649
Ca±on City, CO	47,347	46,824	46,145	32,273	523	679	1.1	1.5	1,299	1,241	4.7	27,440	26,477
Fremont County, CO	47,347	46,824	46,145	32,273	523	679	1.1	1.5	1,299	1,241	4.7	27,440	26,477
Canton, IL	36,962	37,069	38,250	38,080	-107	-1,181	-0.3	-3.1	1,246	1,196	4.2	33,723	32,280
Fulton County, IL	36,962	37,069	38,250	38,080	-107	-1,181	-0.3	-3.1	1,246	1,196	4.2	33,723	32,280
Carbondale, IL	60,365	60,218	59,612	61,067	147	606	0.2	1.0	2,005	1,961	2.2	33,213	32,495
Jackson County, IL	60,365	60,218	59,612	61,067	147	606	0.2	1.0	2,005	1,961	2.2	33,213	32,495
Carlsbad–Artesia, NM	54,152	53,829	51,658	48,605	323	2,171	0.6	4.2	2,249	2,200	2.2	41,539	40,803
Eddy County, NM	54,152	53,829	51,658	48,605	323	2,171	0.6	4.2	2,249	2,200	2.2	41,539	40,803
Cedar City, UT	46,740	46,163	33,779	20,789	577	12,384	1.2	36.7	1,100	1,049	4.9	23,541	22,665
Iron County, UT	46,740	46,163	33,779	20,789	577	12,384	1.2	36.7	1,100	1,049	4.9	23,541	22,665

[1]The April 1, 2000, Population Estimates base reflects modifications to the Census 2000 population as documented in the Count Question Resolution program and geographic program revisions.
[2]The April 1, 1990, census counts include corrections processed through August 1997, results of special censuses and test censuses, and do not include adjustments for census coverage errors.
[3]Based on the April 1, 2010, census counts and the July 1, 2011, estimates.
[4]Based on the April 1, 2010, census counts and the April 1, 2000, estimates base.
[5]Based on resident population estimated as of April 1, 2010 and July 1, 2011 of the year shown.

Table D-1.   Population and Personal Income—*Continued*

Micropolitan statistical area component counties	Population 2011 estimate (July 1)	2010 census count (April 1)	2000 estimates base (April 1)[1]	1990 estimates base (April 1)[2]	Net change 2010–2011[3]	Net change 2000–2010[4]	Percent change 2010–2011[3]	Percent change 2000–2010[4]	Personal Income Total (million dollars) 2011	Total 2010	Percentage change, 2010–2011	Per capita[5] 2011	Per capita 2010
Cedartown, GA	41,211	41,475	38,127	33,815	-264	3,348	-0.6	8.8	1,090	1,051	3.7	26,456	25,405
Polk County, GA	41,211	41,475	38,127	33,815	-264	3,348	-0.6	8.8	1,090	1,051	3.7	26,456	25,405
Celina, OH	40,838	40,814	40,924	39,443	24	-110	0.1	-0.3	1,551	1,429	8.6	37,992	35,004
Mercer County, OH	40,838	40,814	40,924	39,443	24	-110	0.1	-0.3	1,551	1,429	8.6	37,992	35,004
Central City, KY	31,272	31,499	31,839	31,318	-227	-340	-0.7	-1.1	889	824	7.9	28,429	26,169
Muhlenberg County, KY	31,272	31,499	31,839	31,318	-227	-340	-0.7	-1.1	889	824	7.9	28,429	26,169
Centralia, IL	39,335	39,437	41,691	41,561	-102	-2,254	-0.3	-5.4	1,312	1,285	2.1	33,356	32,593
Marion County, IL	39,335	39,437	41,691	41,561	-102	-2,254	-0.3	-5.4	1,312	1,285	2.1	33,356	32,593
Centralia, WA	75,901	75,455	68,600	59,358	446	6,855	0.6	10.0	2,368	2,279	3.9	31,192	30,189
Lewis County, WA	75,901	75,455	68,600	59,358	446	6,855	0.6	10.0	2,368	2,279	3.9	31,192	30,189
Chambersburg, PA	150,811	149,618	129,313	121,082	1,193	20,305	0.8	15.7	5,169	4,916	5.2	34,277	32,803
Franklin County, PA	150,811	149,618	129,313	121,082	1,193	20,305	0.8	15.7	5,169	4,916	5.2	34,277	32,803
Charleston–Mattoon, IL	65,012	64,921	64,448	62,314	91	472	0.1	0.7	2,171	2,059	5.4	33,393	31,681
Coles County, IL	53,916	53,873	53,196	51,644	43	677	0.1	1.3	1,773	1,687	5.0	32,876	31,281
Cumberland County, IL	11,096	11,048	11,253	10,670	48	-205	0.4	-1.8	398	372	7.2	35,900	33,635
Chester, SC	32,916	33,140	34,068	32,170	-224	-928	-0.7	-2.7	929	900	3.3	28,237	27,171
Chester County, SC	32,916	33,140	34,068	32,170	-224	-928	-0.7	-2.7	929	900	3.3	28,237	27,171
Chillicothe, OH	78,249	78,064	73,345	69,330	185	4,719	0.2	6.4	2,356	2,212	6.5	30,110	28,306
Ross County, OH	78,249	78,064	73,345	69,330	185	4,719	0.2	6.4	2,356	2,212	6.5	30,110	28,306
Claremont, NH	43,462	43,742	40,458	38,592	-280	3,284	-0.6	8.1	1,632	1,576	3.6	37,559	36,042
Sullivan County, NH	43,462	43,742	40,458	38,592	-280	3,284	-0.6	8.1	1,632	1,576	3.6	37,559	36,042
Clarksburg, WV	94,523	94,196	92,144	91,509	327	2,052	0.3	2.2	3,311	3,154	5.0	35,033	33,446
Doddridge County, WV	8,171	8,202	7,403	6,994	-31	799	-0.4	10.8	167	162	3.0	20,412	19,785
Harrison County, WV	69,436	69,099	68,652	69,371	337	447	0.5	0.7	2,687	2,552	5.3	38,703	36,869
Taylor County, WV	16,916	16,895	16,089	15,144	21	806	0.1	5.0	457	440	3.9	27,030	26,049
Clarksdale, MS	25,913	26,151	30,622	31,665	-238	-4,471	-0.9	-14.6	845	802	5.3	32,607	30,702
Coahoma County, MS	25,913	26,151	30,622	31,665	-238	-4,471	-0.9	-14.6	845	802	5.3	32,607	30,702
Clearlake, CA	64,323	64,665	58,309	50,631	-342	6,356	-0.5	10.9	2,147	2,067	3.9	33,375	31,921
Lake County, CA	64,323	64,665	58,309	50,631	-342	6,356	-0.5	10.9	2,147	2,067	3.9	33,375	31,921
Cleveland, MS	33,771	34,145	40,633	41,875	-374	-6,488	-1.1	-16.0	1,084	1,038	4.5	32,106	30,451
Bolivar County, MS	33,771	34,145	40,633	41,875	-374	-6,488	-1.1	-16.0	1,084	1,038	4.5	32,106	30,451
Clewiston, FL	39,089	39,140	36,210	25,773	-51	2,930	-0.1	8.1	1,106	1,087	1.7	28,285	27,773
Hendry County, FL	39,089	39,140	36,210	25,773	-51	2,930	-0.1	8.1	1,106	1,087	1.7	28,285	27,773
Clinton, IA	49,015	49,116	50,149	51,040	-101	-1,033	-0.2	-2.1	1,928	1,779	8.4	39,340	36,220
Clinton County, IA	49,015	49,116	50,149	51,040	-101	-1,033	-0.2	-2.1	1,928	1,779	8.4	39,340	36,220
Clovis, NM	49,649	48,376	45,044	42,207	1,273	3,332	2.6	7.4	1,978	1,797	10.1	39,844	36,710
Curry County, NM	49,649	48,376	45,044	42,207	1,273	3,332	2.6	7.4	1,978	1,797	10.1	39,844	36,710
Coffeyville, KS	34,911	35,471	36,252	38,816	-560	-781	-1.6	-2.2	1,192	1,129	5.6	34,133	31,913
Montgomery County, KS	34,911	35,471	36,252	38,816	-560	-781	-1.6	-2.2	1,192	1,129	5.6	34,133	31,913
Coldwater, MI	45,197	45,248	45,787	41,502	-51	-539	-0.1	-1.2	1,270	1,208	5.1	28,098	26,747
Branch County, MI	45,197	45,248	45,787	41,502	-51	-539	-0.1	-1.2	1,270	1,208	5.1	28,098	26,747
Columbia, TN	81,509	80,956	69,498	54,812	553	11,458	0.7	16.5	2,567	2,449	4.9	31,498	30,167
Maury County, TN	81,509	80,956	69,498	54,812	553	11,458	0.7	16.5	2,567	2,449	4.9	31,498	30,167
Columbus, MS	59,671	59,779	61,586	59,308	-108	-1,807	-0.2	-2.9	2,023	1,901	6.4	33,905	31,786
Lowndes County, MS	59,671	59,779	61,586	59,308	-108	-1,807	-0.2	-2.9	2,023	1,901	6.4	33,905	31,786
Columbus, NE	32,593	32,237	31,662	29,820	356	575	1.1	1.8	1,289	1,176	9.6	39,552	36,432
Platte County, NE	32,593	32,237	31,662	29,820	356	575	1.1	1.8	1,289	1,176	9.6	39,552	36,432
Concord, NH	146,579	146,445	136,225	120,240	134	10,220	0.1	7.5	6,383	6,137	4.0	43,548	41,910
Merrimack County, NH	146,579	146,445	136,225	120,240	134	10,220	0.1	7.5	6,383	6,137	4.0	43,548	41,910
Connersville, IN	24,285	24,277	25,588	26,015	8	-1,311	0.0	-5.1	694	666	4.2	28,590	27,414
Fayette County, IN	24,285	24,277	25,588	26,015	8	-1,311	0.0	-5.1	694	666	4.2	28,590	27,414
Cookeville, TN	106,498	106,042	93,417	78,306	456	12,625	0.4	13.5	3,202	3,086	3.7	30,065	29,029
Jackson County, TN	11,371	11,638	10,984	9,297	-267	654	-2.3	6.0	348	337	3.3	30,621	28,937
Overton County, TN	22,169	22,083	20,118	17,636	86	1,965	0.4	9.8	566	548	3.3	25,514	24,773
Putnam County, TN	72,958	72,321	62,315	51,373	637	10,006	0.9	16.1	2,288	2,202	3.9	31,362	30,341
Coos Bay, OR	62,791	63,043	62,779	60,273	-252	264	-0.4	0.4	2,037	1,939	5.1	32,443	30,767
Coos County, OR	62,791	63,043	62,779	60,273	-252	264	-0.4	0.4	2,037	1,939	5.1	32,443	30,767
Corbin, KY	35,823	35,637	35,865	33,326	186	-228	0.5	-0.6	1,057	1,033	2.3	29,500	28,973
Whitley County, KY	35,823	35,637	35,865	33,326	186	-228	0.5	-0.6	1,057	1,033	2.3	29,500	28,973
Cordele, GA	23,710	23,439	21,996	20,011	271	1,443	1.2	6.6	630	605	4.1	26,565	25,834
Crisp County, GA	23,710	23,439	21,996	20,011	271	1,443	1.2	6.6	630	605	4.1	26,565	25,834
Corinth, MS	37,052	37,057	34,558	31,722	-5	2,499	0.0	7.2	1,032	992	4.0	27,844	26,746
Alcorn County, MS	37,052	37,057	34,558	31,722	-5	2,499	0.0	7.2	1,032	992	4.0	27,844	26,746
Cornelia, GA	43,279	43,041	35,902	27,622	238	7,139	0.6	19.9	1,172	1,130	3.7	27,075	26,227
Habersham County, GA	43,279	43,041	35,902	27,622	238	7,139	0.6	19.9	1,172	1,130	3.7	27,075	26,227
Corning, NY	99,033	98,990	98,726	99,088	43	264	0.0	0.3	3,692	3,554	3.9	37,278	35,917
Steuben County, NY	99,033	98,990	98,726	99,088	43	264	0.0	0.3	3,692	3,554	3.9	37,278	35,917
Corsicana, TX	48,054	47,735	45,124	39,926	319	2,611	0.7	5.8	1,591	1,508	5.5	33,112	31,546
Navarro County, TX	48,054	47,735	45,124	39,926	319	2,611	0.7	5.8	1,591	1,508	5.5	33,112	31,546
Cortland, NY	49,363	49,336	48,599	48,963	27	737	0.1	1.5	1,578	1,514	4.3	31,972	30,692
Cortland County, NY	49,363	49,336	48,599	48,963	27	737	0.1	1.5	1,578	1,514	4.3	31,972	30,692

[1]The April 1, 2000, Population Estimates base reflects modifications to the Census 2000 population as documented in the Count Question Resolution program and geographic program revisions.
[2]The April 1, 1990, census counts include corrections processed through August 1997, results of special censuses and test censuses, and do not include adjustments for census coverage errors.
[3]Based on the April 1, 2010, census counts and the July 1, 2011, estimates.
[4]Based on the April 1, 2010, census counts and the April 1, 2000, estimates base.
[5]Based on resident population estimated as of April 1, 2010 and July 1, 2011 of the year shown.

Table D-1. Population and Personal Income—*Continued*

Micropolitan statistical area component counties	2011 estimate (July 1)	2010 census count (April 1)	2000 estimates base (April 1)[1]	1990 estimates base (April 1)[2]	Net change		Percent change		Total (million dollars)		Percentage change, 2010–2011	Per capita[5]	
					2010–2011[3]	2000–2010[4]	2010–2011[3]	2000–2010[4]	2011	2010		2011	2010
Coshocton, OH	36,955	36,901	36,655	35,427	54	246	0.1	0.7	1,099	1,049	4.7	29,730	28,426
Coshocton County, OH	36,955	36,901	36,655	35,427	54	246	0.1	0.7	1,099	1,049	4.7	29,730	28,426
Crawfordsville, IN	38,441	38,124	37,629	34,436	317	495	0.8	1.3	1,270	1,184	7.3	33,045	31,068
Montgomery County, IN	38,441	38,124	37,629	34,436	317	495	0.8	1.3	1,270	1,184	7.3	33,045	31,068
Crescent City, CA	28,659	28,610	27,507	23,460	49	1,103	0.2	4.0	780	755	3.3	27,220	26,383
Del Norte County, CA	28,659	28,610	27,507	23,460	49	1,103	0.2	4.0	780	755	3.3	27,220	26,383
Crossville, TN	56,632	56,053	46,802	34,736	579	9,251	1.0	19.8	1,692	1,623	4.2	29,871	28,875
Cumberland County, TN	56,632	56,053	46,802	34,736	579	9,251	1.0	19.8	1,692	1,623	4.2	29,871	28,875
Crowley, LA	61,982	61,773	58,861	55,882	209	2,912	0.3	4.9	2,038	1,958	4.1	32,883	31,660
Acadia Parish, LA	61,982	61,773	58,861	55,882	209	2,912	0.3	4.9	2,038	1,958	4.1	32,883	31,660
Cullman, AL	80,536	80,406	77,483	67,613	130	2,923	0.2	3.8	2,466	2,448	0.7	30,616	30,416
Cullman County, AL	80,536	80,406	77,483	67,613	130	2,923	0.2	3.8	2,466	2,448	0.7	30,616	30,416
Culpeper, VA	47,476	46,689	34,262	27,791	787	12,427	1.7	36.3	1,702	1,602	6.3	35,850	34,192
Culpeper County, VA	47,476	46,689	34,262	27,791	787	12,427	1.7	36.3	1,702	1,602	6.3	35,850	34,192
Danville, KY	53,281	53,174	51,058	45,686	107	2,116	0.2	4.1	1,500	1,451	3.4	28,146	27,259
Boyle County, KY	28,550	28,432	27,697	25,590	118	735	0.4	2.7	876	847	3.5	30,686	29,729
Lincoln County, KY	24,731	24,742	23,361	20,096	-11	1,381	0.0	5.9	624	604	3.2	25,212	24,416
Daphne–Fairhope–Foley, AL	186,717	182,265	140,415	98,280	4,452	41,850	2.4	29.8	7,100	6,654	6.7	38,024	36,311
Baldwin County, AL	186,717	182,265	140,415	98,280	4,452	41,850	2.4	29.8	7,100	6,654	6.7	38,024	36,311
Decatur, IN	34,370	34,387	33,625	31,095	-17	762	0.0	2.3	1,016	952	6.8	29,566	27,647
Adams County, IN	34,370	34,387	33,625	31,095	-17	762	0.0	2.3	1,016	952	6.8	29,566	27,647
Defiance, OH	38,884	39,037	39,500	39,350	-153	-463	-0.4	-1.2	1,296	1,221	6.1	33,323	31,299
Defiance County, OH	38,884	39,037	39,500	39,350	-153	-463	-0.4	-1.2	1,296	1,221	6.1	33,323	31,299
Del Rio, TX	49,106	48,879	44,856	38,721	227	4,023	0.5	9.0	1,508	1,451	3.9	30,702	29,589
Val Verde County, TX	49,106	48,879	44,856	38,721	227	4,023	0.5	9.0	1,508	1,451	3.9	30,702	29,589
Deming, NM	25,281	25,095	25,016	18,110	186	79	0.7	0.3	742	717	3.4	29,338	28,520
Luna County, NM	25,281	25,095	25,016	18,110	186	79	0.7	0.3	742	717	3.4	29,338	28,520
DeRidder, LA	36,129	35,654	32,986	30,083	475	2,668	1.3	8.1	1,073	1,028	4.4	29,705	28,684
Beauregard Parish, LA	36,129	35,654	32,986	30,083	475	2,668	1.3	8.1	1,073	1,028	4.4	29,705	28,684
Dickinson, ND	25,993	24,982	23,524	23,940	1,011	1,458	4.0	6.2	1,441	1,198	20.3	55,442	47,674
Billings County, ND	816	783	888	1,108	33	-105	4.2	-11.8	63	45	39.8	76,798	58,006
Stark County, ND	25,177	24,199	22,636	22,832	978	1,563	4.0	6.9	1,378	1,153	19.6	54,750	47,346
Dillon, SC	31,758	32,062	30,722	29,114	-304	1,340	-0.9	4.4	750	746	0.5	23,616	23,219
Dillon County, SC	31,758	32,062	30,722	29,114	-304	1,340	-0.9	4.4	750	746	0.5	23,616	23,219
Dixon, IL	35,467	36,031	36,062	34,392	-564	-31	-1.6	-0.1	1,235	1,173	5.3	34,815	32,623
Lee County, IL	35,467	36,031	36,062	34,392	-564	-31	-1.6	-0.1	1,235	1,173	5.3	34,815	32,623
Dodge City, KS	34,568	33,848	32,458	27,463	720	1,390	2.1	4.3	1,117	1,067	4.7	32,309	31,296
Ford County, KS	34,568	33,848	32,458	27,463	720	1,390	2.1	4.3	1,117	1,067	4.7	32,309	31,296
Douglas, GA	51,277	50,731	45,022	35,805	546	5,709	1.1	12.7	1,263	1,201	5.1	24,627	23,549
Atkinson County, GA	8,413	8,375	7,609	6,213	38	766	0.5	10.1	186	177	5.4	22,165	21,138
Coffee County, GA	42,864	42,356	37,413	29,592	508	4,943	1.2	13.2	1,076	1,025	5.1	25,110	24,022
Dublin, GA	57,924	58,414	53,434	48,317	-490	4,980	-0.8	9.3	1,629	1,591	2.4	28,121	27,252
Johnson County, GA	9,975	9,980	8,560	8,329	-5	1,420	-0.1	16.6	208	200	4.3	20,901	20,041
Laurens County, GA	47,949	48,434	44,874	39,988	-485	3,560	-1.0	7.9	1,420	1,392	2.1	29,622	28,737
DuBois, PA	81,445	81,642	83,382	78,097	-197	-1,740	-0.2	-2.1	2,621	2,503	4.7	32,181	30,634
Clearfield County, PA	81,445	81,642	83,382	78,097	-197	-1,740	-0.2	-2.1	2,621	2,503	4.7	32,181	30,634
Dumas, TX	21,954	21,904	20,121	17,865	50	1,783	0.2	8.9	748	674	10.9	34,060	30,673
Moore County, TX	21,954	21,904	20,121	17,865	50	1,783	0.2	8.9	748	674	10.9	34,060	30,673
Duncan, OK	45,197	45,048	43,182	42,299	149	1,866	0.3	4.3	1,733	1,584	9.4	38,344	35,128
Stephens County, OK	45,197	45,048	43,182	42,299	149	1,866	0.3	4.3	1,733	1,584	9.4	38,344	35,128
Dunn, NC	119,256	114,678	91,025	67,833	4,578	23,653	4.0	26.0	3,488	3,319	5.1	29,247	28,666
Harnett County, NC	119,256	114,678	91,025	67,833	4,578	23,653	4.0	26.0	3,488	3,319	5.1	29,247	28,666
Durango, CO	51,917	51,334	43,941	32,284	583	7,393	1.1	16.8	2,256	2,178	3.6	43,453	42,346
La Plata County, CO	51,917	51,334	43,941	32,284	583	7,393	1.1	16.8	2,256	2,178	3.6	43,453	42,346
Durant, OK	43,089	42,416	36,534	32,089	673	5,882	1.6	16.1	1,245	1,196	4.1	28,891	28,085
Bryan County, OK	43,089	42,416	36,534	32,089	673	5,882	1.6	16.1	1,245	1,196	4.1	28,891	28,085
Dyersburg, TN	38,192	38,335	37,279	34,854	-143	1,056	-0.4	2.8	1,235	1,186	4.1	32,333	30,950
Dyer County, TN	38,192	38,335	37,279	34,854	-143	1,056	-0.4	2.8	1,235	1,186	4.1	32,333	30,950
Eagle Pass, TX	55,405	54,258	47,297	36,378	1,147	6,961	2.1	14.7	1,229	1,146	7.3	22,188	21,006
Maverick County, TX	55,405	54,258	47,297	36,378	1,147	6,961	2.1	14.7	1,229	1,146	7.3	22,188	21,006
East Liverpool–Salem, OH	107,570	107,841	112,075	108,276	-271	-4,234	-0.3	-3.8	3,291	3,051	7.9	30,590	28,287
Columbiana County, OH	107,570	107,841	112,075	108,276	-271	-4,234	-0.3	-3.8	3,291	3,051	7.9	30,590	28,287
Easton, MD	38,025	37,782	33,812	30,549	243	3,970	0.6	11.7	2,119	2,009	5.4	55,721	53,050
Talbot County, MD	38,025	37,782	33,812	30,549	243	3,970	0.6	11.7	2,119	2,009	5.4	55,721	53,050
East Stroudsburg, PA	169,882	169,842	138,687	95,681	40	31,155	0.0	22.5	5,362	5,172	3.7	31,566	30,416
Monroe County, PA	169,882	169,842	138,687	95,681	40	31,155	0.0	22.5	5,362	5,172	3.7	31,566	30,416

[1]The April 1, 2000, Population Estimates base reflects modifications to the Census 2000 population as documented in the Count Question Resolution program and geographic program revisions.
[2]The April 1, 1990, census counts include corrections processed through August 1997, results of special censuses and test censuses, and do not include adjustments for census coverage errors.
[3]Based on the April 1, 2010, census counts and the July 1, 2011, estimates.
[4]Based on the April 1, 2010, census counts and the April 1, 2000, estimates base.
[5]Based on resident population estimated as of April 1, 2010 and July 1, 2011 of the year shown.

Table D-1.　Population and Personal Income—*Continued*

Micropolitan statistical area component counties	Population								Personal Income				
	2011 estimate (July 1)	2010 census count (April 1)	2000 estimates base (April 1)[1]	1990 estimates base (April 1)[2]	Net change		Percent change		Total (million dollars)		Percentage change, 2010–2011	Per capita[5]	
					2010–2011[3]	2000–2010[4]	2010–2011[3]	2000–2010[4]	2011	2010		2011	2010
Edwards, CO	59,281	59,507	49,471	27,935	-226	10,036	-0.4	20.3	2,738	2,620	4.5	46,195	44,146
Eagle County, CO	51,854	52,197	41,659	21,928	-343	10,538	-0.7	25.3	2,521	2,414	4.5	48,618	46,358
Lake County, CO	7,427	7,310	7,812	6,007	117	-502	1.6	-6.4	217	207	5.2	29,274	28,346
Effingham, IL	34,280	34,242	34,264	31,704	38	-22	0.1	-0.1	1,299	1,239	4.8	37,882	36,208
Effingham County, IL	34,280	34,242	34,264	31,704	38	-22	0.1	-0.1	1,299	1,239	4.8	37,882	36,208
El Campo, TX	41,314	41,280	41,188	39,955	34	92	0.1	0.2	1,469	1,363	7.8	35,556	32,945
Wharton County, TX	41,314	41,280	41,188	39,955	34	92	0.1	0.2	1,469	1,363	7.8	35,556	32,945
El Dorado, AR	41,427	41,639	45,629	46,719	-212	-3,990	-0.5	-8.7	1,754	1,682	4.3	42,335	40,486
Union County, AR	41,427	41,639	45,629	46,719	-212	-3,990	-0.5	-8.7	1,754	1,682	4.3	42,335	40,486
Elizabeth City, NC	64,197	64,094	53,150	47,649	103	10,944	0.2	20.6	1,948	1,865	4.5	30,349	29,042
Camden County, NC	10,014	9,980	6,885	5,904	34	3,095	0.3	45.0	374	355	5.2	37,353	35,524
Pasquotank County, NC	40,696	40,661	34,897	31,298	35	5,764	0.1	16.5	1,167	1,122	4.0	28,673	27,566
Perquimans County, NC	13,487	13,453	11,368	10,447	34	2,085	0.3	18.3	407	387	5.3	30,207	28,688
Elk City, OK	22,288	22,119	19,799	18,812	169	2,320	0.8	11.7	816	724	12.7	36,616	32,864
Beckham County, OK	22,288	22,119	19,799	18,812	169	2,320	0.8	11.7	816	724	12.7	36,616	32,864
Elko, NV	51,470	50,805	46,942	35,010	665	3,863	1.3	8.2	2,062	1,887	9.3	40,070	37,033
Elko County, NV	49,491	48,818	45,291	33,463	673	3,527	1.4	7.8	1,987	1,822	9.1	40,150	37,215
Eureka County, NV	1,979	1,987	1,651	1,547	-8	336	-0.4	20.4	75	65	15.8	38,071	32,569
Ellensburg, WA	41,629	40,915	33,362	26,725	714	7,553	1.7	22.6	1,375	1,314	4.7	33,031	32,010
Kittitas County, WA	41,629	40,915	33,362	26,725	714	7,553	1.7	22.6	1,375	1,314	4.7	33,031	32,010
Emporia, KS	36,581	36,480	38,965	37,753	101	-2,485	0.3	-6.4	1,141	1,088	4.8	31,186	29,858
Chase County, KS	2,817	2,790	3,030	3,021	27	-240	1.0	-7.9	145	141	3.0	51,481	50,452
Lyon County, KS	33,764	33,690	35,935	34,732	74	-2,245	0.2	-6.2	996	947	5.1	29,493	28,149
Enid, OK	60,670	60,580	57,813	56,735	90	2,767	0.1	4.8	2,415	2,273	6.2	39,803	37,419
Garfield County, OK	60,670	60,580	57,813	56,735	90	2,767	0.1	4.8	2,415	2,273	6.2	39,803	37,419
Enterprise–Ozark, AL	100,570	100,199	92,744	89,873	371	7,455	0.4	8.0	3,373	3,281	2.8	33,538	32,648
Coffee County, AL	50,526	49,948	43,615	40,240	578	6,333	1.2	14.5	1,852	1,793	3.3	36,653	35,732
Dale County, AL	50,044	50,251	49,129	49,633	-207	1,122	-0.4	2.3	1,521	1,489	2.2	30,393	29,574
Escanaba, MI	37,105	37,069	38,520	37,780	36	-1,451	0.1	-3.8	1,194	1,148	4.0	32,175	30,967
Delta County, MI	37,105	37,069	38,520	37,780	36	-1,451	0.1	-3.8	1,194	1,148	4.0	32,175	30,967
Espanola, NM	40,446	40,246	41,190	34,365	200	-944	0.5	-2.3	1,168	1,150	1.6	28,888	28,504
Rio Arriba County, NM	40,446	40,246	41,190	34,365	200	-944	0.5	-2.3	1,168	1,150	1.6	28,888	28,504
Eufaula, AL–GA	29,583	29,970	31,636	27,627	-387	-1,666	-1.3	-5.3	790	783	0.9	26,719	26,183
Barbour County, AL	27,119	27,457	29,038	25,417	-338	-1,581	-1.2	-5.4	727	720	0.9	26,807	26,295
Quitman County, GA	2,464	2,513	2,598	2,210	-49	-85	-1.9	-3.3	63	63	0.9	25,757	24,960
Eureka–Arcata–Fortuna, CA	134,761	134,623	126,518	119,118	138	8,105	0.1	6.4	4,489	4,321	3.9	33,308	32,067
Humboldt County, CA	134,761	134,623	126,518	119,118	138	8,105	0.1	6.4	4,489	4,321	3.9	33,308	32,067
Evanston, WY	20,985	21,118	19,742	18,705	-133	1,376	-0.6	7.0	878	870	0.9	41,833	41,209
Uinta County, WY	20,985	21,118	19,742	18,705	-133	1,376	-0.6	7.0	878	870	0.9	41,833	41,209
Fairmont, MN	20,689	20,840	21,802	22,914	-151	-962	-0.7	-4.4	942	905	4.1	45,532	43,459
Martin County, MN	20,689	20,840	21,802	22,914	-151	-962	-0.7	-4.4	942	905	4.1	45,532	43,459
Fairmont, WV	56,586	56,418	56,598	57,249	168	-180	0.3	-0.3	2,056	1,948	5.6	36,338	34,486
Marion County, WV	56,586	56,418	56,598	57,249	168	-180	0.3	-0.3	2,056	1,948	5.6	36,338	34,486
Fallon, NV	24,637	24,877	23,982	17,938	-240	895	-1.0	3.7	1,042	998	4.4	42,281	40,222
Churchill County, NV	24,637	24,877	23,982	17,938	-240	895	-1.0	3.7	1,042	998	4.4	42,281	40,222
Faribault–Northfield, MN	64,409	64,142	56,665	49,183	267	7,477	0.4	13.2	2,102	2,013	4.4	32,631	31,323
Rice County, MN	64,409	64,142	56,665	49,183	267	7,477	0.4	13.2	2,102	2,013	4.4	32,631	31,323
Farmington, MO	65,577	65,359	55,641	48,904	218	9,718	0.3	17.5	1,829	1,751	4.5	27,886	26,730
St. Francois County, MO	65,577	65,359	55,641	48,904	218	9,718	0.3	17.5	1,829	1,751	4.5	27,886	26,730
Fergus Falls, MN	57,252	57,303	57,159	50,714	-51	144	-0.1	0.3	2,106	1,987	6.0	36,781	34,699
Otter Tail County, MN	57,252	57,303	57,159	50,714	-51	144	-0.1	0.3	2,106	1,987	6.0	36,781	34,699
Fernley, NV	51,871	51,980	34,501	20,001	-109	17,479	-0.2	50.7	1,444	1,397	3.4	27,835	26,805
Lyon County, NV	51,871	51,980	34,501	20,001	-109	17,479	-0.2	50.7	1,444	1,397	3.4	27,835	26,805
Findlay, OH	75,056	74,782	71,295	65,536	274	3,487	0.4	4.9	2,966	2,773	7.0	39,523	37,106
Hancock County, OH	75,056	74,782	71,295	65,536	274	3,487	0.4	4.9	2,966	2,773	7.0	39,523	37,106
Fitzgerald, GA	27,352	27,172	27,415	24,894	180	-243	0.7	-0.9	746	716	4.2	27,260	26,261
Ben Hill County, GA	17,673	17,634	17,484	16,245	39	150	0.2	0.9	470	455	3.3	26,606	25,810
Irwin County, GA	9,679	9,538	9,931	8,649	141	-393	1.5	-4.0	275	260	5.7	28,454	27,089
Forest City, NC	67,538	67,810	62,899	56,956	-272	4,911	-0.4	7.8	1,732	1,674	3.5	25,640	24,697
Rutherford County, NC	67,538	67,810	62,899	56,956	-272	4,911	-0.4	7.8	1,732	1,674	3.5	25,640	24,697
Forrest City, AR	27,970	28,258	29,329	28,497	-288	-1,071	-1.0	-3.7	738	708	4.3	26,373	25,121
St. Francis County, AR	27,970	28,258	29,329	28,497	-288	-1,071	-1.0	-3.7	738	708	4.3	26,373	25,121
Fort Dodge, IA	37,660	38,013	40,235	40,342	-353	-2,222	-0.9	-5.5	1,486	1,334	11.5	39,467	35,200
Webster County, IA	37,660	38,013	40,235	40,342	-353	-2,222	-0.9	-5.5	1,486	1,334	11.5	39,467	35,200
Fort Leonard Wood, MO	53,175	52,274	41,165	41,307	901	11,109	1.7	27.0	2,215	2,035	8.8	41,655	38,540
Pulaski County, MO	53,175	52,274	41,165	41,307	901	11,109	1.7	27.0	2,215	2,035	8.8	41,655	38,540

[1]The April 1, 2000, Population Estimates base reflects modifications to the Census 2000 population as documented in the Count Question Resolution program and geographic program revisions.
[2]The April 1, 1990, census counts include corrections processed through August 1997, results of special censuses and test censuses, and do not include adjustments for census coverage errors.
[3]Based on the April 1, 2010, census counts and the July 1, 2011, estimates.
[4]Based on the April 1, 2010, census counts and the April 1, 2000, estimates base.
[5]Based on resident population estimated as of April 1, 2010 and July 1, 2011 of the year shown.

Table D-1. Population and Personal Income—*Continued*

Micropolitan statistical area component counties	Population								Personal Income				
	2011 estimate (July 1)	2010 census count (April 1)	2000 estimates base (April 1)[1]	1990 estimates base (April 1)[2]	Net change		Percent change		Total (million dollars)		Percentage change, 2010–2011	Per capita[5]	
					2010–2011[3]	2000–2010[4]	2010–2011[3]	2000–2010[4]	2011	2010		2011	2010
Fort Madison–Keokuk, IA–MO	42,640	43,001	45,468	46,234	-361	-2,467	-0.8	-5.4	1,392	1,310	6.3	32,654	30,482
Lee County, IA.........................	35,621	35,862	38,052	38,687	-241	-2,190	-0.7	-5.8	1,169	1,103	6.0	32,827	30,780
Clark County, MO	7,019	7,139	7,416	7,547	-120	-277	-1.7	-3.7	223	207	7.8	31,779	28,987
Fort Morgan, CO	28,175	28,159	27,171	21,939	16	988	0.1	3.6	944	860	9.7	33,489	30,722
Morgan County, CO	28,175	28,159	27,171	21,939	16	988	0.1	3.6	944	860	9.7	33,489	30,722
Fort Payne, AL..........................	71,375	71,109	64,452	54,651	266	6,657	0.4	10.3	1,826	1,873	-2.5	25,586	26,340
DeKalb County, AL	71,375	71,109	64,452	54,651	266	6,657	0.4	10.3	1,826	1,873	-2.5	25,586	26,340
Fort Polk South, LA...................	52,107	52,334	52,531	61,961	-227	-197	-0.4	-0.4	2,287	2,102	8.8	43,887	39,867
Vernon Parish, LA	52,107	52,334	52,531	61,961	-227	-197	-0.4	-0.4	2,287	2,102	8.8	43,887	39,867
Fort Valley, GA.........................	27,823	27,695	23,668	21,189	128	4,027	0.5	17.0	829	789	5.1	29,801	28,411
Peach County, GA	27,823	27,695	23,668	21,189	128	4,027	0.5	17.0	829	789	5.1	29,801	28,411
Frankfort, IN..............................	33,104	33,224	33,866	30,974	-120	-642	-0.4	-1.9	1,062	984	7.9	32,076	29,630
Clinton County, IN	33,104	33,224	33,866	30,974	-120	-642	-0.4	-1.9	1,062	984	7.9	32,076	29,630
Frankfort, KY............................	71,037	70,706	66,798	58,714	331	3,908	0.5	5.9	2,455	2,354	4.3	34,554	33,268
Anderson County, KY	21,644	21,421	19,111	14,571	223	2,310	1.0	12.1	672	643	4.5	31,048	29,938
Franklin County, KY................	49,393	49,285	47,687	44,143	108	1,598	0.2	3.4	1,783	1,711	4.2	36,091	34,720
Fredericksburg, TX....................	25,114	24,837	20,814	17,204	277	4,023	1.1	19.3	1,194	1,123	6.4	47,550	45,079
Gillespie County, TX	25,114	24,837	20,814	17,204	277	4,023	1.1	19.3	1,194	1,123	6.4	47,550	45,079
Freeport, IL...............................	47,563	47,711	48,979	48,052	-148	-1,268	-0.3	-2.6	1,759	1,682	4.6	36,980	35,254
Stephenson County, IL............	47,563	47,711	48,979	48,052	-148	-1,268	-0.3	-2.6	1,759	1,682	4.6	36,980	35,254
Fremont, NE..............................	36,773	36,691	36,160	34,500	82	531	0.2	1.5	1,408	1,312	7.3	38,292	35,771
Dodge County, NE	36,773	36,691	36,160	34,500	82	531	0.2	1.5	1,408	1,312	7.3	38,292	35,771
Fremont, OH..............................	60,734	60,944	61,792	61,963	-210	-848	-0.3	-1.4	2,015	1,918	5.0	33,170	31,490
Sandusky County, OH	60,734	60,944	61,792	61,963	-210	-848	-0.3	-1.4	2,015	1,918	5.0	33,170	31,490
Gaffney, SC...............................	55,540	55,342	52,537	44,506	198	2,805	0.4	5.3	1,492	1,439	3.7	26,856	25,964
Cherokee County, SC..............	55,540	55,342	52,537	44,506	198	2,805	0.4	5.3	1,492	1,439	3.7	26,856	25,964
Gainesville, TX..........................	38,396	38,437	36,363	30,777	-41	2,074	-0.1	5.7	1,757	1,591	10.4	45,765	41,392
Cooke County, TX	38,396	38,437	36,363	30,777	-41	2,074	-0.1	5.7	1,757	1,591	10.4	45,765	41,392
Galesburg, IL............................	70,735	70,626	74,571	75,574	109	-3,945	0.2	-5.3	2,397	2,289	4.7	33,893	32,406
Knox County, IL......................	52,917	52,919	55,836	56,393	-2	-2,917	0.0	-5.2	1,771	1,710	3.6	33,471	32,297
Warren County, IL	17,818	17,707	18,735	19,181	111	-1,028	0.6	-5.5	626	579	8.1	35,144	32,732
Gallup, NM................................	73,664	71,492	74,798	60,686	2,172	-3,306	3.0	-4.4	1,774	1,721	3.1	24,079	23,964
McKinley County, NM..............	73,664	71,492	74,798	60,686	2,172	-3,306	3.0	-4.4	1,774	1,721	3.1	24,079	23,964
Garden City, KS	37,083	36,776	40,523	33,070	307	-3,747	0.8	-9.2	1,239	1,161	6.8	33,417	31,390
Finney County, KS	37,083	36,776	40,523	33,070	307	-3,747	0.8	-9.2	1,239	1,161	6.8	33,417	31,390
Gardnerville Ranchos, NV	46,886	46,997	41,259	27,637	-111	5,738	-0.2	13.9	2,451	2,367	3.5	52,266	50,356
Douglas County, NV	46,886	46,997	41,259	27,637	-111	5,738	-0.2	13.9	2,451	2,367	3.5	52,266	50,356
Georgetown, SC.........................	59,991	60,158	55,797	46,302	-167	4,361	-0.3	7.8	2,304	2,226	3.5	38,403	37,015
Georgetown County, SC	59,991	60,158	55,797	46,302	-167	4,361	-0.3	7.8	2,304	2,226	3.5	38,403	37,015
Gettysburg, PA..........................	101,434	101,407	91,292	78,274	27	10,115	0.0	11.1	3,384	3,272	3.4	33,360	32,251
Adams County, PA	101,434	101,407	91,292	78,274	27	10,115	0.0	11.1	3,384	3,272	3.4	33,360	32,251
Gillette, WY..............................	46,618	46,133	33,698	29,370	485	12,435	1.1	36.9	2,218	2,176	2.0	47,584	47,067
Campbell County, WY	46,618	46,133	33,698	29,370	485	12,435	1.1	36.9	2,218	2,176	2.0	47,584	47,067
Glasgow, KY..............................	52,342	52,272	48,070	42,964	70	4,202	0.1	8.7	1,459	1,395	4.6	27,867	26,689
Barren County, KY..................	42,269	42,173	38,033	34,001	96	4,140	0.2	10.9	1,231	1,173	5.0	29,128	27,838
Metcalfe County, KY...............	10,073	10,099	10,037	8,963	-26	62	-0.3	0.6	227	222	2.5	22,574	21,906
Gloversville, NY........................	55,180	55,531	55,073	54,191	-351	458	-0.6	0.8	1,960	1,895	3.4	35,529	34,164
Fulton County, NY	55,180	55,531	55,073	54,191	-351	458	-0.6	0.8	1,960	1,895	3.4	35,529	34,164
Granbury, TX.............................	60,121	59,672	47,909	34,341	449	11,763	0.8	24.6	2,416	2,304	4.9	40,187	38,483
Hood County, TX	51,670	51,182	41,100	28,981	488	10,082	1.0	24.5	2,105	2,005	5.0	40,740	39,048
Somervell County, TX.............	8,451	8,490	6,809	5,360	-39	1,681	-0.5	24.7	311	298	4.3	36,809	35,068
Grand Island, NE.......................	73,551	72,726	68,305	63,044	825	4,421	1.1	6.5	2,786	2,578	8.0	37,877	35,377
Hall County, NE	59,477	58,607	53,534	48,925	870	5,073	1.5	9.5	2,220	2,075	7.0	37,324	35,312
Howard County, NE	6,342	6,274	6,567	6,057	68	-293	1.1	-4.5	259	224	15.3	40,780	35,800
Merrick County, NE	7,732	7,845	8,204	8,062	-113	-359	-1.4	-4.4	307	279	10.2	39,751	35,521
Grants, NM................................	27,658	27,213	25,595	23,794	445	1,618	1.6	6.3	718	693	3.6	25,965	25,373
Cibola County, NM	27,658	27,213	25,595	23,794	445	1,618	1.6	6.3	718	693	3.6	25,965	25,373
Grants Pass, OR........................	82,987	82,713	75,726	62,649	274	6,987	0.3	9.2	2,498	2,397	4.2	30,103	28,933
Josephine County, OR............	82,987	82,713	75,726	62,649	274	6,987	0.3	9.2	2,498	2,397	4.2	30,103	28,933
Great Bend, KS..........................	27,841	27,674	28,205	29,382	167	-531	0.6	-1.9	1,080	1,003	7.6	38,785	36,236
Barton County, KS..................	27,841	27,674	28,205	29,382	167	-531	0.6	-1.9	1,080	1,003	7.6	38,785	36,236
Greeneville, TN..........................	69,339	68,831	62,909	55,832	508	5,922	0.7	9.4	2,242	2,140	4.8	32,331	31,086
Greene County, TN	69,339	68,831	62,909	55,832	508	5,922	0.7	9.4	2,242	2,140	4.8	32,331	31,086
Greensburg, IN..........................	25,944	25,740	24,555	23,645	204	1,185	0.8	4.8	891	840	6.1	34,354	32,592
Decatur County, IN.................	25,944	25,740	24,555	23,645	204	1,185	0.8	4.8	891	840	6.1	34,354	32,592
Greenville, MS...........................	50,406	51,137	62,977	67,935	-731	-11,840	-1.4	-18.8	1,583	1,531	3.4	31,412	29,986
Washington County, MS..........	50,406	51,137	62,977	67,935	-731	-11,840	-1.4	-18.8	1,583	1,531	3.4	31,412	29,986
Greenville, OH...........................	52,809	52,959	53,309	53,617	-150	-350	-0.3	-0.7	1,813	1,708	6.1	34,325	32,238
Darke County, OH...................	52,809	52,959	53,309	53,617	-150	-350	-0.3	-0.7	1,813	1,708	6.1	34,325	32,238

[1]The April 1, 2000, Population Estimates base reflects modifications to the Census 2000 population as documented in the Count Question Resolution program and geographic program revisions.
[2]The April 1, 1990, census counts include corrections processed through August 1997, results of special censuses and test censuses, and do not include adjustments for census coverage errors.
[3]Based on the April 1, 2010, census counts and the July 1, 2011, estimates.
[4]Based on the April 1, 2010, census counts and the April 1, 2000, estimates base.
[5]Based on resident population estimated as of April 1, 2010 and July 1, 2011 of the year shown.

Table D-1.   Population and Personal Income—*Continued*

Micropolitan statistical area component counties	Population								Personal Income				
	2011 estimate (July 1)	2010 census count (April 1)	2000 estimates base (April 1)[1]	1990 estimates base (April 1)[2]	Net change		Percent change		Total (million dollars)		Percentage change, 2010–2011	Per capita[5]	
					2010–2011[3]	2000–2010[4]	2010–2011[3]	2000–2010[4]	2011	2010		2011	2010
Greenwood, MS	42,234	42,914	48,716	46,578	-680	-5,802	-1.6	-11.9	1,343	1,283	4.7	31,808	29,932
Carroll County, MS	10,373	10,597	10,769	9,237	-224	-172	-2.1	-1.6	359	336	7.1	34,634	31,699
Leflore County, MS	31,861	32,317	37,947	37,341	-456	-5,630	-1.4	-14.8	984	948	3.8	30,888	29,352
Greenwood, SC	69,835	69,661	66,271	59,567	174	3,390	0.2	5.1	2,123	2,056	3.2	30,398	29,495
Greenwood County, SC	69,835	69,661	66,271	59,567	174	3,390	0.2	5.1	2,123	2,056	3.2	30,398	29,495
Grenada, MS	21,706	21,906	23,263	21,555	-200	-1,357	-0.9	-5.8	656	627	4.6	30,231	28,668
Grenada County, MS	21,706	21,906	23,263	21,555	-200	-1,357	-0.9	-5.8	656	627	4.6	30,231	28,668
Guymon, OK	21,312	20,640	20,107	16,419	672	533	3.3	2.7	729	658	10.8	34,214	31,552
Texas County, OK	21,312	20,640	20,107	16,419	672	533	3.3	2.7	729	658	10.8	34,214	31,552
Hammond, LA	122,571	121,097	100,588	85,709	1,474	20,509	1.2	20.4	3,889	3,726	4.4	31,732	30,681
Tangipahoa Parish, LA	122,571	121,097	100,588	85,709	1,474	20,509	1.2	20.4	3,889	3,726	4.4	31,732	30,681
Hannibal, MO	38,998	38,948	37,915	36,158	50	1,033	0.1	2.7	1,329	1,272	4.5	34,091	32,661
Marion County, MO	28,717	28,781	28,289	27,682	-64	492	-0.2	1.7	982	940	4.4	34,200	32,693
Ralls County, MO	10,281	10,167	9,626	8,476	114	541	1.1	5.6	347	332	4.7	33,785	32,570
Harriman, TN	53,838	54,181	51,910	47,227	-343	2,271	-0.6	4.4	1,892	1,835	3.1	35,142	33,923
Roane County, TN	53,838	54,181	51,910	47,227	-343	2,271	-0.6	4.4	1,892	1,835	3.1	35,142	33,923
Harrisburg, IL	24,981	24,913	26,733	26,551	68	-1,820	0.3	-6.8	830	800	3.7	33,214	32,081
Saline County, IL	24,981	24,913	26,733	26,551	68	-1,820	0.3	-6.8	830	800	3.7	33,214	32,081
Harrison, AR	45,315	45,233	42,556	35,963	82	2,677	0.2	6.3	1,347	1,290	4.4	29,722	28,514
Boone County, AR	37,051	36,903	33,948	28,297	148	2,955	0.4	8.7	1,131	1,086	4.2	30,524	29,416
Newton County, AR	8,264	8,330	8,608	7,666	-66	-278	-0.8	-3.2	216	204	5.6	26,127	24,520
Hastings, NE	37,702	37,906	38,190	36,748	-204	-284	-0.5	-0.7	1,563	1,390	12.4	41,449	36,679
Adams County, NE	31,216	31,364	31,151	29,625	-148	213	-0.5	0.7	1,233	1,125	9.6	39,483	35,879
Clay County, NE	6,486	6,542	7,039	7,123	-56	-497	-0.9	-7.1	330	265	24.5	50,910	40,516
Havre, MT	16,397	16,096	16,673	17,654	301	-577	1.9	-3.5	630	581	8.4	38,444	35,981
Hill County, MT	16,397	16,096	16,673	17,654	301	-577	1.9	-3.5	630	581	8.4	38,444	35,981
Hays, KS	28,742	28,452	27,507	26,004	290	945	1.0	3.4	1,194	1,099	8.7	41,552	38,624
Ellis County, KS	28,742	28,452	27,507	26,004	290	945	1.0	3.4	1,194	1,099	8.7	41,552	38,624
Heber, UT	24,417	23,530	15,215	10,089	887	8,315	3.8	54.7	670	631	6.2	27,442	26,608
Wasatch County, UT	24,417	23,530	15,215	10,089	887	8,315	3.8	54.7	670	631	6.2	27,442	26,608
Helena, MT	75,699	74,801	65,765	55,434	898	9,036	1.2	13.7	2,948	2,820	4.5	38,940	37,583
Jefferson County, MT	11,381	11,406	10,049	7,939	-25	1,357	-0.2	13.5	446	428	4.2	39,223	37,516
Lewis and Clark County, MT	64,318	63,395	55,716	47,495	923	7,679	1.5	13.8	2,501	2,391	4.6	38,890	37,595
Helena–West Helena, AR	21,442	21,757	26,445	28,830	-315	-4,688	-1.4	-17.7	671	647	3.8	31,314	29,861
Phillips County, AR	21,442	21,757	26,445	28,830	-315	-4,688	-1.4	-17.7	671	647	3.8	31,314	29,861
Henderson, NC	45,307	45,422	42,954	38,892	-115	2,468	-0.3	5.7	1,342	1,296	3.6	29,621	28,560
Vance County, NC	45,307	45,422	42,954	38,892	-115	2,468	-0.3	5.7	1,342	1,296	3.6	29,621	28,560
Hereford, TX	19,595	19,372	18,561	19,153	223	811	1.2	4.4	703	623	12.8	35,880	31,989
Deaf Smith County, TX	19,595	19,372	18,561	19,153	223	811	1.2	4.4	703	623	12.8	35,880	31,989
Hilo, HI	186,738	185,079	148,677	120,317	1,659	36,402	0.9	24.5	5,929	5,682	4.3	31,749	30,651
Hawaii County, HI	186,738	185,079	148,677	120,317	1,659	36,402	0.9	24.5	5,929	5,682	4.3	31,749	30,651
Hilton Head Island–Beaufort, SC	189,879	187,010	141,615	101,912	2,869	45,395	1.5	32.1	7,539	7,170	5.1	39,703	38,145
Beaufort County, SC	164,684	162,233	120,937	86,425	2,451	41,296	1.5	34.1	6,861	6,520	5.2	41,662	40,001
Jasper County, SC	25,195	24,777	20,678	15,487	418	4,099	1.7	19.8	678	649	4.3	26,896	26,022
Hobbs, NM	65,423	64,727	55,511	55,765	696	9,216	1.1	16.6	2,479	2,241	10.7	37,898	34,607
Lea County, NM	65,423	64,727	55,511	55,765	696	9,216	1.1	16.6	2,479	2,241	10.7	37,898	34,607
Homosassa Springs, FL	140,031	141,236	118,085	93,513	-1,205	23,151	-0.9	19.6	4,575	4,424	3.4	32,675	31,316
Citrus County, FL	140,031	141,236	118,085	93,513	-1,205	23,151	-0.9	19.6	4,575	4,424	3.4	32,675	31,316
Hood River, OR	22,493	22,346	20,411	16,903	147	1,935	0.7	9.5	797	760	4.9	35,441	33,856
Hood River County, OR	22,493	22,346	20,411	16,903	147	1,935	0.7	9.5	797	760	4.9	35,441	33,856
Hope, AR	31,558	31,606	33,542	31,722	-48	-1,936	-0.2	-5.8	925	868	6.6	29,314	27,494
Hempstead County, AR	22,541	22,609	23,587	21,621	-68	-978	-0.3	-4.1	655	613	7.0	29,075	27,123
Nevada County, AR	9,017	8,997	9,955	10,101	20	-958	0.2	-9.6	270	255	5.6	29,912	28,425
Houghton, MI	38,811	38,784	38,317	37,147	27	467	0.1	1.2	1,076	1,038	3.6	27,713	26,732
Houghton County, MI	36,638	36,628	36,016	35,446	10	612	0.0	1.7	995	963	3.4	27,169	26,244
Keweenaw County, MI	2,173	2,156	2,301	1,701	17	-145	0.8	-6.3	80	76	5.7	36,886	35,001
Hudson, NY	62,550	63,096	63,094	62,982	-546	2	-0.9	0.0	2,628	2,516	4.4	42,007	39,919
Columbia County, NY	62,550	63,096	63,094	62,982	-546	2	-0.9	0.0	2,628	2,516	4.4	42,007	39,919
Humboldt, TN	49,935	49,683	48,152	46,315	252	1,531	0.5	3.2	1,520	1,458	4.2	30,436	29,340
Gibson County, TN	49,935	49,683	48,152	46,315	252	1,531	0.5	3.2	1,520	1,458	4.2	30,436	29,340
Huntingdon, PA	45,875	45,913	45,586	44,164	-38	327	-0.1	0.7	1,335	1,276	4.6	29,108	27,711
Huntingdon County, PA	45,875	45,913	45,586	44,164	-38	327	-0.1	0.7	1,335	1,276	4.6	29,108	27,711

[1]The April 1, 2000, Population Estimates base reflects modifications to the Census 2000 population as documented in the Count Question Resolution program and geographic program revisions.
[2]The April 1, 1990, census counts include corrections processed through August 1997, results of special censuses and test censuses, and do not include adjustments for census coverage errors.
[3]Based on the April 1, 2010, census counts and the July 1, 2011, estimates.
[4]Based on the April 1, 2010, census counts and the April 1, 2000, estimates base.
[5]Based on resident population estimated as of April 1, 2010 and July 1, 2011 of the year shown.

Table D-1. Population and Personal Income—*Continued*

Micropolitan statistical area component counties	Population								Personal Income				
	2011 estimate (July 1)	2010 census count (April 1)	2000 estimates base (April 1)[1]	1990 estimates base (April 1)[2]	Net change		Percent change		Total (million dollars)		Percentage change, 2010–2011	Per capita[5]	
					2010–2011[3]	2000–2010[4]	2010–2011[3]	2000–2010[4]	2011	2010		2011	2010
Huntington, IN	37,211	37,124	38,075	35,427	87	-951	0.2	-2.5	1,199	1,146	4.6	32,225	30,898
Huntington County, IN	37,211	37,124	38,075	35,427	87	-951	0.2	-2.5	1,199	1,146	4.6	32,225	30,898
Huntsville, TX	68,087	67,861	61,758	50,917	226	6,103	0.3	9.9	1,737	1,671	3.9	25,508	24,547
Walker County, TX	68,087	67,861	61,758	50,917	226	6,103	0.3	9.9	1,737	1,671	3.9	25,508	24,547
Huron, SD	17,550	17,398	17,023	18,253	152	375	0.9	2.2	843	704	19.8	48,057	40,433
Beadle County, SD	17,550	17,398	17,023	18,253	152	375	0.9	2.2	843	704	19.8	48,057	40,433
Hutchinson, KS	64,607	64,511	64,790	62,389	96	-279	0.1	-0.4	2,173	2,077	4.6	33,642	32,169
Reno County, KS	64,607	64,511	64,790	62,389	96	-279	0.1	-0.4	2,173	2,077	4.6	33,642	32,169
Hutchinson, MN	36,432	36,651	34,898	32,030	-219	1,753	-0.6	5.0	1,325	1,271	4.2	36,359	34,706
McLeod County, MN	36,432	36,651	34,898	32,030	-219	1,753	-0.6	5.0	1,325	1,271	4.2	36,359	34,706
Indiana, PA	89,298	88,880	89,605	89,994	418	-725	0.5	-0.8	3,091	2,938	5.2	34,613	32,822
Indiana County, PA	89,298	88,880	89,605	89,994	418	-725	0.5	-0.8	3,091	2,938	5.2	34,613	32,822
Indianola, MS	29,296	29,450	34,369	35,129	-154	-4,919	-0.5	-14.3	790	757	4.3	26,969	25,742
Sunflower County, MS	29,296	29,450	34,369	35,129	-154	-4,919	-0.5	-14.3	790	757	4.3	26,969	25,742
Iron Mountain, MI–WI	30,625	30,591	32,560	31,421	34	-1,969	0.1	-6.0	1,144	1,091	4.8	37,344	35,714
Dickinson County, MI	26,185	26,168	27,472	26,831	17	-1,304	0.1	-4.7	984	939	4.8	37,594	35,940
Florence County, WI	4,440	4,423	5,088	4,590	17	-665	0.4	-13.1	159	152	5.0	35,870	34,374
Jackson, WY–ID	31,714	31,464	24,250	14,612	250	7,214	0.8	29.7	2,327	2,192	6.2	73,372	69,626
Teton County, ID	10,166	10,170	5,999	3,439	-4	4,171	0.0	69.5	261	249	5.0	25,705	24,490
Teton County, WY	21,548	21,294	18,251	11,173	254	3,043	1.2	16.7	2,066	1,943	6.3	95,861	91,153
Jacksonville, IL	40,814	40,902	42,153	42,041	-88	-1,251	-0.2	-3.0	1,394	1,350	3.2	34,143	33,022
Morgan County, IL	35,543	35,547	36,616	36,397	-4	-1,069	0.0	-2.9	1,206	1,173	2.7	33,922	33,033
Scott County, IL	5,271	5,355	5,537	5,644	-84	-182	-1.6	-3.3	188	176	6.5	35,634	32,948
Jacksonville, TX	51,140	50,845	46,659	41,049	295	4,186	0.6	9.0	1,479	1,411	4.8	28,923	27,728
Cherokee County, TX	51,140	50,845	46,659	41,049	295	4,186	0.6	9.0	1,479	1,411	4.8	28,923	27,728
Jamestown, ND	21,062	21,100	21,908	22,241	-38	-808	-0.2	-3.7	911	850	7.2	43,271	40,286
Stutsman County, ND	21,062	21,100	21,908	22,241	-38	-808	-0.2	-3.7	911	850	7.2	43,271	40,286
Jamestown–Dunkirk–Fredonia, NY	134,368	134,905	139,750	141,895	-537	-4,845	-0.4	-3.5	4,255	4,112	3.5	31,664	30,503
Chautauqua County, NY	134,368	134,905	139,750	141,895	-537	-4,845	-0.4	-3.5	4,255	4,112	3.5	31,664	30,503
Jasper, IN	54,927	54,734	52,511	49,125	193	2,223	0.4	4.2	2,120	1,999	6.0	38,588	36,532
Dubois County, IN	42,199	41,889	39,674	36,616	310	2,215	0.7	5.6	1,718	1,610	6.7	40,718	38,436
Pike County, IN	12,728	12,845	12,837	12,509	-117	8	-0.9	0.1	401	390	3.0	31,525	30,324
Jennings, LA	31,694	31,594	31,435	30,722	100	159	0.3	0.5	992	948	4.7	31,311	29,966
Jefferson Davis Parish, LA	31,694	31,594	31,435	30,722	100	159	0.3	0.5	992	948	4.7	31,311	29,966
Jesup, GA	30,327	30,099	26,565	22,356	228	3,534	0.8	13.3	883	840	5.1	29,118	27,879
Wayne County, GA	30,327	30,099	26,565	22,356	228	3,534	0.8	13.3	883	840	5.1	29,118	27,879
Juneau, AK	32,164	31,275	30,711	26,752	889	564	2.8	1.8	1,552	1,480	4.9	48,242	47,109
Juneau City and Borough, AK	32,164	31,275	30,711	26,752	889	564	2.8	1.8	1,552	1,480	4.9	48,242	47,109
Kahului–Wailuku, HI	156,674	154,834	128,094	100,374	1,840	26,740	1.2	20.9	5,686	5,397	5.4	36,272	34,789
Maui County, HI	156,674	154,834	128,094	100,374	1,840	26,740	1.2	20.9	5,686	5,397	5.4	36,272	34,789
Kalispell, MT	91,301	90,928	74,471	59,218	373	16,457	0.4	22.1	3,275	3,134	4.5	35,875	34,487
Flathead County, MT	91,301	90,928	74,471	59,218	373	16,457	0.4	22.1	3,275	3,134	4.5	35,875	34,487
Kapaa, HI	67,701	67,091	58,463	51,177	610	8,628	0.9	14.8	2,472	2,356	4.9	36,520	35,054
Kauai County, HI	67,701	67,091	58,463	51,177	610	8,628	0.9	14.8	2,472	2,356	4.9	36,520	35,054
Kearney, NE	53,278	52,591	49,141	44,076	687	3,450	1.3	7.0	2,145	1,969	9.0	40,264	37,395
Buffalo County, NE	46,690	46,102	42,259	37,447	588	3,843	1.3	9.1	1,789	1,675	6.8	38,327	36,307
Kearney County, NE	6,588	6,489	6,882	6,629	99	-393	1.5	-5.7	356	293	21.3	53,989	45,122
Keene, NH	76,918	77,117	73,825	70,121	-199	3,292	-0.3	4.5	3,144	3,023	4.0	40,875	39,227
Cheshire County, NH	76,918	77,117	73,825	70,121	-199	3,292	-0.3	4.5	3,144	3,023	4.0	40,875	39,227
Kendallville, IN	47,553	47,536	46,275	37,877	17	1,261	0.0	2.7	1,445	1,369	5.5	30,378	28,820
Noble County, IN	47,553	47,536	46,275	37,877	17	1,261	0.0	2.7	1,445	1,369	5.5	30,378	28,820
Kennett, MO	31,974	31,953	33,155	33,112	21	-1,202	0.1	-3.6	1,019	952	7.0	31,855	29,822
Dunklin County, MO	31,974	31,953	33,155	33,112	21	-1,202	0.1	-3.6	1,019	952	7.0	31,855	29,822
Kerrville, TX	49,783	49,625	43,653	36,304	158	5,972	0.3	13.7	2,119	2,022	4.8	42,572	40,706
Kerr County, TX	49,783	49,625	43,653	36,304	158	5,972	0.3	13.7	2,119	2,022	4.8	42,572	40,706
Ketchikan, AK	13,593	13,477	14,070	13,828	116	-593	0.9	-4.2	702	677	3.6	51,631	50,046
Ketchikan Gateway Borough, AK	13,593	13,477	14,070	13,828	116	-593	0.9	-4.2	702	677	3.6	51,631	50,046
Key West, FL	73,873	73,090	79,589	78,024	783	-6,499	1.1	-8.2	4,354	4,130	5.4	58,941	56,415
Monroe County, FL	73,873	73,090	79,589	78,024	783	-6,499	1.1	-8.2	4,354	4,130	5.4	58,941	56,415
Kill Devil Hills, NC	34,307	33,920	29,967	22,746	387	3,953	1.1	13.2	1,325	1,259	5.3	38,633	37,004
Dare County, NC	34,307	33,920	29,967	22,746	387	3,953	1.1	13.2	1,325	1,259	5.3	38,633	37,004
Kingsville, TX	32,633	32,477	31,963	30,734	156	514	0.5	1.6	1,108	1,029	7.8	33,966	31,612
Kenedy County, TX	437	416	414	460	21	2	5.0	0.5	22	18	23.9	51,037	42,945
Kleberg County, TX	32,196	32,061	31,549	30,274	135	512	0.4	1.6	1,086	1,011	7.5	33,734	31,464
Kinston, NC	59,339	59,495	59,648	57,274	-156	-153	-0.3	-0.3	1,900	1,850	2.7	32,022	31,144
Lenoir County, NC	59,339	59,495	59,648	57,274	-156	-153	-0.3	-0.3	1,900	1,850	2.7	32,022	31,144

[1]The April 1, 2000, Population Estimates base reflects modifications to the Census 2000 population as documented in the Count Question Resolution program and geographic program revisions.
[2]The April 1, 1990, census counts include corrections processed through August 1997, results of special censuses and test censuses, and do not include adjustments for census coverage errors.
[3]Based on the April 1, 2010, census counts and the July 1, 2011, estimates.
[4]Based on the April 1, 2010, census counts and the April 1, 2000, estimates base.
[5]Based on resident population estimated as of April 1, 2010 and July 1, 2011 of the year shown.

Table D-1. Population and Personal Income—*Continued*

Micropolitan statistical area component counties	Population								Personal Income				
	2011 estimate (July 1)	2010 census count (April 1)	2000 estimates base (April 1)[1]	1990 estimates base (April 1)[2]	Net change		Percent change		Total (million dollars)		Percentage change, 2010–2011	Per capita[5]	
					2010–2011[3]	2000–2010[4]	2010–2011[3]	2000–2010[4]	2011	2010		2011	2010
Kirksville, MO..............................	29,933	30,038	29,147	28,813	-105	891	-0.3	3.1	812	789	2.8	27,113	26,280
Adair County, MO....................	25,552	25,607	24,977	24,577	-55	630	-0.2	2.5	698	682	2.4	27,321	26,649
Schuyler County, MO	4,381	4,431	4,170	4,236	-50	261	-1.1	6.3	113	107	5.8	25,902	24,155
Klamath Falls, OR..........................	66,299	66,380	63,775	57,702	-81	2,605	-0.1	4.1	1,986	1,902	4.5	29,961	28,669
Klamath County, OR...............	66,299	66,380	63,775	57,702	-81	2,605	-0.1	4.1	1,986	1,902	4.5	29,961	28,669
Kodiak, AK...................................	13,872	13,592	13,913	13,309	280	-321	2.1	-2.3	610	572	6.5	43,951	41,966
Kodiak Island Borough, AK	13,872	13,592	13,913	13,309	280	-321	2.1	-2.3	610	572	6.5	43,951	41,966
Laconia, NH.................................	60,223	60,088	56,325	49,216	135	3,763	0.2	6.7	2,529	2,433	3.9	41,995	40,494
Belknap County, NH	60,223	60,088	56,325	49,216	135	3,763	0.2	6.7	2,529	2,433	3.9	41,995	40,494
La Follette, TN	40,512	40,716	39,854	35,079	-204	862	-0.5	2.2	1,133	1,098	3.1	27,965	27,003
Campbell County, TN..............	40,512	40,716	39,854	35,079	-204	862	-0.5	2.2	1,133	1,098	3.1	27,965	27,003
La Grande, OR..............................	25,791	25,748	24,530	23,598	43	1,218	0.2	5.0	826	779	6.1	32,033	30,244
Union County, OR	25,791	25,748	24,530	23,598	43	1,218	0.2	5.0	826	779	6.1	32,033	30,244
LaGrange, GA...............................	67,764	67,044	58,779	55,532	720	8,265	1.1	14.1	2,196	2,027	8.4	32,410	30,176
Troup County, GA....................	67,764	67,044	58,779	55,532	720	8,265	1.1	14.1	2,196	2,027	8.4	32,410	30,176
Lake City, FL.................................	67,485	67,531	56,513	42,613	-46	11,018	-0.1	19.5	1,904	1,864	2.1	28,209	27,563
Columbia County, FL...............	67,485	67,531	56,513	42,613	-46	11,018	-0.1	19.5	1,904	1,864	2.1	28,209	27,563
Lamesa, TX....................................	13,751	13,833	14,985	14,349	-82	-1,152	-0.6	-7.7	366	424	-13.6	26,625	30,579
Dawson County, TX.................	13,751	13,833	14,985	14,349	-82	-1,152	-0.6	-7.7	366	424	-13.6	26,625	30,579
Lancaster, SC...............................	77,908	76,652	61,351	54,516	1,256	15,301	1.6	24.9	2,049	1,935	5.9	26,302	25,143
Lancaster County, SC..............	77,908	76,652	61,351	54,516	1,256	15,301	1.6	24.9	2,049	1,935	5.9	26,302	25,143
Laramie, WY.................................	36,889	36,299	32,014	30,797	590	4,285	1.6	13.4	1,360	1,279	6.3	36,864	35,105
Albany County, WY	36,889	36,299	32,014	30,797	590	4,285	1.6	13.4	1,360	1,279	6.3	36,864	35,105
Las Vegas, NM..............................	29,301	29,393	30,126	25,743	-92	-733	-0.3	-2.4	919	896	2.5	31,366	30,523
San Miguel County, NM	29,301	29,393	30,126	25,743	-92	-733	-0.3	-2.4	919	896	2.5	31,366	30,523
Laurel, MS	84,852	84,823	83,107	79,145	29	1,716	0.0	2.1	2,758	2,661	3.7	32,507	31,353
Jasper County, MS...................	16,777	17,062	18,149	17,114	-285	-1,087	-1.7	-6.0	482	479	0.8	28,754	28,191
Jones County, MS....................	68,075	67,761	64,958	62,031	314	2,803	0.5	4.3	2,276	2,182	4.3	33,432	32,144
Laurinburg, NC.............................	35,861	36,157	35,998	33,763	-296	159	-0.8	0.4	1,017	1,006	1.1	28,364	27,881
Scotland County, NC	35,861	36,157	35,998	33,763	-296	159	-0.8	0.4	1,017	1,006	1.1	28,364	27,881
Lawrenceburg, TN........................	42,115	41,869	39,926	35,303	246	1,943	0.6	4.9	1,099	1,051	4.5	26,093	25,020
Lawrence County, TN..............	42,115	41,869	39,926	35,303	246	1,943	0.6	4.9	1,099	1,051	4.5	26,093	25,020
Lebanon, MO	35,636	35,571	32,513	27,158	65	3,058	0.2	9.4	977	932	4.8	27,424	26,162
Laclede County, MO	35,636	35,571	32,513	27,158	65	3,058	0.2	9.4	977	932	4.8	27,424	26,162
Lebanon, NH–VT...........................	174,595	174,724	167,387	155,133	-129	7,337	-0.1	4.4	7,645	7,330	4.3	43,788	41,953
Grafton County, NH.................	88,923	89,118	81,743	74,929	-195	7,375	-0.2	9.0	4,048	3,882	4.3	45,522	43,563
Orange County, VT...................	29,006	28,936	28,226	26,149	70	710	0.2	2.5	1,053	1,010	4.2	36,309	34,893
Windsor County, VT.................	56,666	56,670	57,418	54,055	-4	-748	0.0	-1.3	2,544	2,437	4.4	44,894	43,028
Levelland, TX................................	22,892	22,935	22,716	24,199	-43	219	-0.2	1.0	860	834	3.1	37,566	36,474
Hockley County, TX.................	22,892	22,935	22,716	24,199	-43	219	-0.2	1.0	860	834	3.1	37,566	36,474
Lewisburg, PA...............................	44,847	44,947	41,624	36,176	-100	3,323	-0.2	8.0	1,423	1,349	5.4	31,721	30,111
Union County, PA....................	44,847	44,947	41,624	36,176	-100	3,323	-0.2	8.0	1,423	1,349	5.4	31,721	30,111
Lewisburg, TN...............................	30,881	30,617	26,767	21,539	264	3,850	0.9	14.4	792	762	3.9	25,647	24,849
Marshall County, TN................	30,881	30,617	26,767	21,539	264	3,850	0.9	14.4	792	762	3.9	25,647	24,849
Lewistown, PA..............................	46,858	46,682	46,486	46,197	176	196	0.4	0.4	1,407	1,346	4.5	30,017	28,824
Mifflin County, PA...................	46,858	46,682	46,486	46,197	176	196	0.4	0.4	1,407	1,346	4.5	30,017	28,824
Lexington, NE...............................	26,398	26,370	26,508	21,868	28	-138	0.1	-0.5	922	842	9.5	34,916	31,859
Dawson County, NE.................	24,388	24,326	24,365	19,940	62	-39	0.3	-0.2	813	750	8.4	33,320	30,762
Gosper County, NE..................	2,010	2,044	2,143	1,928	-34	-99	-1.7	-4.6	109	92	18.5	54,274	44,906
Lexington Park, MD......................	107,484	105,151	86,211	75,974	2,333	18,940	2.2	22.0	4,821	4,538	6.2	44,849	42,911
St. Mary's County, MD	107,484	105,151	86,211	75,974	2,333	18,940	2.2	22.0	4,821	4,538	6.2	44,849	42,911
Liberal, KS....................................	23,328	22,952	22,510	18,743	376	442	1.6	2.0	714	669	6.8	30,619	29,037
Seward County, KS	23,328	22,952	22,510	18,743	376	442	1.6	2.0	714	669	6.8	30,619	29,037
Lincoln, IL....................................	30,140	30,305	31,183	30,798	-165	-878	-0.5	-2.8	1,058	982	7.8	35,094	32,426
Logan County, IL.....................	30,140	30,305	31,183	30,798	-165	-878	-0.5	-2.8	1,058	982	7.8	35,094	32,426
Lincolnton, NC	78,932	78,265	63,780	50,319	667	14,485	0.9	22.7	2,705	2,561	5.6	34,275	32,668
Lincoln County, NC	78,932	78,265	63,780	50,319	667	14,485	0.9	22.7	2,705	2,561	5.6	34,275	32,668
Lock Haven, PA............................	39,208	39,238	37,914	37,182	-30	1,324	-0.1	3.5	1,251	1,156	8.3	31,912	29,647
Clinton County, PA..................	39,208	39,238	37,914	37,182	-30	1,324	-0.1	3.5	1,251	1,156	8.3	31,912	29,647
Logansport, IN.............................	38,828	38,966	40,930	38,413	-138	-1,964	-0.4	-4.8	1,229	1,156	6.3	31,648	29,685
Cass County, IN......................	38,828	38,966	40,930	38,413	-138	-1,964	-0.4	-4.8	1,229	1,156	6.3	31,648	29,685
London, KY	59,355	58,849	52,715	43,438	506	6,134	0.9	11.6	1,607	1,562	2.9	27,082	26,479
Laurel County, KY	59,355	58,849	52,715	43,438	506	6,134	0.9	11.6	1,607	1,562	2.9	27,082	26,479

[1]The April 1, 2000, Population Estimates base reflects modifications to the Census 2000 population as documented in the Count Question Resolution program and geographic program revisions.
[2]The April 1, 1990, census counts include corrections processed through August 1997, results of special censuses and test censuses, and do not include adjustments for census coverage errors.
[3]Based on the April 1, 2010, census counts and the July 1, 2011, estimates.
[4]Based on the April 1, 2010, census counts and the April 1, 2000, estimates base.
[5]Based on resident population estimated as of April 1, 2010 and July 1, 2011 of the year shown.

Table D-1. Population and Personal Income—*Continued*

Micropolitan statistical area component counties	2011 estimate (July 1)	2010 census count (April 1)	2000 estimates base (April 1)[1]	1990 estimates base (April 1)[2]	Net change 2010–2011[3]	Net change 2000–2010[4]	Percent change 2010–2011[3]	Percent change 2000–2010[4]	Total (million dollars) 2011	Total (million dollars) 2010	Percentage change, 2010–2011	Per capita[5] 2011	Per capita[5] 2010
Los Alamos, NM	18,222	17,950	18,343	18,115	272	-393	1.5	-2.1	1,106	1,068	3.6	60,719	59,237
Los Alamos County, NM	18,222	17,950	18,343	18,115	272	-393	1.5	-2.1	1,106	1,068	3.6	60,719	59,237
Lufkin, TX	87,669	86,771	80,130	69,884	898	6,641	1.0	8.3	2,930	2,792	5.0	33,423	32,094
Angelina County, TX	87,669	86,771	80,130	69,884	898	6,641	1.0	8.3	2,930	2,792	5.0	33,423	32,094
Lumberton, NC	135,517	134,168	123,339	105,170	1,349	10,829	1.0	8.8	3,365	3,285	2.4	24,834	24,431
Robeson County, NC	135,517	134,168	123,339	105,170	1,349	10,829	1.0	8.8	3,365	3,285	2.4	24,834	24,431
Macomb, IL	32,582	32,612	32,913	35,244	-30	-301	-0.1	-0.9	1,060	1,010	5.0	32,538	30,958
McDonough County, IL	32,582	32,612	32,913	35,244	-30	-301	-0.1	-0.9	1,060	1,010	5.0	32,538	30,958
Madison, IN	32,249	32,428	31,705	29,797	-179	723	-0.6	2.3	963	937	2.8	29,872	28,957
Jefferson County, IN	32,249	32,428	31,705	29,797	-179	723	-0.6	2.3	963	937	2.8	29,872	28,957
Madisonville, KY	46,909	46,920	46,519	46,126	-11	401	0.0	0.9	1,506	1,425	5.7	32,099	30,381
Hopkins County, KY	46,909	46,920	46,519	46,126	-11	401	0.0	0.9	1,506	1,425	5.7	32,099	30,381
Magnolia, AR	24,401	24,552	25,603	25,691	-151	-1,051	-0.6	-4.1	811	773	5.0	33,253	31,536
Columbia County, AR	24,401	24,552	25,603	25,691	-151	-1,051	-0.6	-4.1	811	773	5.0	33,253	31,536
Malone, NY	51,551	51,599	51,134	46,540	-48	465	-0.1	0.9	1,536	1,490	3.1	29,794	28,879
Franklin County, NY	51,551	51,599	51,134	46,540	-48	465	-0.1	0.9	1,536	1,490	3.1	29,794	28,879
Manitowoc, WI	80,976	81,442	82,887	80,421	-466	-1,445	-0.6	-1.7	3,119	2,960	5.4	38,519	36,391
Manitowoc County, WI	80,976	81,442	82,887	80,421	-466	-1,445	-0.6	-1.7	3,119	2,960	5.4	38,519	36,391
Marble Falls, TX	43,117	42,750	34,147	22,677	367	8,603	0.9	25.2	1,756	1,663	5.6	40,734	38,863
Burnet County, TX	43,117	42,750	34,147	22,677	367	8,603	0.9	25.2	1,756	1,663	5.6	40,734	38,863
Marinette, WI–MI	65,586	65,778	68,710	65,468	-192	-2,932	-0.3	-4.3	2,216	2,111	5.0	33,783	32,115
Menominee County, MI	23,930	24,029	25,326	24,920	-99	-1,297	-0.4	-5.1	763	719	6.0	31,871	29,965
Marinette County, WI	41,656	41,749	43,384	40,548	-93	-1,635	-0.2	-3.8	1,453	1,392	4.4	34,881	33,352
Marion, IN	69,793	70,061	73,403	74,169	-268	-3,342	-0.4	-4.6	2,243	2,147	4.5	32,141	30,667
Grant County, IN	69,793	70,061	73,403	74,169	-268	-3,342	-0.4	-4.6	2,243	2,147	4.5	32,141	30,667
Marion, OH	66,212	66,501	66,217	64,274	-289	284	-0.4	0.4	2,131	2,030	5.0	32,179	30,533
Marion County, OH	66,212	66,501	66,217	64,274	-289	284	-0.4	0.4	2,131	2,030	5.0	32,179	30,533
Marion–Herrin, IL	66,622	66,357	61,296	57,733	265	5,061	0.4	8.3	2,243	2,189	2.5	33,674	32,964
Williamson County, IL	66,622	66,357	61,296	57,733	265	5,061	0.4	8.3	2,243	2,189	2.5	33,674	32,964
Marquette, MI	67,694	67,077	64,634	70,887	617	2,443	0.9	3.8	2,204	2,111	4.4	32,555	31,433
Marquette County, MI	67,694	67,077	64,634	70,887	617	2,443	0.9	3.8	2,204	2,111	4.4	32,555	31,433
Marshall, MN	25,891	25,857	25,425	24,789	34	432	0.1	1.7	1,045	999	4.6	40,343	38,603
Lyon County, MN	25,891	25,857	25,425	24,789	34	432	0.1	1.7	1,045	999	4.6	40,343	38,603
Marshall, MO	23,280	23,370	23,756	23,523	-90	-386	-0.4	-1.6	865	785	10.1	37,154	33,568
Saline County, MO	23,280	23,370	23,756	23,523	-90	-386	-0.4	-1.6	865	785	10.1	37,154	33,568
Marshall, TX	66,296	65,631	62,110	57,483	665	3,521	1.0	5.7	2,743	2,514	9.1	41,371	38,234
Harrison County, TX	66,296	65,631	62,110	57,483	665	3,521	1.0	5.7	2,743	2,514	9.1	41,371	38,234
Marshalltown, IA	40,980	40,648	39,311	38,276	332	1,337	0.8	3.4	1,492	1,388	7.5	36,420	34,098
Marshall County, IA	40,980	40,648	39,311	38,276	332	1,337	0.8	3.4	1,492	1,388	7.5	36,420	34,098
Marshfield–Wisconsin Rapids, WI	74,785	74,749	75,555	73,605	36	-806	0.0	-1.1	2,929	2,812	4.2	39,172	37,588
Wood County, WI	74,785	74,749	75,555	73,605	36	-806	0.0	-1.1	2,929	2,812	4.2	39,172	37,588
Martin, TN	34,980	35,021	34,895	31,972	-41	126	-0.1	0.4	1,038	977	6.3	29,679	27,904
Weakley County, TN	34,980	35,021	34,895	31,972	-41	126	-0.1	0.4	1,038	977	6.3	29,679	27,904
Martinsville, VA	67,300	67,972	73,346	73,104	-672	-5,374	-1.0	-7.3	2,026	1,983	2.2	30,097	29,210
Henry County, VA	53,741	54,151	57,930	56,942	-410	-3,779	-0.8	-6.5	2,026	1,983	2.2	30,097	29,210
Martinsville city, VA	13,559	13,821	15,416	16,162	-262	-1,595	-1.9	-10.3	(6)	(6)	(6)	(6)	(6)
Maryville, MO	23,468	23,370	21,912	21,709	98	1,458	0.4	6.7	636	608	4.6	27,114	26,011
Nodaway County, MO	23,468	23,370	21,912	21,709	98	1,458	0.4	6.7	636	608	4.6	27,114	26,011
Mason City, IA	51,482	51,749	54,356	54,724	-267	-2,607	-0.5	-4.8	2,109	1,956	7.9	40,975	37,838
Cerro Gordo County, IA	43,938	44,151	46,447	46,733	-213	-2,296	-0.5	-4.9	1,811	1,692	7.0	41,225	38,366
Worth County, IA	7,544	7,598	7,909	7,991	-54	-311	-0.7	-3.9	298	264	13.0	39,521	34,770
Mayfield, KY	37,519	37,121	37,028	33,550	398	93	1.1	0.3	1,104	1,052	4.9	29,429	28,287
Graves County, KY	37,519	37,121	37,028	33,550	398	93	1.1	0.3	1,104	1,052	4.9	29,429	28,287
Maysville, KY	31,531	31,360	30,892	29,695	171	468	0.5	1.5	845	813	3.9	26,798	25,923
Lewis County, KY	13,878	13,870	14,092	13,029	8	-222	0.1	-1.6	295	286	3.2	21,251	20,606
Mason County, KY	17,653	17,490	16,800	16,666	163	690	0.9	4.1	550	528	4.2	31,158	30,135
McAlester, OK	45,625	45,837	43,953	40,950	-212	1,884	-0.5	4.3	1,514	1,456	4.0	33,191	31,800
Pittsburg County, OK	45,625	45,837	43,953	40,950	-212	1,884	-0.5	4.3	1,514	1,456	4.0	33,191	31,800
McComb, MS	53,470	53,535	52,539	50,210	-65	996	-0.1	1.9	1,482	1,438	3.1	27,713	26,866
Amite County, MS	13,064	13,131	13,599	13,328	-67	-468	-0.5	-3.4	376	360	4.5	28,802	27,464
Pike County, MS	40,406	40,404	38,940	36,882	2	1,464	0.0	3.8	1,106	1,077	2.6	27,361	26,668
McMinnville, TN	39,927	39,839	38,276	32,992	88	1,563	0.2	4.1	1,094	1,060	3.2	27,396	26,601
Warren County, TN	39,927	39,839	38,276	32,992	88	1,563	0.2	4.1	1,094	1,060	3.2	27,396	26,601
McPherson, KS	29,241	29,180	29,554	27,268	61	-374	0.2	-1.3	1,212	1,121	8.2	41,457	38,455
McPherson County, KS	29,241	29,180	29,554	27,268	61	-374	0.2	-1.3	1,212	1,121	8.2	41,457	38,455
Meadville, PA	88,740	88,765	90,366	86,166	-25	-1,601	0.0	-1.8	2,794	2,657	5.2	31,485	29,868
Crawford County, PA	88,740	88,765	90,366	86,166	-25	-1,601	0.0	-1.8	2,794	2,657	5.2	31,485	29,868
Menomonie, WI	43,971	43,857	39,858	35,909	114	3,999	0.3	10.0	1,426	1,350	5.6	32,426	30,740
Dunn County, WI	43,971	43,857	39,858	35,909	114	3,999	0.3	10.0	1,426	1,350	5.6	32,426	30,740

[1]The April 1, 2000, Population Estimates base reflects modifications to the Census 2000 population as documented in the Count Question Resolution program and geographic program revisions.
[2]The April 1, 1990, census counts include corrections processed through August 1997, results of special censuses and test censuses, and do not include adjustments for census coverage errors.
[3]Based on the April 1, 2010, census counts and the July 1, 2011, estimates.
[4]Based on the April 1, 2010, census counts and the April 1, 2000, estimates base.
[5]Based on resident population estimated as of April 1, 2010 and July 1, 2011 of the year shown.
[6]Independent city of Martinsville is included with Henry County; data not available separately.

Table D-1.   Population and Personal Income—*Continued*

Micropolitan statistical area component counties	Population 2011 estimate (July 1)	2010 census count (April 1)	2000 estimates base (April 1)[1]	1990 estimates base (April 1)[2]	Net change 2010–2011[3]	Net change 2000–2010[4]	Percent change 2010–2011[3]	Percent change 2000–2010[4]	Total (million dollars) 2011	Total (million dollars) 2010	Percentage change, 2010–2011	Per capita[5] 2011	Per capita[5] 2010
Meridian, MS	107,364	107,449	106,569	103,224	-85	880	-0.1	0.8	3,345	3,196	4.7	31,156	29,768
Clarke County, MS	16,743	16,732	17,955	17,313	11	-1,223	0.1	-6.8	445	427	4.3	26,603	25,497
Kemper County, MS	10,146	10,456	10,453	10,356	-310	3	-3.0	0.0	278	251	10.5	27,363	24,119
Lauderdale County, MS	80,475	80,261	78,161	75,555	214	2,100	0.3	2.7	2,622	2,518	4.1	32,582	31,394
Merrill, WI	28,602	28,743	29,641	26,993	-141	-898	-0.5	-3.0	957	933	2.6	33,463	32,439
Lincoln County, WI	28,602	28,743	29,641	26,993	-141	-898	-0.5	-3.0	957	933	2.6	33,463	32,439
Mexico, MO	25,566	25,529	25,853	23,599	37	-324	0.1	-1.3	816	787	3.6	31,899	30,876
Audrain County, MO	25,566	25,529	25,853	23,599	37	-324	0.1	-1.3	816	787	3.6	31,899	30,876
Miami, OK	31,860	31,848	33,194	30,561	12	-1,346	0.0	-4.1	1,025	992	3.4	32,179	31,140
Ottawa County, OK	31,860	31,848	33,194	30,561	12	-1,346	0.0	-4.1	1,025	992	3.4	32,179	31,140
Middlesborough, KY	28,725	28,691	30,060	31,506	34	-1,369	0.1	-4.6	737	720	2.4	25,656	25,083
Bell County, KY	28,725	28,691	30,060	31,506	34	-1,369	0.1	-4.6	737	720	2.4	25,656	25,083
Midland, MI	84,063	83,629	82,874	75,651	434	755	0.5	0.9	3,652	3,399	7.4	43,446	40,647
Midland County, MI	84,063	83,629	82,874	75,651	434	755	0.5	0.9	3,652	3,399	7.4	43,446	40,647
Milledgeville, GA	53,817	55,149	54,776	48,438	-1,332	373	-2.4	0.7	1,465	1,417	3.4	27,227	25,997
Baldwin County, GA	44,417	45,720	44,700	39,530	-1,303	1,020	-2.8	2.3	1,267	1,227	3.3	28,533	27,245
Hancock County, GA	9,400	9,429	10,076	8,908	-29	-647	-0.3	-6.4	198	190	4.2	21,059	20,062
Minden, LA	41,288	41,207	41,831	41,989	81	-624	0.2	-1.5	1,416	1,370	3.3	34,292	33,225
Webster Parish, LA	41,288	41,207	41,831	41,989	81	-624	0.2	-1.5	1,416	1,370	3.3	34,292	33,225
Mineral Wells, TX	28,115	28,111	27,026	25,055	4	1,085	0.0	4.0	942	908	3.7	33,497	32,323
Palo Pinto County, TX	28,115	28,111	27,026	25,055	4	1,085	0.0	4.0	942	908	3.7	33,497	32,323
Minot, ND	72,067	69,540	67,392	67,609	2,527	2,148	3.6	3.2	3,255	2,973	9.5	45,171	42,499
McHenry County, ND	5,505	5,395	5,987	6,528	110	-592	2.0	-9.9	197	209	-5.9	35,784	38,782
Renville County, ND	2,490	2,470	2,610	3,160	20	-140	0.8	-5.4	113	118	-4.6	45,209	47,673
Ward County, ND	64,072	61,675	58,795	57,921	2,397	2,880	3.9	4.9	2,946	2,646	11.3	45,976	42,616
Mitchell, SD	23,027	22,835	21,880	20,497	192	955	0.8	4.4	1,070	972	10.1	46,464	42,485
Davison County, SD	19,651	19,504	18,741	17,503	147	763	0.8	4.1	868	802	8.2	44,148	41,057
Hanson County, SD	3,376	3,331	3,139	2,994	45	192	1.4	6.1	202	170	19.3	59,943	50,844
Moberly, MO	25,346	25,414	24,663	24,370	-68	751	-0.3	3.0	828	788	5.2	32,687	30,985
Randolph County, MO	25,346	25,414	24,663	24,370	-68	751	-0.3	3.0	828	788	5.2	32,687	30,985
Monroe, WI	36,891	36,842	33,647	30,339	49	3,195	0.1	9.5	1,414	1,327	6.6	38,324	35,977
Green County, WI	36,891	36,842	33,647	30,339	49	3,195	0.1	9.5	1,414	1,327	6.6	38,324	35,977
Montrose, CO	41,011	41,276	33,432	24,423	-265	7,844	-0.6	23.5	1,269	1,228	3.3	30,933	29,828
Montrose County, CO	41,011	41,276	33,432	24,423	-265	7,844	-0.6	23.5	1,269	1,228	3.3	30,933	29,828
Morehead City, NC	67,373	66,469	59,383	52,407	904	7,086	1.4	11.9	2,639	2,532	4.2	39,174	37,950
Carteret County, NC	67,373	66,469	59,383	52,407	904	7,086	1.4	11.9	2,639	2,532	4.2	39,174	37,950
Morgan City, LA	54,210	54,650	53,500	58,086	-440	1,150	-0.8	2.1	2,031	1,950	4.1	37,462	35,734
St. Mary Parish, LA	54,210	54,650	53,500	58,086	-440	1,150	-0.8	2.1	2,031	1,950	4.1	37,462	35,734
Moscow, ID	37,704	37,244	34,935	30,617	460	2,309	1.2	6.6	1,199	1,150	4.3	31,809	30,816
Latah County, ID	37,704	37,244	34,935	30,617	460	2,309	1.2	6.6	1,199	1,150	4.3	31,809	30,816
Moses Lake, WA	91,265	89,120	74,698	54,798	2,145	14,422	2.4	19.3	2,829	2,645	7.0	30,999	29,483
Grant County, WA	91,265	89,120	74,698	54,798	2,145	14,422	2.4	19.3	2,829	2,645	7.0	30,999	29,483
Moultrie, GA	45,645	45,498	42,053	36,645	147	3,445	0.3	8.2	1,241	1,193	4.1	27,196	26,200
Colquitt County, GA	45,645	45,498	42,053	36,645	147	3,445	0.3	8.2	1,241	1,193	4.1	27,196	26,200
Mountain Home, AR	41,536	41,513	38,386	31,186	23	3,127	0.1	8.1	1,343	1,290	4.1	32,335	31,075
Baxter County, AR	41,536	41,513	38,386	31,186	23	3,127	0.1	8.1	1,343	1,290	4.1	32,335	31,075
Mountain Home, ID	26,346	27,038	29,130	21,205	-692	-2,092	-2.6	-7.2	927	909	1.9	35,173	33,569
Elmore County, ID	26,346	27,038	29,130	21,205	-692	-2,092	-2.6	-7.2	927	909	1.9	35,173	33,569
Mount Airy, NC	73,714	73,673	71,219	61,704	41	2,454	0.1	3.4	2,209	2,140	3.2	29,962	29,029
Surry County, NC	73,714	73,673	71,219	61,704	41	2,454	0.1	3.4	2,209	2,140	3.2	29,962	29,029
Mount Pleasant, MI	70,622	70,311	63,351	54,624	311	6,960	0.4	11.0	1,975	1,876	5.3	27,960	26,678
Isabella County, MI	70,622	70,311	63,351	54,624	311	6,960	0.4	11.0	1,975	1,876	5.3	27,960	26,678
Mount Pleasant, TX	32,596	32,334	28,118	24,009	262	4,216	0.8	15.0	930	916	1.6	28,542	28,202
Titus County, TX	32,596	32,334	28,118	24,009	262	4,216	0.8	15.0	930	916	1.6	28,542	28,202
Mount Sterling, KY	44,802	44,396	40,195	34,345	406	4,201	0.9	10.5	1,177	1,127	4.4	26,273	25,347
Bath County, KY	11,742	11,591	11,085	9,692	151	506	1.3	4.6	293	281	4.2	24,925	24,170
Menifee County, KY	6,317	6,306	6,556	5,092	11	-250	0.2	-3.8	144	140	2.7	22,752	22,173
Montgomery County, KY	26,743	26,499	22,554	19,561	244	3,945	0.9	17.5	741	706	4.9	27,696	26,619
Mount Vernon, IL	47,138	47,284	48,666	45,519	-146	-1,382	-0.3	-2.8	1,591	1,522	4.5	33,747	32,218
Hamilton County, IL	8,425	8,457	8,621	8,499	-32	-164	-0.4	-1.9	292	273	7.1	34,674	32,244
Jefferson County, IL	38,713	38,827	40,045	37,020	-114	-1,218	-0.3	-3.0	1,299	1,249	3.9	33,546	32,213
Mount Vernon, OH	61,275	60,921	54,500	47,473	354	6,421	0.6	11.8	1,956	1,834	6.6	31,917	30,060
Knox County, OH	61,275	60,921	54,500	47,473	354	6,421	0.6	11.8	1,956	1,834	6.6	31,917	30,060
Murray, KY	37,544	37,191	34,177	30,735	353	3,014	0.9	8.8	1,122	1,070	4.9	29,889	28,688
Calloway County, KY	37,544	37,191	34,177	30,735	353	3,014	0.9	8.8	1,122	1,070	4.9	29,889	28,688
Muscatine, IA	54,184	54,132	53,905	51,499	52	227	0.1	0.4	2,035	1,896	7.3	37,559	35,049
Louisa County, IA	11,369	11,387	12,183	11,592	-18	-796	-0.2	-6.5	404	365	10.5	35,508	32,116
Muscatine County, IA	42,815	42,745	41,722	39,907	70	1,023	0.2	2.5	1,631	1,531	6.6	38,104	35,830
Muskogee, OK	71,003	70,990	69,451	68,078	13	1,539	0.0	2.2	2,246	2,156	4.2	31,639	30,320
Muskogee County, OK	71,003	70,990	69,451	68,078	13	1,539	0.0	2.2	2,246	2,156	4.2	31,639	30,320
Nacogdoches, TX	65,466	64,524	59,203	54,753	942	5,321	1.5	9.0	1,927	1,867	3.3	29,441	28,873
Nacogdoches County, TX	65,466	64,524	59,203	54,753	942	5,321	1.5	9.0	1,927	1,867	3.3	29,441	28,873

[1]The April 1, 2000, Population Estimates base reflects modifications to the Census 2000 population as documented in the Count Question Resolution program and geographic program revisions.
[2]The April 1, 1990, census counts include corrections processed through August 1997, results of special censuses and test censuses, and do not include adjustments for census coverage errors.
[3]Based on the April 1, 2010, census counts and the July 1, 2011, estimates.
[4]Based on the April 1, 2010, census counts and the April 1, 2000, estimates base.
[5]Based on resident population estimated as of April 1, 2010 and July 1, 2011 of the year shown.

Table D-1. Population and Personal Income—*Continued*

Micropolitan statistical area component counties	Population								Personal Income				
	2011 estimate (July 1)	2010 census count (April 1)	2000 estimates base (April 1)[1]	1990 estimates base (April 1)[2]	Net change		Percent change		Total (million dollars)		Percentage change, 2010–2011	Per capita[5]	
					2010– 2011[3]	2000– 2010[4]	2010– 2011[3]	2000– 2010[4]	2011	2010		2011	2010
Natchez, MS–LA	52,943	53,119	54,587	56,184	-176	-1,468	-0.3	-2.7	1,611	1,536	4.9	30,433	28,933
Concordia Parish, LA	20,876	20,822	20,247	20,828	54	575	0.3	2.8	562	539	4.3	26,936	25,897
Adams County, MS	32,067	32,297	34,340	35,356	-230	-2,043	-0.7	-5.9	1,049	997	5.2	32,709	30,891
Natchitoches, LA	39,442	39,566	39,080	37,254	-124	486	-0.3	1.2	1,195	1,165	2.6	30,307	29,413
Natchitoches Parish, LA	39,442	39,566	39,080	37,254	-124	486	-0.3	1.2	1,195	1,165	2.6	30,307	29,413
New Bern, NC	128,003	126,802	114,751	102,541	1,201	12,051	0.9	10.5	4,674	4,469	4.6	36,511	35,130
Craven County, NC	104,786	103,505	91,436	81,812	1,281	12,069	1.2	13.2	3,836	3,670	4.5	36,610	35,310
Jones County, NC	10,020	10,153	10,381	9,361	-133	-228	-1.3	-2.2	351	337	4.1	34,983	33,140
Pamlico County, NC	13,197	13,144	12,934	11,368	53	210	0.4	1.6	487	463	5.2	36,883	35,249
Newberry, SC	37,721	37,508	36,108	33,172	213	1,400	0.6	3.9	1,120	1,092	2.6	29,697	29,061
Newberry County, SC	37,721	37,508	36,108	33,172	213	1,400	0.6	3.9	1,120	1,092	2.6	29,697	29,061
New Castle, IN	49,264	49,462	48,508	48,139	-198	954	-0.4	2.0	1,439	1,379	4.4	29,214	27,851
Henry County, IN	49,264	49,462	48,508	48,139	-198	954	-0.4	2.0	1,439	1,379	4.4	29,214	27,851
New Castle, PA	90,535	91,108	94,643	96,246	-573	-3,535	-0.6	-3.7	3,031	2,907	4.2	33,475	31,956
Lawrence County, PA	90,535	91,108	94,643	96,246	-573	-3,535	-0.6	-3.7	3,031	2,907	4.2	33,475	31,956
New Iberia, LA	73,400	73,240	73,266	68,297	160	-26	0.2	0.0	2,775	2,613	6.2	37,805	35,664
Iberia Parish, LA	73,400	73,240	73,266	68,297	160	-26	0.2	0.0	2,775	2,613	6.2	37,805	35,664
New Philadelphia–Dover, OH	92,508	92,582	90,914	84,090	-74	1,668	-0.1	1.8	2,806	2,646	6.1	30,337	28,583
Tuscarawas County, OH	92,508	92,582	90,914	84,090	-74	1,668	-0.1	1.8	2,806	2,646	6.1	30,337	28,583
Newport, TN	35,544	35,662	33,565	29,141	-118	2,097	-0.3	6.2	913	886	3.0	25,696	24,885
Cocke County, TN	35,544	35,662	33,565	29,141	-118	2,097	-0.3	6.2	913	886	3.0	25,696	24,885
Newton, IA	36,547	36,842	37,213	34,795	-295	-371	-0.8	-1.0	1,259	1,154	9.1	34,457	31,357
Jasper County, IA	36,547	36,842	37,213	34,795	-295	-371	-0.8	-1.0	1,259	1,154	9.1	34,457	31,357
New Ulm, MN	25,734	25,893	26,911	26,984	-159	-1,018	-0.6	-3.8	1,009	953	5.8	39,204	36,836
Brown County, MN	25,734	25,893	26,911	26,984	-159	-1,018	-0.6	-3.8	1,009	953	5.8	39,204	36,836
Nogales, AZ	47,676	47,420	38,381	29,676	256	9,039	0.5	23.6	1,194	1,152	3.6	25,037	24,271
Santa Cruz County, AZ	47,676	47,420	38,381	29,676	256	9,039	0.5	23.6	1,194	1,152	3.6	25,037	24,271
Norfolk, NE	48,302	48,271	49,538	46,726	31	-1,267	0.1	-2.6	1,875	1,708	9.8	38,812	35,334
Madison County, NE	34,931	34,876	35,226	32,655	55	-350	0.2	-1.0	1,305	1,213	7.6	37,372	34,728
Pierce County, NE	7,216	7,266	7,857	7,827	-50	-591	-0.7	-7.5	305	268	13.9	42,209	36,843
Stanton County, NE	6,155	6,129	6,455	6,244	26	-326	0.4	-5.1	265	227	16.7	43,000	37,001
North Platte, NE	37,456	37,590	35,939	33,932	-134	1,651	-0.4	4.6	1,578	1,408	12.0	42,118	37,480
Lincoln County, NE	36,142	36,288	34,632	32,508	-146	1,656	-0.4	4.8	1,524	1,370	11.3	42,175	37,770
Logan County, NE	762	763	774	878	-1	-11	-0.1	-1.4	39	28	36.9	50,845	36,911
McPherson County, NE	552	539	533	546	13	6	2.4	1.1	15	10	42.7	26,304	18,844
North Vernon, IN	28,196	28,525	27,554	23,661	-329	971	-1.2	3.5	886	832	6.6	31,435	29,200
Jennings County, IN	28,196	28,525	27,554	23,661	-329	971	-1.2	3.5	886	832	6.6	31,435	29,200
North Wilkesboro, NC	68,984	69,340	65,632	59,393	-356	3,708	-0.5	5.6	2,178	2,095	4.0	31,575	30,230
Wilkes County, NC	68,984	69,340	65,632	59,393	-356	3,708	-0.5	5.6	2,178	2,095	4.0	31,575	30,230
Norwalk, OH	59,496	59,626	59,487	56,238	-130	139	-0.2	0.2	1,881	1,787	5.2	31,612	29,980
Huron County, OH	59,496	59,626	59,487	56,238	-130	139	-0.2	0.2	1,881	1,787	5.2	31,612	29,980
Oak Harbor, WA	78,971	78,506	71,558	60,195	465	6,948	0.6	9.7	3,022	2,881	4.9	38,268	36,624
Island County, WA	78,971	78,506	71,558	60,195	465	6,948	0.6	9.7	3,022	2,881	4.9	38,268	36,624
Oak Hill, WV	45,699	46,039	47,579	47,952	-340	-1,540	-0.7	-3.2	1,338	1,271	5.3	29,277	27,615
Fayette County, WV	45,699	46,039	47,579	47,952	-340	-1,540	-0.7	-3.2	1,338	1,271	5.3	29,277	27,615
Ocean Pines, MD	51,514	51,454	46,543	35,028	60	4,911	0.1	10.6	2,266	2,147	5.5	43,987	41,717
Worcester County, MD	51,514	51,454	46,543	35,028	60	4,911	0.1	10.6	2,266	2,147	5.5	43,987	41,717
Ogdensburg–Massena, NY	111,690	111,944	111,931	111,974	-254	13	-0.2	0.0	3,268	3,144	3.9	29,256	28,089
St. Lawrence County, NY	111,690	111,944	111,931	111,974	-254	13	-0.2	0.0	3,268	3,144	3.9	29,256	28,089
Oil City, PA	54,683	54,984	57,565	59,381	-301	-2,581	-0.5	-4.5	1,839	1,757	4.6	33,628	31,988
Venango County, PA	54,683	54,984	57,565	59,381	-301	-2,581	-0.5	-4.5	1,839	1,757	4.6	33,628	31,988
Okeechobee, FL	40,140	39,996	35,910	29,627	144	4,086	0.4	11.4	1,037	1,008	2.9	25,831	25,164
Okeechobee County, FL	40,140	39,996	35,910	29,627	144	4,086	0.4	11.4	1,037	1,008	2.9	25,831	25,164
Olean, NY	79,832	80,317	83,955	84,234	-485	-3,638	-0.6	-4.3	2,770	2,667	3.9	34,696	33,234
Cattaraugus County, NY	79,832	80,317	83,955	84,234	-485	-3,638	-0.6	-4.3	2,770	2,667	3.9	34,696	33,234
Oneonta, NY	61,917	62,259	61,676	60,390	-342	583	-0.5	0.9	2,069	1,987	4.1	33,414	31,939
Otsego County, NY	61,917	62,259	61,676	60,390	-342	583	-0.5	0.9	2,069	1,987	4.1	33,414	31,939
Ontario, OR–ID	53,692	53,936	52,193	42,472	-244	1,743	-0.5	3.3	1,426	1,360	4.9	26,568	25,209
Payette County, ID	22,624	22,623	20,578	16,434	1	2,045	0.0	9.9	653	619	5.6	28,869	27,329
Malheur County, OR	31,068	31,313	31,615	26,038	-245	-302	-0.8	-1.0	773	742	4.3	24,892	23,677
Opelousas–Eunice, LA	83,552	83,384	87,700	80,312	168	-4,316	0.2	-4.9	2,914	2,779	4.9	34,881	33,277
St. Landry Parish, LA	83,552	83,384	87,700	80,312	168	-4,316	0.2	-4.9	2,914	2,779	4.9	34,881	33,277
Orangeburg, SC	91,910	92,501	91,582	84,804	-591	919	-0.6	1.0	2,662	2,591	2.8	28,965	28,057
Orangeburg County, SC	91,910	92,501	91,582	84,804	-591	919	-0.6	1.0	2,662	2,591	2.8	28,965	28,057
Oskaloosa, IA	22,530	22,381	22,335	21,532	149	46	0.7	0.2	811	724	12.0	36,013	32,339
Mahaska County, IA	22,530	22,381	22,335	21,532	149	46	0.7	0.2	811	724	12.0	36,013	32,339
Ottawa–Streator, IL	154,092	154,908	153,098	148,331	-816	1,810	-0.5	1.2	5,766	5,511	4.6	37,417	35,608
Bureau County, IL	34,606	34,978	35,503	35,688	-372	-525	-1.1	-1.5	1,303	1,236	5.5	37,663	35,391
LaSalle County, IL	113,518	113,924	111,509	106,913	-406	2,415	-0.4	2.2	4,227	4,050	4.4	37,237	35,571
Putnam County, IL	5,968	6,006	6,086	5,730	-38	-80	-0.6	-1.3	235	226	4.3	39,408	37,555
Ottumwa, IA	35,421	35,625	36,051	35,696	-204	-426	-0.6	-1.2	1,144	1,087	5.2	32,297	30,515
Wapello County, IA	35,421	35,625	36,051	35,696	-204	-426	-0.6	-1.2	1,144	1,087	5.2	32,297	30,515

[1]The April 1, 2000, Population Estimates base reflects modifications to the Census 2000 population as documented in the Count Question Resolution program and geographic program revisions.
[2]The April 1, 1990, census counts include corrections processed through August 1997, results of special censuses and test censuses, and do not include adjustments for census coverage errors.
[3]Based on the April 1, 2010, census counts and the July 1, 2011, estimates.
[4]Based on the April 1, 2010, census counts and the April 1, 2000, estimates base.
[5]Based on resident population estimated as of April 1, 2010 and July 1, 2011 of the year shown.

Table D-1.　Population and Personal Income—*Continued*

Micropolitan statistical area component counties	Population 2011 estimate (July 1)	2010 census count (April 1)	2000 estimates base (April 1)[1]	1990 estimates base (April 1)[2]	Net change 2010–2011[3]	Net change 2000–2010[4]	Percent change 2010–2011[3]	Percent change 2000–2010[4]	Personal Income Total (million dollars) 2011	Total (million dollars) 2010	Percentage change, 2010–2011	Per capita[5] 2011	Per capita[5] 2010
Owatonna, MN	36,534	36,576	33,680	30,729	-42	2,896	-0.1	8.6	1,445	1,396	3.5	39,554	38,206
Steele County, MN	36,534	36,576	33,680	30,729	-42	2,896	-0.1	8.6	1,445	1,396	3.5	39,554	38,206
Owosso, MI	69,841	70,648	71,687	69,770	-807	-1,039	-1.1	-1.4	2,055	1,961	4.8	29,422	27,781
Shiawassee County, MI	69,841	70,648	71,687	69,770	-807	-1,039	-1.1	-1.4	2,055	1,961	4.8	29,422	27,781
Oxford, MS	48,472	47,351	38,744	31,826	1,121	8,607	2.4	22.2	1,568	1,488	5.3	32,345	31,325
Lafayette County, MS	48,472	47,351	38,744	31,826	1,121	8,607	2.4	22.2	1,568	1,488	5.3	32,345	31,325
Paducah, KY–IL	99,090	98,762	98,765	94,595	328	-3	0.3	0.0	3,728	3,537	5.4	37,624	35,815
Massac County, IL	15,442	15,429	15,161	14,752	13	268	0.1	1.8	492	466	5.6	31,843	30,161
Ballard County, KY	8,253	8,249	8,286	7,902	4	-37	0.0	-0.4	299	281	6.5	36,228	33,968
Livingston County, KY	9,531	9,519	9,804	9,062	12	-285	0.1	-2.9	311	298	4.4	32,672	31,264
McCracken County, KY	65,864	65,565	65,514	62,879	299	51	0.5	0.1	2,626	2,493	5.3	39,872	38,042
Pahrump, NV	43,351	43,946	32,485	17,781	-595	11,461	-1.4	35.3	1,372	1,346	1.9	31,656	30,723
Nye County, NV	43,351	43,946	32,485	17,781	-595	11,461	-1.4	35.3	1,372	1,346	1.9	31,656	30,723
Palatka, FL	74,041	74,364	70,423	65,070	-323	3,941	-0.4	5.6	2,047	2,007	2.0	27,644	27,024
Putnam County, FL	74,041	74,364	70,423	65,070	-323	3,941	-0.4	5.6	2,047	2,007	2.0	27,644	27,024
Palestine, TX	58,308	58,458	55,109	48,024	-150	3,349	-0.3	6.1	1,689	1,567	7.8	28,966	26,830
Anderson County, TX	58,308	58,458	55,109	48,024	-150	3,349	-0.3	6.1	1,689	1,567	7.8	28,966	26,830
Pampa, TX	23,571	23,464	23,631	24,992	107	-167	0.5	-0.7	927	863	7.4	39,314	36,905
Gray County, TX	22,755	22,535	22,744	23,967	220	-209	1.0	-0.9	885	828	6.9	38,903	36,876
Roberts County, TX	816	929	887	1,025	-113	42	-12.2	4.7	41	35	19.2	50,759	37,593
Paragould, AR	42,720	42,090	37,331	31,804	630	4,759	1.5	12.7	1,226	1,173	4.5	28,709	27,819
Greene County, AR	42,720	42,090	37,331	31,804	630	4,759	1.5	12.7	1,226	1,173	4.5	28,709	27,819
Paris, TN	32,352	32,330	31,115	27,888	22	1,215	0.1	3.9	991	949	4.4	30,629	29,340
Henry County, TN	32,352	32,330	31,115	27,888	22	1,215	0.1	3.9	991	949	4.4	30,629	29,340
Paris, TX	50,074	49,793	48,499	43,949	281	1,294	0.6	2.7	1,657	1,585	4.5	33,092	31,780
Lamar County, TX	50,074	49,793	48,499	43,949	281	1,294	0.6	2.7	1,657	1,585	4.5	33,092	31,780
Parsons, KS	21,511	21,607	22,835	23,693	-96	-1,228	-0.4	-5.4	754	716	5.2	35,029	33,223
Labette County, KS	21,511	21,607	22,835	23,693	-96	-1,228	-0.4	-5.4	754	716	5.2	35,029	33,223
Payson, AZ	53,144	53,597	51,335	40,216	-453	2,262	-0.8	4.4	1,692	1,629	3.9	31,846	30,445
Gila County, AZ	53,144	53,597	51,335	40,216	-453	2,262	-0.8	4.4	1,692	1,629	3.9	31,846	30,445
Pecos, TX	13,757	13,783	13,137	15,852	-26	646	-0.2	4.9	323	304	6.2	23,505	22,047
Reeves County, TX	13,757	13,783	13,137	15,852	-26	646	-0.2	4.9	323	304	6.2	23,505	22,047
Pella, IA	33,335	33,309	32,052	30,001	26	1,257	0.1	3.9	1,161	1,086	6.8	34,823	32,664
Marion County, IA	33,335	33,309	32,052	30,001	26	1,257	0.1	3.9	1,161	1,086	6.8	34,823	32,664
Pendleton–Hermiston, OR	87,894	87,062	81,543	66,874	832	5,519	1.0	6.8	2,780	2,621	6.1	31,632	30,037
Morrow County, OR	11,169	11,173	10,995	7,625	-4	178	0.0	1.6	425	389	9.1	38,029	34,706
Umatilla County, OR	76,725	75,889	70,548	59,249	836	5,341	1.1	7.6	2,356	2,232	5.5	30,701	29,349
Peru, IN	36,611	36,903	36,082	36,897	-292	821	-0.8	2.3	988	926	6.8	27,000	25,168
Miami County, IN	36,611	36,903	36,082	36,897	-292	821	-0.8	2.3	988	926	6.8	27,000	25,168
Phoenix Lake–Cedar Ridge, CA	54,953	55,365	54,501	48,456	-412	864	-0.7	1.6	2,016	1,933	4.3	36,680	34,997
Tuolumne County, CA	54,953	55,365	54,501	48,456	-412	864	-0.7	1.6	2,016	1,933	4.3	36,680	34,997
Picayune, MS	55,718	55,834	48,621	38,714	-116	7,213	-0.2	14.8	1,585	1,524	4.0	28,453	27,309
Pearl River County, MS	55,718	55,834	48,621	38,714	-116	7,213	-0.2	14.8	1,585	1,524	4.0	28,453	27,309
Pierre, SD	20,294	19,988	19,253	17,270	306	735	1.5	3.8	950	869	9.4	46,836	43,291
Hughes County, SD	17,292	17,022	16,481	14,817	270	541	1.6	3.3	803	743	8.1	46,451	43,503
Stanley County, SD	3,002	2,966	2,772	2,453	36	194	1.2	7.0	147	126	17.3	49,052	42,077
Pierre Part, LA	23,153	23,421	23,388	22,753	-268	33	-1.1	0.1	841	811	3.7	36,324	34,713
Assumption Parish, LA	23,153	23,421	23,388	22,753	-268	33	-1.1	0.1	841	811	3.7	36,324	34,713
Pittsburg, KS	39,220	39,134	38,242	35,582	86	892	0.2	2.3	1,159	1,120	3.5	29,542	28,599
Crawford County, KS	39,220	39,134	38,242	35,582	86	892	0.2	2.3	1,159	1,120	3.5	29,542	28,599
Plainview, TX	36,498	36,273	36,602	34,671	225	-329	0.6	-0.9	1,026	1,034	-0.7	28,120	28,413
Hale County, TX	36,498	36,273	36,602	34,671	225	-329	0.6	-0.9	1,026	1,034	-0.7	28,120	28,413
Platteville, WI	51,210	51,208	49,597	49,266	2	1,611	0.0	3.2	1,719	1,625	5.8	33,569	31,732
Grant County, WI	51,210	51,208	49,597	49,266	2	1,611	0.0	3.2	1,719	1,625	5.8	33,569	31,732
Plattsburgh, NY	81,945	82,128	79,894	85,969	-183	2,234	-0.2	2.8	2,789	2,766	0.8	34,029	33,669
Clinton County, NY	81,945	82,128	79,894	85,969	-183	2,234	-0.2	2.8	2,789	2,766	0.8	34,029	33,669
Plymouth, IN	47,050	47,051	45,128	42,182	-1	1,923	0.0	4.3	1,512	1,404	7.7	32,137	29,859
Marshall County, IN	47,050	47,051	45,128	42,182	-1	1,923	0.0	4.3	1,512	1,404	7.7	32,137	29,859
Point Pleasant, WV–OH	58,268	58,258	57,026	56,132	10	1,232	0.0	2.2	1,695	1,650	2.7	29,097	28,316
Gallia County, OH	30,970	30,934	31,069	30,954	36	-135	0.1	-0.4	981	953	3.0	31,680	30,763
Mason County, WV	27,298	27,324	25,957	25,178	-26	1,367	-0.1	5.3	714	698	2.4	26,167	25,542
Ponca City, OK	46,159	46,562	48,080	48,056	-403	-1,518	-0.9	-3.2	1,657	1,584	4.6	35,894	34,098
Kay County, OK	46,159	46,562	48,080	48,056	-403	-1,518	-0.9	-3.2	1,657	1,584	4.6	35,894	34,098
Pontiac, IL	38,885	38,950	39,678	39,301	-65	-728	-0.2	-1.8	1,649	1,520	8.5	42,417	39,100
Livingston County, IL	38,885	38,950	39,678	39,301	-65	-728	-0.2	-1.8	1,649	1,520	8.5	42,417	39,100

[1]The April 1, 2000, Population Estimates base reflects modifications to the Census 2000 population as documented in the Count Question Resolution program and geographic program revisions.
[2]The April 1, 1990, census counts include corrections processed through August 1997, results of special censuses and test censuses, and do not include adjustments for census coverage errors.
[3]Based on the April 1, 2010, census counts and the July 1, 2011, estimates.
[4]Based on the April 1, 2010, census counts and the April 1, 2000, estimates base.
[5]Based on resident population estimated as of April 1, 2010 and July 1, 2011 of the year shown.

Table D-1.   Population and Personal Income—*Continued*

Micropolitan statistical area component counties	2011 estimate (July 1)	2010 census count (April 1)	2000 estimates base (April 1)[1]	1990 estimates base (April 1)[2]	Net change 2010–2011[3]	Net change 2000–2010[4]	Percent change 2010–2011[3]	Percent change 2000–2010[4]	Total (million dollars) 2011	Total (million dollars) 2010	Percentage change, 2010–2011	Per capita[5] 2011	Per capita[5] 2010
Poplar Bluff, MO	43,082	42,794	40,867	38,765	288	1,927	0.7	4.7	1,491	1,421	5.0	34,612	33,189
Butler County, MO	43,082	42,794	40,867	38,765	288	1,927	0.7	4.7	1,491	1,421	5.0	34,612	33,189
Portales, NM	20,446	19,846	18,018	16,702	600	1,828	3.0	10.1	666	619	7.7	32,595	30,887
Roosevelt County, NM	20,446	19,846	18,018	16,702	600	1,828	3.0	10.1	666	619	7.7	32,595	30,887
Port Angeles, WA	71,838	71,404	64,525	56,210	434	6,879	0.6	10.7	2,596	2,506	3.6	36,138	35,048
Clallam County, WA	71,838	71,404	64,525	56,210	434	6,879	0.6	10.7	2,596	2,506	3.6	36,138	35,048
Portsmouth, OH	79,277	79,499	79,195	80,327	-222	304	-0.3	0.4	2,290	2,215	3.4	28,888	27,851
Scioto County, OH	79,277	79,499	79,195	80,327	-222	304	-0.3	0.4	2,290	2,215	3.4	28,888	27,851
Pottsville, PA	147,513	148,289	150,336	152,585	-776	-2,047	-0.5	-1.4	4,830	4,652	3.8	32,744	31,381
Schuylkill County, PA	147,513	148,289	150,336	152,585	-776	-2,047	-0.5	-1.4	4,830	4,652	3.8	32,744	31,381
Price, UT	21,318	21,403	20,422	20,228	-85	981	-0.4	4.8	701	670	4.6	32,886	31,246
Carbon County, UT	21,318	21,403	20,422	20,228	-85	981	-0.4	4.8	701	670	4.6	32,886	31,246
Prineville, OR	20,839	20,978	19,182	14,111	-139	1,796	-0.7	9.4	635	603	5.3	30,496	28,872
Crook County, OR	20,839	20,978	19,182	14,111	-139	1,796	-0.7	9.4	635	603	5.3	30,496	28,872
Pullman, WA	45,077	44,776	40,740	38,775	301	4,036	0.7	9.9	1,369	1,277	7.2	30,379	28,509
Whitman County, WA	45,077	44,776	40,740	38,775	301	4,036	0.7	9.9	1,369	1,277	7.2	30,379	28,509
Quincy, IL–MO	77,314	77,314	78,771	76,323	0	-1,457	0.0	-1.8	2,871	2,742	4.7	37,130	35,453
Adams County, IL	67,159	67,103	68,277	66,090	56	-1,174	0.1	-1.7	2,575	2,464	4.5	38,345	36,702
Lewis County, MO	10,155	10,211	10,494	10,233	-56	-283	-0.5	-2.7	295	278	6.4	29,094	27,227
Raymondville, TX	22,095	22,134	20,082	17,705	-39	2,052	-0.2	10.2	585	552	5.9	26,462	24,900
Willacy County, TX	22,095	22,134	20,082	17,705	-39	2,052	-0.2	10.2	585	552	5.9	26,462	24,900
Red Bluff, CA	63,601	63,463	56,039	49,625	138	7,424	0.2	13.2	1,755	1,675	4.8	27,592	26,325
Tehama County, CA	63,601	63,463	56,039	49,625	138	7,424	0.2	13.2	1,755	1,675	4.8	27,592	26,325
Red Wing, MN	46,217	46,183	44,127	40,690	34	2,056	0.1	4.7	1,959	1,846	6.1	42,377	39,951
Goodhue County, MN	46,217	46,183	44,127	40,690	34	2,056	0.1	4.7	1,959	1,846	6.1	42,377	39,951
Rexburg, ID	50,992	50,778	39,286	34,611	214	11,492	0.4	29.3	1,049	993	5.6	20,564	19,530
Fremont County, ID	13,128	13,242	11,819	10,937	-114	1,423	-0.9	12.0	322	307	4.9	24,545	23,178
Madison County, ID	37,864	37,536	27,467	23,674	328	10,069	0.9	36.7	726	686	5.9	19,184	18,245
Richmond, IN	68,643	68,917	71,097	71,951	-274	-2,180	-0.4	-3.1	2,122	2,037	4.1	30,909	29,584
Wayne County, IN	68,643	68,917	71,097	71,951	-274	-2,180	-0.4	-3.1	2,122	2,037	4.1	30,909	29,584
Richmond–Berea, KY	101,257	99,972	87,454	72,311	1,285	12,518	1.3	14.3	2,822	2,701	4.5	27,866	26,955
Madison County, KY	84,188	82,916	70,872	57,508	1,272	12,044	1.5	17.0	2,414	2,308	4.6	28,677	27,760
Rockcastle County, KY	17,069	17,056	16,582	14,803	13	474	0.1	2.9	407	393	3.7	23,865	23,033
Rio Grande City–Roma, TX	61,715	60,968	53,597	40,518	747	7,371	1.2	13.8	1,187	1,130	5.0	19,235	18,457
Starr County, TX	61,715	60,968	53,597	40,518	747	7,371	1.2	13.8	1,187	1,130	5.0	19,235	18,457
Riverton, WY	40,579	40,123	35,804	33,662	456	4,319	1.1	12.1	1,598	1,502	6.4	39,389	37,299
Fremont County, WY	40,579	40,123	35,804	33,662	456	4,319	1.1	12.1	1,598	1,502	6.4	39,389	37,299
Roanoke Rapids, NC	76,066	76,790	79,456	76,520	-724	-2,666	-0.9	-3.4	2,249	2,173	3.5	29,561	28,367
Halifax County, NC	54,173	54,691	57,370	55,516	-518	-2,679	-0.9	-4.7	1,608	1,551	3.7	29,674	28,430
Northampton County, NC	21,893	22,099	22,086	21,004	-206	13	-0.9	0.1	641	622	3.0	29,282	28,212
Rochelle, IL	53,115	53,497	51,032	45,957	-382	2,465	-0.7	4.8	1,898	1,774	7.0	35,741	33,189
Ogle County, IL	53,115	53,497	51,032	45,957	-382	2,465	-0.7	4.8	1,898	1,774	7.0	35,741	33,189
Rockingham, NC	46,611	46,639	46,564	44,511	-28	75	-0.1	0.2	1,285	1,269	1.2	27,560	27,201
Richmond County, NC	46,611	46,639	46,564	44,511	-28	75	-0.1	0.2	1,285	1,269	1.2	27,560	27,201
Rockland, ME	39,708	39,736	39,618	36,310	-28	118	-0.1	0.3	1,540	1,468	4.9	38,777	36,985
Knox County, ME	39,708	39,736	39,618	36,310	-28	118	-0.1	0.3	1,540	1,468	4.9	38,777	36,985
Rock Springs, WY	44,175	43,806	37,613	38,823	369	6,193	0.8	16.5	2,291	2,093	9.5	51,860	47,977
Sweetwater County, WY	44,175	43,806	37,613	38,823	369	6,193	0.8	16.5	2,291	2,093	9.5	51,860	47,977
Rolla, MO	45,020	45,156	39,825	35,248	-136	5,331	-0.3	13.4	1,409	1,350	4.3	31,287	29,831
Phelps County, MO	45,020	45,156	39,825	35,248	-136	5,331	-0.3	13.4	1,409	1,350	4.3	31,287	29,831
Roseburg, OR	107,490	107,667	100,399	94,649	-177	7,268	-0.2	7.2	3,356	3,229	3.9	31,222	29,987
Douglas County, OR	107,490	107,667	100,399	94,649	-177	7,268	-0.2	7.2	3,356	3,229	3.9	31,222	29,987
Roswell, NM	65,890	65,645	61,382	57,849	245	4,263	0.4	6.9	1,998	1,908	4.7	30,319	29,010
Chaves County, NM	65,890	65,645	61,382	57,849	245	4,263	0.4	6.9	1,998	1,908	4.7	30,319	29,010
Ruidoso, NM	20,454	20,497	19,411	12,219	-43	1,086	-0.2	5.6	661	632	4.6	32,309	30,820
Lincoln County, NM	20,454	20,497	19,411	12,219	-43	1,086	-0.2	5.6	661	632	4.6	32,309	30,820
Russellville, AR	84,391	83,939	75,608	63,642	452	8,331	0.5	11.0	2,399	2,312	3.8	28,423	27,494
Pope County, AR	62,331	61,754	54,469	45,883	577	7,285	0.9	13.4	1,808	1,739	4.0	29,007	28,105
Yell County, AR	22,060	22,185	21,139	17,759	-125	1,046	-0.6	4.9	591	573	3.1	26,772	25,791
Ruston, LA	63,179	63,009	57,906	57,604	170	5,103	0.3	8.8	1,933	1,885	2.6	30,602	29,875
Jackson Parish, LA	16,323	16,274	15,397	15,859	49	877	0.3	5.7	469	458	2.5	28,722	28,090
Lincoln Parish, LA	46,856	46,735	42,509	41,745	121	4,226	0.3	9.9	1,465	1,428	2.6	31,256	30,496
Rutland, VT	61,289	61,642	63,400	62,142	-353	-1,758	-0.6	-2.8	2,527	2,424	4.2	41,233	39,383
Rutland County, VT	61,289	61,642	63,400	62,142	-353	-1,758	-0.6	-2.8	2,527	2,424	4.2	41,233	39,383
Safford, AZ	45,753	45,657	42,036	34,562	96	3,621	0.2	8.6	1,206	1,153	4.7	26,366	25,351
Graham County, AZ	37,147	37,220	33,489	26,554	-73	3,731	-0.2	11.1	937	903	3.7	25,215	24,339
Greenlee County, AZ	8,606	8,437	8,547	8,008	169	-110	2.0	-1.3	270	249	8.2	31,333	29,848
St. Marys, GA	50,410	50,513	43,664	30,167	-103	6,849	-0.2	15.7	1,616	1,519	6.4	32,058	29,961
Camden County, GA	50,410	50,513	43,664	30,167	-103	6,849	-0.2	15.7	1,616	1,519	6.4	32,058	29,961

[1]The April 1, 2000, Population Estimates base reflects modifications to the Census 2000 population as documented in the Count Question Resolution program and geographic program revisions.
[2]The April 1, 1990, census counts include corrections processed through August 1997, results of special censuses and test censuses, and do not include adjustments for census coverage errors.
[3]Based on the April 1, 2010, census counts and the July 1, 2011, estimates.
[4]Based on the April 1, 2010, census counts and the April 1, 2000, estimates base.
[5]Based on resident population estimated as of April 1, 2010 and July 1, 2011 of the year shown.

Table D-1. Population and Personal Income—*Continued*

Micropolitan statistical area component counties	Population 2011 estimate (July 1)	2010 census count (April 1)	2000 estimates base (April 1)[1]	1990 estimates base (April 1)[2]	Net change 2010–2011[3]	Net change 2000–2010[4]	Percent change 2010–2011[3]	Percent change 2000–2010[4]	Total (million dollars) 2011	Total (million dollars) 2010	Percentage change, 2010–2011	Per capita[5] 2011	Per capita[5] 2010
St. Marys, PA	31,751	31,946	35,112	34,878	-195	-3,166	-0.6	-9.0	1,158	1,103	5.0	36,472	34,611
Elk County, PA	31,751	31,946	35,112	34,878	-195	-3,166	-0.6	-9.0	1,158	1,103	5.0	36,472	34,611
Salina, KS	61,963	61,697	59,760	54,935	266	1,937	0.4	3.2	2,434	2,304	5.6	39,276	37,254
Ottawa County, KS	6,119	6,091	6,163	5,634	28	-72	0.5	-1.2	205	187	9.7	33,490	30,638
Saline County, KS	55,844	55,606	53,597	49,301	238	2,009	0.4	3.7	2,229	2,117	5.3	39,910	37,978
Salisbury, NC	138,019	138,428	130,340	110,605	-409	8,088	-0.3	6.2	4,112	4,015	2.4	29,792	29,020
Rowan County, NC	138,019	138,428	130,340	110,605	-409	8,088	-0.3	6.2	4,112	4,015	2.4	29,792	29,020
Sanford, NC	58,752	57,866	49,040	41,370	886	8,826	1.5	18.0	1,928	1,863	3.5	32,815	32,176
Lee County, NC	58,752	57,866	49,040	41,370	886	8,826	1.5	18.0	1,928	1,863	3.5	32,815	32,176
Sault Ste. Marie, MI	38,797	38,520	38,543	34,604	277	-23	0.7	-0.1	1,047	1,020	2.6	26,977	26,417
Chippewa County, MI	38,797	38,520	38,543	34,604	277	-23	0.7	-0.1	1,047	1,020	2.6	26,977	26,417
Sayre, PA	62,917	62,622	62,761	60,967	295	-139	0.5	-0.2	2,105	1,924	9.4	33,462	30,725
Bradford County, PA	62,917	62,622	62,761	60,967	295	-139	0.5	-0.2	2,105	1,924	9.4	33,462	30,725
Scottsbluff, NE	37,728	37,660	37,770	36,877	68	-110	0.2	-0.3	1,386	1,281	8.2	36,737	33,949
Banner County, NE	684	690	819	852	-6	-129	-0.9	-15.8	39	27	43.3	56,545	38,780
Scotts Bluff County, NE	37,044	36,970	36,951	36,025	74	19	0.2	0.1	1,347	1,254	7.4	36,372	33,858
Scottsboro, AL	53,291	53,227	53,926	47,796	64	-699	0.1	-1.3	1,630	1,590	2.5	30,591	29,901
Jackson County, AL	53,291	53,227	53,926	47,796	64	-699	0.1	-1.3	1,630	1,590	2.5	30,591	29,901
Scottsburg, IN	23,987	24,181	22,960	20,991	-194	1,221	-0.8	5.3	673	650	3.4	28,041	26,898
Scott County, IN	23,987	24,181	22,960	20,991	-194	1,221	-0.8	5.3	673	650	3.4	28,041	26,898
Seaford, DE	200,330	197,145	156,638	113,229	3,185	40,507	1.6	25.9	7,009	6,770	3.5	34,988	34,208
Sussex County, DE	200,330	197,145	156,638	113,229	3,185	40,507	1.6	25.9	7,009	6,770	3.5	34,988	34,208
Searcy, AR	78,167	77,076	67,165	54,676	1,091	9,911	1.4	14.8	2,316	2,216	4.5	29,624	28,655
White County, AR	78,167	77,076	67,165	54,676	1,091	9,911	1.4	14.8	2,316	2,216	4.5	29,624	28,655
Sebring, FL	98,630	98,786	87,366	68,432	-156	11,420	-0.2	13.1	2,940	2,839	3.6	29,809	28,751
Highlands County, FL	98,630	98,786	87,366	68,432	-156	11,420	-0.2	13.1	2,940	2,839	3.6	29,809	28,751
Sedalia, MO	42,178	42,201	39,403	35,437	-23	2,798	-0.1	7.1	1,342	1,303	3.0	31,806	30,818
Pettis County, MO	42,178	42,201	39,403	35,437	-23	2,798	-0.1	7.1	1,342	1,303	3.0	31,806	30,818
Selinsgrove, PA	39,819	39,702	37,546	36,680	117	2,156	0.3	5.7	1,236	1,186	4.2	31,031	29,775
Snyder County, PA	39,819	39,702	37,546	36,680	117	2,156	0.3	5.7	1,236	1,186	4.2	31,031	29,775
Selma, AL	43,332	43,820	46,365	48,130	-488	-2,545	-1.1	-5.5	1,240	1,209	2.6	28,615	27,598
Dallas County, AL	43,332	43,820	46,365	48,130	-488	-2,545	-1.1	-5.5	1,240	1,209	2.6	28,615	27,598
Seneca, SC	74,418	74,273	66,215	57,494	145	8,058	0.2	12.2	2,379	2,305	3.2	31,964	30,977
Oconee County, SC	74,418	74,273	66,215	57,494	145	8,058	0.2	12.2	2,379	2,305	3.2	31,964	30,977
Seneca Falls, NY	35,198	35,251	33,342	33,683	-53	1,909	-0.2	5.7	1,189	1,142	4.1	33,783	32,435
Seneca County, NY	35,198	35,251	33,342	33,683	-53	1,909	-0.2	5.7	1,189	1,142	4.1	33,783	32,435
Sevierville, TN	91,466	89,889	71,170	51,050	1,577	18,719	1.8	26.3	2,933	2,787	5.2	32,065	30,910
Sevier County, TN	91,466	89,889	71,170	51,050	1,577	18,719	1.8	26.3	2,933	2,787	5.2	32,065	30,910
Seymour, IN	42,966	42,376	41,335	37,730	590	1,041	1.4	2.5	1,415	1,337	5.9	32,941	31,386
Jackson County, IN	42,966	42,376	41,335	37,730	590	1,041	1.4	2.5	1,415	1,337	5.9	32,941	31,386
Shawnee, OK	70,280	69,442	65,521	58,760	838	3,921	1.2	6.0	2,345	2,209	6.1	33,366	31,720
Pottawatomie County, OK	70,280	69,442	65,521	58,760	838	3,921	1.2	6.0	2,345	2,209	6.1	33,366	31,720
Shelby, NC	97,489	98,078	96,287	84,958	-589	1,791	-0.6	1.9	3,027	2,904	4.2	31,046	29,625
Cleveland County, NC	97,489	98,078	96,287	84,958	-589	1,791	-0.6	1.9	3,027	2,904	4.2	31,046	29,625
Shelbyville, TN	45,509	45,058	37,586	30,411	451	7,472	1.0	19.9	1,403	1,352	3.8	30,832	29,940
Bedford County, TN	45,509	45,058	37,586	30,411	451	7,472	1.0	19.9	1,403	1,352	3.8	30,832	29,940
Shelton, WA	61,019	60,699	49,405	38,341	320	11,294	0.5	22.9	1,852	1,792	3.3	30,345	29,496
Mason County, WA	61,019	60,699	49,405	38,341	320	11,294	0.5	22.9	1,852	1,792	3.3	30,345	29,496
Sheridan, WY	29,239	29,116	26,560	23,562	123	2,556	0.4	9.6	1,485	1,417	4.8	50,803	48,631
Sheridan County, WY	29,239	29,116	26,560	23,562	123	2,556	0.4	9.6	1,485	1,417	4.8	50,803	48,631
Show Low, AZ	107,398	107,449	97,470	77,674	-51	9,979	0.0	10.2	2,744	2,660	3.2	25,554	24,725
Navajo County, AZ	107,398	107,449	97,470	77,674	-51	9,979	0.0	10.2	2,744	2,660	3.2	25,554	24,725
Sidney, OH	49,307	49,423	47,910	44,915	-116	1,513	-0.2	3.2	1,675	1,578	6.2	33,980	31,972
Shelby County, OH	49,307	49,423	47,910	44,915	-116	1,513	-0.2	3.2	1,675	1,578	6.2	33,980	31,972
Sierra Vista–Douglas, AZ	133,289	131,346	117,755	97,624	1,943	13,591	1.5	11.5	4,763	4,536	5.0	35,738	34,438
Cochise County, AZ	133,289	131,346	117,755	97,624	1,943	13,591	1.5	11.5	4,763	4,536	5.0	35,738	34,438
Sikeston, MO	39,136	39,191	40,422	39,376	-55	-1,231	-0.1	-3.0	1,417	1,340	5.8	36,219	34,166
Scott County, MO	39,136	39,191	40,422	39,376	-55	-1,231	-0.1	-3.0	1,417	1,340	5.8	36,219	34,166
Silver City, NM	29,380	29,514	31,002	27,676	-134	-1,488	-0.5	-4.8	965	894	8.0	32,854	30,389
Grant County, NM	29,380	29,514	31,002	27,676	-134	-1,488	-0.5	-4.8	965	894	8.0	32,854	30,389
Silverthorne, CO	27,972	27,994	23,548	12,881	-22	4,446	-0.1	18.9	1,304	1,237	5.5	46,627	44,037
Summit County, CO	27,972	27,994	23,548	12,881	-22	4,446	-0.1	18.9	1,304	1,237	5.5	46,627	44,037
Snyder, TX	16,919	16,921	16,361	18,634	-2	560	0.0	3.4	642	581	10.5	37,970	34,294
Scurry County, TX	16,919	16,921	16,361	18,634	-2	560	0.0	3.4	642	581	10.5	37,970	34,294
Somerset, KY	63,657	63,063	56,217	49,489	594	6,846	0.9	12.2	1,849	1,795	3.0	29,043	28,402
Pulaski County, KY	63,657	63,063	56,217	49,489	594	6,846	0.9	12.2	1,849	1,795	3.0	29,043	28,402
Somerset, PA	77,405	77,742	80,023	78,218	-337	-2,281	-0.4	-2.9	2,597	2,475	4.9	33,549	31,858
Somerset County, PA	77,405	77,742	80,023	78,218	-337	-2,281	-0.4	-2.9	2,597	2,475	4.9	33,549	31,858
Southern Pines–Pinehurst, NC	89,352	88,247	74,769	59,000	1,105	13,478	1.3	18.0	3,438	3,271	5.1	38,477	36,930
Moore County, NC	89,352	88,247	74,769	59,000	1,105	13,478	1.3	18.0	3,438	3,271	5.1	38,477	36,930

[1]The April 1, 2000, Population Estimates base reflects modifications to the Census 2000 population as documented in the Count Question Resolution program and geographic program revisions.
[2]The April 1, 1990, census counts include corrections processed through August 1997, results of special censuses and test censuses, and do not include adjustments for census coverage errors.
[3]Based on the April 1, 2010, census counts and the July 1, 2011, estimates.
[4]Based on the April 1, 2010, census counts and the April 1, 2000, estimates base.
[5]Based on resident population estimated as of April 1, 2010 and July 1, 2011 of the year shown.

Table D-1.   Population and Personal Income—*Continued*

Micropolitan statistical area component counties	Population								Personal Income				
	2011 estimate (July 1)	2010 census count (April 1)	2000 estimates base (April 1)[1]	1990 estimates base (April 1)[2]	Net change		Percent change		Total (million dollars)		Percentage change, 2010–2011	Per capita[5]	
					2010–2011[3]	2000–2010[4]	2010–2011[3]	2000–2010[4]	2011	2010		2011	2010
Spearfish, SD	24,312	24,097	21,802	20,655	215	2,295	0.9	10.5	846	811	4.3	34,799	33,540
Lawrence County, SD	24,312	24,097	21,802	20,655	215	2,295	0.9	10.5	846	811	4.3	34,799	33,540
Spencer, IA	16,590	16,667	17,372	17,585	-77	-705	-0.5	-4.1	741	659	12.5	44,683	39,579
Clay County, IA	16,590	16,667	17,372	17,585	-77	-705	-0.5	-4.1	741	659	12.5	44,683	39,579
Spirit Lake, IA	16,899	16,667	16,424	14,909	232	243	1.4	1.5	772	711	8.6	45,680	42,635
Dickinson County, IA	16,899	16,667	16,424	14,909	232	243	1.4	1.5	772	711	8.6	45,680	42,635
Starkville, MS	47,741	47,671	42,902	38,375	70	4,769	0.1	11.1	1,353	1,294	4.5	28,340	27,151
Oktibbeha County, MS	47,741	47,671	42,902	38,375	70	4,769	0.1	11.1	1,353	1,294	4.5	28,340	27,151
Statesboro, GA	72,881	70,217	55,983	43,125	2,664	14,234	3.8	25.4	1,774	1,698	4.4	24,335	24,018
Bulloch County, GA	72,881	70,217	55,983	43,125	2,664	14,234	3.8	25.4	1,774	1,698	4.4	24,335	24,018
Statesville–Mooresville, NC	161,202	159,437	122,660	93,205	1,765	36,777	1.1	30.0	5,409	5,089	6.3	33,556	31,852
Iredell County, NC	161,202	159,437	122,660	93,205	1,765	36,777	1.1	30.0	5,409	5,089	6.3	33,556	31,852
Staunton–Waynesboro, VA	118,629	118,502	108,988	97,687	127	9,514	0.1	8.7	4,086	3,895	4.9	34,442	32,870
Augusta County, VA	73,549	73,750	65,615	54,557	-201	8,135	-0.3	12.4	4,086	3,895	4.9	34,442	32,870
Staunton city, VA	23,769	23,746	23,853	24,581	23	-107	0.1	-0.4	(7)	(7)	(7)	(7)	(7)
Waynesboro city, VA	21,311	21,006	19,520	18,549	305	1,486	1.5	7.6	(7)	(7)	(7)	(7)	(7)
Stephenville, TX	38,266	37,890	33,001	27,991	376	4,889	1.0	14.8	1,207	1,129	6.9	31,532	29,743
Erath County, TX	38,266	37,890	33,001	27,991	376	4,889	1.0	14.8	1,207	1,129	6.9	31,532	29,743
Sterling, CO	22,619	22,709	20,504	17,567	-90	2,205	-0.4	10.8	785	745	5.4	34,725	32,785
Logan County, CO	22,619	22,709	20,504	17,567	-90	2,205	-0.4	10.8	785	745	5.4	34,725	32,785
Sterling, IL	58,388	58,498	60,653	60,186	-110	-2,155	-0.2	-3.6	2,178	2,067	5.4	37,306	35,362
Whiteside County, IL	58,388	58,498	60,653	60,186	-110	-2,155	-0.2	-3.6	2,178	2,067	5.4	37,306	35,362
Stevens Point, WI	70,084	70,019	67,182	61,405	65	2,837	0.1	4.2	2,494	2,419	3.1	35,585	34,538
Portage County, WI	70,084	70,019	67,182	61,405	65	2,837	0.1	4.2	2,494	2,419	3.1	35,585	34,538
Stillwater, OK	77,988	77,350	68,190	61,507	638	9,160	0.8	13.4	2,523	2,415	4.5	32,356	31,180
Payne County, OK	77,988	77,350	68,190	61,507	638	9,160	0.8	13.4	2,523	2,415	4.5	32,356	31,180
Storm Lake, IA	20,406	20,260	20,411	19,965	146	-151	0.7	-0.7	846	750	12.8	41,466	36,910
Buena Vista County, IA	20,406	20,260	20,411	19,965	146	-151	0.7	-0.7	846	750	12.8	41,466	36,910
Sturgis, MI	61,136	61,295	62,422	58,913	-159	-1,127	-0.3	-1.8	1,823	1,717	6.2	29,826	28,024
St. Joseph County, MI	61,136	61,295	62,422	58,913	-159	-1,127	-0.3	-1.8	1,823	1,717	6.2	29,826	28,024
Sulphur Springs, TX	35,371	35,161	31,960	28,833	210	3,201	0.6	10.0	1,159	1,109	4.5	32,766	31,452
Hopkins County, TX	35,371	35,161	31,960	28,833	210	3,201	0.6	10.0	1,159	1,109	4.5	32,766	31,452
Summerville, GA	25,736	26,015	25,470	22,236	-279	545	-1.1	2.1	607	594	2.1	23,576	22,863
Chattooga County, GA	25,736	26,015	25,470	22,236	-279	545	-1.1	2.1	607	594	2.1	23,576	22,863
Sunbury, PA	94,558	94,528	94,556	96,771	30	-28	0.0	0.0	3,151	3,005	4.9	33,328	31,839
Northumberland County, PA	94,558	94,528	94,556	96,771	30	-28	0.0	0.0	3,151	3,005	4.9	33,328	31,839
Susanville, CA	34,200	34,895	33,828	27,598	-695	1,067	-2.0	3.2	987	949	3.9	28,855	27,272
Lassen County, CA	34,200	34,895	33,828	27,598	-695	1,067	-2.0	3.2	987	949	3.9	28,855	27,272
Sweetwater, TX	15,269	15,216	15,802	16,594	53	-586	0.3	-3.7	503	479	4.9	32,914	31,419
Nolan County, TX	15,269	15,216	15,802	16,594	53	-586	0.3	-3.7	503	479	4.9	32,914	31,419
Tahlequah, OK	47,845	46,987	42,521	34,049	858	4,466	1.8	10.5	1,394	1,354	3.0	29,135	28,708
Cherokee County, OK	47,845	46,987	42,521	34,049	858	4,466	1.8	10.5	1,394	1,354	3.0	29,135	28,708
Talladega–Sylacauga, AL	81,664	82,291	80,321	74,109	-627	1,970	-0.8	2.5	2,517	2,443	3.0	30,820	29,784
Talladega County, AL	81,664	82,291	80,321	74,109	-627	1,970	-0.8	2.5	2,517	2,443	3.0	30,820	29,784
Tallulah, LA	12,004	12,093	13,728	12,463	-89	-1,635	-0.7	-11.9	309	295	4.6	25,709	24,364
Madison Parish, LA	12,004	12,093	13,728	12,463	-89	-1,635	-0.7	-11.9	309	295	4.6	25,709	24,364
Taos, NM	32,917	32,937	29,979	23,118	-20	2,958	-0.1	9.9	1,024	986	3.9	31,119	29,921
Taos County, NM	32,917	32,937	29,979	23,118	-20	2,958	-0.1	9.9	1,024	986	3.9	31,119	29,921
Taylorville, IL	34,865	34,800	35,372	34,418	65	-572	0.2	-1.6	1,345	1,223	9.9	38,569	35,144
Christian County, IL	34,865	34,800	35,372	34,418	65	-572	0.2	-1.6	1,345	1,223	9.9	38,569	35,144
The Dalles, OR	25,234	25,213	23,791	21,683	21	1,422	0.1	6.0	880	821	7.2	34,878	32,491
Wasco County, OR	25,234	25,213	23,791	21,683	21	1,422	0.1	6.0	880	821	7.2	34,878	32,491
The Villages, FL	97,756	93,420	53,345	31,577	4,336	40,075	4.6	75.1	2,720	2,518	8.0	27,824	26,699
Sumter County, FL	97,756	93,420	53,345	31,577	4,336	40,075	4.6	75.1	2,720	2,518	8.0	27,824	26,699
Thomaston, GA	26,977	27,153	27,597	26,300	-176	-444	-0.6	-1.6	738	702	5.1	27,346	25,913
Upson County, GA	26,977	27,153	27,597	26,300	-176	-444	-0.6	-1.6	738	702	5.1	27,346	25,913
Thomasville, GA	44,702	44,720	42,737	38,943	-18	1,983	0.0	4.6	1,595	1,517	5.2	35,687	33,885
Thomas County, GA	44,702	44,720	42,737	38,943	-18	1,983	0.0	4.6	1,595	1,517	5.2	35,687	33,885
Thomasville–Lexington, NC	162,697	162,878	147,246	126,688	-181	15,632	-0.1	10.6	5,389	5,162	4.4	33,121	31,692
Davidson County, NC	162,697	162,878	147,246	126,688	-181	15,632	-0.1	10.6	5,389	5,162	4.4	33,121	31,692
Tiffin, OH	56,469	56,745	58,683	59,733	-276	-1,938	-0.5	-3.3	1,779	1,684	5.7	31,506	29,722
Seneca County, OH	56,469	56,745	58,683	59,733	-276	-1,938	-0.5	-3.3	1,779	1,684	5.7	31,506	29,722
Tifton, GA	41,461	40,118	38,407	34,998	1,343	1,711	3.3	4.5	1,227	1,177	4.2	29,585	29,218
Tift County, GA	41,461	40,118	38,407	34,998	1,343	1,711	3.3	4.5	1,227	1,177	4.2	29,585	29,218

[1] The April 1, 2000, Population Estimates base reflects modifications to the Census 2000 population as documented in the Count Question Resolution program and geographic program revisions.
[2] The April 1, 1990, census counts include corrections processed through August 1997, results of special censuses and test censuses, and do not include adjustments for census coverage errors.
[3] Based on the April 1, 2010, census counts and the July 1, 2011, estimates.
[4] Based on the April 1, 2010, census counts and the April 1, 2000, estimates base.
[5] Based on resident population estimated as of April 1, 2010 and July 1, 2011 of the year shown.
[7] Independent city of Staunton and Waynesboro included with Augusta County; data not available separately.

Table D-1. Population and Personal Income—*Continued*

Micropolitan statistical area component counties	Population								Personal Income				
	2011 estimate (July 1)	2010 census count (April 1)	2000 estimates base (April 1)[1]	1990 estimates base (April 1)[2]	Net change		Percent change		Total (million dollars)		Percentage change, 2010–2011	Per capita[5]	
					2010–2011[3]	2000–2010[4]	2010–2011[3]	2000–2010[4]	2011	2010		2011	2010
Toccoa, GA	25,960	26,175	25,435	23,436	-215	740	-0.8	2.9	793	773	2.6	30,553	29,542
Stephens County, GA	25,960	26,175	25,435	23,436	-215	740	-0.8	2.9	793	773	2.6	30,553	29,542
Torrington, CT	188,789	189,927	182,193	174,092	-1,138	7,734	-0.6	4.2	10,032	9,564	4.9	53,139	50,404
Litchfield County, CT	188,789	189,927	182,193	174,092	-1,138	7,734	-0.6	4.2	10,032	9,564	4.9	53,139	50,404
Traverse City, MI	144,411	143,372	131,342	106,497	1,039	12,030	0.7	9.2	5,211	4,967	4.9	36,085	34,641
Benzie County, MI	17,443	17,525	15,998	12,200	-82	1,527	-0.5	9.5	542	523	3.7	31,079	29,829
Grand Traverse County, MI	88,349	86,986	77,654	64,273	1,363	9,332	1.6	12.0	3,260	3,106	5.0	36,894	35,685
Kalkaska County, MI	17,160	17,153	16,571	13,497	7	582	0.0	3.5	466	439	6.1	27,137	25,615
Leelanau County, MI	21,459	21,708	21,119	16,527	-249	589	-1.1	2.8	944	900	4.9	43,978	41,465
Troy, AL	32,915	32,899	29,605	27,595	16	3,294	0.0	11.1	1,128	1,107	1.9	34,269	33,579
Pike County, AL	32,915	32,899	29,605	27,595	16	3,294	0.0	11.1	1,128	1,107	1.9	34,269	33,579
Truckee–Grass Valley, CA	98,612	98,764	92,033	78,510	-152	6,731	-0.2	7.3	4,370	4,192	4.3	44,313	42,441
Nevada County, CA	98,612	98,764	92,033	78,510	-152	6,731	-0.2	7.3	4,370	4,192	4.3	44,313	42,441
Tullahoma, TN	100,344	100,210	93,024	79,962	134	7,186	0.1	7.7	3,232	3,105	4.1	32,210	31,007
Coffee County, TN	53,016	52,796	48,014	40,343	220	4,782	0.4	10.0	1,802	1,736	3.8	33,998	32,879
Franklin County, TN	40,917	41,052	39,270	34,923	-135	1,782	-0.3	4.5	1,210	1,162	4.2	29,579	28,341
Moore County, TN	6,411	6,362	5,740	4,696	49	622	0.8	10.8	219	208	5.6	34,213	32,654
Tupelo, MS	137,388	136,268	125,251	107,833	1,120	11,017	0.8	8.8	4,397	4,186	5.0	32,003	30,673
Itawamba County, MS	23,332	23,401	22,770	20,017	-69	631	-0.3	2.8	698	664	5.1	29,915	28,377
Lee County, MS	84,156	82,910	75,755	65,579	1,246	7,155	1.5	9.4	2,898	2,758	5.1	34,432	33,207
Pontotoc County, MS	29,900	29,957	26,726	22,237	-57	3,231	-0.2	12.1	801	764	4.9	26,798	25,452
Tuskegee, AL	21,182	21,452	24,105	24,928	-270	-2,653	-1.3	-11.0	586	572	2.4	27,644	26,556
Macon County, AL	21,182	21,452	24,105	24,928	-270	-2,653	-1.3	-11.0	586	572	2.4	27,644	26,556
Twin Falls, ID	100,687	99,604	82,626	68,718	1,083	16,978	1.1	20.5	3,222	3,027	6.4	32,001	30,287
Jerome County, ID	22,682	22,374	18,342	15,138	308	4,032	1.4	22.0	715	668	7.1	31,543	29,736
Twin Falls County, ID	78,005	77,230	64,284	53,580	775	12,946	1.0	20.1	2,507	2,359	6.2	32,134	30,446
Ukiah, CA	87,553	87,841	86,265	80,345	-288	1,576	-0.3	1.8	3,170	3,050	3.9	36,211	34,733
Mendocino County, CA	87,553	87,841	86,265	80,345	-288	1,576	-0.3	1.8	3,170	3,050	3.9	36,211	34,733
Union, SC	28,679	28,961	29,881	30,337	-282	-920	-1.0	-3.1	770	746	3.3	26,859	25,814
Union County, SC	28,679	28,961	29,881	30,337	-282	-920	-1.0	-3.1	770	746	3.3	26,859	25,814
Union City, TN–KY	38,545	38,620	40,202	39,988	-75	-1,582	-0.2	-3.9	1,237	1,159	6.7	32,088	29,997
Fulton County, KY	6,755	6,813	7,752	8,271	-58	-939	-0.9	-12.1	208	188	10.4	30,749	27,578
Obion County, TN	31,790	31,807	32,450	31,717	-17	-643	-0.1	-2.0	1,029	971	6.0	32,372	30,516
Urbana, OH	39,795	40,097	38,890	36,019	-302	1,207	-0.8	3.1	1,246	1,166	6.9	31,300	29,131
Champaign County, OH	39,795	40,097	38,890	36,019	-302	1,207	-0.8	3.1	1,246	1,166	6.9	31,300	29,131
Uvalde, TX	26,535	26,405	25,926	23,340	130	479	0.5	1.8	860	806	6.6	32,404	30,469
Uvalde County, TX	26,535	26,405	25,926	23,340	130	479	0.5	1.8	860	806	6.6	32,404	30,469
Valley, AL	33,939	34,215	36,583	36,876	-276	-2,368	-0.8	-6.5	984	934	5.4	28,994	27,352
Chambers County, AL	33,939	34,215	36,583	36,876	-276	-2,368	-0.8	-6.5	984	934	5.4	28,994	27,352
Van Wert, OH	28,601	28,744	29,659	30,464	-143	-915	-0.5	-3.1	1,036	939	10.3	36,207	32,731
Van Wert County, OH	28,601	28,744	29,659	30,464	-143	-915	-0.5	-3.1	1,036	939	10.3	36,207	32,731
Vermillion, SD	14,051	13,864	13,537	13,186	187	327	1.3	2.4	606	555	9.1	43,106	40,048
Clay County, SD	14,051	13,864	13,537	13,186	187	327	1.3	2.4	606	555	9.1	43,106	40,048
Vernal, UT	33,163	32,588	25,224	22,211	575	7,364	1.8	29.2	1,037	941	10.2	31,278	29,014
Uintah County, UT	33,163	32,588	25,224	22,211	575	7,364	1.8	29.2	1,037	941	10.2	31,278	29,014
Vernon, TX	13,404	13,535	14,676	15,121	-131	-1,141	-1.0	-7.8	463	457	1.5	34,571	33,808
Wilbarger County, TX	13,404	13,535	14,676	15,121	-131	-1,141	-1.0	-7.8	463	457	1.5	34,571	33,808
Vicksburg, MS	48,346	48,773	49,644	47,880	-427	-871	-0.9	-1.8	1,779	1,721	3.4	36,792	35,256
Warren County, MS	48,346	48,773	49,644	47,880	-427	-871	-0.9	-1.8	1,779	1,721	3.4	36,792	35,256
Vidalia, GA	36,499	36,346	34,337	31,451	153	2,009	0.4	5.9	1,087	1,048	3.7	29,771	28,766
Montgomery County, GA	9,065	9,123	8,270	7,379	-58	853	-0.6	10.3	238	229	3.9	26,251	25,081
Toombs County, GA	27,434	27,223	26,067	24,072	211	1,156	0.8	4.4	849	819	3.6	30,934	29,998
Vincennes, IN	38,500	38,440	39,256	39,884	60	-816	0.2	-2.1	1,398	1,322	5.7	36,312	34,431
Knox County, IN	38,500	38,440	39,256	39,884	60	-816	0.2	-2.1	1,398	1,322	5.7	36,312	34,431
Wabash, IN	32,608	32,888	34,960	35,069	-280	-2,072	-0.9	-5.9	1,091	1,032	5.8	33,469	31,407
Wabash County, IN	32,608	32,888	34,960	35,069	-280	-2,072	-0.9	-5.9	1,091	1,032	5.8	33,469	31,407
Wahpeton, ND–MN	22,837	22,897	25,136	25,664	-60	-2,239	-0.3	-8.9	1,036	939	10.3	45,346	40,986
Wilkin County, MN	6,592	6,576	7,138	7,516	16	-562	0.2	-7.9	280	267	4.7	42,437	40,632
Richland County, ND	16,245	16,321	17,998	18,148	-76	-1,677	-0.5	-9.3	756	672	12.5	46,527	41,129
Walla Walla, WA	59,588	58,781	55,180	48,439	807	3,601	1.4	6.5	2,102	1,998	5.2	35,276	33,913
Walla Walla County, WA	59,588	58,781	55,180	48,439	807	3,601	1.4	6.5	2,102	1,998	5.2	35,276	33,913
Walterboro, SC	38,611	38,892	38,264	34,377	-281	628	-0.7	1.6	1,132	1,099	2.9	29,311	28,251
Colleton County, SC	38,611	38,892	38,264	34,377	-281	628	-0.7	1.6	1,132	1,099	2.9	29,311	28,251

[1]The April 1, 2000, Population Estimates base reflects modifications to the Census 2000 population as documented in the Count Question Resolution program and geographic program revisions.
[2]The April 1, 1990, census counts include corrections processed through August 1997, results of special censuses and test censuses, and do not include adjustments for census coverage errors.
[3]Based on the April 1, 2010, census counts and the July 1, 2011, estimates.
[4]Based on the April 1, 2010, census counts and the April 1, 2000, estimates base.
[5]Based on resident population estimated as of April 1, 2010 and July 1, 2011 of the year shown.

Table D-1.   Population and Personal Income—*Continued*

Micropolitan statistical area component counties	Population								Personal Income				
	2011 estimate (July 1)	2010 census count (April 1)	2000 estimates base (April 1)[1]	1990 estimates base (April 1)[2]	Net change		Percent change		Total (million dollars)		Percentage change, 2010–2011	Per capita[5]	
					2010–2011[3]	2000–2010[4]	2010–2011[3]	2000–2010[4]	2011	2010		2011	2010
Wapakoneta, OH	45,838	45,949	46,611	44,585	-111	-662	-0.2	-1.4	1,772	1,660	6.7	38,647	36,118
Auglaize County, OH	45,838	45,949	46,611	44,585	-111	-662	-0.2	-1.4	1,772	1,660	6.7	38,647	36,118
Warren, PA	41,441	41,815	43,863	45,050	-374	-2,048	-0.9	-4.7	1,379	1,305	5.7	33,268	31,243
Warren County, PA	41,441	41,815	43,863	45,050	-374	-2,048	-0.9	-4.7	1,379	1,305	5.7	33,268	31,243
Warrensburg, MO	53,439	52,595	48,258	42,514	844	4,337	1.6	9.0	1,584	1,500	5.6	29,639	28,454
Johnson County, MO	53,439	52,595	48,258	42,514	844	4,337	1.6	9.0	1,584	1,500	5.6	29,639	28,454
Warsaw, IN	77,336	77,358	74,057	65,294	-22	3,301	0.0	4.5	2,903	2,727	6.5	37,541	35,253
Kosciusko County, IN	77,336	77,358	74,057	65,294	-22	3,301	0.0	4.5	2,903	2,727	6.5	37,541	35,253
Washington, IN	31,978	31,648	29,820	27,533	330	1,828	1.0	6.1	1,055	989	6.7	32,989	31,167
Daviess County, IN	31,978	31,648	29,820	27,533	330	1,828	1.0	6.1	1,055	989	6.7	32,989	31,167
Washington, NC	47,691	47,759	44,958	42,283	-68	2,801	-0.1	6.2	1,561	1,476	5.8	32,737	30,887
Beaufort County, NC	47,691	47,759	44,958	42,283	-68	2,801	-0.1	6.2	1,561	1,476	5.8	32,737	30,887
Washington Court House, OH	28,985	29,030	28,433	27,466	-45	597	-0.2	2.1	993	931	6.6	34,264	32,056
Fayette County, OH	28,985	29,030	28,433	27,466	-45	597	-0.2	2.1	993	931	6.6	34,264	32,056
Watertown, SD	33,420	33,130	31,437	27,672	290	1,693	0.9	5.4	1,382	1,212	14.1	41,365	36,534
Codington County, SD	27,442	27,227	25,897	22,698	215	1,330	0.8	5.1	1,134	1,017	11.5	41,322	37,318
Hamlin County, SD	5,978	5,903	5,540	4,974	75	363	1.3	6.6	248	195	27.3	41,566	32,934
Watertown–Fort Atkinson, WI	83,943	83,686	74,021	67,783	257	9,665	0.3	13.1	2,939	2,836	3.7	35,016	33,877
Jefferson County, WI	83,943	83,686	74,021	67,783	257	9,665	0.3	13.1	2,939	2,836	3.7	35,016	33,877
Watertown–Fort Drum, NY	117,910	116,229	111,738	110,943	1,681	4,491	1.4	4.0	5,355	4,986	7.4	45,418	42,735
Jefferson County, NY	117,910	116,229	111,738	110,943	1,681	4,491	1.4	4.0	5,355	4,986	7.4	45,418	42,735
Wauchula, FL	27,887	27,731	26,938	19,499	156	793	0.6	2.9	694	669	3.8	24,898	24,054
Hardee County, FL	27,887	27,731	26,938	19,499	156	793	0.6	2.9	694	669	3.8	24,898	24,054
Waycross, GA	55,244	55,070	51,119	48,799	174	3,951	0.3	7.7	1,509	1,463	3.1	27,309	26,510
Pierce County, GA	18,770	18,758	15,636	13,328	12	3,122	0.1	20.0	528	509	3.7	28,147	27,080
Ware County, GA	36,474	36,312	35,483	35,471	162	829	0.4	2.3	980	953	2.8	26,878	26,215
Weatherford, OK	27,750	27,469	26,142	26,897	281	1,327	1.0	5.1	1,007	898	12.2	36,300	32,634
Custer County, OK	27,750	27,469	26,142	26,897	281	1,327	1.0	5.1	1,007	898	12.2	36,300	32,634
West Plains, MO	40,665	40,400	37,238	31,447	265	3,162	0.7	8.5	1,121	1,085	3.3	27,555	26,741
Howell County, MO	40,665	40,400	37,238	31,447	265	3,162	0.7	8.5	1,121	1,085	3.3	27,555	26,741
West Point, MS	20,456	20,634	21,979	21,120	-178	-1,345	-0.9	-6.1	602	573	5.1	29,417	27,822
Clay County, MS	20,456	20,634	21,979	21,120	-178	-1,345	-0.9	-6.1	602	573	5.1	29,417	27,822
Whitewater, WI	102,931	102,228	93,759	75,000	703	8,469	0.7	9.0	3,585	3,413	5.0	34,830	33,339
Walworth County, WI	102,931	102,228	93,759	75,000	703	8,469	0.7	9.0	3,585	3,413	5.0	34,830	33,339
Willimantic, CT	118,151	118,428	109,091	102,525	-277	9,337	-0.2	8.6	4,625	4,461	3.7	39,141	37,658
Windham County, CT	118,151	118,428	109,091	102,525	-277	9,337	-0.2	8.6	4,625	4,461	3.7	39,141	37,658
Williston, ND	24,374	22,398	19,761	21,129	1,976	2,637	8.8	13.3	1,978	1,236	60.1	81,170	54,772
Williams County, ND	24,374	22,398	19,761	21,129	1,976	2,637	8.8	13.3	1,978	1,236	60.1	81,170	54,772
Willmar, MN	42,173	42,239	41,203	38,761	-66	1,036	-0.2	2.5	1,804	1,732	4.1	42,769	40,993
Kandiyohi County, MN	42,173	42,239	41,203	38,761	-66	1,036	-0.2	2.5	1,804	1,732	4.1	42,769	40,993
Wilmington, OH	41,927	42,040	40,543	35,444	-113	1,497	-0.3	3.7	1,343	1,300	3.3	32,027	31,020
Clinton County, OH	41,927	42,040	40,543	35,444	-113	1,497	-0.3	3.7	1,343	1,300	3.3	32,027	31,020
Wilson, NC	81,452	81,234	73,814	66,061	218	7,420	0.3	10.1	2,702	2,590	4.3	33,170	31,829
Wilson County, NC	81,452	81,234	73,814	66,061	218	7,420	0.3	10.1	2,702	2,590	4.3	33,170	31,829
Winfield, KS	36,272	36,311	36,291	36,915	-39	20	-0.1	0.1	1,196	1,136	5.4	32,982	31,293
Cowley County, KS	36,272	36,311	36,291	36,915	-39	20	-0.1	0.1	1,196	1,136	5.4	32,982	31,293
Winona, MN	51,378	51,461	49,985	47,828	-83	1,476	-0.2	3.0	1,801	1,705	5.6	35,049	33,173
Winona County, MN	51,378	51,461	49,985	47,828	-83	1,476	-0.2	3.0	1,801	1,705	5.6	35,049	33,173
Woodward, OK	20,034	20,081	18,486	18,976	-47	1,595	-0.2	8.6	827	711	16.3	41,287	35,629
Woodward County, OK	20,034	20,081	18,486	18,976	-47	1,595	-0.2	8.6	827	711	16.3	41,287	35,629
Wooster, OH	114,611	114,520	111,564	101,461	91	2,956	0.1	2.6	3,526	3,354	5.1	30,765	29,290
Wayne County, OH	114,611	114,520	111,564	101,461	91	2,956	0.1	2.6	3,526	3,354	5.1	30,765	29,290
Worthington, MN	21,397	21,378	20,832	20,098	19	546	0.1	2.6	889	818	8.7	41,549	38,268
Nobles County, MN	21,397	21,378	20,832	20,098	19	546	0.1	2.6	889	818	8.7	41,549	38,268
Yankton, SD	22,612	22,438	21,652	19,252	174	786	0.8	3.6	870	794	9.5	38,458	35,345
Yankton County, SD	22,612	22,438	21,652	19,252	174	786	0.8	3.6	870	794	9.5	38,458	35,345
Yazoo City, MS	27,886	28,065	28,149	25,506	-179	-84	-0.6	-0.3	733	696	5.2	26,280	24,852
Yazoo County, MS	27,886	28,065	28,149	25,506	-179	-84	-0.6	-0.3	733	696	5.2	26,280	24,852
Zanesville, OH	86,237	86,074	84,585	82,068	163	1,489	0.2	1.8	2,685	2,546	5.5	31,140	29,553
Muskingum County, OH	86,237	86,074	84,585	82,068	163	1,489	0.2	1.8	2,685	2,546	5.5	31,140	29,553

[1]The April 1, 2000, Population Estimates base reflects modifications to the Census 2000 population as documented in the Count Question Resolution program and geographic program revisions.
[2]The April 1, 1990, census counts include corrections processed through August 1997, results of special censuses and test censuses, and do not include adjustments for census coverage errors.
[3]Based on the April 1, 2010, census counts and the July 1, 2011, estimates.
[4]Based on the April 1, 2010, census counts and the April 1, 2000, estimates base.
[5]Based on resident population estimated as of April 1, 2010 and July 1, 2011 of the year shown.

APPENDIXES

APPENDIX A
SOURCE NOTES AND EXPLANATIONS

This appendix presents General Notes on population and economic and government censuses followed by source notes and explanations of the data items presented in table sets A through D of this publication. These table sets vary in both geographic and data coverage.

Each table set begins with the table number and title, followed by the source citation, and related definitions and other explanatory text on the source.

GENERAL NOTES

Population

Decennial censuses. The population statistics for 2010 and earlier are based on results from the censuses of population and housing, conducted by the U.S. Census Bureau as of April 1 in each of those years. As provided by Article 1, Section 2, of the U.S. Constitution, adopted in 1787, a census has been taken every 10 years since 1790. The original purposes of the census were to apportion the seats in the U.S. House of Representatives based on the population of each state and to derive an equitable tax on each state for the payment of the Revolutionary War debt. Through the years, the nation's needs and interests have become more complex, and the content of the decennial census has changed accordingly. At present, census data not only are used to apportion seats in the House and to aid legislators in the realignment of legislative district boundaries but are also used in the distribution of billions of federal dollars each year and are vital to state and local governments and to private firms for such functions as market analysis, site selection, and environmental impact studies.

The decennial censuses before 2010 used both short- and long-form questionnaires to gather information. The short form asked a limited number of basic questions. These questions were asked of all people and housing units and are often referred to as 100 percent questions because they were asked of the entire population. In 2010, these became the only questions because the long-form questionnaire has been replaced by the American Community Survey. The population items include sex, age, race, Hispanic or Latino, household relationship, and group quarters. Housing items include occupancy status, vacancy status, tenure (owner occupied or renter occupied), and mortgage status. The long form of the earlier censuses asked more detailed information on a sample basis and included the 100 percent questions as well as questions on education, employment, income, ancestry, homeowner costs, units in a structure, number of rooms, etc. For information about the 2010 census, see www.census.gov/2010census/ . For information about the 2000 census, see www.census.gov/main/www/cen2000.html .

Persons enumerated in the census were counted as inhabitants of their usual place of residence, which generally means the place where a person lives and sleeps most of the time. This place is not necessarily the same as the legal residence, voting residence, or domicile. In the vast majority of cases, however, the use of these different bases of classification would produce substantially the same statistics, although appreciable differences may exist for a few areas.

The implementation of this usual-residence practice has resulted in the establishment of residence rules for certain categories of persons whose usual place of residence is not immediately apparent (for example, college students were counted at their college residence). As in the above example, persons were not always counted as residents of the place where they happened to be staying on census day. However, persons without a usual place of residence were counted where they were enumerated.

For links to information on procedures and concepts used for the 2010 Census of Population and Housing, as well as a facsimile of the questionnaires and descriptions of the data products resulting from the census, see U.S. Census Bureau, see www.census.gov/2010census/data/ .

Population estimates. The U.S. Census Bureau annually produces estimates of resident population for each state and county using a component of population change method at the county level. To produce the state population estimates, all county populations within each state are summed.

The Census Bureau develops county population estimates with a component of population change method in which they use administrative records and other data to estimate the household and group quarters population. For the household population, the components of population change are births, deaths, net domestic migration, and net international migration. The Census Bureau measures change in the nonhousehold, or group quarters, population by the net change in the population living in group quarters facilities.

A major assumption underlying this approach is that changes in selected administrative and other data sources closely approximate the components of population change. Therefore, Census Bureau demographers separately estimate each component of population change based on administrative records, including registered births and deaths, federal income tax returns, Medicare enrollees, and military movement. The Census Bureau also separately estimates net international migration using information from the American Community Survey (ACS), the decennial census, and other data sources.

Most administrative record data sources lag the current estimate year by as much as 2 years. As a result, the Census Bureau projects the data for the current year based on past years' data. As updated data become available, the Census Bureau revises the projected input data so that each vintage's estimates are always based on the most recent data available.

The Census Bureau produces the estimate of each county's population, starting with the base population from either the 2010 census (for the July 1, 2010, estimates) or the revised population estimate for the prior year (for the July 1, 2011, and later estimates). The Census Bureau then adds or subtracts the demographic components of population change calculated for that time period. The Census Bureau will then add the estimates of net domestic migration, net international migration and the net change in the group quarters population.

State and county estimates may also incorporate other changes due to corrections made since the 2010 census. The corrections occur outside the component estimation framework and are the result of successful local challenges or special censuses.

The results of the 2010 census are used as the base population for subsequent annual population estimates. The enumerated resident population in the 2010 census is the starting point for the post-2010 population estimates. The Census Bureau will modify this enumerated population in two ways to produce the April 1, 2010, population

estimates base. First, they reconcile the Census 2010 race categories with the race categories that appear in their administrative records data by recoding the "Some other race" 2010 census responses to one or more of the five 1997 Office of Management and Budget (OMB) race categories: White, Black or African American, American Indian and Alaska Native, Asian, and Native Hawaiian and Other Pacific Islander. Second, they update the population estimates base to reflect changes to the 2010 census population due to the Count Question Resolution program, legal boundary updates and other geographic program revisions.

The birth and death components are estimated using data from two sources. Where possible, members of the Federal State Cooperative Program for Population Estimates (FSCPE) provide summary data on all registered births and deaths to residents of their respective states and counties from 2010 to the most recent calendar year. The National Center for Health Statistics (NCHS) also provides birth and death data, but these data are not as current as those available from members of the FSCPE. However, the NCHS data include individual record data on each registered birth and death by state, county, month, sex, race, Hispanic origin, and age (for deaths). Where FSCPE vital data are not available, only NCHS data is used.

County birth totals from FSCPE and NCHS sources are controlled to the national NCHS birth total for the corresponding year. Then the county-level sex, race, and Hispanic origin distribution of NCHS births for that year is applied to these totals to derive births for each demographic group for all U.S. counties. Estimates of annual deaths for demographic groups are calculated in similar fashion. The Census Bureau reconciles county death totals from the two data sources to the NCHS national death total for the corresponding year and assigns the county-level age, sex, race, and Hispanic origin distribution of NCHS deaths for that year. Since they produce estimates for July 1 of each year, the Census Bureau uses the NCHS month-of-occurrence information to derive births and deaths for the July 1 to June 30 period for each year.

The Census Bureau produces separate population estimates for the populations under age 65 and age 65 and over, mainly because different data are used to measure the domestic migration of these two populations. To determine the net domestic migration for the population under the age of 65, the Census Bureau uses data derived from federal income tax returns supplied by the Internal Revenue Service (IRS). The data used is limited to filers and their dependents under 65.

To calculate net domestic migration rates the Census Bureau will subtract the out-migrants from the in-migrants for each county to produce the number of net migrants. Then, they will divide the number of IRS-based net migrants in each county by the number of individuals represented on the tax returns in the first year in each county.

To determine the net migration for the age of 65 and over, the Census Bureau uses Medicare enrollment data as of each July 1 from 1999 to 2005 for each county. Due to data consistency issues in the Medicare data after 2005, the Census Bureau projects the number of Medicare enrollees as of July 1 for each county from 2006 to 2008 based on prior trends in Medicare enrollment. Because not all U.S. residents age 65 and over receive or are eligible to receive Medicare benefits, the Census Bureau will use the year-to-year change in the Medicare enrollment to calculate a domestic net migration rate. Assumed is that the year-to-year change in enrollment represents the total change in the age 65 and over population in each county. Since independent estimates for deaths and international migration are available for the population of age 65 and over, as well as the number of individuals turning 65 years old, the Census Bureau will benchmark these components to the Medicare data and remove that change from the total population change to determine the amount of change that, by default, must be due to net domestic migration. Then, the Census Bureau calculates a Medicare-based net migration rate for each county by dividing the net domestic migration estimate by the total number of Medicare enrollees at the beginning of the time period.

International migration is considered any change of residence across the borders of the United States (50 states and District of Columbia). The net international migration component of the population estimates combines four parts: (a) net international migration of the foreign born, (b) net migration between the United States and Puerto Rico, (c) net migration of natives to and from the United States, and (d) net movement of the armed forces population between the United States and overseas.

Net international migration of the foreign-born population is estimated in two parts, immigration and emigration. The estimate of immigration utilizes information from the American Community Survey (ACS) on the reported residence of the foreign-born population in the prior year. The foreign born who reported being abroad in the year prior to the survey are considered immigrants.

Group quarters population data are used from two sources to estimate the change in the group quarters (GQ) populations: (1) Census 2010 group quarters population

by single year of age and facility type (that is, correctional institutions, juvenile facilities, nursing homes, other institutional facilities, university dormitories, military barracks, other non-institutional facilities) for each sub-county area (for example, cities and towns) and (2) a time series of individual GQ records from the Group Quarters Report (GQR) prepared by the FSCPE members.

For further elaboration and explanation regarding Census Bureau methodology for population estimates, including information on net international migration, group quarters population, and estimations of the county populations, see www.census.gov/popest/methodology/2012-nat-st-co-meth.pdf .

American Community Survey

The American Community Survey (ACS) is a nationwide survey designed to provide communities with a fresh look at how they are changing. It was designed to eliminate the need for the long form in the 2010 census. The ACS collects information from U.S. households similar to what was collected on the 2000 census long form, such as income, commute time to work, home value, veteran status, and other important data. As with the official U.S. census, information about individuals will remain confidential.

The ACS collects and produces population and housing information every year instead of every 10 years. About three million households are surveyed each year. Collecting data every year reduces the cost of the official decennial census and provides more up-to-date information throughout the decade about trends in the U.S. population at the local community level. The ACS began in 1996 and has expanded each subsequent year.

Each year, 1-year estimates are available for geographic areas with a population of 65,000 or more. This includes the nation, all states, and the District of Columbia, all congressional districts, approximately 800 counties, and 500 metropolitan and micropolitan statistical areas, among others. In 2008, the ACS released its first multiyear estimates based on ACS data collected from 2005 through 2007. These 3-year estimates are available for geographic areas with a population of 20,000 or more, including the nation, all states and the District of Columbia, all congressional districts, approximately 1,800 counties, and 900 metropolitan and micropolitan statistical areas, among others. For areas with a population less than 20,000, 5-year estimates are available. The first 5-year estimates, based on the ACS data collected from 2005 through 2009, were released in 2010. Since then, 1-year, 3-year, and 5-year estimates are released every year.

More information on the American Community Survey can be found at www.census.gov/acs/www .

Economic Censuses

The economic census is the major source of facts about the structure and functioning of the nation's economy. It provides essential information for government, business, industry, and the general public. It furnishes an important part of the framework for such composite measures as the gross domestic product estimates, input/output measures, production and price indexes, and other statistical series that measure short-term changes in economic conditions. Title 13 of the U.S. Code (Sections 131, 191, and 224) directs the Census Bureau to take the economic census every 5 years, covering years ending in "2" and "7." The economic censuses form an integrated program at 5-year intervals since 1967 and before that for 1963, 1958, and 1954. Prior to that time, the individual censuses were taken separately at varying intervals. Beginning with the 1997 Economic Census data, the census presents data based on the North American Industry Classification System.

The economic censuses are collected on an establishment basis. An establishment is generally a single physical location where business is conducted or where services or industrial operations are performed (for example, factory, mill, store, hotel, movie theater, mine, farm, airline terminal, sales office, warehouse, or central administrative office). A company operating at more than one location is required to file a separate report for each store, factory, shop, or other location. Each establishment is assigned a separate industry classification based on its primary activity and not that of its parent company. Establishments responding to the establishment survey are classified into industries on the basis of their principal product or activity (determined by annual sales volume) in accordance with the *North American Industry Classification System— United States, 2007* manual available from the National Technical Information Service.

More detailed information about the scope, coverage, classification system, data items, and publications for each of the economic censuses and related surveys is published in the *Guide to the Economic Censuses and Related Statistics*. More information on the methodology, procedures, and history of the 2007 Economic Census is available at www.census.gov/econ/census07/www/user_guide.html .

Data from the 2007 Economic Census were released through the Census Bureau's American FactFinder, the Census Bureau's online system for access and dissemination of data.

North American Industry Classification System (NAICS) Sector

The North American Industry Classification System (NAICS) was developed under the direction and guidance of the Office of Management and Budget (OMB) as the standard for use by federal statistical agencies in classifying business establishments for the collection, tabulation, presentation, and analysis of statistical data describing the U.S. economy. Use of the standard provides uniformity and comparability in the presentation of these statistical data. NAICS is based on a production-oriented concept, meaning that it groups establishments into industries according to similarity in the processes used to produce goods or services. Previous census data were presented based on the Standard Industrial Classification (SIC) system developed in 1937. Due to this change, comparability between census years and data found in previous books will be limited.

There are 20 NAICS sectors, which are subdivided into 100 subsectors (three-digit codes), 317 industry groups (four-digit codes), and, as implemented in the United States, 1,904 industries (five- and six-digit codes). While many of the individual NAICS industries correspond directly to industries as defined under the SIC system, most of the higher-level groupings do not. For the 2007 version of NAICS, six of the twenty NAICS sectors have been changed from the 2002 version. For more information regarding the classification changes made from 2002 to 2007, see www.census.gov/eos/www/naics/ .

The **Agriculture, Forestry, Fishing, and Hunting** (NAICS 11) sector comprises establishments primarily engaged in growing crops, raising animals, harvesting timber, and harvesting fish and other animals from a farm, ranch, or their natural habitats.

The establishments in this sector are often described as farms, ranches, dairies, greenhouses, nurseries, orchards, or hatcheries. A farm may consist of a single tract of land or a number of separate tracts, which may be held under different tenures. For example, one tract may be owned by the farm operator and another rented. It may be operated by the operator alone or with the assistance of members of the household or hired employees, or it may be operated by a partnership, corporation, or other type of organization. When a landowner has one or more tenants, renters, croppers, or managers, the land operated by each is considered a farm.

The sector distinguishes two basic activities: agricultural production and agricultural support activities. Agricultural production includes establishments performing the complete farm or ranch operation, such as farm owner-operators, tenant farm operators, and sharecroppers. Agricultural support activities include establishments that perform one or more activities associated with farm operation, such as soil preparation, planting, harvesting, and management, on a contract or fee basis.

Excluded from the Agriculture, Forestry, Fishing, and Hunting sector are establishments primarily engaged in agricultural research and establishments primarily engaged in administering programs for regulating and conserving land, mineral, wildlife, and forest use. These establishments are classified in Industry 54171, Research and Development in the Physical, Engineering, and Life Sciences; and Industry 92412, Administration of Conservation Programs, respectively.

For information on the subsectors of Agriculture, Forestry, Fishing, and Hunting (NAICS 11), see www.census.gov/eos/www/naics/ .

The **Mining, Quarrying, and Oil and Gas Extraction** sector (NAICS 21) comprises establishments that extract naturally occurring mineral solids, such as coal and ores; liquid minerals, such as crude petroleum; and gases, such as natural gas. The term mining is used in the broad sense to include quarrying, well operations, beneficiating (e.g., crushing, screening, washing, and flotation), and other preparation customarily performed at the mine site or as a part of mining activity.

The Mining, Quarrying, and Oil and Gas Extraction sector distinguishes two basic activities: mine operation and mining support activities. Mine operation includes establishments operating mines, quarries, or oil and gas wells on their own account or for others on a contract or fee basis. Mining support activities include establishments that perform exploration (except geophysical surveying) and/or other mining services on a contract or fee basis (except mine site preparation and construction of oil/gas pipelines).

Establishments in the Mining, Quarrying, and Oil and Gas Extraction sector are grouped and classified according to the natural resource mined or to be mined. Industries include establishments that develop the mine site, extract the natural resources, and/or those that beneficiate (i.e., prepare) the mineral mined. Beneficiation is the process whereby the extracted material is reduced to particles that can be separated into mineral and waste, the former suitable for further processing or direct use. The operations that take place in beneficiation are primarily mechanical, such as grinding, washing, magnetic separation, and centrifugal separation. In contrast, manufacturing

operations primarily use chemical and electrochemical processes, such as electrolysis and distillation. However, some treatments, such as heat treatments, take place in both the beneficiation and the manufacturing (that is, smelting/refining) stages. The range of preparation activities varies by mineral and the purity of any given ore deposit. While some minerals, such as petroleum and natural gas, require little or no preparation, others are washed and screened, while yet others, such as gold and silver, can be transformed into bullion before leaving the mine site.

Mining, beneficiating, and manufacturing activities often occur in a single location. Separate receipts will be collected for these activities whenever possible. When receipts cannot be broken out between mining and manufacturing, establishments that mine or quarry nonmetallic minerals, and then beneficiate the nonmetallic minerals into more finished manufactured products are classified based on the primary activity of the establishment. A mine that manufactures a small amount of finished products will be classified in Sector 21, Mining, Quarrying, and Oil and Gas Extraction. An establishment that mines whose primary output is a more finished manufactured product will be classified in Sector 31–33, Manufacturing.

For information on the subsectors of Mining, Quarrying, and Oil and Gas Extraction (NAICS 21), see www.census.gov/eos/www/naics/ .

The **Utilities** sector (NAICS 22) comprises establishments engaged in the provision of the following utility services: electric power, natural gas, steam supply, water supply, and sewage removal. Within this sector, the specific activities associated with the utility services provided vary by utility: electric power includes generation, transmission, and distribution; natural gas includes distribution; steam supply includes provision and/or distribution; water supply includes treatment and distribution; and sewage removal includes collection, treatment, and disposal of waste through sewer systems and sewage treatment facilities.

Excluded from this sector are establishments primarily engaged in waste management services classified in Subsector 562, Waste Management and Remediation Services. These establishments also collect, treat, and dispose of waste materials; however, they do not use sewer systems or sewage treatment facilities.

For information on the subsectors of Utilities (NAICS 22), see www.census.gov/eos/www/naics/ .

The **Construction** sector (NAICS 23) comprises establishments primarily engaged in the construction of buildings or engineering projects (for example, highways and utility systems). Establishments primarily engaged in the preparation of sites for new construction and establishments primarily engaged in subdividing land for sale as building sites also are included in this sector.

Construction work done may include new work, additions, alterations, or maintenance and repairs. Activities of these establishments generally are managed at a fixed place of business, but they usually perform construction activities at multiple project sites. Production responsibilities for establishments in this sector are usually specified in (1) contracts with the owners of construction projects (prime contracts) or (2) contracts with other construction establishments (subcontracts).

Establishments primarily engaged in contracts that include responsibility for all aspects of individual construction projects are commonly known as general contractors, but also may be known as design-builders, construction managers, turnkey contractors, or (in cases where two or more establishments jointly secure a general contract) joint-venture contractors. Construction managers that provide oversight and scheduling only (that is, agency) as well as construction managers that are responsible for the entire project (that is, at risk) are included as general contractor type establishments. Establishments of the "general contractor type" frequently arrange construction of separate parts of their projects through subcontracts with other construction establishments.

Establishments primarily engaged in activities to produce a specific component (for example, masonry, painting, and electrical work) of a construction project are commonly known as specialty trade contractors. Activities of specialty trade contractors are usually subcontracted from other construction establishments, but especially in remodeling and repair construction, the work may be done directly for the owner of the property.

Establishments primarily engaged in activities to construct buildings to be sold on sites that they own are known as operative builders, but also may be known as speculative builders or merchant builders. Operative builders produce buildings in a manner similar to general contractors, but their production processes also include site acquisition and securing of financial backing. Operative builders are most often associated with the construction of residential buildings. Like general contractors, they may subcontract all or part of the actual construction work on their buildings.

There are substantial differences in the types of equipment, work force skills, and other inputs required by establishments in this sector. To highlight these differences and variations in the underlying production functions, this sector is divided into three subsectors.

Subsector 236, Construction of Buildings, comprises establishments of the general contractor type and operative builders involved in the construction of buildings. Subsector 237, Heavy and Civil Engineering Construction, comprises establishments involved in the construction of engineering projects. Subsector 238, Specialty Trade Contractors, comprises establishments engaged in specialty trade activities generally needed in the construction of all types of buildings. Force account construction is construction work performed by an enterprise primarily engaged in some business other than construction for its own account and use, using employees of the enterprise. This activity is not included in the construction sector unless the construction work performed is the primary activity of a separate establishment of the enterprise. The installation and the ongoing repair and maintenance of telecommunications and utility networks are excluded from construction when the establishments performing the work are not independent contractors. Although a growing proportion of this work is subcontracted to independent contractors in the Construction Sector, the operating units of telecommunications and utility companies performing this work are included with the telecommunications or utility activities.

For information on the subsectors of Construction (NAICS 23), see www.census.gov/eos/www /naics/ .

The **Manufacturing** sector (NAICS 31–33) comprises establishments engaged in the mechanical, physical, or chemical transformation of materials, substances, or components into new products. The assembling of component parts of manufactured products is considered manufacturing, except in cases where the activity is appropriately classified in Sector 23, Construction.

Establishments in the Manufacturing sector are often described as plants, factories, or mills and characteristically use power-driven machines and materials-handling equipment. However, establishments that transform materials or substances into new products by hand or in the workers home and those engaged in selling to the general public products made on the same premises from which they are sold, such as bakeries, candy stores, and custom tailors, may also be included in this sector. Manufacturing establishments may process materials or may contract with other establishments to process their materials for them. Both types of establishments are included in manufacturing.

The materials, substances, or components transformed by manufacturing establishments are raw materials that are products of agriculture, forestry, fishing, mining, or quarrying as well as products of other manufacturing establishments. The materials used may be purchased directly from producers, obtained through customary trade channels, or secured without recourse to the market by transferring the product from one establishment to another, under the same ownership.

The new product of a manufacturing establishment may be finished in the sense that it is ready for utilization or consumption, or it may be semifinished to become an input for an establishment engaged in further manufacturing. For example, the product of the alumina refinery is the input used in the primary production of aluminum; primary aluminum is the input to an aluminum wire drawing plant; and aluminum wire is the input for a fabricated wire product manufacturing establishment.

The subsectors in the Manufacturing sector generally reflect distinct production processes related to material inputs, production equipment, and employee skills. In the machinery area, where assembling is a key activity, parts and accessories for manufactured products are classified in the industry of the finished manufactured item when they are made for separate sale. For example, a replacement refrigerator door would be classified with refrigerators and an attachment for a piece of metal working machinery would be classified with metal working machinery. However, components, input from other manufacturing establishments, are classified based on the production function of the component manufacturer. For example, electronic components are classified in Subsector 334, Computer and Electronic Product Manufacturing and stampings are classified in Subsector 332, Fabricated Metal Product Manufacturing.

Manufacturing establishments often perform one or more activities that are classified outside the Manufacturing sector of NAICS. For instance, almost all manufacturing has some captive research and development or administrative operations, such as accounting, payroll, or management. These captive services are treated the same as captive manufacturing activities. When the services are provided by separate establishments, they are classified to the NAICS sector where such services are primary, not in manufacturing.

The boundaries of manufacturing and the other sectors of the classification system can be somewhat blurry. The establishments in the manufacturing sector are engaged in the transformation of materials into new products. Their output is a new product. However, the definition of what constitutes a new product can be somewhat subjective. As clarification, the following activities are considered

manufacturing in NAICS: Milk bottling and pasteurizing; Grinding of lenses to prescription; Water bottling and processing; Wood preserving; Fresh fish packaging (oyster shucking, electroplating, plating, metal heat fish filleting); Treating and polishing for the trade; Apparel jobbing (assigning of materials lapidary work for the trade, to contract factories or shops for fabricating signs and advertising displays, fabrication or other contract operations); Rebuilding or remanufacturing as well as contracting on materials owned by others; Machinery (i.e., automotive parts); Printing and related activities; Ship repair and renovation; Ready-mixed concrete production; Machine shops; Leather converting; and Tire retreading.

Conversely, there are activities that are sometimes considered manufacturing, but which for NAICS are classified in another sector (i.e., not classified as manufacturing). They include: (1) Logging, classified in Sector 11, Agriculture, Forestry, Fishing, and Hunting, is considered a harvesting operation; (2) The beneficiating of ores and other minerals, classified in Sector 21, Mining, Quarrying, and Oil and Gas Extraction, is considered part of the activity of mining; (3) The construction of structures and fabricating operations performed at the site of construction by contractors, is classified in Sector 23, Construction; (4) Establishments engaged in breaking of bulk and redistribution in smaller lots, including packaging, repackaging, or bottling products, such as liquors or chemicals; the customized assembly of computers; sorting of scrap; mixing paints to customer order; and cutting metals to customer order, classified in Sector 42, Wholesale Trade or Sector 44–45, Retail Trade, produce a modified version of the same product, not a new product; and (5) Publishing and the combined activity of publishing and printing, classified in Sector 51, Information, perform the transformation of information into a product whereas the value of the product to the consumer lies in the information content, not in the format in which it is distributed (i.e., the book or CD-ROM).

For information on the subsectors of Manufacturing (NAICS 31–33), see www.census.gov/eos/www /naics/ .

The **Wholesale Trade** sector (NAICS 42) comprises establishments engaged in wholesaling merchandise, generally without transformation, and rendering services incidental to the sale of merchandise. The merchandise described in this sector includes the outputs of agriculture, mining, manufacturing, and certain information industries, such as publishing.

The wholesaling process is an intermediate step in the distribution of merchandise. Wholesalers are organized to sell or arrange the purchase or sale of (a) goods for resale (i.e., goods sold to other wholesalers or retailers), (b) capital or durable nonconsumer goods, and (c) raw and intermediate materials and supplies used in production.

Wholesalers sell merchandise to other businesses and normally operate from a warehouse or office. These warehouses and offices are characterized by having little or no display of merchandise. In addition, neither the design nor the location of the premises is intended to solicit walk-in traffic. Wholesalers do not normally use advertising directed to the general public. Customers are generally reached initially via telephone, in-person marketing, or specialized advertising that may include Internet and other electronic means. Follow-up orders are either vendor-initiated or client-initiated, generally based on previous sales, and typically exhibit strong ties between sellers and buyers. In fact, transactions are often conducted between wholesalers and clients that have long-standing business relationships.

This sector comprises two main types of wholesalers: merchant wholesalers that sell goods on their own account and business-to-business electronic markets, agents, and brokers that arrange sales and purchases for others generally for a commission or fee.

1. Establishments that sell goods on their own account are known as wholesale merchants, distributors, jobbers, drop shippers, and import/export merchants. Also included as wholesale merchants are sales offices and sales branches (but not retail stores) maintained by manufacturing, refining, or mining enterprises apart from their plants or mines for the purpose of marketing their products. Merchant wholesale establishments typically maintain their own warehouse where they receive and handle goods for their customers. Goods are generally sold without transformation, but may include integral functions, such as sorting, packaging, labeling, and other marketing services.

2. Establishments arranging for the purchase or sale of goods owned by others or purchasing goods, generally on a commission basis are known as business-to-business electronic markets, agents and brokers, commission merchants, import/export agents and brokers, auction companies, and manufacturers' representatives. These establishments operate from offices and generally do not own or handle the goods they sell.

Some wholesale establishments may be connected with a single manufacturer and promote and sell the particular manufacturers' products to a wide range of other wholesalers or retailers. Other wholesalers may be connected to a retail chain, or a limited number of retail chains, and only provide a variety of products needed by that particular retail operation(s). These wholesalers may obtain the products from a wide range of manufacturers. Still other wholesalers may not take title to the goods, but act as agents and brokers for a commission.

Although, in general, wholesaling normally denotes sales in large volumes, durable nonconsumer goods may be sold in single units. Sales of capital or durable nonconsumer goods used in the production of goods and services, such as farm machinery, medium and heavy-duty trucks, and industrial machinery, are always included in Wholesale trade. For information on the subsectors of the Wholesale Trade sector (NAICS 42), see www.census.gov/eos/www/naics/ .

The **Retail Trade** sector (NAICS 44–45) comprises establishments engaged in retailing merchandise, generally without transformation, and rendering services incidental to the sale of merchandise. The retailing process is the final step in the distribution of merchandise; retailers are, therefore, organized to sell merchandise in small quantities to the general public. This sector comprises two main types of retailers: store and nonstore retailers.

Store retailers operate fixed point-of-sale locations, located and designed to attract a high volume of walk-in customers. In general, retail stores have extensive displays of merchandise and use mass-media advertising to attract customers. They typically sell merchandise to the general public for personal or household consumption, but some also serve business and institutional clients. These include establishments, such as office supply stores, computer and software stores, building materials dealers, plumbing supply stores, and electrical supply stores. Catalog showrooms, gasoline stations, automotive dealers, and mobile home dealers are treated as store retailers.

In addition to retailing merchandise, some types of store retailers are also engaged in the provision of after-sales services, such as repair and installation. For example, new automobile dealers, electronics and appliance stores, and musical instrument and supplies stores often provide repair services. As a general rule, establishments engaged in retailing merchandise and providing after-sales services are classified in this sector.

The first 11 subsectors of retail trade are store retailers. The establishments are grouped into industries and industry groups typically based on one or more of the following criteria:

1. The merchandise line or lines carried by the store; for example, specialty stores are distinguished from general-line stores.

2. The usual trade designation of the establishments. This criterion applies in cases where a store type is well recognized by the industry and the public, but difficult to define strictly in terms of merchandise lines carried; for example, pharmacies, hardware stores, and department stores.

3. Capital requirements in terms of display equipment; for example, food stores have equipment requirements not found in other retail industries.

4. Human resource requirements in terms of expertise; for example, the staff of an automobile dealer requires knowledge in financing, registering, and licensing issues that are not necessary in other retail industries.

Nonstore retailers, like store retailers, are organized to serve the general public, but their retailing methods differ. The establishments of this subsector reach customers and market merchandise with methods, such as the broadcasting of "infomercials," the broadcasting and publishing of direct-response advertising, the publishing of paper and electronic catalogs, door-to-door solicitation, in-home demonstration, selling from portable stalls (street vendors, except food), and distribution through vending machines. Establishments engaged in the direct sale (nonstore) of products, such as home heating oil dealers and home delivery newspaper routes are included here.

The buying of goods for resale is a characteristic of retail trade establishments that particularly distinguishes them from establishments in the agriculture, manufacturing, and construction industries. For example, farms that sell their products at or from the point of production are not classified in retail, but rather in agriculture. Similarly, establishments that both manufacture and sell their products to the general public are not classified in retail, but rather in manufacturing. However, establishments that engage in processing activities incidental to retailing are classified in retail. This includes establishments, such as optical goods stores that do in-store grinding of lenses, and meat and seafood markets.

Wholesalers also engage in the buying of goods for resale, but they are not usually organized to serve the general public. They typically operate from a warehouse or office and neither the design nor the location of these premises is intended to solicit a high volume of walk-in traffic. Wholesalers supply institutional, industrial, wholesale, and retail clients; their operations are, therefore, generally organized to purchase, sell, and deliver merchandise in larger quantities. However, dealers of durable nonconsumer goods, such as farm machinery and heavy-duty trucks, are included in wholesale trade even if they often sell these products in single units.

For information on the subsectors of Retail Trade (NAICS 44–45), see www.census.gov/eos/www /naics/ .

The **Transportation and Warehousing** sector (NAICS 48–49) includes industries providing transportation of passengers and cargo, warehousing and storage for goods, scenic and sightseeing transportation, and support activities related to modes of transportation. Establishments in these industries use transportation equipment or transportation related facilities as a productive asset. The type of equipment depends on the mode of transportation. The modes of transportation are air, rail, water, road, and pipeline.

The Transportation and Warehousing sector distinguishes three basic types of activities: subsectors for each mode of transportation, a subsector for warehousing and storage, and a subsector for establishments providing support activities for transportation. In addition, there are subsectors for establishments that provide passenger transportation for scenic and sightseeing purposes, postal services, and courier services.

A separate subsector for support activities is established in the sector because, first, support activities for transportation are inherently multimodal, such as freight transportation arrangement, or have multimodal aspects. Secondly, there are production process similarities among the support activity industries.

One of the support activities identified in the support activity subsector is the routine repair and maintenance of transportation equipment (for example, aircraft at an airport, railroad rolling stock at a railroad terminal, or ships at a harbor or port facility). Such establishments do not perform complete overhauling or rebuilding of transportation equipment (that is, periodic restoration of transportation equipment to original design specifications) or transportation equipment conversion (that is, major modification to systems). An establishment that primarily performs factory (or shipyard) overhauls, rebuilding, or conversions of aircraft, railroad rolling stock, or a ship is classified in Subsector 336, Transportation Equipment Manufacturing, according to the type of equipment.

Many of the establishments in this sector often operate on networks, with physical facilities, labor forces, and equipment spread over an extensive geographic area.

Warehousing establishments in this sector are distinguished from merchant wholesaling in that the warehouse establishments do not sell the goods.

Excluded from this sector are establishments primarily engaged in providing travel agent services that support transportation and other establishments, such as hotels, businesses, and government agencies. These establishments are classified in Sector 56, Administrative and Support and Waste Management and Remediation Services. Also, establishments primarily engaged in providing rental and leasing of transportation equipment without operator are classified in Subsector 532, Rental and Leasing Services.

For information on the subsectors of Transportation and Warehousing sector (NAICS 48–49) see www.census.gov/eos/www/naics/ .

The **Information** sector (NAICS 51) comprises establishments engaged in the following processes: (a) producing and distributing information and cultural products, (b) providing the means to transmit or distribute these products as well as data or communications, and (c) processing data.

The main components of this sector are the publishing industries, including software publishing, and both traditional publishing and publishing exclusively on the Internet; the motion picture and sound recording industries; the broadcasting industries, including traditional broadcasting and those broadcasting exclusively over the Internet; the telecommunications industries; Web search portals, data processing industries, and the information services industries.

The expressions "information age" and "global information economy" are used with considerable frequency today. The general idea of an "information economy" includes both the notion of industries primarily producing, processing, and distributing information, as well as the idea that every industry is using available information and information technology to reorganize and make themselves more productive.

For the purposes of NAICS, it is the transformation of information into a commodity that is produced and distributed by a number of growing industries that is at issue. The Information sector groups three types of establishments: (1) those engaged in producing and distributing information and cultural products; (2) those that provide the means to transmit or distribute these products as well as data or communications; and (3) those that process data. Cultural products are those that directly express attitudes, opinions, ideas, values, and artistic creativity; provide entertainment; or offer information and analysis concerning the past and present. Included in this definition are popular, mass-produced products as well as cultural products that normally have a more limited audience, such as poetry books, literary magazines, or classical records.

The unique characteristics of information and cultural products, and of the processes involved in their production and distribution, distinguish the Information sector from the goods-producing and service-producing sectors. Some of these characteristics are:

1. Unlike traditional goods, an "information or cultural product," such as a newspaper online or television program, does not necessarily have tangible qualities, nor is it necessarily associated with a particular form. A movie can be shown at a movie theater, on a television broadcast, through video-on-demand, or rented at a local video store. A sound recording can be aired on radio, embedded in multimedia products, or sold at a record store.

2. Unlike traditional services, the delivery of these products does not require direct contact between the supplier and the consumer.

3. The value of these products to the consumer lies in their informational, educational, cultural, or entertainment content, not in the format in which they are distributed. Most of these products are protected from unlawful reproduction by copyright laws.

4. The intangible property aspect of information and cultural products makes the processes involved in their production and distribution very different from goods and services. Only those possessing the rights to these works are authorized to reproduce, alter, improve, and distribute them. Acquiring and using these rights often involves significant costs. In addition, technology is revolutionizing the distribution of these products. It is possible to distribute them in a physical form, via broadcast, or online.

5. Distributors of information and cultural products can easily add value to the products they distribute. For instance, broadcasters add advertising not contained in the original product. This capacity means that unlike traditional distributors, they derive revenue not from sale of the distributed product to the final consumer, but from those who pay for the privilege of adding information to the original product. Similarly, a directory and mailing list publisher can acquire the rights to thousands of previously published newspaper and periodical articles and add new value by providing search and software and organizing the information in a way that facilitates research and retrieval. These products often command a much higher price than the original information.

The distribution modes for information commodities may either eliminate the necessity for traditional manufacture, or reverse the conventional order of manufacture-distribution.

A newspaper distributed online, for example, can be printed locally or by the final consumer. Similarly, it is anticipated that packaged software, which at the time of the 2007 economic census was mainly bought through the traditional retail channels, is now available mainly online. The NAICS Information sector is designed to make such economic changes transparent as they occur, or to facilitate designing surveys that will monitor the new phenomena and provide data to analyze the changes.

Many of the industries in the NAICS Information sector are engaged in producing products protected by copyright law or in distributing them (other than distribution by traditional wholesale and retail methods). Examples are traditional publishing industries, software and directory and mailing list publishing industries, and film and sound industries. Broadcasting and telecommunications industries and information providers and processors are also included in the Information sector because their technologies are so closely linked to other industries in the Information sector.

For information on the subsectors of Information sector (NAICS 51), see www.census.gov/eos /www/naics/ .

The **Finance and Insurance** sector (NAICS 52) comprises establishments primarily engaged in financial transactions (transactions involving the creation, liquidation, or change in ownership of financial assets) and/or in facilitating financial transactions. Three principal types of activities are identified:

1. Raising funds by taking deposits and/or issuing securities and, in the process, incurring liabilities. Establishments engaged in this activity use raised funds to acquire financial assets by making loans and/ or purchasing securities. Putting themselves at risk, they channel funds from lenders to borrowers and transform or repackage the funds with respect to maturity, scale, and risk. This activity is known as financial intermediation.

2. Pooling of risk by underwriting insurance and annuities. Establishments engaged in this activity collect fees, insurance premiums, or annuity considerations; build up reserves; invest those reserves; and make contractual payments. Fees are based on the expected incidence of the insured risk and the expected return on investment.

3. Providing specialized services facilitating or supporting financial intermediation, insurance, and employee benefit programs.

In addition, monetary authorities charged with monetary control are included in this sector.

The subsectors, industry groups, and industries within the NAICS Finance and Insurance sector are defined on the basis of their unique production processes. As with all industries, the production processes are distinguished by their use of specialized human resources and specialized physical capital. In addition, the way in which these establishments acquire and allocate financial capital, their source of funds, and the use of those funds provides a third basis for distinguishing characteristics of the production process. For instance, the production process in raising funds through deposit taking is different from the process of raising funds in bond or money markets. The process of making loans to individuals also requires different production processes than does the creation of investment pools or the underwriting of securities.

Most of the Finance and Insurance subsectors contain one or more industry groups of (1) intermediaries with similar patterns of raising and using funds and (2) establishments engaged in activities that facilitate, or are otherwise related to, that type of financial or insurance intermediation. Industries within this sector are defined in terms of activities for which a production process can be specified, and many of these activities are not exclusive to a particular type of financial institution. To deal with the varied activities taking place within existing financial institutions, the approach is to split these institutions into components performing specialized services. This requires defining the units engaged in providing those services and developing procedures that allow for their delineation. These units are the equivalents for finance and insurance of the establishments defined for other industries.

The output of many financial services, as well as the inputs and the processes by which they are combined, cannot be observed at a single location and can only be defined at a higher level of the organizational structure of the enterprise. Additionally, a number of independent activities that represent separate and distinct production processes may take place at a single location belonging to a multilocation financial firm. Activities are more likely to be homogeneous with respect to production characteristics than are locations, at least in financial services. The classification defines activities broadly enough that it can be used both by those classifying by location and by those employing a more top-down approach to the delineation of the establishment.

Establishments engaged in activities that facilitate, or are otherwise related to, the various types of intermediation have been included in individual subsectors, rather than in a separate subsector dedicated to services alone because these services are performed by intermediaries, as well as by specialist establishments, the extent to which the activity of the intermediaries can be separately identified is not clear.

The Finance and Insurance sector has been defined to encompass establishments primarily engaged in financial transactions—that is, transactions involving the creation, liquidation, change in ownership of financial assets—or in facilitating financial transactions. Financial industries are extensive users of electronic means for facilitating the verification of financial balances, authorizing transactions, transferring funds to and from transactors accounts, notifying banks (or credit card issuers) of the individual transactions, and providing daily summaries. Since these transaction-processing activities are integral to the production of finance and insurance services, establishments that principally provide a financial transaction processing service are classified to this sector, rather than to the data processing industry in the Information sector.

Legal entities that hold portfolios of assets on behalf of others are significant and data on them are required for a variety of purposes. Thus for NAICS, these funds, trusts, and other financial vehicles are the fifth subsector of the Finance and Insurance sector. These entities earn interest, dividends, and other property income, but have little or no employment and no revenue from the sale of services. Separate establishments and employees devoted to the management of funds are classified in Industry Group 5239, Other Financial Investment Activities.

For information on the subsectors of Finance and Insurance sector (NAICS 52), see www.census.gov/eos/www/naics/ .

The **Real Estate and Rental and Leasing** sector (NAICS 53) comprises establishments primarily engaged in renting, leasing, or otherwise allowing the use of tangible or intangible assets, and establishments providing related services. The major portion of this sector comprises establishments that rent, lease, or otherwise allow the use of their own assets by others. The assets may be tangible, as is the case of real estate and equipment, or intangible, as is the case with patents and trademarks.

This sector also includes establishments primarily engaged in managing real estate for others, selling, renting and/or buying real estate for others, and appraising real estate. These activities are closely related to this sector's main activity, and it was felt that from a production basis they would best be included here. In addition, a substantial proportion of property management is self-performed by lessors.

The main components of this sector are the real estate lessors industries (including equity real estate investment trusts (REITs)); equipment lessors industries (including motor vehicles, computers, and consumer goods); and lessors of nonfinancial intangible assets (except copyrighted works).

Excluded from this sector are establishments primarily engaged in renting or leasing equipment with operators. Establishments renting or leasing equipment with operators are classified in various subsectors of NAICS depending on the nature of the services provided (for example, transportation, construction, agriculture). These activities are excluded from this sector because the client is paying for the expertise and knowledge of the equipment operator, in addition to the rental of the equipment. In many cases, such as the rental of heavy construction equipment, the operator is essential to operate the equipment.

For information on the subsectors of the Real Estate and Rental and Leasing sector (NAICS 53), see www.census .gov/eos/www/naics/ .

The **Professional, Scientific, and Technical Services** sector (NAICS 54) comprises establishments that specialize in performing professional, scientific, and technical activities for others. These activities require a high degree of expertise and training. The establishments in this sector specialize according to expertise and provide these services to clients in a variety of industries and, in some cases, to households. Activities performed include: legal advice and representation; accounting, bookkeeping, and payroll services; architectural, engineering, and specialized design services; computer services; consulting services; research services; advertising services; photographic services; translation and interpretation services; veterinary services; and other professional, scientific, and technical services.

This sector excludes establishments primarily engaged in providing a range of day-to-day office administrative services, such as financial planning, billing and recordkeeping, personnel, and physical distribution and logistics. These establishments are classified in Sector 56, Administrative and Support and Waste Management and Remediation Services.

For information on the subsectors of Professional, Scientific, and Technical Services sector (NAICS 54), see www .census.gov/eos/www/naics/ .

The **Management of Companies and Enterprises** sector (NAICS 55) comprises (1) establishments that hold the securities of (or other equity interests in) companies and enterprises for the purpose of owning a controlling interest or influencing management decisions or (2) establishments (except government establishments) that administer, oversee, and manage establishments of the company or enterprise and that normally undertake the strategic or organizational planning and decision-making role of the company or enterprise. Establishments that administer, oversee, and manage may hold the securities of the company or enterprise.

Establishments in this sector perform essential activities that are often undertaken, in-house, by establishments in many sectors of the economy. By consolidating the performance of these activities of the enterprise at one establishment, economies of scale are achieved.

Government establishments primarily engaged in administering, overseeing, and managing governmental programs are classified in Sector 92, Public Administration. Establishments primarily engaged in providing a range of day-to-day office administrative services, such as financial planning, billing and recordkeeping, personnel, and physical distribution and logistics are classified in Industry 56111, Office Administrative Services.

For information on the subsectors of Management of Companies and Enterprises sector (NAICS 55), see www .census.gov/eos/www/naics/ .

The **Administrative and Support and Waste Management and Remediation Services** sector (NAICS 56) comprises establishments performing routine support activities for the day-to-day operations of other organizations. These essential activities are often undertaken in-house by establishments in many sectors of the economy. The establishments in this sector specialize in one or more of these support activities and provide these services to clients in a variety of industries and, in some cases, to households. Activities performed include: office administration, hiring and placing of personnel, document preparation and similar clerical services, solicitation, collection, security and surveillance services, cleaning, and waste disposal services.

The administrative and management activities performed by establishments in this sector are typically on a contract or fee basis. These activities may also be performed by establishments that are part of the company or enterprise. However, establishments involved in administering, overseeing, and managing other establishments of the company or enterprise, are classified in Sector 55, Management of Companies and Enterprises. Establishments in Sector 55 normally undertake the strategic and organizational planning and decision-making role of the company or enterprise. Government establishments engaged in administering, overseeing, and managing governmental programs are classified in Sector 92, Public Administration.

For information on the subsectors of Administrative and Support and Waste Management and Remediation Services sector (NAICS 56), see www.census.gov/eos/www/ naics/ .

The **Educational Services** sector (NAICS 61) comprises establishments that provide instruction and training in a wide variety of subjects. This instruction and training is provided by specialized establishments, such as schools, colleges, universities, and training centers. These establishments may be privately owned and operated for profit or not for profit, or they may be publicly owned and operated. They may also offer food and/or accommodation services to their students.

Educational services are usually delivered by teachers or instructors that explain, tell, demonstrate, supervise, and direct learning. Instruction is imparted in diverse settings, such as educational institutions, the workplace, or the home, and through diverse means, such as correspondence, television, the Internet, or other electronic and distance-learning methods. The training provided by these establishments may include the use of simulators and simulation methods. It can be adapted to the particular needs of the students, for example, sign language can replace verbal language for teaching students with hearing impairments. All industries in the sector share this commonality of process, namely, labor inputs of instructors with the requisite subject matter expertise and teaching ability.

For information on the subsectors of the Educational Services sector (NAICS 61), see www.census.gov/eos/www/ naics/ .

The **Health Care and Social Assistance** sector (NAICS 62) comprises establishments providing health care and social assistance for individuals. The sector includes both health care and social assistance because it is sometimes difficult to distinguish between the boundaries of these two activities. The industries in this sector are arranged on a continuum starting with those establishments providing medical care exclusively, continuing with those providing health care and social assistance, and finally finishing with those providing only social assistance. The services provided by establishments in this sector are delivered by trained professionals. All industries in the sector share this commonality of process, namely, labor inputs of health practitioners or social workers with the requisite expertise. Many of the industries in the sector are defined based on the educational degree held by the practitioners included in the industry.

Excluded from this sector are aerobic classes in Subsector 713, Amusement, Gambling, and Recreation Industries and nonmedical diet and weight reducing centers in Subsector 812, Personal and Laundry Services. Although these can be viewed as health services, these services are not typically delivered by health practitioners.

For information on the subsectors of the Health Care and Social Assistance sector (NAICS 62), see http://www .census.gov/eos/www/naics/ .

The **Arts, Entertainment, and Recreation** sector (NAICS 71) includes a wide range of establishments that operate facilities or provide services to meet varied cultural, entertainment, and recreational interests of their patrons. This sector comprises (1) establishments that are involved in producing, promoting, or participating in live performances, events, or exhibits intended for public viewing; (2) establishments that preserve and exhibit objects and sites of historical, cultural, or educational interest; and (3) establishments that operate facilities or provide services that enable patrons to participate in recreational activities or pursue amusement, hobby, and leisure-time interests.

Some establishments that provide cultural, entertainment, or recreational facilities and services are classified in other sectors. Excluded from this sector are: (1) establishments that provide both accommodations and recreational facilities, such as hunting and fishing camps and resort and casino hotels are classified in Subsector 721, Accommodation; (2) restaurants and night clubs that provide live entertainment in addition to the sale of food and beverages are classified in Subsector 722, Food Services and Drinking Places; (3) motion picture theaters, libraries and archives, and publishers of newspapers, magazines, books, periodicals, and computer software are classified in Sector 51, Information; and (4) establishments using transportation equipment to provide recreational and entertainment services, such as those operating sightseeing buses, dinner cruises, or helicopter rides, are classified in Subsector 487, Scenic and Sightseeing Transportation.

For information on the subsectors of the Arts, Entertainment, and Recreation sector (NAICS 71), see www.census .gov/eos/www/naics/ .

The **Accommodation and Food Services** sector (NAICS 72) comprises establishments providing customers with lodging and/or preparing meals, snacks, and beverages for immediate consumption. The sector includes both accommodation and food services establishments because the two activities are often combined at the same establishment.

Excluded from this sector are civic and social organizations, amusement and recreation parks, theaters, and other recreation or entertainment facilities providing food and beverage services.

For information on the subsectors of the Accommodation and Food Services sector (NAICS 72), see www.census .gov/eos/www/naics/ .

The **Other Services** (except Public Administration) sector (NAICS 81) comprises establishments engaged in providing services not specifically provided for elsewhere in the classification system. Establishments in this sector are primarily engaged in activities, such as equipment and machinery repairing, promoting or administering religious activities, grantmaking, advocacy, and providing dry cleaning and laundry services, personal care services, death care services, pet care services, photofinishing services, temporary parking services, and dating services.

Private households that engage in employing workers on or about the premises in activities primarily concerned with the operation of the household are included in this sector.

Excluded from this sector are establishments primarily engaged in retailing new equipment and also performing repairs and general maintenance on equipment. These establishments are classified in Sector 44–45, Retail Trade.

For information on the subsectors of the Other Services (except Public Administration) sector (NAICS 81), see www.census.gov/eos/www/naics/ .

The **Public Administration** sector (NAICS 92) consists of establishments of federal, state, and local government agencies that administer, oversee, and manage public programs and have executive, legislative, or judicial authority over other institutions within a given area. These agencies also set policy, create laws, adjudicate civil and criminal legal cases, provide for public safety and for national defense. In general, government establishments in the Public Administration sector oversee governmental programs and activities that are not performed by private establishments. Establishments in this sector typically are engaged in the organization and financing of the production of public goods and services, most of which are provided for free or at prices that are not economically significant.

Government establishments also engage in a wide range of productive activities covering not only public goods and services but also individual goods and services similar to those produced in sectors typically identified with private-sector establishments. In general, ownership is not a criterion for classification in NAICS. Therefore, government establishments engaged in the production of private-sector-like goods and services should be classified in the same industry as private-sector establishments engaged in similar activities.

As a practical matter, it is difficult to identify separate establishment detail for many government agencies. To the extent that separate establishment records are available, the administration of governmental programs is classified in Sector 92, Public Administration, while the operation of that same governmental program is classified elsewhere in NAICS based on the activities performed. For example, the governmental administrative authority for an airport is classified in Industry 92612, Regulation and Administration of Transportation Programs, while operating the airport is classified in Industry 48811, Airport Operations. When separate records for multi-establishment companies are not available to distinguish between the administration of a governmental program and the operation of it, the establishment is classified in Sector 92, Public Administration.

Examples of government-provided goods and services that are classified in sectors other than Public Administration include: schools, classified in Sector 61, Educational Services; hospitals, classified in Subsector 622, Hospitals; establishments operating transportation facilities, classified in Sector 48–49, Transportation and Warehousing; the operation of utilities, classified in Sector 22, Utilities; and the Government Printing Office, classified in Subsector 323, Printing and Related Support Activities.

For information on the subsectors of Public Administration sector (NAICS 92), see www.census.gov/eos/www/naics/ .

Census of Governments

A Census of Governments is taken at 5-year intervals as required by law under Title 13, U.S. Code, Section 161. The purpose of the Census of Governments is to provide periodic and comprehensive statistics about governments and governmental activities for all state and local governments in the U.S. Local governments include counties, cities, townships, special districts, and school districts. Data are obtained on government organizations, finances, and employment. Organization data include location, type, and characteristics of local governments and officials. Finances and employment data are the same as in comparable annual surveys and include revenue, expenditure, debt, assets, employees, payroll, and benefits. The U.S. Code, Title 13, requires this census and provides for voluntary responses. The 2007 census, similar to those taken since 1957, covers three major subject

fields—government organization, public employment, and government finances.

The concept of local governments as defined by the Census Bureau covers three general-purpose governments (county, municipal, and township) and two limited-purpose governments (school district and special district). For information on the history, methodology, and concepts for the Census of Governments, see the *Governments Finance and Employment Classification Manual* at www.census.gov/govs/classification/ .

The term "full-time equivalent employment" refers to a computed statistic representing the number of full-time employees that could have been employed if the reported number of hours worked by part-time employees had been worked by full-time employees. This statistic is calculated separately for each function of a government by dividing the "part-time hours paid" by the standard number of hours for full-time employees in the particular government and then adding the resulting quotient to the number of full-time employees.

Revenue includes all amounts of money received by a government from external sources during its fiscal year (i.e., those originating "outside the government"), net of refunds and other correcting transactions, other than issuance of debt, sale of investments, and agency or private trust transactions. Under this definition, revenue excludes amounts transferred from other funds or agencies of the same government. General revenue covers all government revenue except liquor stores revenue, insurance trust revenue, and utility revenue. Taxes are compulsory contributions exacted by a government for public purposes except employee and employer assessments for retirement and social insurance purposes, which are classified as insurance trust revenue. All tax revenue is classified as general revenue and comprises amounts received (including interest and penalties but excluding protested amounts and refunds) from all taxes imposed by a government. Local government tax revenue excludes any amounts from shares of state imposed and collected taxes, which are classified as intergovernmental revenue. Property taxes are taxes conditioned on ownership of property and measured by its value. This category includes general property taxes related to property as a whole, real and personal, tangible or intangible, whether taxed at a single rate or at classified rates, and taxes on selected types of property, such as motor vehicles or on certain or all intangibles. Direct expenditure includes payments to employees, suppliers, contractors, beneficiaries, and other final recipients of government payment; that is, all expenditure other than intergovernmental expenditure, while general expenditure covers all government expenditure other than the specifically enumerated kinds of expenditure classified as utility expenditure, liquor stores expenditure, and employee retirement or other insurance trust expenditure.

Census of Agriculture

The Census Bureau took a census of agriculture every 10 years from 1840 to 1920; since 1925, this census has been taken roughly once every 5 years. The 1997 Census of Agriculture was the first one conducted by the National Agricultural Statistics Service of the U.S. Department of Agriculture. Over time, the definition of a farm has varied. For recent censuses (including the 2007 census), a farm has been defined as any place from which $1,000 or more of agricultural products were produced and sold or normally would have been sold during the census year. The census of agriculture is the leading source of facts and statistics about the Nation's agricultural production. It provides a detailed picture of U.S. farms and ranches every five years and is the only source of uniform, comprehensive agricultural data for every state and county or county equivalent in the United States.

PART A—STATES

Part A, States, presents 84 tables with 1,362 items of data for each state, the United States as a whole, and the District of Columbia. These tables are numbered A-1 through A-84.

A number of the statistics in Tables A-1 through A-84 are also presented for metropolitan areas in Tables B-1 through B-14, for metropolitan area component counties in Tables C-1 through C-4, and for micropolitan areas in Table D-1.

Table A-1. Area and Population

Sources: Area—U.S. Census Bureau, 2010 Census of Population and Housing, Summary Population and Housing Characteristics, Series CPH-1-1, Table 8; www.census.gov/prod/cen2010/cph-1-1.pdf; Population—U.S. Census Bureau, Table 1: Annual Estimates of the Population for the United States, Regions, States, and Puerto Rico: April 1, 2000 to July 1, 2012 (NST-EST2012-01); Rank—Table 2: Cumulative Estimates of Population Change for the United States, Regions, States and Puerto Rico and Region and State Rankings: April 1, 2010 to July 1, 2012 (NST-EST2012-02); Population change—U.S. Census Bureau, Table 4: Cumulative Estimates of the Components of Population Change for the United States, Regions and States: April 1, 2010 to July 1, 2012

(NST-EST2012-04); www.census.gov/popest/data/state/totals/2012/index.html .

Survey, Census, or Data Collection Method: Based on the "component of population change method" and the Census of Population and Housing; for information, see Appendix B, Limitations of the Data and Methodology, and Internet site www.census.gov/popest/methodology/index.html .

Land area. The Census Bureau provides land area for the decennial censuses. Area was calculated from the specific set of boundaries recorded for the entity (in this case, states and counties) in the Census Bureau's geographic database.

Land area measurements may disagree with the information displayed on census maps and in the TIGER® file because, for area measurement purposes, features identified as "intermittent water" and "glacier" are reported as land area. TIGER® is an acronym for the new digital (computer-readable) geographic database that automates the mapping and related geographic activities required to support the Census Bureau's census and survey programs; TIGER® stands for Topologically Integrated Geographic Encoding and Referencing system.

The accuracy of any area measurement figure is limited by the inaccuracy inherent in (1) the location and shape of the various boundary features in the database and (2) rounding affecting the last digit in all operations that compute and/or sum the area measurement. Identification of land and inland, coastal, and territorial is for statistical purposes and does not necessarily reflect legal definitions thereof.

Population data for 2012 and revised population data for 2000 through 2010 were used to calculate rates or describe various population characteristics in Tables A-2 through A-84.

The 2010 decennial population counts are from the census questionnaires that were asked of all people and housing units. For more information on the decennial census and population estimates, see General Notes.

Persons enumerated in the census were counted as inhabitants of their usual place of residence, which generally means the place where a person lives and sleeps the majority of the time. This place is not necessarily the same as the legal residence, voting residence, or domicile. In the vast majority of cases, however, the use of these different bases of classification would produce substantially the same statistics, although appreciable differences may exist for a few areas.

The implementation of this usual-residence practice has resulted in the establishment of residence rules for certain categories of persons whose usual place of residence is not immediately apparent (for example, college students were counted at their college residence). As in the above example, persons were not always counted as residents of the place where they happened to be staying on census day. However, persons without a usual place of residence were counted where they were enumerated.

Rank numbers are assigned on the basis of area size for the rank of area and by population size for rank of population, with each state placed in descending order, largest to smallest. Where ties—two or more states with identical area populations—occur the same rank is assigned to each of the tied states. In such cases, the following rank number(s) is omitted so that the lowest rank is usually equal to the number of states ranked.

Persons per square mile, also known as population density, is the average number of inhabitants per square mile of land area. These figures are derived by dividing the total number of residents by the number of square miles of land area in the specified geographic area. To determine population per square kilometer, multiply the population per square mile by .386103.

Net change represents the increase or decrease between the 2 years shown.

Percent change represents the increase or decrease between the 2 years shown as a percentage of the beginning population.

Refer to the General Notes on **population estimates** for explanations of **international migration** and **domestic migration**.

Table A-2. Population, by Age Group and Sex

Sources: U.S. Census Bureau, Intercensal Estimates of the Resident Population by Sex and Age for States: April 1, 2000 to July 1, 2010; www.census.gov/popest/data/intercensal/state/ST-EST00INT-02.html ; and Population Estimates, Historical Estimates, 2010s; www.census.gov/popest/data/historical/2010s/index.html . Refer to the General Notes on population estimates for explanations of population by age and sex.

Survey, Census, or Data Collection Method: Based on the Census of Population and Housing; for information, see

Appendix B, Limitations of the Data and Methodology; www.census.gov/popest/methodology/index.html .

Table A-3. Population by Race and Hispanic Origin

Sources: U.S. Census Bureau, State Characteristics, Vintage 2011; www.census.gov/popest/data/state/asrh/2011/index.html ; 2010 Census of Population and Housing, 2010 Demographic Profile, DP-1, accessed through American FactFinder, http://factfinder2.census.gov .

Race. The racial classifications used by the Census Bureau adhere to the October 30, 1997, *Federal Register* Notice entitled "Revisions to the Standards for the Classification of Federal Data on Race and Ethnicity" issued by the Office of Management and Budget (OMB); see Internet site www.whitehouse.gov/omb/rewrite/fedreg/omb-dir15.html . These standards govern the categories used to collect and present federal data on race and ethnicity. The OMB requires federal agencies to use a minimum of five race categories: White, Black or African American, American Indian and Alaska Native, Asian, and Native Hawaiian and Other Pacific Islander. For respondents unable to identify with any of these five race categories, the OMB approved including a sixth category, "Some other race," on the Census 2000 questionnaire.

The question on race for Census 2000 was different from past census in several ways. Most significant was that respondents were given the option of selecting one or more race categories to indicate their racial identities. Because of these changes, the Census 2000 data on race are not directly comparable with data from the 1990 census or earlier censuses. Caution is recommended when interpreting changes in the racial composition of the U.S. population over time.

Population estimates by race and Hispanic origin are calculated using a distributive cohort component method. Previously developed resident state population estimates by age and sex and residential national population estimates by age, sex, race, and Hispanic origin are used as a base. Estimated post-censal changes in the corresponding populations are applied with a cohort component model. These distributions are applied to the original state age-sex and national characteristics estimates. For further information, see Internet site www.census.gov/population/www/socdemo/race/racefactcb.html .

White refers to people having origins in any of the original peoples of Europe, the Middle East, or North Africa. It includes people who indicated their race or races as White or wrote in entries such as Irish, German, Italian, Lebanese, Near Easterner, Arab, or Polish.

Black or African American refers to people having origins in any of the Black racial groups of Africa. It includes people who indicated their race or races as Black, African American, or Negro or wrote in entries such as African American, Afro American, Nigerian, or Haitian.

American Indian and Alaska Native refers to people having origins in any of the original peoples of North and South America (including Central America) and who maintain tribal affiliation or community attachment. It includes people who indicated their race or races by marking this category or writing in their principal or enrolled tribe, such as Rosebud Sioux, Chippewa, or Navajo.

Asian refers to people having origins in any of the original peoples of the Far East, Southeast Asia, or the Indian subcontinent. It includes people who indicated their race or races as Asian Indian, Chinese, Filipino, Korean, Japanese, Vietnamese, or Other Asian or wrote in entries such as Burmese, Hmong, Pakistani, or Thai.

Native Hawaiian and Other Pacific Islander refers to people having origins in any of the original peoples of Hawaii, Guam, Samoa, or other Pacific Islands. It includes people who indicated their race or races as Native Hawaiian, Guamanian or Chamorro, Samoan, or Other Pacific Islander or wrote in entries such as Tahitian, Mariana Islander, or Chuukese.

Two or more races. People may have chosen to provide two or more races either by checking two or more race response check boxes, by providing multiple write-in responses, or by some combination of check boxes and write-in responses. The race response categories shown on the questionnaire were collapsed into the five minimum race groups by the OMB.

Hispanic or Latino. People who identify with the terms "Hispanic" or "Latino" are those who classify themselves in one of the specific Hispanic or Latino categories listed on the questionnaire, such as Mexican, Puerto Rican, or Cuban, as well as those who indicate that they are other Spanish, Hispanic, or Latino. Origin can be viewed as the heritage, nationality group, lineage, or country of birth of the person or the person's parents or ancestors before their arrival in the United States. People who identify their origin as Spanish, Hispanic, or Latino may be any race.

The concept of race, as used by the Census Bureau, reflects self-identification by people according to the race or races with which they most closely identify. These categories are sociopolitical constructs and should not be interpreted as being scientific or anthropological in nature.

Furthermore, the race categories include both racial and national-origin groups.

Traditional and current data collection and classification treat race and Hispanic origin as two separate and distinct concepts in accordance with guidelines from the OMB. Race and Hispanic origin are two separate concepts in the federal statistical system. People who are Hispanic may be any race, and people in each race group may be either Hispanic or non-Hispanic. Also, each person has two attributes, their race (or races) and whether or not they are Hispanic. The overlap of race and Hispanic origin is the main comparability issue. For example, Black Hispanics (Hispanic Blacks) are included in both the number of Blacks and in the number of Hispanics. For further information, see Census Bureau webpage www.census.gov/population/www/socdemo/compraceho.html and www.census.gov/population/cen2000/phc-2-a-B.pdf .

Survey, Census, or Data Collection Method: Based on the Census of Population and Housing; for information, see Appendix B, Limitations of the Data and Methodology, and Internet site www.census.gov/popest/methodology/index.html .

Table A-4. Population, by Residence

Sources: Core-based statistical area population—U.S. Census Bureau, "Intercensal Estimates of the Resident Population for Counties: April 1, 2000 to July 1, 2010"; www.census.gov/popest/data/intercensal/county/CO-ES-T00INT-01.html . Urban population—U.S. Census Bureau, 2010 Census of Population and Housing, Population and Housing Unit Counts CPH-2; and U.S. Census Bureau, 2010 Census Redistricting Data (P.L. 94-171) Summary File; www.census.gov/prod/www/decennial.html and factfinder2.census.gov .

The U.S. Office of Management and Budget (OMB) defines Metropolitan and Micropolitan Statistical Areas according to published standards that are applied to the Census Bureau data. The general concept of a Metropolitan or Micropolitan Statistical Area (collectively referred to as Core Based Statistical Areas, or CBSAs) is that of an area containing a recognized population nucleus and adjacent communities that have a high degree of integration with that nucleus.

A **Metropolitan Statistical Area** is defined by OMB as a CBSA associated with at least one urbanized area that has a population of at least 50,000. The Metropolitan Statistical Area comprises the central county or counties containing the core, plus adjacent outlying counties having a high degree of social and economic integration with the central county as measured through commuting. A core is a densely settled concentration of population, comprising either an urbanized area or urban cluster.

A **Micropolitan Statistical Area** is defined as a CBSA associated with at least one urban cluster that has a population of at least 10,000, but less than 50,000. The micropolitan area comprises the central county or counties containing the core, plus adjacent outlying counties having a high degree of social and economic integration with the central county as a measure through commuting.

For more information on metropolitan and micropolitan statistical areas, see OMB Bulletin No. 08-01, found at Internet site www.census.gov/population/www/metroareas/metrodef.html .

The metropolitan and micropolitan statistical area population estimates are based upon the county estimates. The county estimates methodology is available at: http://www.census.gov/popest/methodology/index.html .

The Census Bureau classifies as **urban** all territory, population, and housing units located within an urbanized area (UA) or an urban cluster (UC).

An **urbanized area** consists of a central place and adjacent densely settled territory that together contain at least 50,000 people, generally with an overall population density of at least 1,000 people per square mile.

An **urbanized cluster** consists of a central place and adjacent densely settled territory that together contain at least 2,500 people, generally with an overall population density of at least 1,000 people per square mile. Under certain conditions, the Census Bureau will consider less densely settled territories as part of an UA or UC. All territories located outside of UAs and UCs are classified as rural. Geographic entities such as metropolitan areas and counties often contain both urban and rural territory. For more information, see http://www.census.gov/geo/maps-data/maps/ua2kmaps.html .

Survey, Census, or Data Collection Method: Based on the "component of population change method" and the Census of Population and Housing; for information, see Appendix B, Limitations of the Data and Methodology; also see www.census.gov/popest/methodology/ and www.census.gov/2010census/ .

Table A-5. Households

Sources: For 2010 data, U.S. Census Bureau, Profile of General Population and Housing Characteristics: 2010;

2010 Census Summary File 1 (SF1) 100 percent data. For 2000 data, U.S. Census Bureau, Census 2000 Summary File 1 (SF1) 100 percent data. All data accessed by American Factfinder; http://factfinder2.census.gov .

A **household** consists of all the people who occupy a housing unit. A house, an apartment or other group of rooms, or a single room, is regarded as a housing unit when it is occupied or intended for occupancy as separate living quarters; that is, when the occupants do not live and eat with any other persons in the structure and there is direct access from the outside or through a common hall. A household includes the related family members and all the unrelated people, if any, such as lodgers, foster children, wards, or employees who share the housing unit. A person living alone in a housing unit, or a group of unrelated people sharing a housing unit such as partners or roomers, is also counted as a household. The count of households excludes group quarters.

People per household (or average household size) is a measure obtained by dividing the number of people in households by the total number of households (or householder).

A **family household** is a household maintained by a householder who is in a family (as defined above) and includes any unrelated people (unrelated subfamily members and/or secondary individuals) who may be residing there. The number of family households is equal to the number of families. The count of family household members differs from the count of family members, however, in that the family household members include all people living in the household, whereas family members include only the householder and his/her relatives.

The expression "husband-wife" or "**married-couple**" before the term "household," "family," or "subfamily" indicates that the household, family, or subfamily is maintained by a husband and wife.

Female householder, no husband present includes a family with a female who maintains a household with no husband of the householder lives alone or with nonrelatives only.

Own child category is a never-married child under 18 years old who is a son or daughter of the householder by birth, marriage, or adoption.

For more information regarding household data, see Internet site www.census.gov/population/www/socdemo/hh-fam.html .

Beginning in 2008, two types of estimates were made available by the American Community Survey (ACS):

1-year estimates (based on data collected in a single year) and 3-year estimates (based on data collected in three consecutive years). In 2010 a third type of estimate was introduced—5-year estimates (based on data, collected in five consecutive years) describe the average characteristics for that time period. Information about the interpretation and use of three- and five-year estimates is available on the ACS website, at www.census.gov/acs/www/Downloads/library/2008/2008_Beaghen_01.pdf .

Survey, Census, or Data Collection Method: Based on the Census of Population and Housing; for information, see Appendix B, Limitations of the Data and Methodology; www.census.gov/2010census/news/press-kits/summary-file-1.html .

Table A-6. Marital Status, 2010

Sources: U.S. Census Bureau, American Community Survey; www.census.gov/acs/www/   ; All data accessed by American Factfinder2; http://factfinder2.census.gov .

Marital status refers to how people responded when asked if they were now married, widowed, divorced, separated, or never married. Couples who live together (unmarried people, people in common-law marriages) were allowed to report the marital status they considered the most appropriate.

Never married includes all people who have never been married, including people whose only marriage(s) was annulled.

Now married, except separated includes people whose current marriage has not ended through widowhood, divorce, or separation (regardless of previous marital history). The category also includes couples who live together or people in common-law marriages if they consider this category the most appropriate.

Separated includes people legally separated or otherwise absent from their spouse because of marital discord. This category also includes people who have been deserted or who have parted because they no longer want to live together but who have not obtained a divorce.

Widowed includes widows and widowers who have not remarried.

Divorced includes people who are legally divorced and who have not remarried. Those without a final divorce decree are classifed as "separated."

Survey, Census, or Data Collection Method: Based on the American Community Survey; for information, see Appendix B, Limitations of the Data and Methodology, and www.census.gov/acs/www/methodology/methodology_main/ .

Table A-7. Residence 1 Year Ago, People Obtaining Legal Permanent Resident Status, and Language Spoken at Home

Sources: Residence 1 year ago—U.S. Census Bureau, 2011 American Community Survey; table B07001, "Geographical Mobility in the Past Year by age for Current Residence in the United States," using American FactFinder2; http://factfinder2.census.gov . People obtaining legal permanent resident status—U.S. Department of Homeland Security, Office of Immigration Statistics, 2011 Yearbook of Immigration Statistics, and prior years, table 4, and Supplemental table 1 (www.dhs.gov/yearbook-immigration-statistics). Language—U.S. Census Bureau, 2011 American Community Survey, table B06007, "Place of Birth by Language Spoken at Home and Ability to Speak English in the United States," using American FactFinder2; http://factfinder2.census.gov .

Residence 1 year ago. The American Community Survey asked those participants who had moved from another residence in the United States 1 year earlier to report the city, town, or post office, the name of the U.S. county, state, and ZIP Code where they lived 1 year ago. People living outside of the United States were asked to report the name of the foreign country or U.S. Island Area where they were living 1 year ago. "Residence 1 year ago" is used in conjunction with location of current residence to determine the extent of residential mobility of the population and the resulting redistribution of the population across the various states, metropolitan areas, and regions of the country. When no information on previous residence was reported for a person, information for other family members, if available, was used to assign a location of residence 1 year ago. All cases of nonresponse or incomplete response that were not assigned a previous residence based on information from other family members were allocated to the previous residence of another person with similar characteristics who provided complete information.

Language other than English includes anyone responding yes when asked if they sometimes or always spoke a language other than English at home. This category does not include the speaking of a language only at school or if speaking is limited to a few expressions or slang. People reporting they did speak another language at home were asked to identify the language spoken.

People obtaining legal permanent resident status refers to an alien admitted to the United States as a lawful permanent resident. Permanent residents are also commonly referred to as immigrants; however, the Immigration and Nationality Act (INA) broadly defines an immigrant as any alien in the United States, except one legally admitted under specific nonimmigrant categories (INA section

101(a) (15)). An illegal alien who entered the United States without inspection, for example, would be strictly defined as an immigrant under the INA but is not a permanent resident alien. Lawful permanent residents are legally accorded the privilege of residing permanently in the United States. They may be issued immigrant visas by the Department of State overseas or adjusted to permanent resident status by the Department of Homeland Security in the United States.

Survey, Census, or Data Collection Method: Based on the American Community Survey; for information, see Appendix B, Limitations of the Data and Methodology; www.census.gov/acs/www/methodology/methodology_main/ . People obtaining legal permanent resident status—Based on U.S. application Citizenship and Immigration Services (USCIS)-based case management systems that compile information supplied by aliens on the forms they are required to submit when applying for a legal status; for information, see Internet site www.dhs.gov/yearbook-immigration-statistics .

Table A-8. Place of Birth, 2011

Sources: U.S. Census Bureau, American Community Survey; "DP-2: Selected Social Characteristics in the United States, 2011; 1 year estimates" and table C05006, "Place of Birth for the Foreign-Born Population," using American FactFinder2; http://factfinder2.census.gov .

Place of birth. Participants of the American Community Survey were asked where they were born and were asked to select from two categories: (1) in the United States or (2) outside the United States. Respondents selecting category 1 were then asked to report the name of the state while respondents selecting category 2 were then asked to report the name of the foreign country, or Puerto Rico, Guam, etc. People not reporting a place of birth were assigned the state or country of birth of another family member, or were allocated the response of another individual with similar characteristics. People born outside the United States were asked to report their place of birth according to current international boundaries. Since numerous changes in boundaries of foreign countries have occurred in the last century, some people may have reported their place of birth in terms of boundaries that existed at the time of their birth or migration, or in accordance with their own national preference.

The **foreign-born** population includes anyone who was not a U.S. citizen at birth. This includes respondents who indicated they were a U.S. citizen by naturalization or not a U.S. citizen. This excludes people born in the United States, Puerto Rico, or a U.S. Island Area such as Guam or the U.S. Virgin Islands, or people born in a foreign country to a U.S. citizen parent(s).

Survey, Census, or Data Collection Method: Based on the American Community Survey; for information, see Appendix B, Limitations of the Data and Methodology, and Internet site www.census.gov/popest/methodology/index.html .

Table A-9. Live Births and Birth Rates

Sources: U. S. National Center for Health Statistics, *National Vital Statistics Reports (NVSR), Births: Final Data for 2010*, Vol. 61, No. 1; www.cdc.gov/nchs/data/nvsr/nvsr61/nvsr61_01_tables.pdf, and *Births: Preliminary Data for 2011*, Vol. 61, No. 5; www.cdc.gov/nchs/data/nvsr/nvsr61/nvsr61_05_tables.pdf , and earlier reports.

The National Vital Statistics System (NVSR) is an intergovernmental data system with the purpose of collecting and disseminating the nation's official vital statistics. These data are provided through contracts between NCHS and vital registration systems operated in the various jurisdictions legally responsible for the registration of vital events—births, deaths, marriages, divorces, and fetal deaths. In the United States, legal authority for the registration of these events resides individually with the 50 States, 2 cities (Washington, DC, and New York City), and 5 territories (Puerto Rico, the Virgin Islands, Guam, American Samoa, and the Commonwealth of the Northern Mariana Islands). These jurisdictions are responsible for maintaining registries of vital events and for issuing copies of birth, marriage, divorce, and death certificates.

Data shown in this report are based on 100 percent of the birth certificates filed in all states and the District of Columbia (D.C.). More than 99 percent of births occurring in this country are registered. The data are provided to the Centers for Disease Control and Prevention's National Center for Health Statistics (NCHS) through the Vital Statistics Cooperative Program (VSCP).

Birth statistics are limited to events occurring during the year. The data are by place of residence and exclude events occurring to nonresidents of the United States. Births that occur outside the United States are excluded. Preliminary data for 2011 are based on a substantial proportion of births for that year.

Birth rates represent the number of births per 1,000 resident population estimated as of July 1 for 2011 and enumerated as of April 1 for 2010 and 2000 (decennial census years). A "low birth weight" is considered between 1,500 and 2,500 grams (with "very low birth weight" anything less than 1,500 grams).

National estimates of births to unmarried women are based on two methods of determining marital status. For 2010 and 2011, birth certificates in 49 states and the

District of Columbia included a direct question about the mother's marital status. A birth is inferred as nonmarital if a paternity acknowledgment was filed or if the father's name is missing from the birth certificate (listed in respective priority-of-use order). For 2000, marital status was inferred in Michigan and New York. Women age 15 to 19 are considered teenagers.

Survey, Census, or Data Collection Method: Based on the National Vital Statistics System; for information, see Appendix B, Limitations of the Data and Methodology, and Internet site www.census.gov/popest/methodology/index .html and www.cdc.gov/nchs/nvss/birth_methods.htm .

Table A-10. Births and Birth Rates by Race and Hispanic Origin and Fertility Rate: 2010

Source: U. S. National Center for Health Statistics, National Vital Statistics Reports (NVSR), *Final Data for 2010*, Vol. 61, No. 1; www.cdc.gov/nchs/nvss.htm .

Births by race. For information on how the National Vital Statistics System, the National Center for Health Statistics (NCHS) collects and publishes data, see appendix entry for Table A-9.

Race and Hispanic origin are reported separately on birth certificates. Race categories are consistent with 1977 Office of Management and Budget standards. Thirty-eight states and the District of Columbia reported multiple-race data for 2010 that were bridged to single-race categories for comparability with other states.

Birth fertility rates are the number of live births per 1,000 women aged 15–44 years.

Survey, Census, or Data Collection Method: Based on the National Vital Statistics System; for information, see Appendix B, Limitations of the Data and Methodology, and www.cdc.gov/nchs/nvss.htm .

Table A-11. Deaths and Death Rates, by Race and Hispanic Origin

Sources: Death for all races and infant deaths—U.S. National Center for Health Statistics and National Vital Statistics Reports (NVSR); www.cdc.gov/nchs/nvss.htm , Deaths for all races—*Preliminary data for 2011*, Vol. 61, No. 6; *Final data for 2010 and Infant Deaths*, Vol. 61, No. 4; Number of deaths by race—Center for Disease Control and Prevention; CDC Wonder data base; http://wonder .cdc.gov/ .

Deaths. Preliminary mortality data are based on records of deaths that occurred in calendar year 2011, which were

received from state vital statistics offices and processed by the Centers for Disease Control and Prevention's National Center for Health Statistics (NCHS). The data are based on death records comprising more than 98 percent of the demographic and medical files for all deaths in the United States in 2011 and 2010. The records are weighted to independent control counts for 2011. Comparisons are made with 2010 final data.

Death statistics are limited to events occurring during the year. The data are by place of residence and exclude events occurring to nonresidents of the United States. Deaths that occur outside the United States are excluded. Death rates represent the number of deaths per 1,000 resident population estimated as of April 1 for 2010 (decennial census year) and July 1 for all other years.

Infant mortality rates are calculated by dividing the preliminary number of infant deaths that occurred during the year by the number of live births for the same period and are presented as rates per 1,000 live births.

Survey, Census, or Data Collection Method: Based on the National Vital Statistics System; for information, see Appendix B, Limitations of the Data and Methodology, and Internet sites www.cdc.gov/nchs/nvss.htm and www.cdc. gov/nchs/data/nvsr/nvsr61/nvsr61_06.pdf .

Table A-12. Age-Adjusted Death Rates by Cause, 2010

Source: U. S. National Center for Health Statistics, National Vital Statistics Reports (NVSR): *Deaths: Final Data for 2010*, Vol. 61, No. 4, table 19; www.cdc.gov/nchs/ data/nvsr/nvsr61/nvsr61_04.pdf .

Death rates by cause. Mortality statistics by cause of death are compiled in accordance with World Health Organization (WHO) regulations, which specify that member nations classify causes of death according to the current revision of the International Statistical Classification of Diseases and Related Health Problems (ICD). Effective with deaths occurring in 1999, the United States began using the Tenth Revision of this classification. Tabulations of cause-of-death statistics are based solely on the underlying cause of death. The underlying cause is defined by the WHO as "the disease or injury which initiated the train of events leading directly to death, or the circumstances of the accident or violence which produced the fatal injury." The underlying cause is selected from the conditions entered by the physician in the cause of death section of the death certificate. When more than one cause or condition is entered by the physician, the underlying cause is determined by the sequence of conditions on the certificate,

provisions, of the ICD, and associated selection rules and modifications.

Age-adjusted rates are mortality rates adjusted for the different age distributions of separate populations. Certain causes of death can be more probable with a certain age group and will distort an area's risk of suffering from certain injuries or diseases. An age-adjusted rate will control the impact a particular age group will have on the death rate of an area and will allow the user to compare mortality risks between areas with different age groups or in a time series. Age-adjusted rates should be viewed as relative indexes rather than actual measures of mortality risk. The age-adjusted rates provided by the National Vital Statistics Reports (NVSR) were computed by the direct method of applying age-specific death rates to the U.S. standard population age distribution.

Survey, Census, or Data Collection Method: Based on the National Vital Statistics System; for information, see Appendix B, Limitations of the Data and Methodology, and www.cdc.gov/nchs/nvss.htm .

Table A-13. Marriages and Divorces—Number and Rate

Sources: Number of marriages and divorces—U.S. National Center for Health Statistics, National Vital Statistics Reports (NVSR), *Births, Marriages, Divorces, and Deaths: Provisional Data for 2009,* annual volume 58, Number 25; and prior reports; www.cdc.gov/nchs/nvss .htm . Marriage and divorce rates—U.S. National Center for Health Statistics, National Vital Statistics System; www.cdc.gov/nchs/mardiv.htm .

Marriage and divorce. Information on the total numbers and rates of marriages and divorces at the national and state levels are published in the NCHS National Vital Statistics Reports. The collection of detailed data was suspended beginning in January 1996 (see *Federal Register* Notice, December 15, 1995). Beginning with the June 2003 data, detailed state tables of marriage and divorce levels have been included in the monthly reports of provisional data published in the NCHS National Vital Statistics Reports. Before 2003, these data were available in the "Detailed Statistical Tables section of NCHS's Data Warehouse" website.

Marriage and divorce data provided by NVSR are counts of all events occurring in the state that were received in the registration offices during a 1-month period. The yearly figures are derived from summing all 12 months. Divorce figures include reported annulments. There is considerable variability among the states in the procedures that are used to submit the counts of marriages and divorces to NCHS and in the extent to which the states update their counts of marriages and divorces as new information is received. Therefore, counts vary in their completeness.

Survey, Census, or Data Collection Method: Based on the National Vital Statistics System; for information, see Appendix B, Limitations of the Data and Methodology, and www.cdc.gov/nchs/nvss.htm .

Table A-14. Health Care Services, Physicians, and Nurses

Sources: Health care services—U.S. Census Bureau, *County Business Patterns, annual;* www.census.gov/econ/ cbp/index.html . Physicians—Kaiser Family Foundation, State Health Facts Organization; www.statehealthfacts .org/ ; KFF source: special data request on State Licensing Information from Redi-Data, Inc. Nurses—Bureau of Labor Statistics, Occupational Employment Statistics, *Occupational Employment and Wages; May 2012 Wage and Employment Statistics*; www.bls.gov/oes/ home.htm#data .

County Business Patterns (CBP) is an annual series that provides subnational economic data by industry. The series is useful for studying the economic activity of small areas, analyzing economic changes over time, and as a benchmark for statistical series, surveys, and databases between economic censuses. CBP covers most of the country's economic activity. The series excludes data on self-employed individuals, employees of private households, railroad employees, agricultural production employees, and most government employees.

CBP data are extracted from the Business Register, the Census Bureau's file of all known single- and multi-establishment companies. The Annual Company Organization Survey and quinquennial economic censuses provide individual establishment data for multi-location firms. Data for single-location firms are obtained from various programs conducted by the Census Bureau, such as the economic censuses, the Annual Survey of Manufactures, and Current Business Surveys, as well as from administrative records of the Internal Revenue Service (IRS), the Social Security Administration (SSA), and the Bureau of Labor Statistics (BLS).

An **establishment** is a single physical location at which business is conducted or services or industrial operations are performed. It is not necessarily identical with a company or enterprise, which may consist of one or more establishments. When two or more activities are carried on at a single location under a single ownership, all activities generally are grouped together as a single establishment. The entire establishment is classified on the basis of its major activity and all data are included in that classification. Establishment counts represent the number of locations with paid employees any time during the year.

Paid **employment** consists of full- and part-time employees, including salaried offices and executives of corporations, who are on the payroll in the pay period including March 12. Included are employees on paid sick leave, holidays, and vacations; not included are proprietors and partners of unincorporated businesses.

Total **payroll** includes all forms of compensation, such as salaries, wages, reported tips, commissions, bonuses, vacation allowances, sick-leave pay, employee contributions to qualified pension plans, and the value of taxable fringe benefits. For corporations, it includes amounts paid to officers and executives; for unincorporated businesses, it does not include profit or other compensation of proprietors or partners. Payroll is reported before deductions for social security, income tax, insurance, union dues, and so on.

Health Care Services combines Ambulatory Health Care Services (NAICS 621), Hospitals (NAICS 622), and Nursing and Residential Care Facilities (NAICS 623). For more information on health care services 2007, NAICS 62), see General Notes or www.census.gov/eos/www/ naics/index.html .

Survey, Census, or Data Collection Method: Health care services—Based on tabulations of data extracted from the U.S. Census Bureau's Business Register; www.census .gov/econ/cbp/methodology.htm and Bureau of Labor Statistics, Survey Methods and Reliability Statement for the May 2012 Occupational Employment Statistics Survey, www.bls.gov/oes/current/methods_statement.pdf .

Table A-15. Health Care, Employment, and Type of Health Insurance

Sources: Health care employment—U.S. Census Bureau, Equal Employment Opportunity Tabulation, American Community Survey, 2006–2010. www.census.gov/people/ eeotabulation/data/eeotables20062010.html . Health insurance—U.S. Census Bureau, American Community Survey, 2009–2011; www.census.gov/acs/www/ .

Survey, Census, or Data Collection Method: Based on the U.S. Census Bureau, Industry and Occupations and EEO websites, www.census.gov/people/io/ and www.census .gov/people/eeotabulation/ .

Employment in health care occupations is from the Equal Employment Opportunity Tabulation of the American Community Survey, 2006–2010. Civilians age 15 and older were asked to describe the type of work they did and their primary work activities as well as the location of their workplace. Table A-15 includes civilians age 16 and older who were employed during the week before their interview. The data refer to the person's job during the previous week. For those who worked two or more jobs, the data refer to the job where the person worked the greatest number of hours. The numbers for each state represent the number who worked in that state, not necessarily residents of that state. The occupations include a selection of health care professionals and technicians.

Health Insurance Coverage presents the number of individuals of all ages who are covered by the first six types of health insurance and those who are not covered by any health insurance.

Health insurance coverage in the ACS and other Census Bureau surveys define coverage to include plans and programs that provide comprehensive health coverage. Plans that provide insurance for specific conditions or situations such as cancer and long-term care policies are not considered coverage. Likewise, other types of insurance like dental, vision, life, and disability insurance are not considered health insurance coverage.

Respondents were instructed to report their current coverage and to mark "yes" or "no" for each of the eight types of insurance:

a. Insurance through a current or former employer or union (of this person or another family member)

b. Insurance purchased directly from an insurance company (by this person or another family member)

c. Medicare, for people 65 and older, or people with certain disabilities

d. Medicaid, Medical Assistance, or any kind of government-assistance plan for those with low incomes or a disability

e. TRICARE or other military health care

f. VA (including those who have ever used or enrolled for VA health care)

g. Indian Health Service

h. Any other type of health insurance or health coverage plan (respondents who answered "yes" to this question were asked to provide their other coverage type in a write-in field and their responses were later edited into the other fields).

People were considered insured if they reported at least one "yes" in categories "a" through "f."

People who had no reported health insurance coverage, or those whose only health coverage was Indian Health Service, were considered uninsured. The types of health insurance are not mutually exclusive; people may be covered by more than one at the same time.

Table A-16. Health Risks, Chronic Conditions, and Cardiovascular Disease

Source: U.S. Centers for Disease Control and Prevention, Atlanta, GA. Behavioral Risk Factor, Surveillance System; www.cdc.gov/brfss/index.htm .

Health conditions. The Behavioral Risk Factor Surveillance System (BRFSS) is a collaborative project of the Centers for Disease Control and Prevention (CDC) and U.S. states and territories. The BRFSS, administered and supported by CDC's Behavioral Surveillance Branch, is an ongoing data collection program designed to measure behavioral risk factors for the adult population (18 years of age or older) living in households. As of 2001, all 50 states, the District of Columbia, Puerto Rico, Guam, and the Virgin Islands participate in the BRFSS. The objective of the BRFSS is to collect uniform, state-specific data on preventive health practices and risk behaviors that are linked to chronic diseases, injuries, and preventable infectious diseases that affect the adult population. Data are collected from a random sample of adults (one per household) through a cross-sectional telephone survey conducted by state health departments with technical and methodological assistance provided by the CDC. Data are collected monthly by state health departments through telephone surveys with more than 350,000 adults interviewed each year.

BRFSS data are directly weighted for the probability of selection of a telephone number, the number of adults in a household, and the number of telephones in a household. A final poststratification adjustment is made for nonresponse and noncoverage of households without telephones. The weights for each relevant factor are multiplied together to get a final weight.

Survey, Census, or Data Collection Method: Based on the Behavioral Risk Factor Surveillance System (BRFSS); www.cdc.gov/brfss/index.htm .

Table A-17. People With and Without Health Insurance Coverage

Sources: U.S. Census Bureau, Current Population Reports; Income, Poverty, and Health Insurance Coverage in the United States: 2011, P60-243; www.census.gov/hhes/www/hlthins/index.html ; detailed tables, Table HI06: Health Insurance Coverage Status by State for all People, 2011; www.census.gov/hhes/www/cpstables/032012/health/toc.htm ; and Health Insurance Historical Tables, HIB series; HIB-4 and HIB-5; www.census.gov/hhes/www/hlthins/data/historical/HIB_tables.html .

Health insurance coverage. The Annual Social and Economic Supplement (ASEC) to the Current Population Survey (CPS) asks about health insurance coverage in the previous calendar year. The survey asks separate questions about the major types of health insurance, and people who answer "no" to each of the coverage questions are then asked to verify that they were in fact not covered by any type of health insurance. For reporting purposes, the Census Bureau broadly classifies health insurance coverage as private coverage or government coverage. Private health insurance is a plan provided through an employer or a union or purchased by an individual from a private company. Government health insurance includes the federal programs Medicare, Medicaid, and military health care; the Children's Health Insurance Program (CHIP); and individual state health plans. People were considered "insured" if they were covered by any type of health insurance for part or all of the previous calendar year. They were considered "uninsured" if they were not covered by any type of health insurance at any time in that year. Research shows health insurance coverage is underreported in the CPS ASEC for a variety of reasons. Children are considered anyone age 17 and younger. For more information, consult source, www.census.gov/hhes/www/hlthins/hlthins.html .

Survey, Census, or Data Collection Method: The Annual Social and Economic Supplement to the Current Population Survey; www.census.gov/hhes/www/hlthins/hlthins .html .

Table A-18. Immunizations, HIV, AIDS, STDs, and Lyme Disease

Sources: National Center for Disease Control and Prevention: Children immunized—Q1:2011–Q4:2011 and Q1:2010–Q4:2010, *National Immunization Survey among Children 19–35 Months of Age by State*; www.cdc.gov/vaccines/stats-surv/imz-coverage.htm ; 65 and over influenza vaccine, www.cdc.gov/flu/fluvaxview/interactive.htm ; AIDS and HIV—*HIV Surveillance Report*, 2011; vol.23, www.cdc.gov/hiv/pdf/statistics_2011_HIV_Surveillance_Report_vol_23.pdf ; STDs—Sexually Transmitted Disease Surveillance, www.cdc.gov/std/stats11/tables.htm ; and Lyme Disease, www.cdc.gov/lyme/stats/ .

Children immunized. The National Immunization Survey (NIS) collects data on child immunization in the United States through telephone surveys followed by mail surveys. The study collects data by interviewing households in all 50 States, the District of Columbia, and 27 urban areas. Telephone interviews are selected by random chance. The NIS data provide current, population-based, state and local area estimates of vaccination coverage produced by a standard methodology. Each quarter, estimates of vaccination coverage levels are calculated and valid comparisons of state efforts to deliver vaccination services are made. To assure the accuracy and precision of the estimates, immunization data for surveyed children are also collected through a mail survey of their pediatricians, family physicians, and other health care providers. In the past year, the NIS Provider Study Immunization History Questionnaire was sent to approximately 30,000 medical providers. Types of immunizations, dates of administration, and additional data about facility characteristics are requested from immunization providers identified during the telephone survey of households. The NIS estimates of vaccination coverage reflect a comparison of information provided by both immunization providers and households. The NIS is now conducted for the CDC by the National Opinion Research Center (NORC) at the University of Chicago. For more information, see Internet site www.cdc.gov/vaccines/stats-surv/imz-coverage.htm#nis .

Influenza vaccine for adults aged 65 and over. For information regarding the National Center for Chronic Disease Prevention and Health Promotion Behavioral Risk Factor Surveillance System, see appendix entry for Table A-16.

Living with HIV. Surveillance of HIV Infection (Not AIDS) includes data from case reports from 53 areas that had laws or regulations requiring confidential reporting by name for adults, adolescents, and children with confirmed HIV infection (not AIDS) as of December 31, 2011. After the removal of personal identifying information, data from these reports were submitted to CDC. Because states initiated reporting on different dates, the length of time that reporting has been in place influences the number of HIV infection cases reported.

The completeness of reporting of HIV infection is estimated at more than 80 percent, yet data on HIV infection should still be interpreted with caution. HIV surveillance reports may not be representative of all persons infected with HIV because not all infected persons have been tested and therefore the data offers a minimum estimate of the number of persons known to be HIV infected. The designation "adults and adolescents" refers to persons aged 13 years and older; the designation "children" refers to persons less than 13 years of age. For 2011 data on persons living with HIV/AIDS, HIV infection (not AIDS), or AIDS, the age-group assignment is based on the person's age as of December 31, 2011. For which concerns deaths of persons with AIDS, age-group assignment is determined by the person's age at the time of death.

Living with AIDS. All fifty states, the District of Columbia, and U.S. dependent areas report AIDS cases to CDC by using a uniform surveillance case definition and case report form. Consult source for guidelines used when defining AIDS. Although the completeness of reporting of AIDS cases to state and local health departments differs by geographic region and patient population, studies conducted by state and local health departments indicate that the reporting of AIDS cases in most areas of the United States is more than 85 percent complete.

Sexually transmitted disease (STD) cases. Cases of nationally notifiable STDs are reported to the CDC by the STD control programs and health departments in the 50 states, the District of Columbia, selected cities, 3,140 U.S. counties, U.S. dependencies and possessions, and independent nations in free association with the United States. Although most areas generally adhere to the same case definitions for STDs, there may be differences in the policies and systems for collecting surveillance data. Comparisons of case numbers and rates among areas should be interpreted with caution. However, since case definitions and surveillance activities within a given area remain relatively stable, trends should be minimally affected by these differences.

Survey, Census, or Data Collection Method: Influenza vaccine—Based on the Behavioral Risk Factor Surveillance System (BRFSS) survey; www.cdc.gov/brfss/. AIDS and HIV—Based on confidential name-based registries of state and local health departments; www.cdc.gov/hiv/topics/surveillance/resources/reports/index.htm#technical . STDs—Based on state and local STD case reports from a variety of public and private sources; www.cdc.gov/std/stats11/trends-2011.pdf and www.cdc.gov/nchstp/od/nchstp.html . Lyme disease; www.cdc.gov/lyme/stats/index.html .

Table A-19. Public and Private School Fall Enrollment

Source: Total enrollment—U.S. Census Bureau, 2009–2011 American Community Survey; B14003, "Sex by School Enrollment by Type of School by Age for the Population 3 Years and Over"; Public school enrollment—U.S. National Center for Education Statistics, Common Core of Data, Elementary/Secondary Information System; http://nces.ed.gov/ccd/elsi/ .

Total (public and private) enrollment data are provided by the American Community Survey. For information on the American Community Survey, see General Notes. For information on how to interpret a 3-year estimate, see appendix entry for Table A-5.

Total enrollment rate is the average percent of people aged 3–4 or 5–17 years who are enrolled in public or private school based on enumerated resident population for the ages of 3–4 or 5–17 as of July 1.

Public enrollment data are from the Common Core of Data (CCD), which is the National Center for Education Statistics' (NCES) primary database on elementary and secondary public education in the United States. The CCD, collected annually, is a comprehensive, national statistical database of all public elementary and secondary schools and school districts and contains data that are comparable across all states.

Data are collected for a particular school year via an online reporting system open to state education agencies during the school year. Beginning with the 2006–2007 school year, nonfiscal CCD data are collected through the Department of Education's Education Data Exchange Network (EDEN). Since the CCD is a universe collection, CCD data are not subject to sampling errors. However, nonsampling errors could come from two sources: nonresponse and inaccurate reporting.

Survey, Census, or Data Collection Method: Total enrollment (public and private) based on the American Community Survey, see www.census.gov/acs/www/methodology/methodology_main/ ; Public school enrollment based on the NCES Common Core of Data (CCD); http://nces.ed.gov/ccd/ .

Table A-20. Public Elementary and Secondary Schools—Finances and Teachers , 2011–2012

Source: *Rankings & Estimates: Rankings of the States 2012 and Estimates of School Statistics 2013*, used with permission of the National Education Association, 2013. All rights reserved. (copyright).

Revenue receipts are available for current expenses, other non-day-school programs operated by the public schools, capital outlay, and debt service for public schools. Included among revenue receipts are all appropriations from general funds of federal, state, county, and local governments; receipts from taxes levied for school purposes; income from permanent school funds and endowments; and income from leases of school lands and miscellaneous sources (interest on bank deposits, tuition, gifts, school lunch charges, and so on).

Total expenditures for public schools include current expenditures for elementary and secondary day schools, capital outlays, and interest payments.

Current expenditures include those expenditures for operating local public day schools, excluding interest on school debt and capital outlay. These expenditures include such items as salaries for school personnel, fixed charges, student transportation, school books and materials, and energy costs.

Capital outlay refers to an expenditure that results in the acquisition of fixed assets or additions to fixed assets that are presumed to have benefits for more than one year. The expenditure is for land or existing buildings, improvements of grounds, construction of buildings, additions to buildings, remodeling of buildings, or initial, additional, and replacement equipment.

Data on classroom **teachers' salaries** are revised periodically by the National Education Association. Teachers at the elementary and secondary school levels include grades kindergarten through 6 and 7 through 12, respectively.

Average salary is the arithmetic mean of the salaries of elementary and secondary school teachers. This figure is the average gross salary before deductions for social security, retirement, health insurance, and so on.

The **pupil–teacher ratio** includes teachers for students with disabilities and other special teachers, although these teachers are generally excluded from class size calculations. The student count for the pupil–teacher ratio includes all students enrolled in the fall of the school year. Pupil–teacher ratios are based on data reported by types of schools rather than by instructional programs within schools and only includes schools that reported both enrollment and teacher data. Ratios are based on data reported by schools and may differ from data reported in other tables that reflect aggregate totals reported by states.

Survey, Census, or Data Collection Method: Based on the National Center for Education Statistics (NCES) Common

Core of Data (CCD); www.nces.ed.gov/ccd/ . For information on the number of teachers, salary, receipts, and expenditures, contact sources; www.nea.org/index.html .

Table A-21. Public High School Graduates and Educational Attainment

Sources: Public high school graduates—U.S. National Center for Education Statistics, *Digest of Education Statistics*, www.nces.ed.gov/ . Attainment and those completing high school—U.S. Census Bureau, 2009–2011 American Community Survey, tables B15001, "Sex by Age by Educational Attainment for the Population 18 Years and Over," and B15002, "Sex by Educational Attainment for the Population 25 Years and Over," using American FactFinder2, http://factfinder2.census.gov/ .

Data for **public high school graduates** include graduates of regular day school programs but exclude other programs and people receiving high school equivalency certificates.

Data for **high school completers** include those people who graduated from high school with a diploma, as well as those who completed high school through equivalency programs.

Data on **educational attainment** are derived from questions asked of all respondents to the American Community Survey, and data presented here are tabulated for people 25 years old and over. Respondents are classified according to the highest degree or the highest level of school completed. Persons currently enrolled in school are asked to report the level of the previous grade attended or the highest degree received.

High school graduate refers to respondents who received a high school diploma or the equivalent, such as passing the test of General Educational Development (G.E.D.), and did not attend college.

Some college, but no degree refers to respondents who have attended college for some amount of time but have no degree.

Associate's degree refers to people whose highest degree is an associate's degree, which generally requires 2 years of college-level work and is either in an occupational program that prepares them for a specific occupation, or an academic program primarily in the arts and sciences. The course work may or may not be transferable to a bachelor's degree.

Advanced degree refers to a graduate or professional degree.

For information regarding how to interpret 3-year estimates, see appendix entry for Table A-5.

Survey, Census, or Data Collection Method: Public high school graduates—Based on the National Center for Education Statistics (NCES) Common Core of Data (CCD); www.nces.ed.gov/ccd/ . Attainment—Based on the American Community Survey; for information see Appendix B, Limitations of the Data and Methodology, and www.census .gov/acs/www/methodology/methodology_main/ .

Table A-22. Institutions of Higher Education

Source: Fall enrollment and degrees conferred—U.S. National Center for Education Statistics, *Digest of Education Statistics*; www.nces.ed.gov/ . Appropriations—State Higher Education Executive Officers Association, Boulder, CO, tables 4 and 5 (copyright); www.sheeo.org .

Higher education is identified by the National Center for Education Statistics (NCES) as the study beyond secondary school at an institution that offers programs terminating in an associate, baccalaureate, or higher degrees. The data shown are based upon the Integrated Postsecondary Education Data System (IPEDS), established as the core postsecondary education data collection program for NCES. IPEDS is a system of surveys designed to collect data from all primary providers of postsecondary education in such areas as enrollment, program completions, faculty, staff, and finances. See the sources for methodological details.

Appropriations refer to money set aside by formal legislative action for a specific use.

Educational appropriations is defined by the SHEEO as the equation: Net State Support plus Local Tax Appropriations minus Research, Agricultural, and Medical (RAM) appropriations. See the source for further information.

Full-time equivalent enrollment (FTE) is a measure of enrollment equal to one student enrolled full-time for one academic year, based on all credit hours, including summer sessions. The data capture FTE enrollment in public institutions of higher education in those credit or contact hours associated with courses that apply to degree or certificate, excluding noncredit continuing education, adult education, or extension courses.

Net tuition data exclude discounts, waivers, and state-appropriated aid to students attending in-state public institutions and exclude medical student tuition.

Degrees conferred refer to awards conferred by a college, university, or other postsecondary education institution as official recognition for the successful completion of a program of studies.

Survey, Census, or Data Collection Method: Fall enrollment and degrees conferred—Based on the Integrated Postsecondary Education Data System (PEDS), "Fall Enrollment" surveys; http://nces.ed.gov/ipeds/ . Appropriations—For information, see www.sheeo.org .

Table A-23. Violent Crimes and Crime Rates

Source: U.S Department of Justice, Federal Bureau of Investigation, Crime in the United States; www.fbi.gov/about-us/cjis/ucr/ .

Data presented on crime are through the voluntary contribution of crime statistics by law enforcement agencies across the United States. The Uniform Crime Reporting (UCR) program provides periodic assessments of crime in the nation as measured by offenses coming to the attention of the law enforcement community. UCR program contributors compile and submit their crime data in one of two means: either directly to the FBI or through the state UCR programs.

Caution is advised when comparing data between areas based on these respective Crime Index figures. Assessing criminality and law enforcement's responses from area to area should encompass many elements (for example, population density and urbanization, population composition, stability of population, modes of transportation, commuting patterns and highway systems, economic conditions, cultural conditions, family conditions, climate, effective strength and emphasis of law enforcement agencies, attitudes of citizenry toward crime, and crime reporting practices). These elements may have a significant impact on crime reporting. Also, not all law enforcement agencies provide data for all 12 months of the year and some agencies fail to report at all. Data in this publication are presented as reported to the FBI.

Data presented reflect the Hierarchy Rule, which requires that only the most serious offense in a multiple-offense criminal incident be counted. In descending order of severity, the violent crimes are murder and nonnegligent manslaughter, forcible rape, robbery, and aggravated assault, followed by the property crimes of burglary, larceny-theft, and motor vehicle theft. The Hierarchy Rule does not apply to the offense of arson.

Violent crimes include four crime categories: (1) Murder and nonnegligent manslaughter, as defined in the UCR program, is the willful (nonnegligent) killing of one human being by another. This offense excludes deaths caused by negligence, suicide, or accident; justifiable homicides; and attempts to murder or assaults to murder. (2) Forcible rape is the carnal knowledge of a female forcibly and against her will. Assaults or attempts to commit rape by force or threat of force are also included; however, statutory rape (without force) and other sex offenses are excluded. (3) Robbery is the taking or attempting to take anything of value from the care, custody, or control of a person or persons by force or threat of force or violence and/or by putting the victim in fear. (4) Aggravated assault is an unlawful attack by one person upon another for the purpose of inflicting severe or aggravated bodily injury. This type of assault is usually accompanied by the use of a weapon or by means likely to produce death or great bodily harm. Attempts are included since an injury does not necessarily have to result when a gun, knife, or other weapon is used, which could and probably would result in a serious personal injury if the crime were successfully completed.

Rates are based on Census Bureau resident population enumerated as of April 1 for decennial census years and estimated as of July 1 for other years.

Survey, Census, or Data Collection Method: Based on the Uniform Crime Reporting Program; www.fbi.gov/ucr/guidelines/guidelines.htm .

Table A-24. Property Crimes and Crime Rates

Source: U.S. Department of Justice, Federal Bureau of Investigation, Crime in the United States, www.fbi.gov/ucr/ucr.htm .

For information on the Uniform Crime Reporting (UCR) program and comparability of data, see appendix entry for Table A-23.

In general, property crimes include four crime categories:

(1) Burglary is the unlawful entry of a structure to commit a felony or theft. (2) Larceny-theft is the unlawful taking, carrying, leading, or riding away of property from the possession or constructive possession of another. It includes crimes such as shoplifting, pocket picking, purse snatching, thefts from motor vehicles, thefts of motor vehicle parts and accessories, bicycle thefts, and so on, in which no use of force, violence, or fraud occurs. This crime category does not include embezzlement, "con" games, forgery, worthless checks, and motor vehicle theft. (3) Motor vehicle theft is the theft or attempted theft of a motor vehicle. This definition excludes the taking of a motor vehicle for temporary use by those persons having lawful access. (4) Arson is any willful or malicious burning

or attempt to burn, with or without intent to defraud, a dwelling house, public building, motor vehicle or aircraft, personal property of another, and so on. Only fires determined through investigation to have been willfully or maliciously set are classified as arson. Fires of suspicious or unknown origins are excluded.

Survey, Census, or Data Collection Method. Based on the Uniform Crime Reporting Program; for information, see www.fbi.gov/ucr/guidelines/guidelines.htm .

Table A-25. Juvenile Arrests, Child Abuse Cases, and Prisoners

Sources: Juvenile arrests—U.S. Department of Justice, Office of Justice Programs, *Juvenile Arrests 2010*, Puzzanchera, C. and Kang, W. (2013). "Easy Access to FBI Arrest Statistics 1994–20," www.ojjdp.gov/ojstatbb/ezaucr/ ; and *2009*, www.ojjdp.gov/pubs/236477.pdf . Child abuse and neglect—U.S. Department of Health and Human Services, Administration for Children and Families, Child Maltreatment, 2011, tables 2.1 and 3.2 (Washington, DC; U.S. Government Printing Office, 2011); www.acf.hhs.gov/sites/default/files/cb/cm11.pdf#page=28 . Prisoners under jurisdiction—U.S. Department of Justice, Office of Justice Programs Bureau of Justice Statistics, Prisoners in 2011 Series NCJ 239808 and earlier reports; www.bjs.gov/index.cfm?ty=pbdetail&iid=4559 . Prisoners executed and under death sentence—U.S. Bureau of Justice Statistics, Capital Punishment 2010, Series NCJ 236510 and earlier reports; www.bjs.gov/index.cfm?ty=pbdetail&iid=2236 .

Juvenile arrest rates are based on analysis of arrest data from FBI reports and population from the Census Bureau. Rates are calculated by dividing the number of arrests of persons under age 18 for every 100,000 persons ages 10–17. The reporting coverage for the total United States is 78 percent and includes all states reporting arrests of persons under age 18. Arrest rates are calculated by dividing the number of youth arrests made in the year by the number of youth living in reporting jurisdictions. While juvenile arrest rates in part reflect juvenile behavior, many other factors can affect the size of these rates. Consequently, comparisons of juvenile arrest rates across states should be made with caution.

Child abuse and neglect data are collected and analyzed through the National Child Abuse and Neglect Data System (NCANDS) by the Children's Bureau, Administration on Children, Youth, and Families in the Administration for Children and Families, U.S. Department of Health and Human Services. The number of investigations includes assessments and is based on the total number of investigations that received a disposition. The number of children subject of an investigation of assessment is based on the total number of children for whom an alleged maltreatment was substantiated, indicated, or assessed to have occurred or the child was at risk of occurrence.

Victims are defined as children subjects of a substantiated, indicated, or alternative response–victim maltreatment.

Each state has its own definitions of child abuse and neglect based on minimum standards set by federal law. Federal legislation provides a foundation for states by identifying a minimum set of acts or behaviors that define child abuse and neglect. The *Federal Child Abuse Prevention and Treatment Act* (CAPTA), (42 U.S.C.A. §5106g), as amended by the *Keeping Children and Families Safe Act of 2003*, defines child abuse and neglect as: Any recent act or failure to act on the part of a parent or caretaker which results in death, serious physical or emotional harm, sexual abuse or exploitation; or an act or failure to act which presents an imminent risk of serious harm.

Within the minimum standards set by CAPTA, each state is responsible for providing its own definitions of child abuse and neglect. Most states recognize four major types of maltreatment: neglect, physical abuse, sexual abuse, and psychological maltreatment.

Data for **prisoners under federal and state jurisdiction** were collected by the Bureau of Justice Statistics as provided by the National Prisoner Statistics program. Adults convicted of criminal activity may be given a prison or jail sentence. The data represent all persons under the jurisdiction of federal and state authorities rather than those in custody of those authorities. Jurisdiction refers to the legal authority over a prisoner, regardless of where the prisoner is held.

Data on **prisoners executed** are for persons executed under crime authority.

Data on **prisoners under death sentence** are collected annually for the Bureau of Justice Statistics as part of the National Prisoner Statistics Program. Data are obtained from the departments of corrections in each of the 50 states and the District of Columbia. The following states and the District of Columbia did not have the death penalty as of December 31, 2012: Alaska, Connecticut, Hawaii, Illinois, Iowa, Maine, Massachusetts, Michigan, Minnesota, New Jersey, New Mexico, New York, North Dakota, Rhode Island, Vermont, West Virginia, and Wisconsin.

The data exclude prisoners under sentence of death who remained within local correctional systems pending exhaustion of the appellate process or who had not been committed to prison.

Survey, Census, or Data Collection Method. Juvenile arrests—Based on analysis of arrest data from FBI reports and population data from the U.S. Census Bureau; www.ojjdp.gov/ojstatbb/ezaucr/asp/methods.asp . Child abuse and neglect—Based on the National Child Abuse and Neglect Data System (NCANDS); www.acf.hhs.gov/sites/default/files/cb/cm11.pdf#page=28 . Prisoners—Based on the National Prisoner Statistics (NPS) system; www.bjs.gov/index.cfm?ty=dcdetail&iid=262#Methodology .

Table A-26. State and Local Justice Employment and Expenditures

Sources: U.S. Department of Justice Statistics, Justice Expenditure and Employment Extracts, 2009, preliminary; NCJ 237913, www.bjs.gov/index.cfm?ty=pbdetail&iid=4335 ; and for 2000, www.bjs.gov/index.cfm?ty=pbdetail&iid=1028 .

Justice expenditure and employment data are extracted from the Census Bureau's Annual Government Finance Survey and Annual Survey of Public Employment.

Full-time employees include those persons whose hours of work represent full-time employment in their employer government.

Expenditure refers to all amounts of money paid out other than for retirement of debt, investment in securities, extensions of loans, or agency transactions. It includes only external cash payments and excludes any intragovernmental transfers and noncash transactions. It also includes any payments financed from borrowing, fund balances, intergovernmental revenue, and other current revenue.

Police protection is the function of enforcing the law, and preserving order and traffic safety and apprehending those who violate the law, whether these activities are performed by a police department, a sheriff's department, or a special police force maintained by an agency whose primary responsibility is outside the justice system but that has a police force to perform these activities in its specialized area (geographic or functional). Data for police protection cover all activities concerned with the enforcement of law and order, including coroners' offices, police-training academies, investigation bureaus, and local jails, "lockup," or other detention facilities not intended to serve as correctional facilities.

Judicial and legal services covers all civil and criminal activities associated with courts, including prosecution and public defense.

Data for **corrections** cover all activities pertaining to the confinement and correction of adults and minors accused or convicted of criminal offenses. Any pardon, probation, and parole activities also are included here.

Survey, Census, or Data Collection Method. Juvenile arrests—Based on the U.S. Census Bureau's Annual Government Finance Survey and Annual Survey of Public Employment; www.bjs.gov/index.cfm?ty=pbdetail&iid=4335 .

Table A-27. Civilian Labor Force and Employment

Source: U.S. Bureau of Labor Statistics, Current Population Survey, Geographic Profile of Employment and Unemployment, 2012 Annual Averages (preliminary), and previous editions; www.bls.gov/gps/ .

The Geographic Profile of Employment and Unemployment presents annual averages from the Current Population Survey (CPS) for census regions and divisions, the 50 states and the District of Columbia, 50 large metropolitan areas, and 17 central cities. The CPS is a sample survey of about 60,500 households conducted by the Census Bureau for the Bureau of Labor Statistics (BLS) and is the regular monthly survey from which the national unemployment rate is derived.

The **civilian noninstitutionalized population** includes persons 16 years of age and older residing in the 50 states and the District of Columbia who are not inmates of institutions (for example, penal and mental facilities, homes for the aged), and who are not on active duty in the armed forces.

The **civilian labor force** comprises all civilians 16 years old and over classified as employed or unemployed. Employed persons are all civilians who, during the survey week, did any work at all as paid employees, in their own business, profession, or on their own farm or who worked 15 hours or more as unpaid workers in an enterprise operated by a member of the family. It also includes all those who were not working but who had jobs or businesses from which they were temporarily absent because of illness, bad weather, vacation, labor-management disputes, job training, or personal reasons, whether they were paid for the time off or were seeking other jobs. Each employed person is counted only once regardless of how many jobs he or she may have.

Survey, Census, or Data Collection Method: Based on the Current Population Survey (CPS); for information, see Appendix B, Limitations of the Data and Methodology, and www.bls.gov/gps/notescps.htm .

Table A-28. Civilian Labor Force and Unemployment

Source: U.S. Bureau of Labor Statistics, Current Population Survey, Geographic Profile of Employment and

Unemployment, 2012 Annual Averages (preliminary), and previous editions; see www.bls.gov/gps/ .

For information on the Geographic Profile of Employment and Unemployment, see appendix entry for Table A-27.

Unemployed persons are all civilians 16 years old and over who had no employment during the survey week, were available for work, except for temporary illness, and had actively pursued employment some time during the prior 4 weeks. Active efforts include sending out resumes, placing or answering advertisements, and contacting potential employers regarding employment opportunities. Those engaged in passive methods of job seeking are not classified as unemployed. Persons who were laid off or were waiting to report to a new job within 30 days did not need to be looking for work to be classified as unemployed. The unemployment rate for all civilian workers represents the number of unemployed as a percent of the civilian labor force.

Survey, Census, or Data Collection Method: Based on the Current Population Survey (CPS); for information, see Appendix B, Limitations of the Data and Methodology, and www.bls.gov/gps/notescps.htm .

Table A-29. Employed Civilians, by Occupation, 2011

Source: U.S. Bureau of Labor Statistics, Local Area Unemployment Statistics, Geographic Profile of Employment and Unemployment, 2011; www.bls.gov/opub/gp/laugp.htm .

For information on the Geographic Profile of Employment or what constitutes an employed person, see appendix entry for Table A-27.

An **occupation** is a set of activities or tasks that employees are paid to perform. Employees who perform essentially the same tasks are in the same occupation, whether or not they work in the same industry. Some occupations are concentrated in a few particular industries; other occupations are found in many industries. These data are based on the occupational classifications derived from Census 2000. For information concerning the occupations, see Internet site www.bls.gov/cps/cpsoccind.htm .

Survey, Census, or Data Collection Method: Based on the Current Population Survey (CPS); for information, see Appendix B, Limitations of the Data and Methodology, and www.bls.gov/gps/notescps.htm .

Table A-30. Private Industry Employment and Wages

Source: U.S. Bureau of Labor Statistics, Employment and Wages, Annual Averages; www.bls.gov/cew/home.htm .

Data from the Quarterly Census of Employment and Wages (QCEW) program (ES-202 program for employment and average annual pay) are the product of a federal-state cooperative program. The QCEW program derives its data from quarterly tax reports submitted to State Employment Security Agencies by over eight million employers subject to state unemployment insurance (UI) laws and from federal agencies subject to the Unemployment Compensation for Federal Employees (UCFE) program. This includes 99.7 percent of all wage and salary civilian employment. The summaries are a result of the administration of state unemployment insurance programs that require most employers to pay quarterly taxes based on the employment and wages of workers covered.

The QCEW program is an employer reported measure and therefore associated with filled jobs, whether full or part-time, and place of work. If a person holds two jobs, the person would be counted twice in QCEW data. Programs which measure full-time equivalent positions or vacant positions target a different concept, as do household reported measures, which more typically show number of people with jobs, regardless of how many, and keep track of them by place or residence. The QCEW program, by definition, measures employment covered by unemployment insurance laws. In excluding self-employed jobs, and others, it differs significantly from those programs that include that employment.

Average annual wages per employee for any given industry are computed by dividing total annual wages by annual average employment. A further division by 52 yields average weekly wages per employee. Annual pay data only approximate annual earnings, because an individual may not be employed by the same employer all year or may work for more than one employer at a time. Average weekly or annual pay is affected by the ratio of full-time to part-time workers, as well as by the numbers of individuals in high- and low-paying occupations. When comparing average pay levels among states and industries, data users should take these factors into consideration. For example, industries characterized by high proportions of part-time workers will show average weekly wage levels appreciably less than the weekly pay levels of regular full-time employees in these industries. The opposite is true of industries with low proportions of part-time workers and of industries that typically schedule heavy weekend and overtime work. Average wage data also may be influenced by work stoppages, labor turnover, retroactive payments, seasonal factors, and bonus payments.

Survey, Census, or Data Collection Method: Based on the Quarterly Census of Employment and Wages (QCEW) program (ES-202); www.bls.gov/cew/home.htm .

Table A-31. Industry Employment and Wages

Sources: U.S. Bureau of Labor Statistics, Quarterly Census of Employment and Wages Database, State and County Wages; and Employment and Wages, Annual Averages, 2011; www.bls.gov/cew/data.htm   and www.bls.gov/cew/cewbultn11.htm .

See the text for Table A-30 for explanations of employment and annual pay data for the Quarterly Census of Employment and Wages program. Refer to General Notes to see information on different industries defined using the North American Industry Classification System (NAICS).

Survey, Census, or Data Collection Method: Based on the Quarterly Census of Employment and Wages (QCEW) program (ES-202); www.bls.gov/cew/cewover.htm .

Table A-32. Union Membership

Source: Hirsch, Barry T. and Macpherson, David A., from the Current Population Survey, Union Membership and Coverage Database, Industrial and Labor Relations Review, Vol. 6, No.2, January 2003, pp. 349–54; database updated regularly at www.unionstats.com/ (copyright).

Union membership data refer to wage and salary workers who report that they are members of a labor union or an employee association similar to a union. These data are based on the Current Population Survey (CPS) and represent union members by place of residence. For information on the CPS, see appendix entry for A-27 and General Notes. Contact the source for information on the methodology used.

Survey, Census, or Data Collection Method. Based on the Current Population Survey, 2012, published January 26, 2013. For information, see Appendix B, Limitations of the Data and Methodology, and Internet sites http://bnaplus.bna.com/LaorReports.aspx and www.unionstats.com .

Table A-33. Median Income of Households in Constant (2011) Dollars and Distribution by Income Level, 2009–2011

Source: U.S. Census Bureau, American Community Survey, "Selected Economic Characteristics in the United States: 2009–2011." Data accessed using American FactFinder; http://factfinder2.census.gov .

Median income divides the income distribution into two equal parts: one-half of the cases falling below the median income and one-half above the median. For households

and families, the median income is based on the distribution of the total number of households and families including those with no income. The median income for individuals is based on individuals 15 years old and over with income. Median income for households, families, and individuals is computed on the basis of a standard distribution. Median income is rounded to the nearest whole dollar. Median income figures are calculated using linear interpolation if the width of the interval containing the estimate is $2,500 or less. If the width of the interval containing the estimate is greater than $2,500, Pareto interpolation is used.

Income of households includes the income of the householder and all other individuals 15 years old and over in the household, whether they are related to the householder or not. Because many households consist of only one person, average household income is usually less than average family income. Although the household income statistics cover the past 12 months, the characteristics of individuals and the composition of households refer to the time of interview. Thus, the income of the household does not include amounts received by individuals who were members of the household during all or part of the past 12 months if these individuals no longer resided in the household at the time of interview. Similarly, income amounts reported by individuals who did not reside in the household during the past 12 months but who were members of the household at the time of interview are included. However, the composition of most households was the same during the past 12 months as at the time of interview.

For the definition of a **household**, or how to interpret 3-year estimates, see appendix entry for Table A-5.

Survey, Census, or Data Collection Method: Based on the American Community Survey; The 2009–2011 ACS 3-year estimates represent the average characteristics over the 3-year period. Due to differences in data collection time periods, multi-year estimates are not comparable with single year estimates. For more information, see Appendix B, Limitations of the Data and Methodology, and also www.census.gov/acs/www/guidance_for_data_users/estimates/ .

Table A-34. Family Income and Families and Individuals below Poverty, 2009–2011

Source: U.S. Census Bureau, American Community Survey, "Selected Economic Characteristics in the United States: 2009–2011." and Tables C17001 and C17013. Data accessed using American FactFinder; http://factfinder2.census.gov .

In compiling statistics on family income, the incomes of all members 15 years old and over related to the householder are summed and treated as a single amount. Although the family income statistics cover the past 12 months, the characteristics of individuals and the composition of families refer to the time of enumeration. Thus, the income of the family does not include amounts received by individuals who were members of the family during all or part of the past 12 months if these individuals no longer resided with the family at the time of enumeration. Similarly, income amounts reported by individuals who did not reside with the family during the past 12 months but who were members of the family at the time of enumeration are included. However, the composition of most families was the same during the past 12 months as at the time of enumeration. See appendix entry for Table A-33 for information on **Median income**.

Poverty status is determined using thresholds arranged in a two-dimensional matrix. The matrix consists of family size cross-classified by presence and number of family members under age 18 years old. Unrelated individuals and two-person families are further differentiated by age of reference person. To determine a person's poverty status, one compares the person's total family income in the last 12 months with the poverty threshold appropriate for that person's family size and composition. If the total income of that person's family is less than the threshold appropriate for that family, then the person is considered poor or "below the poverty level," together with every member of his or her family. If a person is not living with anyone related by birth, marriage, or adoption, then the person's own income is compared with his or her poverty threshold. The total number of people below the poverty level was the sum of people in families and the number of unrelated individuals with incomes in the last 12 months below the poverty level.

For information regarding how to interpret 3-year estimates, see appendix entry for Table A-5.

Survey, Census, or Data Collection Method: Based on the American Community Survey; The 2009–2011 ACS 3-year estimates represent the average characteristics over the 3-year period. Due to differences in data collection time periods, multi-year estimates are not comparable with single year estimates. For more information, see Appendix B, Limitations of the Data and Methodology, and also www.census.gov/acs/www/guidance_for_data_users/estimates/ .

Table A-35. Housing—Units and Characteristics

Source: U.S. Census Bureau, American Community Survey, "Selected Housing Characteristics in the United States, 2009–2011." Data accessed using American FactFinder; http://factfinder2.census.gov .

A **housing unit** is a house, apartment, mobile home or trailer, group of rooms, or single room occupied or, if vacant, intended for occupancy as separate living quarters. Separate living quarters are those in which the occupants do not live and eat with any other persons in the structure and that have direct access from the outside of the building through a common hall. For vacant units, the criteria of separateness and direct access are applied to the intended occupants whenever possible.

Units in structure. A structure is a separate building that either has open spaces on all sides or is separated from other structures by dividing walls that extend from ground to roof. In determining the number of units in a structure, all housing units, both occupied and vacant, are counted. Stores and office space are excluded. The statistics are presented for the number of housing units in structures of specified type and size, not for the number of residential buildings.

Mobile Homes include both occupied and vacant mobile homes to which no permanent rooms have been added. Mobile homes used only for business purposes or for extra sleeping space and mobile homes for sale on a dealer's lot, at the factory, or in storage are not counted in the housing inventory.

1-Unit, Detached are any 1-unit structure detached from any other house, that is, with open space on all four sides. Such structures are considered detached even if they have an adjoining shed or garage. A one-family house that contains a business is considered detached as long as the building has open space on all four sides. Mobile homes to which one or more permanent rooms have been added or built also are included.

1-Unit, Attached include any 1-unit structure that has one or more walls extending from ground to roof separating it from adjoining structures. In row houses (sometimes called townhouses), double houses, or houses attached to nonresidential structures, each house is a separate, attached structure if the dividing or common wall goes from ground to roof.

Year structure built refers to when the building was first constructed, not when it was remodeled, added to, or converted. Housing units under construction are included as vacant housing if they meet the housing unit definition— that is, all exterior windows, doors, and final usable floors are in place. For mobile homes, houseboats, RVs, etc., the manufacturer's model year was assumed to be the year built. The data relate to the number of units built during the specified periods that were still in existence at the time of enumeration.

A housing unit is classified as **occupied** if it is the current place of residence of the person or group of people living in it at the time of enumeration, or if the occupants are only temporarily absent from the residence for 2 months or less; that is, away on vacation or a business trip. If all the people staying in the unit at the time of the interview are staying there for 2 months or less, the unit is considered to be temporarily occupied, and classified as "vacant." The occupants may be a single family, one person living alone, two or more families living together, or any other group of related or unrelated people who share living quarters. Occupied rooms or suites of rooms in hotel, motels, and similar places are classified as housing units only when occupied by permanent residents, that is, people who consider the hotel as their current place of residence or have no current place of residence elsewhere. If any of the occupants in rooming or boarding houses, congregate housing, or continuing care facilities live separately from others in the building and have direct access, their quarters are classified as separate housing units.

Data on **vehicles available** show the number of passenger cars, vans, and pickup or panel trucks of one-ton capacity or less kept at home and available for the use of household members. Vehicles rented or leased for 1 month or more, company vehicles, and police and government vehicles are included if kept at home and used for nonbusiness purposes. Dismantled or immobile vehicles are excluded. Vehicles kept at home but used only for business purposes also are excluded.

House heating fuel data refer to occupied housing units. The data show the type of fuel used most to heat the house, apartment, or mobile home. Utility gas includes gas piped through underground pipes from a central system to serve the neighborhood. Electricity is generally supplied by means of above or underground electric power lines.

Refer to the General Notes to see information on the American Community Survey (ACS). For information regarding how to interpret 3-year estimates, see appendix entry for Table A-5.

Survey, Census, or Data Collection Method: Based on the American Community Survey; The 2009–2011 ACS 3-year estimates represent the average characteristics over the 3-year period. Due to differences in data collection time periods, multi-year estimates are not comparable with single year estimates. For more information, see

Appendix B, Limitations of the Data and Methodology, and also www.census.gov/acs/www/guidance_for_data_users/estimates/ .

Table A-36. Owner- and Renter-Occupied Units— Value and Gross Rent

Source: U.S. Census Bureau, American Community Survey, "Selected Housing Characteristics in the United States: 2009–2011." Data accessed using American Fact-Finder; http://factfinder2.census.gov .

A housing unit is **owner-occupied** if the owner or co-owner lives in the unit even if it is mortgaged or not fully paid for. The owner or co-owner must live in the unit. The unit is owner-occupied if someone who lives in the household is purchasing the house with a mortgage or some other debt arrangement such as a deed of trust, trust deed, contract to purchase, land contract, or purchase agreement. The unit also is considered owned with a mortgage if it is built on leased land and there is a mortgage on the unit. Mobile homes occupied by owners with installment loan balances also are included in this category.

Value is the respondent's estimate of how much the property (house and lot, mobile home and lot, or condominium unit) would sell for if it were for sale. If the house or mobile home was owned or being bought, but the land on which it sits was not, the respondent was asked to estimate the combined value of the house or mobile home and the land.

Median value divides the value distribution into two equal parts: one-half of the cases falling below the median value of the property and one-half above the median.

Renter Occupied includes all occupied housing units that are not owner occupied, whether they are rented for cash rent or occupied without payment of cash rent. "No cash rent" units are generally provided free by friends or relatives or in exchange for services such as resident manager, caretaker, minister, or tenant farmer. Housing units on military bases also are classified as "No cash rent." "Rented for cash rent" includes units in continuing care, sometimes called life care arrangements. These arrangements usually involve a contract between one or more individuals and a health services provider guaranteeing the individual shelter, usually a house or apartment, and services, such as meals or transportation to shopping or recreation.

Gross rent is the contract rent plus the estimated average monthly cost of utilities (electricity, gas, and water and sewer) and fuels (oil, coal, kerosene, wood, etc.) if these are being paid for by the renter (or paid for the renter by someone else).

The **median rent** divides the rent distribution into two equal parts: one-half of the cases falling below the median contract rent and one-half above the median.

Refer to the General Notes to see information on the American Community Survey (ACS). For information regarding how to interpret 3-year estimates, see appendix entry for Table A-5.

Survey, Census, or Data Collection Method: Based on the American Community Survey; The 2009–2011 ACS 3-year estimates represent the average characteristics over the 3-year period. Due to differences in data collection time periods, multi-year estimates are not comparable with single year estimates. For more information, see Appendix B, Limitations of the Data and Methodology, and also www.census.gov/acs/www/guidance_for_data_users/estimates/ .

Table A-37. Home Ownership and Vacancy Rates

Source: Homeownership and vacancy rates—U.S. Census Bureau, "Housing Vacancies and Home Ownership Annual Statistics: 2012"; www.census.gov/housing/hvs/ .

Vacancy rates and **homeownership rates** are based on data obtained from the Current Population Survey/Housing Vacancy Survey (CPS/HVS). Beginning in 2003, new weighting procedures based on the 2000 decennial census were implemented. The CPS/HVS includes the civilian noninstitutionalized population. This universe includes civilians in households, people in noninstitutional group quarters other than military barracks, and military in households living off post or with their families on post (as long as at least one household member is a civilian adult). The universe excludes other military in households and in group quarters (barracks) and people living in institutions. The weighting is controlled to independent counts of housing units for the month of the estimate. The sample size consists of approximately 71,000 addresses per month. A unit is in sample for 4 consecutive months, out for 8 months, back in sample for 4 months, and then retired from the sample. A housing unit is vacant if no one is living in it at the time of the interview, unless its occupants are only temporarily absent. In addition, a vacant unit may be one that is owned entirely by persons who have a usual residence elsewhere.

Rental vacancy rate is the proportion of the rental inventory that is vacant for rent.

The **homeowner vacancy rate** is the proportion of the homeowner inventory that is vacant for sale. The proportion of owner households to occupied households is termed the homeownership rate. It is computed by dividing the number of owner households by the number of occupied households.

The CPS/HVS uses different methodological standards than the American Community Survey and the American Housing Survey. Caution is urged when comparing data produced by each survey. For more information, see Internet site www.census.gov/hhes/www/housing/factsheets.html .

Survey, Census, or Data Collection Method: Homeownership and vacancy rates—Based on the Current Population Survey/Housing Vacancy Survey (CPS/HVS); for information, see Appendix B, Limitations of the Data and Methodology, and Internet site www.census.gov/housing/hvs/methodology/ .

Table A-38. Cost of Living Indicators—Housing, Public University, Energy Expenditures, and Sales Taxes

Sources: Housing prices—Federal Housing Finance Agency, "Monthly Interest Rate Survey"; www.fhfa.gov/ . Public University—U.S. National Center for Education Statistics, Digest of Education Statistics, annual; http://nces.ed.gov/programs/digest/;Energyexpenditures—U.S. Energy Information Administration, State Energy Data System(SEDS);www.eia.doe.gov/emeu/states/_seds.html; State tax rates—Federation of Tax Administrators; www.taxadmin.org/fta/rate/tax_stru.html ; Gasoline state tax rates—U.S. Department of Transportation, Federal Highway Administration, Highway statistics series; www.fhwa.dot.gov/policyinformation/ .

Data on **housing prices** are collected through the Federal Housing Finance Board's Monthly Interest Rate Survey (MIRS). This survey provides monthly information on interest rates, loan terms, and house prices by property type, by loan type, and by lender type, as well as information on 15- and 30-year fixed-rate loans. The sample consists of mortgage lenders who were asked to report the terms and conditions on all single-family, fully amortized, purchase-money, nonfarm loans that they close during the last 5 business days of the month. The survey excludes FHA-insured and VA-guaranteed loans, multifamily loans, mobile home loans, and loans created by refinancing another mortgage.

The **average costs per full-time-equivalent student in public colleges and universities** data shown are based upon the Integrated Postsecondary Education Data System (IPEDS), established as the core postsecondary education data collection program for NCES. IPEDS is a system of surveys designed to collect data from all primary providers of postsecondary education in such areas as enrollment, program completions, faculty, staff, and finances. See the sources for methodological details.

Energy expenditure data refers to money directly spent by consumers to purchase energy. Expenditures equal the amount of energy used by the consumer times the price per unit paid by the consumer. In the calculation of the amount of energy used, process fuel and intermediate products are not included. Population estimates used to calculate per capita data are provided by the Census Bureau's population estimates. See Internet site www.census.gov/popest/estimates.html .

The Federation of Tax Administrators collects data on **state tax rates** from various sources. The data shown are as of January 1 of the year shown. States may change these tax rates any time during the year.

The annual *Highway Statistics* publication is produced by the Office of Highway Policy Information, Federal Highway Administration. **Tax rates for gasoline** are shown as of December 31 for each year. Tax rates include inspection fees and environmental cleanup fees when these fees are targeted at highway fuel use, and include local taxes when these taxes are uniform across all the counties in the State. Consult source for information regarding methodology.

Survey, Census, or Data Collection Method: Housing prices—Based on the Finance Board Monthly Interest Rate Survey (MIRS); www.fhfb.gov/ ; Public university—Based on the Integrated Postsecondary Education Data System (IPEDS) "Fall Enrollment" surveys; for information, see Appendix B, Limitations of the Data and Methodology, and http://nces.ed.gov/ipeds/ ; Energy expenditures—Based on the State Energy Data System (SEDS); for information, see Technical Notes at www.eia.doe.gov/emeu/states/_seds.html ; State tax rates; www.taxadmin.org/ .

Table A-39. Personal Income

Source: U.S. Bureau of Economic Analysis, Regional Economic Accounts; www.bea.gov/regional/index.htm .

Personal income data are based on the Regional Economic Accounts; see Appendix B for additional information. Personal Income is the income that is received by all persons from all sources. It is calculated as the sum of wage and salary disbursements, supplements to wages and salaries, proprietors' income with inventory valuation and capital consumption adjustments, rental income of persons with capital consumption adjustment, personal dividend income, personal interest income, and personal current transfer receipts, less contributions for government social insurance. The personal income of an area is the income that is received by, or on behalf of, all the individuals who live in the area; therefore, the estimates of personal income are presented by the place of residence of the income recipients.

Disposable income is total personal income minus personal current taxes. It is personal income that is available for spending or saving.

For information regarding current vs. chained-dollars, see appendix entry to Table A-42.

Survey, Census, or Data Collection Method: Based on the Regional Economic Accounts. For more information, see www.bea.gov/regional/methods.cfm .

Table A-40. Personal Income Per Capita

Source: U.S. Bureau of Economic Analysis, Regional Economic Accounts; www.bea.gov/regional/index.htm .

For information on **personal and disposable personal income**, see appendix entry for Table A-39.

Per capita personal income is calculated as the total personal income of the residents of an area divided by the population of the area. It is the average income of a person if the population's total income was distributed evenly. The Bureau of Economic Analysis uses the Census Bureau's annual midyear population estimates.

For explanations of current versus constant dollars, see appendix entry for Table A-42.

Survey, Census, or Data Collection Method: Based on the Regional Economic Accounts. For more information, see www.bea.gov/regional/methods.cfm .

Table A-41. Earnings by Industry, 2012

Source: Source: U.S. Bureau of Economic Analysis, Regional Economic Accounts; www.bea.gov/regional/index.htm .

The components of **earnings** are wage and salary disbursements, other labor income, and proprietors' income. Wage and salary disbursements are defined as monetary remuneration of employees, including corporate officers; commissions, tips, and bonuses; and "pay-in-kind" that represents income to the recipient. They are measured before such deductions as social security contributions and union dues. All disbursements in the current period are covered. "Pay-in-kind" represents allowances for food, clothing, and lodging paid in kind to employees, which represent income to them, valued at the cost to the employer. Other labor income consists of employer contributions to privately administered pension and welfare funds and a few small items such as directors' fees, compensation of prison inmates, and miscellaneous judicial fees. Proprietors' income is the monetary income and income in-kind of proprietorships and partnerships, including the independent professions and of tax-exempt cooperatives. Refer to General Notes for information on specific industries.

Survey, Census, or Data Collection Method: Based on the Regional Economic Accounts. For more information, see www.bea.gov/regional/methods.cfm .

Table A-42. Gross Domestic Product, by State and Selected Large Industry

Source: Bureau of Economic Analysis, Survey of Current Business, annual; http://www.bea.gov/regional/index.htm .

Total Gross Domestic Product (GDP) by state is the value added in production by the labor and capital located in a state. GDP for a state is derived as the sum of the gross state product originating in all industries in a state. In concept, an industry's GDP by state, referred to as its "value added," is equivalent to its gross output (sales or receipts and other operating income, commodity taxes, and inventory change) minus its intermediate inputs (consumption of goods and services purchased from other U.S. industries or imported). GDP by state is therefore the state counterpart of the nation's gross domestic product (GDP), BEA's featured measure of U.S. output.

GDP by state for the nation differs from GDP for the following reasons: GDP by state excludes and GDP includes the compensation of federal civilian and military personnel stationed abroad and government consumption of fixed capital for military structures located abroad and for military equipment, except office equipment and GDP by state and GDP have different revision schedules.

Current-dollar estimates are the market value of an item and reflect the prices of the period being measured.

Chained dollars are a measure used to express real prices, or prices that have been adjusted to account for inflation in order to represent a dollar's purchasing power. A chain-dollar estimate is a measure used to approximate the chained-typed index level and is calculated by taking the current-dollar level of a series in the base period and multiplying it by the change in the chained-type quantity index number for the series since the base period.

A chained-type index is an index based on the linking (chaining) of indexes to create a time series. Annual chained-type Fisher indices are used in BEA's national income and product accounts (NIPAs) whereby Fisher ideal price indices are calculated using the weights of adjacent years. Those annual changes are then multiplied (chained) together, forming the chained-type index time series. Chained-dollar estimates correctly show growth rates for a series in the respective base period.

Survey, Census, or Data Collection Method: Based on the Regional Economic Accounts; www.bea.gov/regional/methods.cfm/ .

Table A-43. Science and Engineering Indicators

Sources: Engineers, life and physical scientists, and computer specialist—U.S. Census Bureau, Equal Employment Opportunity Tabulation, American Community Survey, 2006–2010; www.census.gov/people/eeotabulation/data/eeotables20062010.html . Research and Development, and S&E doctorates awarded—National Science Foundation, Science and Engineering State Profiles; www.nsf.gov/statistics/states/ .

The Division of Science Resources Statistics (SRS) of the National Science Foundation (NSF) compiles science and engineering (S&E) data that summarize state-specific data on personnel and finances. The SRS survey databases include doctoral scientists and engineers, S&E doctorates awarded, S&E graduate students and post-doctorates, federal research and development (R&D) obligations by agency and performer, total and industrial R&D expenditures, and academic R&D expenditures. See the source for further detailed information on these topics.

The indicator for engineers, life and physical scientist, and computer specialist represent the extent to which a state's workforce includes trained engineers. The indicator for **engineer** encompasses the standard occupational codes for engineering fields such as aerospace, agricultural biomedical, chemical, civil, computer hardware, electrical and electronics, environmental, industrial, marine and naval architectural, materials, mechanical, mining and geological, nuclear, and petroleum. Engineers design and operate production processes and create new products and services.

Life scientists are identified from standard occupational codes that include agricultural and food scientists, biological scientists, conservation scientists and foresters, and medical scientists.

Physical scientists are identified from standard occupational codes that include astronomers, physicists, atmospheric and space scientists, chemists, materials scientists, environmental scientists, and geoscientists, and postsecondary teachers in these subject areas.

Computer specialists are identified from 10 standard occupational codes that include computer and information scientists, programmers, software engineers, support specialist, systems analysts, database administrators, and network and computer system administrators.

As defined by the Organization for Economic Cooperation and Development, **research and development** (R&D) comprises creative work "undertaken on a systematic basis to increase the stock of knowledge—including knowledge of man, culture, and society—and the use of this stock of knowledge to devise new applications."

Federal R&D obligations represent the amounts for orders placed, contracts awarded, services received, and similar transactions during a given period, regardless of when the funds were appropriated and when future payment of money is required.

Federal obligations for R&D include all direct, incidental, or related costs resulting from, or necessary to, performance of R&D and costs of R&D plant as defined below, regardless of whether the R&D is performed by a federal agency (intramurally) or by private individuals and organizations under grant or contract (extramurally). R&D excludes routine product testing, quality control, mapping and surveys, collection of general-purpose statistics, experimental production, and the training of scientific personnel.

Survey, Census, or Data Collection Method: For information on engineers, life and physical scientists, and computer specialists, see www.census.gov/acs/www/ . For all other data, see www.nsf.gov/statistics/seind12/ .

Table A-44. Employer Establishment Births and Deaths and Business Bankruptcies

Sources: U.S. Small Business Administration, State Dynamic Data; www.sba.gov/advocacy/847 ; and Administrative Office of the U.S. Courts, "Bankruptcy Statistics"; www.uscourts.gov/bnkrpctystats/statistics.htm .

Firms are an aggregation of all establishments owned by a parent company with some annual payroll. Employer **firm births** represent an employing unit which is determined, for the first time, as meeting the definition of "employer" in the state unemployment compensation law or a previously terminated employing unit, which again is determined as meeting the definition of employer. Employer **firm deaths** refer to the voluntary or involuntary closure of a firm or establishment.

Bankruptcy is a condition in which a business cannot meet its debt obligations and petitions a federal district court for either reorganization of its debts or liquidations of its assets. In the action the property of a debtor is taken over by a receiver or trustee in bankruptcy for the benefit of the creditors. This action is conducted as prescribed by the National Bankruptcy Act and may be voluntary or involuntary. See the above source for more methodological information.

Survey, Census, or Data Collection Method: For information, see www.sba.gov/advocacy/847 and www.uscourts .gov/bnkrpctystats/bankrupcystats.htm .

Table A-45. Employer Firms and Nonemployer Establishments

Sources: Employer firms—U.S. Small Business Administration, Office of Advocacy, "Statistics of U.S. Businesses and Nonemployer Statistics: Firm Size Data provided by U.S. Census Bureau"; www.sba.gov/advocacy/849/12162 . Nonemployer establishments—U.S. Census Bureau, "Nonemployer Statistics"; www.census.gov/econ/nonemployer/index.html .

The Census Bureau provides the Office of Advocacy of the U.S. Small Business Administration with data on employer firm size in the Statistics of U.S. Businesses (SUSB). A **firm** is defined as the aggregation of all establishments owned by a parent company (within a geographic location and/or industry) that have some annual payroll. A firm may be located in one or more places. SUSBs employer data contain the number of firms, number of establishments, employment, and annual payroll for employment size of firm categories by location and industry. The employer data consist of static and dynamic data. Data are static or a "snapshot" of firms at a point in time. Industries are defined according to the North American Industry Classification System (NAICS) thereafter.

SUSB data for 1998–2002 uses NAICS 1997, and SUSB data for 2003 and beyond use NAICS 2002. The SUSB total falls short of the total number of firms because it excludes farms and businesses without employees. (Because employment is measured in March, SUSB does have a firm size category of zero for firms that had no employees in March but had positive employment at some point during the year.)

A **nonemployer** business is one that has no paid employees, has annual business receipts of $1,000 or more ($1 or more in the construction industries), and is subject to federal income taxes. Nonemployer businesses are generally small, such as real estate agents and independent contractors. Nonemployers constitute nearly three-quarters of all businesses, but they contribute only about 3 percent of overall sales and receipts data.

For information regarding annual payroll and employment, see appendix entry for Table A-14.

Survey, Census, or Data Collection Method: Employer firms—Statistics of U.S. Businesses and Nonemployer Statistics database; for information, see www.sba.gov/advocacy/847 . Nonemployer establishments—Business income tax returns filed with the Internal Revenue Service; for more information, see www.census.gov/epcd/nonemployer/view/covmeth.htm .

Table A-46. Private Nonfarm Establishments, Employment, and Payroll

Source: U.S. Census Bureau, "County Business Patterns"; www.census.gov/econ/cbp/index.html . Data excludes governmental establishments except for wholesale liquor establishments, retail liquor stores, federally chartered savings institutions, federally chartered credit unions, and hospitals. Establishments without a fixed location or having an unknown county location within a state are included under a "state-wide" geography classification. For state data, a firm is defined as an aggregation of all establishments owned by a parent company within a state. Establishments are nonfarm locations with active payroll in any quarter.

For information regarding establishments, employment, and annual payroll, see appendix entry for Table A-14.

Survey, Census, or Data Collection Method: Based on tabulations of data extracted from the U.S. Census Bureau's Business Register; for information, see www.census.gov/econ/cbp/overview.htm .

Table A-47. Foreign Direct Investment in the United States and U.S. Exports

Sources: U.S. affiliates—Bureau of Economic Analysis, International Economic Accounts, Operations of Multinational Companies, Foreign Direct Investment in the U.S.; www.bea.gov/international/ . U.S. exports—U.S. Census Bureau, Foreign Trade Statistics, State export data; www.census.gov/foreign-trade/statistics/state/ . U.S. agricultural exports—U.S. Department of Agriculture, Economic Research Service, U.S. Agricultural Trade database; www.ers.usda.gov/data/stateexports/ .

Foreign direct investment data in the United States are based on a survey of operations of nonbank U.S. affiliates that are majority-owned by foreign direct investors.

A **U.S. affiliate** is a U.S. business enterprise in which there is foreign direct investment; that is, in which a single foreign person owns or controls, directly or indirectly, 10 percent or more of the voting securities of an incorporated U.S. business enterprise. "Person" is broadly defined to include any individual, corporation, branch, partnership, associated group, association, estate trust, or other organization and any government. A "foreign person" is any person that resides outside the United States; that is, outside the 50 states, the District of Columbia, the Commonwealth of Puerto Rico, and all U.S. territories and possessions.

Gross book value is the book value of land and other property, plant, and equipment (PPE). PPE is measured at the original-cost value; that is, the values shown represent the actual cost of assets at the time they were acquired including all costs incurred in making the assets usable (such as transportation and installation). PPE consists of land, mineral rights, buildings, structures, machinery, and equipment (production, office, and transportation equipment). Excluded are inventories, intangible assets, and PPE not used in the production of products. Employment represents the number of full-time and part-time employees on the payroll at year-end. If the employment of a parent or an affiliate was unusually high or low because of temporary factors (such as a strike) or large seasonal variations, the number that reflected normal operations or an average for the year is shown.

The Census Bureau basic goods data are compiled from the documents collected by the U.S. Customs Service and reflect the movement of goods between foreign countries and the 50 states, the District of Columbia, Puerto Rico, the U.S. Virgin Islands, and U.S. Foreign Trade Zones. They include government and nongovernment shipments of goods, and exclude shipments between the United States and its territories and possessions, transactions with U.S. military, diplomatic and consular installations abroad, U.S. goods returned to the United States by its armed forces, personal and household effects of travelers, and in-transit shipments.

Export statistics consist of goods valued at more than $2,500 per commodity shipped by individuals and organizations (including exporters, freight forwarders, and carriers) from the United States to other countries. Exports are valued at the F.A.S. (free alongside ship) value of merchandise at the U.S. port of export, based on the transaction price including inland freight, insurance, and other charges incurred in placing the merchandise alongside the carrier at the U.S. port of exportation. Data on the value of U.S. agricultural exports by state of production are estimated by the Economic Research Service (ERS) using the customs district-level export data compiled by the Census Bureau and the state-level agricultural production data supplied by the National Agricultural Statistics Service (NASS). From these approximations a state that is the largest producer of an agricultural commodity will also account for the largest share of U.S. exports of that commodity.

U.S. agricultural commodity exports are often produced in inland states. From the farm, a commodity is sold to a local elevator, which in turn may sell it to a larger elevator located at a major transportation hub, which then moves the commodity to a port. As the commodity passes through several states before being exported, the state-of-origin often is lost or the product commingled with similar product from other states. Frequently, the state from which the commodity began its export journey, not necessarily the state in which the commodity was produced, is reported by the exporter. To more accurately reflect the situation for inland agricultural producing states, ERS calculates U.S. state agricultural exports based on a state's share of production of the exported commodity.

Survey, Census, or Data Collection Method: U.S. affiliates—Based on the Bureau of Economic Analysis 2007 Benchmark Survey; www.bea.gov/methodologies/index. htm#international_meth ; U.S. exports—Based on documents collected by the U.S. Customs Service; www.census.gov/foreign-trade/statistics/state/ ; U.S. agricultural exports—Based on Custom District-level export data compiled by the U.S. Census Bureau and State-level agricultural production data supplied by the U.S. Department of Agriculture's National Agricultural Statistical Service (NASS); www.ers.usda.gov/Data/StateExports/Methodology.aspx .

Table A-48. Farms and Farm Earnings

Sources: Farms—U.S. Department of Agriculture, National Agricultural Statistics Service, Farms, Land in Farms, and Livestock Operations, annual; www.nass.usda.gov/ and http://usda.mannlib.cornell.edu/MannUsda/view DocumentInfo.do?documentID=1259 . Earnings—U.S. Bu-

reau of Economic Analysis, Regional Economic Accounts, State Annual Personal Income and Employment; www .bea.gov/regional/index.htm .

A **farm** is any place from which $1,000 or more of agricultural products were produced and sold, or normally would have been sold, during the year. Government payments are included in sales. Ranches, institutional farms, experimental and research farms, and Indian Reservations are included as farms. Places with the entire acreage enrolled in the Conservation Reserve Program (CRP), Wetlands Reserve Program (WRP), or other government programs are counted as farms.

The acreage designated as "**land in farms**" consists primarily of agricultural land used for crops, pasture, or grazing. It also includes woodland and wasteland not actually under cultivation or used for pasture or grazing, provided it was part of the farm operator's total operation. Large acreages of woodland or wasteland held for nonagricultural purposes are not included. Land in farms includes Conservation Reserve, Wetlands Reserve Programs, or other government programs.

Average acreage per farm was calculated by dividing the total land in farms for an area by the number of farms in that area.

Farm earnings comprises the net income of sole proprietors, partners, and hired laborers arising directly from the current production of agricultural commodities, either livestock or crops. It includes net farm proprietors' income and the wages and salaries, pay-in-kind, and supplements to wages and salaries of hired farm laborers; but specifically excludes the income of nonfamily farm corporations.

Survey, Census, or Data Collection Method: Farms—Based on the National Agricultural Statistics Service (NASS) June Agricultural Survey; for information, see http://usda.mannlib.cornell.edu/MannUsda/viewDocument Info.do?documentID=1259 ; Earnings—Based on the Regional Economic Accounts; www.bea.gov/regional/methods.cfm .

Table A-49. Farm Finances and Income

Source: U.S. Department of Agriculture, Economic Research Service, United States and State Farm Income Data; www.ers.usda.gov/Data/farmincome/finfidmu.htm .

The **value of agricultural sector production** is the sum of the value of crop production, the value of livestock production, and revenues from services and forestry in the value added table, which can be found at www.ers.usda .gov/data/farmincome/finfidmu.htm . The value of crop production and livestock production encompass cash receipts, home consumption, and inventory change. Revenues from services and forestry includes machine hire and custom work income, sales of forestry products from farms, farm-related income, and gross imputed rental value of farm dwellings. The income and expenses associated with operators' dwellings are included in this account.

Net value added represents the total value of the farm sector's production of goods and services, less payments to other (nonfarm) sectors of the economy. It reflects production agriculture's addition to the national economic product. It also represents the sum of the economic returns to all the providers of factors of production; farm employees, lenders, landlords, and farm operators.

Farm marketings represent quantities of agricultural products sold by farmers multiplied by prices received per unit of production at the local market. Information on prices received for farm products is generally obtained from surveys of firms (such as grain elevators, packers, and processors) purchasing agricultural commodities directly from producers. In some cases, the price information is obtained directly from the producers.

Net farm income is that portion of the net value added by agriculture to the national economy earned by farm operators. Farm operators typically benefit most from the increases and assimilate most of the declines arising from short-term, unanticipated weather and market conditions. Net farm income is a value of production measure indicating the farm operators' share of the net value added to the national economy within a calendar year, independent of whether it is received in cash or a noncash form such as increases/decreases in inventories and imputed rental for the farm operator's dwelling.

Survey, Census, or Data Collection Method: Based on the Agricultural Resource Management Survey (ARMS); www.ers.usda.gov/data-products/arms-farm-financial-and-crop-production-practices.aspx#.UYKQD0oltKU .

Table A-50. Farm Marketings and Government Payments

Sources: Government Payments—U.S. Department of Agriculture, Economic Research Service, "Farm Income: Data Files"; www.ers.usda.gov/Data/farmincome/FinfidmuXls .htm ; Crops & livestock farm marketings—U.S. Department of Agriculture, Economic Research Service, "Farm Income: Cash Receipts"; www.ers.usda.gov/Data/farmincome/FinfidmuXls.htm ; Principal commodities—U.S.

Department of Agriculture, Economic Research Service, "Farm Income: Cash Receipts"; www.ers.usda.gov/Data/farmincome/FinfidmuXls.htm .

Government payments consist of direct cash payments received by the farm operators. It includes disaster payments, loan deficiency payments from prior participation, payments from Conservation Reserve Programs (CRP), the Wetlands Reserve Programs (WRP), other conservation programs, and all other federal farm programs under which payments were made directly to farm operators. Commodity Credit Corporation (CCC) proceeds and federal crop insurance payments were not tabulated in this category.

For information regarding farm marketings, see appendix entry for Table A-49.

Survey, Census, or Data Collection Method: Based on the Agricultural Resource Management Survey (ARMS); www.ers.usda.gov/data-products/arms-farm-financial-and-crop-production-practices.aspx#.UYKQD0oltKU .

Table A-51. Natural Resource Industries and Minerals

Sources: Natural resource industries—U.S. Census Bureau, County Business Patterns, annual; www.census.gov/econ/cbp/index.html ; Nonfuel minerals—U.S. Geological Survey, Mineral Commodities Summaries, annual; minerals.usgs.gov/minerals/pubs/mcs/ ; Crude petroleum—U.S. Energy Information Administration, Petroleum Supply Annual, and Petroleum Marketing Annual; www.eia.gov/petroleum/supply/annual/volume1/ . Natural gas—U.S. Energy Information Administration, Natural Gas Annual; www.eia.gov/naturalgas/annual/ ; Coal—U.S. Energy Information Administration, Annual Coal Report, www .eia.gov/coal/annual/ .

Natural Resource Industries as presented here includes Agriculture, Forestry, Fishing, and Hunting (NAICS 11), Mining (NAICS 21), Wood Product Manufacturing (NAICS 321), and Paper Manufacturing (NAICS 322). For information on establishments, employment, and payroll, see the appendix entry for Table A-14. For detailed information on industry sectors and subsectors, see the General Notes of this appendix for the North American Industry Classification System (NAICS). Both Wood Product Manufacturing and Paper Manufacturing are subsectors of Manufacturing.

Nonfuel mineral production. The U.S. Geological Survey (USGS) collects information about the quantity and quality of all mineral resources. See the source listed for more detailed information on nonfuel mineral production.

The Energy Information Administration (EIA) collects monthly crude oil production data on an ongoing basis. Data on crude oil production for states are reported to the EIA by state government agencies.

Crude Oil is a mixture of hydrocarbons that exists in liquid phase in natural underground reservoirs and remains liquid at atmospheric pressure after passing through surface separating facilities. Crude oil is refined to produce a wide array of petroleum products.

Crude oil value is the product of quantity and first domestic purchase price as reported by the Petroleum Marketing Annual. The first purchase of crude oil is an equity (not custody) transaction commonly associated with a transfer of ownership of crude oil associated with the physical removal of the crude oil from a property for the first time (also referred to as a lease sale). A first purchase normally occurs at the time and place of ownership transfer where the crude oil volume sold is measured and recorded on a run ticket or other similar physical evidence of purchase. The volume purchased and the cost of such transaction is not measured farther from the wellhead than the point at which the value for landowner royalties is established, if there was a separate landowner. For the most current prices of crude oil, see EIA's Petroleum Navigator found at http://tonto.eia.doe.gov/dnav/pet/pet_sum_top.asp .

Natural gas is a gaseous mixture of hydrocarbon compounds, the primary one being methane. The EIA obtains data on natural gas using Survey Form EIA-895, "Monthly and Annual Quantity and Value of Natural Gas Production Report."

Natural gas quantity represents wellhead marketed production, which is the gross withdrawals less gas used for repressuring, quantities vented and flared, and nonhydrocarbon gases removed in treating or processing operations. Includes all quantities of gas used in field and processing plant operations.

Natural gas value is the imputed wellhead value of marketed production. It is the product of the average wellhead price and the marketed production. The prices used for this publication were derived from EIA's Natural Gas Navigator; http://tonto.eia.doe.gov/dnav/ng/ng_sum_top.asp .

Coal is a readily combustible black or brownish-black rock whose composition, including inherent moisture, consists of more than 50 percent by weight and more than 70 percent by volume of carbonaceous material. The EIA obtains data on coal using the U.S. Department of Labor, Mine Safety and Health Administration, Form 7000-2, "Quarterly Mine Employment and Coal Production Report" and Energy Information Administration Form EIA-7A, "Coal Production Report." Coal production data include both underground and surface mines and are provided in short-tons. A short-ton is a unit of weight equal to 2,000 pounds.

Coal value is the product of quantity and the national average sales price for both underground and surface mine production.

Survey, Census, or Data Collection Method: Natural resource industries—Based on tabulations of data extracted from the U.S. Census Bureau's Business Register; www.census.gov/econ/cbp/methodology.htm; Nonfuel minerals—Based on U.S. Geological Survey Mineral Industry Surveys; http://minerals.usgs.gov/minerals/ ; Crude petroleum—Based on the Petroleum Supply Reporting System (PSRS); http://eia.doe.gov / ; Natural gas—Based on Energy Information Administration Survey Form EIA-895, "Monthly and Annual Quantity and Value of Natural Gas Production Report"; www.eia.doe.gov/oil_gas/natural_gas/data_publications/natural_gas_annual/nga.html ; Coal—Based on U.S. Department of Labor, Mine Safety and Health Administration, Form 7000-2, *Quarterly Mine Employment and Coal Production Report* and Energy Information Administration Form EIA-7A, *Coal Production Report*; www.eia.doe.gov/cneaf/coal/page/acr/acr.pdf .

Table A-52. Agricultural Census

Source: U.S. Department of Agriculture, National Agricultural Statistics Service, *2007 Census of Agriculture*, Vol. 1; www.nass.usda.gov/index.asp and www.agcensus.usda.gov/Publications/2007/Full_Report/Volume_1,_Chapter_2_US_State_Level/ .

Market value of agricultural products sold represents the gross market value before taxes and production expenses of all agricultural products sold or removed from the place in 2007 regardless of who received the payment. It is equivalent to total sales and it includes sales by the operators as well as the value of any shares received by partners, landlords, contractors, or others associated with the operation. It includes value of direct sales and the value of commodities placed in the Commodity Credit Corporation (CCC) loan program. Market value of agricultural products sold does not include payments received for participation in other federal farm programs. Also, it does not include income from farm-related sources such as custom work and other agricultural services or income from nonfarm sources. The value of crops sold in 2007 or 2002 does not necessarily represent the sales from crops harvested in 2007 or 2002. Data may include sales from crops produced in earlier years and may exclude some crops produced in the stated years but held in storage and not sold. Sales figures are expressed in current dollars.

Farms by combined government payments and market value of agricultural products sold represent the value of products sold plus government payments. Total value of products sold combines total sales not under production contract and total sales under production contract. Government payments consist of government payments received from the Conservation Reserve Program (CRP), Wetlands Reserve Program (WRP), Farmable Wetlands Program (FWP), or Conservation Reserve Enhancement Program (CREP) plus government payments received from federal, state, and local programs other than the CRP, WRP, FWP, and CREP, and Commodity Credit Corporation loans.

The term **operator** designates a person who operates a farm, either doing the work or making day-to-day decisions about such things as planting, harvesting, feeding, and marketing. The operator may be the owner, a member of the owner's household, a hired manager, a tenant, a renter, or a sharecropper. If a person rents land to others or has land worked on shares by others, he/she is considered the operator only of the land which is retained for his/her own operation.

For an explanation of farms, land in farms, and the average size of farms, see appendix entry for Table A-48. For explanation for government payments, see appendix entry for Table A-50.

Survey, Census, or Data Collection Method: Based on the 2007 Census of Agriculture; for information, see Appendix B, Limitations of the Data and Methodology, and Internet site www.nass.usda.gov/Census_of_Agriculture/index.asp .

Table A-53. Utilities

Sources: Private utilities—U.S. Census Bureau, County Business Patterns, annual www.census.gov/econ/cbp/index.html . Public water systems—Environmental Protection Agency, Safe Drinking Water Information System; www.epa.gov/safewater/data/getdata.html .

Private utilities. Refer to General Notes to see information on the private utilities industry defined using the North American Industry Classification System (NAICS). See the appendix entry for Table A-14 for information on establishments, employees, and annual payroll. For information on what constitutes residential, see appendix entry for Table A-54.

Data on **water systems** are obtained by the Environmental Protection Agency through the Safe Drinking Water Information System/Federal Version (SDWIS/FED), a database designed and implemented to meet the EPAs needs in the oversight and management of the Safe Drinking Water Act (SDWA). The database contains data submitted by states and EPA regions in conformance with reporting requirements established by statute, regulation, and guidance. Community systems include any public water system that supplies water to the same population year-round.

Nontransient noncommunity systems include any public water system that regularly supplies water to at least 25 of the same people at least 6 months per year, but not year-round. Transient noncommunity systems include any public water system that provides water in a place such as a gas station or a campground where people do not remain for long periods of time.

Table A-54. Energy Consumption

Source: U.S. Energy Information Administration, "State Energy Data"; www.eia.gov/state/seds/

Energy consumption is the use of energy as a source of heat or power or as an input in the manufacturing process. Data on energy consumption are from the State Energy Data System (SEDS), which is maintained and operated by the Energy Information Administration (EIA). SEDS has two principal objectives: (1) to provide state energy consumption, price, and expenditure estimates to members of Congress, federal and state agencies, and the general public and (2) to provide the historical series necessary for EIAs energy models. For methodological and technical information on SEDS, see www.eia.doe.gov/emeu/states/_seds_tech_notes.html .

An **end-use sector** is a firm or individual that purchases products for its own consumption and not for resale (for example an ultimate consumer).

The **residential sector** is the energy-consuming sector that consists of living quarters for private households. Common uses of energy associated with this sector include space heating, water heating, air conditioning, lighting, refrigeration, cooking, and running a variety of other appliances. The residential sector excludes institutional living quarters.

The **commercial sector** is the energy-consuming sector that consists of service-providing facilities and equipment of: businesses; federal, state, and local governments; and other private and public organizations, such as religious, social, or fraternal groups. The commercial sector includes institutional living quarters. It also includes sewage treatment facilities. Common uses of energy associated with this sector include space heating, water heating, air conditioning, lighting, refrigeration, cooking, and running a wide variety of other equipment. Note: This sector includes generators that produce electricity and/or useful thermal output primarily to support the activities of the above-mentioned commercial establishments.

Industrial sector: An energy-consuming sector that consists of all facilities and equipment used for producing, processing, or assembling goods. The industrial sector encompasses the following types of activity: Manufacturing (NAICS codes 31–33); Agriculture, Forestry, Fishing, and Hunting (NAICS code 11); Mining, including oil and gas extraction (NAICS code 21); and Construction (NAICS code 23). Overall energy use in this sector is largely for process heat and cooling and powering machinery, with lesser amounts used for facility heating, air conditioning, and lighting. Fossil fuels are also used as raw material inputs to manufactured products. Note: This sector includes generators that produce electricity and/or useful thermal output primarily to support the above-mentioned industrial activities.

Transportation sector: An energy-consuming sector that consists of all vehicles whose primary purpose is transporting people and/or goods from one physical location to another. Included are automobiles; trucks; buses; motor cycles; trains, subways, and other rail vehicles; aircraft; and ships, barges, and other waterborne vehicles. Vehicles whose primary purpose is not transportation (for example, construction cranes and bulldozers, farming vehicles, and warehouse tractors and forklifts) are classified in the sector of their primary use. In this report, natural gas used in the operation of natural gas pipelines is included in the transportation sector.

Petroleum is a broadly defined class of liquid hydrocarbon mixtures. Included are crude oil, lease condensate, unfinished oils, refined products obtained from the processing of crude oil, and natural gas plant liquids. Note: Volumes of finished petroleum products include nonhydrocarbon compounds, such as additives and detergents, after they have been blended into the products.

For information on natural gas, see appendix entry for Table A-51.

Hydroelectric Power is the production of electricity from the kinetic energy of falling water.

Nuclear electric power (nuclear power) is the electricity generated by the use of the thermal energy released from the fission of nuclear fuel in a reactor.

Table A-55. Energy Expenditures

Source: U.S. Energy Information Administration, "State Energy Data" www.eia.doe.gov/emeu/states/_seds.html .

Energy expenditures refer to the money directly spent by consumers to purchase energy. Expenditures equal the amount of energy used by the consumer times the price per unit paid by the consumer. In the calculation of the amount of energy used, process fuel and intermediate products are not included.

Motor gasoline includes conventional gasoline; all types of oxygenated gasoline, including gasohol; and reformulated gasoline, but excludes aviation gasoline.

Data on energy expenditures are from the State Energy Data System (SEDS), which is maintained and operated by the Energy Information Administration (EIA). For more information about the SEDS, end-use sector, or the various types of energy, see the appendix entry for Table A-54.

Survey, Census, or Data Collection Method: Based on the State Energy Data System (SEDS); for information, see "Technical Notes and Documentation," www.eia.doe.gov/emeu/states/_seds.html .

Table A-56. Construction

Sources: Employment—U.S. Bureau of Labor Statistics, Current Employment Statistics Program; www.bls.gov/sae/home.htm . Earnings—U.S. Bureau of Economic Analysis, Regional Economic Accounts, State Annual Personal Income and Employment; www.bea.gov/regional/index.htm . Establishments—U.S. Census Bureau, County Business Patterns, annual; www.census.gov/econ/cbp/index.html . New housing units—U.S. Census Bureau, Construction Reports, "New Residential Construction," www.census.gov/construction/nrc/ .

Construction. Refer to General Notes of this appendix to see information on the Construction industry defined using the North American Industry Classification System (NAICS).

Data for **nonfarm employment** are based on the Current Employment Statistics (CES) survey of payroll records covering over 390,000 businesses on a monthly basis. Employment is defined as the total number of persons on establishment payrolls employed full- or part-time who received pay for any part of the pay period, which includes the 12th day of the month. Temporary and intermittent employees are included, as are any workers who are on paid sick leave, on paid holiday, or who work during only part of the specified pay period. A striking worker who only works a small portion of the survey period, and is paid, would be included as employed under the CES definitions. Persons on the payroll of more than one establishment are counted in each establishment. Data exclude proprietors, self-employed, unpaid family or volunteer workers, farm workers, and domestic workers. Persons on layoff the entire pay period, on leave without pay, on strike for the entire period, or who have not yet reported for work are not counted as employed.

For information on earnings, see appendix entry for Table A-41.

Value of construction contracts includes new structures and additions. The data represent values of construction in states in which the work was actually done. Refer to the source for information about the data and methodology used to obtain the data.

Statistics on **housing units authorized by building permits** include housing units issued in local permit-issuing jurisdictions by a building or zoning permit. Not all areas of the country require a building or zoning permit. The statistics only represent those areas that do require a permit. Current surveys indicate that construction is undertaken for all but a very small percentage of housing units authorized by building permits. A major portion typically gets under way during the month of permit issuance and most of the remainder begin within the three following months. Because of this lag, the housing unit authorization statistics do not represent the number of units actually put into construction for the period shown, and should therefore not be directly interpreted as "housing starts."

Survey, Census, or Data Collection Method: Employment—Current Employment Statistics (CES) Survey; www.bls.gov/opub/hom/homch2_a.htm . Earnings—Based on the Regional Economic Accounts; "State Personal Income Methodologies," at www.bea.gov/regional/methods.cfm. Establishments—Based on tabulations of data extracted from the U.S. Census Bureau's Business Register; www.census.gov/econ/cbp/methodology.htm . New housing units—Based on a survey of local building permit officials using Form C-404; www.census.gov/construction/nrc/ .

Table A-57. Manufactures

Sources: Employment and average hourly earnings of production workers—U.S. Bureau of Labor Statistics, Current Employment Statistics Program; www.bls.gov/sae/home.htm . Earnings—U.S. Bureau of Economic Analysis, Regional Economic Accounts; www.bea.gov/regional/index.htm . Establishments—U.S. Census Bureau, County Business Patterns, annual; www.census.gov/econ/cbp/index.html . Value of shipments—U.S. Census Bureau, Annual Survey of Manufactures, Geographic Area Statistics; www.census.gov/manufacturing/asm/index.html .

Manufactures. Refer to General Notes of this appendix to see information on the Manufacturing industry defined using the North American Industry Classification System (NAICS). See the notes and explanations for Table A-56 for information on employment. For information regarding earnings, see appendix entry for Table A-41. For information on establishments, see appendix entry for Table 14.

Average hourly earnings are on a "gross" basis. They reflect not only changes in basic hourly and incentive wage rates, but also such variable factors as premium pay for overtime and late-shift work and changes in output of workers paid on an incentive plan. They also reflect shifts in the number of employees between relatively high-paid and low-paid work and changes in workers' earnings in individual establishments. Averages for groups and divisions further reflect changes in average hourly earnings for individual industries. Averages of hourly earnings differ from wage rates. Earnings are the actual return to the worker for a stated period; rates are the amount stipulated for a given unit of work or time. The earnings series do not measure the level of total labor costs on the part of the employer because the following are excluded: benefits, irregular bonuses, retroactive items, payroll taxes paid by employers, and earnings for those employees not covered under production worker, construction worker, or non-supervisory employee definitions.

Value of shipments includes the received or receivable net selling values, free on board plant (exclusive of freight and taxes), of all products shipped, both primary and secondary, as well as all miscellaneous receipts, such as receipts for contract work performed for others, installation and repair, sales of scrap, and sales of products bought and sold without further processing. Included are all items made by or for the establishments from material owned by it, whether sold, transferred to other plants of the same company, or shipped on consignment. The net selling value of products made in one plant on a contract basis from materials owned by another was reported by the plant providing the materials. In the case of multiunit companies, the manufacturer was requested to report the value of products transferred to other establishments of the same company at full economic or commercial value, including not only the direct cost of production but also a reasonable proportion of "all other costs" (including company overhead) and profit.

Table A-58. Manufactures Summary and Export-Related Shipments and Employment

Sources: Manufactures summary—U.S. Census Bureau, Annual Survey of Manufactures, Geographic Area Statistics. Accessed through American FactFinder; www.census.gov/manufacturing/asm/index.html . Export-related—U.S. Census Bureau, Exports from Manufacturing Establishments; www.census.gov/manufacturing/exports/index.html .

Employees includes all full-time and part-time employees on the payrolls of operating manufacturing establishments during any part of the pay period that included the 12th of the months specified on the report form. Included are employees on paid sick leave, paid holidays, and paid vacations; not included are proprietors and partners of unincorporated businesses. These individuals consist of all full-time and part-time employees who are on the payrolls of establishments who worked or received pay for any part of the pay period including the 12th of March, May, August, and November.

Payroll includes the gross earnings of all employees on the payrolls of operating manufacturing establishments paid in the calendar year. Payroll includes all forms of compensation, such as salaries, wages, commissions, dismissal pay, bonuses, vacation and sick leave pay, and compensation in kind, prior to such deductions as employees' social security contributions, withholding taxes, group insurance, union dues, and savings bonds. The total includes salaries of offices of corporations. It excludes payments to proprietors or partners of unincorporated concerns. Also excluded are payments to members of armed forces and pensioners carried on the active payrolls of manufacturing establishments, and employers' social security contributions or other nonpayroll labor costs, such as employees' pension plans, group insurance premiums, and workers' compensation.

Production workers are the number of workers (up through the line-supervisor level) engaged in fabricating, processing, assembling, inspecting, receiving, storing, handling, packing, warehousing, shipping (but not delivering),

maintenance, repair, janitorial and guard services, product development, auxiliary production for plant's own use (for example, power plant), recordkeeping, and other services closely associated with these production operations at the establishment. Employees above the working-supervisor level are excluded from this item.

Production worker hours include all hours worked or paid for at the manufacturing plant, including actual overtime hours (not straight-time equivalent hours). It excludes hours paid for vacations, holidays, or sick leave when the employee is not at the establishment.

Value added by manufactures measures manufacturing activity derived by subtracting the cost of materials, supplies, containers, fuel, purchased electricity, and contract work from the value of shipments (products manufactured plus receipts for services rendered). The result of this calculation is adjusted by the addition of value added by merchandising operations (that is, the difference between the sales value and the cost of merchandise sold without further manufacture, processing, or assembly) plus the net change in finished goods and work-in-process between the beginning- and end-of-year inventories. For those industries where value of production is collected instead of value of shipments, value added is adjusted only for the change in work-in-process inventories between the beginning and end of year. For those industries where value of work done is collected, the value added does not include an adjustment for the change in finished goods or work-in-process inventories. This item avoids the duplication in the figure for value of shipments that results from the use of products of some establishments as materials by others.

The estimates for **export-related** data are provided by the Census Bureau's 2009 Exports from Manufacturing Establishments report. The report relies upon 3 major information sources: (1) the Census Bureau's 2009 Annual Survey of Manufactures; (2) detailed data from the Census Bureau's 2009 edition of U.S. International Trade in Goods and Services; and (3) the Bureau of Economic Analysis' Input-Output (I/O) Accounts of the U.S. Economy for 2008. The data from each source is manipulated and converted so that they are comparable. The user should bear in mind that conversions and adjustments for such differences are imperfect, and a potential source of error in the figures presented in this report. These estimates are preliminary because I/O data for 2009 are not available when the estimates are calculated. Final estimates of export-related employment for 2009 will incorporate I/O data for 2009. A short description of the methodology is as follows: exports as reported by manufacturers on the 2009 Annual Survey of Manufactures (ASM) were allocated to the industry and state of that manufacturer. These export totals then were compared to the U.S. International Trade in Goods and Services, as reported by exporting firms. Because many manufacturers do not know whether or not their products are exported, the export data from the 2009 Annual Survey of Manufactures were adjusted to the totals from the U.S. International Trade in Goods and Services, with differences allocated to industries and states. These data then represented the "direct" exports of manufactured goods, by industry and by state. Refer to the source for further discussion of methodology.

Employment related to direct exports is not collected in the Annual Survey of Manufactures. However, the total value of shipments, as well as total employment, are estimated for each industry in each state. Using these data from the Annual Survey of Manufactures, employment related to direct exports was calculated by multiplying the total employment of each industry in each state by the ratio of the estimated total freight on board value of exports for that industry in that state to total shipments for that industry in that state. As with the estimates of exports, there are no measures available regarding the possible range of error associated with this estimating technique.

Survey, Census, or Data Collection Method: Manufactures summary—Based on the Annual Survey of Manufactures; for information, see Appendix B, Limitations of the Data and Methodology, and www.census.gov/manufacturing/asm/index.html . Export-related—Based on tabulations of data from 3 sources: the Annual Survey of Manufactures, the U.S. Census Bureau's U.S. International Trade in Goods and Services and the Bureau of Economic Analysis' Input-Output (I/O) Accounts of the U.S. Economy; www.census.gov/manufacturing/exports/index.html .

Table A-59. Major Manufacturing Sectors: 2011

Source: U.S. Census Bureau, *Annual Survey of Manufactures*, Geographic Area Statistics. Accessed through American FactFinder; www.census.gov/manufacturing/asm/index.html .

Refer to General Notes of this appendix to see information on the Manufacturing industry and major sectors defined using the North American Industry Classification System (NAICS). See appendix entry for Table A-14 for information on the County Business Patterns. See the notes and explanations for Table A-58 for information on employment and value of shipments.

Survey, Census, or Data Collection Method: Value of Shipments—Based on the *Annual Survey of Manufactures*; for information, see Appendix B, Limitations of the Data and Methodology, and www.census.gov/manufacturing/asm/how_the_data_are_collected/index.html . Employment—Based on tabulations of data extracted from the U.S. Census Bureau's Business Register; www.census.gov/econ/cbp/index.html .

Table A-60. Information Industries

Sources: Employment—U.S. Bureau of Labor Statistics; State and Metro Area Employment, Hours, & Earnings; SAE Databases: Employment, Hours, and Earnings-State and Metro Area; www.bls.gov/sae/home.htm/ or www.bls.gov/sae/eetables/sae_annavg112.pdf or www.data.bls.gov/cgi-bin/dsrv?sm . Earnings—U.S. Bureau of Economic Analysis, Regional Economic Accounts, State Annual Personal Income and Employment; www.bea.gov/regional/index.htm . Establishments—U.S. Census Bureau, County Business Patterns, annual; www.census.gov/econ/cbp/index.html .

Refer to General Notes to see an explanation of the Information industry defined using the North American Industry Classification System (NAICS). See notes and explanations for Table A-56 for information on employment. For information on earnings, see appendix entry for Table A-41. For information on establishments, see appendix entry for Table A-14.

Survey, Census, or Data Collection Method: Employment—Based on the Current Employment Statistics (CES) survey; for information, see Appendix B, Limitations of the Data and Methodology, see Internet site www.bls.gov/opub/hom/homch2_a.htm . Earnings—Based on the Regional Economic Accounts, State Annual Personal Income and Employment; see Internet site www.bea.gov/regional/methods.cfm . Establishments—Tabulations of data extracted from the U.S. Census Bureau's Business Register, see Internet site www.census.gov/econ/cbp/methodology.htm .

Table A-61. Wholesale and Retail Trade

Sources: Employment—U.S. Bureau of Labor Statistics, Current Employment Statistics Program; www.bls.gov/sae/home.htm . Earnings—U.S. Bureau of Economic Analysis, Regional Economic Accounts, State Annual Personal Income and Employment; www.bea.gov/regional/index.htm . Establishments—U.S. Census Bureau, County Business Patterns, annual; www.census.gov/econ/cbp/index.html .

Refer to General Notes to see information on the Wholesale Trade and Retail Trade industries defined using the North American Industry Classification System (NAICS). See the notes and explanations for Table A-56 for information on employment and Table A-14 for information on establishments. For information on earnings, see appendix entry for Table A-41.

Survey, Census, or Data Collection Method: Employment—Based on the Current Employment Statistics (CES) survey; for information, see Appendix B, Limitations of the Data and Methodology, and see www.bls.gov/opub/hom/ . Earnings—Based on the Regional Economic Accounts; for information, see "State Personal Income Methodologies" at www.bea.gov/regional/methods.cfm . Establishments—Based on tabulations of data extracted from the U.S. Census Bureau's Business Register; www.census.gov/econ/cbp/index.html .

Table A-62. Retail Trade Earnings, 2011

Source: Earnings—U.S. Bureau of Economic Analysis, Regional Economic Accounts, State Annual Personal Income and Employment; www.bea.gov/regional/index.htm .

Refer to General Notes to see information on the Retail Trade industry defined using the North American Industry Classification System (NAICS). For more detailed information on subsectors of the Retail Trade industry, see www.census.gov/cos/www/naics.html .

Survey, Census, or Data Collection Method: Earnings—Based on the Regional Economic Information System; for information, see "State Personal Income Methodologies" at www.bea.gov/regional/methods.cfm .

Table A-63. Transportation and Commuting

Sources: Employment—U.S. Bureau of Labor Statistics, Current Employment Statistics Program; www.bls.gov/sae/home.htm . Earnings—U.S. Bureau of Economic Analysis, Regional Economic Accounts, State Annual Personal Income and Employment; www.bea.gov/regional/index.htm . Establishments—U.S. Census Bureau, County Business Patterns, annual, www.census.gov/econ/cbp/index.html . Workers 16 and over, commuting—U.S. Census Bureau, 2009–2011, American Community Survey; table DP03, "Selected economic characteristics"; Data accessed using American FactFinder2; www.census.gov/acs/www/ . Vehicle miles of travel—U.S. Federal Highway Administration, *Highway Statistics*, annual; www.fhwa.dot.gov/policy/ohpi/hss/hsspubs.cfm . Railroad and waterborne shipments—U.S. Bureau of Transportation

Statistics, *State Transportation Statistics*, annual; www.bts.gov/publications/state_transportation_statistics/ .

Refer to General Notes to see information on the Transportation and Warehousing industry defined using the North American Industry Classification System (NAICS). See the notes and explanations for Table A-56 for information on employment and Table A-41 for information on earnings. For information on establishments, see appendix entry for Table A-14.

Vehicle miles of travel data are collected by the Federal Highway Administration (FHWA). Vehicle miles of travel are miles of travel by all types of motor vehicles as determined by the states on the basis of actual traffic counts and established estimating procedures.

Railroad shipment data are developed by the Association of American Railroads (AAR) from the Surface Transportation Board's Carload Waybill Sample. The sample contains detailed information on the origination and termination of carloads by commodity and carrier for virtually all U.S. freight railroads. Normal statistical variations and limited sampling of very small railroads may cause limited distortions.

Waterborne shipment data are compiled by the U.S. Army Corps of Engineers and include detailed data on the movements of vessels and commodities at the ports and harbors on the waterways and canals of the United States and its territories. Data on foreign commerce are supplied to the Corps of Engineers by the Census Bureau, U.S. Customs, and purchased from the Journal of Commerce, Port Import Export Reporting Service. The tonnage figures of shipments represent short tons (2,000 pounds).

For information regarding how to interpret 3-year estimates, see appendix entry for Table A-5. For information on commute data provided by American Community Survey, consult source.

Survey, Census, or Data Collection Method: Employment—Based on Current Employment Statistics (CES) survey; for information, see Appendix B, Limitations of the Data and Methodology, and www.bls.gov/opub/hom/homch2_a.htm . Earnings—Based on the Regional Economic Information System; www.bea.doc.gov/bea/regional/articles/ . Establishments—Based on tabulations of data extracted from the U.S. Census Bureau's Business Register; www.census.gov/econ/cbp/index.html . Workers 16 and over—Based on the American Community Survey; The 2009–2011 ACS 3-year estimates represent the average characteristics over the 3-year period. Due to differences in data collection time periods, multi-year estimates are not comparable with single year estimates. For more information, see Appendix B, Limitations of the Data and Methodology, and also www.census.gov/ acs/www/Downloads/Accuracy_of_the_Data_MYE .pdf . Vehicle miles of travel—Based on the Highway Performance Monitoring System (HPMS); www.fhwa.dot .gov/policy/ohpi/hss/hsspubs.cfm . *Railroad shipments*— Based on the Association of American Railroads (AAR) database;www.fhwa.dot.gov/policy/ohpi/hpms/index.cfm. Waterborne shipments—Based on the U.S. Army Corps of Engineers' (Corps) Navigation Data Center (NDC) database; www.bts.gov/publications/state_transportation _statistics/ .

Table A-64. Motor Vehicle and Motorcycle Registrations, Highway Mileage, Bridges, and Drivers Licenses

Sources: Registrations, highway mileage, and driver's licenses—U.S. Federal Highway Administration, *Highway Statistics*, annual; www.fhwa.dot.gov/policy/ohpi/hss/ hsspubs.cfm . Bridges—U.S. Federal Highway Administration, Office of Bridge Technology; www.fhwa.dot.gov/ bridge/britab.cfm .

Vehicle registration. Data are collected by the Federal Highway Administration (FHWA) from state motor vehicle registration agencies. Accordingly, registration practices and dates vary. For uniformity, data have been adjusted to a calendar-year basis as registration years in states differ. Registration data include publicly, privately, and commercially owned vehicles.

Highway mileage. Total includes roads and streets in the functional systems that are assigned to groups according to the character service they are intended to provide. The functional systems are (1) **arterial highways** that generally handle the long trips, (2) **collector facilities** that collect and disperse traffic between the arterials and the lower systems, and (3) **local roads and streets** that primarily serve direct access to residential areas.

Interstate system connects, as directly as practicable, the nation's principal metropolitan areas, cities, and industrial centers.

Bridges. Data are based on the National Bridge Inventory (NBI). The NBI is a compilation of data supplied by states as required by the National Bridge Inspection Standards for bridges located on public roads. The database is maintained in a format prescribed by the Recording and Coding Guide for the Structure Inventory and Appraisal of the Nation's Bridges. Bridges are structurally deficient if they have been restricted to light vehicles, require immediate rehabilitation to remain open, or are closed. Bridges are functionally obsolete if they have deck geometry, load-carrying capacity, clearance or approach roadway alignment that no longer meet the criteria for the system of which the bridge is carrying a part.

Drivers licenses. Each state and the District of Columbia administers its own driver licensing system. Since 1954, all states have required drivers to be licensed, and since 1959, all states have required examination before licensing. Tests of knowledge of state driving laws and practices, vision, and driving proficiency are now required for new licensees.

Survey, Census, or Data Collection Method: Registrations and drivers licenses—Based on data provided to the U.S. Federal Highway Administration by individual states, Highway mileage—Based on the Highway Performance Monitoring System (HPMS); www.fhwa.dot.gov/ policyinformation/statistics/2011/ . Bridges—Based on the National Bridge Inventory (NBI); for information; www.fhwa.dot.gov/bridge/nbi.htm .

Table A-65. Traffic Fatalities and Seat Belt Use

Sources: Traffic fatalities and alcohol-involved crashes— U.S. National Highway Traffic Safety Administration. *Traffic Safety Facts, Annual Report*; www-nrd.nhtsa.dot .gov/CATS/index.aspx . Seat belts—U.S. Department of Transportation, National Highway Traffic Safety Administration, *Seat Belt Use in 2011—Use Rates in the States and Territories*; www-nrd.nhtsa.dot.gov/CATS/ index.aspx and www-nrd.nhtsa.dot.gov/Pubs/811651.pdf .

Traffic fatalities. The National Highway Traffic Safety Administration (NHTSA) has a cooperative agreement with an agency in each state's government to provide information on all qualifying fatal crashes in the state. These agreements are managed by regional contracting Officer's Technical Representatives located in the 10 NHTSA regional offices.

A fatal crash involves a motor vehicle in transport on a traffic way in which at least one person dies within 30 days of the crash.

Traffic fatality rate is per 100 million vehicle miles traveled.

Traffic fatalities in alcohol-involved crashes include both drivers and occupants. Only the BAC of the operator is considered when classifying data as alcohol-involved.

Blood alcohol content (BAC) is measured as a percentage by weight of alcohol in the blood (grams/deciliter). A positive BAC level (0.01 g/dl and higher) indicates that alcohol was consumed by the person tested.

Seat belt use. Data for states are based on observational surveys conducted in accordance with Section 157, Title 23, U.S. Code. For national figures, data are based on the National Occupant Protection Use Survey (NOPUS). Motorists observed in the survey were counted as "belted" if they appeared to have a shoulder belt across the front of their body.

Survey, Census, or Data Collection Method: Traffic fatalities and persons killed in alcohol involved crashes—Based on the Fatality Analysis Reporting System (FARS); for information, see Appendix B, Limitations of the Data and Methodology and www.nhtsa.gov/FARS . Safety belts—For states, based on surveys conducted in accordance with Section 157, Title 23, U.S. Code; for national figures, based on the National Occupant Protection Use Survey (NOPUS); see www-nrd.nhtsa.dot.gov/Pubs/811651.pdf .

Table A-66. Communications

Sources: Mobile wireless subscribers—Federal Communications Commission, Local Telephone Competition: Status as of December 31, 2011; www.fcc.gov/wcb/iatd/comp.html . Percent of households using Internet—U.S. Department of Commerce, National Telecommunications and Information Administration, Exploring the Digital Nation: Computer and Internet Use at Home and Networked Nation: Broadband in America 2007; www.ntia.doc.gov/report/2011/exploring-digital-nation-computer-and-internet-use-home and www.ntia.doc.gov/reports/2008/NetworkedNation.html . Revenue—Federal Communications Commission, Trends in Telephone Service; www.fcc.gov/wcb/iatd/trends.html .

Internet access. The Federal Communications Commission (FCC) provides data for households with telephones, computers, and Internet access based on the Current Population Survey (CPS) conducted by the Census Bureau. The CPS is a nationwide monthly survey of civilian non-institutionalized population 15 years old and over that uses a sample of 50,000.

Mobile wireless subscribership. The FCC's local competition and broadband data gathering program collects data on mobile wireless telephone subscribership and high-speed connections from telecommunications carriers twice a year using FCC Form 477.

Revenue. On April 1, 2000, the Federal Communications Commission required carriers first filed an FCC Form 499-A Telecommunications Reporting Worksheet to report previous year revenue data for TRS, USF, North American Numbering Planning Administration, and local number portability contribution purposes. The FCC Form 499-A superseded the older reporting requirements and is now filed to satisfy carrier registration requirements at the FCC as well. State-level telephone revenues are estimated using data from various editions of Telecommunications Industry Revenues, Statistics of Communications Common Carriers, Local Telephone Competition, and access filings to the FCC. The carriers also file quarterly data reported on form 499Q.

Survey, Census, or Data Collection Method: Households with Internet access—Based on the Current Population Survey; for information, see Appendix B, Limitations of the Data and Methodology, and the following document at www.census.gov/prod/2002pubs/tp63rv.pdf . Mobile wireless subscribers—Based on the Federal Communications Commission's Local Competition and Broadband Data Reporting Program (FCC Form 477); www.fcc.gov/wcb/iatd/comp.html . Revenue—Based on FCC Form 499-A and FCC Form 499-Q; www.fcc.gov/wcb/iatd/trends.html .

Table A-67. Financial Activities

Sources: Employment—U.S. Bureau of Labor Statistics, Current Employment and Statistics Program; www.bls.gov/sae/home.htm . Earnings—U.S. Bureau of Economic Analysis, Regional Economic Accounts, State Annual Personal Income and Employment; www.bea.gov/regional/index.htm . Establishments—U.S. Census Bureau, County Business Patterns, annual; www.census.gov/econ/cbp/index.html . FDIC-Insured financial institutions, number and assets—U.S. Federal Deposit Insurance Corporation, Statistics on Banking, annual; www2.fdic.gov/SDI/SOB/ . FDIC-insured financial institutions offices and deposits—U.S. Federal Deposit Insurance Corporation, Summary of Deposits, summary tables; www2.fdic.gov/sod/index.asp . Credit unions—National Credit Union Administration, *Year-end Statistics for Federally Insured Credit Unions*, annual; www.ncua.gov/ . Life insurance—American Council of Life Insurers, Washington, DC, *Life Insurers Fact Book, 2012*; table 10.4; www.acli.com (copyright).

Refer to General Notes of this appendix to see information on the Finance and Insurance industry and Real Estate and Rental and Leasing industry defined using the North American Industry Classification System (NAICS).

For information on employment, see appendix entry for Table A-56.

For information on earnings, see appendix entry for Table A-41. For information on establishments, see appendix entry for Table A-14.

FDIC-insured financial institutions includes both FDIC-insured commercial banks and FDIC-insured savings institutions. Also includes insured U.S. branches of foreign banks. The category of FDIC-insured commercial banks includes all commercial banks insured by the Federal Deposit Insurance Corporation (FDIC) either through the Bank Insurance Fund (BIF) or through the Savings Association Insurance Fund (SAIF). These institutions are regulated by and submit financial data to one of the three federal commercial bank regulators. The category of FDIC-insured savings institutions includes all institutions insured by either the FDIC Savings Association Insurance Fund (SAIF) operating under state or federal banking codes applicable to thrift institutions. These institutions are regulated by and submit financial data to the Office of Thrift Supervision or the FDIC.

The term "offices" includes both main offices and branches. Banking office is defined to include all offices and facilities that actually hold deposits, and does not include loan production offices, computer centers, and other nondeposit installations, such as automated teller machines (ATMs). Several institutions have designated home offices that do not accept deposits; these have been included to provide a more complete listing of all offices. The figures for each geographical area only include deposits of offices located within that area.

A credit union is a not-for-profit financial institution owned and operated by its members. Each credit union serves the specific field of membership it decides upon. Credit union data are collected by the National Credit Union Administration (NCUA) using the Year-End Call Report.

Life insurance. The American Council of Life Insurers (ACLI) publishes life insurance data by tabulating NAIC statutory data. Annuity refers to a financial contract that offers tax-deferred savings and a choice of payout options to meet the owner's income needs in retirement: income for life, income for a certain period of time, or a lump sum.

Survey, Census, or Data Collection Method: Employment—Based on the Current Employment Statistics (CES) survey; for information, see Appendix B, Limitations

of the Data and Methodology, and www.bls.gov/opub/hom/homch2_a.htm . Earnings—Based on the Regional Economic Accounts; for information, see "State Personal Income Methodologies" at www.bea.gov/regional/methods.cfm . Establishments—Based on tabulations of data extracted from the U.S. Census Bureau's Business Register; www.census.gov/econ/cbp/methodology.htm . Credit unions—Credit unions provided the data for the Year-end Statistics for Federally Insured Credit Unions by completing the Year-End Call Report. For information, see www.ncua.gov/ . FDIC-Insured financial institutions number and assets—Based on Federal Financial Institution Examination Council (FFIEC) Call Reports and the Office of Thrift Supervision (OTS) Thrift Financial Reports; for information, see www2.fdic.gov/sdi/sob/disclaimer.asp . FDIC-insured financial institutions offices and deposits—Based on surveys of every FDIC-insured bank and savings association as of June 30 each year conducted by the Federal Deposit Insurance Corporation (FDIC) and the Office of Thrift Supervision (OTS); www2.fdic.gov/sod/sodPublications.asp?barItem=5 . Life insurance—Based on American Council of Life Insurers (ACLI) tabulations of National Association of Insurance Commissioners (NAIC) statutory data; for information, see http://www.acli.com .

Table A-68. Professional and Business Services and Education and Health Services

Sources: Employment—U.S. Bureau of Labor Statistics, Current Employment Statistics Program; www.bls.gov/sae/home.htm . Earnings—U.S. Bureau of Economic Analysis, Regional Economic Accounts, State Annual Personal Income and Employment; www.bea.gov/regional/index.htm . Establishments—U.S. Census Bureau, County Business Patterns, annual; www.census.gov/econ/cbp/index.html .

Professional and Business Services includes Professional, Scientific, and Technical Services; Management of Companies and Enterprises; and Administrative and Support and Waste Management and Remediation Services.

Education and Health Services includes Educational Services and Health Care and Social Assistance. Refer to General Notes to see information on the above industries defined using the North American Industry Classification System (NAICS).

For information on employment, see appendix entry for Table A-56. For information on earnings, see appendix entry for Table A-41. For information on establishments, see appendix entry for Table A-14.

Survey, Census, or Data Collection Method: Employment—Current Employment Statistics (CES) survey; www.bls.gov/opub/hom/homch2_a.htm . Earnings—Based on the Regional Economic Information System; for information, see "State Personal Income Methodologies" at www.bea.gov/regional/methods.cfm . Establishments—Based on tabulations of data extracted from the U.S. Census Bureau's Business Register; for information, see www.census.gov/econ/cbp/methodology.htm .

Table A-69. Leisure and Hospitality Services

Sources: Employment—U.S. Bureau of Labor Statistics; State and Metro Area Employment, Hours, & Earnings; SAE Databases: Employment, Hours, and Earnings-State and Metro Area; www.bls.gov/sae/home.htm/ or www.bls.gov/sae/eetables/sae_annavg112.pdf or http://data.bls.gov/cgi-bin/dsrv?sm . Earnings—U.S. Bureau of Economic Analysis, Regional Economic Accounts, State Annual Personal Income and Employment; www.bea.gov/regional/index.htm . Establishments—U.S. Census Bureau, County Business Patterns, annual; www.census.gov/econ/cbp/index.html .

Refer to General Notes to see information on Arts, Entertainment, and Recreation Services and Accommodation and Food Services industries defined using the North American Industry Classification System (NAICS). For information on employment, see appendix entry for Table A-56. For information on earnings, see appendix entry for Table A-41. For information on establishments, see appendix entry for Table A-14.

Survey, Census, or Data Collection Method: Employment—Current Employment Statistics (CES) Survey; www.bls.gov/opub/hom/homch2_a.htm . Earnings—Based on the Regional Economic Accounts, State Annual Personal Income and Employment; www.bea.gov/regional/methods.cfm . Establishments—Tabulations of data extracted from the U.S. Census Bureau's Business Register; www.census.gov/econ/cbp/methodology.htm .

Table A-70. Travel and Tourism Indicators

Sources: International visitors for pleasure by primary state of destination—U.S. Department of Homeland Security, Office of Immigration Statistics, *2012 Year Book of Immigration Statistics*, Nonimmigrant Admissions, www.dhs.gov/yearbook-immigration-statistics . National parks—U.S. National Park Service, *Statistical Abstract*, annual, and unpublished data, https://irma.nps.gov/App/ . State parks—The National Association of State Park Directors, Raleigh, NC, *Annual Information Exchange Report, 2011–2012*, and earlier years; http://naspd1.org/ .

International visitors for pleasure: The Yearbook of Immigration Statistics is a compendium of tables that provides data on foreign nationals who, during a fiscal year, were granted lawful permanent residence (for example, admitted as immigrants or became legal permanent residents), were admitted into the United States on a temporary basis (for example, tourists, students, or workers), applied for asylum or refugee status, or were naturalized. A nonimmigrant is defined by Section 101(a)(15) of the Immigration and Nationality Act (INA) as an alien who is not an immigrant and is admitted in one of the nonimmigrant alien classes of admission. Nonimmigrant admissions refer to number of events (that is, entries into the United States) rather than persons. As such, one nonimmigrant may enter the United States more than once, and each entry would count as a separate admission record.

Visitors to national parks. A visit is defined as the entry of any person, except National Park Service (NPS) personnel, onto lands or waters administered by the NPS. A visit may occur as a recreation visit or a nonrecreation visit.

A same-day reentry, negligible transit, and an entry to a detached portion of the same park on the same day are considered to be a single visit. Visits are reported separately for two contiguous parks.

Data on visitors to state parks are collected by the National Association of State Park Directors (NASPD), composed of 50 state park directors. In some states, park agency has under its control forests, fish, and wildlife areas, and/or other areas. In other states, park agency is responsible for state parks only. These data include overnight visitors.

Survey, Census, or Data Collection Method: International visits for pleasure by primary state of destination—Based on the Visitors Arrival Program (I-94 Form), www.tinet.ita.doc.gov/cat/f-2004-45-540.html ; National parks—Based on the National Park Service, U.S. Department of the Interior, Natural Resource Stewardship and Science, Integrated Resource Management Application (IRMA), https://irma.nps.gov/App/ ; State parks, http://naspd.indstate.edu/index.html .

Table A-71. Government

Sources: Employment—U.S. Bureau of Labor Statistics, Current Employment Statistics Program, (CES), "State and Metro Area Employment, Hours, and Earnings Database"; www.bls.gov/sae/data.htm or www.bls.gov/sae/eetables/sae_annavg112.pdf . Earnings—U.S. Bureau of Economic Analysis, Regional Economic Accounts, State Annual Personal Income and Employment; www.

bea.gov/regional/index.htm . Federal tax collections—Internal Revenue Service, Data Book, Publication 55B; www.irs.gov/uac/SOI-Tax-Stats-IRS-Data-Book ; State tax collections—U.S. Census Bureau, *Federal, State and Local Governments, Tax Collections, State Government Tax Collections*, annual; www.census.gov/govs/statetax/ .

For information on **earnings**, refer to appendix entry for Table A-41. Government employment covers only civilian workers. Government enterprises are government agencies that cover a substantial portion of their operating costs by selling goods and services to the public and that maintain separate accounts. For additional information regarding employment, refer to the notes and explanations for Table A-56.

Data on **federal tax collections** are provided by the Internal Revenue Service (IRS) through the Statistics of Income (SOI) program. This program pulls data electronically from the master file and augments the data with items captured from the hard copies of taxpayers' returns. The IRS processes about 200 million tax returns each year, and SOI uses approximately half a million of these for statistics. Classification by state is based on the individual's address (or, in the case of businesses, the location of the principal office or place of business). However, some individuals may use the address of a tax attorney or accountant. Sole proprietors, partners in a partnership, or shareholders in an "S" corporation may use their business addresses. Such addresses could have been located in a state other than the state in which the individual resided. Similarly, taxes withheld reported by employers located near a state boundary might include substantial amounts withheld from salaries of employees who reside in a neighboring state. Also, while taxes of corporations may be paid from the principal office, the operations of these corporations may be located in one or more other state(s).

State tax collections data are collected by the Census Bureau through an Annual Survey of State Government Tax Collection. These statistics are of all 50 state governments in the United States and are for state governments only. They should not be interpreted as state area data (state plus local government tax collections combined). The state government tax data presented by the Census Bureau may differ from data published by state governments because the Census Bureau may be using a different definition of which organizations are covered under the term "state government." For the purpose of State Government Tax Collections statistics, the term "state government" refers not only to the executive, legislative, and judicial branches of a given state, but it also includes

agencies, institutions, commissions, and public authorities that operate separately or somewhat autonomously from the central state government but where the state government maintains administrative or fiscal control over their activities as defined by the Census Bureau. The tax revenue data pertain to state fiscal years that end on June 30, in all but four states (Alabama and Michigan, September 30; New York, March 31; and Texas, August 31). Amounts shown for these four states reflect the different timing of their respective fiscal years.

Survey, Census, or Data Collection Method: Employment—Based on the Current Employment Statistics (CES) survey; for information, see Appendix B, Limitations of the Data and Methodology, and www.bls.gov/opub/hom/pdf/homch2.pdf . Earnings—Based on the Regional Economic Accounts; for information, see "State Personal Income Methodologies" at www.bea.gov/regional/methods.cfm . Federal tax collections—Based on the IRS's Statistics of Income (SOI) program; for information, see www.irs.gov/taxstats/index.html . State tax collections—Based on surveys to appropriate state government offices directly involved with state-administered taxes; for information, see www.census.gov/govs/statetax/ .

Table A-72. State Government Employment and Finances

Sources: Employment—U.S. Census Bureau, State Government Employment and Payroll Data; www.census.gov/govs/apes/index.html . Finances—U.S. Census Bureau, "State Government Finances"; www.census.gov/govs/state/ .

The Census Bureau collects data on **state government employment** by conducting an Annual Survey of Government Employment. Alternatively, every 5 years, in years ending in a "2" or "7," a Census of Governments, including an employment portion, is conducted. For both the census and the annual surveys, the employment detail is equivalent.

Employment refers to all persons gainfully employed by and performing services for a government.

Employees include all persons paid for personal services performed, including persons paid from federally funded programs, paid elected or appointed officials, persons in a paid leave status, and persons paid on a per-meeting, annual, semi-annual, or quarterly basis. Unpaid officials, pensioners, persons whose work is performed on a fee basis, and contractors and their employees are excluded from the count of employees.

Full-time equivalent employment refers to a computed statistic representing the number of full-time employees who could have been employed if the reported number of hours worked by part-time employees had been worked by full-time employees. This statistic is calculated separately for each function of a government by dividing the "part-time hours paid" by the standard number of hours for full-time employees in the particular government and then adding the resulting quotient to the number of full-time employees.

Finance data are collected by the Census Bureau through the Annual Survey of Government Finances, which covers all state and local governments in the United States. The survey content includes the entire range of government finance activities: revenue, expenditure, debt, and assets.

Revenue includes all amounts of money received by a government from external sources during its fiscal year net of refunds and other correcting transactions, other than issuance of debt, sale of investments, and agency or private trust transactions. Revenue excludes amounts transferred from other funds or agencies of the same government. Revenue comprises amounts received by all agencies, boards, commissions, or other organizations categorized as dependent on the government concerned. Stated in terms of the accounting procedures from which these data originate, revenue covers receipts from all accounting funds of a government, other than intragovernmental service (revolving), agency, and private trust funds.

General revenue comprises all revenue except that classified as liquor store, utility, or insurance trust revenue. Generally, the basis for this distinction is not the fund or administrative unit established to account for and control a particular activity, but rather the nature of the revenue source involved. Within general revenue are four main categories: taxes, intergovernmental revenue, current charges, and miscellaneous general revenue.

Intergovernmental revenue comprises monies from other governments, including grants, shared taxes, and contingent loans and advances for support of particular functions or for general financial support; any significant and identifiable amounts received as reimbursement for performance of governmental services for other governments; and any other form of revenue representing the sharing by other governments in the financing of activities administered by the receiving government. All intergovernmental revenue is reported in the general government sector, even if it is used to support activities in other sectors (such as utilities). Intergovernmental revenue excludes amounts received from the sale of property,

commodities, and utility services to other governments (which are reported in different revenue categories). It also excludes amounts received from other governments as the employer share or for support of public employee retirement or other insurance trust funds of the recipient government, which are treated as insurance trust revenue.

Taxes are compulsory contributions exacted by a government for public purposes, other than for employee and employer assessments and contributions to finance retirement and social insurance trust systems and for special assessments to pay capital improvements. Tax revenue comprises gross amounts collected (including interest and penalties) minus amounts paid under protest and amounts refunded during the same period. It consists of all taxes imposed by a government whether the government collects the taxes itself or relies on another government to act as its collection agent.

Expenditure includes all amounts of money paid out by a government during its fiscal year—net of recoveries and other correcting transactions—other than for retirement of debt, purchase of investment securities, extension of loans, and agency or private trust transactions. Under this definition, expenditure relates to external payments of a government and excludes amounts transferred to funds or agencies of the same government (other than payments to intragovernmental service funds).

Expenditure includes payments from all sources of funds, including not only current revenues but also proceeds from borrowing and prior year fund balances. Note, however, that the Census Bureau's finance statistics do not relate expenditure to their source of funding. Expenditure includes amounts spent by all agencies, boards, commissions, or other organizations categorized as dependent on the government concerned.

General expenditure comprises all expenditure except that classified as liquor store, utility, or insurance trust expenditure. As noted above, it includes all such payments regardless of the source of revenue from which they were financed. General government expenditures are classified by function and character and object.

Intergovernmental expenditure is defined as amounts paid to other governments for performance of specific functions or for general financial support. Includes grants, shared taxes, contingent loans and advances, and any significant and identifiable amounts or reimbursement paid to other governments for performance of general government services or activities. By definition, it excludes amounts paid to other governments for purchase of commodities, property, or utility services and for any tax levied as such on facilities of the government.

Direct expenditure comprises all final expenditures paid to current employees, former employees (retirees) and to private sector entities outside of the government itself (e.g., all expenditure other than intergovernmental expenditure).

Education expenditures cover the operation, maintenance, and construction of public schools and facilities for elementary and secondary education (kindergarten through high school), vocational-technical education, and other educational institutions except those for higher education. Covers operations by independent governments (school districts) as well as those operated as integral agencies of state, county, municipal, or township governments. Also covers financial support of public elementary and secondary schools.

Public welfare expenditures are those cash payments made directly to individuals contingent upon their need, other than those under federal categorical assistance programs.

Highway expenditures include maintenance, operation, repair, and construction of highways, streets, roads, alleys, sidewalks, bridges, tunnels, ferry boats, viaducts, and related nontoll structures.

For more information, see the Governments Finance and Employment Classification Manual at www.census.gov/govs/classification/index.html .

Survey, Census, or Data Collection Method: Employment—Based on the Annual Survey of Government Employment; www.census.gov/govs/www/apestechdoc.html .Finances—Annual Survey of Government Finances; www.census.gov/govs/state/ .

Table A-73. State Government Tax Collections: 2012 and Federal Aid to State and Local Governments

Sources: Tax collections—U.S. Census Bureau, "State Government Tax Collections"; www.census.gov/govs/statetax/ . Federal aid—U.S. Census Bureau, Federal Aid to States for Fiscal Year 2010, and previous editions; www.census.gov/prod/www/governments.html and www .census.gov/govs/www/taxgen.html .

Data on **state government tax collections** are collected by the Census Bureau by conducting an Annual Survey of

State Government Tax Collection. The data are on the fiscal year tax collections of all 50 state governments in the United States and are for state governments only. They should not be interpreted as state area data (state plus local government tax collections combined). See appendix entry for Table A-71 for more information.

Property taxes include three types, all having in common the use of value as a basis for the tax. General property taxes, relating to property as a whole, taxed at a single rate or at classified rates according to the class of property. Property refers to real property (for example, land and structures) as well as personal property; personal property can be either tangible (for example, automobiles and boats) or intangible (for example, bank accounts and stocks and bonds). Special property taxes, levied on selected types of property (for example, oil and gas properties, house trailers, motor vehicles, and intangibles) and subject to rates not directly related to general property tax rates. Taxes based on income produced by property as a measure of its value on the assessment date. For more information on Taxes, see appendix entry for Table A-71 and A-72.

Sales and gross receipts taxes are taxes on goods and services, measured on the basis of the volume or value of their transfer, upon gross receipts or gross income there from, or as an amount per unit sold; and related taxes based upon use, storage, production, importation, or consumption of goods and service.

General sales and gross receipts taxes are applicable with only specified exceptions to sales of all types of goods and services or to all gross receipts, whether at a single rate or at classified rates, and sales use taxes.

Individual income tax includes tax on individuals measured by net income and tax on special types of income (for example, interest, dividends, income from intangible property).

Corporation net income tax includes taxes on corporations and unincorporated businesses, measured by net income, whether on corporations in general or on specific kinds of corporations, such as financial institutions.

For more information, see the Governments Finance and Employment Classification Manual at www.census.gov/govs/classification/index.html .

Federal aid to state and local governments. All amounts of federal government grants and other payments to state and local governments represent actual cash outlays made during the fiscal year. Federal government executive department and agency provides annual data on grants and other payments to governmental units. The data are collected from federal agencies by the Census Bureau.

Data on federal aid include the following: direct cash grants to state and local government units, payments for grants-in-kind, such as purchases of commodities distributed to state or local government institutions (for example, school programs); payments to nongovernment entities when such payments result in cash or in-kind services passed on to state and local governments; payments to regional commissions and organizations that are redistributed to the state or local level; federal government payments to state or local governments for research and development that is an integral part of the provision of public services; and shared revenues.

Survey, Census, or Data Collection Method: Tax collections—Based on the Annual Survey of State Government Tax Collection; www2.census.gov/govs/statetax/statetax techdoc2012.pdf ; Federal aid—Based on a survey of federal government departments and agencies; www.census .gov/prod/www/abs/fas.html .

Table A-74. State Resources, Expenditures, and Balances

Sources: National Association of State Budget Officers, Washington, DC, *2012 State Expenditure Report, Fiscal 2010–2012 Data*, and *Fiscal Survey of the States, Fall 2012* (copyright).

The general fund is the predominant fund for financing a state's operations and represents the primary component of discretionary expenditures of revenue derived from general sources, which have not been earmarked for specific items. Components of state spending within the general fund include elementary and secondary education, Medicaid, higher education, corrections, transportation, and public assistance, among other expenditures.

State general funds support most ongoing broad-based state services, as opposed to long-term state capital projects, and are available for appropriation to support any governmental activity.

These funds exclude special funds earmarked for particular purposes, such as highway trust funds, which are supported by fuel taxes and motor license fees.

Federal funds are funds received directly from the federal government. For more information on federal funds, see appendix entry for Table A-75.

Resources include funds budgeted, adjustments, and balances from the previous year. Expenditures may or may not include budget stabilization fund transfers, depending on state accounting practices. Refer to the source for more detail.

Survey, Census, or Data Collection Method: Based on surveys completed by Governors' state budget offices in the 50 states; www.nasbo.org/ .

Table A-75. Federal Government

Sources: Employment—U.S. Bureau of Labor Statistics, Current Employment Statistics Program, SAE Databases, Employment, Hours, and Earnings: State and Metro Area; www.bls.gov/sae/home.htm . Earnings—U.S. Bureau of Economic Analysis, Regional Economic Accounts, State Annual Personal Income and Employment; www.bea.gov/regional/index.htm ; Federal funds and grants—U.S. Census Bureau, *Consolidated Federal Funds Report*, annual, terminated after release of 2010 data; www.census.gov/govs/cffr/ .

Federal employment. In general, employment data refer to persons who worked during, or received pay for, any part of the pay period that includes the 12th of the month, which is standard for all federal agencies collecting employment data from business establishments.

National employment figures for federal government establishments, however, represent the number of persons who were paid for the last full pay period of the calendar month; intermittent federal government workers are counted if they performed any service during the month. For more information regarding employment, see appendix entry for Table A-56.

Congressional staff and the U.S. Postal Service are included in federal earnings. For more information regarding earnings, see appendix entry for Table A-41.

Total **federal funds and grants** includes federal government expenditures for grants to state and local governments, salaries and wages, procurement, direct payment for individuals, and other programs for which data are available by state. Data for these items come from a variety of sources within the federal government and represent actual expenditures of the federal government during the fiscal year.

Defense Department data are computed from Defense Department grants to state and local governments, salaries and wages, retired military pay, procurement, and research grants. Per capita for defense is based on resident population estimated as of July 1.

Direct payment for individuals data are compiled from amounts reported by the federal agencies for the Federal Assistance Award Data System (FAADS). The FAADS is a quarterly report of financial assistance awards made by each federal agency. Coverage includes grants, direct payments to individuals and others, insurance, and loans.

All amounts of federal government grants to state and local governments represent actual cash outlays made during the fiscal year. This includes direct cash grants to state and local government units; payments for grants-in-kind, such as purchases of commodities distributed to state and local government institutions; payments to non-government entities when such payments result in cash or in-kind services passed on to state or local governments; payments to regional commissions and organizations that are redistributed to the state or local level; federal government payments to state and local governments for research and development that is an integral part of the provision of public service; and federal revenues shared with state and local governments. Direct payments include, but is not limited to, social security payments, federal retirement and disability benefits, veteran benefits, Medicare benefits, excess earned income tax credits, unemployment compensation, food stamp payments, housing assistance, agricultural assistance, and federal employees life and health insurance. For a complete listing of federal government expenditures for direct payments consult the source.

Survey, Census, or Data Collection Method: Employment—Based on the Current Employment Statistics (CES) survey; for information, see Appendix B, Limitations of the Data and Methodology, and Internet site www.bls.gov/opub/hom/homch2_a.htm . Earnings—Based on the Regional Economic Accounts; www.bea.gov/regional/methods.cfm . Federal funds and grants—Based on information systems in various federal government agencies; www.census.gov/econ/overview/go1300.html .

Table A-76. Federal Individual Income Tax Returns

Sources: Tax returns—U.S. Internal Revenue Service, *Statistics of Income Bulletin*, quarterly; www.irs.gov/taxstats/index.html . Property and land—U.S. General Services Administration, Federal Real Property Profile, annual; www.gsa.gov/graphics/ogp/FY_2010_FRPP_Report_Final.pdf .

For information on federal individual income tax returns, see appendix entry for Table A-71 or consult the source.

Data on **federally owned property and federal lands** are collected through the General Services Administration's

(GSA's) Federal Real Property Profile (FRPP) reporting system. Contributing agencies provide data annually based on their real property holdings as of September 30. Land acreage is divided into urban and rural categories. Leased land is usually not reported if it is included with a building lease.

Buildings are roofed and walled structures built for permanent use. Buildings owned by the government, whether or not located on government-owned land, are included in the data. Buildings under construction are included only if they were available for use as of September 30 of the year shown.

Survey, Census, or Data Collection Method: Tax returns—Based on the IRS's Statistics of Income (SOI) program; for information; www.irs.gov/taxstats/index.html ; Property and land—Based on annual agency reports; www.gsa.gov/ .

Table A-77. Social Security, Supplemental Nutrition Assistance Programs, and School Lunch Programs

Sources: Social Security—U.S. Social Security Administration, *Annual Statistical Supplement of the Social Security Bulletin*; www.ssa.gov/policy/docs/statcomps/oasdi_sc/2011/index.html and www.ssa.gov/policy/data_type.html . Federal food stamp and national school lunch programs—U.S. Department of Agriculture, Food and Nutrition Service, Supplemental Nutrition Assistance Program, Annual State Level Data; www.fns.usda.gov/fns/data.htm .

Social security. The Old-Age, Survivors, and Disability Insurance Program (OASDI) provides monthly benefits for retired and disabled insured workers and their dependents and to survivors of insured workers. To be eligible for benefits, a worker must have had a specified period of employment in which OASDI taxes were paid. The data were derived from the Master Beneficiary Record (MBR), the principal administrative file of social security beneficiaries. Data for total recipients and retired workers include persons with special age-72 benefits. Special age-72 benefit represents the monthly benefit payable to men who attained age 72 before 1972 and for women who attained age 72 before 1970 and who do not have sufficient quarters to qualify for a retired-worker benefit under either the fully or the transitionally insured status provision.

As of October 1, 2008, **Supplemental Nutrition Assistance Program** (SNAP) is the new name for the federal Food Stamp Program. SNAP is the federal name for the program. State programs may have different names. SNAP provides low-income households with electronic benefits that can be used at most grocery stores. The U.S. Department of Agriculture administers SNAP at the federal level through its Food and Nutrition Service (FNS). State agencies administer the program at state and local levels, including determination of eligibility and allotments, and distribution of benefits.

The average monthly benefit was about $133 per person and about $278 per household in Fiscal Year (FY) 2012. Consult source for more information on program.

The **National School Lunch Program** covers public and private elementary and secondary schools and residential child care institutions. Costs include federal cash reimbursements at rates set by law for each meal served and commodity costs. The Food and Nutrition Service administers the program at the federal level. At the state level, the National School Lunch Program is usually administered by state education agencies, which operate the program through agreements with school food authorities. Consult source for more information on program.

Survey, Census, or Data Collection Method: Social security—Based on a 10 percent sample of administrative records; www.ssa.gov/policy/ . Federal food stamp and national school lunch programs—Based on administrative records; www.fns.usda.gov/pd/ .

Table A-78. Social Insurance Programs and Workers' Compensation

Sources: SSI—U.S. Social Security Administration, *Annual Statistical Supplement to the Social Security Bulletin*; www.ssa.gov/policy/docs/statcomps/ . TANF—U.S. Administration for Children and Families, Temporary Assistance for Needy Families (TANF) Program, TANF Caseload data and Financial Data; www.acf.hhs.gov/programs/ofa/programs/tanf/data-reports . State unemployment insurance—U.S. Employment and Training Administration, *Unemployment Insurance Financial Data Handbook*, annual; www.ows.doleta.gov/unemploy/hb394.asp . Workers' compensation—National Academy of Social Insurance, Washington, DC, *Workers' Compensation: Benefits, Coverage, and Costs*, annual; www.nasi.org/publications2763/publications.htm .

The **Supplemental Security Income** (SSI) program provides cash payments in accordance with nationwide eligibility requirements to people with limited income and resources who are aged, blind, or disabled. An aged person is defined as an individual who is 65 years old or over. A blind person is anyone with vision of 20/200 or less with the use of correcting lens in the better eye or with tunnel vision of 20 degrees or less. The disabled classification refers to any person unable to engage in any substantial gainful activity by reason of any medically determinable physical or mental impairment expected to result in death or that has lasted or can be expected to last for a continuous period of at least 12 months. For a child under 18 years, eligibility is based on disability or severity comparable with that of an adult, since the criterion of substantial gainful activity" is inapplicable for children.

The **Temporary Assistance for Needy Families** (TANF) program is a time-limited program that assists families with children when the parents or other responsible relatives cannot provide for the family's basic needs. The federal government provides grants to states to run the TANF program so that the states decide on the design of the program, the type and amount of assistance payments, the range of other services to be provided, and the rules for determining who is eligible for benefits. Prior to TANF, the cash assistance program to families was called Aid to Families with Dependent Children (1980–1996). Under the new welfare law (Personal Responsibility Reconciliation Act of 1996), the program became TANF.

Unemployment insurance is presently administered by the U.S. Employment and Training Administration and each state's employment security agency. The program provides unemployment benefits to eligible workers who are unemployed through no fault of their own (as determined under state law) and meet other eligibility requirements of state law. Unemployment insurance payments (benefits) are intended to provide temporary assistance to unemployed workers who meet the requirements of state law. Each state administers a separate unemployment insurance program within guidelines established by federal law. Eligibility for unemployment insurance, benefit amounts, and the length of time benefits are available are determined by the state law under which unemployment insurance claims are established. In the majority of states, benefit funding is based solely on a tax imposed on employers.

Workers' compensation provides protection to workers disabled from work-related injury or illness. The program includes protection under the laws of 50 states, the District of Columbia, and two federal programs (the Federal Employees compensation Act and the Longshoremen's and Harbor Workers' Compensation Act). Payments represent compensation and medical benefits and include insurance losses paid by private insurance carriers, disbursements of state funds, and self-insurance payments.

Survey, Census, or Data Collection Method: SSI—Based on Social Security Administration administrative records; www.ssa.gov/policy/docs/statcomps/ssi_asr/index.html   .

TANF—For information, see www.acf.hhs.gov/programs/ofa/programs/tanf . State unemployment insurance—For information, see www.doleta.gov/ . Workers' compensation—For information, see www.nasi.org/ .

Table A-79. Government Transfer Payments to Individuals

Source: U.S. Bureau of Economic Analysis, "Regional Accounts Data, Annual State Personal Income"; www.bea.gov/regional/index.htm .

Personal current transfer receipts are personal income that are payments to persons for which no current services are performed. It consists of payments to individuals and to nonprofit institutions by federal, state, and local governments and by businesses. Government transfer payments to individuals consist of: retirement and disability insurance benefits, medical benefits, income maintenance benefits, unemployment insurance compensation, veteran's benefits, federal education and training assistance, and other transfer receipts of individuals from governments.

Retirement and disability insurance benefits consist of Old-Age, Survivors, and Disability (OASDI) benefits; railroad retirement and disability benefits; federal and state workers' compensation; temporary disability benefits; Black Lung benefits; and Pension Benefit Guaranty benefits.

Medical payments include medical benefits, public assistance medical care, and military medical insurance benefits. Medicare benefits are federal government payments made through intermediaries to beneficiaries for the care provided to individuals under the Medicare program. Public assistance medical care benefits are received by low-income individuals. These payments consist mainly of the payments made through intermediaries to the vendors for care provided to individuals under the federally assisted, state-administered Medicaid program and State Children's Health Insurance Program (SCHIP) and under the general assistance medical programs of state and local governments.

Military medical insurance benefits are vendor payments made under the TriCare Management Program, formerly called the Civilian Health and Medical Plan of the Uniformed Services program, for the medical care of dependents of active duty military personnel and of retired military personnel and their dependents at nonmilitary medical facilities.

Income maintenance benefits consist largely of supplemental security income payments, family assistance, food stamp payments, and other assistance payments, including general assistance.

Unemployment insurance benefits are made up of state unemployment compensation; unemployment compensation of federal civilian employees, railroad employees, and veterans; and trade adjustment allowances. State unemployment compensation are benefits consisting mainly of the payments received by individuals under state-administered unemployment insurance (UI) programs, but they include the special benefits authorized by federal legislation for periods of high unemployment. The provisions that govern the eligibility, timing, and amount of benefit payments vary among the states, but the provisions that govern the coverage and financing are uniform nationally. Unemployment compensation of federal civilian employees are benefits received by former federal employees under a federal program administered by the state employment security agencies. Unemployment compensation of railroad employees are benefits received by railroad workers who are unemployed because of sickness or because work is unavailable in the railroad industry and in related industries, such as carrier affiliates. This UI program is administered by the Railroad Retirement Board (RRB) under a federal program that is applicable throughout the nation. Unemployment compensation of veterans are benefits that are received by unemployed veterans who have recently separated from military service and who are not eligible for military retirement benefits. The compensation is paid under a federal program that is administered by the state employment security agencies. Trade adjustment allowances are the payments received by workers who are unemployed because of the adverse economic effects of international trade arrangements.

Veterans' benefits include veterans' pension and disability benefits, veterans' readjustment benefits, veterans' life insurance benefits, and other assistance to veterans (federal government payments received by paraplegics and by certain other disabled veterans to purchase automobiles and other conveyances, state and local government payments of assistance to indigent veterans, and the state and local government payments of bonuses to veterans).

Federal education and training assistance consists of federal fellowships, higher education student assistance, Job Corps payments, and interest payments on guaranteed student loans. Federal fellowships consist of the payments to outstanding science students who receive National Science Foundation (NSF) grants, the subsistence payments to the cadets at the six state maritime academies, and the payments for all other federal fellowships. Higher education student assistance consists of the federal payments, called Pell Grants, for an undergraduate education for students with low incomes. Job Corps payments are primarily the allowances for living expenses received by economically disadvantaged individuals who are between the ages of 16 and 21 and who are enrolled in the designated vocational and educational training programs. These benefits also include the adjustment allowances received by trainees upon the successful completion of their training. Interest payments on guaranteed student loans are made by the Department of Education to commercial lending institutions on behalf of the individuals who receive low-interest, deferred-payment loans from these institutions in order to pay the expenses of higher education.

Other transfer receipts of individuals from governments consist largely of Bureau of Indian Affairs payments, education exchange payments, Alaska Permanent Fund dividend payments, compensation of survivors of public safety officers, compensation of victims of crime, disaster relief payments, compensation for Japanese internment, and other special payments to individuals.

Survey, Census, or Data Collection Method: Based on the Regional Economic Accounts. For more information, see "State Personal Income and Employment Methodologies" at www.bea.gov/regional/pdf/spi2011.pdf/ .

Table A-80. Medicare, Medicaid, and Children's Health Insurance Program

Sources: Medicare enrollment—U.S. Centers for Medicare and Medicaid Services, Data Compendium, www.cms.gov/Research-Statistics-Data-and-Systems/Statistics-Trends-and-Reports/DataCompendium/2011_Data_Compendium.html . Medicaid—U.S. Centers for Medicare and Medicaid Services, Medicaid Eligibles, Beneficiaries, and Payments, Fiscal Year 2009; www.cms.gov/Research-Statistics-Data-and-Systems/Computer-Data-and-Systems/MedicaidDataSourcesGenInfo/MSIS-Tables-Items/CMS1254726.html . CHIP—U.S. Centers for Medicare and Medicaid Services, Children's Health Insurance Program, CHIP Enrollment by State, www.medicaid.gov/medicaid-chip-program-information/by-topics/childrens-health-insurance-program-chip/childrens-health-insurance-program-chip.html .

Medicare. Since July 1966, the federal Medicare program has provided two coordinated plans for nearly all people age 65 and over: (1) a hospital insurance plan, which covers hospital and related services and (2) a voluntary supplementary medical insurance plan, financed partially by monthly premiums paid by participants, which partly covers physicians' and related medical services. Since July 1973, such insurance also applies to disabled beneficiaries

of any age after 24 months of entitlement to cash benefits under the social security or railroad retirement programs and to persons with end-stage renal disease.

Medicaid is a health insurance program for certain low-income people. These include: certain low-income families with children; aged, blind, or disabled people on supplemental security income; certain low-income pregnant women and children; and people who have very high medical bills. Medicaid is funded and administered through a state-federal partnership. Although there are broad federal requirements for Medicaid, states have a wide degree of flexibility to design their program. States have authority to establish eligibility standards, determine what benefits and services to cover, and set payment rates. All states, however, must cover these basic services: inpatient and outpatient hospital services; doctors' services, family planning, and periodic health checkups; and diagnosis and treatment for children.

Center for Medicare and Medicaid Service (CMS) administers the Children's Health Insurance Program (CHIP). Children began receiving insurance through CHIP in 1997 and the program helped states expand health care coverage to more than 5 million of the nation's uninsured children. The program was reauthorized on February 4, 2009, when the president signed into law the Children's Health Insurance Program Reauthorization Act of 2009 (CHIPRA or Public Law 111-3). CHIPRA finances the Children's Health Insurance Program (CHIP) through Fiscal Year (FY) 2013.

The Children's Health Insurance Program is jointly financed by the federal and state governments and is administered by the states. Within broad federal guidelines, each state determines the design of its program, eligibility groups, benefit packages, payment levels for coverage, and administrative and operating procedures. CHIP provides a capped amount of funds to states on a matching basis.

Federal payments under Title XXI to states are based on state expenditures under approved plans effective on or after October 1, 1997.

Survey, Census, or Data Collection Method: Medicare—For information, see www.cms.gov/Research-Statistics-Data-and-Systems/Research-Statistics-Data-and-Systems.html . Medicaid—Based on the Medicaid Statistical Information System (MSIS) and CMS-64 reports; see www.cms.hhs.gov/MedicaidDataSourcesGenInfo/02_MSISData.asp . CHIP—Based on the CHIP Statistical Enrollment Data System (SEDS); for information, see www.cms.hhs.gov/NationalCHIPPolicy/ .

Table A-81. Department of Defense and Veterans

Sources: Department of Defense—U.S. Department of Defense, DoD Personnel and Procurement Statistics, Personnel, Publications, Atlas/Data Abstract for the United States and Selected Areas, annual; http://siadapp .dmdc.osd.mil/ . Veterans—U.S. Department of Veterans Affairs, National Center for Veterans Analysis and Statistics; www.va.gov/vetdata/Veteran_Population.asp .

The **Department of Defense** (DoD) is responsible for providing the military forces of the United States. It includes the Office of the Secretary of Defense, the Joint Chiefs of Staff, the Army, the Navy, the Air Force, and the defense agencies. The President serves as Commander in Chief of the armed forces; from him, the authority flows to the Secretary of Defense and through the Joint Chiefs of Staff to the commanders of unified and specified commands (for example, U.S. Strategic Command).

DoD personnel data include active duty military, civilian, and Reserve and National Guard. Expenditures include payroll outlays, contracts, and grants. Payroll outlays consist of active duty military pay, civilian pay, Reserve and National Guard pay, and retired military pay. Contracts include supply and equipment contracts, Research, Development, Test, and Evaluation (RDT&E) contracts, service contracts, construction contracts, and civil function contracts. Consult the source for more information.

Veterans. The Office of Policy in the Department of Veterans Affairs (VA) is responsible for administering a range of programs and analyses concerning veteran surveys, demographics, and population estimates. Within the Office of Policy, the Office of the actuary (OACT) develops estimates and projections of the veteran population and their characteristics.

The Department of Veterans Affairs (VA) provides official estimates and projections of the veteran population using the Veteran Population Model (VetPop). The model is updated periodically for improved methodology, more recent data, and changing needs. For each year from April 1, 2000, to September 30, 2036, VetPop generates the number of veterans by selected characteristics: at the state and/or national levels—by age, gender, period of service, race/ethnicity, rank (Officer/Enlisted), and branch of service; at the county level—by age and gender. Veteran's data is derived from a combination of Census 2000, Defense Manpower Data Center (DMDC) losses, and GORGO, the projection model used by Department of Defense's Office of the Actuary.

A veteran is someone 18 years and older (there are a few 17-year-old veterans) who is not currently on active duty, but who once served on active duty in the U.S. Army, Navy, Air Force, Marine Corps, or Coast Guard, or who served in the Merchant Marine during World War II.

There are many groups whose active service makes them veterans including: those who incurred a service-connected disability during active duty for training in the Reserves or National Guard, even though that service would not otherwise have counted for veteran status; members of a national guard or reserve component who have been ordered to active duty by order of the president or who have a full-time military job. The latter are called AGRs (Active Guard and Reserve). No one who has received a dishonorable discharge is a veteran.

Survey, Census, or Data Collection Method: Department of Defense—For information, see http://siadapp.dmdc .osd.mil/ .Veterans—Based on the U.S. Department of Veterans Affairs administrative data; for information, see www.va.gov/vetdata/Veteran_Population.asp .

Table A-82. Elections

Sources: Voting-age population—U.S. Census Bureau, "Estimates of the Total Resident Population and Resident Population Age 18 Years and Older for the United States, States, and Puerto Rico: July 1, 2012," SCPRC-EST2012-18 +POP-RES; www.census.gov/popest/data/state/asrh/2012/ files/SCPRC-EST2012-18+POP-res.pdf . "Estimates of the Resident Population by Selected Age Groups for the United States, States, and Puerto Rico: July 1, 2008," SC-EST2008-01; www.census.gov/popest/data/state/asrh/2008/ tables/SC-EST2008-01.csv . Percent of voting-age population voting for president, electoral votes, votes for President and votes for senators—U.S. Congress, Clerk of the House, Statistics of the Presidential and Congressional Election, biennial; http://history.house.gov/Institution/ Election-Statistics/Election-Statistics/ .

The **voting-age population** relates to people 18 years old and over in all states and the District of Columbia. Data include armed forces stationed in each state, aliens, and the institutionalized population.

Votes cast for president. The Constitution specifies how the president and vice president are selected. Each state elects, by popular vote, a group of electors equal in number to its total of members of the Congress. The 23rd Amendment, adopted in 1961, grants the District of Columbia three presidential electors, a number equal to that of the least populous state. A majority vote of all electors is necessary to elect the president and vice president. If no candidate receives a majority, the House of Representatives, with each state having one vote, is empowered to elect the president and vice president, again, with a majority of votes required.

Votes cast for U.S. senators. The U.S. Senate is composed of 100 members, two from each state, who are elected to serve for a term of 6 years. One-third of the Senate is elected every 2 years. Senators were originally chosen by the state legislatures. The 17th Amendment to the Constitution, adopted in 1913, prescribed that senators be elected by popular vote.

Survey, Census, or Data Collection Method: Voting-age population—Based on the Census of Population and Housing; for information, see Appendix B, Limitations of the Data and Methodology, and www.census.gov/popest/topics/methodology/2004_st_char_meth.html ; Percent of voting-age population voting for president and popular votes—See http://history.house.gov/Institution/Election-Statistics/Election-Statistics/ .

Table A-83. Composition of the Congress and Public Officials

Sources: Votes—U.S. House of Representatives, Office of the Clerk, Statistics of the Presidential and Congressional Election of November 6, 2012; http://clerk.house.gov/member_info/electionInfo/2012election.pdf . Composition of the Congress—Office of the Clerk, Official List of Members by State, www.memberguide.gpoaccess.gov/ . Blacks—Joint Center for Political and Economic Studies, Washington, DC, Black Elected Officials: A Statistical Summary, 2002 and 2012 (copyright). See http://jointcenter.org/ . Hispanics—National Association of Latino Elected and Appointed Officials (NALEO) Educational Fund, Los Angeles, CA. National Directory of Latino Elected Officials, formerly published as the National Roster of Hispanic Elected Officials (copyright); www.naleo.org/ . Women—Center for American Women and Politics, Eagleton Institute of Politics, Rutgers University, New Brunswick, NJ, information releases (copyright); www.cawp.rutgers.edu/ .

In each state, totals for votes cast for representatives represent the sum of votes cast in each congressional district or votes cast for representatives-at-large in states where only one member is elected. In all years, there are numerous districts within the state where either the Republican or Democratic party had no candidate. In some states, the Republican and Democratic vote includes votes cast for the party candidate by endorsing parties. Refer to the notes and explanations for Table A-82 for information on senators.

Black elected officials. As of January 2001, no Black elected officials had been identified in Hawaii, Montana, North Dakota, or South Dakota. The total includes U.S. and state legislatures and elected state administrators, city and county offices, law enforcement, and education officials not shown separately.

Hispanic public officials data include U.S. representatives, state executives and legislators, county and municipal officials, judicial and law enforcement officials, and education and school boards.

Data for **women holding state public offices** cover women in statewide elective executive offices and state legislatures, county commissions, mayoralties, townships, and local councils.

Survey, Census, or Data Collection Method: For information on methodology, consult the following sources: Votes, http://clerk.house.gov/member_info/election.aspx; Composition of the Congress, clerk.house.gov/member_info/index.aspx ; Black officials, http://jointcenter.org/DB/ ; Hispanic officials, www.naleo.org/ ; Women holding offices, www.cawp.rutgers.edu/ .

Table A-84. Composition of Governors and State Legislatures

Source: The Council of State Governments, Lexington, KY, *The Book of the States 2012* (copyright); http://knowledgecenter.csg.org/drupal/view-content-type/1502 .

Data for **votes cast for governor** represent total votes cast, including scattered votes. The percentage of votes cast for the leading party represents the percentage of the total votes cast for the party with a majority or plurality.

Data shown for **composition of state legislatures** reflect election results in year shown for most states and to odd-year elections the previous years in a few states. The figures reflect the immediate results of elections, including holdover members in state houses that do not have all of their members running for reelection. Lower house refers to the body consisting of state representatives. Upper house refers to the body consisting of U.S. state senators.

Survey, Census, or Data Collection Method: Votes for governor—For information, see www.cqpress.com/gethome.asp .

PART B—METROPOLITAN AREAS

Table B consists of 14 tables (B-1 through B-14) with 159 data items for 366 metropolitan statistical areas (MSAs), including 11 metropolitan statistical areas with metropolitan divisions and 29 metropolitan divisions. They are presented alphabetically in each of the 14 tables.

All summaries, including historical data, are presented for the areas as currently defined. Where possible, the original figures have been retabulated to reflect the status of metropolitan area boundaries as of December 1, 2009. For more information on these areas, see Appendix C, Geographic Concepts and Codes.

Table B-1. Area and Population

Sources: Area—U.S. Census Bureau, 2010 Census Summary File 1, Geographic Identifiers, Table G001; see http://factfinder2.census.gov/ ; Population—U.S. Census Bureau, Historical Estimates Data for 1990 and 2000; see www.census.gov/popest/data/historical/index.html; Current Estimates Data for 2010 and 2011; see www.census .gov/popest/data/historical/2010s/vintage_2011/metro .html.

Total area. Area measurement data provide the size, in square units, of geographic entities for which the Census Bureau tabulates and disseminates data. Area is calculated from the specific boundary recorded for each entity (in this case, states and counties) in the Census Bureau's geographic database.

Area measurements may disagree with the information displayed on the Census Bureau maps and in the MAF .TIGER® database because, for area measurement purposes, features identified as "intermittent water" and "glacier" are reported as land area. The accuracy of any area measurement data is limited by the accuracy inherent in (1) the location and shape of the various boundary information in the database, (2) the location and shapes of the shorelines of water bodies in that database, and (3) rounding affecting the last digit in all operations that compute and/or sum the area measurements. Identification of land and inland, coastal, and territorial is for statistical purposes and does not necessarily reflect legal definitions thereof.

Population numbers for 2010, 2000, and 1990 are counts of the resident population on April 1 of those decennial census years. The April 1 estimates base population may differ from the April 1 census count due to legal boundary updates, other geographic program changes, and Count Question Resolution actions.

Population estimates for 2011 measure the estimated population from the calculated number of people living in an area as of July 1. The Census Bureau develops county population estimates with a component of population

change method in which they use administrative records and other data to estimate the household and group quarters population. For the household population, the components of population change are births, deaths, net domestic migration, and net international migration. They measure change in the nonhousehold, or group quarters, population by the net change in the population living in group quarters facilities.

A major assumption underlying this approach is that changes in selected administrative and other data sources closely approximate the components of population change. Therefore, Census Bureau demographers separately estimate each component of population change based on administrative records, including registered births and deaths, federal income tax returns, Medicare enrollees, and military movement. They also separately estimate net international migration using information from the American Community Survey (ACS), the decennial census, and other data sources.

Most administrative record data sources lag the current estimate year by as much as 2 years; therefore, the Census Bureau projects the data for the current year based on past years' data. As updated data become available, they revise the projected input data so that each vintage's estimates are always based on the most recent data available.

For more information on the method used for these estimates, see Appendix B, Limitations and Methodology, and the website at www.census.gov/popest/methodology/ index.html .

Rank numbers are assigned on the basis of population size, with each metropolitan area placed in descending order, largest to smallest. Where ties occur—two or more areas with identical populations—the same rank is assigned to each of the tied metropolitan areas. In such cases, the following rank number(s) is omitted so that the lowest rank is usually equal to the number of metropolitan areas ranked.

People per square mile of land area, also known as population density, is the average number of inhabitants per square mile of land area. These figures are derived by dividing the total number of residents by the number of square miles of land area in the specified geographic area.

Table B-2. Components of Population Change

Sources: U.S. Census Bureau, Population Estimates, Cumulative Estimates of Components of Resident Population Change for Metropolitan and Micropolitan Statistical Areas: April 1, 2010 to July 1, 2011; www.census

.gov/popest/data/historical/2010s/vintage_2011/metro .html .

The Census Bureau develops county population estimates with a component of population change method in which they use administrative records and other data to estimate the household and group quarters population. For the household population, the components of population change are births, deaths, net domestic migration, and net international migration. They measure change in the non-household, or group quarters, population by the net change in the population living in group quarters facilities.

A major assumption underlying this approach is that changes in selected administrative and other data sources closely approximate the components of population change. Therefore, Census Bureau demographers separately estimate each component of population change based on administrative records, including registered births and deaths, federal income tax returns, Medicare enrollees, and military movement. They also separately estimate net international migration using information from the American Community Survey (ACS), the decennial census, and other data sources.

Most administrative record data sources lag the current estimate year by as much as 2 years; therefore, the Census Bureau projects the data for the current year based on past years' data. As updated data become available, they revise the projected input data so that each vintage's estimates are always based on the most recent data available.

The Census Bureau produces the estimate of each county's population, starting with the base population from either the 2010 census (for the July 1, 2010, estimates) or the revised population estimate for the prior year (for the July 1, 2011, and later estimates). They then add or subtract the demographic components of population change calculated for that time period. Basically, they add the estimated number of births and subtract the estimated number of deaths for the time period. Next, they add the estimates of net domestic migration, net international migration, and the net change in the group quarters population. The definitions of these concepts follow.

The Census Bureau produces separate population estimates for the populations under age 65 and age 65 and over, mainly because different data are used to measure the domestic migration of these two populations. For the population under age 65, they use person-level data from individual federal tax returns to estimate net domestic migration. They use Medicare enrollment data to calculate measures of migration for the population age 65 and over because this population is not always well represented

on tax returns. County total population estimates are the sum of the estimates of the population under age 65 and age 65 years and over.

State and county estimates may also incorporate other changes due to corrections made since the 2010 census. The corrections occur outside the component estimation framework and are the result of successful local challenges or special censuses.

Natural increase. Births minus deaths. The rate of natural increase expresses natural increase during a time period as a percentage of an area's population at the midpoint of the time period.

Net international migration. Any change of residence across the borders of the United States (50 states and District of Columbia). The Census Bureau makes estimates of net international migration for the nation, states, and counties. They estimate net international migration in four parts: (1) net international migration of the foreign born, (2) net migration between the United States and Puerto Rico, (3) net migration of natives to and from the United States, and (4) net movement of the armed forces population between the United States and overseas. The largest component, net international migration of the foreign born, includes lawful permanent residents (immigrants), temporary migrants (such as students), humanitarian migrants (such as refugees), and people illegally present in the United States. Currently, they do not estimate these components individually.

Net Domestic Migration. The difference between domestic in-migration to an area and domestic out-migration from the same area during a time period. Domestic in- and out-migration consist of moves where both the origin and the destination are within the United States (excluding Puerto Rico).

Percentage population change is the difference between the population of an area at the beginning and end of a time period, expressed as a percentage of the beginning population.

Table B-3. Population by Age, Race, and Sex

Source: U.S. Census Bureau, "*Annual County Resident Population Estimates by Age, Sex, Race and Hispanic Origin: April 1, 2010 to July 1, 2011*," see www.census.gov/ popest/data/counties/asrh/2011/index.html .

Age, sex, and race estimates are based on the distributed cohort component method. For an overview, see www .census.gov/popest/methodology/index.html .

Age. The age classification is based on the age of the person in complete years as of July 1. The age of the person usually was derived from their date of birth information.

Median age represents the age that divides the age distribution into two equal parts, one-half of the cases falling below the median age and one-half falling above the median. This measure is rounded to the nearest tenth.

Race. The concept of race, as used by the Census Bureau, reflects self-identification by people according to the race or races with which they most closely identify. These categories are sociopolitical constructs and should not be interpreted as being scientific or anthropological in nature. Furthermore, the race categories include both racial and national-origin groups. Caution must be used when interpreting changes in the racial composition of the U.S. population over time. The racial classifications used by the Census Bureau adhere to the December 15, 2000 (revised from October 30, 1997), *Federal Register Notice* entitled, "Revisions to the Standards for the Classification of Federal Data on Race and Ethnicity" issued by the OMB, www.census.gov/population/race/ . These standards govern the categories used to collect and present federal data on race and ethnicity. The OMB required federal agencies to use a minimum of five race categories: White, Black or African American, American Indian and Alaska Native, Asian, and Native Hawaiian and Other Pacific Islander. For respondents unable to identify with any of these five race categories, the OMB approved including a sixth category "Some other race."

The Census 2010 question on race included three areas where respondents could write in a more specific race group. The response categories and write-in answers can be combined to create the five minimum OMB race categories plus "Some other race." People who responded to the question on race by indicating only one race are referred to as the race alone population or the group that reported only one race category.

White. A person having origins in any of the original peoples of Europe, the Middle East, or North Africa. It includes people who indicate their race as "White" or report entries such as Irish, German, Italian, Lebanese, Near Easterner, Arab, or Polish.

Black or African American. A person having origins in any of the Black racial groups of Africa. It includes people who indicate their race as "Black, African American, or Negro," or who provide written entries such as African American, Afro American, Kenyan, Nigerian, or Haitian.

American Indian and Alaska Native. A person having origins in any of the original peoples of North and South America including Central America, and who maintain tribal affiliation or community attachment. It includes people who classify themselves as described below.

American Indian. Includes people who indicate their race as "American Indian," entered the name of an Indian tribe, or report such entries as Canadian Indian, French-American Indian, or Spanish-American Indian.

Alaska Native. Includes written responses of Eskimos, Aleuts, and Alaska Indians as well as entries such as Arctic Slope, Inupait, Yupik, Alutiiq, Egeik, and Pribilovian. The Alaska tribes are the Alaskan Athabascan, Tlingit, and Haida.

Asian. A person having origins in any of the original peoples of the Far East, Southeast Asia, or the Indian subcontinent including Cambodia, China, India, Japan, Korea, Malaysia, Pakistan, the Philippine Islands, Thailand, and Vietnam. It includes "Asian Indian," "Chinese," "Filipino," "Korean," "Japanese," "Vietnamese," and "Other Asian."

Asian Indian includes people who indicate their race as "Asian Indian" or identify themselves as Bengalese, Bharat, Dravidian, East Indian, or Goanese. *Chinese* includes people who indicate their race as "Chinese" or who identify themselves as Cantonese or Chinese American. In some census tabulations, written entries of Taiwanese are included with Chinese while in others they are shown separately. *Filipino* includes people who indicate their race as "Filipino" or who report entries such as Philipano, Philipine, or Filipino American. *Japanese* includes people who indicate their race as "Japanese" or who report entries such as Nipponese or Japanese American. *Korean* includes people who indicate their race as "Korean" or who provide a response of Korean American. *Vietnamese* includes people who indicate their race as "Vietnamese" or who provide a response of Vietnamese American.

Native Hawaiian and Other Pacific Islander. A person having origins in any of the original peoples of Hawaii, Guam, Samoa, or other Pacific Islands. It includes people who indicate their race as "Native Hawaiian," "Guamanian or Chamorro," "Samoan," and "Other Pacific Islander."

Native Hawaiian includes people who indicate their race as "Native Hawaiian" or who identify themselves as "Part Hawaiian" or "Hawaiian." *Guamanian or Chamorro* includes people who indicate their race as such, including written entries of Chamorro or Guam. *Samoan* includes people who indicate their race as "Samoan" or who identify themselves as American Samoan or Western

Samoan. *Other Pacific Islander* includes people who provided a write-in response of a Pacific Islander group such as Tahitian, Northern Mariana Islander, Palauan, Fijian, or a cultural group, such as Melanesian, Micronesian, or Polynesian.

Hispanic or Latino origin. People who identify with the terms "Hispanic" or "Latino" are those who classify themselves in one of the specific Hispanic or Latino categories listed on the questionnaire—"Mexican," "Puerto Rican," or "Cuban"—as well as those who indicate that they are "other Spanish, Hispanic, or Latino." Origin can be viewed as the heritage, nationality group, lineage, or country of birth of the person or the person's parents or ancestors before their arrival in the United States. People who identify their origin as Spanish, Hispanic, or Latino may be of any race.

Table B-4. Migration and Commuting, 2009–2011

Source: U.S. Census Bureau, American Community Survey, "C07201: Geographical Mobility in the Past Year for Current Residence—Metropolitan Statistical Area Level in the United States, 2009–2011"; "B08604: Worker Population for Workplace Geography, 2009–2011"; "B08016: Place of Work for Workers 16 years Old and Over—Metropolitan Statistical Area Level, 2009–2011"; "B08134 and B08135: Aggregate Travel Time to Work and Means of Transportation to Work by Travel Time to Work, 2009–2011" http://factfinder2.census.gov .

Residence one year ago. For the American Community Survey, people who had moved from another residence in the United States or Puerto Rico 1 year earlier were asked to report the exact address (number and street name); the name of the city, town, or post office; the name of the U.S. county or municipio in Puerto Rico; state or Puerto Rico; and the ZIP Code where they lived 1 year ago. People living outside the United States and Puerto Rico were asked to report the name of the foreign country or U.S. Island Area where they were living 1 year ago.

The tabulation category, "Same house," includes all people 1 year and over who did not move during the 1 year as well as those who had moved and returned to their residence 1 year ago. The category, "Different house in the United States" includes people who lived in the United States 1 year ago but in a different house or apartment from the one they occupied at the time of interview. These movers are then further subdivided according to the type of move. In most tabulations, movers within the United States are divided into three groups according to their previous residence: "Different house, same county," "Different county, same state," and "Different state." The last

group may be further subdivided into region of residence 1 year ago. An additional category, "Abroad," includes those whose previous residence was in a foreign country, Puerto Rico, American Samoa, Guam, the Northern Marianas, or the U.S. Virgin Islands, including members of the armed forces and their dependents.

Place of Work. Data were tabulated for workers 16 years old and over, that is, members of the armed forces and civilians who were at work during the reference week. Data on place of work refer to the geographic location at which workers carried out their occupational activities during the reference week.

In the American Community Survey, the exact address (number and street name) of the place of work was asked, as well as the place (city, town, or post office); whether the place of work was inside or outside the limits of that city or town; and the county, state, or foreign country, and ZIP Code. If the respondent's employer operated in more than one location, the exact address of the location or branch where he or she worked was requested. When the number and street name were unknown, a description of the location, such as the building name or nearest street or intersection, was to be entered. People who worked at more than one location during the reference week were asked to report the location at which they worked the greatest number of hours. People who regularly worked in several locations each day during the reference week were requested to give the address at which they began work each day. For cases in which daily work did not begin at a central place each day, the respondent was asked to provide as much information as possible to describe the area in which he or she worked most during the reference week.

Means of Transportation to Work. Means of transportation to work refers to the principal mode of travel or type of conveyance that the worker usually used to get from home to work during the reference week.

People who used different means of transportation on different days of the week were asked to specify the one they used most often, that is, the greatest number of days. People who used more than one means of transportation to get to work each day were asked to report the one used for the longest distance during the work trip. The category, "Car, truck, or van," includes workers using a car (including company cars but excluding taxicabs), a truck of one-ton capacity or less, or a van.

Private Vehicle Occupancy. Private vehicle occupancy refers to the number of people who usually rode to work in the vehicle during the reference week. The category,

"Drove alone," includes people who usually drove alone to work as well as people who were driven to work by someone who then drove back home or to a nonwork destination.

Mean Travel Time to Work (in minutes). Mean travel time to work (in minutes) is the average travel time that workers usually took to get from home to work (one way) during the reference week. This measure is obtained by dividing the total number of minutes taken to get from home to work (the aggregate travel time) by the number of workers 16 years old and over who did not work at home. The travel time includes time spent waiting for public transportation, picking up passengers and carpools, and time spent in other activities related to getting to work. The aggregate travel time to work used to calculate mean travel time to work is rounded to the nearest tenth of a minute.

Table B-5. Population Characteristics, 2009–2011

Source: U.S. Census Bureau, American Community Survey, "DP02. Selected Social Characteristics in the United States: 2009–2011" http://factfinder2.census.gov .

Household. A household includes all the people who occupy a housing unit as their usual place of residence.

Family household. A family includes a householder and one or more people living in the same household who are related to the householder by birth, marriage, or adoption. All people in a household who are related to the householder are regarded as members of his or her family. A family household may contain people not related to the householder, but those people are not included as part of the householder's family in census tabulations. Thus, the number of family households is equal to the number of families, but family households may include more members than do families. A household can contain only one family for purposes of census tabulations. Not all households contain families since a household may comprise a group of unrelated people or one person living alone.

Single-parent household. A household with a male householder with no wife present or a female householder with no husband present.

Foreign-born population. The Census Bureau separates the U.S. resident population into two groups based on whether or not a person was a U.S. citizen at the time of birth. Anyone born in the United States or U.S. Island Area (such as Puerto Rico) or born abroad to a U.S. citizen parent is a U.S. citizen at the time of birth and consequently included in the *native population*. The term *foreign-born population*

refers to anyone who is not a U.S. citizen at birth. This includes naturalized U.S. citizens, legal permanent resident aliens (immigrants), temporary migrants (such as students), humanitarian migrants (such as refugees), and people illegally present in the United States.

Language Spoken at Home by the Respondent. The American Community Survey asked about languages spoken at home in an effort to measure the current use of languages other than English. This category included persons 5 years old and over and excluded respondents who spoke a language other than English exclusively outside of the home.

Table B-6. Enrollment, Teachers, and Educational Attainment

Sources: Enrollment, number of teachers, and high school completers—National Center for Education Statistics, Common Core of Data, www.nces.ed.gov/ccd/bat/ ; Educational attainment—U.S. Census Bureau, American Community Survey, "DP02. Selected Social Characteristics in the United States: 2009–2011" http://factfinder2 .census.gov .

Enrollment, teachers, and high school completers. The Common Core of Data (CCD) is the Department of Education's primary database on public elementary and secondary education in the United States. CCD is a comprehensive, annual, national statistical database of all public elementary and secondary schools and school districts, which contains data that are designed to be comparable across all states.

The objectives of the CCD are twofold: first, to provide an official listing of public elementary and secondary schools and school districts in the nation, which can be used to select samples for other NCES surveys. And second, to provide basic information and descriptive statistics on public elementary and secondary schools and schooling in general.

The CCD survey annually collects data about all public elementary and secondary schools, all local education agencies, and all state education agencies throughout the United States. CCD contains three categories of information: general descriptive information on schools and school districts; data on students and staff; and fiscal data. Most of the data are obtained from administrative records maintained by the state education agencies (SEAs).

The number of students enrolled in public schools is provided by the schools. The number of teachers is provided by the Local Education Agencies and represents full-time equivalent teachers. The number of high school completers includes all students who have received diplomas, as well as individuals who received a certificate of attendance or other certificate of completion in lieu of a diploma during the previous school year and subsequent summer school.

Educational Attainment. Educational attainment data in this table include persons who are 25 years old and over. In the American Community Survey, respondents are classified according to the highest degree or the highest level of school completed. The question included instructions for persons currently enrolled in school to report the level of the previous grade attended or the highest degree received. The category "High School Graduate or Higher" includes people whose highest degree was a high school diploma or its equivalent, people who attended college but did not receive a degree, and people who received an associate's, bachelor's, master's, or professional or doctorate degree. People who reported completing the 12th grade but not receiving a diploma are not included. The category "Bachelor's degree or higher" includes those who received a bachelor's, master's, or professional or doctorate degree.

Table B-7. Median Income, Household Income Distribution, and Poverty Status, 2009–2011

Source: U.S. Census Bureau, American Community Survey, "DP03. Selected Economic Characteristics in the United States: 2009–2011"; http://factfinder2.census.gov .

Income. Total income is the sum of the amounts reported separately for wage or salary income; net self-employment income; interest, dividends, or net rental or royalty income or income from estates and trusts; Social Security or Railroad Retirement income; Supplemental Security Income (SSI); public assistance or welfare payments; retirement, survivor, or disability pensions; and all other income. Receipts from the following sources are not included as income: capital gains, money received from the sale of property (unless the recipient was engaged in the business of selling such property); the value of income "in kind" from food stamps, public housing subsidies, medical care, employer contributions for individuals, etc.; withdrawal of bank deposits; money borrowed; tax refunds; exchange of money between relatives living in the same household; gifts and lump-sum inheritances, insurance payments, and other types of lump-sum receipts.

Median income divides the income distribution into two equal parts: one-half of the cases falling below the median income and one-half above the median. For households

and families, the median income is based on the distribution of the total number of households and families including those with no income. The median income for individuals is based on individuals 15 years old and over with income. Median income for households, families, and individuals is computed on the basis of a standard distribution. Median income is rounded to the nearest whole dollar. Median income figures are calculated using linear interpolation if the width of the interval containing the estimate is $2,500 or less. If the width of the interval containing the estimate is greater than $2,500, Pareto interpolation is used.

Income of households includes the income of the householder and all other individuals 15 years old and over. In compiling statistics on family and household income, the incomes of all persons 15 years old and over in the household (or family) are summed and treated as a single amount. Although the income statistics cover the past 12 months, the characteristics of individuals and the composition of families refer to the time of enumeration. Thus, the income of the family or household does not include amounts received by individuals who were members of the family or household during all or part of the past 12 months if these individuals no longer resided with the family at the time of enumeration. Similarly, income amounts reported by individuals who did not reside with the family or in the household during the past 12 months but who were members of the family or household at the time of enumeration are included. However, the composition of most families and most households was the same during the past 12 months as at the time of interview.

Poverty status is determined using thresholds arranged in a two-dimensional matrix. The matrix consists of family size cross-classified by presence and number of family members under age 18 years old. Unrelated individuals and two-person families are further differentiated by age of reference person. To determine a person's poverty status, one compares the person's total family income in the last 12 months with the poverty threshold appropriate for that person's family size and composition. If the total income of that person's family is less than the threshold appropriate for that family, then the person is considered poor or "below the poverty level," together with every member of his or her family. If a person is not living with anyone related by birth, marriage, or adoption, then the person's own income is compared with his or her poverty threshold. The total number of people below the poverty level was the sum of people in families and the number of unrelated individuals with incomes in the last 12 months below the poverty level. The average poverty threshold for a family of four in 2011 was $23,021. See www.census .gov/hhes/www/poverty/data/threshld/ for detailed poverty thresholds.

Table B-8. Health Insurance, Medicare, Social Security, and Supplemental Security Income

Sources: Persons with no health insurance—U.S. Census Bureau, American Community Survey, "DP03. Selected Economic Characteristics in the United States: 2009–2011." Persons with a disability—U.S. Census Bureau, American Community Survey, "DP02. Selected Social Characteristics in the United States: 2009-2011"; http://factfinder2.census .gov. Medicare program enrollment—Centers for Medicare and Medicaid Services, CMS Statistics: Medicare Enrollment, www.cms.hhs.gov/MedicareEnrpts/. Social security— U.S. Social Security Administration, Office of Research and Statistics, OASDI Beneficiaries by State and County, www .ssa.gov/policy/docs/statcomps/oasdi_sc/2011/index.html. Supplemental security income—U.S. Social Security Administration, Office of Research, Evaluation, and Statistics, SSI Recipients by State and County, www.ssa.gov/policy/ docs/statcomps/ssi_sc/2011/index.html .

Health Insurance. In the American Community Survey, respondents were instructed to report their current coverage for each of eight types of health insurance: Insurance through a current or former employer or union (of this person or another family member); Insurance purchased directly from an insurance company (by this person or another family member); Medicare, for people 65 and older, or people with certain disabilities; Medicaid, Medical Assistance, or any kind of government-assistance plan for those with low incomes or a disability; TRICARE or other military health care; VA (including those who have ever used or enrolled for VA health care); Indian Health Service; or any other type of health insurance or health coverage plan.

Disability status. Disability is defined as the product of interactions among individuals' bodies; their physical, emotional, and mental health; and the physical and social environment in which they live, work, or play. Disability exists where this interaction results in limitations of activities and restrictions to full participation at school, at work, at home, or in the community. For example, disability may exist where a person is limited in their ability to work due to job discrimination against persons with specific health conditions; or disability may exist where a child has difficulty learning because the school cannot accommodate the child's deafness. In an attempt to capture a variety of characteristics that encompass the definition of disability, the ACS identifies serious difficulty with four basic areas of functioning—hearing, vision, cognition, and ambulation.

Medicare enrollment. When first implemented in 1966, Medicare covered only most persons age 65 and over.

By the end of 1966, 3.7 million persons had received at least some health care services covered by Medicare. In 1973, other groups became eligible for Medicare benefits: persons who are entitled to social security or Railroad Retirement disability benefits for at least 24 months; persons with end stage renal disease (ESRD) requiring continuing dialysis or kidney transplant; and certain otherwise noncovered aged persons who elect to buy into Medicare.

Medicare consists of two primary parts: Hospital Insurance (HI), also known as Part A, and Supplementary Medical Insurance (SMI), also known as Part B. Health care services covered under Medicare's Hospital Insurance include, inpatient hospital care, skilled nursing facility care, home health agency care, and hospice care. SMI coverage is optional and requires payment of a monthly premium.

Social security. The Old-Age, Survivors, and Disability Insurance Program (OASDI) provides monthly benefits for retired and disabled insured workers and their dependents and to survivors of insured workers. To be eligible for benefits, a worker must have had a specified period of employment in which OASDI taxes were paid. A worker becomes eligible for full retirement benefits at age 65 through 67 (depending on the year of birth), although reduced benefits may be obtained at age 62; the worker's spouse is under the same limitations. Survivor benefits are payable to dependents of deceased insured workers. Disability benefits are payable to an insured worker under age 65 with a prolonged disability and to that person's dependents on the same basis as dependents of a retired worker. Also, disability benefits are payable at age 50 to the disabled widow or widower of a deceased worker who was fully insured at the time of death. A lump-sum benefit is generally payable on the death of an insured worker to a spouse or minor children.

The data were derived from the Master Beneficiary Record (MBR), the principal administrative file of social security beneficiaries. Data for total recipients and retired workers include persons with special age-72 benefits. Special age-72 benefit represents the monthly benefit payable to men who attained age 72 before 1972 and for women who attained age 72 before 1970 and who do not have sufficient quarters to qualify for a retired-worker benefit under either the fully or the transitionally insured status provision.

Supplemental security income. The Supplemental Security Income (SSI) program provides cash payments in accordance with nationwide eligibility requirements to people with limited income and resources who are aged, blind, or disabled. Under the SSI program, each person living in his or her own household is provided a cash payment from the federal government that is sufficient, when added to the person's countable income (the total gross money income of an individual less certain exclusions), to bring the total monthly income up to a specified level (the federal benefit rate). If the individual or couple is living in another household, the guaranteed level is reduced by one-third.

An aged person is defined as an individual who is 65 years old or over. A blind person is anyone with vision of 20/200 or less with the use of correcting lens in the better eye or with tunnel vision of 20 degrees or less. The disabled classification refers to any person unable to engage in any substantial gainful activity by reason of any medically determinable physical or mental impairment expected to result in death or that has lasted or can be expected to last for a continuous period of at least 12 months. For a child under 18 years, eligibility is based on disability or severity comparable with that of an adult, since the criterion of "substantial gainful activity" is inapplicable for children.

Table B-9. Housing Units and Building Permits

Sources: Housing units—U.S. Census Bureau, "Housing Unit Estimates for Counties: April 1, 2010 to July 1, 2011," www.census.gov/popest/data/housing/totals/2011/index.html. Building permits—U.S. Census Bureau, "Annual New Privately Owned Residential Building Permits" Permits by county or metropolitan area 2010–2011; www.census.gov/construction/nrc/ .

Housing unit estimates are developed by using building permits, mobile home shipments, and estimates of housing unit loss to measure housing unit change since the last census. For more information see www.census.gov/popest/methodology/index.html .

Building permits data are based on reports submitted by local building permit officials in response to a Census Bureau mail survey. They are obtained using Form C-404, "Report of New Privately Owned Residential Building or Zoning Permits Issued." Data are collected from individual permit offices, most of which are municipalities; the remainder are counties, townships, or New England and Middle Atlantic-type towns. Currently, there are 20,000 permit-issuing places. When a report is not received, missing data are either (1) obtained from the Survey of Use of Permits, which is used to collect information on housing starts, or (2) imputed.

The data relate to new private housing units intended for occupancy on a housekeeping basis. They exclude mobile homes (trailers), hotels, motels, and group residential structures, such as nursing homes and college dormitories. They also exclude conversions of and alterations to existing buildings. A housing unit consists of a room or group of rooms intended for occupancy as separate living quarters by a family, by a group of unrelated persons living together, or by a person living alone.

Table B-10. Housing Units: 2009–2011

Source: U.S. Census Bureau, American Community Survey, "DP04. Selected Housing Characteristics: 2009–2011." http://factfinder2.census.gov/ .

A housing unit is a house, apartment, mobile home or trailer, group of rooms, or single room occupied or, if vacant, intended for occupancy as separate living quarters. Separate living quarters are those in which the occupants do not live and eat with any other persons in the structure and which have direct access from the outside of the building or through a common hall. A housing unit is classified as occupied if it is the usual place of residence of the person or group of people living in it at the time of census enumeration or if the occupants are only temporarily absent; that is, away on vacation or business. All occupied housing units are classified as either owner occupied or renter occupied. A housing unit is owner occupied if the owner or co-owner lives in the unit even if it is mortgaged or not fully paid for. All occupied housing units that are not owner occupied, whether they are rented for cash rent or occupied without payment of cash rent, are classified as renter occupied.

One-unit detached is a one-unit structure detached from any other house, that is, with open space on all four sides. Such structures are considered detached even if they have an adjoining shed or garage. A one-family house that contains a business is considered detached as long as the building has open space on all four sides. Mobile homes to which one or more permanent rooms have been added or built also are included.

Ownership rate is computed by dividing the number of owner-occupied housing units by the number of occupied housing units. A housing unit is **owner-occupied** if the owner or co-owner lives in the unit even if it is mortgaged or not fully paid for. The owner or co-owner must live in the unit. The unit is owner-occupied if someone who lives in the household is purchasing the house with a mortgage or some other debt arrangement such as a deed of trust, trust deed, contract to purchase, land contract, or purchase agreement. The unit also is considered owned with a mortgage if it is built on leased land and there is a mortgage on the unit. Mobile homes occupied by owners with installment loan balances also are included in this category.

Selected monthly owner costs were obtained for owner-occupied units. Selected monthly owner costs are the sum of payments for mortgages, deeds of trust, contracts to purchase, or similar debts on the property (including payments for the first mortgage, second mortgages, home equity loans, and other junior mortgages); real estate taxes; fire, hazard, and flood insurance on the property; utilities (electricity, gas, and water and sewer); and fuels (oil, coal, kerosene, wood, etc.). It also includes, where appropriate, the monthly condominium fee for condominiums and mobile home costs (installment loan payments, personal property taxes, site rent, registration fees, and license fees). Selected monthly owner costs were tabulated for all owner-occupied units, and usually are shown separately for units "with a mortgage" and for units "not mortgaged." Table B-10 includes only those units with a mortgage.

To inflate selected monthly owner costs from previous years, the dollar values are inflated to the latest year's dollar values by multiplying by a factor equal to the average annual Consumer Price Index (CPI-U-RS) factor for the current year, divided by the average annual CPI-U-RS factor for the earliest year.

Median Selected Monthly Owner Costs are determined by dividing the monthly owner costs distribution into two equal parts: one-half of the cases falling below the median monthly owner costs and one-half above the median.

Median monthly rent refers to the **gross rent**, which is the contract rent plus the estimated average monthly cost of utilities (electricity, gas, and water and sewer) and fuels (oil, coal, kerosene, wood, etc.) if these are paid by the renter (or paid for the renter by someone else). Gross rent is intended to eliminate differentials that result from varying practices with respect to the inclusion of utilities and fuels as part of the rental payment.

The estimated costs of water and sewer, and fuels are reported on a 12-month basis but are converted to monthly figures for the tabulations.

Vehicles available. The question on vehicles available was asked at occupied housing units. These data show the number of passenger cars, vans, and pickup or panel trucks of one-ton capacity or less kept at home and available for the use of household members. Vehicles rented or leased for one month or more, company vehicles, and police and government vehicles are included if kept at home and used for nonbusiness purposes. Dismantled or immobile vehicles are excluded. Vehicles kept at home but used only for business purposes also are excluded.

Table B-11. Personal Income and Earnings, by Place of Work

Source: U.S. Bureau of Economic Analysis, Regional Economic Accounts, Local Area Personal Income and Employment; www.bea.gov/regional/index.htm .

Personal income is the income that is received by all persons from all sources. It is calculated as the sum of wage and salary disbursements, supplements to wages and salaries, proprietors' income with inventory valuation and capital consumption adjustments, rental income of people with capital consumption adjustment, personal dividend income, personal interest income, and personal current transfer receipts, less contributions for government social insurance.

The personal income of an area is the income that is received by, or on behalf of, all the individuals who live in the area; therefore, the estimates of personal income are presented by the place of residence of the income recipients.

Personal income differs by definition from money income, which is prepared by the Census Bureau, in that money income is measured before deduction of personal contributions for social insurance and does not include imputed income, lump-sum payments, and income received by quasi-individuals. Money income does include income from private pensions and annuities and from interpersonal transfer, such as child support; therefore it is not comparable to personal income. Total personal income is adjusted to place of residence.

About 90 percent of the state and county estimates of personal income are based on census data and on administrative-records data that are collected by other federal agencies. The data from censuses are mainly collected from the recipient of the income. The most important sources of census data for the state and county estimates are the census of agriculture and the census of population and housing that are conducted by the Census Bureau. The data from administrative records may originate either from the recipients of the income or from the source of the income. These data are a byproduct of the administration of various federal and state government programs. The most important sources of these data are as follows: the state unemployment insurance programs of the Employment and Training Administration, Department of Labor; the social insurance programs of the Social Security Administration and the Health Care Financing

Administration, Department of Health and Human Services; the federal income tax program of the Internal Revenue Service, Department of the Treasury; the veterans benefit programs of the Department of Veterans Affairs; and the military payroll systems of the Department of Defense. The remaining 10 percent of the estimates are based on data from other sources. For example, the estimates of the components of farm proprietors' income, a component of personal income, are partly based on the state estimates of farm income and the county estimates of case receipts, crop production, and livestock inventory that are prepared by the Department of Agriculture, which uses sample surveys, along with census data and administrative-records data, to derive its estimates.

Total **earnings** cover wage and salary disbursements, supplements to wages and salaries, and proprietor's income. Wage and salary disbursements consists of the monetary remuneration of employees, including corporate officers salaries and bonuses, commissions, pay-in-kind, incentive payments, and tips. It reflects the amount of payments disbursed, but not necessarily earned during the year. It is measured before deductions, such as social security contributions and union dues. Wage and salary disbursements includes stock options of nonqualified plans at the time that they have been exercised by the individual. Stock options are reported in wage and salary disbursements. The value that is included in wages is the difference between the exercise price and the price that the stock options were granted. Supplements to wages and salaries consists of employer contributions for employee pension and insurance funds and of employer contributions for government social insurance. Proprietor's income is the current-production income (including income in kind) of sole proprietorships and partnerships and of tax-exempt cooperatives. Corporate directors' fees are included in proprietors' income, but the imputed net rental income of owner-occupants of all dwellings is included in rental income of persons. Proprietors' income excludes dividends and monetary interest received by nonfinancial business and rental incomes received by persons not primarily engaged in the real estate business; these incomes are included in dividends, net interest, and rental income of persons, respectively.

Table B-12. Employees and Earnings, by Selected Major Industries, 2011

Source: U.S. Bureau of Economic Analysis, Regional Economic Accounts, Local Area Personal Income and Employment; www.bea.gov/regional/index.htm .

The estimates of employment and earnings from 2011 are based on the 2007 North American Industry Classification System (NAICS). For more information on NAICS, please visit www.census.gov/eos/www/naics/index.html .

The BEA employment series for states and local areas comprises estimates of the number of jobs, full-time plus part-time, by place of work. Full-time and part-time jobs are counted at equal weight. Employees, sole proprietors, and active partners are included, but unpaid family workers and volunteers are not included.

Earnings by place of work is the sum of wage and salary disbursements, supplements to wages and salaries, and proprietors' income.

Table B-13. Civilian Labor Force and Banking

Sources: Civilian labor force—U.S. Bureau of Labor Statistics (BLS), *Local Area Unemployment Statistics, Annual Averages*; www.bls.gov/lau/. Banking—U.S. Federal Deposit Insurance Corporation (FDIC); www2.fdic.gov/sod/index.asp .

Civilian Labor Force

Civilian labor force data are the product of a federal-state cooperative program in which state employment security agencies prepare labor force and unemployment estimates under concepts, definitions, and technical procedures established by the BLS. These data for substate areas are produced by the BLS primarily for use in allocating funds under various federal legislative programs. Users of these data are cautioned that, because of the small size of many of the areas, as well as limitations of the data inputs, the estimates are subject to considerable, but nonquantifiable, error. An explanation of the technical procedures used to develop monthly and annual local area labor force estimates appears monthly in the Explanatory Note for state and area unemployment data in the BLS periodical, *Employment and Earnings*. Additional information may also be found at the BLS website at www.bls.gov/opub/hom/ .

The civilian labor force comprises all persons in the civilian noninstitutional population classified as either employed or unemployed. Employed persons are persons 16 years and over in the civilian noninstitutional population who, during the reference week (a) did any work at all (at least 1 hour) as paid employees; worked in their own business, profession, or on their own farm, or worked 15 hours or more as unpaid workers in an enterprise operated by a member of the family; and (b) all those who were not working but who had jobs or businesses from which they were temporarily absent because of vacation, illness, bad weather, childcare problems, maternity or paternity leave, labor-management dispute, job training, or other family or personal reasons, whether or not they were paid for the time off or were seeking other jobs. Each employed person is counted only once, even if he or she holds more than one job. Excluded are persons whose only activity consisted of work around their own house (painting, repairing, or own home housework) or volunteer work for religious, charitable, and other organizations.

Unemployed people are all civilians aged 16 years and older who had no employment during the reference week, were available for work, except for temporary illness, and had made specific efforts to find employment sometime during the 4-week period ending with the reference week. Persons who were waiting to be recalled to a job from which they had been laid off need not have been looking for work to be classified as unemployed. The unemployment rate for all civilian workers represents the number of unemployed as a percent of the civilian labor force.

Banking

The FDIC and OTS collect deposit data on each office of every FDIC-insured bank and saving association as of June 30 of each year in the Summary of Deposits (SOD) survey. The FDIC surveys all FDIC-insured commercial banks, savings banks, and U.S. branches of foreign banks, and the OTS surveys all savings associations. Data presented here exclude U.S. branch offices of foreign banks. For all counties, individual banking offices—not the combined totals of the bank—are the source of the data.

Insured **savings institutions** include all FDIC-insured (OTS-Regulated and FDIC-Regulated) financial institutions that operate under federal or state banking charters. The number of **banking offices** in any given area includes every location at which deposit business is transacted. Banking office is defined to include all offices and facilities that actually hold deposits, but to exclude loan production offices, computer centers, and other non-deposit installations, such as automated teller machines (ATMs). The term "offices" includes both main offices and branches. An institution with four branches operates a total of five offices.

Table B-14. Federal Government Expenditures and Private Business Establishments and Employment

Sources: Federal government expenditures—U.S. Census Bureau, *Consolidated Federal Funds Report,* www.census.gov/govs/cffr/ (The CFFR has been terminated. 2010 was the final year); Private nonfarm business—County Business Patterns, www.census.gov/econ/cbp/index.html .

Data on federal expenditure and obligations are obtained from a report prepared by the Census Bureau in accordance with the Consolidated Federal Funds Report (CFFR) Act of 1982 (P.L. 97-326). The data are for federal fiscal years beginning October 1 and ending the following September 30. Dollar amounts reported can reflect expenditures or obligations. In some cases, dollar amounts are negative, representing de-obligations of financial assistance that had previously been awarded. The Federal Financial Statistics Program, including the CFFR was recently terminated. This book includes data for 2010, the final year.

Direct payments for individuals include Social Security benefits, federal government retirement, Medicare, Supplemental Security Income, food stamps, educational and housing assistance, and other categories not shown separately. All data represent actual expenditures during the fiscal year.

Salaries and wages represent actual federal expenditures during the fiscal year; the geographic distribution of these amounts by state and county was estimated based upon place of employment.

Defense contract awards cover procurement awards given by the Defense Department. Amounts represent the value of obligations for contract actions and do not reflect actual federal government expenditures. In general, only current-year contract actions are included; however, multiple-year obligations may be reported for contract actions of less than three years' duration.

County Business Patterns (CBP) is an annual series that provides subnational economic data by industry. The series is useful for studying the economic activity of small areas; analyzing economic changes over time; and as a benchmark for statistical series, surveys, and databases between economic censuses. CBP covers most of the country's economic activity. The series excludes data on self-employed individuals, employees of private households, railroad employees, agricultural production employees, and most government employees. The County Business Patterns program has been tabulated on a North American Industry Classification System (NAICS) basis since 1998. Data for 1997 and earlier years are based on the Standard Industrial Classification (SIC) system. For more information on the relationship between the two systems, see Concordances www.census.gov/eos/www/naics/concordances/concordances.html .

CBP data are extracted from the Business Register, the Census Bureau's file of all known single and multi-establishment companies. The Annual Company Organization Survey and quinquennial economic censuses provide individual establishment data for multi-location firms. Data for single-location firms are obtained from various programs censuses, the Annual Survey of Manufactures, and Current Business Surveys, as well as from administrative records of the Internal Revenue Service (IRS), the Social Security Administration (SSA), and the Bureau of Labor Statistics (BLS).

An **establishment** is a single physical location at which business is conducted or services or industrial operations are performed. It is not necessarily identical with a company or enterprise, which may consist of one or more establishments. When two or more activities are carried on at a single location under a single ownership, all activities generally are grouped together as a single establishment. The entire establishment is classified on the basis of its major activity and all data are included in that classification. Establishment-size designations are determined by paid employment in the mid-March pay period. The size group "1 to 4" includes establishments that did not report any paid employees in the mid-March pay period but paid wages to at least one employee at some time during the year.

Establishment counts represent the number of locations with paid employees any time during the year. This series excludes governmental establishments except for wholesale liquor establishments (NAICS 4248), retail liquor stores (NAICS 44531), federally-chartered savings institutions (NAICS 522120), federally-chartered credit unions (NAICS 522130), and hospitals (NAICS 622).

Annual payroll includes all forms of compensation, such as salaries, wages, reported tips, commissions, bonuses, vacation allowances, sick-leave pay, employee contributions to qualified pension plans, and the value of taxable fringe benefits. For corporations, it includes amounts paid to officers and executives; for unincorporated businesses, it does not include profit or other compensation of proprietors or partners. Payroll is reported before deductions for social security, income tax, insurance, union dues, etc.

Paid employment consists of full- and part-time employees, including salaried officers and executives of corporations, who are on the payroll in the pay period including March 12. Included are employees on paid sick leave, holidays, and vacations; not included are proprietors and partners of unincorporated businesses.

PART C—METROPOLITAN AREAS WITH COMPONENT COUNTIES

Table C consists of 4 tables (C-1 through C-4) with 50 data items for 366 metropolitan statistical areas (MSAs), 29 metropolitan divisions (in 11 large metropolitan statistical areas), and 1,100 counties within the metropolitan areas. They are presented alphabetically in each of the 4 tables, with counties listed alphabetically within each metropolitan area.

All summaries, including historical data, are presented for the areas as currently defined. Where possible, the original figures have been retabulated to reflect the status of metropolitan area boundaries as of December 1, 2009. For more information on these areas, see Appendix C, Geographic Concepts and Codes.

Table C-1. Population and Population Characteristics

Sources: Population and change—U.S. Census Bureau, Historical Estimates Data, county estimates base for April 1, 1990 and April 1, 2000 www.census.gov/popest/data/historical/index.html. For 2010–2011, compiled from Current Estimates Data, www.census.gov/popest/data/counties/totals/2011/index.html. Age—U.S. Census Bureau, County Population Estimates by Age, Sex, Race and Hispanic Origin, www.census.gov/popest/data/counties/asrh/2011/index.html .

Population numbers for 2010, 2000, and 1990 are counts of the resident population on April 1 of those decennial census years. The April 1 estimates base population may differ from the April 1 census count due to legal boundary updates, other geographic program changes, and Count Question Resolution actions.

Population estimates for 2011 measure the estimated population from the calculated number of people living in an area as of July 1. The Census Bureau develops county population estimates with a component of population change method in which they use administrative records and other data to estimate the household and group quarters population. For the household population, the components of population change are births, deaths, net domestic migration, and net international migration. They measure change in the nonhousehold, or group quarters, population by the net change in the population living in group quarters facilities.

A major assumption underlying this approach is that changes in selected administrative and other data sources closely approximate the components of population change. Therefore, Census Bureau demographers separately estimate each component of population change based on administrative records, including registered births and deaths, federal income tax returns, Medicare enrollees, and military movement. They also separately estimate net international migration using information from the American Community Survey (ACS), the decennial census, and other data sources.

Most administrative record data sources lag the current estimate year by as much as 2 years, therefore, the Census Bureau projects the data for the current year based on past years' data. As updated data become available, they revise the projected input data so that each vintage's estimates are always based on the most recent data available.

For more information on the method used for these estimates, see Appendix B, Limitations and Methodology, and the website at www.census.gov/popest/methodology/index.html .

Age. The age classification is based on the age of the person in complete years as of July 1, 2011. The age of the person usually was derived from their date of birth information.

Table C-2. Population Characteristics and Housing Units

Sources: Population—U.S. Census Bureau, County Population Estimates by Age, Sex, Race and Hispanic Origin, www.census.gov/popest/data/counties/asrh/2011/index .html . Housing—U.S. Census Bureau, County-Level Housing Unit Estimates, April 1, 2010 to July 1, 2011, www.census .gov/popest/data/housing/totals/2011/index.html . For 2000, U.S. Census Bureau, "Intercensal Estimates of Housing Units for Counties" April 1, 2000 to July 1, 2010, www .census.gov/popest/data/intercensal/housing/hu2010.html .

Race. The concept of race, as used by the Census Bureau, reflects self-identification by people according to the race or races with which they most closely identify. These categories are sociopolitical constructs and should not be interpreted as being scientific or anthropological in nature. Furthermore, the race categories include both racial and national-origin groups. Caution must be used when interpreting changes in the racial composition of the U.S. population over time. The racial classifications used by the Census Bureau adhere to the December 15, 2000 (revised from October 30, 1997), *Federal Register Notice* entitled, "Revisions to the Standards for the Classification of Federal Data on Race and Ethnicity" issued by the OMB, www.census.gov/population/race/ . These standards govern the categories used to collect and present federal data on race and ethnicity. The OMB required federal agencies to use a minimum of five race categories: White, Black or African American, American Indian and Alaska Native, Asian, and Native Hawaiian and Other Pacific Islander. For respondents unable to identify with any of these five race categories, the OMB approved including a sixth category, Some other race.

The Census 2010 question on race included three areas where respondents could write in a more specific race group. The response categories and write-in answers can be combined to create the five minimum OMB race categories plus "Some other race." People who responded to the question on race by indicating only one race are referred to as the race alone population or the group that reported only one race category.

White. A person having origins in any of the original peoples of Europe, the Middle East, or North Africa. It includes people who indicate their race as White or report entries such as Irish, German, Italian, Lebanese, Near Easterner, Arab, or Polish.

Black or African American. A person having origins in any of the Black racial groups of Africa. It includes people who indicate their race as Black, African American, or Negro, or who provide written entries such as African American, Afro American, Kenyan, Nigerian, or Haitian.

Asian. A person having origins in any of the original peoples of the Far East, Southeast Asia, or the Indian subcontinent including Cambodia, China, India, Japan, Korea, Malaysia, Pakistan, the Philippine Islands, Thailand, and Vietnam. It includes Asian Indian, Chinese, Filipino, Korean, Japanese, Vietnamese, and Other Asian.

Asian Indian includes people who indicate their race as Asian Indian or identify themselves as Bengalese, Bharat, Dravidian, East Indian, or Goanese. *Chinese* includes people who indicate their race as Chinese or who identify themselves as Cantonese or Chinese American. In some census tabulations, written entries of Taiwanese are included with Chinese while in others they are shown separately. *Filipino* includes people who indicate their race as Filipino or who report entries such as Philipano, Philipine, or Filipino American. *Japanese* includes people who indicate their race as Japanese or who report entries such as Nipponese or Japanese American. *Korean* includes people who indicate their race as Korean or who provide a response of Korean American. *Vietnamese* includes people who indicate their race as Vietnamese or who provide a response of Vietnamese American.

American Indian and Alaska Native. A person having origins in any of the original peoples of North and South America including Central America, and who maintain tribal affiliation or community attachment. It includes people who classify themselves as described below.

American Indian. Includes people who indicate their race as American Indian, entered the name of an Indian tribe, or report such entries as Canadian Indian, French-American Indian, or Spanish-American Indian.

Alaska Native. Includes written responses of Eskimos, Aleuts, and Alaska Indians as well as entries such as Arctic Slope, Inupait, Yupik, Alutiiq, Egeik, and Pribilovian. The Alaska tribes are the Alaskan Athabascan, Tlingit, and Haida.

Native Hawaiian and Other Pacific Islander. A person having origins in any of the original peoples of Hawaii, Guam, Samoa, or other Pacific Islands. It includes people who indicate their race as Native Hawaiian, Guanamian or Chamorro, Samoan, and Other Pacific Islander.

Native Hawaiian includes people who indicate their race as Native Hawaiian or who identify themselves as "Part Hawaiian" or Hawaiian. *Guamanian or Chamorro* includes people who indicate their race as such, including written entries of Chamorro or Guam. *Samoan* includes people who indicate their race as Samoan or who identified themselves as American Samoan or Western Samoan. *Other Pacific Islander* includes people who provided a write-in response of a Pacific Islander group such as Tahitian, Northern Mariana Islander, Palauan, Fijian, or a cultural group, such as Melanesian, Micronesian, or Polynesian.

Hispanic or Latino origin. People who identify with the terms Hispanic or Latino are those who classify themselves in one of the specific Hispanic or Latino categories listed on the questionnaire—Mexican, Puerto Rican, or Cuban—as well as those who indicate that they are "Other Spanish, Hispanic, or Latino." Origin can be viewed as the heritage, nationality group, lineage, or country of birth of the person or the person's parents or ancestors before their arrival in the United States. People who identify their origin as Spanish, Hispanic, or Latino may be of any race.

Housing unit estimates are developed by using building permits, mobile home shipments, and estimates of housing unit loss to measure housing unit change since the last census. For more information, see www.census.gov/popest/methodology/index.html .

Table C-3. Personal Income and Earnings, by Industry

Sources: Personal income and earnings—U.S. Bureau of Economic Analysis, Regional Economic Accounts, Local Area Personal Income and Employment, www.bea.gov/regional/index.htm. Population for per capita income—U.S. Census Bureau; For 2005, compiled from Population Estimates, Intercensal Estimates of the Resident Population of Counties: April 1, 2000 to July 1, 2010, www.census.gov/popest/data/historical/2000s/index.html . For 2011, compiled from Current Estimates Data, www.census.gov/popest/data/counties/totals/2011/index.html.

Personal income is the income that is received by all persons from all sources. It is calculated as the sum of wage and salary disbursements, supplements to wages and salaries, proprietors' income with inventory valuation and capital consumption adjustments, rental income of people with capital consumption adjustment, personal dividend income, personal interest income, and personal current transfer receipts, less contributions for government social insurance.

The personal income of an area is the income that is received by, or on behalf of, all the individuals who live in the area; therefore, the estimates of personal income are presented by the place of residence of the income recipients.

Personal income differs by definition from money income, which is prepared by the Census Bureau, in that money income is measured before deduction of personal contributions for social insurance and does not include imputed income, lump-sum payments, and income received by quasi-individuals. Money income does include income from private pensions and annuities and from interpersonal transfer, such as child support; therefore it is not comparable to personal income. Total personal income is adjusted to place of residence.

About 90 percent of the state and county estimates of personal income are based on census data and on administrative-records data that are collected by other federal agencies. The data from censuses are mainly collected from the recipient of the income. The most important sources of census data for the state and county estimates are the census of agriculture and the census of population and housing that are conducted by the Census Bureau. The data from administrative records may originate either from the recipients of the income or from the source of the income. These data are a byproduct of the administration of various federal and state government programs. The most important sources of these data are as follows: the state unemployment insurance programs of the

Employment and Training Administration, Department of Labor; the social insurance programs of the Social Security Administration and the Health Care Financing Administration, Department of Health and Human Services; the federal income tax program of the Internal Revenue Service, Department of the Treasury; the veterans benefit programs of the Department of Veterans Affairs; and the military payroll systems of the Department of Defense. The remaining 10 percent of the estimates are based on data from other sources. For example, the estimates of the components of farm proprietors' income, a component of personal income, are partly based on the state estimates of farm income and the county estimates of case receipts, crop production, and livestock inventory that are prepared by the Department of Agriculture, which uses sample surveys, along with census data and administrative-records data, to derive its estimates.

Total **earnings** cover wage and salary disbursements, supplements to wages and salaries, and proprietor's income. Wage and salary disbursements consist of the monetary remuneration of employees, including corporate officers salaries and bonuses, commissions, pay-in-kind, incentive payments, and tips. It reflects the amount of payments disbursed, but not necessarily earned during the year. It is measured before deductions, such as social security contributions and union dues. Wage and salary disbursements includes stock options of nonqualified plans at the time that they have been exercised by the individual. Stock options are reported in wage and salary disbursements. The value that is included in wages is the difference between the exercise price and the price that the stock options were granted. Supplements to wages and salaries consists of employer contributions for employee pension and insurance funds and of employer contributions for government social insurance. Proprietor's income is the current-production income (including income-in-kind) of sole proprietorships and partnerships and of tax-exempt cooperatives. Corporate directors' fees are included in proprietors' income, but the imputed net rental income of owner-occupants of all dwellings is included in rental income of persons. Proprietors' income excludes dividends and monetary interest received by nonfinancial business and rental incomes received by persons not primarily engaged in the real estate business; these incomes are included in dividends, net interest, and rental income of persons, respectively.

The estimates of earnings from 2011 are based on the 2007 North American Industry Classification System (NAICS). For more information on NAICS visit www.census.gov/eos/www/naics/index.html .

Earnings by place of work is the sum of Wage and Salary Disbursements, supplements to wages and salaries and proprietors' income.

Table C-4. Labor Force and Private Business Establishments and Employment

Sources: Civilian labor force—U.S. Bureau of Labor Statistics, Local Area Unemployment, Annual Averages; www.bls.gov/lau/ . Private nonfarm businesses—U.S. Census Bureau, County Business Patterns; www.census.gov/econ/cbp/ .

Civilian Labor Force

Civilian labor force data are the product of a federal-state cooperative program in which state employment security agencies prepare labor force and unemployment estimates under concepts, definitions, and technical procedures established by the BLS. These data for substate areas are produced by the BLS primarily for use in allocating funds under various federal legislative programs. Users of these data are cautioned that, because of the small size of many of the areas, as well as limitations of the data inputs, the estimates are subject to considerable, but nonquantifiable, error. An explanation of the technical procedures used to develop monthly and annual local area labor force estimates appears monthly in the Explanatory Note for state and area unemployment data in the BLS periodical, *Employment and Earnings*. Additional information may also be found at the BLS website at www.bls.gov/opub/hom/ .

The civilian labor force comprises all persons in the civilian noninstitutional population classified as either employed or unemployed. Employed persons are persons 16 years and over in the civilian noninstitutional population who, during the reference week, (a) did any work at all (at least 1 hour) as paid employees; worked in their own business, profession, or on their own farm, or worked 15 hours or more as unpaid workers in an enterprise operated by a member of the family; and (b) all those who were not working but who had jobs or businesses from which they were temporarily absent because of vacation, illness, bad weather, childcare problems, maternity or paternity leave, labor-management dispute, job training, or other family or personal reasons, whether or not they were paid for the time off or were seeking other jobs. Each employed person is counted only once, even if he or she holds more than one job. Excluded are persons whose only activity consisted of work around their own house (painting, repairing, or own home housework) or volunteer work for religious, charitable, and other organizations.

Unemployed people are all civilians aged 16 years and older who had no employment during the reference week, were available for work, except for temporary illness, and had made specific efforts to find employment sometime during the 4-week period ending with the reference week. Persons who were waiting to be recalled to a job from which they had been laid off need not have been looking for work to be classified as unemployed. The unemployment rate for all civilian workers represents the number of unemployed as a percent of the civilian labor force.

County Business Patterns (CBP) is an annual series that provides subnational economic data by industry. The series is useful for studying the economic activity of small areas; analyzing economic changes over time; and as a benchmark for statistical series, surveys, and databases between economic censuses. CBP covers most of the country's economic activity. The series excludes data on self-employed individuals, employees of private households, railroad employees, agricultural production employees, and most government employees. The County Business Patterns program has been tabulated on a North American Industry Classification System (NAICS) basis since 1998. Data for 1997 and earlier years are based on the Standard Industrial Classification (SIC) system. For more information on the relationship between the two systems, see Concordances www.census.gov/eos/www/naics/concordances/concordances.html .

CBP data are extracted from the Business Register, the Census Bureau's file of all known single and multi-establishment companies. The Annual Company Organization Survey and quinquennial economic censuses provide individual establishment data for multilocation firms. Data for single-location firms are obtained from various programs censuses, the Annual Survey of Manufactures, and Current Business Surveys, as well as from administrative records of the Internal Revenue Service (IRS), the Social Security Administration (SSA), and the Bureau of Labor Statistics (BLS).

An **establishment** is a single physical location at which business is conducted or services or industrial operations are performed. It is not necessarily identical with a company or enterprise, which may consist of one or more establishments. When two or more activities are carried on at a single location under a single ownership, all activities generally are grouped together as a single establishment. The entire establishment is classified on the basis of its major activity and all data are included in that classification. Establishment-size designations are determined by paid employment in the mid-March pay period. The size group "1 to 4" includes establishments that did not report any paid employees in the mid-March pay period but paid wages to at least one employee at some time during the year.

Establishment counts represent the number of locations with paid employees any time during the year. This series excludes governmental establishments except for wholesale liquor establishments (NAICS 4248), retail liquor stores (NAICS 44531), federally-chartered savings institutions (NAICS 522120), federally-chartered credit unions (NAICS 522130), and hospitals (NAICS 622).

Total payroll includes all forms of compensation, such as salaries, wages, reported tips, commissions, bonuses, vacation allowances, sick-leave pay, employee contributions to qualified pension plans, and the value of taxable fringe benefits. For corporations, it includes amounts paid to officers and executives; for unincorporated businesses, it does not include profit or other compensation of proprietors or partners. Payroll is reported before deductions for social security, income tax, insurance, union dues, and so on. First-quarter payroll consists of payroll during the January-to-March quarter.

Paid employment consists of full- and part-time employees, including salaried officers and executives of corporations, who are on the payroll in the pay period including March 12. Included are employees on paid sick leave, holidays, and vacations; not included are proprietors and partners of unincorporated businesses.

PART D—MICROPOLITAN AREAS WITH COMPONENT COUNTIES

Table D consists of 1 table (D-1) with 13 data items for 576 micropolitan statistical areas and 688 counties within the micropolitan areas. They are presented alphabetically, with counties listed alphabetically within each micropolitan area.

All summaries, including historical data, are presented for the areas as currently defined. Where possible, the original figures have been retabulated to reflect the status of micropolitan area boundaries as of December 1, 2009. For more information on these areas, see Appendix C, Geographic Concepts and Codes.

Table D-1. Population and Personal Income

Sources: Population—U.S. Census Bureau, from 2010 to 2011, "Annual Estimates of the Resident Population: April 1, 2010 to July 1, 2011, www.census.gov/popest/data/counties/totals/2011/files/CO-EST2011-Alldata.csv. For 2000, Population Estimates: Historical Estimates Data (revised data for April 1, 2000, Population Estimates base) www.census.gov/popest/data/intercensal/county/files/CO-EST00INT-TOT.csv. For 1990, Population Estimates: Historical Estimates Data (revised data for April 1, 1990, Population Estimates base) www.census.gov/popest/data/intercensal/st-co/files/CO-EST2001-12-00.pdf. Personal income—U.S. Bureau of Economic Analysis, State and Local Area Personal Income, www.bea.gov/regional/index.htm .

Population numbers for 2010, 2000, and 1990 are counts of the resident population on April 1 of those decennial census years. The April 1 estimates base population may differ from the April 1 census count due to legal boundary updates, other geographic program changes, and Count Question Resolution actions.

Population estimates for 2011 measure the estimated population from the calculated number of people living in an area as of July 1. The Census Bureau develops county population estimates with a component of population change method in which they use administrative records and other data to estimate the household and group quarters population. For the household population, the components of population change are births, deaths, net domestic migration, and net international migration. They measure change in the nonhousehold, or group quarters, population by the net change in the population living in group quarters facilities.

A major assumption underlying this approach is that changes in selected administrative and other data sources closely approximate the components of population change. Therefore, Census Bureau demographers separately estimate each component of population change based on administrative records, including registered births and deaths, federal income tax returns, Medicare enrollees, and military movement. They also separately estimate net international migration using information from the American Community Survey (ACS), the decennial census, and other data sources.

Most administrative record data sources lag the current estimate year by as much as 2 years; therefore, the Census Bureau projects the data for the current year based on past years' data. As updated data become available, they revise the projected input data so that each vintage's estimates are always based on the most recent data available.

For more information on the method used for these estimates, see Appendix B, Limitations and Methodology, and the website at www.census.gov/popest/methodology/index.html .

Personal income is the income that is received by all persons from all sources. It is calculated as the sum of wage and salary disbursements, supplements to wages and salaries, proprietors' income with inventory valuation and capital consumption adjustments, rental income of people with capital consumption adjustment, personal dividend income, personal interest income, and personal current transfer receipts, less contributions for government social insurance.

The personal income of an area is the income that is received by, or on behalf of, all the individuals who live in the area; therefore, the estimates of personal income are presented by the place of residence of the income recipients.

Personal income differs by definition from money income, which is prepared by the Census Bureau, in that money income is measured before deduction of personal contributions for social insurance and does not include imputed income, lump-sum payments, and income received by quasi-individuals. Money income does include income from private pensions and annuities and from interpersonal transfer, such as child support; therefore it is not comparable to personal income. Total personal income is adjusted to place of residence.

About 90 percent of the state and county estimates of personal income are based on census data and on administrative-records data that are collected by other federal agencies. The data from censuses are mainly collected from the recipient of the income. The most important sources of census data for the state and county estimates are the census of agriculture and the census of population and housing that are conducted by the Census Bureau. The data from administrative records may originate either from the recipients of the income or from the source of the income. These data are a byproduct of the administration of various federal and state government programs. The most important sources of these data are as follows: the state unemployment insurance programs of the Employment and Training Administration, Department of Labor; the social insurance programs of the Social Security Administration and the Health Care Financing Administration, Department of Health and Human Services; the federal income tax program of the Internal Revenue Service, Department of the Treasury; the veterans benefit programs of the Department of Veterans Affairs; and the military payroll systems of the Department of Defense. The remaining 10 percent of the estimates are based on data from other sources. For example, the estimates of the components of farm proprietors' income, a component of personal income, are partly based on the state estimates of farm income and the county estimates of case receipts, crop production, and livestock inventory that are prepared by the Department of Agriculture, which uses sample surveys, along with census data and administrative-records data, to derive its estimates.

APPENDIX B
LIMITATIONS OF THE DATA AND METHODOLOGY

INTRODUCTION

The data presented in this *State and Metropolitan Area Data Book* came from many sources. The sources include not only federal statistical bureaus and other organizations that collect and issue statistics as their principal activity, but also governmental administrative and regulatory agencies, private research bodies, trade associations, insurance companies, health associations, and private organizations such as the National Education Association and philanthropic foundations. Consequently, the data vary considerably as to reference periods, definitions of terms and, for ongoing series, the number and frequency of time periods for which data are available.

The statistics presented were obtained and tabulated by various means. Some statistics are based on complete enumerations or censuses while others are based on samples. Some information is extracted from records kept for administrative or regulatory purposes (school enrollment, hospital records, securities registration, financial accounts, social security records, income tax returns, and so on), while other information is obtained explicitly for statistical purposes through interviews or by mail. The estimation procedures used vary from highly sophisticated scientific techniques to crude "informed guesses."

Each set of data relates to a group of individuals or units of interest referred to as the *target universe* or *target population*, or simply as the *universe* or *population*. Prior to data collection the target universe should be clearly defined. For example, if data are to be collected for the universe of households in the United States, it is necessary to define a "household." The target universe may not be completely traceable. Cost and other considerations may restrict data collection to a survey universe based on some available list and that list may be inaccurate or out of date. This list is called a *survey frame* or *sampling frame*.

The data in many tables are based on data obtained for all population units, a census, or on data obtained for only a portion, or sample, of the population units. When the data presented are based on a sample, the sample is usually a scientifically selected probability sample. This is a sample selected from a list or sampling frame in such a way that every possible sample has a known chance of selection and usually each unit selected can be assigned a number, greater than zero and less than or equal to one, representing its likelihood or probability of selection.

For large-scale sample surveys, the probability sample of units is often selected as a multistage sample. The first stage of a multistage sample is the selection of a probability sample of large groups of population members, referred to as primary sampling units (PSUs). For example, in a national multistage household sample, PSUs are often counties or groups of counties. The second stage of a multistage sample is the selection, within each PSU selected at the first stage, of smaller groups of population units, referred to as secondary sampling units. In subsequent stages of selection, smaller and smaller nested groups are chosen until the ultimate sample of population units is obtained. To qualify a multistage sample as a probability sample, all stages of sampling must be carried out using probability-sampling methods.

Prior to selection at each stage of a multistage (or a single-stage) sample, a list of the sampling units or sampling frame for that stage must be obtained. For example, for the first stage of selection of a national household sample, a list of the counties and county groups that form the PSUs must be obtained. For the final stage of selection, lists of households, and sometimes persons within the households, have to be compiled in the field. For surveys of economic entities and for the economic censuses the Census Bureau generally uses a frame constructed from the Census Bureau's Business Register. The Business Register contains all establishments with payroll in the United States including small single establishment firms as well as large multi-establishment firms.

Wherever the quantities in a table refer to an entire universe, but are constructed from data collected in a sample survey, the table quantities are referred to as *sample estimates*. In constructing a sample estimate, an attempt is made to come as close as is feasible to the corresponding universe quantity that would be obtained from a complete census of the universe. Estimates based on a sample will, however, generally differ from the hypothetical census figures. Two classifications of errors are associated with estimates based on sample surveys: (1) *sampling error*—the error arising from the use of a sample, rather than a census, to estimate population quantities, and (2) *nonsampling error*—those errors arising from nonsampling sources. As discussed below, the magnitude of the sampling error for an estimate can usually be estimated from the sample data. However, the magnitude of the nonsampling error for an estimate can rarely be estimated. Consequently, actual error in an estimate exceeds the error that can be estimated.

The particular sample used in a survey is only one of a large number of possible samples of the same size, which could have been selected using the same sampling procedure. Estimates derived from the different samples would, in general, differ from each other. The *standard error* (SE) is a measure of the variation among the estimates derived from all possible samples. The standard error is the most commonly used measure of the sampling error of an estimate. Valid estimates of the standard errors of survey estimates can usually be calculated from the data collected in a probability sample. For convenience, the standard error is sometimes expressed as a percent of the estimate and is called the relative standard error or *coefficient of variation* (CV). For example, an estimate of 200 units with an estimated standard error of 10 units has an estimated CV of 5 percent.

A sample estimate and an estimate of its standard error or CV can be used to construct interval estimates that have a prescribed confidence that the interval includes the average of the estimates derived from all possible samples with a known probability. To illustrate, if all possible samples were selected under essentially the same general conditions, and using the same sample design, and if an estimate and its estimated standard error were calculated from each sample, then: (1) approximately 68 percent of the intervals from one standard error below the estimate to one standard error above the estimate would include the average estimate derived from all possible samples; (2) approximately 90 percent of the intervals from 1.6 standard errors below the estimate to 1.6 standard errors above the estimate would include the average estimate derived from all possible samples; and (3) approximately 95 percent of the intervals from two standard errors below the estimate to two standard errors above the estimate would include the average estimate derived from all possible samples.

Thus, for a particular sample, one can say with the appropriate level of confidence (e.g., 90 percent or 95 percent) that the average of all possible samples is included in the constructed interval. Example of a confidence interval: an estimate is 200 units with a standard error of 10 units. An approximately 90 percent confidence interval (plus or minus 1.6 standard errors) is from 184 to 216.

All surveys and censuses are subject to nonsampling errors. Nonsampling errors are of two kinds *random and nonrandom*. Random nonsampling errors arise because of the varying interpretation of questions (by respondents or interviewers) and varying actions of coders, keyers, and other processors. Some randomness is also introduced when respondents must estimate. Nonrandom nonsampling errors result from total nonresponse (no usable data obtained for a sampled unit), partial or item nonresponse (only a portion of a response may be usable), inability or unwillingness on the part of respondents to provide correct information, difficulty interpreting questions, mistakes in recording or keying data, errors of collection or processing, and coverage problems (overcoverage and undercoverage of the target universe). Random nonresponse errors usually, but not always, result in an understatement of sampling errors and thus an overstatement of the precision of survey estimates. Estimating the magnitude of nonsampling errors would require special experiments or access to independent data and, consequently, the magnitudes are seldom available.

Nearly all types of nonsampling errors that affect surveys also occur in complete censuses. Since surveys can be conducted on a smaller scale than censuses, nonsampling errors can presumably be controlled more tightly. Relatively more funds and effort can perhaps be expended toward eliciting responses, detecting and correcting response error, and reducing processing errors. As a result, survey results can sometimes be more accurate than census results.

To compensate for suspected nonrandom errors, adjustments of the sample estimates are often made. For example, adjustments are frequently made for nonresponse, both total and partial. Adjustments made for either type of nonresponse are often referred to as *imputations*. Imputation for total nonresponse is usually made by substituting for the questionnaire responses of the nonrespondents the "average" questionnaire responses of the respondents. These imputations usually are made separately within various groups of sample members, formed by attempting to place respondents and nonrespondents together that have "similar" design or ancillary characteristics. Imputation for item nonresponse is usually made by substituting for a missing item the response to that item of a respondent having characteristics that are "similar" to those of the nonrespondent.

For an estimate calculated from a sample survey, the *total error* in the estimate is composed of the sampling error, which can usually be estimated from the sample, and the nonsampling error, which usually cannot be estimated from the sample. The total error present in a population quantity obtained from a complete census is composed of only nonsampling errors. Ideally, estimates of the total error associated with data given in these tables should be given. However, due to the unavailability of estimates of nonsampling errors, only estimates of the levels of sampling errors, in terms of estimated standard errors or coefficients of variation, are available. To obtain estimates of the estimated standard errors from the sample of interest, obtain a copy of the referenced report, which appears at the end of each table.

Source of Additional Material: The Federal Committee on Statistical Methodology (FCSM) is an interagency committee dedicated to improving the quality of federal statistics, http://www.fcsm.gov/ .

Principal databases: Beginning below are brief descriptions of 18 of the sample surveys, censuses, and administrative collections that provide a substantial portion of the data contained in this publication.

U.S. DEPARTMENT OF AGRICULTURE

National Agriculture Statistics Service (NASS)

Census of Agriculture

Universe, Frequency, and Types of Data: Complete count of U.S. farms and ranches conducted once every 5 years with data at the national, state, and county level. Data published on farm numbers and related items/characteristics.

Type of Data Collection Operation: Complete census for number of farms; land in farms; farm income; agriculture products sold; farms by type of organization; total cropland; irrigated land; farm operator characteristics; livestock and poultry inventory and sales; and selected crops harvested. Market value of land, buildings, and products sold, total farm production expenses, machinery and equipment, and fertilizer and chemicals.

Data Collection and Imputation Procedures: Data collection is by mailing questionnaires to all farmers and ranchers. Producers can return their forms by mail or online. Nonrespondents are contacted by telephone and correspondence follow-ups. Imputations were made for all nonresponse item/characteristics and coverage adjustments were made to account for missed farms and ranches. The response rate for the 2007 census was 85.2 percent.

Estimates of Sampling Error: Weight adjustments were made to account for the undercoverage and whole-unit nonresponse of farms on the Census Mail List (CML). These were treated as sampling errors.

Other (Nonsampling) Errors: Nonsampling errors are due to incompleteness of the census mailing list, duplications on the list, respondent reporting errors, errors in editing reported data, and imputation for missing data. Evaluation studies are conducted to measure certain nonsampling errors such as list coverage and classification error. It is a reasonable assumption that the net effect of nonmeasurable errors is zero (the positive errors cancel the negative errors).

Sources of Additional Material: U.S. Department of Agriculture, National Agricultural Statistics Service (NASS), 2007 Census of Agriculture, Appendix A-1 Census of Agriculture Methodology, Appendix B-1 General Explanation and Census of Agriculture Report Form.

Multiple Frame Surveys

Universe, Frequency, and Types of Data: Surveys of U.S. farm operators to obtain data on major livestock inventories, selected crop acreage and production, grain stocks, and farm labor characteristics, farm economic data, and chemical use data. Estimates are made quarterly, semiannually, or annually depending on the data series.

Type of Data Collection Operation: Primary frame is obtained from general or special purpose lists, supplemented by a probability sample of land areas used to estimate for list incompleteness.

Data Collection and Imputation Procedures: Mail, telephone, or personal interviews used for initial data collection. Mail nonrespondent follow-up by phone and personal interviews. Imputation based on average of respondents.

Estimates of Sampling Error: Estimated CVs range from 1 percent to 2 percent at the U.S. level for crop and livestock data series and 3 to 5 percent for economic data. Regional CVs range from 3 to 6 percent, while state estimate CVs run 5 to 10 percent.

Other (Nonsampling) Errors: In addition to the above, replicated sampling procedures used to monitor effects of changes in survey procedures.

Sources of Additional Material: U.S. Department of Agriculture, National Agricultural Statistics Service (NASS), USDA's National Agricultural Statistics Service: *The Fact Finders of Agriculture*, March 2007.

U.S. BUREAU OF LABOR STATISTICS

Current Employment Statistics (CES) Program

Universe, Frequency, and Types of Data: Monthly survey drawn from a sampling frame of over 8 million unemployment insurance tax accounts in order to obtain data by industry on employment, hours, and earnings.

Type of Data Collection Operation: The CES sample included about 145,000 businesses and government agencies, which represent approximately 557,000 individual worksites.

Data Collection and Imputation Procedures: Each month, the state agencies cooperating with the Bureau of Labor Statistics (BLS), as well as BLS Data Collection Centers, collect data through various automated collection modes and mail. BLS Washington staff prepares national estimates of employment, hours, and earnings while states use the data to develop state and area estimates.

Estimates of Sampling Errors: The relative standard error for total nonfarm employment is 0.1 percent. A birth/death model adjusts for the impact of business openings and closings. From April through December 2012, the cumulative birth/death model added 755,000 employees.

Other (nonsampling) Errors: Estimates of employment adjusted annually to reflect complete universe. Average adjustment is 0.2 percent over the last decade, with an absolute range from less than 0.1 percent to 0.6 percent.

Sources of Additional Material: U.S. Bureau of Labor Statistics, Employment & Earnings Online. See www.bls .gov/opub/ee/home.htm .

U.S. DEPARTMENT OF COMMERCE

U.S. BUREAU OF ECONOMIC ANALYSIS (BEA)

Regional Economic Accounts

Universe, Frequency, and Types of Data: The Regional Economic Accounts website contains estimates of personal income and its components and employment for local areas such as states, counties, metropolitan areas, and micropolitan areas.

Type of Data Collection Operation: The estimates of personal income are primarily based on administrative records data, census data, and survey data.

Data Collection and Imputation Procedures: The data are collected from administrative records, which may come from the recipients of the income or from the sources of the income. These data are a byproduct of the administration of various federal and state government programs. The most important sources of these data are—the state unemployment insurance programs of the Bureau of Labor Statistics (BLS), the social insurance programs of the Centers for Medicare and Medicaid Services, federal income tax program of the Internal Revenue Service, veterans benefit programs of the U.S. Department of Veterans Affairs, and military payroll systems of the U.S. Department of Defense.

The data from censuses are mainly collected from the recipients of income. The most important sources for these data are the Census of Agriculture at the U.S. Department of Agriculture (USDA) and the Census of Population and Housing conducted by the U.S. Census Bureau. Other sources may include estimates of farm proprietors' income by the USDA, wages and salaries from County Business Patterns from the Census Bureau, and the Quarterly Census of Employment and Wages by the Department of Labor.

Estimates of Sampling Error: Not applicable, except component variables may be subject to error.

Other (Nonsampling) Errors: Nonsampling errors in the administrative data sets may affect personal income estimates.

Sources of Additional Material: Methodological information on other Bureau of Economic Analysis (BEA) datasets such as "State Personal Income" and "Gross State Product" may be found at www.bea.gov/regional/ methods.cfm .

U.S. CENSUS BUREAU

American Community Survey (ACS)

Universe, Frequency, and Types of Data: Nationwide survey to obtain annual data about demographic, social, economic, and housing characteristics of housing units and the people residing in them. It covers the household population and, beginning in 2006, also includes the group quarters population living in prisons, nursing homes, college dormitories, and other group quarters.

Type of Data Collection Operation: Housing unit address sampling is performed twice a year in both August and January. First-phase of sampling defines the universe for the second stage of sampling through two steps. First, all addresses that were eligible for the second phase sampling within the past 4 years are excluded from eligibility. This ensures that no address is in sample more than once in any 5-year period. The second step is to select a 20 percent systematic sample of "new" units, i.e., those units that have never appeared on a previous Master Address File (MAF) extract. All new addresses are systematically assigned to either the current year or to one of four back-samples. This procedure maintains five equal partitions of the universe. The second-phase sampling is done on the current year's partition and results in approximately 3,000,000 housing unit addresses in the United States and 36,000 in Puerto Rico. Group quarter sampling is performed separately from the housing unit sampling. The sampling begins with separating the small (15 persons or fewer) and the large (more than 15 persons) group quarters. The target sampling rate for both groups is a 2.5 percent sample of the group quarters population. It results in approximately 200,000 group quarters residents being selected in the United States, and an additional 1,000 in Puerto Rico.

Data Collection and Imputation Procedures: The American Community Survey is conducted every month on independent samples. Each housing unit in the independent monthly samples is mailed a prenotice letter announcing the selection of the address to participate, a survey questionnaire package, and a reminder postcard. These sample units addresses receive a second (replacement) questionnaire package if the initial questionnaire has not been returned by mid-month. Sample addresses for which a questionnaire is not returned in the mail and a telephone number is not available are forwarded to telephone centers for follow-up. Interviewers attempt to contact and interview these mail nonresponse cases by telephone. Sample addresses that are still unresponsive after 2 months of attempts are forwarded for a possible personal visit. Unresponsive addresses are subsampled at rates between 1 in 3 and 2 in 3. Those addresses selected through this process are assigned to Field Representatives (FRs), who visit the addresses, verify their existence, determine their occupancy status, and conduct interviews. Collection of group quarters data is conducted by FRs only. Their methods include completing the questionnaire while speaking to the resident in person or over the telephone, or leaving paper questionnaires for residents to complete for themselves and then pick them up later. This last option is used for data collection in federal prisons. If needed, a personal interview can be conducted with a proxy, such as a relative or guardian. After data collection is completed, any remaining incomplete or inconsistent information on the questionnaire is imputed during the final automated edit of the collected data.

Estimates of Sampling Error: The data in the ACS products are estimates and can vary from the actual values that would have been obtained by conducting a census of the entire population. The estimates from the chosen sample addresses can also vary from those that would have been obtained from a different set of addresses. This variation causes uncertainty, which can be measured using statistics such as standard error, margin of error, and confidence interval. All ACS estimates are accompanied by margins of error to assist users.

Other (Nonsampling) Errors: Nonsampling Error—In addition to sampling error, data users should realize that other types of errors may be introduced during any of the various complex operations used to select, collect, and process survey data. An important goal of the ACS is to minimize the amount of nonsampling error introduced through coverage issues in the sample list, nonresponse from sample housing units, and transcribing or editing data. One way of accomplishing this is by finding additional sources of addresses, following up on nonrespondents, and maintaining quality control systems.

Sources of Additional Material: U.S. Census Bureau, American Community Survey website at www.census .gov/acs; U.S. Census Bureau, American Community Survey Accuracy of the Data documents at http://www.census.gov/acs/www/UseData/Accuracy/Accuracy1.htm .

Annual Survey of Manufactures (ASM)

Universe, Frequency, and Types of Data: The Annual Survey of Manufactures is conducted annually, except for years ending in "2" and "7", for all manufacturing establishments having one or more paid employees. The purpose of the ASM is to provide key intercensal measures of manufacturing activity, products, and location for the public and private sectors. The ASM provides statistics on employment, payroll, worker hours, payroll supplements, cost of materials, value added by manufacturing, capital expenditures, inventories, and energy consumption. It also provides estimates of value of shipments for 1,800 classes of manufactured products.

Type of Data Collection Operation: The ASM includes approximately 50,000 establishments selected from the census universe of 328,500 manufacturing establishments. Approximately 15,400 large establishments are selected with certainty, and the remaining establishments are selected with probability proportional to a composite measure of establishment size. The survey is updated from two sources: Internal Revenue Service (IRS) administrative records are used to include new single-unit manufacturers and the Company Organization Survey identifies new establishments of multi-unit forms.

Data Collection and Imputation Procedures: Survey is conducted by mail with phone and mail follow-ups of nonrespondents. Imputation (for all nonresponse items) is based on previous year reports, or for new establishments in the survey, on industry averages.

Estimates of Sampling Error: Estimated relative standard errors for number of employees, new expenditures, and for value added totals are given in annual publications. For U.S.-level industry statistics, most estimated relative standard errors are 2 percent or less, but vary considerably for detailed characteristics.

Other (Nonsampling) Errors: The unit response rate is about 85 percent. Nonsampling errors include those due to collection, reporting, and transcription errors, many of which are corrected through computer and clerical checks.

Sources of Additional Material: U.S. Census Bureau, *Annual Survey of Manufactures*, www.census.gov/manufacturing/asm/index.html .

State Government Tax Collections (STC)

Universe, Frequency, and Types of Data: The universe for the State Tax Collections Survey covers the 50 state governments only. No local governments are included in the universe for each state. The data have been collected annually since 1939. Statistics on the State Government Tax Collections Survey include measurement of tax by category: Property Tax, Sales and Gross Receipts Taxes, License Taxes, Income Taxes, and Other Taxes. Each tax category is broken down into subcategories (e.g., motor fuel sales, alcoholic beverage sales, motor vehicle licenses, alcoholic beverage licenses). There are currently 25 different tax codes that state tax revenue may fall into.

Type of Data Collection Operation: Most of the data in this report were gathered by a mail canvass of appropriate state government offices that are directly involved with state-administered taxes. There are approximately one hundred offices that are canvassed to collect data from all fifty states. Follow-up procedures include the use of mail, telephone, and e-mail until data are received.

Data Editing and Imputation Procedures: Data are processed from several collection methods including direct response to survey forms from state government officials, as well as from the compilation of administrative records

and supplemental sources. Regardless of the collection method, these data are edited using ratio edits of the current year's value to the prior year's value. The fifty state governments provide the Census Bureau with administrative records from their central accounting systems. These administrative records are unique to each state as each state is legally organized differently from every other state and, as such, each state has a unique organizational and accounting structure. It is the responsibility of the Census Bureau to classify the different accounting and organizational structures into uniform tax categories so that entities with different methods of government accounting can be presented on a comparable basis. The records represent the core, or central, state government and are limited to tax revenue. Data on state government tax revenues are compiled from state administrative records by Census Bureau employees, according to the Census Bureau's classification methodology. When state records do not include full tax revenue detail or reporting units do not respond, supplemental data sources from external financial reports or the Census Bureau's *Annual Survey of State Government Finances and Quarterly Summary of State and Local Government Tax Revenue* are required to complete the datasets. This procedure is called imputation. Supplemental records are merged with data from the state governments. Although every effort is made to obtain financial information from all state government entities, financial statements may not be available at the time the Census Bureau closes the processing, or governmental entities may not respond to the Census Bureau's requests. Every year the data are subject to revisions as new data become available.

Estimates of Sampling Error: These data are not subject to sampling error because this is a complete enumeration of all 50 state governments.

Other (Nonsampling) Errors: Despite efforts made in all phases of collection, processing, and tabulation to minimize errors, the survey is subject to nonsampling errors such as the inability to obtain data for every variable for all units, inaccuracies in classification, mistakes in keying and coding, and coverage errors.

Sources of Additional Material: For further information, see the *Government Finance and Employment Classification Manual*, www.census.gov/govs/classification/ and the *2007 Census of Governments*, www.census.gov/govs/cog/ .

Annual Survey of Public Employment and Payroll (ASPEP)

Universe, Frequency, and Types of Data: The population of interest for this survey includes the civilian employees of all federal government agencies (except the Central Intelligence Agency, the National Security Agency, and the Defense Intelligence Agency), all agencies of the 50 state governments, and 89,476 local governments (i.e., counties, municipalities, townships, special districts, and school districts) including the District of Columbia. Data have been collected annually since 1957. A census is conducted every 5 years (years ending in "2" and "7"). A sample of state and local governments is used to collect data in the intervening years. A new sample is selected every 5 years (in years ending in "4" and "9"). The survey provides data on full-time and part-time employment, part-time hours worked, full-time equivalent employment, and payroll statistics by governmental function (i.e., elementary and secondary education, higher education).

Type of Data Collection Operation: Data collected for the Annual Survey of Government Employment are public record and are not confidential, as authorized by Title 13, U.S. Code, Section 9. Census Bureau staff compiled federal government data from records of the U.S. Office of Personnel Management (OPM). These data are based on the Monthly Report of Federal Civilian Employment. Census Bureau staff collected some state government data through special arrangements, referred to as central collection agreements, wherein data for multiple state agencies or school districts are reported by a central respondent generally in an electronic file. Forty-five of the state governments provided data from central payroll records for all or most of their agencies/institutions. Data for agencies and institutions for the remaining state governments were obtained by mail canvass questionnaires. Local governments were also canvassed using a mail questionnaire. All respondents receiving the mail questionnaire had the option of responding electronically using the website developed for reporting data.

Data Editing and Imputation Procedures: Editing is a process that ensures survey data are accurate, complete, and consistent. Efforts are made at all phases of collection, processing, and tabulation to minimize errors. Although some edits are built into the Internet data collection instrument and the data entry programs, the majority of the edits are performed post collection. Edits consist primarily of two types: (1) *consistency edits* and (2) *historical ratio edits* of the current year's reported value to the prior year's value. The *consistency edits* check the logical relationships of data items reported on the form. For each function where employees are reported, the *historical ratio edits* compare data from two different time periods.

Not all respondents answer every item on the questionnaire. There are also questionnaires that are not returned despite efforts to gain a response. Imputation is the process of filling in missing or invalid data with reasonable values in order to have a complete data set for analytical purposes. For nonresponding governments, the imputations were based on recently reported historical data from either a prior year annual survey or the most recent Census of Governments. These data were adjusted by a growth rate that was determined by the growth of responding units that were similar (in size, geography, and type of government) to the nonrespondent. If there was no recent historical data available, the imputations were based on the data from a randomly selected responding donor that was similar to the nonrespondent. In cases where good secondary data sources exist, the data from those sources were used.

Estimates of Sampling Error: The intercensal data come from a sample rather than a census of all possible units. The particular sample that was selected is one of a larger number of possible samples of the same size and sample design that could have been selected. Each sample would have yielded different estimates. The estimated coefficients of variation, which are provided for each estimate on www.census.gov/govs , are an estimate of this sampling variability.

Other (Nonsampling) Errors: Although every effort is made in all phases of collection, processing, and tabulation to minimize errors, the data are subject to nonsampling errors such as inability to obtain data for every variable from all units in the population of interest, inaccuracies in classification, response errors, misinterpretation of questions, mistakes in keying and coding, and coverage errors. The data processing section describes our efforts to mitigate errors due to nonresponse, keying, reporting errors, etc.

Sources of Additional Material: For further information, see the *Government Finance and Employment Classification Manual* www.census.gov/govs/classification/ and the *2007 Census of Governments*, www.census.gov/govs/cog/ .

Annual Finance Survey (AFS)

Universe, Frequency, and Types of Data: The population of interest for this survey contains the 50 state governments and 89,476 local governments (counties, municipalities, townships, special districts, and school districts) including the District of Columbia. In years ending in "2" and "7" the entire universe is canvassed. In intervening years, a sample of the population of interest is surveyed. The survey coverage includes all state and local governments in the United States.

The survey collects financial data. Revenue data include taxes (i.e., property, sales, tobacco, motor vehicle, licensing and permit), charges, interest, and other earnings. Expenditure data include total by function (i.e., education, highways, airports, water and sewerage, health, hospitals, corrections, fire and police protection), and by accounting category (i.e., current operations and capital outlays). Debt data include issuance, retirement, and amounts outstanding. Financial assets data include securities and other holdings, by type.

Type of Data Collection Operation: The data collection for the state and local finance survey (both census and sample survey) is made up of three modes to obtain data: mail canvass, internet collection, and central collection from state sources. Collection methods vary by state and type of government. Administrative data are compiled for most state government agencies and the 48 largest and most complex county and municipal governments. The survey melds several government finance surveys, including the Survey of Local Government Finances, Survey of Public-Employee Retirement Systems, Integrated Post-secondary Educational Data System (IPEDS) from the National Center for Education Statistics (NCES), State Government Finances Survey, and the Survey of Public Elementary-Secondary Education Finances.

Data Editing and Imputation Procedures: Not all respondents answer every item on the questionnaire. There are also questionnaires that are not returned despite efforts to gain a response. Imputation is the process of filling in missing or invalid data with reasonable values in order to have a complete data set for analytical purposes. For nonresponding governments, imputations for missing units are based on recently reported historical data from either a prior year annual survey or the most recent census, adjusted by a growth rate. If no historical data are available, data from a randomly selected similar unit are used for the imputation.

Editing is a process that ensures data are accurate, complete, and consistent. Efforts are made at all phases of collection, processing, and tabulation to minimize errors. Although some edits are built into the internet data collection instrument and the data entry programs, the majority of the edits are performed post collection. Data are checked for internal consistency within the questionnaire and for historical accuracy.

Estimates of Sampling Error: In census years, all of the units in the population are surveyed, and there is no sampling error. In the intercensal years, the population is sampled, and the estimates are subject to sampling error. The coefficient of variation is a measure of sampling variability expressed as a percentage of the estimated total. Generally, the estimated coefficients of variation for

state and local government revenues, expenditures, debt, or assets are under 3 percent in each state. Coefficients of variation for the estimates are given in the tables on the website www.census.gov/govs/estimate/index.html .

Other (Nonsampling) Errors: Although every effort is made in all phases of collection, processing, and tabulation to minimize errors, the data are subject to nonsampling errors such as inability to obtain data for every variable from all units in the population of interest, inaccuracies in classification, response errors, misinterpretation of questions, mistakes in keying and coding, and coverage errors.

Sources of Additional Material: For more information on the survey, see www.census.gov/govs/estimate/index.html . On that site, see the *Survey Methodology* and *Government Finance and Employment Classification Manual.*

FEDERAL PROGRAMS

Consolidated Federal Funds Report (CFFR)
Federal Aid to States (FAS)
Federal Assistance Award Data System (FAADS)

Universe, Frequency, and Types of Data: The federal statistics included in these tables come from three sources. The Consolidated Federal Funds Report (CFFR) covers all states, the District of Columbia, and U.S. outlying areas. CFFR data were obtained from federal government expenditures or obligations to government agencies. Thirty-three departments and agencies of the executive branch of the federal government with grant making authority are generally reporting quarterly to FAADS.

The Federal Assistance Award Data System is authorized by Title 31, Section 6102(a), U.S. Code. Reporting covers approximately 600 federal assistance programs. While primarily concerned with assistance to state and local governments, all major programs providing transfer payments to individuals, discretionary project grants, loans, or insurance are also covered. The CFFR reports have been prepared annually by the Census Bureau since 1983 as authorized by Titles 13 and 31, U.S. Code and a 1982 designation by the Office of Management and Budget. Data are obtained on the amount of virtually all federal expenditures, including grants, loans, direct payments, insurance, procurement, salaries and wages, and other awards (such as price supports and research awards). Data collected for CFFR come from the following sources: U.S. Department of Defense, FAADS, Federal Procurement Data System, Office of Personnel Management, and the U.S. Postal Service. Selected data from the information on payments to state or local governments reported by federal agencies come from the FAS report.

The Census Bureau's Federal Financial Statistics program was terminated in 2012. The 2010 CFFR data in this book are from the final release of CFFR data.

Type of Data Collection Operation: FAADS is a repository of data on federal financial assistance award transactions; the administrative data are compiled quarterly. The CFFR aggregates this quarterly data and supplements the data with additional records from the federal agencies to get the complete array of variables reported by CFFR. FAS uses imported electronic data files that have been completed by the various federal agencies.

Data Editing and Imputation Procedures: When respondents submit the data, sometimes there are errors due to a misinterpretation of the request, a keying error, an inadvertent misclassification, etc. To mitigate these types of errors, the Census Bureau edits the data by verifying the data totals and geographic coding.

Estimates of Sampling Error: These data are not subject to sampling error because this is a complete enumeration of all governments in the universe.

Other (Nonsampling) Errors: Coverage errors occur when there is a failure to cover the entire population of interest for a survey. Since we may not have a complete list of agencies, we may have some coverage error. When data are missing due to nonresponse, the Census Bureau imputes for the missing data items in order to have a complete data set for analytical purposes. Errors may also arise in our geographic coding due to agency data entry input errors. These errors are mitigated by following editing procedures. Routine edits applied to FAADS data are primarily intended to identify and correct keying or calculation errors made by respondents.

Sources of Additional Material: For more information on the federal data, see www.census.gov/govs/cffr/; for links to information on the Consolidated Federal Funds Report, www.census.gov/govs/www/faads.html; for information on the Federal Assistance Award Data System, www.census.gov/prod/2011pubs/fas-10.pdf; and for information on the most recent Federal Aid to States. Because these programs have been terminated, the websites provide links to related data sources.

2007 Economic Census

(Industry Series, Geographic Area Series, and Subject Series Reports) (for NAICS sectors 21 to 81).

Universe, Frequency, and Types of Data. Conducted every 5 years to obtain data on number of establishments, number of employees, payroll, total sales/receipts/revenue, and other industry-specific statistics. The universe is all establishments with paid employees excluding agriculture, forestry, fishing and hunting, and government. (Nonemployer Statistics, discussed separately, covers those establishments without paid employees.)

Type of Data Collection Operation: All large employer firms were surveyed (i.e., all employer firms above payroll-size cutoffs established to separate large from small employers) plus, in most sectors, a sample of the small employer firms.

Data Collection and Imputation Procedures: Mail questionnaires were used with both mail and telephone follow-ups for nonrespondents. Businesses also had the option to respond electronically. Data for nonrespondents and for small employer firms not mailed a questionnaire were obtained from administrative records of other federal agencies or imputed.

Estimates of Sampling Error: Not applicable for basic data such as sales, revenue, receipts, payroll, etc., for sectors other than Construction (NAICS 23). Estimates of sampling error for construction industries are included with the data as published on the Census Bureau website.

Other (Nonsampling) Errors: Establishment response rates by NAICS sector in 2002 ranged from 80 percent to 89 percent. Nonsampling errors may occur during the collection, reporting, keying, and classification of the data.

Sources of Additional Material: U.S. Census Bureau, see www.census.gov/econ/census07/www/methodology/ .

Census of Population

Universe, Frequency, and Types of Data: Complete count of U.S. population conducted every 10 years since 1790. Data obtained on number and characteristics of people in the United States.

Type of Data Collection Operation: The 2010 census consisted of one form for 100 percent of the population. On this 2010 questionnaire and on the 100 percent questionnaire of the 1990 and 2000 censuses, the 100 percent items included: age, date of birth, sex, race, Hispanic origin, relationship to householder, homeownership, and mortgage status. In 1980, approximately 19 percent of the housing units were included in the sample that received a longer questionnaire; in 1990 and 2000, approximately 17 percent were included in the sample. By 2010, the sample had been eliminated and replaced the ongoing American Community Survey.

Data Collection and Imputation Procedures: In 1980, 1990, 2000, and 2010, mail questionnaires were used extensively with personal interviews in the remainder. Extensive telephone and personal follow-up for nonrespondents was done in the censuses. Imputations were made for missing characteristics.

Estimates of Sampling Error: The 2010 census included no sampling. In prior censuses, sampling errors for data were estimated for all items collected by sample and varied by characteristic and geographic area. The coefficients of variation (CVs) for national and state estimates were generally very small.

Other (Nonsampling) Errors: Since 1950, evaluation programs have been conducted to provide information on the magnitude of some sources of nonsampling errors such as response bias and undercoverage in each census. Results from the evaluation program for the 1990 census indicated that the estimated net undercoverage amounted to about 1.5 percent of the total resident population. For the 2000 census, the evaluation program indicated a net overcount of 0.5 percent of the resident population.

Sources of Additional Material: U.S. Census Bureau, The Coverage of Population in the 1980 Census, PHC80-E4; *Content Reinterview Study: Accuracy of Data for Selected Population and Housing Characteristics as Measured by Reinterview*, PHC80-E2; *1980 Census of Population,* Vol. 1, (PC80-1), Appendixes B, C, and D. *Content Reinterview Survey: Accuracy of Data for Selected Population and Housing Characteristics as Measured by Reinterview*, 1990, CPH-E-1; Effectiveness of Quality Assurance, CPH-E-2; Programs to Improve Coverage in the 1990 Census, 1990, CPH-E-3. For 2000 census evaluations, see www.census. gov/pred/www . For 2010 census evaluations, see www .census.gov/2010census/about/cpex.php .

County Business Patterns

Universe, Frequency, and Types of Data: County Business Patterns is an annual tabulation of basic data items extracted from the Business Register, a file of all known single- and multi-location employer companies maintained and updated by the U.S. Census Bureau. Data include number of establishments, number of employees, first quarter and annual payrolls, and number of establishments by employment size class. Data are excluded for self-employed individuals, private households, railroad employees, agricultural production workers, and most government employees.

Type of Data Collection Operation: The annual Company Organization Survey provides individual establishment data for multi-location companies. Data for single-establishment companies are obtained from various Census Bureau programs, such as the Annual Survey of Manufactures and Current Business Surveys, as well as from administrative records of the Internal Revenue Service, the Social Security Administration, and the Bureau of Labor Statistics.

Estimates of Sampling Error: Not applicable.

Other (Nonsampling) Error: The data are subject to nonsampling errors, such as inability to identify all cases in the universe; definition and classification difficulties; differences in interpretation of questions; errors in recording or coding the data obtained; and estimation of employers who reported too late to be included in the tabulations and for records with missing or misreported data.

Sources of Additional Materials: U.S. Census Bureau, County Business Patterns, www.census.gov/econ/cbp/index.html .

Current Population Survey (CPS)

Universe, Frequency, and Types of Data: Nationwide monthly sample designed primarily to produce national and state estimates of labor force characteristics of the civilian noninstitutionalized population 16 years of age and older.

Type of Data Collection Operation: Multi-stage probability sample that currently includes 72,000 households from 824 sample areas. Sample size increased in some states to improve data reliability for those areas on an annual average basis. A continual sample rotation system is used. Households are in sample 4 months, out for 8 months, and in for 4 more. Month-to-month overlap is 75 percent; year-to-year overlap is 50 percent.

Data Collection and Imputation Procedures: For first and fifth months that a household is in sample, personal interviews; other months, approximately 85 percent of the data collected by phone. Imputation is done for item nonresponse. Adjustment for total nonresponse is done by a predefined cluster of units, by state, metropolitan status and CBSA size; for item nonresponse imputation varies by subject matter.

Estimates of Sampling Error: The national total estimates of the civilian labor force and of employment have monthly CVs of about .2 percent and annual average CVs of about .1 percent. Unemployment is a much smaller characteristic and consequently has substantially larger CVs than the civilian labor force or employment. The national unemployment rate, the most important CPS statistic, has a monthly CV of about 2 percent and an annual average CV of about 1 percent. Assuming a 6 percent unemployment rate, states have annual average CVs of about 8 percent. CVs for subnational areas, such as states, tend to be larger and vary by area.

Other (Nonsampling) Errors: Estimates of response bias on unemployment are available. Estimates of the unemployment rate from reinterviews range from –2.4 percent to 1.0 percent of the basic CPS unemployment rate (over a 30-month span from January 2004 through June 2006). Eligible CPS households are approximately 82 percent of the assigned households, with a corresponding response rate of 92 percent.

Sources of Additional Material: U.S. Census Bureau and Bureau of Labor Statistics, Current Population Survey: Design and Methodology, (Technical Paper 66), available on the Internet www.census.gov/prod/2006pubs/tp-66.pdf and the Bureau of Labor Statistics, www.bls.gov/cps/ and the *BLS Handbook of Methods*, Chapter 1, available at www.bls.gov/opub/hom/homch1_a.htm .

Monthly Survey of Construction

Universe, Frequency, and Types of Data: Survey conducted monthly of newly constructed housing units (excluding mobile homes). Data are collected on the start, completion, and sale of housing. (Annual figures are aggregates of monthly estimates.)

Type of Data Collection Operation: A multi-stage probability sample of approximately 900 of the 20,000 permit-issuing jurisdictions in the United States was selected. Each month in each of these permit offices, field representatives list and select a sample of permits for which to collect data. To obtain data in areas where building permits are not required, a multi-stage probability sample of 80 land areas (census tracts or subsections of census tracts) was selected. All roads in these areas are canvassed and data are collected on all new residential construction found. Sampled buildings are followed up until they are completed (and sold, if for sale).

Data Collection and Imputation Procedures: Data are obtained by telephone inquiry and/or field visit. Nonresponse/undercoverage adjustment factors are used to account for late reported data.

Estimates of Sampling Error: Estimated CV of 5 percent to 6 percent for estimates of national totals of units started, but may be higher than 20 percent for estimated totals of more detailed characteristics, such as housing units in multiunit structures.

Other (Nonsampling) Errors: Response rate is over 90 percent for most items. Nonsampling errors are attributed to definitional problems, differences in interpretation of questions, incorrect reporting, inability to obtain information about all cases in the sample, and processing errors.

Sources of Additional Material: All data are available at www.census.gov/const/www/newresconstindex.html . Further documentation of the survey is also available at that site.

Nonemployer Statistics

Universe, Frequency, and Types of Data: Nonemployer statistics are an annual tabulation of economic data by industry for active businesses without paid employees that are subject to federal income tax. Data showing the number of firms and receipts by industry are available for the United States, states, counties, and metropolitan areas. Most types of businesses covered by the Census Bureau's economic statistics programs are included in the nonemployer statistics. Tax-exempt and agricultural-production businesses are excluded from nonemployer statistics.

Type of Data Collection Operation: The universe of nonemployer firms is created annually as a byproduct of the Census Bureau's Business Register processing for employer establishments. If a business is active but without paid employees, then it becomes part of the potential nonemployer universe. Industry classification and receipts are available for each potential nonemployer business. These data are obtained primarily from the annual business income tax returns of the Internal Revenue Service (IRS). The potential nonemployer universe undergoes a series of complex processing, editing, and analytical review procedures at the Census Bureau to distinguish nonemployers from employers and to correct and complete data items used in creating the data tables.

Estimates of Sampling Error: Not applicable.

Other (Nonsampling) Errors: The data are subject to nonsampling errors, such as industry misclassification as well as errors of response, keying, nonreporting, and coverage.

Sources of Additional Material: U.S. Census Bureau, Nonemployer Statistics, www.census.gov/econ/nonemployer/index.html .

Population Estimates

Universe, Frequency, and Types of Data: The U.S. Census Bureau annually produces estimates of total resident population for each state and county. County population estimates are produced with a component of population change method, while the state population estimates are solely the sum of the county populations.

Type of Data Collection Operation: The Census Bureau develops county population estimates with a demographic procedure called an "administrative records component of population change" method. A major assumption underlying this approach is that the components of population change are closely approximated by administrative data in a demographic change model. In order to apply the model, Census Bureau demographers estimate each component of population change separately. For the population residing in households the components of population change are births, deaths, and net migration, including net international migration. For the nonhousehold population, change is represented by the net change in the population living in group quarters facilities.

Estimates of Sampling Error: Not applicable.

Other (Nonsampling) Errors: Not available.

Sources of Additional Material: U.S. Census Bureau, "Methodology for the United States Resident Population Estimates by Age, Sex, Race, and Hispanic Origin and the State and County Total Resident Population Estimates" at www.census.gov/popest/methodology/index.html .

U.S. DEPARTMENT OF EDUCATION

National Center for Education Statistics Integrated Postsecondary Education Data Survey (IPEDS), Completions

Universe, Frequency, and Types of Data: Annual survey of all Title IV (federal financial aid) eligible postsecondary institutions to obtain data on earned degrees and other formal awards, conferred by field of study, level of degree, sex, and by racial/ethnic characteristics (every other year prior to 1989, then annually).

Type of Data Collection Operation: Complete census.

Data Collection and Imputation Procedures: Data are collected through a web-based survey in the fall of every year. Missing data are imputed by using data of similar institutions.

Estimates of Sampling Error: Not applicable.

Other (Nonsampling) Errors: For 2010–2011, the response rate for degree-granting institutions was 100 percent.

Sources of Additional Material: U.S. Department of Education, National Center for Education Statistics (NCES), *Postsecondary Institutions and Price of Attendance in 2011–12; Degrees and Other Awards Conferred: 2010–11; and 12-Month Enrollment: 2010–11: First Look (Provisional Data)*. See www.nces.ed.gov/ipeds/ .

U.S. FEDERAL BUREAU OF INVESTIGATION

Uniform Crime Reporting (UCR) Program

Universe, Frequency, and Types of Data: Monthly reports on the number of criminal offenses that become known to law enforcement agencies. Data are also collected on crimes cleared by arrest or exceptional means; age, sex, and race of arrestees and for victims and offenders for homicides, number of law enforcement employees, on fatal and nonfatal assaults against law enforcement officers, and on hate crimes reported.

Type of Data Collection Operation: Crime statistics are based on reports of crime data submitted either directly to the FBI by contributing law enforcement agencies or through cooperating state UCR Programs.

Data Collection and Imputation Procedures: States with UCR programs collect data directly from individual law enforcement agencies and forward reports, prepared in accordance with UCR standards, to the FBI. Accuracy and consistency edits are performed by the FBI.

Estimates of Sampling Error: Not applicable.

Other (Nonsampling) Errors: During 2011, law enforcement agencies active in the UCR Program represented 97.8 percent of the total population. The coverage amounted to 98.8 percent of the U.S. population in metropolitan statistical areas, 92.3 percent of the population in cities outside metropolitan areas, and 93.1 percent in nonmetropolitan counties.

Sources of Additional Material: U.S. Department of Justice, Federal Bureau of Investigation, *Crime in the United States,* annual, *Hate Crime Statistics,* annual, *Law Enforcement Officers Killed and Assaulted,* annual, www.fbi.gov/about-us/cjis/ucr .

U.S. INTERNAL REVENUE SERVICE

Individual Income Tax Returns

Universe, Frequency, and Types of Data: Annual study of unaudited individual income tax returns, Forms 1040, 1040A, and 1040EZ, filed by U.S. citizens and residents. Data provided on various financial characteristics by size of adjusted gross income, marital status, and by taxable and nontaxable returns. Data by state, based on the population of returns filed, also include returns from 1040NR, filed by nonresident aliens plus certain self-employment tax returns.

Type of Data Collection Operation: Stratified probability sample of 308,946 returns for tax year 2010. The sample is classified into sample strata based on the larger of total income or total loss amounts, the size of business plus farm receipts, and other criteria such as the potential usefulness of the return for tax policy modeling. Sampling rates for sample strata varied from 0.01 percent to 100 percent.

Data Collection and Imputation Procedures: Computer selection of sample of tax return records. Data adjusted during editing for incorrect, missing, or inconsistent entries to ensure consistency with other entries on return.

Estimates of Sampling Error. Estimated CVs for tax year 2010: adjusted gross income less deficit 0.09 percent; salaries and wages 0.17 percent; and tax-exempt interest received 1.25 percent. (State data not subject to sampling error.)

Other (Nonsampling) Errors: Processing errors and errors arising from the use of tolerance checks for the data.

Sources of Additional Material: U.S. Internal Revenue Service, *Statistics of Income, Individual Income Tax Returns,* annual, (Publication 1304). www.irs.gov/uac/SOI-Tax-Stats-Individual-Income-Tax-Returns-Publication-1304-%28Complete-Report%29.

NATIONAL CENTER FOR HEALTH STATISTICS (NCHS)

National Vital Statistics System

Universe, Frequency, and Types of Data: Annual data on births and deaths in the United States.

Type of Data Collection Operation: Mortality data based on complete file of death records, except 1972, based on 50 percent sample. Natality statistics 1951–1971, based on 50 percent sample of birth certificates, except a 20 percent to 50 percent sample in 1967, received by NCHS.

Data Collection and Imputation Procedures: Reports based on records from registration offices of all states, District of Columbia, New York City, Puerto Rico, Virgin Islands, Guam, American Samoa, and Northern Marianas.

Estimates of Sampling Error: For recent years, there is no sampling for these files; the files are based on 100 percent of events registered.

Other (Nonsampling) Errors: It is believed that more than 99 percent of the births and deaths occurring in this country are registered.

Sources of Additional Material: U.S. National Center for Health Statistics, *Vital Statistics of the United States,* Vol. I and Vol. II annual, and the *National Vital Statistics Reports.* See the NCHS website at www.cdc.gov/nchs/nvss.htm .

NATIONAL HIGHWAY TRAFFIC SAFETY ADMINISTRATION (NHTSA)

Fatality Analysis Reporting System (FARS)

Universe, Frequency, and Types of Data: FARS is a census of all fatal motor vehicle traffic crashes that occur throughout the United States including the District of Columbia and Puerto Rico on roadways customarily open to the public. The crash must be reported to the state/jurisdiction and at least one directly related fatality must occur within 30 days of the crash.

Type of Data Collection Operation: One or more analysts, in each state, extract data from the official documents and enter the data into a standardized electronic database.

Data Collection and Imputation Procedures: Detailed data describing the characteristics of the fatal crash, the vehicles and persons involved are obtained from police crash reports, driver and vehicle registration records, autopsy reports, highway department, etc. Computerized edit checks monitor the accuracy and completeness of the data. The FARS incorporates a sophisticated mathematical multiple imputation procedure to develop a probability distribution of missing blood alcohol concentration (BAC) levels in the database for drivers, pedestrians, and cyclists.

Estimates of Sampling Error: Since this is census data, there are no sampling errors.

Other (Nonsampling) Errors: FARS represents a census of all police-reported crashes and captures all data reported at the state level. FARS data undergo a rigorous quality control process to prevent inaccurate reporting. However, these data are highly dependent on the accuracy of the police accident reports. Errors or omissions within police accident reports may not be detected.

Sources of Additional Material: The FARS Coding and Validation Manual, ANSI D16.1 *Manual on Classification of Motor Vehicle Traffic Accidents* (Sixth Edition), www .nhtsa.gov/FARS .

Geographic Concepts

STATES

States are the major political units of the United States. The District of Columbia is treated as a state equivalent in this publication. Tables A-1 through A-84 present data for the United States, the 50 states, and the District of Columbia. For census purposes, states are often grouped into geographic regions and divisions. However, Table A only uses an alphabetical state presentation.

METROPOLITAN AND MICROPOLITAN STATISTICAL AREAS

The U.S. Office of Management and Budget (OMB) defines metropolitan and micropolitan statistical areas according to published standards that are applied to U.S. Census Bureau data. The general concept of a metropolitan or micropolitan statistical area is that of a core area containing a substantial population nucleus, together with adjacent communities having a high degree of economic and social integration with that core. The term "core based statistical area" (CBSA) refers collectively to metropolitan and micropolitan statistical areas.

The major purpose of CBSAs is to enable all federal agencies to use the same geographic definitions in tabulating and publishing data for metropolitan and micropolitan areas. The definitions are designed to serve a wide variety of statistical and analytical purposes; adoption of the area for any specific purpose should be judged in terms of appropriateness for that purpose. While the definitions have been developed for statistical use by federal agencies, state and local governments as well as private business firms have often found the definitions helpful in presenting data for metropolitan and micropolitan areas.

The official 2000 Standards for Defining Metropolitan and Micropolitan Statistical Areas may be found on the OMB website at www.whitehouse.gov/sites/default/files/omb/fedreg/metroareas122700.pdf . OMB Bulletin 10-02, which was issued on December 1, 2009, provides the listing of metropolitan and micropolitan statistical areas found in this publication; this document and related documents may be found at www.whitehouse.gov/sites/default/files/omb/assets/bulletins/b10-02.pdf . Metropolitan areas presented in tables B-1 through B-14 and C-1 through C-4 and micropolitan areas presented in table D-1 of this publication are those county-based areas defined originally as of June 6, 2003, and updated on December 1, 2009. A series of maps showing these areas appears on pages 414 to 425.

As this book goes to press, the Office of Management and Budget has just released new metropolitan and micropolitan area definitions based on the 2010 census. Most federal data sources will now begin to use the new definitions.

Historical development. In 1910, the Census Bureau introduced "metropolitan districts" as an area classification. This marked the first use by the Census Bureau of a unit for reporting population data for large cities, together with their suburbs. Originally, only cities of at least 200,000 population were designated as the core of a metropolitan district. By 1940, the concept had been expanded to apply to a city of 50,000 or more inhabitants. The metropolitan district was generally defined to include contiguous minor civil divisions (MCDs) and incorporated places having a population density of at least 150 persons per square mile; therefore, the boundaries did not necessarily follow county lines.

A major limitation of the metropolitan district concept, from the standpoint of statistical presentation, was that not many data items beyond those available from the census of population and housing were available for MCDs and smaller places. The applicability of the metropolitan district concept also was limited because other generally similar area classifications were in use (e.g., the industrial areas of the census of manufactures and the labor market areas of the Labor Department's Employment and Training Administration), which were defined in different ways.

The standard metropolitan area (SMA) concept was developed in 1949 by the Bureau of the Budget (now OMB), with the advice of the newly established Federal Committee on Standard Metropolitan Areas, to overcome the above difficulties. It was designed so that a wide variety of statistical data on metropolitan areas might be presented for a uniform set of geographic areas. The SMAs consisted of one or more contiguous counties containing at least one city of 50,000 or more inhabitants. Additional counties had to meet certain criteria of metropolitan character and of social and economic integration with the central county in order to be included in an SMA.

Changes in the official criteria have been made at the time of each census since 1950. None of these changes have involved significant deviations from the basic metropolitan concept. Several modifications have been made in the rules for determining how large a city must be to have a metropolitan division defined. Criteria changes also have been made to reflect changing national conditions. For example, the 1949 rule specified that a county must have less than 25 percent of its workers engaged in agriculture. However, with a rapidly decreasing proportion of the population engaged in farming, this requirement has been eliminated because practically no counties are still affected by it. In 1959, the designation "standard metropolitan area" was changed to "standard metropolitan statistical area" (SMSA) to emphasize the nature and purpose of the areas. The SMSA designation was changed to the MSA/CMSA/PMSA designations in June 1983. The term "core based statistical area" (CBSA) was adopted in 2000 and refers collectively to metropolitan and micropolitan statistical areas.

The metropolitan and micropolitan statistical areas used in this book are based on application of 2000 standards that appeared in the *Federal Register* on December 27, 2000, to 2000 decennial census data. Metropolitan and micropolitan statistical area definitions were announced by OMB effective June 6, 2003, and subsequently updated. The lists of metropolitan and micropolitan statistical areas definitions may be found at www.census.gov/population/metro/ .

New definitions based on the 2010 census were released through OMB Bulletin 13-01 dated February 28, 2013. These new definitions will be used in future releases of federal statistical data, but are not used in this book.

Defining metropolitan and micropolitan statistical areas. The 2000 standards provide that each CBSA must contain at least one urban area of 10,000 or more population. Each metropolitan statistical area must have at least one urbanized area of 50,000 or more inhabitants. Each micropolitan statistical area must have at least one urban cluster of at least 10,000 but less than 50,000 population.

Under the standards, the county (or counties) in which at least 50 percent of the population resides within urban areas of 10,000 or more population, or that contain at least 5,000 people residing within a single urban area of 10,000 or more population, is identified as a "central county" (counties). Additional "outlying counties" are included in the CBSA if they meet specified requirements of commuting to or from the central counties. Counties or equivalent entities form the geographic "building blocks" for metropolitan and micropolitan statistical areas throughout the United States and Puerto Rico.

If specified criteria are met, a metropolitan statistical area containing a single core with a population of 2.5 million or more may be subdivided to form smaller groupings of counties referred to as "metropolitan divisions."

Principal cities and metropolitan and micropolitan statistical area titles. The largest city in each metropolitan or micropolitan statistical area is designated a "principal city." Additional cities qualify if specified requirements are met concerning population size and employment. The title of each metropolitan or micropolitan statistical area consists of the names of up to three of its principal cities and the name of each state into which the metropolitan or micropolitan statistical area extends. Titles of metropolitan divisions also typically are based on principal city names but in certain cases consist of county names.

Defining New England city and town areas. In view of the importance of cities and towns in New England, the 2000 standards also provide for a set of geographic areas that are defined using cities and towns in the six New England states. The New England city and town areas (NECTAs) are defined using the same criteria as metropolitan and micropolitan statistical areas and are identified as either metropolitan or micropolitan, based, respectively, on the presence of either an urbanized area of 50,000 or more population or an urban cluster of at least 10,000 but less than 50,000 population. If the specified criteria are met, a NECTA containing a single core with a population of at least 2.5 million may be subdivided to form smaller groupings of cities and towns referred to as New England city and town area divisions. NECTAs are not included in this book.

Changes in definitions over time. Changes in the definitions of these statistical areas since the 1950 census have consisted chiefly of:

- The recognition of new areas as they reached the minimum required city or urbanized area population

- The addition of counties (or cities and towns in New England) to existing areas as new decennial census data showed them to qualify.
- In some instances, formerly separate areas have been merged, components of an area have been transferred from one area to another, or components have been dropped from an area. The large majority of changes have taken place on the basis of decennial census data. However, Census Bureau data serve as the basis for intercensal updates in specified circumstances.

Because of these historical changes in geographic definitions, users must be cautious in comparing data for these statistical areas from different dates. For some purposes, comparisons of data for areas as defined at given dates may be appropriate; for other purposes, it may be preferable to maintain consistent area definitions. Historical metropolitan area definitions are available for 1999, 1993, 1990, 1983, 1981, 1973, 1970, 1963, 1960, and 1950.

Special metropolitan area notes found in this publication. This report includes metropolitan and micropolitan statistical areas and metropolitan divisions defined by the Office of Management and Budget as of June 6, 2003, and updated in December 2009. There are 366 metropolitan statistical areas and 576 micropolitan statistical areas in the United States. In addition, there are eight metropolitan statistical areas and five micropolitan statistical areas in Puerto Rico not covered in this publication.

There are two metropolitan areas that we want to specially note for users. First, the Denver, CO, metropolitan area had the special case involving the newly created county of Broomfield. Broomfield County, CO, was formed from parts of Adams, Boulder, Jefferson, and Weld Counties, CO, on November 15, 2001, and is coextensive with Broomfield city. For purposes of defining and presenting data for metropolitan statistical areas, Broomfield City is treated as if it were a county at the time of the 1990 and 2000 censuses. The other area is the St. Louis, MO-IL area. A portion of Sullivan city in Crawford County, MO, is legally part of the St. Louis, MO-IL MSA. Census 2000 tabulations and intercensal estimates for the St. Louis, MO-IL metropolitan statistical area do not include this small area.

COUNTIES

The primary political divisions of most states are termed "counties," which are the basic building blocks for metropolitan areas. In Louisiana, these divisions are known as "parishes." In Alaska, which has no counties, the county equivalents are the organized "boroughs" and the "census areas" that are delineated for statistical purposes by the State of Alaska and the Census Bureau. In four states (Maryland, Missouri, Nevada, and Virginia), there are one or more cities that are independent of any county organization and thus constitute primary divisions of their states. These cities are known as "independent cities" and are treated as equivalent to counties for statistical purposes. The District of Columbia has no primary divisions, and the entire area is considered equivalent to a county for statistical purposes.

Tables C-1 through C-4 present data for the 366 metropolitan statistical areas, 29 metropolitan divisions, and their 1,100 component counties defined as of December 2009. Table D-1 presents data for the 576 micropolitan statistical areas and their 688 counties likewise defined as of December 2009.

Metropolitan and Micropolitan Statistical Areas: November 2007 - Alaska, Idaho, Montana, Oregon, Washington, Wyoming

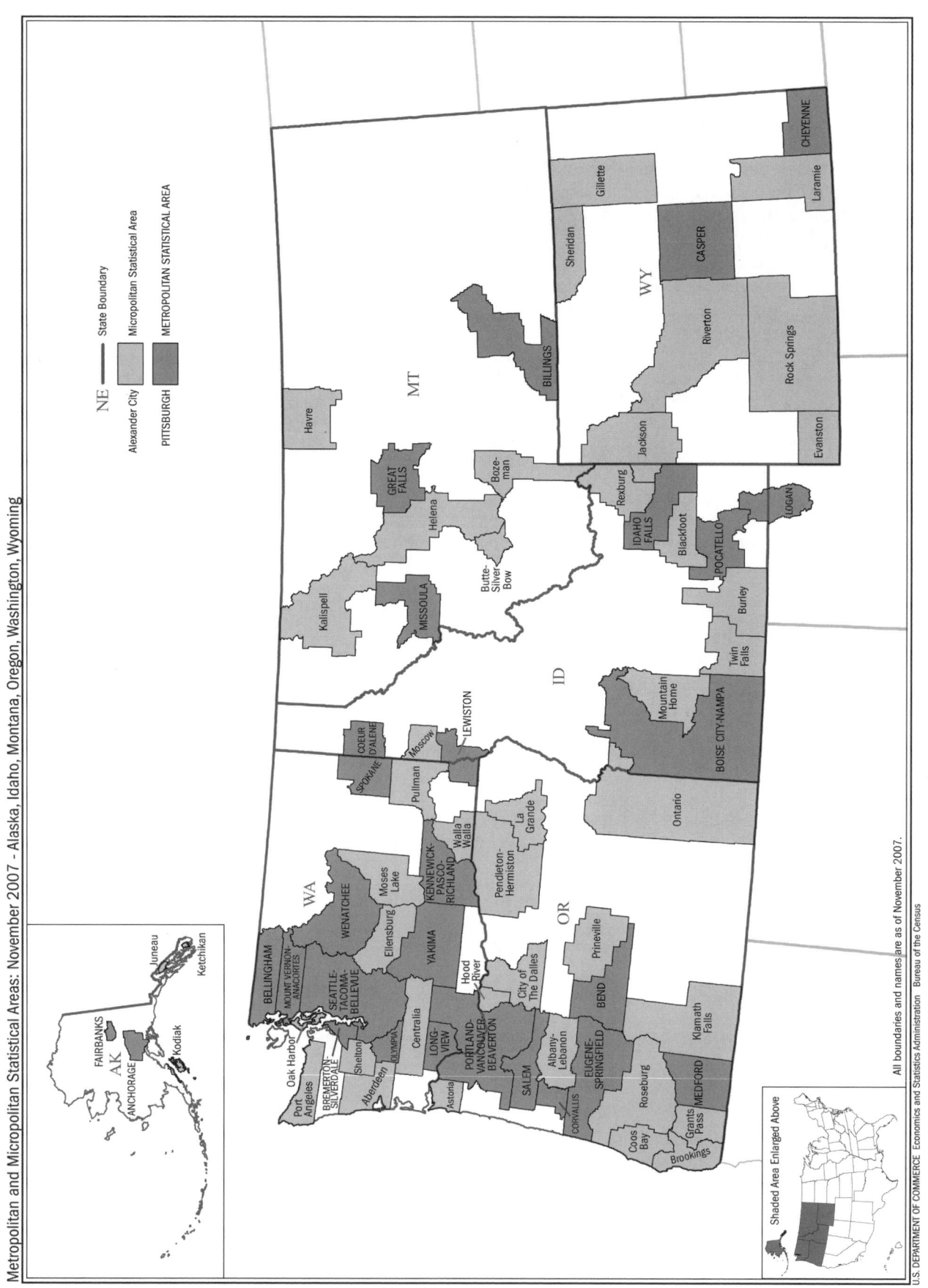

U.S. DEPARTMENT OF COMMERCE Economics and Statistics Administration Bureau of the Census

All boundaries and names are as of November 2007.

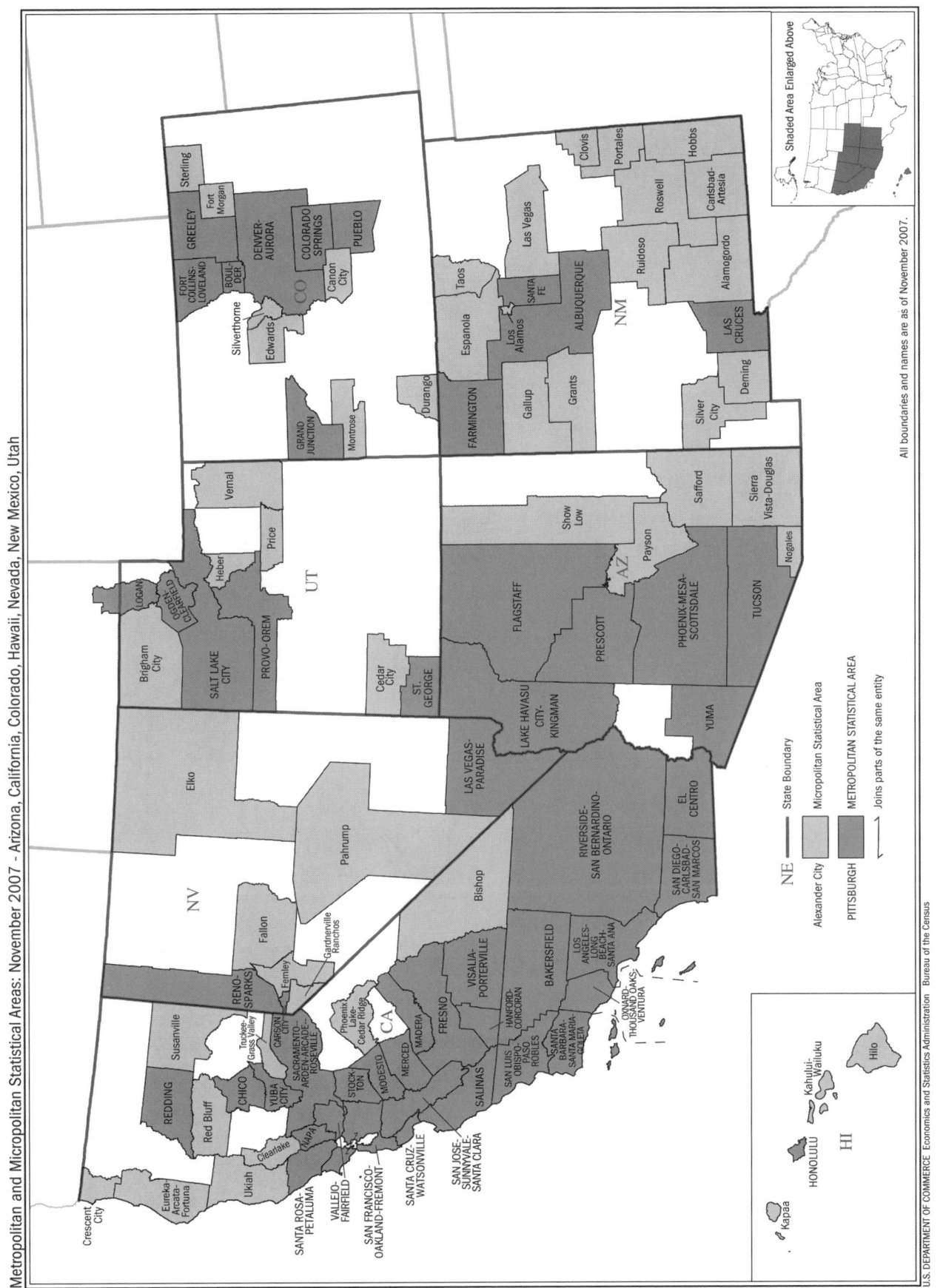

Metropolitan and Micropolitan Statistical Areas: November 2007 - Arizona, California, Colorado, Hawaii, Nevada, New Mexico, Utah

U.S. DEPARTMENT OF COMMERCE Economics and Statistics Administration Bureau of the Census

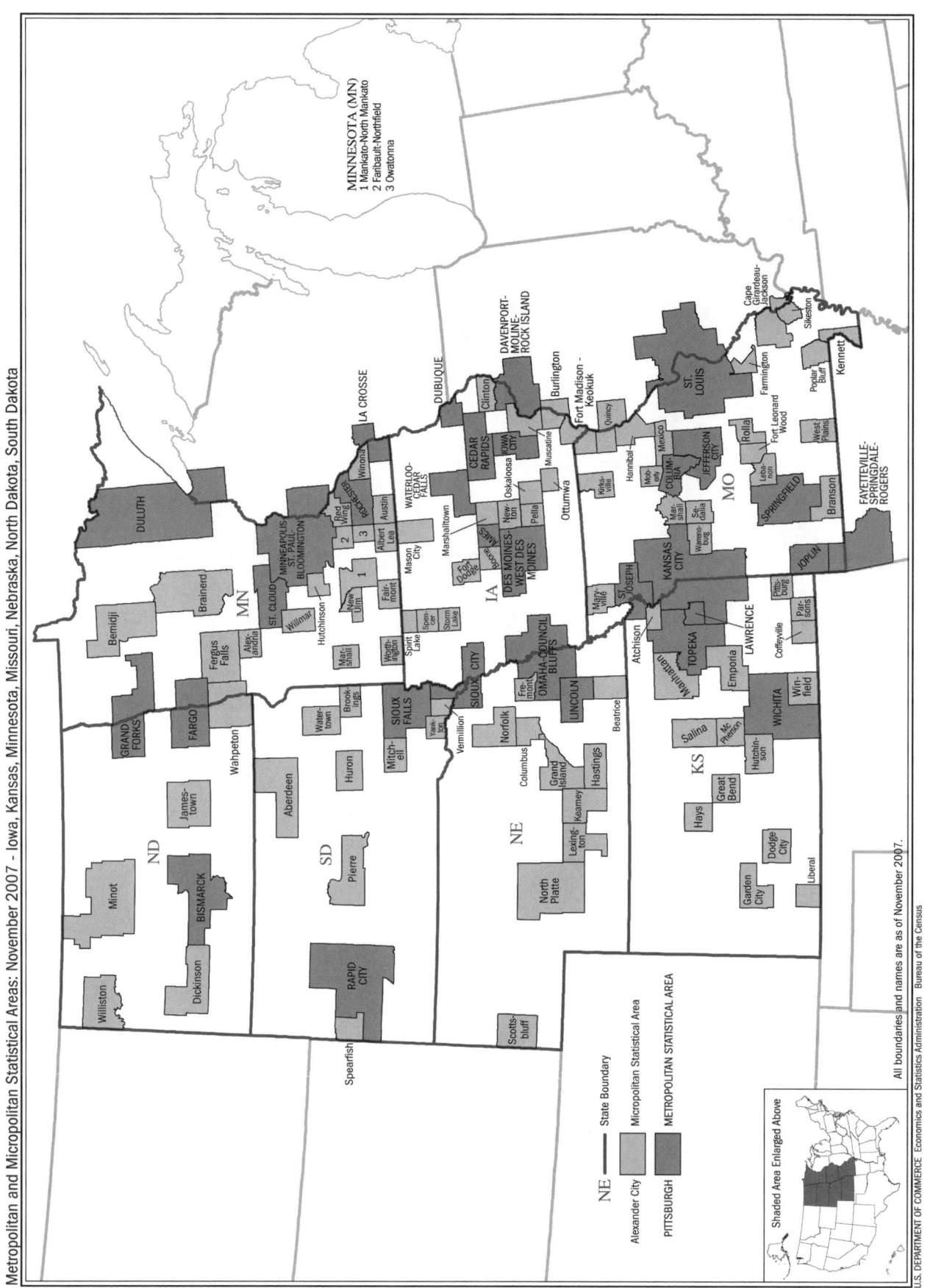

Metropolitan and Micropolitan Statistical Areas: November 2007 - Iowa, Kansas, Minnesota, Missouri, Nebraska, North Dakota, South Dakota

MINNESOTA (MN)
1 Mankato-North Mankato
2 Faribault-Northfield
3 Owatonna

NE ⎯⎯ State Boundary
Alexander City   Micropolitan Statistical Area
PITTSBURGH   METROPOLITAN STATISTICAL AREA

Shaded Area Enlarged Above

U.S. DEPARTMENT OF COMMERCE Economics and Statistics Administration Bureau of the Census   All boundaries and names are as of November 2007.

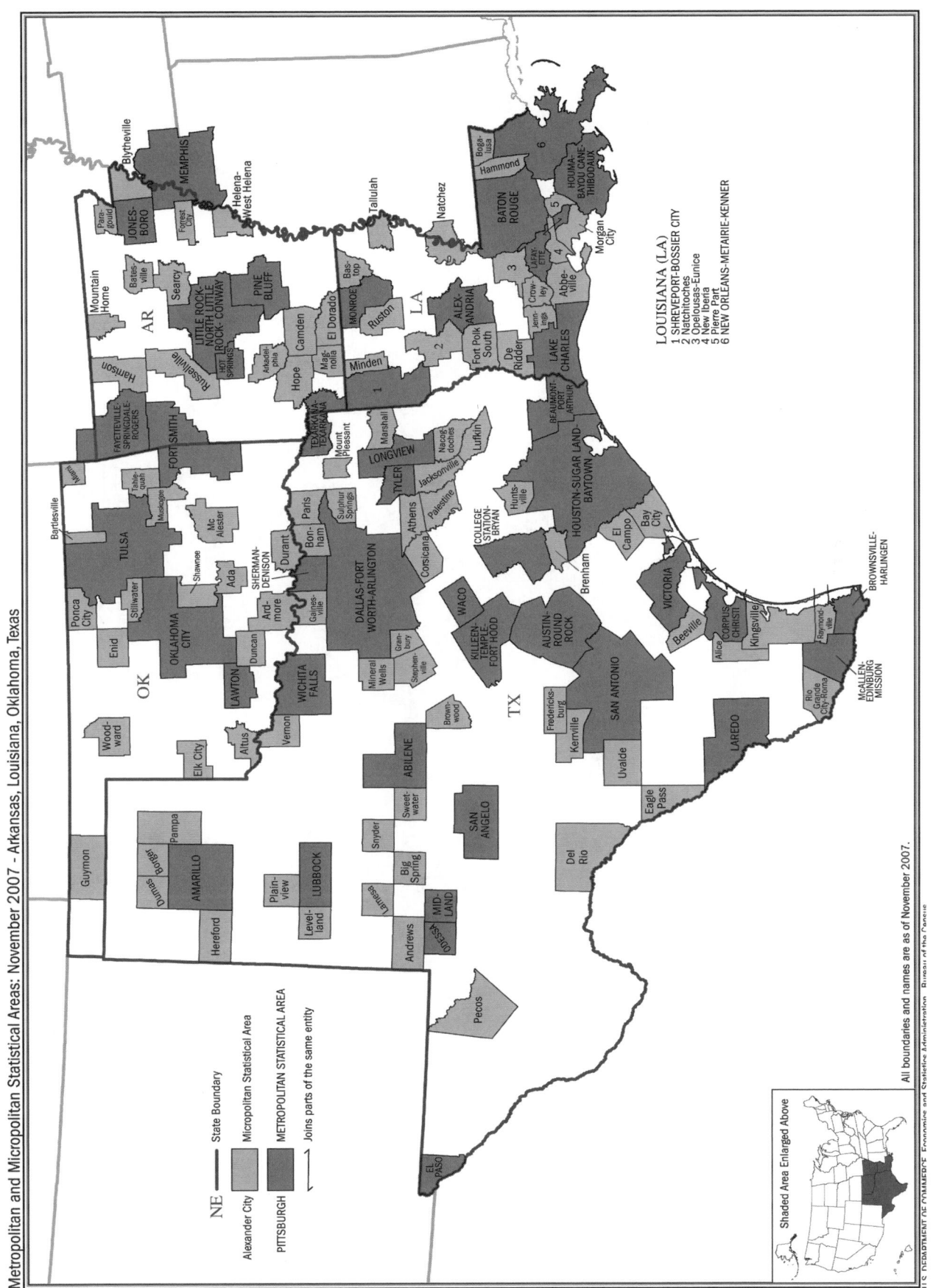

Metropolitan and Micropolitan Statistical Areas: November 2007 - Arkansas, Louisiana, Oklahoma, Texas

LOUISIANA (LA)
1 SHREVEPORT-BOSSIER CITY
2 Natchitoches
3 Opelousas-Eunice
4 New Iberia
5 Pierre Part
6 NEW ORLEANS-METAIRIE-KENNER

NE — State Boundary

Alexander City   Micropolitan Statistical Area

PITTSBURGH   METROPOLITAN STATISTICAL AREA

↑ Joins parts of the same entity

Shaded Area Enlarged Above

All boundaries and names are as of November 2007.

U.S. DEPARTMENT OF COMMERCE, Economics and Statistics Administration, Bureau of the Census

Metropolitan and Micropolitan Statistical Areas: November 2007 - Illinois, Indiana, Kentucky, Michigan, Ohio, Wisconsin

NE

State Boundary
Micropolitan Statistical Area
METROPOLITAN STATISTICAL AREA

Alexander City
PITTSBURGH

MICHIGAN (MI)
1 MUSKEGON-NORTON SHORES
2 Mount Pleasant
3 SAGINAW-SAGINAW TOWNSHIP NORTH
4 HOLLAND-GRAND HAVEN
5 LANSING-EAST LANSING
6 NILES-BENTON HARBOR
7 SOUTH BEND-MISHAWAKA
8 Coldwater

OHIO (OH)
1 SANDUSKY
2 CLEVELAND-ELYRIA-MENTOR
3 MANSFIELD
4 Ashland
5 CANTON-MASSILLON
6 New Philadelphia-Dover
7 Bellefontaine
8 Wapakoneta
9 SPRINGFIELD
10 Wilmington
11 Washington Court House

KENTUCKY (KY)
1 Madisonville
2 Central City
3 ELIZABETHTOWN
4 LOUISVILLE - JEFFERSON COUNTY
5 Campbellsville
6 Richmond-Berea
7 Middlesborough

WISCONSIN (WI)
1 Menomonie
2 Iron Mountain
3 Marshfield – Wisconsin Rapids
4 OSHKOSH-NEENAH
5 Manitowoc
6 SHEBOYGAN
7 MILWAUKEE-WAUKESHA-WEST ALLIS
8 Watertown-Fort Atkinson
9 JANESVILLE
10 Whitewater

ILLINOIS (IL)
1 BLOOMINGTON-NORMAL
2 KANKAKEE-BRADLEY
3 DECATUR
4 Charleston-Mattoon
5 Marion-Herrin
6 Harrisburg

INDIANA (IN)
1 MICHIGAN CITY-LA PORTE
2 ELKHART-GOSHEN
3 Kendallville
4 Angola
5 Logansport
6 Wabash
7 Huntington
8 Decatur
9 ANDERSON
10 Richmond
11 Connersville
12 Greensburg
13 Vincennes
14 Washington
15 North Vernon
16 Scottsburg
17 Madison

All boundaries and names are as of November 2007

Shaded Area Enlarged Above

U.S. DEPARTMENT OF COMMERCE Economics and Statistics Administration Bureau of the Census

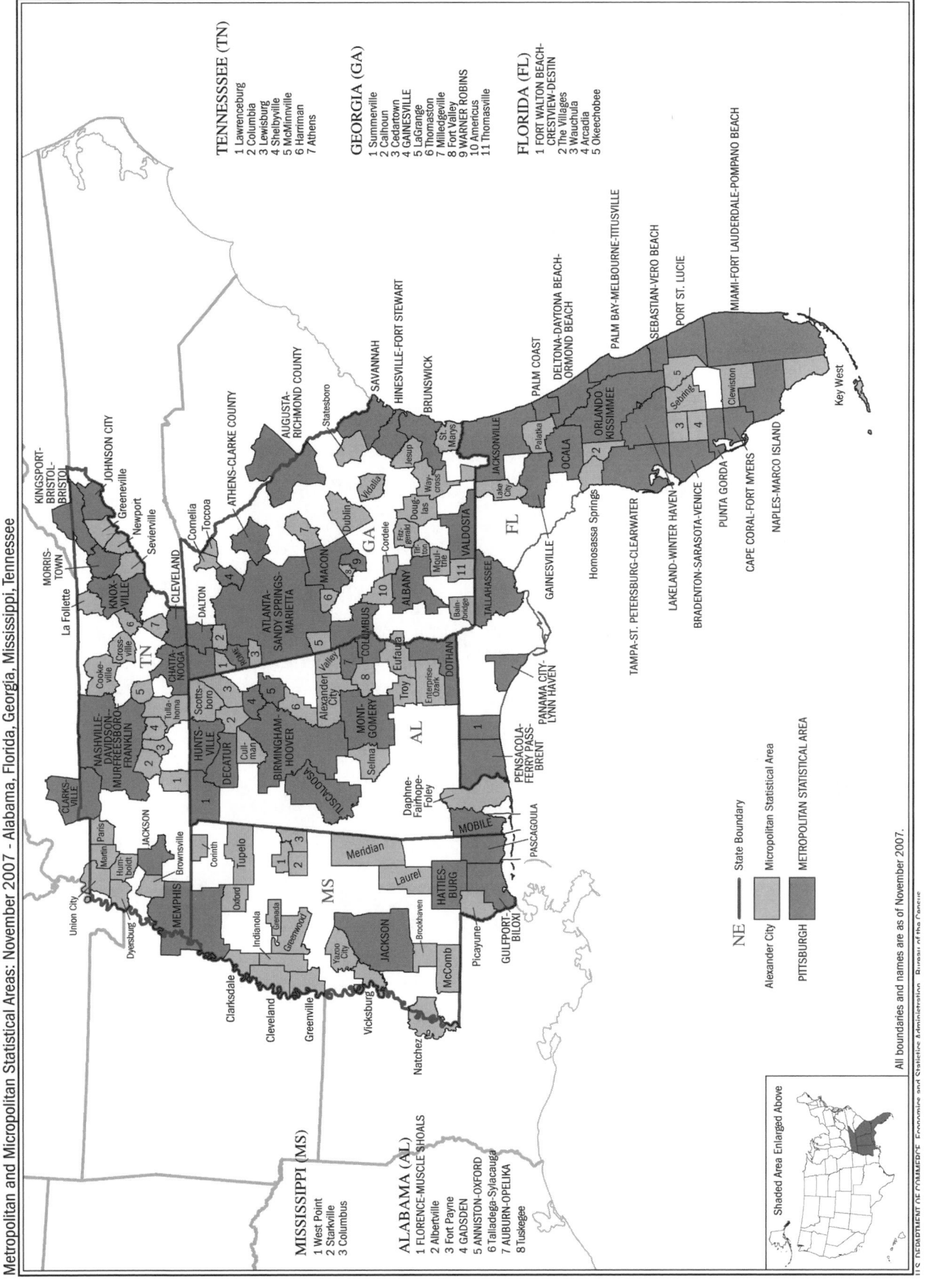

Metropolitan and Micropolitan Statistical Areas: November 2007 - Alabama, Florida, Georgia, Mississippi, Tennessee

TENNESSSEE (TN)
1 Lawrenceburg
2 Columbia
3 Lewisburg
4 Shelbyville
5 McMinnville
6 Harriman
7 Athens

GEORGIA (GA)
1 Summerville
2 Calhoun
3 Cedartown
4 GAINESVILLE
5 LaGrange
6 Thomaston
7 Milledgeville
8 Fort Valley
9 WARNER ROBINS
10 Americus
11 Thomasville

FLORIDA (FL)
1 FORT WALTON BEACH-CRESTVIEW-DESTIN
2 The Villages
3 Wauchula
4 Arcadia
5 Okeechobee

MISSISSIPPI (MS)
1 West Point
2 Starkville
3 Columbus

ALABAMA (AL)
1 FLORENCE-MUSCLE SHOALS
2 Albertville
3 Fort Payne
4 GADSDEN
5 ANNISTON-OXFORD
6 Talladega-Sylacauga
7 AUBURN-OPELIKA
8 Tuskegee

NE   —— State Boundary

Alexander City   Micropolitan Statistical Area

PITTSBURGH   METROPOLITAN STATISTICAL AREA

All boundaries and names are as of November 2007.

U.S. DEPARTMENT OF COMMERCE, Economics and Statistics Administration, Bureau of the Census

Shaded Area Enlarged Above

Metropolitan and Micropolitan Statistical Areas: November 2007 - Connecticut, Maine, Massachusetts, New Hampshire, New Jersey, New York, Pennsylvania, Rhode Island, Vermont

NE —— State Boundary

Alexander City ▒ Micropolitan Statistical Area

PITTSBURGH ▓ METROPOLITAN STATISTICAL AREA

Shaded Area Enlarged Above

All boundaries and names are as of November 2007.

U.S. DEPARTMENT OF COMMERCE Economics and Statistics Administration Bureau of the Census

Metropolitan and Micropolitan Statistical Areas: November 2007 - Delaware, District of Columbia, Maryland, North Carolina, South Carolina, Virginia, West Virginia

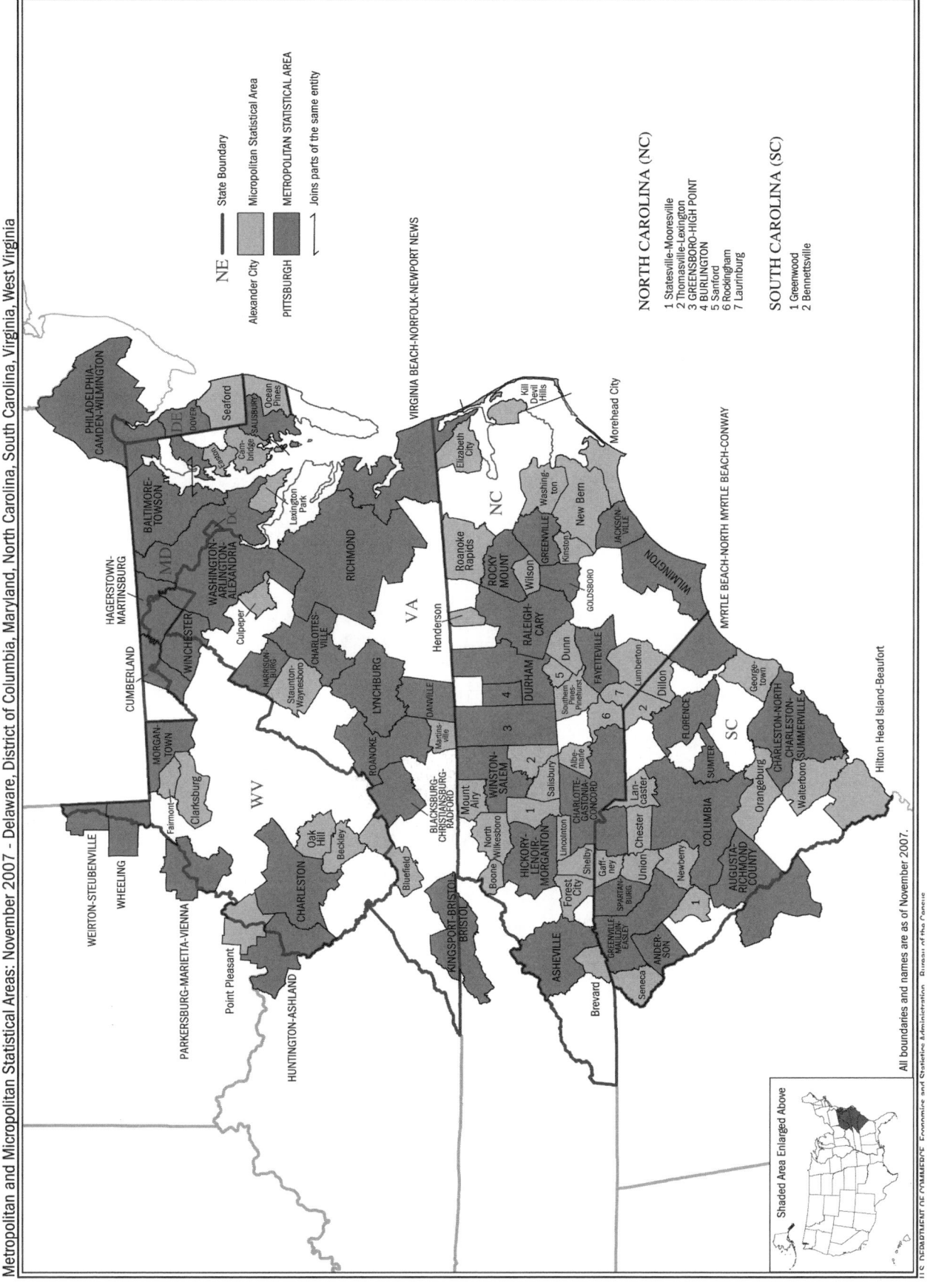

NE ⎯⎯⎯ State Boundary

Alexander City — Micropolitan Statistical Area

PITTSBURGH — METROPOLITAN STATISTICAL AREA

↑ Joins parts of the same entity

NORTH CAROLINA (NC)

1 Statesville-Mooresville
2 Thomasville-Lexington
3 GREENSBORO-HIGH POINT
4 BURLINGTON
5 Sanford
6 Rockingham
7 Laurinburg

SOUTH CAROLINA (SC)

1 Greenwood
2 Bennettsville

All boundaries and names are as of November 2007.

U.S. DEPARTMENT OF COMMERCE, Economics and Statistics Administration, Bureau of the Census

Shaded Area Enlarged Above

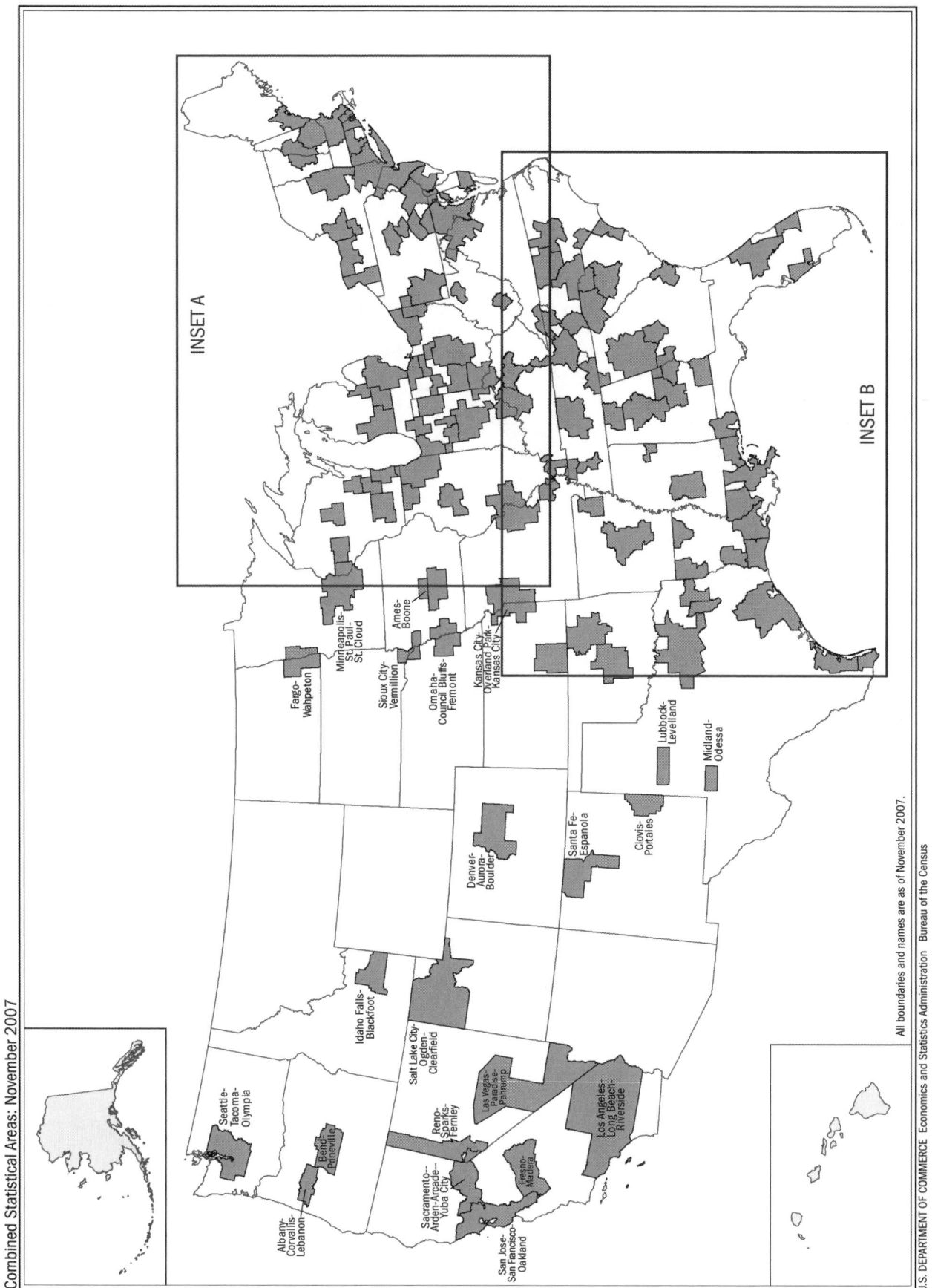

Combined Statistical Areas: November 2007

INSET A

INSET B

Fargo-
Wahpeton

Minneapolis-
St.Paul-
St.Cloud

Ames-
Boone

Sioux City-
Vermillion

Omaha-
Council Bluffs-
Fremont

Kansas City-
Overland Park-
Kansas City

Lubbock-
Levelland

Midland-
Odessa

Santa Fe-
Espanola

Clovis-
Portales

Denver-
Aurora-
Boulder

Idaho Falls-
Blackfoot

Salt Lake City-
Ogden-
Clearfield

Seattle-
Tacoma-
Olympia

Bend-
Prineville

Reno-
Sparks-
Fernley

Las Vegas-
Paradise-
Pahrump

Los Angeles-
Long Beach-
Riverside

Albany-
Corvallis-
Lebanon

Sacramento-
Arden-Arcade-
Yuba City

Fresno-
Madera

San Jose-
San Francisco-
Oakland

All boundaries and names are as of November 2007.

U.S. DEPARTMENT OF COMMERCE Economics and Statistics Administration Bureau of the Census

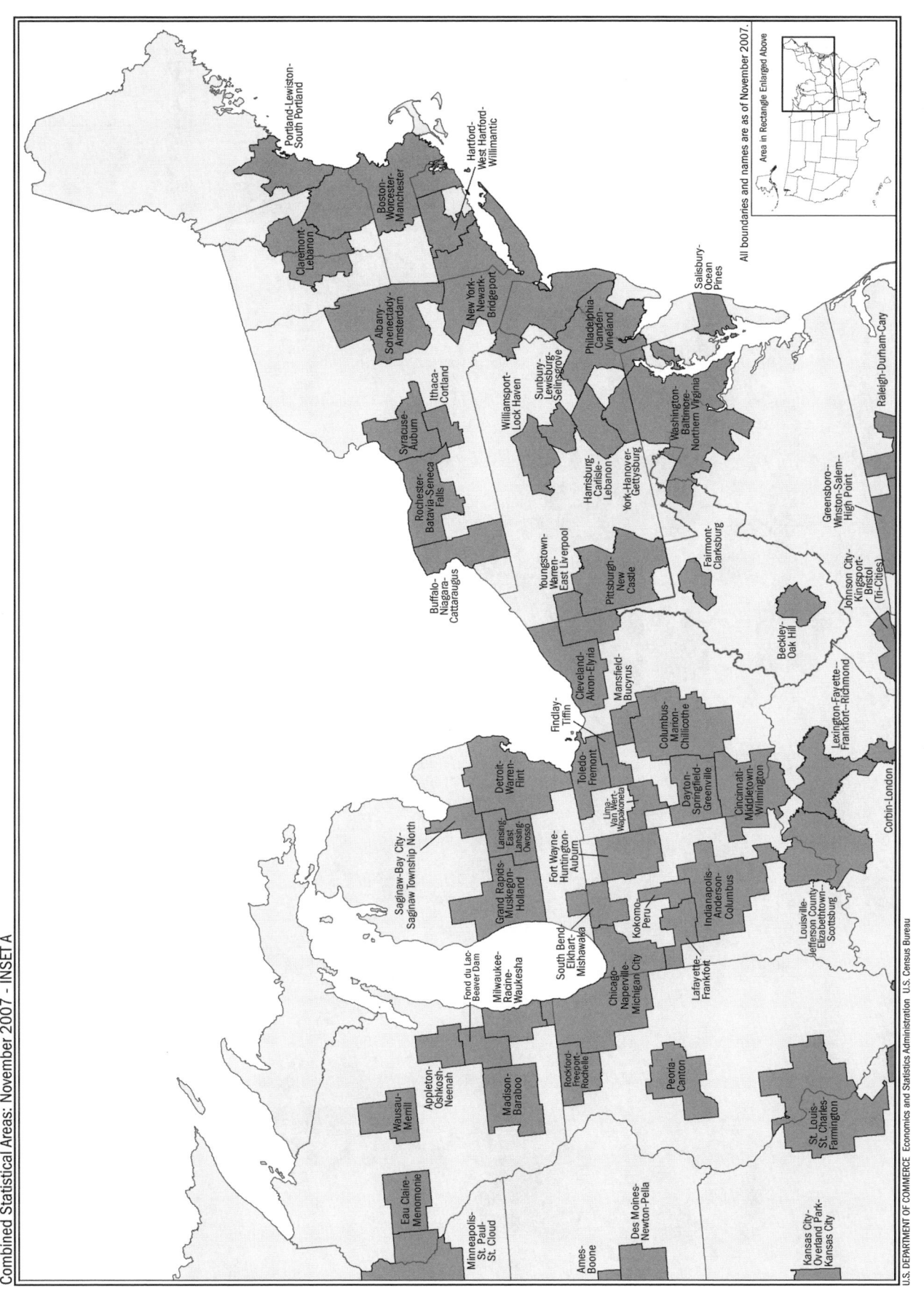

Combined Statistical Areas: November 2007 - INSET A

All boundaries and names are as of November 2007.

Area in Rectangle Enlarged Above

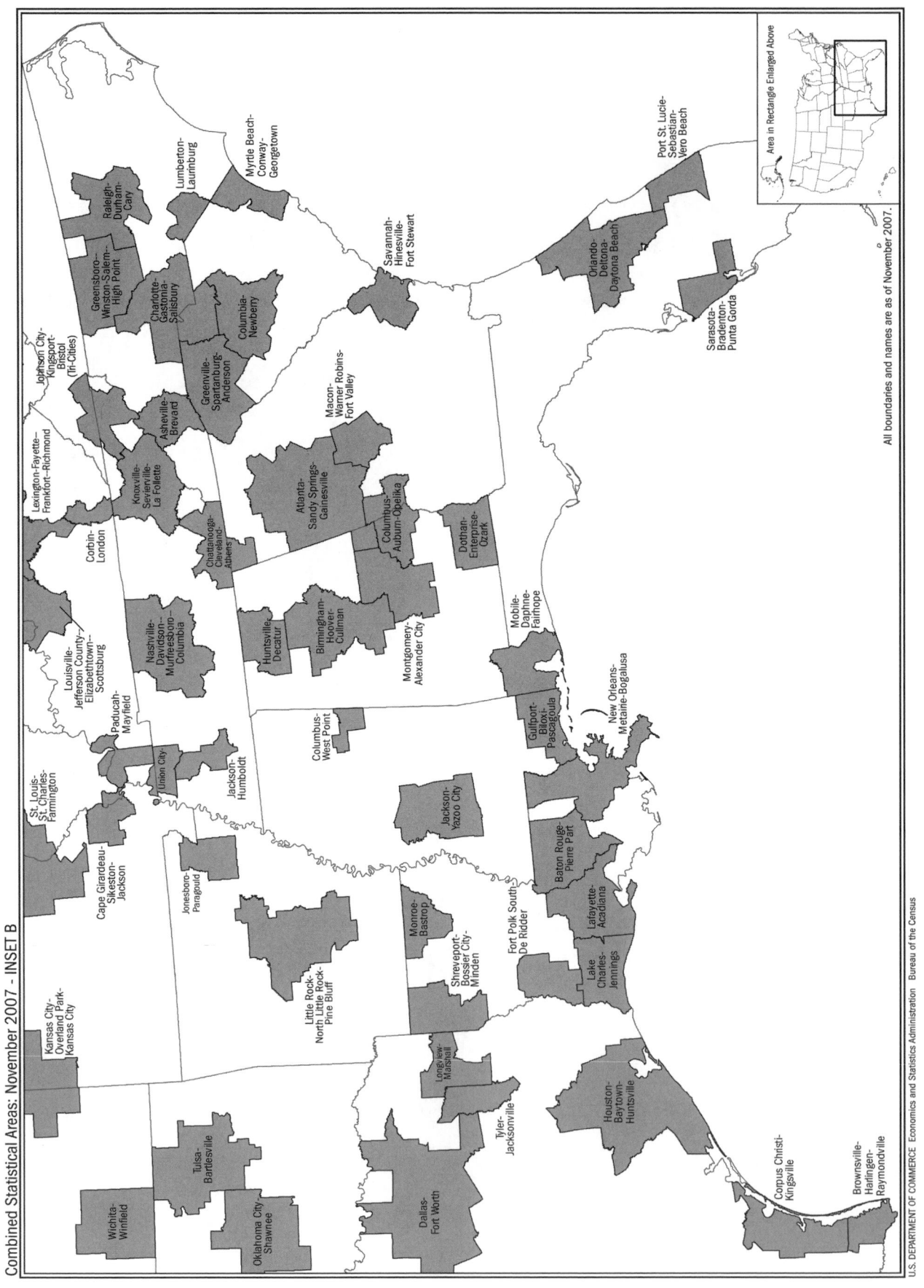

Combined Statistical Areas: November 2007 - INSET B

Area in Rectangle Enlarged Above

All boundaries and names are as of November 2007.

Port St. Lucie-Sebastian-Vero Beach

Myrtle Beach-Conway-Georgetown

Lumberton-Laurinburg

Raleigh-Durham-Cary

Greensboro-Winston-Salem-High Point

Charlotte-Gastonia-Salisbury

Columbia-Newberry

Savannah-Hinesville-Fort Stewart

Orlando-Deltona-Daytona Beach

Sarasota-Bradenton-Punta Gorda

Johnson City-Kingsport-Bristol (Tri-Cities)

Greenville-Spartanburg-Anderson

Macon-Warner Robins-Fort Valley

Lexington-Fayette—Frankfort--Richmond

Asheville-Brevard

Knoxville-Sevierville-La Follette

Atlanta-Sandy Springs-Gainesville

Columbus-Auburn-Opelika

Dothan-Enterprise-Ozark

Corbin-London

Chattanooga-Cleveland-Athens

Louisville-Jefferson County-Elizabethtown--Scottsburg

Nashville-Davidson--Murfreesboro--Columbia

Huntsville-Decatur

Birmingham-Hoover-Cullman

Montgomery-Alexander City

Mobile-Daphne-Fairhope

New Orleans-Metairie-Bogalusa

Paducah-Mayfield

Columbus-West Point

Gulfport-Biloxi-Pascagoula

St. Louis-St. Charles-Farmington

Union City

Jackson-Humboldt

Jackson-Yazoo City

Baton Rouge-Pierre Part

Cape Girardeau-Sikeston-Jackson

Jonesboro-Paragould

Monroe-Bastrop

Lafayette-Acadiana

Kansas City-Overland Park-Kansas City

Little Rock-North Little Rock-Pine Bluff

Shreveport-Bosser City-Minden

Fort Polk South-De Ridder

Lake Charles-Jennings

Longview-Marshall

Houston-Baytown-Huntsville

Tyler-Jacksonville

Tulsa-Bartlesville

Corpus Christi-Kingsville

Brownsville-Harlingen-Raymondville

Wichita-Winfield

Oklahoma City-Shawnee

Dallas-Fort Worth

Metropolitan and Micropolitan New England City and Town Areas (NECTAs): November 2007

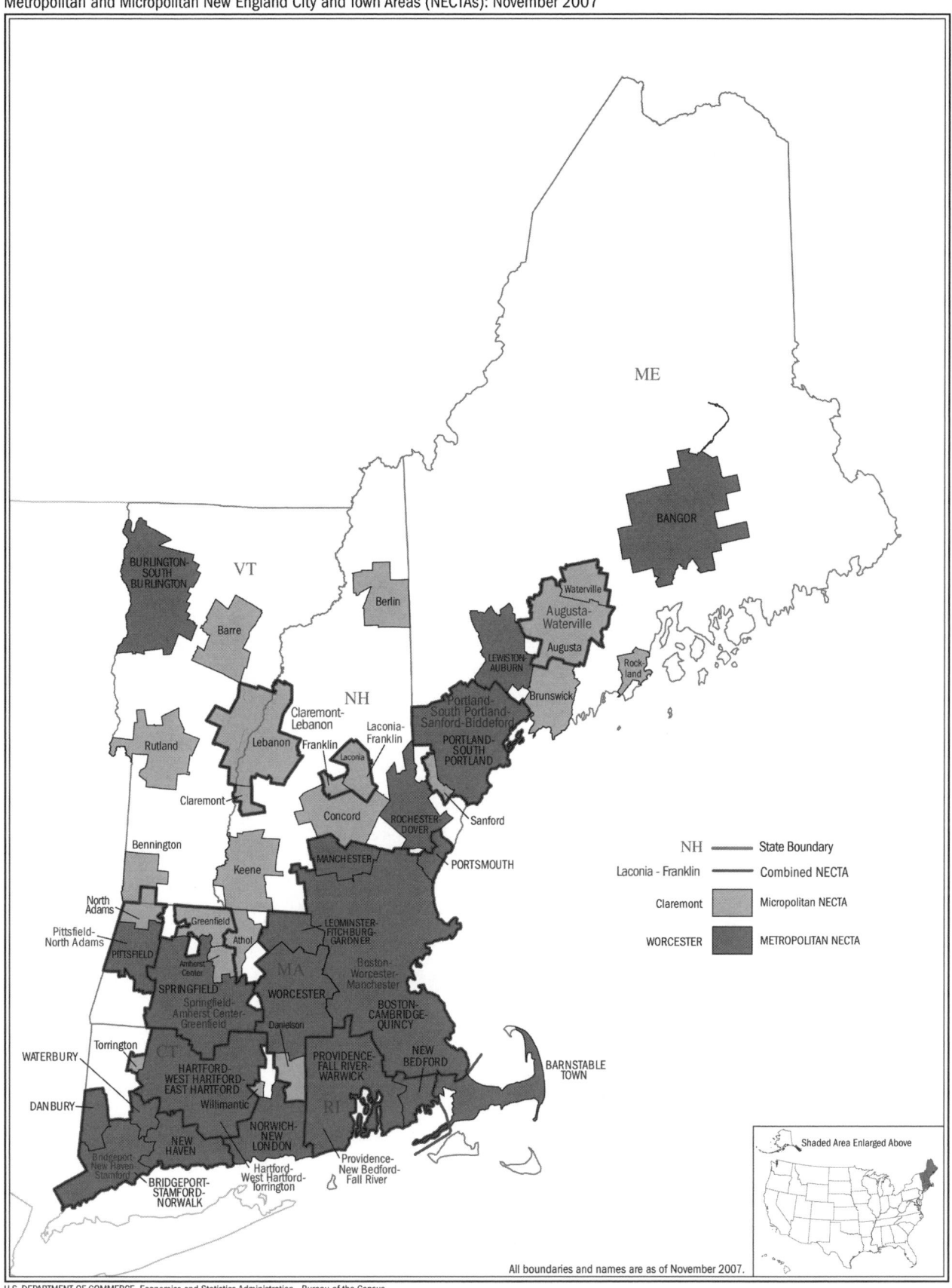

All boundaries and names are as of November 2007.

Shaded Area Enlarged Above

The bibliography below includes the most recent statistical abstracts for states. For some states, a near equivalent has been listed in substitution for, or in addition to, a statistical abstract. All sources contain statistical tables on a variety of subjects for the state as a whole, its component parts, or both. Internet sites also contain statistical data.

Alabama
University of Alabama
Center for Business and Economic Research
P.O. Box 870221
Tuscaloosa, AL 35487-0221
Phone: 205-348-6191. Fax: 205-348-2951
Internet site: http://cber.cba.ua.edu

Alabama Economic Outlook, 2013. Revised annually
http://cber.cba.ua.edu/publications.html

Alaska
State of Alaska, Department of Commerce
Community and Economic Development
550 West 7th Avenue, Suite 1770
Anchorage, AK 99501-3569
Phone: 907-465-2500. Fax 907-269-8125
Internet site: http://commerce.alaska.gov/

The Alaska Economic Performance Report, 2009. Online.
www.dced.state.ak.us/pub/2009_Performance_Report_web.pdf

Arizona
Arizona Commerce Authority
333 North Central Avenue
Suite 1900
Phoenix, AZ 85004
Phone: 800.542.5684
Internet site: www.azcommerce.com/data/az-at-a-glance

University of Arizona
Economic and Business Research Center
1130 East Helen Street, McClelland Hall, Room 103
P.O. Box 210108
Tucson, AZ 85721-0108
Phone: 520-621-2155. Fax: 520-621-2150
Internet site: http://ebr.eller.arizona.edu

Arizona—*Continued*
Arizona's Economy. Quarterly Online, Spring 2013
http://azeconomy.eller.arizona.edu/azeconomyissues/AEspring13.pdf

Arizona Economic Outlook. Online
http://ebr.eller.arizona.edu/forecasting/index.asp

Arkansas
University of Arkansas at Little Rock
Institute for Economic Advancement
College of Business
2801 South University Avenue
Little Rock, AR 72204-1099
Phone: 501-569-8519. Fax: 501-569-8538
Internet site: www.aiea.ualr.edu/publications/70-arkansas-statistical-abstract.html

Arkansas State and County Economic Data, 2010.
Annual
www.aiea.ualr.edu/pubs/2010/10-05%20AR%20Economic%20Profile%202010.pdf

Arkansas Personal Income Handbook, 2011
www.aiea.ualr.edu/pubs/2011/PIH/11-09%20AR%20personal%20income%202011.pdf

Arkansas Statistical Abstract, 2008
www.aiea.ualr.edu/images/08-01_AR_Statistical_Abstract_2008.pdf

California
California Department of Finance
915 L Street
Sacramento, CA 95814
Phone: 916-445-3878
Internet site: www.dof.ca.gov/index.php

California Statistical Abstract, 2009. Annual. Online only
www.dof.ca.gov/html/fs_data/STAT-ABS/Toc_xls.htm

Colorado
University of Colorado at Boulder Government
    Publications
Library, 184 UCB
1720 Pleasant Street
Boulder, CO 80309-0184
Phone: 303-492-8705
Internet site: http://ucblibraries.colorado.edu/govpubs/
    index.htm

Colorado by the Numbers. Online only
www.colorado.edu/libraries/govpubs/online.htm

Colorado Office of Economic Development and
    International Trade
1625 Broadway, Suite 2700
Denver, CO 80202
Phone: 303-892-3840. Fax: 303-892-3848
Internet site: www.colorado.gov/cs/Satellite/OEDIT/
    OEDIT/1162927366334

Connecticut
Connecticut Department of Economic and Community
    Development
505 Hudson Street
Hartford, CT 06106-7106
Phone: 860-270-8000
Internet site: www.ct.gov/ecd/site/default.asp

The Connecticut Economic Digest
www.ct.gov/ecd/cwp/view.asp?a=1106&q
    =303286&ecdNav=|

Connecticut Town Profiles, 2012
www.cerc.com/TownProfiles/default.asp

The Connecticut Economy
http://cteconomy.uconn.edu

Delaware
Delaware Economic Development Office
99 Kings Highway
Dover, DE 19901
Phone: 302-739-4271. Fax: 302-739-5749
Internet site: http://dedo.delaware.gov

2013 Delaware Data Book. Online
http://dedo.delaware.gov/dedo_pdf/NewsEvents_pdf/
    publications/DEDO_Data_Book_March_2013.pdf

District of Columbia
Business Resource Center
64 New York Avenue NW, Suite 3149
Washington, DC 20002
Phone: 202-671-1552
Internet site: http://brc.dc.gov/resources/facts.asp
Market Facts and Statistics. Online only.

Florida
University of Florida
Bureau of Economic and Business Research
P.O. Box 117145
Gainesville, FL 32611-7145
Phone: 352-392-0171, ext. 219. Fax: 352-392-4739
Internet site: www.bebr.ufl.edu

Print versions of the *Florida Statistical Abstract*, the
Florida County Perspective, and the *Florida County
Rankings* were discontinued in 2011. However, most
data from these publications are available online at:
www.bebr.ufl.edu/data

Georgia
University of Georgia
Terry College of Business
Selig Center for Economic Growth
Athens, GA 30602-6269
Phone: 706-542-8100. Fax: 706-542-3835
Internet site: http://terry.uga.edu/selig

Georgia Statistical Abstract, 2012–2013
Georgia Economic Outlook, 2013
The Multicultural Economy 2012
www.terry.uga.edu/about/centers-institutes/selig/
    publications

Hawaii
State of Hawaii, Department of Business
Economic Development and Tourism
P.O. Box 2359
Honolulu, HI 96804
Phone: 808-586-2480
Internet site: www.hawaii.gov/dbedt

The State of Hawaii Data Book 2010. Annual.
    Periodically updated.
http://dbedt.hawaii.gov/economic

Idaho
Idaho Department of Commerce
P.O. Box 83720
Boise, ID 83720-0093
Phone: 208-334-2470. Fax: 208-334-2631
Toll free: 800-842-5858
Internet site: http://commerce.idaho.gov

Economic Indicators and Community Demographics.
  Online
http://commerce.idaho.gov/business/economic-indicators

Illinois
Illinois Department of Commerce and Economic
  Opportunity
100 W. Randolph
Chicago, IL 60601
Phone: 312-814-7179
Internet site: www.ildceo.net/dceo

Illnois Economic Indicators
www.ildceo.net/dceo/Bureaus/Facts_Figures/Illinois_
  Economic_Indicators

Indiana
Indiana University, Kelley School of Business
Indiana Business Research Center
100 South College Avenue, Suite 240
Bloomington, IN 47404
Phone: 812-855-5507
Internet site: www.stats.indiana.edu
STATS Indiana. Online only

Iowa
Iowa State University, University Extension
Regional Capacity Analysis Program
17 East Hall, Ames, IA 50011
Phone: 515-294-9903. Fax: 515-294-0592

State Library of Iowa, State Data Center of Iowa
Internet site: www.seta.iastate.edu

Ola Babcock Miller Building
1112 East Grand
Des Moines, IA 50319-0233
Phone: 800-248-4483. Fax: 515-242-6543
Internet site: www.iowadatacenter.org

Kansas
University of Kansas, Institute for Policy and Social
  Research
1541 Lilac Lane, 607 Blake Hall
Lawrence, KS 66045-3129
Phone: 785-864-3701. Fax: 785-864-3683
Internet site www.ipsr.ku.edu
Kansas Statistical Abstract, 2011. 46th ed. Online only

Kentucky
Kentucky Cabinet for Economic Development
Old Capitol Annex, 300 West Broadway
Frankfort, KY 40601-1975
Phone: 800-626-2930. Fax: 502-564-3256
Internet site www.thinkkentucky.com

Kentucky Deskbook of Economic Statistics, 2009.
Online only
http://dspace.kdla.ky.gov:8080/jspui/
  bitstream/10602/2500/3/2009_Deskbook_Part1.pdf

Kentucky Economic Development Guide
http://businessclimate.com/kentucky-economic
  -development/magazine

Louisiana
Louisiana State Census Data Center
Division of Administration
Office of Information Technology
P.O. Box 94095
Baton Rouge, LA 70804
Phone: 225-219-9470. Fax: 225-219-9465
Internet site: www.louisiana.gov/Explore/
  Demographics_and_Geography

Maine
Maine State Planning Office
38 State House Station
Augusta, ME 04333-0038
Phone: 800-662-4545. Fax: 207-287-6489
Internet site www.maine.gov/spo

Maryland
Maryland Department of Planning
301 West Preston Street, Room 702
Baltimore, MD 21201
Phone: 410-767-4450

Maryland State Data Center
Internet site: www.mdp.state.md.us/msdc

2011 Maryland Statistical Handbook
www.mdp.state.md.us/msdc/md_statistical_
  handbook11.pdf

Massachusetts
MassCHIP, Massachusetts Department of Public Health
Executive Office of Health and Human Services
One Ashburton Place
11th Floor
Boston, MA 02108
Phone: 617-573-1600

Instant Topics. Online only
www.mass.gov/eohhs/researcher/community-health/
  masschip/topics

Michigan
Michigan Economic Development Corporation
300 North Washington Square
Lansing, MI 48913
Phone: 1-888-522-0103
Internet site: www.michigan.org/medc/miinfo

Sources of Economic and Demographic Data
www.michiganadvantage.org/County-Profiles
   -Population-and-Demographics

Minnesota
Minnesota Department of Employment and Economic
   Development (DEED)
1st National Bank Building
332 Minnesota Street, Suite E200
Saint Paul, MN 55101-1351
Phone: 800-657-3858

*Minnesota Department of Employment and Economic
   Development.* Online only.
Internet site: www.positivelyminnesota.com

Minnesota State Demographic Center
658 Cedar Street, Room 300
Saint Paul, MN 55155
Phone: 651-296-2557
Internet site: www.demography.state.mn.us

Mississippi
Mississippi State University Libraries
P.O. Box 5408
Mississippi State, MS 39762-5408
Phone: 662-325-7668

Mississippi Statistical Resources
Internet site: http://guides.library.msstate.edu/content
   .php?pid=15893&sid=106686

Missouri
University of Missouri-Columbia
Economic and Policy Analysis Research Center
10 Professional Building, Columbia, MO 65211
Phone: 573-882-4805. Fax: 573-882-5563

Missouri Census Data Center. Online only
Internet site: http://mcdc2.missouri.edu

Montana
Montana Department of Commerce
Census and Economic Information Center
301 South Park Avenue, P.O. Box 200500
Helena, MT 59620-0505
Phone: 406-841-2740. Fax: 406-841-2731
Internet site: http://ceic.mt.gov

Nebraska
Nebraska Department of Economic Development
301 Centennial Mall South, P. O. Box 94666
Lincoln, NE 68509-4666
Phone: 800-426-6505. Fax 402-471-3778
Internet site http://info.neded.org

Nevada
Nevada Department of Administration
Division of Budget and Planning
209 East Musser Street, Room 200
Carson City, NV 89701-4298
Phone: 775-684-0222. Fax: 775-684-0260
Internet site: http://admin.nv.gov

Nevada Statistical Abstract. Online only
www.budget.state.nv.us

New Hampshire
New Hampshire Office of Energy and Planning
4 Chenell Drive
Concord, NH 03301-8501
Phone: 603-271-2155. Fax 603-271-2615
Internet site: www.nh.gov/oep/index.htm

New Jersey
State of New Jersey Department of Labor and
   Workforce Development
1 John Fitch Plaza, P.O. Box 110
Trenton, NJ 08625-0110
Phone: 609-984-2595. Fax: 609-984-6833
Internet site: http://lwd.dol.state.nj.us

Labor Market Information. Online only
Internet site: http://lwd.dol.state.nj.us/labor/lpa/LMI_
   index.html

New Mexico
University of New Mexico
Bureau of Business and Economic Research
MSC06 3510
1 University of New Mexico
Albuquerque, NM 87131-0001
Phone: 505-277-2216. Fax 505-277-7066

New Mexico Business, Current Economic Report.
   Monthly. FOR-UNM Bulletin. Quarterly
Internet site: http://bber.unm.edu

New York
Nelson A. Rockefeller Institute of Government
411 State Street
Albany, NY 12203-1003
Phone: 518-443-5522. Fax: 518-443-5788
Internet site: www.rockinst.org

New York State Statistical Yearbook, 2011. 36th ed.
www.rockinst.org/nys_statistics

North Carolina
North Carolina Office of State Budget and Management
116 West Jones Street
Raleigh, NC 27603-8005
Phone: 919-807-4700. Fax: 919-733-0640
Internet site: www.osbm.state.nc.us

How North Carolina Ranks, 2012. Online only
www.rockinst.org/nys_statistics

North Dakota
North Dakota Department of Commerce
Economic Development & Finance Division
P.O. Box 2057
Bismarck, North Dakota 58502-2057
Phone: 701-328-5300. Fax: 701-328-5320
www.business.nd.gov

Ohio
Ohio Department of Development
Office of Policy Strategic Research and Strategic
   Planning
77 South High Street, P.O. Box 1001
Columbus, OH 43216-1001
Phone: 614-466-5017
Internet site: www.odod.state.oh.us/research

Oklahoma
University of Oklahoma
Michael F. Price College of Business
Center for Economic and Management Research
307 West Brooks, Room 3
Norman OK 73019-4004
Phone: 405-325-2931, Fax: 405-325-7688
Internet site: http://cemr.ou.edu/cemr/cemr_publications
   .aspx

Statistical Abstract of Oklahoma
www.ou.edu/price/cemr/cemr_publications.html

Oregon
Oregon State Archives
800 Summer Street, NE
Salem, OR 97310
Phone: 503-373-0701. Fax: 503-378-4118
Internet site: www.sos.state.or.us/

Oregon Blue Book. 2013–2014. Biennial
www.sos.state.or.us/bbook

Pennsylvania
Penn State Harrisburg
Pennsylvania State Data Center
Institute of State and Regional A airs
777 West Harrisburg Pike,
Middletown, PA 17057-4898
Phone: 717-948-6336. Fax: 717-948-6754
Internet site: http://pasdc.hbg.psu.edu

Pennsylvania Statistical Abstract, 2012.
Also Available on CD-ROM.
http://pasdc.hbg.psu.edu/Publications/
   PennsylvaniaAbstract/tabid/1018/Default.aspx

Pennsylvania State Facts, 2013
http://pasdc.hbg.psu.edu/sdc/pasdc_files/pastats/PA_
   Facts_2013.pdf

Rhode Island
Rhode Island Economic Development Corporation
315 Iron Horse Way, Suite 101
Providence, RI 02908
Phone: 401-278-9100. Fax 401-273-8270
Internet site: www.riedc.com/r/index.html

Rhode Island Economic Development Corporation
www.riedc.com/data-and-publications/economy-and
   -workforce

South Carolina
South Carolina Budget and Control Board
Office of Research and Statistics
1919 Blanding Street, Columbia, SC 29201
Phone: 803-898-9960
Internet site: www.bcb.sc.gov/BCB/BCB-index.phtm

South Carolina Statistical Abstract, 2012
Also available on CD-ROM.
http://abstract.sc.gov

South Dakota
South Dakota Governor's Office on Economic
   Development
711 E. Wells Ave.
Pierre, South Dakota 57501
Phone: 605-367-4518
Internet site: www.sdreadytowork.com/

Tennessee
University of Tennessee
Center for Business and Economic Research
College of Business Administration
916 Volunteer Boulevard
Knoxville, TN 37996-0570
Phone: 865-974-5441. Fax: 865-974-3100
Internet site: http://cber.bus.utk.edu/Default.htm

Tennessee State Data Center
http://tndata.utk.edu

Texas
Texas Almanac, University of North Texas
History Department
1155 Union Circle #310650
Denton, TX 76203-5017
Phone: 940-369-5200

Texas Almanac
Internet site www.texasalmanac.com

Texas State Data Center and Office of the State
   Demographer
Institute for Demographic and Socioeconomic Research
University of Texas at San Antonio
One UTSA Circle
San Antonio, TX 78249-0704
Phone: 210-458-6543. Fax: 210-458-6541
Internet site: http://txsdc.utsa.edu

Utah
Governor's Office of Planning and Budget
Demographic and Economic Analysis, 150
P.O. Box 132210
Salt Lake City, UT 84114-2210
Phone 801-538-1027. Fax: 801-538-1547

Spring 2013 Data Guide
2013 Economic Outlook
Internet site: www.governor.utah.gov/dea

Vermont
Department of Labor
Economic and Labor Market Information
P.O. Box 488
Montpelier, VT 05601-0488
Phone: 802-828-4202. Fax: 802-828-4050

Economic and Labor Market Information
Internet site: www.vtlmi.info

Virginia
Weldon Cooper Center for Public Service
P.O. Box 400206
Charlottesville, VA 22904-4206
434-982-5522. Fax: 434-982-5524
Internet site: www.coopercenter.org

Washington
Washington State Office of Financial Management
P.O. Box 43113
Olympia, WA 98504-3113
Phone: 360-902-0555
Internet site www.ofm.wa.gov

Washington State Data Book, 2011. Online only
www.ofm.wa.gov/databook/default.asp

West Virginia
West Virginia University
College of Business and Economics
Bureau of Business and Economic Research
P.O. Box 6025, Morgantown, WV 26506
Phone: 304-293-7831
Internet site: www.be.wvu.edu/bber/index.htm

2010 West Virginia County Data Profiles.
www.be.wvu.edu/demographics/demographicprofiles
   .htm

West Virginia Economic Outlook, 2013. Annual
www.be.wvu.edu/bber/pdfs/WV_Economic_
   Outlook_2013.pdf

Wisconsin
Wisconsin Legislative Reference Bureau
One East Main Street, Suite 200
Madison, WI 53703
608-266-0341. Fax: 608-266-5648

2011–2012 Wisconsin Blue Book. Biennial
Internet site: www.legis.state.wi.us/lrb/pubs/bluebook
   .htm

Wyoming
Department of Administration and Information
Economic Analysis Division
2800 Central Avenue, Suite 206
Cheyenne, WY 82002-0060
307-777-7504. Fax: 307-632-1819
Internet site: http://eadiv.state.wy.us

The Equality State Almanac, 2010
http://eadiv.state.wy.us/Almanac/Almanac.html

Wyoming 2013 – Just the Facts
http://eadiv.state.wy.us/Wy_facts/facts2013.pdf

KEY FEDERAL WEBSITES WITH STATE-LEVEL INFORMATION

Many federal government agencies publish state-level information. The sites listed below have large concentrations of state-level information on easy-to-locate websites.

U.S. BUREAU OF ECONOMIC ANALYSIS
Gross State Product and Personal income at
www.bea.gov/regional/index.htm

U.S. BUREAU OF LABOR STATISTICS
Current Employment Statistics at
www.bls.gov/sae/home.htm

Geographic Profile of Employment and Unemployment at
www.bls.gov/gps/home.htm

State occupational injuries, illnesses, and fatalities at
www.bls.gov/iif/oshstate.htm

U.S. CENSUS BUREAU
American Community Survey data at
www.census.gov/acs/www

Annual Survey of Manufactures at
www.census.gov/manufacturing/asm/index.html

Building permits at
www.census.gov/construction/bps

County Business Patterns at
www.census.gov/econ/cbp/index.html

Economic Census 2012 data at
www.census.gov/econ

Foreign trade at
www.census.gov/foreign-trade/statistics/state

Population and Housing unit estimates at
www.census.gov/popest

State and County QuickFacts profiles at
http://quickfacts.census.gov/qfd/index.html

State government finances at
www.census.gov/govs/state

State government employment and payroll at
www.census.gov/govs/apes

U.S. DEPARTMENT OF AGRICULTURE
Economic Research Service
Agricultural Exports at
www.ers.usda.gov/Data/StateExports

Farm Income Wealth and Statistics at
www.ers.usda.gov/Data/farmincome

State Fact Sheets at
www.ers.usda.gov/StateFacts

National Agricultural Statistics Service
Census of Agriculture at
www.agcensus.usda.gov/ and
www.nass.usda.gov/Publications/index.asp

U.S. DEPARTMENT OF HEALTH AND HUMAN SERVICES
Centers for Disease Control and Prevention
Behavioral Risk Factor Surveillance System at
www.cdc.gov/brfss/

Fast Stats A to Z at
www.cdc.gov/nchs/fastats/map_page.htm

Substance Abuse and Mental Health Services
  Administration
State-level data at
www.samhsa.gov

ENERGY INFORMATION ADMINISTRATION
Energy consumption at
www.eia.doe.gov/emeu/states/_seds.html

General state information at
http://tonto.eia.doe.gov/state

ENERGY INFORMATION ADMINISTRATION—
Continued

State Electricity Profiles at
www.eia.gov/state

NATIONAL CENTER OF EDUCATION
STATISTICS
State Education Data Profiles at
http://nces.ed.gov/programs/stateprofiles/

NATIONAL SCIENCE FOUNDATION
Science and Engineering State Profiles at
www.nsf.gov/statistics/states

U.S. DEPARTMENT OF TRANSPORTATION
Federal Highway Administration
Highway statistics at
www.fhwa.dot.gov/policy/ohpi/hss/index.cfm

Federal Highway Administration
State traffic safety information at
www.fhwa.dot.gov

INDEX